Webster's
New Dictionary
&
Thesaurus

Promotional Sales Books, Inc.

Contents

About This Dictionary

In order to make this dictionary a valuable "tool" for anyone concerned with the English language, the lexicographers who have compiled this book have tried to make it easy-to-use as well as contemporary. It would be of little use to you to have a dictionary that featured thousands of foreign, obscure, and antiquated terms. Thus, these words have been trimmed down to the basics — words that may still be in use after hundreds of years as well as those foreign words that you may encounter on a steady basis (**du jour**). In addition, we have included many of the more contemporary words that have come into use throughout the last several years, especially in the fields of science and computers. Words and terms such as **desktop publishing** and acronyms such as **ASCII** and **DOS** are important inclusions that assure the contemporary nature of this dictionary.

To use this dictionary, it is necessary for you to understand how it is organized. We've organized the words in paragraphs, featuring the root word in a larger, bold typeface. The words that are derived from this root word, or those that are related to it, are also in bold type. Thus, the word **execute** will include derivative words such as **execution**, **executioner**, and **executive**. If there are alternative spellings for the words, they are included. If there are unique plural forms of the word, these are included also.

In the next section is a list of abbreviations which appear throughout this dictionary. This includes the parts of speech, in order for you to recognize how the entry word is used. (Since this is not a grammar book, you will have to look elsewhere to determine what a *noun* is in contrast to a *verb transitive*.) You will find the word **lady** as a *noun* (*n.*) and the word **lag** as a *verb intransitive* (*v.i.*). However, the word **laggard** is a *noun* and an *adjective*, and the differing definitions are provided.

For many of the words where there may be a question of how to pronounce them, there are accent marks (′) to show syllable emphasis as well as pronunciation guides. For example, look at the word **banquet**.

banq′uet (bang′-kwet) *n*. feast. -*v.i.* feast. -*v.t.* give a feast to -**banq′ueter**
n. [F., dim of *banc*, bench]

This is a complete entry. First you are provided with the root
word; **banquet**. In order for you to know that the accent is on the
first syllable, there is an accent mark (′). Following the root word is
a pronunciation guide in parentheses. The first syllable is pronounced
like the word *bang*; the second sounds like *kwet*. The parts of speech
follow. This word can be used in several ways: as a *noun*, *verb
intransitive*, *verb transitive*. The associated word is **banqueter**,
which is a *noun* . Finally, the derivation of the word is given, the
diminutive (dim) of the French word *banc*.

We do not provide the accent marks with words of one syllable,
or those with a silent *e* at the end of the word.

Most pronunciation guides are self-explanatory. For example,
the second syllable in the word **baroque** is pronounced as a *k*, and
the pronunciation guide provides the letter (-k-). As a guide for you,
following are the common pronunciations that we use:

ch	chip	ng	French nasal sound
CH	chord	ng	ring
g	go	s	sweet
hw	where	th	thin
j	juice, gene	TH	this

As you saw from the example above, the derivation or etymology
of the main word is provided at the end of most entries in square
brackets. Like the rest of this dictionary, we've tried to make it easy
to use and in most cases have given the primary origin for a word,
usually the Latin or Anglo-Saxon derivation. From time to time,
where it would enhance your understanding of the derivation of the
word, a somewhat more detailed explanation is provided.

Finally, when entries contain prefixes, we have offered only a
handful of the words that can be created by the use of the prefix. A
prefix such as **anti-** can be used to create hundreds of words. We have
offered only a few, but suggest that you see the words without the
prefix.

Abbreviations Used In This Book

a.	adjective	*lit.*	literally
abbrev.	abbreviation	*maths.*	mathematics
adv.	adverb	*med.*	medicine
alg.	algebra	*mil.*	military
arch.	archaic	*mod.*	modern
archit.	architecture	*mus.*	music
astron.	astronomy	*myth.*	mythology
avoir.	avoirdupois	*n.*	noun
bot.	botany	*n. masc.*	noun masculine
cap.	capital	*naut.*	nautical
cp.	compare	*obj.*	objective
char.	character	*obs.*	obsolete
chem.	chemistry	*opp.*	opposite
colloq.	colloquial	*orig.*	origin (-ally)
comp.	comparative	*p.p.*	past participle
compute.	computers	*p.t.*	past tense
conj.	conjunction	*perh.*	perhaps
contr.	contraction	*pert.*	pertaining to
const.	construction	*philos.*	philosophy
corrupt.	corruption, corrupted	*phot.*	photography
dial.	dialect, dialectal	*phys.*	physics
dem. pron.	demonstrative pronoun	*pl.*	plural
dim.	diminutive	*poet.*	poetry, poetical
e.g.	for instance	*polit.*	politics
elec.	electricity	*poss.*	possessive
esp.	especially	*pref.*	prefix
euph.	euphemism	*prep.*	preposition
fem.	feminine	*pres. p.*	present participle
fig.	figuratively	*print.*	printing
fort.	fortification	*prob.*	probably
fr.	from	*pron.*	pronoun
gen.	generally	*pros.*	prosody
geog.	geography	*prov.*	provincial
geol.	geology	*psych.*	psychology
gram.	grammar	*q.v.*	which see
hist.	history	*redupl.*	reduplication
ident.	identical	*reflex.*	reflexive
i.e.	that is	*rhet.*	rhetoric
imit.	imitation, imitative	*rel. pron.*	relative pronoun
impers.	impersonal	*sing.*	singular
infin.	infinitive	*sl.*	slang
intens.	intensive	*superl.*	superlative
interj.	interjection	*surg.*	surgery
lang.	language	*trans.*	transitive

trig.	trigonometry	*v.i.*	verb intransitive
ult.	ultimately	*v.s.*	(*vide supra*) see above
usu.	usually	*v.t.*	verb transitive
v.	verb	*zool.*	zoology
var.	variant, variation		
v. aux.	auxiliary verb		

Word Derivations

AF.	Anglo-French	ME.	Middle English
Afr.	African	Med. L.	Medieval Latin
Am. Amer.	American	Mex.	Mexican
Arab.	Arabic	Mod. L.	Modern Latin
Aram.	Aramaic	Mongol.	Mongolian
Austr.	Australian	N.	North
Braz.	Brazilian	Norw.	Norwegian
Can. F.	Canadian French	O.	Old
Carib.	Caribbean	OE.	Old English
Celt.	Celtic	OF.	Old French
Chin.	Chinese	OHG.	Old High German
Dan.	Danish	ON.	Old Norse
Du.	Dutch	ONF.	Old North French
E.	English	Pers.	Persian
F.	French	Peruv.	Peruvian
Flem.	Flemish	Port.	Portuguese
G.	Greek	Rom.	Romany
Gael.	Gaelic	Russ.	Russian
Ger.	German	S.	South
Heb.	Hebrew	Sans.	Sanskrit
Hind.	Hindustani	Sc.	Scottish, Scots
Hung.	Hungarian	Scand.	Scandinavian
Ice.	Icelandic	Slav.	Slavonic
Ind.	Indian	Sp.	Spanish
Ir.	Irish	Sw.	Swedish
It.	Italian	Teut.	Teutonic
Jap.	Japanese	Tibet.	Tibetan
L.	Latin	Turk.	Turkish
LL.	Low or Late Latin	U.S.	United States
M.	Middle	VL.	Vulgar Latin
Malay	Malay	W.	Welsh, West

A

a, an *a.* one; any. [OE, an, one]

aard'vark *n.* S. African ant-bear. [Du. *aarde*, earth, *Larken*, pig]

A-bomb *n.* atomic bomb.

ab'acus *n-* flat piece at the top of a column; frame with parallel wires on which slide beads for counting. [L. -G. *abax*, tablet, reckoning board]

abalo'ne *n.* shellfish yielding mother-of-pearl. [Sp. Amer.]

aban'don *v.t.* give up altogether.

aban'doned *pp.* and *a.* given up, *esp.* to evil. **-aban'donment** *n.* [F. *abandonner*]

abase' *v.t.* lower, humiliate. **-abase'-ment** *n.* [F. *abaiser.* See **base**]

abash' *v.t.* confuse, make ashamed. [F. *ébahir*, astound]

abate' *v.t.* lessen. *-v.i.* become less. **abate'ment.** [F. *abatire*, beat off]

abbreviate *v.t.* shorten or abridge. **-abbrevia'tion** *n.* [L. *abbreviate*]

ab'dicate *v.t.* give up formally. *-v.i.* give up power or office, *esp.* the throne. **abdica'tion** *n.* [L. *abdicate*]

abdo'men *n.* belly. **-abdom'inal** *a.* [L.]

abduct' *v.t.* carry off, kidnap. **-abduction** *n.* [L *abducere*, lead away]

aberration *n.* wandering, *esp.* mental disorder, 'wandering of wits.' **-aberr'ant** *a.* [L. *aberrare*, wander away]

abet' *v.t.* help in something bad. [OF. *abeter*, egg on]

abey'ance *n.* suspension from use or action. [OF. *abéance*, fr. *aboer*, gape at]

abhor' *v.t.* dislike very strongly; loathe, detest. [L. *abhorrere*, shrink from]

abide' *v.i.* stay, reside; await. *-v.t.* endure, put up with. [OE. *abidan*]

abil'ity *n.* capacity, power, skill. [L. *habilis*, easy to hold]

a'ble *a.* capable, clever, having power or skill. **-a'bly** *adv.* [L. *habilis*, fit]

ab'negate *v.t.* give up, renounce. **abnega'tion** *n.* [L. *abnegare*, deny]

abnorm'al *a.* irregular; not usual; not according to type; exceptional. [L. *ab*, from, *norma*, rule]

aboard' *adv.* on board, on a ship, train or plane. *-prep.* on board of. [board]

abolish *v.t.* do away with. **-aboli'tionist** *n.* one who wishes to do away with, *esp.* an evil, *e.g.*, slavery. [F. *abolir*]

abort' *v.t.* miscarry. **-abor'tion** *n.* something misshapen or unnatural. **-abor'tive** *a.* prematurely born; come to nothing. [L. *aboriri*, miscarry]

about' *adv.* on all sides; nearly; up and down; out, astir. *-prep.* round; near; dealing with. [OE. *onbutan*]

above' *adv.* in a higher place. *-prep.* on top of, higher; more than. [OE. *abufan*]

abroad' *adv.* out of house or country; at large. [ME. *on brede*, on breadth]

abrupt' *a.* hasty; steep; sudden; blunt. **-abrupt'ly** *adv.* **-abrupt'ness** *n.* [L. *abrumpere*, break off]

ab'sent *a.* away, not present. **-(absent')** *v.t.* keep away. **-ab'sence** *n.* **-absentee'** *n.* one away; one who habitually stays away. **-absentee'ism** *n.* practise of a landlord living away from his estate, or a man absenting himself from his work. **ab'sently** *adv.* **-ab'sent-mind'ed** *a.* inattentive, preoccupied. **-ab'sent-mindedness** *n.* [L. *absens*, away]

ab'solute *a.* not limited, unconditional; entire, pure (as absolute alcohol). **ab'solutely** *adv.* **-ab'soluteness** *n.* [L. *ab-solvere*, set free]

absolve' *v.t.* free from, pardon. **-absolu'tion** *n.* [L. *absolvere*, set free]

absorb' *v.t.* suck up, drink in; engage the whole attention of **-absorb'ent** *a.* and *n.* **-absorp'tion** *n.* **-absorp'tive** *a.* [L. *absorbers*, suck away]

abstain *v.i.* keep from, refrain, *esp.* from strong drink. [L. *abstenere*, hold from]

ab'stract *a.* separate; existing only in the mind, not concrete. *-n.* summary, abridgment. **-abstract'** *v.t.* draw from, remove. **-abstract'ed** *a.* absent-minded. **-abstraction** *n.* **-abstract'ly** *adv.* [L. *abstrahere*, draw away]

absurd' *a.* silly, contrary to reason. **-absurd'ity** *n.* **-absurd'ly** *adv.* [L. *absurdus*, fr. *surdus*, deaf]

abundance *n.* great plenty. **-abun'dant** *a.* plentiful. **-abun'dantly** *adv.* [F. *abondance*]

abuse' *v.t.* misuse; miscall, address in rude language. [L. *ab*, away from, *uti*, use]

abut' *v.i.* end on, border on. **-abut'ment** *n.* support, *esp.* for the end of a bridge. [OF. *abouter*, join at the end]

abyss' *n.* very deep gulf or pit. **-abys'mal** (-z-) *a.* **-abys'mally** *adv.* **-abyss'al** *a.* [G. *abyssos*, bottomless]

acad'emy *n.* higher school; society to advance arts or sciences. **-academ'ic** *a.* of an academy; theoretical. **-academ'ically** *adv.* **-academi'cian** *n.* [G. *akademeia*, garden where Plato taught]

accel'erate (aks-) *v.t.* and *i.* increase speed. **-accel'erator** *n.* mechanism to increase speed, *esp.* in an automobile. [L.

accelerate, fr. *celer*, swift]

ac'cent (aks-) *n.* stress of the voice; mark to show such stress; manner of speech peculiar to a district or individual. [F. , fr. L. accentual note or tone]

accept' (aks-) *v.t.* take, receive; admit, believe; agree to [L. *acceptare*, take]

ac'cess (-ks-) *n.* admission; entrance; attack; liberty to approach; means of approach. **-accessibil'ity** *n.* **-access'ible** *a.* easy to approach. **-access'ibly** *adv.* [L. *accedere*, go near to]

accessary *n.* helper, *esp.* in a crime.[*access*]

accessory *a.* additional. *-n.* added or nonessential item of dress or equipment; accomplice, aid in crime (*access*]

ac'cidence (-ks-) *n.* part of grammar dealing with changes in the form of words, *e.g.* , plurals. [for accidents]

ac'cident (-ks-) *n.* something happening by chance; mishap; quality not essential. **-acciden'tal** *a.* happening by chance. *-n.* (*mus.*) sharp, flat or natural, not of the key. **-acciden'tally** *adv.* [F.]

acclaim' *v.t.* applaud, receive with applause. **-acclama'tion** *n.* **-acclam'a-tory** *a.* [L. *acclamare*, shout to]

accomm'odate *v.t.* fit; harmonize; supply. **-accommoda'tion** *n.* lodgings; loan; adjustment or compromise; obligingness. [L. *accommodate*, fit]

accom'pany *v.t.* go with; join with. **accom'paniment** *n.* something which accompanies, *esp.* (*mus.*) the instrumental part which goes with, *e.g.* , a vocal solo. **-accom'panist** *n.* one who plays an accompaniment. [F. *accompagner*]

accom'plice *n.* companion in evil deeds. [Earlier *complice*, fr. L. *complex*, woven together]

accom'plish *v.t.* carry out; finish. **accom'plished** *a.* complete, perfect; socially talented. **-accom'plishment** *n.* completion; a personal ability, talent. [F. *accomplir*]

accord' *v.t.* compose, settle. *-v.i.* agree. *-n.* agreement, harmony. **-accord'-ance** *n.* **-accord'ant** *a.* **-accord'ing** *adv.* [L. *ad*, to, *cor, cordis*, heart]

account' *v.t.* reckon, judge. *-v.i.* give a reason; make a statement of money. *-n.* statement of monies; report, description. **-accountabil'ity** *n.* **-account'able** *a.* responsible. **-account'ant** *n.* professional reckoner, one skilled in accounts. [OF. *aconter*, reckon]

accumulate *v.t.* amass. *-v.i.* grow into a mass, increase. **-accumula'tion** *v.* -

accu'mulator *n.* electrical storage battery. [L. *cumulare*, heap up]

ac'curate *a.* exact, correct. **-ac'curacy** *n.* **-ac'curately** *adv.* **-ac'curateness** *n.* [L. *accurare*, give care to]

accuse' *v.t.* charge with wrongdoing; blame. [L. *accusare*, call to account]

accus'tom *v.t.* make used to, familiarize. **-accus'tomed** *a.* [OF. *acostumer*]

acer'bity *n.* sour, bitterness; severity of manner. [L. *acerbitas*]

ace'tic *a.* derived from or having the nature of vinegar. [L. *acetum*, vinegar]

ache (ak) *n.* continuous pain. *-v.i.* be in pain. **-ach'ing** *a.* [OE. *acan*]

achieve' *v.t.* finish, accomplish, perform successfully. **-achieve'ment** *n.* something accomplished; high exploit; coat of arms. [F. *achever*]

ac'id *a.* sharp, sour. *-n.* sour substance; (*chem.*) one of a class of compounds which combine with bases (alkalis, oxides, *etc.*) to form salts. **-acid'ify** *v.t.* **-acid'ity** *n.* [L. *acidus-acere*, be sour]

acknow'ledge (-nol' -) *v.t.* admit, own, recognize. **-acknow'ledgment** *n.* [ME. *knowlechen*, perceive]

ac'me *n.* highest point. [G. *akme*, point]

ac'ne *n.* skin disease; pimple. [G. *akme*, point]

acous'tic *a.* pertaining to hearing. [G. *akoustikos*]

acquaint' *v.t.* make to know, inform. [OF. *acointier* -L. *ad*, to, *cognitus*, known]

acquiesce' *v.i.* agree in silence; consent. **-acquiescence** *n.* **-acquiescent** *a.* [L. *acquiescere*, rest]

acquire' *v.t.* gain, get. [L. *acquirere*]

acquit' *v.t.* settle, discharge, as a debt; behave (oneself); declare innocent. **acquitt'al** *n.* act of declaring innocent in a court. [F. *acquitter*]

a'cre (a'-ker) *n.* measure of land, 4840 square yards. *-pl.* lands, estates. [OE. *wer*, field]

ac'rid *a.* bitter and hot to the taste; irritating. **-acrid'ity** *n.* **-ac'ridness** *n.* [irreg. formation fr. L. *acer*, sharp]

ac'rimony *n.* bitterness of feelings or language. **-acrimo'nious** *a.* sharp, biting, severe. [L. *acrimonia*]

ac'robat *n.* performer of skilled gymnastic feats. **-acrobat'ic** *a.* **-acrobat'ics** *n. pl.* his art- [G. *akrobatos*, tiptoe walking]

acrophobia *n.* fear of heights. [G. *akron*, point, *phobos*, fear]

across' *adv.* and *prep.* crosswise; from side to side. [For on or in cross]

act *n.* thing done, deed; process of doing;

law or decree; section of a play. -v.t. perform, as in a play. -v.i. exert force; work,
as a mechanism; behave. -ac′ting n. performance of a part; working. -ac′tion n.
-activity; operation; gesture; battle; lawsuit. [F. acte fr. L. agere, do]

act′ual adv. real; existing in the present;
not imaginary or bygone. -actual′ity n.
ac′tually adv. [l. actualis]

ac′tuary n. registrar; one who makes calculations for insurance companies. -
actua′rial a. [L. actuarius, recorder]

ac′umen n. sharpness of wit. [L.]

acute′ a. sharp; sensitive; keen, shrewd;
critical. [L. acutus, sharpened]

ad′age n. old saying, proverb. [F.]

ad′amant n. very hard stone; diamond.
-a. very hard, unbreakable; unyielding. -
adamant′ine a. [G. adamas, invincible,
not to be broken or tamed]

adapt′ v.t. fit; modify; alter for a new use.
[L. adaptare]

add v.t. and i. join; put something on; say
further. -adden′dum (pl. -a) something to
be added. -addi′tion n. -addi′tional a. [L.
addere, put to]

ad′dict n. one given up to something,
usually an evil, e.g. , drug-addict. [L. ad-
dictus;-addicere, make over]

address′ v.t. speak to; direct; dispatch;
mark a destination, as on an envelope. n.
skill; bearing; a speech; direction on a letter. [F. adresser, make straight]

adept′ a. skilled. (-ad′-) n. expert; al-
chemist. [L. adeptus, having attained]

ad′equate a. sufficient, suitable; equal to.
-ad′equacy n. -ad′equately adv. [L.
adæquatus, made equal to]

adhere′ v.i. stick to; become or remain
firm, in an opinion etc. [L. adhærere, stick]

ad′it n. horizontal entrance into a pit or
mine. [L. adire, go in]

adja′cent a. lying close to; contiguous.
[L. adjacere]

adjective n. word added to a noun to show
quality or circumstance. -adjecti′val a. [L.
adjectivus, added]

adjourn′ (a-jurn′) v.t. and i. put off,
postpone; end a meeting; move to another
place. -adjourn′ment n. [F. ajourner, fr.
OF. journ, day]

a′junct a. joined, added. -n. person or ing
added. [L. adjungere, add to]

adjust′ v.t. set right; make exact or
suitable; arrange. [F. ajuster, fr. juste,
right]

admin′ister v.t. manage; look after; dispense, as justice etc.; supply.
admin′istra′tion n. -admin′istrative. a. -

admin′istrator n. [L. administrate]

ad′miral n. naval officer of very high or
great rank. [F. amiral, fr. Arab. amir-al
(bahr), prince of the (sea)]

admire′ v.t. look on with wonder and
pleasure; respect highly; love or esteem.
[L. admirari, wonder at]

admit′ v.t. let in; allow; accept as true;
grant. [L. admittere, send to]

admon′ish v. t. warn; reprove gently; advise. [earlier amonest, OF. amonester, ad-
vise]

adoles′cent a. growing to manhood; not
fully adult. -n. youth. -adoles′cence n. [L.
adolescere, grow up]

adopt′ v.t. take into relationship, esp. as
one's child; take up, as a principle, resolution, idea. [L. adoptare, choose for
oneself]

adore′ v.t. and i. worship; love intensely.
-ador′able a. -adora′tion n. -ador′er n. (L.
adorare, worship, pray to]

adorn′ v.t. beautify, embellish, deck.
-adorn′ment n. [L. adornare]

adre′nal a. near the kidneys. -adre′nal
glands′, two small ductless glands over the
kidneys. -adre′nalin n. secretion of these
glands, taken from animals for use in
medicine; powerful astringent drug. [L.
ad, to, renes, kidneys]

adrift′ a. and adv. floating free; loose;
without aim or direction. [on drift]

ad′ult a. -grown-up, mature. -n. grownup
person. [L. adolescere, adult-, grow]

adul′terate v.t. corrupt; make impure by
mixture. [L. adulterate, corrupt]

advance′ v.t. bring forward; promote; encourage; pay beforehand. -v.i. go forward;
improve in rank or value. [F. avancer, put
forward]

advantage n. gain; superiority. -v.t.
benefit, promote. -advanta′geous a. -
advanta′geously adv. [F. avantage]

adven′ture n. remarkable happening;
enterprise; risk; bold exploit; commercial
speculation. -v.t. and i. risk; take a risk.
-adven′turer n. masc. [F. aventure]

ad′verb n. word added to a verb, adjective
or other adverb to modify the meaning.
-adverb′ial a. [L. adverbium, fr. ad, to,
verbum, word]

ad′verse a. opposed to; hostile; contrary
to desire. -ad′versary n. enemy-
advers′ative a. -ad′versely adv. -
advers′ity n. distress, misfortune. [L. ad-
vertere, turn against]

ad′vertise v.t. and i. make known; give
notice of, esp. in newspapers, bills etc. [F.
avertir, warn]

advice' *n.* opinion given; counsel; iformation, news (*esp.* in *pl.*). [F. *avis*]

advise *v.t.* and *i.* give an opinion to; recommend a line of conduct; inform. [F. *avis*]

ad'vocate *n.* defender; one who pleads the cause of another, *esp.* in a court of law. -*v.t.* uphold, recommend. **ad'vocacy** *n.* - **advoca'tion** *n.* [L. *advocatus*, called in]

a'erate *v.t.* expose to, or mix with, air; charge with carbonic acid or other gas. [L. *aer*, air]

aer'ial *a.* belonging to the air; ethereal: -*n.* elevated wire to send out or receive radio signals. [L. *aer*, air]

a'erie, a'ery, ey'rie *n.* nest of a bird of prey, *esp.* an eagle. [F. *aire*]

aero- *prefix* having to do with air or aircraft. [L. *aer*, air] -**aerobat'ics** *n.* 'stunts' in aviation. -**a'erodrome** *n.* **airfield.** -**aeronaut'ics** *n. pl.* science of air navigation.

aero'bia *n. pl.* bacteria that cannot live without air, [G. *aer*, air, *bios*, life]

aero'bics *n.* any system of sustained exercises designed to increase the amount of oxygen in the blood and strengthen the heart and lungs.

a'erosol *n.* suspension of fine solid or liquid particles in a gas; container for dispensing such.

aesthetic, esthetic *a.* relating to the principles of beauty and taste, and of art. [G. *aisthesthai*, perceive]

affair' *n.* business operation; any small matter; romantic attachment. -*pl.* matters in general; public business. [F. *affaire*, fr. *faire*, do]

affect' *v.t.* acton, influence; move the feelings of, make a show of, make pretense; assume. -**affecta'tion** *n.* show, pretense. -**affec'ted** *a.* making a pretense. **affec'tedly** *adv.* -**affec'ting** *a.* moving the feelings, pathetic. -**affec'tingly** *adv.* - **affec'tion** *n.* fondness, love. **affec'tionate** *a.* loving. -**affec'tionately** *adv.* [L. *affectare*, aim at, fr. *afficere*, apply oneself to]

affiliate *v.t.* adopt; attach, as a society to a federation, *etc.*; attribute to, father on. -**affilia'tion** *n.* [L. *affiliate*]

affinity *n.* relationship; structural resemblance; attraction, *esp.* chemical attraction. -**affin'itive** *a.* [L. *affinitas*]

affirm *v.t.* assert positively; maintain a statement. -*v.i.* make a solemn declaration, *esp.* without oath in a court of law. [L, *affirmare*, make firm]

affix' *v.t.* fasten to, attach. [L. *affigere*, *affix-*, fix to]

afflict' *v.t.* give pain or grief, vex. - **afflic'tion** *n.* distress, that which afflicts. -**afflic'tive** *a.* [L. *affligere*]

af'fluent *a.* wealthy. -*n.* tributary stream. -**af'fluence** *n.* wealth, abundance. [L. *affluere*, flow towards]

afford' *v.t.* be able to buy, or. to sustain the expense of-, **produce,** yield. [earlier *aforth*, OE. *geforthian*, fr. *forth*, forward]

affront' *v.t.* insult openly; meet face to face. -*n.* insult; contemptuous treatment. [F. *affronter*, confront]

aft *adv.* towards or near the stern of a ship. [OE. *æftan*]

af'ter *adv.* behind; later. -*prep.* like or in imitation of-, behind; later than. *a.* behind; later; nearer to the stem of a ship. [OE. *æfter*, farther away]

af'ter- as prefix makes compounds, as **afterbirth** *n.* membrane expelled after a birth. -**af'terclap** *n.* brief, dramatic recrudescence of an affair apparently closed. -**aftercrop** *n.* -**afterdamp** *n.* gas left after an explosion in a coalmine. - **af'termath** *n.* second mowing of grass; sequel, later or secondary results. **af'ternoon** *n.* -**af'terthought** *n.* **af'terwards, af'terward** *adv.* later. [OE. *Eeftanweard*]

again' *adv.* once more; back, in return; besides. [OE. *ongean*]

against' *prep.* opposite; in opposition to; in contact with; in exchange for. [*again*, with *gen.* -*es*, and -*t* added]

age *n.* length of time a person or thing has existed; period of time; period of history; maturity; a long time. -*v.t.* make old. *v.i.* grow old.[OF. *edage*, fr. L. *a!tas*, age]

agen'da *n.* things to be done; program of a business meeting. [L.]

a'gent *n.* person or thing producing an effect; cause; natural force; person authorised to carry on business or affairs for another. -**a'gency** *n.* instrumentality; business or place of business of an agent. [L. *agere*, do]

aggravate *v.t.* make worse; [colloq.] annoy. [L. *aggravate*, make heavy]

aggregate *v.t.* gather into a mass. -*n.* sum total. -**aggrega'tion** *n.* -**ag'gregative** *a.* [L. *aggregate*, form into a rock]

aggres'sion *n.* unprovoked attack. **aggress'** *v.i.* -**aggress'ive** *a.* quarrelsome. [L. *aggredi, aggress-*, advance towards]

aghast *a.* terrified; horror-stricken. [earlier *agast*, fr. OE. *æmstan*, terrify]

ag'ile (-j-) *a.* active, nimble. [F. , fr. L. *agere*, do]

ag'itate (-j-) *v.t.* keep in motion; disturb,

excite; keep in discussion. **-agita'tion** *n.*
-ag'itator *n.* [L. *agitare*]

agnos'tic *n.* one who holds that we know
nothing of things outside the material
world. **-agnos'ticism** *n.* [G. *a*, not, *gnostos*,
knowing]

ago' *adv.* gone; since; past. [earlier *agone*,
p. p. of OE. *agan*, pass]

ag'ony *n.* extreme suffering; violent
struggle; death struggle. **-ag'onize** *v.i.* suffer great pain or sorrow. **-ag'onizing** *a.* [G.
agonia, struggle for victory]

agorapho'bia *n.* morbid fear of crossing
open spaces. [G. agora, market-place,
phobos, fear]

agree' *v.i.* be of one mind; consent; harmonize; determine, settle; suit. [F. *agréer*,
fr. L. *gratus*, pleasing]

ag'riculture *n.* art or practise of cultivating the ground. [L. *agricultural*, tillage of
the field]

ahead' *adv.* in front of. [*a* and *head*]

aid *v.t.* help. **-n.** help, support; something
helpful. [F. *aider* -L. *adjutare*]

AIDS *n.* acronym for acquired immune
(or immuno-) deficiency syndrome.

ail *v.t.* trouble, afflict. **-v.i.** be ill. **-ail'ing**
a. **-ail'ment** *n.* [OE. *eglan*]

aim *v.t.* and *i*. direct effort towards; try to;
give direction to a weapon; strike or throw.
-n. direction; endeavor; purpose. **-aim'less**
a. without object. [OF. *esmer*, estimate]

air *n.* mixture of gases we breathe, the atmosphere; breeze; tune; manner; affected
manner. **-pl.** affected manners. *v.t.* expose;
dry or warm. [G. *aer*, fr. *aein*, blow]

air- used as a prefix makes compounds
denoting things in, of, or having to do with
the air, as **air'balloon** *n.* including broadcasting by radiowaves, as **air'time.** **-air'**
base *n.* **-air' brake** *n.* **air' chamber** *n.*
-air'-condition *v.t.* fit with system to keep
the interior air at requisite temperature *etc.*
-aircraft *n.* **-air'craft carrier** *n.* **-air'crew**
n. **air'duct** *n.* **-air' force** *n.* national organization dealing with military aircraft.
-airgun *n.* gun discharged by force of compressed air. **-air' hole** *n.* **-air' lane** *n.*
aircraft route. **-air' lift** *n.* organized air
transport operation. **-air'line** *n.* organization dealing with transport by airplanes.
-air'man *n.* **-air'plane** *n.* heavier-than-air
flying machine. **-air'port** *n.* station for
passenger aircraft. **air' power** *n.* **-air'tight**
a. not allowing the passage of air. **-air'**
valve *n.* **-air'way** *n.* regular aircraft route.
air'worthy *a.* fit for service in the air.
airwor'thiness *n.*

aisle *n.* wing of a church, or lateral

division of any part of a church; walk between seats in a church. [bad spelling of F.
aile-fr. L. *ala*, wing]

ajar' *adv.* partly open. [ME. *on char*, on
the turn]

alarm' *n.* notice of danger; sudden fright;
call to arms. **-v.t.** warn of danger; frighten.
-alarm'ing *a.* **-alarm'ist** *n.* one given to
prophesying danger. **-alarm-clock'** *n.*
clock which rings a bell at a set hour to
give warning of the time. [OF. *à l'arme*, fr.
It. *all' arme*, to arms (cp. *alert*)]

al'bacore *n.* large kind of tuna fish. [Port.]

al'bum *n.* book of blank leaves, for collecting portraits, stamps, autographs *etc.*
[L. *albus*, white]

albu'men *n.* constituent of animal and
vegetable matter, found nearly pure in
white of egg. [L. , fr. *albus*, white]

al'cohol *n.* liquid made in fermenting
sugar *etc.* , and forming the intoxicating
part of fermented drinks. **-alcohol'ic** *a.*
alcohotiza'tion *n.* **-al'coholize** *v.t.* **-**
al'coholism *n.* a disease, alcohol poisoning. [Arab. *al koh'l*, fine powder used to
darken the eyelids]

alert' *a.* watchful; brisk. **-n.** sudden attack
or surprise; alarm signal. **alert'ness** *n.* [OF.
à l'érte, fr. It. *all'erta*, to the height (watch-
tower). cp. *alarm*]

al'gae *n. pl.* seaweed. **-al'gous** *a.* [L. *alga*]

al'gebra *n.* method of calculating, using
letters to represent the numbers and signs
to show relations between them, making a
kind of abstract arithmetic. **-algebra'ic,**
algebra'ical *a.* **-al'gebraist** *n.* [Arab. *al-
jebr*, joining of broken parts]

a'lias *adv.* otherwise. **-n.** assumed name. [L.]

al'ibi *n.* plea that a person charged with a
crime was somewhere else when it was
conuitted. [L. = other-where]

a'lien *a.* foreign; different in nature; adverse. **-n.** foreigner. [L. *alienus*, foreign]

alike' *a.* like, similar. [ME. *yliche*]

al'iment *n.* food. **-v.t.** feed, support.
aliment'ary *a.* **-alimenta'tion** *n.* [L.
alimentu-alere, nourish]

al'imony *n.* income allowed to a man or
woman legally separated from his or her
spouse. [L. *alimonia*, maintenance]

al'kali *n.* substance which combines with
acid and neutralizes it, forming a salt.
Potash, soda *etc.* are **alkalis. -al'kaline** *a.*
-alkalin'ity *n.* **-al'kalize** *v.t.* **-al'kaloid** *n.*
[Arab. *al-qali*, burnt ashes of certain
plants]

all (awl) *a.* the whole of, every one of. *adv.*
wholly, entirely. **-n.** the whole, everything.
[OE. *all, eall*]

allege' v.t. and i. plead, bring forward as an argument; assert. -**allega'tion** n. [L. allegare, quote]

alle'giance n. duty of a subject to his government or superior; loyalty. [See liege]

alleviate v.t. make light, ease, lessen. [Late L. alleviate, fr. levis, light]

allitera'tion n. beginning of two or more words in close succession with the same sound, as e.g. , Sing a song of Sixpence. [L. ad, to, and littera, letter]

al'locate v.t. place; assign as a share. -**allocation** n. apportionment [VL. allocare, fr. locus place]

allot' v.t. give out; distribute as shares. **allot'ment** n. -**allott'ee** n. [OF. aloter. See lot]

allow' v.t. acknowledge; permit; give, grant. -**allow'able** a. -**allow'ably** adv. -**allow'ance** n. [OF. allouer]

alloy' v.t. mix metals; debase. -n. mixture of two or more metals. [F. aloi, fr. L. alligare, bind]

allure' v.t. entice, win over; fascinate. [lure]

allu'vial a. deposited by rivers. [L. alluvius, washed against]

ally' v.t. join in relationship by treaty, marriage or friendship. -**allied** a. -**al'ly** n. confederate; state or sovereign bound to another by treaty. -pl. **ai'lies**. [F. allier]

almost (awl'-) adv. nearly, all but. [OE. eallmœst]

alms (amz) n. gifts to the poor. [OE. aelmesse, fr. G. eleemosyne, pity; almoner through OF. almosnier]

aloe n. genus of plants of medicinal value, found chiefly in S. Africa. -pl. bitter drug made from the plants; American plant of the amaryllis family [G.]

aloft' adv. on high; overhead; (naut.) at the masthead. [ON, a lopt, in the air]

alone' a. single, solitary. -adv. separately. [all one]

aloud' adv. with loud voice; audibly; not in a whisper. [loud]

al'phabet n. set of letters used in writing a language. -**alphabet'ic, alphabetical** a. in the order of the letters. -**alpha-bet'ically** adv. [G. alpha beta, A, B, the first two G. letters]

alread'y (awl-red'i) adv. before, previously. [all ready, prepared]

al'so (awl'-) adv. further, too; in addition; besides. [OE. eallswa]

al'tar (awl'-) n. raised place, stone, etc. on which sacrifice may be offered; in a Christian Church, table on which the priest consecrates the Eucharist. [L. altare]

al'ter (awl'-) v.t. change, make different. -v.i. become different. [F. altirer, fr. L. alter, other]

al'ternate v.t. cause to occur by turns. v.i. happen by turns. -**alter'nate** a. one after the other, by turns. -**alter'nately** adv. [L. alternate, fr. alter, other]

al'ternator n. generator of alternating current. [L. alter, other]

although' conj. notwithstanding that. [all though]

altim'eter n. instrument for measuring heights. [L. altos, high, and meter]

at'titude n. height. [L. altitudo]

al'to n. (mus.) male voice of highest pitch or female of the lowest; part written for it; contralto part. [It. , fr. L. altus, high]

al'truism n. principle of living and acting for the good of others. -**altruist'ic** a. -**altruist'ically** adv. [F. altruisme]

alum'nus n. graduate or pupil of a school or college. -pl. **alum'ni**. [L. alere, nourish]

al'ways (awl'-) adv. at all times; for ever. -also **always** [all and ways]

amass' v.t. collect in quantity. -**amass'able** a. [F. amasser]

am'ateur (-ur) n. one who carries on an art, study, game etc. for the love of it, not for money. -a. imperfect, like the work of an amateur; not professional. -**amateur'ish** a. -**amateur'ishly** adv. **am'ateurism** n. [F. fr. L. amator, lover]

amaze' v.t. surprise, greatly astound. [OE. amasian]

ambassador n. representative of the highest rank sent by one state to another. [F. ambassadeur]

am'bient a. surrounding, encompassing. -n. air, sky. [L. ambi, about, iens, ient-, going]

ambiguous a. of double meaning; doubtful. -**ambigu'ity** n. [L., fr. amb and agere, lit. , drive both ways]

am'bit n. circuit; space around; sphere of action. [L. ambitus, going round]

ambi'tion n. desire of power, fame, honor; object of that desire. [L. ambitio, going about for votes -ambire, go round]

ambivalence, ambiv'alency n. in one person, opposite emotional reactions to the same thing; -**ambiv'alent** a. [L. ambi, both, valere, be strong]

am'ble v.i. of a horse, move with both legs together one side, then the other; move at an easy pace. -n. this movement. **am'bler** n. [L. ambulate, walk]

am'bulance n. special carriage for the sick or wounded; movable hospital. [F.

earlier *hôpital ambulant*, fr. L. *ambulate*, walk]

am'bush *n.* a lying in wait. -*v.t.* waylay, attack from hiding. [OF. embusche, hiding in the woods]

ame'nable *a.* easy to be led or controlled. [F. *amener*, lead]

a'miable *a.* friendly, kindly. [F. *aimable*, lovable, fr. L. *amare*, love]

am'icable *a.* friendly. -**amicabil'ity** *n.* - **am'icably** *adv.* [Late L. *amicabilis*]

ammo'nia *n.* pungent alkaline gas. [fr. *sal ammoniac*, salt said to have been first obtained in a region named after the god (Jupiter) *Ammon*]

ammuni'tion *n.* cartridges, powder *etc.* for firearms; formerly, all military stores [F. *l'ammunition*, for *in munition*. *See* **munition**]

amne'sia *n.* loss of memory. [G.]

am'nesty *n.* general pardon. [G. *amnesia*, oblivion]

amoeb'a *n.* simplest microscopic animal, a unit mass which constantly changes its shape. [G. *amoibe*, change]

among' (-mu-), **amongst'** *prep.* mixed with, or the number of [OE. *on gemang*, fr. *gemang*, crowd]

am'orous *a.* easily moved to love; in love. [F. *amoreux*]

amount *v.i.* come to, be equal to. -*n.* sum total; result; quantity. [OF. *amonter*, mount up]

am'père *n.* unit of current of electricity, the amount one volt can send through one ohm. [fr. *Ampère*, F. physicist]

am'persand *n.* character &. [and per se, *'land'* by itself]

amphib'ious *a.* living both on land and in water. -**amphib'ian** *n.* (G. *amphi*, on both sides, *bios*, life]

am'ple *a.* big enough, full, spacious. - **am'plify** *v.t.* make bigger, louder *etc.* - **am'plitude** *n.* spaciousness. -**am'ply** *adv.* fully. [F.]

am'putate *v.t.* cut off (a limb *etc.*) am- putation *n.* [L. *amputate*].

amuse' *v.t.* divert; occupy pleasantly; ex- cite a sense of fun. [F. *amuser*, make to muse. *See* **muse**]

an *See* a.

anaero'bia *n. pl.* bacteria able to live without air. **anerob'ic** *a.* [G. *a.* without, *aer*, air, *bios*, life]

an'agram *n.* word or sentence made by arranging in different order the letters of another word or sentence. [G. *anagram- ma*]

analge'sic *n.* anodyne, pain-killer. **anal-**

ge'sia *n.* painlessness. [G. *an*, not, *algein*, feel pain]

anal'ogy *n.* agreement or likeness in cer- tain respects; correspondence. - **anal'ogous** *a.* having similarity or cor- respondence. -**anal'ogously** *adv.* (G. *analogia*]

anal'ysis *n.* separation or breaking up of anything into its elements or component parts. [G. , fr. *lyein*, loose]

an'archy *n.* lack of government in a state; lawlessness; confusion. **anarch'al** *a.* - **anarch'ically** *adv.* **an'archism** *n.* system of certain revolutionaries, aiming at a society with no government, in which each man should be a law to himself. -**an'arch**, **an'archist** *n.* [G. *anarchia*]

anat'omy *n.* dissection of a body; science of the structure of the body; detailed analysis or examination. [G. *ena*, up, *tem- nein*, cut]

an'cestor *n.* forefather. -**anees'tral** *a.* - **an'cestry** *n.* [L. *ante*, before, *cedere*, go]

anch'or (-k-) *n.* implement for chaining a ship to the bottom of the sea. -*v.t.* fasten by an anchor. -*v.i.* cast anchor. **anch'orage** *n.* suitable place for anchoring. [L. *ancoral*]

an'cient *a.* old; belonging to a former age; time-worn. -*n.* old man; one who lived in an earlier age (*esp.* in *pl*) **anciently** *adv.* [F. *ancien*]

an'cilary *a.* subordinate; subservient. [L. *ancilla*, maidservant]

and *conj.* in addition, used to join words and sentences, to introduce a consequence *etc.* [OE. *and, end*]

an'ecdote *n.* very short story, dealing with a single incident. -**anecdot'al** *a.* [G. = *unpublished*]

anem'ia *n.* lack of blood. -**anem'ic** *a.* [G. *an-*, not, *hainia*, blood]

anemom'eter *n.* instrument to measure the strength of wind, a wind-gauge. [G. *anemos*, wind, and meter]

anesthet'ic *a.* causing insensibility. -*n.* drug that does this. -**anesthe'sia** *n.* state of insensibility. -**anes'thetist** *n.* [G. *anais- thetos*, without feeling]

an'gel (anj-) *n.* divine messenger; mini- stering spirit; person with the qualities of such a spirit, as gentleness, purity *etc.* [G. *angelos*, messenger]

ang'er *n.* wrath, strong emotion including a sense of injury and a desire to retaliate. -*v.t.* rouse this emotion in. -**ang'rily** *adv.* **ang'ry** *a.* [ON. *angr*]

angi'na *n.* severe inflammation of the throat; quinsy. -**angi'na pec'toris**, heart disease marked by spasms of severe pain.

[L. , fr. *anguere*, strangle]

ang'le *v.t.* fish. -n. book. **ang'ler** *n.* **angling** *n.* [OE. *angel*]

ang'le *n.* corner; meeting of two lines. **ang'ular** a. **-angular'ity** *n.* [F. , fr. L. *angulus*, corner]

ang'uish (-ng-gw-) *n.* great pain, mental or bodily. [L. *anguere*, strangle]

an'imal *n.* being having life, feeling, power of voluntary motion; beast. -*a.* of or belonging to animals; sensual. **an'imalism** *n.* **-an'imally** adv. [L. *animale*, having breath of life]

an'imate *v.t.* to give life to; enliven; actuate. **-an'imated** *a.* **-anima'tion** *n.* [L. *animare*]

animos'ity *n.* hatred. enmity. **-an'imus** *n.* actuating spirit; enmity. [L. *animus*, spirit]

an'kle *n.* joint between the foot and the leg. **-ank'let** *n.* ornament or ring for the ankle. [OE. *ancleow*]

ankylosaus *n.* any plant-eating dinosaur of the Cretaceous period of the suborder *ankylosauria* which has short legs and armour of bony plates.

annex' *v.t.* add, attach; take possession of, *esp.* territory. **-annexa'tion** *n.* **an'nexe** *n.* something added; supplementary building. [F. *annexer*, fr. L. *nectere*, bind]

anni'hilate (-ni'-hi-) *v.t.* reduce to nothing, destroy. [Late L. *annihilate*, fr. *nihil*, nothing]

anniversary *a.* yearly. -*n.* day on which an event happened or is celebrated. [L. *annus*, year, *vertere*, turn]

an'notate *v.t.* make notes upon. [earlier *annote*; F. *annoter*. See **note**]

announce' *v.t.* make known, proclaim. **-announce'ment** *n.* [F. *annoncer*, fr. L. *nuntius*, messenger]

annoy' *v.t.* trouble, vex; tease. **annoy'ance** *n.* [OF. *enoier*, fr. L. *in odio*, in hatred]

ann'ual *a.* yearly. -*n.* plant which lives only a year; book published every year. **-annualize** *v.t.* to calculate for a shorter period as though on the basis of a full year. **-ann'ually** adv. [Late L. *annualis*, fr. *annus*, year]

annul' *v.t.* reduce to nothing, abolish. [L. *annulare*, reduce to naught, *nullum*]

an'nular *a.* ring-shaped. [L. *annularis*, fr. *annulus*, ring]

an'ode *n.* (*elec.*) positive pole, or point of entry of a current. opposite to **cathode**. [G. *anodos*, way up]

anoint' *v.t.* smear with oil or ointment; consecrate with oil. [OF. *enoindre* -L. *ungere*]

anon'ymous *a.* nameless, *esp.* without an author's name. [G. *anonymos*]

anorex'ia, anorex'y *n.* loss of appetite. [G. *an*, not, *orexis*, longing]

anoth'er *pron.* one other, a different one. [for another]

anoxemia *n.* deficiency or reduction of oxygen in the blood.

an'swer *v.t.* reply to; pay, meet; satisfy; suit. -*v.i.* reply, prove suitable; *n.* reply; solution; acknowledgment. **-an'swerable** *a.* that can be answered; accountable. **-an'swerer** *n.* [OE. *andswarian*, swear back]

ant *n.* small social insect, proverbial for industry, the emmet. **-ant'eater** *n.* S. American animal which feeds on ants by means of a long sticky tongue. **-ant'hill** *n.* mound raised by ants in building their home [OE. *aemette*]

ant- *prefix* for anti- before a vowel, as **antacids antal'akli**. *See* words in **anti-**. **antagonist** *n.* opponent. **-antag'onize** *v.t.* **-antag'onism** *n.* **-antagonis'tic** *a.* hostile. **-antagonis'tically** adv. [G. *agonizesthai*, contend]

antarctic *a.* of the south polar regions. -*n.* these regions [G. *anti-* and *arctic*]

ante- *prefix* before [L. *ante*] found in compound words, as **antechamber** *n.* room leading to a chief apartment. **-antedate'** *v.t.* date before the true time; assign to an earlier date; anticipate. **-antemerid'ian** (*abbrev.* **a.m.**) *a.* before noon; between midnight and noon etc.

antece'dent *a.* going before. -*n.* (*gram.*) noun *etc.* to which a relative pronoun refers. -*n. pl.* one's past history, record. [L. *antecedere*, go before]

antenn'a *n.* (*pl.* **antenn'ae**) insect's feeler; (*radio*) elevated conducting wire, an aerial. [L. = *sail-yard*]

an'ther *n.* top of the pollen-bearing stamen in a flower. (G. *anthos*, flower)

anthol'ogy *n.* collection of choice poems, literary extracts *etc.* **-anthol'ogist** *n.* maker of such. [G. *anthologia*, gathering of flowers]

an'thrax *n.* infectious disease of sheep and cattle, which can be transmitted to man. [G. = *carbuncle*]

an'thropoid *a.* like man (of certain apes). [G. *anthropos*, man]

anthropol'ogy *n.* scientific study of the human race. **-anthropolog'ical** *a.* **anthropol'ogist** *n.* [G. *anthropos*, *logos*, word]

anthropomorph'ism *n.* ascription of human form and qualities to the Deity. [G.

anthropos, man, *morphe*, form]

anti- *prefix* against; ant- before a vowel.
[G. *anti*] Makes compounds as **anti-
air'craft** *a*. **-anticath'olic** *a*. **An'tichrist**
n. **-anticli'max** *n* **-an'tidote** *n*. counter-
poison. **-antinuclear** *a*. opposed to nuclear
weapons. **-antisep'tic** a. and *n*.
antispasmod'ic a. and *n*. **-antitox'in** *n*.
(see word without prefix]

an'tibody *n*. protective substance forming in the blood in response to the presence
of toxins *etc*. [*body*]

an'tic *a*. odd, grotesque. **-n**. grotesque figure or movement, an odd trick. [It. *antico*
-L. *antiquus*, ancient]

antici'pate *v.t.* be beforehand; take or
consider before the due time; foresee;
enjoy in advance; expect. **-anticipa'tion**
n. **-anti'cipative, anticipatory** *a*. [L. *an-
ticipare*, take beforehand]

antiox'idant *n*. substance that inhibits or
slows oxidation and therefore checking
the deterioration it causes to tissue. **-an-
tioxidant.** *a*.

antip'athy *n*. dislike. **-antipathetic** *a*.
[G. *antipatheia*, fr. *pathos*, feeling]

antique' *a*. ancient; old-fashioned **-n**. relic
of former times. [F. , fr. L. *ante*, before]

anti-Semitism *n*. hostility or prejudice
against the Jews. **-an'ti-Sem'itic** *a*.
an'ti-Sem'ite *n*. [*See* Semitic]

antitox'in *n*. substance formed in the
body to counteract a disease or poison; appropriate serum injected into the
bloodstream for the prevention of certain
diseases. (G. *anti-, toxicon*, poison]

ant'ler *n*. deer's horn; branch of that horn.
-ant'lered *a*. [VL. *ante ocularis ramus*
branch before the eye]

an'tonym *n*. word of which the meaning
is the opposite of another. [G. *anti*, against,
and onyma, name]

anx'ious *a*. troubled, uneasy, *esp*. about
something doubtful or in the future. -
anxi'ety *n*. anxiously *adv*. [L. *anxius*, fr.
angere, compress]

an'y *a*. and *pron*. one indefinitely; some.
-an'ybody *n*. **-an'yhow** *adv*. **an'ything** *n*.
-an'yway *adv*. **-an'ywhere** *adv*. [OE.
aenig, fr. *an*, one]

aort'a *n*. great artery which rises from the
left ventricle of the heart and sends its
branches all through the body. **-aort'al** *a*.
[G. *aorte*, what is hung up]

apart' *adv*. separately; aside. [F. *à part*]

apart'heid (a-part-had) *n*. idea of
segregation of races. (*Afrikaans*]

ap'athy *n*. want of feeling; indifference.
[G. *apatheia*]

ape *n*. monkey; monkey with no tail; imitator. **-v.t**. imitate. [OE. *apa*]

ap'erture *n*. opening. [L. *aperture*]

a'pex *n*. (*pl*. **a'pexes, a'pices**] top or peak
of anything. [L. = *summit*]

aphorism *n*. maxim, pithy saying. [G.
aphorismos, definition]

aphrodisiac *a*. exciting to sexual intercourse. [G. *Aphrodite*, goddess of love]

a'piary *n*. place where bees are kept. [L.
apiarium, fr. *apis*, bee]

apiece' *adv*. for each. [orig. two words]

aplenty *a*., *adv*. abundant, enough; in
supply.

apoc'rypha *n*. religious writing of doubtful authenticity. [L. fr. G. *apokryphos*, hidden away]

ap'ogee *n*. point of the sun's or moon's
orbit farthest from the earth; the highest
point. [F. , fr. G. *apo*, off, *ge*, earth]

apol'ogy *n*. something spoken in defense;
acknowledgment of an offence and expression of regret; poor substitute (with for).
[G. *apologia*, speaking away]

ap'oplexy *n*. sudden stroke, causing loss
of sensation and motion, usually through
haemorrhage in the brain. **-apoplec'tic** *a*.
[G. *apoplexia*, disablement]

apos'trophe (-e-fi) *n*. a turning away
from the subject of a speech to address
some person present or absent; mark (')
showing the omission of a letter or letters
in a word. **-apos'trophize** *v.t.* [G. , fr.
strephein, turn]

appara'tus *n*. equipment, instruments,
for performing any experiment or operation. [L. fr. *apparare*, make ready]

appa'rent *a*. seeming; obvious.
appa'rently *adv*. [L. *apparere*, appear]

appari'tion (-i'-shun) *n*. appearance, *esp*.
of a ghost or other remarkable thing. [L.
appar-ere, appear]

appeal' *v.i.* call upon, make earnest request; refer to, have recourse to; refer to a
higher court. **-n**. request, reference, supplication. **-appell'ant** *n*. one who appeals
to a higher court. **-appell'ate** *a*. [F. *ap-
peler*]

appear' *v.i.* become visible; come before;
see, be plain. **-appear'ance** *n*. (OF. *apareir*
-L. *apparere*]

appease' *v.t.* pacify, quiet, allay. [OF. *a
pais*, at peace]

append' *v.t.* join on, add. [L. *appendere*,
hang on]

ap'petite *n*. desire, inclination, *esp*.
desire for food. **-ap'petize** *v.t.* **-appeti'zer**
n. **-appeti'zing** a. **-appeti'zingly** *adv*. [F.
apetit, fr. L. *petere*, seek]

applaud' *v.t.* praise by handclapping; praise loudly. -applaud'er *n.* applauding *a.* -applaud'ingly *adv.* -applause' *n.* [L. *applaudere*, clap]

applied' *a.* used for a practical or utilitarian purpose, as applied art, sci'ence. [*apply*]

apply' *v.t.* lay or place on; administer; bring into operation; devote, employ. -appli'ance *n.* -applicabil'ity *n.* -applicable *a.* -ap'plicably *adv.* -applicant *n.* -applica'tion *n.* [L. *applicare,* bend to]

appoint' *v.t.* fix, settle; name to an office; equip. -appoint'ment *n.* -*n. pl.* equipment. (F. , fr. *à point,* fitly]

appor'tion *v.t.* divide out in shares. [*See* portion]

appraise' *v.t.* set a price on, value. [F. *approcier,* fr. L. *pretium,* price]

appre'ciate (-shi-) *v.t.* estimate justly; be sensible of good qualities in the thing judged. -*v.i.* rise in price. [Late L. *appretiare,* fr. pretium, price]

apprehend' *v.t.* take hold of, seize by authority; recognize, understand; fear. [L. apprehendere, take hold of]

approach' *v.i.* draw near; come near in quality, condition *etc.* -*v.t.* come near to; *n.* a drawing near; means of reaching; approximation. [F. *approcher,* fr. L. *proprius,* nearer]

approba'tion *n.* sanction, approval. [L. *approbate,* test, try]

appro'priate *v.t.* take to oneself -*a.* suitable, fitting. [Late L. *appropriate,* fr. *proprius,* own]

approve' *v.t.* think well of, commend. [F. *approuver*]

approx'imate *a.* nearly resembling; nearing correctness. -*v.t.* bring close. *v.i.* come near. -approx'imately *adv.* -approxima'tion *n.* -approx'imative *a.* [L. *proximus,* nearest]

A'pril *n.* fourth month of the year. [L. *aprilis*]

apropos' *adv.* to the purpose; appropriately; in reference (to). [F. *à propos*]

apse *n.* arched recess at the end of a church. -ap'sidal *a.* [earlier *apsis*, G. *felloe* of a wheel]

apt *a.* suitable; prompt, quick-witted, likely. -apt'itude *n.* -apt'ly *adv.* -apt'ness *n.* [L. *aptus,* fr. *apere,* fasten]

aqua'rium *n.* (*pl.* aqua'riums, aqua'ria) tank or pond for keeping water animals or plants, usually in a natural setting. [L. *aqua,* water]

Aqua'rius *n.* the Water-bearer, 11th sign of the zodiac, which sun enters on 21st January. [constellation *Aquarius* -L. *aqua,* water]

aquat'ic *a.* living or growing in water, or having to do with water. [L. *aqua,* water]

aq'ueduct *n.* artificial channel for water. [L. *aquae ductus,* water conduit]

arach'nida (-k-) *n.* class including spiders, scorpions, mites. -arach'nid *n.* one of these. [G. *arachns,* spider]

ar'biter *n.* judge; umpire. -ar'bitrary *a.* not bound by rules; despotic. -ar'bitrate *v.i.* act as arbiter, , decide a dispute. [L. = *judge*]

ar'bor *n.* garden seat enclosed by branches, plants; shaded walk. [earlier *erber,* fr. OF. *herbier,* herb-garden]

arc *n.* part of a circle or other curve. [L. *arcus,* bow]

arc *n.* luminous electrical discharge between two terminals. -arc'-lamp *n.* arc'-light *n.* lamp that produces high-intensity light by the jumping of electric current in an arc between electrodes *usu.* made of carbon or metal. [L. *arcus,* bow]

arch *n.* curved structure in building, supporting itself over an open space by mutual pressure of the stones. -*v.t.* give, or make into, an arch. -arched' *a.* arch'way *n.* [L. *arcus,* bow]

arch *a.* chief; roguish, sly. -arch'ly *adv.* -arch'ness *n.* -arch-*prefix* chief. [G. *archos,* chief. Meaning of 'roguish' arose from arch-rogue]

archaeol'ogy (-k-) *n.* study of ancient times from remains of art, implements *etc.* -archaeolog'ical *a.* -archaeol'ogist *n.* [G. *archaiologia*]

archa'ic (-k-) *a.* old, primitive. [G. *archaios,* old]

archan'gel (-k-) *n.* angel of the highest order. [*angel*]

arch'er *n.* one who shoots with a bow. arch'ery *n.* [L. *arcus,* bow]

arch'etype (-ki-) *n.* original pattern or model. -arch'etypal *a.* [G. *typos,* model]

archipel'ago *n.* sea full of small islands; group of islands. [G. *archi-,* chief, *pelagos,* sea. The Greek chief sea was the Aegean]

arch'itect (-k-) *n.* master-builder, one who designs buildings; any maker or contriver. [G. *architekton,* chief builder]

archives (-kivz) *n.* place where government records are kept. -*pl.* public records. [G. *archeion,* public office]

arc'tic *a.* of northern polar regions; extremely cold. [G. *arktikos,* fr. *arktos,* bear, constellation of the Great Bear]

ar'dent *a.* fiery; passionate. [L. *ardere,* burn]

ard'uous a. laborious, hard to accomplish. [L. *arduus*, steep]

a'rea n. open space; superficial contents of a figure: extent, scope. [L. open space]

are'na n. space in the middle of an amphitheater; place of public contest; place of action; battlefield. [L. = *sand*]

ar'gon n. inert gas forming part of the air. [G. *argos*, idle]

ar'got n. slang. [F.]

ar'gue v.i. prove; offer reasons; dispute. v.t. prove by reasoning; discuss. [L- *arguere*, prove]

ar'id a. parched, dry; empty, uninteresting. **-arid'ity** n. [L. *aridus*]

A'ries a. the Ram, 1st sign of the zodiac, which sun enters on c. 21st March [L.]

aristoc'racy n. government by the best in birth or fortune. [G. *aristos*, best, *kratos*, power]

arith'metic n. science of numbers; art of reckoning by figures. **-arithmet'ical** a. **arithmet'ically** adv. **-arithmeti'cian** n. [G. *arithrnetike* -*arithmos*, number]

ark n. box, chest; Noah's vessel; place of refuge. [OE. *earc*, L. *arca*, coffer]

arm n. limb extending from shoulder to wrist; anything projecting from the main body, as a branch of the sea, the supporting rail of a chair etc. -v.t. give an arm to. -compounds as **arm'chair** n. **arm'ful** n. **arm'hole** n. **-arm'let** n. band worn on arm. -etc. [OE. *earm*]

arm n. weapon; branch of the army. -pl. weapons; war: the military profession. v.t. supply with weapons. -v.i. take up arms. **-arm'ament** n. **-armed'** a. [L. *arma*, neut. P.]

arm'istice n. truce, suspension of fighting. [F., fr. Mod. L. *armistitium*]

arm'or n. defensive covering or dress; plating of warships. [L. *armare*, arm]

arm'y n. large body of men armed for warfare and under military command; host; great number. [F. *armée*, p. p. of *armer*, fr. L. *armare*, arm]

aro'ma n. sweet smell; peculiar charm. [G. = *spice*]

around' adv. on every side; in a circle. prep. on all sides of. [*round*]

arouse' v.t. awaken. [*rouse*]

arraign' v.t. accuse, indict, put on trial; call to account. [OF. *arainer*; Low L. *arrationare*, reason]

arrange' v.t. set in order; settle, adjust; plan. -v.i. make agreement. **-arrange'ment** n. [F. *arranger*, fr. *rang*, rank]

array' v.t. set in order; dress; equip. adorn. [OF. *aréer*]

arrest' v.t. stop; catch the attention; apprehend by legal authority. -n. seizure by warrant; making prisoner. **-arrest'ment** n. detention of a person arrested pending bail etc. [OF. *arester*]

arrive' v.i. reach a destination; (with *at*) attain an object, achieve success. **arri'val** n. [F. *arriver*]

ar'row n. pointed weapon to be shot with a bow. **-ar'rowy** a. **-ar'row-head** n. metal part of an arrow. [OE. *arwe*]

ar'son n. crime of intentionally setting on fire houses, ships or other property. [OF., fr. L. *ardere*, bum]

art n. skill; human skill as opposed to nature; skill applied to music, painting, poetry etc.; any one of the subjects of this skill; system of rules; profession or craft; contrivance, cunning, trick; -pl. certain branches of learning, languages, history etc. , as distinct from natural science. **art'ful** a. cunning, clever. **-art'fully, -art'fulness** n. **-art'ist** n. one who practises a fine art, esp. painting; one who makes his craft a fine art. **-artis'tically** adv. **-art'istry** n. **-art'less** a. simple, unaffected. **-art'lessly** adv. **-art'less-ness** n. [F. , fr. L. *ars*, fr. a root meaning 'fit together']

arterio'sclero'sis n. hardening of the arteries. [G. *arterial* artery, *skleros*, hard]

ar'tery n. tube carrying blood from the heart; any main channel of communications. **-arte'trial** a. [G. *arterial*]

arteriogram n. x-ray of an artery that has been injected with dye; **-arteriograph**.

arthri'tis n. inflammation of a joint, gout. [G. *arthron*, joint]

art'icle n. clause, head, paragraph, section; literary composition in a journal etc.; rule or condition; commodity or object. -v.t. bind as an apprentice. [L. *artus*, joint]

artic'ulate v.t. joint; utter distinctly; form into words or syllables. -v.i. speak. a. jointed; (of speech) clear, distinct. [L. *articulate*, joint]

artificial (-sh-) a. synthetic; made by art, not natural; affected; feigned.

artill'ery n. cannon; troops who use them. [OF. *artillerie*—*artiller*, arm]

as adv. conj. in that degree, so far, since, because, when, while, in like manner. [worn-down form of *also*]

ascend' v.i. climb, mount up; rise; go back in time. -v.t. walk, climb, mount up. **ascend'ancy** n. control, domination. **ascend'ant** a. rising; above the horizon. -n. superiority. **-aseen'sion** n. **-ascent'** n. rise. [L. *ascendere*, climb up]

ascertain' v.t. and i. get to know, find out.

-ascertain'able *a.* **-ascertain'ment** *n.* [earlier *acertaine*, OF. *acertener*]

ASCII computer code standardized to allow transmission of data between various hardware and software. [*American Standard Code for Information Interchange.*]

ascor'bic ac'id *n.* chemical substance identified with vitamin C. [G. *a-*, and *scorbutic*]

ash *n.* familiar timber tree; its tough, white wood. **-ash'en** *a.* **-mount'ain ash**, rowan. [OE. *Tsc*]

ashamed' *a.* affected with shame. [*See* **shame**]

aside' *adv.* to, or on, one side; privately; apart. *-n.* words spoken in an under-tone not to be heard by someone present. [on side]

ask *v. t.* request, require, question, invite. *-v.i.* make enquiry; make request. [OE. *ascian* or *acsian*]

asleep' *a.* and *adv.* sleeping; at rest. [earlier on sleep]

asp *n.* small venomous snake, vipera aspis of S. Europe. [G. *aspis*]

as'pect *n.* look, view, appearance. [L. *aspecere*, look at]

asphyx'ia *n.* suffocation. [G. *asphygia*, pulse stoppage]

as'pirin *n.* drug used to relieve theumatic and neuralgic pains. [Trademark]

ass *n.* familiar quadruped of the horse family; stupid fellow. (OE. *assa*]

assas'sin *n.* one who kills by treacherous violence, usually for reward. **-assassinate** *v.t.* **-assassina'tion** *n.* [fr. Arab. *hash-shashin*]

assault' *n.* sudden attack; attack of any kind. *-v.t.* make an attack on. [F. *assaut*, VL. *adsaltus.*]

assem'ble *v.t.* bring together, collect; put together, as machinery. *-v.i.* meet together. [F. *assembler*-Late L. *assimulare*, bring together]

assembler language *n.* computer coding system meant to resemble natural language, uses symbols and numerals as equivalents of machine language.

assent' *v.i.* concur, agree. *-n.* acquiescence, agreement. [F. *assentir*]

assert' *v.t.* declare strongly, insist upon. **-asser'tion** *n.* **-asser'tive** *a.* **-asser'tively** *adv.* [L. asserere, claim]

assess' *v.t.* fix the amount (of a tax or fine); tax or fine; fix the value, estimate, *esp.* for taxation. [fr. L. *assidere*, assess-, sit by as judge]

as'sets *n. pl.* property available to pay

debts, *esp.* of an insolvent debtor. *-n. sing.* item of such property; thing of value. [F. *assez*, enough]

assign' (in') *v.t.* allot, apportion, fix; transfer; ascribe. **-assign'able** *a.* **asignation** *n.* appointment to meet, tryst. [L. *assignare*, allot by sign, *signum*]

assist' *v.t.* help, support. *-v.i.* be present. **-assis'tance** *n.* help, relief

asso'ciate *v.t.* join with, unite. *-v.i.* combine, unite. *-n.* companion, partner, ally, friend. *-a.* joined, connected. [L. *associare*, fr. *socius*, companion]

assume' *v.t.* take for granted; put on; claim, arrogate; pretend. *-v.i.* be arrogant. **-assump'tion** *n.* supposition; arrogance. [L. *assumere*, take to oneself]

assure' *v.t.* make safe; insure; tell positively; give confidence. [F. *assurer*, make sure, fr. L. *securus*]

as'terisk *n.* star (*) used in printing. [G. *asterikos*, little star]

as'teroid *n.* small planet. [G. *aster*, star, *eidos*, form]

astigmatism *n.* defect of the eye in which the rays are not brought to a proper focus at one point. **-astigmat'ic** *a.* (G. *a-*, not, *stigma*, point]

astonish, astound' *v.t.* amaze, surprise greatly. **-aston'ishing** *a.* **astonishment** *n.* [OF. *estoner*, VL. *extonere*, thunderstrike; ME, *astoun*, later *astound*; fr. p. p. *astoned* came a new verb *astony*, later *astonish*. See **stun**]

as'tral *a.* of the stars, starry; belonging to the spirit-world. [L. *astralis*]

astrology *n.* science (formerly synonymous with astronomy) pert. to the influence of the stars on human and terrestrial affairs. [G. *astrologia*, knowing of the stars (*aster*, star)]

astron'omy *n.* science or study of the heavenly bodies. [G. *astron*, star, *nomos*, law]

astute' *a.* crafty, cunning; shrewd, acute. **-astute'ly** *adv.* **-astute'ness** *n.* [L. *astutus*, fr. *astus*, crafty]

asy'lum *n.* refuge, sanctuary; home for the care of the unfortunate. *esp.* lunatics; formerly a refuge for criminals. [fr. G. *a-*, not, *syle*, right of seizure]

at *prep.* near to, by, in; engaged on; in the direction of [OE. *æt*]

a'theism *n.* disbelief in the existence of God. [fr. G. *a-*, not, *theos*, God]

ath'lete *n.* one trained to physical exercises, feats or contests of strength. [G. *athletes*, fr. *athlos*, contest]

Atlan'tic *n.* the ocean between Europe,

Africa and the American Continent; belonging to Atlas (*myth*). [fr. Mount Atlas in N. W. Africa]

at'las *n*. book of maps. [G. *Atlas*, a Titan who bore the world on his shoulders and whose image appeared on the title-page of old map books]

ATM *n*. automatic or automated teller machine operated by customers with magnetized cards to make financial transactions.

atmosphere *n*. mass of gas surrounding a heavenly body, *esp*. the earth. atmospher'ic *a*. -atmospher'ically *adv*. -atmospher'ics *n*. pl. noises in wireless reception due to electrical disturbances from the atmosphere. [G. *atmos*, vapor, *sphaira*, sphere]

at'oll *n*. ring-shaped coral island enclosing a lagoon. [Maldive word]

at'om *n*. smallest particle of matter which enters into chemical combination; any very small particle. -atom'ic *a*. at'om bomb', bomb in which the explosion is caused by atomic energy. atom'ic en'ergy, energy derived from a sustained neutron chain reaction resulting from nuclear fission of the atom. [G. *atomos*, fr. a-, not, *temnein*, cut]

at'rophy *n*. wasting away in a living body with lessening of size and strength, emaciation. -v.i. waste away, become useless. -at'rophied *a*. [G. a-, not, *trephein*, nourish]

attach' *v.t*. fasten, seize, connect, join to. -v.i. adhere. [F. *attacher*, It. *attaccare*. See attack]

attack' *v.t*. fall upon violently; assault, assail; affect (of a disease). -n. assault; seizure. [F. *attaquer*, It. *attaccare*, join; F. and E. sense is fr. *attaccare battaglia*, join battle]

attain' *v.t*. arrive at, reach, gain by effort. [F. *atteindre*]

attempt' *v.t*. try, endeavor, make an effort or attack on. -n. trial, effort. [L. *attentare*, try]

attest' *v.t*. bear witness to, certify. attesta'tion *n*. [L. *attestari*, bear witness]

at'titude *n*. posture, position; behavior, relation of persons expressing thought, feeling *etc*. [L. *aptitudo*, fr. *aptus*, fit]

attorn'ey (-tur'-) *n*. one legally authorized to act for another; a qualified practicioner of law, lawyer. [OF. *atorner* -Low L. *atornare*, appointl]

attract' *v.t*. draw towards, literally or figuratively; entice; cause to approach; charm, fascinate. -attrac'tion *n*. attrac-

tive *a*. -attrac'tively *adv*. - attractiveness *n*. [L. *attrahere*]

attribute *v.t*. ascribe, assign, refer to. [L. *attribuere-tribuere*, pay tribute

ATV *n*. pl. ATVs all-terrain vehicle; a vehicle with special wheels or tires for traversing rough terrain.

auc'tion *n*. public sale in which the bidder offers increase of price over another, and what is sold goes to the highest bidder. [L. *augere*, increase]

aud'ience *n*. act of hearing; judicial hearing; formal interview; assembly of hearers. [F. , fr. L. *audire*, hear]

audiocassette *n*. tape enclosed in a case, used to record and play back sound; a sound tape recording. audiotape.

aud'it *n*. formal examination of accounts; periodical settlement. -v.t. examine (accounts). -aud'itor *n*. [L. *auditus audire*, hear]

audition *n*. sense of hearing; hearing, *esp*. test hearing of a performer.

aud'itory *a*. [L. *audire*, hear]

au'ger *n*. carpenter's tool for boring holes. [an *auger* was ME. a *nauger* OE. *nafugar*. cp. adder]

august' *a*. majestic, dignified. -Aug'ust *n*. eighth month of the year. [L. *augustus*, venerable; Augustus Caesar, 31 B. C. -14 A. D.]

aunt (ant) *n*. father's or mother's sister; uncle's wife. [OF. *ante*, fr. L. *amita*, paternal aunt]

aur'al *a*. of the ear. -aur'ally *adv*. [L. *auris*, ear]

authentic *a*. trustworthy, real, genuine, true. [G. *authentikos*, first-hand, fr. *authentes*, one who does things for himself]

auth'or *n*. originator, constructor; writer of a book; an author's writings. auth'oress *n*. fem. -auth'orship *n*. [L. *auctor*, fr. *augere*, make grow]

author'ity *n*. legal power or right; delegated power; permission; book, person *etc*. settling a question, entitled to be believed; body or board in control, *esp*. in pl. -authoriza'tion *n*. -auth'orize *v.t*. author'itative *a*. -author'itatively *adv*. [L. *auctoritas*, fr. *auctor, v. s.]

autobiog'raphy *n*. biography or life of a person written by himself. [fr. G. *autos*, self, *bios*, life, *graphein*, write]

aut'omation *n*. the automatic control of successive production processes by electronic apparatus. [G. *autos*, self]

automo'bile *n*. a mechanical road vehicle *usu*. with four wheels and for passenger transportation. [G. *autos*, self, and mobile]

autop'sy *n.* personal inspection; postmortem examination. [G. *autopsia*, seeing for oneself -autos, self, *opsis*, sight]

aut'umn (-um) *n.* third season of the year, season of harvest; fall. **-autum'nal** *a.* - **autum'nary** *adv.* [L. *autumnus*]

avail' *v. i.* be of value, of use. -*v.t.* benefit, help. -*n.* benefit, as in *be of little avail, etc.* [F. *valoir*, be worth]

av'arice *n.* greediness of wealth. **avari'cious** *a.* **-avari'ciously** *adv.* [F.]

avenge' *v.t.* take vengeance on behalf of (a person) or on account of (a thing). [OF. *avengier*, fr. L. *vindicate.*]

av'enue *n.* approach; double row of trees, with or without a road; handsome street. [F. , fr. *avenir*, come to]

av'erage *n.* mean value or quantity of a number of values or quantities. -*a.* medium, ordinary. -*v.t.* fix or calculate a mean. *v.i.* exist in or form a mean. [orig. unknown]

avert' *v.t.* turn away, ward off. [L. *avertere*, turn from]

a'viary *n.* place for keeping birds. **a'viarist** *n.* [L. *aviarium*, fr. *avis*, bird]

avia'tion *n.* art of flying by mechanical means. **-a'viator** *n.* **-av'ion** *n.* French word for airplane. [F. , fr. L. *avis*, bird]

avoid' *v.t.* keep clear of, escape; (*law*) annul, invalidate. **-avoid'able** *a.* **avoidance** *n.* [OF. *esvuider*, empty out]

AWACS *n.* acronym for airborne warning and control system

await' *v.t.* wait or stay for; be in store for. [ONF. *awatier. See* **wait**]

awake', awa'ken *v.t.* rouse from sleep, stir. -v.i.cease from sleep; bestir oneself; become aware, not sleeping. [OE. *awæcnan*]

award' *v.t.* adjudge. -*n.* judgment of an arbiter, final decision. [fr. OF. *eswarder.*]

aware' *a.* informed, conscious. awareness *n.* [OE. *sewer*]

away' *adv.* absent, apart, at a distance. [OE. *onweg*, on the way]

awe *n.* dread mingled with reverence. - **aw'ful** *a.* inspiring awe; dreadful; very bad. [ON. *agi*, fear]

awhile' *adv.* for a time. [*See* **while**]

awk'ward *a.* clumsy, ungainly; difficult to deal with; embarrassed. **-awk'wardly** *adv.* **-awk'wardness** *n.* [orig. *adv.* , with suffix -*ward* on *old awk*, backhanded]

awl *n.* pointed tool for boring small holes, *esp.* in leather. [OE. *æl*]

awry' *adv.* crookedly, perversely. *a.*

crooked, distorted; wrong. [earlier *onwry. See* **wry**]

ax, axe *n.* tool with iron blade for hewing or chopping. [OE. *æx*]

ax'iom *n.* self-evident truth; received principle. **-axiomat'ic** *a.* [G. *axioma*, fr. *axioein*, take for granted]

ax'is *n.* straight line round which a body revolves; line or column about which parts are arranged; (politics) German-Italian (Nazi-Fascist) alliance in World War II. [L. = *pivot*]

ax'le *n.* rod on which a wheel turns. [ON. *äxul-tre*]

az'imuth *n.* arc between zenith and horizon; its angular distance from the meridian. [Arab. *as-sumut*, the way]

AZT *n.* azidothymidine, a drug used to treat the AIDS virus. [Trademark]

az'ure *a.* clear blue, sky-colored. -*n.* delicate blue; the sky. [orig. the *lapis lazuli*, fr. Arab. *azward*, Pers. *lajward*, Place in Turkestan, where it was procured]

B

bab'ble *v.i.* speak like a baby; talk idly. -*v.t.* utter idly. -*n.* chatter, idle talk. - **bab'bler** *n.* **-bab'bling, bab'ble ment** *n.* [imit. of infant speech]

ba'bel *n.* confusion of sounds; scene of confusion. [Tower of *Babel* (Gen. xi), understood as confusion, but prob. Assyr. *bab-ilu*, gate of the gods]

baboon' *n.* species of large monkey, with long face and dog-like tusks. [F. *babouin*]

ba'by *n.* infant child. **-babe** *n.* [earlier *baban.* imit. of baby speech]

bacil'lus *n.* (pl. **bacil'li**) microbe, minute organism causing disease. [Late L. , dim. of *baculus*, rod]

back *n.* hinder part.; situated behind. -*v.t.* support; make recede. -*v.i.* move away to the rear. -*v.* to the rear; to a former condition; in return. **-back'-ground** *n.* space at the back; space behind the chief figures of a picture *etc.* **-back-hand** *n.* stroke with the hand turned backward; writing that slopes to the left. **-back' talk** *n.* insolent rejoinder. **-back'-ward, back'wards** *adv.* to the rear; to the past; from a better to a worse state. *a.* lagging behindhand. [OE. *bæc*]

ba'con *n.* cured pig's flesh. [OE.]

bacte'rium *n.* microbe, disease-germ - **bact'ria** *pl.* **-bacte'rial** *a.* **-bacteri ol'ogist** *n.* **-bacteriol'ogy** *n.* study of bacteria. [G. *bakerion*, little staff]

bad *a.* not good; evil, wicked; faulty. **-bad'ly** *adv.* **-bad'ness** *n.* [ME. *badde*]

badge *n.* mark or sign. (ME. *bage*]

bag *n.* sack, pouch; measure of quantity. -*v.i.* swell out. -*v.t.* put in a bag; kill, seize, as game *etc.* -**bagg′y** *a.* loosely bulging. [ON. *baggi*]

bagg′age *n.* portable luggage of an army; any luggage; saucy or worthless woman. [F. *bagage*]

bail *n.* (law) security given for a person's reappearance in court; one giving such security. -*v.t.* release on security. [OF., fr. *bailler*, give]

bail *v.t.* empty out water from a boat. **bail′ out** *v.i.* drop from an airplane by parachute. -**bail′er** *n.* [obs. *bail*, bucket]

bait *n.* food put on a hook to entice fish; any lure or enticement; refreshment on a journey. -*v.t.* set a lure; feed and water; annoy, persecute. -*v.i.* take refreshment on a journey. [ON. *beita*, cause to bite]

bake *v.t.* cook or harden by dry heat, to cook in oven. -*v.i.* make bread; become scorched. -**ba′ker** *n.* -**ba′kery**. -**ba′ker′s doz′en**, thirteen. [OE. *bacan*]

bal′ance *n.* pair of scales; equilibrium; surplus; sum due on an account; difference of two sums. -*v.t.* weigh; bring to equilibrium; adjust. -*v.i.* have equal weight; be in equilibrium. -**bal′ance-sheet** *n.* list of assets and liabilities. [L. *bilanx- bis*, twice, and *lanx*, platter]

bald (bawld) *a.* hairless (featherless *etc*); plain, meager. [earlier *balled*, fr. Welsh *bal*, white on the brow]

ball (bawl) *n.* anything round; globe, sphere; bullet; game played with ball. [ON. *bollr*]

ball′ast *n.* heavy material put in a ship to give steadiness by added weight. -*v.t.* load thus. [obs. *last*, burden]

ball′et (-ā-) *n.* theatrical dance. [F.]

balloon′ *n.* early form of aircraft, raised by large gas-filled bag; inflated toy. -*v.i.* go up in a balloon; puff out. -**balloon′ist** *n.* [F. *ballon*]

ball′ot *n.* method of voting secretly by putting balls or tickets into a box. -*v.i.* vote by this method. -**ball′ot-box** *n.* [It. *ballotta*, dim. of *balla*, ball]

ban *n.* denunciation, curse; proclamation. -*v.t.* curse, forbid; outlaw. -**banns** *n. pl.* proclamation of marriage. [OE. *bannan*, summon, later curse]

bana′na (-an-) *n.* tall tropical or subtropical tree; its fruit. [Sp. or Port. fr. native Guinea name]

band *n.* strip used to bind; bond. -**ban′dage** *n.* strip of cloth used by surgeons for binding. [*bind*]

band *n.* company, troop; company of musicians. -*v.t.* and *i.* join into a band. [F. *bande*]

bang *n.* heavy blow; sudden loud noise, explosion. -*v.t.* beat, strike violently; slam; make a loud noise. [ON. *banga*, beat, of imit. orig.]

ban′ish *v.t.* condemn to exile; drive away. [F. *bannir*, proclaim outlaw. cp. *ban*]

bank *n.* mound or ridge of earth; margin of a river, lake *etc.*; rising ground in the sea. -*v.t.* and *i.* enclose with a ridge; pile up; of an airplane, tilt inwards in turning. [ME. *banker*]

bank *n.* establishment for keeping, lending, exchanging *etc.* money. -*v.t.* put in a bank. -*v.i.* keep or deal with a bank. -**bank′er** *n.* -**bank′ing** *n.* [fr. It. *banca*, orig. a money-changer's bench]

bank′rupt *n.* one who fails in business, cannot pay his debts. -*a.* insolvent. -**bank′ruptcy** *n.* insolvency. [earlier *bankrout*, fr. It. *banca rotta*, broken bank]

bann′er *n.* flag bearing a device; a country's flag. [F. *bannière*]

banq′uet (bang′-kwet) *n.* feast. -*v.i.* feast. -*v.t.* give a feast to -**banq′ueter** *n.* [F., dim. of *banc*, bench]

baptize′ (-iz′) *v.t.* immerse in or sprinkle with water ceremonially; christen. -**bap′tism** *n.* -**baptis′mal** (-iz′) *a.* **baptis′mally** *adv.* -**bap′tist** *n.* believer in baptism by immersion only. [G. *baptizein*, immerse]

bar *n.* rod of any substance; bank of sand at the mouth of a river; rail in a law-court; body of lawyers; counter where drinks are served; shop where alcoholic drinks are served and consumed. -*v.t.* make fast; obstruct; hinder, shut out (in); except. *prep.* except. -**bar′code′** *n.* a machine-readable arrangement of numbers and parallel line. [F. *barre*]

bar′barous *a.* savage, brutal, uncivilized. -**barba′rian** *n.* -**barbar′ic** *a.* [G. *barbaros*, foreign]

bar′ber *n.* one who shaves beards and cuts hair. [L. *barba*, beard]

bare *a.* uncovered; naked; poor, scanty. *v.t.* make bare. -**bare′ly** *adv.* -**bare′ness** *n.* -**bare′back** *a.* and *adv.* without a saddle.

bar′gain (-gin) *n.* contract or agreement; favourable purchase -*v.i.* make a bargain; chaffer. [OE. *bargagne*]

barge *n.* flat-bottomed freight boat; state or pleasure boat. [fr. L. *barca*, bark, boat]

bark *n.* rind of a tree. -*v.t.* strip the bark from; rub off (skin). [ON. *börkr*]

bark *v.i.* utter a sharp cry, *esp.* of a dog. -*n.*

cry of a dog *etc.* [OE. *beorcan*]

barn *n.* building to store grain, hay *etc.* [OE. *bern* for *bere-ærn*, barley-house]

barom'eter *n.* instrument to measure the weight or pressure of the atmosphere, indicate weather changes. [G. *baros*, weight]

bar'on *n.* title of nobility, in Britain a peer of the lowest rank. **-bar'oness** *fem.* **bar'onage** *n.* **-baro'nial** *a.* **bar'ony** *n.* **bar'on of beef'**, double sirloin. [F.]

baroque' (-k) *a.* in art, extravagantly ornamented; irregularly shaped. [F.]

barr'el *n.* round wooden vessel, made of curved staves bound with hoops; quantity held by such vessel; anything long and hollow, as tube of a gun. *-v.t.* put in a barrel. **-barr'elled** *a.* [F. *baril*]

barr'en *a.* unfruitful, sterile; unprofitable. **-barr'enness** *n.* [OF. *brehaing*]

bar'rier *n.* fence, obstruction; any obstacle. [F. *barrière*, fr. L. *barra*, bar]

barring *prep.* excepting.

bar'rister *n.* in Britain lawyer in the higher law courts. [fr. *bar* of the Inns of Court]

bar'ter *v.i.* traffic by exchange of things. *-v.t.* give (one thing) in exchange for another. *-n.* traffic by exchange. [OF. *barater*, haggle]

base *n.* bottom, foundation; starting point; fixed point. *-v.t.* found, establish. **base''ment** *n.* lowest story of a building; room or rooms in a building which are below ground level. [G. *basis*, step, pedestal]

base *a.* low, mean; despicable. [VL. *bassus*, stumpy]

base'ball *n.* ball game played by two teams of nine players on an open field and in which the runner must complete a circuit of four bases to score; the ball used in this game. [fr. 'prisoners' base', where *base* is for *bars*]

bash'ful *a.* shy, modest, wanting confidence. [*abash*]

BA'SIC *n.* a computer programming language that uses common English terms. [fr. *B*eginner's *A*ll-purpose *S*ymbolic *I*nstruction *C*ode]

ba'sin *n.* deep circular dish; a sink; dock; hollow holding water; land drained by a river. [F. *bassin*]

ba'sis *n.* foundation, groundwork. [G.]

bask (-a-) *v.i.* lie in warmth and sunshine. [ON. *bathask*, bathe]

bas'ket *n.* vessel made of interwoven twigs, rushes *etc.* [orig. doubtful]

bass (bas) *n.* lowest part in music; man's lowest voice; one having such a voice. *-a.* low in the scale, deep. [It. *basso*, base]

bass (bas) *n.* sea-fish of the perch family. [OE. *bærs*]

bassoon' *n.* wood-wind instrument. **-bassoon'ist** *n.* [F. *basson. See* **bass**]

baste *v.t.* drop melted fat over (roasting meat). [OF. *basser*, soak]

bat *n.* heavy stick; flat club, *esp.* as used in baseball, cricket, *etc.* *-v.i.* use the bat in a game. **-bat'ter** *n.* **-bat'ting** *n.* [OE. *batt*, club]

bat *n.* mouse-like flying animal of nocturnal habits. [ME. *bakke*]

bath (-a'-) *n.* water to plunge the body in; act of bathing; vessel for bathing. *-v.t.* wash. [OE. *bæth*]

bathe (-āTH) *v.t.* and *i.* wash. **-ba'ther** *n.* **-ba'thing** *n.* [OE. *bathian*]

bat'ter *v.t.* strike continuously. *-n.* ingredients beaten up with liquid into a paste. **-bat'tering-ram** *n.* former military engine for beating down walls *etc.* [F. *battre*, beat]

bat'tery *n.* number of cannon; place where they are mounted; unit of artillery, men horses and guns; (*law*) assault by beating; (*electr.*) set of voltaic cells in which electric current is stored, [F. *batterie*]

bat'tle *n.* fight between armies. *-v.i.* fight, struggle. [F. *bataille*]

bay *a.* reddish-brown. *-n.* horse of this colour. [fr. L. *badius*]

bay *n.* wide inlet of the sea. [Late L. *baia*]

bay *n.* space between two columns; recess. **-bay'-window** *n.* window in a recess. [F. *baie*, fr. *bayer*, gape]

bay *n.* bark; cry of hounds in pursuit. *v.i.* bark. *v.t.* bark at. [earlier *abay*, OF. *abaier*, bark]

be *v.i.* live; exist; have a state or quality. [OE. *beon*, exist]

beac'on *n.* signal-fire; sea-mark; radio transmitter to guide ships or aircraft; traffic lights. [OE. *beacn*]

beam *n.* long squared piece of wood; ship's widest part; bar of a balance; shaft of light. *-v.t.* emit in rays. *-v.i.* shine. *-a.* (of radio transmission) in a controlled direction. [OE. = *tree*]

bean *n.* any of various kinds of leguminous plants and their seeds. [OE.]

bear (-ā-) *v.t.* carry; support; endure; produce; press (upon). [OE. *beran*]

bear *n.* heavy, partly-carnivorous quadruped; rough fellow; speculator for a fall in stocks. [OE. *bera*]

beard *n.* hair on the chin; similar growth in plants. *-v.t.* defy. [OE.]

beast *n.* animal; four-footed animal; brutal man; **-beast'liness** *n.* **-beast'ly** *a.* [OF. *beste*]

beat v.t. strike repeatedly; overcome. -v.i. throb; sail against the wind. -n. stroke; pulsation; regularly-trodden course. [OE. *beatan*]

beat'ify (be-at'-) v.t. make happy; pronounce in eternal happiness (the first step in canonisation). [L. *beatus*, blessed, *facere*, make]

beaut'y n. loveliness, grace; beautiful person or thing. -beaut'eous a. -beautic'ian n. keeper of a beauty—parlor. [F. *beauté*]

because' adv. and conj. by reason of; on account of. [earlier *by cause*]

become' (-kum') v.i. come to be. -v.t. suit. [OE. *becuman*, fr. *come*]

bed n. couch or place to sleep on; place in which anything rests, in architecture etc.; bottom of a river; layer, stratum; garden plot. -v.t. lay in a bed; plant. [OE. *bedd*]

bee n. insect that makes honey; bee-like association of persons in some activity, as sewing-bee, spelling-bee. -bee'hive n- bee'line n. shortest route. -bees'wax n. [OE. *beo*]

beech n. common tree with smooth silvery bark and small nuts. -beech'en a. - beech'mast n. beech nuts. [OE. *bece*]

beef n. flesh of an ox or cow. -beefy a. fleshy, stolid. [F. *boeuf*, ox]

beer n. fermented alcoholic beverage made from malt and hops. [OE. *beor*]

beet n. plant with a carrot-shaped root, used as a vegetable (red variety) or to extract sugar (white variety). [OE. *bete*]

befit' v.t. be suitable to. -befitt'ing a. -befitt'ingly adv. [*fit*]

before' prep. in front of, in presence of, in preference to; earlier than. -adv. ahead; earlier; in front; in advance. -conj. sooner than. [OE. *beforan*]

beg v.t. ask earnestly, beseech; take for granted, esp. in begging the question, taking for granted what ought to have been proved. -v.i. ask for or live on alms. - beg'gar n. -beg'garly a. -beg'gary n. [OF. *begard*, fr. Med. L. *begardus*, member of a certain mendicant order. The v. is fr. the n.]

begin' v.i. take rise; commence. -v.t. enter on, originate. [OE. *beginnan*]

begrudge' v.t. grudge, envy anyone the possession of something; give unwillingly. [*grudge*]

behave' v.i. bear, carry, conduct (oneself). -beha'viorism n. psychological approach based on the (objective) study of reaction to external stimulus. [*have*]

behind' (-hi'-) prep. in the rear of. -adv. in the rear. [OE. *behiadan*]

behold' v.t. watch, see. -behold'en a. bound in gratitude. -behold'er n. onlooker. [OE. *behealdan*]

be'ing n. existence; creature. [*be*]

bela'ted a. tardy, late. [*late*]

bel'fry n. bell-tower. [OHG. *bergfrid*, guard-peace, watchtower]

belie' v.t. falsify; counterfeit; speak falsely of [OE. *beleogan*, deceive]

believe' v.t. regard as true; trust in. -v.i. have faith; suppose. -belief' n. believable a [ME. *beleven*]

bell n. hollow metal vessel to give a ringing sound when struck; anything shaped like a bell; sound of a bell. -bell'buoy n. [OE. *belle*]

bel'ladonna n. deadly nightshade; narcotic drug made from it. [It. *bella donna*, fair lady]

bel'ly n. part of the body which contains the bowels; stomach. -v.t. and i. swell out. [OE. *belg*]

belong' v.i. be the property or attribute of, be connected with. [earlier *long*, as though 'go along with']

below' adv. beneath; unworthy of. -prep. lower than. [*by low*]

belt n. band; girdle. -v.t. furnish, surround, or mark, with a belt. [OE.]

bend v.t. curve or bow. -v.i. take a curved shape. -n. curve. [OE. *bendan*]

beneath' prep. under, lower than. -adv. in a lower position. [OE. *beneothan*]

benedic'tion n. invocation of the divine blessing. [L. *benedictio*]

ben'efit n. advantage, favor, profit, good. -v.t. do good to. -v.i. receive good. [L. *benefactum*, well done]

benev'olent a. kindly, charitable. -benev'olence n. - benev'olently adv. [L. *bene*, well, *volens*, wishing]

benign' (-in) a. kindly, mild, gentle; favourable. [L. *benignus*]

bent n. kind of wiry grass. [OE. *beonot*- (in place-names)]

bent n. inclination, turn of mind. [*bend*]

bequeath' (-th) v.t. leave by will. -bequest' n. act of bequeathing; legacy. [OE. *becwethan-be-* and *cwethan*, say]

bereave' v.t. rob of -bereave'ment n. [OE. *bereafian*, plunder]

berth n. ship's anchoring place; place to sleep in a ship; employment, situation. v.t. moor. [*bear*, in naut. sense of direction]

beside' prep. by the side of, near; distinct from. -besides' adv. and prep. in addition, otherwise, over and above. [OE. *bi sidan* by the side]

best a. , adv. superlative of good or well.

v.t. defeat. **-best-man** *n.* groomsman at a wedding. [OE. *bet(e)st. See* **better**]

bet *n.* wager. *-v.t.* and *i.* wager. [prob. shortened fr. *abet*]

betray′ *v.t.* give up treacherously; be disloyal to; mislead; reveal, show signs of. [L. *tradere,* hand over]

bett′er *a.* and *adv.* comparative of good and well. *-v.t.* and *i.* improve. [OE. *betera,* compar. of a lost stem **bat-*]

bev′el *n.* slant, diagonal surface; tool for setting off angles. [cp. F. *biveau*]

bev′erage *n.* liquor for drinking. [OF. *bevrage,* fr. *beivre,* L. *bibere,* drink]

beware′ *v.i.* be on one's guard. [*ware*]

bewil′der *v.t.* puzzle, lead astray. [fr. obs. *wildern,* wilderness]

beyond′ *adv.* farther away. *-prep.* on the farther side of; later than; surpassing, out of reach of. [OE. *begeondan*]

bez′el *n.* part of a setting which holds a precious stone. [OF. *bisel*]

bib *n.* cloth put under a child's chin. [ME. *bibben,* fr. L. *bibere,* drink]

Bi′ble *n.* Old and New Testaments, the sacred writings of the Christian Church. **-bib′lical** *a.* [G. *biblia,* books]

bi′centennial *n.* the day celebrating an event exactly 200 years previously. [fr. *bi-,* two, L. *centenarius,* century]

bi′cycle *n.* vehicle with two wheels, one in front of the other, propelled by pedals worked by the rider. **-bi′cyclist** *n.* [F. fr. *bi-,* two, and G. *kyklos,* wheel]

bid *v.t.* offer; command. *-n.* offer, *esp.* of a price at an auction sale. **-bid′der** *n.* **-bid′ding** *n.* [confusion of OE. *beodan,* offer, and *biddan,* request]

bienn′ial (bi-en′-) *a.* happening every two years; lasting two years. *-n.* plant which lives two years. **-bienn′iatly** *adv.* [L. *biennium,* two years]

big *a.* large, great; pregnant; haughty. **-big′ness** *n.* [orig. unknown]

big′amy *n.* crime of having two husbands or two wives at once. **-big′amist** *n.* [*bi-,* two, and G. *gamos,* marriage]

big′ot *n.* one blindly or obstinately devoted to a party or creed. **-big′oted** *a.* **-big′otry** *n.* narrow zeal. [F.]

bilat′eral (bi-) *a.* two-sided. [*lateral*]

bile *n.* fluid secreted by the liver; (*fig.*) anger, bitter temper. **-bil′ious** *a.* **bil′iousness** *n.* [L. *bilis*]

biling′ual (bi) *a.* having or written in two languages. **-biling′ualism** *n.* [fr. *bi-,* two, and L. *lingua,* tongue]

bill *n.* bird's beak. *-v.i.* join bills, as doves; caress. [OE. *bile*]

bill *n.* note of charges; banknote; draft of proposed law; advertisement; commercial document. *-v.t.* announce by advertisement. **-bill′board** *n.* a large surface designed to exhibit bills for advertising **bill′fold** *n.* a folding pouch designed to carry paper money and other small personal belongings. [Late L. *billa, bulla,* seal]

bill′iards (-ly-) *n.* game played on a table with balls and cues. (F. *bille,* ball, *billard,* cue]

bill′ion *n.* a thousand millions. [F.]

bin *n.* receptacle for storing corn, wine *etc.,* or for refuse. [OE. *binn,* manger]

bi′nary *a.* twofold. *-n.* double star, two stars revolving round the same center of gravity. [L. *bini,* two by two]

bind (-i-) *v.t.* tie fast; tie round, gird, tie together; unite; put (a book) into a cover. [OE. *bindan*]

binoc′ular *a.* adapted to both eyes. *-n.* telescope made for two eyes (*usu.* in *pl.*). (L. *bini,* two together, *oculus,* eye]

bi′o- *prefix* meaning life. [G. *bios*] forms compounds as **-biochemistry** *n.* chemistry of living things. **-biodynam′ics** *n.*

biodegrad′able *a.* capable of decomposition by natural means. [L. *gradus,* degree]

biog′raphy *n.* story of a person's life. **biog′rapher** *n.* **-biograph′ical** *a.* **biograph′ically** *adv.* (G. *graphein,* write]

biol′ogy *n.* science of life. **-biolog′ical** *a.* **-biolog′ically** *adv.* **-biol′ogist** *n.* [G. *logos,* discourse]

bion′ics *n.* study of relation of biological and electronic processes **-bion′ic** *a.* having physical functions augmented by electronic equipment. [fr. G. *bios,* life, and elec*tronic*]

bio′rhythm *n.* a cyclically recurring pattern of physiological states in an organism or organ, believed by some to affect physical and mental states and behavior. **-bio′rhythmic** *adv.* [G. *rhythmos,* rhythm]

bipart′ite *a.* composed of two parts or parties. [*part*]

birch *n.* tree with smooth white bark; rod for punishment, made of birch twigs. *-v.t.* flog. [OE. *birce*]

bird *n.* feathered animal. [OE. *bridd*]

birth *n.* bearing or being born of; offspring; parentage. [ON. *byrth*]

bisect′ *v.t.* cut in equal halves. **bisect′or** *n.* [L. *bi-,* two, *secare,* cut]

bit *n.* fragment, piece, bite; in computing, smallest unit of information. [OE. *bita*]

bit *n.* biting part of a tool; mouthpiece of a horse's bridle. *-v.t.* put the bit in. [OE. *bite, bite*]

bitch *n.* female dog. [OE. *bicce*]

bite *v.t.* cut into with the teeth; cut into generally; corrode. -*n.* act of biting; wound made by biting; mouthful. [OE. *bitan*]

bitt'er *a.* harsh-tasting; sharp, painful; stinging. [OE. *biter*]

bi'valve *a.* having a double shell. *n.* mollusk with such a shell. [L. *bi*-, two, *valva*, valve]

black *a.* without light; dark; of the darkest color. -*n.* darkest color; black paint or fabric; a person of a black-skinned race. -**black'en** *v.t.* and *i.* -**black'-mar'ket** *n.* illicit dealings in rationed goods. [OE. *blæc*]

bladd'er *n.* membraneous bag to contain liquid, *esp.* as part of the body; inflated bag. [OE. *blæddre*]

blade *n.* leaf; leaf-like part of anything; edge of a tool; sword; dashing fellow; flat of an oar. [OE. *blæd*, blade (of oar)]

blame *v.t.* find fault with; censure. -*n.* censure, culpability. [F. *blâmer* - G. *blasphemein*, speak ill of]

bland *a.* smooth in manner. -**bland'ish** *v.t.* -**bland'ishment** *n.* [L. *blandus*]

blank *a.* without marks or writing; empty; vacant, confused; (of verse) without rhyme. -*n.* empty space; lottery ticket not drawing a prize; void. -*v.* in sport, to prevent another team from scoring any points. -**blank'ly** *adv.* [F. *blanc*, white]

blank'et *n.* woollen bed-covering. -*v.t.* cover with a blanket; cover. [F. *blanc*]

blare *v.i.* roar; trumpet. -*n.* trumpet sound; roar. [*imit.*]

blast (-ast) *n.* current of air; gust of wind; explosion. -*v.t.* blow up; blight, ruin. [OE. *blæst*, strong gust]

blaze *n.* bright flame of fire; brightness; outburst; white mark on animal's face. *v.i.* burn fiercely, brightly; burn with passion etc. [OE. *blæse*, torch]

bleak *a.* cold and cheerless; exposed; originally pale. [ON. *bleikr*]

bleed *v.i.* lose blood. -*v.t.* draw blood from; extort money from. [OE. *bledan*]

blend *v.t.* mix. -*n.* mixture. [ON. *blanda*, mix]

bless *v.t.* consecrate; give thanks to; invoke happiness on; make happy. **bless'edness** *n.* -**bless'ing** *n.* [OE. *bletsian*, consecrate (with blood)]

blind *a.* lacking sight; heedless, random; dim; closed at one end; concealed, as *blind corner*. -*v.t.* deprive of sight. -*n.* something cutting off light; screen for a window; pretext. [OE.]

blindside *v.t.* to attack by surprise; to attach someone's weak spot.

blink *v.i.* look with half-closed eyes; wink; shine unsteadily. -*v.t.* shut the eyes to, shirk. -*n.* gleam; glimpse; glance. [OE. *blencan*, deceive]

bliss *n.* perfect happiness. [OE. *bliths*, fr. *blithe*]

blis'ter *n.* bubble on the skin; plaster to produce one. -*v.t.* raise a blister. [OF. *blestre*]

blizz'ard *n.* blinding storm of wind and snow. [orig. uncertain]

block *n.* solid piece of wood, a stump; any compact mass; obstacle; stoppage; pulley with frame; group of houses; stupid person. -*v.t.* obstruct, stop up; shape on a block; sketch. -**blockade** *n.* shutting of a place by siege. -*v.t.* close by siege. [F. *bloc*]

blood *n.* (blud) red fluid in the veins of men and animals; race, kindred; good parentage; temperament; passion. -*v.t.* draw blood from; harden to blood-shed. -**blood count** *n.* amount of red and white corpuscles in given quantity of blood. -**blood-transfusion** *n.* transference of blood of one person to another of same blood group. -**blood'vessel** *n.* [OE. *blod*]

bloom *n.* flower of a plant; blossoming; prime, perfection; glow; powdery deposit on fruit. -*v.i.* be in flower; flourish. -**bloom'ing** *a.* [ON. *blom*]

bloss'om *n.* flower; flower-bud. -*v.i.* flower. [OE. *blostm*]

blot *n.* spot, stain; blemish; disgrace. -*v.i.* spot, stain; obliterate; dry with blotting paper. [orig. uncertain]

blow *v.i.* make a current of air; pant; sound a blast. -*v.t.* drive air upon or into; drive by current of air; sound; spout (of whales); boast; fan, -*n.* blast. [OE. *blawan*]

blow *v.i.* blossom. [OE. *blowan*]

blow *n.* stroke or knock; sudden calamity, [orig. uncertain]

blue *a.* of the color of the sky or shades of that color; livid; (*sl.*) depressed. -*n.* the color; paint, clothing *etc.* of that color. -*v.t.* make blue; dip in blue liquid. -**blue-pen'cil** *v.t.* correct or edit. -**blue'-print** *n.* copy of a drawing made by the action of light on sensitised paper. [F. *bleu*]

bluff *a.* steep; abrupt; rough and hearty blunt, frank. -*n.* cliff, high steep bank. [obs. Du. *blaf*]

bluff *v.t.* deceive by pretence of strength. [cp. Du. *verbluffen*]

blun'der *v.i.* flounder; make a stupid mistake. -*n.* gross mistake. [ME. *blondren*, confuse]

blunt *a.* having dull edge or point; abrupt of speech. -*v.t.* dull. [orig. unknown]

blush *v.i.* become red in the face; be ashamed. -*n.* red glow on the face; flush of color. [OE. *blyscan*, shine]

boar *n.* male of the swine. [OE. *bar*]

board *n.* broad, flat piece of wood; table, meals; authorized body of men; thick stiff paper. -*pl.* theater, stage. -*v.t.* cover with planks; supply food daily; enter a ship; attack -*v.i.* take daily meals. -**board'ing-school** *n.* -**on board'**, in or into a ship. [OE. *bord*, plank, table, side of ship]

boast *n.* brag, vaunt. -*v.i.* brag. -*v.t.* brag of, have to show. [AF. *bost*, clamor]

boat *n.* small open vessel; ship generally. -*v.i.* sail about in a boat. [OE. *bat*]

bob *n.* pendant; slight blow; knot of hair, ribbon *etc.*; weight of a plumb-line *etc. v.i.* move up and down. -*v.t.* move jerkily; cut (women's hair) short. -**bobbed** *a.* [orig. uncertain]

bobb'in *n.* small round stick on which thread is wound. [F. *bobine*]

bod'y *n.* whole frame of a man or animal; main part of such frame; main part of anything; substance; mass; person; number of persons united or organized; matter, opposed to spirit. -*v.t.* give form to. [OE. *bodig*]

bog *n.* wet, soft ground. -*v.t.* entangle in such ground. [Ir. Gael. *bogach*, fr. *bog*, soft]

boil *n.* inflamed swelling. [OE. *byl*]

boil *v.i.* bubble up from the action of heat; be agitated, seethe; be cooked by boiling. -*v.t.* cause to bubble up; cook by boiling. -**boil'er** *n.* vessel for heating water or generating steam. -**boil'ingpoint** *n.* [F. *bouillir*]

bold *a.* daring, fearless; presumptuous; well-marked, prominent. -**bold'ly** *adv.* -**bold'ness** *n.* [OE. *bald*]

bol'ster *n.* long pillow; pad, support. *v.t.* support, uphold. [OE.]

bolt *n.* bar or pin; arrow; rush, running away; discharge of lightning. -*v.t.* fasten with a bolt; swallow hastily. -*v.i.* rush away; break from control. [OE. = heavy arrow]

bomb (bom) *n.* explosive projectile usually dropped from aircraft; grenade. *v.t.* attack with bombs. -**bombard'** *v.t.* shell. -**bomb'er** *n.* bomb-dropping airman, airplane. [L. *bombus*, a humming]

bond *n.* that which binds; link, union; written promise to pay money or carry out a contract. -*v.t.* bind; store goods until duty is paid on them. [*band*]

bone *n.* hard substance forming the skeleton of animals; piece of this. -*v.t.* take out bone. [OE. *ban*]

bo'nus *n.* extra payment. [L. *bonum*, something good]

book *n.* collection of sheets of paper bound together; literary work; main division of a work. -*v.t.* enter in a book. [OE. *boc*, beech, *boc stæf*, beech-staff, letter]

boom *n.* long spar; barrier. [Du.]

boom *v.i.* hum; roar. -*n.* hum or roar. [ME. *bommen*]

boom *n.* sudden commercial activity; prosperity. -*v.i.* become active, prosperous. -*v.t.* push into prominence. [orig. uncertain]

boost *v.t.* help forward; push, advertise forcefully. -*n.* help forward; advertisement. [orig. unknown]

boot *n.* covering for the foot and lower leg. [F. *botte*]

booth *n.* hut or stall. [ON. *buth*]

bor'der *n.* margin; frontier; limit, boundary; flowerbed adjoining a walk, lawn *etc.* -*v.t.* put on a margin, edging; adjoin. -*v.i.* resemble. -*v.i.* resemble (with on); be adjacent (with upon). -**bor'derer** *n.* [F. *bordure*, edge]

bore *v.t.* pierce, making a hole; weary. -*n.* hole; size or cavity of a gun; wearisome person. -**bore'dom** *n.* -**bo'rer** *n.* [OE. *borian*, pierce]

bor'row *v.t.* and *i.* obtain on loan or trust; adopt from abroad. -**bor'rower** *n.* [OE. *borgian*, fr. *borg*, pledge]

boss *n.* employer; person in charge. [Du. *baas*]

bot'any *n.* science of plants. -**botan'ic, botanical** *a.* -**bot'anize** *v.i* -**bot'anist** *n.* [G. *botane*, plant]

both *a.* the two. -*adv.* and *conj.* as well; for the one part. [ME. *bathe*]

both'er (-TH-) *v.t.* pester, perplex. -*v.i.* fuss, be troublesome. -*n.* trouble, fuss. [orig. unknown]

bot'tle *n.* vessel for holding liquids; contents of such vessel. -*v.t.* put in a bottle. [F. *bouteille*]

bott'om *n.* lowest part; bed of a sea, river *etc.* sitting part of the human body; ship; staying power, stamina. -*v.t.* put a bottom to; base. [OE. *botm*]

bot'ulism *n.* form of food poisoning. [L. *botulus*, sausage]

bough (bow) *n.* branch of a tree. [OE. *bog*, arm, shoulder]

boul'der *n.* large stone rounded by action of water. [ME. *bulderston*]

bounce *v.i.* bound, like a ball; throw oneself about; boast, exaggerate. -*n.* leap, spring, rebound; boast. [ME. *bunsen*, thump]

boun'ty n. gift; premium. [F. *bonté*- L. *bonitatem-bonus*, good]

bow n. bend, bent line; rainbow; weapon for shooting arrows; looped knot of ribbon *etc.*; instrument for playing violin. -**bow'man** n. archer. [OE. *bogs*]

bow v.i. bend the body in respect, assent *etc.*; submit. -v.t. bend downwards; cause to stoop; crush. -n. inclination in respect. [OE. *bugan*]

bow'el (-ow'-) n. intestines. -pl. entrails; interior; seat of emotions; pity, feeling. [OF. *bouel*]

bowl (-ō-) n. round vessel, a deep basin; drinking-cup; hollow part of anything. [OE. *bolle*]

box n. tree yielding hard smooth wood; its wood; case, generally with a lid; contents of such case; small house or lodge; driver's seat; compartment. -v.t. put in a box; confine. [OE., fr. L.]

box n. blow. -v.t. cuff. -v.i. fight with the fists, *esp.* with gloves on. -**box'er** n. one who so fights; a breed of dog. [orig. uncertain]

boy n. male child; lad; young man; native servant. [ME. *boi*]

brace n. clasp, clamp; pair, couple; strut, support; carpenter's tool for turning boring instruments. -pl. suspenders. -v.t. stretch, strain, string up, support, make firm. [OF. *brasse, pl.* two arms]

brack'et n. support for a shelf -pl. in printing, the marks [ ] used to enclose words. -v.t. enclose in brackets; couple, connect; (*artillery*) range by dropping shells nearer and farther than a mark. [earlier *bragget*, fr. F. *brogue*]

brag v.i. boast, bluster. -n. boastful language. [OF. *braguer*]

braille (brāl) n. system of printing for the blind; letters used, consisting of raised dots. [Louis *Braille*, inventor]

brain n. nervous matter in the skull; intellect. -v.t. dash out the brain. -**brain'less** a. -**brain'y** a. [OE. *brægen*]

brake n. instrument for retarding the motion of a wheel; wagonette. -v.t. apply a brake to. [OF. *brac* -L. *brachium*, arm]

bram'ble n. prickly shrub, the blackberry. -**bram'bly** a. [OE. *bræmbel*]

branch (-a-) n. limb of a tree; anything like a limb; subdivision, section; subordinate department of a business. -v.i. bear branches; divide into branches; diverge. [F. *branche*]

brand n. burning piece of wood; mark made by a hot iron; trade-mark; sword; class of goods; mark of infamy. -v.t. burn with an iron; mark. [OE.]

bran'dy n. spirit distilled from wine. (Du. *brandewijn*, burnt wine]

brash n. rash, eruption; belching of acid water from stomach; hedge-clippings; rock, ice fragmental. loud, arrogant, ambitious; brittle. [F. *brèche*]

brass n. alloy of copper and zinc; brass memorial tablet in a church; (*sl.*) money; impudence. -**brass'y** a. [OE. *bræs*]

brave a. bold, courageous; splendid; finely dressed. -n. Indian warrior. -v.t. defy, meet boldly. -**brave'ly** adv. -**bra'very** n. [F.]

brawl v.i. quarrel noisily; flow noisily. n. noisy quarrel. -**brawl'er** n. [F. *brailler*, be noisy]

brawn n. muscle; thick flesh; strength; preparation of chopped meat. -**brawn'y** a. [OF. *braon*, fleshy part]

breach n. break, opening; breaking of rule, duty, law, promise; quarrel. -v.t. make a gap in. [F. *breche*]

bread (-ed) n. food made of flour or meal baked; food; livelihood. [OE.]

break (brāk) v.t. part by force; shatter, crush, bruise, burst, destroy, frustrate; make bankrupt; discard; loosen, dissolve; tell with care. -v.i. become broken, shattered; divided; open, appear; crack, give way; part, fall out. -n. fracture; gap, opening; dawn; separation, interruption. [OE. *brecan*]

breast (-est) n. human chest; woman's mammary gland; affection; any protuberance. -v.t. face, oppose; mount. [OE. *breost*]

breath (-eth) n. air taken into and put out from the lungs; life; power of breathing; very slight breeze. -**breathe** (-èTH) v.i. inhale and exhale air from the lungs; live; pause, rest. -v.t. inhale and exhale; utter softly; exercise. [OE. *bræth*, exhalation]

breed v.t. generate, bring forth; give rise to; rear. -v.i. be produced, - be with young. -n. offspring produced; race, kind. [OE. *bredan*, keep warm, cherish]

breeze n. gentle wind; wind; rumor; quarrel; something easily achieved. -**breez'ily** adv. -**breez'y** a. windy; bright, lively. [F. *brise*]

brew (-ōō-) v.t. prepare a beverage by fermentation, as beer from malt *etc.*, or by infusion, as tea *etc.*; plot, contrive. -v.i. be in preparation. [OE. *breowan*]

bribe n. gift to corrupt; allurement. -v.t. influence by a bribe; win over; pervert. -**bri'ber** n. -**bri'bery** n. [F. = fragment, broken meats]

brick *n.* oblong mass of hardened clay; any oblong block. -*v.t.* lay or pave with bricks. [F. *brique*]

bride *n.* woman about to be, or just, married. [OE. *bryd*]

bridge *n.* structure for crossing a river *etc.*; raised narrow platform on a ship; upper part of the nose; part of a violin supporting the strings. -*v.t.* make a bridge over. [OE. *brycg*]

bri′dle *n.* headgear of horse-harness; curb or restraint. -*v.t.* put a bridle on; restrain -*v.i.* throw up the head. -**bri′dle-path** *n.* [OE. *bridel*]

brief *a.* short; concise. -*n.* summary of a case for the use of counsel; papal letter. -*n. pl.* underpants. [F. *bref*]

bright *a.* shining, full of light; lively; cheerful; clever. -**bright′en** *v.t.* and *i.* -**bright′ly** *adv.* -**bright′ness** *n.* [OE. *beorht*]

brill *n.* white-spotted flat-fish like turbot. [orig. unknown]

brill′iant (-lya-) *a.* and *n.* shining; sparkling; splendid. [F. *brillant*]

brine *n.* salt water; pickle. -**bri′ny** *a.* salt. -*n.* (*sl.*) the sea. [OE. *bryne*]

bring *v.t.* fetch; carry with one; cause to come. [OE. *bringan*]

brink *n.* edge of a steep place; utmost edge of anything. [ME. *brenk*]

brisk *a.* active, lively, sharp. -*v.t.* enliven. -*v.i.* cheer up -**brisk′ly** *adv.* -**brisk′ness** *n.* [W. *brysg*]

bris′tle (-is′l) *n.* short, stiff hair. -*v.i.* stand erect -*v.t.* erect like bristles. [ME. *brustel*]

broad (-awd) *a.* wide, ample, open; outspoken; coarse; general; tolerant; of pronunciation, dialectal. -**broad′en** *v.t.* and *i.* -**broad′ly** *adv.* -**broad′-mind′ed** *a.* tolerant, not narrow in ideas. [Sp. *brocado*]

broil *v.t.* cook over hot coals or direct heat; grill. -*v.t.* be heated. -**broiler** *n.* apparatus for cooking under direct heat, [F. *broiler*, burn]

bro′ker *n.* one employed to buy and sell for others; dealer; one who values goods distrained for rent. - **bro′kerage** *n.* payment to a broker. [OF. *brocheor*]

brontosaur′us *n.* extinct giant lizard. [G. *bronte*, thunder, *sauros*, lizard]

bronze *n.* alloy of copper and tin. -*a.* the appearance of bronze to. -**bronzed** *a.* coated with, or colored bronze; sunburnt. [F.]

broth *n.* decoction of meat, usually with vegetables. [OE.]

broth′el *n.* house of prostitutes. [ME. = vile person, fr. OE. *breothan*, go to ruin]

broth′er (-uTH′-) *n.* son of the same parents; anyone closely united with another. -**broth′erhood** *n.* relationship; fraternity, company. [OE. *brothor*]

brow *n.* ridge over the eyes; forehead; edge of a hill. -**brow′beat** *v.t.* bully. [OE. *bru*, eye-lid, eyebrow]

browse *v.i.* feed on shoots and leaves; study desultoriy, as books. [fr. obs. *n. browse*, young shoots]

bruise (-ōōz) *v.t.* injure by a blow or pounding; oppress. -*n.* contusion; discolored lump raised on the body by a blow. -**bruis′er** *n.* boxer, prizefighter. [OF. *bruiser*]

brunt *n.* shock of an attack; chief stress of anything. [orig. a blow; orig. uncertain]

brush *n.* small shrubs; thicket; backwoods. [F. *brousse*, faggots]

brush *n.* utensil for sweeping; tool of hair used by painters; bushy tail; skirmish, fight; bundle of wires, or anything like a broom. -*v.t.* remove dust, clean with a brush; touch lightly. -*v.i.* move lightly. [F. *brousse*, faggots]

bubb′le *n.* hollow globe of liquid, blown out with air; anything empty; swindle. -*a.* deceptive; transient. -*v.i.* form bubbles, rise in bubbles. -**bubb′ly** *a.* [earlier *burble*, of imit. orig.]

buck′et *n.* vessel, usually round with an arched handle, for water *etc.* -**buck′etful** *n.* [OE. *buc*, pitcher]

buck′le *n.* metal instrument with rim and tongue, for fastening straps, bands *etc.* -*v.t.* fasten with a buckle. -*v.i.* warp, bend. [F. *boucle*, boss of shield]

bud *n.* first shoot of a plant, leaf *etc.*; unopened flower. -*v.i.* begin to grow -*v.t.* graft. [ME. *bodde*]

budge *v.i.* move, stir. [F. *bouger*]

budg′et *n.* bag and its contents; annual financial statement; collection of things. -*v.t.* prepare a financial statement. [OF. *bougette*, wallet]

buff′alo *n.* any of several species of large oxen. [Port. *bufalo* - G. *bous*, bull]

bug *n.* small blood-sucking insect; any insect. [OE. *budda*, beetle]

bu′gle *n.* hunting-horn; instrument like a trumpet. [for *bugle-horn* fr. L. *buculus*, fr. *bos*, ox]

build (bild) *v.t.* erect, as a house, bridge *etc.*; form, construct. -*v.i.* depend (on). -*n.* make, form. [OE. *byldan*]

bulb *n.* rounded stem or shoot of the onion and other plants; anything resembling this, as electric light bulb. -*v.i.* form, bulbs. -**bulb′ous** *a.* [L. *bulbus*, onion]

bulk *n.* size, volume; greater part; cargo.

-*v.i.* be of weight or importance. -
bulk'iness *n*. -**bulk'y** *a*. large; unwieldy.
[ON. *bulki*, heap, cargo]

bull (-ŏŏ-) *n*. male of cattle; male of
various other animals; speculator for a rise
in stocks. -**bull'ock** *n*. castrated bull -
bull's-eye *n*. boss in glass; lantern; middle
part of a target. [ME. *bole*]

bull (-ŏŏ-) *n*. Papal edict, bearing Pope's
seal. [L. *bulla*, seal]

bull'et (-ŏŏ-) *n*. metal ball discharged from
a rifle, pistol *etc*. [F. *boulet*, cannonball]

bull'etin (-ŏŏ-) *n*. official report; brief official statement reporting on an event;
news report. [F. fr. L. *bulla*, seal]

bull'ion *n*. uncoined gold or silver, in
mass. [F. *bouillon*, boiling]

bull'y *n*. rough, overbearing fellow. -*v.t.*
intimidate, overawe; ill-treat. [orig. uncer-
tain]

bump *n*. heavy blow, dull in sound; swelling caused by a blow; protuberance. -*v.t.*
strike against. - [imit.]

bunch *n*. number of things tied or growing
together; cluster; tuft, knot. -*v.t.* put
together in a bunch. -*v.i.* draw together into
a cluster. [orig. uncertain]

bun'dle *n*. package; number of things tied
together. -*v.t.* tie in a bundle; send (off)
without ceremony. -*v.i.* pack and go (with
off *etc*.) [*bind*]

bunk *n*. box or recess for sleeping in. *esp*.
in a ship's cabin [Du. *bank*, bench]

bunk'er *n*. receptacle for coal, *esp*. in a
ship; sandy hollow on a golf-course. [perh.
ON. *bunke*, ship's hold]

buoy *n*. floating mark anchored in the sea;
something to keep a person afloat. -*v.t.*
mark with a buoy; keep from sinking; sup-
port. -**buoy'ancy** *n*. -**buoy'ant** *a*. [L. *boia*,
chain (by which the buoy was secured)]

burd'en *n*. load; weight; cargo; anything
difficult to bear. -*v.t.* load, encumber. -
burden'some *a*. [OE. *byrthen*]

burd'en *n*. chorus of a song; chief theme.
[F. *bourdon*, humming tone]

bu'reau *n*. writing-desk; office, *esp*. for
public business. [F. = *office*, earlier *desk*,
and earlier still its cloth covering; OF.
burel, a coarse cloth]

bureauc'racy (-ok'-) *n*. government by
officials; body of officials. -**bu'reaucrat**
n. - **bureaucrat'ic** *a*. [*bureau* and G.
kratein, govern]

bur'glar *n*. one who breaks into a house
by night with intent to steal. [prob. fr. OE.
burg, dwelling]

burn *n*. small stream. [OE. *burne*]

burn *v.t.* destroy or injure by fire. -*v.i.* be

on fire, literally or figuratively; shine; be
consumed by fire. -*n*. injury or mark
caused by fire. -**burn'er** *n*. -**burn'ing** *a*.
[OE. *burnan*]

burr'ow (-ō) *n*. hole of a rabbit *etc*. -*v.i.*
make holes in the ground, as a rabbit; bore;
conceal oneself. (var. of borough; OE.
beorgan, protect]

burst *v.i.* fly asunder; break into pieces;
break open violently; break suddenly into
some expression of feeling. -*v.t.* shatter;
break violently. -*n*. a bursting explosion;
outbreak; spurt; (*sl.*) drunken spree. [OE.
berstan]

bur'y (ber'-i) *v.t.* put underground; put in
a grave. -**bur'ial** *n*. [OE. *brygan*]

bus'by *n*. fur hat worn by hussars. [orig.
uncertain]

bush *n*. shrub; woodland, thicket; backwoods, interior of S. Africa and Australia.
[ME. *bush*, *busk*]

bush'el *n*. dry measure of eight gallons.
[OF. *boissel*, dim. of *boiste*, box]

bust *n*. sculpture representing the head
and shoulders of the human body; upper
part of the body. [F. *buste*]

bus'y *a*. actively employed; diligent; meddling; occupied. -*v.t.* occupy. -**bus'ily** *adv*.
-**bus'iness** (biz'-nis) *n*. affairs, work, occupation. [OE. *bysig*]

but *prep*. and *conj*. without; except; only;
yet; still; besides. [OE. *butan*, *beutan*, out-
side]

butch'er *n*. one who kills animals for food,
or sells meat. -*v.t.* slaughter, murder. [F.
boucher fr. *bouc*, goat]

butt *n*. target; object of ridicule. [F. *but*,
end, aim]

butt *n*. thick end of anything; stump. [orig.
uncertain]

butt *v.t.* and *i*. strike with the head; push.
-*n*. blow with the head, as of a sheep. [F.
bouter, thrust]

butt'er *n*. oily substance produced from
cream by churning. -*v.t.* spread with butter;
flatter grossly. [OE. *butere*, fr. L. *buty-
rum*]

butt'ock *n*. rump, protruding hinder part
(*usu*. in *pl*.). [prob. dim of *butt*, thick end]

butt'on *n*. knob or stud, *esp*. for fastening
dress; badge; bud. -*v.t.* fasten with buttons.
[F. *bouton*, bud]

buy (bi) *v.t.* get by payment; obtain in exchange for something; bribe. -**buy'er** *n*.
[OE. *bycgan*]

buzz *v.i.* make a humming sound. -*n*. humming; sound of bees. -**buzz'er** *n*. signalling
device. [imit.]

by *prep*. near; beside; with, through. *adv*.

near, close; out of the way; beyond. **-by'-and-by,** soon. **-by'gone** *a.* past. **-by'-pass** *n.* road to divert traffic from busy main road. **-by'-product** *n.* **-by'-way** *n.* [OE. *bi*]

byte *n.* in computing, sequence of bits processed as a single unit of information. [perh. *bite*]

C

cab *n.* carriage for public transport; taxicab; covered part of a vehicle or machine (*esp.* a locomotive, truck or tractor) which accommodates the driver. [F. *cabriolet*, light carriage]

cab'aret *n.* small tavern; restaurant entertainment. [F.]

cab'bage *n.* green vegetable with large round head. [fr. L. *caput*, head]

cab'in *n.* hut, small room, *esp.* in a ship. *-v.t.* shut up, confine. [F. *cabane*, hut]

cabinet *n.* case of drawers for things of value; private room; committee of politicians governing a country. [dim. of *cabin*]

ca'ble *n.* strong rope; submarine telegraph line; message sent by such line. *-v.t* .and *i.* telegraph by cable. **-cablegram** *n.* [Late L. *capulum*, halter]

cache (-ash) *n.* hidden store; secret hiding-place. [F. *cacher*, hide]

cacophony *n.* disagreeable sound, discord of sounds. **-cacoph'onous** a. [G. *kakophonia*, ill sound]

CAD *n.* (*compute*.) use of computers to prepare and test mechanical designs and engineering and architectural drawings. [computer *a*ssisted *d*esign]

caesarean, cesarean *n.* (birth) delivery by incision. [confusion of L. *caedre, caes-*, cut, with *Caesar*]

caffeine *n.* alkaloid in tea and coffee. [F. *cafeine*]

cage *n.* place of confinement; box with bars, *esp.* for keeping animals or birds. *-v.t.* put in a cage, confine. [F., fr. L. *caves*, hollow]

cake *n.* piece of dough baked; fancy bread; flattened hard mass. *-v.t.* and *i.* make into a cake. [ON. *kaka*]

calculate' *v.t.* reckon, compute. *-v.i.* make reckonings. **-cal'culable** *a.* **-calculating** *a.* **-calcula**é**tion** *n.* **-calculator** *n.* a person who calculates; a machine which carries out calculations. **-cal'culus** *n.* stone in the body; method of mathematical calculation. [L. *calculus*, pebble]

cal'dron, caul'dron *n.* large kettle or boiler. [fr. L. *calidus*, hot]

cal'endar *n.* table of months and days; list

of documents, register. [L. *calendae*, first days of months]

calf (kaf) *n.* young of the cow, also of various other animals; leather made of calfs skin. **-calves** (kavz) *pl.* **-calve** *v.i.* give birth to a calf. [OE. *cealf*]

calf (kaf) *n.* fleshy hinder part of the leg below the knee. [ON. *kalfi*]

caliber *n.* size of the bore of a gun; capacity; character. [F.]

call (kawl) *v.t.* announce; name; summon. *-v.i.* shout; pay a short visit. *-n.* shout; animal's cry; visit; invitation. **-call'er** *n.* visitor. **-call'ing** *n.* vocation, occupation. [ON. *kalla*, cry loudly]

call'ous *a.* hardened, unfeeling. **-callos'ity** *n.* hard lump on the skin. [L. *callosus*, thick-skinned]

calm *n.* stillness, want of wind. *-a.* still, quiet. *-v.t.* and *i.* become, make, still or quiet. **-calm'ly** *adv.* **-calm'ness** *n.* [F. *calme*]

cal'orie, cal'ory *n.* unit of heat; unit expressing the heat or energy potential of food when digested. **-calorific** *a.* heatmaking. **-calorim'eter** *n.* heat-meas uring instrument. [fr. L. *color*, heat]

cam *n.* device to change a rotary motion to a reciprocating one. [*comb*]

CAM *n.* (*compute*) application of computers to certain manufacturing tasks. [computer *a*ided *m*anufacturing]

cam'el *n.* animal of Asia and Africa, with a hump (or two humps) on its back, used as a beast of burden. [G. *kamelos*]

cam'era *n.* apparatus used to make photographs; judge's private room. [L. *chamber*]

camp *n.* tents of an army; military quarters; travellers' resting-place. *-v.i.* form or lodge in a camp. **-camp'er** *n.* **-camp'ing** *n.* [L. *campus*, field]

campaign' *n.* time in which an army keeps the field; series of operations. *-v.i.* serve in a war. [L. *campania*, open country]

camp'us *n.* college grounds. [L. = field]

can *v.i.* be able; having the power; be allowed. [pres. of OE. *cunnan*, know]

can *n.* vessel, usually of metal, for holding liquids. *-v.t.* put, or preserve, in a can. **-cannery** *n.* factory where foods are canned. [OE. *canne*]

canal' *n.* artificial watercourse, duct in the body. **-canaliza'tion** *n.* **-can'alize** *v.t.* cut canal through; convert into canal; direct (thoughts *etc.*) into particular channel. [L. *canalis*, water-pipe]

can'cel *v.t.* cross out; annul, abolish, suppress. **-cancella'tion** *n.* [L. *cancellare*, mark lattice-wise]

can'cer *n.* malignant growth or tumor; the Crab, 4th sign of the zodiac, which sun enters about midsummer. [L. = crab]

can'did *a.* frank, open, impartial. - **can'didly** *adv.* -**can'didness** *n.* -**can'dor** *n.* [L. *candidus*, white]

candidate *n.* one who seeks an office, appointment, privilege *etc.* [L. *candidatus*, one wearing a white toga]

can'dle *n.* stick of wax with a wick; light. -**can'dlepower** *n.* unit, standard for measuring light. [L. *candela*]

can'dy *n.* (sweetmeat of) crystallized sugar. -*v.t.* preserve with sugar. -*v.i.* become encrusted with sugar. -**can'died** *a.* [fr. *silgar*-candy, F. *sucre candi*, fr. Arab. *qand*, sugar]

cane *n.* stem of a small palm or large grass; walking-stick. -*v.i.* beat with a cane. [G. *kanna*, reed]

ca'nine *a.* like or pertaining to the dog. [L. *canes*, dog]

cann'on *n.* ancient (unrifled) piece of ordnance; modem weapon used in aircraft. [F. *canon*, fr. L. *canna*, reed, tube]

cann'y *a.* shrewd; cautious; crafty. - **cann'ily** *adv.* -**cann'iness** *n.* [*See* can]

can'on *n.* law, rule, *esp.* of the church; standard; body of books accepted as genuine; list of saints. [G. *kanon*, rule]

can'opy *n.* covering over a throne, bed *etc.* -*v.t.* cover with a canopy. [G. *konopeion*, couch with mosquito curtains, fr. *konops*, gnat]

cant *n.* inclination from the level. -*v.t.* and *i.* tilt. [Med. L. *cantus*, edge, corner]

can'ticle *n.* hymn. [L. *canere*, sing]

cantilever *n.* large bracket supporting balcony *etc.* [Sp. *can*, support; F. *lever*, raise]

can'yon *n.* deep gorge, ravine. [Sp. *cañon*]

cap *n.* covering for the head; lid, top or other covering. -*v.t.* put a cap on; confer a degree upon; outdo; raise the cap in respect. [OE. *ceppe*, hood]

ca'pable *a.* able, gifted; having the capacity, power. -**capabil'ity** *n.* [F.]

capa'city (-as'-) *n.* power of holding or grasping; room; volume; character; ability, power of mind. -**capa'cious** *a.* roomy. [F. *capacité*- L. *capere*, hold]

capillary *a.* hair-like. -*n.* tube with very small bore, *esp.* a small vein. [L. *capillaris*, fr. *capillus*, hair]

cap'ital *n.* headpiece of a column; chief town; large-sized letter; money, stock, funds. *a.* affecting life; serious; chief, leading; excellent. [L. *capitalis*, fr. *caput*, head]

Cap'itol *n.* temple of Jupiter in Rome; house of Congress or state legislature in U.S. [L. *Capitolium*]

capitulate *v.i.* surrender on terms. - **capitula'tion** *n.* [Med. L. *capitulate*, draw terms under 'heads'; fr. *caput*, head]

Capricorn *n.* the Goat, 10th sign of zodiac, which sun enters in midwinter. [L. *caper*, goat, *cornu*, hom]

capsize *v.t.* upset.-*v.i.* be upset over turned. [orig. uncertain]

cap'sule *n.* seed vessel of a plant; gelatin case for a dose of medicine. [L. *capsular* dim. of *capsa*, case]

cap'tain *n.* leader, chief; commander of a vessel, company of soldiers. [F. *capitaine*. (fr. L. *caput*, head)]

cap'tion *n.* title, of an article, picture *etc.* [orig. a law term meaning arrest. [fr. L. *capere*, take]

cap'tive *n.* one taken prisoner, kept in bondage.; taken, imprisoned. -**captivate** *v.t.* fascinate. -**cap'tivating** *a.* -**capti'vity** *n.* [L. *captivus*]

cap'ture *n.* seizure, taking. -*v.t.* seize, catch, make prisoner. -**cap'tor** *n.* [L. *captura*, fr. *capere*, take]

car *n.* wheeled vehicle, railroad or tramway carriage; automobile. [L. *carrus*]

car'apace *n.* upper shell of tortoise *etc.* [F. -Sp. *carapacho*]

car'at *n.* small weight used for gold, diamonds *etc.*; proportional measure of twenty-fourths used to state the fineness of gold. [G. *keration*, carob fruit, small weight]

car'bon *n.* non-metallic element, substance of pure charcoal, found in all organic matter. -**car'bon diox'ide**, gas exhaled from the lungs. -**car'bon monoxides** odorless poisonous gas from car exhausts *etc.* [L. *carbo*]

car'buretor *n.* apparatus for mixing oi] vapor and air in an engine. [*carbon*]

car'cass, car'case *n.* dead body of an animal; orig. skeleton. [F. *carcasses*]

carcinoma *n.* cancerous growth. - **carcino'sis** *n.* spread of cancer in body. [G. *karkinōma*, crab]

card *n.* pasteboard; small piece of pasteboard with a figure for playing games, or with a name and address *etc.*; dial of a compass. -**card'board** *n.* pasteboard. [G. *chartes*, leaf of papyrus]

car'diac *a.* pert.to heart; heart stimulant or cordial. -**car'diograph** *n.* instrument recording heart movements.-**car'diogram** *n.* graph of these. -**car'dioid** *a.* heart-shaped. [G. *kardia*, heart] car′digan n. knitted woollen jacket, waistcoat.[7th Earl of *Cardigan*]

car′dinal a. chief, principal. -n. prince of the R.C. Church; member of the pope's council. -**cardinal points**, North, South, East and West. [G. *cardinals*, essential, fr. *cardo*, hinge]

care n. anxiety; pains, heed; charge, oversight.-v.i. be anxious; be disposed (to); have regard or liking (for). [OE. *caru, n., cearian* v., sorrow]

career′ n. course through life; course of action, height of activity; course, running. -v.i. run or move at full speed. [F. *carriare*, racecourse]

caress′ v.t.fondle, embrace, treat with affection. -n. act or expression of affection. [L. *carus*, dear]

car′et n. mark inserted to show where something has been omitted. [L. *caret*, there is wanting]

car′go n. ship's load. [Sp. *cargar*, load]

carn′age n. slaughter. [L. *caro*, flesh]

car′nal a. fleshly, sensual; worldly. [L. *carnalis*, of the flesh]

car′nival n. revel; season of revelry before Lent. [F. *carnaval*]

carnivorous a. flesh-eating. **carn′i**- **vore** n. -pl. **carnivore**. [L. *carnivorus*]

car′ol n. song of joy or praise. -v.i. and t.sing or warble. -**car′olhng** n. [OF. *carole*]

carouse′ n. drinking-bout.-v.i. hold a drinking bout.-**carous′al** n. -**carous′er** n. [fr. phrase drink carouse, Ger. *gar aus*, quite out]

carp n. freshwater fish. [P. *carpe*]

carp v.i. catch at small faults or errors; cavil. [ON. *karpa*, chatter, influenced by L. *carpere*, pluck]

carpenter n. worker in timber, as in building, *etc.* car′pentry n. [L. *carpentari, carpentum*, chariot]

car′pet n. cloth floor-covering. -v.t. cover a floor. [Med. L. *carpita*, patchwork]

carriage n. act or cost of carrying; vehicle; bearing, conduct.-**carr′iage**- **horse** n. [ONF. *cariage*, fr. *carier*, carry]

carr′ion n. rotting dead flesh. a. [ONF. *caroigne*]

carr′y v.t.convey, transport; capture; effect; behave. -v.i. reach, of a projectile, sound. -n. range. [ONF. *carier*, fr. *car*, vehicle]

cart n. two-wheeled vehicle without springs. -v.t. convey in such vehicle; carry. -**cart′age** n. -**cart′er** n. -**cart′-wright** n. [ON. *kartr*]

cartilage n. firm elastic tissue in the body of vertebrates; gristle. **cartila′ginous** (-aj)

a. [L. *cartilage*]

car′ton n. pasteboard container. [F.]

cartridge n. case containing the charge for a gun. [F. *cartouche*, fr. It.*cartoccio*, roll of paper, fr. *carta*, card]

carve v.t. cut; hew, sculpture, engrave; cut up (meat). -**carv′er** n. **car′very** n. an eating establishment at which customers pay a set price and may then have unrestricted helpings of food from a variety of meats, salads, and other vegetables. -**carv′ing** n. [OE. *coerfan*, cut]

case n. instance; state of affairs; condition; lawsuit; grounds for a suit. [orig. 'what befalls'; F. *cas*, fr. L. *cadere*, fall]

case n. box, sheath, covering; any receptacle; box and its contents. -v.t. put in a case -**case′harden** v.t. a process to harden steel by combining it with carbon. -**case′-hardening** n. [ONF. *casse*, fr. L. *capere*, hold]

cash n. money, coin. -v.t. turn into or exchange for money. -**cashier′** n. -**cash′book** n. -**cash′less** adv. functioning, operated, or performed without using coins or banknotes for money transactions but instead using credit cards or electronic transfer of funds. -**cash′ register** n. recording till. [orig. 'moneybox'; It.*cassa*, fr. L. *capere*, hold]

cashier′ v.t. discharge, dismiss in disgrace. [L. *cassare*, make void]

casi′no n. building with gamingtables, public dance-halls *etc.* [It.]

cask′et n. small case or box for jewels *etc.*; coffin, *usu.* of ornate kind. [F. *cassette*, small case]

cassette′ n. plastic container for film, magnetic tape *etc.* [OF. *casse*, case]

cast (-a-) v.t. throw or fling; shed; throw down; allot, as parts in a play; found, as metal. -v.i. cast about, look around. -n. throw; thing thrown; distance thrown; squint; mold; manner, quality, tinge, color, degree; set of actors. [ON. *kasta*]

caste n. section of society in India; social rank. [Port. *caste*, race]

castigate v.t. chastise; punish or rebuke severely. -**castiga′tion** n. -**cas′tigator** n. [L. *castigate*]

cas′trate v.t. remove the testicles, deprive of the power of generation. -**castra′tion** n. [L. *castrate*]

cas′ual (-zh-) a. accidental; unforeseen; occasional; unmethodical. -**cas′ually** adv. -**cas′ualty** n. accident; loss in war. [L. *casualis*, fr. *cadere*, fall]

cat n. tame or wild animal of the genus Felis; spiteful woman; piece of wood tapered at both ends; nine-lashed whip. -

catt'y *a.* -cat'-fish *n.* fish with features like cat.-cat'gut *n.* cord made of intestines of animals. [ONF. -Late L. *cattus*]

cat'aclism *n.* upheaval. [G. *kataklysrnos*]

cat'acomb *n.* underground gallery for burial. [Late L. *Catacumbas*]

catalogue, cat'alog (-og) *n.* descriptive list.-*v.t.* make a list of; enter in a catalogue. [G. *katalogos*, fr. *legein*, choose]

catal'ysis *n.* chemical change effected by catalyst.-cat'alyst *n.* substance producing chemical change in another sub stance without itself changing. [G. *kata*, down, *luein*, loose]

cat'aract *n.* waterfall; defect in an eye, causing blindness. [G. *katarhaktes*]

catastrophe *n.* climax of a tragedy; great disaster. [G. *katastrophe*]

catch *v.t.* take hold of, seize; understand. -*v.i.* be contagious; get entangled. -*n.* seizure; anything that holds, stops *etc.*; that which is caught; form of musical composition; advantage taken or to be gained; hidden difficulty or drawback. -catchword *n.* cue; popular phrase. [ONF. *cachier*]

category *n.* class or order; division. -categorical *a.* positive; what may be affirmed of a class. -categor'ically *adv.* -cat'egorize *v.t.* [G. *kategoria*, assertion]

ca'ter *v.i.* provide food, entertainment *etc.* -ca'terer *n.* -ca'tering *n.* [ME. *acatour*, buyer, fr. OF. *achater*, buy]

cathedral *n.* principal church of a diocese. -*a.* pertaining to a cathedral. [orig. *a.* in cathedral church, fr. G. *kathedra*, seat (*i.e.*, of the bishop)]

cath'ode *n.* negative pole in electricity. [G. *kata*, down, *hodos*, way]

cath'olic *a.* universal; including the whole body of Christians; relating to the Roman Catholic Church. -*n.* adherent of the R.C. Church. [G. *katholikos*, universal]

catt'le *n.* beasts of pasture, *esp.* oxen, cows. -sometimes horses, sheep . [L. *capitale*, stock, fr. *caput*, head]

caul *n.* membrane covering head of some infants at birth; openwork head covering. [OF. *cale*, small cap]

cause *n.* that which produces an effect; reason; origin; motive, purpose; lawsuit; party principle. -*v.t.* bring about, make to exist.-caus'al *a.* -causa'tion *n.* -cause'less *a.* [L. *causa*]

caust'ic *a.* burning; bitter, severe. -*n.* corrosive substance. -caus'tically *adv.* [G. *kaustikos*]

cauterize *v.t.* burn with a caustic or hot iron. -cauteriza'tion *n.* [G. *kauterion*, hot iron]

ca'ution *n.* heedfulness, care; warning. -*v.t.* warn. -cau'tionary *a.* -cau'tioner *n.* -cau'tious *a.* -cau'tiously *adv.* -cau'tiousness *n.* [L. *cautio*, fr. *cavere*, beware]

cave *n.* hollow place in the earth; den. -cav'ern *n.* deep cave. -cav'ernous *a.* -cav'ernously *adv.* -cav'ity *n.* hollow opening. (L. *cavus*, hollow]

caviar' *n.* salted sturgeon roe; (*fig.*) some thing too fine for the vulgar taste. [Turk. *khavyar*]

cease *v.i.* stop, give over. -*v.t.* discontinue. -cease'less *a.* -cease'lessly *adv.* [F. *cesser*-L. *cessare*, give over]

cede' *v.t.* yield, give up, *esp.* of territory. [L. *cedere*, yield]

cei'ling *n.* inner roof, *usu.* plastered; upper limit.-ceil *v.t.* [F. *ceil*, heaven, fr. L. *call*, canopy]

celebrate *v.t.* make famous; mark by ceremony (event of festival); perform with due rites. -cel'ebrant *n.* -cel'ebrated *a.* famous. -celebra'tion *n.* -celeb'rity *n.* fame; famous person. [L. *celebrate*]

cel'ery *n.* vegetable with long white eatable stalks. [F. *cgleri*]

celestial *a.* heavenly, divine. [L. *cælestis*, fr. *cxlum*, heaven]

cell *n.* small room; small cavity; unit-mass of living matter. -cell'ular *a.* -cell'ude *n.* [L. *cella*]

cell'ar *n.* underground room for storage. [L. *cellarium*, set of cells]

celluloid *n.* synthetic substance made from cellulose; substitute for bone, ivory, *etc.* [Trademark] . [L. *cella*]

cement' *n.* mortar; anything used for sticking together. -*v.t.* unite with cement; unite firmly. [F. *ciment*]

cem'etery *n.* burying-ground. [fr. G. *koimeterion*, sleeping-place]

cen'sor *n.* supervisor of morals; one who examines plays, books, news *etc.* before publication. -censo'rial *a.* -censo'rious *a.* fault-finding. censo'riously *adv.* -censo'riosness *n.* -cen'sorship *n.* [L. = judge of morals]

cen'sure *n.* blame; reproof. -*v.t.* blame, reprove. cen'surable *a.* -cen'surably *adv.* [L. *censure*, judgment]

cen'sus *n.* official counting of the inhabitants of a country; any official counting. [L.]

cent *n.* hundred; hundredth part of a dollar. per cent', in, to, by each hundred. [L. *centum*]

centenn'ial *n.* hundred years; celebration of a hundredth anniversary. -*a.* pertaining to a hundred. -centena'rian n. one a hundred years old. a. lasting a, or happening every, hundred years. -cente'nary n. centennial. [L. centenarius]

cen'ter n. mid-point of anything; pivot, axis; point to which, or from which, things move or are drawn. -cen'tral a. [L. centrum]

centigrade a. having a hundred degrees. [L. centum, hundred, gradus, degree]

centimeter n. one hundredth part of meter. [L. centum, hundred]

centipede n. small segmented animal with many legs. [L. centipeda-centum, hundred, pes, ped-, foot]

cen'tury n. hundred years; unit of one hundred. [L. centenarius]

ce'real a. pertaining to corn. -n. grain used as food (usu. pl.). [L. cerealis, fr. Ceres, goddess of agriculture]

cer'ebral a. pertaining to the brain. -cerebra'tion n. brain action. cer'ebrospi'nal a. [fr. L. cerebrum, brain]

cer'emony n. sacred rite; formal observance; usage of courtesy; formality. [L. cærimonia]

cer'tain a. sure, settled, fixed, inevitable; some, one; of moderate (quantity, degree etc.). cer'tainly adv. cer'tainty n. -cer'titude n. [F., fr. L. certus]

cer'tify v.t. make known as certain; declare formally. -certifica'tion n. -certif'icate n. written declaration. -v.t. give a written declaration. -cer'tifier n. [L. cerius, sure, facere, make]

chafe v.t. make hot by rubbing; fret or wear by rubbing; irritate. -cha'fing-dish n. -cha'fing-gear n. [F. chauffer]

chain n. series of links or rings each passing through the next; fetter; anything that binds; connected series of things or events; surveyor's measure. -v.t. fasten with a chain; confine. makes compound nouns as -chain-arm'or, chain'-mail, chain'-shot, chain'stitch etc. [F. chatne, fr. L. catena]

chair n. movable seat; seat of authority; professor's seat, or his office; iron support for a rail on a railway. -v.t. carry in triumph. -chair'nian n. one who presides. chair'manship n. [F. chaire, fr. G. kathedra]

chalk (chawk) n. white substance, carbonate of lime. -v.t. rub or mark with chalk. -v.i. mark with chalk; keep a reckoning. chalk'iness n. -chalk'y a. [OE. cealc, L. calx, lime]

challenge v.t. call to fight; call to account; dispute; claim; object to. -chall'engeable a. chall'enger n. [L. calumnia, false accusation]

cha'mber n. room; room for an assembly; assembly or body of men; compartment; cavity. -cha'mberlain n. officer appointed by a king etc. for domestic and ceremonial duties. -cha'mber-maid n. servant with care of bedrooms. -cha'mber-pot, cha'mber n. vessel for urine. [F. chambre, fr. L. camera, vault]

cham'pion n. one who fights for another; one who defends a cause; in sport etc., one who excels all others; hero. -v.t. fight for, maintain. -cham'pionship n. [F., fr. Late. L. campio, fighter in the arena]

chance (-a-) n. that which happens; fortune; risk; opportunity; possibility; probability. -v.t. risk. -v.i. happen- a. casual, unexpected. [F., fr. OF. cheoir, fall; orig. 'fall' of dice]

change v.t. alter or make different; put for another; exchange, interchange. -v.i. alter; put on different clothes. -n. alteration, variation; variety; conversion of money; small money; balance received on payment. -change'ling n. child substituted for another by the fairies. [F. changer]

chann'el n. bed of a stream; deeper part of a strait, bay, harbor; groove; means of passing or conveying. -v.t. groove, furrow. [L. canalis]

chant v.t. and i. sing. -n. song; church melody. -chant'er n. -chant'ry n. -endowment or chapel for singing masses. -chant'y (sh-) n. sailor's song. [F. chanter, fr. L. cantare, sing]

cha'os (ka) n. disorder, confusion; state of the universe before the Creation. [G.]

chap'el n. subordinate place of worship, as one attached to a garrison, house, prison etc., and not a cathedral or parish church; division of a church with its own altar. [orig. sanctuary where was deposited the cappella, or sacred cloak, of St.Martin]

chap'lain n. clergyman attached to a chapel, regiment, ship of war, institution etc. -chap'laincy n. [F. chapelain. See chapel]

chap'ter n. division of a book; section, heading; assembly of the clergy of a cathedral etc. organized branch of a society, fraternity. [L. capitulum, dim. of caput, head; the church chapter was a meeting at which a chapter was read]

char v.t. scorch, burn, reduce to charcoal. [fr. charcoal]

character (ka-) n. letter, sign, or any distinctive mark; essential feature; nature; total of qualities making up an individuality; moral qualities; reputation of possessing them; statement of the qualities of a person who has been in one's service;

person noted for eccentricity; personality in a play or novel. [G. *character*, tool for stamping]

char'coal *n.* black residue of wood, bones *etc.* by smothered burning; charred wood. **char'coal-burner** *n.* [orig. uncertain]

charge *v.t.* fill; load; lay a task on, enjoin, command; deliver an injunction; bring an accusation against; ask as a price; fill with electricity. -*v.i.* make an onset.-*n.* that which is laid on; cost, price; load for a gun *etc.*; command, exhortation; accusation; accummulation of electricity. -*pl.* expenses. -**charge'able** *a.* **char'ger** *n.* officer's horse. [F. *charger*, Low L. *carricare*, load]

char'iot *n.* two-wheeled war vehicle drawn by horses; state carriage. -**charioteer'** *n.* [F., fr. *char*, car]

charity *n.* love, kindness; disposition to think kindly of others; practical kindliness, alms-giving. **char'itable** *a.* -**charitably** *adv.* [F. *charitg*, fr. L. *caritas-carus*, dear]

charm *n.* magic spell; thing worn to avert evil; anything that fascinates; attractiveness. -*v.t.* bewitch; delight, attract.- charmed *a.* -**charm'er** *n.* -**charm'ing** *a.* -**charm'ingly** *adv.* [F. *charme*, fr. L. *carmen*, song, incantation]

chart *n.* map of the sea; diagram or tabulated statement. -**chart'-house** *n.* (Nautical). [L. *charta*, paper]

chart'er *n.* writing in evidence of a grant of privileges *etc.*; patent. -*v.t.* establish by charter; let or hire. [L. *chartula*, dim. of *charta*, paper]

chase *v.t* hunt, pursue; drive from, into *etc.* -*n.* pursuit, hunting; thing hunted; hunting-ground. [F. *chasser*]

chase *v.t* decorate with engraving. -**cha'ser** *n.* **cha'sing** *n.* [for *enchase*, F. *enchdsser*, enshrine]

chasm (kazm) *n.* deep cleft; abyss. [G. *chasma*]

chassis *n.* framework, wheels and machinery of a motor-car; underframe of an airplane. [F.]

chaste *a.* pure; modest; virtuous; (*art*) in good taste. -**chaste'ly** *adv.* -**chas'tity** *n.* [L. *castus*, pure]

chastise' *v.t* inflict punishment on; reduce to order. **chas'tisement** *n.* [*chaste*]

chat *v.t* talk idly or familiarly. -*n.* familiar talk; idle talk; genus of small birds, as stonechat, whinchat *etc.* -**chatt'ily** *adv.* **chatt'y** *a.* [*chatter*]

chatt'el *n.* any movable property (*usu.* in *pl.*). [fr. Late L. *capitale*, goods, property. *See* cattle]

cheap *a.* low in price; inexpensive; easily

obtained; of little value or estimation. [OE. *ceap*, a bargain]

cheat *v.t.* deprive of by deceit, defraud; impose upon. -*v.i.* practise deceit.-*n.* fraud. [for *escheat*, confiscate]

check *v.t.* stop; restrain; hinder; repress; control; examine. -*n.* threatening the king at chess; repulse; stoppage; restraint; token, ticket; order for money; bill; a mark (√) indicating approval of the affirmative. [F. *échec*, fr Pers. *shah*, king (in danger)]

cheek *n.* side of the face below the eye; impudence. -*v.t.* address impudently. -**cheek'ily** *adv.* -**cheek'y** *a.* [OE. *ceace*, cheek, jaw]

cheer *n.* mood; mirth, joy; food; shout of approval. -*v.t.* comfort; gladden; encourage, *esp.* by shouts. -*v.i.* shout applause. [F. (bonne) *chère*-Low L. *cara*, face]

cheese *n.* curd of milk coagulated, separated from the whey and pressed. [OE. *ciese*, fr. L. *caseus*]

chef (*sl.*) *n.* head cook. [F. *chef de cuisine*]

chemistry (k-) *n.* science which treats of the properties of substances and their combinations and reactions. -**chem'ical** *a.* -**chem'ically** *adv.* -**chem'ist** *n.* [*See* alchemy]

cher'ish *v.t.* treat with affection; protect; encourage. [F. *chérir*]

chess *n.* game of skill played by two persons with 32 'pieces' on a board of 64 squares. -**chess'board** *n.* -**chess'men** *n.pl.* the pieces used in chess. [F. of *echec*. *See* check]

chest *n.* box; coffer; upper part of the trunk of the body. [OE. *cist*, fr. L. *cista*]

chew *v.t.* grind with the teeth. -**chew'ing-gum** *n.* [OE. *ceowan*]

chick *n.* short for chicken; young of birds, *esp.* of the domestic fowl. -**chick'enheart'ed** *a.* -**chick'en-pox** *n.* mild contagious fever. [OE. *cicen*]

chic'ory *n.* salad plant of which the root is ground and mixed with coffee. [fr. G. *kichora*, endive]

chief *n.* head or principal person. -*a.* principal, foremost, leading. -**chiefly** *adv.* [F. *chef*, fr. L. *caput*, head]

child (-i-) *n.* infant; bov or girl; son or daughter. **child'ren** *n.pl.* **child'bed** *n.* state of a woman giving birth to a child. -**child'birth** *n.* -**child'hood** *n.* -**child'ish** *a.* -**child'ishly** *adv.* -**child'less** *a.* -**child'like** *a.* [OE. *cild*]

chill *n.* coldness; cold with shivering; anything that damps, discourages. [OE. *ciele*, cold]

chim'ney n. passage for smoke. - **chim'ney-sweep** n. [L. *caminus*, furnace]

chin n. part of the face below the mouth. [OE. *cin*]

chi'na n. fine earthenware. [fr. *China*]

chink n. cleft, crack. [OE. *cinu*]

chip v.t. chop or cut into small pieces; break little pieces from; shape by cutting off pieces. -v.i. break off. -n. small piece broken off, thin fried slices of potato; counter used as a token in gambling and games; tiny wafer of silicon forming an integrated circuit in a computer. [related to *chop*]

chiropractic n. and a. treatment of diseases by manipulating joints, *esp.* of the spine. -**chiroprac'tor** n. [G. *cheir*, hand, *praktikos*, concerned with action]

chis'el (-zl) n. cutting tool, usually a bar of steel with an edge across the main axis. -v.t. cut or carve with a chisel. [ONF., fr. L. *cmdere*, cut]

chlo'rine n. yellowish-green gas with a suffocating action on the lungs. **chlo'rate** n. -**chlo'ride** n. -**chlo'rinate** v.t. [G. *chlaros*, yellowish-green]

chlorophyll (kl-) n. coloring matter of plants. [G. *chloros*, green, *phyllon* leaf]

chocolate n. paste of cacao-tree seeds; sweetmeat or drink made from it.-a. dark brown. [Mex. *chocolatl*]

choice n. act or power of choosing; alternative; something chosen. -a. select, fine, worthy of being chosen. -**choice'ly** adv. [F. *choisir*, choose]

choke v.t. throttle; stop up; smother, stifle; obstruct.-v.i. suffer choking. -n. act or noise of choking; device to regulate flow of gas etc. [OE. *aceocian*]

choose v.t. take one thing rather than another; select.-v.i. will, think fit. [OE. *ceosan*]

chop v.t. cut with a blow; cut in pieces. n. hewing blow; slice of meat containing a rib. [ME., related to *chap* and *chip*]

chord (k-) n. harmonious simultaneous union of musical notes. [*accord*]

chor'us n. band of singers; combination of voices singing together; refrain. -v.t. sing or say together. [L., fr. G. *choros*, band of singers]

Christian (kris tyan) n. follower of Christ.-a. following Christ; relating to Christ or his religion. -**chris'ten** (krisén) v.t. baptize, give a name to. **chris'tendom** (-an-) n. all Christian countries. - **chris'tianize** v.t -**Christian'ity** n. religion of Christ. -**Christ'mas** n. festival of the birth of Christ. -**Chris'tian** name, name

given at christening, individual name. - **Chris'tian Sci'ence**, religious system founded by Mary Baker Eddy, in America. [G. *christos*, anointed]

chromosome n. microscopic body found in cell during division. [G. *chrome*, color]

chron'ic (k-) a. lasting a long time. - **chron'icle** n. record of events in order of time. -v.t. record. -**chron'icler** n. - **chronological** a. -**chronolo'gically** adv. **chronol'ogist** n. -**chronol'ogy** n. - **chronom'eter** n. instrument for measuring time exactly. -**chronomet'rical** a. - **chronom'etry** n. [G. *chronos*, time]

chrysalis n. resting state of an insect between grub and fly; case from which it emerges. [G. *chrysallis*, fr. *chrysos*, gold (fr. the gold-colored sheath of butterflies)]

church n. building for Christian worship; whole body of Christians; clergy; body or md of Christians. -v.t. give thanks on behalf of (a woman) after childbirth etc. [OE. *eirice*, fr. G. *kyriakon*, of the Lord]

churn n. vessel for making butter. -v.t. shake up (a liquid). [OE. *cyrin*]

ci'der n. drink made from apples. [F. *cidre*-G. *sikera*, strong drink]

cigar' n. roll of tobacco-leaves for smoking. **cigarette'**, **cigaret'** n. fine lycut tobacco rolled in paper for smoking. [Sp. *cigarro*; F. *cigarette*]

cin'der n. piece of glowing coal; partly burnt coal. [OE. *sinder*, slag]

cir'cle (ser-kl) n. perfectly round figure; ring; company of persons gathered round another, or round an object of interest; seance; class or division of society. -v.t. surround. -v.i. move round. -**cir'cular** a. round; moving round. -n. letter sent to several (a circle of) persons. [L. *circulus*, dim. of *circus*, ring]

cir'cuit (-kit) n. a moving round; area; round of visitation, *esp.* of judges; district; path of an electric current. -**circu'itous** a. -**circu'itously** adv. [L. *circuitus*, a going round]

circumcise v.t. cut off the foreskin of - **circumcis'ion** n. [L. *circumcidere*, cut round]

circumference n. boundary line, *esp.* of a circle. [L. *circumferential* periphery]

circumflex n. accent (^) on a vowel or syllable -a. bending or winding round. [L. *flectere*, *flexum*, to bend]

circumspect a. watchful, prudent. [L. *circumspicere*, look around]

cir'cumstance n. detail; event, matter of fact.-pl. state of affairs; condition in life; surroundings or things accompanying a certain action. **-circumstan'tial** *a.* depending on details; particular as to details; indirect. [L. *eir-cumstare*, stand round]

cirr'us *n.* high fleecy cloud. [L. = curl]

cit'izen *n.* inhabitant of a city; townsman; member of a state. **-citizenship** *n.* [fr. OF. *citeain*]

civ'ic *a.* pertaining to a city or citizen. **-civics** *n.* science of municipal and national life of service. [L. *civicus*, citizen]

civ'il *a.* relating to citizens or the state; refined, polite, not barbarous; not military; (*law*) not criminal. **-civil'ian** *n.* non-military person. **-civiliza'tion** *n.* **civ'ilize** *v.t.* refine, bring out barbarism. **-civ'ilized** *a.* **-civil'ity** *n.* politeness. **-civ'illy** *adv.* [L. *civilis*]

claim *v.t.* call for; demand as a right.-*n.* demand for a thing supposed due; right; thing **claimed. -claim'ant** *n.* **-clam'ant** *a.* demanding attention. [L. *clamare*, shout]

clam *n.* bivalve shellfish. [OE. = fetter]

clamp *n.* tool for holding or pressing. *v.t.* fasten with clamps. [Du. *clamp*]

clan *n.* tribe or collection of families under a chief, and of supposed common ancestry; sect, group. [Gael. *clann*]

clap *n.* hard, explosive sound; slap. -*v.i.* strike with this noise; strike the open hands together; applaud. -*v.t.* strike together; pat; applaud; thrust suddenly, impose abruptly. [imit.]

clar'ify *v.t.* make clear; purify **-clarification** *n.* [L. *clarificare*]

clash *n.* loud noise, as of weapons striking together; conflict, collision. -*v.i.* make a clash; come into conflict.-*v.t.* strike together to make a clash. [imit.]

clasp *n.* hook or other means of fastening; embrace; military decoration. -*v.t.* fasten; embrace, grasp. **-clasp-knife** *n.* [orig. uncertain]

class *n.* rank of society; division of pupils; division by merit; quality; any division, order, kind, sort.-*v.t.* assign to the proper division. **-classifica'tion** *n.* **-class'ify** *v.t.* arrange methodically in classes. [L. *classes*, division of the Roman people]

class'ic, classical *a.* of the first rank of Greek and Roman authors; of the highest rank; refined, chaste; famous. [*See* class]

clause (-z) *n.* part of a sentence; article; n a formal document. [F., fr. L. *clausa*]

claustrophobia *n.* morbid fear of enclosed spaces. [L. *clausus-claudere*, shut; G. *phobos*, fear]

clavichord (-k-) *n.* obsolete musical instrument like a spinet. [Mod. L. *clavichor-dium*, key string]

clay *n.* stiff viscous earth; earth generally; human body. **clay'ey** *a.* [OE. *clæg*]

clean *a.* free from dirt, stain or any defilement; pure; guiltless; trim, shapely. *adv.* so as to leave no dirt; entirely. -*v.t.* free from dirt.-**clean'er** *n.* **-clean'liness** (klen-) *n.* -**clean'ly** (klen'-) *a.* **-clean'ly** *adv.* cleanness *n.* **-cleanse** (klenz) *v.t.* [OE. *claene*]

clear *a.* free from cloud; pure, undimmed, bright; free from obstruction or difficulty; plain, distinct; without defect or drawback; transparent.-ado. wholly, quite. *v.t.* make clear; acquit; pass over or through; make as profit; free from cloud; obstruction, difficulty; free by payment of dues. -*v.i.* become clear, bright, free, transparent. **-clearinghouse** *n.* place where cheques are exchanged. **-clear'ing-station** *n.* place from which wounded are removed; place where items are kept prior to being removed. **clear-sight'ed** *a.* [F. *clair*, fr. L. *clarus*]

cleat *n.* wedge; (*naut.*) block to which ropes are made fast; porcelain insulation. [*See* clod, clot]

clef *n.* mark to show the pitch in music. [F., fr. L. *clavis*, key]

cleft *n.* opening made by cleaving; crack, fissure. [*cleave*]

clench *v.t.* make fast; set firmly together; grasp; drive home. [OE. *-clencan*, in *be-ciencan*, make to cling]

clere'story *n.* upper part of a church with a row of windows. [*clear* ('lighted') *storey*]

clergy *n.* appointed m; nisters of the Christian church. **-cler'gyman** *n.* [L. *clericus. See* clerk]

clev'er *a.* able, skillful, adroit.**clev'erly** *adv.* **-clev'erness** *n.* [orig. uncertain]

cli'ent *n.* customer, one who employs a professional man. **-clientele'** *n.* body of clients. [L. *cliens*]

cliff *n.* steep rock face. [OE. *clil*]

climate *n.* the average weather conditions of a region. [G. *klinw, klimatos*, slope]

cli'max *n.* highest point, culmination; arrangement of language to rise in dignity and force; point of greatest excitement, tension, in a play, story *etc.* [G. *klimax*, ladder]

climb *v.t* and *i.* mount by clutching, grasping, pulling; creep up, mount, ascend. **climb'er** *n.* **-climb'ing** *n.* [OE. *climban*]

clinch *v.* clench (*q.v.*).

cling *v.i.* stick fast, be attached; remain by. [OE. *clingan*]

clinic *n.* relating to practical instruction in

medicine in hospitals. -*n*. place or meeting for medical examination or teaching (also *clinique'*). -**clin'ical** *a*. **clin'ically** adv. [G. kline, bed]

clip *v.t.* grip, clutch, hug. -*n*. device for gripping. [OE. *clyppan*]

clip *v.t.* cut with scissors or shears; cut short.-*n*. the wool shorn at a place or in a season. -**clip'ping** *n*. something clipped off, *esp*. article cut out of a publication. **clipp'er** *n*. [ON. *kappa*]

cloak *n*. loose outer garment; disguise, pretext.-*v.t.* cover with a cloak; disguise, conceal. [earlier *cloke*, fr. Late L. *clocca*, bell (shape of garment)]

clock *n*. instrument for measuring time; ornament on the side of a stocking. [orig. 'bell;' fr. Late. L. *clocca*]

clog *n*. obstruction, impediment, wooden-soled shoe; *v.t.* gather in a mass and cause stoppage; choke up. -**clog'-dance** *n*. [orig. unknown]

close (-a) *a*. shut up; confined; secret; unventilated, stifling; reticent; niggardly; compact; crowded; strict, searching. *adv*. nearly, tightly. -*n*. shut-in place; precinct of a cathedral. -**close'ly** adv. -**close'ness** *n*. -**close'-up** *n*. photograph or film sequence taken at short range. [L. *claudere*, close]

close (-z) *v.t.* shut; stop up; finish. -*v.i.* come together, grapple. -*n*. end. [L. *claudere*]

clos'et (-z-) *n*. small private room; a cabinet, recess or cupboard for storage of e.g. household utensils or clothes. -*v.t.* shut up in a closet; conceal. [OF. dim. of *clas*, fr. L. *claudere*]

clot *n*. mass or lump. -*v.t.* form into lumps. [OE. *clod*-, in compounds]

cloth (-th) *n*. woven fabric. **clothes** (-TH-) *n. pl.* dress; bed-coverings. -**clothe** *v.t.* put clothes on. **clo'thier** *n*. **clo'thing** *n*. [OE. *clath*]

cloud *n*. vapor floating in the air; state of gloom; great number or mass. -*v.t.* overshadow, dim, darken. -*v. i.* become cloudy. -**cloud'less** *a*. -**cloud'y** *a*. [OE. *clud*, mass]

clown *n*. rustic; jester. **clown'ish** *a*. [perh. fr. Du. *kloen*, clew, hoyden]

cloy *v.t.* weary by sweetness, sameness *etc*. [earlier *accloy*, fr. F. *enclouer, prick,* spike with a nail]

club *n*. thick stick; bat; one of the suits at cards; association for a common object.-*v.t.* strike with a club; put together. -*v.i.* join for a common object. [ON. *klubba*]

cluck *n*. noise of a hen. -*v.i.* make that noise. [OE. *cloccian*]

clue *n*. ball of thread; thread used as a guidance, trail; indication, *esp*. of the solution of a mystery. [OE. *cliwen*, ball of thread]

clus'ter *n*. group, bunch. -*v.t.* and *i*. gather, grow in a cluster. [OE. *clyster*]

clutch *v.t.* grasp eagerly, snatch. -*v.i.* make a snatch at.-*n*. grasp, tight grip; device for connecting and disconnecting parts of machinery, *e.g.* a motor engine. [OE. *clyccan*]

clutt'er *n*. litter, confusion. -*v.t.* and *i*. [*clot*]

coach *n*. large four-wheeled carriage; passenger car on a railroad [F. *coche*]

coagulate *v.t.* and *i*. curdle, form into a mass. [L. *coagulate*]

coal *n*. glowing ember; mineral consisting of carbonized vegetable matter, used as fuel. -*v.t.* supply with coal. -*v.i.* take in coal. [OE. *col*]

coarse *a*. rough, harsh; unrefined; indecent; gross. [ME. *cars*, fr. AF. *cros*, F. *gros*]

coast *n*. sea-shore. -*v.i.* and t.sail by the coast. -**coast'er** *n*. [L. *costa*, rib]

coat *n*. outer garment; animal's fur or feathers; covering; layer.-*v.t.* clothe, cover with a layer. -**coat-of-arms** *n*. heraldic bearings. [OF. *cote* fr. L. L. *cotta*]

co'balt *n*. a metal; blue pigment made from it. [Ger. *kobalt*, fr. *kobold*, demon]

COB'OL *n*. computer programming language for general commercial use. [fr. common business oriented language]

cob'web *n*. spider's web. [ME. *coppeweb*, fr. *coppe,* spider]

cocaine' *n*. alkaloid drug used as an anaesthetic. [*coca*, American shrub]

cock *n*. male bird; tap for liquids; hammer of a gun; its position drawn back; upward turn. -*v.t.* set or turn assertively; draw back (gun hammer). [OE. *cocc*]

co'co *n*. tropical palm. -**co'conut** *n*. very large hard nut from the cocopalm. 1Sp. = ugly-face, bogey (fr. marks at end of the shell)]

co'coa *n*. powder made from the seed of the cacao, a tropical tree; drink made from the powder. [corrupt.of *cacao*. fr. Mex. *cacauatl*]

cocoon' *n*. sheath of an insect in the chrysalis stage. [F. *cocon*, L. *concha*, shell]

co'da *n*. passage completing and rounding off a musical composition. [L. *canda*, tail]

code *n*. collection of laws; system of signals. -**codifica'tion** *n*. -**co'dify** *v.t* [F. fr. L. *cortex*, set of tablets; book]

cod'icil *n*. addition to a will. [L. *codicillus*, dim. of *codex. See* **code**]

coff'ee *n*. seeds of a shrub originally from Arab; drink made from these seeds. [Turk, *qahveh*, Arab. *qahweh*, wine]

coff'in *n*. box for a dead body. -*v.t.* put into a coffin. [L. *cophinus*, G. *kophinos*, basket]

cog *n*. one of a series of teeth on a wheel. [ME. *cogge*]

co'gent *a*. forcible, convincing. -co'gency *n*. -co'gently *adv*. [L. *cogere*, constrain-*co*, together, *agere*, drive]

cog'itate *v.i*. think, reflect.-*v.t*. plan. - cogita'tion *n*. [L. *cogitare*]

cogni'tion *n*. perception; act of knowing. [L. *cognoscere, cognit*-, know]

cognizance *n*. knowledge, awareness, observation. [L. *cognoscere*, know]

coil *v.t*. lay in rings; twist into a winding shape. -*v.i*. twist; take up a winding shape. -*n*. series of rings. [OF. *coiner*, collect]

coin *n*. piece of money; money. -*v.t*. make into money, stamp; invent.-coin'age *n*. [L. *cuneus*, wedge (a stamping die being like a wedge)]

coincide' *v.i*. happen together; agree exactly. -coin'cidence *n*. coincident; coincidental *a*. [Med. *coincidere*, fall together. *See* incident]

coi'tion *n*. sexual intercourse. [L. *coitio*]

cold *a*. lacking heat; indifferent, apathetic; dispiriting. -*n*. lack of heat; common ailment marked by nasal catarrh *etc*. -cold'ly *adv*. -cold'ness *n*. -cold feet, (*sl*.) fear, timidity. -cold stor'age *n*. storing perishable goods at artificially reduced temperatures. cold war, diplomatic, economic but non-military hostility. [OE. *ceald*]

col'ic *n*. severe intestinal pain. [fr. G. *kolon*, lower intestine]

collaborate *v.i*. work with another, *esp*. in literature. -collabora'tion *n*. -collaborator *n*. one who works thus; native who collaborates with the enemy in an occupied country. [L. *collaborare*, fr. *laborare*, work]

collapse' *v.i*. fall together, give way; lose strength, fail. -*n*. act of collapsing. collaps'ible *a*. [L. *labi, laps*-, slip]

collate' *v.t*. compare carefully; appoint to a benefice. -colla'tion *n*. bringing together for comparison; light repast. [L. *collatus*, fr. *conferre*, bring together]

collateral *a*. accompanying; subordinate; of the same stock but a different line. -*n*. kinsman. [L. *latus*, side]

colleague' *n*. associate, companion in an office, employment. [L. *college*]

collect' *v.t*. gather, bring together. -*v.i*. come together. -collec'ted *a*. gathered; calm. [L. *colligere, collect*-, gather together]

coll'ege *n*. society of scholars; place of higher education; association. -colle'gian *n*. -colle'giate *a*. [L. *collegium*, fr. *legere*, gather]

collide' *v.i*. strike or dash together; come into conflict. -colli'sion *n*. [L. *collidere*, fr. *laedere*, hurt]

co'lon *n*. mark (:) indicating a division of a sentence. [G. *kolon*, limb, part of a sentence]

co'lon *n*. lower intestine.

col'ony *n*. body of people who settle in a new country; country so settled. [L. *colonia*, fr. *colere*, till]

coluss'us *n*. huge statue; very big man. - coloss'al *a*. huge. [L.]

col'or (kul'-er) *n*. hue, tint; complexion; paint or anything giving color; race, when associated with skin-color. -*pl*. flags. -*v.t*. stain, dye, paint, give color to; disguise; misrepresent.-*v.i*. become colored; blush. -col'orblind'ness *n*. the inability to distinguish between certain colors. [L. *color*]

col'umn (-um) *n*. long vertical cylinder, pillar; division of a page; body of troops; anything like these. -colum'nar *a*. - col'umnist (-um-ist) *n*. writer of a periodical column. [L. *columna*-G. *kolone*, hill]

co'ma *n*. stupor, unnatural sleep. - co'matose *a*. [G. *koma*]

comb *n*. toothed instrument for arranging hair, or ornamenting it; cock's crest; mass of honey-cells. -*v.t*. apply a comb to. [OE. *comb*, Ice. *kambri*]

combine' *v.t*. and *i*. join together; ally. - com'bine *n*. group of companies or political associates. -combina'tion *n*. [Late L. *combinare*, put two-and-two (*bini*) together]

combus'tion *n*. burning. [Late L. *combustion* fr. *comburere*, burn]

come (kum) *v.i*. approach, arrive, move towards; reach; happen (to); originate (from); get to be, become; turn out to be. [OE. *cuman*]

com'edy *n*. drama dealing with the lighter side of life, ending happily, or treating its subject humorously; play of this kind. - come'dian *n*. player in comedy. [I. *comoedia*]

com'fort (kum'-) *v.t*. console, cheer, gladde -*n*. consolation; well-being; ease; means of consolation or ease. -comfort-able *a*. -com'fortably *adv*. com'forter *n*. one who comforts; baby's 'dummy'. [Late L. *confortare*, strengthen]

com'ic *a.* relating to comedy; funny, laughable. **-com'icala. -com'ically** *adv.* [G. *komikos*]

comm'a *n.* mark (,) separating short parts of a sentence. [G. *komma*, piece cut off, short clause]

command' *v.t.* order; rule; compel; have in oneś power; overlook; dominate. *-v.i.* exercise rule. *-n.* order, rule; power of controlling, ruling, dominating, overlooking; post of one commanding; his district. **commandant'** *n.* **-commandeer'** *v.t.* seize for military service. **-command'er** *n.* **- command'ment** *n.* [L. *mandare*, enjoin]

commem'orate *v.t.* celebrate, keep in memory by ceremony. **-commemora'tion** *n.* **-commem'orative** *a.* [L. *commemorate. See* **memory**]

commence' *v.t.* and *i.* begin. **- commence'ment** *n.* the act of commencing; ceremony at which degrees or diplomas are conferred. [F. *commencer*-L. *com* and *initiare*, begin]

commend' *v.t.* praise; commit, entrust. **- commendable** *a.* praiseworthy. [L. *commendare*]

comm'ent *n.* note, collection of notes; remark; criticism. *-v.i.* make remarks, notes, criticisms. **-comm'entator** *n.* [L. *commentari*]

comm'entary *n.* series of comments; book of notes or comments on another book. **-runn'ing commentary,** comments on a game *etc.* as it proceeds. [*comment*]

comm'erce *n.* buying and selling; dealings, intercourse. **-commer'cial** *a.* **-commercialize** *n.* [L. commercium, fr. *merx*, merchandise]

commis'sion *n.* doing, committing; something entrusted to be done; payment by a percentage for doing something; delegate -d authority; body entrusted with some special duty. *-v.t.* give an order for; authorize, give power to. **-commis'sioner** *n.* [L. *commission* fr. *committere*, entrust]

commit' *v.t.* entrust, give in charge; perpetrate, be guilty of, compromise, entangle. **-committee'** *n.* person to whom something is committed. **-commit'ment** *n.* **-committ'al** *n.* [L. *committere*, entrust]

committ'ee *n.* body appointed or elected for some special business, usually from some large body. [orig. one person entrusted with a duty *etc.* [fr. L. *committere*, entrust]

commodity *n.* article of trade, anything meeting a need. [L. *commodus, fit*]

comm'on *a.* shared by or belonging to all, or several; public, general; ordinary, usual,

frequent; inferior, vulgar. *-n.* land belonging to a community, unenclosed land not belonging to a private owner. *pl.* ordinary people; the lower house of the British Parliament; rations, food provided daily. [L. *communis*]

commo'tion *n.* stir, disturbance, tumult. [L. *movere, mot-,* move]

commune' *v.i.* have intimate intercourse. **- commu'nicable** *a.* **-commu'nicant** *n.* one who receives Communion. **- commu'nicate** *v.t.* impart, give a share. *v.i.* give or exchange information; receive Communion. **-communica'tion** *n.* act of giving, *esp.* information; information, letter, message. **-commu'nion** *n.* fellowship; body with a common faith; sharing. **- Commu'nion** *n.* participation in the sacrament of the Lord's Supper; that sacrament, Eucharist. [L. *communes*, common]

commu'nity *n.* state; body of people with something in common, *e.g.*, district of residence, religion; joint ownership. **- comm'une** *n.* small administrative district; organization where property and responsibilities are shared in common. **- commu'nal** *a.* common, shared by a number. **comm'unism** *n.* doctrine that all goods, means of production *etc.* should be the property of the community. [L. *communes*, common]

commute' *v.t.* exchange; change (a punishment *etc.*) into something less; change (a duty *etc.*) for a money payment; (*elec.*) reverse current. **commuta'tion** *n.* [L. *mutare*, change]

com'pact *n.* agreement, covenant. [L. *compacisci*, agree together]

compact' *a.* neatly arranged or packed; solid, concentrated; terse. **com'pact** *n.* pocket-sized vanity case. **-compact disk** digital disk on which music, video, or computer data is encoded and read by a laser device. **-compact'ly** *adv.* **-compact'ness** *n.* [L. *compingere, compact-,* join together]

compan'ion *n.* mate, follow, comrade, associate. **compan'ionable** *a.* **compan'ionship** *n.* [L. *companio*, mess mate, fr. *panes*, bread]

com'pany *n.* assembly; society; association of people for trade *etc.*; ship's crew; part of a battalion. [*companion*]

compare' *v.t.* notice or point out the likenesses and differences of anything; liken or contrast; make the comparative and superlative of an adjective or adverb. *- v.i.* be like; compete with. **-com'parable** *a.* **- compar'ative** *a.* that may be compared; not absolute; relative, partial. **-**

compar'atively adv. **-compar'ison** n. [L. comparare]

compart'ment n. division or part divided off, a section; division of a railway car etc. [L. com and partiri, share, fr. pars, share]

com'pass (kum'-) n. instrument for showing the north; instrument for describing circles (usu. in pl.); circumference, measurement round; space, area, scope, reach. -v.t. contrive; surround; attain. [VL. compassare, go round, fr. passus, step]

compassion (-shun) n. pity, sympathy. **compassionate** a. **-compas'sionately** adv. [L. com, with, pati, pass-, suffer]

compatible a. consistent, agreeing with. **-compatibil'ity** n. **compat'ibly** adv. [Med. L. compatibilis, sharing in suffering, fr. pati, suffer]

compel' v.t. force, oblige, bring about by force. **-compul'sion** n. **compul'sory** a. [L. compellere, drive together]

com'pensate v.t. make up for; counterbalance. **-compensa'tion** n. [L. compensate, weigh together]

compete' v.i. strive, vie (with). **-competi'tion** n. **-compet'itive** a. **compet'itor** n. [L. competere, seek in common]

competent a. able, skillful; properly qualified; proper, due, legitimate, suitable, sufficient. **-com'petence**, **com'petency** n. **-com'petently** adv. [L. competere, be convenient]

compile' v.t. make up (e.g., a book) from various sources or materials; put together. **-compila'tion** n. **-compi'ler** n. [L. compilare, plunder]

compiler n. (compute.) computer program that translates a program written in high-level language into machine languge that the compute can execute.

complacent a. self-satisfied. **com'plaisance** n. obligingness, willingness to please. **com'plaisant** a. [L. complacere, please greatly]

complain' v.i. grumble; bring a charge, make known a grievance; (with of) make known that one is suffering from. **complain'ant** n. **-complaint'** n. statement of a wrong, a grievance; an illness. [L. plangere, beat the breast]

complete a. full, finished, ended, perfect. -v.t. finish; make whole, full, perfect. **-complement** n. something completing a whole; full allowance, equipment, etc. **complement'ary** a. **-complete'ly** adv. **complete'ness** n. **-comple'tion** n. [L. cornplere, complete, fill up]

com'plex a. intricate, compound, involved-n. psychological abnormality, obsession. **-complex'ity** n. [L. complectere, plait together]

complicate v.t. make intricate, involved, difficult. **-complica'tion** n. [L. eomplicare, fold together]

compliment n. remark neatly expressing praise. -pl. expression of courtesy, formal greetings. -v.t. praise, congratulate. **complement'ary** a. [Sp. cumplimiento, a 'fulfilling' of an act of courtesy; same word as complement]

comply' v.i. consent, yield, do as asked. **-compli'ance** n. **compli'ant** a. [It. complire, fr. Sp. cumplir, satisfy requirements, fr. L. complere, fill up]

component n. part, elemental. composing, making up. [L. componere, put together]

compose' v.t. make up; write, invent; arrange, put in order; settle, adjust; calm. **-composed'** a. calm. **compo'ser** n. author of a musical work. **-com'posite** a. compound, not simple. **-compo'sure** n. calmness. [F. composer]

compound' v.t. mix, make up, put together; compromise, make a settlement of debt by partial payment; condone. -v.i. come to an arrangement, make terms. **com'pound** a. not simple; composite, mixed. -n. mixture, joining; substance, word etc. made up of parts. [L. componere, put together]

comprehend' v.t. understand, take in; include, comprise. [L. comprehendere, grasp]

compress' v.t. squeeze together; make smaller in size, bulk. **-com'press** n. pad of wet lint etc. applied to a wound, inflamed part etc. **compress'ible** a. **compres'sion** n. [L. premere, press-, press]

comprise' v.t. include, contain. [F. compris, pp. of comprendre, comprehend]

compromise n. meeting halfway, coming to terms by giving up part of a claim. -v.t. expose to risk or suspicion. v.i. come to terms. [L. compromittere, put before an arbiter]

compute' v.t. reckon, estimate. **computa'tion** n. **-comput'er** n. a machine, usu. electronic, capable of carrying out calculations and other complex functions at high speeds. **-comput'erize** v.t. equip with, perform by a computer. [L. computare]

com'rade n. mate, companion, friend. **com'radeship** n. [Sp. camorada, roomful, later room-mate; fr. L. camera, room]

con v.t. direct the steering of a ship. **conn'ing-tower** n. [earlier cond, condy, fr. F. conduire, guide]

con v.t. trick, swindle. -n. [fr. *confidence* trick]

con'cave a. hollow, rounded inwards. -**concav'ity** a. [L. *cavus*, hollow]

conceal' v.t. hide, keep secret. **concealment** n. [L. *celare*, hide]

concede' v.t. admit, grant; yield. -**conces'sion** n. -**concess'ive** a. [L. *cedere*, *cess-*, give away]

conceit' n. vanity, overweening opinion of oneself; far-fetched comparison. -**conceit'ed** a. conceive **conceive'** v.t. become pregnant with; take into the mind, think of, imagine; understand. -**conceiv'able** a. -**conceiv'ably** adv. [F. *concevoir*, fr. L. *concipere*]

concentrate v.t. reduce to small space; increase in strength; gather to one point.- v.i. come together; devote all attention. -**concentra'tion** n. -**concentra'tion camp**, camp for political prisoners etc. [L. *concentrum*]

concentric a. having a common center. [L. *cum* and *centrum*, center]

con'cept n. idea, abstract notion. -**concep'tual** a. -**concep'tion** n. conceiving, idea [L. *concipere*, conceive]

concern' v.t. to relate or belong to; to interest, affect, trouble, involve. -n. affair, importance, business, establishment. **concern'ing** prep. respecting. [L. *cernere*, have regard to]

concert' v.t. arrange, plan together. -**con'cert** n. musical entertainment; harmony, agreement. **concert'ed** a. mutually arranged. **concer'to** (cher-) n. musical composition for solo instrument and orchestra. **concerti'na** n. musical instrument with bellows and keys. [F. *concerted*]

conciliate v.t. pacify, gain friendship. [L. *conciliate*, bring together in council]

concise' a. brief, in few words. -**concise'ly** adv. -**concise'ness** n. concision (-sizhn) n. [L. *concisus*, fr. *cædere*, cut]

conclude' v.t. end, finish; settle; v.i. come to an end; infer, deduce; decide. **conclu'sion** (-oo'shn) n. -**conclu'sive** a. decisive, convincing. -**conclu'sively** adv. [L. *concludere*]

concoct' v.t. make a mixture, prepare with various ingredients; make up; devise, as a plan. -**concoc'tion** n. [L. *concoquere*, boil together]

conc'ord n. agreement. -**concord'ance** n. agreement; an index to the words of a book. **concord'ant** a. [L. *Concordia*]

con'crete a. solid; consisting of matter, facts, practice, etc.; not abstract.-n. mixture of sand, cement, etc., used in building

-**concrete'ly** adv. [L. *concrescere*, *concretum*, grow together]

concubine n. woman living with a man as his wife, but not married to him. **concu'binage** n. [fr. L. *con*, together, and *cubare*, lie]

concur' v.i. agree, express agreement; happen together. -**concur'rence** n. **concur'rently** adv. [L. *concurrere*, run together]

concussion (-shn) n. violent shock; injury by blow, fall, etc. [L. *concussion*, shaking together]

condemn' v.t. blame; find guilty; doom; find unfit for use. **condem'natory** a. **condemna'tion** n. [L. *condemnare*]

condense' v.t. concentrate, make more solid; turn from gas into liquid; compress. - v.i. turn from gas to liquid. **condensa'tion** n. **conden'ser** n. (*elec.*) apparatus for storing electrical energy for reducing vapors to liquid form; lens, mirror for focusing light. [L. *condensare*]

condescend' v.i. stoop, deign; be gracious; patronize. **condecen'sion** n. [Late L. *condescendere*, come down]

condition n. thing on which a statement or happening or existing depends; stipulation; state of circumstances of anything. -v.t. be essential to the happening or existence of; stipulate; make fit (for). -**condi'tioned reflex** n. response automatically produced by stimulus repeatedly applied. [L. *condicio*, discussion]

condominium n. joint rule; an apartment in a house consisting of individually owned apartments; an apartment in such a house. *abbrev.* **con'do**. [L]

condone' v.t. overlook, forgive, treat as not existing. [L. *condonare*, remit]

conduct' v.t. lead, direct, manage. -**con'duct** n. behavior; management. -**conduc'tor** n. **conduc'tion** n. **conduc'tive** a. -**conductiv'ity** n. power to conduct heat, electricity. [L. *conducere*]

cone n. solid figure with a circular base and tapering to a point; any object in this shape; fruit of the pine, fir, etc. -**con'ic**, **con'ical** a. **co'nifer** n. tree bearing cones. **coniféerous** a. [G. *konos*, peak]

confection n. prepared delicacy, sweetmeat; made-up millinery, etc. -**confectioner** n. dealer in cake, pastry, sweets, etc. -**confec'tionery** n. [L. *conficere*, make up]

confederate a. united in a league-n. ally; accomplice. -v.t. and i. unite. [L. *confœderatus*, fr. *fœdus*, *fœderis*, treaty, league]

confer' v.t. grant, give. - v.i. talk with, take

advice. -confer'ment *n*. -con'ference *n*. [L. *conferre*, bring together]

confess' *v.t.* admit, own, acknowledge, declare; (of a priest) to hear the sins of. *v.i.* acknowledge; declare one's sins orally to a priest. -confes'sor *n*. priest who hears confessions; person who keeps his faith under pesecution, but without martyrdom; one who confesses. [L. *confiteri, confessus*, acknowledge]

confide' *v.i.* trust (in). *v.t.* entrust. - confidant' *n*. one entrusted with smrets. -con'fidence *n*. trust; boldness, assurance; intimacy. con'fident *a*. -con'fidently *adv*. [L. *fidere*, trust]

configuration *n*. shape, aspect; outline. [L. *figurare*, fashion]

confine' *v.t.* shut up, imprison; keep within bounds; keep in house, bed. -con'fines *n.pl.* boundaries. -confine'ment *n*. restraint, imprisonment; child bed. [L. *confinis*, bordering]

confirm' *v.t.* make strong, settle; make valid, ratify; make sure, verify; administer confirmation to. -confirma'tion *n*. making strong, valid, certain, *etc.*; rite administered by a bishop to confirm baptized persons in the vows made for them at baptism. [L. *confirmare*]

confiscate *v.t.* seize by authority. - confisca'tion *n*. confiscatory *a*. [L. *confiscare*, seize for the treasury, *liscus*. cp. *fiscal*]

con'flict *n*. struggle, trial of strength; variance. -conflict' *v.t.* be at odds with, inconsistent with; clash. [L. *conflictusfligere*, strike]

conform' *v.t.* and *i.* comply, adapt to rule, pattern, custom, *etc.* [L. *conformare*, give same shape]

confront' (-unt') *v.t.* face; bring face to face with. -confronta'tion *n*. [F. *confronter*, fr. front, brow]

confuse' *v.t.* disorder, mix mentally. - confu'sion *n*. [*See* confound]

congenial *a*. suitable, to one's liking; of kindred disposition. -conge' nially *adv.* - congenial'ity *n*. [Mod. L. *congenialis*, suiting one's genius]

conglomerate *a*. gathered into a ball. -*v.t.* and *i.* -*n*. rock of rounded pebbles cemented together-puddingstone. conglomera'tion *n*. confused mass. [L. *conglomerate*]

congratulate *v.t.* felicitate, offer expression of pleasure at another's good fortune, success, *etc.* -congratula'tion *n*. congratulatory *a*. [L. *congratulari*]

congregate (-ng-g-) *v.i.* flock together; as-

semble. -congrega'tion *n*. assembly, *esp.* for religious worship. [L. *grex, gregis*, herd]

cong'ress (-ng-g-) *n*. meeting; a formal assembly for discussion; a legislative body. congres'sional *a*. [L. *congredi*, congresses, go together]

congruent (-ng-groo-) *a*. fitting together; suitable, accordant. -cong'ruence *n*. cong'ruous *a*. -congru'ity *n*. [L. *congruere*, rush together]

con'jugal *a.* of marriage; between married persons. -conjugal'ity *n*. [L. *conjunx*, spouse, *lit.* joined together]

conjugate *v.t.* inflect a verb in its various forms (past, present, *etc.*). -conjuga'tion *n*. [L. *conjugate*]

conjunction *n*. part of speech joining words, phrases, *etc.*; union; simultaneous happening. -conjunc'ture *n*. combination of circumstances, decisive point. [L. *conjungere*, join together]

conjure' *v.t.* implore solemnly. -con'jure (kunjer) *v.t.* and *i.* produce magic effects by secret natural means; invoke devils. [L. *conjurare*, swear together]

connote *a*. innate, congenital. - conna'tion *n*. connat'ural *a*. of the same nature. [L. *nasci, natus*, be born]

connect' *v.t.* and *i.* join together, unite; associate -connec'tion, conne'xion *n*. - connect'ive *a*. [L. *nectere*, bind]

connote' *v.t.* imply, mean in addition to the chief meaning. connota'tion *n*. [Med. L. *connotare*]

con'quer (-ker) *v.t.* win by war; overcome, defeat.- *v.i.* be victorious. -conqueror (-ke) *n*. -con'quest *n*. [L. *quæxrere*, seek]

con'science (-shens) *n*. mental sense of right and wrong. conscien'tious *a*. [L. *conscientia*, knowledge within oneself]

con'scious (-shus) *a*. aware, awake to one's surroundings and identity, in one's senses. -con'sciously *adv.* con'sciousness *n*. [L. *conscius*, aware]

con'script *n*. one compulsorily enlisted for military service. -conscrip'tion *n*. [L. *conscribere*, write together, enroll]

con'secrate *v.t.* make sacred. -consecra-tion *n*. [L. *consecrate*]

consec'utive *a*. orderly; in unbroken succession; expressing consequence. - consec'utively *adv.* [L. *consequi*, con and *sequi, secutus*, follow]

consent' *v.i.* agree to, comply. -*n*. agreement, acquiescence. [L. *consentire*, feel together]

con'sequence *n*. result, effect, what follows on a cause. con'sequent *a*. -

consequen'tial a. self-important.
con'sequently adv. [L. consequential fr. consequi, follow]

conserve' v.t. keep from change or decay. conser'vancy n. board controlling a river or port, its fisheries etc. -conserva'tion n. -conser'vative a. and n. -conser'vatory n. greenhouse. [L. conser- vare, protect]

consid'er v.t. think over; examine; make allowance for; esteem; be of opinion that. -considera'tion n. -consid'erable a. important; somewhat large. consid'erably adv. -consid'erate a. thoughtful for others; careful. consid'erately adv. [L. considerate]

consist' v.i. be composed of-, agree with, be compatible. consist'ent a. agreeing (with); constant. [L. consistere, stand firm]

consolidate v.t. make firm; combine into a connected whole. -consolida'tion n. [L. consolidate, fr. solidus, solid]

consonant n. sound making a syllable only with a vowel, a non-vowel. -a. agreeing with, in accord. -con'sonance n. [L. consonare, sound with]

con'sort n. ship sailing with another; husband or wife, esp. of a queen or king. -consort' v.i. associate, keep company with. [L. consors, fr. sors, fate]

conspicuous a. striking to the eye, very noticeable; eminent. -conspic'uously adv. [L. conspicere, see clearly]

conspire' v.i. combine for an evil purpose, plot. conspir'ator n. -conspir'acy n. -conspirator'ial a. [L. conspirare, lit. breathe together]

constable n. officer of the peace; governor of a royal fortress; British policeman. [Late L. comes stabuli, count of the stable, marshal]

con'stant a. fixed, unchanging; steadfast; always duly happening or continuing. -con'stantly adv. con'stancy n. [L. constare, stand together]

constellation n. group of stars. [L. constellation, cluster of stars. -stellar, star]

constitute v.t. set up, establish, make into, found, give form to. -constitu'tion n. make, composition; basic physical condition; disposition; body of principles on which a state is governed. -constitu'tional a. relating to a constitution; in harinony with a political constitution. -n. walk taken for health. -constituency n. a body of people entitled to elect a representative in government; the geographical location of this body. [L. constituere, place together]

constrain' v.t. force, compel; urge. -constraint' n. compulsion; restraint; embarrassment. [L. constringere, tighten]

construct' v.t. to make, build, form, put together. -construc'tion n. -construc'tive a. -construc'tively adv. [L. con struere, constructum, pile together, build]

construe' v.t. interpret, analyze, grammatically; translate. [L. construere, pile together]

consult' v.t. and i. seek counsel, advice or information (from). -consul'tant n. one who consults or advises; specialist (in medicine etc,.). consulta'tion n. [L. consultare]

consume' v.t. make away with; use up; eat or drink up; destroy. -consump'tion n. using up; destruction; wasting of the body by tuberculosis. -consump'tive a. [L. consumers, use up]

con'tact n. touching; being in touch; person contacted. -v.t. get into touch with. conta'gion (-jn) a. passing on of disease by touch, contact; physical or moral pestilence. -conta'gious a. [L. tangere, touch]

contain' v.t. hold; have room for; include; restrain (oneself). contain'er n. [L. tenere, hold]

contam'inate v.t. stain, sully, infect. -contaminant n. substance or thing that infects, pollutes, or corrupts. [L. contamen, contagion]

con'template v.t. gaze upon; meditate on; intend, purpose. [L. contemplari; orig. of augurs viewing a templum in the sky. cp. templo]

contem'porary a. existing at, or lasting, the same time; of the same age. -n. one existing at the same time. [L. tempus, tempor, time]

contend' v.i. strive, fight, dispute. con ten'tion n. -conten'tious a. -conten'tiously adv. [L. tendere, stretch]

content' a. satisfied. -v.t. satisfy. -n. satisfaction. -con'tent n. holding capacity; pl. that contained. -content'ment n. [L. continere, contain]

contest' v.t. dispute, debate, fight for. -con'test n. debate; conflict, strife; competition. -contes'tant n. -contes'table a. [L. contestari, call to witness]

con'text n. what comes before and after a passage, words, esp. as fixing meaning. [L. contexere, weave together]

con'tinent a. self-restraining; sexually chaste. -con'tinence n. [L. continere, hold together]

con'tinent n. large continuous mass of land, a main division of the earth. -The

Con'tinent, European mainland.
continen'tal a. [L. continere, hold together]

contin'ue v.t. and i. go on, carry on, last, remain, keep in existence, prolong, resume. -contin'ual a. -contin'ually adv. continuance n. -continua'tion n. - contin'uity n. contin'uous a. - contin'uously adv. [L. continuare]

contort' v.t. twist out of normal shape; writhe. contor'tion n. [L. contorquere, contortum, twist together]

con'tour (-oor) n. outline of shape of anything, esp. mountains, coast, etc. -contour (line) n. line on a map showing uniform elevation. [F., fr. contourner, follow the outline]

contraception n. birth-control; prevention of conception, usu. by artificial means. -contracep'tive a. and n. [L. contra and conception]

con'tract n. bargain, agreement; formal writing recording an agreement; agreement enforceable by law. -contract' v.i. enter into an agreement; become smaller. -v.t. agree upon; incur, become involved in; make smaller; shorten. [L. contrahere, draw together]

contradict' v.t. deny; be at variance with. -contradic'tory a. -contradic'tion n. [L. contradicere, speak against]

con'trary a. opposed; opposite, other. n. something the exact opposite of another. adv. in opposition. -con'trarily adv. - contrari'ety n. -con'trariwise adv. [L. contraries]

contrast' (-a-) v.t. bring out differences; set in opposition for comparison. - v.i. show great difference. -con'trast n. striking difference; something showing a marked difference; placing, comparison, to bring out differences. [Late L. contrastare, stand against]

contribute v.t. give or pay to a common fund; help to a common result.- v.i. give or pay or help in a common fund or effort. -contribu'tion n. -contrib'utor n. contrib'utory a. contrib'utive a. [L. contribuere. See tribute]

con'trite a. sorrowing for wrong-doing. - contri'tion n. -con'tritely adv. [L. conterere, contrit-, bruise]

contrive' v.t. devise, invent, design; succeed in bringing about. -contri'ver n. - contri'vance n. [F. controuver]

control' v.t. command, dominate, regulate; direct, check, test.-n. domination; restraint; direction; check; (spiritualism) medium's spirit-guide. -pl. controlling levers etc. of car, plane; -control'lable a.

-controlled substance n. drug whose possession and use is restricted by law. [OF. contre-rolle, duplicate register]

controversy n. dispute, debate, esp. a dispute in the press and of some duration. [L. controversus, turned against]

convalescent a. recovering from illness. -n. person recovering from sickness. convales'cence n. [L. convalescere, grow strong]

convene' v.t. call together. - v.i. assemble. -conven'er n. one who calls a meeting; chairman of a committee. [L. convenire, come together]

convenient a. handy; favorable to needs, comfort; well-adapted to one's purpose. -conve'niently adv. -conve'nience n. [L. convenire, come together]

convention n. a calling together; assembly; treaty, agreement; rule or practice based on agreement; accepted usage, esp. one grown quite formal; deadening. - conven'tional a. -conven'tionally adv. - conventionality n. [convene]

converge' v.i. approach, tend to meet. - conver'gent a. conver'gence n. (Late L. convergere, incline together]

converse' v.i. talk (with). -con'verse n. talk. -con'versant a. familiar with, versed in. [L. conversari, dwell with]

convert' v.t. apply to another purpose; change, transform; cause to adopt a religion, an opinion. -con'vert n. converted person. -convert'ible a. being capable of transformation. -n. automobile with a collapsible roof. [L. converters, turn about]

con'vex a. curved outwards, like any part of the surface of an egg; opposite of concave. -convex'ity n. [L. conuexus]

convey' v.t. carry, transport; impart, communicate; make over, transfer. - convey'ance n. carriage, vehicle; (law) transfer of property. -convey'ancer n. one skilled in the legal forms of transferring property. -convey'ancing n. [OF. conveier, fr. L. via, way; orig. escort]

convict' v.t. prove or declare guilty. - con'vict n. criminal undergoing penal servitude. convic'tion n. a convicting, verdict of guilty; a being convinced, firm belief, state of being sure. -convince' v.t. bring to a belief, satisfy by evidence or argument. [L. convincere, fr. vincere, vanquish]

convoy v.t. escort for protection, as ships, war supplies, etc. -con'voy n. party (of ships, troops, etc.) conveying or convoyed. [same as convey]

convulse' v.t. shake violently; affect with

violent involuntary contractions of the musdes. -convul′sive *a.* -convul′sively *adv.* -convul′sion *n.* [L. *convel- lere,* fr. *vellere, vulsum,* pluck]

cook *n.* one who prepares food for the table. - *v.i.* act as cook; undergo cooking. - *v.t.* prepare (food) for the table, *esp.* by heat; (*sl.*) falsify accounts, *etc.*, **cookbook** book of cooking recipes. [OE *coc,* fr. L. *coquus*]

cool *a.* moderately cold; unexcited, calm; lacking friendliness or interest.-*v.t.* **and** *i.* make or become cool. -*n.* cool time, place, *etc.* [OE. *col*]

coop *n.* cage or pen for fowls. -*v.t.* shut up in a coop; confine. -**coop′er** *n.* one who makes casks. **coop′erage** *n.* [L. *cupa,* vat, cask]

cooperate *v.i.* work together. - **co′operation** *n.* working together; production **or** distribution by cooperators who share the profits. -**co′operative** *a.* - **co′operator** *n.* [fr. L. *co-,* together, and *opus,* work]

coordinate *a.* equal in degree, status, *etc.* -*v.t.* place in the same rank; bring into order as parts of a whole. -*n.* coordinate thing; any set of numbers defining the location of a point. -**co′ordination** *n.* [L. *ordo, ordin-,* order]

cop *n.* conical ball of thread or spindle. [OE. *cop, copp*]

cope *v.i.* contend, deal with. [perh. fr. F. *coupler,* grapple]

copp′er *n.* reddish malleable ductile metal; bronze money, bronze coin; large vessel for boiling clothes. -*v.t.* cover with copper. -**copp′ersmith** *n.* one who works in copper. [L. *Cyprium aes,* bronze from Cyprus, G. *Kypros*]

cop′ula *n.* word acting as a connecting link in a sentence; connection. -**cop′ulate** *v.i.* unite sexually. -**copula′ tion** *n.* - **cop′ulative** *a.* [L. *copula bond,* couple, fr. *co-,* together, *apere,* fit]

cop′y *n.* imitation; single specimen of a book; piece of writing for a learner to imitate; matter for printing. -*v.t.* make a copy of, imitate. - **cop′yright** *n.* legal exclusive right to print and publish a book, article, work of art, *etc.* -*a.* protected by copyright *v.t.* protect by copyright. -**cop′yist** *n.* [L. *copia,* abundance]

cor′al *n.* hard substance made by sea polyps and forming pink or red or white growths, islands, reefs; ornament or toy of coral. -**cor′alline** *a.* [L. *corallum*]

cord *n.* thin rope or thick string; rib on cloth, ribbed fabric; electrical wire with protective coating; measure of cut wood,

usually 128 cub. ft.-*v.t.* fasten or bind with cord. -**cord′age** *n.* **cord′uroy** *n.* ribbed cotton stuff. -*a.* -**cord′uroy road′,** swamp road of transverse logs. [G. *chortle,* gut; *corduroy* is of unknown origin]

cordial *a.* hearty, sincere, warm. -*n.* stimulating medicine or drink cordially. [L. *car, cordis,* heart]

cord′on *n.* a chain of troops or police; ornamental cord; fruit-tree grown as a single stem. [F. dim of *corde,* cord]

cord′uroy. See **cord.**

core *n.* horny seed-case of apple and other fruits; central or innermost part of anything. [perh. fr. L. *car,* heart]

Corin′thian (-th-) *a.* of Corinth; of the Corinthian order of architecture, ornate Greek. -*n.* native of Corinth; man of fashion. [*Corinth*]

cork *n.* bark of cork-oak; piece of it, *esp.* a round piece used as a stopper. -*v.t.* stop up with a cork; stop up generally. **cork′y** *a.* light, buoyant. -**cork′screw** *n.* tool for pulling out corks. [Sp. *alcorque,* cork-shoe, slipper; of Arab. orig.]

corn *n.* grain, fruit or cereals; a grain; maize. -*v.t.* preserve (meat) with salt. - **corn′ball** *n.* person given to mawkish or unsophisticated behavioral. another word for corny. **corn′crake** *n.* bird, the landrail. -**corn′flower** *n.* blue flower growing in cornfields. -**corn row** *n.* hairstyle of narrow braids plaited in rows close to the scalp. -**corn′starch** *n.* maize flour. [OE. *corn*]

corn *n.* horny growth on foot or toe. [OF., fr. L. *cornu,* horn]

corn′ea *n.* horny membrane covering the front of the eye. [for L. *cornea tela,* horny web]

corn′er *n.* part of a room where two sides meet; remote or humble place; point where two walls, streets, *etc.* meet; angle, projection; buying up of the whole existing stock of a commodity. -*v.t.* drive into a position of difficulty, or one leaving no escape; establish a monopoly- [L. *cornu,* horn]

coroll′a *n.* flower's inner envelope of petals. [L. dim. of *corona,* crown]

cor′ollary *n.* proposition that follows without proof from another proved; natural consequence. [L. *corolla,* a garland]

coro′na *n.* crown, top; top part of a cornice; sun's luminous envelope; moon's halo during a solar eclipse. -**cor′onary** *a.* of a crown; of the crown of the head; as a circle; relating to the arteries which supply blood to the heart. [L. *corona,* crown]

cor'oner *n.* officer who holds inquests on bodies of persons supposed killed by violence, accident, *etc.* **-cor'onership** *n.* [A.F. *corouner*, fr. *coroune*, crown]

corp'oral *n.* non-commissioned officer below a sergeant. [OF. *corporal*, fr. L. *corpus*, body]

corporation *n.* body of persons legally authorised to act as an individual; authorities of a town or city; (*colloq.*) rotundity of figure. **-cor'porate** *a.* [fr. L. *corporale*, to embody]

corps *n.* military force, body of troops. [F. = body; L. *corpus*]

corpse *n.* dead body of human being. [L. *corpus*]

corp'ulent *a.* bulky of body, fat. **-cor'pulence** *n.* [L. *corpulentus*, fr. *corpus*]

corpuscle (-usl) *n.* minute organism or particle, *esp.* the red and white corpuscles of the blood. [L. *corpusculum*, dim. of *corpus*, body]

correct' *v.t.* set right; rebuke, punish; counteract; neutralize. *-a.* right, exact, accurate, in accordance with facts or a standard. [L. *corrigere, correct-*, fr. *regere*, rule]

corr'elate *v.t.* bring into mutual relation. *-n.* either of two things or words necessarily implying the other. **-correlation** *n.* [*relate*]

corr'espond' *v.i.* exchange letters; answer or agree with in some respect. **-correspond'ence** *n.* **correspon'dent** *n.* [*respond*]

corrob'orate *v.t.* confirm, support (a statement, *etc.*). **-corrobora'tion** *n.* **corrob'orative** *a.* [L. *corroborate*, strengthen]

corrode' *v.t.* eat away, eat into the surface of (by chemical action, disease, *etc.*). **corro'sive** *a.* **-corro'sion** *n.* [L. *rodere, ros*, gnaw]

corr'ugated *a.* wrinkled, bent into ridges. **-corruga'tion** *n.* [L. *corrugatus*, fr. *ruga*, wrinkle]

corrupt' *v.t.* make rotten; pervert, make evil; bribe. *- v.i.* rot. *a.* tainted with vice or sin; influenced by bribery; spoilt by mistakes, altered for the worse (of words, literary passages, etc.) [L. *corrumpere, corrupt-*, lit. break up]

cor'sage *n.* bodice of a woman's dress; flowers *etc.* to wear on it. [OF.]

cortisone *n.* synthetic hormone, used *esp.* in treatment of rheumatoid arthritis. [fr. L. *cortex*, covering (of the kidneys)]

cosine *abbrev.* **cos** (kos) *n.* (*trigonometry*) in a right-angled triangle, the cosine of an acute angle is the ratio of its adjacent side to the hypotenuse. [*co-* for complement, and L. *sinus*, a bay]

cosmetic *n.* a preparation to beautify the skin. [G. *kosmos*, order, adornment]

cos'mic (kos'-) *a.* relating to the universe; of the vastness of the universe. **-cos'mic rays**, shortest known electromagnetic waves. **-cosmol'ogy** *n.* the science or the study of the universe. **-cosmolog'ical** *a.* **-cosmol'ogist** *n.* **-cosmog'raphy** *n.* description or mapping of the universe. **-cosmog'rapher** *n.* **-cosmograph'ic** *a.* **-cosmopol'itan** *a.* relating to all parts of the world **-cos'mos** *n.* universe; ordered system, as opposed to chaos. [G. *kosmos*, order (the name given by Pythagoras to the universe)]

cost *v.t.* entail the payment, or loss, or sacrifice of; have as price. *-n.* price; expenditure of time, labor, *etc.* *-pl.* expenses of a lawsuit. **-cost'ing** *n.* system of calculating cost of production. **-cost'ly** *a.* of great price or value; involving much expenditure, loss, *etc.* **-cost'liness** *n.* [L. *constare*, fr. *stare*, stand]

cos'tal *a.* of, pert. to *-ribs.* **-cos'tate** *a.* ribbed. [L. *costa*, rib]

cos'tume *n.* style of dress; outer clothes; set of outer clothes for a woman; theatrical clothes. **-costu'mier** *n.* [It. *costume*, custom, fashion]

cot *n.* swinging bed an board ship; light or folding bed. [Hind. *khat*]

cott'age *n.* small house. **-cott'ager** *n.* [AF. *cotage*, fr. OE. *cot*]

cott'on *n.* plant; the white downy fibrous covering of its seeds; thread, cloth made of this fibre. **-cott'on-wool** *n.* wadding of raw cotton. [Arab, *qutn*]

cott'on *v.i.* take (to); agree (with). [orig. unknown]

couch *v.t.* put into (words); lower (a lance) for action; cause to lie down. *-v.i.* lie down, crouch. *-n.* piece of furniture for reclining on by day, sofa; bed, or what serves for one. [F. *coucher*, OF. *colchier*, fr. L. *collocare*, place together]

cough (kof) *v.i.* expel air from the lungs with sudden effort and noise, often to remove an obstruction. *-n.* act of coughing; ailment or affection of coughing. [imit.origin]

council *n.* any deliberative or administrative body; one of its meetings. **-coun'cilor, councillor** *n.* [L. *concilium*, assembly]

coun'sel *n.* deliberation or debate; advice; intentions; barrister or barristers. *- v.t.* advise, recommend. **-coun'selor, counsellor** *n.* [L. *consilium*, plan]

count *v.t.* reckon, calculate, number; include; consider to be. - *v.i.* be reckoned in; depend or rely (on); be of importance. *n.* reckoning; item in a list of charges or indictment; act of counting. -**count'less** *a.* -**count'ing-house** *n.* room or building or actions. [L. *computare,* reckon]

count *n.* European nobleman of rank corresponding to British earl. -**count'ess** *n. fem.* wife or widow of a count or earl. [L. *comes, commit-,* a companion]

count'er *n.* table of a bank, shop, *etc.,* on which money is paid, *etc.;* disk or other object used for counting, *esp.* in card games; token. [F. *comptoir,* fr. L. *computare,* count]

count'er *n.* curved part of the stern of a ship. [orig. uncertain]

count'er *adv.* in the opposite direction; contrary. - *v.t.* oppose, contradict. -**counter culture** *n.* alternative lifestyle that opposes tradition and social norms. [*See* counter- *prefix*]

count'er *n.* fencing, *etc.,* parry. - *v.t.* and *i.* parry. [for *counter-parry*]

counter- *prefix* used to make compounds with meaning of reversed, opposite, rival, retaliatory. [L. *contra,* against]. -**counteract'** *v.t.* neutralize or hinder. -**counterac'tion** *n.* -**count'er-attack** *v.t.* and *i.* and *n.* attack after an enemy's advance. -**count'er-attraction** *n.* -**counterbal'ance** *n.* weight balancing or neutralizing another. -**count'er-claim** *n.* (*esp.* in *law*) claim to off-set an opponent's -**count'er-clock'wise** *adv.* and *a.* -**counterfeit** *a.* sham, forged false. -*n.* imitation, forgery. -*v.t.* imitate with intent to deceive; forge. -**counterfeiter** *n.* [F. *fait,* made]

counterpart *n.* something so like another as to be mistaken for it; something complementary or correlative of another. [*counter* and *part*]

coun'try *n.* region, district; territory of a nation, land of birth, residence, *etc.;* rural districts as opposed to town; nation. **country music** *n.* popular folk music of S.W and S.E. U.S. *usu.* accompanied by guitar, banjo, and other stringed instruments; cowboy music (also **country and western music**). -**coun'tryside** *n.* any rural district or its inhabitants. - **coun'trified** *a.* rural in manner or appearance. [F. *controe,* Late L. *contrata,* (land) spread before one, *contra*]

coun'ty *n.* division of a country or state. [F. *comté,* fr. *comte,* count]

coup'le *n.* two, a pair; leash for two hounds. -*v.t.* tie (hounds) together; connect, fasten together; associate, connect in the mind. -*v.i.* join, associate. -**coup'ler** *n.* -**coup'ling** *n.* **coup'let** *n.* pair of lines of verse, *esp.* rhyming and of equal length. [F., fr. L. *copula,* bond]

cou'pon *n.* detachable ticket entitling the holder to something, *eg.* periodical payment of interest, entrance to a competition, share of rationed goods, *etc.* [F., fr. *couper,* cut]

cou'rage (ku'-) *n.* bravery, boldness. **coura'geous** *a.* -**coura'geously** *adv.* [F., fr. L. *cor,* heart]

cou'rier *n.* express messenger; attendant on travelers. [F. *courrier,* fr. L. *currere,* run]

course *n.* movement or run in space or time; direction of movement; successive development, sequence; line of conduct or action; series of lectures, exercises, *etc.;* any of the successive parts of a dinner. - *v.t.* hunt. *v.i.* run swiftly, gallop about - **cours'er** *n.* swift horse. [F. *cours,* fr. L. *currere,* run]

court *n.* space enclosed by buildings, yard; number of houses enclosing a yard opening on to a street; section of a museum, *etc.;* area marked offer enclosed for playing various games; retinue and establishment of a sovereign; assembly held by a sovereign; body with judicial powers, place where they sit, one of their sittings; attention, homage, flattery. - *v.t.* seek; woo, try to win or attract. **cour'teous** *a.* polite. -**cour'teously** *adv.* -**cour'tesy** *n.* -**court'ly** *a.* ceremoniously polite; characteristic of a court. -**court'liness** *n.* -**court- mar'tial** *n.* court of naval or military officers for trying naval or military offenses. - **court'ship** *n.* wooing. -**court'yard** *n.* space enclosed by buildings. [L. *cohors, cohort-;* cognate with *hortus,* garden]

cous'in (kuz'-) *n.* sons or daughter of an uncle or aunt; person related to another by descent from one ancestor through two of his or her children. [Med. L. *cosinus*]

cove *n.* small inlet of coast, sheltered small bay. [OE. *cofa,* recess]

cov'enant (ku-) *n.* contract, mutual agreement; compact.- *v.t.* agree to by a covenant.- *v.i.* enter into a covenant. [L. *convenire,* come together]

cov'er (ku-) *v.t.* be over the whole top of, enclose; include; shield; protect; screen; counterbalance.-*n.* lid, wrapper, envelope, binding, screen, anything which covers. -**cov'ert** *a.* secret, veiled. -*n.* thicket, place sheltering game. -**cov'ertly** *adv.* [F. *coucrir,* L. *cooperire*]

cov'et (ku-) *v.t.* long to possess, *esp.* what

belongs to another. -co'vetous *a.* - co'vetousness *n.* [L. *cupiditare*, desire]

cow *n.* female ox; female of elephant, whale, *etc.* -cow'bane *n.* water hemlock. -cow'boy *n.* cattleman on a ranch. -cow'- catcher *n.* fender on locomotive for clearing line. [OE. *cu*]

cow *v.t.* frighten into submission, overawe. [ON. *kuga*, oppress]

cow'ard *n.* one given to fear, fainthearted. -cow'ardly *a.* -cow'ardice *n.* [F. *couard*, fr. L. *cauda*, tail]

cow'er *v.i.* crouch, shrinking, in fear or cold. [cp, Ger. *kauern*]

cowl *n.* monk's hooded cloak; its hood; hooded top for chimney; (engine) bonnet. [L. *cucullus*, hood of a cloak]

cox'swain (kok'sn), **cox** *n.* steerer of a boat, *esp.* one in permanent charge of a boat. [earlier *cock-swain*]

coy *a.* shy; slow to respond, *esp.* to lovemaking. -coy'ly *adv.* -coy'ness *n.* [F. *coi*, fr. L. *quietus*]

coyo'te *n.* N. American prairiewolf. [Mex. *coyote*]

CPU *n.* (*compute.*) portion of the computer that performs calculations and controls its primary functions. [*central processing unit*]

crab *n.* edible crustacean with ten legs, of which the front pair are armed with strong pincers, noted for sidelong and backward walk. - *v.i.* (of aircraft) fly sideways. - crabb'ed *a.* perverse; badtempered, irritable; of writing, hard to read. [OE. *crabba*; the *a.* fr. the crooked walk of the creature]

crack *v.t.* break, split partially; break with sharp noise; cause to make a sharp noise, as of whip, rifle, *etc.* - *v.i.* make a sharp noise; split; of the voice, lose clearness when changing from -boy's to man's. *n.* sharp explosive noise; split, fissure; flaw. -(*sl.*) sharp witty retort, wisecrack. -*a.* special, smart, of great reputation for skill or fashion. -crack'er *n.* explosive firework; a thin dry cake. [OE. *cracian*; of imit.orig.]

cra'dle *n.* infant's bed on rockers; *fig.* earliest resting-place or home; supporting framework. - *v.t.* lay in, or hold as in, a cradle; cherish in early stages. [OE. *cradol*]

craft *n.* skill, cunning; manual art; skilled trade; members of a trade. -crafts'man *n.* -crafts'manship *n.* -crafty *a.* cunning. - craf'tily *adv.* [OE. *cræft*]

craft *n.* vessel of any kind for carriage by water or air; ship; ships collectively. [fr. small craft for vessels of small craft, power]

crag *n.* steep rugged rock. [*Celt.*]

cram *v.t.* fill quite full; stuff, force; pack tightly; feed to excess; prepare quickly for examination. -*n.* close-packed state; rapid preparation for examination; information so got; (*sl.*) lie. [OE. *crammian*, fr. *crimman*, insert]

cramp' *n.* painful muscular contraction; clamp for holding masonry, timber, *etc.*, together. - *v.t.* hem in, keep within too narrow limits. [OF. *crampe*]

crane *n.* large wading bird with long legs, neck and bill; machine for moving heavy weights. -*v.i.* stretch the neck for better seeing. [OE. *cran*]

cra'nium *n.* skull -cra'nial *a.* [Low L. G. *kranion*, skull]

crank *n.* arm at right angles to an axis, for turning a main shaft, changing reciprocal into rotary motion, *etc.*; fanciful turn of speech; fad; faddist. - *v.t.* and *i.* turn, wind. -crank'y *a.* shaky; crotchety. [OE. *crane*]

crann'y *n.* small opening, chink. - crann'ied *a.* [F. *cran*, notch]

crash *n.* violent fall or impact with loud noise; burst of mixed loud sound, *e.g.* of thunder, breaking crockery; sudden collapse or downfall. -*v.i.* make a crash: fall, come with, strike with, a crash; collapse; of an airplane, come to earth by, or with, an accident. [imit. origin]

crash *n.* coarse linen for towels. [Russ. *krashenina*, colored linen]

crass *a.* grossly stupid; gross. [L. *crassus*, thick, fat]

crate' *n.* open-work case of wooden bars or wicker. [Du. *krat*, basket]

cra'ter *n.* mouth of a volcano; bow-shaped cavity, esp. one made by the explosion of a large shell, a mine, *etc.* [G. *krater*, mixingbowl]

crave *v.t.* and *i.* have a very strong desire for, long for; ask. -cra'ving *n.* [OE. *crafi*, *an*, demand as a right]

cra'ven *a.* cowardly, abject. -*n.* coward. [OF. *craventer*, overthrow]

crawl *v.i.* move along the ground on the belly or on the hands and knees; move very slowly; move stealthily or abjectly; swim with the crawl-stroke. -*n.* crawling motion; very slow walk; racing stroke at swimming. -crawl'er *n.* [ON. *krafla*, claw]

cray'on *n.* stick or pencil of colored chalk; picture made with crayons. [F. *crayon*, pencil, fr. *craie*, chalk]

cra'zy *a.* rickety, failing to pieces; full of cracks; insane, extremely foolish; madly eager (for). -craze *v.t.* make crazy. -*n.*

general or individual mania. [F. *craser*, break]

cream *n.* oily part of milk; best part of anything. - *v.i.* form cream. -*v.t.* take cream from; take the best part from. **-cream'y** *a.* **-cream'ery** *n.* butter and cheese factory; shop for milk and cream. [L. *chrisma*, fr. G. *chrism*, anoint]

create' *v.t.* bring into being; give rise to; make. **-crea'tion** *n.* **-creative** *a.* **-crea'tor** *n.* **-crea'ture** *n.* anything created; living being; dependent, tool. [L. *create*]

cre'dence *n.* belief, credit; side-table for the elements of the Eucharist before consecration. **-creden'tials** *n.pl.* letters of introduction, *esp.* those given to an ambassador. [L. *credere*, believe]

cred'it *n.* belief, trust; good name; influence or honor or power based on the trust of others; trust in another's ability to pay; allowing customers to take goods for later payment; money at one's disposal in a bank, *etc.*; side of a book on which such sums are entered, - *v.t.* believe; put on the credit side of an account; attribute, believe that a person has. **-cred'ible** *a.* worthy of belief. **-cred'ibly** *adv.* **-credibil'ity** *n.* - **cred'itable** *a.* bringing honor. - **cred'itably** *adv.* **-cred'itor** *n.* one to whom a debt is due. **-credit'worthy** *a.* (of an individual or business enterprise) adjudged as meriting credit on the basis of such factors as earning power previous record of debt repayment, *etc.* **-cred'ulous** *a.* too ready to believe. **-credu'lity** *n.* [L. *credere*, believe]

creed *n.* a system of religious belief; summary of Christian doctrine; system of beliefs, opinions, principles, *etc.* [L. *credo*, I believe]

creek *n.* narrow inlet on the sea-coast. [ON. *kriki*, bend, nook]

creel *n.* basket, *esp.* angler's fishhawker's basket. [origin uncertain. cp. OF. *creil*, hurdle; *crates*, wickerwork]

creep *v.i.* make way along the ground, as a snake; move with stealthy, slow movements; go about abjectly; of skin or flesh, to feel a shrinking, shivering sensation, due to fear or repugnance. **creep'er** *n.* creeping or climbing plant. **-creep'y** *a.* uncanny, unpleasant; causing the flesh to creep. [OE. *creopan*]

cremation *n.* burning as a means of disposing of corpses; this process. **-cremate'** *v.t.* **-crem'atory, cremator'ium** *n.* place for cremation. [L. *cremare*, burn]

Cre'ole *n.* native of the West Indies or Sp. America descended from European ancestors; a person descended from French or Spanish ancestors settled in the U.S. Gulf states; languages associated with these cultures. [F. *croole*]

cres'cent *n.* moon as seen on the first or last quarter; any figure of this shape; row of houses on a curve. -*a.* growing, increasing. [L. *crescere*, grow]

crest *n.* comb or tuft on an animal's head; plume or top of a helmet; top of mountain, ridge, wave, *etc.*; badge above the shield of a coat of arms, also used separately on seals, plate, *etc.* - *v.i.* crown. -*v.t.* reach the top of. **-crest'fallen** *a.* cast down by defeat or failure. [L. *crest*]

cretaceous (-shus) *a.* chalky; (*geol.*) of the upper Mesozoic rocks. [L. *creta*, chalk]

cret'in *n.* deformed idiot. **-cret'inism** *n.* **-cret'inous** *a.* [Swiss *crestin*, Christian]

crev'ice (-is) *n.* cleft, fissure. **-crevasse'** *n.* deep open chasm in a glacier. [F. *crevasse*]

crew *n.* ship's or boat's company, excluding passengers; gang or set. fearlier crue, accrue, reinforcement. [fr. L. *crescere*, grow]

crew'el *n.* woolen embroidery yarn. [orig. uncertain]

crew neck *n.* rounded, close-fitting neckline on a sweater, shirt, or other top.

crib *n.* barred rack for fodder; child's bed *usu.* with high or with barred sides; cards thrown out at cribbage; a plagiarism; a translation. -*v.t.* confine in small space; copy unfairly. **-cribb'age** *n.* card game. [OE. *cribb*, ox-stall]

crick *n.* spasm or cramp, *esp.* in the neck. [orig. uncertain]

crick'et *n.* chirping insect. [F. *criquet*, fr. *criquer*, creak, crackle]

crime *n.* violation of the law (usually of a serious offense): wicked or forbidden act; (military) offence against regulations. -*v.t.* charge (in army) with an offence against the regulations. **-crim'inal** *a.* and *n.* - **crim'inally** *adv.* **-criminal'ity** *n.* - **criminol'ogy** *n.* study of crime and criminals. [L. *crimen*]

crim'son (-z-) *a.* of rich deep red. -*n.* the color. -*v.t.* and *i.* turn crimson. [O. Sp. *cremesin*, fr. Arab. *qirmiz, kermes*, cochineal insect]

cringe *v.i.* shrink, cower; behave obsequiously. [ME. *crengen*, succumb]

cripp'le *n.* one not having a normal use of the limbs, a disabled or deformed person. -*v.t.* maim or disable; diminish the resources of. [OE. *crypel*]

cri'sis *n.* turning point or decisive moment, *esp.* in illness; time of acute danger or suspense. [G. *krisis*, decision]

crite′rion *n.* -(crite′ria *pl*). stan dard of judgment; standard; rule. [G.]

crit′ic *n.* one who passes judgment; writer expert in judging works of literature, art, *etc.* -**crit′ical** *a.* skilled in, or given to, judging; fault-finding; of great importance, decisive. -**crit′icism** *n.* -**crit′ically** *adv.* -**crit′icize** *v.t.* -**critique′** *n.* critical essay, carefully written criticism. [G. *kritikos, krinein,* judge]

croak *v.t.* utter a deep hoarse cry, as a raven, frog; talk dismally. -*n.* such cry. - **croak′er** *n.* [imit. origin]

cro′chet *n.* kind of knitting done with a hooked needle. -*v.t.* and *i.* do such work. [F. dim. of *croc,* hook]

crock *n.* earthenware jar or pot; broken piece of earthenware; old broken-down horse. -(*sl.*) broken-down or unfit person. -**crock′ery** *n.* earthenware. [OE. *crocc,* pot]

croc′odile (krok′-) *n.* large amphibious reptile. -**croc′odile-tears,** hypocritical pretense of grief, the crocodile being fabled to shed tears while devouring human victims. [G. *krokodeilos,* lizard]

Croe′sus *n.* very wealthy man. [*Crcesus,* king of Lydia]

crone *n.* withered old woman. [perh. fr. Ir. *crion,* withered]

cro′ny *n.* intimate friend [earlier *chrony,* contemporary. [G. *chronos,* time]

crook *n.* hooked staff, any hook, bend, sharp turn; (*sl.*) cheat; criminal. - *v.t.* bend into a hook or curve. -**crook′ed** *a.* bent, twisted; deformed; dishonest. [ON. *krokr*]

croon *v.t.* sing in an undertone; hum. - **croo′ner** *n.* entertainer who croons sentimental songs. [cp. Du. *kreunen,* groan]

crop *n.* year's produce of cultivation of any plant or plants, in a farm, field, country, *etc.*; harvest, *lit.* or *lig.*; pouch in a birde̓s gullet; stock of a whip; hunting whip; cutting of the hair short, closely-cut head of hair. - *v.t.* and *i.* poll or clip; bite or eat down; raise produce or occupy land with it. [OE. *cropp,* head of herb, ear of corn, *etc.*]

croquette′ *n.* meat or fish ball, cake; rissole. [F.]

cross *n.* stake with a transverse bar, used for crucifixion. -**the Cross,** that on which Christ suffered; model or picture of this; symbol of the Christian faith; affliction; intermixture of breeds, hybrid. -*v.t.* place so as to intersect; make the sign of the cross on or over; pass across, over; meet and pass; mark with lines across, thwart, oppose; modify breed of animals or plants by intermixture. - *v.i.* intersect, pass over. -*a.* transverse; intersecting; contrary; adverse; out of temper. -**cross′bow** *n.* bow fixed across a wooden shoulder-stock. - **cross′coun′try** *a.* across fields or land. **cross′eyed** *a.* squinting. -**cross-exam′ine** *v.t.* examine a witness already examined by the other side.[L. *crux*]

crouch *v.i.* bend low for hiding, or to spring, or servilely. [orig. uncertain]

croup *n.* throat disease of children. [Sc. orig. a verb, *croak*]

crow *n.* large black carrion-eating bird. [OE. *crawe,* imit. of *cry*]

crow (-ō) *v.i.* utter the cock's cry; utter joyful sounds; exult. -*n.* cry of the cock. [OE. *crawan*]

crowd *v.i.* flock together. -*v.t.* cram, force, thrust, pack; fill with people. -**crowd out,** exclude by excess already in. -*n.* throng, large number, mass. [OE. *crudan,* press, push]

crown *n.* monarch's headdress; wreath for the head; royal power; formerly, British coin of five shillings; various foreign coins; top of the head; summit or topmost part; completion or perfection of anything. [L. *corona*]

CRT *n.* (*compute.*) output device the converts electric signals into visual form by beans of a controlled electron beam; computer screen. [cathode *ray tube*]

cru′cial *a.* decisive, critical. [fr. L. *crux,* cross, in the sense of fingerpost at crossroads, decision-point]

cru′cify *v.t.* put to death on a cross. - **crucifix′ion** *n.* **cru′cifix** *n.* image of Christ on the cross. [L. *cruci figere* (*p.p. fixus*) fix on a cross]

crude *a.* in the natural **or** raw state; rough, unfinished, rude. -**crude′ly** *adv.* -**cru′dity** *n.* [L. *crudus,* raw]

cru′el *a.* delight in or callous to others' pain; merciless. -**cru′elty** *n.* -**cruelly** *adv.* [F. *cruel,* L. *crudetis*]

cru′et *n.* small stoppered bottle for vinegar, oil, *etc.*; stand holding such bottles, mustard-pots, *etc.* [OF. *cruie,* pot, F. *cruche,* jar]

cruise (-ooz) *v.i.* sail about without precise destination. -*n.* cruising voyage. -**cruise control** *n.* device that maintains the speed of a vehicle at a setting chosen by the driver. -**cruis′er** *n.* warship of less displacement and greater speed than a battleship. [Du. *kruisen,* fr. *kruis,* cross]

crumb *n.* small particle, fragment; soft part of bread. -*v.t.* reduce to, or cover with crumbs. -**crum′ble** *v.t.* and *i.* break into small fragments; decay. [OE. *cruma*]

crusad'e *n.* medieval Christian war to recover the Holy Land; campaign against evil. - *v.i.* engage in a crusade. -**crusa'der** *n.* [F. *croisade*, and Sp. *cruzada*, marked with a cross]

crush *v.t.* compress so as to break, bruise, crumple; break to small pieces; defeat utterly, overthrown. act of crushing; crowded mass of persons, *etc.* [OF. *cruissir*]

crust *n.* hard outer part of bread; similar hard outer casing on anything. - *v.t.* and *i.* cover with or form a crust. -**crust'y** *a.* having or like a crust, short-tempered. -**crust'ily** *adv.* [L. *crusta*, rind]

crustacean (-shn) *n.* hard-shelled animal, *e.g.* crab, lobster shrimp. -**crusta'ceous** (-shus) *a.* [L. *crusta*, rind]

crutch *n.* staff with a cross-piece to go under the armpit for the use of cripples; forked support. [OE. *crycc*]

crux (kruks) *n.* the most important point; (*fig.*) a cause of extreme difficulty or perplexity. [L. *crux, crucis*, a cross]

cry *v.i.* utter a call; shout; weep, wail. -*v.t.* utter loudly, proclaim. -*n.* loud utterance; scream, wail, shout; the characteristic call of an animal; watch-word; fit of weeping. [F. *crier*]

crypt *n.* vault, *esp.* under a church. -**cryp'tic** *a.* secret, mysterious. -**cryp'togram** *n.* piece of cipher-writing. [G. *krypte*, vault; *cryptein*, hide]

crys'tal *n.* clear transparent mineral; very clear glass; cut-glass vessels; form assumed by many substances with a definite internal structure and external shape of symmetrically arranged plane surfaces. -**crys'tal-set'**, wireless set in which a small crystal rectifies current. -**crystalline** *a.* -**crys'tal** *v.t.* and form into crystals; become definite. [G. *krystallos*, clear ice]

cub *n.* young of the fox and other animals; junior Boy Scout. - *v.t.* and *i.* bring forth (cubs). [perh. fr. Ir. *cuib*, whelp]

cube *n.* regular solid figure contained by six equal squares; cubemultiplying a number by itself twice. -*v.t.* multiply thus. -**cu'bic** *a.* three-dimensional; of the third power. -**cu'bical** *a.* cube-shaped. -**cu'bism** *n.* style of art in which objects are presented to give the appearance of an assemblage of geometrical shapes. -**cu'bist** *n.* (G. *kybos*, a die]

cu'bicle *n.* small separate sleeping compartment in a dormitory. [L. *cubare*, lie]

cu'bit *n.* an old measure of length, about 18 inches. [L. *cubitus*, forearm, from elbow to finger-tips]

cuck'old *n.* husband of unfaithful wife. [OF. *eucu*, cuckoo)

cu'ckoo *n.* migratory bird named from its call. [imit. orig.]

cud'dle *v.t.* hug. -*v.i.* lie close and snug, nestle. [orig. uncertain]

cue *n.* pigtail; long tapering stick used by a billiard player. -**cue'ist** *n.* [F. *queue*, tail]

cue *n.* last words of an actor's speech as signal to another to act or speak; hint or example for action. [earlier 'q.,' for L. *quando*, when (to come in)]

cuff *n.* ending of a sleeve; wristband. [ME. *cuffe*]

cuff *v.t.* strike with the hand. -*n.* blow with the hand. [F. *coiffer*]

cuisine' *n.* cookery; kitchen department. [F.]

culinary *a.* of, or for, cooking. [L. *culinarius*, fr. *culina*, kitchen]

cull *v.t.* gather, select. [L. *colligere*, collect]

culminate *v.i.* reach the highest point; come to a climax. -**culmina'tion** *n.* [L. *culmen*, summit]

culpable *a.* blameworthy. -**culpabil'ity** *n.* -**cul'pably** *adv.* [L. *culpa*, fault]

cul'prit *n.* offender, one guilty of an offense; (*law*) prisoner about to be tried. [fr. OF. *cul. prest*, contr. of *culpable prest*, ready (to be proved) guilty]

cult *n.* system of religious worship; pursuit of, or devotion to, some object. [L. *cultus*, fr. *colere*, cultivate]

cultivate *v.t.* raise (*crops*) on land; develop, improve, refine; devote attention to, practice, frequent. [L. *cultura*]

culture *n.* cultivation; state of manners, taste, and intellectual development at a time or place. **cul'tured pearl'**, artificially grown real pearl. -**cul'tured** *a.* refined, showing culture. -**cul'tural** *a.* [Late L. *cultivate*, fr. *colere*, till]

culvert *n.* tunneled drain for the passage of water, under a road, *etc.* [orig. unknown]

cumulative *a.* representing the surn of items added by degrees; of shares, entitled to arrears of interest before other shares receive current interest. [L. *cumulus*, heap]

cu'mulus *n.* cloud shaped in rounded white masses. -**cu'muli** *pl.* [L. *cumulus*, heap]

cunn'ing *n.* skill, dexterity; selfish cleverness; skill in deceit or evasion; -*a.* having such qualities, crafty, sly. -**cunn'ingly** *adv.* [OE. *cunnan*, know]

cup *n.* small drinking vessel of china or earthenware with a handle at one side; any small drinking vessel; contents of a cup; various cup-shaped formations. cavities, sockets, *etc.* -**cup'board** *n.* closed cabinet, recess, or case with shelves, *esp.* one for crockery or provisions. [OE. *cuppe*; a cupboard was originally a table or sideboard]

Cu'pid *n.* Roman god of love. [L.]

curator *n.* person in charge of something, *esp.* a museum, library, *etc.* -**cura'torship** *n.* [L. fr. *curare*, care]

curb *n.* chain or strap passing under a horse's lower jaw and giving powerful control with reins; any check or means of restraint; stone edging to a footpath or sidewalk. -*v.t.* apply a curb to (a horse); restrain. -**curb'stone** *n.* [F. *courber*, fr. L. *curvare*, bend]

curd *n.* coagulated milk. -**curd'le** *v.t.* and *i.* turn into curd, coagulate; of blood, to shrink with horror, *etc.* -**curd'y** *a.* (ME. *crudde*, prob. fr. OE. *crudan*, press]

cure *v.t.* heal, restore to health; remedy; preserve (fish, skins, *etc.*). -*n.* remedy; course of medical treatment; successful treatment, restoration to health. cure of souls, care of a parish or congregation. [L. *curate*, fr. *cura*, care]

cu'rious *a.* eager to know, inquisitive; prying; puzzling, strange, odd; minutely accurate. **cu'riously** *adv.* -**curios'ity** *n.* eagerness to know; inquisitiveness; strange or rare thing. -**cu'rio** *n.* curiosity of the kind sought for collections. [L. *curiosus*, inquisitive caring for, fr. *cura*, care]

cu'rium *n.* radioactive inert gaseous element. [Marie and Pierre *Curie*]

curl *v.t.* bend into spiral or curved shape. -*v.i.* take spiral or curved shape or path. -*n.* spiral lock of hair; spiral or curved state or form or motion. -**cur'ly** *a.* -**curl'ing** *n.* game like bowls played with large rounded stones on ice. [ME. *crul*, curly]

curr'ent *a.* in circulation or general use; going on, not yet superseded; fluent, running. -*n.* body of water or air in motion; flow of a river, *etc.*; tendency, drift, transmission of electricity through a conductor. -**curr'ently** *adv.* -**curr'ency** *n.* time during which anything is current; money in use; state of being in use. [L. *currere*, run]

curriculum *n.* (**curricula** *pl.*) course of study at school, college *etc.* [L., fr. *currere*, run]

curr'y *n.* preparation of a mixture of spices; dish flavored with it. -*v.t.* prepare a dish with curry. [Tamil *kari*, relish]

curse *n.* utterance intended to send a person or thing to destruction or punishment; expletive in the form of a curse; affliction,

bane, scourge. - *v.t.* and *i.* utter a curse, swear at, afflict. [OE. *curs*]

cursor *n.* (*compute.*) flashing pointer on CRT that can be moved by keys or mouse.

curt *a.* short, brief, rudely brief. **curt'ness** *n.* -**curt'ly** *adv.* [L. *curtus*, short]

curtail' *v.t.* cut short, diminish. -**curtail'ment** *n.* [L. *curtus*, short]

cur'tain (-tin) *n.* cloth hung as a screen; screen separating audience and stage in a theater; end to an act or scene. -*v.t.* provide or cover with a curtain. -**curt'ain-fire** *n.* barrage. -**curt'ain** raiser *n.* short play coming before the main one. [Late L. *cortina*]

curve *n.* line of which no part is straight, bent line. -*v.t.* bend into a curve. - *v.i.* have or assume a curved form or direction. -**curv'ature** *n.* a bending; a bent shape. -**curvet'** *n.* horse's trained movement like a short leap over nothing. -*v.i.* to make this movement; frisk. -**curvilin'ear** *a.* of bent lines. [L, *curvus*, bent, *curvare*, bend]

cu'shion (*n.* bag filled with soft stuffing or air, to support or ease the body; pad, elastic lining of the sides of a billiard table. -*v.t.* provide or protect with a cushion. [F. *coussin*]

cusp *n.* point; horn of the moon; crown of a tooth; the meeting-point of two intersecting curves; the point of change; small architectural ornament. [L. *cuspis*, point]

cus'tody *n.* safe-keeping, guardianship, imprisonment. -**custo'dian** *n.* keeper, caretaker, curator. [L. *custodial* fr. *custos*, keeper]

cus'tom *n.* fashion, usage, habit; busi ness patronage; *pl.* duties levied on imports. -**cus'tomary** *a.* -**cus'tomarily** *adv.* -**cus'tomer** *n.* one who enters a shop to buy, *esp.* one who deals regularly with it. -**cus'tomize** *v.t.* to build or alter to particular specifications. [OF. *coustume*, fr. L. *consuetudo*]

cut *v.t.* sever or penetrate or wound or divide or separate with pressure of an edge or edged instrument; pare or detach or trim or shape by cutting; divide; intersect; reduce, abridge; ignore (a person); strike (with a whip, *etc.*) -*n.* act of cutting; stroke, blow (of knife, whip, *etc.*); fashion, shape; incision; engraving; piece cut off, division. -**cutting edge** *n.* lead or forefront of a field; state-of-the-art. [orig. uncertain]

cute *a.* (*sl.*) shrewd; cunning; engaging, attractive. [*acute*]

cut'ler *n.* one who makes, repairs or deals in knives and cutting implements. -**cut'lery** *n.* knives, scissors. [OF. *coutelier*, fr. *coutel*, knife]

cut'let *n.* small piece of meat broiled or fried. [F. *cotelette*, double dim. of *cote*, rib, L. *costa*]

cyan'ogen *n.* poisonous gas, compound of carbon and nitrogen. -**cy'anide** *n.* compound of cyanogen. -**cyano'sis** *n.* blue jaundice. [G. *kyanos*, dark blue]

cy'cle (si'-) *n.* recurrent series or period; rotation of events; complete series or period; development following a course of stages; series of poems, etc.; bicycle. -*v.i.* move in cycles; use a bicycle. -**cy'clic, cy'clical** *a.* -**cy'clist** *n.* bicycle-rider. **cyclom'eter** *n.* instrument for measuring circles or recording distance travelled by a wheel, *esp.* of a bicycle. [G. *kyklos*, circle]

cy'clone *n.* a system of winds moving round a center of low pressure; a circular storm. -**cyclon'ic** *a.* [G. *kyklos*, circle]

cyl'inder (sil'-) *n.* roller-shaped solid or hollow body, of uniform diameter; piston chamber of an engine. -**cylin'drical** *a.* [G. *kylindein*, roll]

cym'bal (sim'-) *n.* one of a pair of cymbals. -*pl.* musical instrument consisting of two round brass plates struck together to produce a ringing or clashing sound. [G. *kymbalon*]

cyn'ic (sin'-) *n.* one of a sect of Greek philosophers affecting contempt of luxury and bluntness of speech; cynical person. -**cyn'ical** *a.* skeptical of goodness; given to showing up human weakness, seeing the more unworthy motive in others. in showing or admitting motives more commonly concealed. -**cyn'icism** *n.* [G. *kynikos*, doglike]

cy'press *n.* coniferous tree with very dark foliage; its wood; its foliage as a symbol of mourning. [L. *cupressus*]

cyst (si-) *n.* bladder or sac containing morbid matter. [G. *kystis*, bladder]

cytochemistry *n.* study of the chemical composition of cells.

Czar, Tzar, Tsar (zar) *n.* emperor or king *esp.* of Russia 1547-1917, or of Bulgaria in the Middle Ages and after 1908. [L. *Cæsar*]

Czech' (check) *n.* member, language of western branch of Slavs. [*Polish*]

D

dab *v.t.* strike feebly; apply with momentary pressure, *esp.* anything wet and soft. -*n.* slight blow or tap; smear; small flat roundish mass; small flat fish. [orig. uncertain]

dab'ble *v.i* splash about; be a desultory student or amateur (in). -**dab'bler** *n.* [obs. Du. *dabbelen*]

dace *n.* freshwater fish. [ME. *darce*]

dac'tyl *n.* (*pros.*) foot of three syllables, long-short-short. [L. *dactylus*, finger]

da'do *n.* lower part of a room wall when lined or painted separately. [It.]

daff'odil *n.* a yellow narcissus. [for earlier *affodil*, F. *aspodéle*]

daft *a.* foolish, crazy; fey; feeble-minded. [OE. *gedoefte*, meek, gentle]

dagg'er *n.* short, edged, stabbing weapon. [Med. L. *daggarius*]

dahl'ia (dal'-) *n.* garden plant with large, handsome flowers. [Dahl, Sw. botanist]

dail'y *a.* done, occurring, published, *etc.*, every day. -*adv.* every day, constantly. *n.* daily newspaper. [*day*]

dain'ty *n.* choice morsel, delicacy. -*a.* choice, delicate; pretty and neat; hard to please, fastidious. [OF. *deintie*, fr. L. *dignitas*, worthiness]

dair'y (daré-) *n.* place for dealing with milk and its products. [ME. *dey*, a woman, servant]

da'is (da-is) *n.* low platform, usually at one end of a hall. [F. fr. L. *discus*, table]

dais'y (-z-) *n.* small wild flower with yellow center and white petals. [OE. *dæges eage*, day's eye]

dais'ywheel *n.* a component of a computer printer in the shape of a wheel with many spokes that prints characters using a disk with characters around the circumference as the print element. [*daisy* and *wheel*]

Dalai Lam'a head of Buddhist priesthood of Tibet. [Mongol. *datai*, ocean, *lama*, high-priest]

dale *n.* valley. [OE. *dxl*]

dall'y *v.i.* spend time in idleness or amusement or love-making; loiter. -**dall'iance** *n.* [OF. *dallier*, chaff]

dam *n.* mother, usually of animals. [var. of *dame*]

dam *n.* barrier to hold back a flow of waters. -*v.t.* supply, or hold with a dam. [Du.]

dam'age *n.* injury, harm -*pl.* sum claimed or adjudged in compensation for harm or injury. -*v.t.* do harm to, injure. [L. *damnum*, hurt, loss]

dam'ask *n.* figured woven material of silk or linen, *esp.* white table linen with design shown up by the light; color of the damask-rose, a velvety red. *a.* made of damask; colored like damask-rose. -*v.t.* weave with figured designs. [*Damascus*]

dame *n.* noble lady. [F., fr. L. *domina, fem.* of *dominus*, lord]

damn (-in) v.t. condemn to hell; be the ruin of, give a hostile reception to. -v.i. curse. -interj. expression of annoyance, impatience, etc. **dam'nable** a. deserving damnation, hateful, annoying. -**damna' tion**, n. -**dam'natory** a. [L. damnare, condemn to a penalty]

damp a. moist; slightly moist. -n. diffused moisture; in coal-mines, a dangerous gas. -v.t. make damp; deaden, discourage. -**damp'er** n. anything that discourages or depresses; silencing-pad in a piano; plate in a flue to control draught. [Du. damp, steam]

dance (-a-) v.i. move with rhythmic steps, leaps, gestures, etc., usually to music; be in lively movement, bob up and down. v.t. perform (a dance); cause to dance. n. rhythmical movement; arrangement of such movements; tune for them; dancing party. -**dan'cer** n. [F. danser]

dandelion n. yellow-flowered wild plant. [F. dent de lion, lion's tooth, from the edge of the leaf]

dand'ruff n. dead skin in small scales among the hair. [ON, hrufa, scab]

dan'dy n. a man who pays undue attention to dress; fashion; fop. [orig. uncertain]

dan'ger (dan'-j-) n. liability or exposure to injury or harm; risk, peril; oriainallv meaning, subjection. -**dan'gerous** a. -**dan'gerously** adv. [F. fr. L. dominium, rule]

dan'gle (dang'gl) v.t. and i. hang loosely and swaying. [related to ding]

dank a. oozy, unwholesomely damp. [orig. uncertain]

dapp'er a. neat and precise, esp. in dress. [Du. dapper, brave, sprightly]

dare v.t. venture, have the courage (to); defy. **dar'ing** a. bold. -n. adventurous courage. **dare'devil** a. reckless. -n. reckless person. [OE. dearr]

dark a. having little or no light; gloomy; deep in tint; dim, secret, mysterious, unenlightened; wicked. -n. absence of light or color or knowledge. [OE. deorc]

darling n. one much loved or very lovable. -v. beloved or prized. [OE. deorling, dim. of dear]

darn v.t. mend by filling (hole, etc.) with interwoven yarn. -n. place so mended. -**darn'ing** n. [orig. uncertain]

dart n. light javelin or other pointed missile: darting motion. -pl. indoor game, throwing darts at target. v.t. cast, throw rapidly (a dart, glance, etc.). -v.i. go rapidly or abruptly, like a missile. [F. dard]

Darwin'ian a. of, pert. to Darwin and his theory of evolution. [Charles Darwin]

dash v.t. smash, throw, thrust, send with violence; cast down; tinge, flavor. -v.i. move or go with great speed or violence. n. rush, onset; vigor; smartness; small quantity, tinge; stroke (-) between words. -**dash'ing** a. spirited, showy. [prob. imit. orig.]

data See **datum**.

date n. stone-fruit of a date palm. [G. daktylos, finger]

date n. statement on a document of its time, or time and place of writing, time of an occurrence; period of a work of art, etc.; season, time; appointment. -v.t. mark with a date; refer to a date; court. -v.i. exist (from); betray time or period of origin. [L. data. given]

da'tum n., **da'ta** pl. thing given, known, or assumed as the basis for a reckoning, reasoning, etc. -n. pl. collection of information, statistics etc. on a given subject. -**da'ta base** n. a systematized collection of data that can be accessed immediately and manipulated by a data-processing system for a specific purpose. **da'ta pro'cessing** n. the process of converting information into a form that can be machine-read so that it can be stored, used and updated by a computer. [L.]

daub v.t. coat, plaster, paint roughly. n. smear; rough picture. [F. dauber, fr. L. dealbare, plaster, fr. albus, white]

daught'er (dawt'-) n. female child, female descendant. -**daught'er-in-law** n. wife of a son. -**daught'erly** a. [OE. dohtor]

daunt v.t. frighten, esp. into giving up a purpose. -**daunt'less** a. not to be daunted. [F. dompter, L. domitare, tame]

dawn v.i. begin to grow light; to appear, begin. -n. first light, daybreak, first gleam or beginning of anything. -**dawn'ing** n. [earliest is dawning, fr. ON. daga, become day]

day n. time during which the sun is above the horizon; period of 24 hours; point or unit of time; daylight; time, period. -**dail'y** a., adv. and n. (see also under **daily**). -**day'- dream**, n. reverie. **day'light** n. natural light, dawn; (fig.) publicity, enlightenment. -**day'light-sa'ving** n. system of regulating the clock to maximize the daylight hours. [OE. dæg]

daze v.t. stupefy, stun, bewilder. -n. stupefied or bewildered state. [ON. dasa]

daz'zle v.t. blind or confuse or overpower with brightness, light, brilliant display or prospects. -n. brightness that dazzles the vision. [daze]

DBMS *n.* (*compute.*) computer programs that contruct, maintain, manipulate, and provide access to a database [database *m*anagement *s*ystem]

deac'on *n.* one in the lowest degree of holy orders; official of a free church. [G. *diakonos,* servant]

dead (ded) *a.* no longer alive; benumbed; obsolete; extinguished; lacking luster or movement or vigor; sure, complete. -*n.* dead person or persons (gen. in *pl.,* the dead). -**dead' beat** *a.* exhausted -*n.* one who consistently fails to pay debts; loafer. -**dead'en** *v.t.* -**dead'-end** *n.* blind alley; cul-de sac. -**dead'heat** *n.* race in which competitors finish exactly even. -**dead'ly** *a.* fatal; death-like. -**dead of night,** time of greatest sillness and **darkness.** -**dead'reck'oning** *n.* reckoning of ship's position by log and compass alone. [OE.]

deaf (def) *a.* wholly or partly without hearing; unwilling to hear. **deaf'ness** *n.* -**deaf'en** *v.t.* [OE.]

deal *v.t.* to distribute, give out. -*v.i.* to do business (with, in), deal with, handle, act in regard to. -*n.* a share; distribution; quantity. -**deal'er** *n.* one who deals; a trader. [OE. *n. dæl*]

dean *n.* head of a cathedral chapter; university or college official. **dean'ery** *n.* dean's house or appointment. [OF. *deien,* fr. L. *decanus;* orig. chief of ten monks]

dear *a.* beloved; costly, expensive. -*n.* beloved one. *adv.* at a high price. -**dear'ly** *adv.* -**dear'ness** *n.* -**dearth** (derth) *n.* scarcity. [OE. *deore*]

death (deth) *n.* dying; end of life; end, extinction; annihilation; personified power that annihilates, kills. -**death'less** *a.* immortal or destined to be immortal. -**death'ly** *a.* and *adv.* like death. -**death'mask,** plaster-cast of face after death. -**death'-rate,** annual proportion of deaths to population. -**death'-trap,** unsafe place, vessel, mine *etc.* -**death-warrant,** execution order. **death'watch** *n.* ticking beetle. [OE.]

debacle' (di-bakl') *n.* utter collapse, rout, disaster. [F.]

debate' *v.t.* discuss, dispute about. -u.*i.* engage in discussion; consider; reason out (with oneself). -*n.* discussion, controversy. **deba'table** *a.* -**deba'ter** *n.* [F. *débattre*]

debauch' (-tsh) *v.t.* lead awav from virtue; spoil, vitiate; seduce. -*n.* bout of sensual indulgence. **debauchee'** (-osh-) *n.* -debauch'ery *n.* [F. *dobaucher*]

debenture *n.* bond of a company or corporation. [L. debere, owe]

debility *n.* feebleness, *esp.* of health. -debil'itate *v.t.* [L. *debilitas,* weakness]

deb'it *n.* entry in an account of a sum owed; side of the book in which such sums are entered. -*v.t.* charge, enter as due. [L. *debere,* owe]

debonair' *a.* genial, pleasant. [F. *débonnaire.* orig. (of hawks) well-bred]

deb'ris *n.* fragments, rubbish. [F. *débris,* fr. *briser,* break]

debt (det) *n.* what is owed; state of owing. -**debt'or** *n.* [L. *debere,* owe]

debug *v.t.* (*compute.*) detect, trace, and eliminate mistakes in computer software.

debut' *n.* first appearance in public. **de'butant** *n.* (-ante fem.). [F.]

dec'ade *n.* period often years; set often. [G. *dekas,* group of ten]

dec'adent (or de-ca'-) *a.* declining, failing away. -**dec'adence** (or de-ca') *n.* [F. *decadent*]

dec'agon *n.* figure of ten angles. -**decag'onal** *a.* -**dec'agram** *n.* ten grams. -**decahedron** *n.* solid of ten faces. -**decahe'dral** *a.* -**dec'aliter** *n.* ten liters. -**dec'alogue** *n.* the ten commandments. **dec'ameter** *n.* ten meters. [G. *deka,* ten]

decant' *v.t.* pour off (liquid, wine, etc,) to leave sediment behind. -**decant'er** *n.* stoppered bottle for wine or spirits. [L. *canthus,* lip of jug]

decapitate *v.t.* behead. -**decapita'tion** *n.* [L. *caput,* head]

decay' *v.t.* and *i.* rot, decompose; fall off, decline. -*n.* rotting; a falling away, break up. [OF. *decair,* fr. *de* and L. *cadere,* fall]

decease' *n.* death. -*v.i.* die. -**deceased'** *a.* dead. -n, person lately dead. [L. *decessus,* departure]

deceive' *v.t.* mislead, persuade of what is false. [F. décevoir]

decelerate *v.t.* and *i.* retard the speed of; slow down. [L. *de,* away from, *celer,* speed]

Decem'ber *n.* twelfth month. [L. *decem* (formerly) = tenth month]

de'cent *a.* seemly, not immodest; respectable; passable. -**de'cency** *n.* -**de'cently** *adv.* [L. *decere.* be fitting]

decentralize *v.t.* transfer (government functions *etc.*) from main center to local centers. [L. *de,* away from, and center]

deception *n.* deceiving; being deceived; trick. -**decep'tive** *a.* misleading, apt to mislead. [F. *deception*]

decibel *n.* l/10th of bel; approx. smallest change in sound detectable by human ear. [*bel*]

decide' *v.t.* settle, determine, bring to

resolution; give judgment. -v.i. determine, resolve. -deci'ded a. settled; resolute. - deci'dedly adv. certainly, undoubt edly. decis'ion (-zhn) n. [L. decidere]

decid'uous a. of leaves, horns, etc., falling periodically; of trees, losing leaves annually. [L. decidere, fall down]

dec'imal (des-) a. relating to tenths; pro ceeding by tens. -n. decimal fraction. - dec'imal system, system of weights and measures in which the value of each denomination is ten times the one below it. [L. decem, ten]

dec'imate v.t. kill a tenth or large proportion of. -decima'tion n. [L. decem, ten]

deci'pher v.t. turn from cipher into ordinary writing; make out the meaning of deci'pherable a. [cipher]

deck n. platform covering the whole or part of a ship's hull; pack of cards. -v.t. array, decorate. deck'-chair n. light folding chair of wood and canvas. [Du. dek, roof, covering]

declaim' v.i. and t. speak in oratorical style. -declama'tion n. declam'atory a. [L. declamare, cry out]

declare' (-at') v.t. announce formally; state emphatically; show; name (as liable to customs duty). -v.i. take sides (for). [L. declarare, make clear]

decline' v.i. slope or bend or sink downward; decay; refuse; make the caseendings of nouns. -n. gradual decay, loss of vigor; wasting disease. - declen'sion n. a falling off, a declining; group of nouns. -declina'tion n. downward slope or angle. [L. declinare, bend away]

decode' v.t. decipher a code message. [L. de, from, and code]

decompose' (de-, -oz) v.t. separate into elements. -v.i. rot. [compose]

décor' n. scenery on stage. [F.]

dec'orate v.t. beautify by additions; invest (with an order, medal, etc.). -decora'tion n. -dec'orative a. -dec'orator n. esp. a tradesman who paints and papers houses, [L. decorare, make fitting]

decor'um n. seemly behavior, usage required by decency or good manners. - deco'rous a. -deco'rously adv. [L.]

decoy' n. bird or person trained or used to entrap others; bait, enticement. [first in decay-duck; coy fr. Du. kooi, cage]

decrease' v.t. and i. diminish, make or grow less. -de'crease n. a lessening. [L. decrescere-de, from, crescere, grow]

decree' n. authoritative order; edict. v.t. order with authority, [L. decretum]

decrepit a. old and feeble. -decrepitude n. [L. decrepitus, fr. crepare creak]

decriminalize v.t. to remove the legal penalties from (some previously illegal act or practice); make no longer illegal. - decrim-inali'zation n. [crime]

decry' v.t. cry down, disparage. [cry]

dedicate v.t. devote to God's service; set aside entirelv for some purpose; inscribe or address (a book, etc.) [L. dedicare]

deduce' v.t. draw as a conclusion from facts. -deduct' v.t. take away, subtract. - deduction n. deducting; amount subtracted; deducing; conclusion deduced; inference from general to particular. [L. deducere, lead down]

deed n. act; action or fact; legal document. [OE. deed]

deem v.t. judge, consider, hold to be true. [OE. deman]

deep a. extending far down or in or back; at or of a given depth; far down or back; profound; heartfelt; of color, dark and rich; of sound, low and full. -n. deep place. -adv. far down, etc. -deep'en v.t. -deep'ly adv. [OE. deop]

deer n. family of ruminant animals with deciduous horns in the male. -deerhound n. large rough-coated greyhound. [OE. deor, wild animal]

deface' v.t. mar the appearance of; blot out. -deface'ment n. [face]

defame' v.t. speak ill of, dishonor by slander or rumor. -defama'tion n. defam'atory a. [L. diffamare]

default' n. failure to act or appear or pay. -in default of, in the absence of v.t. and i. fail to pay. -default'er n. esp. a soldier punished for failure to comply with regulations. [fault]

defeat' n. overthrow; lost battle or encounter; frustration. -v.t. overcome. [F. dofait, undone]

def'ecate v.t. clear of impurities. defeca-tion n. [L. defcecare]

defect' n. lack, falling short, blemish, failing. -defec'tion n. abandonment of a leader or cause. defect'ive a. incomplete, faulty. -n. one mentally or physically lacking. [L. deficere, undo]

defend v.t. protect, guard, uphold. - defense' n. -defend'er n. -defens'ive a. serving for defense. -n. position or attitude of defense. [L. defenders, ward off]

defer' v.t. put off. -v.i. procrastinate. defer'ment n. [L. differre, set aside]

defer' v.i. submit in opinion or judgment (to another). -def'erence n. respect for another inclining one to accept his views, etc. [L. *deferrer*, submit]

defi'cient (-ish'nt) *a.* wanting or falling short in something. **-def'icit** *n.* amount by which a sum of money is too small. [L. *deficere*, fail]

de'file *n.* narrow pass; march in file. *-v.i.* march in file. [F. *déliler*, march past]

defile' *v.t.* make dirty, pollute. defilement *n.* [OE. *fylan*, foul]

define' *v.t.* mark out, show clearly the form; lay down clearly, fix the bounds or limits of, state contents or meaning of **defi'nable** *a.* -defini'tion *n.* def'inite (-it) *a.* exact, precise, defined. def'initely *adv.* -defin'itive *a.* conclusive, to be looked on as final. -defin'itively *adv.* [F. *dgfinir*]

deflate' *v.t.* release air from (something inflated); remove excess of paper money in circulation. **-defla'tion** *n.* **-defla'tor** *n.* [coinage fr. *inflate*]

deflect' *v.i.* and *i.* make to turn, or turn, from a straight course. **-deflec'tion** *n.* [L. *deflectere*, bend aside]

deform' *v.t.* spoil the shape of, make ugty. **-deform'ity** *n.* **-deforma'tion** *n.* [L. *deformis*, ill-formed, ugly]

defraud' *v.t.* cheat. [*fraud*]

defray' *v.t.* provide the money for (expenses, *etc.*). [F. *defrayer*]

deft *a.* skillful, neat-handed. **-deft'ly** *adv.* **-deft'ness** *n.* [OE. *gedxfte*, gentler]

defunct' *a.* dead. [L. *defungi*, accomplish, *oneés* duty, finish]

defy' *v.t.* set at naught; challenge to do, *esp.* something beyond expected power; offer insuperable difficulties. **defi'ance** *n.* **-defi'ant** *a.* **-defi'antly** *adv.* [F. *défier* -Low L. *dffidare*, renounce faith]

degenerate *v.i.* fall away from the qualities proper to race or kind. *a.* fallen away in quality. *-n.* [L. *degenerate*]

degrade' *v.t.* reduce to a lower rank; dishonor; debase. **degrada'tion** *n.* **degra'ded** *a.* [L. *gradus*, degree, step]

degree' *n.* step or stage in a process or scale or series; relative rank, order, condition, manner, way; university rank; unit of measurement of angles or temperature; form in the comparison of *a.* and *adv.* [F. *degré*, fr. L. *de* and *gradus*, step]

dehydrate *v.t.* deprive of water; dry by chemical means, as certain food-stuffs. [L. *de*, not, G. *hvdor*, water]

de'ify *v.t.* make a god of, treat as a god. **-deifica'tion** *n.* [fr. L. *deus*, god, and *facere*, make]

deign *v.i.* condescend, think fit. [F. *daigner*, fr. L. *dignari*, think fit]

deindustrializa'tion *n.* the decline in importance of manufacturing industry in the economy of a nation or area. **-deindustrialize** *v.* [*industry*]

de'ism *n.* belief in a god but not in revelation. **-de'ist** *n.* **-deis'tic** *a.* [L. *deus*, god]

de'ity *n.* divine status or attributes, a god; the Supreme Being. [L. *deus*, god]

deject' *v.t.* dispirit, cast down. **-deject'ed** *a.* **-dejec'tion** *n.* [L. *dejicere*]

delay' *v.t.* postpone, hold back. *-v.i.* be tardy, linger. *-n.* act of delaying; fact of being delayed. [F. *délai*]

delectable *a.* delightful. [L. *delectabilis*]

del'egate *v.t.* send as deputy; commit (authority, business, *etc.*) to a deputy. [L. *delegate*]

delete' *v.t.* strike out. **-dele'tion** *n.* **delen'da** *n. pl.* things to be deleted. [L. *delere, deletunt*, destroy]

deleterious *a.* harmful. [G. *deleterios*]

deliberate *v.t.* and *i.* consider, debate. *a.* done on purpose; well-considered: without haste, slow. **delib'erately** *adv.* **-deliberation** *n.* **-delib'erative** *a.* [L. *deliberate*, weigh]

delicate *a.* dainty; tender; fastidious; exquisite; deft; ticklish; sensitive-, modest. **-del'icately** *adv.* **-del'icacy** *n.* [L. *delicatus*, fr. *lacere*, entice]

delicatessen *n.* food that is sold ready-prepared, such as cooked meats, salads, *etc.*; the store where such food is sold. **-del'i** *abbrev.* [Ger.]

delicious (-ish'us) *a.* very delightful or pleasing. **-deli'ciously** *adv.* **-deli'ciousness** *n.* [L. *delicix*, delight]

delight' (-lit') *v.t.* please highlv. *-v.i.* take great pleasure (in). *-n.* great pleasure. **-delight'ful** *a.* [L. *delectare*]

delineate *v.t.* portray by drawing or description. **-delin'eator** *n.* **-delinea'tion** *n.* [L. *delineate*, fr. *linea*, line]

delinquent *n.* offender. **-delin'quency** *n.* [L. *delinquere*, fr. l*inquere*, leave]

delirium *n.* disorder of the mind; raving, as in fever. **-delir'ious** *a.* **-delir'iously** *adv.* with wild excitement. [L.]

deliv'er *v.t.* set free; hand over; launch, send in, deal; give forth; disburden, as a woman at childbirth. **-deliv'ery** *n.* **-deliv'erance** *n.* [fr. L. *liberare*, set free]

dell *n.* wooded hollow. [OE.]

del'ta *n.* tract of alluvial land at the mouth of a river. [fr. its usual shape, the Greek fourth letter, *delta*, Δ]

delude' (-a-) *v.t.* deceive. **-delu'sion** *n.* false belief; hallucination. **-delu'sive** *a.* [L. *deludere*, play false]

del'uge *n.* flood, great flow, rush,

downpour. -v.t. flood. [F. *deluge*]

delve v.t. and i. dig. [OE. *delfan*]

demagogue (-og) n. mob leader or agitator. [G. *dernagogos*, fr. *demos*, people, and *agogos*, leader]

demand' (-a-) v.t. ask as by right, ask as giving an order; call for as due or right or necessary-n. urgent request, claim, requirement; call for (a commodity). [L. *dem, andare*, entrust]

demarcation n. boundary line, its marking out. [Sp. *dernarcacin*]

demean' (-men') v.t. conduct oneself, behave, show specified bearing. -demean'or (-er) n. conduct, bearing. [F. *dérnener*, conduct]

demean' v.t. lower, degrade (oneself). [mean, in sense of low, base]

dement'ed a. mad; beside oneself [L. *dementare*, send out of one's mind]

demerit n. bad point; undesirable quality. [L. *demeritum*, desert]

demise' (-z) n. death; conveyance by will or lease; transfer of sovereignty on death or abdication. -v.t. convey to another. [F. *ettre*, put off]

demo'bilize v.t. disband (troops). -demobiliza'tion n. [*mobilise*]

democ'racy n. government by the people; state so governed. -dem'ocrat n. advocate of democracy. democrat'ic a. -democrat'ically adv. -democ'ratize v.t. -democratiza'tion n. [G. *demokratia, demos*, the people, *Kratein*, rule]

demog'raphy n. study of human population with emphasis on statistical analysis. [G. *demos*, people, *graphein*, draw]

demolish v.t. knock to pieces, destroy, overthrow. demoli'tion n. [L. *demoliri*, fr. *moles*, mass, building]

de'mon n. devil, evil spirit; person of prenatural cruelty or evil character or energy. -demo'niac n. one possessed by a demon. -demoni'acal a. -demon'ic a. of the nature of a devil, or of genius. [G. *daimon*]

dem'onstrate v.t. show by reasoning, prove; describe or explain by specimens or experiment. -v.i. make exhibition of political sympathy; make a show of armed force. -demon'strative a. conclusive; needing outward expression, unreserved; pointing out. [L. *demonstrate*]

demor'alize v.t. deprave morally; deprive of courage and discipline, morale. [F. *démoratiser*]

demote' v.t. reduce in rank; grade downwards. -demo'tion n. [*motion*]

demur' (-mer) v.i. raise objections, make difficulties. -n. hesitation, pause. [AF. *demurer*, stay]

demure' a. reserved, quiet, staid; affecting to be grave or decorous. -demure'ly adv. [AF. *demurer*, stay]

den n. cave or hole of a wild beast; lurking place; small room. [OE. *denn*]

dena'ture v.t. deprive of essential qualities. -dena'tured al'cohol, spirit made undrinkable. [*nature*]

deni'al. See deny.

denigrate v.t. blacken, defame. -denigra'tion n. [L. *nigrare*, blacken]

denizen n. inhabitant. [AF. *deinz*, fr. L. *de intus*, from within]

denominate v.t. give a name to -denomina'tion n. name, *esp.* one applicable to each individual of a class; distinctively named church or sect. -denom'inator n. number written below the line in a fraction, the divisor. [L. *denominate*]

denote' v.t. stand for, be the name of-, mark, indicate, show. -denota'tion n. [L. *denotare*]

denouement n. unravelling of a dramatic plot; final solution of a mystery. [F.]

denounce' v.t. speak violently against; accuse; give notice to withdraw from (a treaty, *etc.*). [F. *dononcer*]

dense a. thick, compact; stupid. -dense'ly adv. -dens'ity n. [L. *densus*]

dent n. hollow or mark left by a blow or pressure. -v.t. make a dent in. [*dint*]

dent'al a. of or relating to teeth or dentistry; pronounced by applying the tongue to the teeth. —dent'ate a. toothed. -dent'istry n. art of a dentist. -denti'tion n. teething; arrangement of teeth. -dent'ure n. set of teeth, *esp.* artificial. [L. *dens*, tooth]

denude' v.t. strip, make bare. -denuda'tion n. *esp.* removal of forest or surface soil by natural agency; erosion. [L. *denudare*]

deny' v.t. declare untrue or non-existent; contradict, reject; disown; refuse to give; refuse. deni'al n. deni'able a. [F. *denier*; L. *denegare*]

deodorize v.t. rid of smell. -deodoriza'tion n. -deo'dorizer n. [*odour*]

depart' v.i. go away; start; die; diverge, stray from. depart'ure n. [F. *dopartir*]

department n. division, branch province. -department'al a. -department'- ally adv. [*depart*]

depend' v.i. rely entirely; live (on); be contingent, await settlement or decision (on); hand down. -depend'able a. reliable. -

depend'ant *n*. one for whose maintenance another is responsible. [L. *dependere*, hang from]

depict' *v.t.* give a picture of. -depic'tion [L. *depingere*, depict]

depil'atory *a*. removing hair. -*n*. substance that does this. -depila'tion *n*. [L. *depilare*, fr. *pilus*, hair]

deplete' *v.t.* empty, exhaust, or nearly. -deple'tion *n*. [L. *deplere*, deplete]

deplore' *v.t.* lament, regret. -deplor'able *a*. -deplor'ably *adv*. [L. *deplorare*]

deploy' *v.i.* of troops, ships, *etc.*, to spread out from column into line. -deploy'ment *n*. [F. *déployer*]

depo'larize *v.t.* deprive of polarity. [*polarize*]

depo'nent *n*. one who makes a statement on oath, a deposition. [L. *deponere*, put down]

depop'ulate *v.t.* deprive of, reduce, population. -depopula'tion *n*. [*populate*]

deport' *v.t.* remove into exile; transport. -deporta'tion *n*. [F. *deporter*]

depose' *v.t.* remove from office, *esp.* of a sovereign. -*v.i.* make a statement on oath, give evidence. -deposi'tion *n*. [F. *doposer*, set down]

depos'it (-z-) *v.t.* set down; give into safe keeping, *esp.* in a bank; pledge for the carrying out of a contract. -*n*. act of depositing; thing deposited; pledge; sediment. -depositor *n*. [L. *depositum*, laid down]

dep'ot *n*. railroad or bus station; storage place for supplies, *esp.* military. [F. *dépôt*]

deprave' *v.t.* make bad, corrupt, pervert. -deprav'ity *n*. wickedness. [L. *pravus*, crooked, wrong]

dep'recate *v.t.* express disapproval of, advise against. -dep'recatory *a*. [L. *deprecari*, pray against]

depre'ciate (-shi-) *v.t.* lower the price or value or purchasing power of; belittle. *v.i.* fall in value. [L. *depretiare*]

depress' *v.t.* lower, in level or activity; affect with low spirits. -depres'sion (-shn) *n*. depressing; hollow; center of low barometric pressure; low spirits; low state of trade. -depress'ible *a*. [L. *deprimere, depress-*, press down]

deprive' *v.t.* strip, dispossess (of). -depriva'tion *n*. [L. *privare*, deprive]

depth *n*. deepness; degree of deepness; deep place, abyss; profundity; intensity. [*deep*]

depute' *v.t.* commit to (a substitute); point as substitute. -dep'uty *n*. substitute, delegate. [L. *deputare*, choose - *lit*. cut off]

derail' *v.t.* make (a train) leave the ails.

-derail'ment *n*. [*rail*]

derange' *v.t.* throw into confusion or isorder; disturb; disorder the mind at; -deranged' *a*. disordered; out of one's mind, insane. -derangement *n*. [F. *ranger*]

derby *n*. a man's hat with dome-shaped crown and narrow brim; horse-race, *usu.* restricted to three-year-olds; race or competition in any sport, *usu.* with specific qualifications. [Earl of *Derby*]

der'elict *a*. abandoned, forsaken, *esp.* of ship. -*n*. thing forsaken, *esp.* a ship; son who has become unable to look after himself *usu.* as a result of alcoholism. -derelic'tion *n*. neglect (of duty). [L. *derelictus*, forsaken]

deride' *v.t.* laugh to scorn. -deris'ion, derisive *a*. -deris'ory *a*. futile. [L. *ridere*, laugh at]

derive' *v.t.* get from; deduce; show the gin of. -*v.i.* issue (from), be descended from). -deriva'tion *n*. -deriv'ative *a*. traceable back to something else. -*n*. thing or word derived from another. [L. *care*, lead water]

dermatol'ogy *n*. (*phys.*) science of the kin. -dermati'tus *n*. inflammation of the skin. [G. *derma*, skin]

derr'ick *n*. hoisting-machine. [*Derrick*, hangman at Tyburn, London, c. 1600]

derr'inger (-j-) *n*. small pistol. [Henry *Derringer*, gunsmith]

descend' *v.i.* come or go down; slope down; swoop on or attack; stoop, condescend; spring from (ancestor, *etc.*); pass to an heir, be transmitted-*v.t.* go or come down. -descend'ant *n*. one descended from another. -descent' *n*. [L. *descendere*, climb down]

describe' *v.t.* give a detailed account of-, trace out (a geometrical figure, *etc.*); pass along (a course, *etc.*). -descrip'tive *a*. -descrip'tion *n*. detailed account; marking out; kind, sort, species. [L. *describere*, write down]

desecrate *v.t.* violate the sanctity of, profane; convert to evil uses. -desecra'tion *n*. -des'ecrator *n*. [opposite of *consecrate*]

desert' (-z-) *n*. (*usu. pl.*) conduct or qualities deserving reward or punishment; what is due as reward or punish ment; merit, virtue. [OF.]

desert' (-z-) *v.t.* abandon, leave. -*v.i.* run away from service, *esp.* of soldiers and sailors. -deser'tion *n*. -desert'er *n*. [L. *deserere*, abandon]

des'ert (-z-) *n*. uninhabited and barren region. -*a*. barren, uninhabited, desolate. [L. *deserere, desert-*, abandon]

deserve' (-z-) *v.t.* show oneself worthy of, have by conduct a claim to. -*v.i.* be worthy (of reward, *etc.*). **-deserv'edly** *adv.* **-deserv'ing** *a.* meritorious. [L. *deservire*, serve well]

desiccate *v.t.* to dry up. **desicea'tion** *n.* [L. *desiccate*, fr. *siccus*, dry]

design' (-zin) *v.t.* plan out; purpose; set apart for a purpose; make working drawings for; sketch. -*n.* project, purpose, mental plan; outline, sketch, working plan; art of making decorative patterns, *etc.* **des'ignate** (dez'-ig-) *v.t.* name, pick out, appoint to office. -*a.* appointed but not yet installed in office. **-designa'tion** *n.* name. [L. *designare*, mark out]

desire' (-z-) *v.t.* wish for, long for; ask for, entreat. -*n.* longing; expressed wish; wish or felt lack; request; thing wished or requested. [F. *dosirer*, fr. L. *desider-are*, long for]

desist' *v.i.* cease, give over. [L. *desistere*, stand back]

desk *n.* sloped board on which a writer rests his paper, a reader his book; table or other piece of furniture designed for the use of a writer or reader. [It. *desco* - L. *discus*, disk, table]

desktop publishing *n.* (*compute.*) use of computers in the preparation of typeset-quality publications, *e.g.* newsletters, reports, books, magazines, etc.

des'olate *n.* solitary; neglected, barren, ruinous; dreary, dismal, forlorn. -*v.t.* depopulate, lay waste; overwhelm with grief. **desola'tion** *n.* [L. *desolare*, leave alone, fr. *solus*, alone]

despair *v.i.* lose all hope. -*n.* loss of all hope; something causing this. despairing *a.* [L. *desperare*, give up hope]

despatch'. *See* **dispatch**.

desperate *a.* leaving no room for hope; hopelessly bad or difficult or dangerous; reckless from despair. **-despera'tion** *n.* **des'perately** *adv.* **-despera'do** *n.* one ready for any lawless deed. [*despair*]

despise' (-z) *v.t.* look down on. **des'picable** *a.* base, contemptible, vile. **des'picably** *adv.* **-despite'** *n.* scorn; ill-will, malice, spite. -prep. in spite of. **-despite'ful** *a.* **-despite'fully** *adv.* [L. *despicere*, look down]

despond' *v.i.* lose heart or hope. **despond'ent** *a.* **-despond'ency** *n.* **despond'ently** *adv.* [L. *despondere* (*animum*) give up (heart)]

des'pot *n.* tyrant, oppressor. [G. *despotes*]

dessert' (-z-) *n.* fruit, *etc.*, served after dinner. [F., fr. *desseruir*, clear away]

destabilize *v.t.* to undermine or subvert (a government, economy, *etc.*) so as to cause unrest or collapse. **-de'stabilization** *n.* (L. *stabilis*, stable]

des'tine (-tin) *v.t.* predetermine, ordain or fix in advance; set apart, devote. **-des'tiny** *n.* power which foreordains; course of events or person's fate, *etc.*, regarded as fixed by this power. **-destina'tion** *n.* place to which a person or thing is bound; intended end of a journey. [L. *destinare*, make fast.]

des'titute *a.* in absolute want, in great need of food, clothing, *etc.* **destitu'tion** *n.* [L. *destitutus*, abandoned]

destroy' *v.t.* make away with, put an end to, reduce to nothingness or uselessness. [L. *destruere*, 'unbuild']

des'ultory *a.* off and on, flitting from one thing to another, unmethodical. [L. *desultor*, circus rider, *lit.* leaper down]

detach' (-tsh) *v.t.* unfasten, disconnect, separate. **-detached'** *a.* standing apart, isolated. [F. *détacher* - See **attach**]

de'tail *n.* item or particular; treatment of anything item by item; small or unimportant part; party or man told off for a duty in the army *etc.* detail' *v.t.* relate with full particulars; appoint for a duty. [F. *detail*]

detain' *v.t.* keep under restraint; keep from going; keep waiting. **-deten'tion** *n.* [L. *detinere*, hold back]

detect' *v.t.* find out or discover the existence or presence or nature or identity of. **-detect'or** *n.* device for detecting electrical waves. **-detec'tion** *n.* **-detect'ive** *a.* employed in or apt for detection. -*n.* policeman or other person employed in detecting criminals. [L. *detegere*, detect, uncover]

détente' (da-tongt') *n.* slackening of tension in international crises. [F.]

deter' *v.t.* make to abstain (from); discourage, frighten. **-deterr'ent** *a.* [L. *deterrere*, frighten off]

detergent *a.* cleansing. -*n.* cleansing substance (for wounds, *etc.*); chemical substance which, added to water, removes dirt from fabrics *etc.* [L. *detergere*, wipe off]

dete'riorate *v.i.* and *t.* become or make worse. **-deteriora'tion** *n.* [L. *deteriorate*, make worse]

deter'mine *v.t.* make up one's mind, decide; fix as known; bring to decision; be the deciding factor in; law, end. -*v.i.* come to an end; come to a decision. **deter'mined** *a.* resolute. **-deter'minism** *n.* theory that human ction is settled by forces independent of will. [L. *determinate*]

detest' v.t. hate, loathe. [L. testari, execrate]

det'onate v.i. and t. explode with a loud report; set off an explosive. **-detona'tion** n. **-detonator** n. esp. a detonating apparatus as the fuse of a bomb, etc. [L. tonare, thunder down]

de'tour n. course which leaves the main route to rejoin it later. [F. detour, a turning aside]

detract' v.t. and i. takeaway (apart) from; belittle. [L. detrahere, detract-, draw away]

det'riment n. harm done, loss, damage. [L. detrimentum]

detri'tus n. gravel, debris, from wearing exposed surfaces. [L.]

deuce n. two at dice, cards, etc.; score of all at tennis. [F. deux, two]

deval'ue, devaluate v.t. reduce in value, esp. currency. **-devalua'tion** n. [value]

dev'astate v.t. lay waste. **-devasta'tion** n. [devastaire]

devel'op v.t. bring to maturity; bring , bring out; evolve. **-v.i.** grow to a maturer state. **-devel'oper** n. esp. photographic chemical; muscle exerciser. **-devel'opment** n. [F. dovelopper]

de'viate v.i. leave the way, turn aside, diverge. **-devia'tion** n. **-de'viator** n. [L. viare]

device' n. contrivance, invention; fancy; scheme, plot; heraldic or semblematic or design. [F. devis]

dev'il n. personified spirit of evil; superhuman evil being, vice; fierceness in fighting; person of great wickedness, cruelty, etc.; one who devils for a lawyer or author; dish or devilled food. **-v.t.** **-dev'il's ad'vocate** n. one appointed to state the disqualifications of a person whom it is proposed to make a saint. [G. diabolos, slanderer]

de'vious a. roundabout; twisting; erring. (L. devius, out of the way)

devise' (-z-) v.t. plan, frame, contrive; plot; leave by will. [F. deviser, fr. L. dividire, divide]

devi'talize v.t. deprive of vitality, vigor. [vital]

devoid' a. empty of, lacking, free from. [obs. v. devoid, empty out; cp. avoid]

devote' v.t. set apart, give up exclusively (to a person, purpose, etc.). **devotee'** n. one devoted, worshipper. **-devo'ted** a. esp. very loyal or loving. [L. deuovere, devot-, vow]

devour' v.t. eat up, consume, destroy. **-devour'er** n. [L. devorare, swallow]

devout' a. earnestly religious; reverent. **-devout'ly** adv. [F. dovot]

dew n. moisture from the air deposited as small drops on cool surfaces between nightfall and morning; any beaded moisture. **-v.t.** wet with, or as with, dew. [OE. deaw]

dexterity n. manual skill, neatness, adroitness. **dex'terous** a. neat-handed, skillful. [L. dexter, on the right hand]

dex'trose n. grape-sugar also made from starch; glucose. [L. dexter]

diabetes n. disease relating to an excess of sugar in the blood caused by the failure of the pancreas to produce insulin; urinary disease. **diabe'tic** a. [G. diabaiein, pass through]

diabol'ic, diabolical a. devilish. [See devil]

diagnosis n. art or act of deciding from symptoms the nature of a disease; guess at the cause of anything. [G.]

diag'onal a. from corner to corner; oblique. **-n.** line from corner to corner. **-diag'onally** adv. [G. diagonios]

di'agram n. drawing, figure in lines, to illustrate something being expounded, as in a geometrical figure, weatherchart, etc. [G. diagramma]

di'al n. plate marked with graduations on a circle or arc on which something may be recorded (e.g., time on a sundial, dial of a clock, etc.); (sl.) face. **-v.t.** indicate on a dial; select a number on a telephone. [L. dies, day]

di'alect n. characteristic speech of a district; a local variety of a language. **-dialect'al** a. [G. dialektos, speech]

dialect'ic(s) n. art of arguing. [G. dialektikos]

di'alogue, dialog n. conversation between two or more; literary work representing this; the conversational part of a novel, play, movie, etc. [G. dialogos, conversation]

dial'ysis n. (dial'yses pl.) (chem.) separation of substances by filtration. [G.]

diamanté' n. fabric covered with sparkling particles; imitation diamond jewelry. [F. diamant, diamond]

diam'eter n. straight line passing from side to side of a figure or body through its centre; thickness; unit of magnifying power. **-diamet'rical** a. exact opposite. **-diamet'rically** adv. [G. diametros, measuring through]

di'amond n. very hard and brilliant precious stone; lozenge-shaped figure; card of the suit marked by (red) lozenges or diamonds. [F. *diamant*]

di'aper *n.* fabric with a small woven pattern; pattern of that kind; towel, *etc.*, of the fabric; a baby's garment, made of cloth or another absorbent material, fitting between its legs and around its waist. -**di'apered** *a.* [OF. *diaspre*]

diaph'anous *a.* transparent; showing through (a mist, *etc.*) [G. *diaphanes*]

di'aphragm (-am) *n.* partition dividing the two cavities of the body, midriff, plate or disk wholly or partly closing an opening. [G. *diaphragms*]

diarrhoe'a *n.* excessive looseness of the bowels. [G. *diarrhoia*]

di'ary *n.* daily record of events or thoughts; book for such record. **di'arist** *n.* [L. *diarium*, daily allowance]

dias'pora *n.* dispersion of Jews from Palestine after Babylonian captivity; Jewish communities that arose after this; dispersion, as of people orig. of one nation. [G. *diaspeirein*, scatter]

di'astase *n.* organic ferment turning starch into sugar. [G. *diastases*, division]

dias'tole *n.* heart's dilating movement, opp. of systole, the contracting movement. [G.]

di'athermy *n.* curative treatment by heating parts of body by electric currents. [G. *dia*, through, *therme*, heat]

diaton'ic *a.* (*mus.*) of the natural major or minor scale. [G. *diatonikos*]

diatribe *n.* bitter speech of criticism, invective. [G. = a wearing away (of time)]

dice. *See* **die.**

dichotomy *n.* division into two. -**dichot'omize**, *v.t.* and *i.* -**dichot'omous** *a.* [G. *dicha*, in two, *temnein*, cut]

dicotyledon *n.* plant with two seed leaves or cotyledon. **dicotyle'donous** *a.* [G. *di-*, twice, *coty*, led on]

dictate' *v.t.* and *i.* say or read for exact reproduction by another on paper; prescribe, lay down. -**dic'tate** *n.* bidding. -**dicta'tion** *n.* **dicta'tor** *n.* one with absolute authority, supreme ruler. [L. *dictare*, say often]

dic'tion *n.* choice and use of words. -**dic'tum** *n.* (dic'ta) *a.* pronouncement, saying. [L. *dictio*, a speaking]

dictionary n. book setting forth, usually in alphabetical order, the words of a language with meanings, derivations, foreign equivalents, *etc.*; book of reference with items in alphabetical order. [Med. L. *dictionarium*, collection of sayings]

didac'tic *a.* instructive; meant, or meaning, to teach. -**didac'ticism** *n.* [G. *dieaktikos*]

die (di) *v.i.* cease to live; come to an end. **die'hard** *n.* one who resists (reform, *etc.*) to the end. [ON. *deyja*]

die (di) *n.* cube with sides marked one to six for games of chance; small cube of bread, *etc.*; (*pl.* **dice**); stamp for embossing, *etc.* (*pl.* **dies**). -**dice** *v.i.* to gamble with dice. -**di'cer** *n.* [F. *de*]

dies'el engine (dee-sl) *n.* oil-fuelled internal combustion engine. [R. *Diesel*]

di'et *n.* kind of food lived on; regulated course of feeding, restricted choice of foods; food. -*v.i.* follow a prescribed diet. -**di'etary** *n.* allowance or character of food, *esp.* in an institution, *etc.* -*a.* relating to diet. -**dietet'ic** *a.* -*n. pl.* science of diet. [G. *diaita*, system of life]

di'et *n.* parliamentary assembly in certain European countries. [Med. L. diets]

diff'er *v.i.* be unlike; disagree. -**diff'erence** *n.* unlikeness; degree or point of unlikeness; disagreement; remainder left after subtraction. **different** *a.* unlike. -**diff'erently** *adv.* -**differen'tial** *a.* varying with circumstances. differential gear *n.* mechanism in an automobile which allows the back wheels to revolve at different speeds when rounding a corner. **differen'tially** *adv.* -**differen'tiate** *v.t.* make different; develop into unlikeness. -*v.i.* discriminate. **differentia'tion** *n.* [L. *differre*, carry apart]

difficulty *n.* hardness to be done or understood; hindrance, obstacle; an obscurity; embarrassment. **difficult** *a.* not easy, hard, obscure; captious, hard to please. [L. *difficultas*]

diff'ident *a.* timid, shy. -**diff'idently** *adv.* -**diff'idence** *n.* [L. *diffidere*, distrust]

diffract' *v.t.* break up, as ray of light. [L. *diffringere, diffract*, break asunder]

diffuse' (-z) *v.t.* spread abroad. -*a.* (-s) loose, verbose. [L. *diffundere, diffus-*, pour apart]

dig *v.i.* work with a spade. -*v.t.* turn up with a spade; hollow out, make a hole in; get by digging; thrust into; delve. -**digg'er** *n.* one who digs; gold-miner; Australian. [OF. *diguer*]

digest' *v.t.* prepare (*food*) in the stomach, *etc.*, for assimilation; bring into handy form by sorting, tabulating, summarizing; reflect on; absorb; endure. -*v.i.* of food, to undergo digestion. **di'gest** *n.* methodical summary, *esp.* of laws. [L. *digerere, digest-*]

dig'it (-j-) *n.* any of the numbers 0 to 9; finger or toe. **dig'ital** *a.* using digits, *esp.* in a display. -**dig'ital recording** *n.* a sound recording process that converts audio signals into a series of pulses that correspond to the voltage level, which then can be stored on tape or on any other memory system. -**digita'lis** *n.* drug made from foxglove. [L. *digitus*, finger]

dig'nity *n.* worthiness, excellence, claim to respect; honorable office or title; stateliness, gravity. -**dig'nify** *v.t.* give dignity to. -**dig'nified** *a.* stately, majestic. -**dig'nitary** *n.* holder of high office. [L. *dignitas -dignus*, worthy]

digress' *v.t.* go aside from the main course, *esp.* deviate from the subject. [L. *digredi*, digress-step aside]

dilapidated *a.* ruinous, falling into decay. -**dilapida'tion** *n.* [L. *dilapidarei*, scatter stones apart]

dilate' (di-) *v.t.* widen, expand. -*v.i.* expand; talk or write at large (on). -**dilatation, dila'tion** *n.* [L. *dilatare*]

dilatory *a.* delaying, slow. [Late L. *dilatorious*, putting off (time)]

dilem'ma *n.* position in fact or argument offering choice only between two or more unwelcome courses. [G.]

dil'igent *a.* unremitting in effort, industrious. **dil'igence** *n.* industry; French stage-coach. [L. *diligere*, delight in]

dill *n.* medicinal herb. [OE. *dile*]

dilute' *a.* reduce (a liquid) in strength by adding water or other matter. -*a.* weakened thus. -**dilu'tion** *n.* [L. *diluere, dilut-*, wash away]

dim *a.* indistinct, faint, not bright. -*v.t.* and *i.* make or grow dim. -**dim'ly** *adv.* -**dim'ness** *n.* [OE. *dimm*, dark]

dime *n.* U. S. 10 cent piece. [F. *disme*]

dimension *n.* measurement, size. -**dimen'sional** *a.* [L. *dimensio*]

dimin'ish *v.t.* and *i.* lessen. **diminution** *n.* **dimin'utive** *a.* very small. -*n.* derivative word implying smallness. [L. *diminuere*, make less]

dim'ple *n.* small hollow in the surface of the skin, *esp.* of the cheek; any small hollow. -*v.t.* and *i.* mark with or break into dimples. [orig. uncertain]

din *n.* continuous roar of confused noises. -*v.t.* repeat to weariness, ram (opinion, *etc.*) into. [OE, *dyne*]

dine *v.i.* take dinner. -*v.t.* give dinner to. -**di'ning-room** *n.* room used for meals. -**di'ner** *n.* one who dines; railroad restaurant-car; inexpensive restaurant. [F. *diner*]

dinghy (ding'gi) *n.* small boat; ship's tender. [Hind. *dingi*]

dinn'er *n.* chief meal of the day. [F. *diner*]

di'nosaur *n.* extinct giant reptile. [G. *deinos*, terrible, *sauros*, lizard]

di'ocese *n.* district or jurisdiction ofa bishop. **dioc'esan** *a.* -*n.* bishop, or clergyman, or the people of a diocese. [F. *diocese*]

diox'ide *n.* oxide with two parts of oxygen to one of a metal. [*oxide*]

dip *v.t.* put partly or for a moment into a liquid; immerse, involve; lower and raise again; take up in a ladle, bucket, *etc.* -*v.i.* plunge partially or temporarily; go down, sink; slope downwards. -*n.* act of dipping; downward slope; hollow. -**dipp'er** *n.* [OE. *dyppan*]

diphtheria *n.* infectious disease of the throat with membranous growth. **diphtherit'ic** *a.* [G. *diphthera*, skin]

diphthong *n.* union of two vowel sounds in a single compound sound. [G. *diphthongos*, having two sounds]

diplo'ma *n.* document vouching for a person's title to some degree, honor, *etc.*, -**diplo'macy** *n.* management of international relations; skill in negotiation; tactful or adroit dealing. **dip'lomat** *n.* one engaged in official diplomacy. [G. -folded paper]

dire *a.* dread, terrible. [L. *dirus*]

direct' *v.t.* put in the straight way; address (a letter, *etc.*); aim, point, turn; control, manage, order. -*a.* straight; going straight to the point; lineal; immediate; frank, straightforward. -**direc'tion** *n.* a directing; body of directors; address, instruction; aim, course of movement. -**direct'or** *n.* one who directs; member of a board managing a company. -**direct'ory** *n.* book of names and addresses, streets, *etc.* [L. *dirigere*, direct-*, make straight]

dirge *n.* song of mourning. [L. *dirige*, in antiphon in Office for the Dead; *Dirige, Domine . . . viam meam,* Direct, O Lord. . . my way]

dirt'y *a.* unclean; soiled; mean. -**dirt** *n.* filth; mud, earth. **dirt' far'mer** *n.* farmer who farms his own land, usu. without the help of hired hands. -**dirt'ily** *adv.* **dirt'iness** *n.* [ON. *drit*, excrement]

dis- *prefix*, indicates negation, opposition, deprivation; in many verbs, it indicates the undoing of the action of the simple verb, *eg.* -**disembark'**, come out from what one embarked in; many verbs, nouns and adjectives in *dis-* mean the exact opposite of the simple word, *e.g.* -**disarrange'**, disorders -**disloy'al**; some verbs in *dis* - mean to deprive of the thing indicated by the simple word, *eg.* -**disembowel**. All such words are omitted, and the meaning should be sought under the simple word to which *dis-* is prefixed. [L.]

disa'ble *v.t.* incapacitate; disqualify; cripple. **disabil'ity** *n.* [*able*]

disaffected *a.* ill-disposed, inclined to sedition, **disaffec'tion** *n.* [*affect*]

disallow' *v.t.* reject the validity of (evidence *etc.*). [*allow*]

disappoint' *v.t.* fail to fulfill (hope) -**disappointment** *n.* [*appoint*]

disarm' *v.t.* li. take away weapons; reduce armaments; conciliate. -**disarm'ament** *n.* [*arm*]

disarray' *v.t.* throw into disorder; derange. -*n.* undress. [*array*]

disas'ter (-a-) *n.* calamity, a sudden or great misfortune. -**disas'trous** *a.* [orig. evil star. L. *astrum*]

disband' *v.t.* and *i.* disperse. [*band*]

disburse' *v.t.* pay out money. -**disbursement** *n.* [F. *bourse*, purse]

disc *See* **disk.**

discard' *v.t.* and *i.* reject, or play as worthless (a card); give up; cast off. [OF. *descarter*, scatter]

discern' *v.t.* make out; distinguish. -**discern'ment** *n.* insight. -**discern'ible** *a.* [L. *discernere*, separate, sift]

discharge' *v.t.* unload; fire off; release; dismiss; let go, pay; emit. -*n.* a discharging; a being discharged; matter emitted; document certifying release, payment, *etc.* [OF. *descharger*, unload]

disci'ple *n.* follower, one who takes another as teacher and model. -**discipleship** *n.* -**dis'cipline** (-in) *n.* training that produces orderliness, obedience, self-control; result of such training in order, conduct, *etc.*; system of rules; maintenance of subordination in an army, school, *etc.* -u-*t.* train; chastise. **disciplin'arian** *n.* -**dis'ciplinary** *a.* [L. *discipulus*, pupil]

disclose' *v.t.* reveal, bring to light. -**disclo'sure** *n.* [*close*]

discon'solate *a.* unhappy, downcast; unconsoled. [*console*]

dis'cord *n.* absence of concord; difference, dissension; disagreement of sounds. [L. *discordia*]

discount' *v.t.* give present value of (a bill of exchange, *etc.*); detract from; allow for exaggeration in. -**dis'count** *n.* deduction made on discounting a bill, receiving payment for an account, *etc.* [OF. *desconter*, count off]

discourage (-kur-) *v.t.* reduce the confidence of; deter from; show disapproval of. -**discour'agement** *n.* [*courage*]

discourse *n.* speech, treatise, sermon; conversation. -**discourse'** *v.i.* speak, converse. -*v.t.* utter. [L. *discursus*, running to and fro]

discov'er (-kuv-) *v.t.* find out, light upon; make known. -**discov'ery** *n.* -**discov'erer** *n.* -**discov'erable** *a.* [*cover*]

discredit *v.t.* refuse to believe; disgrace; damage reputation. -*n.* -**discreditable** *a.* shameful, disgraceful. [*credit*]

discreet' *a.* prudent, knowing when to be silent. -**discreet'ly** *adv.* -**discre'tion** (-eshén) *n.* [*discrete*]

discrete' *a.* separate; disjoined. -**discreteness** *n.* -**discret'ive** *a.* [L. *discretus*, separated]

discrim'inate *v.t.* and *i.* detect or draw distinctions distinguish from or between. -**discrimina'tion** *n.* [L. *discriminare*, divide, discern]

disc'us *n.* a disk which is thrown to perform a track-and-field sport of that name. [G. *diskos*]

discuss' *v.t.* exchange opinions on; debate; consume (food or drink). -**discus'sion** *n.* [L. *discutere, discuss-*, agitate]

disdain' *n.* scorn, contempt. -*v.t.* scorn. [OF. *desdain*; cp. *deign*]

disease' *n.* illness; disorder of health. [OF. *desaise*, discomfort]

disembody *v.t.* remove from body, *esp.* of spirits; disband. -**disembod'ied** *a.* [*embody*]

disgrace' *n.* ignominy; cause of shame; loss of favor-*v.t.* bring shame or discredit upon. -**disgrace'ful** *a.* -**disgrace'fully** *adv.* [*grace*]

disgruntled *a.* dissatisfied; ill-humored. **disgrun'tle** *v.t.* [*grunt*]

disguise' (-giz) *v.t.* change the appearance of, make unrecognizable; conceal, cloak; misrepresent. -*n.* false appearance; dress or device to conceal identity. [OF. *desguiser*, change costume]

disgust' *n.* violent distaste, loathing. *v.t.* affect with loathing. [OF. *desgoust*, now *dogo* (it, distaste)]

dish *n.* shallow vessel for food; portion or variety of food; contents of a dish. -*v.t.* put in a dish; serve up. [OE. *disc*, platter]

dishonor *n.* disgrace; loss of honor -*v.t.* disgrace; to insult; refuse payment on. [*honor*]

disillusion *n.* freeing from illusion. *v.t.* undeceive. illusion -**disinfect'** *v.t.* free from infection or germs; purify. -**disinfect'ant** *a.* ln. germdestroying (agent). [*infect*]

disin'tegrate *v.t.* break up, crumble, fall to pieces. -**disintegra'tion** *n.* [*integrate*]

disin'terested *a.* unbiased, impartial. [*interest*]

disk, disc *n.* thin circular plate; anything disk-like. **-disk jock'ey** *n.* (*sl.*) announcer on a radio program who introduces and plays recorded music. **-disk drive** *n.* in computer technology the unit that controls the mechanism for handling a diskette. **-disk'ette** *n.* floppy disk, used for storing information on a computer. [G. *diskos*, a round plate]

dislodge' *v.t.* eject from a position, lodg ment. [*lodge*]

dis'mal (-z-) *a.* depressing, or depressed; cheerless, dreary. **-dis'mally** *adv.* [ME. in the dismal, L. *dies mali*, evil days]

dismay' *v.t.* dishearten, daunt. *-n.* consternation, horrified amazement. [OF. *desmayer*, deprive of power]

dismember *v.t.* tear or cut limb from limb; divide, partition. **-dismem'berment** *n.* [*member*]

dismiss' *v.t.* send away, disperse, disband; put away from employment, or from the mind. **-dismiss'al** *n.* [L. *mittere, miss-*, send]

disparage *v.t.* speak slightingly of; bring into disrepute. **-dispar'agement** *n.* [OF. *desparagier*, orig. marry unequally]

disparate *a.* essentially different, not related. **-dispar'ity** *n.* inequality. [*parity*]

dispassionate *a.* cool; unbiased. [*passion*]

dispatch *v.t.* send off, send to a destination or on an errand; kill; eat up; finish off, get done with speed. *-n.* a sending off-, efficient speed; an official written message. *-pl.* state papers. [Sp. *despachar*, expedite]

dispel' *v.t.* clear away; banish. [L. *dispellere*, drive apart]

dispense' *v.t.* deal out; make up (a medicine), relax, not insist on; do without; administer. *-v.i.* make up medicines. **-dispens'er** *n.* **-dispens'ary** *n.* place where medicine is made up. **-dispensation** *n.* license or exemption; provision of nature or providence; act of dispensing. **-dispens'able** *a.* [L. *dispen sare*, distribute by weight]

disperse' *v.t.* scatter. **-dispersed'** *a.* scattered; placed here and there. **-disper'sion** *n.* [F. *disperser*]

display' *v.t.* spread out for show; show, expose to view. *-n.* a displaying; show, exhibition; show, ostentation. [OF. *despleier*, L. *displicare*, unfold]

dispose' (-z) *v.t.* arrange; make inclined (to). *-v.i.* ordain, appoint. **-dispose of**, sell, get rid of; have authority over. **-dispo'sal**

n. **-disposi'tion** *n.* arrangement; plan; inclination; east of mind or temper. [F. *disposer*]

dispute' *v.i.* debate, discuss. *-v.t.* call in question; debate, argue; oppose, contest; try to debar from. **dis'putable** *a.* **-dis'putant** *n.* **-disputa'tion** *n.* **-disputa'tious** *a.* [L. *disputare*, discuss]

disrupt' *v.t.* shatter, break in pieces, split. **-disrup'tion** *n.* **-disrup'tive** *a.* [L. *disrumpere*, disrupt-, break asunder]

dissect' *v.t.* cut up (a body, organism) for detailed examination; examine or criticize in detail. **-disse'tion** *n.* **-dissec'tor** *n.* [L. *dissecare*, cut up]

disseminate *v.t.* spread abroad. **-dissemina'tion** *n.* **-dissem'inator** *n.* [L. *disseminate*, scatter seed]

dissent' *v.i.* differ in opinion; express such difference; disagree with the doctrine, *etc.*, of an established church. *n.* such disagreement. **-dissent'er** *n.* **-dissentient** *a.* and *n.* **-dissen'sion** n. [L. *dissentire*, differ in feeling]

dissertation *n.* formal discourse; treatise. [L. *dissertation*]

dissipate *v.t.* scatter, clear away; waste, squander. *-v.i.* disappear, clear away. **-diss'ipated** *a.* corrupted, dissolute. [L. *dissipate*, scatter]

dissociate *v.t.* separate, sever. dissociation *n.* [L. *socius*, companion]

dissolve' *v.t.* absorb or melt in a fluid; break up, put an end to, annul. *-v.i.* melt in a fluid; disappear, vanish; break up, scatter. **-dissol'uble** *a.* **-dissolu'tion** *n.* [L. *dissolvers*, loosen]

dissonant *a.* jarring, discordant in sound. **-diss'onance** *n.* [L. *dissonare*, sound diversely]

dis'tance *n.* amount of space between two things; remoteness; excessive dignity. *-v.t.* leave behind, *esp.* in a race. **-dis'tant** *a.* **-dis'tantly** *adv.* [L. *distans, distantis*, fr. *distare*, stand apart]

distaste' *n.* dislike, aversion; disgust. **-distaste'ful** *a.* offensive to one's taste; unpleasant. [*taste*]

distemper *n.* disordered state of mind or body; disease of dogs. [L. *temperate*, mix, temper]

distend' *v.t.* and *i.* swell out by pressure from within. [L. *tendere*, stretch]

distill' *v.i.* pass over or condense from a still; trickle down. *-v.t.* obtain (a substance or part of it) in a purified state by evaporating and then condensing it. **-distill'ery** *n.* place where these are distilled. [L. *distillate*, trickle down]

distinct' *a.* clear, easily seen, sharp of outline; definite; separate, different. -**distinct'ly** *adv.* -**distinct'ness** *n.* distinction *n.* point of difference; act of distinguishing; eminence, high honor, high quality. -**distinct'ive** *a.* characteristic. -**disting'uish** *v.t.* class; make a difference in; recognize, make out; honor; make prominent or honored (*usu. refl.*). -*v.i.* draw a distinction, grasp a difference. -**disting'uishable** *a.* [L. *distinguere, -distinct-*, prick off]

distort' *v.t.* put out of shape; misrepresent, garble. -**distor'tion** *n.* [L. *distorquere, distort-*, twist apart]

distract' *v.t.* turn aside, divert; bewilder, drive mad. **distrac'tion** *n.* [L. *distrahere, distract-*, pull apart]

distraught' (-awt) *a.* bewildered, crazy. [fr. F. *distrait*, absentminded]

distress' *n.* severe trouble, mental pain; pressure of hunger or fatigue or want; (*law*) -**distraint.** -*v.t.* afflict, give mental pain to. -**distress'ful** *a.* [OF. *destresse*, fr. L. *distringere*, pull asunder]

distribute *v.t.* deal out; spread, dispose at intervals; classify. -**distrib'utive** *a.* -**distribu'tion** *n.* -**distrib'utor** *n.* [L. *distribuereé* cp. *tribute*]

dis'trict *n.* portion of territory; region. [F. = control, region controlled]

disturb' *v.t.* trouble, agitate; unsettle, derange. -**distur'bance** *n.* -**distur'ber** *n.* [L. *disturbare*, disorder]

ditch *n.* long narrow hollow dug in the ground, usually for drainage. -*v.t.* and *i.* make or repair ditches; discard. [OE. *die*]

dit'to same, aforesaid; (used to avoid repetition in lists, *etc.*). [It., fr. L. *dictus*, the said]

diuret'ic (di-fir-) *a.* exciting discharge of urine. -*n.* substance with this property. [G. *diouretikos*]

diur'nal *a.* daily; in, or of, daytime; taking a day. [L. *diurnalis*, fr. *dies*, day]

di'va *n.* distinguished female singer; prima-donna. [L. = *divine*]

dive *v.i.* plunge under the surface of water; descend suddenly; disappear; go deep down into. -*n.* an act of diving; (*sl.*) disreputable place of entertainment. -**di'ver** *n.* [OE. *dufan*, sink, and *dyfan*, dip]

diverge' *v.i.* get further apart, separate. -**diver'gent** *a.* -**diver'gence** *n.* [L. *di-*, apart, and *uergere*, turn]

di'vers (-z) *a.* sundry. -**diverse'** *a.* different, varied. **divers'ify** *v.t.* [*divert*]

divert' *v.t.* turn aside, ward off, cause to turn; amuse, entertain. -**diver'sion** *n.* a turning aside; that which diverts; amusement; entertainment. [L. *divertere*, turn aside]

divest' *v.t.* unclothe, strip, dispossess. [L. *devestire*, undress]

divide' *v.t.* make into two or more parts, split up, separate; classify; cut off; deal out; take or have a share; part into two groups for voting; -**divide** a number by another, find out how many times the former contains the latter. -*v.i.* become divided. -**div'idend** *n.* number to be divided by another; share of profits, of money divided among creditors, *etc.* -**divi'ders** *n. pl.* measuring compasses. -**divis'ible** *a.* -**divis'ion** *n.* (-vizh-n). -**divi'sional** *a.* -**divi'sor** *n.* [L. *dividere, divis-*, to force asunder]

divine' *a.* of, pertaining to, proceeding from, God; sacred; godlike, heavenly. -*n.* theologian; clergyman. -*v.t.* and *i.* guess; predict, tell by inspiration or magic. -**divine'ly** *adv.* -**divin'ity** *n.* quality of being divine; god; theology, [L. *divinus*, of the gods]

divina'tion *n.* divining. -**divi'ner** *n.* -**divi'ning-rod** *n.* switch for detecting underground water or minerals. [*divine*]

divorce' *n.* legal dissolution of marriage; complete separation, disunion. -*v.t.* dissolve a marriage; put away; separate. -**divorcee'** *n.* divorced person. [F.]

div'ot *n.* patch of turf, *esp.* as dislodged accidentally in the game of golf. [Scot.]

divulge' *v.t.* reveal, let out (a secret). [L. *divulgare*, spread among the people, *vulgus*]

dizz'y *a.* feeling dazed, unsteady; causing, or fit to cause, dizziness, as of speed, *etc.* *v.t.* to make dizzy. -**dizz'iness** *n.* -**dizz'ily** *adv.* [OE. *dysig*, foolish]

do *v.t.* perform, effect, transact, bring about, finish, prepare, cook; cheat. *v.i.* act, manage, work, fare, serve, suffice. -*v. aux.* makes negative and interrogative sentences and expresses emphasis. [OE. *don*]

do'cile *a.* willing to obey; easily taught. -**docil'ity** *n.* [L. *docilis-, docere*, teach]

dock *n.* basin with flood-gates for loading or repairing ships. -*v.t.* put in a dock. *v. i.* go into dock. -**dock'yard** *n.* enclosure with docks, for building or repairing ships. -**dock'er** *n.* dock-worker or docklaborer. [O. Du. *dokke*]

dock'et *n.* endorsement showing the contents of a document; memorandum; certificate of payment of customs. -*v.t.* make a memorandum, endorse with a summary. [earlier *dogget*, orig. uncertain]

doc'tor *n.* one holding a University's highest degree in any faculty; medical practitioner. *-v.t.* treat medically; adulterate, garble. **-doc'torate** *n.* **-doc'toral** *a.* [L. *doctrina*, fr. *docere*, teach]

doc'trine *n.* what is taught; teaching of a church, school, or person; belief, opinion, dogma; statement of official government policy. [L. fr. *docere*, teach]

doc'ument *n.* something written furnishing evidence or information. *-v.t.* furnish with proofs, illustrations, cer tificates. **- document'ary** *a.* **-document- a'tion** *n.* [L. *documentum*, example]

dodd'ering *a.* trembling with ague or frailty; useless; pottering. [cp. *dither*]

dodec'agon *n.* twelve-sided, twelve angled plane figure, [G. *dodeka*, twelve, *gonia*, angle]

dodge *v.i.* swerve, make zig-zag movement, *esp.* to avoid a pursuer or gain an advantage; shuffle. play fast and loose. *v.t.* elude by **dodging.** *-n.* an act of dodging; trick, artifice; shift, ingenious method. - **dodg'er** *n.* [orig. unknown]

doe *n.* female of deer, hare, rabbit, antelope *etc.* [OE. *do*]

dog *n.* familiar domestic quadruped; person (in contempt, abuse, or playfully). *-v.t.* follow steadily or closely. [OE, *docga*]

dogg'erel *n.* slipshod, unpoetic or trivial verse. [orig. uncertain]

dog'ma *n.* article of belief, *esp.* one laid down authoritatively by a church; body of beliefs. **-dogmat'ic** *a.* relating to dogma or dogmas; asserting opinions with arrogance. **-dogmat'ically** *adv.* **-dog' matism** *n.* arrogant assertion of opinion. **dog'matist** *n.* **-dog'matize** *v.i.* [G. *dokeiro*, to seem]

dol'drums *n. pl.* region of light winds and calms near the equator; state of depression, dumps. [*dull*]

dole *n.* charitable gift; (*sl.*) a payment from government funds to the unemployed. *-v.t.* (usually dole out) deal out, *esp.* in niggardly quantities. [OE. *dal*]

dole *n.* woe. **-dole'ful** *a.* full of grief; dismal. **-dole'fully** *adv.* [OF. *duel*]

doll'ar *n.* coin of Canada, U.S., and other countries. [Ger. *thaler*]

dol'or (-er) *n.* grief, sadness. **-dol'orous** *a.* **-dol'orously** *adv.* [L. *dolor*]

dol'phin *a.* sea mammal like a porpoise; figure of a curved, large-headed fish common in decoration and heraldry; buoy for mooring. **-dolphinar'ium.** *n.* a pool or aquarium for dolphins, *esp.* one in which they give public displays. [OF. *dalfin*, fr. L. *delphinus*]

domain' *n.* lands held or ruled over; sphere, field of influence, province. [F. *domaine*, fr. L. *dorninium*]

dome *n.* rounded vault forming a roof, large cupola. **-domed** *a.* [F. *dome*]

domes'tic *a.* of or in the home; of the home country, not foreign; home-keeping; of animals, tamed, kept by man. [L. *domesticus*]

dom'icile *n.* person's regular place of living (usually legal). **-domicil'iary** *a.* pert. to the domicile. [F.]

dom'inate *v.t.* rule, control, sway; of heights, to overlook. *-v.i.* control, be the most powerful or influential member or part of something.[L. *dominus*, lord]

Domin'ican *a.* pert. to order of monks of St. Dominic. *-n.* Dominican monk. [*St. Dominic*]

dominion *n.* sovereignty, rule; territory of a government. [L. *dominio*]

dom'ino *n.* cloak with a half-mask for masquerading. *-pl.* game played with small flat pieces, marked on one side with 0 to 6 spots on each half of the face. *-sing.* one of these pieces. (It.]

don *v.t.* put on (clothes). [*do on*]

donate' *v.t.* give. **-dona'tion** *n.* donor *n.* [L. *donare*, give]

don'gle *n.* in computer technology, an electronic device that accompanies a software item to prevent the unauthorized copying of programs. [orig. uncertain]

donk'ey *n.* ass. **-donk'ey-engine** *n.* small hauling or hoisting engine on a ship. [orig. uncertain] ·

doom n. fate, destiny; ruin; judicial sentence, condemnation; Last Judgment. *-v.t.* sentence, condemn; destine to destruction or suffering. **-dooms'day** *n.* day of the Last Judgment. [OE. *dom*]

door *n.* hinged, sliding, or revolving barrier to close the entrance to a room, carriage, *etc.* **-door-to-door** *a.* going from one building or destination to the next, *usu.* selling. **-door'way** *n.* entrance provided, or capable of being provided, with a door. [OE. *dor, duru*]

dopamine *n.* amine ($C_8H_{11}NO_2$) formed in the brain that is an essential neurotransmitter in the central nervous system's regulation of movement and emotions.

dope *v.t.* drug; stupefy with drugs. *-n.* narcotic drugs; stupid person. **-dope'y** *a.* dull-witted. [Du. *doop*, sauce]

dor'ic *n.* a Greek dialect. *-a.* simplest order of Greek architecture. [G. *dorikos*]

dor'mant *a.* not acting, in a state of

suspension. -**dor'mancy** n. -**dorm'er** n. upright window set in a sloping roof - **dor'mitory** n. sleeping-room with a number of beds; building containing sleeping quarters. [L. *dormire*, sleep]

dor'sal a. of or on the back. -**dor'sally** adv. [L. *dorsum*, back]

do'ry n. a flat-bottomed boat. [Miskito, *dori*, dugout]

DOS n. (*compute*.) operating system for a computer. [*disk operating system*]

dose n. amount (of a drug, *etc*.) administered at one time. -v.t. give doses to . -**dos'age** n. [F.]

dot n. small spot or mark. -v.t. mark with a dot or dots; place here and there. **dot ma'trix prin'ter** n. in computer technology, a printer in which each character is produced by a subset of an array of needles at the printhead. [OE. *dott*, speck]

dot (dot) n. dowry. [F.]

dote v.i. be silly or weak-minded; be passionately fond of. -**do'tage** n. feeble minded old age. -**do'tard** n. [AF. *doter*]

dou'ble (dub-) a. of two parts, layers *etc*.; folded; twice as much or many; of two kinds; ambiguous; deceitful. -adv. twice; to twice the amount or extent; in a pair. n. person or thing exactly like, or mistakable for, another; quantity twice as much as another; sharp turn; evasion or shift. v.t. and i. make or become double; increase twofold; fold in two; turn sharply; get round, sail round. [F. *double*, fr. L. *duplus*]

double team v.t. (*sports*) guard, defend against, or block an opposing player with two players.

doubt (dowt) v.t. hesitate to believe, call in question; suspect. -v.i. be wavering or uncertain in belief or opinion. -n. state of uncertainty, wavering in belief; state of affairs giving cause for uncertainty. - **doubt'er** n. -**doubt'ful** a. -**doubt'fully** adv. **doubt'lessly** adv. [L. *dubitare*]

douche n. jet or spray of water applied to the body or some part of it; shower. -v.t. give a douche to. [F.]

dough n. flour or meal kneaded with water. -**dough'y** a. [OE. *dag*]

dour a. grim, stubborn. [F. *dur*]

douse, dowse v.t. plunge into water; souse; strike; extinguish. -v.i. fall into water. [O. Du. *doesen*, beat]

dove (duv) n. bird of the pigeon family. [cp. Du. *duif*]

dow'er n. widow's share for life of her husband's estate; dowry. -v.t. give dowry to; endow. -**dow'ry** n. property which a wife brings to her husband; talent. [F. *douaire*, -L. *dotare*, endow]

down adv. to, or in, or towards, a lower position; with a current or wind; of paying, on the spot. -prep. from higher to lower part of; at a lower part of; along with. - **down'cast** a. looking down; dejected. - **down' link** n. communications path for transmission of information or signals from a spacecraft or satellite to earth. - **down'pour** n. heavy fall of rain. - **down'right** a. plain, straightforward. adv. quite, thoroughly. -**downsize** v.t. to make a smaller version. -**down time** n. time during which a machine or plant is not working because it is incapable of production, as when under repair. [for *adown*, OE. of *dune*, off hill]

down n. fluff or fine hair of young birds; anything like this, soft and fluffy. -**down'y** a. [OE. *dunn*]

dow'ry. See **dower.**

dowse v.i. seek for water, minerals, with aid of divining-rod or -**dows'ing-rod** n. -**dows'er** n. water-diviner. [earlier *dense*, perh. conn. with Ger. *deuter*, indicate]

doze v.i. sleep drowsily, be half asleep. n. nap. [orig. uncertain]

doz'en twelve, a set of twelve. [F. *douzaine*, fr. L. *duo*, two, *decem*, ten]

drab a. of dull light brown; dull, monotonous. -n. drab color. [F. *drop*, cloth]

draft n. detachment of men, *esp*. troops, reinforcements; selection for compulsory military service; design, sketch; rough copy of a document; order for money; act of drinking, quantity drunk at once; one drawing of, or fish taken in, a net; dose; an inhaling; depth of water needed to float a ship; current of air between apertures in a room, *etc*. -a. constituting a preliminary version. -v.t. make an outline sketch or design of, make a preliminary version of something, *esp*. a piece of writing; to conscript for military service. -**drafts'man** n. one who draws plans and designs for buildings, ships *etc*., one skilled in drawing. [*draw*]

drag v.t. pull along with difficulty or friction; trail, go heavily; sweep with a net; protract. -v.i. lag, trail; be tediously protracted. -n. check on progress; checked motion, iron shoe to check a wheel; vehicle; lure for hounds to hunt; kinds of harrow, sledge, net, grapnel, rake; (*fig*.) a tedious person or thing; (*sl*.) transvestite clothing. [var. of *draw*]

drag'on n. mythical fire-breathing monster, like a winged crocodile. - **drag'onfly** n. long-bodied insect with large gauzy wings. -**dragoon'** n. cavalryman, usually of heavy cavalry. *v.t.* subject to military oppression; domineer over, persecute. [F.]

drain *v.t.* draw off (liquid) by pipes, ditches, *etc.*; dry; drink to the dregs; empty, exhaust. *-v.i.* flow off or away; become rid of liquid. *-n.* channel for removing liquid; constant outlet, expenditure, strain. **drain'age** *n.* [OE. *dreahnian*, strain a liquid]

drake *n.* male duck. [orig. uncertain]

dr'a'ma (dra-) stage-play; art of literature of plays; play-like series of events. - **dramat'ic** *a.* of drama; vivid, arresting. **-dramatiza'tion** *n.* **-dram'atisperso'nae** *n.* characters of a play. [G. = *action*]

drape *v.t.* cover, adorn with cloth; arrange in graceful folds. *-n.* curtain **dra'per** *n.* dealer in cloth, linen, *etc.* **-dra'pery** *n.* [F. *drop*, cloth]

dras'tic *a.* strongly effective. [G. *drastikos*, active]

draw *v.t.* pull, pull along, haul; bend (a bow); inhale; entice, attract; bring (upon, out, *etc.*); get by lot; of a ship, require (depth of water); take from (a well, barrel, *etc.*); receive (money); delineate, portray with a pencil, *etc.*; *-v.i.* pull; shrink; attract; make or admit a current of air, *etc.*; write orders for money; come, approach (near). *-n.* act of drawing; casting of lots; unfinished game, a tie. **-draw'bridge** *n* . hinged bridge to pull up. **-draw'er** *n.* one who or that which draws; sliding box in a table or chest. *-pl.* two-legged undergarment. **-draw'ing** *n..* action of the verb; art of depicting in line; sketch so done. [OE. *dragon*; *drawn game*, for *withdrawn*, the stakes being 'withdrawn' for lack of a decision; *drawing-room* for earlier *withdrawing room*]

drawl *v.t.* and *i.* speak slowly in indolence or affectation. *-n.* such speech. [Du. *dralen*]

dread (dred) *v.t.* fear greatly. *-n.* awe, terror. *-a.* feared, awful, revered. **-dread'ful** *a.* **-dreadlocks** *n. pl.* hair worn in the Rastafarian style of long matted or tightly curled strands. [OE. *adrcovdan*]

dream *n.* vision during sleep; fancy, reverie, vision of something ideal. *v.i.* have dreams. *-v.t.* see or imagine in dreams; think of as possible. [ME.]

drear'y *a.* dismal, dull; cheerless. [OE. *dreorig*, gory]

dredge *n.* machinery, appliance for bringing up mud, objects, *etc.*, from the bottom of sea or river. *-v.t.* bring up, clean, deepen, with such appliance. **-dredg'er** *n.* ship for dredging. [cp. *drag*]

dredge *v.t.* sprinkle with flour. [F. *dragée*, sweetmeat]

dregs *n. pl.* sediment, grounds, worthless part. [ON. *dregg*]

drench *v.t.* wet thoroughly, soak; make (an animal) take a dose of medicine. *-n.* dose for an animal; soaking. [OE. *drencan*, make drink]

dress *v.t.* clothe; array for show; trim, smooth, prepare surface of. draw up (troops) in proper line; prepare (food) for the table; put dressing on. *-v.i.* put on one's clothes; form in proper line. *-n.* clothing, clothing for ceremonial evening wear; frock. [F. *dresser*]

drift *n.* being driven by a current; slow current or course; deviation from a course; (also **drift'age**); tendency; speaker's meaning; wind-heaped mass of snow, sand, *etc.*; material driven or carried by water; (in S. Africa) ford. *-v.i.* be carried as by current of air, water; move aimlessly or passively. [*drive*]

drill *n.* boring tool or machine; exercise of soldiers or others in handling of arms and maneuvers; routine teaching. *-v.t.* bore; exercise in military movements or other routine. *-v.i.* practice a routine. [Du. *dril*]

drink *v.t.* and *i.* swallow liquid; absorb; take intoxicating liquor, *esp.* to excess. *n.* liquid for drinking; portion of this; act of drinking; intoxicating liquor; excessive use of it. - **drink'er** *n.* **-drink'able** *a.* [OE. *drincan*]

drip *v.t.* and *i.* or let fall in drops. *-n.* process of dripping; that which falls by dripping. **drip'stone** *n.* projection over round window or door to stop dripping of water. **dripp'ing** *n.* act of dripping; melted fat that drips from roasting meat. [Scand.]

drive *v.t.* force to move in some direction; make move and steer (a vehicle, animal, *etc.*); chase; convey in a vehicle, fix by blows, as a nail; urge, impel. [OE. *drifan*]

drive train *n.* system in a vehicle which delivers power from the transmission to the wheel axles, via the universal joint, drive shaft, and clutch.

driz'zle *v.i.* rain in fine drops *-n.* fine rain. [OE. *dreosan*, fall in drops]

drogue *n.* drag or brake; funnel-shaped device on the end of a feed-hose to facilitate mid-air refuelling of airplanes; small parachute which, when deployed, causes a larger parachute to open, or which is used as a brake. [*drag*]

drone *n.* male of the honey-bee; lazy idler; deep humming; bass pipe of bagpipe, or its note. *-v.t.* and *i.* hum; talk in a monotone. [OE. *dran*, bee]

droop *v.i.* hang down as in weariness, languish, flag. -*v.t.* let hang down. -*n.* drooping condition. [ON. *drupa*]

drop *n.* globule of liquid; very small quantity; fall, descent; thing that falls, as a gallows platform; distance through which a thing falls. -*v.t.* let fall; let fall in drops; utter casually; discontinue. -*v.i.* fall; fall in drops; lapse; come or go casually. [OE. *dropa*]

drought (-owt) *n.* long-continued dry weather; thirst. [OE. *drugoth*]

drown *v.t.* suffocate in water; of sound, *etc.*, to overpower. -*v.i.* be suffocated in water. [OE. *druncnian*, to be drunk, get drowned]

drow'sy (-z-) *a.* half-asleep; lulling; dull, lacking life. -**drow'sily** *adv.* -**drow'siness** *n.* -**drowse** *v.i.* [obs. Du. *droosen*, become sleepy]

drudge *v.i.* work hard at mean or distasteful tasks. -*n.* one who drudges. -**drudg'ery** *n.* [orig. obscure]

drug *n.* medicinal substance; commodity not wanted (usually within the market). *v.t.* mix drugs with; administer a drug to, *esp.* one inducing sleep or unconsciousness. -**drug'store** *n.* retail store which sells medicines and a variety of other articles, such as food, film, household utensils, cosmetics. **drugg'ist** *n.* dealer in drugs, chemist. [F. *drogue*]

drum *n.* musical instrument, made of skin stretched over a round hollow frame or hemisphere, and played by beating with sticks; various things shaped like a drum; part of the ear. -*v.t.* and *i.* play a drum; tap or thump continuously. [imit. orig.]

drunk *a.* overcome by strong drink; fig. under the influence of strong emotion. -**drunk'en** *a.* drunk; often drunk; caused by or showing intoxication. -**drunk'ard** *n.* one given to excessive drinking. -**drunk'enness** *n.* [*drink*]

dry *a.* without moisture; rainless; not yielding milk, or other liquid; not in or under water; cold, unfriendly; caustically witty; having prohibition of alcoholic drink; uninteresting, needing effort to study; lacking sweetness. -*v.t.* remove water, moisture. -*v.i.* become dry, evaporate. -**dry'goods** *n. pl.* drapery, textiles. -**dry'point** *n.* needle for engraving without acid; an engraving so made. [OE. *dryge*]

du'al *a.* twofold; of two, forming a pair. -**dual'ity** *n.* -**du'alism** *n.* recognition of two independent powers or principles, as good and evil, mind and matter. -**dualis'tic** *a.* [L. *dualis*]

dub *v.t.* confer knighthood on; give a title to; give fresh sound-track to (film); smear with grease, dubbin. -**dubb'in, dubbing** *n.* grease for making leather supple. [late OE. *dubbian*]

du'bious *a.* causing doubt, not clear or decided; of suspected character; hesitating. [L. *dubiosus*]

duck *n.* familiar swimming bird; amphibious motor vehicle. drake *n. masc.* -**duck'ling** *n.* duck *v.i.* plunge under water; bend or bob down. -*v.t.* plunge someone under water. [OE. *duce*, diver]

duck *n.* strong linen or cotton fabric. -*pl.* trousers of it. [Du. *doek*, linen]

duct *n.* channel or tube. -**duct'less** *a.* (of giands) secreting directly certain substances essential to health. [L. *ductus*]

ductile *a.* capable of being drawn into wire; flexible and tough; docile. -**ductil'ity** *n.* [L. *ducere*, lead]

dud *n.* (*sl.*) shell that fails to explode; futile person or project or thing. *a.* [orig. uncertain]

dude *n.* someone from the city, *esp.* an Easterner in the West; dandy; guy. [orig. uncertain]

due *a.* that is owing; proper to be given, inflicted, *etc.*; adequate, fitting; usual, ascribable; under engagement to arrive, be present. -*adv.* (with points of the compass), exactly. -*n.* person's fair share; charge fee, *etc.* (*usu.* in *pl.*)-**du'ly** *adv.* [F. *du*, fr. *devoir*, L. *debere*, owe]

du'el *n.* fight with deadly weapons between two persons; keen two-sided contest. -*v.i.* fight in a dual or duels. -**du'ellist** *n.* [F.]

duet' *n.* piece of music for two performers. [It. *duetto*, fr. L. *duo*, two]

du jour *a.* available or served on that particular day; of the day. [F.]

duke *n.* peer of rank next below a prince; sovereign of a small state called a duchy. -**duke'dom** *n.* [L. *dux*, leader]

dul'cimer (-sim-) *n.* stringed instrument played with hammers, an ancestor of the piano. [L. *dulce melos*, sweet tune]

dull *a.* stupid; sluggish; tedious; not keen or clear or bright or sharp or defined; lacking liveliness or variety; gloomy, overcast. -*v.t.* and *i.* make or become dull. —**dul'ly** *adv.* -**dull'ard** *n.* -**dull'ness** *n.* [OE. *dol*, foolish]

dumb *a.* incapable of speech; silent; (*sl.*) stupid. -**dumb'bell** *n.* weight for exercises. -**dumbfound', dumbfound'er** *v.t.* confound into silence. -**dumb'show** *n.* acting without words. -**dumb'ly** *adv.* -

dumb'ness *n*. [OE.]

dumm'y *n*. imaginary card-player; imitation object. (OE.]

dump *v.t.* throw down in a mass; send low-priced goods for sale abroad. -*n*. rubbish-heap; temporary depot of stores or munitions. [orig. uncertain]

dun *a*. of a dull grayish brown. -*n*. this color; horse of dun color. [OE. *dunn*]

dun *v.t.* to make persistent demands, *esp*. for payment of debts. -*n*. one who duns. [orig. uncertain]

dune *n*. mound of dry shifting sand on a coast or desert. -dune buggy *n*. lightweight vehicle with oversize, low-pressure tires used mainly for driving on sand dunes and beaches. [F.]

dung *n*. excrement of animals; manure. *v.t.* to manure. -dung'hill *n*. manure heap. [OE.]

dung'eon (dunjn) *n*. underground cell or vault for prisoners; formerly a tower or keep of a castle. [F. *donion*]

dunk shot *n*. (*sports*) basketball shot in which the player jumps high enough to slam the ball down through the basket with one or both hands.

duodenum *n*. upper part of small intestine, 12 in. long. [L. *duodeni*, twelve]

du'plex *a*. two-fold -*n*. apartment having rooms on two floors; a house consisting of two family units. duplicate *v.t.* make an exact copy of; double. *a*. double; twofold. -*n*. exact copy. [L.]

du'rable *a*. lasting, resisting wear. -durabil'ity *a*. -dura'tion *n*. time a thing lasts. -du'rably *adv*. [L. *durare*, last]

du'ress *n*. restraint, coercion, imprisonment; (*law*) illegal compulsion. [L. *durus*, hard]

du'ring *prep*. throughout, in the time of. [L. *durare*, last]

dusk *n*. dark stage of twilight; partial darkness. -dusk'y *a*. dark; dark colored. -dusk'ily *adv*. [OE. *dor*]

dust *n*. fine particles, powder, of earth or other matter, lying on a surface or blown along by the wind. -*v.t.* sprinkle with powder; rid of dust. -dust'-cov'er *n*. book-jacket. [OE.]

du'ty *n*. what one ought to do, moral or legal obligation; office, function, being occupied in these; tax on goods for the public revenue; respect. -du'ty-free *a*. (of goods) free from duty, tax. [AF. *duet*, what is due]

duvet' *n*. down-quilt. [F.]

dwarf *n*. very undersized person. -*a*. unusually small, stunted. -*v.t.* make stunted; make seem small by contrast.[OE. *dweorg*]

dwell *v.i.* live, make one's abode (in); fix one's attention, write or speak at length (on). -dwell'ing *n*. house. -dwell'er *n*. [OE. *dwellan*, linger]

dwindle *v.i.* grow less, waste away, to grow feeble. [OE. *dwinan*]

dye (di) *v.t.* impregnate (cloth, *etc*.) with coloring matter; color thus. -*n*. coloring matter in solution which may be dissolved for dyeing; tinge, color. -dy'er *n*. [OE. *deagian*, v.; *deag*, n.]

dynam'ics (di) *n. pl.* branch of physics dealing with force as producing or affecting motion; physical or moral forces. -dynam'ic *a*. of or relating to motive force, force in operation. -dynam'ical *a*. -dynam'ically *adv*. -dy'namite *n*. high explosive of nitroglycerin. -*v.t.* blow up with this. -dy'namiter *n*. -dy'namo *n*. machine to convert mechanical into electrical energy, generator of electricity. -dyne *n*. unit of force. [G. *dynamis*, power]

dynasty (din-) *n*. line or family of hereditary rulers. -dyn'ast *n*. -dynast'ic *a*. [G. *dynastes*, prince]

dysentery (dis-) *n*. inflammatory disease of the bowels. [G. *dusenteria*]

dyspepsia *n*. indigestion. -dyspep'tic *a*. and *n*. [G. *dyspepsia*]

dyspnoe'a *n*. difficulty in breathing. [G. *dys*-, ill, *pnoe*, breathing]

dystoc'ia *n*. abnormal, slow, or difficult childbirth, usually because of disordered or ineffective contractions of the uterus. [G. *dys*-, ill, *tokos*, childbirth]

E

each *a*. and *pron*. every one taken separately. [OE. *ælc*]

ea'ger (eg -) *a*. full of keen desire; keen, impatient. -eag'erly *adv*. -eag'erness *n*. [F. *aigre*, sour, keen]

ea'gle (eegl) *n*. large bird of prey with keen sight and strong flight; (golf) hole played in two under par. -ea'glet *n*. young eagle. [F. *aigle*]

ear *n*. organ of hearing, *esp*. external part, sensitiveness to musical sounds; attention. -ear'drum *n*. tympanum. [OE. *eare*]

ear *n*. spike or head of corn. [OE.]

earl (erl) *n*. peer of rank next below a marquis. -earl'dom *n*. [OE. *eorl,* nobleman, warrior]

earl'y (erl -) *a*. and *adv*. in the first part, or near or nearer the beginning, of some portion of time. [OE. *ærlice*]

earn (ern) *v.t.* get for labor, merit, *etc*. -earn'ings *n. pl.* what has been earned. [OE. *earnian*]

earn'est (ern -) *a*. serious, ardent, sincere. -**earn'estness** *n*. -**earn'estly** *adv*. [OE. *eornost*, eagerness]

earth (er-) *n*. ground, soil: dry land; planet or world we live on; mold, soil, mineral; fox's hole. -*v.t*. cover with earth; connect electrically with the earth. -**earth'en** (-th-) *a*. -**earth'ly** *a*. -**earth'y** *a*. -**earth'enware** (-th-) *n*. vessels of baked clay. -**earth'quake** *n*. volcanic convulsion of the surface of the earth. [OE. *eorthe*]

ease (ez) *n*. comfort; freedom from constraint or annoyance or awkwardness or pain or trouble; idleness; informal position or step; relief, alleviation. -*v.t*. and *i*. to relieve of pain; reduce burden; give bodily or mental ease to; slacken, relax. -**ease'ful** *a*. -**ease'ment** *n*. (*law*) right over another's property, as right of way. -**eas'y** *a*. not difficult; free from bodily or mental pain, complaint; not in much demand; fitting loosely. [F. *aise*]

east *n*. part of the horizon where the sun rises; regions towards that. -*a*. on or in or near the east; coming from the east. -*adv*. from, or to, the east. -**east'erly** *a*. and *adv*. from or to the east. -**east'ern** *a*. of or dwelling in the east. -**east'erner** *n*. **east'ward** *a*. and *n*. -**east'ward(s)** *adv*. [OE. *easte*]

East'er *n*. Christian festival of the resurrection of Christ. [OE. *Eastre*, goddess of spring festival]

eas'y. See **ease.**

eat *v.t*. and *i*. chew and swallow; swallow; consume, destroy; gnaw; wear away. -*n*. *pl*. (*sl*.) food ready for consumption, *usu*. of small quantity. -**eat'able** *a*. [OE. *etan*]

eaves (evz) *n*. *pl*. overhanging edges of a roof. -**eaves'dropper** *n*. one who stands under eaves or elsewhere to overhear. -**eaves'dropping** *n*. [OE. *efes*]

ebb *n*. flowing back of the tide; decline. -*v.i*. flow back; decline. [OE. *ebba*]

EBCDIC n. a computer coding system that can represent 256 different characters. [*Extended Binary Coded Decimal Interchange Code*]

eb'ony *n*. hard black wood. -*a*. made of or black as ebony. -**eb'onite** *n*. vuleanite. [L. *ebenus*]

ebullient *a*. boiling; exuberant. [L. *ebullire*, boil out]

eccentric *a*. not placed, or not having the axis placed, centrally; not circular (in orbit); irregular; odd, whimsical. -*n*. mechanical contrivance to change circular into to-and-fro movement, whimsical person [G. *ekkentros*, out of center]

ecclesiastic *a*. of or belonging to the church- clergyman. -**ecclesias'tical** *a*. [G. *ekklesiastikos, ekkiesia*, church]

ech'elon *n*. formation of troops or warships in parallel divisions each with its front clear of the one in front. [F. *echelon*, rung of ladder]

ech'o (ek -) *n*. repetition of sounds by reflection; close imitation. -*v.i*. resound or be repeated by echo. -*v.t*. repeat as an echo; imitate opinions. [G.]

eclec'tic *a*. borrowing one's philosophy from various sources; catholic in views or taste. -*n*. eclectic person. -**eclec'ticism** *n*. [G. *eklektikos*, selective]

eclipse' *n*. blotting out of the sun, moon, *etc*., by another body coming between it and the eye or between it and the source of its light; loss of light or brilliance; obscurity. -*v.t*. cause to suffer eclipse; outshine, surpass. [G. *ekleipsis*, leave out]

ecol'ogy *n*. the science devoted to the system of interrelationships between organisms and their environments; the totality of these interrelationships; activity undertaken to maintain or restore the balance of nature. -**e'cological** *a*. relating to ecology; benefiting the balance of nature. [G. *oikos*, house]

econ'omy *n*. management, administration; thrift, frugal use, structure, organization. -**econom'ic** *a*. on business lines. **econom'ics** *n. pl*. political economy, the science of the production and distribution of wealth. **econom'ical** *a*. saving, frugal; of economics. **econom'ically** *adv*. -**econ'omist** *n*. -**econ'omize** *v.t*. and *i*. [G. *oikonomia*, house -law]

ecru' *n*. and *a*. color of unbleached linen. [F.]

ec'stasy *n*. exalted state of feeling, rapture; trance; frenzy. [G. *ekstasis*]

ecumen'ic(al) *a*. pert. to the universe of the Christian world or church. -**ecumeni'city** *n*. [G. *oiken*, inhabit]

ec'zema *n*. skin disease. [G. *ekzema*]

Ed'en *n*. garden of Adam and Eve; ideal spot. [Heb.]

edge *n*. cutting side of a blade; sharpness; border, boundary. -*v.t*. sharpen give an edge or border to; move gradually. -*v.i*. advance sideways or gradually. -**edge'ways, edge'wise** *adv*. -**ed'gy** *a*. irritable. -**on edge**, nervous, excited. [OE. *ecg*]

ed'ible *a*. eatable. -**edibil'ity** *n*. [L. *edibilis, edere*, eat]

e'dict *n*. order proclaimed by authority, a decree. [L. *edictum*]

ed'ifice (-fis) building, *esp*. a big one. -

ed'ify v.t. improve morally. -**edifica'tion** n. [L. edificare, build]

ed'it v.t. prepare for publication. -**ed'ition** n. form in which a book is published; number of copies of a book, newspaper, etc. ; printed at one time, issue. -**ed'itor** n. [L. edere, give out]

ed'ucate v.t. bring up; train mentallyand morally; provide schooling for; train. [L. educare, educat -]

educe' v.t. bring out, develop; infer. -**edu'cible** deduction n. -**educ'tor** n. [L. educere, lead out]

eel n. snakelike fish. [OE. sæl]

ee'rie, ee'ry a. weird; superstitiously timid. [OE. earg, cowardly]

efface' v.t. wipe or rub out. -**effacement** n. [F. effacer]

effect' n. result, consequence; impression. -pl. property. -v.t. bring about, accomplish. -**effect'ive** a. -**effect'ively** adv. -**effect'ual** a. -**effect'ually** adv. -**effect'uate** v.t. [L. efficere, effect -], bring about]

effem'inate a. womanish, unmanly. -**effem'inacy** n. [L. effeminate, fr. femina, woman]

effervesce' (-es) v.i give off bubbles; issue in bubbles. -**efferves'cent** a. -**efferves'cence** n. [L. effervescere]

effete' a. worn -out, feeble. [L. effetus, exhausted by breeding]

effi'cient a. capable, competent; producing effect. **effi'ciently** adv. -**effi'ciency** n. [L. eflicere, effect]

eff'igy n. image, likeness. [L. effigies, fr. fingere, form]

eff'luent n. flowing out. -n. streamflowing from a larger stream, lake, etc. [L. effluere, flow out]

eff'ort n. exertion, endeavor. [F., fr. L. fortis, strong]

effrontery (-un-) n. brazen impudence. [F. effronto a. lit. without brow (for blushing)]

effu'sion n. a pouring out; literary composition. -**effu'sive** a. gushing, demonstrative. [L. effundere, effus -, pour out]

egg n. oval body produced by the female of birds, etc. , esp. of domestic fowl, and containing the germ of their young. -**egg'-plant** n. plant with an edible, purpleskinned fruit of pearshaped form; the fruit of this plant, aubergine. [ON.]

egg v.t. egg on, encourage, urge. [ON. eggia, fr. egg, edge]

eg'o n. the self, the conscious thinkingsubject. -**egocen'tric** a. selfcentered. -**eg'oism** n. systematic selfishness; theorythat bases morality on self-interest. -**eg'oist** n. -**egois'tic, egois'tical** a. -**eg'otism** n. talking habitually about oneself -, self -conceit. -**eg'otist** n. -**egotis'tic, egotistical** a. [L. = 1]

e'gret n. lesser white heron. [F. aigrette]

eight (at) a. and n. cardinal number, one above seven. eighth (at-th) a. ordinal number. -**eighth'ly** adv. -**eighteen'** a. and n. eight more than ten. -**fig'ure-of-eight** n. skating figure; any figure shaped as 8. [OE. eahta]

eith'er (-TH-) a. and pron. one or theother; one of two; each. -adv. or conj. bringing in first of alternatives or strengthening an added negation. [OE. æther]

ejaculate v.t. and i. exclaim, utter suddenly. [L. ejaculari, shoot forth]

eject' v.t. throw out; expel, drive out. [L. ejicere, eject-, throw out]

elaborate v.t. work out in detail; produce by labor. -a. worked out in detail; highly finished; complicated. -**elaboration** n. [L. elaborate]

elapse' v.i. of time, to pass by. [L. elabi, elaps-, slip away]

elas'tic a. resuming normal shape after distortion; springy; not unalterable or inflexible. -n. cord, fabric, made elastic with interwoven rubber. -**elasti'city** n. [G. elastikos]

ela'tion n. high spirits; pride. -**elate'** v.t. [L. elatus, pp. of efferre, bring out]

el'bow n. outer part of the joint betweenthe upper arm and the forearm. -v.t. thrust, jostle with the elbows. [OE. elnboga]

el'der a. older. -n. person of greater age; old person; official of certain churches. -**el'derly** a. growing old. -**elédest** a. oldest. [old]

elect v.t. choose; choose by vote. -a. chosen; select, choice. -**elec'tion** n. choosing, esp. by voting -**electioneer'** to busy oneself in political elections. -**elect'ive** a. appointed, filled, chosen by election. -**elect'or** n. -**elect'oral** a. -**elect'orate** n. body of electors. [L. eligere, elect-, fr. legere, choose]

electricity (-is'-) n. active condition ofthe molecules of a body or of the etherround it, produced by friction, magnetism, etc. ; force which shows itself in lightning, etc. ; study of this. -**elec'tric** a. of, charged with, worked by, producing, electricity. [G. elektron, amber]

elec'tro- prefix makes compounds meaning of, by, caused by, electricity, as. **elec'tro -biol'ogy** n. science of electrical phenomena in living creatures. -**elec'tro-mag'net** n. -**electrol' ysis** n. electrical decomposition of a chemical compound.

-elec'troscope *n.* instrument to show the presence or kind of electricity. -
elec'trocute *v.t.* cause death by electric shock; execute (criminals) by electricity. [G. *electron*, amber]

elec'trode *n.* terminal of electric circuit; conductor leading current into, out of, water or gas. [G. *hodos,* way]

elec'tron *n.* one of fundamental particles of matter identified with unit of charge of negative electricity and essential component of the atom. -electron'ic *a.* of electrons or electronics; using devices, such as semiconductors, transistors or valves, dependent on action of electrons. -electron'ics *pl. n.* technology concerned with development of electronic devices and circuits; science of behavior and control of electrons. -electron'ic da'ta processing *n.* data processing largely performed by electronic equipment. [G. *electron,* amber]

el'egant *a.* graceful, tasteful; refined. -el'egance *n.* [L. *elegans*]

el'egy *n.* lament for the dead; sad poem. -elegi'ac *a.* plaintive. -*n. pl.* elegiac verses. [G. *elegeia*]

el'ement *n.* component part; substance which cannot be chemically analyzed; proper abode or sphere; resistance wire of electric heater. -*pl.* powers of the atmosphere; rudiments, first principles. -elemental *a.* of the powers of nature; tremendous; not compounded. -element'ary *a.* rudimentary, simple; primary. [L. *elementum*]

el'ephant *n.* big four-footed, thickskinned animal with ivory tusks and a long trunk. [L. *elephas*]

el'evate *v.t.* raise, lift up. -eleva'tion *n.* raising; angle above the horizon, as of a gun; drawing of one side of a building, *etc.* -el'evator *n.* lift or hoist. [L. *elevare*]

elev'en *a.* and *n.* number next above ten, one added to ten; team of eleven persons. -elev'enth *a.* the ordinal number. [OE. *endleofan*]

elic'it (-a-) *v.t.* draw out. [L. *elicere*]

el'igible *a.* fit or qualified to be chosen; suitable, desirable. **eligibil'ity** *n.* [L. *eligibilis -eligere,* fr. *legere,* choose]

eliminate *v.t.* remove, get rid of, set aside. -elimina'tion *n.* [E. *oliminare,* put out of doors]

elite' *n.* pick of (society, *etc.*).

elix'ir *n.* preparation sought by the alchemists to change base metals into gold, or to prolong life; sovereign remedy. [Arab. *al-iksiri*]

elk *n.* large deer. [OE. *eoth*]

ell *n.* measure of length. [OE. *eln*]

ellipse' *n.* an oval; figure made by a plane cutting a cone at a smaller angle with the side than the base makes; *gram.* omission of words needed to complete the grammatical construction or full sense.[L. *ellipsis*]

elocution *n.* art of public speaking, recitation, voice, management. -elocu'tionist *n.* [L. *eloqui,* speak out]

e'longate *v.t.* lengthen. -elonga'tion *n.* [L. *e,* out, *longus,* long]

elope' *v.i.* run away with a lover; escape. -elope'ment *n.* [AF. *aloper*]

eloquence *n.* fluent and powerful use of language. -el'oquent *a.* el'oquently *adv.* [L. *eloqui,* speak out]

else *adv.* besides; otherwise. -*pron.* other. elsewhere' *adv.* in or to some other place. [OE. *elles,* otherwise]

elucidate *v.t.* throw light upon, explain. -elucida'tion *n.* -elu'cidatory *a.* [L. *lucidus,* bright]

elude' *v.t.* escape, slip away from, dodge. [L. *eludere,* play off]

em *n.* (*printing*) the square of any size of type. [m.]

ema'ciate (shi-) *v.t.* to make lean. -emacia'tion *n.* [L. *emaciare,* emaciate, fr. *macies,* leanness]

em'anate *v.i.* issue from, originate. -emana'tion *n.* [L. *emanare,* flow out]

emancipate *v.t.* set free. -emancipa'tion *n.* -eman'cipator *n.* [L. *emancipate,* emancipate]

emasculate *v.t.* castrate; enfeeble, weaken. -emascula'tion *n.* -emas'cu-lative *a.* [L. *emasculate*]

embalm' (-bam) *v.t.* preserve (dead body) from decay with spices, *etc.*; perfume; reverently preserve (*e.g.*, a memory). [*balm*]

embar'go *n.* order stopping the movement of ships; suspension of commerce; ban. -*v.t.* put under an embargo. [Sp.]

embark' *v.t.* and *i.* put, go, on board ship; engage, involve (in). embarka'tion *n.* [F. *embarquer,* cp. bark]

embarrass *v.t.* perplex, put into difficulty; encumber. -embarr'assment *n.* [F. *embarrasser,* orig. put within 'bars']

em'bassy *n.* office or work or residence of an ambassador; deputation. [*ambassador*]

embatt'le *v.t.* provide with battlements. -embatt'led *a.* [*See* battlement]

embellish *v.t.* adorn. -embell'ishment *n.* [F. *embellir*]

em'ber *n.* glowing cinder. [OE. *æmerge*]

embez'zle v.t. divert fraudulently, misappropriate (money in trust, etc.). - embez'zler n. -embez'zlement n. [AF. embesiler, damage, steal]

embitter v.t. make bitter. [bitter]

em'blem n. symbol; heraldic device - emblemat'ic a. emblemat'icall y adv. [G. emblems, inlaid work]

embod'y v.t. give body, concrete expression, to; represent, be an expressionof. embod'iment n. [body]

embold'en v.t. encourage. [bold]

em'bolism n. obstruction of artery by bloodclot. [G. embolismos, what is thrown in]

embrace' v.t. clasp in the arms; seize, avail oneself of, accept. -n. clasping in the arms. [F. embrasser]

embrasure (-zher) n. opening in a wall for a cannon; bevelling of a wall at the sides of a window. [F.]

embroider v.t. ornament with needlework; embellish, exaggerate (a story). - embroi'dery n. [F. broder]

em'bryo n. unborn or undeveloped offspring, germ; undeveloped thing. [G. embryon]

emerge' v.i. come up, out; rise to notice; come out on inquiry. -emer'gency n. sudden unforeseen thing or event needing prompt action. [L. emergere]

em'ery n. hard mineral used for polishing. [F. émeri]

emet'ic a. causing vomiting. -n. medicine doing this. [G. emetikos]

em'igrate v.t. go and settle in another country. -emigra'tion n. em'igrant n. [L. emigrare]

em'inent a. distinguished, notable. - em'inently adv. -em'inence n. distinction; rising ground. -Em'inence, title of cardinal. [L. eminere, stand out]

emit' v.t. give out, put forth. -emitt'er n. -emis'sion a. -em'issary n. one sent out on a mission. -emissiv'ity n. power of emitting. [L. emittere]

emollient a. softening. -n. ointment or other softening application. [L. emollire, soften]

emo'tion n. mental agitation, excited state of feeling. -emo'tional a. given to emotion; appealing to the emotions. [L. emotio, fr. emovere, stir]

em'pathy n. ability to enter fully into another's feelings, experience. [G. en, in, pathos, feeling]

em'peror n. sovereign of an empire. - em'press fem. [L. imperator, fr. imperare, command]

em'phasis n. stress on words; vigor of speech, expression; importance attached. n. -em'phasize v.t. emphat'ic a. forcible; stressed. -emphat'ically adv. tG.]

em'pire n. large territory, esp. an aggregate of states under one supreme control. [F. fr. L. imperium]

empiric a. relying on experiment orexperience, not on theory. -n. empiric scientist, physician. -empir'ically adv. - empir'icism n. [G. ernpeirikos, experienced]

employ' n. use; keep occupied; use theservices of, keep in one's service. -employ'er n. -employee' n. -employ'ment n. [F. employer]

emporium n. center of commerce; (in affected language) store. [L. mart]

empow'er v.t. enable, authorize [power]

emp'ty a. containing nothing; unoccupied; senseless; vain, foolish. -v.t. and i. make or become empty. -n. empty box, basket, etc. -emp'tiness n. [OE. æmettig]

em'ulate v.t. strive to equal or excel; imitate. -em'utator n. emula'tion n. competition, rivalry. -em'ulative a. -em'ulous a. [L. æmulari, rival]

emul'sion n. milky liquid mixture withoily or resinous particles in suspension. [L. mulgere, milk]

en - prefix forms verbs with sense of putin, into, on; as: engulf' v.t. swallow up. -enrage' v.t. to put into a rage. Many such words are omitted and the meaning and derivation should be sought under the simple word. [F. en, L. in]

en (typography) half of an em (q.v.)

ena'ble v.t. make able, authorize; give power or strength. [able]

enact' v.t. make law; play, act. [act]

enam'el n. glasslike coating applied to metal, etc. to preserve the surface; coating of the teeth; any hard outer coating. -v.t. cover with enamel; adorn with colors. [en-, and obs. amel, F. émail, enamel]

enam'or (-er) v.t. inspire with love. [F. enamourer]

encaustic a. burnt in. -n. art of burning colored designs into tiles etc. [G. enkaustikos, burnt in]

encephalitis n. inflammation of the brain. [G. Kephale, head]

enchant' (-a-) v.t. bewitch, delight. - enchant'ment n. [F. enchanter]

encir'cle v.t. surround; embrace; go round. [circle]

enclave' n. portion of territory entirely surrounded by foreign land. [F.]

enclose' v.t. shut; place in with something

else (in a letter, *etc.*); fence, *esp.* common land. -**enclo'sure** (-zher) *n.* [*close*]

encom'pas (-kum-) *v.t.* surround; include. [*compass*]

en'core *interj.* again, once more. -*n.* call for the repetition of a song, *etc.*; the repetition. -*v.t.* call for repetition. [F.]

encounter *v.t.* meet in hostility; meet with. -*n.* hostile or casual meeting. [OF. *encontrer*]

encour'age (-kur-) *v.t.* hearten, inspirit. -**encouragement** *n.* [*courage*]

encroach *v.i.* intrude (on) as a usurper. -**encroach'ment** *n.* [F. *accrocher,* hook on]

encrypt' *v.t.* put (a message) into code; to put (computer data) into a coded form; to distort (a television or other signal) so that it cannot be understood without the appropriate decryption equipment. -**encrypted** *a.* -**en'cryption** *n.* [G. *kryptein,* hide]

encyclope'dia, encyclopae'dia *n.* book of information on all subjects, or on every branch of a subject, usually arranged alphabetically. [fr. G. *enkyklios paideia,* all-round education]

end *n.* limit; extremity; conclusion; fragment; latter part; death; event, issue; purpose, aim. -*v.t.* put an end to. -*v.i.* come to an end. [OE. *ende*]

endang'er *v.t.* expose to danger. -**endangered** *a.* in danger; used *esp.* of animals in danger of extinction. [F. fr. L. *dominium,* rule]

endeav'or (-dev-er) *v.i* try, attempt. -*n.* attempt, effort. [F. *devoir,* duty]

endemic *a.* regularly existing or found in a country or district. -*n.* -**endemic disease.** [G. *en,* in, *demos,* people]

en'dive *n.* curly leaved chicory. (F.)

en'docrine *n.* substance absorbed from the ductless glands into the bloodstream. *a.* -**endocrinol'ogy** *n.* [fr. G. *endon,* within, *krinein,* to separate]

endorse' *v.t.* write (*esp.* sign one's name) on the back of, ratify; confirm. -**endorse'ment** *n.* [F. *endosser,* fr. *dos,* back]

endow' *v.t.* provide a permanent income for; furnish. -**endow'ment** *n.* [OF. *endouer*]

endure' *v.i* last. -*v.t.* undergo; tolerate, put up with. -**endu'rance** *n.* power of enduring. -**endu'rable** *a.* [L. *indurate,* fr. *durus,* hard]

ene'ma, en'ema *n.* rectal injection; instrument for this. [G. *enienai,* send in]

en'emy *n.* hostile person, opponent; armed foe; hostile force or ship. (F. *ennemi,* fr. L. *inimicus*]

en'ergy *n.* vigor, force, activity. -**energet'ic** *a.* -**energet'ically** *adv.* -**en'ergize** *v.t.* give vigor to. [F. *Onergie*]

en'ervate *v.t.* weaken, deprive of vigor. -**enerva'tion** *n.* [L. *enervare,* deprive of sinew]

enfold' *v.t.* enwrap; encompass. [*fold*]

enforce' *v.t.* compel obedience to; impose (action) upon; drive home. -**enforce'ment** *n.* -**enforce'able** *a.* [OF. *enforcier,* strengthen]

engage' *v.t.* bind by contract or promise; hire; order; pledge oneself, undertake; attract, occupy; bring into conflict; interlock. -*v.i.* begin to fight; employ oneself (in); promise. -**engage'ment** *n.* [F. *engager-gage,* pledge]

en'gine *n.* complex mechanical contrivance; machine; instrument of war. -**engineer'** *n.* one who constructs or is in charge of engines, military works, or works of public utility (*e.g.* bridges, roads). -*v.t.* construct as an engineer; contrive. [F. *engin,* fr. L. *ingenium,* skill]

English (ing'gl-) *a.* of England. -*n.* language or people of England and of all peoples who have adopted this language. [OE. *Englise*]

engrave' *v.t.* and *i.* cut in lines on metal for printing; carve, incise; impress deeply. -**engra'ving** *n.* copy of a picture printed from an engraved plate. -**engra'ver** *n.* [*grave*]

engross' *v.t.* write out in large letters or in legal form; absorb (attention). -**engross'ment** *n.* [AF. *engrosser,* fr. *grosse,* large (letter)]

enhance' *v.t.* heighten, intensify, raise in price. -**enhance'ment** *n.* -**enhanc' ive** *a.* [F. *hausser,* rasie]

enig'ma *n.* riddle; puzzling thing or person. -**enigmat'ic, enigmatical** *a.* -**enigmat'ically** *adv.* [G. *ainigma*]

enjoin' *v.t.* command, impose, prescribe. [F. *enjoindre*]

enjoy' *v.t.* take pleasure in; have the use or benefit of. -*v. refl.* be happy.

enlarge' *v.t.* make bigger; set free. -*v.i.* grow bigger; talk at large (with on) -**enlarge'ment** *n.* [*large*]

enlighten (-lit-) *v.t.* instruct, inform. -**enlight'ened** *a.* factually well-informed, tolerant of alternative opinions, and guided by rational thought; privy to or claiming a sense of spiritual or religious revelation of truth. -**enlight'enment** *n.* [*light*]

enlist' *v.t.* and *i.* engage as a soldier or helper; gain (sympathies, *etc.*). -**enlistment** *n.* [*list*]

enli'ven v.t. brighten, make more lively or cheerful. [*life*]

en'mity n. ill -will; hostility. [AF. *enimitg*]

ennui' n. boredom. [F.]

enor'mous a. very big, vast. **-enor'mity** n. gross offense; great wickedness. [L. *enormis*, abnormal]

enough' (e-nuf) a. as much or as many as need be, sufficient. -n. sufficient quantity. adv. sufficiently. **-enow'** a., n. , and adv. enough. [OE. *genog*]

enrich' v.t. make rich; add to. -enrich'ment n. [*rich*]

enroll', enrol' (-ō-) v.t. write the name on a roll or list; engage, enlist, take in as a member; enter, record. **-enroll'ment** n. [F. *enrôler*]

ensconce' v.t. place snugly, comfortably in safety. [*sconce*]

ensem'ble (ong-song-bl) n. effect of any combination regarded as a whole; woman's matching dress; (*mus.*) concerted piece, passage. [F.]

en'sign (-sin) n. naval or military flag; badge, emblem; a commissioned officer of the lowest rank. [F. *enseigne*]

enslave' v.t. make into a slave. **-enslave'ment** n. **-ensla'ver** n. [*slave*]

ensue' v.i follow, happen, after; result from. -v.t. strive for. [F. *ensuiure*, fr. L. *insequi*, follow up]

ensure' v.t. make safe, certain to happen. [F. *assurer*, cp. *assure*]

entab'lature n. in architecture, part resting on capital of column. [L. *tabula*, table]

entan'gle (-ng-gi) v.t. entwine; involve; ensnare. **-entang'lement** n. [tangle]

entente' (ong-tongt) n. a friendly understanding between nations. [F.]

ent'er v.t. go or come into; join (a society, etc.); write in, register. -v.i. go or come in; join; begin: engage. **-en'trance** n. going or coming in; right to enter; fee paid for this; door or passage to enter. **-en'trant** n. one who enters, *esp.* a contest. **-en'try** n. entrance; an entering; item entered, *e.g.* in an account, list. [F. *entrer*]

enterprise n. design, undertaking, usually a bold or difficult one; **-enterprising** a. bold and active in spirit. [F.]

entertain' v.t. receive as guest; amuse; maintain; consider favorably, cherish. **-entertain'er** n. **-entertaining** a. amusing. **-entertain'ment** n. hospitality; amusement; public performance. [F. *entretenir*]

enthu'siasm n. ardent eagerness, zeal. **-enthu'siast** n. **enthusias'tic** a. **-enthusias'tically** adv. **enthuse'** v.i (colloq.) show enthusiasm. [G.

enthousiasmos, inspiration]

entice' v.t. allure; attract or entrap adroitly. **-entice'ment** n. (OF. *enticier*, provoke]

entire' a. whole, complete, not broken. **-entire'ly** adv. **-entire'ty** n. [F. *entier*, fr. L. *integer*, whole]

enti'tle v.t. give a title or claim to. [*title*]

en'tity n. thing's being or existences thing having real existence. [Late L. *entitas*, fr. *esse*, be]

entomology n. study of insects, **-entomol'ogist** n. **-entomological** (-oj' -) a. [G. *entomon*, insect]

entourage' (ong-tŏŏ-razh) n. retinue, suite; surroundings. [F.]

en'trails n. pl. bowels, intestines; inner parts. [F. *entrailles*]

entrance. See **enter.**

entrap' v.t. catch in a trap; lure into a trap; lure into a position which compromises the victim. [*trap*]

entreat' v.t. ask earnestly, beg, implore. entreat'y n. [*treat*]

entrée' n. freedom of access; side dish served between courses; the main course itself. [F.]

entrust' v.t. confide (to); commit, put in charge. [*trust*]

entry. See **enter.**

enumerate v.t. count. **-enumera'tion** n. **-enumerator** n. one who enumerates. [L. *enumerate*, number of]

enunciate v.t. state clearly; pronounce. [L. *eauntiare*]

envel'op v.t. wrap up, enclose. **-envel'opment** n. **en'velope** n. folded, gummed cover of a letter; covering, wrapper. [F. *envelopper*]

envi'ron v.t. surround. **-envi'roriment** n. surroundings; conditions of life or growth. **-envi'rons** n. pl. districts round (a town, etc.). [F. *adv.*]

envisage v.t. view; look at. [*visage*]

en'voy n. messenger; diplomatic minister of rank below an ambassador. (F. *envoyé*, one sent]

en'voy n. short concluding stanza of a poem. [F. *envoi*]

en'vy n. bitter or longing consideration of another's better fortune or success or qualities; object of this feeling. -v.t. feel envy of. **—en'vious** a. **-en'viable** a. [F. *envie*, L. *invidia*]

en'zyme n. digestive ferment; leaven. [G. *zyme*, leaven]

ephem'eral a. short-lived, lasting only for a day, or few days. **-ephem'eron**, **ephem'era** n. ephemeral insect or thing. [G. *ephemeros*] ep'ic *a.* telling in continuous story the achievements of a hero or heroes. -*n.* epic poem. [G. *epikos*]

epicure *n.* one dainty in eating and drinking. [*Epicurus*, of Athens (300 B.C.)]

epidemic *a.* prevalent for a time among a community. -*n.* -epidemic disease. [fr. G. *epi*, upon, *demos*, people]

epidermis *n.* outer skin. -epidermic *a.* [G.]

epiglott'is *n.* cartilage at root of tongue, closing larynx in swallowing. [G. *epi*, upon, *glotta*, tongue]

epigram *n.* short poem with a witty orsatirical ending; pointed saying. [G. *epigramma*, inscription]

epilepsy *n.* disease in which the suffererfalls down in a fit, with foaming and spasms. epilep'tic *a.* subject to epilepsy. -*n.* person who suffers fromepilepsy. [G. *epilepsia*, seizure]

ep'ilogue (-og) *n.* short speech or poemat the end of a play; the concluding part of a book. [G. *epilogos*, peroration]

Epiph'any *n.* festival of the appearance of Christ to the Magi. [G. *epiphania*, manifestation]

episcopal *a.* of a bishop; ruled bybishops. -epis'capacy *n.* government by bishops; body of bisbops. -episcopa'lian *a.* of an episcopal system or churchman. member or adherent of an episcopal church. [*See* bishop]

episeotomy *n.* incision of the perineum to facilitate childbirth.

ep'isode *n.* incident; incidental narrativeor series of events; part of a Greek tragedy between choric songs. -episod'ic, episod'ical *a.* [G. *epeisodion*, coming inbesides]

epistemic a. of or pertaining to knowledge; cognitive. -epistemology *n.* study of the source, nature and limitations of knowledge. -epist'emological *a.* [G. *episteme*, knowledge]

epis'tle (-sl) *n.* letter, *esp.* of the apostles; poem in the form of a letter. -epis'tolary *a.* [G. *epistole*]

ep'itaph *n.* inscription on a tomb. [G. *epitaphion*, fr. *taphos*, tomb]

ep'ithet *n.* adjective expressing a quality or attribute; name full of meaning. -epithet'ic *a.* [G. *epitheton*]

epit'ome (-me) *n.* summary, abridgment. -epitomize *v.t.* epit'omist *n.* [G. , fr. *epitemnein*, cut into]

e'poch (-ok) *n.* beginning of a period; period, era, *esp.* one marked by notable events. -e'pochal *a.* [G. *epoche*, stoppage]

e'qual *a.* same in number, size, merit, *etc.* ; fit or qualified; evenly balanced. -*n.* one equal to another. *v.t.* be equal to. [L. *æqualis*, fr. *æquus*, level]

equanim'ity *n.* calmness, evenness of mind or temper. [L. *æquanimitas*]

equate' *v.t.* state or assume the qualityof -equa'tion *n.* statement of equality between two mathematical expressions; balancing; compensation for inaccuracy. -equa'tor *n.* great circle of the earth eqidistant from the poles. -equator'ial *a.* [L. *æquare*, *equat*-, make equal]

equestrian *a.* of, skilled in, horseriding; mounted on a horse. -*n.* rider orperformer on a horse. [L. *equestris*]

equi- *prefix*, equal, at equal. [L. *æqui*-] -equiangular (-ng-g-) *a.* having equal angles. [*angular*]. -equidis'tant *a.* atequal distances. [*distant*] . -equilat'eral *a.* having equal sides. [*lateral*] *etc.*

equilibrium *n.* state of balance; balanced mind. -equili'brate *v.t.* and *i.* -equil'ibrist *n.* -equil'ibrator *n.* stabilizing plane, fin, of airplane; acrobat, rope-walker. [L. -*equilibrium*, fr. *libra*, scales]

equ'ine *a.* of a horse. [L. *equinus*, fr. *equus*, horse]

e'quinox *n.* time at which the sun crosses the equator and day and night are equal. -*pl.* points at which the sun crosses the equator. -equinoc'tial *a.* [L. *æquinoctium*, fr. *nox*, night]

equip' *v.t.* supply, fit out, array. -equip'ment *n.* -eq'uipage *n.* carriage, horses and attendants; retinue; outfit. [F. *équiper*]

eq'uity *n.* fairness; use of the principles of justice to supplement the law; systemof law so made. eq'uitable *a.* fair, reasonable, just. -eq'uitably *adv.* [L. *æquitas*, fr. *æquus*, equal]

equivalent *a.* equal in value; having the same meaning or result; corresponding. -*n.* equivalent thing, amount, *etc.* -equiv'alence, equivalency *n.* [F. *equivalent*, L. *valens*, *ualentis*, worth]

equivocal *a.* ambiguous, of double or doubtful meaning; questionable, liable to suspicion. [Late L. *quivocare*, call alike]

e'ra *n.* system of time in which years are numbered from a particular event; time of the event; memorable date; period. [L. *æra*, brasses (as counters)]

eradicate *v.t.* root out. -eradica'tion *n.* eradicator *n.* (L. *eradicate*)

erase' *v.t.* rub out; efface. eraser *n.* -era'sure *n.* [L. *eradere*, *eras*-, scrape out]

erect' *a.* upright. -*v.t.* set up; build. -

erect'ile a. **-erec'tion** n. **erect'or** n. [L. erectus, upright]

erg n. unit of work. [G. ergon, work]

er'go adv. therefore. [L.]

er'gonomics n. applied science, concerned with the nature and characteristics of people as they relate to design and activities with the intention of producing more effective results and greater safety.

er'mine n. animal like a weasel with fur brown in summer and white, except for black tail-tip, in winter; its fur usu. white. [OF.]

erne n. eagle, esp. sea-eagle. [OE. earn]

erode' v.t. wear out, eat away. **-ero'sion** n. **-ero'sive** a. [L. erodere, eros-]

erot'ic a. relating to sexual love. [G. erotikos, fr. Eros, god of love]

err v.i make mistakes; be wrong; sin. **-errat'ic** a. irregular in movement, conduct, etc. **erra'tum** (-a-) n. **erra'ta** pl. mistake noted for correction. **-erroneous** a. mistaken, wrong. **-err'or** n. mistake; wrong opinion; sin. **-err'ant** a. wandering in search of adventure; erring.[F. errer, wander]

err'and n. short journey for a simple business; the business; purpose. **-err'and boy** n. [OE. ærende, message]

erratic a. odd, eccentric; following an irregular course. [err]

er'udite a. learned. **-erudi'tion** n. knowledge got by study. [L. eruditas]

erupt' v.i burst out. **-erup'tion** n. bursting out, esp. a volcanic outbreak; rash. **-erupt'ive** a. [L. erurnpere, erupt-]

erythromycin n. antibiotic ($C_{37}H_{67}NO_{13}$) obtained from an actinomycete used in treating bacterial infactions.

escape' v.i get free; get off safely; go unpunished; find a way out. -v.t. elude; come out unawares from. -n. an escaping; leakage. **-escapade'** n. flighty exploit. **-escap'ist** n. one who tries to escape from reality. [ONF. escaper, fr. L. ex, out of, cappa, cloak]

es'cort n. armed guard for a traveler, criminal, ships etc.; person or persons accompanying another for protection or courtesy. **-escort'** v.t. act as escort to. [F. escorte]

ESL abbr. English as a second language.

esoteric a. secret; for the initiated. [G. esoterikos, fr. eso, within]

espionage n. spying; the use of spies [F. espionnage]

espouse' (-z) v.t. marry; support, attach oneself to (a cause, etc.). **-espous'al** n. [OF. espouser]

essay' v.t. try, attempt; test. **-ess'ay** n. literary composition, usually short and in-prose; attempt. **-ess'ayist** n. writer of essays. [F. essayer]

ess'ence n. existence, being; absolute being, reality; all that makes a thing what it is; extract got by distillation; perfume, scent. **-essen'tial** a. of, or constituting, the essence of a thing. -n. indispensable element; chief point. **-essential'ity** n. **-essen'tially** adv. [F.]

estab'lish v.t. set up; settle; found; prove. **-estab'lishment** n. establishing; church system established by law; permanent organized body; full number of a regiment, etc.; household; house of business; public institution. (L. stabilire, fr. stare, stand]

estate' n. landed property; person's property; a class as part of a nation; rank, state, condition. [OF. estat]

esteem' v.t. think highly of, consider; -n. favorable opinion, regard **-esteemed'** a. highly respected. [L. ætimare]

es'timate v.t. form an approximate idea of (amounts, measurements, etc.); form an opinion of, quote a probable price for. -n. approximate judgment of amounts, etc.; the amount, etc., arrived at; opinion; price quoted by a contractor. **-es'timable** a. worthy of regard. **-estima'tion** n. opinion, judgment, esteem. [L. stimare]

estrange' v.t. make unfriendly, put astop to affection. **-estrange'ment** n. [OF. estrangier, make strange]

etcet'era (abbrev. etc.), 'and the rest'. -n. pl. accessories, trimmings. [L.]

etch v.t. make an engraving by eating away the surface of a metal plate with acids, etc. -v.i. practice this art **-etch'ing** n. **etch'er** n. [Du. etsen]

eter'nal a. without beginning or end; everlasting; changeless. **-eter'nally** adv. **eter'nity** n. [L. mternus]

e'ther (-th-) n. substance or fluid supposed to fill all space; the clear sky, region above the clouds; colorless volatile liquid used as an anesthetic. **-ethe'real** a. light, airy; heavenly. **-ethereal'ity** n. [L. ether, upper air]

eth'ic, ethical a. relating to, or treating of, morals. **-eth'ically** adv. **-eth'ics** n. pl. science of morals; moral principles, rules of conduct. [G. ethikos, fr. ethos, character]

eth'nic a. of race. **-ethnog'raphy** n. description of races of men. **-ethnograph'ic** a. **-ethnol'ogy** n. science of races. **ethnolo'gical** a. [G. ethnikos, fr. ethnos, nation]

ethnobot'any n. branch of botany concerned with the use of plants in the customs and folklore of a people.

eth'yl n. base of alcohol, ether, etc. ; type of petrol. [ether]

etiol'ogy n. study of causes, esp. inquiry into the origin of disease. -etiol'ogical a. [G. aitia, cause]

etiquette n. conventional rules of manners; court ceremonial; code of conduct for a profession. [F. Otiquette]

etymology n. tracing, or an account of, a word's formation, origin, development; science of this. -etymolo'gical a. - etymolo'gically adv. -etymol'ogist n. - et'ymon n. primitive word from which a derivative comes. [G, etymologia, fr. etymos, true]

Eu'charist (-k-) n. sacrament of the Lord's Supper; consecrated elements. - eucharis'tic a. [G. eucharistia, thanksgiving]

Euclidian geometry n. theory based on the postulates of Euclid, including that only one line may be drawn through a given point parallel to a given line.

eu'logy n. speech or writing in praise of a person; praise. -eu'logize v.t. -eu'logist n. eologistic a. -eulogis'tically adv. [G. eulogia, praise]

eu'nuch (-k) n. castrated man, esp. one employed in a harem. [G eunouchos, bedguard]

euph'emism n. substitution of a mild word or expression for a blunt one; instance of this. [G. euphemismos, speaking fair]

eu'phony n. pleasantness of sound. [G. euphonia, fr. phone, voice]

Europe'an a./n. (native) of continent of Europe. [G. Europe]

euthanasia n. gentle, easy death; theory that incurables, etc. should be painlessly removed. [G.]

evac'uate v.t. empty; discharge; withdraw from; remove (people) from area. - evacua'tion n. -evacuee' n. evacuated person. [L. vacuus, empty]

evade' v.t. avoid, escape from; elude; frustrate. -eva'sion n. -eva'sive a. - eva'sively adv. [L. euadere, eva]

eval'uate v.t. find or state the value or number of. -evalua'tion n. [value]

evan'gel n. gospel. -evangel'ical a. of or according to the gospel teaching; of the Protestant school which maintains salvation by faith. -evan'gelize v.t. preach to; convert. [G. evangelion, good tidings]

evap'orate v.i turn into vapor; pass off in vapor. -v.t. turn into vapor. [L. eva'porare, fr. vapor, vapour]

eve n. evening before (a festival, etc.); time just before (an event, etc.); evening. [even]

e'ven n. evening. -e'vensong n. evening prayer. [OE. æfen]

e'ven a. flat, smooth; uniform in quality; equal in amount, balanced; divisable by two; impartial. -v.t. make even. adv. invites comparison with something les sstrong included by implication in the stament. [OE. efen]

e'vening (-vn-) n. close of day; of one'slife, old age. [OE. zefnung]

event' n. occurrence of a thing; notable occurrence; issue; result. -event'ful . full of exciting events. -event'ual a. that will happen under certain conditions; resulting in the end. -event'ually adv. -eventual'ity n. possible event. -event'uate v.i. turn out; end. (L. evenire, event -, come out]

ev'er adv. always; constantly; at anytime; by any chance. -ev'erglade n. swamp. - ev'ergreen n. non-deciduousplant, shrub. -a. [OE. æfre]

ev'ery (-vr-) a. each of all; all possible. -ev'erybody n. -ev'eryday a. usual, ordinary. ev'eryone n. -ev'erything n. ev'erywhere adv. in all places. [OE. æfre lis, ever each]

evict v.t. expel by legal process, turnout. [L. evincere, evict -, prove]

ev'ident a. plain, obvious -ev'idently adv. -ev'idence n. sign, indications ground for belief, testimony; in evidence, conspicuous. -v.t. indicate, prove. -evidential a. [L. videre, see]

e'vil a. bad, harmful. -n. what is bad or harmful; sin. -e'villy adv. [OE. yfel]

evince' v.t. show, indicate. -evinc'ible a. -evinc'ive a. [L. evincere, prove]

evis'cerate (-vis-er-) v.t. disembowel. - eviscera'tion n. [L. eviscerate]

evoke' v.t. call up. -evoca'tion n. - evoc'ative a. [L. evocare]

evolve' v.t. develop; unfold, open out; produce. -v.i. develop, esp. by natural process; open out. evolu'tion n. an evolving; development of species fromearlier forms; movement of troops or ships; movement in dancing, etc. [L. evolvere, evolut -, to roll out]

ex', formerly, as in ex-king, etc. [G.]

exacerbate v.t. aggravate, embitter. - exacerba'tion n. [L. exacerbare, cp. acerbity]

exact' (-gz-) a. precise, accurate, strictly correct. -v.t. demand, extort; insist upon; enforce. -exact'ly adv. [L. exigere, exact

-, to weigh, *prove*, forceout]

exagg′erate *v.t.* magnify beyond truth, overstate. [L. *exaggerate*, heap up]

exalt′ (egz-awlt′) *v.t.* raise up; praise; make noble. -exalta′tion *n.* an exalting; rapture. [L. *exaltare*, fr. *altos*, high]

exam′ine *v.t.* investigate; ask questions of, test the knowledge or proficiency of by oral or written questions; inquire into. [L. *examinare*, weigh accurately]

exam′ple *n.* thing illustrating a general rule; specimen; model, pattern; warning, precedent. [L. *exemplum*, sample]

exas′perate (-gz-) *v.t.* irritate, enrage; intensify, make worse. -exaspera′tion *n.* [L. *exasperate*, fr. *asper*, rough]

ex′cavate *v.t.* hollow out; make a hole by digging; unearth. -excava′tion *n.* act of excavating; resulting cavity. -ex′cavator *n.* [L. *excavare*, fr. *cavus*, hollow]

exceed′ *v.t.* be greater than; do morethan authorized, go beyond; surpass. -exceed′ingly *adv.* very. -excess′ *n.* an exceeding; amount by which a thing exceeds; too great an amount; intemperance or immoderate conduct. [L. *excedere, excess* -, to go beyond]

excel′ *v.t.* be very good, pre-eminent. -*v.t.* surpass, be better than. -ex′cellent *a.* very good. -ex′cellence *n.* -ex′cellency *n.* title of ambassadors, *etc.* [L. *excellere*, rise above]

except′ *v.t.* leave or take out; exclude. -*v.i.* raise objection. -*prep.* not including; but. *conj.* unless. -except′ing *prep.* not including. -excep′tion *n.* an excepting; thing excepted, not included in a rule; objection. -excep′tional *a.* unusual. -excep′tionally *adv.* -excep′tionable *a.* open to objection. [L. *exceptus*, taken out]

excerpt (ek′serpt) *n.* quotation; selected passage; extract. -*v.t.* take out; quote. lex, from, *carpere*, to pick]

excess′. *See* **exceed.**

exchange′ *v.t.* give (something) in return for something else. -*v.i.* of an officer, change posts with another. -*n.* giving one thing and receiving another; giving or receiving coin, bills. *etc.* of one country for those of another; thing given for another; building where merchants meet for business. -exchange′able *a.* - exchangeabil′ity *n.* [*change*]

excise′ (-z) *n.* duty charged on homegoods during manufacture or before sale. - exci′sable *a.* liable to excise. [Du. *accijns*]

excise′ *v.t.* cut out, cut away. -excis′ion *n.* [L. *excidere, ercis-*]

excite′ *v.t.* rouse up, set in motion; stimu-

late, move to strong emotion. -exci′table *a.* -exci′tably *adv.* -excitabil′ity *n.* - excite′ment *n.* [L. *excitare*]

exclaim *v.i.* and *t.* cry out. -exclamation *n.* -exclama′tion point *or* mark, *n.* punctuation mark (!) used to indicate an interjection or an element of surprise or stress in an utterance. -exclam′atory *a.* expressing exclamation. [L. *exclamare*, shout out]

exclude′ *v.t.* shut out; debar from. - exclu′sion *n.* -exclu′sive *a.* excluding; inclined to keep out (from society, *etc.*); sole, only; different from all others. - exclu′sively *adv.* [L. *excludere*]

excommu′nicate *v.t.* shut off from the sacraments of the church. [Church L. *excommunicare*, expel from communion]

ex′crement *n.* waste matter discharged from the bowels, dung. [L. *excernere, excret* -, sift out]

excur′sion *n.* journey, ramble, trip, for pleasure; deviation from planned route. [L. *excursiona*, running out]

excuse′ (-z) *v.t.* try to clear from blame; overlook, forgive, gain exemption; set free, remit. -excuse′ (-a) *n.* that which serves to excuse; apology. -excu′sable (-z-) *a.* [L. *excusare*, fr. *causa*, cause]

ex′ecute *v.t.* carry out, perform; sign (adocument); kill (criminals). **execu′tion** *n.* **execu′tioner** *n.* one employed to kill those sentenced to death by law. - **exec′utive** *a.* carrying into effect. -*n.* committee carrying on the business of a society, *etc.*; the administrative branchof government; a person with administrative or managerial control, *esp.* in business. **exec′utor** *n.* person appointed by one making a will to carry out the provisions of the will. [L. *exsequi, exsecut* -, follow out]

exem′plar *n.* model type. -exemp′lary *a.* fit to be imitated, serving as an example. -exemp′larily *adv.* -exemp′lify *v.t.* serve as example of, make an attested copy of -exemplifica′tion *n.* [L. *exemplum*, sample]

exempt′ (-gz-) *a.* freed from, not liable. -*v.t.* free from. exemp′tion *n.* [L. *exemptus*, taken out]

ex′ercise (-z) *n.* employment, use (of limbs, faculty, *etc.*); use of limbs for health; practice for the sake of training; task set for training. -*v.t.* use, employ; give (training, health) exercise to; carryout, discharge; trouble, harass. -*v.i.* take exercise. [L. *exercere*, keep at work]

exert′ (-gz -) *v.t.* bring into activeopera-tion. -exer′tion *n.* [L. *exserere, exsert* -,

exhale' *v.t.* breathe out; give off as vapor. -*v.i.* breathe out; pass of asvapor. - **exhala'tion** *n.* [L. *exhalare,* breathe out]

exhaust' (igz -awst') *v.t.* draw off; use up; empty, treat, discuss, thoroughly; tire out. -*n.* used steam, fluid or gas from an engine; passage for, or coming out of, this. [L. *exhaurire, exhaust -,* drain out]

exhibit (-gz-) *v.t.* show, display; manifest; show publicly in competition. -*n.* thing shown, *esp.* in competition or as evidence in a court. -**exhibi'tion** *n.* display; act of displaying; public show (of works of art, *etc.*); allowance made to a student, scholarship. [L. *exhibere,* holdforth]

exhilarate (-gz-) *v.t.* enliven, gladden. - **exhilara'tion** *n.* [L. *exhilarate,* fr. *hilaris,* happy, merry]

exhort' *v.t.* urge, admonish earnestly. - **exhorta'tion** *n.* -**exhort'er** *n.* [L. *hortari,* encourage]

exhume' *v.t.* unearth; take out again what has been buried. -**exhuma'tion** *n.* [L. *ex,* out of, *humus,* ground]

exigent (-j-) *a.* exacting; urgent. - **ex'igence, exigency** *n.* pressing need; emergency. [L. *exigere,* force out]

ex'ile *n.* banishment, expulsion fromone's own country; long absence abroad; one banished. -*v.t.* banish. [F. *exil*]

exist' (-gz-) *v.i* be, have being, continue to be. -**existen'tialism** *n.* theory of the fortuitous nature of the universe, in which we create our own values. [F. *exister,* fr. L. *ex(s)istere,* make to stand out]

ex'it *n.* actor's departure from the stage; a going out; way out; death. -**ex'it** *v.i sing.* 'goes out'. **ex'eunt** (-i unt) *pl.* 'go out' *n.* stage directions, to indicate the going off of a player or players. (L. *exire,* go out]

ex'odus *n.* departure, *esp.* of a crowd. - **Ex'odus,** second book of Old Testament, relating the departure of the Israelitesfrom Egypt. [G. *exodus,* way out]

exonerate *v.t.* free, declare free, fromblame; exculpate; acquit. - **exonera'tion** *n.* **exon'erative** *a.* [L. *exonerate,* un burden]

exorbitant *a.* very excessive, immoderate. -**exorb'itantly** *adv.* **exorbitance** *n.* [L. *exorbitare,* go out of one's orbit]

ex'orcize, exorcise (-z) *v.t.* cast out (evil spirits) by invocation; free a person of evil spirits. -**ex'orcism** *n.* -**ex'orcist** *n.* [G. *exorkizein,* from ex, out, *horkos,* oath]

exoskeleton *n.* bony outer structure of, e. g. , crab, turtle; any hard or horny outercasing. [G. *exo,* outside, and *skeleton*]

exot'ic *a.* brought in from abroad, not native. -*n.* exotic plant, *etc.* [G. ex*otikos,* fr. *exo,* outside]

expand' *v.t.* and *i.* spread out; enlarge, increase in bulk, develop. -**expan'sion** *n.* - **expan'sive** *a.* wide-spreading; effusive. [L. *expanders*]

expatriate *v.t.* banish. **expatria'tion** *n.* [L. *patria,* country]

expect' *v.t.* look on as likely to happen; look for as due. (L. *exspectare,* look out for]

expectorate *v.t.* and *i.* spit out (phlegm, *etc.*) -**expectora'tion** *n.* [L. *expectorate,* fr. *pectus,* breast]

expedient *a.* fitting, advisable; politic. -*n.* device, contrivance. [*expedite*]

ex'pedite (-lt) *v.t.* help on, hasten. - **expedi'tion** *n.* promptness; journey for a definite purpose; warlike enterprise; bodyof men sent on such enterprise. - **expedi'tionary** *a.* -**expedi'tious** *a.* prompt, speedy. [L. *expedite,* free the foot, help on]

expel' *v.t.* drive, cast out. -**expul'sion** *n.* **expulsive** *a.* [L. *expellere, expuls -]*

expend' *v.t.* spend, pay out; use up. - **expend'iture** *n.* -**expense'** *n.* spending; cost. -*pl.* charges, outlay incurred. - **expens'ive** *a.* costly. [L. *expendere,* fr. *pendere, pens -,* weigh]

experience *n.* observation of facts as a source of knowledge; a being affected consciously by an event; the event. [L. *experiential* fr. *experire,* test thoroughly]

experiment *n.* test, trial; something done in the hope that it may succeed, or totest a theory. -*v.i.* make an experiment. - **experiment'al** *a.* -**experiment'ally** *adv.* [L. *experiri,* test]

ex'pert *a.* practiced, skillful. -*n.* one expert in something; an authority. [L. *experiri,* test]

expire' *v.t.* breathe out. -*v.i.* give out breath; die; die away; come to an end. [L. *ex(s)pirare*]

explain' *v.t.* make clear, intelligible; give details of, account for. -**explana'tion** *n.* **explan'atory** *a.* [L. *explanare,* make smooth]

explic'it (-a-) *a.* stated in detail; stated, not merely implied; outspoken. [L. *explicare,* unfold]

explode' *v.i* go off with a bang; burst violently. -*v.t.* made explode; discredit, expose (a theory, *etc.*). -**explo'sion** *n.* - **explo'sive** *a.* and *n.* [L. *explodere, explos -,* clap out (of theater)]

ex'ploit *n.* brilliant feat, deed. -*v.t.* turnto

advantage; make use of for one's own ends. -exploita'tion n. [F.]

explore' v.t. examine (a country, etc.) by going through it; investigate. - explora'tion n. -explor'atory a. - explor'er n. [L. explorare, announce discovery]

ex'port v.t. send (goods) out of the country. -n. exported article. -expor-ta'tion n. - export'er n. [L. exportare, carry out]

expose' (-z) v.t. leave unprotected; lay open (to); exhibit, put up for sale; unmask; disclose. -expo'sure n. act of exposing, being exposed; (photo. the exposing of the sensitive plate to light; duration of this. [F. exposer]

expostulate v.i make (esp. friendly) remonstrances. [L. expostulate, demand urgently]

expound' v.t. explain, interpret. - expo'nent n. one who expounds; executant; maths. index, symbol showing the power of a factor. -exponen'tial a. - exposi'tion n. explanation, description; exhibition of goods, etc. -expos'itory a. -expos'itor n. [L. exponere, put forth]

express' v.t. put into words; make knownor understood by words; conduct, etc.; squeeze out; send by express. -a. definitely stated, specially designed; of a messenger, specially sent off, of a train, fast and making few stops. -n. express train or messenger. -adv. specially, on purpose; with speed. -express'ly adv. -express'ible a. -expres'sion n. a pressing out; phrase, saying; what the features convey of thought, feeling, etc. -expres'sionism n. theory that art, literature, should be primarily an expression of the artist's personality. [L. expressus, squeezed out, clearly stated]

expulsion. See expel.

expurgate v.t. remove objectionable parts (from a book, etc.). -expurga'tion n. - ex'purgator n. -expurg'atory a. [L. expurgate, make pure]

exquisite (-iz-it) a. of extreme beauty or delicacy; keen, acute; keenly sensitive. -n. dandy. -ex'quisitely adv. [L. exquisitus, sought out]

extant' a. of a document, etc. , still existing. [L. exstare, stand forth]

extempore (-ri) a. and adj. without preparation, off-hand. -extempora'neous a. -extemp'orary a. -extemp'orize v.t. speak without preparation; devise for the occasion. -extemporiza'tion. [L. ex tempore, out of the time]

extend' v.t. stretch out, lengthen; prolong in duration; widen in area, scope; accord,

grant. -v.i. reach; cover an area; have arange or scope; become larger or wider. -exten'sible a. -extensibil'ity n. -exten-sion n. -extens'ive a. wide, large, comprehensive. -extent' n. size, scope; space, area; degree. [L. extenders, extens -, stretch out]

extended family n. nuclear family and close relatives, often living under one roof.

extenuate v.t. make less blameworthy. extenua'tion n. [L. extenuate, make thin, fr. tenuis, thin]

exte'rior a. outer, outward. -n. outside; outward appearance. [L.]

exterminate v.t. root out, destroy utterly. -extermina'tion n. [L. exterminare, drive over the boundary]

extern'al a. outside. extern'ally adv. [L. externus]

extinct' a. quenched, no longer burning; having died out or come to an end. - extinc'tion n. -exting'uish v.t. put out, quench; wipe out. -exting' uishable a. - exting'uisher n. that which extinguishes; cap to put out a candle; apparatus for putting out a fire. [L. extinguere, extinct -, quench]

extol v.t. praise highly; exalt. [L. extollere, lift up]

extort' v.t. get by force or threats; extract illegally. [L. extorquere, extort -, wrench away]

ex'tra a. additional; larger, better than usual. -adv. additionally; more than usually. -n. extra thing; something charged as additional. -extrajudi'cial a. outside court or normal legal practice. [for extraordinary]

extract' v.t. take out, esp. by force; obtain against a person's will; get by pressure, distillation, etc.; deduce, derive; copy out, quote. -ex'tract n. matter got by distillation; concentrated juice; passage from a book. -extrac'tion n. extracting; ancestry. - extract'or n. [L. extrahere, extract -, draw out]

extradi'tion n. delivery, under a treaty, of a foreign fugitive from justice to the authorities concerned. ex'tradite v.t. give or obtain such delivery. extradi'table a. [L. extradition, handing over]

extra'neous a. added from without, not naturally belonging. [L. extraneus]

ex'traordinary a. out of the usual course; additional; unusual, surprising, exceptional. -extraord'inarily adv. [L. extraor-dinarius, fr. extraordinem, outside the order]

extraterrest'rial a. of, or from outside the

earth's atmosphere. [L. *extra*, outside, *terra*, earth]

extra´vagant *a.* wild, absurd; wasteful; exorbitant. [L. *extrauagari*, wander outside the bounds]

extreme´ *a.* at the end, outermost; of a high or the highest degree; severe; going beyond moderation. -*n.* thing at one end or the other, first and last of a series; utmost degree. -**extreme´ly** *adv.* -**extre´mist** *n.* advocate of extreme measures. **extrem´ity** *n.* end. -*pl.* hands and feet; utmost distress; extreme measures. [*extremus*]

ex´tricate *v.t.* disentangle, set free. -**ex´tricable** *a.* -**extrica´tion** *n.* [L. *extricare*, extricate]

ex´trovert *n.* (*psych.*) one whose mind is turned outward away from himself. usually a cheerful and uninhibited person. [L. *extra*, outside, *vertere*, turn]

exub´erant a, prolific, abundant, luxuriant; effusive, high-flown. -**exu´berance** *n.* -**exu´berantly** *adv.* [L. *uber*, fertile]

exude´ *v.i* ooze out. -*v.t.* give off (moisture). -**exuda´tion** *n.* [L. *exsudare*, sweat out]

exult´ *v.i.* rejoice, triumph. -**exulta´tionn.** **exult´ant** *a.* [L. *ex(s)ultare* leap for joy]

eye (i) *n.* organ of sight; look, glance; attention; various things resembling an eye. -*v.t.* look at; observe. -**eye-ball** *n.* pupil. -**eye´brow** *n.* fringe of hair above the eye. -**eye´lash** *n.* hair fringing the eyelid. -**eye´less** *a.* -**eye´let** *n.* small hole for a rope, *etc.* to pass through. -**eye´lid** *n.* lid or cover of the eye. -**eye´sore** *n.* ugly mark, thing that annoys one to see. -**eye´-witness** *n.* one who saw something for himself. [OE. *eager*]

F

fable *n.* tale; legend; short story with a moral, *esp.* one with talking animals as characters. -*v.t.* invent, tell fables about. -**fab´ulist** *n.* writer of fables. -**fab´ulous** *a.* told of in fables; unhistorical; absurd, unbelievable. [L. *fabula*, fr. *fari*, speak]

fab´ric *n.* thing put together; building, frame, structure; woven stuff, texture. -**fabricate** *v.t.* invent (a lie, *etc.*); forge (a document). -**fab´ricator** *n.* -**fabrica´-tion** *n.* [L. *fabrica*, fr. *faber*, smith]

façade´ *n.* front of a building. [F.]

face *n.* front of the head; front, surface, chief side of anything; outward appearance: look; coolness, impudence. *v.t.* meet boldly-. look or front towards; give a covering surface. -*v.i.* turn. -**fa´cer** *n.*

blow in the face; sudden difficulty. [F.]

fac´et (fas´-) *n.* one side of a many-sided body, *esp.* of a cut gem. [F. *facette*, dim. of face]

facetious (fas-e-shus) *a.* waggish, jocose, given to jesting. -**face´tiae** (-se, ´shi) *n. pl.* pleasantries, witticisms. [L. *facetus*, graceful]

fac´ile *a.* easy; working easily; easygoing. -**facil´itate** (-sit-) *v.t.* make easy, help. -**facil´ity** *n.* easiness; dexterity. -*pl.* opportunities, good conditions. [F.]

facsimile (fak-sim´li) *n.* exact copy. **facsimile machine** *n.* (FAX) device that scans a page of text or graphics and converts it into electronic pulses for tranmission to other locations via telephone lines. [L. *fac simile*, make like]

fact *n.* thing known to be true or to have occurred. [L. *factum,* thing done]

fac´tion *n.* political or other party (used alwavs in a bad sense); misguided party spirit. -**fac´tious** *a.* [L. *factio*]

fac´tion *n.* a television program, film, or literary work comprising a dramatized presentation of actual events. [fr. *fact* and fiction]

fac´tor *n.* something contributing to a result; one of numbers that multiplied together give a given number; agent, one who buvs and sells for another. -**fac´tory** *n.* building where things are manufactured; trading station in a foreign country. [L. *facere*, to do]

fac´ulty *n.* ability, aptitude; inherent power; a power of the mind; department of a university; members of a profession; authorization. -**fac´ultative** *a.* optional. [L. *facultas*, power]

fad *n.* pet idea, craze. -**fadd´y** *a.* -**fadd´ist** *n.* [orig. uncertain]

fade *v.i.* wither; lose color; grow dim; disappear gradually. -**fade in´**, -**out´**, gradual appearance, disappearance, of a cinema scene; similar effect with sounds in radio. -**fade´less** *a.* [OF. *fader*]

Fah´renheit (-hit) *a.* of the thermometric scale on which the freezing point of water is 32° and the boiling point, 212° [*Fahrenheit*, Ger. inventor (d. 1736)]

fail *v.i.* be insufficient; run short; lose power; die away; be wanting at need; be unsuccessful; become bankrupt. -*v.t.* disappoint, give no help to. -**fail´-safe** *a.* designed to return to safe condition in the event of a failure or malfunction; (of a nuclear weapon) capable of being deactivated in the event of a failure or accident; unlikely to fail; foolproof. -**fail´ure** *n.* [L.

falterer, to deceive]

faint *a.* feeble; dim; pale; weak; inclined to swoon. -*v.i.* swoon: to fade or decay; lose courage. -*n.* swoon. -**faint′ly** *adv.* [OF. *feint*, sluggish]

fair *n.* periodical gathering for trade, often with amusements added of shows and roundabouts. -**fair′ing** *n.* present from a fair; streamlining of an aircraft. [L. *feria*, holiday]

fair *a.* beautiful; ample; blond; unblemished; of moderate quality or amount; just, honest; of weather, favorable. -*adv.* honestly. [OE. *foeger*]

fair′way *n.* navigable channel in river; roadstead, *etc.* ; (*golf*) main track from green to green, with 'rough' on either side. [*fair*]

fairy (fatr-) *n.* small elemental being with powers of magic. *a.* of fairies; like a fairy, beautiful and delicate. [OF. *faierie*, land of fays]

faith *n.* trust; belief; belief without proof, religion; promise; loyalty. [OF. feid fr. L. *fides*; cp. fidelity]

fake *v.t.* counterfeit; falsify; adulterate. -*n.* sham; counterfeit; dodge or trick. -*a.* [earlier *feak, feague*; Ger. *fegen*, furbish]

fall (-aw-) *v.i.* drop, come down freely; hang down; become lower; come to the ground, cease to stand; perish; collapse; be captured; pass into a condition; become; happen. -*n.* a falling; amount that falls; amount of descent; yielding to temptation; autumn; rope of hoisting tackle. [OE. *feallan*]

fall′acy (fal′-a-si) *n.* misleading argument; flaw in logic; mistaken belief. -**falia′cious** (-a-) *a.* [L. *allere*, deceive]

fall′ible *a.* liable to error. -**fall′ibly** *adv.* -**fallibil′ity** *n.* [F. fr. *Low.* L. *fallibilis*]

fallow a. plowed and harrowed but left without crop; uncultivated. -*n.* fallow land. -*v.t.* break up (land). [OE. *fealg*, harrow]

fallow *a.* pale brown or reddish yellow. -**fall′ow-deer** *n.* [OE. *fealo*]

false (-aw-) *a.* wrong, erroneous; deceptive; faithless; sham; artificial; untrue. -**false′ly** *adv.* -**false′hood** *n.* lie. -**fal′sify** *v.t.* to alter fraudulently; misrepresent; disappoint (hopes, *etc.*). -**falsification** *n.* [L. *falsus*, mistaken, fr. *fallere, fals-*, deceive]

falset′to *n.* forced voice above the natural range. [It. dim. of *falso*, false]

fal′ter (-aw-) *v.i.* stumble; speak hesitatingly; waver. -*v.t.* say hesitatingly. [orig. uncertain]

fame *n.* reputation; renown; rumor. [L. *fama*, report]

familiar *a.* intimate; closely acquainted; well-known, common; unceremonious. -*n.* familiar friend or demon. [L. *familiaris*, fr. *familia* household]

fam′ily *n.* household of parents and their children; group of parents and children, or near relatives; person's children; all descendants of a common ancestor; class, group of allied objects. -**fam′ily-tree′** *n.* lineage of a person, family, in graphic form. [L. *familia*, household, fr. *famulus*, servant]

fam′ine (-in) *n.* extreme scarcity of food; starvation. -**fam′ish** *v.t.* starve. -*v.i.* be very hungry. [F. , fr. L. *fames*, hunger]

fa′mous. *See* **fame.**

fan *n.* instrument for producing a current of air; winnowing machine; propellerblade; thing spread out as a bird's tail; ventilating machine. -*v.t.* winnow, blow, or cool with a fan. [OE. *fann*, fr. L. *vannus*]

fan *n.* enthusiastic follower (of a game, *etc.*), devotee (of a person). -**fan′mail** *n.* letters from one's fans. [for *fanatic*]

fanat′ic *a.* filled with mistaken enthusiasm, esp. in religion. -*n.* fanatic person; zealot. -**fanat′ical** *a.* -**fanat′ically** *adv.* -fanaticism *n.* [L. *fanaticus*]

fan′cy *n.* power of imagination; mental image; notion, whim, caprice; liking, inclination; followers of a hobby. *a.* ornamental, not plain; of whimsical or arbitrary kind. -*v.t.* imagine; be inclined to believe; have or take a liking for. -**fan′cier** *n.* one with liking and expert knowledge. [shortened fr. *fantasy*]

fang *n.* long pointed tooth; snake's poison tooth; root of a tooth. [OE. *fang*, booty, fr. *fon*, seize]

fantasy *n.* power of imagination, *esp.* extravagant; mental image; fanciful invention or design. -**fanta′sia** (-z-) *n.* fanciful musical composition. -**fantas′tic** *a.* quaint, grotesque, extremely fanciful. -**fantas′tically** *adv.* [G. *phantasia*]

far *adv.* at or to a great distance or advanced point; by very much. *a.* distant. -*n.* great distance or amount. -**far′-fetched** *a.* forced, not natural. -**far′sighted** *a.* able to see the future effects of present action; able to see objects clearly only when they are far from the eyes. [OE. *feorr*]

far′ad *n.* unit of electrical capacity. [Michael *Faraday*, 1791-1867]

farce *n.* play meant only to excite laughter; absurd and futile proceeding. [F.]

fare (fer) *n.* money paid by a passenger for conveyance; passenger; food-*v.i.* happen; get on; travel. -farewell′ *interj.* goodbye.

-n. leave-taking. [OE. *faran*, travel]

farm *n*. tract of cultivated land. -*v.t.* pay or take a fixed sum for the proceeds of (a tax, *etc.*); cultivate. [F. *ferme*]

far'ther (-TH-) *a*. more distant. -*adv*. to, at, greater distance. -far'thest *a*. most far. *adv*. to, at, greatest distance. [*far*]

fas'cia *n*. long flat surface of wood or stone in a building; part of shop-front bearing the merchant's name. [L.]

fascinate *v.t.* make powerless by look or presence; charm, attract. -**fascina'tion** *n*. -**fas'cinator** *n*. charmer; headscarf for evening wear. [L. *fascinate*, enchant]

Fas'cist *n*. member of Italian or similar political party aiming at the overthrow of communists, radicals, *etc.*, by violence, and of strong rule by a dictator. [It. fascistic members of a *fascio*, union]

fash'ion (-shun) *n*. make, style; manner; custom, esp. in dress. -*v.t.* shape, make. -**fash'ionable** *a*. in the prevailing mode. -**fash'ionably** *adv*. [F. *façon*]

fast (-a-) *v.t.* go without food or some kinds of food *esp.* as a religious exercise. -*n*. act or appointed time, of fasting. -**fast'day** *n*. [OE. *fæstan*]

fast (-a-) *a*. firm, fixed, steady, permanent; rapid; ahead of true time; dissipated. -*adv*. firmly, tightly; rapidly; in a dissipated way. -**fast'ness** *n*. fast state; fortress. [OE. *fæst*, firm]

fast'en (-sen) *v.t.* attach, fix, secure. -*v.i.* seize (upon) [*fast*]

fastidious *a*. hard to please; easily disgusted. [F. *fastidieux*, L. *fastidiosus*]

fat *a*. plump, thick, solid; containing much fat; fertile. -*n*. oily substance of animal bodies; fat part. -*v.t.* feed (animals) for slaughter. -**fatt'en** *v.t.* and *i*. -**fat'ness** *n*. -**fatt'y** *a*. [OE. *fætt*]

fate *n*. power supposed to predetermine events; goddess of destiny; destiny; person's appointed lot or condition; death or destruction. -*v.t.* preordain. -**fate'ful** *a*. prophetic, fraught with destiny. -**fa'tal** *a*. deadly, ending in death; destructive; very ill-advised, disastrous; inevitable. - **fa'tally** *adj*. -**fatal'ity** n. rule of fate; calamity; death by accident. -**fa'talism** n. belief that everything is predetermined; submission to fate. [L. *fatum*, decree of the gods]

fa'ther *n*. male parent; forefather, ancestor; originator, early leader; priest, confessor; oldest member of a society. -*v.t.* beget; originate; pass as father or author of, act as father to; fix the paternity of - **fa'therhood** *n*. -**fa'ther-in-law** *n*. father of

one's husband or wife. -**fa'therly** *a*. - **fa'therless** *a*. -**fa'therland** *n*. one's country. -**Fa'ther's Day** *n*. day in which the father is honored by the family, *usu*. the third Sunday in June. [OE. *fæder*]

fath'om (-ia'TH-) *n*. (*naut.*) measure of six feet. -*v.t.* sound (water); get to the bottom of, understand. -**fath'omless** *a*. too deep to fathom. -**fath'omable** *a*. [OE. *fæthm*, two arms outstretched]

fatigue *v.t.* weary. -*n*. weariness of body or mind; toil; soldier's non-military duty-*n*. *pl*. informal army clothes. [F. *fatiquer*, L. *fatigare*].

fau'cet (-set) *n*. apparatus for controlling the flow of liquid from a pipe, *esp*. in a kitchen or bathroom; tap [F. *fausseti*]

fault *n*. defect; misdeed; blame, culpability; (*tennis*) ball wrongly served; (*hunting*) failure of scent; (*geol.*) a break in strata. -**fault'y** *a*. -**fault'less** *a*. -**fault'ily** *adv*. -**fault'lessly** *adv*. [F. *faute*]

faun'a *n*. animals of a region or period. [L. *Fauna*, sister of *Faunus*; *v.s.*]

favor (-ver) *n*. goodwill; approval; partiality; especial kindness; badge or knot of ribbons. -*v.t.* regard or treat with favor; oblige; treat with partiality; aid support. -**favorably** *adv*. -**fa'vorite** (-it) *n*. favored person or thing; horse, *etc.*, expected to win race. *a*. chosen, preferred. - **fa'voritism** *n*. practice of showing undue preference. [L. *favor*]

fawn *n*. young fallow-deer. *a*. of a light yellowish-brown. [F. *faon*]

fear *n*. dread, alarm; unpleasant emotion caused by coming evil or danger. -*v.i.* regard with fear; revere; hesitate, shrink from (doing something). [OE. *fær*, sudden peril]

feas'ible (-z-) *a*. practicable, that can be done. -**feas'ibly** *adv*. -**feasibil'ity** *n*. [F. *faisable*, fr. *faire*, do]

feast *n*. banquet, lavish meal; religious anniversary to be kept with joy; annual village festival. -*v.i.* partake of a banquet, fare sumptuously. -*v.t.* regale with a feast. [L. *festa*]

feat *n*. notable deed; surprising trick. [F. *fait*, fr. L. *factum*, deed]

feath'er (feTH'-) *n*. one of the barbed shafts which form the covering of birds. -*v.t.* provide with feathers; turn (an oar) edgeways. -*v.i.* grow feathers; turn an oar. [OE. *fether*]

feat'ure *n*. part of the face (*usu. pl.*); characteristic or notable part of anything. -*v.t.* portray; give prominence to. -**feat'ureless** *a*. flat, undistinguished [OF. *faiture*, shape]

Feb'ruary *n.* second month of the year. [L. *Februarius*]

fe'ces *n.pl.* excrement, bodily waste matter. -**fe'cal** *a.* [L. *faex*, dregs]

fec'und *a.* fertile. [L. *fecundus*, fruitful]

fed'eral *a.* of, or like, the government of states which are united but retain more or less independence within themselves; pert. to the Union in the Civil War. [L. *fœdus, foeder-*, alliance]

fee *n.* payment for services, *esp.* one due to a public official or a professional man; entrance-money. -*v.t.* pay a fee to. [OE. *feoh*, cattle, money]

fee'ble *a.* weak; ineffective; insipid. -**fee'bly** *adv.* [F. *faible*]

feed *v.t.* give food to; supply, support. -*v.i.* take food. -*n.* a feeding; fodder, pasturage; allowance of fodder; material supplied to a machine; part of a machine taking in material. [OE. fedan]

feel *v.t.* examine, search, by touch; perceive, have knowledge of, by touch or in emotions. -*v.i.* use the sense of touch; grope; be conscious; have, be affected by (a sentiment); sympathize. -*n.* sense of touch; impression on it. -**feel'ing** *n.* sense of touch; physical sensation; emotion; sympathy, tenderness; conviction or opinion not solely based on reason. -*pl.* susceptibilities. *a.* sensitive, sympathetic. [OE. *felan*]

feign (fan) *v.t.* pretend, simulate. -*v.i.* pretend. [F. *feindre*, fr. L. *fingere*, invent]

feint (fant) *n.* sham attack or blow meant to deceive an opponent. -*v.i.* make such move. (F. *feinte*]

feli'city (-is'-) *n.* great happiness, bliss; appropriateness of wording. -**feli'citous** *a.* apt, well-chosen; happy. -**feli'citate** *v.t.* congratulate. -**felicita'tion** *n.* (*usu.* in *pl.*), congratulations. [L. *felix, felic-*, happy]

fe'line *a.* of cats; catlike. -**felin'ity** *n.* [L. *felinus*, fr. *felis*, cat]

fell *v.t.* knock down; cut down (a tree). [OE. *fellan*]

fell'ow *n.* comrade, associate; counterpart, like thing; member (of certain learned societies, *etc*); person. -*a.* of the same class, associated. -**fell'owship** *n.* [ON. *felagi*, partner]

fel'on *n.* one who has committed a felony. *a.* cruel, fierce. -**fel'ony** *n.* crime more serious than a misdemeanor. -**felo'nious** *a.* [F. *folon*]

felt *n.* cloth made by rolling and pressing wool with size; thing made of this. -*v.t.* make into, or cover with, felt. [OE.]

fe'male *a.* of the sex which bears offspring; relating to this sex or to women. -*n.* one of this sex. -**fe'male screw'**, screw cut on the inside surface of a screw-hole. [F. *femelle*]

fem'inine (-in) *a.* of women; womanly; (*gram.*) of the gender proper to women's names. -**feminin'ity** *n.* -**fem'inism** *n.* influence of women; advocacy of this, of women's political rights, *etc.* -**fem'inist** *n.* [L. *femininus*]

fem'oral *a.* of the thigh. [Late L. *femoralis*, fr. *femur*, thigh]

fence *n.* art of using a sword; hedge or railing; (*sl.*) receiver of stolen goods. -*v.t.* put a hedge round, enclose. -*v.i.* practice sword-play. -**fen'cing** *n.* [*defence*]

fend *v.t.* ward off, repel. -*v.i.* provide (for oneself, *etc*).. -**fend'er** *n.* bundle of rope, *etc.*, hung over a ship's side to prevent chafing; frame round a hearth; guard of the wheel of an automobile. [*defend*]

fer'ment *n.* leaven, substance causing a thing to ferment; excitement, tumult. -**ferment'** *v.i.* undergo a chemical change with effervescence, liberation of heat and alteration of properties, e. g. process set up in dough by yeast. -*v.t.* subject to this process; stir up, excite. -**fermenta'tion** *n.* [L. *fermentum*]

fero'cious (-ō-shus) *a.* fierce, savage, cruel. -**feroc'ity** (-os'-) *n.* savage cruelty. [L. *ferax, feroc-*]

ferr'et *n.* half-tamed animal like a weasel used to catch rabbits, rats, *etc.* ; -*v.t.* take or clear with ferrets; search out. -*v.i.* search about, rummage. [F. *furet*]

ferr'ic *a.* **ferr'ous** *a.* containing iron. [L. *ferrum*, iron]

ferry *v.t.* and *i.* carry, pass, by boat across a river, strait, *etc.* -*n.* place or a boat for ferrying. -**ferr'yman** *n.* [OE. *ferian*, carry]

fer'tile *a.* fruitful, producing abundantly. -**fertil'ity** *n.* -**fer'tilize** *v.t.* make fertile. -**fer'tilizer** *n.* -**fertiliza'tion** *n.* [L. *fertilis*, fr. *ferre*, bear]

fer'vent *a.* hot, glowing; ardent, intense. -**fer'vently** *adv,* -**fer'vency** *n.* -**fer'vor** (-er) *n.* -**fer'vid** *a.* ardent, impassioned; zealous. -**fer'vidly** *adv.* [L. *fervere*, boil]

fes'tal *a.* of a feast; keeping holiday; gay. -**fes'tive** *a.* of a feast; joyous, gay; jovial. -**fes'tival** *n.* festal days; merrymaking; periodical musical celebration. -**festiv'ity** *n.* gaiety, mirth; occasion for rejoicing. -*pl.* festive proceedings. [L. *festum*, feast]

fes'ter *n.* suppurating condition, sore. -*v.i.* ulcerate, produce matter (in wound); rankle. -*v. t.* cause to fester. [OF. *festre*]

fetch *v.t.* go for and bring; draw forth; be

sold for; charm. -n. trick. -**fetch'ing** a. attractive. [OE. *fetian*]

fet'id a. stinking. [L. *fetidus* from *fetere*, to stink]

fet'ish n. inanimate object worshipped by savages; as enshrining a spirit; anything which is the object of irrational reverence. [F. *fetiche*]

falter n. chain or shackle for the feet; check, restraint. -*pl.* captivity. -*v.t.* chain up; restrain, hamper. [OE. *feter*, fr. *fet*, feet]

fet'tle n. condition, trim. [perh. fr. OE. *fetel*, belt, in sense of girding onself]

fe'tus n. fully-developed young in womb or egg. -**fe'tal** a. [L. = offspring]

feud (fud) n. bitter and lasting mutual hostility, *esp.* between two families or tribes. [OF. *faide*]

feud n. fief. -**feud'al** a. of a fief. -**feud'al system**, medieval political system based on the holding of land from a superior in return for service. -**feud'alism** n. [Med. L. *feudum*]

fe'ver n. condition of illness with high temperature and waste of tissue; nervous excitement. -*v.t.* throw into fever. -**fe'verish** a. -**fe'verishly** adv. -**fe'ver few** n. herb formerly used as a febrifuge. [OE. *fefer*, fr. L. *febris*]

few a. not many. -n. small number. -**few'ness** n. [OE. *feawe*]

fiancé (fe-ong-sa,) n. , **fiancee'** *fem.* one betrothed. a. betrothed, engaged. [F.]

fias'co n. breakdown, ignominious failure. [It. = bottle]

fib n. trivial lie. -*v.i.* tell a fib. -**fibb'er** n. [orig. uncertain]

fi'ber n. filament forming part of animal or plant tissue; substance that can be spun. -**fi'brous** a. -**fi'berglass** n. material made from glass fibers. -**fiber optics** n. cable consisting of glass or plastic fibers able to transmit data in the form of light. [L. *fibre*]

fibro'sis n. overgrowth of fibrous tissue. -**fibrosi'tis** (-i-) n. inflammation of fibrous tissue, kind of rheumatism. [*fibre*]

fib'ula n. outer leg-bone from knee to ankle; buckle; brooch, or clasp. [L.]

fic'kle a. changeable, inconstant. -**fic'kleness** n. [OE. *ficol*, tricky]

fic'tion n. invented statement or narrative; novels, stories collectively; conventionally accepted falsehood. -**ficti'tious** a. not genuine, imaginary; assumed. [L. *fictio*, fr. *fingere*, shape]

fid'dle n. violin; in a ship, a frame to stop things rolling off a table. -*v.i.* play the fiddle; make idle movements, trifle. -**fid'dlestick** n. bow. -*pl.* nonsense. -

fid'dler n. [OE. *fithele*]

fidelity n. faithfulness. [L. *fidelitas*]

fidu'ciary (-sh-) a. held or given in trust; relating to a trustee. -n. trustee. [L. *fiduciarius*, fr. *fides*, faith]

field n. piece of land tilled or used as pasture; enclosed piece of land; battleground; tract of land rich in a specified product (*eg.* gold field); all the players in a game or sport; all competitors but the favorite; surface of a shield, coin, *etc.* ; range, area of operation or study. -*v.i.* and *t.* in certain sports, stop and return a ball. -n. (*compute.*) group of related characters (bytes) treated as a unit. -**field'-day** n. day of maneuvers; day of athletic contests; important occasion. -**field'glass** n. binoculars for outdoor use. -**field'er** n. one who fields at baseball, cricket *etc.* [OE. *feld*]

fiend n. devil. -**fiend'ish** a. fiend-like, devilish. [OE. *feond*, enemy]

fierce a. savage, wild, raging. -**fierce'ness** n. -**fierce'ly** adv. [L. *ferus*, wild]

fi'ery (fi-) a. consisting of fire; blazing, glowing; flashing; irritable; spirited; ardent, eager. [*fire*]

fig n. familiar soft round many-seeded fruit; tree bearing it. [F. *figue*, L. *ficus*]

fight (fit) v.i. contend in battle or in single combat. -*v.t.* contend with; maintain against an opponent; settle by combat; maneuver (ships, troops) in battle. -n. act of fighting, combat, battle; strife. -**fight'er** n. [OE. *feohtan*]

fig'ure (-er) n. form, shape; bodily shape; appearance, *esp.* conspicuous appearance; space enclosed by lines or surfaces; diagram, illustration; likeness, image; pattern; movement in dancing, skating, *etc.*; numerical symbol; amount, number; abnormal form of expression for effect in speech, *e.g.* a metaphor. -*v.i.* use numbers; show, be conspicuous; be estimated; consider. -*v.t.* to calculate, estimate; represent by picture or diagram; to ornament. -**fig'urative** a. metaphorical; full of figures of speech. -**fig'uratively** adv. [F.]

fil'ament n. thread-like body; (*elec.*) wire in lamp. [Late L. *filamentum*]

file n. tool, usually of roughened steel, for smoothing or rubbing down metal or other material. -*v.t.* apply a file to, smooth, rub down, polish. -**fi'ling** n. action of using a file; scrap of metal removed by a file. (OE. *feol*]

file n. stiff wire on which papers are threaded; device for holding papers for reference; papers so arranged. -*v.t.* place in a file. [F. *fit*, thread]

file n. in formation of soldiers, a front-rank man and the man or men immediately behind him. -**in file**, arranged in two lines facing to one end of the rank.- **single**, or -**Indian file**, formation of a single line of men one behind the other. -v.i. march in file. [F. *file*, fr. *filer*, spin out]

fil′ial a. of, or befitting, a son or daughter. -**fil′ially** adv. [L. *filius*, son]

filibuster n. one who deliberately obstructs the passage of legislation, *esp.* by making long speeches; adventurer in irregular warfare, privateer; pirate.-v.i. act as a filibuster. [F. *flibustier*]

fili′form a. thread-like, in form of fine thread. [L. *filum*, thread]

fill v.t. make full; occupy completely, hold, discharge duties of; stop up; satisfy; fulfill. -v.i. become full. -n. full supply; as much as desired. -**fill′er** n. -**fill′ing** n. what is used to pad, complete, stop a hole, *etc.* [OE. *fyllan*]

fill′et, fil′et n. head-band; strip of meat; piece of meat or fish boned, rolled and tied. -v.t. encircle with a fillet; make into fillets. [F. *filet*]

fill′y n. female foal. [ON. *fylja*]

film n. very thin skin or layer; thin sensitized sheet used in photography; sensitized celluloid roll used in cinema photography; cinematographic picture; dimness on the eyes; slight haze; thread. v.t. photograph or represent by moving pictures; cover with a film. -v.i. become covered with a film. -**film′y** a. -**film′star** n. popular actor or actress for films. [OE. *filmen*]

fil′ter n. cloth or other apparatus for straining liquids. -v.t. and i. pass through a filter. -v.i. make a way through. -**filtra′tion** n. (F. *filtre*]

fin n. propelling or steering organ of a fish; erection on tail of an airplane. [OE. *finn*]

fi′nal a. coming at the end; conclusive. -n. game, heat, examination, *etc.* , coming at the end of a series. -**fi′nally** adv. -**final′ity** n. -**finalize** v.t. -**fina′le** n. closing part of a musical composition, opera, *etc.* [L. *finis*, end]

finance′ n. management of money. -pl. money resources. -v.t. find capital for. -v.i. deal with money. -**finan′cial** a. -**finan′cially** adv. -**finan′cier** n. [F.]

find (fi-) v.t. come across, light upon, obtain; recognize; experience, discover; discover by searching; ascertain; declare on inquiry; supply. -n. a finding; something found. -**find′er** n. [OE. *findan*]

fine n. sum fixed as a penalty; sum paid in consideration of a low rent. -**in fine**, to sum up. -v.t. punish by a fine. [Low L. *finis*, fine]

fine a. choice, pure, of high quality, delicate, subtle; in small particles; slender; excellent; handsome; showy; free from rain; fastidious. -n. fine weather. -adv. in fine manner. -v.t. make clear or pure; thin; refine. -v.i. become clear or pure or thinned. -**fine′ly** adv. -**fine′ness** n. -**fi′nery** n. showy dress. [F. *fin*]

fin′ger (-ng-g-) n. one of the jointed branches of the hand; various things like this. -v.t. touch or handle with the fingers. [OE.]

fin′ish v.t. bring to an end, complete, perfect: kill. -v.i. come to an end. -n. end, last stage; decisive result: completed state; anything serving to complete or perfect -**fin′isher** n. [L. *finire*]

fi′nite (fi-nit) a. bounded, limited, conditioned. [L. *finitus*, fr. *finire*]

fiord′, fjord (fyord′) n. narrow inlet of the sea between cliffs. [*Norwegian*]

fir n. coniferious tree; its wood. [ON. *fyra*, cp. Dan. *fyr*, Ger. *föhre*]

fire n. state of burning, combustion, flame, glow; mass of burning fuel; destructive burning, conflagration; ardor, keenness, spirit; shooting of firearms. -v.t. make burn; supply with fuel; bake; inspire; explode; discharge (a firearm); propel from a firearm. -v.i. begin to burn; become excited; discharge a firearm; dismiss from employment. -**fire′arm** n. weapon shooting by explosion, a gun, pistol, cannon. -**fire department** n. organized body of men with appliances to put out fires and rescue those in danger from fire. -**fire-bug** n. incendiary, pyromaniac. -**fire′-engine** n. engine with apparatus for extinguishing fires. -**fire′-escape** n. apparatus for escaping from a burning house. -**fire′fly** n. insect giving out a glow of phosphorescent light. -**fire′irons** n.pl. tongs, poke, and shovel.-**fire′place** n. hearth in a room. -**fire′-plug** n. connection in a water main for a hose. -**fire′-proof** a. resistant to fire, incombustible.-**fire′work** n. device giving spectacular effects by explosions and colored flames. [OE. *fyr*]

firm a. solid, fixed, stable; steadfast; resolute; settled. -v.t. make firm; solidify. -n. commercial house. partners carrying on a business. [L. *firrnus*]

firmament n. vault of heaven. [L. *firmamentum*, fr. *firmare*, make firm]

first a. earliest in time or order; foremost in rank or position. -adv. before others in time, order, *etc.* -**first′-aid** n. help given to an injured person before the arrival of a doctor. **-first'ly** *adv.* **-first' strike** *a.* (of a nuclear missile) intended for use in an opening attack calculated to destroy the enemy's nuclear weapons. [OE. *fyrest*, fr. *ftore*]

fis'cal *a.* of a state treasury; of public revenue, taxation. [L. *fiscus*, purse]

fish *n.* vertebrate cold-blooded animal with gills, living in water; flesh of fish.-*v.i.* try to catch fish; search for; try in a roundabout way to elicit information. -*v.t.* try to catch fish in; draw (up); produce. **-fish'er** *n.* **-fish'erman** *n.* one who lives by fishing. [OE. *fisc*]

fis'sure (-sh-) *n.* cleft, split. **-fis'sile** *a.* capable of splitting; tending to split. - **fis'sion** *n.* splitting; division of living cells into more cells. **-fissip'arous** *a.* reproducing by fission. [L. *fissura*]

fist *n.* clenched hand; handwriting. -*v.t.* strike with the clenched hand. **-fisticuffs** *n. pl.* fighting with fists. [OE. *fyst*]

fit *n.* sudden passing attack of illness; seizure with convulsions, spasms, loss of consciousness, *etc.*, as of epilepsy, hysteria, *etc.*; sudden and passing state, mood. **-fit'ful** *a.* spasmodic capricious. - **fit'fully** *adv.* [OE. *fitt*, conflict]

fit *a.* well-suited, worthy; proper, becoming; ready; in good condition. -*v.t.* be suited to; be properly adjusted to; arrange, adjust, apply, insert; supply, furnish. -*v.i.* be correctly adjusted or adapted, be of the right size. -*n.* way a garment fits; its style; adjustment. **-fit'ly** -*adv.* **-fit'ness** *n.* **-fitt'er** *n.* **-fit'ment** *n.* piece of furniture. **-fitt'ing** *n.* action of fitting; apparatus; fixture. *a.* that fits; becoming, proper. [orig. uncertain]

five *a.* and *n.* cardinal number next after four. **-fifth** *a.* ordinal number. - **fifth'genera'tion** *a.* denoting developments in computer design to produce machines with artifical intelligence. - **five'fold** *a.* and *adv.* **-fifteen'** *a. and n.* ten and five. *-fifteen'th a.* **-fifth'ly** *adv.* - **fifteenth'ly** adv. **-fif'ty** *a.* and *n.* five tens. **-fif'tieth** *a.* **-fives** *n.* ball-game played with the hand or a bat in a court. [OE. *fif*]

fix *v.t.* fasten, make firm or stable; set, establish; appoint, assign, determine; make fast, permanent. -*v.i.* become firm or solidified; determine. -*n.* difficult situation. **-fix'ity** *n.* **-fix'edly** *adv.* **-fixa'tion** *n.* fixing. (*psychoanalysis*) arrest in development. - **fix'ative** *a.* **-fix'ture** *n.* thing fixed in position; thing annexed to a house; date for a sporting event; the event. [L. *ligere, fix-*]

flac'cid (-ks-) flabby. **-flaccid'ity** *n.* [L. *flaccidus*, fr. *flaccus*, flabby]

flag *n.* water plant with sword-shaped leaves, *esp.* the iris. **-flagg'y** *a.* [ME. *flagge, flegge*]

flag *n.* flat slab of stone. -*pl.* pavement of flags. -*v.t.* pave with flags. **-flag'-stone** *n.* [ON. *flaga*]

flag *n.* banner, piece of bunting attached to a staff or halyard as a standard or signal. -*v.t.* inform by flag-signals.-*v.i.* droop, languish. **-flag'-day** *n.* day on which small flags or emblems are sold in the streets for charity. **-flag'-off'icer** *n.* admiral entitled to show a flag as an indication of his rank; commander of a fleet or squadron. - **flag'ship** *n.* ship with an admiral on board. **-flag'staff** *n.* pole on which flag is hoisted. [orig. uncertain]

flag *v.i.* droop, fade; lose vigor. [orig. uncertain]

fla'grant *a.* glaring, scandalous; enormous. **-fla'grantly** *adv.* **-fla'grancy** *n.* [L. *flagrare*, burn]

flail *n.* instrument for threshing corn by hand, long handle with a short thick stick swinging at the end. -*v.t.* [OF. *flaiel*, fr. L. *flagellum*, scourge]

flair *n.* intuitive feeling or special aptitude (with for). (F. = scent]

flak *n.* opposition put up by anti-aircraft defences. [abbrev. of Ger. *fliegerabwehrkanone*]

flake *n.* light fleecy piece, *esp.* of snow; thin broad piece, *esp.* split or peeled off, layer. -*v.t.* break flakes from. -*v.i.* come off in flakes. **-fla'ky** *a.* [orig. uncertain]

flame *n.* burning gas; portion of burning gas, *esp.* above a fire; visible burning; passion, *esp.* love; sweetheart. -*v.i.* give out flames, blaze; burst out in anger, *etc.* **flame'-thrower** *n.* device for throwing jets of flame in battle. **-flam'mable** *a.* capable of being easily ignited and of burning quickly. [L. *flamma*]

flange (-anj) *n.* projecting flat rim collar, or rib. -*v.t.* provide with a flange. [orig. uncertain]

flank *n.* fleshy part of the side between the hips and ribs; side of a building or body of troops. -*v.t.* guard or strengthen on the flank; attack or take in flank; be at, or move along, either side of. [F. *flanc*]

flap *v.t.* strike with something broad, flat and flexible; move (wings) up and down. -*v.i.* sway, swing, flutter. -*n.* act of flapping; broad piece of anything hanging from a hinge or loosely from one side. [imit. orig.]

flare (-ar) *v.i.* blaze with bright unsteady flame. -*n.* act of flaring; bright unsteady flame; signal light used at sea. [orig. uncertain]

flash v.i. break into sudden flame; gleam; burst into view; appear suddenly. -v.t. cause to gleam; emit (light, etc.) suddenly. -n. sudden burst of light or flame; sudden short access; ribbon or badge; display. a. showy; sham. -**flash′y** a. -**flash-back** n. break in book, play, film, to insert what has previously taken place. -**flash′light** n. small battery-operated portable light; apparatus for taking flash photographs. -**flash′point** n. temperature at which oil vapor ignites. [earlier meaning dash, splash; of imit. orig.]

flat a. level; spread out; at full length; smooth; downright; dull, lifeless; below true pitch. -n. what is flat; simpleton; note half a tone below the natural pitch; punctured tire. -**flat′car** n. railroad freight vehicle with no raised sides and no roof. [ON. flatr]

flatt′er v.t. court, fawn on; praise insincerely; inspire a belief, esp. an unfounded one; gratify (senses); represent too favorably. -**flatt′erer** n. -**flatt′ery** n. [F. flatter, 'smooth']

flat′ulent a. generating gases in the intestines; caused by or attended by or troubled with such gases; vain, pretentious, turgid. -**flat′ulence** n. -**flat′ulency** n. [L. flat-, flare, blow]

flaunt v.t. and i. wave proudly; show off. [orig. uncertain]

flautist n. flute-player, flutist. [It. flautista]

fla′vor (-vvr) n. mixed sensation of smell and taste; distinctive taste; undefinable characteristic quality of anything. -v.t. give a flavor to; season. -**flavoring** n. [OF. floor, smell]

flaw n. crack; defect, blemish. -v.t. make a flaw in. -v.i. crack. -**flaw′less** a. [orig. uncertain]

flea (-e) n. small wingless jumping insect which feeds on human and other blood. [OE.]

flee v.i. run away. -v.t. run away from; sbun. [OE. fleon]

fleece n. sheep's wool. -v.t. rob. -**flee′cy** a. [OE. fleos]

fleet n. naval force under an admiral; number of ships, etc., sailing in company; number of automobiles, aircraft, etc., owned by one company. [OE. fleet, ship]

fleet a. swift, nimble. [ON. fljotr]

flesh n. soft part, muscular substance, between skin and bone; this as food; of plants, the pulp; fat; sensual appetites. -**flesh′ings** n. pl. close-fitting flesh-colored theatrical garments. -**flesh-pots** n. pl. high living.

-**flesh′ly** a. carnal, material. -**flesh′y** a. plump, pulpy. -**flesh′ily** adv. [OE. flæsc]

flex′ible a. that may be bent without breaking, pliable; manageable; supple. -**flexibil′ity** n. -**flex′ibly** adv. -**flex′ion, flec′tion** n. bending, bent state. -**flex′time, flex′itime** n. system permitting variation in starting and finishing times of work, providing an agreed number of hours is worked over a specified period. [L. flexibilis]

flight (-it) n. act or manner of flying through the air; swift movement or passage; sally; distance flown; airplane journeys; stairs between two landings; number flying together, as birds. arrows. -**flight′y** a. light-headed, thoughtless, capricious. [fly]

flight (-It) n. a running away. [floe]

flim′sy (-zi) a. very thin; unsubstantial; fragile. -n. very thin paper. -**flim′sily** adv. [Welsh llymsi]

flinch v.i. shrink, draw back. [earlier flench, ME. fleechen]

fling v.t. throw. -v.i. rush, go hastily; kick, plunge. -n. throw; hasty attempt; spell of indulgence; vigorous dance. [orig. uncertain]

flint n. hard stone found in gray lumps with a white crust; piece of this. -**flint′lock** n. gun or its lock discharged by a spark struck from flint. [OE.]

flip n. flick or fillip, very light blow. -v.t. strike or move with a flick; turn over. -v.i. move in jerks; turn over; lose one's mind or composure. -**flip′per** n. limb or fin for swimming. [imit. orig.]

flirt v.t. throw with a jerk, give a brisk motion to. -v.i. play at courtship. -n. jerk, sudden throw; one who plays at courtship. -**flirta′tion** n. [imit. orig.]

float v.i. rest or drift on the surface of a liquid; be suspended freely (in a liquid). -v.t. of a liquid, support, bear along; commerce, get (a company) started. -n. anything small that floats (esp. to support something else, e.g., a fishing net); lowbodied cart; footlight. -**flota′tion** n. act of floating, esp. floating of a company. [OE. flotian]

flock n. number of animals of one kind together; body of people, religious congregation. -v.i. gather in a crowd. [OE. flocc, herd]

flog v.t. beat with a whip, stick, etc. [orig. uncertain]

flood (flud) n. flowing in of the tide; flowing water; overflow of water, inundation. -v.t. inundate; cover or fill with water. -**The**

Flood, great deluge of Noah's time. - **flood'-gate** *n*. gate for letting water in or out. -**flood'-lighting** *n*. illumination of, e. g., exterior of a building, by distant projectors. -**flood'lit** *a*. -**flood-tide** *n*. rising tide. [OE. *flod*]

floor (flor) *n*. lower surface of a room; set of rooms on one level; flat space. -*v.t*. supply with a floor; knock down; confound. [OE. *flor*]

flop *v.i*. sway about heavily; move clumsily; sit or fall with a thump. -*v.t*. throw down with a thud. -*n*. flopping movement or sound. *adv*. with a flop. -**flop'py** *a*. - **flop'py disk** *n*. flexible magnetic disk that stores information and can be used to store data for use in a microprocessor. [imit. orig.]

flop *n*. (*sl*.) failure; something that falls flat. [*flop v. s*.]

flo'ra (flaw'-) *n*. **plants of a region; a list of them.** -**flo'ral** *a*. of flowers. - **flor'iculture** *n*. cultivation of flowers. - **flor'et** *n*. small flower forming part of a composite flower. -**flor'ist** *n*. one who deals in, grows, or studies, flowers. [L. *flos, flor-*, flower]

flor'id *a*. flowery, ornate; ruddy, high-colored. -**florid'ity** *n*. [L. *flos*, flower]

floss *n*. rough silk on a cocoon; silk for embroidery; fluff. -**floss'y** *a*. light and downy. [OF. *flosche*, down]

flound'er *v.i*. plunge and struggle, *esp*. in water or mud; proceed in bungling or hesitating manner. -*n*. act of floundering. [orig. uncertain]

flour *n*. sifted finer part of meal; wheat meal; fine soft powder. -*v.t*. sprinkle with flour. -**flour'y** *a*. -**flour'iness** *n*. [flower of wheat]

flour'ish (flur-) *v.i*. thrive; be in the prime. -*v.t*. brandish, display; wave about. -*n*. ornamental curve in writing; florid expression; waving of hard, weapon, *etc*.; fanfare (of trumpets). [OF. *florir*, to bloom]

flow (flo) *v.i*. glide along as a stream; hang loose; move easily; move in waves; be ample in form; run full; abound. -*n*. act or fact of flowing; quantity that flows; rise of tide; ample supply; outpouring. [OE. *flowan*]

flow'er (flow-) *n*. colored (not green) part of a plant from which the fruit is developed, bloom, blossom; ornamen tation; choicest part, pick. -*v.i*. bloom, or blossom. -*v.t*. ornament with worked flowers. [F. *fleur*, fr. L. *flos, flor-*]

flu *abbrev*. of influenza, *q.v*. **fluc'tuate** *v.i*. vary irregularly, rise and fall; waver, be unstable. -**fluctua'tion** *n*. [L. *fluctuare*, fr.

fluctus, wave]

flue *n*. passage for smoke or hot air, chimney. [orig. unknown]

flu'ent *a*. flowing, copious and ready (in words); graceful (in movement). -**flu'ency** *adv*. -**flu'ency** *n*. [L. *fluere*, flow]

flu'id *a*. flowing easily, not solid. -*n*. fluid substance, gas or liquid. -**fluid'ity** *n*. [L. *fluidus*, fr. *fluere*, flow]

fluke *n*. flat triangular point of an anchor. [orig. uncertain fluke *n*. lucky stroke. -*v.i*. make a fluke. -**flu'ky** *a*. [orig. uncertain]

flunk *v.t*. fail someone in an examination or course. -*v.i*. fail in an examination or course. [orig. uncertain]

flu'or *n*. mineral containing fluorine. - **fluores'cence** *n*. luminous state produced in a transparent body by direct action of light, *esp*. violet and ultra-violet rays; power of rendering ultra-violet rays visible. -**fluores'cent** *a*. -**fluores'cent lighting**, lighting by electric discharge acting on fluorescent coating of tube, lamp. -**fluoresce'** *v.i*. -**flu'orine** *n*. nonmetallic element of the chlorine group. [L. fr. *fluere*, flow]

flush *v.i*. take wing and fly away. -*v.t*. cause to do this. -*n*. number of birds flushed at once. [orig. uncertain]

flush *n*. set of cards all of one suit. [L. *fluxus*, flow]

flush *v.i*. become suffused with blood; turn suddenly red in the face; blush. -*v.t*. cleanse by rush of water; cause to glow or redden. [orig. uncertain]

flute *n*. musical wind instrument, wooden pipe with holes stopped by the fingers or keys and a blow-hole in the side; flute player in a band; groove or channel. -*v.i*. play on a flute. -*v.t*. make grooves in. - **flut'ist, flautist** *n*. one who plays the flute. [F. *flute*]

flutt'er *v.i*. flap wings rapidly without flight or in short flights; move, come down, quiveringly; be excited, agitated. -*v.t*. flap quickly; agitate, -*n*. fluttering, occasional bet, speculation. [OE. *floterian*]

flux *n*. morbid discharge, as of blood; a flowing; flow of the tide; constant succession of changes; substance mixed with metal to help melting. [L. *fluxus*]

fly *n*. two-winged insect; artificial fly of silk, *etc*., used in angling. [OE. *fleoge*]

fly *v.i*. move through the air on wings or in aircraft; pass quickly through the air; float loosely; wave; spring; rush; flee, run away. -*v.t*. cause to fly; set flying; run from. -*n*. a flying; one-horse vehicle for hire; flap on a garment or tent; speed regulator in a machine. -**fly'-wheel** *n.* heavy wheel regulating a machine. -**fly'ing-boat** *n.* airplane fitted with floats instead of landing wheels. [OE. *fleogan*]

foal *n.* young of the horse, ass, or other equine animal. -*v.t.* bear (a foal). -*v.i.* bear a foal. [OE. *fola*]

foam *n.* collection of small bubbles in a liquid; froth; froth of saliva or perspiration. -*v.i.* give out, or form into, foam. -**foam'y** *a.* [OE. *fam*]

fo'cus *n.* point at which rays meet after being reflected or refracted; point of convergence; principal seat or centre. -*v.t.* bring to a focus. -*v.i.* come to a focus. -**fo'cal** *a.* [L. = *hearth*]

fodd'er *n.* dried food for horses, cattle, *etc.* -*v.t.* feed with fodder. [OE. *fodor*]

foe *n.* enemy. [OE. *fah*]

fog *n.* thick mist; unusually dark atmosphere. -*v.t.* cover in fog; puzzle. -**fogg'y** *a.* -**fog'horn** *n.* instrument to warn ships in fog. [orig. uncertain]

foil *n.* small arc or space in the tracery of a window; thin layer; metal in a thin sheet; leaf of metal set under a gem; anything which sets off another thing to advantage; light blunt sword for fencing. [L. *folium*, leaf]

foil *v.t.* baffle, defeat; frustrate. [F. *fouler*, trample]

fold *v.t.* double up; bend part of; clasp (in the arms); interlace (the arms); wrap up. -*v.i.* become folded; be or admit of being folded. -*n.* a folding; space between two thicknesses; coil; winding; line, made by folding, a crease. -**fold'er** *n.* [OE. *fealdan*]

fo'liage *n.* leaves collectively. [F. *feuillage*, fr. *feuille*, (L. *fola*), leaf]

fo'lio *n.* piece of paper numbered only on the front; two pages, or a page, with the opposite side of an account in a ledger; number of words as a unit of length; sheet of printing paper folded once into two leaves or four pages; book of such sheets. **in folio**, made of folios. *a.* made thus. [L. *folirim*, leaf]

folk (fōk) *n.* race of people; people in general. -**folk'-song** *n.* music originating among a people. -**folk'-lore** *n.* traditions, beliefs popularly held; study of these. -**folk'-dance** *n.* traditional dance among the people. [OE. *foic*]

foll'icle *n.* small sac; gland. -**follic'ular** *a.* [L. *folliculus*, dim. *offollis*, bag]

foll'ow *v.t.* go or come after; keep to (a path, *etc.*); accompany, attend on; take as a guide, conform to; engage in; be consequent on; grasp the meaning of. -*v.i.* go or come after; come next; result. -**foll'ower** *n.* -**foll'ow through** *n-* in ball games continuation of stroke after ball is struck. -**foll'ow up** *n.* deepening of impression, pursuing of advantage gained. [OE. *folgian*]

fond *a.* tender, loving; credulous; foolish. -**fond of**, having love or liking for. -**fon'dle** *v.t.* caress. [ME. *fonnen*, be foolish]

font *n.* bowl for baptismal water. [L. *fons, font-*, fountain]

fontanelle' *n.* gap between parietal bones of young child, animal. [F.]

food ('-ŏŏ-) *n.* that which is eaten or meant to be; nourishment. [OE. *foda*]

fool (-ŏŏ-) *n.* silly or empty-headed person; simpleton; jester, clown; dupe. -*v.i.* act as a fool. -*v.t.* delude; dupe; make a fool of, mock. *a.* foolish. -**fool'ish** *a.* -**fool'ishly** *adv.* -**fool'ery** *n.* -**fool'hardy** *a.* foolishly venturesome. -**foolhard'iness** *n.* -**foolproof** *a.* able to withstand careless or inexpert handling. [F. *fol (fou)*]

foot (-oo-) *n.* lowest part of the leg, from the ankle down; lowest part of anything, base, stand; end of a bed, *etc.*; infantry: measure of length of twelve inches; division of a verse. -*v.t.* set foot to; put a foot on (a stocking, *etc.*). -*v.i.* step, tread, dance. -**foot'ing** *n.* firm standing; relations, conditions. -**foot'lights** *n. pl.* row of lights at outer edge of stage. -**foot'man** *n.* liveried servant. -**foot'note** *n.* note at foot of page. [OE. *fot*]

for *prep.* because of, instead of; toward; on account of, , to prevent or heal; in favor of, respecting; during, in search of, in payment of; in the character of. -*conj.* because. [OE.]

for'age *n.* food for cattle and horses, *esp.* of an army. -*v.i.* collect forage, make a roving search. -**for'age cap** *n.* undress cap in army. [F. *fourrage*]

for'ay *n.* raid. -*v.i.* make a raid. [OF. *forreor*, forager]

forbid' *v.t.* order not to; refuse to allow. -**forbidden** *ptp.* prohibited, unlawful. -**forbidd'ing** *a.* uninviting. [OE. *forbeodan*]

force *n.* strength, power; body of troops; body of police; compulsion; mental or moral strength; measurable influence inclining a body to motion. -*v.t.* constrain, compel; break open; urge, strain; drive; produce by effort; hasten the maturity of. -**for'cible** *a.* -**for'cibly** *adv.* -**force'ful** *a.* [F.]

ford *n.* place where a river may be crossed by wading. -**ford'able** *a.* [OE.]

fore- *prefix* meaning previous, before, front. [OE.]

fore *a.* in front. *-n.* front part. **-fore-and-aft** *a.* placed in the line from bow to stern of a ship. **-fore'arm** *n.* arm from wrist to elbow. **-forearm'** *v.t.* arm beforehand. - **fore'bear, for'bear** *n.* ancestor. - **forebode'** *v.t.* betoken. **foreboding** *n.* presentiment. **-forecast'** *v.t.* estimate beforehand, prophesy. **-forecast** *n.* conjecture, guess at a future event. **-fore'head** (for'hed) *n.* part of the face above the eyebrows and between the temples. **-fore'man** *n.* one in charge of work; leader of a jury. **-fore'runner** *n.* one who goes before, a precursor. **-forsee'** *v.t.* see beforehand. **-foreshad'ow** *v.t.* figure beforehand, be a type of. **-fore'sight** *n.* foreseeing; care for the future; front sight of a gun. **-forestall'** *v.t.* be beforehand with. **-fore-tell'** *v.t.* prophesy. **-forewarn'** *v.t.* warn beforehand. **-fore'word** *n.* preface. [*fore-*]

foreclose' *v.t.* take away the power of redeeming (a mortgage); shut out, bar. - **foreclo'sure** *n.* [F. *forclore*]

forego'ing *a.* preceding. **-foregone'** *a.* inevitable; predetermined, as in foregone conclusion. [*go*]

foren'sic *a.* of courts of law. [L. *forensis*, fr. *forum*, market-place]

foren'sics *n.* study and practice of debate and formal argument.

for'est *n.* large wood; the trees in it; tract of land mainly occupied by trees; region kept waste for hunting. **-for'ester** *n.* one who lives in a forest or is employed in charge of one. **-for'estry** *n.* management of forests. [Med. L. *forestis*, unfenced]

forev'er *adv.* constantly; eternally. [*for* and *ever*]

for'feit (-fit) *n.* thing lost by crime or fault; penalty, fine. *-pl.* game. *a.* lost by crime or fault. *-v.t.* lose, have to pay or give up. **-for'feiture** *n.* [F. *forfait*, crime, wrong]

forge *v.t.* shape (metal) by heating in a fire and hammering; invent; make in fraudulent imitation of a thing, to counterfeit. *-n.* smithy; gmith's hearth; workshop for melting or refining metal **for'ger** *n.* **-for'gery** *n.* forged document; the making of it. [F. *forger*, fr. L. *fabricate*]

forget' *v.t.* lose memory of, not to remember. [OE. *forgietan*]

forgive' (giv) *v.t.* pardon, remit. - **forgive'ness** *n.* [OE. *forgiefan*]

fork *n.* pronged farm tool for digging or lifting; pronged instrument for holding food in eating or cooking; division into

branches; point of this division; one of the branches. *-v.i.* branch. *-v.t.* make forkshaped; dig, lift, or throw with a fork. **forked** *a.* [L. *urca*]

form *n.* shape, visible appearance; visible person or animal; structure; nature; species, kind; class in a school; customary way of doing a thing; set order of words; regularly drawn up document, *esp.* a printed one with blanks for particulars; behavior according to rule; condition, good condition; long seat without a back, a bench; hare's nest; frame for type (more often *forme*). *-v.t.* put into shape, mold, arrange, organize; train; shape in the mind, conceive; go to make up, make part of. *-v.i.* come into existence or shape. **-for'mal** *a.* ceremonial, according to rule; explicit; of outward form or routine; according to a rule that does not matter; precise; stiff. - **for'mative** *a.* serving or tending to form; used in forming. [L. *forma*, shape]

formal'dehyde *n.* colorless pungent gas used in solution in water or absorbed into porous materials as antiseptic and disinfectant. [L. *formica*, ant]

form'at (-ma) *n.* size and shape of an object. [F.]

for'mer *a.* earlier in time; of past times; first-named. *-pron.* first-named thing or person or fact. **-for'merly** *adv.* [fr. OE. *superl. formest*, foremost]

for'mic *a.* of or derived from ants. - **for'mic a'cid**, acid originally got from ants. **-for'micant** *a.* with ant-like motion. **-for'micary** *n.* anthill. **-formi-ca'tion** *n.* feeling as of ants crawling on one's skin. [L. *formica*, ant]

formid'able *a.* to be feared; likely to cause difficulty serious. **-for'midably** *adv.* [L. *formido:r*, dread]

for'mula (-a-) *n.* set form of words setting forth a principle, or prescribed for an occasion; recipe; in science, a rule or fact expressed in symbols and figures. - **for'mulary** *n.* collection of formulas. - **for'mulate** *v.t.* express in a formula, or systematically. **-formula'tion** *n.* **-for'-mulator** *n.* -*pl.* **form'ulae, form'ulas.** [L. , *dim.* of *forma*, form]

fornica'tion *n.* sexual intercourse between man and woman. **-for'nicate** *v.i.* [L. *fornix*, brothel]

fort *n.* fortified place. [L. *fortis*, strong]

forte *n.* one's strong point. [F. *fort*, upper half of sword-blade]

forth (-th) *adv.* onwards, into view; onwards in time. **-forthcom'ing** *a.* about to come; ready when wanted. **-forth'right** *n.* straightforward; straightway. **-forthwith'**

adv. at once, immediately. [OE.]

FORT'RAN n. high-level computer programming language for mathematical and scientific purposes. [fr. *formula trans-lation*]

forthright a. candid, straightforward, blunt. [*forth* and *right*]

for'tify v.t. strengthen; provide with defensive works. -**fortifica'tion** n. [L. *fortis*, strong]

fortitude n. courage in adversity or pain. [L. *fortitude*, fr. *fortis*, strong]

fort'ress n. fortified place, military strong-hold. [F. *forteresse*]

for'tune n. chance; luck, good luck, prosperity; wealth, stock of wealth. -**for'tunate** a. lucky, favorable. -**for'tunately** adv. -**for'tune-teller** n. one who predicts a person's future, usually for money. [L. *fortune*]

for'ward a. lying in front of one, onward; prompt; precocious; pert. -n. in football, a player in the first line. -adv. towards the future; towards the front; to the front, into view; at or in the fore part of a ship; onward, so as to make progress. -v.t. help forward; send, dispatch. -**for'wards** adv. forward. -**for'wardly** adv. pertly. forwardness n. [OE. *foreweard*]

foss'il a. petrified in the earth and recognizable as the remains of animals or plants, esp. prehistoric ones; (of persons) antiquated. -n. fossilized thing. -**foss'ilize** v.t. and i. turn into a fossil. [L. *fossilis*, fr. *fodere, foss-*, to dig]

foster v.t. encourage; be favorable to; formerly, to tend, cherish. -**fos'terbrother** n. one related by upbringing not by blood. [OE. *fostor*, feeding, food]

foul a. loathsome, offensive; dirty; charged with harmful matter; clogged, choked; unfair; wet, rough; obscene, disgustingly abusive. -n. collision; (in games) act of unfair play. -adv. unfairly. -v.i. become foul. -v.t. make foul; jam; collide with. -**foul'ly** adv. [OE. *ful*]

found v.t. establish, institute; lay the base of; base, ground. -**founda'tion** n. a founding; base, lowest part of a building; endowed institution. -**found'er** n. -**Founding Fathers** n. pl. American leaders who were members of the American Constitutional Convention of 1787. [F. *fonder*, fr. L. *fundus*, bottom]

found v.t. (of metals), melt and run into a mold. -**found'er** n. -**found'ry** n. workshop for founding. [F. *fondre*, fr. L. *fundare*, pour]

found'er v.i. of a horse, to fall lame, collapse. -vt. cause to do this. [F. *effondrer*, knock out the bottom] **found'er** v.i. of a ship, to sink. [OF. *enfondrir*, engulf]

fount'ain (-in) n. spring; source; jet of water, esp. an ornamental one. [F. *fontaine*, fr. L. *fons, fontis*, spring]

four (fōr) n. and a. cardinal number next after three. -**fourth** a. ordinal number. -**fourth'ly** adv. -**Fourth of July** n. U.S. public holiday celebrating the Declaration of Independence; Independence Day. -**four'teen'** n. and a. four and ten. -**four-post'er** (-ō-) n. bed with four posts for curtains, etc. -**four'some** n. (*golf*) game for four players, two against two. **four-star** a. of the highest military rank; highest quality. **fourth class** a. lowest rate and method of parcel post mailing. [OE. *feower*]

fowl n. domestic cock or hen; bird. -v.i. hunt wild birds. -**fowl'er** n. -**fowl'ing-piece** n. light gun. [OE. *fugol*]

fox n. red bushy-tailed animal, in many places preserved for hunting; cunning person. -v.t. discolor (paper) with brown spots. -v.i. act craftily; sham. -**fox-hole** n. (*sl.*) orig. in World War II small trench for one or two giving protection against snipers or divebombers. -**fox'trot** n. dance. [OE.]

frac'tion n. numerical quantity not an integer; fragment, piece, small part. -**frac'tional** a. [*fracture*]

frac'ture n. breakage. -v.t. and i. break. [L. *frangere, fract-*, break]

frag'ile (-j-) a. breakable. -**fragility** n. [L. *fragilis*, fr. *frangere*, break]

frag'ment n. piece broken off, small portion; incomplete part. -**frag'mentary** a. [L. *fragmentum*]

fra'grant (-ag-) a. sweet-smelling. [L. *fragrans, fragrant-* fr. *fragrare*, smell]

frail a. easily broken, delicate; morally weak, unchaste. -**frail'ty** n. -**frail'ly** adv. [F. *fraiel*, fr. L. *fragilis*]

frail n. rush basket. [F. *fraiel*]

frame v.t. put together, make; adapt; put into words; put into a frame; trump-up a charge against. -n. that in which a thing is set or inserted, as a square of wood round a picture, etc.; structure; constitution; mood. -**frame'-up** n. plot, manufactured evidence. -**frame'work** n. light wooden or other structure; structure into which completing parts can be fitted. [OE. *ramian*, avail]

fran'chise n. person or company granted a license to operate a store, hotel, etc., using the name of the parent company, but

operating in an independent manner.
franchisee *n.* person or company granted a franchise. -**franchise** *n.* right of voting; citizenship. [F. = *freedom*]

frank *a.* candid, outspoken, sincere. -*n.* signature on a letter of a person entitled to send it free of postage charges; letter with this. -*v.t.* mark a letter thus. [F. *franc*, Frank, conqueror, 'free man.' (conquest of Gaul)]

fraternal *a.* of a brother; brotherly. -**frater′nally** *adv.* -**frater′nity** *n.* brotherliness; a brotherhood; club of male students *usu.* living in the same house. -**frat′ernize** *v.i.* associate, make friends. -**frat′ricide** *n.* killing of a brother or sister; the killer. -**frat′ricidal** *a.* [L. *frater*, brother]

fraud *n.* criminal deception; dishonest trick-**fraud′ulence** *n.* -**fraud′ulent** *a.* [L. *fraus, fraud*-]

fray *v.t.* and *i.* wear through by rubbing, make or become ragged at the edge. [F. *frover*, fr. L. *fricare*, rub] -**fray** *n.* fight. [for *affray*]

free *a.* having liberty; not in bondage; not restricted or impeded; released from strict law, literality, tax, obligation, *etc.* ; disengaged; spontaneous; liberal; frank; familiar. -*v.t.* set at liberty, disengage. -**free fall** *n.* unchecked motion of a body in flight. -**free′ly** *adv.* -**free′lance** *n.* medieval mercenary; unattached journalist, artist, *etc.* ; politician independent of party. -**free′load** *v.i.* live off money and gifts provided by others without giving anything in return. -**free market** *n.* market in which prices are not government-regulated but are based on supply and demand. -**free′-will** *n.* spontaneity; freedom of choice. *a.* unrestrained, voluntary. [OE. *freo*, not in bondage]

freeze *v.i.* become ice; become rigid with cold; feel very cold. -*v.t.* turn solid by cold; chill; affect with frost. -*v.t.* and *i.* stop *esp.* if then held in a static position. -**freez′ing-point** *n.* temperature at which water becomes solid. [OE. *freosan*]

freight *n.* hire of a ship; cargo; a load which is being transported; charge for the conveyance of goods. -*v.t.* hire or load (a ship). -**freighter** *n.* -**freight′age** *n.* [earlier *fraught, q. v.*]

fren′zy *n.* fury, delirious excitement. -**fren′zied** *a.* [F. *frénésie*]

fre′quent *a.* happening often; common, habitual; numerous. [L. *frequens*]

fres′co *n.* method of painting in water color on the plaster of a wall before it dries; painting done thus. -*v.t.* -**fres′coed** *a.* . [It.]

fresh a. new; additional; different; recent;

inexperienced; pure; not pickled, salted, *etc.*; not stale; not faded or dimmed; not tired; of wind, strong. -**fresh′ly** *adv.* -**fresh′ness** *n.* -**fresh′en** *v.t.* and *i.* -**fresh′et** *n.* rush of water at a river mouth; flood of river water. -**fresh′man** *n.* member of a college in his first year. [OE. *fersc*, not salt]

fret *n.* pattern of straight lines intersecting; bar to aid the fingering of a stringed instrument. -*v.t.* ornament with carved pattern. -**fret** *v.t.* and *i.* chafe, worry. -*n.* irritation. -**fret′ful** *a.* irritable, easily vexed. [OE. *fretan*, gnaw]

fri′ar *n.* member of a mendicant religious order. -**fri′ary** *n.* convent of friars. [F. *frère*, brother]

fric′tion *n.* rubbing; resistance met with by a body moving over another; unpleasantness, ill-feeling. -**fric′tional** *a.* [L. *fricare, frict*-, rub]

Fri′day *n.* sixth day of the week. -**Good Friday**, Friday before Easter. [OE. *frigedæg*, day of *Freyja*, Norse goddess of love]

friend (frend) *n.* one attached to another by affection and esteem; intimate associate; supporter; Quaker. [OE. *freond*]

frieze *n.* band of decoration on wall of building. [F. *frise*]

fright *n.* sudden fear, grotesque person or thing. -*v.t.* terrify. -**fright′en** *v.t.* terrify. -**fright′ful** *a.* -**fright′ful-ness** *n.* [OE. *fyrhto*]

fri′gid (ii-) *a.* cold; formal; dull. -**fri′gidly** *adv.* -**fridid′ity** *n.* [L. *frigidus*]

frisk *v.i.* frolic. -*n.* frolic. -**frisk′y** *a.* -**frisk′ily** *adv.* [OF. *frisque*, lively]

frivolous *a.* silly, trifling; given to trifling. -**frivol′ity** *n.* [L. *frivolus*]

frock *n.* woman's dress; monk's gown. -*v.t.* invest with the office of priest. -**frock coat** *n.* man's long coat not cut away in front. [F. *froc*]

frog *n.* tailless amphibious animal developed from a tadpole. [OE. *frogga*]

from *prep.* expressing departure, moving away, source, distance, cause, change of state, *etc.* [OE. *from*]

frond *n.* plant organ consisting of stem and foliage, usually with fruit forms, *esp.* in ferns. [L. *frons, frond*-, leaf]

front (-unt) *n.* fore part: forehead. -*v.i.* look, face. -*v.t.* face; oppose. *a.* of or at the front. [L. *frons, front*-, forehead]

front′ier *n.* part of a country which borders on another. [F. *frontiers*]

frost *n.* act or state of freezing; weather in which the temperature falls below the point at which water turns to ice; frozen dew or mist. -v.t. injure by frost; cover with rime; powder with sugar, etc. ; give a slightly roughened surface; turn (hair) white. -frost'y a. -frost'ily adv. -frost'.- bite n. inflammation of the skin due to cold. [OE.]

frown v.i. knit the brows, esp. in anger or deep thought. -n. a knitting of the brows. [OF. froignier]

fru'gal a. sparing, economical, esp. in use of food. -fru'gally adv. -frugal'ity n. [L. frugalis, fr. frux, frug-, fruit]

fruit (frōōt) n. seed and its envelope, esp. an eatable one; vegetable products (usu. in pl.); produce; result, benefit. -v.i. bear fruit. -fruit'ful a. -fruit'less a. - frui'tion n. enjoyment; realization of hopes. -fruit'y a. [L. fructus, fr. frui, fruct-, enjoy]

frustrate' v.t. baffle, disappoint. frustra- tion n. [L. frustrari]

fry n. young fishes. -small fry young or insignificant beings. [F. frai]

fry v.t. cook with fat in a shallow pan. in- ternal parts of animals usually eaten ied. -fry'ing pan n. [F. frire]

fuel (ffi-) n. material for burning. -v.t. rovide fuel for; take in fuel; provide a ource of energy for. [ME. fewel, fr. L. cus, hearth]

fu'gitive (fa-) a. that runs, or has run, ay; fleeting, transient. -n. one who flees; exile, refugee. [L. fugitivus, fr. fugere, fugit-, flee]

fulcrum n. (ful'cra pl.) point on which lever is placed for support. [L.]

fulfill' (fool-) v.t. satisfy; carry out; obey; satisfy the requirements of. -fulfill'ment n. [OE. fullfyllan]

full (fool) a. holding all it can; containing abundance; ample; complete; plump. -adv. very; quite; exactly. -full'y adv. -ful'ness, full'ness n. -full-blown a. of flowers, completely open. [OE.]

fulminate v.i. explode. -v.t. and i. thunder out (blame, etc.). -n. chemical compound exploding readily. -fulmina'tion n. [L. ful- men, thunderbolt]

fum'ble v.i. and t. handle awkwardly, grope about.[lorig, uncertain]

fume n. smoke; vapor; exhalation. -v.i. emit fumes: give way to anger, chafe. [L. lumare, smoke]

fun n. sport, amusement, jest, diversion. -v.i. joke. -funn'y a. [ME, fonnen, be foolish]

func'tion n. work a thing is designed to do; official duty; profession; public occasion or ceremony. -v.i. operate, work. - func'tional a. -func'tionary n. official. [L. functio]

fund n. permanent stock; stock or sum of money. -pl. money resources. -v.t. convert (debt) into permanent form; in- vest money permanently. -fund'ament n. buttocks. -fundament'al a. essen- tial, primary; of, affecting, or serving as, the base. -n. one laying stress on belief in literal and verbal inspiration of the Bible or other traditional creeds. -fundament'alism n. [L. fundus, bot- tom]

fu'neral a. of, or relating to, the burial of the dead. -n. ceremonies at a burial. - fune'real a. fit for a funeral, dismal. [L. funus, funer-, burial]

fun'gus (-ng-g-) n. mushroom or allied plant; spongy morbid growth. -fun'gous a. -fun'gicide n. substance used to destroy fungus. [L.]

funn'el n. cone-shaped vessel or tube; chimney of locomotive or ship; ventilating shaft. [L. fundere, pour]

fur n. short soft hair of certain animals; lining or trimming or garment of dressed skins with such hair; crust or coating resembling this. -v.t. provide with fur. - furr'ier n. one who deals in furs. -furr'y a. [F. v. fourrer, fr. OF. fourre, sheath, cover]

furl v.t. roll up and bind (a sail, an umbrel- la. etc.). [F. ferier]

fur'nace n. apparatus for applying great heat to metals; hot place; closed fireplace for heating a boiler, etc. [F. fournaise]

fur'nish v.t. supply, fit up with; fit up a house with furniture: yield. -fur'niture n. movable contents of a house or room. [F. fournir]

furor' n. burst of enthusiastic popular ad- miration. [It.]

furr'ow n. trench made bv a plow ship's track; rut, groove. -v.t. make furrows in. [OE. furh]

fur'ther (-TH-) adv. more; in addition; at or to a greater extent. a. additional; -v.t. help forward. [OE. furtha a.; furthor adv.]

fu'ry n. wild anger, rage; fierce passion; violence of storm, etc. ; snakehaired avenging deity (usu. pl.). -fu'rious a. - fu'riously adv. [L. furia]

fuse n. tube containing material for setting light to a bomb, firework, etc.; device used as a safety measure which interrupts an electric circuit. [L. fusus, spindle]

fuse v.t. and i. melt with heat; blend by melting. -fu'sible a. -fu'sion n. [L. fundere, fus-, pour]

fu'selage n. spindle-shaped body of an airplane. [L. fusus, spindle]

fuss *n*. needless bustle or concern. -*v.i* make a fuss. -*v.t.* hustle. [orig. uncertain]

fu'tile *a*. useless, ineffectual, frivolous. -**futil'ity** *n*. [L. *futilis*, leaky]

fu'ture *a*. that will be; of, or relating to, time to come. -*n*. time to come; what will happen; tense of a verb indicating this. -**fu'rity** *n*. -**fu'turism** *n*. movement in art marked by complete abandonment of tradition. -**fu'turist** *n*. and *a*. [L. *futurus*, about to be]

fuzz n. fluff. -**fuzz'y** *a*. -**fuzz box** *n*. an electronic device that breaks up the sound passing through it, used *esp*. by guitarists. [imit. of blowing away light particles]

G

gab *n*. talk, chatter; gift of the gab, eloquence. -**gab'ble** *v.i.* and *t*. talk, utter inarticulately or too fast. -*n*. such talk. [imit. orig.]

ga'ble *n*. triangular upper part of the wall at the end of a ridged roof. [OF.]

gad *v.i.* go about idly. -**gad'about** *n*. gadding person. [fr. obs. *gadling*-OE. g, ædeling, comrade]

gadg'et *n*. small fitting or contrivance. [orig. uncertain]

gaff *n*. barbed fishing spear; stick with an iron hook for landing fish; spar for the top of a fore-and-aft sail. -*v.t.* seize (a fish) with a gaff. [F. *gaffe*]

gaffe *n*. tactless or embarrassing blunder. [F.]

gag *n*. thing thrust into the mouth to prevent speech or hold it open for operation; closure in a debate. -*v.t.* apply a gag to; silence. [orig. *v*. strangle; imit. of victim's noises]

gag *n*. words inserted by an actor in his part. -*v.i.* of an actor, to put in words not in his part. [orig. uncertain]

gage *n*. pledge, thing given as security; challenge, or something symbolizing one. -*v.t.* pledge, stake. *See also* **gauge**. [F.]

gal'axy *n*. Milky Way; any other of the stellar universes; brilliant company. **galac'tic** *a*. [G. *gala, galakt-*, milk]

gale *n*. strong wind. [orig. uncertain]

gall'ant *a*. fine, stately, brave; chivalrous; very attentive to women, amatory. *n*. man of fashion; lover, paramour. [F. *galant*]

gall'ery *n*. raised floor over part of the area of a building, *esp*. a church; top floor of seats in a theatre; its occupants; long narrow platform on the outside of a building; passage in a wall, open to the interior of a building; covered walk with side openings, a colonnade; room or rooms for showing works of art; horizontal passage in mining. [F. *galerie*]

gall'ey *n*. one-decked vessel with sails and oars, usually rowed by slaves or criminals; large rowing-boat, *esp*. that used by the captain of a warship; ship's kitchen; printer's tray for set-up type. -**gall'ey-proof** *n*. printer's proof in long slip form. (OF. *galee*)

gall'on *n*. liquid measure of eight pints or four quarts. [ONF. *galon*]

gall'op *v.i.* go at a gallop. -*v.t.* cause to move at a gallop. -*n*. horse's, or other quadruped's, fastest pace, with all four feet off the ground together in each stride; ride at this pace. -**gall'oper** *n*. [F. *galoper*]

gall'ows *n*. structure, usually of two upright beams and a cross-bar, *esp*. for hanging criminals on. [OE. *gealga*]

galvanism *n*. electricity produced by chemical action. -**galvan'ic** *a*. -**galvan'ic batt'ery** *n*. -**gal'vanize** *v.t.* apply galvanism to; stimulate thus; rouse by shock; coat with metal by galvanism. -**galvaniza'tion** *n*. -**galvanom'eter** *n*. instrument for measuring galvanism. [Galvani, It. physicist, (d. 1798)]

gam'bit *n*. chess opening involving the sacrifice of a piece. [It. *gambetto*, wrestler's trip, fr. *gamba*, leg]

gam'ble *v.i.* play games of chance for money stakes; speculate wildly; risk much for great gain. -*n*. risky undertaking. -**gam'bler** *n*. [fr. *game n*.]

game *n*. diversion, pastime, jest; contest for amusement; scheme, plan of action; animals or birds hunted; their flesh, *a*. plucky, spirited. -*v.i.* gamble. -**game'ly** *a*. -**game'ster** *n*. gambler. -**game'cock** *n*. fowl bred for fighting. -**game'keeper** *n*. man employed to breed game, prevent poaching, *etc*. -**gam'y** *a*. having the flavor of hung game; spirited. [OE. *gamen*]

gamete' *n*. sexual reproductive cell. [G. *gamos*, marriage]

gamm'a-rays *n*. *pl*. rays given off by radio-active substances, e. g. , radium. [G. letter *gamma*]

gam'ut *n*. whole series of musical notes; scale; compass of a voice. [Med, L. *gamma*, and *ut*, names of notes]

gang *n*. company, band. -**gang'er** *n*. foreman over a gang of workmen. -**gang'way** *n*. bridge from a ship to the shore; anything similar; passage between rows of seats. [OE. = going, way]

gang'lion (-ng-gl-) *n*. knot on a nerve from which nerve fibers spread out; nerve nucleus. [G. *ganglion*] gang'rene *n.* mortification, decomposition of a part of the body. *-v.t.* affect with this. *-v.i.* be affected with this. **-gang'renous** *a.* [L. *gangraena,* G. *gangraina*]

gape *v.i.* open the mouth wide; stare; yawn. *-n.* yawn; wide opening of the mouth. [ON, *gapa*]

gar'age *n.* building to house automobiles. **-gar'age sale** *n.* sale of personal belongings or household effects held at a person's home, usually in the garage. [F. , fr. *garer,* make safe]

garb *n.* dress, fashion of dress. *-v.t.* dress, clothe. [OF. *garbe,* contour]

garb'age (-ij) *n.* offal; refuse; anything worthless; originally, giblets. [orig. uncertain]

gar'den *n.* ground for growing flowers, fruit, or vegetables. *-v. i.* cultivate a garden. **-gar'dener** *n.* **-gar'den ci'ty,** planned town with parks and planted areas. **-gar'dening** *n.* the planning and cultivation of a garden. [ONF. *gardin*]

gar'gle *v.i.* and *i.* wash the throat with liquid kept moving by the breath. *-n.* liquid used for this. [F. *gargouiller*]

gar'lic *n.* plant with a strong smell and taste, used in cooking. [OE. *garleac,* spear leek]

gar'ment *n.* article of dress. *-pl.* clothes. fF. *garniment,* equipment]

gar'nish *v.t.* adorn, decorate (*esp.* food or literary matter). *-n.* material for this. [F. *garnir*]

garr'et *n.* room on the top floor, an attic. [orig. turret, OF. *garite,* refuge]

garr'ulous *a.* talkative. [L. *garrulus -garrire,* chatter]

gas *n.* elastic fluid such as air, *esp.* one not liquid or solid at ordinary temperature; such fluid, *esp.* coal-gas used for heating or lighting; such fluid or a mixture used as poison in warfare, or found as an explosive in mines, or employed as an anesthetic, *etc.*; gasoline. *-v.t.* project gas over; poison with gas.

gas'oline, gas'olene *n.* liquid from petroleum, used as fuel. [gas]

gasp (-a-) *v.i.* catch the breath with open mouth, as in exhaustion or surprise. *-n.* convulsive catching of the breath. [ON, *geispa,* yawn]

gas'tric *a.* of the stomach. **-gastron'omy** *n.* art of good eating. **-gastronom'ical** *a.* **-gastron'omer, gas'tronome** *n.* judge of cooking. **-gas'teropod** *n.* mollusk, *e. g.* a snail, with organ of locomotion placed ventrally. [G. gaster, belly]

gate *n.* opening in a wall which may be closed by a barrier; barrier for closing it; device for regulating the flow of water; any entrance or way out; entrance-money at, *e.g.* a football-game **-gate'crasher** *n.* one who attends a party, *etc.* without being invited. [OE. *geat*]

gate *n.* (*compute*) electronic circuit which performs logical or mathematical calculations or operations.

gath'er (-TH-) *v.t.* bring together; collect; draw together, pucker; deduce. *-v.i.* come together; collect; form a swelling full of pus. **-gathers** *n. pl.* puckered part of a dress. [OE. *gadrian*]

gaud (gawd) *n.* showy ornament. **-gaud'y** *a.* showy without taste. [orig. uncertain]

gauge, gage *n.* standard measure, as of diameter of wire, *etc.* ; distance between rails of a railway; capacity, extent; instruments for measuring such things as size of wire, rainfall, height of water in a boiler, *etc. -v.t.* measure, test, estimate. [ONF.]

gaunt (gaw-) *a.* lean, haggard, starved-looking. [orig. uncertain]

gav'el *n.* a mallet; chairman's or auctioneer's hammer. [orig. unknown]

gay *a.* light-hearted; showy; dissolute; homosexual. **-gai'ly** *adv.* **-gai'ety** *n.* [F. *gai*]

gaze *v.i.* look fixedly. *-n.* long intent look. [orig. uncertain]

gear *n.* apparatus, tackle, tools; set of wheels working together, *esp.* by engaging cogs; rigging; harness; equipment; clothing; goods, utensils. *-v.t.* provide with gear; put in gear. **-gear'-box, -case** *n.* box, case protecting gearing of bicycle, car. **-gear'-wheel** *n.* wheel with cogs *etc.* for transmitting motion in cycle. [ME. *gere,* fr. ON.]

Gei'ger counter *n.* instrument for measuring density of radio-active field. [Geiger, German physicist]

gelatin gel'atine *n.* transparent substance made by stewing skin, tendons, *etc.* [It. *gelatins,* fr. *gelata,* jelly]

gem *n.* precious stone; thing of great beauty or worth. *-v.t.* adorn with gems. [L. *gemma,* bud, gem]

gem'ini (jem'-i-ni) *n.* constellation containing Castor and Pollux; third sign of the zodiac (the twins) which sun enters c. May 21st. [L. *pl.* of *geminus,* twin]

gen'der *n.* sex, male or female; classification of nouns, corresponding roughly to sexes and sexlessness (in English). [F, *genre,* fr. L. *genus,* gener-, kind]

gene (jen) *n.* one of the biological factors determining heredity. [G. *genos,* race]

gen'eral *a.* not particular or partial; including or affecting or applicable to all or most; not restricted to one department; usual, prevalent; miscellaneous; dealing with main elements only. -*n.* officer in the armed forces of rank above lieutenant general. **-general'ity** *n.* **-gen'eral ize** *v.t.* reduce to general laws. *-v.i.* draw general conclusions. **-generaliza'tion** *n.* **gen'erally** *adv.* [L. *generalis,* fr. *genus,* gener-, kind]

gen'erate *v.t.* bring into being; produce. **-genera'tion** *n.* bringing into being; step in a pedigree; all persons born about the same time; average time in which children are ready to replace their parents (about 30 years). **-gen'erative** *a.* **-gen'erator** *n.* a begetter; apparatus for producing (steam, *etc.*). [L. *generare,* procreate]

generic *a.* belonging to, characteristic of, a class or genus. **-gener'ically** *adv.* [L. *genus, gener-,* race]

gen'erous *a.* noble-minded; liberal, free in giving; copious; of wine, rich. **gen'erously** *adv.* **-generos'ity** *n.* [L. *generosus,* of noble birth]

gen'esis *n.* origin; mode of formation. **-Genesis** *n.* first book of the Old Testament. [G.]

genetics *n.* science dealing with heredity, variation, reproduction. **-genet'ic** *a.* [G. *genesis*]

ge'nial *a.* kindly, jovial; sympathetic; mild, conducive to growth. [L. *genialis*]

gen'ital *a.* of generation. *-n. pl.* external generative organs. [L. *gignere,* genit-, beget]

ge'nius *n.* with high power of mind; person with this; tutelary spirit; prevalent feeling, taste; character, spirit. [L. = a spirit watching over a person from birth, fr. *gignere,* gen-, beget]

genre' (zhong'r) *n.* kind, variety; style of painting homely scenes. [F.]

gen'tile *a.* of race other than Jewish; *-n.* gentile person. [L. *gens, gent-,* race, translating G. *ta ethne,* the nations]

gen'tle *a.* mild, quiet, not rough or severe; courteous; noble; well-born. **-gentil'ity** *n.* social superiority. **-gen'tleman** *n.* chivalrous well-bred man; man of good social position; man of noble birth; man (used as a mark of politeness). **-gent'ry** *n.* people next below the nobility. [F. *gentil*]

gen'uine *a.* real, true, not sham, properly so called. [L. *genuinus,* native]

ge'nus *n.* race, tribe, kind, class. [L.]

geode' *n.* rock cavity lined with crystals; stone containing this. [G. *geodes,* earth]

geography *n.* science of the earth's form,

physical features, climate, population, *etc.*; book on this. **-geog'rapher** *n.* **-geograph'ical** *a.* **-geograph'ically** *adv.* [G. *ge,* earth, *graphein,* write]

geol'ogy *n.* science of the earth's crust, the rocks, their strata, *etc.* **-geol'ogist** *n.* **geolog'ical** *a.* **-geolog'ically** *adv.* **geol'ogize** *v.i.* practice geology. [G. *ge,* earth, *logia,* discourse]

geom'etry *n.* science of the properties and relations of magnitudes in space, as lines, surfaces, *etc.* [G. *ge,* earth, *metron,* measure]

germ *n.* rudiment of a new organism, of an animal or plant; microbe; elementary thing. **-germ'icide** *n.* substance for destroying disease-germs. **-germici'dal** *a.* **-germ'inate** *v.i.* sprout. *-v.t.* cause to sprout. **-germina'tion** *n.* **germ warfare** *n.* warring method in which the weapons are germs released to produce disease among the enemy. [L. *gerrnen,* seed]

germane' *a.* relevant, belonging to a subject. [L. *germanus, v. s.*]

gestation *n.* carrying of young in the womb between conception and birth; period of gestation. [L. *gestatio*]

gesticulate *v.i.* use expressive or lively movements accompanying, or instead of, speech. **-gesticula'tion** *n.* [L. *gestus,* action]

ges'ture *n.* movement to convey some meaning. [Low L. *gestura*]

get (g-) *v.t.* obtain, procure, earn; cause to go or come; bring into a position or state; induce; (in *perf. tense*) be in possession of, have (to do). *-v.i.* reach, attain; become. **get'-away** *n.* escape. [ON. *geta*]

ghett'o *n.* part of a city where members of a particular national or racial group predominate, or are restricted. [it.]

ghost *n.* spirit, dead person appearing again, specter; semblance. **ghost'ly** *a.* [OE. *gast,* spirit]

gi'ant *n.* human being of superhuman size; very tall person, plant, *etc.* *-a.* huge. **gigant'ic** *a.* enormous, huge [F. *goant,* fr. L. *gigas, gigant*]

gift (g-) thing given, present; faculty, power. *-v.t.* endow or present (with). **gift'ed** *a.* talented. [give]

gift wrap *v.t.* to wrap a present in decorative paper and trimmings. **- gift wrap** *n.* **gift wrapping** *n.* **gift wrapper** *n.*

gigabit *n.* (*comp. sci.*) unit of information equal to one billion bits or binary digits

gig'ahertz *n. pl.* **gigahertz** unit of frequency equal to one billion hertz; formerly **gigacycle.** [abbr. *GHz*]

gig'gle (g-) *v.i.* laugh in a half-suppressed way, foolishly or uncontrollably. -*n.* such a laugh. [limit. orig.]

GIGO (*compu. sci.*) term used to stress the fact the computer results are dependant upon the quality of the computer input. [*G*arbage *I*n/*G*arbage *O*ut]

gild (g-) *v.t.* put a thin layer of gold on. **gilt** *a.* **gilded**-*n.* layer of gold put on. [OE. *gyldan*, fr. gold]

gill (g-) *n.* breathing organ in fishes; flesh below a person's jaws and ears. [orig, unknown. cp, Sw. *gill*, Dan. *giaelle*]

gin *n.* snare, trap; kind of crane; machine for separating cotton from seeds. -*v.t.* snare; treat (cotton) in a gin. [F. *engin*, L. *ingenium*, skill]

gin *n.* spirit flavored with juniper. [short for *geneva*, F. *genievre*, fr. L. *juniperus*, juniper]

gin'ger *n.* plant with a hot-tasting spicy root used in cooking, *etc.* ; the root; spirit, mettle; light reddish yellow color. [Late L. *gingiber*, of Eastern orig.]

gin'gerly *a.* such as to avoid noise or injury; cautious. -*adv.* in a gingerly manner. [orig. uncertain]

giraffe' *n.* African ruminant animal, with spotted coat and very long neck and legs. [F. *girafe*, fr. Arab.]

girl female child; young unmarried woman; woman. [ME. *gurie*; of unknown orig.]

girth (g-) *n.* band put round a horse to hold the saddle, *etc.* ; measurement round a thing. -*v.t.* surround, secure, with a girth. [ON. *gjdrth*]

give (g-) *v.t.* bestow, confer ownership of, make a present of, deliver, impart; assign; yield, supply; make over, cause to have. *v.i.* yield, give way. -*n.* yielding, elasticity. (gave *p. t.* -given *p.p.*)-**giv'er** *n.* [OE. *giefan*]

gla'cier *n.* river of ice, a slow-moving mass of ice formed by accumulated snow in mountain valleys. -**gla'cia** (-shal) *a.* of ice, or of glaciers; crystallized. -**glacia'tion** *n.* -**gla'cis** (-se) *n* outer sloping bank of a fortification. [F. , fr. *glace*, ice]

glad *a.* pleased; happy, joyous; giving joy. -*v.t.* make glad. [OE. *glæd*]

glam'or *n.* magic, enchantment. -**glam'orous** *a.* -**glamorize** *n.* make seem glamorous, *esp.* deceptively. [corrupt. of grammar, gramarye, magic]

glance *v.i.* glide off something struck; pass quickly; allude, touch; look rapidly. *v.t.* direct (the eyes) rapidly. -*n.* brief look; flash; sudden oblique movement or blow.

[F. *glacer*, (formerly) slide]

gland *n.* organ separating constituents of the blood, for use or ejection. -**gland'ular** *a.* [L. *glans*, gland-, acorn]

glare *v.t.* shine with oppressive brightness; look fiercely. -*n.* dazzling brightness; fierce look. [ME. *glareni*]

glass (-i-) *n.* hard transparent substance made by fusing sand with; a potash, *etc.* ; things made of it collectively; glass drinking vessel; contents of this; lens; telescope, barometer, or other instrument. *pl.* spectacles. -**glaze** *v.t.* furnish with glass; cover with glassy substance or glaze. -*v.i.* become glassy. -*n.* transparent coating; substance used to give this; glossy surface. -**gla'zier** *n.* one whose trade is to glaze windows. [OE. *glæs*]

glauco'ma *n.* eye disease. [G.]

gleam *n.* slight or passing beam of light; faint or momentary show. -*v.i.* give out gleams. [OE. *glaees*]

glean *v.t.* and *i.* gather, pick up, after reapers in a cornfield; pick up (facts, *etc.*). -**glean'er** *n.* [F. *glaner*]

glide *v.i.* pass smoothly and continuously; go stealthily or gradually; of an airplane, move with engines shut off. -*n.* smooth, silent movement; in music, sounds made in passing from tone to tone. [OE. *glidani*]

glimm'er *v.i.* shine faintly or with flickering. -*n.* such light. [ME. *glimeren*]

glimpse *n.* momentary view; passing flash or appearance. -*v.t.* catch a glimpse of. -*v.i.* glimmer. [gleam]

glis'ten (-is'n) *v.i.* glitter, sparkle, shine. [OE. *glisnian*, shine]

glitt'er *v.i.* shine with bright quivering light, sparkle. -*n.* [ON. *glitra*]

globe *n.* round body, sphere; heavenly sphere, *esp.* the earth; sphere with a map of the earth or the stars; anything of about this shape, as a lampshade, fish-bowl, *etc.* -**glob'al** *a.* -**globe'-trotter** *n.* hasty, sightseeing traveller. -**glob'ule** *n.* small round body; drop. -**glob'ular** *a.* globe-shaped. [L. *globus*, round mass]

gloom *n.* darkness; melancholy, depression. -*v.i.* look sullen, or dark. -*v.t.* make dark or dismal. [cp. *glum*]

glor'y *n.* renown, honorable fame; splendor; heavenly bliss; exalted or prosperous state. -*v.i.* take pride (in). **glor'ify** *v.t.* make glorious, invest with glory. -**glorifica'tion** *n.* -**glor'ious** *a.* **glor'iously** *adv.* [fL. *gloria*]

gloss *n.* surface shine. -*v.t.* put a gloss on. -**gloss'y** *a.* smooth and shining **gloss'iness** *n.* [orig. uncertain]

gloss *n.* marginal interpretation of a word; comment, explanation. *-v.t.* interpret; comment; explain away. **-gloss'ary** *n.* collection of glosses; dictionary or vocabulary of special words. [F. *glose*, fr. G. *glossa*, tongue]

glove (-uv) *n.* covering for the hand. *-v.t.* provide with, or put on, gloves. [OE. *glof*]

glow (-o) *v.i.* give out light and heat without flames; shine; be, or look, very hot, burn with emotion. *-n.* shining heat; feeling of bodily heat; warmth of color; ardor. **-glow'worm** *n.* small luminous insect. [OE. *glowan*]

glu'cose *n.* grape-sugar, dextrose. [G. *glykys*, sweet]

glue (-oo) *n.* hard substance made from horns, hoofs, *etc.* , and used warm as a cement. *-v.t.* fasten with glue. **-glu'ey** *a.* [F. *glu*, bird-lime]

glum *a.* sullen, frowning, dejected. [orig. uncertain] [*gloom*]

glut *v.t.* feed, gratify to the full or to excess; overstock. *-n.* excessive supply. [OF. *gloutir*, swallow]

glutt'on *n.* one who eats too much, a greedy person; one eagerly devouring (books, work, *etc.*). **-glutt'onous** *a.* **glutt'ony** *n.* [F. *glouton*]

glutt'on *n.* carnivorous animal, the wolverine. fglution]

gnarled (narld) *a.* of a tree, knobby, rugged, twisted. [var. of *knurled*]

gnat (n-) *n.* small two-winged fly; mosquito. [OE. gnæt]

gnaw (n-) *v.t.* bite steadily, wear away by biting; corrode. [O. E. *gnagan*]

gnome (n-) *n.* goblin, a fairy living underground. [Mod. L. *gnomus*]

gnos'tic (n-) *a.* of knowledge; having mystical knowledge; pert. to the Gnostics. [G. *gnostikos*]

gnu (nu-) *n.* S. African antelope somewhat like an ox. [*Kaffir nqu*] go *v.i.* move along, make way; be moving; depart; elapse; be kept, put, be able to be put; result; contribute to a result; tend to; become. *-n.* energy, vigor. **-go'er** *n.* **go'gett'er** *n.* pushful, assertive person. [OE. *gan*]

goal *n.* end of a race; object of effort; posts through which the ball or disk is to be driven in football, soccer, hockey *etc.*; act of doing this. [orig. uncertain]

goat *n.* four-footed animal with long hair and horns, and a beard. **-goat'herd** *n.* one who tends goats. **-goat'ee** *n.* beard like a goat's. [OE. *gat*]

god *n.* superhuman being worshipped as having supernatural power; object of worship, idol. **-God** *n.* Supreme Being. **godd'ess** *fem.* **-God'speed,** may God speed (you) and bring (you) success. [OE.]

gold *n.* yellow precious metal; coins of this, wealth; fig. beautiful or precious material or thing; color of gold. *-a.* of like, or having the color of, gold. **-gold'en** *a.* **-gold'smith** *n.* worker in gold. **-gold-standard** *n.* financial arrangement whereby currencies are expressed in fixed terms of gold. [OE.]

golf *n.* game in which a small hard ball is struck with clubs. *-v.i.* play this game. **golf'er** *n.* **-golf course** *n.*, place where golf is played, consisting of tees, greens and fairway. [Du. *kilf*, club]

go'nad *n.* sex gland. [G. *gone*, generation]

gong *n.* metal disk with turned rim which resounds as a bell when struck with a soft mallet; anything used in the same way. [Malay]

gonorrhea *n.* venereal disease. [G. *gonorroia*]

good *a.* right; proper; excellent; virtuous; kind; safe; adequate; sound; valid. *-n.* that which is good; well-being; profit. *-pl.* property, wares. **-good'-breeding** *n.* politeness. **-good-day,** a greeting. **-good fellowship** *n.* sociability, merry company. Good Friday, Friday before Easter commemorating Christ's crucifixion. **-good'-will'** *n.* kindly feeling; heartiness; right of trading as a recognized successor. [OE. *god*]

good-bye' *interj.* farewell. [earlier *godbwye*, for God be with you]

goose *n.* large web-footed bird; its flesh; simpleton; tailor's smoothing iron. **goose'flesh** *n.* bristling state of the skin due to cold or fright [OE. *gosi*]

gore *n.* clotted shed blood. **-gor'y** *a.* **gor'ily** *adv.* [OE. *gor*, blood, filth]

gorge'ous (-jus) *a.* splendid, showy, dazzling. [OF. *gorgias*, swaggering)

gorill'a *n.* anthropoid ape of the largest kind. [orig. unknown]

gos'ling (-z-) *n.* young goose. [dim. of goose]

gos'pel *n.* tidings preached by Jesus; record of his life; any of the four books by the evangelists. [OE. godspel, god spel, good tidings]

goss'ip *n.* idle talk about other persons, esp. regardless of fact; idle talk or writing; one who talks thus; formerly, a familiar friend. *-v.i.* talk gossip. [OE. *godsibb*, God akin, sponsor]

Goth'ic *a.* of Goths; barbarous; in architecture, of the pointed arch style common in Europe 12th-16th cent. ; a printing type. [L. *Gothi*, Goths]

gouge *n*. chisel with a curved cutting edge. -*v.i.* cut with a gouge, hollow (out). [F.]

govern (guv-) *v.t.* rule, direct, guide, control; serve as a precedent for; be followed by (a grammatical case, *etc*.) - **gov'ernment** *n*. rule; control; ruling body of a state; the state. -**gov'ernmental** *a*. [F. *gouverner*, fr. L. *gubernare*, steer]

gown *n*. loose flowing upper garment; woman's frock; official robe, as in a university, *etc*. [OF. *gonne*]

grab *v.t.* grasp suddenly, snatch. -*n*. sudden clutch; greedy proceedings. **grab'bing** *a*. greedy. [orig. uncertain]

grace *n*. charm, attractiveness; easy and refined motion, manners, *etc*. ; ornament, accomplishment; favor; divine favor; short thanksgiving before or after a meal; title of a duke or archbishop. -*v*. *t*. add grace to honor. -**grace'ful** *a*. -**grace'less** *a*. shameless, depraved. -**gra'cious** *a*. indulgent, ben-eficent, condescending. **grace'fully** *adv*. -**gra'ciously** *adv*. [F. *grace*, fr. L. *gratia*, pleasing quality, favor]

grade *n*. step or stage; degree of rank, *etc*. ; class; slope; gradient. -*v.i.* arrange in classes. -**grada'tion** *n*. series of degrees or steps; each of them; arrangement in steps; insensible passing from one shade, *etc*. , to another. -**grade school** *n*. elementary school. -**gra'dient** *n*. degree of slope. - **grad'ual** *a*. taking place by es; moving step by step; slow and steady; not steep. - **grad'ually** *adv*. **grad'uate** *v.i.* receive a university degree diploma; one who has received a university degree or diploma. -**gradua'tion** *n*. [L. *gradus*, step]

graft *n*. shoot of a plant set in a stock of another plant; the process; (SL.) work. *v.t.* insert (a shoot) in another stock; transplant (living tissue in surgery). [earlier graffe, F. *greefe*]

graft *n*. bribery, corruption; profit or advancement obtained by corrupt means. [orig. uncertain]

grail *n*. Holy Grail, platter or cup used by Christ at the Last Supper. [OF. *graal*]

grain *n*. seed or fruit of a cereal plant; wheat and allied plants; small hard particle; unit of weight, ⅟₇₀₀₀th of the pound avoirdupois; texture; arrangement of fibers; formerly cochineal, scarlet dye, dye in general. -*v.t.* paint in imitation of wood grain. -**grainy** *a*. [F. , cp. *granary*]

gram *n*. unit of weight in the metric system. [F. , fr. G. *gramma* letter, small weight]

gramm'ar *n*. science of the structure and usages of a language; book on this; correct use of words. **grammar'ian** (-ar-) *n*. - **gramm'ar school** *n*. elementary school. [G. *gramma*, letter]

grand *a*. chief, of chief importance; splendid, magnificent; lofty; imposing; final. - **grand'child** *n*. child of children. **grand'daughter** *n*. , child of children. **grandee'** *n*. Spanish or Portuguese nobleman. -**grand'eur** *n*. nobility; magnificence; dignity. -**grand'father** *n*. parent of parents. -**grandil'oquence** *n*. -**grandil'oquent** *a*. pompous in speech. -**grandmaster** *n*. head of order of knights or freemasons. -**grand'mother** *fem*, parent of parents. -**grand-slam'** *n*. (cards) taking of every trick in bridge. -**grand'son** *n*. child of children. -**grand'stand** *n*. raised seats for spectators at races, *etc*. [L. *grandis*, great]

granite (-it) *n*. hard crystalline rock, used for building. [It. *granito*]

grant *v.t.* consent to fulfill (a request); permit; bestow, give formally; admit. -*n*. a granting; thing granted. -**grant'or** *n*. **grant'ee** *n*. [AF. *graanter*]

gran'ule *n*. small grain. -**granular** *a*. of, or like, grains. -**gran'ulate** *v.t.* form into grains. [L. *granum*, grain]

grape *n*. fruit of the vine. -**grape'fruit** *n*. large citrus fruit, kind of shaddock. **grape'shot** *n*. bullets as scattering charge for a cannon. -**grape'-sugar** *n*. dext rose. -**grape'-vine** *n*. circulation of news, *etc*. , *esp*. among natives, without obvious means of communication. [F. *grappe* (*de raisin*), bunch (of grapes)]

graphic *a*. of, in, or relating to writing, drawing, painting, *etc*. ; vividly descriptive. -**graph** *n*. graphic formula, diagram showing symbolically a series of connections. -**graph'ically** *adv*. -**graph'ite** *n*. form of carbon (used in pencils). **graphol'ogy** *n*. study of handwriting. [G. *graphein*, write]

grasp *v.t.* seize firmly, clutch; understand. -*v.i.* clutch (at). -*n*. firm hold; mastery. (ME. *graspen*)

grass *n*. herbage, plants grown for cattle to eat, to cover lawns, *etc*. ; plant of this kind. -*v.t.* cover with turf, put down on grass. -**grass'hopper** *n*. jumping, chirping insect. [OE. gærs]

grate *n*. fireplace, frame of bars for holding fuel; framework of crossed bars (also **grating** *n*.). [L. *cratis*, hurdle]

grate'ful *a*. thankful; pleasing. - **grate'fully** *adv*. -**grat'itude** *n*. sense of being thankful for something received. [L. *gratus*, pleasing] grat'ify v.t. do a favor to; indulge. **gratifica'tion** n. [L. gratificare, fr. gratus, pleasing]

gratu'ity n. gift of money. -gratu'itous a. given free, done for nothing; uncalled for. -gratu'itously adv. [Low L. gratuitat-, fr. gratus, pleasing]

grave n. hole dug for a dead body; monument on this; death. [OE. græf]

grave a. serious, weighty; dignified, solemn; plain, dark in color, deep in note. -grave'ly adv. [L. gravis, heavy]

grav'el n. small stones, coarse sand; aggregation of urinary crystals; disease due to this. -v.t. cover with gravel; puzzle. -grav'elly a. [F. gravelle]

grav'ity n. importance; seriousness, heaviness; force of attraction of one body for another, esp. of objects to the earth. grav'itate v.i. move by gravity; sink, settle. -gravita'tion n. [L. gravitate, fr. gravis, heavy]

gra'vy n. juices from meat in cooking; dressing or sauce for food made from these juices. [orig. uncertain]

gray, grey a. between black and white in color, as ashes or lead; clouded; dismal; turning white; aged. -n. gray color; gray horse. -gray'ling n. gray fish. [OE. græg]

graze v.i. and t. feed on grass. [OE. grasiani]

graze v.t. touch lightly in passing; abrade the skin thus. -v.i. move so as to touch lightly. -n. [orig. uncertain]

grease n. soft melted fat of animals; thick oil as a lubricant-v.t. apply grease to. [F. graisse]

great (-at) a. large; big; important; preeminent, distinguished. -as prefix, indicates a degree further removed in relationship, e.g. great-grand'father n. father of a grandfather or grandmother. great'uncle n. uncle of a parent. great'ly adv. -great'ness n. -great'- coat n. overcoat, esp. military. [OE.]

greed'y a. gluttonous, over-eager for food, wealth, etc. -greed n. -greed'ily adv. -greed'iness n. IOE. graedig]

Greek n. native of Greece. -a. of Greece. [G. Graikoi, Greeks]

green a. of color between blue and yellow, colored like growing grass; emerald, etc.; unripe; inexperienced; easily deceived. -n. the color; piece of grass-covered land. (golf) -putting-green, ground about each hole. -green'ery n. vegetation. [OE. grene]

greet v.t. accost or salute; receive; meet. greet'ing n. [OE. gretan]

grenade' n. explosive shell or bomb, thrown by hand or shot from a rifle. grenadier' n. soldier of the Grenadier Guards; formerly, a soldier who threw grenades. [F. = pomegranate]

grid n. frame of bars; grating; grid-iron. [gridiron]

grid n. (elec.) system of power transmission lines; (radio) perforated screen as part of amplifying mechanism. [gridiron]

grief (-ef) n. deep sorrow. -griev'ance n. real or imaginary ground of complaint. grieve v.i. feel grief. -v.t. cause grief to. griev'ous a. painful, oppressive. [F. grever, afflict]

grill n. gridiron; food cooked on one. -v.t. and i. broil on a gridiron. [F. gril]

grim a. stem; of stern or harsh aspect; joyless. -grimly adv. [OE. grimm, fierce]

grime n. soot, dirt. -v.t. soil; befoul. gri'my a. -gri'miness n. [orig. uncertain]

grin v.i. show the teeth. -n. act of grinning; impish smile. [OE. grennian]

grind v.t. crush to powder between hard surfaces; oppress; make sharp or smooth; grate. -v.i. perform the action of grinding; work (esp. study) hard; -n. action of grinding; hard work. -grind'stone n. revolving disk of stone for grinding, etc. -grind'er n. [OE. grindan]

grip n. firm hold, grasp; grasping power; mastery; handle; bag. -v.t. grasp or hold tightly. [OE. gripa]

gripe v.t. grip; oppress; afflict with pains of colic. -n. grip. -pl. colic pains. gri'ping a. [OE. gripan]

groan v.i. make a low deep sound of grief, pain or displeasure; be in pain or overburdened. -n. the sound. [OE. granian]

gro'cer n. dealer in, tea, spices, domestic stores; storekeeper. -gro'cery n. his trade, or, pl. wares. [OF. grossier, wholesaler]

groin n. depression between belly and thigh; edge made by intersection of two vaults; structure of timber, etc. to stop shifting of sand on sea beach. -v.t. build with groins. [orig. uncertain]

gross a. rank; overfed; flagrant; total, not net; thick, solid; coarse; indecent. -n. twelve dozen. -gross'ly adv. -gross out v.t. (sl.) to cause (a person) to feel distaste or strong dislike for (something). [F. gros, fr. L. grossus, thick]

ground (-ow-) n. bottom of the sea; surface of the earth; position, area, on this; soil; special area; reason, motive; surface or coating to work on with paint. -pl. dregs; enclosed land round a house. -v.t. establish; instruct (in elementary principles); place on the ground. -*v.i.* run ashore. [OE. *grund*]

group *n.* number of persons or things near together, or placed or classified together; class; two or more figures forming one artistic design. -*v.t.* arrange in a group. -*v.i.* fall into a group. [P. *groppo*, bunch]

group therapy *n.* (*psych.*) therapeutic technique in which patients are treated as a group, includes supervised, interactive discussion in an attempt to find solutions for problems.

grow *v.i.* develop naturally; increase in size, height, *etc.* ; be produced; become by degrees. -*v.t.* produce by cultivation. -**growth** *n.* growing; increase; what has grown or is growing. [OE, *growan*]

grudge *v.t.* be unwilling to give or allow. -*n.* feeling of ill-will; earlier *grutch*, grumble. [OF. *groucier*]

guarantee' (ga-) *n.* giver of guaranty of security; guaranty. -*v.t.* answer for the fulfillment, or genuineness or permanence of. secure (to) a person; secure (against risk, *etc.*). -**guar'anty** *n.* written or other undertaking to answer for performance of obligation; ground or basis of security. [F. *garantir*, protect]

guard (ga-) *n.* posture of defense; watch; protector; sentry; soldiers protecting anything; official in charge of a train; protection; defense. -*v.t.* protect, defend. -*v.i.* be careful. -**guard'ian** *n.* keeper, protector; person having custody of an infant, *etc.* **guard'ianship** *n.* [F. *garde*]

guess (ges) *v.t.* estimate without calculation or measurement; conjecture, think likely. -*v.i.* form conjectures. -*n.* rough estimate. [ME. *gessen*]

guest (gest) *n.* one entertained at another's house; one living in a hotel. [ON. *gestr*]

guide (gid) *n.* one who shows the way; adviser; book of instruction or infor. mation; contrivance for directing motion. -*v.t.* lead, act as guide to; arrange. **guid'ance** *n.* -**guide'-book** *n.* manual for travellers. -**guide'-post** *n.* signpost. -**guid'ed missile** *n.* projectile, rocket *etc.* directed by remote control. [F.]

guile *n.* cunning, treachery, deceit. [OF.]

guillotine *n.* machine for beheading; machine for cutting paper; drastic curtailment of parliamentary debate. -*v.t.* use a guillotine upon. [F. , Dr. Guillotin suggested its use (1789)]

guilt (gilt) *n.* fact or state of having offended; culpability. -**guilt'y** *a.* having committed an offence. -**guilt'ily** *adv*. . **guilt'less** *a.* -**guilt'iness** *n.* [OE. *gylt*]

guitar' (git-) *n.* musical instrument with six strings. [F. *guitare*, L. *cithara*]

gulf *n.* partly enclosed portion of the sea; chasm, abyss. -**gulf stream** *n.* current of warm water moving from Gulf of Mexico to *n.* Atlantic and Europe. [F. *golfer*]

gum *n.* firm flesh in which the teeth are set. -**gum'boil** *n.* abscess in the gum. [OE. *goma*]

gum *n.* sticky substance issuing from certain trees; this prepared for use to stick papers, *etc.*, together. -*v.t.* stick with gum. -**chew'ing gum** *n.* sticky substance for chewing. [F. *gomme*]

gun *n.* weapon consisting mainly of a metal tube from which missiles are thrown by explosion; cannon, pistol, *etc.* [short for *Gunhilda*, name of a medieval war-engine]

gush *v.i.* flow out suddenly and copiously. -*n.* sudden copious flow; effusiveness. -**gush'er** *n.* gushing person or oil-well. [orig. uncertain]

gut *n.* in *pl.* entrails, intestines; (*sl.*) courage, spirit. -*sing.* material made from guts of animals, as for violin strings, *etc.* ; narrow passage, strait. -*v.t.* remove the guts from (fish); remove or destroy the contents of (a house). [OE. *guttas* (pi.)]

gutt'er *n.* channel for carrying off water from a roof, from the side of a street. -*v.t.* make channels in. -*v.i.* flow in streams; of a candle, melt away by the wax forming channels and running down. [F. *gouttiere*, fr. *goutte*, drop]

guy (gi) *n.* rope or chain to steady or secure something. -*v.t.* to secure with a guy. -**guy'-rope** *n.* [OF. *guier*, guide]

guz'zle *v.t.* and *i.* eat or drink greedily. **guzz'ler** ri. [imit.]

gymna'sium *n.* place fitted up for muscular exercises, athletic training. **gymnast'ic** *a.* of exercise. -*n.* (in *pl*). muscular exercises, with or without apparatus such as parallel bars. **gym'nast** *n.* expert in gymnastics. [G. *gymnasion*, fr. *gymnos*, naked]

gynecology *n.* part of medicine dealing with functions and diseases of women. [G. *gyne*, woman]

gypsy *n.* one of a wandering race of people, orig. from India, *usu.* maintaining a migratory way of life; one who lives in a way that resembles the life of a gypsy. [fr. Egyptian]

gyro *n. pl.* **gyros** a gyroscope. (*sl*) Greek sandwich of roasted lamb or beef stiffed in pita bread with vegetables. -**gyroscope** *n.* instrument consisting of a heavy wheel mounted on a set of rings so that its axis can turn freely in any direction.

H

ha *interj.* exclamation of surprise, pleasure, *etc.* [imit.]

hab'eas cor'pus *n.* writ issued to produce prisoner in court. [L. = *have the body*]

hab'it *n.* settled tendency or practice; constitution; dress (esp. riding-habit). *v.t.* dress. -**habit'ual** *a.* that is a habit, customary. -**habit'ually** *adv.* -**habit'uate,** *v.t.* accustom. -**habitua'tion** *n.* **habit'ué** *n.* constant visitor; resident. -**hab'itude** *n.* customary manner of action. [F.]

hab'itable *a.* fit to live in -**habitation**-*n.* dwelling. -**hab'itat** *n.* natural home of an animal. [L. *habitare,* dwell]

hack *v.t.* cut, mangle, gash. -*n.* notch; bruise. -**hack'er** *n.* person that hacks; (*sl.*) a computer fanatic. [OE. *haccian*]

hack *n.* hired horse; horse for ordinary riding; literary drudge. -*v.t.* **hackney.** [short for *hackney*]

hack'ney *n.* horse for ordinary riding; carriage kept for hire. -*v.t.* make trite or common. [Hackney, Middlesex]

hail *n.* frozen vapor falling in pellets. *v.i.* it hails, hail falls. -*v.t.* pour down. **hailstone** *n.* [OE. *hagol*]

hail *interj.* greeting. -*v.t.* greet; call. -*v.i.* hail from, be arrived from. -*n.* call, shout. [obs. *n.* hail health; ON. *heill*]

hair *n.* filament growing from the skin of an animal, as the covering of a man's head; such filaments collectively. **hair'y** *a.* -**hair'iness** *n.* -**hair'breadth** *n.* breadth of a hair; infinitesimal breadth. -**hair'pin** *n.* pin to secure hair in place. -**hair'pin curve** *n.* v-shaped bend on road. -**hair'-splitting** *a.* drawing over-fine distinctions. [OE. *hær*]

half (haf) *n.* **halves** (havz) *pl.* either of two equal parts of a thing. -*a.* forming a half -*adv.* the extent of half -**half'-blood** *n.* relationship of persons with one common parent. -**half'breed** *n.* one of mixed parentage. -**half'-brother,** -**sister** *n.* brother (sister) by one parent only. **half'caste** *n.* half-breed *esp.* of European and Asiatic parents-**half' title** *n.* (shortened) title of book printed on page before title page. [OE. *healf*]

hall (hawl) *n.* large room; house of a landed proprietor; building belonging to a guild; entrance passage. -**hall'mark** *n.* mark used to indicate standard of tested gold and silver. -*v.t.* stamp with this. [OE. *heall*]

Hallowe'en' *n.* All Hallows Eve, (Oct. 31) [OE. *halgian.* hallow]

hallucinate *v.t.* produce illusion in the mind of. -**hallucina'tion** *n.* illusion; see,

hear, something that is not present. [L. *hallucinari,* wander in mind]

halt (hawlt) *n.* stoppage on a march or journey. -*v.i.* make a halt. -*v.t.* bring to a halt. [Ger.]

halt'er *n.* rope or strap with headstall to fasten horses or cattle; noose for hanging criminals. -*v.t.* fasten with a halter. [OE. *hælfter*]

ham *n.* hollow of the knee; back of the thigh; hog's thigh salted and dried. **ham'string** *n.* tendon at the back of the knee. -*v.t.* cripple by cutting this. [OE. *hamm*]

hamburger *n.* ground beef formed into cakes, fried or broiled and *usu.* served in a bun. [Hamburg, Germany]

hamm'er *n.* tool, usually with a heavy head at the end of a handle, for beating, driving nails, *etc.*; machine for the same purposes; contrivance for exploding the charge of a gun; auctioneer's mallet. -*v.t.* and *i.* beat with, or as with, a hammer. [OE. *hamor*]

hamp'er *n.* large covered basket. [OF. *hanapier,* case for *hanaps,* goblets]

hamp'er *v.t.* impede, obstruct the movements of. -*n.* in a ship, cumbrous equipment. [orig. uncertain]

hand *n.* extremity of the arm beyond the wrist; side, quarter, direction; style of writing; cards dealt to a player; measure of four inches; manual worker; person as a source. -*v.t.* lead or help with the hand; deliver; pass; hold out. -**hand'bag** *n.* bag for carrying in the hand. -**hand'bill** *n.* small printed notice for distribution by hand. -**hand'book** *n.* short treatise. -**hand'iwork** *n.* thing done by any one in person. **hand'kerchief** *n.* small square of fabric carried in the pocket for wiping the nose, *etc.,* or worn round the neck. [OE.]

handicap *n.* race or contest in which the competitors' chances are equalized by starts, weights carried, *etc.*; condition so imposed; disability. -*v.t.* impose such conditions. -**handicapper** *n.* [*hand* in *cap;* orig. lottery game]

han'dle *n.* part of a thing made to hold it by; fact that may be taken advantage of -*v.t.* touch, feel, with the hands; manage, deal with; deal in. [OE. *handle n. handlian v. t.*]

hand'some (-ns-) *a.* of fine appearance; generous. -**hand'somely** *adv.* [*hand; orig.* pleasant to handle]

hang *v.t.* fasten to an object above, suspend; kill by suspending from gallows; attach or set up (wallpaper, doors, *etc.*). *v.i.* be suspended; cling. -**hangdog** *a.* of sneaking aspect. -**hangman** *n*. executioner. [OE. *hangian*]

hang'ar (-ng-) *n*. shed for aircraft. [F.]

hang'er *n*. that by which a thing is suspended *e.g.* **coat-hanger.** [*hang*]

Han'ukkah, Chan'ukah *n*. eight-day Jewish festival of lights beginning on the 25th of Kislev and commemorating the rededication of the temple by Judas Maccabeus in 165 B. C. [fr. Heb. literally: a dedication]

hap *n*. chance. -*v.i.* happen. -**hap'less** *a*. unlucky. -**haphaz'ard** *a*. random, without design. -*adv.* by chance. -**hap'ly** *adv.* perhaps. -**happ'en** *v.i.* come about, occur. [ON. *happ*, luck]

happ'y *a*. glad, content; lucky, fortunate; apt. [*hap*]

har'ass *v.t.* worry, trouble; attack repeatedly. -**har'assed** *a*. [F. *harasser*]

har'bor (-ber) *n*. place of shelter for ships; shelter, -*v.t.* give shelter to. -*v.i.* take shelter. [ME. *herberwe*]

hard *a*. firm, resisting pressure, solid; difficult to understand; harsh, unfeeling; difficult to bear; stingy; heavy; strenuous; of water, not making lather well with soap. -*adv.* vigorously; with difficulty; close. -**hard-bitt'en** *a*. tough in a fight. **hard'-boiled** *a*. (*sl.*) tough thick-skinned. -**hard'en** *v.t.* and *i*. -**hard up'**, short of cash. -**hard'ware** *n*. small ware of metal. -**hardware** (*compute.*) computer equipment used to process data; physical equipment, e.g. printer, disk drive, *etc.* [OE. *heard*]

hard copy *n*. (*compute.*) paper printout of data from computer; physical form of data originating from the computer, originally viewed on the monitor.

hard'y *a*. robust, vigorous; able to endure hardship; bold; of plants, able to grow in the open all the year round. [F. *hardi*, bold]

harm *n*. damage, hurt. [OE. *hearm*]

har'mony *n*. agreement; combination of musical notes to make chords; melodious sound. -**harmo'nious** *a*. -**harmon'ica** *n*. various musical intruments. -**har'monize** *v.t.* bring into harmony. -*v.i.* be in harmony. -**har'monist** *n*. -**harmoniza'tion** *n*. [G. *harmonia*]

harp *n*. musical instrument of strings played by the hand. -*v.i.* play on a harp; dwell on continuously. -**harp'sichord** *n*. stringed instrument with keyboard, an ancestor of the piano. [OE. *hearpe*]

harsh *a*. rough, bitter, unpleasing to the touch or taste: severe; unfeeling. -**harshly** *adv.* [ME. *harsk*]

har'vest *n*. season for gathering in grain; the gathering; the crop; product of an action. -*v.t.* gather in. -**har'vester** *n*. **har'vest home** *n*. festival at end of harvest. -**harvest-queen** *n*. image of Ceres. [OE. *hærfest*]

hash *v.t.* cut up small. -*n*. dish of hashed meat. [F. *hacher*, chop]

hashish *n*. narcotic drug prepared from Indian hemp. [Arab.]

haste *n*. speed, quickness; hurry. *v.i.* hasten. -**hast'en** (-sen) *v.i.* come or go quickly or hurriedly. -*v.t.* hurry; accelerate. [OF.]

hat *n*. covering for the head, usually with a brim. -**hatt'er** *n*. dealer in, or maker of, hats. [OE. *hætt*]

hatch *n*. lower half of a divided door; hatchway; trapdoor over it. -**hatch'way** *n*. opening in the deck of a ship for cargo, *etc.* [OE. *hæc*]

hatch *v.t.* bring forth young birds from the shell; incubate. -*v.i.* come forth from the shell. -*n*. a hatching; the brood hatched. -**hatch'ery** *n*. hatching place for fish. [ME. *hacchen*]

hate *v.t.* dislike strongly; bear malice to. -*n*. **hatred.** -**hate'ful** *a*. -**hate'fully** *adv.* -**ha'tred** *n*. emotion of extreme dislike. active ill-will. [OE. *hatian*, hate]

haul *v.t.* pull, drag. -*v.i.* of wind, to shift. -*n*. a hauling; draught of fishes; acquisition. -**haul'age** *n*. carrying of loads; charge of this. [*hale*]

have (hav) *v.t.* hold or possess; be possessed or affected with; be obliged (to do); engage in, carry on; obtain; (as auxiliary forms perfect and other tenses). [OE. *habban*]

ha'ven *n*. harbor; refuge. [OE. *hæfn*]

hav'oc *n*. pillage, devastation, ruin. [orig. to cry *havoc*, gave the signal for pillage; OF. *havo*]

hawk *n*. bird of prey. -*v.t.* and *i*. hunt with hawks. [OE. *hafoc*]

hay *n*. grass mown and dried. -**hay'stack** *n*. large pile of hay with ridged or pointed top. [OE. *hieg*]

haz'ard *n*. game at dice; chance, a chance; risk, danger; (*golf*) bunker or other hindrance. -*v.t.* expose to risk; run the risk of. -**haz'ardous** *a*. risky, perilous. [F. *hasard*]

haze *n*. misty appearance in the air, often due to heat; mental obscurity. -**ha'zy** *a*. misty. [orig. uncertain]

he *pron.* male person or animal already referred to. -*n*. a male. [OE.]

head (hed) *n*. upper part of a man's or animal's body, containing mouth, sense organs and brain; upper part of anything; chief part; leader; progress; title, heading; headland. -*v.t.* provide with a head; get the lead of. -*v.i.* face, front. **-head'ache** (-ak) *n.* continuous pain in the head. **-headlight** *n.* front light of automobile or other vehicle. **-head'lines** *n. pl.* headings in newspaper. **-headquar'ters** *n. pl.* residence of commander-in-chief, center of operations.**-head'stone** *n.* tombstone. **-head'strong** *a.* self-willed. [OE. *heafod*]

heal *v.t.* restore to health, make well, cure. -*v.t.* become sound. **-health** *n.* soundness of body; condition of body; toast drunk in a person's honor. [OE.*hælan*]

heap *n.* number of things lying one on another; great quantity. -*v.t.* pile up; load (with gifts, *etc.*). [OE.]

hear *v.t.* perceive with the ear; listen to; try (a case); get to know. -*v.i.* perceive sound; learn. **-hear'er** *n.* **-hear'say** *n.* rumor. *a.* not based on personal knowledge. [OE. *hieran*]

heart (hart) *n.* hollow organ which makes the blood circulate; seat of the emotions and affections; mind, soul; courage; middle of anything; playing card marked with a figure of a heart, one of these marks. **-heartache** *n.* grief, anguish. **-heart'burn** *n.* sharp, burning feeling at heart, caused by gastric acidity. **-heart'felt** *a.* very sincere. **-heart'less** *a.* unfeeling. **-heart'rending** *a.* extremely sad, agonizing. **heart'y** *a.* friendly; vigorous; in good health; satisfying the appetite. **-heart'ily** *adj*. [OE. *heorth*]

heat *n.* hotness; sensation of this; hot weather or climate; warmth of feeling, anger, *etc.*; sexual excitement in animals; race (one of several) to decide the persons to compete in a deciding course. -*v.t.* make hot. -*v.i.* become hot. **-heat'edly** *adv.* [OE. *hæte*]

heave *v.t.* lift with effort; throw something heavy), utter (a sigh). -*v.i.* swell, rise. -*n.* a heaving. **-heave to'.** (of a ship) come to a stop. [OE. *hebban*]

heav'en *n.* sky; abode of God: God; place of bliss. **-heav'enly** *a.* of, like heaven; divine. [OE. *hæfon*]

heav'y (hev-) *a.* of great weight; striking or failing with force; sluggish; difficult; severe; sorrowful; serious; dull; over compact. [OE. *hefig*]

He'brew *n.* Jew, Jewish language. **hebra'ic** *a.* [I. *Hebraeus*]

hedge *n.* fence of bushes. -*v.t.* surround with a hedge. -*v.i.* make or trim hedges; bet on both sides; secure against loss; shift, shuffie. [OE. *hecg*]

heed *v.t.* take notice of, care for.[OE. *hedani*]

heel *n.* hinder part of the foot; part of a shoe supporting this; (*colloq*) unpleasant person. [OE. *hela*]

heel *v.i.* of a ship, to lean to one side. *v.t.* cause to do this.-*n.* a heeling. [OE. *hieldan*, incline]

hegem'ony *n.* leadership. political domination. **-hegemon'ic** *a.* [G. *hegemon*, leader]

height *n.* measure from base to top: quality of being high; high position, highest degree; hill-top. **-height'en** *v.t.* make higher; intensity. [OE. *hiehthu*]

heir *n.* person legally entitled to succeed to property or rank. [L. *heres*]

hel'ical *a.* spiral. **-helicop'ter** *n.* aircraft made to rise vertically by the pull of an air-screw or screws, revolving horizontally. [G. *helix*, spiral; *pteron*, wing]

he'lium *n.* gaseous element, first discovered in the sun's atmosphere by Lockyer in 1868. [G. *helios*, sun]

hell *n.* abode of the damned; place or state of wickedness, or misery, or torture; abode of the dead generally; gambling resort. **hell'ish** *a.* [OE.]

helm *n.* tiller or wheel for turning the rudder of a ship. [OE. *helma*]

help *v.t.* aid, assist; serve (food, with food); remedy, prevent.-*n.* aid, assistance; an aid, support. **-help'er** *n.* [OE. *helpan*]

hemisphere *n.* half sphere; half of the celestial sphere; half of the earth. **hemispher'ical** *a.* [G. *hemi-*, half]

hemoglobin *n.* red coloring matter of the blood. [G. *haima*, blood, *globus*, ball]

hemophilia *n.* tendency to excessive bleeding from slight injuries. **hemophil'iac** *n.* [G. *haima*, blood]

hemorrhage *n.* bleeding. [G. *haumorragia*, fr. *haima*, blood]

hen *n.* female of the domestic fowl and other birds. [OE. *henn*]

hepat'ic *a.* pert. to the liver. **-hepatit'is** *n.* disease or condition relating to inflammation of the liver. [L. *hepar*, liver]

hep'tagon *n.* plane figure with seven sides, angles. **-heptag'onal** *a.* **-hep'tarchy** (-ki) *n.* rule by seven. **-hep'tateuch** (-tuk) *n.* first seven books of the Old Testament. [G. *hepta*, seven]

her *pron.* obj., *possess.,* of *she.* **-herself'**, emphatic, reflex, of *she, her;* in her proper character. [OE. *hire,* fr. *heo* she]

herb *n.* plant with a soft stem which dies down after flowering; plant of which parts are used for medicine, food or scent. [L. *herba*, grass]

here *adv.* in this place; at or to this point. [OE. *her*]

heredity *n.* tendency of an organism to transmit its nature to its descendants. - **hereditary** *a.* descending by inheritance; holding office by inheritance; that can be transmitted from one generation to another. [L. *heres, hered-*, heir]

her'esy *n.* opinion contrary to the orthodox opinion. [G. *hairesis*, sect, school of thought]

her'mit *n.* person living in solitude, *esp.* from religious motives. **-her'mitage** *n.* his abode. **-her'mit-crab'** *n.* kind of crab living in discarded mollusk shells. [G. *eremites*, fr. *eremia*, desert]

hern'ia *n.* protrusion of an internal organ through the wall of tissue that encloses it; rupture. [L.]

he'ro *n.* illustrious warrior; one greatly regarded for achievements or qualities chief man in a poem, play, or story; demigod. [G. *heros*, demigod, hero]

her'oin *n.* strongly addictive narcotic drug derived from morphine. [Ger. trade-name]

her'pes *n.* any of several skin diseases, including shingles (herpes zoster) and cold sores (herpes simplex). [G. *herpein*, creep.]

hertz *n.* (*radio*) unit of frequency. [H. Hertz, 1857-94]

hes'itate *v.i.* hold back, feel, show, indecision; be reluctant. **-hes'itant** *a.* **hes'itantly** *adv.* **-hes'itancy** *n.* indecision, doubt. **-hesita'tion** *n.*[L. *hæsitare*, fr. *hærere, hæs-*, stick fast]

heteroge'neous *a.* composed of diverse elements. **-heterogene'ity** *n.* [G. *heteros*, other, *genos*, kind]

hew *v.t.* and *i.* chop or cut with ax or sword. **-hew'er** *n.* [OE. *heawan*]

hexagon *n.* figure with six sides, angles. **-hexag'onal** *a.* **-hexam'eter** *n.* verse line of six feet. [G. *hex*, six]

hibernate *v.i.* pass the winter, *esp.* in torpor. **-hiberna'tion** *n.* [L. *hibernare* hibernat, fr. *heims* winter]

hide *n.* skin, raw or dressed. [OE. *hyd*]

hide *n.* old measure of land. [OE. *hid*]

hide *v.t.* put or keep out of sight; conceal, keep secret. *-v.i.* conceal oneself. **hid'den** *a.* [OE. *hydan*]

hierarch (-k) *n.* chief priest. **-hi'erarchy** *n.* graded priesthood or other organization. **-hierarch'ical** *a.* **-hi'eroglyph** *n.* figure of an object standing for a word or sound as in ancient Egyptian writing. [C *hieros*, holy]

high *a.* of great or specified extent upwards; far up; of great rank, quality or importance; of roads, main; of meat, tainted; of a season, well advanced; of sound, acute in pitch. *-adv.* far up; strongly, to a great extent; at or to a high pitch; at a high rate. **-high'brow** *a.* intellectual-*n.* **-high'-explosive** *n.* powerful explosive as lyddite, t. n. t. *-a.* **-high'lands** *n. pl.* mountainous country. **-high'ly** *adv.* **-high seas** *n.* ocean. **-high-spirited** *a.* courageous, daring. **high'strung** *a.* super-sensitive. **-high-water** *n.* high tide. **-high'way** *n.* main road; ordinary route. **-high'wayman** *n.* robber on the road, *esp.* a mounted one. [OE. *heah*]

hike *v.t.* hoist, shoulder. *-v.i.* tramp, camp out, *esp.* carrying one's equipment. *-n.* ramble, walking-tour. **-hi'ker** *n.* [orig. uncertain]

hill *n.* natural elevation, small mountain; mound. **-hill'ock** *n.* little hillbilly *a.* **-hill'iness** *n.* [OE. *hyll*]

hilt *n.* handle of a sword, *etc.* [OE.]

him *pron.* , *obj.* of *he*. **-himself'**, emphatic and reflex. of *he, him*; in his proper character, sane. **-his**, *possess.* of *he*. [OE.]

hind'er *v.t.* obstruct, bamper. **-hind'rance** *n.* obstacle. [OE. *hinder*, behind]

hinge (-j) *n.* movable joint, as that on which a door bangs. *-v.t.* attach with, or as with, a hinge. *-v.i.* turn on, depend on. [ME. *heng*]

hint *n.* slight indication, covert suggestion. *-v.t.* give a hint of. *-v.i.* make a hint. [OE. *hentan*, pursue]

hip *n.* projecting part of thigh; the hip joint. [OE. *hype*]

hippo'potamus *n.* large African animal living in rivers. [G. *hippos*, horse, *potamus*, river]

hire *n.* payment for the use of a thing; wages; a hiring or being hired. *-v.t.* take or give on hire. [OE. *hyr*, wages]

his'tory *n.* study of past events; record of these; past events; train of events, public or private; course of life or existence; systematic account of phenomena. **historical** *a.* of, or based on history; belonging to the past. **-histor'ically** *adv.* [G. *historia* narrative]

hit *v.t.* strike with a blow or missile; affect injuriously; find; suit. *-v.i.* strike; light (upon). *-n.* blow; success, *esp.* relating to music, theater *etc.* [ON. *hitta*, meet with]

hitch *v.t.* raise or move with a jerk; fasten with a loop, *etc.* *-v.i.* be caught or fastened. *-n.* jerk; fastening, loop or knot; difficulty, obstruction. [orig. uncertain]

hive *n.* box in which bees are housed. *v.t.*

gather or place (bees) in a hive. -*v.i.* enter a hive. [OE. *kvf*]

hoard *n.* stock, store, *esp.* hidden away. -*v.t.* amass and hide away; store. [OE, *hord*, treasure]

hoax *v.t.* deceive by an amusing or mischievous story. -*n.* such deception. [contr. of *hocus*]

hobble *v.i.* walk lamely. -*v.t.* tie the legs together of (horse, *etc.*). -*n.* limping gait; rope for hobbling. [orig. uncertain]

hobb'y *n.* formerly a small horse; favorite occupation as a pastime. [*Hob*, for Robert]

hock'ey *n.* game played with a ball or disk and curved sticks. [OF. *hoquet,* crook]

hoe *n.* tool for scraping up weeds, breaking ground, etc.—*v. t.* break up or weed with a hoe. [F. *houe*]

hog *n.* pig, *esp.* one required for fattening; greedy or dirty person. -**hogs'head** *n.* large cask; liquid measure of 52½ gallons. [OE. *hogg*]

hold *v.t.* keep fast, grasp; support in or with the hands, *etc.*; maintain in a position; have capacity for: own, occupy; carry on; detain; celebrate; keep back; believe. -*v.i.* cling; not give way; abide (by), keep (to); last, proceed, be in force; occur. -*n.* grasp; fortress. [OE. *healda*n]

hole *n.* hollow place, cavity; perforation, opening. -*v.t.* perforate, make a hole in. [OE. *hol, a.* hollow]

Holerith card *n.* (*compute.*) card containing data represented by 12 rows and 80 columns of punch positions.

holiday *n.* day or period of rest from work, or of recreation; originally a religious festival. [*holy day*]

holl'ow *n.* cavity, hole, valley. -*a.* having a cavity, not solid; empty; false; not fulltoned. -*v.t.* make a hollow in; bend hollow. [OE *holh*]

holocaust *n.* burnt sacrifice; great slaughter or sacrifice. [G. *holos,* whole]

holograph *n.* document wholly written by the signer. -**holog'raphy** *n.* science of using lasers to produce a photographic record. -**hol'ogram** *n.* photographic record produced by illuminating the object with light (as from a laser), *esp.* in order to produce a three-dimensional image. [G. *holos,* whole]

ho'ly *a.* belonging to, or devoted to, God; free from sin, divine. -**ho'lily** *adv.*-**ho'liness** *n.* quality of being holy; title of the Pope. [OE. *halig*]

home *n.* dwelling-place; fixed residence; native place; institution for the infirm, *etc.* -*a.* of or connected with home; not foreign.

-*adv.* to or at one's home: to the point aimed at. -**home'less** *a.* -**home'-sick** *a.* depressed by absence from home. -**home'spun** *a.* spun or made at home. -*n.* cloth made of home-spun yarn: anything plain or homely. [OE. *ham*]

homicide *n.* killing of a human being; the killer. -**hom'icidal** *a.* [L. *homicide,* man slayer]

homogeneous *a.* of the same nature: formed of uniform parts. -**homogene'ity** *n.* -**homog'enize** *v.t.* make uniform, blend. [G. *homos,* same, *genos,* kind]

hom'onym *n.* word of the same form as another but of different sense. [G. *homos,* same, *onoma,* name]

homosexuality *n.* sexuality between members of same sex. [G. *homos,* same]

hon'est (on-) *a.* upright, just; free from fraud; unadulterated. [L. *honestus*]

hon'ey *n.* sweet fluid collected by bees. -**hon'eycomb** *n.* structure of wax in hexagonal cells in which bees place honey, eggs, *etc.* -*v.t.* fill with cells of perforations. -**hon'eymoon** *n.* month after marriage; holiday taken by a newly-wedded pair. -**hon'eysuckle** *n.* climbing plant, woodbine. [OE. *hunig*]

hon'or (on-er) *n.* high respect; renown; reputation; sense of what is right or due; chastity; high rank or position; source or cause of honor; court-card. -*pt.* mark of respect; distinction in examination. -*v.t.* respect highly; confer honor on; accept or pay (a bill, *etc.*) when due. -**hon'orary** *a.* conferred for the sake of honor only; holding a position without pay or usual requirements; giving services without pay. [F. *honneur,* fr. L. *honos,* honor-]

hood (hood) *n.* cover for the head and neck, often part of a cloak; cover for the engine of an automobile. -*v.t.* put a hood on. -**hood'wink** *v.t.* deceive. [OE. *hod*]

hook *n.* bent piece of metal, *etc.* for catching hold, hanging up, *etc.*; curved cutting tool. -*v.t.* catch or secure with a hook. [OE. *hoe*]

hoop *n.* band of metal, *etc.* for binding a cask; circle of wood or metal for trundling as a toy; circle of flexible material for expanding a woman's skirt. [OE. *hop*]

hoot *n.* cry of an owl; cry of disapproval. -*v.t.* assail with hoots. -*v.i.* utter hoots. -**hoot'er** *n.* siren. [imit.]

hop *n.* climbing plant with bitter cones used to flavor beer, *etc.* -*pl.* the cones. [Du.]

hop *v.i.* spring (of person on one foot; of animals, on all feet at once). -*n.* act or the action of hopping. -(*sl.*) dance. [OE. *hopian*]

hope *n*. expectation of something desired; thing that gives, or an object of, this feeling. -*v.i.* feel hope. -*v.t.* expect and desire. [OE. *hopian*]

horizon *n*. boundary of the part of the earth seen from any given point; line where earth (or sea) and sky seem to meet; boundary of mental outlook. **-horizon'tal** *a*. parallel with the horizon, level. **horizon'tally** *adv*. [G. = *bounding*]

hor'mone *n*. internal glandular secretion stimulating growth, action of organs, *etc*. [G *hormaein*, stir up]

horn *n*. hard projection on the heads of certain animals, *e.g.*, cows; substance of it; various things made of it, or resembling a horn; wind instrument originally made of a horn. [OE.]

horr'or *n*. terror; intense dislike or fear; something causing this. **-horr'ible** *a*. exciting horror, hideous, shocking. **horr'ibly** *adv*. **-horr'id** *a*. horrible. **horr'idly** *adv*. **-horr'ify** *v.t.* move to horror. **-horrif'ic** *a*. [L. *horrere*, bristle]

horse *n*. familiar four-footed animal used for riding and draught; cavalry; vaulting-block; frame for support. -*v.t.* provide with a horse or horses; carry or support on the back. **-horse'-lat'itudes** *n. pl.* regions of calm in the Atlantic Ocean. **-horse laugh** *n*. rough boisterous laugh. **-horse'man** *n*. (skilled) rider. **-horse'-play** *n*. rough play. **-horse'-power** *n*. unit of rate of work of an engine, *etc.*; 550 foot-pounds per second. **-horse'radish** *n*. plant with a pungent root. **-horse'shoe** *n*. iron shoe for a horse; thing so shaped. [OE. *hors*]

hose *n*. stockings; flexible tube for conveying water. -*v.t.* water with a hose. **-ho'siery** *n*. his goods. [OE. *hosa*]

hos'pital *n*. institution for the care of the sick; charitable institution. [OF.]

hospitality *n*. friendly and liberal reception of strangers or guests. **hospitable** *a*. **-hos'pitably** *adv*. **-hos'pitaller** *n*. one of charitable religious order. **-hospitalize** *v.t.* place in a hospital as a patient. [*host*]

host *n*. one who entertains another; the keeper of an inn. **-hostess** *fem*. [L. *hospes, hospit-*, host, guest]

host *n*. bread consecrated in the Eucharist. [L. *hostia*, victim]

hos'tage *n*. person taken or given as a pledge; person seized for the purposes of extortion. [OE. *ostage*]

hos'tile *a*. of an enemy; opposed. [L. *hostis, hostil-*, enemy]

hot *a*. of high temperature, very warm, giving or feeling heat; pungent; angry; severe. **-hot air** *n*. (*sl*.) nonsense. empty talk. **-hot'-bed** *n*. glass-covered bed for forcing plants; atmosphere favorable to growth. **-hot'-blooded** *a*. ardent, passionate; irritable. **-hot'-dog** *n*. hot sausage in a long roll. [OE. *hat*]

hotel' *n*. large or superior inn. **hotel'-keeper** *n*. **-hotel'ier** *n*. [F. *hotel*]

hound *n*. hunting dog. *v.t.* chase (as) with hounds. [OE. *hund*]

hour (owr) *n*. twenty-fourth part of a day; time of day; appointed time -*pl*. fixed times for prayer; the prayers; book of them. **-hour'ly** *adv*. every hour; frequently. -*a*. frequent; happening every hour. **-hour'-glass** *n*. sand-glass running an hour. [F, *heure*. fr. L. *hora*]

house *n*. building for human habitation; building for other specified purpose; inn; legislative or other assembly; family: business firm; school boarding-house. -*v.t.* receive, store in a house; furnish with houses. -*v.i.* dwell, take shelter. **-house'boat** *n*. boat fitted for living in on a river, *etc*. **-house'warming** *n*. party to celebrate the entry into a new house. [OE. *hus*]

how *adv*. in what way; by what means; in what condition; to what degree; (in direct or dependent question). **-howev'er** *adv*. in whatever manner, to whatever extent; all the same. [OE. *hu*]

howl *v.i.* utter long, loud cry. -*n*. such cry. [imit.]

hub *n*. middle part of a wheel, from which the spokes radiate; central point of activity. [orig. uncertain]

hud'dle *v.t.* and *i*. heap, crowd together confusedly. -*n*. confused heap. [orig. uncertain]

hue *n*. color, complexion. [OE. *hiw*]

hug *v.t.* clasp tightly in the arms; cling; keep close to. -*n*. strong clasp. [orig. uncertain]

huge *a*. very big. **-huge'ly** *adv*. very much. [OF. *ahuge*]

hull *n*. shell, husk; body of a ship. -*v.t.* remove shell or husk; send a shot into the hull of (a ship). [OE. *hulu*, husk]

hu'man *a*. of man, relating to, or characteristic of the nature of man. **-hu'manly** *adv*. **-humane'** *a*. benevolent, kind; tending to refine. **-humanitar'ian** *n*. philanthropist. -*a*. of, or holding the views of a humanitarian. **-human'ity** *n*. human nature; human race. **-human'ities** *n. pl.* polite learning *esp*. Latin and Greek. [L. *humanus*]

hum'ble *a*. not proud, lowly, modest. *v.t.*

bring low, abase. **-hum'bly** *adv*. [L. *humilis*, fr. *humus*, ground]

hu'mid *a*. moist, damp. **-humid'ity** *n*. [L. *humidus*, fr. *humere*. be moist]

humiliate *v.t.* lower the dignity of, abase, mortify. **-humilia'tion** *n*. [L. *humiliare*, *humiliat-*]

hu'mor *n*. state of mind, mood; temperment; faculty of saying, or perceiving what excites amusement; transparent fluid of an animal or plant. *-v.t.* gratify, indulge. [L. *humor*, moisture]

hump *n*. normal or deforming lump, *esp*. on the back. *-v.t.* make hump-shaped. [orig. uncertain]

hun'dred *n*. and *a*. cardinal number, ten times ten; subdivision of a county. **hun'dredth** *a*. ordinal number. **hun'dredfold** *a*. and *adv*. **hun'dredweight** *n*. weight of 112 lbs., twentieth part of a ton. [OE.]

hun'ger *n*. discomfort or exhaustion caused by lack of food; strong desire. *-v.i.* feel hunger. **-hung'ry** *a*. **hung'rily** *adv*. [OE. *hungor*]

hunt *v.i.* go in pursuit of wild animals or game. *-v.t.* pursue (game, *etc*.); do this over (a district); use (dogs, horses) in hunting; search for. *-n*. hunting; hunting district or society. [OE. *huntian*]

hurricane *n*. violent storm, tempest. **hurr'icane-lamp** *n*. lamp made to be carried in wind. [Sp. *huracan*]

hurr'y *n*. undue haste; eagerness. *-v.i.* move or act in great haste. *-v.t.* cause to act with haste; urge to haste. **-hurr'iedly** *adv*. [orig. uncertain]

hurt *v.t.* injure, damage, give pain to, wound *-n*. wound, injury, harm. **hurt'ful** *a*. [F. *heurter*, dash against]

hus'band (-z-) *n*. man married to a woman. *-v.t.* economize. [OE. *husbonda*, master of the house]

hush *v.t.* silence. *-v.i.* be silent. *-n*. silence. -also *interj*. [imit.]

husk *n*. dry covering of certain seeds and fruits; worthless outside part. *-v.t.* remove the husk from. [orig. uncertain]

hustle *v.t.* push about, jostle. *-v.i.* push one's way, bustle. *-n*. bustle. [Du. *hutselen*, shake up]

hut *n*. small mean dwelling; temporary wooden house. [F. *huttle*]

hy'brid *n*. offspring of two plants or animals of different species; mongrel. *-a*. cross-bred. **-hy'bridize** *v.t.* and *i*. **-hy'-bridism** *n*. [L. *hybrida*]

hydro- *prefix*. [G. *hydor*, water] in **hydrant** *n*. water-pipe with a nozzle for a hose. **-hydraul'ic** *a*. relating to the conveyance of water; worked by water power. *-n*. (in *pl*.) science of water conveyance or water-power. **-hydroelec'tric** *a*. of electricity obtained from water power or steam. **hy'drogen** *n*. colorless gas which combines with oxygen to form water. **-hy'drophone** *n*. instrument for detecting sound through water. **-hydropon'ics** *n*. *pl*. science of cultivating plants in water without using soil. **-hydrostat'ic** *a*. of hydrostatics. Also many other compounds.

hy'giene *n*. principles of health; sanitary science. [G. *hygies*, healthy]

hymn (him) *n*. song of praise, *esp*. to God. *-v.t.* praise in song. **-hym'nal** *a*. of hymns. *-n*. book of hymns. [G. *hymnos*]

hyperbola *n*. curve produced when a cone is cut by a plane making a larger angle with the base than the side makes. [G. *hyperbole*, hyper, beyond, *ballein*, throw]

hy'phen *n*. a short stroke joining two words or syllables. **hyphenate** *v.t.* to connect by a hyphen. [G. *hypo-*, under, *hen*, one]

hypno'sis (hip-) *n*. state like deep sleep in which the subject acts on external suggestion. **-hypnot'ic** *a*. of hypnosis. *n*. person under hypnosis; thing producing it. **-hyp'notism** *n*. production of hypnosis. **-hyp'notist** *n*. **-hyp'notize** *v.t.* IG. *hypnos*, sleep]

hypochon'dria *n*. morbid depression. [G. *hypochondria*, parts below the costal cartilages (as the seat of melancholy)]

hypoc'risy *n*. assuming of a false appearance of virtue; insincerity **hypocrite** *n*. **-hypocrit'ical** *a*. **-hypocrit'ically** *adv*. [G. *hypokrisis*, acting a part]

hypoderm'ic *a*. introduced beneath the skin. [G. *hypo*, under, *derma*, skin]

hypot'enuse *n*. side of a right-angled triangle opposite the right angle. [G. *hypoteinousa*, 'subtending']

hypoth'esis *n*. supposition as a basis for reasoning; assumption. **-hypothet'ical** *a*. **-hypothet'ically** *adv*. [fr. G. *hypo*, under, and *tithenai*, place]

hyste'ria (his-) *n*. disturbance of (a woman's) nervous system with convulsions, disturbance of mental faculties, *etc*.; morbid excitement. **-hyster'ical** *a*. **-hyster'ically** *adv*. **-hyster'ics** *n*. *pl*. fits of hysteria. [G. *hystera*, womb]

I

I *pron*. pronoun of the first person singular. [OE. *ic*]

iamb'us, i'amb *n*. metrical foot of a short

followed by a long syllable. -**iamb'ic** *a.*
[G. *iambos*]

Ibe'rian *a.* of Spain and Portugal. [*Iberia*]

i'bex *n.* wild goat with large horns. [L.]

i'bis *n.* stork-like wading bird. [G.]

ice *n.* frozen water; frozen confection. -*v.t.*
cover with ice; cool with ice: cover with
sugar. -**ice'-age** *n.* glacial period. -**ice'ax**
n. climber's ax for ice. -**ice'berg** *n.* large
floating mass of ice. -**ice'-blink** *n.* reflection in air of distant ice. -**ice'-bound** *a.*
bound, surrounded by ice. -**icecap** *n.*
frozen region at N., S. Pole. -**ice'-cream**
a. frozen flavored cream or similar substance. [OE. *is*]

ichthyol'ogy (ikth-) *n.* branch of zoology
treating of fishes. -**ichthyosaur'us** *n.*
prehistoric marine animal. [G. *ichthys*,
fish, *sauros*, lizard]

id *n.* (*psych.*) instinctive impulses of the
individual. [L. = it]

ide'a *n.* notion in the mind; way of thinking; vague belief, plan, aim. -**ide'al** *a.* existing only in idea; visionary; perfect. -*n.*
perfect type. -**ide'ally** *adv.* **ide'alism** *n.* imaginative treatment; philosophy that the
object of external perception consists of
ideas. -**ide'alist** *n.* -**ide'alize** *v.t.* represent
or look upon as ideal. [G. = *look*;
semblance]

ident'ity *n.* absolute sameness; individuality. -**ident'ical** *a.* the very same.
-**ident'ically** *adv.* -**ident'ify** *v.t.* establish
the identity of; associate (oneself) within,
separably; treat as identical. -
identifica'tion *n.* [L. *idem*, same]

ideol'ogy *n.* science of ideas; system of
ideas; abstract speculation. -**ideol'ogist** *n.*
[*idea* and G. *logia*, discourse]

id'iom *n.* one's language; way of expression natural to a language; expression
peculiar to it. -**idiomat'ic** *a.* characteristic
of a language; marked by the use of idioms,
colloquial. -**idiomat'ically** *adv.* [*See* idiot]

id'iot *n.* mentally deficient person. -
id'iocy *n.* state of being an idiot. -**idiot'ic**
a. -**idiot'ically** *adv.* [G. *idios*, own,
peculiar]

i'dle *a.* doing nothing; lazy; useless, vain,
groundless. -*v.i.* be idle. -*v.t.* pass time in
idleness. [OE. *idel*, useless]

i'dol *n.* image of a deity as an object of
worship; false god; object of excessive
devotion. -**idol'ator** *n.* worshipper of
idols. -**i'dolize** *v.i.* make an idol of; love or
venerate to excess. [G. *eidolon*, image]

if *conj.* on the condition or supposition that;
whether. [OE. *gif*]

ig'loo *n.* Eskimo snow-hut. [Eskimo]

ig'neous *a.* fiery; resulting from fire. -
ignite' *v.t.* set on fire. -*v.t.* take fire. -
igni'tion *n.* device for igniting explosive
mixture in internal-combustion engine.[L.
ignis, fire]

ignore' *v.t.* disregard, leave out of account.
-**ig'norance** *n.* lack of knowledge. [L. *ig-
norare*, not to know]

il- *prefix*, for in- before '*l*', negatives the
idea of the simple word: e.g. **ille'gal** *a.* not
legal. -**illeg'ible** *a.* not legible; *etc. etc.*
Such words are not given where the meaning and derivation are clear from the
simple word.

ill *a.* out of health; bad, evil; faulty. -*n.* evil,
harm; *adv.* not well; faultily, unfavorably.
-**ill'-bred** *a.* bad-mannered. -**ill'favored**
a. ugly. -**ill'-feeling** *a.* resentment, unpleasantness. -**ill-natured** *a.* bad-
tempered. -**ill'ness** *n.* -**ill-timed** *a,* inopportune. -**ill-will** *n.* enmity. [ON. *illr*]

illegiti'mate *a.* illegal; born out of wedlock. -*n.* bastard. -**illegit'imacy** *n.* [L. *il-
legitirnus*]

illit'erate *a.* unable to read or write. -
illit'eracy *n.* [L. *il-*, not, -*litteratus*]

illu'minate *v.t.* light up; decorate with
lights; decorate with gold and colors. [L.
illuminare, throw into light, *lumen*]

illu'sion *n.* deceptive appearance, belief,
or statement. [L. *illudere*, *illus-*, mock]

ill'ustrate *v.t.* make clear, *esp.* by ex-
amples or drawings; adorn with pictures.
-**illus'trious** *a.* famous. [L. *illustrare*,
throw into brightness]

im'age *n.* statue; semblance; type; simile,
metaphor; counterpart; optical counterpart, as in a mirror. -*v.t.* make an image of,
reflect. -**im'agery** *n.* images; use of
rhetorical figures. [L. *imago, imagin-*,
image]

imag'ine (-j-) *v.t.* picture to oneself; conjecture; think. -**imag'inable** *a.* -**imag'-
inary** *a.* existing only in fancy. -
imagina'tion *n.* faculty of making mental
images; fancy. [image]

im'itate *v.t.* take as model; mimic, copy.
[L. *imitari*]

im- *prefix,* for *in-* before '*m*', negatives the
idea of the simple word: *e.g.,* **imm'ature**
a. not mature. -**immo'bile** *a.* not mobile,
etc., etc. Such words are not given where
the meaning and derivation are clear from
the simple word.

immate'rial *a.* not composed of matter;
unimportant. [L. *im-* and *materialis*]

imme'diate *a.* occurring at once; direct,
not separated by others. -**imme'diately**
adv. -**imme'diacy** *n.* [Med. L. *immediatus*]

immense' *a.* huge, vast, immeasurable. [L. *immensus*, unmeasured]

immerse' *v.t.* dip, plunge, into a liquid. [L. *immergere, immers-*]

imm'igrate *v.i.* come into a country as a settler. **-immigra'tion** *n.* **-imm'igrant** *n.* *-a.* [L. *immigrate, iminigrat-*]

imm'inent *a.* close at hand. [L. *imminere, imminent-*, overhang]

immob'ilize *v.t.* put out of action; deprive of mobility. [*mobile*]

immor'tal *a.* not mortal, undying, everlasting. **-immor'talize** *v.t.* render immortal; make famous for ever. [L. *immortalis*]

immune' *a.* secure, exempt; proof (against a disease, *etc.*). [L. *immunis*, exempt, orig, from public service, *munus*]

im- *prefix*, for *in-* before '*p*', negatives the idea of the simple word: *e.g.*, **impal'pable** *a.* not palpable, untouchable. **-impar'tial** *a.* not partial, fair; *etc., etc.* Such words are not given where the meaning and derivation are clear from the simple word.

im'pact *n.* collision, or the impulse resulting therefrom. [L. *impingere, impact-*, dash against]

impair' *v.t.* weaken, damage. **impair'ment** *n.* [F. *empirer,* make worse]

impale' *v.t.* transfix, *esp.* on a stake, to put to death; combine (two coats of arms) by placing them side by side with a line between. **-impale'ment** *n.* [F. *empaler,* fr. *pal,* stake]

impart' *v.t.* give a share of; communicate. [L. *impartire,* fr. *pars,* part]

impar'tial *a.* unbiased. [L. *im-*, and *pars, partis*]

im'passe *n.* position, situation from which there is no escape; deadlock. [F.]

impass'ible *a.* not liable to pain or suffering. [L. *pati, pass-,* suffer]

impas'sioned *a.* deeply moved; showing deep feeling. [*passion*]

impeach' *v.t.* call in question; accuse; accuse of treason. [orig. hinder, F. *empecher,* prevent]

impecc'able *a.* incapable of sin or error. [L. *impeccabilis,* fr. *peccare,* sin]

impede' *v.t.* hinder. [L. *impedire,* shackle]

imper'ative *a.* expressing command; obligatory. *-n.* imperative mood. **imper'atively** *adv.* [L. *imperare,* command]

imper'fect *a.* not perfect, having flaws; (*Gram.*) of tense denoting continuous action in the past [L *imperfectus*]

impe'rial *a.* of an empire; of an emperor; majestic. [L. *imperium,* rule, empire]

imper'sonate *v.t.* play the part of. -

impersona'tion *n.* **-imper'sonator** *n.* one who impersonates another, *esp.* on the stage. [*person*]

im'petus *n.* force with which a body moves; impulse. [L. = attack]

implant' *v.t.* insert, fix. [*plant*]

im'plement *n.* tool, instrument, utensil. *-v.t.* (im-ple-ment') carry (a contract, *etc.*) into effect. [L. *implore,* fill up]

im'plicate *v.t.* involve, include; entangle; imply. **-implica'tion** *n.* **-implic'it** (-s-) *a.* implied but not expressed; involved in a general principle, exclusive of individual judgment. **-implic'itly** (-s-) *adv.* **-imply'** *v.t.* involve the truth of, mean. [L. *implicare,* entangle]

implore' *v.t.* entreat earnestly. [L. *implorare,* fr. *plorare,* weep]

import' *v.t.* bring in, introduce (*esp.* goods from a foreign country); imply, mean; express; be of consequence to. **-im'port** *n.* thing imported; meaning; importance. [L. *importare,* fr. *portare,* carry]

impose' *v.t.* lay (a tax, duty, *etc.*) upon. *v.i.* be impressive take advantage, practice deceit (on). **-imposi'tion** *n.* **-impos'ter** *n.* deceiver, one who assumes a false character. [F. *imposer*]

im'potent *a.* powerless, ineffective. [*potent*]

impov'erish *v.t.* make poor or weak. **impov'erishment** *n.* [OF. *enipourir*]

impreg'nable *a.* proof against attack. [F. *imprenable,* fr. *prendre,* take]

impreg'nate *v.t.* make pregnant; saturate. **-impregna'tion** *n.* [*pregnant*]

impress' *v.t.* imprint, stamp; fix; affect deeply. **-im'press** *n.* act of impressing; mark impressed. **-impres'sion** *n.* impress; printed copy; total of copies printed at once; effect produced, *esp.* on mind or feelings; notion, belief. **-impres'sionism** *n.* method of painting or writing to give general effect without detail. [L. *imprimere, irnpress-,* fr. *premere,* press]

impress' *v.t.* press into service. **impress'ment** *n.* [*press*]

imprint' *v.t.* impress; stamp; publisher's name on the title page of a book. **-im'print** *n.* impression, stamp. [*print*]

impris'on (-z-) *v.t.* put in prison. **imprls'onment** *n.* [*prison*]

improve' *v.t.* make better; make good use of. *-v.i.* become better. [A.F. *emprower,* turn to profit, OF. *prou,* profit]

im'provise *v.t.* compose or utter extempore; get up, arrange, extempore. **improvisa'tion** *n.* [F. *improviser*]

im'pudent *a.* pert, insolent, saucy. [L. *im-*

pudens, impudent-, shameless]

im′pulse *n.* sudden application of force; motion caused by it; sudden inclination to act; incitement. -**impul′sion** *n.* impulse, usually in the first sense. -**impul′sive** *a.* given to acting without reflection. -**impul′sively** *adv.* [L. *impellere, impuls-*, cp. *impel*]

impu′nity *n.* freedom from injurious consequences. (L. *impunitas*]

impute′ *v.t.* set to the account of, ascribe. -**imputabil′ity** *n.* -**imputa′tion** *n.* [L. *imputare,* fr. *putare,* reckon]

in *prep.* expresses inclusion within limits of space. time, circumstances, *etc.* -*adv.* in or into some state, place, *etc.* [OE.]

in- *prefix* negatives the idea of the simple word; *e.g.,* **inact′ive** *a.* not active; **incapable** *a.* not capable, *etc., etc.* Such words are omitted where the meaning and derivation may easily be inferred from the simple word. [L. *in-*, not]

inane′ *a.* empty, void; foolish, silly. -**inan′ity** *n.* -**inani′tion** *n.* being empty, exhaustion. [L. *inanis,* empty]

inaug′urate *v.t.* admit to office; begin, initiate, *esp.* with ceremony. [L. *inaugurate,* take auguries before action]

incandes′cent *a.* glowing with heat, shining; of artificial light; produced by glowing filament. -**incandes′cence** *n.* -**incandesce′** *v.i.* and *t.* [L. *candescere,* begin to glow, *candere*]

incarcerate *v.t.* imprison, shut up. -**incarcera′tion** *n.* -**incar′cerator** *n.* [L. *in,* in, *carcer,* prison]

incense′ *v.t.* enrage; incite, urge. [L. *incendere, incens-*]

in′cense *n.* gum or spice giving a sweet smell when burned; its smoke; flattery. *v.t.* burn incense to; perfume with incense. [L. *incendere, incens-*, kindle]

incen′tive *a.* arousing. -*n.* something that arouses to feeling or action. [L. *incentivus,* setting the tune]

incess′ant *a.* unceasing; continual; without intermission. -**incessantly** *adv.* [L. *cessare,* cease]

in′cest *n.* sexual intercourse of kindred within forbidden degrees. -**incest′uous** *a.* [L. *incestus,* impure, unchaste]

inch (-sh) *n.* one-twelfth of a foot. [OE. *ynce,* L. *uncia,* twelfth part]

in′cident *n.* event, occurrence. -*a.* naturally attaching to; striking, falling (upon). -**in′cidence** *n.* falling on, or affecting. -**incident′al** *a.* casual, not essential. -**incident′ally** *adv.* [L. *incidere,* fall in]

incin′erate *v.t.* consume by fire. -

incin′erator *n.* -**incinera′tion** *n.* [Med. L. *incinerare,* reduce to ashes]

incip′ient *a.* beginning. -**incip′ience** *n.* -**incip′iently** *a.* [L. *incipere,* begin]

incite′ *v.t.* urge, stir up. -**incite′ment** *n.* [L. *incitare,* rouse]

incline′ *v.t.* bend, turn from the vertical; dispose. -*v.i.* slope; be disposed. -**in′cline** *n.* slope. -**inclina′tion** *n.* [F. *incliner,* cp. *decline*]

include′ *v.t.* reckon in; comprise. -**inclu′sion** *n.* -**inclu′sive** *a.* -**inclu′sively** *adv.* [L. *includere,* shut in]

incog′nito *adv.* with identity concealed or not avowed. -*a.* concealing or not avowing identity. -*n.* this condition. [It., fr. L. *incognitus,* unknown]

incohe′rent *a.* unable to be understood. [*in-* and L. *cohaerere*]

in′come *n.* receipts, *esp.* annual, from work, investments, *etc.* -**in′come-tax** *n.* direct tax on income. [*in* and *come*]

increase′ *v.i.* become greater in size, number, *etc.* -*v.t.* make greater. -**in′crease** *n.* growth, enlargement, multiplication. -**in′crement** *n.* increase; profit. [L. *increscere,* fr. *crescere,* grow]

incrim′inate *v.t.* charge with crime; involve in an accusation. -**incrim′in-atory** *a.* [L. *crimen,* crime]

in′cubate *v.t.* hatch (eggs). -*v.i.* sit on eggs; of disease germs, pass through the stage between infection and appearance of symptoms. [L. *incubare*)

incumb′ent *a.* lying, resting on, -*n.* present holder of an office. -**incumb′cncy** *n.* office or tenure of an incumbent. [L. *incumbere,* lie upon]

incur′ *v.t.* fall into, bring upon oneself [L. *incurrere,* run into]

incur′sion *n.* invasion, inroad. [*incur*]

indeed′ *adv.* in truth, really. [*in deed*]

indel′ible *a.* that cannot be blotted out, or effaced; permanent. [L. *delere,* wipe out]

indem′nity *n.* security against loss; compensation, *esp.* exacted by a victorious country after war. -**indem′nify** *v.t.* compensate. -**indemnifica′tion** *n.* [L. *indemnis,* unharmed]

indent′ *v.t.* make notches or holes in; draw up a document in duplicate; make an order (upon some one *for*); requisition, order by indent; (*print.*) give relatively wider margin to (line, passage). -**in′dent** *n.* notch; an order, requisition. -**indenta′tion** *n.* -**indent′ure** *n.* indented document ′sealed agreement, *esp.* one binding apprentice to master. *v.t.* bind by indenture. [Med. L. *iridetitare,* give a serrated edge]

indepen'dent *a.* not subject to others; self-reliant; free; valid in itself; politically of no party. **-inde'pen'dence** or **indepen'dency** *n.* being independent; self-reliance; self-support. [L. *depinigere*, depend]

in'dex *n.* (**in'dexes, in'dices** *pl.*) forefinger, anything that points out. an indicator; alphabetical list of references, usually at the end of a book. *-v.t.* provide a book with an index; insert in an index. **-in'dicate** *v.t.* point out, state briefly. [L. *indicare*, fr. *dicare*, make known]

In'dian *a.* of India, the Indies; or the aborigines of America. [L. *India - Indus*, the Indus]

indict' *v.t.* accuse, *esp.* by legal process. [OF. *enditer*, fr. L. *dictare*, proclaim]

indiff'erent *a.* impartial; careless; unimportant neither good nor bad, tolerable; having no inclination for or against. [*different*]

indi'genous *a.* born in or natural to a country. [L. *indigena*, native]

indig'nant *a.* moved bv anger and scorn; angered by injury. **-indig'nantly** *adv.* **-indigna'tion** *n.* contemptuous resentment. **-indig'nity** *n.* unworthy treatment; insult. [L. *indignari*, be angry at something unworthy, *indignus*]

individ'ual *a.* single; characteristic of a single person or thing. *-n.* single person. **-individ'ually** *adv.* **-individual'ity** *n.* individual existence or character. **-individ'ualism** *n.* social theory of free action of individuals. **-individ'ualist** *n.* [L. *iridividuus*. undivided, single]

indom'itable *a.* unsubduable. **-indom'itably** *adv.* [L. *domare, domit-*, tame]

induce' *v.t.* persuade; bring about; infer; produce (electricity) by induction. **-induce'ment** *n.* incentive, attraction. **induct'** *v.t.* instal in office. **-induc'tion** *n.* inducting; general inference from particular instances. [L. *inducere, induct-*, lead in]

indulge *v.t.* gratify; give free course to; take pleasure in freely. [L. *indulgere*, be courteous]

in'dustry *n.* diligence; habitual hard work; branch of manufacture or trade. **-indus'trious** *a.* diligent. **-indus'trial** *a.* of industries, trades. **-indus'trialism** *n.* factory system. **-indus'trialize** *v.t.* [L. *industria*]

inept' *a.* absurd, out of place, irrelevant; fatuous. **-inept'itude** *n.* [L. *ineptus*, fr. *aptus*, cp. *apt*]

inert' *a.* without power of action or resistance; slow, sluggish. **-iner'tia** (-shya) *n.* property by which matter continues in its existing state of rest or motion in a straight line unless that state is changed by external force; inability to exert oneself. **-inert'ly** *adv.* **-inert'ness** *n.* [L. *iners, inert-*, sluggish]

inev'itable *a.* unavoidable, not to be escaped. [L. *inevitabilis*, fr. *euitare*, avoid]

inex'orable *a.* unrelenting. **-inex'orably** *adv.* [L. *exorare*, entreat]

infall'ible *a.* never wrong, certain, unfailing. [*in-*, and Low L. *fallibilis*]

in'fant *n.* small child; person under the age of one, a minor. **-in'fancy** *n.* **-infant'icide** *n.* murder of new-born child; person guilty of this. **-in'fantile** *a.* childish. [L. *infans, infant-*, unable to speak]

in'fantry *n.* foot soldier. [It. *infanteria*]

infect' *v.t.* make noxious; affect (with disease). **-infec'tion** *n.* **-infec'tious** *a.* catching. [L. *inficere, infect-*, dip in]

infer' *v.t.* deduce by reasoning, conclude. **-inference** *n.* **-inferen'tial** *a.* **-infer'-able** *a.* [L. *inferre*, bring in]

infe'rior *a.* lower; of poor quality. *-n.* one lower (in rank, *etc.*). **-inferior'ity** *n.* **-inferior'ity complex** (*psych.*) suppressed sense of inferiority. resulting in undue self-assertion; (*colloq.*) sense of inferiority. [L. comp. of *inferus*, low]

in'fidel *n.* unbeliever. *-a.* unbelieving. **-infidel'ity** *n.* disbelief (in religion); disloyalty. [L. *infidelis*, fr. *fides*, faith]

infilt'rate *v.i.* percolate, trickle through. *-v.t.* cause to pass through pores. [*See* **filter**]

in'finite *a.* boundless. **-infinites'imal** *a.* extremely or infinitely small. **-in'finitely** *adv.* **-infin'ity** *n.* **-infin'itive** *a. gram.* in the mood expressing the notion of the verb without limitation bv any particular subject. [L. *infinitus*, unbounded]

infirm' *a.* physically, mentally, weak, irresolute. **-infirm'ity** *n.* **-infirm'ary** *n.* hospital. [L. *infirm us*, cp. *firm*]

inflate' *v.t.* blow up with air or gas; raise (price) artificially; increase (currency of a state) abnormally. **-infla'tion** *n.* [L, *flare, flat-*, blow]

inflex'ible *a.* unbending, unyielding; stern. [L. *in-, flexibilis*, yielding]

inflict' *v.t.* impose, deliver forcibly, cause to be borne. **-inflic'tion** *n.* inflicting; boring experience. [L. *infligere, inflict-*.]

in'fluence *n.* agent or action working invisibly (upon); moral power (over, with); thing or person exercising this. *-v.t.* exert influence upon. **-influen'tial** *a.* **-influ-**

en'tially adv. [L. fluere, flow]

inform' v.t. tell; inspire. -v.i. bring a charge against. -inform'ant n. one who tells. - informa'tion n. telling; what is told, knowledge. -informa'tion techno'logy n. the technology of the production, storage, and communication of information using computers and microelectronics. - inform'ative a. -inform'er n. one who brings a charge. [L. informare, give form to]

infuriate v.t. fill with fury. [fury]

inge'nious a. clever at contriving; cleverly contrived. -ingenu'ity n. skill in planning, invention. -inge'niously adv. [L. ingenium, natural ability]

in'génue n. artless young girl, esp. as a stage type. [F.]

ingen'uous a. frank, artless, innocent. [L. ingenuus, free-born, frank]

ingra'tiate v. refl. work oneself into a position of favor. [L. in gratiam, into favor]

ingre'dient n. component part of a mixture. [L. ingredi, step in]

inhab'it v.t. dwell in. -inhab'itable a. - inhab'itant n. [L. habitare, dwell]

inhale' v.t. breathe in. -v.i. breathe in air. -inhala'tion n. [L. inhalare]

inher'it v.t. take as heir; derive from parents. -v.i. succeed as heir. [L. heres, heir]

inhib'it v.t. forbid; forbid to exercise clerical functions; hinder (action). [L. inhibere, inhibit-, hold in]

ini'tial (-ish-) a. of the beginning, occurring at the beginning. -n. initial letter. v.t. mark, sign, with one's initials. -ini'tiate v.t. set on foot, begin; admit, esp. into a secret society. -n. initiated person. - initia'tion n. -ini'tiative n. first step, lead; power of acting independently. -a. originating. -ini'tiatory a. [L. initialis, fr. initium, beginning]

inject v.t. force in (fluid, medicine, etc.), as with a syringe; fill thus. -injec'tion n. [L. injicere, inject-, throw in]

injunc'tion n. judicial order to restrain; authoritative order; exhortation. [Late L. injunctio, cp. enjoin]

in'jury n. wrong, damage, harm. -in'jure v.t. do wrong to, damage. [L. injuria, fr. jus, jur-, law]

ink a. fluid used for writing; paste used for printing. -v.t. mark with ink; cover or smear with it. -ink'bottle n. [ME. enke. G. enkhaustos, burnt in]

ink'ling n. hint, slight knowledge or suspicion. [ME. inklen, whisper]

in-law n. relative by marriage as mother-in-law. [in and law]

in'lay v.t. embed; decorate thus. -n. inlaid work. [in and lay]

in'mate n. occupant, inhabitant esp. in institution. [in and mate]

inn n. public house for the lodging or refreshment of travelers. -inn'keeper n. [OE.]

inn'ocent a. free from guilt; guileless; harmless. -n. innocent person, esp. a young child; idiot. [L. nocere, harm]

innoc'uous a. harmless. [See innocent]

inn'ovate v.t. bring in changes, new things. -inn'ovator n. -innova'tion n. [L. innocare, fr. novus, new]

inord'inate a. excessive. [L. inordinatus, unordered, cp. order]

inorgan'ic a. not organic or organized; of substance without carbon. [in-, and L. organcus]

in'put n. power or information supplied to machine; work or money put into an enterprise. [in and put]

in'quest n. legal or judicial inquiry, esp. into cause of sudden, violent, death. [OF. enqueste, inquiry]

insane' a. mad. -insan'ity n. [L. insanus]

inscribe' v.t. write (in or on something); mark; trace (figure) within another; dedicate. -inscrip'tion n. inscribing, words inscribed on a monument, coin, etc. [L. inscribere, inscript-]

in'sect n. small invertebrate animal with six legs, body divided into segments and two or four wings. -insect'icide n. preparation for killing insects. -insectiv'orous a. insect-eating. [L. insectum, cut into (from the segments)]

insem'inate v.t. sow; impregnate. - insemina'tion n. [in-, and L. seminare, to sow]

insert' v.t. place or put (in, into, between); introduce (into written matter, etc.). - inser'tion n. [L. inserere, fr. serere, sert-, join]

in'side n. inner side, surface, or part. -a. of, in, or on, the inside. -adv. in or into the inside. -prep. within, on the inner side. [in and side]

in'sidious a. stealthy, treacherous. - insid'iously adv. [L. insidiosus, fr. insidere, lie in wait]

in'sight n. mental penetration. [sight]

insig'nia n. pl. badges or emblems of an honor or office. [L. =distinguished things; fr. signurn, sign]

insin'uate v.t. bring or get (something into something) gradually or subtly; hint. -

insinua'tion n. [L. *insinuate*, introduce tortuously. cp. *sinuous*]

insist' v.i. dwell on, maintain, demand persistently. [L. *insistere*, fr. *sistere*, stand]

in'solent a. insulting, offensively contemptuous. **-in'solently** adv. **-in'solence** n. [L. *insolens*; orig. unaccustomed]

inspect' v.t. examine closely or officially. **-inspec'tion** n. **-inspec'tor** n. [L. *inspicere, inspect-*, look into]

inspire' v.t. breathe in; infuse thought or feeling into; arouse, to create. **-inspira'tion** n. breath; influence, *esp.* divine influence. [L. *inspirare*]

install' v.t. place (person in an office, *etc.*) with ceremony; establish, have put in. installa'tion n. [F. *installer*, put in a stall]

install'ment (-awl-) n. payment of part of a debt; any of parts of a whole delivered in succession; installation. [earlier *estallment*, fr. OF, *estaler*, fix]

in'stance n. example; particular case; request; place in a series. -v.t. cite. **-in'stant** a. urgent; belonging to the current month; immediate. -n. moment, point of time. [L. *instantia*, fr. *instare*, be present, urge]

instead' (-ed) adv. in place (of). [*stead*]

in'step n. top of the foot between toes and ankle. [orig. uncertain]

instill' v.t. put in by drops; drop slowly (into the mind). [L. *stillare*, drop]

in'stinct n. inborn impulse or propensity; unconscious skill; intuition; involuntary impulse. **-instinct'** a. charged, full. **-instinct'ive** a. **-instinct'ively** adv. [L. *instinctus*, fr. *instinguere*, urge]

in'stitute v.t. establish, found; appoint; set going. -n. society for promoting some public object, *esp.* scientific; its building. **-institu'tion** n. instituting; established custom or law; institute. **-institu'tional** a. **-in'stitutor** n. [L. *instituere, institute*, set up]

instruct' v.t. teach, inform, give directions to. **-instruc'tion** n. [L. instruere, instruct-, build]

in'strument n. tool or implement, *esp.* for scientific purposes; person or thing made use of; contrivance for producing music; legal document. **-instrument'al** a. **-instrument'alist** n. player of musical instrument. [L. *instrumentum*, fr. *instruere*, build]

in'sular a. of an island; of islanders. [L. *insula*, island]

in'sulin (-sŏi-) n. extract used in the treatment of diabetes and mental diseases. [L. *insula*, island]

insult' v.t. assail with abuse in act or word.

-in'sult n. scornful abuse, affront. [L. *insultare*, jump at]

insure' v.t. secure the payment of a sum in event of loss, death, *etc.*, by a contract and payment of sums called premiums; make such contract about; make safe (against); make certain. [var. of e**nsure**]

intact' a. untouched; whole, uninjured. [L. *tangere, tact-*, touch]

intang'ible a. not perceptible to touch, elusive. **-intangibil'ity** n. [*in-*, and L. *tangibilis*]

in'teger (-j-) n. whole number. **-in'tegral** (-g-) a. **-in'tegrate** v.t. combine into a whole. **-integra'tion** n. **-integ'rity** n. original perfect state; honesty, uprightness. [L. = *untouched*]

intell'igent a. having or showing good intellect; quick at understanding. **-intelligently** adv. **-intell'igence** n. intellect; quickness of understanding; information. news. **-intell'igible** a. that can be understood. [L. *intelligens, intelligent-*]

intend' v.t. design, purpose, mean. [L. *intenders, intens-, intent-*, bend the mind on, fr. *tendere*, stretch]

intense' a. very strong or acute **-intens'ify** v.t. **-intens'ive** a. giving emphasis; aiming at increased productiveness. **-intens'ively** adv. [See intend]

intent' n. purpose. -a. eager; resolved, bent. **-intent'ly** adv. **-inten'tion** n. purpose, aim. **-inten'tional** a. **-intent'ness** n. [See intend]

inter' v.t. bury. **-inter'ment** n. [F. *enterrer*, fr. *terre*, earth]

inter' *prefix* meaning between, among, mutually; forms compounds, *e.g.*, **intercolo'nial** a. between colonies. [L. *inter*, between]

interac'tive language n. (*compute.*) means or method by which programmers communicate while executing a program.

intercede' v.i. plead. **-intercession** n. **-intercess'or** n. [L. *cedere, cess-*, go]

intercept' v.t. cut off, seize in transit. **-intercep'tion** n. [L. *capere, capt-*, take]

in'tercourse n. mutual dealings; communication; connection. [OF. *entrecours*, fr. *entrecourre*, run between]

in'terest n. concern, curiosity; thing exciting this; money paid for use of borrowed money; legal concern; right; advantage; personal influence. -v. t. excite interest; cause to feel interest. **-interesting** a. **-in'terestingly** adv. [L. *interesse*, be a concern to]

interfere' v.i. meddle; clash; of rays, *etc.*, strike together. [L. *ferire*, strike]

in'terim *n.* meantime. *-a.* temporary, intervening. [L. = meanwhile]

inte'rior *a.* situated within; inland. *-n.* inside, inland. [L. comp. of *interns,* fr. L. *intra,* within]

interjec'tion *n.* word thrown in, or uttered abruptly. **-interject'** *v.t.* [L. *interjectio,* fr. *jicere, ject-,* throw]

interme'diate *a.* coming between two; interposed. **-interme'diary** *n.* one acting between two parties, go-between. [L. *medius,* middle]

intermit' *v.t.* and *i.* stop for a time. **-intermis'sion** *n.* **-intermitt'ent** *a.* ceasing at intervals. [L. *mittere,* put, send]

inter'nal *a.* in, of, the interior; of home (as opposed to foreign) affairs. **-inter'nal-combus'tion en'gine,** engine driven by explosions of gas within its cylinder. [L. *internus*]

interna'tional (-nash-) *a.* between nations. *-n.* international (games, *etc.*) contest; one taking part in such. [*national*]

inter'pret *v.t.* explain; explain to oneself; translate for another's benefit; in art, render, represent. **-inter'preter** *n.* **-interpretation** *n.* [L. *interpretari*]

inter'preter *n.* (*compute.*) computer program which converts information from progamming language into machine language.

interr'ogate *v.t.* question *esp.* closely or officially. **-interroga'tion** *n.* **-interrog'ative** *a.* questioning; used in asking a question. [L. *rogare,* ask]

intersect' *v.t.* cut into or through; divide; cross (each other). **-intersec'tion** *n.* **-intersec'tional** *a.* [L. *secare, sect-,* cut]

in'terval *n.* pause, break, intervening time or space; difference of pitch between any two musical tones. [L. *intervallum,* orig. space between ramparts]

in'terview *n.* meeting, *esp.* formally arranged; meeting of a journalist and person whose views he wishes to publish. *-v.t.* have an interview with. **-in'terviewer** *n.* [F. *entrevue,* fr. *voir,* see]

intest'ate *a.* not having made a will. *-n.* intestate person. [L. *testari, testat-,* make a will]

in'timate *a.* familiar, closely acquainted; close. *-n.* intimate friend. **-in'timacy** *n.* **-in'timate** *v.t.* make known; announce. **-intima'tion** *v.i.* [L. *intimatus*]

in'timidate *v.t.* force or deter by threats. **-intimida'tion** *n.* **-intim'idator** *n.* [Late L. *intimidate,* fr. *timidus,* timid]

in'to *prep.* expresses motion to a point within. [*in to*]

intone' *v.t.* recite in monotone or singing voice. **-intona'tion** *n.* modulation of voice; intoning. [Church L. *intoniare,* fr. *tonus,* tone]

intox'icate *v.t.* make drunk; excite beyond self-control. [G. *toxicon,* arrow poison]

in'tricate *a.* involved, puzzlingly entangled. [L. *intricatus,* entangled]

intrigue' *n.* underhand plotting or plot; secret love affair. *-v.i.* carry on an intrigue. *-v.t.* whet the interest of, fascinate. **-intri'guer** *n.* [F., fr. L. *intricare,* entangle, *v.s.*]

introduce' *v.t.* bring in, forward; make known formally; bring to notice; insert. **-introduc'tion** *n.* preface to a book. **-introduc'tory** *a.* [L. *introducere,* lead in]

introspec'tion *n.* examination of one's own thoughts. [L. *introspicere, introspect-,* look within]

introvert' *v.t.* turn inwards. *-n.* (in'-) (*psych.*) introspective person, one whose mind is turned within. **-introversion** *n.* [L. *vertere,* turn]

intrude' *v.i.* thrust in without invitation or right. *-v.t.* force in. **-intru'sion** *n.* **-intru'sive** *a.* [L. *intruders, intrus-,* thrust in]

intui'tion (-ish-) *n.* immediate or direct apprehension by the mind without reasoning; immediate insight. **-intu'itive** *a.* **-intu'itively** *adv.* [Med. L. *intuitio,* fr. *inteuri, intuit-,* look upon]

invade' *v.t.* enter with hostile intent; assail; encroach on. **-inva'der** *n.* **-inva'sion** *n.* [L. *invadere, invas,* go in]

inval'id *a.* not valid, of no legal force. [L, *invalidus* fr. *validus,* strong]

inval'uable *a.* above price. [*valuable*]

invent' *v.t.* devise, originate. [L. *invenire, invent-,* come upon, discover]

in'ventory *n.* list of goods, *etc.* *-v.t.* enter in an inventory. [L. *inventarium*]

invert' *v.t.* turn upside down; reverse the position or relations of. **-in'verse** *a.* inverted. *-n.* opposite. **-inverse ratio,** the ratio of reciprocals. [L. *invertere, invers-,*]

inver'tebrate *a/n.* (animal) with no backbone; spineless, weak. [L. *in-,* and *vertebra*]

invest' *v.t.* lay out (money); clothe; endue; cover as a garment; lay siege to. **-invest'iture** *n.* formal installation of person in office or rank. **-invest'ment** *n.* investing; money invested; stocks and shares bought. **-invest'or** *n.* [L. *inuestire,* clothe]

invest'igate *v.t.* inquire into. [L. *investgare,* fr. *vestigare,* track]

invin'cible *a.* unconquerable.

invincibil'ity n. [L. vincere, conquer]

invite' v.t. request courteously; attract, tend to call forth. -**invita'tion** n. -**invi'ting** a. enticing, attractive. **invitingly** adv. [L. invitare]

in'voice n. list of goods sent, with prices. -v.t. make an invoice of. [pl. of obs, invoy, F. envoi, sending]

invol'untary a. without power of will or choice; unintentional. [L. involuntarius]

involve' v.t. wrap up, entangle, implicate; imply, entail. -**in'volute** a. intricate; rolled spirally. -**involu'tion** n. [L. involvere, fr. volvere, volut-, roll]

in'ward adv. towards the inside, centre. -a. internal; in the heart, mind. -**in'wardly** adv. -**in'wardness** n. inner meaning. [OE. innanweard]

I/O n. equipment or data used to communicate with a computer [Input/Output]

i'odine n. non-metallic element of the chlorine group, used in medicine. [G. iodes, violet-colored, fr. color of its vapor]

i'on n. electrically charged atom or group of atoms. [G. = going]

ion'ic a. of Iona in Greece, pert. to style of architecture characterized by column with ramshorn volute at top. [Ionia]

ire n. anger, wrath. -**irate** a. angry. -iras'cible a. hot-tempered. -**irascibil'ity** n. -iras'ciblyadv. [L. ira]

i'ris n. genus of plants with sword-shaped leaves and showy flowers: circular membrane of the eye containing the pupil; formerly, rainbow. -**irides'cent** a. showing colors like a rainbow; changing color with change of position. -**irides'cence** n. [G. = rainbow]

i'ron n. metal, much used for tools, utensils, etc. , and the raw material of steel: tool, etc. , of this metal; smoothing iron; (golf) iron-headed club. [OE. iren]

i'rony n. speech in which the meaning is the opposite of that actually expressed; words used with an inner meaning. -iron'ical a. -iron'ically adv. [G. eironeia, dissimulation, affected ignorance]

ir- prefix for in - before 'r'. Many words are omitted in which the prefix simply negatives the idea of the simple word, as in irregular a. not regular, etc. irra'diate v. t. shine upon, throw light upon. -irradia'tion n. [L. radius, ray]

irr'igate v.t. water by channels or streams. [L. irrigare, irrigate, fr. rigare, moisten]

irri'tate v.t. excite to anger; excite, inflame, stimulate. [L. irritare, irritat]

is v. 3rd. pers. sing. pres. of be. [OE.]

Is'lam, Is'lamism n. the Muslim religion; the entire Muslim world. -**Islamic** a. [Ar. , slam -salama, to submit to God]

i'sland (-il-) piece of land surrounded by water; anything like this. -**i'slander** n. dweller on an island. [earlier iland, OE. iegland]

ism n. doctrine, theory, practice, esp. of a faddy or extravagant nature. [Suffix -ism, G. -ismos]

i'so pref. equal. [G. isos]

i'solate v.t. place apart or alone. [L. insula, island]

isos'celes a. of a triangle, having two of its sides equal. [G. isosceles, fr. isos, equal, and skelos, leg]

i'sotope (-tōp) n. element chemically identical with others, but having a different nuclear mass, hence atomic weight. [G. topos, place]

iss'ue n. going or passing out; outlet; offspring, children; outcome, result; question, dispute; a sending or giving out officially or publicly; number or amount so given out. -v.i. go out; result in; arise (from). -v.t. emit, give out, send out. [OF. issir, go out, L. exire]

it pron. neuter pronoun of the third person. -**itself'** pron. reflex and emphatic of it. [OE. hit]

ital'ic a. of type, sloping. -**ital'ics** n. pl. this type, now used for emphasis, foreign words, etc. -**ital'icize** v.t. put in italics. [L. Italicus, Italian]

itch v.i. feel an irritation in the skin; be anxious or keen to. -n. irritation in the skin; impatient desire. -**itch'y** a. [OE. giccan]

i'tem n. any of a list of things; detail; entry in an account or list. [L. adv = in like manner]

it'erate v.t. repeat. [L. iterare-iterum, again]

itin'erant a. travelling from place to place; travelling on circuit. -**itin'eracy** n. -itin'erary n. record of travel; route, line of travel; guide-book. [L. iter, itiner-, journey]

i'vory n. hard white substance of the tusks of elephants, etc. [F. iuoire]

i'vy n. climbing evergreen plant. -**i'vied** a. overgrown with ivy. [OE. ifig]

J

jab v.t. poke roughly, thrust abruptly. -n. poke. [var. of job]

jack n. sailor; boy, servant; knave in a pack of cards; various mechanical appliances, esp. for raising heavy weights; flag or ensign; various small things; added to names of animals. [F. , Jacques, James, but in E.

a pet form of John]

jack n. leather coat; leather bottle for liquor. [F. *Jacque*]

jack'al n. wild animal closely allied to the dog. [Pers. *shagal*]

jack'ass n. male donkey; stupid fellow [Jack = the *male*, and *ass]*

jack'et n. sleeved outer garment, a short coat; outer casing. [F. *jaquette*]

jade n. sorry nag, worn-out horse; in contempt, a woman. -*v.t.* tire out; weary. [orig. uncertain]

jade n. ornamental stone, usually green. [Sp. *(piedra de) ijada, colie* (stone), as supposed to cure pain]

jag n. sharp projection, e. g., point of rock. **-jagg'ed** a. [orig. unknown]

jail n. building for confinement of criminals or suspects; -*v.t.* send to, confine in prison. [OF. *gaole*, prison]

jam *v.t.* squeeze; cause to stick and become unworkable; pack together; interfere with. -*v.i.* stick and become unworkable. -*n.* fruit preserved by boiling with sugar; blockage, *esp.* traffic; musical improvisation by a group of musicians. [orig. uncertain]

jan'itor n. caretaker, doorkeeper. [L.]

Jan'uary n. first month of the year. [L. *januarius*, of Janus]

jar n. vessel of glass, earthenware, *etc.* [Arab. , *iarrah*, earthen vessel]

jar *v.i.* make a grating noise; vibrate gratingly, wrangle -*v.t.* cause to vibrate. -*n.* jarring sound; shock, *etc.* [imit.]

jaundice (-dis) n. disease marked by yellowness of the skin. **-jaun'diced** a. jealous, of soured outlook. [F. *jaunisse*, fr. *jaune*, yellow]

jaw n. one of the bones in which the teeth are set. -*pl.* mouth; gripping part of vice, *etc.* [F. *joue*, cheek]

jazz n. syncopated music and dance. -*v.i.* indulge in jazz. -*a.* discordant or bizarre in color, *etc.* **-jazz up'** (*sl.*) liven. [orig. unknown]

jeal'ous a. suspiciously watchful; distrustful of the faithfulness (of); envious; anxiously solicitous (for). -jeal'ousy n. **jeal'ously** adv. [F. *jaloux*]

Jeho'vah n. Hebrew name for God. [Heb. *Yahweh*]

jerk n. sharp, abruptly stopped movement, twitch, start, sharp pull. -*v.t.* and i. move, or throw, with a jerk; sneer. [orig. unknown]

jet n. hard black mineral capable of a brilliant polish. [G. *gagates*]

jet n. stream of liquid, gas, *etc.* , *esp.* shot from a small hole; the small hole; spout,

nozzle; aircraft driven by jet propulsion. -*v.t.* and i. spurt out in jets. [F. , fr. *jeter*, to throw]

jet'sam n. goods thrown out to lighten a ship and later washed ashore. **-jett'ison** *v.t.* throw overboard thus. [OF. *jetaison*, fr. *jeter*, throw]

jew'el n. precious stone; personal ornament containing one; precious thing. **jew'eler,** n. dealer in jewels. **-jew'elry** n. [OF. *goiel*]

jib n. ship's triangular staysail. [var. of *gybe*]

jig n. lively dance; music for it; various mechanisms or fittings. -*v.i.* dance a jig; make jerky up-and-down movements. [orig. uncertain]

jilt *v.t.* cast off (a over) after encouraging. -*n.* one who does this. [earlier *jillet,* dim. of Jill]

job n. piece of work; employment; unscrupulous transaction. -*v.i.* do odd jobs: deal in stocks. [orig. uncertain]

jock'ey a. professional rider in horseraces. -*v.t.* cheat; maneuver. [dim. of Jock, var. of Jack]

jog *v.t.* move or push with a jerk. -*v.i.* walk or ride with jolting pace; take exercise. -*n.* a jogging. **-jog'ger** n. person who runs at a jog trot over some distance for exercise, usually regularly. [orig. uncertain]

join *v.t.* put together. fasten, unite. -*v.i.* become united or connected. -*n.* a joining; place of joining. **-join'er** n. one who joins; maker of furniture and light woodwork. **-joint** n. arrangement by which two things fit or are joined together: share of or by two or more. -*v.t.* connect by joints: divide at the joints. **-joint'ly** adv. [F. *joindre*, fr. L. . *jungere, junct-*, join]

joist n. parallel beam stretched from wall to wall on which to fix floor or ceiling. [OF. *giste*, fr. L. *jacere*, lie]

joke n. thing said or done to cause laughter, something not in earnest. *v.i.* make jokes. *v.t.* banter. **-jo'ker** n. [L. *jocus*, jest]

jolt n. jerk; throwing up or forwards. as from a seat -*v.t.* and i. move or shake with jolts. [orig. uncertain]

jos'tle *v.t.* and i. knock or push against. -*n.* a jostling. [OF, jouster]

jot n. small amount. -*v.t.* write (down) briefly. [G. *iota*]

joule n. unit of electrical energy; unit of heat. [J. P. Joule, 1818-1891]

jour'nal n. daily record; logbook; daily newspaper or other periodical; part of an axle or shaft resting on the bearings. -**journalese'** n. jargon of journalists. -

jour'nalism n. editing, or writing in, periodicals. -jour'nalist n. journalis'tic a. [F. journal, fr. L. diurnalis]

jour'ney (jur-) n. a going to a place; distance traveled. -t. t. travel. -jour'neyman n. one who has learned a trade and works as an artisan paid by the day: hireling. [See journal]

joy n. gladness, pleasure; cause of this. - joy'-ride n. (sl.) pleasurable, reckless (and often unlawful) drive in a vehicle. [F. joie]

Juda'ic(al) a. of Jews. Ju'daism n. doctrine of Jews. [G, Joudaios, Jew]

judge (juj) n. officer appointed to try and decide cases in law court; one who decides a dispute, question. contest; -judg'ment n. sentence of a court; opinion; faculty of judging: misfortune regarded as a sign of divine displeasure. -judi'cious a. sensible, prudent. -judi'ciously adv, . - judi'ciary n. courts of law, system of courts and judges. [L. judex, n. judicare, v. , fr. jus, law]

jug n. deep vessel for liquids; contents of one. -v.t. stew (esp. a hare) in a jug or jar (jugged p.t./p.p. jugg'ing pres.p.); (sl.) imprison. [orig. uncertain]

jug'gle v.i. play conjuring tricks, amuse by sleight of hand; practice deceit. -v.t. trick or cheat (out of). -n. a juggling. [OF. joglere, L. joculari, jest]

jug'ular a. of or in the neck or throat. [L. jugulum, collar-bone]

juice n. liquid part of vegetable, fruit, meat; (coll.) gasoline or other source of power. -juic'y a. [L. jus, broth]

July' n. seventh month of the year. [L. birth-month of Julius Caesar]

jump v.i. spring from the ground. -v.t. pass by jumping. -n. leap, sudden upward movement. -jump'er n. -jump'y a. nervous. [of It. orig.]

junc'tion n. joining; place of joining; railway station where lines join. [L. jungere, junct-, join]

June n. sixth month of the year. [L. Junius]

jung'le (-ng-gl) n. tangled vegetation; land covered with it, esp. in India and the tropics; tangled mass. -jung'ly a. [Hind. jangal, Sans. jangala, desert]

junk n. old rope; salt meat; old odds and ends. [orig. unknown]

junk n. sailing vessel of the Chinese seas. [Port. junco]

junt'a n. council in Spain, Italy; group of persons, esp. military, holding power after a revolution. [Sp.]

Ju'piter n. Roman chief of gods; largest of the planets. [L.]

jur'y n. body of persons sworn to render a verdict in a court of law; body of judges in a competition. -jur'or n. one who serves on a jury. [L. jurare, swear, fr. jus, law]

just a. upright, fair; proper, right, equitable. -adv. exactly, barely. -just'ly adv. -justice (-is) n. quality of being just. fairness; judicial proceedings; judge, magistrate. -just'ify v.t. show to be right or true or innocent; be sufficient grounds for. [L. justus, fr. jus, law, right]

jut v.i. project. -n. projection. [jet]

ju'venile a. young; of, or for, the youthful. -n. young person, child. juvenil'ia n. pl. early, youthful, writings. [L. juvenilis- juvenis, young]

juxtapose' (-z) v.t. put side by side. - juxtaposi'tion n. [L. juxta, beside]

K

Kai'ser n. emperor, esp. of Germany. [L. Caesar]

kangaroo' n. Australian pouched mammal with very strong hind legs for jumping. [orig. uncertain]

keen a. sharp, vivid, acute, eager, strong. -keenly adv. [OE. cene]

keep v.t. observe, carry out; retain possession of, not lose; maintain; detain; cause to continue; reserve; manage. -v.i. remain good; remain; continue. -n. maintenance, food; central tower of a castle, a stronghold. -keep'er n. -keep'ing n. care, charge. possession; harmony, agreement. -keep'sake n. thing treasured for giver's sake. [OE. cepan]

keg n. small cask. [ON. kaggi, cask]

kenn'el n. house of shelter for dogs. -v.t. put into a kennel. [F. chenit, fr. L. canis, dog]

ker'osene n. lamp-oil or burning oil from petroleum or coal and shale. [G. keros, wax]

key n. instrument for moving the bolt of a lock; fig. anything that 'unlocks'; music, a set of related notes, lever to play a note of piano, organ, etc. -key'pad n. small keyboard with push buttons; a data input device consisting of a limited number of keys, each with nominated functions. [OE. caeg]

kick v.i. strike out with the foot; be recalcitrant; recoil. -v.t. strike with the feet. -n. blow with the foot; recoil. [ME. kiken, of unknown orig.]

kid n. young goat; leather of its skin; (sl.) child. v.t. (sl.) to hoax. [ON. kith]

kid'nap v.t. steal (a child), abduct (a person). -kid'naper n. [kid, child, nap, nab]

kid'ney *n*. either of the pair of organs which secretes the urine; nature, kind. [orig. uncertain]

kill *v.t.* deprive of life, slay. [ME. *kellen]*

kil'ogram *n*. weight of 1,000 grams. - **kil'ometer** *n*. -**kil'oliter** *n*. -**kil'owatt** *n*. electrical power of 1,000 watts. [G. *chilioi,* thousand]

kin *n*. family, relatives. -*a*. related by blood. [OE. *cynn]*

kind *n*. genus, sort, variety, class. -*a*. having a sympathetic nature, considerate, good, benevolent. [OE. *gecynd,* nature]

kin'dergarten n. school for teaching young children by games, *etc*. [Ger. = children's garden; (coined by Froebel)]

kin'dle *v.t.* set on fire. -*v.i.* catch fire. [ON. *kynd*a]

king *n*. male sovereign ruler of an independent state; piece in the game of chess; card in each suit with a picture of a king. -**king'dom** *n*. state ruled by a king. realm, sphere. [OE. *ying]*

kiss *n*. caress with the lips. -*v.t.* -*v.i.* exchange kisses. [OE. *cyssan]*

kit *n*. wooden tub; outfit; personal effects, *esp*. of traveller. -**kit'-bag** *n*. bag for soldier's or traveler's kit. [orig. uncertain]

kitch'en *n*. room used for cooking. - **kitch'en-garden** *n*. garden for vegetables, fruit. -**kitch'enmaid** *n*. **kitch'ener** *n*. cooking-range. **kitchenette** *n*. small compact kitchen. [OE. *cycene]*

kitt'en *n*. young cat. [var. of F. *chaton,* dim. of *chat,* cat]

knack (n-) *n*. toy, trifle; acquired faculty for doing something adroitly; trick. [orig. uncertain]

knee (n-) *n*. joint between the thigh and lower leg; corresponding joint in animals; part of a garment covering the knee. [OE. *cneow]*

kneel (n-) *v.i.* fall or rest on the knees. [OE. *cneowlian.* cp. knee]

knife (n-) *n*. (knives *pl*.) cutting blade in a handle. -*v.t.* cut or stab with a knife. **knife'board** *n*. board for cleaning knives [OE. *cnif]*

knight (nit) *n*. person of a rank below baronet, given the right to prefix Sir to his name; military follower, a champion; piece in the game of chess. -*v.t.* make (person) a knight. [OE. *cniht,* youth]

knit (n-) *v.t.* form a fabric by putting together a series of loops in wool, or other yarn; make close or compact. -*v.i.* unite. [OE *cynttan]*

knock (n-) *v.t.* strike, hit. -*n*. blow, rap. - **knock'er** *n*. who or what knocks; metal appliance for knocking on a door. -**knock'-kneed** *a*. having incurved legs. -**knock-'out** *n*. boxer's finishing blow. [OE. *cnocian]*

knot (n-) *n*. twisting together of parts of two or more strings, ropes, *etc*. , to fasten them together; cockade, cluster; hard lump, *esp*. of wood where a branch joins or has joined in; measure of speed of ships, *e.g*., ten knots means ten nautical miles per hour; difficulty. -*v.t.* tie with or in knots. [OE. *enotta]*

know *v.t.* be aware of, have information about, be acquainted with, recognize, have experience, understand. -*v.i.* have information or understanding. -**know'able** *a*. - **know'ing** *a*. that knows; cunning, shrewd. -**know'ingly** *adv*. -**knowledge** (nol-) *n*. knowing; what one knows; all that is or may be known, -**knowl'edgeable** (nolij-) *a*. intelligent, well-informed. [OE. *cnawan]*

knuc'kle (nuc-kl) *n*. bone at a finger joint. -*v.i.* knuckle down, to put the knuckles on the ground in playing marbles; yield -*v.t.* strike with the knuckles. [ME. *knokel]*

ko'sher *a*. of food, *etc*. . fulfilling the Jewish law. -*n*. kosher food or shop. [Heb. *kosher,* right]

ku'dos *n*. credit, prestige. [G.]

L

la'bel *n*. slip of paper, metal. *etc*., fixed to an object to give some information about it. -*v.t.* affix a label to; (fig.) a descriptive phrase associated with a person. [OF, narrow strip]

la'bial *a*. of the lips; pronounced with the lips. -*n*. sound so pronounced: letter representing it. [L. *labium,* lip]

la'bor (-her) *n*. exertion of the body or mind; task; pains of childbirth workmen collectively. -*v.i.* work hard; strive; maintain normal motion with difficulty; *esp*. of a ship, be tossed heavily. -*v.t.* elaborate; stress to excess. -**La'bor Day** *n*. (in the U.S. and Canada) a public holiday in honor of labor, held on the firit Monday in September. -**la'borer** *n*. one who labors, *esp*. a man doing manual work for wages. -**laborious** *a*. hard-working: toilsome. **labor'iously** *adv;* - **lab'oratory** n. place set apart for scientific investigations or for manufacture of chemicals. [L. *labor,* toil]

labyrinth *v.i.* network of passages in which it is hard to find the way, a maze. **labyrin'thine** *a*. [G. *labyrinthos]*

lace *n*. cord to draw edges together, *e. g*., to tighten shoes, stays, *etc*.; ornamental braid; fine open work fabric, often of elaborate pattern. -v.t.. fasten with laces: intertwine; flavor with spirit. [L. *laqueus*, noose]

lack *n.* deficiency, want. -v.t. be without, or poorly supplied with, [of Teutonic original]

lack'ey *n.* footman; menial attendant; obsequious person. -v.t. be, or play the, lackey to. [F. *laquais*]

laconic *a.* using, or expressed in, few words. **-lacon'ically** *adv.* **-lacon'icism** *n.* [G. *Lakonikos*, Spartan]

lac'quer *n.* hard varnish made from lac. -v.t. coat with lacquer. [Port. *lacre*, sealing-wax, fr. *lac*, *q.v.*]

lacrosse' *n.* ball-game played with long-handled rackets. [F. *(jeu de) la crosse*, the crook]

lac'tic *a.* of milk. **-lacta'tion** *n.* secreting of milk. **-lae'teal** *a.* of milk. **-lac'tose** *n.* milk sugar. **-lac'tic a'cid**, acid got from sour milk, [L. *lac*, *lact-*, milk]

lad *n.* boy, young fellow; stripling. [ME., *servant*]

ladd'er *n.* appliance consisting of two poles connected by cross-bars (rungs) used as means of ascent. [OE. *hlaeder*]

la'dle *n.* spoon with a long handle and large bowl. -v.t. lift out with a ladle. **la'dleful** *n.* [OE. *hladan*]

la'dy *n.* woman of good breeding or social position; title of woman of rank; formerly, mistress, wife, love; polite term for any woman. **-our Lady**, Virgin Mary. **la'dylike** *a.* **-la'dyship** *n.* [OE. *hloefdige*, loaf-kneader]

lag *v.i.* go too slow, fall, behind. -n. (*sl.*) convict. **-lagg'ard** *n.* one who lags. -a. loitering, slow. [orig. obscure]

lagoon' *n.* salt-water lake, often one enclosed by a reef or an atoll. [F. *lagu ne*, fr. L. *locus*. lake]

lair (lar) *n.* resting-place of a wild animal. [OE. *leger*, couch]

laissez-faire (les-a-fer) *n.* leaving alone; principle of non-intervention. [F.]

lake *n.* large body of water surrounded by land. **-lake'let** *n.* small lake. **-lake'-dwelling,** *n.* prehistoric dwelling built on piles in a lake. [OE. *lac*, L. *locus*]

lamb (lam) *n.* young of the sheep; its meat; innocent or helpless creature. -v.i. of a sheep, to give birth to a lamb. **lambing** *n.* birth of lambs; shepherd's work tending the ewes and newborn lambs at this time. **-lamb'like** *a.* meek. [OE.]

lambaste' *v.t.* thrash; criticize, scold severely. [*lanz* and *baste*]

lame *a.* crippled in a limb, *esp.* leg or foot; limping; of an excuse, *etc.*, unconvincing.

v.t. make lame. **-lame duck** *n.* disabled person; useless political official. [OE. *lama*]

lament' *n.* passionate expression of grief, song of grief. -v.t. and *i.* feel or express sorrow (for). **-lamenta'tion** *n.* **-lam'entable** *a.* deplorable. [L. *lamentum*, cry of mourning]

lamp *n.* vessel holding oil to be burnt at a wick for lighting; various other appliances as sources of light. **lamp'black** *n.* pigment made from soot. [G. *lampas*]

lampoon' *n.* venomous satire on an individual, -v.t. write lampoons against. [F. *lampon*, fr. *lampons*, 'let us guzzle' refrain to scurrilous songs]

lamp'rey *n.* fish like an eel with a sucker mouth. [F. *lamproie*]

lance (-a-) *n.* horseman's spear. -v.t. pierce with a lance or lancet. **-lan'cet** *n.* pointed two-edged surgical knife. **lan'cer** *n.* cavalry soldier armed with a lance. [F.]

land *n.* solid part of the earth's surface; ground, soil; country; property consisting of land. -pl. estates. -v.i- come to land, disembark. -v.t. bring to land. **-land'ing** *n.* act of landing; platform between flights of stairs. **-land'locked** *a.* enclosed by land. **-land'lord** *n.* **-land'lady** *fem.* person who lets land or houses, *etc.*; master or mistress of an inn, boardinghouse, *etc.* **-land'lubber** *n.* person ignorant of the sea and ships. [OE.]

landscape *n.* piece of inland scenery; picture of it. **-land'scape-painter** *n.* **land'scape-gard'ening** *n.* laying out of grounds picturesquely. [Du. *landschap*]

lane *n.* narrow road or street; passage in a crowd of people. [OE.]

lang'uage (-ng-gw-) *n.* speech; words used by a people; words used in a branch of learning; style of speech. [F. *langage*, fr. L. *lingua*, tongue]

lang'uish (ng-gw-) *v.i.* be or become weak or faint; be in depressing or painful conditions; droop, pine. **-lang'uid** *a.* weak, faint, spiritless, dull. **-lang'uidly** *adv.* **-lang'uor** (-gur) *n.* faintness; want of energy or interest; tender mood; softness of atmosphere. **-lang'uorous** *a.* [F. *languir*]

lant'ern *n.* transparent case for a lamp or candle; erection on a dome or roof to admit light. **-lant'horn** *n.* lantern. **lant'ern-jaws** *n. pl.* long thin jaws, giving concave effect. [L. *lanterns*]

lap *n.* fold, flap; front of a woman's skirt as used to hold anything; seat or receptacle made by a sitting person's thighs; single turn of wound thread, *etc.*; round of a racecourse. -v.t. enfold, wrap round. **lap'dog** *n.* small pet dog. [OE. *lappa*]

lap *v.t.* drink by scooping up with the tongue; of waves, *etc.*, to make a sound like an animal lapping. [OE. *lapian*]

lapa'roscope *n.* medical instrument consisting of a tube that is inserted through the abdominal wall and illuminated to enable a doctor to view the internal organs. **lapa'roscopy** *n.* [G. *lapara*, flank]

lapel' *n.* part of the front of a coat folded back toward the shoulders. [*lap*]

lapse *n.* slip; mistake; fall from virtue; passing (of time, *etc.*). *-v.i.* fall away; come to an end, *esp.* through some failure. [L. *lapsus*, slip]

lap'wing *n.* plover. [OE. *hleapewince*]

lard *n.* prepared pig's fat. *-v.t.* insert strips of bacon; intersperse or decorate (speech with strange words, *etc.*) [F. = *bacon*]

lard'er *n.* store-room for meat and other food. [OF. *lardier*, bacon-tub]

large *a.* broad in range or area; great in size, number, *etc.*; liberal; generous. **large'ly** *adv.* [L. *largus*, copious]

lark *n.* frolic, spree. *-v.i.* indulge in one. **lark'y** *a.* [ME. *laik*, sport; ON. *leikr*]

lar'va *n.* (**lar'vae** *pl.*) insect in the stage between grub and caterpillar. **-lar'val** *a.* [L. = *ghost, mask*]

lar'ynx *n.* part of the throat containing the vocal chords. **-laryngi'tis** *n.*- inflammation of this. [G.]

la'ser *n.* device for concentrating electromagnetic radiation or light of mixed frequencies into an intense, narrow concentrated beam. [fr. *l*ight *a*mplication by *s*timulaued *e*mission of *r*adiation]

lash *n.* stroke with a whip; flexible part of a whip. *-v.t.* strike with a whip thong, *etc.* *-t.i.* aim a violent blow of a whip, *etc.* [orig. uncertain]

lash *v.t.* fasten or bind with cord, *etc.* [OF. *lachier*, lace]

lass'o *n.* rope with a noose for catching cattle, *etc.*, by throwing the noose over the head. *-v.t.* catch with a lasso. [Sp. *lazo*, fr. L. *laqueus*, noose]

last *n.* model of foot on which shoemaker shapes boots, *etc.* [OE. *loeste*]

last *a.* and *adv.* last person or thing. **last'ly** *adv.* **-last'post** (*mil.*) bugle call at retiring hour, sounded also at military funerals. [OE. *latost*, fr. late]

last *v.i.* continue, hold out, remain alive or unexhausted. [OE. *loestan*, follow, continue]

latch *v.t.* fasten with a latch. *-n.* fastening for a door, consisting of a bar, a catch for it. and a lever to lift it, small lock with spring action. *-latch'key* *n.* [OE. *loeccan*, catch]

late *a.* after the proper time, backward; far on in a period of time; that was recently but now is not; recently dead; recent in date; of a late stage of development. *-adv.* after the proper time; recently; at or till a late hour. *-late'ly* *adv.* not long since. [OE. *loet*, tardy]

lat'eral *a.* of or at the side. **-lat'erally** *adv.* [L. *laterals*, fr. *latus*, later-, side]

la'tex (la-) *n.* milky plant-juice. [L.]

lath (lath) *n.* strip of wood. **-lath'y** *a.* like a lath; tall and thin. [OE. *loett*]

lathe *n.* machine for spinning an object while it is being cut or shaped. [orig. uncertain]

lath'er (-TH-) *n.* froth of soap and water; frothy sweat. *-v.t.* cover (chin) with lather. *-v.i.* form a lather. [OE. leather, foam, washing-soda]

Lat'in *a.* of the ancient Romans; of or in their language; speaking a language descended from theirs; of such people. *-n.* language of the ancient Romans. **latin'ity** *n.* manner of writing Latin; Latin style. **-lat'inism** *n.* word of idiom imitating Latin. [L. *Latinus*, of Latium (the part of Italy which included Rome)]

lat'itude *n.* freedom from restriction; scope. (*geog.*) angular distance on a meridian reckoned North or South from the equator. *-pl.* regions, climes. [L. *latus*, wide]

latrine' (-en) *n.* camp or barracks substitute for a toilet; any such toilet. [L. *latrina*, for *lavatrina*, lavatory]

laud *n.* praise, song of praise. *-v.t.* **laud'able** *a.* **-laud'ably** *adv.* **-lauda'tion** *n.* [L. *laus*, laud-]

laugh *v.i.* make the sounds instinctively expressing amusement or merri ment or scorn. *-n.* sound or act of laughing. **laugh'able** *a.* funny. **laugh'ter** *n.* laughing. [OE. hliehhan]

launch *v.t.* hurl; set going; set afloat. *v.i.* enter on a course. *-n.* the setting afloat of a vessel. [F. *lancer*]

launch *n.* largest boat carried by a warship; large power-driven boat. [Sp. *lancha*]

laundress *n.* washerwoman. **-laun'dry** *n.* place for washing clothes, *esp.* as a business. **-laun'der** *v.t.* wash and iron, *etc.* **launderette, laundromat** *n.* self-service laundry. [ME. *lavander*, L. *lavare*, wash]

la'va (la-) *n.* matter thrown out by volcanoes in fluid form and solidifying as it cools. [It., fr. L. *lavare*, wash]

lav'ender *n.* shrub with fragrant flowers; color of the flowers, a pale blue tinged with lilac. [Med. L. *livendula*]

lav'ish *a.* giving or spending profusely; very or too abundant. -*v.t.* spend, give, profusely. [OE. *lavasse*, deluge of rain]

law *n.* rule binding on a community; system of such rules; branch of this system; knowledge of it, administration of it; general principle deduced from facts; invariable sequence of events in nature. **law'ful** *a.* allowed by the law. -**law'yer** *n.* professional expert in law. -**law'-abiding** *a.* obedient to the laws. -**law'suit** *n.* carrying on of a claim in a court. [OE. *lagu*]

lawn *n.* fine linen. [*laon*, in France]

lawn *n.* stretch of carefully tended turf in a garden, *etc.* -**lawn'-mower** *n.* machine for cutting grass. -**lawn'-tennis** *n.* game played on a flat ground with a net across the middle. [earlier, *launde*, glade, fr. F. *lande*, moor]

lawyer. *See* law.

lay *v.t.* deposit on a surface, cause to lie; produce eggs. -**lay'er** *n.* one who lays; thickness of matter spread on a surface; one of several such; shoot fastened down to take root. -*v.t.* propagate plants by making layers. -**lay off**, cease; discontinue or suspend. [OE. *lecgan*]

lay *n.* minstrel's song, ballad. [F. *lai*]

lay *a.* not clerical; of or done by persons not clergymen; non-professional. -**lay'-man** *n.* [G. *laikos*, of the people]

layette' (-et) *n.* clothes needed for a newborn child. [F. dim. of *laie*, box]

la'zy *a.* averse to work, indolent. -**la'zily** *adv.* -**la'ziness** *n.* -**laze** *v.i.* indulge in laziness. [orig. uncertain]

lea *n.* piece of meadow or open ground. [OE. *leah*, track of ground]

leach *v.t.* and *i.* remove or be removed from substance by percolating liquid; lose soluble substances by action of percolating liquid. -*n.* act or process of leaching; substance that is leached or constituents removed by leaching; porous vessel for leaching. [perh. *retch*, muddy ditch]

lead (led) *n.* soft, heavy grey metal; plummet or lump of this used for sounding depths of water; graphite in a pencil. -*pl.* piece of roof covered with the metal; strips of it used to widen spaces in printing, *etc.* -*v.t.* cover, weight or space with lead. -**lead'en** *a.* of or resembling lead. -**lead'-pencil** *n.* drawing, writing, implement of graphite enclosed in wood. [OE.]

lead (led) *v.t.* guide, conduct; persuade; serve as a way, conduct people. -*v.i.* be or go or play the first. -*n.* leading; example; front place. -**lead'er** *n.* one who leads; article in a newspaper expressing editorial views. -also reading artéicle. -**lead'ership** *n.* -**lead'ing question** *n.* question worded to prompt the answer desired; question which demands exploration of considerations not yet taken into account. [OE. *lcedan*]

leaf *n.* (**leaves** *pl.*) part of a plant's foliage consisting usually of a green blade on a stem; two pages of a book, *etc.*; thin sheet; flap or movable part of a table, *etc.* -**leaf'let** *n.* small leaf; single sheet, often folded, of printed matter for distribution, a hand-bill. [OE.]

league *n.* measure of road distance, about three miles. [OF. *legue*]

league (leg) *n.* agreement for mutual help; parties to it; federation of clubs, *etc.* -*v.t.* and *i.* combine in a league. **leag'uer** *n.* member of a league.

leak *n.* hole or break through which a liquid undesirably passes in or out. -*v.i.* let liquid in or out of; of a liquid, to find its way through a leak. [cp. Ger. *lech*]

lean *a.* not fat; thin. -*n.* lean part of meat, mainly muscular tissue. -**lean'ness** *n.* [OE. *hloene*]

lean *v.i.* bend or incline; tend (toward). *v.t.* cause to lean, prop (against). [OE. hliniani

leap *v.i.* spring from the ground. -*v.t.* spring over. -*n.* jump. -**leap'-frog** *n.* game in which a player vaults over another bending down. -**leap'-year** *n.* year with February 29th as an extra day. [OE. *hleapan*]

learn *v.t.* gain skill or knowledge by study, practice or being taught. -*v.i.* gain knowledge; be taught; find out. **learn'ed** *a.* showing or requiring learning. [OE. *leornian*]

lease *n.* a contract by which land or property is given for a stated time by an owner to a tenant, usually for a rent. -*v.t.* take or give the use of by a lease. -**lease'hold** *n.* -**less'or** *n.* granter of a lease. -**less'ee** *n.* one to whom a lease is granted. [OF. *lais*, fr. *laisser*, leave]

leash *n.* thong for holding dogs; set of three animals. [F. *laisse*]

least *a.* smallest. -*n.* smallest one. -*adv.* in smallest degree. [OE. *læst*]

leath'er (leTH'-) *n.* skin of an animal prepared for use. -**leath'ern** *a.* of leather. -**leath'ery** *a.* tough. [OE. *lether*]

leave *v.t.* go away from; deposit; allow to remain; depart without taking; bequeath. -*v.i.* go away, set out. (left, p.t./p.p. - leaving, press). [OE. *loefan*]

leave *n.* permission; permission to be absent from duty. [OE. *leaf*]

lec'tern *n.* reading-desk in church. [OF. *letrin*, fr. L. *legere*, to read]

lect'ure *n.* discourse for the instruction of an audience; speech of reproof. *-v.i.* reprove. *-v.i.* deliver a discourse. **lect'urer** *n.* **-lect'ureship** *n.* appoint ment as lecturer. [L. *lecture*, reading]

ledge *n.* narrow flat surface projecting from a wall, cliff, *etc.*; ridge or rock below the surface of the sea. [ME. *legge*]

ledg'er *n.* book of debit and credit accounts, chief account book of a firm. [orig. a (church) book lying permanently in one place, fr. ME. *liggen*, lie]

lee *n.* shelter; side of anything, *esp.* a ship, away from the wind. **-lee'-shore** *n.* shore on lee-side of ship. **-lee-side** *n.* sheltered side (of ships, *etc.*). [OE. *hleo*]

leech *n.* blood-sucking worm; (formerly) physician. [OE. *loece*]

leer *v.i.* glance with malign, sly, or immodest expression. *-n.* such glance. [orig. uncertain]

lees *n. pl.* sediment of wine, *etc.* [F. *lie*]

left *a.* denotes the side, limb, *etc.*, opposite to the right; (see right). *-n.* left hand or part. *-(pol.)* Socialist, democratic, party; their more extreme sections. **-left'ist** *n. adj.* on or towards the left. **-left'-handed** *a.* having more power, skill, in the left hand. [OE. *lyft*, weak]

leg *n.* one of the limbs on which a person or animal walks, runs, or stands; support resembling this; part of a garment covering a leg. **-legg'ing** *n.* (usu. in *pl.*) covering of leather or other material for the leg. [ON. *leggr*]

leg'acy *n.* anything left by a will; thing handed down to a successor. [L. *legare*, bequeath, fr. *lex, leg-*, law]

le'gal *a.* of, appointed or permitted by, or based on, law. **-le'gally** *adv.* **-legal'ity** *n.* **-le'galize** *v.t.* to make legal. **legalization** *n.* **-le'gal ten'der**, money which can legally be used in paying a debt. [L. *legalis*, fr. *lex*, law]

legatee' *n.* one who receives a legacy. [irregularly fr. *legacy*]

leg'end *n.* traditional story or myth; traditional literature; inscription. legendary *a.* [L. *legenda*, be read]

legible (-j-) *a.* easily read. **-legibil'ity** *n.* **-leg'ibly** *adv.* [L. *legere*, read]

le'gion *n.* body of infantry in the Roman army; various modern military bodies; association of veterans; large number. **le'gionary** *a.* and *n.* [L. *legio*, fr. *legere*, levy]

leg'islator (-j-) *n.* maker of laws. -

leg'lslature *n.* body that makes laws. [L. *legislator*, proposer of laws]

legit'imate (-j-) *a.* lawful, proper, regular; born in wedlock. [L. *legitimus*, fr. *lex, leg-*, law]

lei'sure *n.* freedom from occupation, spare time. [F. *loisir*, fr. L. *licere*, be lawful]

lem'on *n.* pale-yellow fruit with acid juice; tree bearing it; its color. **lemonade'** *n.* drink made from lemon juice. **-lem'ony** *a.* [F. *limon*, lime]

lend *v.t.* give the temporary use of, let out for hire or interest; give, bestow. **-lends** itself to, is adapted to. **-lend'er** *n.* [OE. *laenan*]

length (-th) *n.* quality of being long; measurement from end to end; long stretch; piece of a certain length. **length'en** *v.t.* and *i.* **-length'wise** *a.* and *adv.* **-length'y** *a.* **-length'ily** *adv.* **-at length**, at last. [OE. *lengthu*]

le'nient *a.* mild, being without severity. [L. *lenis*, mild]

lens (-z) it. **len'ses** *pl.* piece of glass with one or both sides curved, used for concentrating or dispersing light in cameras, spectacles, telescopes, *etc.*; combination of such glasses in an instrument. **-lentic'ula** *n.* small lens; freckle. **-lentic'ular** *a.* like a lens; double-convex. **-also len'tiform** *a.* **-len'toid** *a.* lens-shaped. [L. *lentil* (fr. its shape)]

Lent *n.* period of fasting from Ash Wednesday to Easter-Eve (40 days). [OE. *lencten*, Spring]

lent'il *n.* eatable seed of a leguminous plant. **-leintic'ular** *a.* like lentil. [F. *lentille*, dim. fr. L. *lens*, lentil]

Le'o *n.* the lion, 5th sign of Zodiac, which sun enters c. 22nd July; constellation. **le'onine** *a.* like a lion. [L. *leo*, lion]

leop'ard (lep') *n.* large carnivorous animal with spotted coat. **-leop'ardess** fem. [G. *leopardos*, lionpard]

lep'er *n.* one suffering from leprosy; outcast. **-lep'rosy** *n.* disease forming silvery scales on the skin and eating away parts affected. **-lep'rous** *a.* [G. *lepis*, scale]

les'bian *a.* homosexual (of women). **lesbianism** *n.* [island of Lesbos]

le'sion *n.* wound, injury. [L. *laedere*, hurt]

less *a.* comp. of little; not so much. *-adv.* to smaller extent or degree. *-pron.* less amount or number. *-prep.* after deductions, minus. **-less'en** *v.t.* make less, diminish. **-less'er** *a.* [OE. *laessa*, less]

less'on *n.* portion of Scripture read in church; something to be learnt by a pupil; part of a course of teaching; experience that teaches. -*v.t.* teach, discipline. [F. *lecon*, L. *lectio*, reading]

let *v.t.* allow, enable, cause to; allow to escape; grant use of for rent, lease. -*v.i.* be leased. [OE. *loetan*]

let *v.t.* hinder. -*n.* hindrance; in games, an obstruction of a ball or player cancelling the stroke. -let alone', not to mention; not interfere with. -let down', disappoint, desert, fail. -let go', cease to hold. -let off, withhold punishment. -let on' (*sl.*) pretend; disclose (secret, *etc.*; let out', make a way of escape for. [OE. *lettan*]

le'thal *a.* deadly, fatal. [L. *lethalis*]

leth'argy *n.* drowsiness, apathy, want of energy or interest. -lethar'gic *a.* - lethargically *adv.* [G. *lethargia*]

lett'er *n.* one of the symbols with which words are written; a written message. -pl. literature, knowledge of books. *v.t.* mark with letters. -lett'ered *a.* learned. lett'erpress *n.* matter printed from type [F. *lettre*, fr. L. *littera*]

lett'uce (-tis) *n.* salad plant with milky juice. [L. *lactuca*, fr. *lac*, milk]

leu'cocyte *n.* white corpuscle of blood or lymph. [G. *leukos*, whiter]

leukemia, leukaem'ia *n.* a progressive blood disease characterized by an excessive number of white corpuscles. [G. *leukos*, white]

Levant' *n.* eastern part of the Mediterranean and the adjoining countries; wind of those regions. -Levant'ine *n.* [F. *levant*, rising, east]

lev'el *n.* instrument for showing or testing a horizontal line or surface; horizontal passage in a mine; social or moral standard. -*a.* horizontal; even in surface; even in style, quality, *etc.* -*v.t.* make level, bring to the same level; lay low; aim (a gun). -level-head'ed *a.* not apt to be carried away by emotion or excitement. [L. *libella*, dim. of *libra*, balance]

le'ver *n.* bar used to apply force at one end by pressure exerted at the other, a point in between resting against a fixed support. -le'verage *n.* action or power of a lever. [L. *levare*, raise]

levitation *n.* power of raising a solid body into the air by annulling gravitational pull. -lev'itate *v.t.* and *i.* to make lighter. [L. *levis*, light]

lev'y *n.* act of collecting taxes or enrolling troops; amount or number levied. -*v.t.* raise or impose by compulsion. [F. *lever*, raise]

lewd *a.* indecent. [OE. *loewede*, lay, layman]

lex'icon *n.* dictionary. -lexicog'raphy *n.* compiling of dictionaries. -lexicog'rapher *n.* [G. *lexikon* (*biblion*), word (book)]

li'able *a.* subject (to), exposed (to), answerable. -liabil'ity *n.* state of being liable. -*pl.* debts. [F. *lier*, bind]

liai'son *n.* connecting link; illicit love. [F.]

liar. *See* lie.

li'bel *n.* written, published, statement damaging to a person's reputation. -*v.t.* write, publish, a libel against. [L. *libellus*, dim. of *liber*, book]

lib'eral *a.* generous; open-minded; of a political party, favoring changes making towards democracy. -*n.* one of such a party. [L. *liber*, free]

lib'erty *n.* freedom. -lib'erate *v.t.* set free. [L. *liber*]

libidinous *a.* lustful. -libi'do *n.* (*psych.*) emotional urge behind human activities, *e. g.*, sex. [L. *libido*, lust]

Li'bra *n.* the Balance 7th. sign of zodiac, which sun enters c. Sept. 22nd, zodiacal constellation; pound weight. [L.]

li'brary *n.* collection of books; place where the books are kept; reading or writing room in a house. -librar'ian *n.* keeper of a library. -librar'ianship *n.* [L. *liber*, book]

librett'o *n.* book of words of an opera. librett'ist *n.* [It. = little book]

li'cense *n.* leave, permission; formal permission; document giving it; excessive liberty; dissoluteness; writer's or artist's transgression of the rules of his art (often poetic license). -li'cense *v.t.* grant a license to. -licen'tious *a.* sexually immoral. [L. *licentia*, fr. *licere*, allowed]

lice *See* louse.

lick *v.t.* pass the tongue over; (*sl.*) beat. *n.* act of licking. [OE. *liccian*]

lid *n.* movable cover; cover of the eye, the eyelid. -lidd'ed *a.* [OE. *hlid*]

lie *v.i.* be horizontal or at rest; be situated; recline. -*n.* direction; state (of affairs, *etc.*). [OE. *licgan*]

lie *v.i.* make a false statement. -*n.* untrue statement. -li'ar *n.* [OE, *leogan*]

lien *n.* right to hold property until a claim is met. [F. = *bond*]

lieu *n.* in lieu of, instead of. lieuten'ant *n.* substitute; junior army or navy officer. [F. fr. L. *locus*, place]

life *n.* lives *pl.* active principle of the existence of animals and plants, animate existence; time of its lasting; history of such an existence; manner of living; vigor, vivacity. -life'-belt *n.* -life'-jacket *n.* life'-preserv'er *n.* devices to keep one afloat in water. **-life-blood** *n*. blood on which life depends. **-life'boat** *n*. boat for rescuing shipwrecked persons. **-life'buoy** *n*. buoy to support a person in water. **-life'-class** *n*. art class with living models. **-life'-cycle** *n*. successive stages of an organism through a complete generation. **-life-guard** *n*. body-guard. rescuer of bathers in difficulties. **life'less** *a*. [OE. *lif*]

lift *v.t*. raise to a higher position. *-v.i*. rise. *-n*. act of lifting; journey as a pass enger in someone else's vehicle, given free of charge; in Britain, elevator. [ON. *lypta*]

lig'ament *n*. band of tissue joining bones. **-lig'ature** *n*. thread for tying up an artery. [L. *ligare*, bind]

light *a*. of, or bearing, little weight; gentle; easy, requiring little effort; trivial. *-adv*. in a light manner. **-light'** *v.i*. get down from a horse or vehicle; come by chance (upon). **-light'en** *v.t*. reduce or remove a load, *etc*. **-light'-fing'ered** *a*. thievish. **-light'-hand'ed** *a*. having a light touch. —**light'-headed** *a*. delirious, giddy. [OE. *leoht*]

light *n*. natural agent by which things are visible; source of this; window; mental vision; light part of anything. *-a*. bright; pale, not dark-*v.t*. set burning; give light to. *-v.i*. take fire; brighten. **light'en** *v.t*. give light to. **-light'ning** *n*. visible discharge of electricity in the atmosphere. **-light'house** *n*. tower with a light to guide ships. [OE. *leoht*]

lighter *n*. large boat used for loading and unloading ships. [*light*]

like *a*. similar, resembling. *-adv*. in the manner of. *-pron*. similar thing. **-like'ly** *a*. probably true; hopeful, promising. *adv*. probably. **-like'ness** *n*. qualitv of being like: portrait. **-like'wise** *adv*. in like manner. [OE. *gelic*, similar]

like *v.t*. to find agreeable. *-v.i*. to be pleasing. **-like'able** *a*. [OE. lician, please]

li'lac *n*. shrub bearing pale violet flowers; their color. *-a*. of this color. [OF. Pers. *lilak*, blue]

lilt *v.t*. and *i*. sing merrily. *-n*. rhythmical effect in music. [ME. *lulten*, strike up loudly]

lil'y *n*. bulbous flowering plant. **lilia'ceous** *a*. **-li'ly of the valley**, plant with fragrant small white bells. [L. *liliurn*]

limb *n*. arm or leg; branch of a tree. [OE. *tim*]

limb *n*. edge of the sun or moon. [L. *limbus*, edge]

lim'ber *n*. detachable front part of a gun-carriage. *-v.t*. attach the limber to (a gun). [orig. uncertain]

limber *a*. lithe, supple. [orig. uncertain]

lime *n*. sticky substance used for catching birds; alkaline earth from which mortar is made. *-v.t*. smear, or catch, with lime. treat (land) with lime. [OE. *lim*]

lime *n*. acid fruit like a lemon. [F.]

limit *n*. boundary; utmost extent or duration. *-v.t*. restrict, bound. **-limita'tion** *n*. **-lim'itable** *a*. [L. *limes, limit-*, boundary]

limousine' (-zen) *n*. closed type of automobile with the top projecting over the driver's seat. [F. fr. hood worn by natives of province of Limousin]

limp *a*. without firmness or stiffness. [orig. uncertain]

limp *v.i*. walk lamely. *-n*. limping gait. [orig. uncertain]

line *n*. linen thread; any cord or string; wire; stroke made with a pen, *etc*.; long narrow mark; continuous length without breadth; row; series; course; province of activity; trade or business. *-v.t*. cover inside; mark with a line or lines; bring into line. **-li'ning** *n*. covering for the inside of a garment, *etc*. **-lin'eage** *n*. descent from, or the descendants of an ancestor. [OE.]

lin'en *a*. made of flax. *-n*. cloth made of flax; linen articles collectively. [L. *linum*, flax]

li'ner *n*. large passenger ship or airplane. [*line*]

ling'er (-ng-g) *v.i*. tarry, loiter; remain long. [OE. *lengan*, prolong]

linge'rie *n*. linen goods, *esp*. women's underwear. [F.]

liniment *n*. embrocation. [L. *linimentum*, fr. *linere*, smear]

link *n*. ring of a chain; connection. *-v.t*, join with, or as with, a link. *-v.i*. be so joined. **-link'up** *n*. establishing of a connection or union between objects, groups, organizations, *etc*.; connection or union established. [of ON. orig.]

link *n*. torch. [orig. uncertain]

links *n. pl*. undulating ground near sea; golfcourse. [OE. *hlinc*]

lino'leum *n*. floorcloth surfaced with hardened linseed oil. **-linocut** *n*. engraving on linoleum instead of wood; print from this. [L. *linum*, flax, *oleum*, oil]

li'notype *n*. machine for producing lines of words cast in one piece; line of type so cast. [line-of-type]

lin'seed *n*. flax seed. [L. *linum*, flax]

lint *n*. soft material of fluffed-up linen; fluff, scraps of thread. [ME. *linnet*]

lint'el *n*. top piece of a door or window. [OF.]

li'on *n*. large animal of the cat tribe; person

of importance. **-li'oness** *fem.* **li'onize** *v.t.* treat as a celebrity. [F., fr. L. leo, leon-]

lip *n.* either edge of the mouth; edge or margin; (*sl.*) insolence. **-lipp'ed** *a.* **-lip'-service** *n.* insincere devotion. **-lip'stick** *n.* cosmetic in stick form for coloring lips. [OE. *lippa*]

lipo- *prefix* fat, as in **lipoid'** *a.* fat-like. [G. *lipos*, fat]

liq'uid *a.* fluid, not solid or gaseous: bright, clear. **-n.** a liquid substance. **liq'uefy** *v.t.* and *i.* [L. *liquere*, be clear]

liquidate *v.t.* pay (debt); arrange the affairs of, and dissolve (a company *sl.*) put out of action, wipe out. [L. *liquere*, be clear]

liq'uor (lik'er) *n.* liquid, *esp.* alcoholic one for drinking. **-liqueur'** (likur) *n.* alcoholic liquor flavored and sweetened. [L. *liquere*, be clear]

liq'uorice, licorice (-kur-is) *n.* black substance used in medicine and as a sweetmeat; plant or its root, from which the substance is obtained. [fr. G. *glykus*, sweet, and *rhiza*, root]

lisp *v.t.* and *i.* speak with faulty pronunciation of the sibilants; speak falteringly. *n.* a lisping. [OE. *awlyspian*] list *n.* border or edge of cloth; strips of cloth, *esp.* used as material for slippers. *pl.* space for tilting. [OE. *lisle*]

list *n.* roll or catalogue. **-v.t.** write down in a list. [list, *v.s.*] **list** *v.i.* desire; of a ship, incline, lean to one side. **-n.** desire; inclination of a ship. **-list'less** *a.* indifferent, languid. **list'lessly** *adv.* (OE. *lystan*, please]

list'en (lis'en) *v.i.* try to hear, give attention in order to hear. **-listen-in** *v.i.* listen to a radio broadcast. **-list'ener** *n.* (OE. *hlystan*]

lit'any *n.* form of prayer. [G. *litaneia*]

lit'er *n.* measure of capacity in the French decimal system, equal to 2. 11 pints. [F.]

lit'eral *a.* of letters; exact as to words; according to the sense of actual words, not figurative or metaphorical. **-lit'erally** *adv.* [L. *litera*, letter]

lit'erary *a.* of, or learned in, literature. **li'terate** *a.* educated. **-lit'eracy** *n.* **-litera'tim** *adv.* letter for letter. **-lit'erature** *n.* books and writings of artistic value; production of these; profession of writers. [L. *litera*, letter]

lith'o- *prefix* pertaining to stone, as in **lith'ocarp** *n.* fossil fruit. **-lith'oglyph** *n.* engraving on stone, *esp.* on a gem. - **lith'ophyl** *n.* fossil leaf **-lith'ophyte** *n.* coral polyp. [G. *lithos*, stone]

lithog'raphy *n.* the making of drawings on stone for printing. **-lith'ograph** *n.* print

so produced. **-v.t.** print thus. [G. *lithos*, stone, *graphein*, write]

lit'igate *v.i.* go to law. **-lit'igant** *a.* and *n.* **-litiga'tion** *n.* **-litig'ious** (-j-) *a.* fond of going to law. **-litig'iousness** *n.* [L. *litigare*, fr. lis, lit-, lawsuit]

lit'mus *n.* blue coloring-matter turned red by acids. **-lit'mus-paper** *n.* (ON. *litmose*, lichen (used in dyeing)]

litt'er *n.* portable couch; kind of stretcher for the wounded; straw, *etc.*, as bedding for animals; fragments lying about, untidy refuse of paper, *etc.*; young of an animal produced at a birth. **-v.t.** strew (a place) with litter; bring forth. [F. *litiere*, fr. *lit*, bed]

lit'tle *a.* small, not much. **-n.** small quantity. **-adv.** slightly. [OE. *lytel*]

lit'urgy *n.* form of public worship. **litur'gical** *a.* **-lit'urgist** *n.* state. [G. *leitourgia*, public worship]

live (liv) *v.i.* have life; pass one's life, continue in life; dwell; feed. **-liv'ing** *n.* state of being in life; means of earning livelihood; church benefice. [OE. *lifian*]

live (liv) *a.* living; flaming. **-live-stock** domestic animals *esp.* horses, cattle, pigs. **-live'-wire** *n.* wire carrying an electric current; (*sl.*) energetic person. [from alive]

livelihood *n.* means of living. [OE. *liflad*, life-course]

live'ly *a.* brisk, active, vivid. **-live'liness** *n.* [OE. *liflic*, like life]

liv'er *n.* organ which secretes bile. *a.* liver-colored, reddish-brown. **-liv'erish** *a.* of liver; irritable. [OE. *lifer*]

liv'ery *n.* allowance of food for horses; distinctive dress of a person's servants. [F. *livrée*, handed over (orig. of any allowance)]

liz'ard *n.* four-footed, five-toed reptile with scaly body; saurian. [L. *lacertus*]

lla'ma *n.* Peruvian animal used as a beast of burden; its wool. [Peruv.]

load *n.* burden; amount usually carried at once. **-v.i.** put a load on or into; charge (a gun); weigh down. [OE. *lad*, way, journey]

loaf *n.* loaves *pl.* mass of bread as baked; cone of sugar. [OE. *hlaf*] **loaf** *v.i.* idle. **-loaf'er** *n.* [orig. uncertain loam *n.* fertile soil. [OE. *lam*]

loan *n.* thing lent; an act of lending. **-v.t.** lend. [ON. *lan*]

loath, loth (-th) *a.* unwilling. **-loath'ly** *a.* **-loath'some** *a.* disgusting. **-loathe** (-TH) *v.t.* abhor. [OE. *lath*, repulsive]

lobb'y *n.* corridor into which rooms open; pressure group, *esp.* one seeking influence on government. **-v.t.** and *i.* exert pressure in this way. [med. L. *lobium*]

lobe *n.* soft hanging part of the ear; any similar flap. [G. *lobos*, lobe of ear]

lob'ster *n.* shellfish with long tail and claws, which turns scarlet when boiled. [OE. *loppestre*]

lo'cal *a.* relating to place; of or existing in a particular place. **-local'ity** *n.* place, situation; district. **-lo'cally** *adv.* **-lo'calize** *v.t.* **-locate'** *v.t.* attribute to a place; find the place of. **-loca'tion** *n.* a placing; situation. [L. *locus.* place]

lock *n.* tress of hair. [OE. *loc*]

lock *n.* appliance for fastening a door, lid, *etc.*; mechanism for discharging a firearm; enclosure in a river or canal for moving boats from one level to another; close crowd of vehicles. *-v.t.* fasten with a lock; join firmly; embrace closely-*v.i.* become fixed or united. **-lock'er** *n.* small cup board with a lock. **-lock'jaw** *n.* tetanus. **-lookout** *n.* exclusion of workmen by employers as a means of coercion. **-lock'smith** *n.* one who makes and mends locks. **-lock'et** *n.* small pendant of precious metal for a portrait, *etc.* -lock-up *n.* place for housing prisoners, cars, *etc.* [OE. *loc*]

locomo'tive *a.* having the power of moving from place to place. *-n.* engine moving from place to place by its own power; railway engine. **-locomo'tion** *n.* action or power of moving from place to place. [fr. L. *loco*, from a place, and *moveri*, be moved]

lo'cust *n.* destructive winged insect; carob-tree; its fruit, resembling a bean in shape. [L. *locusta*, lobster]

lode *n.* vein of ore. [*See* **load**]

lodge *n.* house for a shooting or hunting party; house at the gate of an estate; meeting-place of a branch of freemasons, *etc.*; the branch. *-v.t.* house; deposit. *-v.i.* live in another's house at a fixed charge; become fixed after being thrown. [F. *loge*]

loft *n.* attic; room over a stable; gallery in a church. *-v.t.* send (a golf-ball) high. **loft'y** *a.* of great height; elevated. **loft'ily** *adv.* [ON. *lopt*, sky]

log *n.* unhewn portion of a felled tree; apparatus for measuring the speed of a ship; journal kept on board ship, *etc.*, a **log'-book** *n.* *-v. t.* record, *usu.* as written data on a regular basis. **-log'ger** *n.* a lumberjack. [orig. uncertain]

log'arithm *n.* one of a series of arithmetical functions tabulated for use in calculation. **-logarith'mic** *a.* [G. *logos*, word, ratio, *arithmos*, number]

log'ic *n.* art of reasoning. **-log'ical** *a.* relating to logic; according to reason; able to reason well. [G. *logos*, word]

loin *n.* part of the body on either side between ribs and hip. [OF. *loigne*, fr. L. *lumlus*]

loi'ter *v.i.* waste time on the way, hang about. **-loi'terer** *n.* [Du. *leuteren*]

loll *v.i.* sit or lie lazily; of the tongue, hang out. *-v.t.* hang out (the tongue). [imit. orig.]

lollipop *n.* a sweet. [child language]

lone *a.* solitary. **-lone'ly** *a.* alone; feeling sad because alone. **-lone'liness** *n.* **lone'some** *a.* [for *alone*]

long *a.* having length, *esp.* great length. *adv.* for a long time. **-long-headed** *a.* shrewd, intelligent. *-long-run* *n.* outcome, result. **-longshoreman** *n.* dock laborer. [OE. *long*]

long *v.i.* have a keen desire. **-long'ing** *n.* [OE. *langian*, grow long]

longevity (-j-) *n.* long existence of life. **longe'vial** *a.* [L. *longaevus-aevum*, age]

longitude *n.* distance of a place east or west from a standard meridian. **longitu'dinal** *a.* of length or longitude. [L. *longus*, long]

look *v.i.* direct or use the eyes; face; take care; seem; hope. *-n.* a looking; expression; aspect. **-look'alike** *n.* a person, *esp.* a celebrity, or thing that is the double of another. **-look'ing glass** *n.* mirror. **-look af'ter**, take care of. **-look alive'**, hasten. **-look'-out** *n.* watch; place for watching; watchman. [OE. *locian*]

loom *n.* machine for weaving. [OE. *geloma*, tool] **loom** *v.i.* appear dimly, *esp.* with vague or enlarged appearance, or (fig.) out of the future. [orig. unknown]

loop *n.* figure made by a curved line crossing itself; similar rounded shape in a cord or rope, *etc.*, crossed on itself. *v.t.* form into a loop. *-v.i.* form a loop. [orig. uncertain]

loose *a.* not tight or fastened or fixed or exact or tense; slack; vague; dissolute. *v.t.* set free; unfasten; make slack. *-v.i.* shoot, let fly. **-loose'ly** *adv.* **-loos'en** *v.t.* make loose. **-loose'ness** *n.* [ON. *lauss*]

loot *n.* and *v.t.* plunder. [Hind. *lut*]

lop *v.t.* cut away twigs and branches; chop off. [OE. *loppian*] **lop** *v.i.* hang; imply. **lop'-ear** *n.* drooping ear; rabbit with such ears. **lopsi'ded** *a.* with one side lower than the other, badly balanced. [orig. uncertain]

lord *n.* feudal superior; one ruling others; owner; God; title of peers of the realm. *v.i.* domineer. [OE. *hlafweard*, loaf-ward]

lore *n.* learning; body of facts and traditions. [OE. *lar*]

lose *v.t.* be deprived of, fail to retain; let

slip; fail to get; be late for; be defeated in. -v.i. suffer loss. **-loss** n. a losing; what is lost; harm or damage resulting from losing. **-los'er** n. **-lost** a. [OE. *losian*, be lost]

lot n. one of a set of objects used to decide something by chance (to cast lots); fate, destiny; item at an auction; collection; large quantity. [OE. *hlot*]

lo'tion n. liquid for washing wounds, improving the skin, etc. [L. *lotio*]

lott'ery n- gamble in which part of the money paid for tickets is distributed to some owners of tickets selected by chance. [*lot*]

lott'o n. game of chance. [*lot*]

loud a. strongly audible; noisy; obtrusive. **-loud'ly** adv. **-loud'speak'er** n. device for magnifying sound. [OE. *hlud*]

lounge v.i. loll; move lazily. -n. place for, or a spell of, lounging; deep chair or sofa. [orig. uncertain]

louse n. lice pl. parasitic insect. **-lous'y** a. infested with lice; (fig.) bad, mean. [OE. *lus*]

lou'ver, lou'vre n. set of boards or slats set parallel and slanting to admit air without rain; ventilating structure of these. [OF. *lover*]

love (luv) n. warm affection; sexual passion; sweetheart; score of nothing. -v.t. have love for. -v.i. be in love. **-lov'able** a. **-love'less** a. **-love'lorn** a. forsaken by, or pining for, a lover. **-love'ly** a. beautiful, delightful. **-lov'er** n. **-love'-apple** n. tomato. **-love'-bird** n. small green parrot. [OE. *lufu*]

low a. not tall or high or elevated; humble; commonplace; vulgar; dejected; not loud. **-low'er** v.t. cause or allow to descend; diminish; degrade. **-low'land** n. low-lying country. **-low'ly** a. modest, humble. **-low'liness** n. **-low'brow** n. person not an intellectual. -a. **-low' down** a. mean, despicable. -n. inside information. [OE. *lah*]

loy'al a. faithful; true to allegiance. [F., fr. L. *legalis*, legal]

loz'enge n. diamond figure; small sweetmeat or tablet of medicine, formerly of this shape. [F. *losange*]

lub'ricate v.t. oil or grease; make slippery. **-lu'bricant** n. substance used for this. **-lubrica'tion** n. [L. *lubricate*, fr. *lubricus*, slippery]

lu'cid a. clear; easily understood. **lucid'ity** n. **-lu'cidly** adv. **-lu'cifer** n. morning star; Satan; match. [L. *lucidus*, fr. *lux*, light]

luck n. fortune, good or ill; chance. **luck'y** a. having good luck. **-luck'less** a. **-luck'ily** adv. fortunately. [Du. *luk*]

luge n. light Alpine sleigh for one. -v.i. [F.]

lugg'age n. traveler's baggage. [orig. uncertain]

lug'sail n. oblong sail fixed on a yard which hangs slanting on a mast. **-lugg'er** n. vessel with such sails. [orig. uncertain]

lull v.t. soothe with sounds, sing to sleep; make quiet. -v.i. become quiet. -n. brief time of quiet in storm or pain. **-lull'aby** (-bi) n. lulling song or sounds. [imit. origin]

lum'bar a. relating to the loins. **lumba'go** n. rheumatism in the loins. [L. *lumbus*, loin]

lum'ber v.i. move heavily; obstruct. -n. disused articles, useless rubbish; timber, esp. in planks. [orig. obscure]

lu'minous a. bright, shedding light. **lu'minary** n. heavenly body giving light; person noted for learning. **luminos'ity** n. [L. *lumen, lumin-*, light]

lump n. shapeless piece, mass; swelling; sum covering various items. -v.t. throw together in one mass or sum. -v.i. move heavily. **-lump'ish** a. clumsy; stupid. **lump'y** a. [orig. uncertain]

lu'nar a. of the moon. **-lunar caustic**, nitrate of silver. [L. *luna*, moon]

lu'natic a. insane. -n. insane person. **lu'nacy** n. [L. *luna*, moon]

lunch n. meal taken in the middle of the day. **-lunch'eon** (-shn) n. lunch; midday banquet. [orig. uncertain]

lung n. light, spongy air-breathing organ. [OE. *lungen*]

lunge v.i. thrust with a sword, etc. -n. such thrust, or thrusting movement. [F. *allonger*, lengthen, stretch out]

lurch n. leave in the lurch, leave in difficulties, abandon (a comrade) [obs. card game of lurch]

lurch n. sudden roll to one side. -v.i. make a lurch. [orig. uncertain]

lure n. falconer's apparatus for recalling a hawk; something which entices, a bait. -v.i. recall (a hawk); entice. [F. *leurre*]

lu'rid a. ghastly, pale, glaring. **-lu'ridly** adv. [L. *luridus*, yellowish]

lurk v.i. lie hidden; be latent. **-lurk'er** n. **-lurk'ing** a. [orig. uncertain]

lush a. of grass, etc., luxuriant and juicy. -n. (sl.) habitually drunken person. [orig. uncertain]

lust n. sensual desire; passionate desire. v.i. have passionate desire. **-lust'ful** a. **lust'y** a. healthy, vigorous. **-lust'ily** adv. [OE. = *pleasure*]

lus'ter *n.* gloss, shine; splendid reputation, glory; glossy material. **-lus'trous** *a.* [L. *lustrare,* shine]

lux'ury *n.* possession and use of costly and choice things for enjoyment; enjoyable but not necessary thing; comfortable surroundings. **-luxu'rious** *a.* **-luxu'riously** *adv.* **-luxu'riate** *v.i.* indulge in luxury; grow rank; take delight (in). **-luxu'riant** *a.* growing profusely; abundant. **-luxu'riantly** *adv.* **-luxu'riance** *n.* [L. *luxuria*]

lye *n.* water made alkali with wood ashes, *etc.*, for washing. [OE. *leag*]

lymph *n.* colorless animal fluid; matter from cowpox used in vaccination. **-lymphat'ic** *a.* of lymph; flabby, sluggish. *-n.* vessel in the body conveying lymph. [L. *lympha,* water]

lynch *n.* lynch law, procedure of a self appointed court trying and executing an accused person. *-v.t.* put to death without proper trial. [orig. uncertain]

lynx *n.* animal of cat tribe noted for keen sight. **-lynx-eyed** *a.* quick-sighted. [G.]

lyre *n.* instrument like a harp. **-lyr'ic**, **lyr'ical** *a.* relating to the lyre; meant to be sung; of short poems, expressing the poet's own thoughts and feelings; describing a poet who writes such poems. **-lyr'ic** *n.* lyric poem. **-lyricist** *n.* lyric poet. [G. *Tyra*]

M

maca'bre (-a-ber) *a.* gruesomely imaginative. [F.]

macaro'ni *n.* Italian paste of wheat in long tubes. [It. *maccheroni*]

macaroon' *n.* small cake containing ground almonds. [It. *maccherone*]

mache'te *n.* W. Indian cutlass. [Sp.]

Machiavell'ian (mak-i-a-vell'-yan) *a.* crafty, unprincipled, in politics; dictated by expediency. [*Machiavelli,* It. statesman (d. 1527)]

machination (-kin-) *n.* plotting, intrigue. **-mac'hinate** *v.i.* lay plots.

machine' (-shen) *n.* apparatus combining the action of several parts, to apply mechanical force for some purpose; person like a machine from regulation or sensibility; controlling organization; bicycle, vehicle, automobile. *-v.t.* sew, print with a machine. **-machi'nery** *n.* parts of a machine collectively; machines. **-machi'nist** *n.* one who makes or works machines. **-machine'-gun** *n.* gun firing repeatedly and continuously by means of a loading and firing mechanisms [G. *mechane*]

mach'o (-ch-) *a.* denoting or exhibiting pride in characteristics believed to be typically masculine, as physical strength, sexual appetite, *etc.* *-n.* man who displays such characteristics. [Sp. = male]

mack'erel *n.* sea-fish with blue and silver barred skin. [F. *maquereau*]

macro- prefix great, long, as in **macroblot'ic** *a.* long-lived. **macrop'terous** *a.* long-winged. **macru'rous** *a.* long-tailed. [G. *makros,* long, large]

macroscopic *a.* visible to the naked eye, opp. to microscopic. [G. *makros,* large, *skopeein,* to look at]

mad *a.* suffering from mental disease, insane; wildly foolish; excited; angry. [OE.]

mad'am *n.* polite form of address to a woman. [F. *madame,* my lady]

madd'er *n.* climbing plant; its root; dyestuff made from this. [OE. *mædere*]

madonn'a *n.* Virgin Mary; picture or statue of the Virgin Mary. [It.]

Maf'ia *n.* international secret criminal organization. [it.]

magazine' *n.* storehouse for explosives and the military stores; a periodical with stories and articles by different writers; an appliance for supplying cartridges automatically to a gun. [F. *magasn,* store, shop]

mag'ic (-j-) *n.* art of influencing events by controlling nature or spirits, any mysterious agency of power; witchcraft, conjuring. [G. *magos]*

magistrate (-j-) *n.* civil officer administering the law. **-magiste'rial** *a.* at or referring to a magistrate or master; dictatorial. **-mag'istracy** *n.* office of a magistrate; magistrates collectively. [L. *magister,* master]

magnanimous *a.* great souled, above resentment, *etc.* **-magnanim'ity** *n.* [fr. L. *magnus,* great, *animus,* soul]

magne'sium *n.* metallic chemical element. **-magne'sia** *n.* white powder compound of this used in medicine. [*Magnesia,* in Greece]

mag'net *n.* piece of iron having the properties of attracting iron and pointing north and south when suspended; lodestone. **-magnet'ic** *a.* **-magnet'ically** *adv.* **-mag'netism** *n.* magnetic phenomena; the science of this; personal chann or power of attracting others. [G. *magnes,* Magnesian stone. (*u.s.*)]

magnificent *a.* splendid, stately, imposing, excellent. **-magnif'icently** *a.* **-magnificence** *n.* [*magnify]*

mag'nify *v.t.* exaggerate; make greater;

increase the apparent size, as with a lens; praise. [L. *magnus*, great, *facere*, make]

mag'nitude *n.* size; extent; amount; importance. [L. *magnitudae*]

mag'num *n.* wine bottle holding two quarts. [L. *magnus*, great]

mahog'any *n.* tropical American tree; its reddish-brown wood. [W. Ind.]

maid'en *n.* young unmarried woman. -*a.* unmarried; of, or suited to, a maiden; having a blank record. -**maid** *n.* young unmarried woman; woman servant. [OE. *mægden*, girl]

mail *n.* armor made of interlaced rings or overlapping plates. -**mail'ed** *a.* covered with mail. [L. *macula*, mesh]

mail *n.* bag of letters; letters conveyed at one time; official despatch of letters. -*v.t.* send by mail. -**mail'box** *n.* public box for depositing mail that is being sent out; box at a house or business to which mail is delivered for the occupier. -**mail'man** *n.* one who delivers mail. [OF. *male*, leather bag]

maim *v.t.* cripple, mutilate. [OF. *mahaignier*, mutilate]

main *n.* open sea, chief matter; strength, power. -*a.* chief, principal, leading. -**main-deck** *n.* ship's chief deck. -**main'land** *n.* stretch of land which forms the main part of the country. -**main'ly** *adv.* -**main'mast** *n.* chief mast in a ship. -**main'sail** *n.* lowest sail of a mainmast. -**main' spring** *n.* chief spring of a watch or clock. -**main'stay** *n.* rope from top of mainmast to deck; chief support. -**main'-yard** *n.* lower yard on main-mast. [OE. *mægen*, strength]

main'frame *n.* in a large computer, the central processing unit.

maintain' *v.t.* carry on; preserve; support, sustain, keep up; keep supplied; affirm. -**maintain'able** *a.* -**main'tenance** *n.* [L. *manu tenere*, hold with the hand]

maize *n.* Indian corn, a cereal. [Sp. *maiz*, fr. Cuban]

maj'esty *n.* stateliness; kingship or queenship. -**majes'tic** *a.* -**majes'tically** *adv.* [L. *majestas*]

major *a.* greater; out of minority. -*n.* one out of minority; officer in the army, ranking below lieutenant-colonel. -**major'ity** *n.* state of having reached the full legal age; the greater number; the larger party voting together; excess of the vote on one side. [L. = greater]

make *v.t.* construct; produce; bring into being-, establish; appoint; amount to; cause to do something; accomplish; reach; earn. -*v.i.* tend; contribute, of the title, to

raise. -*n.* style of construction, form, manufacture. -**make-up** *n.* constituents; style; cosmetics. **make'-believe** *v.i.* pretend. -*n.* -a. [OE. *macian*]

mal- prefix ill, badly, miss; not [L. male, ill] . -**maladjust'ment** *n.* faulty adjustment. -**maladministra'tion** *n.* faulty administration. -**maladroit'** *a.* clumsy, not dexterous. -**mal'content** *a.* actively discontented. -*n.* malcontent person. -**malev'olent** *a.* full of ill-will. -**malev'olence** *n.* -**malforma'tion** *n.* faulty information. -**malnutri'tion** *n.* faulty, inadequate. nutrition. -**malprac'tice** *n.* wrong-doing. -**mal'treat** *v.t.* treat ill, handle roughly. -**maltreat'ment** *a.*

mal'ady *n.* disease. [F. *maladie*]

malaise' *n.* vague discomfort, uneasiness. as in fever. [OF.]

mal'apropism *n.* laughable misuse of words. (Mrs. Malaprop, char. in play)

malar'ia (-Ar-) *n.* fever due to mosquito bites. -**malar'ial** *n.* -**malar'ious** *n.* [It. *maléaria*, bad air]

male *a.* of the begetting sex; of man or male animals. -*n.* male person or animal. [F. *mdle*, fr. L. *masculus*]

mal'ice *n.* action of ill-will. [L. *malitia*]

malign (-lin) *a.* hurtful. -*v.t.* slander, misrepresent. -**malig'nant** *a.* feeling extreme ill-will; of a disease, very virulent. [L. *malignus*]

maling'erer *n.* one who pretends illness to escape duty. -**maling'er** *v.i.* [OF. *malingreux*, beggar with artificial sores]

mall (mawl, mal) *n.* level shaded walk or avenue; urban shopping area with a variety of shops. [L. *malleus*, hammer]

mall'eable *a.* capable of being hammered into shape. -**malleabil'ity** *n.* [L. *malleus*, hammer]

mall'et *n.* hammer, usually of wood. [F. *maillet*, *malleus*, hammer]

malt *n.* grain used for brewing. -*v.t.* make into malt. [OE. *mealt*]

mamm'al *a.* animal of the type feeding their young with their milk. -**mamma'lian** *a.* [L. *mamma*, breast]

mamm'oth *n.* extinct animal like an elephant. [Russ. *mamont*]

man *n.* (men *pl.*) human being; person: human race; adult human male; man- servant; piece used in a game, *e.g.*, chess. -*v.t.* supply (a ship, *etc.*), with necessary men. -**man'ful** *a.* brave, resolute. -**man'fully** *adv.* -**man'hole** *n.* opening through which a man may pass. -**man'hood** *n.* -**mankind'** *n.* human beings in general. -**man'like** *a.* **man'ly** *a.* -**man'liness** *n.* -**mann'ish** *a.*

manlike. -**man'hand'le** v.t. move by man-power; (sl.) knock about. [OE. mann]

man'acle n. fetter for the hand. -v.t. hand-cuff. [L. manicula, small sleeve]

man'age v.t. carry on, conduct; succeed in doing; handle; persuade. -v.i. conduct af-fairs. [It. maneggiare, train horses]

mandarin n. Chinese official; small sweet orange. [Port. mandarim]

man'date a. command of, or commission to act for another. **man'datary** n. holder of a mandate. **man'datory** a. [L. man-datum]

man'dible n. lower jaw bone; either part of a bird's beak. [OF. fr. L. mandere, chew]

man'dolin(e) n. stringed musical instru-ment like a lute. [F.]

mane n. long hair at the back of the neck of a horse, lion, etc. [OE. manu]

maneuv'er n. movement of troops or ships in war, stratagem. -v.t. cause to per-form maneuvers. -v.i. perform maneuvers; employ stratagems, to work adroitly. [F.]

mange n. skin disease of dogs, etc. - **ma'ngy** a. [OF. manjue, itch]

man'ger (manjer) n. eating trough in a stable or byre. [F. mangeoire]

mang'le (mang'gl) v.t. hack, mutilate, spoil. (AF. mahangler]

man'grove n. swamp-growing tropical tree whose drooping shoots take root. [orig. uncertain]

ma'nia n. madness; prevailing craze. - **ma'niac** a. affected by mania. -n. mad per-son. -**mani'acal** a, [G.]

man'icure n. treatment of the nails and hands; person doing this professionally. -v.t. apply such treatment to. [L. manus hand, cura, care]

manifest a. clearly revealed, visible, un-doubted. -v.t. make manifest. -n. list of cargo for the Customs. -**manifesta'tion** n. -**manifes'to** n. declaration of policy by a sovereign or commander or body of per-sons; any formal declaration of overall political intent. [L. manifestos]

man'ifold a. numerous, varied. -n. pipe with several outlets. -v.t. make copies of (a document). [many and fold]

manipulate v.t. handle; deal with skillful-ly; manage craftily. [L. manipulus, hand-ful]

mannequin (or mann'ekin) n. live model employed by dressmakers, etc. [F.]

mann'er n. way a thing happens or is done; sort or kind; custom; style. -pl. social be-havior. [F. manière]

man'or n. unit of land in the feudal period. -**man'or-house** n. residence of the lord of the manor. -**manor'ial** a. [F. manoir, L. manere, dwell]

man'sion n. large dwelling-house. [L. mansio]

man'tel n. structure enclosing a fireplace. -**man'telpiece** n. mantel or mantel-shelf. [var. of mantle]

man'tis n. locustlike insect. -**praying man'tis** n. mantis that crosses its forelegs as if in prayer. [G.]

man'tle n. loose cloak; covering; hood fixed round a gas jet for incandescent light. -v.t. cover; conceal. -v.i. become covered with scum; of the blood, rush to the checks; of the face, blush. -**mant'let** n. short mantle; moveable bullet-proof screen. [L. mantellum, cloak]

man'ual a. of or done with the hands. -n. handbook, text book; organ keyboard. [L. manualis-manus, hand]

manufacture n. making of articles or materials, esp. in large quantities for sale. -v.t. produce (articles), work up (materials) into finished articles. -**manufac'turer** n. owner of a factory. [F. fr. L. manu facere, make by hand]

manure' v.t. enrich land. -n. dung or other substances used for fertilizing land. [F. manceuvrer]

manuscript a. written by hand. -n. book, document, etc., written by hand; copy of mat-ter to be printed. [Med. L. manuscriptum]

man'y (men'i) a. numerous. -n. large num-ber. [OE. manig]

map n. flat representation of the earth or some part of it, or of the heavens. -v.t. make a map of. [L. mappa, cloth]

ma'ple n. tree of the sycamore family, one kind yielding sugar. [OE. mapel]

mar v.t. spoil, impair. [OE. mierran]

mar'athon n. long-distance race. [Marathon, Greece]

maraud' v.t. and i. make a raid for plunder. -maraud'er n. [F. marauder]

mar'ble n. kind of lime stone capable of taking a polish; slab of this; small ball used in a game called marbles. -v.t. color so as to resemble veined marble. [L. marmor]

March n. third month of the year. [L. mar-tius (mensis), (month) of Mars]

march n. border or frontier. -v.i. border. [F. marche] **march** v.i. walk with a military step; start on a march; go. -v.t. cause to march or go. -n. action of marching; dis-tance marched in a day; tune to accompany marching. lF. marcher, walk]

mare n. female of the horse or other equine animal. -**mare's nest** n. fancied discovery. [OE. mere] mar'garine (-g-) *n.* vegetable substance imitating butter, and containing vegetable and animal oils. [F.]

mar'gin (-j-) *n.* border or edge; amount allowed beyond what is absolutely necessary; blank space round a printed page. [L. *margo, margin-*]

marinade' *v.t.* soak (meat, fish) in wine spices, *etc.*, before cooking. -*n.* the marinading liquor. [F.]

marine' *a.* of the sea or shipping; used at sea. -*n.* shipping collectively; soldier serving on board a ship. -mar'iner *n.* sailor. [L. *mare*, sea]

marionette' *n.* puppet worked with strings. [F.]

mar'ital *a.* relating to a husband or marriage. [L. *maritus,* husband]

mar'itime *a.* bordering on the sea; connected with seafaring or navigation. [L. *maritimus,* fr. *mare,* sea]

mark *n.* something set up to be aimed at; sign or token; inscription; line, dot, scar, or any visible trace or impression. -*v.t.* make a mark on; indicate, be a distinguishing mark of, watch. -*v.i.* take notice. marks'man *n.* one skilled in shooting. -mark'er *n.* [OE. *mearc*]

mark *n.* German coin; various old coins. [orig. uncertain]

mark'et *n.* place or assembly for buying and selling; demand for goods; place or center for trade. -*v.t.* bring to or sell in a market. -mark'etable *a.* [L. *mercari, mercat-,* trade]

marl'ine (-in) *n.* two-strand cord. [Du. *marlijn,* fr. *marren,* bind]

marmalade *n.* orange preserve. [F. *marmalade*]

maroon' *n.* fugitive slave in the West Indies; marooned person. -*v.t.* leave on a desert island. [Sp, *cimarron,* wild]

marquee' (-ke) *n.* roof-like structure or awning, *usu.* at the entrance of a building; large tent. [F. *marquise,* lit. *marchioness*]

marquetry (-ket-) *n.* inlaid work of wood, ivory *etc.* [F. *marqueterie*]

marquise, mar'quess *n.* nobleman of rank next below a duke. -mar'quisate *n.* [OF. *marchis,* L. *marca,* boundary]

ma'rrow *n.* fatty substance inside bones. [OE. *me rg*]

ma'rry *v.t.* join as husband and wife; take as husband or wife. -*v.i.* take a husband or wife. -mar'riage (-rij) *n.* state of being married: act of marrying. [F. *marier,* L. *maritare*]

Mars' *n.* Roman god of war; 2nd nearest planet to earth. -martian *a.* of Mars. -*n.*

supposed dweller in Mars. [L. *Mars, Mart*]

marsh *n.* low-lying wet land. -marshmall'ow *n.* herb growing near marshes; soft candy *orig.* made from this. [OE. *mersc*]

marsh'al *n.* high officer of state; military rank; chief officer of a district. -*v.t.* arrange in due order; conduct with ceremony. [F. *maréchal,* orig. a horse-servant]

marsupial *n.* animal that carries its young in a pouch, *e. g.* the kangaroo. [G. *marsupion,* small bag]

mart *n.* market place or market hall; auction room. [Du. *markt,* market]

mar'tial (-shal) *a.* relating to war; warlike. [L. *Mars,* god of war]

martinet' *n.* strict disciplinarian. [orig. uncertain]

mar'tyr (-ter) *n.* one put to death for refusing to give up a belief or cause, *esp.* the Christian faith; one who suffers in some cause; one in constant suffering. -*v.t.* make a martyr of. [G. = *witness*]

mar'vel *n.* wonderful thing. -*v.i.* wonder. -mar'velous *a.* [F. *merueille*]

Marx'ist (-ks-) *a.* of Karl Marx, Socialist (d. 1883) of his works or doctrine. -Marxism *n.* Marx's doctrine of materialist conception of history.

marzipan' *n.* paste of sugar and ground almonds. [Ger.]

masca'ra *n.* eyelash cosmetic. [Sp.]

mas'cot *n.* thing supposed to bring good luck. [F. *mascotte*]

masculine (-lin) *a.* of males; manly, vigorous; (*gram.*) of the gender to which names of males belong. [L. *masculinus*]

mask (-d-) *n.* covering for the face; disguise or pretense. -*v.t.* cover with mask; hide, disguise. -masque *n.* form of amateur theatrical performance; masquerade. -masquerade *n.* masked ball. -*v.i.* go about in disguise. [F. *masque*]

masochism *n.* form of sexual perversion which delights in endurance of pain. -mas'ochist *n.* [Sacher-*Masoch,* novelist]

ma'son *n.* worker in stone; freemason. [F. *macon*]

mass *n.* service of the Eucharist. [L. *missa,* fr. *mittere,* send]

mass *n.* quantity of matter; dense collection of this; large quantity. -the mass'es, the populace. -*v.t.* and *i.* form into a mass. -mass'ive *a.* having great size and weight. -mass' production, large-scale production. [G. *maza,* barley cake]

mass'acre (-ker) *n.* general slaughter; indiscriminate killing, *esp.* of unresisting people. -*v.t.* make a massacre of. [F.]

mass'age *a.* rubbing and kneading the muscles, *etc.,* as curative treatment. *v.t.* apply this treatment to. **-mass'eur** *n.* - **mass'euse** *fem.,* one who practises massage. [F. fr. G. *massein,* knead]

mast *n.* (*naut.*) of timber, steel *etc.,* pole for supporting sails, derricks *etc.* [OE. *mcest*]

mast *n.* fruit of beech, oak, *etc.,* used as food for pigs. [OE. *mæst*]

mast'er (ma-) *n.* one who employs another; head of a household; owner; one in control; captain of a merchant ship; teacher; artist of great reputation. *-v.t.* overcome; acquire knowledge of, or skill in. **-mast'erful** *a.* imperious, self- willed. **-mast'erly** *a.* skillfully done. **-mast'ery** *n.* victory, authority. **-mast'erpiece** *n.* finest work of artist or craftsman. [L. *magister*]

masticate *v.t.* chew. **-mastica'tion** *n.* [L. *masticate,* chew gum]

mastiff *n.* large dog used as watch-dog. [OF. *mastin* (*a.*), domestic]

mast'odon *n.* extinct elephant. [G. *mastos,* breast, *odous, odon-,* tooth]

mast'oid *a.* breast-shaped,*esp.* of the bone behind the ear. *-n.* this bone; sinusitis of the mastoid. [G. *mastos,* breast]

mat *n.* small carpet or strip of plaited rushes, *etc.*;thick tangled mass. *-v.t.* and *i.* form into such a mass. **-matt'ing** *n.* fabric of mats. [L. *matta*]

mat'ador *n.* man who kills the bull in a bull fight. [Sp. fr. L. *mactare,* to kill]

match *n.* person or thing exactly corresponding to another; one able to contend equally with another; trial of skill; marriage; person regarded as eligible for marriage. *-v.t.* join in marriage; meet equally in contest; place in contest with; get something corresponding to (a color, pattern, *etc.*). *-v.i.* correspond. **-match'less** *a.* unequalled. [OE. *gernæcca*]

match *n.* small stick with a head of combustible material, which bursts into flame when rubbed; fuse. [F. *meche,* wick]

mate *n.* comrade, husband or wife; officer in a merchant ship immediately below the captain. *-v.t.* marry. *-v.i.* keep company. [Du. *maat*]

mate'rial *a.* of matter or body; unspiritual; essential, important. *-n.* stuff from which anything is made; stuff or fabric. - **materialism** *n.* opinion that nothing exists except matter. **-mate'rialist** *a.* and *n.* - **materialis'tic** *a.* **-mate'rialize** *v.t.* make material. *-v.i.* come into existence. - **materially** *adv.* [L.*materia,* matter]

mater'nal *a.* of or related through a mother. **-matern'ity** *n.* motherhood. [L. *mater,* mother]

mathematics *n. pl.* science of space and number. [*mathernatike,* fr. G. *manthanein,* learn]

mat'inee *n.* morning and afternoon performance. [F. *matins,* morning]

matriarch *n.* mother as ruler of family. [L. *mater,* mother]

matricide *n.* killing of one's own mother; the killer. [L. *mater,* mother]

matriculate *v.t.* enter on a college or university register. *-v.i.* enter one's name on such register; pass an examination entitling one to do this. [Med. L. *matricula,* register of numbers]

matrimony n. marriage. **-matrimo'nial** *a.* [L. *matrimoniurn, mater,* mother]

mat'rix *n.* mold for casting. [L.]

ma'tron *n.* married woman; woman superintendent of a hospital, school, *etc.* **ma'tronly** *a.* [L. *matrona*]

matt'er *n.* substance of which a thing is made up; physical or bodily substance in general; pus; substance of a book, *etc.*; affair; reason, cause of trouble. *-v.i.* be of importance. [F. *matiere* fr. L. *materia*]

matt'ress *n.* stuffed flat case used as or under a bed; a frame with stretched wires for supporting a bed. [OF. *materas*]

mature' *a.* ripe, completely developed, grown. *-v.t.* bring to maturity. - *v.i.* come to maturity; of a bill, become due. **matu'rity** *n.* [L. *maturus,* ripe]

maud'lin *a.* weakly sentimental. [L. *magdalena,* Mary Magdalen, fr. pictures showing her weeping]

maul, mawl *n.* heavy wooden hammer, - **maul** *v.t.* beat or bruise; handle roughly. [L. *mialleus,* hammer]

mausole'um *n.* stately building as a tomb. [L. fr. *Mausolus,* King of Caria]

maxill'a *n.* jawbone. **-maxill'ary** *a.* of the jaw or jawbone. [L.]

max'im *n.* short pithy saying; axiom; rule of conduct. [F. *maxime*]

max'im *n.* a machine-gun. [Sir H. Vaxitn, inventor]

max'imum *n.* greatest possible size or number. *-a.* greatest. **-maximize** *v.t.* [L. = greatest]

May *n.* fifth month of the year; hawthorn; its flowers. *-v.i.* take part in May-day festivities. [L. *Maius,* fr. *Maia,* goddess of growth]

may *v. aux.* express possibility, permission, opportunity, *etc.* **-may'be** *adv.* possibly, perhaps. [OE. *mæg*]

mayonnaise' *n.* sauce of egg-yolk, olive-oil, lemon-juice, *etc.* [F.]

may'or *n.* head of a municipality. -
may'oral *a.* -**may'oralty** *n.* office or time
of office, of a mayor. [L. *major*, greater]

maze *n.* labyrinth; network of paths or
lines. -*v.t.* stupefy. [cp. *amaze*]

me *pron.* objective case singular of the 1st
personal pronoun I. [OE.]

mead *n.* alcoholic drink made from honey.
[OE. *meodu*]

mea'ger *a.* lean, thin, scanty. [F. *maigre*,
thin]

meal *n.* grain ground to powder. -**meal'y**
a. [OE. melo]

meal *n.* occasion of taking food; food
taken. [OE. *mael*, time fixed]

mean *a.* inferior; shabby; small-minded;
niggardly, miserly; bad-tempered.
mean'ly *adv.* -**mean'ness.** (OE. *gemaene*]

mean *a.* intermediate in time; quality, *etc.*
-*n.* anything which is intermediate. *pl.* that
by which something is done; money
resources. -**mean'time** *n.* **meanwhile** *n.*
time between one happening and another.
-*adv.* during this time. [OF. *meien*]

mean *v.t.* intend, design; signify; import.
-**mean'ing** *n.* sense, significance. -*a.* expressive. [OE. *mænan*]

meas'les (mez'ls) *n.pl.* infectious disease
with red spots. -**meas'ly** *a.* of measles;
poor, wretched. [ME. *maseles*]

meas'ure (mezh-er) *n.* size or quantity;
vessel, rod, line, *etc.*, for ascertaining size
or quantity; unit of size or quantity; poeti-
cal rhythm; order or tune; musical time;
slow dance; course or plan of action; law.
-*v.t.* ascertain size or quantity of-, estimate;
bring into competition (with). *v.i.* be (so
much) in size or quantity. [F. *mesure*]

meat *n.* food; flesh of animals used as food.
-**meat'y** *a.* [OE. *mete*]

mechan'ic (-k-) *a.* relating to a machine.
-*n.* one employed in working with
machinery; skilled workman. -*pl.* branch
of science dealing with motion and tendency of motion. -**mechan'ical** *a.* concerned
with machines or manual operation;
worked or produced by, or as though by, a
machine; like a machine; relating to
mechanics. -**mechan'ically** *adv.* [G.
mechane, machine]

med'al *n.* piece of metal usually round or
star-shaped with an inscription, *etc.*, and
used as a reward or memento. -**medall'ion**
n. large medal; various things like this in
decorative work. -**med'alist** *n.* winner of
a medal; maker of medals. [L. *metallum*,
metal]

med'dle *v.i.* interfere, busy one's self with
unnecessarily. -**meddlesome** *a.* [AF. *med-*

lar, OF. *mesler* (mod. *méler*) mix]

me'dial *a.* middle; average. -**me'dian** *a.*
[L. *medius*, middle]

me'diate *v.i.* go between in order to reconcile. -*v.t.* bring about by mediation. -*a.* not
immediate, depending on something intermediate. -**media'tion** *a.* **me'diator** *a.*
[Late L. *mediare*]

medicine *n.* art of healing by remedies and
the regulation of diet: remedy or mixture
of drugs. -**med'ical** *a.* -**med'ically** *adv.* -
med'icament *n.* remedy. **med'icate** *v.t.*
impregnate with medicinal substances. -
medic'inal *a.* having healing properties,
curative. [L. *medicinal* fr. *medicus*,
physician]

Medieval *a.* relating to the Middle Ages.
[fr. L. *medius*, middle, and *ævum*, age]

me'diocre *a.* neither bad nor good, ordinary. -**medioc'rity** *n.* [L. *mediocris*]

meditate *v.t.* think about; plan. -*v.i.* be occupied in thought. -**medita'tion** *n.* -
med'itative *a.* reflective. -**med'itatively**
adv. [L. *meditari*]

Meditera'nean *n.* the sea between
Europe and Africa. [L. *medius*, middle,
terra, earth]

me'dium *n.* (**me'diums, me'dia** *pl.*) middle quality or degree; intermediate substance conveying force; surroundings; environment; means, agency; (spirit.) person
as medium for spirit manifestations. -*a.*
between two qualities, degrees, moderate,
etc. [L.]

med'ley *n.* miscellaneous mixture;
jumble. [OF. *mesler*, mix]

meek *a.* submissive, humble. -**meek'ly**
adv. -**meek'ness** *n.* [ON. *miukr,* soft]

meet *a.* fit, suitable. -**meet'ly** *adv.*
meet'ness *n.* IOE. *gemæte*]

meet *v.t.* come face to face with; encounter; satisfy, pay. -*v.i.* come face to
face; assemble; come into contact. -*n.*
meeting for a hunt. -**meet'ing** *n.* assembly.
[OE. *metan*]

meg'a- *prefix* great. [G. *mesas, mesa-,*
great] -**meg'afog** *n.* fog-signal fitted with-
megaphones. -**megalith'ic** *a.* consisting of
great stones. -**megaloma'nia** *n.* a passion
for great things. -**meg'aphone** *n.* an instrument for carrying the sound of the voice to
a distance. -**meg'astar** *n.* a very well-
known personality in the entertainment
business.

meio'sis *n.* rhetorical understatement opposite of hyperbole. [G. *meiosiss*, diminu-
tion]

meg'abyte *n.* (*compute.*) about 1 million
bytes; 1,024 Kbytes

mel'ancholy *n.* sadness, dejection, gloom. -*a.* gloomy, dejected. - **melancho'lia** *n.* mental disease accompanied by depression. -**melanchol'ic** *a.* [G. *melangcholia*, black bile]

mell'ow *a.* ripe; juicy; (*colloq.*) partly drunk. -*v.t.* and *i.* make or become mellow. [ME. *melwe*, ripe]

mel'odrama *n.* play full of sensational happenings and ending happily. **melodramatic** *a.* [F. *mélodrame*]

mel'ody *n.* sweet sound; series of musical notes arranged to make a tune. [G. *melos*, song]

mel'on *n.* various gourds eaten as fruit, *esp.* watermelon. [G. *melon*, apple]

melt *v.i.* become liquid by heat; be dissolved; become softened; waste away. -*v.t.* cause to soften or dissolve or become liquid by heat. -**melt'down** *n.* (in nuclear reactor) the melting of the fuel rods as a result of a defect in the cooling system, with the possible escape of radiation into the environment. [OE. *meltan*]

mem'ber *n.* limb; any part of a complicated structure; any of the individuals making up a body or society. -**mem' bership** *n.* [L. *membrum*, limb]

mem'brane *n.* thin flexible tissue in a plant or animal body. [L. *membrane*]

mem'oir *a.* record of events; autobiography or biography. [F. *mémoire*, memory]

mem'ory *n.* faculty of recollecting or recalling to mind; recollection; length of time one can remember. -**memor'ial** *a.* of or preserving memory. -*n.* something which serves to keep in memory; statement in a petition. -**memor'ialize** *v.t.* commemorate; petition. -**memor'ialist** *n.* - **mem'orize** *v.t.* commit to memory. **mem'orable** *a.* worthy of being remembered. -**mem'orably** *adv.* -**memoran'dum**, **mem'o** *n.* note to help the memory; note of a contract; informal letter. [L. *memor*, mindful]

men'ace *n.* threat. -*v.t.* threaten. [F., fr. L. *minari*, threaten]

mend *v.t.* repair, correct, put right. -*v.i.* improve, *esp.* in health. -*n.* [*amend*]

menial *a.* relating to a servant in a house; servile. -*n.* household servant. [ME. *meinie*, household]

meningi'tis *n.* inflammation of membranes of brain. [G. *méninx*, membrane]

menopause *n.* cessation of menstruation. [G. *men*, month, *pausis*, cessation]

men'sal *a.* monthly. -**men'ses** *n. pl.* monthly discharge from uterus. -

men'strual *a.* -**menstrua'tion** *n.* approximately monthly discharge of blood and cellular debris from womb of nonpregnant woman. -**men'struate** *v.i.* [L. mensis, month]

menstruation. *See* **mensal.**

ment'al *a.* relating to or done by the mind. -**ment'ally** *adv.* -**mental'ity** *n.* quality of mind. [L. *mens, ment-*, mind]

mentation *n.* activities of the mind; thinking.

men'thol *n.* kind of camphor extracted from peppermint. [L. *mentha*, mint]

men'tion (-shun) *n.* reference to or remark about (person or thing). -*v.t.* refer to, speak of. [L. *mentio*]

men'tor *n.* wise and trusted adviser. [G. *Mentor*, counselor of the son of Ulysses]

men'u *n.* bill of fare. [F. = detailed]

mercenary (-s-) *a.* hired; working simply for reward. -*n.* hired soldier in foreign service. [L. *merces*, reward]

mer'chant *n.* wholesale trader. **mer'chandise** *n.* things in which he deals. - **mer'chantman** *n.* trading ship. [F. *Marchand*]

mer'cury *n.* liquid white metal, quicksilver. -**Mercury**, Roman god of eloquence, messenger of the gods; planet nearest to the sun. -**mercu'rial** *a.* lively, sprightly of, or containing mercury. [L. *Mercurius*, orig. god of merchandiser]

mer'cy *n.* quality of compassion, clemency; a refraining from the infliction of suffering by one who has the right or power to inflict it. -**mer'ciful** *a.* **mer'ciless** *a.* [L. *merces*, reward]

mere *a.* only; not of more value or size, *etc.*, than name implies. -**mere'ly** *adv.* [L. *merus*, unmixed]

merge *v.i.* lose identity, mix in. -*v. t.* cause to lose identity or to be absorbed. -**mer'ger** (-j-) *n.* a being absorbed into something greater; a combining of business firms. [L. *mergere*, dip]

merid'ian *a.* relating to noon, or the position of the sun at noon. -*n.* noon; highest point reached by a star, *etc.*; period of greatest splendor; imaginary circle in the sky passing through the celestial poles: circle of the earth passing through the poles and a place stated. [L. *meridies*, mid-day]

mer'it *n.* excellence, worth; quality of deserving well. -*pl.* excellences or defects. -*v.t.* deserve. -**merito'rious** *a.* deserving well. [L. *meritum*]

mer'maid *n.* imaginary sea creature having the upper part of a woman and the tail of a fish. [obs. *mere*, sea]

mer'ry a. joyous, cheerful. -merr'ily adv.
-merr'iment n. -merr'ythought n. forked
bone between the head and breast of a bird.
-merr'y-go-round n. revolving machine
with wooden horses, model automobiles
etc. [OE. myrge]

mesh n. one of the open spaces of a net.
-v.t. catch in meshes. [OE. masc]

mess n. portion of food; state of untidy
confusion; company of people who
regularly eat together; place where they do
this. -v.i. take one's meals thus; busy one's
self untidily. -v.t. make a mess of, to muddle. [OF. mes, fr. mettre, put]

message n. communication from one person to another. -mess'enger n. message-
bearer. [F. fr. L. mittere, miss-, send]

Messi'ah n. promised deliverer of the
Jews; Christ. -Messian'ic a. [Heb.
mashiah, anointed

meta- prefix over, beyond; also expressing
change. [G.]

metabolism n. process of chemical
change in a living organism. -metabol'ic
a. [G. metabole, change]

met'al n. any of a number of chemical elements usually bright and easy to melt, e.g.
gold, iron, etc., broken stone used for
macadam roads. -metall'ic a. -
met'allurgy n. art of refining metals. -
met'allurgist n. [G. metallon, mine]

metamer n. (chem.) compound that has
the same molecular weight and same
elements in the same proportion as another
compound, but differs in structure.

metamorphosis n. change of shape, substance, character, etc. [G. morphe, form]

metaphor n. (rhet.) transference of a term
to something it does not literally apply to;
substance of this. -metaphor'ical a. [G.
pherein, carry]

metaphysics n.pl. theory of being and
knowing. -metaphys'ical a. [fr. books of
Aristotle, called in G. ta meta ta physika,
'the (works) after the physics,' referring to
position but later mistaken for 'Works
beyond or above physics']

me'teor n. shining body appearing temporarily in the sky; shooting star. --
meteor'ic a. -me'teorite n. fallen meteor.
-meteorol'ogy n. science of weather. -
meteorolog'ical a. -meteorol'ogist n. [G.
meteoros a., lofty]

me'ter n. instrument for measuring, esp. gas
or electricity consumption; verse, rhythm;
unit of length in the French decimal system,
39.37 inches. -met'ric a. of this system. -
met'rical a. of measurement or of poetic
meter. [G. metron, measurer]

methane n. a light colorless gas, marsh-
gas. [G. methan]

meth'od n. a way of doing something; orderliness, system. -method'ical a. -
Meth'odist n. member of any of the churches originated by John Wesley and G.
Whitefield. -Meth'odism n. -meth'od-ize
v.t. reduce to order. [G. methodos, inves-
tigation]

meth'yl n. base of wood spirit; many other
organic compounds. -meth'ylate v.t. mix
with methyl. [fr. G. methy, wine, hyle,
wood]

meticulous a. (over) particular about
details. [L. meticulosus, timid]

met'ric. See meter.

metronome n. (music) device for beating
time at the required tempo. [F. metronome]

metropolis n. (metropolises) pl. chief
city of a state. [G. meter, mother, polis,
city]

mezzanine n. (archit.) in a building, low
story between two higher ones. [It. mez-
zanine]

mi'ca n. mineral found in glittering scales
or plates. [L. = crumb]

micro- prefix small. [G. mikros] -
mi'crochip n. a small piece of semiconductor material carrying many integrated
circuits. -mi'crocomputer n. a small computer in which the central processing unit
is contained in one or more silicon chips.
-mi'crocosm n. world of man; man as an
epitome of the universe. -microcos'mic a.
-mi'crofilm n. minute film of book or
manuscript. -micro'meter n. instrument
for making very small measurements. -
mi'crophone n. instrument for recording
or making sounds louder, e.g., as part of a
telephone or of broadcasting apparatus.
micropro'cessor n. integrated circuit acting as central processing unit in a small
computer. -mi'croscope n. instrument by
which a very small body is magnified and
made, visible. -microscop'ic a. relating to
a microscope; so small as to be only visible
through a microscope. -mi'crosurgery n.
intricate surgery performed on cells, tissues, etc., using a specially designed
operating microscope and miniature
precision instruments. -mi'crobe n.
minute plant or animal, esp. one causing
disease or fermentation. [F., fr. G. mikros,
small bios, life]

mid- prefix intermediate, that is in the middle. -mid'day n. noon or about then. -
midd'ling a. medium, mediocre, fair. -
mid'land n. middle part of a country.
-mid'night n. twelve o'clock at night. -
mid'rib n. rib along center of leaf. -

mid'ship n. middle part of ship. -
mid'shipman n. junior naval officer attending service academy. -**mid'summer** n.
summer solstice; middle part of the summer. -**Mid'summer Day** n. June 24th. -
mid'way a. and adv. half-way. [OE. midd]

mid'dle a. equal distance from, or between. two extremes; medium, intermediate. -n. middle point or part. -
mid'dleman n. trader handling goods between producer and consumer. -**Mid'dle A'ges**, roughly, period from 5th to 15th c.
-**mid'dle weight** n. and a. (jockey, boxer) between light and heavy weight. [OE. middel]

midst n. in the midst of, surrounded by, among. -prep. among. [ME. middes]

mid'wife n. woman who assists others in childbirth. [OE. mid, with, wif, woman]

might (mit) n. power, strength. -**might'y** a. -**might'ily** adv. [OE. miht]

mi'graine (me-) n. severe sick headache, often affecting one side of head. [F., fr. G. hemi, half, kranion, skull]

mi'grate v.i. move from one place to another. -**mi'grant** a. and n. -**migra'tion** n. -**mi'gratorya**. [L. migrare]

mild (-i-) a. gentle, merciful, indulgent; not strongly flavored. -**mild'ly** a. -
mild'ness n. [OE. milde]

mil'dew n. destructive fungus on plants or things exposed to damp. -v.i. become tainted with mildew. -v.t. affect with mildew. IOE. meledeaw, honey dew]

mile n. measure of length, 1760 yards. -
mi'leage n. distance in miles. -**mile'stone** n. stone at mile intervals to mark distances.
[L. mille (passuum) thousand (paces)]

mil'itary a. of, or for, soldiers or armies or warfare. -n. soldiers. -**mil'itant** a.
engaged in warfare; combative. -n.
militant person.-**mili'tia** (-ish-a) n. force of citizens, not professional soldiers, which may be called on at need for military service. [L. miles, milit-, soldier]

milk n. white fluid with which animals feed their young. -v.t. draw milk from. -
milk'maid n. woman working with cows or in a dairy. -**milk'-teeth** n. first set of animal teeth. -**milk'weed, milk'wort** n.
plants producing milky juice. -**milk'y** a.
containing or like milk. -**Milk'y Way**, the galaxy. [OE. meolc]

mill n. machinery for grinding corn, etc.;
building containing this; various manufacturing machines; factory. -v.t. put through a mill; pound. -**mill'er** n. -**mill'race** n.
stream of water driving a mill wheel. -
mill'stone n. one of a pair of flat circular stones used for grinding. -**mill'wright** n.

builder and repairer of mills. [OE. myln]

millennium n. period of a thousand years; period of Christ's reign on earth at his Second Coming. -**millenn'ial** a. [L. mille, thousand]

mill'epede, millipede n. many-legged wormlike insect. [L. mille, thousand, ped, foot]

mill'et n. small grain of an Indian cereal plant: the plant. [F.]

milligram n. thousandth part of a gram.
-**mill'imeter** n. -**mill'iliter** n. [L. mille, thousand]

mill'iner n. one who makes up or deals in women's hats, ribbons, etc. -**mill'inery** n.
[for Milaner, orig. a dealer in articles of Milan (Italy)]

mill'ion n. thousand thousands. [L. mille, thousand]

millisecond n. one thousandth of a second (abbr. ms, msec)

mime n. jester; old form of dramatic representation, esp. one not using words. -
mim'eograph n. form of duplicating machine. -**mim'ic** a. imitated, feigned, esp. to amuse. -n. one skilled in amusing imitation. -v.t. imitate, ludicrously or closely. -**mim'icry** n. [G. mimos, buffoon]

mince v.t. cut or chop small; utter with affected carefulness. -v.i. walk in an affected manner. -n. minced-meat. [OF. mincier, small]

mind (-i-) n. thinking faculties as distinguished from the body, intellectual faculties; memory; attention; intentions taste.
-v.t. attend to; care for; keep in memory.
-**mind'ed** a. disposed. -**mind'ful** a. taking thought; keeping in memory. [OE. gemynd]

mine pron. that belonging to me. [OE. min, gen. of I, me]

mine n. deep hole for digging out coal, metals, etc.; underground gallery with a charge of explosive; large shell or canister of explosive placed in the sea to destroy ships. -v.t. dig from a mine; make a mine in or under. -v.i. make or work in a mine.
-**mine'-field** n. area of sea sown with mines. -**mine'-layer** n. ship used for laying mines. -**mine'-sweeper** n. ship used to clear away mines. [F.]

min'eral a. got by mining; inorganic. -n.
mineral substance. -**min'eral-water** n.
water containing some mineral, etc., natural or artificial kinds used for drinking.
[F.]

mini n. anything that is very short or small; a miniature. n. garment usu. a skirt, that is very short and falls well above the knees.

min'iature n. small painted portrait; book or model on a small scale. -a. small scale. -min'iaturist n. painter of miniatures. [It. miniatura, fr. miniare, paint in red lead]

min'imize v.t. bring to, estimate at, the smallest possible amount. -min'imum n. lowest size, quantity. -a. smallest in size, quantity. [L.minimus, smallest]

min'ister n. person in charge of a department of the State; diplomatic representative; clergyman. -v.t. supply. -v.i. serve; contribute; be serviceable or helpful. [L. = servant]

mink (-ngk)n. weasellike animal; its valuable fur. [cp. Low Ger. mink, otter]

minn'ow n. small freshwater fish. [F. menuise, small fish]

mi'nor a. lesser; smaller; underage. -n. person under the legal age. -minor'ity n. state of being a minor; lesser number; smaller party voting together. [L.]

Min'otaur n. mythical monster, half bull, half-man. [G. Minos, in Crete, and tauros. bull]

mint n. place where money is coined. -v.t. to coin money. [L. moneta]

mint n. aromatic plant used in cooking. [G. mintha]

min'uend n. number from which another is to be subtracted. [L. minure, lessen]

mi'nus prep. less, with the deduction of. -a. quantities, negative. [L.]

minute' (mi-nfit) a. very small; very precise. -minute'ly adv. - minu'tiae n. pl. trifles, precise details. [L. minutus, small]

min'ute n. 60th part of an hour or of a degree or angle; moment; memorandum. -pl. record of the proceedings of a meeting, etc. -v.t. make a minute of, record in minutes. [minute (v.s.)]

miracle n. supernatural event; marvel. [F., fr. L. mirus, wonderful]

mirage' n. deceptive image in the atmosphere, e.g. of a lake in the desert. [F. fr. se mirer, be reflected]

mire n. bog, deep mud—v.t. stick in, dirty with mud. [ON. myrr]

mirr'or n. polished surface for reflecting images. -v.t. reflect an image of [OF. mireor, L. mirari, contemplate]

mirth n. merriment. -mirth'ful a. [OE. myrgth-merg, merry]

mis- prefix meaning amiss, wrongly; makes compounds, e.g. misapply' v.t. apply wrongly. -misman'agement n. bad management. Such words are not given where the meaning and derivation may easily be found from the simple word.

misadventure n. mishap, accident, bad luck. [OF. mesaventure]

misalliance n. improper or degrading marriage. [alliance]

misanthrope n. hater of mankind. [G. misein, hate, anthropos, man]

misappropriate v.t. embezzle, put to wrong use. [mis- and Low L. appropriare]

misbehave v.i. to behave improperly. -misbehavior n. [mis- and behave]

miscegenation n. interbreeding of races; marriage or sexual relations between two people of different race. [L. miscue, mix, genus, race]

miscellaneous a. mixed, assorted. -miscell'any n. collection of assorted writings in one book, literary medley. [L. miscellaneous, fr. miscere, mix]

mis'chief (-chif) n. source of harm or annoyance; annoying conduct. -mis'chievous a. having harmful effect; disposed to or full of mischief. [OF. meschief, fr. meschever, come to grief]

misconduct n. bad behavior; wrong management. [mis- and conduct]

misconstrue' v.t. to interpret wrongly. -misconstruction n. [mis- and construe]

mis'deed n. evil deed; crime. [OE. misdaed]

misdemeanor n. (law) offense less than a felony. [demeanor]

mi'ser (-z-) n. one who hoards instead of using money; stingy person. -mi'serly a. [L. = wretched]

miserable a. very unhappy, wretched; mean; disappointing. -mis'ery n. great unhappiness; distress, poverty. [L. miser]

misfire' v.i. to fail to explode; (fig.) to produce no effect. [mis- and fire]

mis'fit n. a bad fit; a person unable to adapt himself to his surroundings. [misand fit]

misfortune n. bad luck; calamity. [mis and fortune)]

misgiving n. doubt, mistrust. -misgive' v.t. [ME. give = suggest]

mis'hap n. accident, calamity. [hap]

mislead' v.t. to lead astray; to deceive - p.p. misled' -mislead'ing a. deceptive, [mis- and lead]

misno'mer n. wrong name; use of one. [OF. mesnorner, fr. L. norninare, name]

misog'amy n. hatred of marriage. -misog'amist n. [G. misein, gamos, marriage]

misog'yny (-j-) n. hatred of women. -misog'ynist n. [G. misein, gyne, woman]

misquote' v.t. to quote wrongly. -misquota'tion n. an incorrect quotation. [mis- and quotation]

misrepresent' v.t. to give a false description on account of -**misrepresenta'tion** n. [*mis-* and *represent*]

Miss n. title of an unmarried woman or girl; girl. [short for mistress]

miss v.t. fail to hit, reach, find, catch, notice; not be in time for; omit, notice, regret absence of. -n. fact of missing. -**miss'ing** a. lost, absent, [OE. *missan*]

miss'al n. mass-book. [Church L. *missale*, fr. *missa*, mass]

miss'ile (-il) that which may be thrown or shot to do damage. -**guid'ed miss'ile** n. air rocket or other explosive weapon which is guided to the target either from the ground, or by its own internal mechanism. [L. *missiles*, fr. *mittere miss-*, send]

mis'sion (mish'un) n. sending or being sent on some service; party of persons sent; person's calling in life. **missionary** n. of religious missions. -n. one who goes on religious missions. [L. *mission*]

mist n. water vapor in fine drops. [OE. = *darkness*]

mistake' v.t. not to understand; form a wrong opinion about; take (a person or thing) for another. -v.i. be in error. -n. error in thought or action. [*take*]

mis'ter n. courteous form of address to a man (written *Mr.*). [*master*]

mis'tress n. woman who employs other persons; woman with mastery or control; woman teacher; object of a man's illicit love; mode of address to a woman (written *Mrs.*, pron. *miséiz*). [OF. maistresse, fém. of maistre, master]

mistrust' v.t. to feel no confidence in; to look on with suspicion. -n. want of trust. [*mis-* and *trust*]

misunderstand' v.t. to take a wrong meaning from. [*mis* and *understand*]

mitt'en n. glove without separate fingers. [F. *mitaine*]

mix v.t. put together or combine or blend, mingle. -v.i. be mixed; associate. -**mix'er** n. one that mixes; person at ease in any society. -**mix'ture** n. [L. *mixtus*, mixed, fr. *miscere*, mix]

mnemon'ic (n-) a. helping the memory. -n. something intended to help the memory. -pl. art of improving the memory. [G. *mnemon*, mindful]

moan n. low murmur, usually indicating pain. -v.t. bewail. -v.i. utter a moan. [OE. *muan*]

moat n. deep wide ditch round a town or building. -v.t. surround with a moat. [ME. *mote*, mound]

mob n. disorderly crowd of people; mixed assembly. -v.t. attack in a mob, hustle or ill-treat. [abbrev. fr. L. *mobile* (*vulgus*), fickle (crowd)]

mo'bile (-bil) a. capable of movement; easily moved or changed. -**mobil'ity** n. **mo'bilize** v.t. prepare (forces) for active service. -v.i. an army, prepare for active service. -**mobiliza'tion** n. [L. *mobilis*]

mocc'asin n. Native Amer. soft shoe, usually of deerskin; shoe or slipper of similar shape; poisonous water snake. [*Native American*]

mock v.t. make fun of, hold up to ridicule; disappoint. -v.i. scoff. -n. act of mocking; laughing stock. -a. sham, imitation. -**mock'ing-bird** n. N. Amer. bird which mimics other birds' notes. [F. *moquer*]

mode n. method, manner, fashion. -**mo'dish** a. in the fashion. [F.]

mod'el n. representation of an object made to scale; pattern; person or thing worthy of imitation; person employed by an artist to pose, or by a dressmaker to show off clothes. -v.t. work into shape; make according to a model. [F. *modèle*]

modem n. (*compute.*) device used to connect computer terminals to telephone transmission lines. [*modulator/demodulator*)

mod'erate (-it) a. not going to extremes, not excessive. medium. -n. person of moderate views. -v.t. and i. make or become less violent or excessive. -**modera'tion** n. -**mod'erator** n. go-between or mediator; president of a Presbyterian body. [L. *moderatus*]

mod'ern a. of present or recent times; new fashioned. -n. person living in modern times. -**mod'ernism** n. of modern character or views. [F. *moderne*, Late L. *modernus*]

mod'est a. unassuming, retiring, not overrating one's qualities or achievements. -**mod'esty** n. [L. *modestus*]

mod'ify (fi) v.t. make small changes in, tone down. -**modifica'tion** n. [L. *modificare*, limit]

mod'ulate v.t. regulate; vary in tone. -v.i. change the key of music. **modulation** n. [L. *modulari*, measure]

mo'hair n. fine cloth of goat's hair. [Arab. *mukhayyar*]

Mohamm'edan, Muhammadan a. of Mohammed or his religion; Muslim; Islamic. -n. believer in Mohammed. [*Mohammed*]

moist a. damp, slightly wet. -**moist'en** v.t. -**mois'ture** n. liquid, *esp.* diffused or in drops. [OF. *moiste*]

mo'lar a. of teeth, serving to grind. -n.

molar tooth. [L. *molaris*, fr. *mola*, millstone]

molass'es (-ez) *n*. drainings of raw sugar, treacle. [L. *mel*, honey]

mold (mold) *n*. pattern for shaping; hollow object in which metal is cast; character, form. -*v.t.* shape or pattern. **mold'er** *v.i.* crumble, decay, rot. -**mold'ing** *n*. molded object; decoration, *esp.* a long strip of ornamental section. [F. *moule*]

mold *n*. growth caused by dampness. -**mold'y** *a*. [ME. *moulen*, become mildewed]

mole *n*. small burrowing animal. [earlier *mouldwarp*, 'earth-thrower']

mol'ecule *n*. one of the uniform small particles, composed of atoms, of which a homogeneous substance is made up. -**molec'ular** *a*. [F., fr. L. *moles*, mass]

molest' *v.t.* interfere with, meddle with so as to annoy or injure. -**molesta'tion** *n*. [L. *molestare*]

mortify *v.t.* calm down. [L. *mollificare*, make soft]

mollusks, moll'usc *n*. soft-bodied and usually hard-shelled animal. [L. *molluscus-mollis, soft]*

molt *v.i.* change feathers. -*v.t.* shed (feathers). -*n*. action of molting. [OE. *mutian*, fr. L. *mutare*, change]

molt'en *a*. melted. [old *pp.* of *melt*]

moment *n*. very short space of time. -**mo'mentary** *a*. lasting a moment. -**mo'mentarily** *adv*. -**moment'ous** *a*. important. -**moment'um** *n*. force of moving body. [L. *momentum*, movement]

mon'arch (-k) *n*. sovereign ruler of a state. -**mon'archy** *n*. state ruled by a sovereigns his rule. [G. *monos*, alone, *archein*, ruler]

monastery *n*. house occupied by a religious order. -**monast'ic** *a*. relating to monks, nuns, or monasteries. -**monast'icism** *n*. [Late G. *monasterion*, fr. *monazein*, live alone]

Mon'day (mun'da) *n*. second day of the week. [OE. *monandæg*, moon day]

mon'ey (mun'-) *n*. current coin; medium of exchange. -**mon'etary** *a*. -**mon'etarism** *n*. theory that inflation is caused by an excess quantity of money in an economy; economic policy based on this theory and on a belief in the efficiency of free market forces. -**money market** *n*. financial system for the trade of low-risk, short-term securigites. [F. *monnaie. See* mint]

mon'itor *n*. one who gives warning or advice; senior pupil in a school charged with special duties and authority; small warship with heavy guns; kind of lizard. [L. fr.

monere, monit-, admonish]

monk (monk) *n*. one of a religious community of men living apart under vows. -**monk'ish** *a*. -**monk's-hood** *n*. poisonous plant, the aconite. [OE. *munic*, Late G. *monachos*, solitary]

monk'ey (munk'i) *n*. animal closely allied to man; imitative or mischievous child. -*v.i.* play tricks. -**monk'ey-wrench** *n*. wrench with movable jaw. [G. *Moneke*, son of Martin the Ape, in 15th c. version of Reynard the Fox]

mono- *prefix*. [G. *monos*, alone, single] -**monochrome** *n*. representation in one color. -*a*. of only one color. -**monochromatic** *a*. -**mon'ocle** *n*. single eyeglass. -**monog'amy** *n*. custom of being married to only one person at a time. -**mon'ogram** *n*. two or more letters interwoven. -**mon'ograph** *n*. short book on a single subject. -**mon'olith** *n*. prehistoric monument, a single large stone. -**mon'ologue, mon'olog** *n*. dramatic composition with only one speaker. -**monop'oly** *n*. exclusive possession of a trade, privilege, *etc*. -**monop'olize** *v.t.* -**monop'olist** *n*.-**mon'orail** *n*. railway having cars running on or suspended from a single rail. -**mon'osyllable** *n*. word of one syllable. -**monosyliab'ic** *a*. -**mon'otheism** *n*. belief that there is only one God. **mon'otheist** *n*. -**mon'otone** *n*. continuing on one note. -**monot'onous** *a*. lacking in variety, wearisome. -**monot'ony** *n*. -**mon'otype** *n*. machine for casting and setting printing type in individual letters.

monsoon' *n*. seasonal wind of the Indian Ocean; other periodical winds. [Arab. *mausim*, lit. season]

mon'ster *n*. misshapen animal or plant; person of great wickedness huge animal or thing. -*a*. huge. [L. *monstrum*, marvel]

month (munth) *n*. one of the twelve periods into which a year is divided; period of the revolution of the moon. -**month'ly** *a*. happening, payable, *etc*., once a month. -*adv*. once a month. -*n*. **monthly** magazine. [OE. *monath*; fr. *moon*]

mon'ument *n*. anything that commemorates; written record. -**monument'al** *a*. of or serving as a monument; vast, stupendous. [L. *monumentum*]

mood *n*. state of mind and feelings. -**mood'y** *a*. changeable in mood; gloomy. -**mood'ily** *adv*. -**mood'iness** *n*. [OE. *mod*]

mood *n*. (*gram.*) group of forms indicating function of verb. [var. of *mode*]

moon *n*. satellite revolving round the earth; satellite of a planet. -*v.i.* go about dreamily. -**moon'light** *n*. -**moon'shine** *n*.

nonsense; smuggled liquor. **-moon'stone** *n.* precious stone. **-moon'-struck** *a.* lunatic. [OE. *mona*]

moor *n.* tract of waste land, often hilly and heath-clad; land preserved for grouse shooting. [OE. *mor*]

moor *v.t.* fasten (a ship) with chains, ropes or cable and anchor. *-v.i.* secure a ship thus. **-moorings** *n.* [orig. uncertain]

moose *n.* Amer. elk. [Algonkin, *mus*]

moot *v.t.* bring for discussion. *-a.* open to argument. *-n.* (*hist.*) meeting, as town-moot. folk-*moot*. [OE. *mot*]

mop *n.* bundle of yarn, cloth, *etc.*, fastened to the end of a stick and used for cleaning. *-v.t.* clean or wipe with a mop or with any absorbent stuff. [OF. *mappe*, L. *mappa*, napkin]

mope *v.i.* be depressed, dull or dispirited. [Du. *moppen*, sulk]

mor'al *a.* concerned with right and wrong conduct; of good conduct. **-moral victory** *n.* failure or defeat that inspirits instead of crushing the loser. **-morale'** *n.* discipline and spirit of an army or other body of persons. -mor'alist *n.* teacher of morals. -moral'ity *n.* good moral conduct; moral goodness or badness; kind of medieval drama, containing a moral lesson. -mor'alize *v.t.* interpret morally. *-v.i.* write or think on moral aspects of things. -mor'ally *adv.* [L. *moralis*]

morass' *n.* marsh, bog. [Du. *moeras*]

moratorium *n.* government's authority to delay payment of debts during national emergency; suspension of activity, *esp.* during a period of reconsideration. [L. *mora*, delay]

mor'bid *a.* unwholesome, sickly. **-mor'bidly** *adv.* **-morbid'ity** *n.* [L. *morbidus*, from *morbus*, disease]

more *a.* greater in quantity or number. *-adv.* to a greater extent; in addition. *-pron.* greater or additional amount or number. **-moreo'ver** *adv.* besides. [OE. *mora*]

morgue' (morg) *n.* mortuary in which dead bodies are placed for identification, *etc.* [F.]

moribund *a.* dying. [L. *moribundus*]

Mor'mon *n.* member of the Church of Jesus Christ of Latter-Day Saints, founded in U.S.A. by Joseph Smith (1805-1844) in 1830. [fr. *Mormon*, alleged author of *The Book of Mormon*]

morn *n.* morning. **-morn'ing** *n.* early part of the day. **-morn'ing glo'ry** *n.* convotvulus. [OE. *morgen*]

mo'ron *n.* adult with mental capacity of a child. [G. *moros*, foolish]

morose' *a.* sullen, unsociable. [L. *morosus*, moody]

morph'ia, morph'ine *n.* narcotic part of opium. [G. *Morpheus*, god of sleep]

morphology *n.* science of the forms of living organisms. [G. *morphe*, form]

Morse *a.* **Morse-code** *n.* system of signalling in which the letters of the alphabet are represented by various combinations of dots and dashes, short and long flashes, *etc.* [*Morse*, inventor (d. 1872)]

mor'sel *n.* mouthful; fragment. [L. *morsus*, bite]

mort'al *a.* subject to death; fatal. *-n.* mortal creature. **-mortal'ity** *n.* being mortal; great loss of life; death rate. **-mort'ally** *adv.* [L. *mors*, *mort-*, death]

mort'ar *n.* vessel in which substances are pounded; short gun throwing at high angles; mixture of lime, sand, and water for holding bricks and stones together. [L. *mortarium*]

mort'gage (morg-aj) *n.* conveyance of property as security for debt with provision that the property be reconveyed at payment within an agreed time. *-v.t.* convey by mortgage. [OF. = dead pledger]

morti'cian (-ish-) *n.* funeral undertaker. [L. *mors, mort-*, death]

mort'ify *v.i.* subdue by self-denial; humiliate. [L. *mortificare*, make dead]

mort'ise (-is) *n.* hole made in a piece of wood, *etc.*, to receive the tongue at the end of another piece called a tenon. *-v.t.* make a mortise in; fasten by mortise and tenon. [F. *mortaise*]

mort'uary *a.* of or for burial. *-n.* building where dead bodies are kept for a time. [L. *mortuarius-mors*, death]

mosa'ic *n.* picture or pattern made by fixing side by side small bits of colored stone, glass, *etc.*; this process of decoration. [F. *mosaique*]

Mos'lem. *See* **Mus'lim.**

mosque (mosk) *n.* Islamic place of worship. [Arab. *masjid*]

mosqui'to (-ke-to) *n.* various kinds of gnat. [Sp., fr. L. *musca*, fly]

moss *n.* swamp; small plant growing in masses on a surface. *-v.t.* cover with moss. [OE. *mos*]

most *a.* greatest in size, number, degree. *-n.* greatest amount, degree. *-adv.* in the greatest degree. **-most'ly** *adv.* for the most part. [OE. *moest*]

mot' (mo) *n.* pithy or witty saying. **-mot juste**, right word. [F.]

mote *n.* speck of dust. [OE. *mot*]

moth' *n.* nocturnal insect of butterfly family. -**moth′eaten** a. [OE. moththe]

moth′er (muTH-) n. female parent; head of a religious community of women. -a. inborn. -v.t. act as a mother to. -**moth′erhood** n. -**moth′erly** a. -**moth′er-in-law** n. mother of one's wife or husband. -**moth′erboard** n. (in an electronic system) a printed circuit board through which signals between all other boards are routed. -**moth′er of pearl′** n. iridescent substance forming the lining of certain shells. -**Moth′er's Day** n. day in which the mother is honored by the family, usu. the second Sunday in May. [OE. moder]

mo′tion n. process or action or way of moving; proposal in a meeting; application to a judge. -v.t. direct by a sign. -**mo′tionless** a. [L. motio, fr. movere, mot-, move]

mot′tle n. blotch on a surface; arrangement of blotches. -v.t. mark with blotches. -**mott′led** a. blotchy. [prob. from motley, (v.s.)]

mo′tor n. that which imparts movement; machine to supply motive power. **mo′torize** v.t. mechanize. -**mo′tor-boat** (-bus, -launch, etc.) n. one moved by an engine carried inside it. -**mo′torcade** n. formal procession of motor vehicles. -**mo′torist** n. user of an automobile. [motion]

mott′o n. (mott′oes pl.) saying adopted as a rule of conduct; short inscribed sentence; word or sentence accompanying a heraldic crest. [It.]

mound n. heap of earth or stones; small hill. [orig. uncertain]

mount n. hill; that on which anything is supported or fitted; horse. -v.i. go up; get on horseback; rise. -v.t. go up; get on the back of, set on a mount; furnish with a horse. -**mount′ain** n. hill of great size. -**mountaineer′** n. one who lives among or climbs mountains. [L. mons, mont-, hill]

mourn -v.i. feel or show sorrow. -v.t. grieve for. -**mourn′ing** n. act of mourning; conventional signs of grief for a death; clothes of a mourner. [OE. murnan]

mouse n. (mice pl.) small rodent animal. -v.i. catch mice. [OE. mus]

mouse n. (compute.) input device that is moved about on a tabletop or pad and directs a pointer (cursor) on a video screen

mousse′ n. dish of frozen whipped cream; similar cold dishes. [F.]

mouth (-th; pl. -THz) n. opening in the head, used for eating, speaking, etc.; opening into anything hollow; outfall of a river, entrance to harbor, etc. -(-TH) v.t. take into the mouth; declaim. -v.i. declaim. [OE.

muth]

move -v.t. change the position of-, stir; propose. -v.i. change places; take action. -n. a moving; motion making towards some goal. -**mov′able** a. and n. **move′ment** n. process or action of moving; moving parts of a machine; main division of a piece of music. -**mov′ie** n. (sl.) motion picture, film. [L. movere]

mow v.t. cut (grass, etc.); cut down, kill. -v.i. cut grass. [OE. mawan]

much a. in quantity. -n. large amount; important matter. -adv. in a great degree, nearly. [ME. muche]

mu′cus n. viscous secretion of the mucous membrane. -**mu′cous** a. -**mu′cous membrane**, lining of body cavities, canals. [L.]

mud a. wet and soft earth. -**mud′dle** v.t. confuse; bewilder; mismanage. -v.i. be busy in a fumbling way. -n. confusion. -**mudd′y** a. [of Teutonic orig.]

muff′in n. light round flat cake, toasted and buttered. [orig. uncertain]

muffle v.t. wrap up; of sound, deaden. -**muff′ler** n. scarf to cover neck and throat; device which deadens sound, esp. as attached to the exhaust system of an automobile, etc. [F. emmoufler, swathe]

mug n. drinking cup. -(sl.) face; fool. -v.i. study hard; to attack or threaten with the intention of robbing, usu. in the street. -**mugg′er** n. one who robs in this way. [fr. mugan]

mugg′y a. damp and stifling. [dial. mug, mist, fr. ON. mugga]

Muhammadan. See **Mohammedan.**

mulch n. straw, leaves, etc., spread as a protection for the roots of plants. -v.t. protect in this way. [orig. uncertain]

mule n. cross between horse and ass; obstinate person. -**muleteer′** n. mule driver. -**mu′lish** a. [L. mulus]

mule n. heelless slipper. [F.]

mull v.t. heat (wine or ale) with sugar and spices. [orig. uncertain]

mult-, multi- prefix much, many. [L. multus, much] -**multian′gular** (-ng-g-) a. many-angled. -**multicult′ural** a. consisting of, relating to, or designed for the cultures of several different races. -**multidisciplinary** a. of, or relating to, or involving many disciplines or branches of learning. **multieth′nic** a. consisting of, relating to, or designed for various different races. -**multifa′rious** a. manifold, varied. -**mul′tiform** a. many forms. -**multilat′eral** a. many-sided. -**mul′tiple!** a. having many parts. -n. quantity which contains another

an exact number of times. -mul'tiplicand
n. number to be multiplied by another. -
multiplica'tion n. -multiplicity, variety,
greatness in number. -mul'tiply v.t. make
many; find the sum of a given number
taken a stated number of times. -v.i. increase in number or amount. -mul'titude
n. great number; great crowd. -
multitu'dinous a. very numerous.

mum' a. silent. [imit.]

mum'ble v.i. and t. speak indistinctly.
[ME. momelen]

mumm'y n. embalmed body. -munim'ify
v.t. [Arab. mumiyah]

mumps n. pl. contagious disease marked
by swelling in the glands of the neck. [obs.
mump, grimace]

mundane a. worldly; ordinary. [L. mun-
danus]

municipal (-is'-) a. belonging to the affairs of a city or town. -municipal'ity n.
city or town with local self-government;
its governing body. [L. municipium, town
with rights of Roman citizenship]

muni'tion (-ish'-) n. (usually pt.) military
stores. [L. munitio]

mu'ral a. of or on a wall. -n. wall painting.
[L. murus, wall]

mur'der n. the unlawful and deliberate
killing of a human being. -v.t. to kill thus.
[OE. morthor]

mur'mur v.i. make a low continuous
sound; complain. -v.t. utter in a low voice.
-n. sound or act of murmuring. [L. mur-
murare]

mus'cle (mus'l) n. part of the body which
produces movement by contracting; part
of the body made up of muscles. -
mus'cular a. [F.]

Muse (-z) n. one of the nine goddesses inspiring learning and the arts. [L. musa]

muse (-z) v.i. be lost in thought. -n. state
of musing. [F. muser]

muse'um n. place to show objects illustrating the arts, history, etc. [L.]

mush n. pulp; boiled corn meal; (fig.) sentimentality. [mash]

mush'room n. kind of edible fungus. -a.
of rapid growth. [F. mousseron]

mu'sic (-z-) n. art of expressing or causing
an emotion by melodious and harmonious
combination of notes; the laws of this;
composition in this art; such composition
represented on paper. -mu'sical a. -
mu'sically adv. -musi'cian n. -mu'sical n.
colorful light drama with songs, music. [G.
mousike (techne), (art of the) muses]

musk n. a scent obtained from a gland of
the musk-deer; various plants with a

similar scent. [F. musc]

musk'et n. infantryman's gun, esp. unrifled. -musketeer' n. -musk'etry n. use
of firearms. [F. mousquet]

Mus'lim, Mos'lem n.   follower   of
Mohammed. -a. of the Islamic religion.
[Arab. salama, submit to God]

mus'lin (-z-) n. fine cotton fabric. [orig. fr.
Mosul, in Mesopotamia]

muss'el n. bivalve shellfish. [L. musculus,
little mouse]

must n. unfermented wine. [L. mustum]

must v. aux. be obliged to, or certain to.
[OE. moste]

mustache (mus-tash) n. hair on the upper
lip. [F.]

mus'tang n. wild horse of American
prairies. [Sp. mestengo]

mustard n. powdered seeds of a plant used
in paste as a condiment; the plant. [OF.
moustarde]

must'er v.t. and i. assemble. -n. assembly,
esp. for exercise, inspection. [L.
monstrare, show]

must'y a. moldy. [orig. uncertain]

mute a. dumb; silent. -n. dumb person;
hired mourner; clip, etc. to deaden sound
of musical instruments. [L. mutus]

mu'tilate v.t. deprive of a limb or other
part; damage. -mutila'tion n. -mu'til-
ator n. [L. mutilare]

mu'tiny n. rebellion against authority, esp.
against the officers of a disciplined body.
-v.i. commit mutiny. -mu'tinous a. -
mutineer' n. [F. mutiner]

mutt'er v.i. speak with the mouth nearly
closed, indistinctly. -v.t. utter in such tones.
-n. act of muttering. [imit.]

mu'tual a. done, possessed, etc., by each
of two with respect to the other. mu'tually
adv. common to both. [L. mutuus]

muz'zle n. projecting mouth and nose of
an animal; thing put over these to prevent
biting; end of a firearm bv which the
projectile leaves. -v.t. put a muzzle on. [OF.
musel, snout]

my poss. a. belonging to me. -myself'
pron. emphatic and reflex, of I, me. [for
mine]

myeli'tis n. inflammation of the spinal
cord. [G. myelos. marrow]

myo'pia n. short-sightedness. -my'opic a.
[G. myein, close, ops, eye]

myeso'tis n. various small flowering
plants including the forget-me-not.
(myosote). [G. mys., mouse, ous, ot-, ear]

myr'iad (mir-) n. ten thousand; endless
number. -a. innumerable. [G. myrias,
myriad-]

myrrh (mer) *n.* aromatic gum of the balsamodendron. [G. *myrrha*]

myrtle *n.* evergreen shrub. [OF. *myrtille*, myrtle-berry]

mys'tery (mis-) *n.* obscure or secret thing; state of being obscure; religious rite; miracle-play. -**myst'ic** *a.* of hidden meaning, *esp.* in a religious sense. -*n.* one who seeks direct communication with God by self-surrender or contemplation. -**myst'ify** *v.t.* bewilder. [G. *mysterion*, secret]

myth (mith) *n.* tale with supernatural characters or events; imaginary person or object. -**myth'ical** *a.* -**mythol'ogy** *n.* myths collectively; study of these. [G. *mythos*, fable]

N

nab *v.t.* (*sl.*) seize, catch, [orig. uncertain. *cp. nap*]

nacelle' (-sel') *n.* streamlined part of an aircraft that houses engine, crew, passengers, and cargo. [L. *navicella*, little ship]

na'cre (na-ker) *n.* mother-of-pearl. [F.]

na'dir *n.* point opposite the zenith. [Arab. *niazir*, opposite]

nag *n.* small horse for riding; horse. [orig. uncertain]

nag *v.t.* and *i.* worry, be worrying, by constant fault-finding. [Sw. *nagga*, peck]

nail *n.* horny shield of the ends of the fingers; claw; small metal spike for fixing wood, *etc.* -*v.t.* fix with a nail. [OE. *nægel*]

naive' *a.* simple, unaffected. [F.]

na'ked *a.* bare, unclothed. -**na'kedness** *n.* -**na'kedly** *adv.* [OE. *nacod*]

name *n.* word by which a person, thing. *etc.* is denoted; reputation. -*v.t.* give a name to; call by a name; appoint: mention. -**name'less** *a.* -**name'ly** *adj.*, . that is to say. -**name'sake** *n.* person having the same name as another. [OE. *nama*]

nann'y *n.* female goat (also **nann'ygoat**); children's nurse. [*name*]

nap *n.* roughish surface cloth made by projecting fibers. [Du. *nop*]

nap *v.i.* take a short sleep. -*n.* short sleep. [OE. *knappian*]

nape *n.* back of the neck; hollow there. [OE. *hnoepp*, bowl]

naph'tha *n.* flammable oil distilled from coal, *etc.* -**naph'thalene** *n.* disinfectant. [G.]

nap'kin *n.* square piece of linen for wiping fingers or lips at table; similar such pieces of cloth or absorbent material. [F. *nappe*, cloth]

narcissus *n.* bulbous plant with a white scented flower; (*psychoanalysis*) one who loves himself. [G. *narkissos*]

narcotic *n.* drug causing sleep, insensibility or hallucination. -**a.** -**narco'sis** *n.* stupefying effect of narcotic. [G. *narkotikos*]

narrate' *v.t.* relate, tell (story). -**narration** *n.* -**narr'ative** *n.* account or story. [L. *narrare*]

narr'ow *a.* of little breadth. -*n.* *pl.* narrow part of a strait. -*v.t.* and *i.* make, become, narrow. -**narr'owly** *adv.* -**narr'owminded** *a.* bigoted. -**narr'owness** *n.* [OE. *nearu*]

na'sal (-z-) *a.* of the nose. -*n.* sound uttered through the nose. -**na'salize** *v.t.* make nasal in sound. [L. *nasus*, nose]

nas'ty *a.* foul, disagreeable. -**nast'ily** *adv.* -**nas'tiness** *n.* [orig. uncertain]

na'tal *a.* relating to birth. [L. *natalis*]

na'tion (-shun) *n.* people or race organized as a state. -**na'tional** (nash-) *a.* **nationally** *adv.* -**national'ity** *n.* national quality or feeling; facts of belonging to a particular nation. -**nat'ionalist** *n.* one who supports national rights. -**nat'ionalize** *v.t.* convert into the property of a nation. [L. *natio*]

na'tive (-tiv) *a.* born in a particular place; originating from that country; found in a pure state; of one's birth. -*n.* one born in a place; oyster reared in an artificial bed. -**nativ'ity** *n.* -**Nativ'ity** *n.* birth of Christ; Christmas. [L. *natiuus- nasci*, *nãt-*, be born]

na'ture *n.* innate or essential qualities of a thing; class, sort; life force; disposition; power underlying all phenomena in the material world; material world as a whole. -**nat'ural** *a.* of, according to, occurring in, provided by, nature. -*n.* half-witted person; (*music*) sign restoring sharp or flat note to its natural pitch. **nat'urally** *adv.* -**nat'uralist** *n.* one who studies plants and animals. -**nat'uralize** *v.t.* admit to citizenship; accustom to a new climate. -**naturaliza'tion** *n.* [L. *aatura*, fr. *nasci*, *not-*, to be born]

naught (nawt) *n.* nothing, zero. *a.* bad, useless. -**naught'y** *a.* wayward, not behaving well. [OE. *nawiht*, no whit]

nau'sea *n.* sickness. -**nau'seate** *v.t.* affect with sickness; reject with loathing. -**nau'seous** *a.* [L. = seasickness]

nautical *a.* of seamen or ships. [G. *nautes*, sailor]

nautilus *n.* shellfish with a membrane which acts as a sail. [G. *nautilos*, sailor]

naval. *See* **navy.**

nave *n.* main body of a church building. [L. *nauis*, ship]

na'vel *n.* small pit on the abdomen. [OE. *nafela*, dim. of *nafu*, nave, hub]

navigate *v.i.* sail. -*v.t.* sail over; direct the steering of a ship. -**nav'igator** *n.* one who navigates; worker digging a canal. -**navv'y** *n.* laborer (navigator in second sense). [L. *navigare*, fr. *nauis*, ship]

na'vy *n.* fleet; warships of a country with their crews and organization. -**na'val** *a.* [OF. *navie- navis*, ship]

Nazi *n.* German National Socialist Party; member of this; one holding views similar to this. *a.* [contr. of Ger. *National sozialist*]

Nean'derthal man (ne-an'-der-tal), primitive type of prehistoric man. [fr. skull found in the *Neanderthal*, valley near Dusseldorf]

near *adv.* at or to a short distance. -*prep.* close to. -*a.* close at hand, close; closely related; stingy; of horses, vehicles, *etc.* , left. -*v.t.* and *i.* approach. -**near'ly** *adv.* closely; almost. -**near'ness** *n.* - **near'sighted** *a.* able to see objects clearly only if they are near to the eyes.

neat *a.* pure, undiluted; simple and elegant; cleverly worded; deft. -**neat'ly** *adv.* -**neat'ness** *n.* [F. *net*, clean]

neb'ula *n.* star-cluster. -**neb'ular** *a.* - **neb'ulous** *a.* cloudy; vague. [L. = *mist*]

necessary (nes'-) *a.* needful, requisite, that must be done. -*n.* needful thing. **nec'essarily** *adv.* -**necess'ity** *n.* compel, give power or state of affairs; a being needful; needful thing; poverty. **necessitate** *v.t.* make necessary. [L. *aecessarius*]

neck *n.* part of the body joining the head to the shoulders; narrower part of a bottle, *etc.*; narrow piece of anything between wider parts. -**neck'erchief** (chif) *n.* kerchief for the neck. -**neck'lace** *n.* ornament round the neck. -**neck'tie** *n.* narrow strip of tailored material worn about the neck and tied at the front. [OE. *hnecca*, nape of neck]

necrol'ogy *n.* list of deaths, obituaries. [G. *nekros*, dead body]

nec'tar *n.* drink of the gods; the honey of flowers. -**nect'arine** *a.* -*n.* variety of peach. [G. *nektar*]

née (nā) *a.* born, preceding maiden surname of a married woman. [F.]

need *n.* want, requirement; necessity; poverty. -*v.t.* want, require. [OE. *nied*]

need'le *n.* pointed pin with an eye and no head, for passing thread through cloth, *etc.*; knitting pin; magnetized bar of a compass; obelisk. [OE. ntdl]

neg'ative *a.* expressing denial or refusal; wanting in positive qualities; not positive. -*n.* negative word or statement; in photography, a picture made by the action of light on chemicals in which the lights and shades are reversed. -*v.t.* disprove, reject. -**negate'** *v.t.* deny. -**nega'tion** *n.* [L. *negativus, negare*, deny]

neglect' *v.t.* disregard, take no care of; fail to do; omit through carelessness. -*n.* fact of neglecting or being neglected. **neglect'ful** *a.* [L. *neglegere, neglect-*, not to pick up]

negotiate *v.i.* discuss with a view to finding terms of agreement. -*v.t.* arrange by conference; transfer (bill, *etc.*); get over (an obstacle). [L. *negotiari, negotium*, business]

Ne'gro *n.* member of the black African race. [Sp., fr. L. *niger, negr-*, black]

neigh *v.i.* of a horse, to utter its cry. -*n.* the cry. [OE. *hnægan*]

neigh'bor (nq'bur) *n.* one who lives, stands, *etc.* near another. -**neigh'boring** *a.* situated near by. -**neigh'borhood** *n.* district; people of a district; region round about. [OE. *neahgebur*, 'nigh boor', near by farmer]

nei'ther *a.* and *pron.* not either. -*adv.* not on the one hand; not either. -*conj.* nor yet. [OE. *nahwæther*, not whether]

neo- *pref.* new. [G. *neos*, new]

neolith'ic *a.* of the later stone age. - **neol'ogism** *n.* new coined word or phrase. -**neontol'ogy** *n.* study of still-existing races of animals. -**neoter'ic** *a.* modern. - **ne'ophyte** *n.* new convert; beginner.

ne'on *n.* rare atmospheric gas. -**ne'on lighting**, produced by passing an electric current through a tube containing neon. [G. *neos*, new]

neph'ew *n.* brother's or sister's son, [F. *neveu*, fr. L. *nepos*]

ne'potism *n.* favoritism. [It. *nepotismo*, fr. *nepote*, nephew. (orig. because of favors bestowed by a pope on his nephews)]

Nep'tune *n.* Roman god of the sea; one of the outermost planets of the Solar system. [G. *Neptunus*]

nerve *n.* sinew, tendon; fiber or bundle of fibers conveying feeling, impulses to motion, *etc.*, between the brain and other parts of the body; assurance, coolness in danger. (*sl.*) impudence. -*pl.* irritability, unusual sensitiveness to fear, annoyance, *etc.* -*v.t.* give courage or strength to. -**nerve'less** *a.* -**nerv'ous** *a.* of the nerves; vigorous; excitable, timid. -**nerv'ously** *adv.* -**nerv'ousness** *n.* -**nerv'y** *a.* brash; courageous. [L. *nervus*, sinew]

nest *n.* place in which a bird lays and hatches its eggs; animal's breeding place; any snug retreat. -*v.i.* make or have a nest. -**nes'tle** (-sl) *v.i.* settle comfortably, usually pressing in or close to something. - **nest'ling** *n.* bird too young to leave the nest. [OE.]

net *n.* open-work fabric of meshes of cord, *etc.*; piece of it used to catch fish, *etc.* -*v.t.* to cover with, or catch in, a net. -*v.i.* make net. -**net'ting** *n.* string or wire net. - **net'work** *n.* intricate system-*e.g.*, of transport systems. -**network** (*compute.*) system of computers or terminals interconnected by communication circuits. [OE. *nett*]

net, nett *a.* left after all deductions; clear profit. -*v.t.* gain as clear profit. [F. clean]

nett'le *n.* plant with stinging hairs on the leaves. -*v.t.* irritate, provoke. [OE. *netele*]

neuralgia *n.* pain in the nerves, *esp.* of face and head. -**neural'gic** *a.* -**neurasthe'nia** *n.* nervous debility. -**neurasthen'ic** *a.* - **neuri'tis** *n.* inflammation of nerves. - **neuro'sis** *n.* nervous disorder. -**neurot'ic** *a.* suffering from neurosis; abnormally sensitive. -*n.* neurotic person. [G. *neuron*, nerve]

neut'er *a.* neither masculine nor feminine. -*n.* neuter word; neuter gender. [L. = neither]

neut'ral *a.* taking neither side in a war; dispute, *etc.*; without marked qualities; belonging to neither of two classes. -*n.* neutral state, or a subject of one. **neutral'ity** *n.* impartiality. -**neut'ralize** *v.t.* make ineffective; counterbalance. [L. = neither]

neut'ron *n.* electrically uncharged particle of the atom. -**neut'ron bomb** *n.* nuclear bomb designed to destroy people but not buildings. [L. *neuter,* neither]

nev'er *adv.* at no time. -**nevertheless'** *adv.* for all that. [OE. *nœfre*]

new *a.* not existing before, fresh; lately come into some state or existence. *adv.* (usually new-) recently, fresh. - **newfang'led** (-ng-gld) *a.* of new fashion. **new'ly** *adv.* -**new'ness** *n.* -**news** *n.* report of recent happenings, fresh information. -**news'-dealer** *n.* one who deals in newspaper, magazines *etc.* -**news'paper** *n.* periodical publication containing news. [OE. *niave*, new; cp. F. *nouvelles*]

next *a.* nearest; immediately following. - *adv.* on the first future occasion. [OE. niehst, superl. of neah, high]

nex'us *n.* connecting link. [L.]

nib *n.* pen-point. -*pl.* crushed cocoa beans.

[earlier *neb*, beak, OE. *nebb*]

nib'ble *v.t.* take little bites of. -*v.i.* take little bites. -*n.* little bite. [fr. *nip*]

nice *a.* hard to please; careful, exact; difficult to decide; minute; subtle, fine; (*sl.*) pleasant, friendly, kind, agreeable, *etc.* - **nice'ly** *adv.* -**ni'cety** *n.* precision; minute distinction or detail. [OF. *nice*, foolish]

nick *v.t.* make a notch in, indent; just catch in time. -*n.* notch; exact point of time. [orig. uncertain]

nick'el *n.* silver-white metal much used in alloys and plating; five cent piece. [Sw. abbrev. fr. Ger. *kupfernickel*, copper nickel (ore)]

nick'name *n.* name added to or replacing an ordinary name. -*v.t.* give a nickname to. [earlier, a *nickname* was an *eke-name*; fr. *eke*, also, [OE. *ecan*, cp. *newt*]

nic'otine- *n.* poisonous oily liquid in tobacco. [F. fr. J. *Nicot*, who sent tobacco plants to France (1560)]

niece *n.* brother's or sister's daughter. [F. niece, fr. L. neptis]

night (nit) *n.* time of darkness between day and day; end of daylight; dark. **night'-blind'ness** *n.* inability to see in a dim light. -**night'-club** *n.* club open at night for dancing, entertainment. -**night'fall** *n.* end of day. -**night'ingale** *n.* small bird which sings usually at night. -**night'ly** *a.* happening or done every night; of the night. - **night'ly** *adj.* every night, by night. - **night'mare** *n.* feeling of distress during sleep; bad dream. -**night'shade** *n.* various plants of the potato family, some of them with poisonous berries. -**night'-shift** *n.* night duty; relay of workmen on night duty. -**night'stick** *n.* policeman's club. [OE. *nihl*]

ni'hilism *n.* denial of all reality; rejection of all religious and moral principles: opposition to all constituted authority or government. -**ni'hilist** *n.* [L. *nihil*, nothing]

nil *n.* nothing, zero. [contr. of L. *nihil*]

nim'ble *a.* active, quick. [OE. *niman*, take, capture]

nim'bus *n.* cloud of glory, halo; raincloud or storm-cloud. [L. = cloud]

nine *a.* and *n.* cardinal number next above eight. -**ninth** (-i-) *a.* -**ninth'ly** *adv.* - **nine'teen** *a.* and *n.* nine and ten. - **nine'teenth** *a.* -**nine'ty** *a.* and *n.* nine tens. -**nine'tieth** *a.* [OE. *nigon*]

ninja *n.* member of secret Japanese feudal organization.

nip *v.t.* pinch sharply; detach by pinching; check growth (of plants) thus. -*n.* pinch;

check to growth; sharp coldness of weather. [orig. uncertain]

nipp'le *n.* point of a breast, teat. [orig. uncertain]

Nirva'na *n.* in Buddhism, attainment of union with the divine by the conquest of personal desires and passions. [Sanskrit = extinction]

ni'trogen *n.* colorless, tasteless gaseous element forming four-fifths of the atmosphere. **-nitrog'enous** (-j-) *a.* of or containing nitrogen. [G. *nitron*]

nitroglycerin *n.* high explosive produced by interaction of glycerin and nitric or sulfuric acids. [G. *nitron*]

no *a.* not any. *-adv.* expresses a negative reply to question or request. **-no'body** *n.* no person; person of no importance. **-noth'ing** (nuth'-) *n.* not anything. *a.* for earlier none; *adv.* [OE. *na*]

no'ble *a.* distinguished by deeds, character, rank or birth; of lofty characters impressive; excellent. *-n.* member of the nobility. **-nobil'ity** *n.* class holding special rank, usually hereditary, in a state; a noble being. **-no'bly** *adv.* **no'bleman** *n.* [L. *nobilis*]

nocturnal *a.* of, in, or by night; active by night. **-noc'tule** *n.* night-flying list. **-noc'turne** *n.* dreamy piece of music; night scene. [L. *nocturnus,* fr. *nox, noct-,* night]

nod *v.i.* bow the head slightly and quickly in assent, command, *etc.* , let the head droop with sleep, err through carelessness or inattention. *-v.t.* incline (the head) thus. *-n.* an act of nodding. [orig. uncertain]

Noël *n.* Christmas; Christmas carol. [F.]

no-fault *a.* pertaining to automobile insurance which guarantees that an accident victim is compensated for damages by their insurance company without determination of blame.

no-frills *a.* (*sl.*) basic; plain; reduced to the essentials; without extras or special features.

noise *n.* clamor, din; any sound. *-v.t.* rumor. **-noise'less** *a.* **-nois'y** *a.* **-nois'ily** *adv.* (F.]

nom'ad *a.* roaming from pasture to pasture; not having a fixed place of dwelling. *-n.* member of a nomad tribe; wanderer. **-nomad'ic** *a.* [G. *nomas, nomad-*]

nomenclature *n.* system of names or naming. [L. *nomen,* name]

nom'inal *a.* of a name or names; existing only in name. **-nom'inally** *adv.* **nom'inate** *v.t.* propose as a candidate appoint to an office. **-nom'inator** *n.* **nomina'tion** *n.* **-nominee'** *n.* [L. *nominalis,* fr. *nomen,* name]

non- *prefix* makes compounds that negative the idea of the simple word, *e.g.,* **-noncom'batant** *n.* one who does not fight. The meaning and derivation of those not given should be sought by reference to the simple word. [L. = note]

nonagenarian (-ār-) *a.* between ninety and a hundred years old. *-n.* person of such age. [L. *nonagenarius,* fr. *nonageni,* ninety each]

nonchalant (-sh-) *a.* unconcerned. **non'chalantly** *adv.* **-non'chalance** *n.* [F.]

noncommittal *a.* not committing or pledging oneself to opinion, *etc.* [*non-,* and L. *committere*]

nonconformist *n.* one who does not conform to the established church. **nonconform'ity** *n.* [*conform*]

non'descript *a.* not easily described. indeterminate. [*describe*]

none (nun) *pron.* no one. *-a.* no. *-adv.* in no way.[OE. *nan* for *ne an,* not one]

nonentity *n.* non-existence; nonexistent thing; person of no importance [*entity*]

noninvasive *a.* not entering the body by penetration, *esp.* surgery and diagnostic procedures.

nonplus' *n.* state of perplexity, deadlock. *-v.t.* bring to a nonplus. [L. *non plus,* not more]

non'sense *n.* words or actions that are foolish or meaningless; **-nonsen'sical** *a.* [*non-* and *sense*]

non'violence *n.* the belief or practice of peaceful methods in pursuit of any goal; lack or absence of violence.

nood'le *n.* (*cookery*) hardened paste of flour and eggs, used in soup. [Ger. *nudel*]

nook *n.* sheltered corner. [cp. Gael. *niue*]

noon *n.* midday. [L. *nona (hora),* ninth (hour)]

noose *n.* running loop; snare. *-v.t.* to catch in a noose. [L. *nodus,* knot]

nor *conj.* and not. [ME. *nother*]

norm *n.* rule; pattern; type. **-nor'mal** *a.* perpendicular; conforming to type, ordinary. **-normal'ity** *n.* **-nor'mally** *adv.* **normal'ize** *v.t.* to render normal; bring into conformity with standard; heat (steel) above critical temperature and allow it to cool in air to relieve internal stresses. **normal'ization** *n.* [L. *norma,* carpenter's square]

Norse *a.* of Norway. *-n.* Norwegian people or language.

north (-th) *n.* region or cardinal point opposite to the midday sun; part of the world, of a country, *etc.* , towards this point. *-adv.* towards or in the north. *-a.* to, from, or inthe north. -nor'therly (-TH-) *a.* -nor'-thern *a.* -nor'therner *n.* -northwards *adv.* [OE.]

Norwe'gian *a.* of, *pert.* to Norway. -*n.* [OE. *Northweg*]

nose *n.* organ of smell, used also in breathing. -*v.t.* detect by smell. -*v.i.* smell. [OE. *nosu*]

nostal'gia *n.* home-sickness. [G. *nostos*, return home, *algos*, pain]

nos'tril *n.* one of the openings of the nose. [OE. nosthvri, nose-hole]

not *adv.* expressing negation. [*nought*]

no'table *a.* worthy of note, remarkable. -no'tably *adv.* -notabil'ity *n.* eminent person. [*note*]

nota'tion *n.* representing of numbers, quantities, *etc.* , by symbols; set of such symbols. [L. *notare, notat-*, note]

notch *n.* small V-shaped cut or indention. - *v.t.* make a notch in; score. [F. *oche*]

note *n.* symbol standing for a musical sound; single tone; mark, sign; brief written message, memorandum, letter; fame, regard. -*v.t.* observe; set down. -no'ted *a.* well known. [L. *nota*, mark; *notare*, note]

nothing (nuth'-) *n.* no thing; not anything. *adv.* not at all. [*no thing*]

no'tice (-tis) *n.* warning, intimation, announcement; bill, *etc.* , with an announcement. -*v.t.* mention; observe; give attention to. -no'ticeable *a.* [L. *notus*, known]

no'tify (-i) *v.t.* report, give notice of or to. -notifica'tion *n.* [L. *notilicare*]

no'tion *n.* idea, opinion, belief-, fancy. (*colloq.*) desire, whim. [F. fr. L. *notio*]

notorious *a.* known for something bad; well known. -notori'ety *n.* [Low L. *notorius*]

nought (nawt) *n.* nothing; cipher (0) [OE. *nowiht*]

noun (nown) *n.* word used as a name of person, or thing. [L. *nomen*, name]

nourish (nur'-) *v.t.* supply with food; keep up. -nour'ishment *n.* [F. *nourrir*, fr. L. *nutrire*, feed]

no'va *n.* (novae *pl.*) new star. [L.]

nov'el *a.* new, strange. -*n.* fictitious tale published as a book. -nov'elist *n.* writer of novels. [L. *novus*, new]

November *n.* eleventh month of the year. [L. *novem*, nine]

nov'ice *n.* candidate for admission to a religious order; one new to anything. -novi'tiate, novi'ciate (-vish-) [L. *novitius*, fr. *novus*, new]

now *adv.* at the present time. now'adays *adv.* in these times. [OE. *nu*]

no'where *adv.* not anywhere; (*sl.*) far behind; defeated. [*no* and *where*]

nox'ious (-ksh) *a.* hurtful, harmful, dangerous. [L. *noxa*, harm]

noz'zle *n.* pointed spout, *esp.* at the end of a hose. [dim. of *nose*]

nu'ance (-ong-s) shade of difference. [F.]

nu'bile *a.* marriageable. [L. *nubere*, marry]

nu'cleus *n.* center, kernel; beginning meant to receive additions; head of a comet; central part of an atom. -nu'clear *a.* of, pert. to atomic nucleus. -nu'clear bomb *n.* bomb whose force is due to uncontrolled nuclear fusion or nuclear fission. -nu'clear disarmament *n.* elimination of nuclear weapons from country's armament. -nu'clear en'ergy *n.* energy released by nuclear fission. -nu'clear fam'ily *n.* primary social unit consisting of parents and their offspring. -nu'clear fis'sion *n.* disintegration of the atom. -nu'clear fu'sion *n.* reaction in which two nuclei combine to form nucleus with release of energy (also fu'sion). -nu'clear phy'sics *n.* branch of physics concerned with structure of nucleus and particles of which it consists. -nu'clear reac'tion *n.* change in structure and energy content of atomic nucleus by interaction with another nucleus, particle. [L. = *kernel*]

nude *a.* naked. -nu'dity *n.* [L. *nudus*]

nudge *v.t.* touch with the elbow. -*n.* such touch. [orig. uncertain]

nugg'et *n.* rough lump of native gold. [orig. uncertain]

nuisance *n.* something offensive or annoying. [F. *noire, nuis-*, harm]

null *a.* of no effect, void. [L. *nullus*, none]

numb (num) *a.* deprived of feeling, *esp.* by cold. -*v.t.* [OE. *numen*]

num'ber *n.* sum or aggregate; word or symbol saying how many; single issue of a paper, *etc.* , issued in regular series; classification as to singular or plural; rhythm; metrical feet or verses; company or collection. -*v.t.* count; class, reckon; give a number to; amount to. -nu'meral *a.* of or expressing number. -*n.* sign or word denoting a number. -nu'merate *v.t.* count. -*a.* able to count. -numera'tion *n.* -nu'merator *n.* top part of a fraction, figure showing how many of the fractional units are taken. -numer'ical *a.* of, or in respect of, number, or numbers. -nu'merous *a.* many. [L. *numerus*]

numismat'ic *a.* of coins. -*n.* in *pl.* study of coins. -numis'matist *n.* [L. *numisma*, current coin]

nun *n.* woman living in a convent under religious vows. **-nunn'ery** *n.* convent of nuns. [Church L. *nonna, fem.* of *nonnus,* monk]

nup'tial *a.* of or relating to marriage or a marriage. *-n.* in *pl.* marriage. [L. *nupti—,* wedding]

nurse n. person trained for the care of the sick or injured; woman tending another's child. *-v.t.* act as a nurse to. **-nurs'ery** *n.* room for children; rearing place for plants. **-nurs'ing-home** *n.* private hospital. [L. nutrix, foster-mother]

nur'ture *n.* bringing-up. *-v.t.* bring up. [F. *nourriture,* nourishment]

nut *n.* fruit consisting of a hard shell and kernel: small block with a hole to be screwed on a bolt. *-v.i.* gather nuts. [OE. *hnutu*]

nutriment *n.* food. **-nutri'tion** (-trish'n) *n.* the receiving or supply of food; food. **-nutri'tious** *a.* good in effects as food. **-nu'tritive** *a.* [L. *nutrire,* nourish]

ny'lon *n.* synthetic filament of great strength and fineness, made into fabrics, *etc. -pl.* nylon stockings. (*New York, London*)

nymph *n.* legendary semi-divine maiden living in the sea, woods, mountains, *etc.* [G. *nymphe,* bride]

O

oaf *n.* changeling; dolt. [ON. *alfr,* elf]

oak *n.* familiar forest tree. **-oak'en** *a.* **-oak-apple** *n.* insect-gall on the oak. [OE. *ac*]

oar *n.* wooden lever with a broad blade worked by the hands to propel a boat. [OE. *ar*]

oa'sis *n.* fertile spot in the desert. [G. of Egypt, orig.]

oat *n.* grain of a common cereal plant (*usu. pl.*); the plant. [OE. *ate*]

oath *n.* confirmation of the truth of a statement by the naming of something sacred; act of swearing. [OE. *ath*]

ob'durate *a.* stubborn. **-ob'duracy** *n.* [L. *obduratus-durare, durat-,* harden]

obedient. *See* **obey.**

obeis'ance *n.* bow, curtsy. [F. *obéissance,* obedience]

obese' *a.* very fat. **-obe'sity** *n.* corpulence. [L. *obesus*]

obey *v.t.* do the bidding of-, be moved by. [L. *oboedire*]

ob'fuscate *v.t.* confuse; make dark or obscure. [L. *obfuscare,* darken]

obit'uary *n.* notice or record of a death or deaths. [Med. L. *obituarius,* fr. *obitus,* departure]

ob'ject *n.* material thing; that to which feeling or action is directed; end or aim; word dependent on a verb or preposition. **-object'** *v.t.* state in opposition. *-v.i.* feel dislike or reluctance to something. **-objective** *a.* external to the mind. *-n.* thing or place aimed at. [Med, L. *objectum,* thrown in the way]

oblige' *v.t.* bind morally or legally to do a service to; compel. **-obliga'tion** *n.* binding promise; debt of gratitude; indebtedness for a favor; duty. [L. *obligare,* fr. *ligare,* bind]

oblique' *a.* slanting; indirect. **-obliq'uity** *n.* **-oblique'ly** a*dv.* [F., fr. L *obliquus-liquis,* slanting]

oblit'erate *v.t.* blot out. **-oblitera'tion** *n.* [L. *obliterare,* fr. *literà,* letter]

obliv'ion *n.* forgetting or being forgotten. **-obliv'ious** *a.* [L. *oblivio]*

ob'long *a.* rectangular with adjacent sides unequal. *-n.* oblong figure. [L. *oblongus*]

obnox'ious (-okshus) *a.* offensive, disliked. [L. *obnoxius,* exposed to harm]

o'boe *n.* wood wind instrument. **o'boist** *n.* [F. *hautbois,* hautboy]

obscene' *a.* indecent; offensive. **obscen'ity** *n.* [L. *obscænus*]

obscure' *a.* dark, dim; indistinct; unexplained; humble. *-v.t.* dim; conceal; make unintelligible. [L. *obscurus*]

obse'quious *a.* servile, fawning. [L. *obsequiosus,* compliant]

observe' (-z-) *v.t.* keep, follow; watch; note systematically; notice; remark. *v.i.* make a remark. **-observ'able** *a.* **-observ'ance** *n.* paying attention; keeping. **-observa'tion** *n.* action or habit of observing; noticing; remark. **-observ'atory** *n.* a building scientifically equipped for the observation of stars, *etc.* [L. *observare,* fr. *servare,* guard]

obsess' *v.t.* haunt, fill the mind. **-obses'sion** *n.* **-obsess'ional** *a.* [L. *obsidere, obsess,* besiege]

ob'solete *a.* no longer in use, out of date. **-obsoles'cent** *a.* going out of use. [L. *obsolescere,* grow out of use]

ob'stacle *n.* thing in the way; hindrance to progress. [L. *obstaculum*]

obstet'ric *a.* of midwifery. *-n.* in *pl.* midwifery. [L. *obstetrix,* midwife]

ob'stinate *a.* stubborn. [L. *obstinatus]*

obstruct' *v.t.* hinder; block up. **obstruc'tion** *n.* [L. *obstruere, obstruct-,* build up against]

obtain *v.t.* get. *-v.i.* be customary. **obtain'able** *a.* [L. *obtinere*]

obtuse' *a.* not sharp or pointed; greater

than a right angle; stupid. -**obtuse'ly** adv. [L. obtusus, blunt]

ob'verse n. side of a coin or medal with the chief design. -a. turned towards one. [L. obversus, turned towards]

ob'vious a. clear, evident. [L. obvius, what meets one in the way]

occa'sion n. opportunity; reason, need; immediate but subsidiary cause; time when a thing happens. -v.t. cause. - **occa'sional** a. happening or found now and then. -**occa'sionally** adv. sometimes, now and then. [L. occasio]

occult' a. secret, mysterious. -v.t. hide from view. [L. occultus, fr. occulere, hide]

occ'upy v.t. take possession of; inhabit; fill; employ. -**occ'upancy** n. fact of occupying; residing. -**occ'upant** n. - **occupa'tion** n. seizure; possession; employment. -**occ'upier** n. [L. occupare, take possession of]

occur' v.i. happen; come to mind. - **occurr'ence** n. [L. occurrere, run against]

o'cean n. great body of water surrounding the land of the globe; large division of this; sea. -**ocean'ic** a. [G. okeanos, stream encircling the world]

OCR n. (compute.) ability of certain light sensitive machines to recognize printed letters, numbers, and special characters, and translate them into computer terms. [optical character recognition]

oct-', oc'ta-, oc'to- prefix eight. - **oc'tagon** n. figure with eight angles. - **octag'onal** a. -**octang'ular** a. having eight angles. -**oc'tave** n. group of eight days; eight lines of verse; note eight degrees above or below a given note; this space. -**Octo'ber** n. tenth month of the year. (Roman eighth.) -**octogena'rian** a. of an age between eighty and ninety. -n. a person of such age. -**oc'topus** n. a mollusk with eight arms covered with suckers. -**octet** n. group of eight. [G. and L. okto, eight]

oc'ular a. of the eye or sight. -**oc'ularly** adv. -**oc'ulate** a. -**oc'ulist** n. eye surgeon. [L. oculus, eye]

odd a. that is one in addition when the rest have been divided into two equal groups; not even; not part of a set; strange, queer. -**odd'ity** n. quality of being odd; odd person or thing. -**odd'ments** n. pl. odd things. -**odds** n. pl. difference, balance; advantage to one of two competitors; advantage conceded in betting; likelihood. [ON. odda(tala), odd (number)]

ode n. lyric poem of lofty style. [G.]

o'dor n. smell. -**o'dorize** v.t. fill with scent. [L. odor]

oen'ophile n. lover or connoisseur of wines. [G. oinos, wine, philos, loving]

of prep. denotes removal, separation, ownership, attribute, material, quality, etc. [OE.]

off adv. away. -prep. away from. -a. distant; of horses, vehicles, etc. , right. **off'chance** n. remote possibility. **off'col'or**, indisposed, not at one's best. -**off'shoot** n. branch from main stem. **off'spring** n. children, issue. -**off'ing** n. more distant part of the sea visible to an observer. [var. of of]

off'al n. parts cut out in preparing a carcase for food; refuse. [= off-fall]

offend' v.t. displease. -v.i. do wrong. - **offense'** n. -**offend'er** n. -**offen'sive** a. causing displeasure. -n. position or movement of attack. [L. offendere, strike against]

off'er v.t. present for acceptance or refusal; propose; attempt. -v.i. present itself-n. offering, bid. [L. offerre]

off'ice n. service; duty; official position; form of worship; place for doing business; corporation carrying on business. -**off'icer** n. one in command in an army, navy, air force, etc. -v.t. supply with officers. - **offi'cial** (fish'-) a. having or by authority. -n. one holding an office, esp. in a public body. -**offi'cialism** n. undue official authority or routine. -**offi'cialdom** n. officials collectively; their work, usually in a contemptuous sense. -**offi'ciate** v.i. to perform the duties of an office; perform a service. -**offi'cious** (-ish'us) a. meddlesome, importunate in offering service. - **offi'ciousness** n. [L. officium, duty]

o'gle v.i. make eyes. -v.t. make eyes at. n. amorous glance. [Low Ger. oegeln, eye]

ohm n. unit of electrical resistance. [Ohm, Ger. physicist (d. 1854)]

oil n. light flammable viscous liquid, obtained from various plants, animal substances, and minerals. -v.t. apply oil to. -v.i. of a ship etc. , take in oil fuel. **oil'-cake** n. cattle food made from linseed etc. -**oil'-cloth** n. oil-coated canvas, linoleum. - **oil'skin** n. material made waterproof with oil. -**oil'y** a. [L. oleum]

oint'ment n. greasy preparation for healing the skin. [OF. oignement]

okay', OK adv. and a. all right. -v.t. pass as correct. [perh. abbrev. for orl korrect]

old a. advanced in age, having lived or existed long; belonging to an earlier period. -**old'en** a. old. -**old-fash'ioned** a. in the style of an earlier period, out of date; fond of old ways. [OE. eald]

olfac'tory *a.* of smell. **-olfac'tion** *n.* [L. *olfacere*, cause to smell]

ol'igarchy (-ki) *n.* government by a few. [G. *oligarchia*, fr. *oligos*, few]

ol'ive (-iv) *n.* evergreen tree; its oil-yielding fruit. *-a.* gray-green in color. [L. *oliva*]

Olym'pic *a.* of Olympus. **-Olym'pic Games'**, great athletic festival of ancient Greece; (*mod.*) international sports meeting held every four years. [G.]

o'mega *n.* last letter of Greek alphabet; end. [G.]

om'elet, om'elette *n.* dish of fried eggs with seasoning, *etc.* [F. *omelette*]

o'men *n.* prophetic object or happening. **-om'inous** *a.* portending evil. [L.]

omit' *v.t.* leave out, neglect. **-omis'sion** *n.* [L. *omittere*]

omni- all. [L. *omnis*, all] **-om'nibus** *n.* road vehicle travelling on a fixed route and taking passengers at any stage; several books bound in one volume. *-a.* serving or containing several objects. [L. = for all] **-omnip'otent** *a.* all powerful. **- omnip'otence** *n.* **-omnipres'ent** *a.* everywhere at the same time. **omnipres'cence** *n.* **-omnis'cient** (shient) *a.* knowing everything. **-omnis'cience** *n.* **-omniv'orous** *a.* devouring all foods. [L. *ominis*, all]

on *prep,* above and touching, at, near, towards, *etc.* *-adv.* so as to be on, forwards, continuously, *etc.* **-on'ward** *a.* and *adv.* **-on'wards** *adv.* [OE.]

once (wuns) *adv.* one time; ever; formerly. [ME. *ones*, fr. *one*]

one (wun) *a.* lowest cardinal number; single; united; only, without others; identical. *-n.* number or figure 1; unity; single specimen. *-pron.* particular but not stated person; any person. **-oneself'** *pron.* **-one'-**sided *a.* lop-sided; biased. **-one-sidedness** *n.* **-one'ness** *n.* [OE. *an*]

on'erous *a.* burdensome. [L. *onerosus*]

on'ion (un'yun) *n.* plant with a bulb of pungent flavor. [L. *unio*]

on'ly *a.* that is the one specimen. *adv.* solely, merely, exclusively. *conj.* but, excepting that. [OE. *anlic*, one like]

onomatopoe'ia *n.* formation of a word by using sounds that resemble or suggest the object or action to be named. [G. *onomatopoiia*]

on'set *n.* assault, attack; start. [*on. set*]

ontol'ogy *n.* science of being, of the real nature of things. [G. *on*, being]

o'nus *n.* responsibility. [L. = *burden*]

ooze *n.* wet mud, slime; sluggish flow. *v.i.* pass slowly through, exude. [OE. *was*, juice; *wase*, mud]

o'pal *n.* white or bluish stone with iridescent reflections. **-opales'cent** *a.* showing changing colors. [G. *oppallios*]

opaque' *a.* not transparent. **-opa'city** *n.* [L. *opacus*]

o'pen *a.* not shut or blocked up; without lid or door; bare; not enclosed or covered or limited or exclusive; frank; free. *-v.t.* set open, uncover, give access to; disclose, lay bare; begin; make a hole in. *-v.i.* become open. *-n.* clear space, unenclosed country. [OE.]

op'era *n.* musical drama. **-operat'ic** *a.* **-op'era-glass** *n.* binoculars for viewing stage performance. [It. L. = work]

opera'ting system *n.* (*compute.*) software that controls the execution of computer programs.

opera'tion *n.* working, way a thing works; scope; act of surgery. **-op'erate** *v.i.* **-op'erative** *a.* workingman. *n.* mechanic. **-op'erator** *n.* [L. *operation* fr. *opus*, work]

ophthal'mia *n.* inflammation of the eye. **-ophthal'mic** *n.* **-ophthalmol'ogist** *n.* specialist in eye infections. [G.]

opin'ion *n.* what one thinks about some thing; belief, judgment. **-opine'** *v.t.* think; utter an opinion. **-opin'ionated, opiniona-**tive *a.* stubborn in holding an opinion. [L. *opinio*]

o'pium *n.* sedative and narcotic drug made from the poppy. **-o'piate** *v.t.* mix with opium. *-n.* opiated drug. [L.]

oppo'nent *n.* adversary. *a.* opposed, adverse. [L. *opponere*, place against]

opportune *a.* seasonable, well timed. **-opportu'nity** *n.* favorable time or condition. [L. *opportunus*]

oppose' (-z) *v.t.* set against; contrast; resist, withstand. *-past p.* adverse. **-oppo'ser** *n.* **-opp'osite** (-zit) *a.* contrary facing, diametrically different. **-opposi'tion** (-ish) *n.* a being opposite; resistance; party opposed to that in power. [F. *opposer*]

oppress' *v.t.* govern with tyranny; weigh down. [L. *opprimere, oppress-*, press down]

op'tic *a.* of the eye or sight. *-n.* eye; in *pl.* science of sight or light. **-op'tical** *a.* **opti'cian** (-ish-) *n.* maker of, dealer in, optical instruments. [G. *optikos*]

op'timism *n.* belief that the world is the best possible world; doctrine that good must prevail in the end; disposition to look on the bright side. [L. *optimus*, best]

op'tion *n.* choice. **-op'tional** *a.* [L. *optio*, fr. *optare*, choose]

op'ulent *a.* rich; profuse. **-op'ulence** *n.* [L. *opulentus*, wealthy]

o'pus *n.* (**op'era** *pl.*) musical composition of a particular composer, usually numbered in sequence. [L.]

or *conj.* introduces alternatives; if not. [ME. *other*, (mod. *either*)]

or'acle *n.* place where divine utterances were supposed to be given; answer there given, often ambiguous; wise or mysterious adviser. [L. *oraculum*, orate, speak]

or'al *a.* by mouth; spoken. **-or'ally** *adv.* [L. *os*, *or-*, mouth]

or'ange (-inj) *n.* familiar bright reddish-yellow round fruit; tree bearing it; color of the fruit. *-a.* of the color of an orange. [Pers. *narang*]

or'ator *n.* maker of a speech, skillful speaker. **-ora'tion** *n.* formal speech. - **orator'ical** *a.* of an orator or oration. - **or'atory** *n.* speeches; eloquent language; small chapel. **-orator'io** *n.* semi-dramatic composition of sacred music. [L. *orare*, speak]

orb *n.* globe, sphere. **orbed'**, **orbic'ular**, **orbic'ulate(d)** *a.* spherical. **-orb'it** *n.* cavity holding the eye; track of a heavenly body. **-or'bital** *a.* pert. to orbit. [L. *orbis*, circle]

orch'ard *n.* enclosure containing fruit trees. [OE. *ortgeard*]

or'chestra *n.* band of musicians; place occupied by such band in a theater, *etc.*; the forward section of seats on the main floor of a theater. **-or'chestrate**, *v.t.* compose or arrange music for an orchestra. - **orchestra'tion** *n.* [G. = dancing space for chorus]

or'chid, (-k-) *n.* various flowering plants. [Med. L. *orchideæ*]

ordain' *v.t.* admit to Christian ministry; confer holy orders upon; decree, destine. [OF. *ordener*, fr. L. *ordo*, order]

ord'inance *n.* decree, rule, municipal regulation; ceremony. [L. *ordinare*]

or'deal *n.* method of trial by requiring the accused to undergo a dangerous physical test; trying experience. [OE. *ordal*, judicial test]

or'der *n.* rank, class, group; monastic society; sequence, succession, arrangement; command, pass, instruction. *-v.t.* arrange; command; require. **-or'derly** *a.* methodical. *-n.* soldier following an officer to carry orders; soldier in a military hospital acting as attendant. **-or'derliness** *n.* [F. *ordre*-L. *ordo*, *ordin-*]

or'dinal a. showing number or position in a series, as first, second etc. [*order*]

or'dinary *a.* usually commonplace. *-n.* bishop in his province; public meal supplied at a fixed time and price. [L. *ordo*, *ordin-*, order]

ore *n.* native mineral from which metal is extracted. [OE. *ora*]

oreg'ano *n.* herb, variety of marjoram. [G. *origanon*, wild marjoram]

or'gan *n.* musical instrument of pipes worked by bellows and played by keys; member of an animal or plant carrying out a particular function; means of action; newspaper. **-organ'ic** *a.* of the bodily organs; affecting bodily organs; having vital organs; organized, systematic. - **organ'ically** *adv.* **-or'ganism** *n.* organized body or system. **-or'ganist** *n.* one who plays an organ. **-or'ganize** *v.t.* furnish with news; give a definite structure; get up, arrange, put into working order. [G. *organon*, instrument]

or'gasm *n.* paroxysm of emotion, *esp.* sexual; climax of sexual arousal. [G. *orgasmos*, swelling]

or'gy (-ji) *n.* drunken or licentious revel. **-orgias'tic** *a.* [G. *orgia*, *pl.* , secret rites]

or'ient *n.* the East; luster of the best pearls. *-a.* rising; Eastern; of pearls, from the Indian seas. *-v.t.* place so as to face the east; find one's bearings. **-orien'tal** *a.* and *n.* **-orienta'tion** *n.* **-orien'talist** *n.* expert in Eastern languages and history. **-or'ientate** *v.t.* relate to the points of the compass; take bearings of. [L. *oriens*, *orient-*, rising]

or'ifice *n.* opening, mouth of a cavity. [Late L. *orifium*]

or'igin *n.* beginning, source, parentage. - **original** (-ij-) *a.* primitive, earliest; new, not copied or derived; thinking or acting for oneself, eccentric. *-n.* pattern, thing from which another is copied; eccentric person. **-ori'ginally** *adv.* **-original'ity** *n.* **-ori'ginate** *v.t.* bring into existence. [L. *origo*, *origin-*, fr. *oriri*, rise]

Ori'on *n.* constellation containing seven very bright stars, three of which form Orion's belt. [Orion, a hunter placed among the stars at his death]

or'nament *n.* decoration. *-v.t.* adorn. - **ornate'** *a.* highly decorated, elaborate. [L. *orna mentum*]

ornithol'ogy *n.* science of birds. - **ornitholo'gical** *a.* **-ornithol'ogist** *n.* [G *ornis*, *ornith-*, bird]

or'phan *n.* child bereaved of one or both of its parents. **-or'phanage** *n.* institution for the care of orphans. **-or'phanhood** *n.* [G. *orphanos*, bereaved]

ortho- *prefix* right. [G. *orthos*, right] -
or´thodox *a.* holding accepted views or
doctrine; conventional. **-or´thodoxy** *n.* -
orthog´raphy *n.* correct spelling. **-or-**
thopedic, -orthopaed´ic *a.* for curing de-
formity.

or´yx *n.* kind of straight-horned antelope.
[G. = *pickax*]

os´cillate *v.i.* swing to and fro; vary between extremes; set up wave motion in
wireless apparatus. **-oscilla´tion** *n.* -
os´cillator *n.* one that oscillates, *esp.* a person setting up unauthorized wireless
waves from a radio receiving set. [L. *os-*
cillare, swing]

os´culate *v.t.* and *i.* kiss. **-oscula´tion** *n.*
-oscula´tory *a.* [L. *osculari*, fr. *as*, mouth]

osmo´sis *n.* intermixing of fluids by percolation through a dividing membrane. [G.
osmos, impulse]

os´prey *n.* fishing eagle; egret plume. [L.
ossifraga, 'bone-breaker']

osten´sible *n.* professed, used as a blind.
-osten´sibly *adv.* **-ostenta´tion** *n.* show,
display. [L. *ostendere*, show]

osteop´athy *n.* art of treating diseases by
removing structural derangement by
manipulation, *esp.* of spine. **-os´teopath** *n.*
one skilled in this art. [G. *osteon*, bone, and
patheia, suffering]

os´tracize *v.t.* exclude from society, exile.
-os´tracism *n.* [G. *ostrakizein*]

os´trich *n.* large swift-running flightless
African bird. [OF. *austruche*]

oth´er (uTH´-) *a.* not this, not the same;
alternative, different. *-pron.* other person
or thing. **-oth´erwise** (-iz) *adv.* differently,
[OE.]

ott´er *n.* furry aquatic fish-eating animal.
[OE. *otor*]

ott´oman *n.* cushioned seat without back
or arms. [*Othman*, founder of a Turk.
dynasty]

ought (awt) *v. aux.* expressing duty or
obligation or advisability. [*owe*]

ounce *n.* weight, twelfth of the Troy
pound, sixteenth of the avoirdupois pound.
[L. *uncia*]

ounce *n.* snow-leopard. [F. *once*]

our *pron.* belonging to us. [OE. *ure*]

out *adv.* from within, from among, away,
not in the usual or right state. **-out´ing** *n.*
pleasure excursion. **-out´side** *n.* outer side,
exterior. *n*, exterior; external. *adv.* on the
outer side. *-prep.* beyond. **-out´ward** *a.*
and *adv.* **-out´wards** *adv.* **-out´wardly** *adv.*
[OE. *ut*]

out- as *prefix* makes many compounds
with the sense of beyond, in excess, *etc.*,
e.g. **outflank´** *v.t.* get beyond the flank.
-out´put *n.* quantity put out, *etc.* These are
not given where the meaning and derivation may easily be found from the simple
word.

out´age *n.* quantity of something lost
during storage or transportation; failure,
interruption, *esp.* in the supply of electric
current; period or time during such a
failure. [*out*]

out´back *n.* (Australia) remote open
country. [*out* and *back*]

out´cast *n.* homeless person; vagabond,
pariah. [ME.]

outclass´ *v.t.* excel, surpass. [*out* and
class]

out´come *n.* result, consequence. [ME.]

out´law *n.* one placed beyond the protection of the law, an exile. **-out´lawry** *n.* [ON.
utlagi]

out´post *n.* post, station beyond main company. [*out* and *post*]

out´rage *n.* violation of others' rights;
gross or violent offense or indignity. *-v.t.*
injure, violate, ravish, insult. [F.]

out´rigger *n.* frame outside a ship's gun-
wale; frame on the side of a rowing boat
with a rowlock at the outer edge. [earlier
outlegger, Du. *uitlegger*, 'outlyer']

outskirts *n. pl.* environs; parts farthest
from the center. [*out* and *skirts*]

out´set *n.* beginning, start. [*out* and *set*]

out´take *n.* unreleased take from a recording session, film, or television program.
[*out* and *take*]

o´val *a.* egg-shaped, elliptical. *-n.* oval figure or thing. **-o´vary** *n.* egg-producing
organ. [L. *ovum*, egg]

ova´tion *n.* enthusiastic burst of applause.
[L. *ovatio*]

ov´en (uv-) *n.* heated iron box or other
receptacle for baking in. [OE. *ofn*]

o´ver *adv.* above, above and beyond, going
beyond in excess, too much, past, finished,
in repetition, across, *etc. -prep.* above, on,
upon, more than, in excess of, along,
across, *etc. a.* upper, outer. [OE. *ofer*]

o´ver- as *prefix* makes compounds with
meaning of too, too much, in excess,
above, *e.g.* **o´verdo** *v.t.* do too much. These
words are not given where the meaning and
derivation may be found from the simple
word.

overbear´ *v.t.* bear down, dominate, overwhelm. **-overbear´ing** *a.* domineering,
haughty. [*over* and *bear*]

overboard´ *adv.* over ship's side into
water. [*over* and *board*]

overcast´ *a.* dull and heavy, (of sky)

clouded. [*over* and *cast*]

overhaul' *v.t.* come up with in pursuit; examine and set in order. -*n.* thorough examination, *esp.* for repairs. [*haul*]

o'verhead *a.* over one's head, above. *adv.* above. -**o'verhead charg'es**, costs, business expenses apart from cost of production. [*over* and *head*]

o'verpass *n.* elevated level to allow free flow of traffic over traffic moving in another direction.

oversee' *v.t.* look, see over. -**over-seer'** *n.* supervisor of work. [OE. *oferseon*]

o'versight *n.* error, *esp.* of omission. [ME.]

o'vert *a.* open, unconcealed. -**o'vertly** *adv.* [OF. = opened]

overthrow' *v.t.* vanquish; overturn; remove from office; throw too far. -*n.* ruin, disaster; defeat.

overtime *adv./n.* (work) done after regular hours. [*over* and *time*]

o'verture *n.* opening of negotiations; proposal; introduction of an opera, *etc.* [OF. = opening]

overwhelm' *v.t.* flow over, submerge, overbear. -**overwhelm'ing** *a.* resistless. [*over* and *whelm*]

oviparous *a.* egg-laying. [L. *ovum, parere*, bring forth]

o'void *a.* egg-shaped. [L. *ovum*, egg, G. *cidos*, form]

owe *v.t.* be bound to repay, be indebted for. -**ow'ing** *a.* owed, due. -**owing to**, caused by. [OE. *agan*, own]

owl *n.* night bird of prey. -**owl'et** *n.* young owl. -**owl'ish** *a.* solemn and dull. [OE. *ule*]

own *a.* emphasizes possession. -*v.t.* possess; acknowledge. -*v.i.* confess. [OE. *agen, a.* , one's own, *agnian, v.*]

ox *n.* **ox'en** *pl.* large cloven-footed and usually horned animal used for draft, milk, and meat, a bull or cow. [OE. *oxa*]

ox'ygen *n.* gas in the atmosphere which is essential to life, burning; *etc.* -**ox'ide** *n.* compound of oxygen. -**ox'idize** *v.t.* cause to combine with oxygen; cover with oxide, make rusty. -*v.i.* combine with oxygen, rust. -**ox'yacet'ylene** *a.* involving, using mixture of oxygen and acetylene. [G. *oxys,* sour]

oxymoron *n.* (*rhet.*) figure of speech combining incongruous terms. [G. *oxys*, sharp, *moros*, foolish]

oy'ster *n.* bivalve mollusk or shellfish, usually eaten alive. [G. *ostreon*]

o'zone *n.* condensed form of oxygen with a pungent odor; refreshing influence. [G. *ozein*, smell]

P

pab'ulum *n.* food, nourishment. [L.]

pace *n.* step; length of a step; walk or speed of stepping; speed. -*v.i.* step. -*v.t.* cross or measure with steps; set the speed for. -**pa'cer** *n.* -**pace'maker** *n.* one that sets the pace at which something happens or should happen; electronic device surgically implanted in those with heart disease. [L. *passus*]

pach'yderm (-k-) *n.* thick-skinned animal, *e.g.* an elephant. [G. *pachydermos*]

pacif'ic *a.* quiet; tending to peace. -**pac'ify** (-s-) *v.t.* calm; establish peace. -**pacif'icist, pa'cifist** *n.* advocate of the abolition of war; one who refuses to help in war. -**pac'ificism** *n.* (L. *pacifus,* peacemaking, fr. *pax, pac-*, peace]

pack *n.* bundle; company of animals, large set of people or things; set of playing cards; packet; mass of floating ice. -*v.t.* make into a bundle; put together in a box, *etc.*; arrange one's luggage for traveling; fill with things; order off. -**pack'age** *n.* parcel. -**pack'et** *n.* small parcel. -**pack'-horse** *n.* horse for carrying bundles of goods. [Du. *pak*]

pact *n.* covenant of agreement. -also **pac'tion**. [L. *pactus*, contract]

pad *n.* piece of soft stuff used as a cushion; shin-guard; sheets of paper fastened together in a block; foot or sole of various animals. -*v.t.* make soft, fill in, protect, *etc.*, with a pad or padding. -**padd'ing** *n.* stuffing; literary matter put in simply to increase quantity. [orig. uncertain]

pad'dle *n.* short oar with a broad blade at one or each end; blade of a paddle wheel. -*v.i.* move by paddles; roll gently. -*v.t.* propel by paddles. -**pad'dle-wheel** *n.* wheel with crosswise blades which strike the water successively to propel a ship. [orig. unknown]

pad'dle *v.i.* walk with bare feet in shallow water. [orig. uncertain]

pad'lock *n.* detachable lock with a hinged hoop to go through a staple or ring. -*v.t.* fasten with padlock. [orig. uncertain]

pa'gan *a.* heathen. -*n.* heathen. -**pa'ganism** *n.* [L. *paganus*, rustic]

page *n.* boy servant, attendant. [F.]

page *n.* one side of a leaf of a book. -*v.t.* number the pages of -**pa'ginate** *v.t.* number the pages of. -**pagina'tion** *n.* [L. *pagina-pangere*, fasten]

pa'geant (paj'-ent) *n.* procession, dramatic show, of persons in costume, usually illustrating history, brilliant show.

-pa'geantry n. [orig. uncertain]

pail n. large round open vessel for carrying liquids etc.; bucket. -pail'ful n. [orig. uncertain]

pain n. bodily or mental suffering; penalty. -v.t. inflict pain upon. [L. poena, penalty]

paint n. coloring matter prepared for putting on a surface with brushes. -v.t. portray, color, coat, or make a picture of, with paint; describe. [F. peint, p.p- of peindre]

paint'er n. rope for fastening bow of a boat to a ship, etc. [L. pendere, hang]

pair (pŏr) n. set of two, esp. existing or generally used together. -v.t. arrange in a pair or pairs. -v.i. come together in pair or pairs. [L. par, equal]

paja'mas n. pl. sleeping suit of loose trousers and jacket. [Pers. pae, jamah, leg garment]

pal'ace n. official residence of a king, bishop, etc.; stately mansion. [L. palatium]

pal'ate n. roof of the mouth; sense of taste. -pal'atable a. agreeable to eat. [L. palatum]

pale a. faint in color, dim, whitish. -v.i. grow white. [L. pallidus]

paleo- prefix ancient. [G. palaios).- paleolith'ic a. of the early part of the Stone Age. -paleontol'ogy n. study of ancient life (through fossils, etc.). paleozool'ogy n. study of fossil animals.

pal'ette n. artist's flat board for mixing colors on. -palette-knife n. [F.]

palisade' n. fence of pointed stakes. esp. for defense. -v.t. enclose with one. [F. palissade, fr. pal, stake]

pall (pawl) i. become tasteless or tiresome. -v.t. to cloy, dull. [for appal]

pall'et n. straw bed, small bed, portable platform for storing or moving goods. [A. F. paillette, fr. paille, straw]

pall'id a. pale. -pall'or n. paleness. [L. pallidus, pale]

palm (pim) n. flat of the hand: tropical tree; leaf of the tree as a symbol of victory. -v.t. conceal in the palm of the hand; pass off by trickery. -palm'istry n. fortune-telling from the lines on the palm of the hand. [L. palma]

pal'pitate v.t. throb. -palpita'tion n. [L. palpare, palpitarè, freq. of feel]

pam'pas n. pl. vast grassy plains of S. America. [Sp.]

pam'per v.t. over-indulge. [orig. uncertain]

pamph'Iet n. thin paper cover book, stitched but not bound. -pamphleteer' n. writer of pamphlets. [OF. Pamphilet, title of a medieval poem (taken as type of a small book)]

pan n. broad, shallow vessel. -pan'cake n. thin cake of fried batter. -pan'cake landing, awkward flat landing of aircraft. - pan'handle v.i. beg for food or money in the street. [OE. panne]

panace'a n. universal remedy. [G. panakeia, all-healing]

pan'creas n. large gland secreting a digestive fluid, sweetbread. -pancreat'ic a. - pan'creatin n. pancreatic secretion. [G. pan. all, kreas, flesh]

pandem'ic a. universal. -n. widespread epidemic disease. [G. pas, pan, all, demos, people]

pan'der n. go-between in illicit love affair; procurer. v.t. minister basely. [fr. Pandarus, prince who acted as agent between Troilus and Cressida]

pane n. piece of glass in a window. [F pan. flat section]

pan'el n. compartment of a surface, usually raised or sunk, e.g. in a door; strip of different material in a dress; thin board with a picture on it; list of jurors, doctors, etc. -v.t. decorate with panels. -pan'eling n. paneled work. [OF. = small pane]

pan'ic n. sudden and infectious fear. -a. of such fear; due to uncontrollable general impulse. [G. panikos, of Pan]

pan'oply n. full suit of armor; complete, magnificent array. [G. panoplia-pan-, all, hoplon, weapon]

panoram'a n. picture arranged round a spectator or unrolled before him; wide or complete view. -panoram'ic a. (G. pan-, all, horama, view]

pan'sy (-zi) n. flowering plant; a species of violet. [F. pensèe, thought]

pant v.i. gasp for breath. -n. gasp. - pant'ing adv. [orig. uncertain]

pan'theism n. identification of God with the universe. -pan'theist n. -pan'theon n. temple of all the gods; building for memorials of a nation's great dead. [G. pan-, all, theos, a god]

pan'tomime n. dramatic entertainment in dumb show; Christmas-time dramatic entertainment. -pantomim'ic a. [G. pantomimes, all mimic]

pan'try n. room for storing food or utensils. [F. paneterie- L. panis, bread]

pants n. pl. trousers. [pantaloons]

pa'pacy n. office of the Pope; papal system. -pa'pist a. of, or relating to, the Pope. -pa'pist n. -papist'ic a. [Med. L. papatia, see pope]

pa'per n. material made by pressing pulp

of rags, straw, wood, *etc.* , into thin flat sheets; sheet of paper written or printed on; newspaper; article or essay. -*pl.* documents, *etc*. -*v.t.* cover with paper. -**pap'ier mâ'ché** *n*. paper pulp shaped by molding and dried hard. [G. *papyros*, Nile rush from which paper was made]

papoose' *n*. N. Amer. Indian child. [native]

par *n*. equality of value or standing; equality between market and nominal value. -**par'ity** *n*. equality. [L. = equal]

par'able *n*. allegory, story pointing a moral. [G. *parabole*, comparison]

parab'ola *n*. curve formed by cutting cone with plane parallel to its slope. [G. *para*, beside, *ballein*, throw]

parab'ole *n*. parable, sustained simile. [*See* **parabola**]

parachute' (-sh-) *n*. apparatus extending like an umbrella to enable a person to come safely to earth from a great height. [L. *parare*, ward off, and chute]

parade' *n*. display; muster of troops; parade ground. -*v.t.* muster; display. -*v.i.* march with display. [F.]

par'adigm (-dim) *n*. model, example. [G. *paradeigma*]

par'adise *n*. garden of Eden; Heaven; state of bliss. [G. *paradeisos*, pleasureground]

par'adox *n*. statement that seems absurd but may be true. -**paradox'ical** *a*. [G. *paradoxos*, contrary to opinion]

par'affin *n*. wax or oil distilled from shale, wood, *etc*. [fr. L. *parum*, little, and affinis, related (because of its lack of affinity with other bodies)]

par'agon *n*. pattern or model. [OF.]

par'agraph *n*. section of a chapter or book; short record. -*v.t.* arrange in para graphs. [G. *paragraphos*, written beside (orig. of the sign indicating the new section)]

par'allel *a*. continuously at equal distances; precisely corresponding. -*n*. line of latitude; thing exactly like another; comparison. -*v.t.* represent as similar, compare. -**par'allelism** *n*. [G. *parallelos*, beside one another]

parallel'ogram *n*. four-sided plane figure with opposite sides equal and parallel. [L.]

par'allel out'put *n*. (*compute.*) form of computer output in which all characters on a line are transmitted at the same instant.

paral'ysis *n*. incapacity to move or feel, due to damage to the nerve system. -**par'alyze** *v.t.* [G. *paralysis*, cp. **palsy**]

paramed'ical *a*. of persons working in various capacities in support of medical

profession. [G. *para*, beside, L. *medicus*, physician]

par'amount *a*. supreme. [F. *par amont*, upwards]

par'anoia *n*. kind of mental disease. -**parano'ic** *n*. [G. *para*, beside, *noein*, to think]

parapherna'lia *n*. *pl*. personal belongings, trappings, odds and ends of equipment. [Med. L.]

paraphrase *n*. expression of a meaning of a passage in other words. -*v.t.* put the meaning of in other words. [G. *paraphrases*, beside phrase]

par'asite *n*. self-interested hanger-on; animal or plant living in or on another. [G. *parasitos*]

par'atroops *n*. *pl*. airborne troops to be dropped by parachute. -**par'atrooper** *n*. [*parachute* and *troops*]

par'boil *v.i.* scald the surface in boiling water, boil partly; scorch. [OF. *parboillir*, boil thoroughly]

par'buckle *n*. rope for raising or lowering round objects, the middle being secured at the higher level and the ends passed under and round the object. -*v.t.* raise or lower in this way. [orig. uncertain]

par'cel *n*. packet of goods, specially one enclosed in paper; quantity dealt with at one time; piece of land. -*v.t.* divide into parts; make up in a parcel, [F. *parcelle*, small part]

parch *v.t.* and *i*. dry by exposure to heat, roast slightly, make or become hot and dry. [ME. *perche*, contr. of perish]

parch'ment *n*. skin prepared for writing; manuscript of this. [*pergamum*, in Asia Minor (where first used)]

par'don *v.t.* forgive. -*n*. forgiveness. [F. *pardonner*]

pare (păr) *v.t.* trim by cutting away the edge or surface of [F. *parer*, make ready]

paregor'ic *a*. soothing. -*n*. soothing medicine; tincture of opium. [G. *paregorikos*, comforting]

par'ent *n*. father or mother. [L. *parere*, bring forth]

paren'thesis *n*. **paren'theses** *pl*. *n*. word, phrase, or sentence inserted in a passage independently of the grammatical sequence and usually marked off by brackets, dashes, or commas. -*pl*. round brackets, ( ), used for this. -**parenthet'ic** *a*. [G.]

par'iah (pã-ri-a) *n*. Indian of no caste; social outcast. [Tamil, *parairyar*]

par'ish *n*. district under a priest; subdiv ision of a county. -**parish'ioner** *n*. inhabitant of a parish. [F. *paroisse*]

par'ity check *n.* (*compute.*) system for detecting errors during transmission between computers, checking whether the number of bit (0s or 1s) is odd or even.

park *n.* large enclosed piece of ground, usually with grass or woodland, attached to a country house or set aside for public use. [F. *parc*]

parl'ance *n.* way of speaking. **-parl'ey** *n.* meeting between leaders or representatives of opposing forces to discuss terms. *v.i.* hold a discussion about terms. [F. *parler*, speak]

parl'iament *n.* legislature of the United Kingdom; any legislative assembly. [F. *parlement-parler*, speak]

parl'or *n.* sitting-room or room for receiving company in a small house; private room in an inn; store selling some special service or goods. [F. *parloir* fr. *parler*, speak]

paro'chial (-k-) *a.* of a parish; narrow, provincial. **-paro'chialism** *n.* concentration on the local interests. (Late L. *parochial* parish)

par'ody *n.* composition in which author's characteristics are made fun of by imitation; burlesque; feeble imitation. *-v.t.* write a parody of. **-par'odist** *n.* [G. *parodia*]

parole' *n.* early freeing of prisoner on condition he is of good behavior; word of honor. *-v.t.* place on parole. [F.]

par'onym *n.* word with same derivation; word with same sound but differing spelling and meaning, *e.g.*, moat, mote. [G. *para*, beside, *onoma*, name]

par'oxysm *n.* sudden violent attack of pain, rage, laughter, *etc.* [G. *paroxysmos para*, beyond, *oxys*, sharp]

par'quet (-ka) *n.* flooring of wooden blocks. *-v.t.* lay a parquet. [F.]

parr'icide *n.* murder or murderer of one's own parent. [L. *parricida*]

parr'ot *n.* bird with short hooked beak, some varieties of which can be taught to imitate speech; unintelligent imitator. [dim. of F. *Pierre*, Peter]

parr'y *v.t.* ward off. *-n.* act of parrying, *esp.* in fencing. [F. *parer*]

parse (-z) *v.t.* describe (a word) or analyze (a sentence) in terms of grammar. [fr. school question, L. *quæ pars orationis?* What part of speech?]

par'simony *n.* stingyness; undue economy. **-parsimo'nious** *a.* [L. *parsimonia*, fr. *parcere*, spare]

par'sley *n.* herb used for seasoning, *etc.* [G. *petroselinon*, rock parsley]

par'snip *n.* plant with a yellow root cooked as a vegetable. [L. *pastinaca*, fr. *pastinare*, dig up]

par'son *n.* clergyman of a parish or church; clergyman. **-par'sonage** *n.* parson's house. [*person*]

part *n.* portion, section, share; duty; character given to an actor to play; interest. *-v.t.* divide; separate; distribute. *-v.i.* separate from. [L. *pars, part-*, part]

par'tial *a.* prejudiced; fond of; being only in part. **-partial'ity** *n.* **-par'tially** *adv.* [L. *partialis*]

partic'ipate (-is-) *v.t.* and *i.* share in. **-partic'ipant** *n.* **-partic'ipator** *n.* **-participa'tion** *n.* **-part'iciple** *n.* adjective made by inflection from a verb and keeping the verb's relation to dependent words. **-particip'ial** *a.* [L. *participate*, fr. *pars*, part, and *capere*, take]

part'icle *n.* minute portion of matter; least possible amount; minor part of speech. [L. *particular* dim. of *pars*, part]

partic'ular *a.* relating to one, not general; considered apart from others; minute; exact, fastidious. *-n.* detail or item. *-pl.* details. [L. *particularist*]

partisan' (-z-) *n.* adherent of a party. *-a.* adherent to a faction. [F.]

parti'tion *n.* division; dividing wall. *-v.t.* divide. [L. *partition*]

part'ner *n.* member of a partnership; one that dances with another; husband or wife. **-part'nership** *n.* association of persons for business, *etc.* [OF. *parconier*]

part'ridge *n.* small game bird of the grouse family. [G. *perdix*]

part'y *n.* number of persons united in opinion; side; social assembly. *-a.* of, or belonging to, a faction. **-part'y col'ored** *a.* differently colored in different parts, variegated. [F. *parti*]

pass (-ki-) *v.t.* go by, beyond, through, *etc.*; exceed; be accepted by. *-v.i.* go; be transferred from one state to another; elapse; undergo examination successfully. *-n.* way, *esp.* a narrow and difficult way; passport; condition; successful result from a test. **-pass'able** *a.* **-past** *a.* ended. *-n.* bygone times. *-adv.* by; along. *-prep.* beyond; after. [L. *passus*, step]

pass'age *n.* journey; voyage; fare; part of a book, *etc.*; encounter. **-pass'enger** *n.* traveler, *etc.* by some conveyance. **-pass'port** *n.* document granting permission to pass. **-pass'word** *n.* in warfare, secret word to distinguish friend from foe. [F.]

pas'sion *n.* suffering; strong feeling; wrath; object of ardent desire. **passionate**

a. easily moved to anger; moved by strong emotions. [L. *passio*]

pass'ive *a-* suffering; submissive; denoting the grammatical mood of a verb in which the action is suffered by the subject. [L. *pati, pass,* suffer]

Pass'over *n.* feast of the Jews to commemorate the time when God, smiting the first-born of the Egyptians, passed over the houses of Israel. [*pass over*]

paste *n.* soft composition, as of flour and water; fine glass to imitate gems. -*v.t.* fasten with paste. -**past'y** *n.* pie enclosed in paste. -*a.* like paste. -**pa'stry** *n.* articles of food made chiefly of paste. **paste'board** *n.* stiff, thick paper. [G. *barley* porridge]

pas'tel *n.* crayon; art of crayon-drawing; a drawing in this medium. -**pas'tellist** *n.* -**pas'tel-shades** *n. pl.* delicate colors. [F.]

pasteurize *v.t.* sterilize (milk *etc.*) by heating. [Louis *Pasteur* d. 1895]

pas'time (-ā-) *n.* that which serves to make time pass agreeably, recreation. [*pass* and *time*]

pas'tor *n.* minister of the gospel. -**past'oral** *a.* relating to shepherds or rural life; relating to the office of pastor. -*n.* poem describing rural life. -**past'orate** *n.* office or jurisdiction of a spiritual pastor. [L. = *shepherd*]

past'ure (-ā-) *n.* grass for food of cattle; ground on which cattle graze. -*v.t.* feed on grass. -*v.i.* graze. -**past'urage** *n.* business of grazing cattle; pasture. [L. *pascere, past-,* feed]

pat *n.* light, quick blow; small mass as of butternut. tap. [imit. orig.]

patch *n.* piece of cloth sewed on a garment; spot or plot; plot of ground. -*v.t.* mend; repair clumsily. -**patch'y** *a.* full of patches. [OF. *pieche,* piece]

pa'tent *a.* open; evident; manifest; open to public perusal; as letters patent. -*n.* deed securing to a person the exclusive right to an invention. -*v.t.* secure a patent. [L. *patens,* patent-, fr. *patere,* lie open]

pater'nal *a.* of a father; fatherly. [L. *pater,* father]

path (-ā-) *n.* way or track; course of action. [OE. *pæth*]

pathol'ogy *n.* science of the causes and nature of diseases. -**patholog'ical** *a.* pert. to science of disease; due to disease, morbid, unhealthy, diseased. [G. = *suffering*]

pa'thos *n.* power of exciting tender emotions. -**pathet'ic, pathet'ical** *a.* affecting or moving one's emotions. (G. = feeling]

pa'tient (-shent) *a.* bearing trials without murmuring. -*n.* person under medical treatment. -**pa'tience** *n.* quality of enduring. [L. *pati,* suffer]

pa'triarch (-k) *n.* father and ruler of a family, *esp.* in Biblical history; venerable old man. -**patriarch'al** *a.* [G. *patriarches,* head of a family]

patri'cian (-shan) *n.* noble of ancient Rome; person of noble birth. [fr. L. *patricius,* one sprung from the *patres conscripti,* or senators]

pat'riot *n.* one that loves and serves his country. -*a.* **patriotic. -patriot'ic** *a.* inspired by love of one's country. [G. *patriotes,* fellow-countryman]

patrol' *n.* marching round as a guard; small body patroling. -*v.i.* go round on guard, or reconnoitering. [F. *patrouiller*]

pa'tron *n.* man under whose protection another has placed himself, guardian saint; one that has the disposition of a church-living, *etc.* -**pat'ronage** *n.* special countenance or support; right of presentation to a church-living, *etc.* -**pat'ronize** *v.t.* assume the air of a superior towards; frequent as a customer. [L. *patronus*]

patt'er *v.i.* tap in quick succession; make a noise, as the sound of quick, short steps; pray or talk rapidly. -*n.* quick succession of small sounds. [frequentative of *pat*]

patt'ern *n.* model for imitation; specimen. [L. *patronus*]

pau'per *n.* poor person, *esp.* one supported by the public. -**pau'perism** *n.* state of being destitute of the means of support. [L. = poor]

pause *n.* stop or rest. -*v.i.* cease for a time. [G. *pausis*]

pave *v.t.* form a surface with stone or brick. -**pave'ment** *n.* paved floor or footpath; material for paving. [L. *pavire,* ram down]

pawn *n.* goods deposited as security for money borrowed. -*v.t.* pledge. -**pawn'-broker** *n.* one that lends money on goods pledged. [OF. *pan*]

pawn *n.* piece in a game, *esp.* chess. [OF. *paon,* fr. L. *pedo, pedon-,* footsoldier]

pay *v.t.* give money, *etc.* , for goods received or services rendered; compensate. -*v.i.* be remunerative. -*n.* wages. -**pay'able** *a.* justly due. -**pay'ment** *n.* discharge of a debt. [F. *payer*]

pea *n.* fruit, growing in pods, of a leguminous plant; the plant. -**pea'nut** *n.* groundnut. [G. *pison*]

peace *n.* calm; repose; freedom from war; quietness of mind. -**peace'keeping** *n.* a maintenance of peace, *esp.* the prevention of further fighting between hostile forces in an area. [L. *pax, pac-*]

peach *a.* stone-fruit of delicate flavor; tree which bears this. [F. *pêche*]

pea'cock *n.* bird, remarkable for the beauty of its plumage and fan-like spotted tail. [L. *pavo* and *cock*]

peak *n.* pointed end of anything, *esp.* the sharp top of a hill; maximum point in a curve or record. [var. of *pike*]

peal *n.* loud sound, or succession of loud sounds; chime; set of bells. *-v.i.* sound loudly. [for *appeal*]

pear *n.* tree yielding sweet, juicy fruit; the fruit. [L. *pirum*]

peas'ant (pez'-) *n.* rural laborer; rustic. *-a.* rural. [F. *paysan-pays*, country]

peat *n.* decomposed vegetable substance, dried and used for fuel. [Celt. orig.]

peb'ble *n.* small, roundish stone; transparent and colorless rock-crystal. [OE. *popelstan*]

pecan' *n.* N. American tree; its nut-also **pecan'-nut.** [Chin.]

peck *n.* fourth part of a bushel; great deal. [AF. *pek*]

peck *v.t.* and *i.* pick or strike with the beak; eat with beak. [var. of *pick*]

pec'toral *a.* of the chest. *-n.* medicine for chest ailments; breast-plate; cross worn over chest. [L. *pectoralis*]

pecu'liar *a.* one's own; particular; strange. **-peculiar'ity** *n.* something that belongs to, or is found in, one person or thing only. [L. *peculiaris*]

ped'agogue (-gog) *n.* schoolmaster; pedantic or narrow-minded teacher. [G. *paidogogos*, 'boy-leader']

ped'al *a.* of a foot. *-n.* something to transmit motion from the foot. *-v.i.* use a pedal. [L. *pedalis*, fr. *pes*, foot]

ped'ant *n.* one who overvalues, or insists unreasonably on, petty details of book-learning, grammatical rules, *etc.* **-pedant'ic** *a.* [F. *pédant*]

ped'estal *n.* base of a column, pillar, *etc.* [F. *pédestal*; L. *pes, pedis*, foot]

pedes'trian *a.* going on foot. *-n.* one that walks on foot. **-pedes'trianism** *n.* the practice of walking. [L. *pedester, pedestr-*, fr. *pes*, foot]

pediat'rics *n.* treatment of children's diseases. **-pedia'trician** *n.* [G. *paidos*, child]

ped'igree *n.* register of ancestors; genealogy. [AF. *pe de gru*, crane's foot]

ped'lar, pedd'ler *n.* one who travels about hawking small commodities. **-ped'dle** *v.t.* and *i.* [OE. *ped*, basket]

pedom'eter *n.* instrument which records the distance walked by a person. [L. *pes, pedis*, a foot, [G. *metron*, a measure]

pe'dophilia *n.* sexual perversion of which children are the object of desire. [G. *paidos*, child, *philos*, loving]

peel *v.t.* strip off the skin, bark or rind. *-v.i.* come off, as the skin or rind. *-n.* rind, skin. [F. *peler*]

peep *v.i.* cry, as a chick; chirp. *-n.* cry of a young chicken. [imit. orig.]

peer *n.* one of the same rank; nobleman. **-peer'less** *a.* unequaled; matchless. **-peer'age** *n.* rank of a peer; body of peers. [L. *par*, equal]

peer *v.i.* peep; look narrowly, as with shortsighted eyes. [Teutonic orig.]

peev'ish *a.* fretful; querulous. [orig. uncertain]

peg *n.* wooden nail or pin. *-v.t.* fasten with pegs. [orig. uncertain]

pel'ican *n.* large water-fowl, remarkable for the enormous pouch beneath its bill. [G. *pelekan*]

pell'et *n.* little ball. [F. *pelote*]

pelt *v.t.* strike with missiles. *-v.i.* throw missiles; fall persistently, as rain. [orig. uncertain]

pelt *n.* hide or skin. [L. *pellis*]

pel'vis *n.* bony cavity at lower end of the body. [L. = *basin*]

pen *n.* instrument for writing. *-v.t.* compose and commit to paper; write. **pen-knife** *n.* pocket-knife. **-pen'name** *n.* one skilled in hand-writing, author. **pen'manship** *n.* [L. *penna*, feather]

pen *n.* small enclosure, as for sheep. *-v.t.* shut up. **-pent** *a.* closely confined; shut up. [OE. *penn*]

pe'nal *a.* relating to, incurring, or inflicting, punishment. **-pen'alty** *n.* punishment for a crime or offense. **-pe'nalize** *v.t.* lay under penalty. [L. *penalis, poena*, punishment]

pen'ance *n.* suffering submitted to as an expression of penitence. [OF. *penéance*, L. *pœnitentia*]

pen'cil *n.* small brush used by painters; instrument, as of graphite, for writing, *etc.* *-v.t.* paint or draw; mark with a pencil. [L. *penicillum*, little tail]

pend'ant *n.* hanging ornament. *-a.* suspended; hanging; projecting. **-pend'ing** *prep.* during. *-a.* awaiting decision. [L. *pendere*, hang]

pen'dent *a.* pendant, hanging. [L. *pendere*, hang]

pend'ulum *n.* suspended weight swinging to and fro, *esp.* as a regulator for a clock. [L. *pendulus*, hanging]

pen'etrate *v.t.* enter into; pierce; arrive at the meaning of. **-pen'etrable** *a.* capable of being pierced. [L. *penetrare*]

pen'guin *n.* swimming bird, unable to fly. [Welsh *pen gwyn*, white head]

penicill'in *n.* extract of the mold *penicillium notatum*, used to prevent growth of bacteria. [L. *penicillus*, little tail]

penin'sula *n.* land nearly surrounded by water. [L. *paene*, almost, *insula*, island]

pe'nis *n.* male organ of generation. [L.]

pen'itent *a.* affected by a sense of guilt. -*n.* one that repents of sin. -**pen'itence** *n.* sorrow for sin; repentance. -**peniten'tiary** -*n.* prison. [L. *pænitere*, repent]

penn'ant *n.* narrow piece of bunting, *esp* . a long narrow flag, on a lance, *etc.* -also **pennon.** [L. *penna*, plume]

penn'y *n.* **penn'ies** *pl.* (denoting the number of coins). -**pence** *pl.* (amount of pennies in value), copper coin; cent; 100th part of a pound. -**penn'iless** *a.* having no money. [OE. *pennig*]

pen'sion *n.* allowance for past services; annuity paid to retired public officers, soldiers, *etc.* -*v.t.* grant a pension to. - **pen'sioner** *n.* [L. *pensio-pendere, pens*, weigh]

pen'sive *a.* thoughtful with sadness, wistful. [F. *pensif*, L. *pensare*, weigh]

pent'agon *n.* plane figure having five sides and five angles. -**Pent'agon** *n.* headquarters of the Department of Defense; the U.S. military leadership. -**pentag'onal** *a.* -**pent'ateuch** (-k) *n.* the first five books of the Old Testament. [G. *pente*, five]

pent'house *n.* shed standing with its roof sloping against a higher wall; structure or dwelling built on the roof of a building. [F. *appentis*, L. *appendicium*, appendage]

penulti'mate *n.* second last. [L. *paene*, almost, *ultimus*, last]

penum'bra *n.* imperfect shadow; partial shade between shadow and full light. - **penum'bral** *a.* [L. *paene*, almost, *umbra*, shadow]

pen'ury *n.* want; extreme poverty. **penu'rious** *a.* niggardly. [L. *penuria*]

peo'ple *n.* body of persons that compose a community, nation; persons generally. -*v.t.* stock with inhabitants. [F. *peuple*, nation; L. *populus*]

pepp'er *n.* fruit of a climbing plant, which yields a pungent aromatic spice. -*v.t.* sprinkle with pepper; pelt with shot. - **pepp'ery** *a.* having the qualities of pepper; irritable. -**pepp'ermint** *n.* aromatic plant. [G. *peperi*]

peram'bulate *v.t.* walk through or over, traverse. -*v.i.* walk about. [L. *perambulare*, per, through, *ambulare*, walk]

perceive' *v.t.* obtain knowledge of through the senses; observe; understand. - **perceiv'able** *a.* -**percep'tible** *a.* discernible. [L. *percipere*]

percent'age *n.* proportion or rate per hundred. -**per cent**, in each hundred. [L. *per centum*, by the hundred]

percen'tile *n.* one of 99 actual or notional values of a variable dividing its distribution into 100 groups with equal frequencies; centile. [L. *per centum*, by the hundred]

per'colate *v.t.* and *i.* pass through small interstices, as a liquor; filter. -**percola'tion** *n.* [L. *percolate*]

percus'sion *n.* collision; vibratory shock. -**percus'sion instrument**, musical instrument played by striking, *e. g.* drum or cymbal. [L. *percussio*]

per'egrinate *v.i.* travel from place to place. [L. *peregrinus*, foreigner]

perempt'ory *a.* authoritative; forbidding debate; final; absolute. [L. *peremptorius*, destructive]

perenn'ial *a.* lasting through the years; perpetual; (*bot.*) continuing more than two years. [L. *perennis*]

per'fect *a.* complete; finished. -*n.* tense denoting a complete act. -*v.t.* finish; make skillful. -**perfec'tion** *n.* state of being perfect. [L. *perfectus*, done thoroughly]

per'fidy *n.* treachery. [L. *perfidia*, faithlessness]

per'forate *v.t.* pierce. -**perfora'tion** *n.* hole bored through anything. [L. *perforare-per*, through, *forare*, bore]

perform' *v.t.* bring to completion; fulfill; represent on the stage. -*v.i.* act a part; play, as on a musical instrument. **perform'ance** *n.* -**perform'er** *n.* one who performs, *esp.* actor or other entertainer. [OF. *par- fournir*, furnish through]

per'fume *n.* agreeable scent; fragrance. - *v.t.* scent. [L. *perfumare*, perfume]

perfunct'ory *a.* done indifferently, careless. -**perfunct'orily** *adv.* [L. *perfungi, perfunct-*, get done with]

perhaps' *adv.* it may be; possibly. [E. *hap*, chance]

pericard'ium *n.* membrane, enclosing heart. [G. *peri*, around, *kardia*, heart]

perigee *n.* point on moon or planet's orbit, at which it is nearest earth. [G. *peri*, around, *ge*, earth]

per'il *n.* danger; exposure to injury. - **per'ilous** *a.* full of peril. [L. *periculum*]

perim'eter *n.* outer boundary of a plane figure. [G. *perimetros*]

pe'riod *n.* time in which a heavenly body

makes a revolution; particular portion of time; complete sentence. punctuation mark at the end of a sentence (.). -**period'ic** a. recurring at regular intervals. -**period'ical** a. relating to a period; periodic. -n. publication issued at regular intervals. [G. *periodos*, circuit]

peripatet'ic a. walking about. [G. *peripatetikos*]

periph'ery n. circumference; surface; outside. [G. *peri*, around, *pherein*, carry]

periph'erals n. pl. (*compute.*) any hardware device separate and distinct from the main computer. also **periph'eral equipment**.

per'iscrope n. an instrument, used *esp.* in submarines, for giving a view of objects that are on a different level. [G. *peri-*, round, and *skopein*, to look]

per'ish v.i. die, waste away. **per'ishable** a. [L. *perire*]

peritoni'tis n. inflammation of the peritoneum. [G. *peritoneion*]

per'jure (-jer) v.t. forswear. -v.i. bear false witness. [L. *perjurare*]

perk v.t. and i. smarten; become cheerful; toss head. -**perky** a. smart, cheeky. [orig. uncertain]

per'manent a. continuing in the same state; lasting. -**per'manent wave**, lasting artificial hair-wave. [L. *permanere*]

per'meate v.t. pass through the pores of, saturate. -**per'meable** a. admitting of the passage of fluids. [L. *permeate, permeate*, pass through]

permit' v.t. allow; give leave to; give leave. -(per'-) n. written permission. -**permis'sion** n. leave; liberty. - [L. *permittere, permiss-*]

permute' v.t. interchange. -**permuta'tion** n. mutual transference; (*alg.*) change in the arrangement of a number of quantities. [L. *permutare*, change thoroughly]

perni'cious (-nish'-) a. having the quality of destroying or injuring; hurtful. [L. *perniciosus*]

perox'ide n. oxide with largest proportion of oxygen. [L. *per*, intens., and *oxide*]

perpendic'ular a. exactly upright; at right angles to the plane of the horizon; at right angles to a given line or surface. [L. *perpendicularis*]

per'petrate v.t. commit (something bad). [L. *perpetrare*, accomplish]

perpet'ual a. continuous, lasting for ever. -**perpet'ually** adv. -**perpet'uate** v.t. make perpetual; not to allow to be forgotten. [L. *perpetualis*]

perplex' v.t. puzzle; complicate. perplex'-ity n. puzzled or tangled state. [L. *perplexus*, entangled]

per'quisite (-it) n. casual payment in addition to salary belonging to an employment. [L. *perquisitum*, thing eagerly sought]

per'secute v.t. oppress for the holding of an opinion; subject to persistent ill treatment. [L. *persequi*, persecute, pursue]

persevere' v.i. persist, maintain an effort. -**perseve'rance** n, [L. *perseverare*]

persimm'on n. N. American tree bearing edible plum-like fruit; the fruit. [*Algonkin*]

persist' v.i. continue in a state or action in spite of obstacles or objections. **persist'ent** a. -**persist'ence** n. [L. *persistere*, fr. *sistere*, stand]

per'son n. individual human being; individual divine being; character in a play, *etc.*; in grammar a classification, or one of the classes, of pronouns, and verb-forms according to the person speaking, spoken to, or spoken of. -**per'sonable** a. good-looking. -**per'sonal** a. individual, private, of one's own; of or relating to grammatical person. -**personal'ity** n. distinctive character. -**per'sonally** adv. in person. -**per'sonalty** n. personal property. -**person'ify** v.t. represent as a person; typify. **personifica'tion** n. -**personnel'** n. staff employed in a service or institution. [L. *persona*, char. in a play]

perspec'tive (-iv) n. art of drawing on a flat surface to give the effect of solidity and relative distances and sizes; drawing in perspective; mental view. -**in perspective**, in due proportion. [L. *perspicere, perspect-*, look through]

perspire' v.i. sweat. -**perspira'tion** n. [L. *perspirare*, breathe through]

persuade' (-sw-) v.t. convince; bring (any one to do something) by argument, *etc.* -**persuasion** n. -**persua'sive** a. [L. *persuadere, persuas-*]

pertain' v.i. belong, relate. -**pert'inent** a. to the point. [L. *pertinere*, belong]

pertinacity (-as'-) n. -**pertina'cious** a. obstinate, persistent. [L. *pertinax*]

perturb' v.t. disturb gradually; alarm. [L. *perturbare*]

peruse' v.t. read, *esp.* in a slow or careful manner. -**peru'sal** n. [orig. uncertain]

pervade' v.t. spread through. -**perva'sion** n. -**perva'sive** a. [L. *pervadere, pervas*, go through]

pervert' v.t. turn to a wrong use; lead astray. -**per'vert** a. one who has turned to error, *esp.* in religion, morals *etc.*; abnormal person in matters of sex. -**perverse'** a.

obstinately or unreasonably wrong, wayward, *etc*. **-perver'sity** *n*. [L. *pervertere, perverse*, turn away]

pess'imism *n*. theory that everything turns to evil; tendency to see the worst side of things. [L. *pessimus*, worst]

pest *n*. troublesome or harmful thing or person; plague. **-pestif'erous** *a*. bringing plague; harmful, deadly. **-pest'ilent** *a*. troublesome; deadly. **-pest'ilence** *n*. deadly plague. [L. *pestis*]

pest'er *v.t*. annoy, trouble or vex persistently. [OF. *empestrer*]

pet *n*. animal or person kept or regarded with affection. *-v.t*. make a pet of. **pet** *n*. fit of ill-temper or sulking. **-pett'ish** *a*. [orig. uncertain]

pet'al *n*. colored flower leaf. [G. *petalon*, thin plate]

petit *a*. petité, *fem*. , small, dainty. [F.]

peti'tion (-ish'-) *n*. request, *esp*. one presented to a sovereign or government. *v.t*. present a petition to. [L. *petitio*]

pet'rify *v.t*. turn into stone; paralyze with fear, *etc*. **-petrifac'tion** *n*. [L. *petra*, rock]

petro'leum *n*. mineral oil. **-pet'rol** *n*. refined petroleum; gasoline. **-petro'leum jelly**, soft paraffin, vaseline. [fr. L. *petra*, rock, and *oleum*, oil]

petti'coat *n*. woman's underskirt. [orig. *petty coat*, small coat]

pett'y *a*. unimportant, trivial; on a small scale. **-pett'y off'icer** *n*. non-commissioned naval officer. [F. *petit*, small]

pet'ulant *a*. given to small fits of temper. **-pet'ulance**. [L. *petulans, petulant-*, *pert*, wanton]

petu'nia *n*. plant with funnel-shaped flowers allied to tobacco. *-a*. purplish pink. [Amer. Ind. *petun*, tobacco]

pew *n*. fixed seat in a church. [OF. *puie*, fr. G. *podium*, pedestal]

pew'ter *n*. alloy of tin and lead; ware made of this. [OF. *peutre*]

phag'ocyte (fag'o-sit) *n*. white blood corpuscle, leucocyte, devouring microbes. [G. *phagein*, eat, *kytos*, cell]

pharmaceut'ic *a*. relating to pharmacy. *n*. in *pl*. science of pharmacy. **pharmaceut'ical** *a*. **-pharmaco-poe'ia** *n*. official book with a list and directions for the use of drugs. **-phar'-macy** *n*. preparation and dispensing of drugs; drugstore. **-phar'macist** *n*. [G. *pharmakon*, poison, drug]

pharynx (far'ingks) *n*. tube or cavity that connects the mouth with the gullet. [E. *pharynx. -yngos*]

phase (-z) *n*. aspect of the moon or a planet;

stage of development. **-pha'sic** *a*. [G. *phasis*]

phase. See **faze**.

pheas'ant (fez'-) *n*. game-bird. [G. Phasis, river in Colchis (where the bird first came from)]

phenomenon *n*. **phenomena** *pl*. anything appearing or observed; remarkable person or thing. **-phenom'enal** *a*. (*colloq*.) exceptional. [G. *phainein*, show]

phil- *prefix* loving. [G. *philein*, love]; **philan'der** *v.i*. amuse oneself with lovemaking. **-philan'thropy** *n*. love of mankind; practise of doing good to one's fellow men. **-philanthrop'ic** *a*. **philan'thropist** *n*. **-philat'ely** *n*. stamp collecting. **-philat'elist** *n*. **-philatel'ic** *a*. **-philol'ogy** *n*. science of the structure and development of languages. **-philos'ophy** *n*. pursuit of wisdom; study of realities and general principles; system of theories on the nature of things or on conduct. **philos'opher** *n*. one who studies, or possesses, or originates, philosophy.

phlebitis *n*. inflammation of a vein. [G. *phleps, phlep-*, vein]

phlebotomy *n*. bleeding, blood-letting. **phlebot'omist** *n*. [G. *phleps*, vein]

phlegm (flem) *n*. viscid secretion of the mucus membrane, ejected by coughing, *etc*.; calmness, sluggishness. [G. *phlegma*, inflammation]

pho'bia *n*. morbid fear, dislike. [G. *Phobos*, fear]

phoenix *n*. legendary bird supposed to be only one of its kind and after living for centuries to burn (fire) and rise renewed from the ashes; unique thing. [G. *Phoiinix*, purple red.]

phone *n*. , *a*. , and *v.i*. abbrev. of telephone. [G. *phone*, voice, sound]

pho'ney *a*. not genuine. [orig. uncertain]

phon'ic(al) *a*. of sound, phonetic. [G. *phone*, voice, sound]

phono- *prefix*. [G. *phone*, voice]. **phonet'ic** *a*. of, or relating to, vocal sounds. *-n*. in *pl*. the science of vocal sounds. **-phoneti'cian** *n*. **-pho'nograph** *n*. instrument recording and reproducing sounds.

phosphorus *n*. non-metallic element which appears luminous in the dark. **phosphores'cence** *n*. faint glow in the dark. [G. *phos*, light]

pho'to- *prefix* light. [G. *phos*, phot-, light]. **-pho'to-electri'city** *n*. electricity produced or affected by the action of light. **-pho'tograph** *n*. picture made by the chemical action of light on a sensitive film.

-*v.t.* take a photograph of. -**photog'rapher** *n.* -**photograph'ic** *a.* -**photog'raphy** *a.* -**pho'tostat** *n.* photographic apparatus for obtaining exact copies of manuscript, drawing, *etc.* **photosyn'thesis** *n.* (*bot.*) formation of complex compounds by the action of light on chlorophyll. -**photogenic** *a.* able to photograph well and attractively. [G. *phos. phot-*, light, and *gignesthai*]

phrase (-z) *n.* mode of expression; small group of words; pithy expression. -*v.t.* express in words. -**phraseology** (-i-ol'-) *n.* manner of expression, choice of words. [G. *phrasis*]

phrenol'ogy *n.* study of the shape of the skull; theory that mental powers are indicated by the shape of the skull. -**phrenol'ogist** *n.* [G. *phren*, mind]

phys'ics (-iz'–) *n.* medicine. -*pl.* science of the properties of matter and energy. -*v.t.* dose with medicine. -**phys'ical** *a.* relating to physic, or physics, or the body. -**physically** *adv.* -**physi'cian** *n.* qualified medical practitioner. -**phys'icist** *n.* student of physics. -**physiog'nomy** *n.* judging character by face; the face. -**physique'** (-ek) *n.* bodily structure and development. [G. *physis*, nature]

pian'o *a.* and *adv.* in a low tone or voice. -*n.* pianoforte. -**pian'oforte** (-ta) *n.* musical instrument with strings which are struck by hammers worked by a keyboard. -**pi'anist** *n.* performer on the pianoforte. [It. *piano*, soft, *forte*, loud]

pic'ador *n.* mounted bull-fighter armed with a lance, who excites the bull. [Sp. *pica*, a pike]

picc'olo *n.* small flute. [IT. = little]

pick *n.* tool consisting of a curved iron crossbar and a wooden shaft for breaking up hard ground or masonry. -**pick'ax** *n.* pick. [orig. *piker*]

pick *v.t.* break the surface of, skin with something pointed; gather; choose, select carefully; find an occasion for. -*n.* act of picking; choicest part. -**pick'ings** *n. pl.* odds and ends of profit. [OE. *pycan*]

pick'et *n.* prong or pointed stake: small body of soldiers on police duty; party of trade unionists posted to deter would-be workers during a strike. -*v.t.* tether to a peg; post as a picket; beset with pickets. [F. *piquet*]

pic'kle (pik'l) *n.* brine or other liquid for preserving food; sorry plight; troublesome child. -*pl.* pickled vegetables. -*v.t.* preserve in pickle. [Du. *pekel*]

pic'nic *n.* pleasure excursion including a meal out of doors. -*v.i.* take part in a picnic. [F. *pique-nique*]

pic'ture *n.* drawing or painting or photograph; representation; image. -*v.t.* represent in, or as in, a picture. -**pictor'ial** *a.* of, in, with, painting or pictures; graphic. -*n.* newspaper with many pictures. -**pictor'ially** *adv.* -**picturesque'** (-esk) *a.* such as would be effective in a picture; striking, vivid. [L. *pictura-pingere, pict-*, paint]

pie *n.* a magpie, wood-pecker; dish of meat, fruit, *etc.*, covered with pastry; mass of printer's type in confusion, *etc.* [L. *pica*]

piece *n.* separate part or fragment; single object; literary or musical composition, *etc.* -*v.t.* mend, put together. -**piece'work** *n.* work paid by amount done regardless of time taken. [F. *piece*]

pier *n.* piece of solid upright masonry, *esp.* supporting a bridge or between two windows; structure running into the sea as a landing stage, *etc.* -**pier**- glass *n.* tall mirror. [Med. L. *pera*]

pierce *v.t.* make a hole in; make a way through. [F. *percer*]

pi'ety *n.* godliness, devoutness; dutifulness. -**pi'etism** *n.* affected or exaggerated piety. [L. *pietas*]

pig *n.* swine; oblong mass of smelted metal. -*v.i.* of a sow, to produce a litter; herded together in a dirty untidy way. -**pig'tail** *n.* plait of hair hanging from the back of the head. [of Teut. orig.]

pi'geon *n.* bird of many wild and domesticated varieties, often trained to carry messages, *etc.* -**pi'geon'hole** *n.* compartment for papers. [F.]

pig'ment *n.* coloring matter, paint or dye. [L. *pigmentum*]

pike *n.* spear formerly used by infantry; peaked hill; large freshwater fish; turnpike or tollgate. [OE. *pic*]

pile *n.* beam driven into the ground, *esp.* as a foundation for building in water or wet ground. [L. *pilum*, dart]

pile *n.* nap of cloth, *esp.* of velvet, carpet. [L. *pilus*, hair]

piles *n.* (in *pl.*) tumors of veins of rectum; hemorrhoids. [L. *pila*, ball]

pil'fer *v.t.* steal in small quantities. -**pil'ferage** *n.* [OF. *pelfrer*]

pil'grim *n.* one who walks to sacred place; wanderer. -**pil'grimage** *n.* [L. *peregrinus*]

pill *n.* pellet of medicine. [L. *pila*, ball]

pill'age *n.* seizing goods by force; *esp.* in war; plunder. -*v.t.* and *i.* plunder. [F.]

pill'box *n.* (*mil. sl.*) small concrete fort or blockhouse. [*pill* and *box*]

pill'ory *n.* frame with holes for head and hands in which an offender was confined and exposed to pelting and ridicule. -*v.t.* set in pillory; expose to ridicule and abuse. [F. *pilori*]

pill'ow *n.* cushion for the head, especially in bed. -*v.t.* lay on a pillow. [L. *pulvinus*]

pi'lot *n.* person qualified to take charge of a ship entering or leaving a harbor, or where knowledge of local waters is needed; steersman; navigator of an airplane; guide. -*v.t.* act as pilot to. -**pi'lot stud'y** *n.* a small-scale experiment or set of observations undertaken to decide how and whether to launch a full-scale project. [F. *pilote*]

pimp *n.* procurer; pander. -*v.i.* pander. [orig. unknown]

pimpernel *n.* plant with small scarlet or blue or white flowers closing in dull weather. [F. *pirnprenelle*]

pim'ple *n.* small pustular spot on the skin. -**pim'ply** *a.* [orig. uncertain]

pin *n.* short thin piece of stiff wire with a point and head for fastening soft materials together; wooden or metal peg or rivet. -*v.t.* fasten with a pin or pins; seize and hold fast. -**pin'-cushion** *n.* pad into which pins are stuck. - [OE. *pinn*, peg]

pin'afore *n.* washing apron or overall. [because pinned afore the dress]

piñata *n.* papier-maché or clay form filled with candy or toys, hung at parties and festivities to be broken open with a stick.

pince'-nez *n.* eye-glasses held on the nose by a spring catch. [F.]

pincers *n. pl.* tool for gripping, composed of two limbs crossed and pivoted. [F. *pincer*]

pinch *v.t.* nip, squeeze. -*n.* nip; stress: as much as can be taken up between finger and thumb. [ONF. *pinchier*]

pine *n.* evergreen coniferous tree. -**pine'apple** *n.* tropical fruit. [L. *pinus*]

pine *v.i.* waste away with grief, want, *etc.* [OE. *pinian*, fr. *pin*, pain]

ping'-pong *n.* table-tennis. [imit.]

pin'ion *n.* wing. -*v.t.* disable by binding wings, arms. [L. *penna*, feather]

pinn'acle *n.* pointed turret on a buttress or roof; mountain peak; highest pitch or point. [L. *pinna*, point]

pint (pint) *n.* liquid and dry measure, half a quart. [F. *pinte*]

pioneer' *n.* one of an advanced body preparing a road for troops; explorer; one who first originates. -*v.i.* act as pioneer or leader. [F. *pionier*, fr. *pion*, foot soldier]

pi'ous *n.* devout. [L. *pius*]

pip *n.* seed in a fruit. [short for *pippin*]

pipe *n.* tube of metal or other material;

musical instrument, a whistle; shrill voice, or bird's note; tube with a small bowl at the end for smoking tobacco; wine cask. -*v.i.* and *t.* play on a pipe. [OE.]

pipp'in *n.* various sorts of apples. [F. *pepin*, seed]

pi'quant *a.* pungent; stimulating. [F. *piquer*, string, prick]

pique *v.t.* irritate; hurt the pride of; stimulate. -*n.* feeling of injury or baffled curiosity. [F.]

pi'qué *n.* stiff ribbed cotton fabric. [F.]

pi'rate *n.* sea-robber; publisher, *etc.*, who infringes copyright. -*v.t.* publish or reproduce regardless of copyright. [G. *peirates*, fr. *peiran*, attack]

pirouette' *n.* spinning round on the toe. -*v.i.* do this. [F.]

Pisc'es *n. pl.* the Fishes, 12th sign of the zodiac, which the sun enters c. Feb. 19. -**pis'cine** *a.* of or like a fish. [L. *piscis*, fish]

pist'il *n.* female organ of a flower consisting of ovary, style, stigma. [L. *pistillum*, pestle]

pist'ol *n.* small gun used with one hand. -*v.t.* shoot with a pistol. [F. *pistolet*]

pist'on *n.* plug fitting a cylinder and working up and down, *e.g.* as in a steam engine, *etc.* -**piston-rod** *n.* rod connecting piston with other parts of machinery. [F.]

pit *n.* deep hole in the ground; coal mine or its shaft; depression in any surface; in a theater, section for musicians in front of the stage; enclosure in which animals were set to fight. -*v.t.* set to fight; mark with small scars. -**pit'fall** *n.* covered pit for catching animals or men; concealed danger. [L. *puteus*, well]

pit *n.* stone of a fruit. [OE. *pitha*]

pitch *n.* dark sticky substance obtained from tar or turpentine. -*v.t.* coat with this. -**pitch'-blende** *n.* an oxide of uranium. [L. *pix, pic-*]

pitch *v.t.* set up; cast or throw. -*v.i.* fix upon; fall headlong; of a ship to plunge lengthwise. -*n.* act of pitching; degree height, station; slope; degree of acuteness of sounds. -**pitch'er** *n.* -**pitch'fork** *n.* fork for lifting and pitching hay, *etc.* -*v.t.* throw with, or as with, a pitchfork. [orig. uncertain]

pitch'er *n.* large jug. [OF. *pichier*]

pith *n.* tissue in the stems and branches of certain plants; essential substance, most important part. -**pith'y** *a.* consisting of pith; terse, concise. -**pith'ily** *adv.* [OE. *pitha*]

pitt'ance *n.* small allowance; inadequate wages. [F. *pitance*, orig. = pity]

pitu'itary *a.* mucous. **-pitu'itary gland,** small ductless gland situated beneath the brain. [L. *pituitarius*]

pit'y *n.* sympathy or sorrow for others' suffering; regrettable fact. *-v.t.* feel pity for. **-pit'iful** *a.* full of pity; contemptible. [F. *pitie* fr. L. *pietas*, piety]

piv'ot *n.* shaft or pin on which something turns; central fact; important factor. *-v.t.* furnish with a pivot. *-v.i.* to turn on one. [F.]

pix'el *n.* any of a number of very small picture elements that make up a picture, as on a visual display unit. [fr. *pix* (pictures) and *elements*]

pix'y, pix'ie *n.* fairy. [orig. uncertain]

placate' *v.t.* conciliate, pacify. **-plac'able** *a.* [L. *placare*]

place *n.* particular part of space, spot; position; town, village, residence, buildings; office or employment. *-v.t.* put in a particular place. [F.]

placen'ta (pla-sen'ta) *n.* organ connecting the parent with the unborn mammal; that portion of a plant to which the seeds are attached. [L. *placenta*, a flat cake]

pla'cer *n.* deposit yielding gold after washing. [Sp.]

pla'cid (-as'-) *a.* calm; not easily agitated. **-placid'ity** *n.* [L. *placidus*]

pla'giary *n.* one who publishes borrowed or copied literary work as original; act of so doing. [L. *plagiarius*, kidnapper]

plague (plāg) *n.* pestilence; affliction. *-v.t.* trouble or annoy. **-pla'guy** *a.* **-pla'guily** *adv.* [L. *plaga*, stroke]

plaid *n.* long Scottish-Highland shawl. [Gael. *plaide*, blanket, fr. *peallaid*, sheepskin]

plain *a.* flat, level; unobstructed, not intricate; easily understood; simple, ordinary; unadorned; not beautiful. *-n.* tract of level country. *adv.* clearly. **-plain'ly** *adv.* **-plain'-dealing** *n.* honesty, candidness. **-plain'-speaking** *n.* outspokenness, frankness. [L. *planus*, smooth]

plait (plat) *n.* fold; braid of hair, straw, *etc.* *-v.t.* form into plaits. [OF. *pleit*]

plan *n.* drawing representing a thing's horizontal section; diagram, map; project, design; way of proceeding. *-v.t.* make a plan of; make a design; arrange beforehand. [F. fr. L. *planus*, level]

plane *n.* carpenter's tool for smoothing wood. *-v.t.* make smooth with one. [L. *planus*, level]

plane *a.* perfect, flat, or level; smooth surface. [var. of *plain*]

plane *n.* abbrev. of airplane; wing of an airplane or glider. *-v.t.* glide in an airplane. [F. *planer*, hover]

plan'et *n.* heavenly body revolving round the sun. **-plan'etary** *a.* [G. *planetes*, wanderer]

planeta'rian *n.* apparatus showing movement of sun, moon, stars and planets by projecting lights on inside of dome; building in which the apparatus is housed. [G. *planetes*, wanderer]

plank *n.* long flat piece of sawn timber. [Late L. *planca*]

plank'ton *n.* general term for free-floating organisms in sea or lake, *etc.* [G. *plangktos*, wandering]

plant *n.* member of the vegetable kingdom, living organism feeding on inorganic substances; equipment or machinery needed for a manufacture. *-v.t.* set in the ground. **-planta'tion** *n.* wood of planted trees; estate for cultivation of tea, tobacco, *etc.*; formerly, a colony. [L. *planta*]

plant'ain *n.* tropical tree like a banana; its fruit. [Sp. *plantano*]

plaque' (plak) *n.* ornamental plate or tablet; plate of clasp or brooch. [F.]

plast'er *n.* mixture of lime, sand, *etc.*, to spread on walls, *etc.*; piece of fabric spread with a medicinal or adhesive substance for application to the body. *-v.t.* apply plaster to. **-plast'erer** *n.* [G. *plassein*, mold]

plast'ic *a.* produced by molding; easily molded; molding shapeless matter. [G. *plastikos-plassein*, mold]

plas'tics *n. pl.* name for various synthetic or natural substances capable of being molded into shape, *e.g.*, casein, bitumen, resins. [*plastic*]

plate *n.* flat thin sheet of metal, glass, *etc.*; utensils of gold or silver; shallow round dish from which food is eaten. *-v.t.* cover with a thin coating of gold, silver, or other metal. [G. *platus*, broad, flat]

plat'eau *n.* level high land. [F.]

plat'en *n.* plate by which paper is pressed against type in a printing press; roller in a typewriter. [G. *platus*, broad, flat]

plat'form *n.* raised level surface or floor. [F. *plate-forme*, flat form]

plat'itude *n.* commonplace remark. [F. *plat*, flat]

plat'inum *n.* white heavy malleable metal. **-plat'inotype** *n.* photographic process or print in which platinum is used. [Sp. *platina*, dim. of *plate*, silver]

Platon'ic *a.* of, pert. to Plato and his philosophy; (of love) spiritual, friendly. [*Plato*]

platoon' *n.* small body of soldiers employed as a unit; sub-division of an infantry company. [F. *peloton*]

platt'er *n.* a flat dish. [AF. *plater*]

plaud'it *n.* act of applause. [L. *plaudere*, clap the hands]

plaus'ible *a.* something fair or reasonable; fair-spoken. **-plausibil'ity** *n.* [L. *plausibilis*]

play (plā) *v.i.* move with light or irregular motion, flicker, *etc.*; amuse oneself; take part in a game; perform on a musical instrument. *-v.t.* use or work (an instrument); take part in (a game); contend with in a game; perform (music), perform on (an instrument); act; act the part of *-n.* brisk or free movement; activity; sport; amusement; gambling; dramatic piece or performance. **-play'er** *n.* **-play'fellow, play'mate** *n.* friend, companion in play.- **play'thing** *n.* toy. **-play'wright** *n.* author of plays. [OE. *plegian*]

plea *n.* that is pleaded; excuse; statement of a prisoner or defendant. **-plead** *v.i.* address a court of law; make an earnest appeal. *-v.t.* bring forward as an excuse or plea. [F. *plaid*]

pleach' *v.t.* interweave the branches of (a hedge, *etc.*). [OF. *presser*]

please *v.t.* be agreeable to. *-v.i.* like; be willing. **-pleas'ance** (plez'-) *n.* delight; pleasure-ground. **-pleas'ure** *n.* enjoyment; satisfaction; will, choice. - **pleas'urable** *a.* giving pleasure. - **pleas'ant** *a.* pleasing, agreeable. [F. *plaire*, *plais-* fr. L. *placere*]

pleat *n.* three-fold band on a garment *etc.* , made by folding the material on itself. *v.i.* make a pleat in. [*plait*]

plebe'ian *a.* belonging to the common people; low or rough. *-n.* one of the common people. [L. *plebs*, common people]

pleb'iscite *n.* a decision by direct voting of a whole people. [F.]

pledge *n.* thing given as security; toast; promise. *-v.t.* give over as security; engage; drink the health of. [OF. *plege*]

Plei'stocene *a.* of Glacial period or formation. [G. *pleistos*, most, *kainos*, new]

plent'y *n.* quite enough; abundance. - **plent'eous** *a.* **-plent'iful** *a.* abundant. [OF. *plente-*L. *plenus*, full]

pleth'ora *n.* excess of red corpuscles in the blood; oversupply. **-plethor'ic** *a.* [G. *plethein*, become full]

pleu'ra *n.* membrane enclosing lung. - **pleu'ral** *a.* [G. *pleura*, side]

pleur'isy *n.* inflammation of membrane round the lungs. [G. *pleura*, side]

pli'able *a.* easily bent or influenced. - **pliabil'ity** *n.* **-pli'ant** *a.* pliable. **-pli'ancy** *n.* [F.]

pli'ers *n. pl.* small pincers with a flat grip. [L. *plicare*, bend]

plight *n.* state (usually of a distressing kind); predicament. [OE. *plit*, fold or plait]

plinth *n.* square slab as the base of a column, *etc.* [G. *plinthos*, brick]

plod *v.i.* walk or work doggedly. [imit. orig.]

plot *n.* small piece of land; plan or essential facts of a story, play, *etc.*; secret design, conspiracy. *-v.t.* make a map of; devise secretly. *-v.i.* take part in conspiracy. [OE.]

plotter *n.* (*compute.*) output device that converts electronic signals into figures, lines, or curves; printing device.

plow *n.* implement for turning up the soil. *-v.t.* turn up with a plow, furrow. - **plow'share** *n.* cutting blade of plow. [ON. *plogr*]

pluck *v.i.* pull or pick off, strip the feathers from; reject in an examination. *-n.* plucking; beast's heart, lungs, *etc.*; courage. [OE. *pluecian*]

plug *n.* something fitting into and filling a hole; tobacco pressed hard; piece of this for chewing. *-v.t.* stop with a plug. *-(sl.)* push; advertise persistently. [Du. = *bung*]

plum *n.* stone fruit; tree bearing it. **plum-cake, plum-pudding** *n.* rich cake, pudding full of raisins, other fruits and spices. [OE. *plume*, L. *prune*]

plumb (-m) *n.* ball of lead attached to a string and used for sounding, finding the perpendicular, *etc.* *-a.* perpendicular. *-adv.* perpendicularly; exactly. *-v.t.* find the depth of, set exactly upright. **-plumb'er** (-mer) *n.* one who works in lead, *etc.* and repairs water pipes *etc.* [L. *plumbuimi*, lead]

plume *n.* feather; ornament consisting of feathers or horse-hair. *-v.t.* furnish with plumes; strip of feathers; boast. **-plu'mage** *n.* feathers of a bird. [L. *pluma*, feather]

plump *a.* of rounded form, moderately fat. [Du. *plomp*, blunt]

plun'der *v.t.* rob systematically; take by open force. *-v.i.* rob. *-n.* violent robbery; property so obtained, spoils. [Ger. *plundern*, pillage]

plunge *v.t.* put forcibly (into). *-v.i.* throw oneself (into); enter or move forward with violence. *-n.* plunge, dive. **-plun'ger** *n.* [F. *plonger*]

pluper'fect *a.* of a tense, expressing action completed before a past point of time. [L. *plus quam perfectum*, more than perfect]

plus *prep.* with addition of (usually indicated by the sign +). *-a.* to be added; positive. [L. *plus*, more]

plur'al *a.* more than one; denoting more than one person or thing. *-n.* word in its plural form. **-plu'ralism** *n.* holding more than one appointment, vote, *etc.* [L. *plus, plur-*, more]

plush *n.* fabric like velvet, but with a long soft nap. [F. *peluche*]

Plu'to *n.* outermost of the planets so far discovered. **-Pluto'nian** *a.* pert. to Pluto; dark subterranean; igneous. [G. *Plouton*, god of the underworld]

plutocracy *n.* government by the rich, wealthy class. **-plu'tocrat** *n.* wealthy person. **-plutocrat'ic** *a.* [G. *ploutokratia*, power by wealth]

plutonium *n.* element produced by radioactive decay of neptunium. [*Pluto*]

ply *n.* fold, thickness. [L. *plicare*, fold]

ply *v.t.* wield, work at; supply pressingly. *-v.i.* go to and fro. [*apply*]

pneumatic *a.* of, or coated by, or inflated with, wind or air. **-pneumo'nia** *n.* inflammation of the lungs. [G. *pneuma*, breath]

poach *v.i.* cook (an egg) by dropping without the shell into boiling water. [F. *pocher*, pocket]

poach *v.t.* hunt (game) illegally. *-v.i.* trespass for this purpose. **-poach'er** *n.* [orig. uncertain]

pock *n.* pustule as in smallpox, *etc.* **pockmarks, pock'pit** *n.* mark or small hole left on skin after smallpox *etc.* [OE. *poc*]

pock'et *n.* small bag inserted in a garment; cavity filled with ore, *etc.*; mass of water or air differing in some way from that surrounding it. *-v.t.* put into one's pocket; appropriate. **-pock'etbook** *n.* small bag or case for holding money, papers *etc.* [F. *poche*, cp. *poke*]

pod *n.* long seed-vessel, as of peas, beans, *etc.* *-v.i.* form pods. *-v.t.* shell. [orig. uncertain]

po'em *n.* imaginative composition in verse. **-po'et** *n.* writer of poems. **-po'etess** *fem.* **-po'etry** *n.* art or work of a poet. **-po'esy** *n.* poetry. [G. *poiein*, make]

pog'ram *n.* concerted rising (against, *e.g.*, the Jews), with massacre and pillage. [Russ.]

poign'ant (poin'-) *a.* pungent, stinging, moving, vivid. **-poign'ancy** *n.* [F. *poindre, poign-*, fr. L. *pungere*, prick]

point *n.* dot or mark; punctuation mark; item, detail; unit of value; position, degree, stage; moment; essential object or thing; sharp end; headland; movable rail, changing a train to other rails; one of the direction marks of a compass; striking or effective part or quality; act of pointing. *-v.t.* sharpen; give value to (words, *etc.*); fill up joints with mortar; aim or direct. *-v.i.* show direction or position by extending a finger, stick, *etc.*; direct attention; of a dog, to indicate the position of game by standing facing it. **-point'-blank'** *a.* aimed horizontally; at short range. *adv.* with level aim (there being no necessity to elevate for distances), at short range. [L. *puncture*, fr. *pungere*, prick]

poise *v.t.* place or hold in a balanced or steady position. *-v.i.* be so held; hover. *-n.* balance, equilibrium, carriage (of body, *etc.*). [OF. *pois*, weight]

poi'son (-z-) *n.* substance which kills or injures when introduced into living organism. *-v.t.* give poison to; infect; pervert, spoil. **-poi'soner** *n.* **-poi'sonous** *a.* [F.]

poke *v.t.* push or thrust with a finger, stick, *etc.*; thrust forward. *-v.i.* make thrusts; to pry. *-n.* act of poking; card game. **-po'ker** *n.* metal rod for poking a fire. **-po'ky** *n.* bag; pouch. [ONF. *paque*; F. *poche*, ofteut. orig.]

pol'aroid *n.* type of plastic which polarizes light; camera that develops print very quickly inside itself. [Trademark]

pole *n.* long rounded piece of wood; measure of length, 5½ yards; measure of area, 30¼ square yards. *-v.t.* propel with a pole. [OE. *pal*, fr. L. *palus*]

pole *n.* each of the two points about which the stars appear to revolve; each of the ends of the axis of the earth; each of the opposite ends of a magnet, electric cell, *etc.* **-po'lar** *a.* **-polar'ity** *n.* **-po'larize** *v.t.* give magnetic polarity to; affect light so that its vibrations are kept to one plane. **-polariza'tion** *n.* **-pole'-star** *n.* north star; guide, lodestar. [G. *polos*, pivot]

pole'cat *n.* small animal of the weasel family; skunk. [F. *poule*, hen (fr. its preying on *poultry*)]

polem'ic *a.* controversial. *-n. pl.* war of words; art of controversy; branch of theology dealing with differences in doctrines. **-polem'ical** *a.* [G. *polemos*, war]

police' *n.* public order; civil force which maintains public order. *-v.t.* keep in order. **-police'man** *n.* [G. *polis*, city]

pol'icy *n.* a contract of insurance. [It. *polizza*, invoice]

pol'icy *n.* political wisdom; course of action adopted, *esp.* in state affairs; prudent procedure. [OF. *policie* fr. G. *politeia*, government]

po'liomyelitis, po'lio *n.* inflammation of

the spinal cord; infantile paralysis. [G. *polios*, gray, *myelos*, marrow]

pol'ish *v.t.* make smooth and glossy; refine. -*n.* act of polishing; gloss; refinement of manners; substance used in polishing. [L. *polire*, make to shine]

polite' *a.* refined; having refined manners, courteous. -**polite'ly** *adv.* -**polite'ness** *n.* [L. *politus*]

pol'itic (pol'-it-ic) *a.* wise, shrewd, expedient, cunning. -*n.* in *pl.* art of government; political affairs or life. -**polit'ical** *a.* of the state or its affairs. -**politi'cian** *n.* one engaged in politics. [fr. G. *polites*, a citizen]

pol'itics *n.* science and art of civil government; political principles or opinions; political methods. -**pol'itic** *a.* prudent; crafty, scheming. -**political** *a.* [*v.s.*]

pol'ka *n.* quick, round dance; music for it. -*v.i.* dance a polka. [Polish]

poll *n.* head or top of the head, counting of voters; voting; number of votes recorded. -*v.t.* cut off the top of; take the votes of, receive (votes). *v.i.* to vote. -**poll'-tax** *n.* tax on each head, or person. [of Teut. orig.]

poll'en *n.* fertilizing dust of a flower. -**pollina'tion** *n.* transferring of pollen to stigma by insects, *etc.* [L. = fine dust]

pollute *v.t.* make foul: desecrate. -**pollu'tion** *n.* [L. *polluere, pollut-*]

po'lo *n.* game like hockey played by men on ponies, four-a-side. -**wa'ter po'lo,** ballgame played in water. [Balti = ball]

polonaise' *n.* Polish dance; music for it; gown looped up over hooped petticoat, [F. = Polish]

poltergeist *n.* (*psych. research*) spirit, ghost, throwing things about and causing unexplained noises. [Ger.]

poly- *prefix.* many. [G. *polus,* many] -**polyan'dry** *n.* polygamy in which one woman has more than one husband. -**pol'ychrome** *a.* many colors. -*n.* work of art in many colors. -**polychromat'ic** *a.* -**polyeth'ylene** *n.* tough thermoplastic material. -**polyg'amy** *n.* custom of being married to several persons at a time. -**polyg'amist** *n.* -**pol'yglot** *a.* speaking, writing, or written in several languages. -**pol'ygon** *n.* figure with many angles or sides. -**polyg'onal** *a.* -**polygynyn.** polygamy in which one man has more than one wife. -**polyhe'dron** *n.* solid figure contained by many faces. -**pol'ytheism** *n.* belief in many gods. -**pol'ytheist** *n.* -**polytheist'ic** *a.*

pom'egranate *n.* large fruit with thick rind containing many seeds in a red pulp;

the tree. [OF. *pome grenade*]

pomp *n.* splendid display or ceremony. -**pomp'ous** *a.* self-important; puffed up; of language, inflated. -**pompos'ity** *n.* [G. *pompe,* solemn procession]

pon'cho *n.* blanket worn orig. by S. American Indians. [Sp.]

pond *n.* small body of still water, *esp.* for watering cattle, *etc.* [same as *pound*]

pon'der *v.t.* and *i.* meditate, think over; -**pond'erable** *a.* capable of being weighed. -**pond'erous** *a.* heavy, unwieldy. [L. *pondus, ponder-,* weight]

pon'tiff *n.* Pope; high priest. **pontifical** *a.* pompous and dogmatic. -**pontif'icate** *v.i.* . [L. *pontifex,* high priest]

pontoon' flat bottomed boat or metal drum for use in supporting a temporary bridge. [L. *ponto,* punt]

po'ny *n.* horse of a small breed. [Gael. *poniadh*]

poo'dle *n.* variety of pet dog with long curly hair often clipped fancifully. [Ger. *pudel,* orig. water dog]

pool *n.* small body of still water (*esp.* of natural formation); deep place in a river. [OE. *pol*]

pool *n.* collective stakes in various games; variety of billiards; combination of capitalists to fix prices and divide business; common fund. -*v.t.* throw into a common fund. [F. *poule,* hen]

poor *a.* having little money; unproductive, inadequate, insignificant, unfortunate. -**poor'ly** *a.* not in good health. [L. *pauper*]

pop *n.* abrupt small explosive sound. *v.i.* make such sound; go or come unexpectedly or suddenly. -*v.t.* put or place suddenly. **pop-corn** *n.* Indian corn puffed up through exposure to heat. [imit. orig.]

pop *n.* music of general appeal, *esp.* to young people. -*a.* popular. [fr. *popular*]

Pope *n.* bishop of Rome as head of the Roman Catholic Church. [G. *pappas,* father]

pop'lar *n.* tree noted for slender tallness and tremulous leaves. [L. *populus*]

pop'lin *n.* corded fabric of silk and worsted. [It. *papalina (fem.),* papal, because made at Avignon (seat of the Pope, 1309-1408)]

popp'y *n.* bright flowered plant which yields opium. [OE. *popig,* L. *papaver*]

pop'ulace *n.* common people. -**pop'ular** *a.* of or by the people; finding general favor. -**popular'ity** *n.* being generally liked. -**pop'ularize** *v.t.* make popular. -**populate** *v.t.* fill with inhabitants. -**population** *n.* inhabitants; the number of them. -**pop'ulous** a. thickly populated. [L. *populus*]

por'celain n. fine earthenware, china. [F. *porcelaine*]

porch n. covered approach to the entrance of a building; a veranda. [F. *porche*, fr. L. *porticos*, colonnade]

por'cupine n. rodent animal covered with long pointed quills. [OF. *porc esp in*, "Spiny pig"]

pore n. minute opening, *esp.* in the skin. -**por'ous** a. full of pores; allowing a liquid to soak through. -**poros'ity, porousness** n. [G. *poros*]

pore v.i. fix the eyes or mind upon; study attentively. [ME. *pouren*]

pork n. pig's flesh as food. -**pork'er** n. pig raised for food. -**pork'y** a. fleshy; fat. [L. *porcus*, pig]

pornog'raphy n. indecent art, literature. [G. *porne*, whore, *graphein*, write, draw]

por'poise (-pus) n. blunt-nosed sea animal about five feet long. [OF. *porpeis*, pig-fish]

porridge n. soft food of oatmeal or other meal boiled in water. [var. of *pottage*]

port n. harbor or haven; town with a harbor. [L. *portus*]

port n. city gate; opening in the side of a ship. [L. *porta*, a gate]

port n. strong red wine. [*Oporto*]

port n. bearing. -v.t. carry (a rifle) slanting upwards in front of the body. -**port'able** a. easily carried. -**port'age** n. carrying or transporting. -**port'ly** a. large and dignified in appearance. [L. *portare*, carry]

port'al n. large door or gate. [OF.]

portend' v.t. foretell; be an omen of. **port'ent** n. omen, marvel. -**portent'ous** a. [L. *portendere*, foretell]

port'er n. door keeper. [L. *porta*, gate]

port'er n. person employed to carry burdens, *esp.* at airports *etc.*; railway sleeping-car attendant; a dark beer. [L. *portare*, carry]

portfolio n. case for papers, *etc.*; office of a minister of state. [corrupt. of It. *portafogli*, carry leaves]

port'hole n. small opening in the side or superstructure of a ship for light and air. [L. *porta*, a gate]

por'tion n. part or share; destiny; lot; dowry. -v.t. divide into shares; give dowry to. -**por'tionless** a. [L. *portio*]

portray' v.t. make a picture of, describe. -**port'rait** n. likeness. [L. *protrahere*, draw forth]

pose v.t. lay down; place in an attitude. -v.i. assume an attitude, give oneself out as. -n. attitude, *esp.* one assumed for effect. -

poseur' (-ur) n. one who poses for effect. [F. *poser*]

posh a. (*sl.*) stylish, smart. -v.t. spruce up. [perh. port *out*, starboard *home*, the fashionable sides of the ship to travel to India during the British Raj]

posi'tion n. way a thing is placed; situation, attitude; state of affairs; office for employment; strategic point. [L. *ponere, posit-*, lay down]

pos'itive a. firmly laid down; definite; absolute, unquestionable; confident; over-confident; not negative; greater than zero. -n. positive degree; in photography, print in which the lights and shadows are not reversed. [L. *positivus, posit-*]

poss'e n. a force, body (of police or others with legal authority). [L. *posse*, be able]

possess' (-zes') v.t. own; of an evil spirit, have the mastery of. -**posses'sion** n. -**possess'ive** a. of or indicating possession n. possessive case in grammar. -**possessor** n. [L. *possidere, possess-*]

poss'ible a. that can or may be, exist, happen, be done. -**possibil'ity** n. - **poss'ibly** adv. [L. *possibilis*]

post n. upright pole of timber or metal fixed firmly, usually as a support for something. -v.t. display; stick up (on a post, notice board, *etc.*). -**post'er** n. placard; advertising bill. [L. *postis*]

post (pōst) n. official carrying of letters or parcels; collection or delivery of these; point, station or place of duty; place where a soldier is stationed; place held by a body of troops, fort; office or situation. -v.t. put into the official box for carriage by post; transfer (entries) to a ledger; supply with latest information; station (soldiers, *etc.*) in a particular spot. v.i. travel with post horses. -adv. in haste. -**post'age** n. charge for carrying a letter, *etc.* -**post'al** a. - **post'card** n. card with message sent by post. -**post'man** n. man who collects or delivers the post. **post'mark** n. official mark with the name of the office, *etc.*, stamped on letters. -**post'-master** n. official in charge of a post office. **post-office** n. office which receives and transmits mail; government department in charge of conveying of mail. -**postproduction** n. editing of a film or recording that takes place after the artists' taping is complete. [L. *ponere, posit-*, place]

post-, later, after. [L. *post*, after]. - **postdate'** v.t. give a date later than the actual date. -**post-grad'uate** a. carried on after graduation. -**poste'rior** (post-) a. later; hinder. -**poster'ity** n. descendants; later generations. -**post'ern** n. back or private door. -post'humous a. born after the father's death; published after the author's death; occurring, conferred, etc. , after death. -postmortem a. taking place after death. -n. medical examination of a dead body. -postpone' v.t. put off to a later time. -postpone'ment n. -post'script n. addition to a letter or book.

postmerid'ian a. of the afternoon. -n. afternoon, cont. p. m. [L. post, after]

post o'bit a. taking effect after death. -n. bond given by borrower securing repayment on death of one from whom he has expectations. [L. post, after, obitus, death]

postulate v.t. claim, demand, take for granted. -n. something taken for granted. [L. postulare, demand]

pos'ture n. attitude, position. [L. positura, fr. ponere, place]

po'sy n. bunch of flowers; verse accompanying it. [shortened fr. poesy]

pot n. round vessel; cooking vessel. -v.t. put into or preserve in a pot. [OE. pott]

po'table a. drinkable. [L. potare, drink]

pot'ash n. alkali used in soap, etc.; crude potassium carbonate. -potass'ium n. white metal. [orig. pot ashes]

pota'to n. plant with tubers grown for food. -(pl.) potatoes. -pota'to-bug n. Colorado beetle. [Sp. patata]

po'tent a. powerful. -po'tency n. -po'tentate a. ruler. -poten'tial a. latent, may or might but does not now exist or act. -n. amount of potential energy or work. [L. potens, pres. p. of posse, be able]

po'tion n. a draught; dose of medicine or poison. [L. potio-potare, drink]

potpourri' n. mixture of rose petals, spices, etc.; musical or literary medley. [F.]

pott'er n. maker of earthenware vessels. -pott'ery n. place where earthenware is made; earthenware; art of making it. [pot]

pouch n. small bag. -v.t. put into one. [F. poche, pocket]

pound n. weight, 12 oz. troy, 16 ozs. avoirdupois; unit of money, 100 pence. -pound'age n. payment or commission of so much per pound (money); charge of so much per pound (weight). [OE. pund, L. pondus, weight]

pound v.t. crush to pieces or powder; thump; cannonade. [OE. punian]

pour (pawr) v.i. come out in a stream, crowd, etc. -v.t. give out thus; cause to run out. [orig. unknown]

pout v.i. thrust out the lips. -v.t. thrust out (the lips). -n. act of pouting. -pout'er n. pigeon with the power of inflating its crop. [orig. uncertain]

pov'erty n. the condition of being poor; poorness, lack. [F. pauvreté]

pow'der n. solid matter in fine dry particles; medicine in this form; gunpowder. -v.t. apply powder to, reduce to powder. -pow'dery a. [F. poudre]

pow'er n. ability to do or act; authority; person or thing having authority. -pow'erful a. -pow'erless a. -pow'erhouse; power station n. building where electrical power is generated. [OF. poeir]

prac'tice v.t. do habitually; put into action; work at; exercise oneself in. -v.i. exercise oneself, exercise a profession. -n. habitual doing; action as distinguished from theory; habit; exercise in an art or profession. -prac'tical a. relating to action or real existence; given to action rather than theory; that is (something) in effect though not in name. -prac'tically adv. virtually, almost; in actuality, rather than in theory. -practi'tioner n. one engaged in a profession. [G. praktikos, concerned with action]

pragmat'ic a. of the affairs of a state; concerned with practical consequences; officious, dogmatic. [G. pragmatikos, skilled in business]

prair'ie n. large tract of grass-land without trees. [F. = meadow]

praise v.t. express approval or admiration of, glorify. -n. commendation; fact or state of being praised. -praise'worthy a. [OF. preisier]

prance v.i. walk with bounds; strut about. -n. a prancing. [orig. uncertain]

prank n. frolicsome trick or escapade. [orig. uncertain]

prate v.i. talk idly, chatter; give away a secret. -n. chatter. -prat'tle v.i. and v.t. utter childishly. -n. childish chatter. -pratt'ler n. [Du. praten]

prawn n. edible sea crustacean like a shrimp. [orig. unknown]

pray v.t. ask earnestly. -v.i. offer prayers, especially to God. -pray'er n. earnest entreaty; action or practice of praying to God. -pray'erful a. [OF. preier fr. L. precari]

pre- prefix, makes compounds with the meaning of before, or beforehand; e.g. predeter'mine v.t. determine beforehand. [L. prae-, pre-, before]

preach v.i. deliver a sermon. -v.t. set forth in religious discourse. -preach'er n. [F. precher, fr. L. praedicare, fr. dicare, to proclaim]

pream'ble n. introductory part; preface. [L. proeambulus, going before]

precar'ious *a.* insecure, unstable, perilous. [L. *precarius*, uncertainly possessed]

precau'tion *n.* preventive measure; cautious foresight. **-precautionary** *a.*

precede' *v.t.* go or come before in rank, order, time, *etc.* *-v.i.* go or come before. **-pre'cedence** *n.* higher or more honorable place; right to this. **-prec'edent** (pres'-) *n.* previous case or occurrence taken as a rule. [L. *praecedere*, go before]

pre'cept *n.* rule for conduct; maxim. **-precept'or** *n.* teacher. [L. *praecipere*, *praecept*-, take before, order]

pre'cinct *n.* ground attached to a sacred or official building; limit or boundary; division of a city as relates to policing, voting *etc.* [Med. L. *praecinctum*, enclosure]

prec'ious (presh'us) *a.* of great value, highly valued; affected, overrefined. **prec'iously** *adv.* **-prec'iousness** *n.* **precios'ity** *n.* over-refinement in art or literature. [L. *pretiosus*, valuable]

precip'itate *v.t.* throw headlong; hasten the happening of; in chemistry, cause to be deposited in solid form from a solution. *-a.* over-sudden, rash. *-n.* substance chemically precipitated. [L. *praecipitare*]

precise' *a.* exact, strictly; worded; particular; careful in observance. [L. *praecisus*, cut off in front]

preclude' *v.t.* prevent. [L. *praecludere*]

precocious *a.* developed too soon, *esp.* mentally. **-preco'city** (-os-) *n.* [L. *praecox*, *precoc*, early ripe]

precogni'tion *n.* knowledge beforehand. [pre-, and L. *cognoscere*, *cognit*-, know]

precursor *n.* forerunner. [L.]

pred'atory *a.* relating to plunder; given to plundering; rapacious. **-preda'cious** *a.* of animals, living by capturing prey. [L. *praeda*, booty]

pred'ecessor *n.* one who precedes another in an office, *etc.* [Late L. *praedecessor*, fr. *decessor*, one who withdraws]

predes'tine *v.t.* destine, ordain beforehand. **-predes'tinate** *v.t.* foreordain by unchangeable purpose. **-predes'tined** *a.* **-predestina'tion** *n.* doctrine that man's fate is unalterably fixed. [pre-, and L. *destinare*, make fast]

pred'icate *v.t.* affirm or assert. *-n.* that which is predicated; in grammar, a statement made about a subject. [L. *praedicare*, proclaim]

predict' *v.t.* foretell. **-predic'tion** *n.* [L. *praedicere*, *predict*-, say before]

predom'inate *v.i.* be the main or control-

ling element. **-predom'inance** *n.* **predom'inant** *a.* [*dominate*]

pre-em'inent *a.* excelling all others. **-pre-em'inently** *adv.* outstandingly. **pre'-em'inence** *n.* [*eminent*]

prefab'ricate *v.t.*. make beforehand parts (of a house *etc.*) to be assembled at a chosen site. **-prefab** *n.* (*sl.*) prefabricated house. [L. *fabricari*, fabricate, construct]

pref'ace *n.* introduction to a book, *etc.* *-v.t.* introduce. **-prefatory** *a.* [L. *prae fatio*, speaking beforehand]

pre'fect *n.* person put in authority; Roman official; head of a department; schoolboy with responsibility for maintaining discipline. [L. *praefectus*]

prefer *v.t.* like better; promote. **preferable** *a.* **-pref'erably** *adv.* **- preference** *n.* **- preferen'tial** *a.* giving or receiving a preference. [L. *praeferre*, bear before]

pre'fix *n.* preposition or particle put at the beginning of a word or title. **-prefix'** *v.t.* put as introduction; put before a word to make a compound. [*fix*]

preg'nant *a.* with child; full of meaning. **-preg'nancy** *n.* [L. *praegnans*]

prehensile *a.* capable of grasping. [L. *prehendere*, *prehens*-, seize]

prejudice (is) *n.* judgment or bias decided beforehand; harm likely to happen to a person or his rights as a result of others' action or judgment; prepossession (usually unfavorable). *-v.t.* influence unfairly; injure. **-prejudi'cial** *a.* harmful; detrimental. [L. *praejudicium*]

prelim'inary *a.* preparatory, introductory. *-n.* introductory or preparatory statement or action. [F. *préliminaire*, fr. L. *limen*, threshold]

prel'ude *n.* performance, event, *etc.*, serving as an introduction; in music, introductory movement. *-v.i.* and *t.* serve as prelude. [L. *ludere*, play]

premature *a.* happening or done before the proper time. [*mature*]

premeditate *v.t.* think out beforehand. [*meditate*]

premenstrual *a.* of or occurring before a menstrual period. **-pre'menstrual ten'sion** or **syn'drome** *n.* any of various symptoms, including *esp.* nervous tension, that may be experienced as a result of hormonal changes in the days before a menstrual period starts. [pre-, and L. *menstruus*, monthly]

prem'ier *a.* chief, foremost. *-n.* prime minister. [F. = first]

prem'ise (prem'is) *n.* in logic, a proposition from which an inference is drawn. *-pl.*

in law, beginning of a deed; house or buildings with its belongings. -**premise'** (-iz) *v.t.* state by way of introduction. -prem'iss *n.* (logical) premise. [L. *praemittere, prerni,* send in front]

pre'mium *n.* reward; sum paid for insurance; bonus; excess over nominal value. [L. *praemium,* booty, reward]

preocc'upy (-pi) *v.t.* occupy to the exclusion of other things. -**preoccupa'tion** *n.* mental concentration with the appearance of absentmindedness. [*occupy*]

prep *n.* (schoolboy *sl.*) preparation (of lessons). -**prep school,** *contr.* for preparatory school.

prepare' *v.t.* make ready; make. -*v.i.* get ready. -**prepara'tion** *n.* -**prepar'atory** *a.* [L. *praeparare,* make ready before]

preposi'tion *n.* part of speech; a word marking the relation between two other words. -**preposi'tional** *a.* [L. *praeponere, praeposit-,* put before]

prepos'terous *a.* utterly absurd. [L. *praeposterus,* lit. 'before behind']

prep'py *a.* characteristic of or denoting a fashion style of neat, understated, and often expensive clothes, suggesting that the wearer is well off, upper class, and conservative. -*n.* a person exhibiting such style. [fr. preparatory school]

prerog'ative *n.* peculiar power or right, *esp.* as vested in a sovereign. [L. *praerogative,* right to vote first]

pre'science (pre'-shi-ens) *n.* foreknowledge. -**pres'cient** (pre'-shi-ent) *a.* [L. *pre scientia,* knowledge]

prescribe' *v.t.* and *i.* order, appoint; order the use of (a medicine). -prescription *n.* prescribing; thing prescribed; written statement of it; in law, uninterrupted use as the basis of a right or title; such title. -**prescrip'tive** *a.* [L. *praescribere, praescript-,* write before]

pres'ent *a.* that is here, now existing or happening. -*n.* -**pres'ently** *adv.* soon. -**pres'ence** *n.* a being present; personal appearance. [L. *praesens, pres. p. of praeesse,* be before]

present' *v.t.* introduce formally; show; point or aim; give, offer. -**pres'ent** *n.* gift. -**present'able** *a.* fit to be seen. -**presenta'tion** *n.* -**present'ment** *n.* [L. *praesentare,* place before]

preserve' (-z-) *v.t.* keep from harm or injury or decay. -*n.* jam; place where game is kept for shooting. -**preserva'tion** *n.* -**preserv'ative** *a.* and *n.* [L. *servare,* protect]

preside' (-z-) *v.i.* be chairman; superin-

tend. -pres'ident *n.* head of a society, company, republic. -**pres'idency** *n.* -**presiden'tial** *a.* [L. *praesidere,* fr. *sedere,* sit]

press *v.t.* subject to push or squeeze; urge steadily or earnestly. -*v.i.* bring weight to bear. -*n.* crowd; machine for pressing, *esp.* a printing machine; printing house; its work or art; newspapers collectively; large cupboard. -**press'ing** *a.* urgent. -**pres'sure** *n.* and *v.t.* -**press'urize** *v.t.* apply pressure to; maintain normal atmospheric pressure inside the cabin during high-altitude flying, *etc.* -**press'urized** *a.* [L. *pressare,* frequent, of *premere*]

press *v.t.* force to serve in the navy or army; take for royal or public use. [earlier *prest* fr. L. *praestare,* furnish]

prestidig'itator (-j-) *n.* magician, conjurer. [F. *prestidigitateur*]

prestige' *n.* reputation, or influence depending on it. [F. = magic]

presume' (-z-) *v.t.* take for granted. -*v.i.* take liberties. -**presu'mable** *a.* -**presumably** *adv.* -**presump'tion** *n.* -**presump'tuous** *a.* forward, taking liberties. [L. *praesumere, praesumpt-,* take before]

pretend' *v.t.* feign, make believe. -*v.i.* lay claim, feign. -**pretense'** *n.* -**pretend'er** *n.* -**preten'tion** *n.* -**preten'tious** *a.* making claim to special (and *usu.* unjustified) merit or importance. [L. *praetendere,* hold before, put forward]

prett'y (prit'-i) *a.* having beauty that is attractive rather than imposing; charming, *etc.* *adv.* fairly, moderately. -**prett'ily** *adv.* [OE. *praettig,* tricky]

prevail' *v.i.* gain the mastery; be in fashion or generally established. [L. *praevalere-valere,* be powerful]

prevent' *v.t.* stop from happening. [L. *praevenire, praevent-,* come before]

pre'vious *a.* preceding; happening before. -**pre'viously** *adv.* [L. *praevius,* fr. *via,* way]

prey *n.* that is hunted and killed by carnivorous animals; victim. -*v.i.* prey upon; treat as prey, afflict. [OF. *preie,* fr. L. *praeda,* booty]

priapic *a.* overly concerned with masculinity or virility. [Greek god, *Priapus,* god of procreation]

price *n.* that for which a thing is bought or sold. -*v.t.* fix or ask a price of. -**price'less** *a.* invaluable. [F. *prix,* fr. L. *pretium,* reward, value]

prick *n.* slight hole made by pricking; a pricking or being pricked. -*v.t.* pierce slightly with a sharp point; mark by a prick;

erect (the ears). [OE. *prica,* point]

pride *n.* too high an opinion of oneself, haughtiness; feeling of elation or great satisfaction; something causing this. *-v. refl.* take pride. [OE. *pryto*]

pride *n.* company (of lions). [*pride*]

priest *n.* official minister of a religion; clergyman. [OE. *preost*]

prig *n.* self-righteous person who professes superior culture, morality, *etc.* - **prigg'ish** *a.* [orig. uncertain]

prim *a.* very restrained, formally prudish. [orig. uncertain]

pri'mal *a.* of the earliest age; first, original. -**pri'mary** *a.* chief, of the first stage, decision, *etc.* [L. *primus,* first]

pri'mates *n. pl.* first order of mammals, including man and the higher apes. [L. *primus,* first]

prime *a.* first in time, quality, *etc.* **Prime Min'ister,** the leader of a government. -*n.* office for the first canonical hour of the day; first or best part of anything. [L. *primus,* first]

prime *v.t.* fill up, *e.g.,* with information; prepare (a gun, explosive charge, *etc.*), for being let off by laying a trail of powder; prepare canvas for paint with preliminary coating of oil, *etc.* [orig. uncertain]

prim'er *n.* elementary school book. [*prime*]

prime'val *a.* of the earliest age of the world. [L. *primaevus*]

primitive *a.* of an early, undeveloped kind. [L. *primitivus*]

prim'ordial *a.* existing at or from the beginning. [L. *primus,* first, *ordo,* order]

prince *n.* ruler or chief; son of a king or queen. -**prin'cess** *fem.* -**prince'ly** *a.* - **prince'ling** *n.* young prince; petty ruler. [L. *princess, princip-,* first, chief]

prin'cipal *a.* chief in importance. -*n.* head of certain institutes, *esp.* schools or colleges, person for whom another is agent or second; sum of money lent and yielding interest; chief actor. -**principal'ity** *n.* territory or dignity of a prince. [L. *principalis*]

prin'ciple *n.* fundamental truth or element; moral rule or settled reason of action; uprightness. [L. *principium*]

print *v.t.* impress; reproduce (words, pictures, *etc.*), by pressing inked types on blocks to paper, *etc.* , produce in this way; stamp (a fabric) with a colored design. -*n.* impression mark left on a surface by something that has pressed against it; printed cotton fabric, printed lettering; photograph; written imitation of printed type. -**print'er** *n.* one engaged in printing. [OF. *preinte* fr. L. *premere,* press]

pri'or *a.* earlier. -*adv.* prior to, before. -*n.* chief of a religious house or order. - **pri'oress** *fem.* -**prior'ity** *n.* precedence in time or importance. -**prior'itze** *v.t.* arrange (items to be attended to) in order of their relative importance; give priority to or establish as a priority. -**pri'ory** *n.* monastery or nunnery under a prior or prioress. [L. = superior, former]

prism *n.* solid whose two ends are similar, equal, of parallel rectilinear figures and whose sides are parallelograms; transparent body of this form usually with triangular ends by which light can be reflected [G. *prisma,* piece sawn off]

pris'on (-z-) *n.* jail. -**pris'oner** *n.* one kept in prison; one captured in war. [F. fr. *prehendere, prehens-,* seize]

pri'vate *a.* not public, reserved for or belonging to or concerning an individual only; of a soldier, not holding any rank. -*n.* private soldier. -**pri'vacy** *n.* **privately** *adv.* [L. *privatus,* set apart]

privilege *n.* right or advantage belonging to a person or class; an advantage or favor that only a few obtain. -*v.t.* give an advantage to. [L. *privilegium,* private law, fr. *lex,* law]

priv'y *a.* private, confidential. -*n.* latrine. -**Privy Council,** a body of persons appointed by the sovereign, *esp.* in recognition of great public services. -**priv'ily** *adv.* [F. *priue,* fr. L. *privatus,* private]

prize *n.* reward for success in competition; thing striven for; thing that is won, *e.g.,* in a lottery, *etc.* -**prize'-fight** *n.* boxing match with money prize. -**prize'-money** *n.* money from the sale of prizes. -**prize'-ring** *n.* arena in which prize fight takes place. -*v.t.* value highly. [OF. *pris,* fr. L. *pretium*]

prize *n.* ship or property captured in naval warfare. [F. *prise,* capture]

prob'able *a.* likely. [L. *probabilis-probare,* prove]

pro'bate *n.* a proving of a will; certificate of this. [L. *probare, probat-,* prove]

probation *n.* testing of a candidate before admission to full membership of some body; system of releasing offenders, *esp.* juvenile ones, or first offenders, so that their punishment may be canceled by a period of good behavior. [F.]

probe *n.* blunt rod for examining a wound. -*v.t.* explore with a probe; examine into. [L. *probare,* prove]

pro'bity *n.* honesty, uprightness. [L. *probitas-probus,* good]

prob'lems *n.* question or difficulty set for or needing a solution. [G. *problema*, thing thrown before]

probos'cis (-sis) *n.* trunk or long snout, *e.g.*, of an elephant. [G. *proboskis*, 'food instrument']

proceed' *v.i.* go forward; be carried on; go to law. **-proce'dure** *n.* act or manner of proceeding; method of conducting business proceedings; conduct. **-pro'ceeds** *n.pl.* price or profit. **-pro'cess** *n.* state of going on, series of actions or changes; method of operation; action of law; outgrowth. **-proces'sion** *n.* body of persons going along in a fixed or formal order. **processional** *a.* [L. *procedere, process-*, to go forward]

proclaim' *v.t.* announce, make public. **proclama'tion** *n.* [L. *proclamare*]

procrastinate *v.i.* put off, delay. [L. *procrastinate*, fr. *cras*, to-morrow]

procreate *v.t.* beget; bring into being. **-procrea'tion** *n.* [L. *procreare*]

procure' *v.t.* obtain; bring about. **procu'rable** *a.* **-procura'tor** *n.* Roman official in a province; one who manages another's affairs. **-procura'tion** *n.* appointment or hority of a procurator. **procure'ment** *n.* act or an instance of procuring; act of buying. [L. *procurare*, bring about, get as agent]

prod *v.t.* poke with something pointed. **-***n.* a prodding. [orig. uncertain]

prod'igal *a.* wasteful. **-***n.* spendthrift. [L. *prodigere*, squander]

prod'igy (-ji) *n.* marvel; person with some marvellous gift. [L. *prodigium*]

produce' *v.t.* bring forward; bring into existence, make; stage, or prepare to stage (a play, *etc.*); extend in length. **-prod'uce** *n.* that which is yielded or made.**-produ'cer** *n.* one who grows or makes produce; one who produces plays. *etc.* **-produ'cer goods**, raw materials, *etc.* used in production. **-prod'uct** *n.* result of a process of manufacture; number resulting from a multiplication. **-produc'tion** *n.* producing; things produced. **-produc'tive** *a.* **-productiv'ity** *n.* [L. *producere, product-*, bring forth]

profane' *a.* not sacred; blasphemous, irreverent. **-***v.t.* pollute, desecrate. profanation *n.* **-profan'ity** *n.* profane talk or behavior. [L. *profanus*]

profess' *v.t.* assert; lay claim to; have as one's profession or business; teach as a professor. **-profess'edly** *adv.* avowedly. **profession** *n.* a professing, vow of religious faith, entering a religious order; calling or occupation, *esp.* learned or scientific or artistic. **-profes'sional** *a.* of a profession. **-***n.* paid player. **-profess'or** *n.* teacher of the highest rank in a university. **-professo'rial** *adv.* **- professorship** *n.* **-profess'orate** *n.*, professorship. **-professor'iate** *n.* body of professors of a university. [L. *profiteri, profess-*, own or acknowledge]

profi'cient (ish'-) *a.* skilled. **-***n.* one who is skilled. **-profi'ciency** *n.* [L. *proficere*, be useful]

pro'file (-fil) *n.* outline of anything as seen from the side. [It. *proffilo*]

profit *n.* benefit obtained; money gains. **-***v.t.* and *i.* benefit. **-profitable** *a.* yielding profit. **-profitless** *a.* [F. fr. L. *profectus*, progress, profit]

profound' *a.* deep; very learned. **- profun'dity** *n.* [L. *profundus*]

profuse' *a.* abundant, prodigal. **- profusion** *n.* [L. *profusus*, poured out]

pro'geny *n.* descendants. **-progenitor** *n.* ancestor. [L. *progenies*]

progno'sis *n.* forecast, *esp.* of the course of a disease from observation of its symptoms. **-prognost'icate** *v.t.* foretell. [G.]

pro'grams *n.* plan, detailed notes of intended proceedings; broadcast on radio or television; syllabus or curriculum; detailed instructions for computer. **-***v.t.* feed program into (*computer*); arrange detailed instructions for (*computer*) **pro'grammer** *n.* [G. *programma*, public written notice]

pro'gress *n.* onward movement; development; state journey. **-progress'** *v.i.* go forward [L. *progressus*]

prohibit *v.t.* forbid. **-prohibi'tion** *n.* forbidding by law of the sale of intoxicants. **-prohibi'tionist** *n.* **-prohib'itive** *a.* tending to forbid. **-prohib'itory** *a.* [L. *prohibere*, prohibit-]

proj'ect *n.* plan. **-project'** *v.t.* throw; plan; cause to appear on a distant background. **-***v.i.* stick out. **-project'ile** *a.* capable of being thrown. **-***n.* heavy missile, *esp.* shell from big gun. **-projec'tion** *n.* [L. *projectum*, thrown forward]

proletariat, proletariats (-tär-) *n.* lowest class of a community, common people. **-proletar'ian** *a.* [L. *proles*, offspring with which Roman proletarius served the state]

prolif'erate *v.i.* and *t.* reproduce by process of budding or cell division; increase in numbers in a similar way. **-prolif'eration** *n.* [L. *proles*, progeny, *ferre*, bear]

prolif'ic *a.* fruitful; producing much, [L. *proles*, offspring, *ferre*, bear]

prolong' *v.t.* lengthen out. **-prolonga'tion** *n.* [L. *longus*, long]

promenade' *n.* leisurely walk; lace made or used for this. *-v.i.* take a leisurely walk; go up and down. [F.]

prom'inent *a.* sticking out; distinguished; eminent. **-prom'inence** *n.* [L. *prominere*, jut out]

promis'cuous *a.* mixing without distinction, indiscriminate; having a number of sexual partners without formal attachment. **-promiscu'ity** *n.* [L. *propiscuus*, fr. *miscere*, mix]

prom'ise (-is) *n.* undertaking to do or not do something. *-v.t.* make a promise *-v.i.* make a promise. **-prom'issory** *a.* containing a promise. [L. *promittere, promiss-*, send forth]

promote' *v.t.* move up to a higher rank or sition; help forward; begin the process of forming or making. **-promo'ter** *n.* - **promo'tion** *n.* [L. *promovere, promot-*, move forward]

prompt *a.* done at once; ready. *-v.t.* and *i.* suggest, help out (an actor or speaker) by reading his next words or suggesting words. **-prompt'er** *n.* [L. *promptus*, pp. of *promere*, put forth]

prone *a.* lying face or front downward; inclined to. [OF. fr. L. *pronus*]

pro'noun *n.* word used to represent a noun. **-pronom'inal** *a.* [L. *pronomen*]

pronounce' *v.t.* utter formally; form with the organs of speech. *-v.i.* give an opinion or decision. **-pronounce'able** *a.* - **pronounced'** *a.* strongly marked, decided. **-pro-nounce'ment** *n.* declaration. - **pronun-cia'tion** *n.* way a word, *etc.* , is pronounced. [F. *prononcer*, L. *pronuntiare*, proclaim]

proof *n.* something which proves; test or demonstration; standard of strength of spirits; trial impression from type or an engraved plate. *-a.* of proved strength; giving impenetrable defense against. - **proof mark** *n.* mark on a proved, or tested, gun. **-proof'-reader** *n.* reader and corrector of printer's proofs. [F. *preuve. See* **prove**]

prop *n.* pole, beam, *etc.* , used as a support. *-v.t.* support, hold up. [Du.]

propaganda *n.* association or scheme for propagating a doctrine; attempt, or material used, to propagate a doctrine. - **propagand'ist** *n.* [L. *propagandus*]

propagate *v.t.* reproduce or breed; spread by sowing, breeding, example, instruction,

persuasion. *etc.* *-v.i.* breed or multiply. - **propaga'tion** *n.* [L. *propagare*, propagate, fr. *propago*, slip for transplanting]

propel' *v.t.* cause to move forward. - propell'er *n.* revolving shaft with blades for driving a ship or airplane. **propulsion** *n.* [L. *propellers, propuls-*]

prop'er *a.* own, peculiar, individual; of a noun, denoting an individual person or place; fit, suitable; strict; conforming to etiquette, decorous. **-prop'erly** *adv.* [L. *proprius*, own]

prop'erty *n.* owning; being owned; that is owned; quality or attribute belonging to something; article used on the stage in a play, *etc.* [F. *propriété*]

proph'et *n.* inspired teacher or revealer of the Divine Will; one who foretells future events. **-proph'etess** *fem.* **-proph'ecy** (-si) *n.* prediction or prophetic utterance. - **proph'esy** (-si) *v.i.* utter predictions. *-v.t.* foretell. **-prophet'ic** *a.* **-prophet'ically** *adv.* [G. *prophetes*, fore-speaker]

prophylactic (pro-) *a.* done or used to ward off disease. *-n.* prophylactic medicine or measure. [G. *prophylaktikos*, guarding, before]

proportion *n.* share; relation; comparison; relative size or number; due relation between connected things or parts. - *v.t.* arrange proportions of. [L. *proportio-portio*, share]

propose' *v.t.* put forward for consideration; present (someone) for office, membership *etc.*; propose a toast to be drunk. *-v.i.* offer marriage. **-propo'sal** *n.* - **propo'ser** *n.* [L. *proporere, proposit-*]

proposition *n.* statement or assertion; suggestion of terms. [L. *propositio*]

proprietor *n.* owner. [F. *propriété*]

propriety *n.* fitness; properness; correct conduct. [L. *proprietarius*, fr. *proprietas*, property]

proscribe' *v.t.* outlaw, condemn. - **proscrip'tion** *n.* [L. *proscribere*]

prose *n.* speech or writing not verse. *-v.t.* talk or write prosily. **-prosa'ic** *a.* commonplace. **-pro'sy** *a.* tedious, dull. - pro'sily *adv.* **-pro'siness** *n.* [L. *prosus*, straightforward]

prosecute *v.t.* carry on, bring legal proceedings against. [L. *prosequi*, fr. *sequi, secut-*, to follow]

pros'pect *n.* view; mental view; that is to be expected. *-v.t.* and *i.* explore, *esp.* for gold. **-prospect'ive** *a.* future. - **prospect'ively** *adv.* **-prospect'or** *n.* - **prospect'us** *n.* circular describing a company, school, *etc.* [L. *prospicere*, prospect-, look forward]

pros'per *v.i.* do well. -*v.t.* cause to do well. -**prosper'ity** *n.* good fortune, well-being. -**pros'perous** *a.* flourishing; rich. -**pros'perously** *adv.* [L.]

prostitute *n.* woman who hires herself for sexual intercourse. -*v.t.* make a prostitute of; sell basely, put to an infamous use. -**prostitu'tion** *n.* [L. *prostituere, prostitut-*, offer for sale]

prostrate *a.* lying full length; overcome; exhausted. -*v.t.* throw down; overthrow; exhaust; lay flat; bow (oneself) to the ground. -**prostra'tion** *n.* [L. *pro*, forward, *sternere, strat-*, strew]

protagonist *n.* leading actor in a play; leading figure in a cause, debate, *etc.* [G. *protos*, first, *agonistes*, combatant]

protect' *v.i.* defend or guard. -**protec'tion** *n.* -**protect'ive** *a.* -**protec'tionist** *n.* one who advocates protecting industries by taxing competing imports. -**protector** *n.* one who protects; regent. -**protect'orate** *n.* office or period of a protector of a state; relation of a state to a territory that it protects and controls; such territory. [L. *protegere, protect-*, cover in front]

prot'égé (-āzha-) *n.* -**pro'tégée** *fem.* person who is under the care and protection of another. (F.]

pro'tein *n.* kinds of organic compound, which form the most essential part of the food of living creatures. **protein'ic** *a.* [G. *protos*, first]

protest' *v.i.* assert formally; make a declaration against. -**pro'test** *n.* declaration of objection. -**Prot'estant** *a.* belonging to any branch of the Western Church outside the Roman communion. -*n.* member of such church. -**Prot'estantism** *n.* -**protesta'tion** *n.* [L. *protestari*, testify]

pro'tocol *n.* draft of terms signed by the parties as the basis of a formal treaty; rules of diplomatic etiquette. [G. *protokollon*, first leaf]

pro'ton *n.* electrically positive nucleus containing same quantity of electricity, but greater mass, than the electron, [G. *proton*, first]

protoplasm *n.* physical basis of all living organisms, a colorless, formless substance resembling albumen. -**protoplas'mic** *a.* [G. *protos*, first, *plasma,* form]

prototype *n.* original type or model. [G. *protos*, first, and *type*]

protozo'a *n.* lowest class of animals. [G. *protos*, first, *zöon*, animal]

protract' *v.t.* lengthen; draw to scale. -**protrac'tion** *n.* -**protract'or** *n.* instrument for setting out angles on paper. [L. *protrahere, protract-*, draw forward]

protrude' *v.i.* and *t.* stick out. -**protru'sion** *n.* [L. *protudere*]

proud *a.* feeling or displaying pride, that is the cause of pride; stately. -**proud'ly** *adv.* [OE. *prud*]

prove *v.t.* demonstrate, test; establish the validity of (a will, *etc.*). -*v.i.* turn out (to be, *etc.*). [F. *prouver,* fr. L. *probare*]

prov'erb *n.* short pithy saying in common use, *esp.* one with a moral. **proverb'ial** *a.* [L. *proverbium*]

provide' *v.i.* make preparation. -*v.t.* supply or equip, get in what will be required. -**provi'ded** (that) *conj.* on condition that. -**prov'ident** *a.* thrifty; showing foresight. -**prov'idence** *n.* foresight, economy; kindly care of God or nature. -**provi'sional** *a.* temporary. -**provi'so** *n.* condition. [L. *providere, provis-*, foresee]

prov'ince *n.* division of a country; a sphere of action. -*pl.* any part of the country outside the capital. -**provin'cial** *n.* one belonging to a province. -*a.* narrow, lacking in polish. -**provin'cialism** *n.* [L. *provincia*]

provoke' *v.t.* bring about, irritate. [L. *provocare,* call forth]

prov'ost *n.* head of certain colleges, or administrative assistant to the president. [OF. fr. Late L. *propositus,* placed before]

prow *n.* bow of a ship. [F. *proue*]

prow'ess *n.* bravery, fighting capacity. [F. *prouesse,* gallantry]

prowl *v.i.* roam stealthily, *esp.* in search of prey, *etc.* [ME. *prollen*]

prox'y *n.* authorized agent or substitute; writing authorizing a substitute. [fr. *procuracy. See* **procure**]

prude *n.* woman who affects excessive propriety with regard to relations of the sexes. [F.]

pru'dent *a.* careful, discreet, exercising forethought. -**pru'dence** *n.* -**pruden'-tial** *a.* [L. *prudens, prudent-*, far-seeing]

prune *n.* dried plum. [F.]

prune *v.t.* cut out dead parts, excessive branches, *etc.* [OF. *prooignier*]

pru'rient *a.* given to or springing from lewd thoughts. -**pru'rience** *n.* [L. *pruriens, pr. p.* of *prurire,* itch]

pry *v.i.* look curiously; make furtive or inquisitive enquiries. [ME. *prien*]

psalm *n.* sacred song. -**psalm'ist** *n.* writer of psalms. [G. *psalmos,* twanging of strings]

pseudo- *prefix,* sham. -**pseu'donym** *n.* false name. [G. *pseudes,* false] psy'chic (si'kik) a. of the soul or mind; that appears to be outside the region of physical law. -psychi'atrist n. one who treats mental diseases. -psy'chical a. psychic. - psy'cho-anal'ysis n. theory that the mind can be divided into conscious and unconscious elements; medical practice based on this. -psy'choan'alyst n. -psychol'ogy n. study of the mind. -psycholo'gical a. - psychol'ogist n. -psychosomat'ic a. pert. to mind and body as one unit, of physical disease having emotion as origin. - psy'chother'apy n. treatment of disease by mental influence. [G. psyche, breath, soul]

ptero- (ter-) prefix. winged. (G. pteron, wing) -pterocar'pous a. having winged seeds. -pterodac'tyl n. prehistoric large flying reptile with bat-like wings.

pto'maine (t-) n. poisonous alkaloid found in putrefying animal or vegetable matter. [G. ptoma, dead body]

pu'berty n. sexual maturity. [L. pubertas]

pub'lic a. of or concerning the public as a whole; not private; open to general observation or knowledge. -n. community or its members. -publica'tion n. -pub'licist n. writer on public concerns. -publi'city n. being generally known; notoriety. - pub'licly adv. [L. publicus, fr. populus, people]

pub'lish v.t. make generally known; prepare and issue for sale (books, music, etc.). -pub'lisher n. [public]

puc'ker v.t. and i. gather into wrinkles. -n. wrinkle. [fr. poke, bag]

pud'dle n. small muddy pool; rough cement for lining ponds, etc. -v.t. line with puddle; produce wrought iron. [OE. pudd, ditch]

pu'erile a. childish. [L. puer, boy]

puer'peral a. of, caused by childbirth. - puerperium n. state of a woman during and immediately after childbirth. [L. puer, child, parere, bear]

puff n. short blast of breath of wind, etc.; its sound; piece of pastry; laudatory notice, piece of advertisement. -v.i. blow abruptly; breathe hard. -v.t. send out in a puff, blow up; advertise; smoke hard. -puff'y a. - puff'-add'er n. poisonous African snake. [imit. orig.]

pu'gilist n. boxer. L. pugil, boxer]

pugna'cious a. given to fighting. pugna'city n. (L. pugnax, pugnac-,]

pulchritude n. beauty. [L. pulchritude]

pull (pool) v.t. pluck or tug at; draw or haul; propel by rowing. -n. an act of pulling; force exerted by it; draught of liquor. [OE. pullian, snatch]

pull'ey (poo-) n. wheel with a groove in the rim for a cord, used to raise weights by a downward pull. [F. poulie]

pul'monary a. of, or affecting the lungs. [L. pulmo, lung]

pulp n. soft moist vegetable or animal matter. -v.t. reduce to pulp. [L. pulpa]

pul'pit (poo-) n. erection or platform for a preacher. (L. pulpitum, a stage]

pulse n. throbbing of the arteries, esp. in the wrist; vibration. -pulsate' v.i. throb, quiver. -pulsa'tion n. [L. pulsus]

pulverize v.t. reduce to powder. [L. pulvis, pulver-, powder]

pu'ma n. large American carnivorous animal of the cat family. [Peruv.]

pump n. appliance in which the piston and handle are used for raising water, or putting in or taking out air or liquid, etc. -v.t. raise, put in, take out, etc., with a pump. -v.i. work a pump. [orig. uncertain]

pump n. light shoe. [Du. pampoesje]

pun n. play on words. -v.i. make one. - pun'ster n. [orig. uncertain]

punch n. tool for perforating or stamping; blow with the fist; (sl.) energy, drive. -v.t. stamp or perforate with a punch; strike with the fist; drive (of cattle). [F. poincon, awl, fr. pungere, pierce]

punch n. drink made of spirit, or wine with water or milk, lemon, spice, etc. -punch-bowl n. [Hindu panch, five (ingredients)]

punc'tual a. in good time, not late. [L. punctus, point]

punctuate v.t. to put in punctuation marks. -punctua'tion n. putting in marks, e.g. commas, colons, etc., in writing to assist in making the sense clear. [L. punctus, point]

punc'ture n. an act of pricking; a hole made by pricking. -v.t. to prick a hole in. [L. punctura]

pun'dit n. one learned in Hindu philosophy; any learned person. [Hind. pandit]

pungent a. biting; irritant. [L. pungens, pungent-, fr. pungere, prick]

pun'ish v.t. cause to suffer for an offense, inflict a penalty on. -(sl.) treat roughly. - pun'ishable a. -pun'ishment n. - pu'nitive a. inflicting or intending to inflict punishment. [L. punire]

punk a. crumbling, decayed; worthless. - n. young, inexperienced person; petty gangster; style of rock music characterized by a savage rejection of convention; one who follows such a style. [orig. uncertain]

puny a. small and feeble. [OF. puisne, fr. L. post natus, younger] pu'pa n. pu'pae pl. chrysalis. [L. = doll]

pu'pil n. person being taught; opening in the middle of the eye. -pu'pillary a. [L. pupillus, child]

pupp'et n. figure of a human being often with jointed limbs controlled by wire, a marionette. [OF. poupette, doll]

pupp'y n. young dog; conceited young man. -pup n. puppy. [F. poupée, doll]

pur'chase v.t. buy. -n. buying; what is bought; leverage, grip, good position for applying force. [F. pourchasser, to obtain by pursuit]

pure a. unmixed, untainted; simple; spotless; faultless; innocent. -pure'ly adv. pu'rify v.t. and i. -purifica'tion n purifica'tory a. -pu'rism n. excessive insistence on correctness of language. - pu'rist n. -pu'rity n. state of being pure. [L. purus, clean, pure]

purge v.t. make clean, clear out. -n. aperient. -purg'atory n. place for spiritual purging; state of pain or distress. [L. purgare]

purl n. edging of gold or silver wire or of small loops; stitch that forms a rib in knitting. -v.t. ornament with purls. -v.i. knit in purl. [It. pirlare, twirl]

purloin v.t. steal. [OF. porloignier, remove, fr. loin, far]

pur'ple n. color between crimson and violet. a. of this color. -v.t. make purple. [G. Porphyra, shell-fish that gave Tyrian purple]

purport' v.t. mean; be intended to seem. -pur'port n. meaning, apparent meaning. [OF. porporter, embody]

pur'pose (-pos) n. intention, design, aim. -v.t. intend. -pur'posely adv. [OF. porpos, fr. porposer, propose]

purse n. small bag for money. -v.t. contract in wrinkles. -v.i. become wrinkled and drawn in. -pur'ser n. officer who keeps accounts, etc. , on a ship. [G. pyrsa, hide, leather]

pursue' v.t. run after; aim at; engage in. -v.i. go in pursuit; continue. pursu'ance n. carrying out. -pursu'ant adv. accordingly. -pursu'er n. -pursuit' n. running after, attempt to catch; occupation. [F. poursuivre, fr. L. prosequi, follow]

pur'view n. scope or range. [AF. purveu est, it is provided (words used to introduce new enactment in a law)]

pus n. matter formed or discharged in a sore or inflammation. -pu'rulent a. forming pus. -pu'rulence n. [L.]

push (poosh) v.t. move or try to move away by pressure. -v.i. make one's way. -n. an act of pushing; persevering self assertion.

-push'ful a. given to pushing oneself. [F. pousser]

pusillanimous a. cowardly. pusillanim'ity n. [fr. L. pusillus, very small, and animus, spirit]

pus'tule n. small pimple containing pus. [L. pustula]

put (poot) v.t. place or set; express; put on, don (clothes); assume (airs) -put out, annoy; disconcert; eject. -put-up a. concocted. -put up with, tolerate. [Late OE. putian]

pu'trid a. rotten. -pu'trefy v.t. and i. make or become rotten. [L. putrid us]

putt (put) v.t. throw (a weight or shot) from the shoulder; strike (a gold ball) along the ground in the direction of the hole. -putt'er n. golf club for putting. [var. of put]

putt'y n. paste of whiting and oil used by glaziers; polishing powder of calcined tin used by jewelers. -v.t. fix or fill with putty. [F. potée]

puz'zle n. bewildering or perplexing question, problem, or toy. -v.t. perplex. -v.i. think in perplexity. [fr. ME. opposal, question, interrogation]

pyg'my, pig'my n. dwarfed. dwarf. [G. pygmaios, fr. pygme, measure of length, 13½ inches]

py'lon n. gateway to Egyptian temple; steel erection to mark out an airfield or carry power cables etc. [G. = gateway]

pyr'amid n. solid figure with sloping sides meeting at an apex; solid structure of this shape, esp. the ancient Egyptian monuments (usually with a square base); group of persons or things highest in the middle. -pyram'idal a. [G. pyramis, pyramid-,]

pyre n. pile of wood for burning a dead body. -pyrol'ogy n. science of heat. [G. pyr, fire]

pyri'tes n. term for sulfides of various metals (e.g. iron) in gold-colored crystals. [L.]

pyromania n. uncontrollable impulse and practice of setting things on fire. pyroman'iac n. [G. pyr, fire, and mania]

Pythagore'an a. of, pert. to Pythagoras or his doctrine of transmigration of souls.

py'thon (-th-) n. large nonpoisonous snake that crushes its prey. -py'thoness n. Apollo's priestess at Delphi; witch. [G. Python, name of a serpent killed by Apollo]

Q

qua (qua) conj. as, in capacity of [L.]

quack n. harsh cry of the duck; pretender to medical or other skill. -v.i. of a duck, to utter its cry. [imit.]

quadr-, four. [L. *quattuor*]. **-quad'rangle** *n.* four-sided figure; four sided court in a building. *contr.* quad. **-quadrang'ular** *a.* **-quad'rant** *n.* quarter of a circle; instrument for taking angular measurements. **-quadrate'** *v.t.* make square.

quaff *v.i.* drink deeply. *-v.t.* drink, drain. [orig. uncertain]

quag, quag'mire *n.* marshy tract with quaking surface. [*quake*]

quail *n.* small bird of the partridge family. [OF. *quaille*]

quaint *a.* interestingly old-fashioned or odd. **-quaint'ly** *adv.* [OF. *cointe*]

quake *v.i.* shake or tremble (from fear, apprehension). **-Qua'ker** *n.* member of the Society of Friends, a Christian religious sect. [OE. *cwacian*]

qual'ify (kwol'-) *v.t.* ascribe a quality to, describe; make competent; moderate. *-v.i.* make oneself competent, *esp.* by passing an examination. **-qualific'ation** *n.* qualifying, thing that qualifies. **-qual'ity** *n.* attribute, characteristic, property; degree of excellence; rank. **-qual'itative** *a.* relating to quality. [L. *qualis*, of what kind]

qualm (kwam) *n.* sudden feeling of sickness; misgiving; scruple. [Du.]

quandary state of perplexity, puzzling situation. [orig. uncertain]

quan'tity (kwon'-) *n.* size, number, amount; specified or considerable amount. **quan'titative** *a.* **-quan'tum** *n.* desired or required amount. [L. *quantus*, how much]

quarantine *n.* isolation to prevent infection. *-v.t.* put in quarantine. [L. *quadriginta*, forty (ref to days of isolation)]

quark *n.* in physics, any of several hypothetical particles thought to be fundamental units of matter. [word coined by Murray Gell-Mann, physicist]

quarr'el (kwor'-) *n.* angry dispute; breakup of friendship. *-v.i.* fall out with; find fault with. [F. *querelle fr.* L. *queri*, complain]

quarr'y *n.* object of a hunt. [F. *curée*]

quarr'y *n.* place where stone is got from the ground for building, *etc. -v.t.* and *i.* get from a quarry. [L. *quadrare*, square (stones)]

quart (kwort) *n.* quarter of a gallon, or two pints. [*quarter*]

quar'ter *n.* fourth part; region, district; mercy. *-pl.* lodgings. *-v.t.* divide into quarters. **-quart'erdeck** *n.* part of upper deck used by officers. **-quartet'** *n.* music for four performers; group of four musicians. [L. *quartus*, fourth]

quartz (kworts) *n.* stone of silica, often containing gold. [Ger. quarz]

quasar *n.* extremely distant starlike object emitting powerful radio waves. [Fr. *quasi* stellar]

quash (kwosh) *v.t.* annul, *esp.* by legal procedure. [F. *casser*, break]

qua'si *conj.* and *adv.* almost; in a sense; in appearance. [L. *quam si*, as if]

quat'rain *n.* four-lined stanza, with alternate rhymes. [F.]

qua'ver *v.i.* tremble, shake, say or sing in quavering tones. *-n.* trill; musical note half the length of a crotchet. [orig. uncertain]

queen *n.* wife of a king; female sovereign; piece of the game of chess; perfect female bee, wasp, *etc.*; court card. **-queen'ly** *a.* [OE. *cwen*]

queer *a.* odd, strange. **-queer'ly** *adv.* [Ger. quer, athwart, across]

quell *v.t.* crush, put down, suppress; allay. [OE. *cwellan*, kill]

quench *v.t.* extinguish, put out; slake. [OE. *cwencan*, quench]

que'ry *n.* question; mark of interrogation. *-v.t.* question, ask; mark with a query. [L. *quaere*, seek]

quest *n.* search. *-v.i.* search. [L. *qusit*-, to seek]

ques'tion (-chn) *n.* sentence seeking for an answer; problem; debate, strife. *-v.t.* ask questions of, interrogate; dispute. **ques'tionable** *a.* doubtful, *esp.* [F.]

quick *a.* rapid, swift, keen, brisk; living. *-n.* sensitive flesh. *-adv,.* rapidly. **-quick'ly** *adv.* **-quick'en** *v.t.* give life to; make speedier, stir up. *-v.t., i.* become living; become faster. **-quick'sand** *n.* loose wet sand which swallows up animals, ships, *etc.* [OE. *cwic*, living]

qui'et *a.* undisturbed; with little or no motion or noise. *-n.* state of peacefulness, absence of noise or disturbance. *-v.t.* and *i.* make or become quiet. [L. *quies, quiet*-, *n.* quiet]

quill *n.* hollow stem of a large feather; spine of a porcupine; pen, fishing-float, *etc.* , made of a feather-quill. [orig. uncertain]

quilt *n.* padded coverlet. *-v.t.* stitch (two pieces of cloth) with padding between. [L. *culcita*, cushion]

quinine' *n.* bitter drug made from the bark of a tree and used to cure fever, *etc.* [Peruv. *kina*, bark]

quintes'sence *n.* purest form or essential feature. **-quintessen'tial** *a.* [Med. L. *quinta essentia*, substance of the heavenly bodies; (outside the 'four elements')]

quintet', quintette' *n.* musical piece for

five singers, players; the singers, players. [It. *quintetto*]

quin'tuple *a.* multiplied by five, greater by five times, composed of five parts. [L. *quintus*, fifth]

quip *n.* smart saying, epigram. [L. *quippe*, forsooth (ironical)]

quirk *n.* fanciful turn; quibble; evasion. -**quirk'y** *a.* full of twists; peculiar. (orig. unknown]

quit *a.* free, rid. -*v.t.* leave, go away on equal or even terms by repayment, *etc.* **quitt'ance** *n.* receipt, discharge. -**quitt'er** *n.* shirker; deserter. [L. *quietus*, discharge]

quite *a.* wholly, completely. [*quit*]

quiv'er *n.* a carrying-case for arrows. (OF. *cuivre*, ult. of Teut. orig.]

quiv'er *v.i.* shake or tremble. -*n.* an act of quivering. [*quaver*]

quixot'ic *a.* showing enthusiasm for visionary ideals, generous, helpful, against one's own interests. [Don Quixote, hero of novel of Cervantes (d. 1616)]

quiz *v.t.* make fun of, look at curiously or critically. -*n.* entertainment in which general or specific knowledge of players is tested by questions; examination, interrogation. -**quizz'ical** *a.* questioning; mocking. [orig. uncertain]

quor'um *n.* number that must be present in a meeting to make its transactions valid. [L. = *of whom*]

quo'ta *n.* share to be contributed or received. [L. *quot*, how many]

quote *v.t.* copy or repeat passages from; refer to, *esp.* to confirm a view; state a price for. -**quota'tion** *n.* -**quota'tion mark** *n.* marks of punctuation ("-") indicating the beginning and end of quotation. -**quo'table** *a.* -**quo'tably** *adv.* [Med. L. *quotare*, distinguish by numbers]

quo'tient (-shent) *n.* number resulting from dividing one number by another. [L. *quotiens*, how many times]

R

rabb'et *n.* groove cut in edge of plank allowing another to fit into it. -*v.t.* cut rabbet in. [OF. *rabat*, abatement]

rabb'i *n.* Jewish teacher, doctor of law; pastor of congregation. -**rabbin'ic**, **rabbinical** *a.* -**rabbin'ics** *n.* the study of rabbinic literature of the post-Talmudic period.]

rabb'it *n.* small rodent animal which resembles the hare. -*v.i.* hunt rabbits. [orig. uncertain]

rab'ble *n.* crowd of vulgar, noisy people; mob. [orig. unknown]

rab'id *a.* raging; mad. -**ra'bies** *n.* canine madness. [L. *rabere*, to be mad]

race *n.* descendants of a common ancestor; one of the distinct varieties of the human species; peculiar breed, as of horses. *etc.* -**ra'cial** *a.* of race or lineage. -**rac'ialism**, **rac'ism** *n.* belief in innate superiority of particular race, antagonism towards members of different race based on this belief [F.]

race *n.* running; act of running in competition for a prize; strong current of water, *esp.* leading to a water-wheel. -*pl.* meeting for the sport of horse-racing. -*v.t.* contend with in a race. -*v.i.* run swiftly. **ra'cer** *n.* -**race'course** *n.* ground on which horse races are run. -**race'horse** *n.* horse bred for racing only. [ON. *ras*]

rack *v.t.* stretch or strain; stretch on the rack or wheel; torture. -*n.* instrument for stretching anything. [Du. *rak; n.* fr. *rekken*, stretch]

rack'et *n.* bat used in tennis, badminton, *etc.* -*pl.* ball game played in a paved court surrounded by four walls. -**rack'et-court** *n.* [F. *raquette*]

rack'et *n.* loud noise, uproar; (*sl.*) dishonest enterprise; organized fraud or roguery. -**rack'eteer** *n.* gangster, swindler. -*v.i.* make a noise. [Gael. *racaid*]

ra'dar *n.* device for finding range and direction by ultrahigh-frequency point-to-point radio waves, which reflect back to their source and reveal position and nature of objects sought [*radio angle detection and ranging*]

ra'diate *v.t.* emit rays. -*v.t.* emit in rays. -**radia'tion** *n.* transmission of heat, light *etc.* from one body to another; particles, rays emitted in nuclear decay; act of radiating. -**ra'diance** *n.* brightness. -**ra'diant** *a.* -**ra'diator** *n.* that which radiates, *esp.* heating apparatus for a room, or a part of an engine for cooling it. [L. *radius*, ray, wheel-spoke]

radical *a.* of a root; fundamental; thorough. -*n.* politician desiring thorough reforms. -**rad'icalism** *n.* [L. *radix, radic-*, root]

ra'dio *n.* use of electromagnetic waves for broadcasting, communication etc; device for receiving, amplifying radio signals; broadcasting, content of radio program. *v.t.* transmit (message *etc.*) by radio. **radioac'tive** *a.* emitting invisible rays that penetrate matter. -**radioactiv'ity** *n.* -**radiocarbon da'ting** technique for determining age of organic materials based on their content of radioisotope ¹⁴C acquired from atmosphere when they formed part of living plant. **ra´dio frequency** any frequency that lies in range 10 kilohertz to 300, 000 megahertz and can be used for broadcasting; frequency transmitted by particular radio station. **-ra´diograph** *n.* image produced on sensitized film or plate by radiation. **-radiographer** *n.* - **radiography** *n.* production of image on film or plate by radiation. **-radiois´otope** *n.* radioactive isotope. **-radiol´ogist** *n.* **radiol´ogy** *n.* science of use of rays in medicine **-radio´ther´apy** *n.* diagnosis and treatment of disease by x-rays.

ra´dium *n.* rare metal named from its radioactive power. [*radiate*]

ra´dius *n.* straight line from center to circumference of a circle or sphere. **ra´dial** *a.* of a ray or rays; of a radius; of radium. [*radiate*]

raf´fle *n.* lottery in which an article is assigned by lot to one of those buying tickets. **-v.t.** dispose of by raffle. [orig. dicing game, F. *rafle*]

raft *n.* number of logs or planks, *etc.* , of wood tied together and floating. [ON. *raptr*, beam]

rag *n.* fragment of cloth; torn piece. **ragg´ed** *a.* shaggy; torn; clothed in frayed or torn clothes; wanting smoothness. **rag´time** *n.* music with strong syncopation. [OE. *ragg*]

rage *n.* violent anger or passion; fury. **-v.i.** speak or act with fury; be widely and violently prevalent. **-the rage**, the fashion. [F. fr. L. *rabies*, madness]

raid *n.* rush, attack; foray. **-v.t.** make a raid on. **-raid´er** *n.* [var. of *road*, cp. inroad]

rail *n.* horizontal bar, *esp.* as part of a fence, railway line, *etc.* **-v.t.** enclose with rails. **-rail´ing** *n.* fence of rails. **-rail** *n.* road with lines of iron rails on which trains run. **-rail** *n.* [OF. *reille* fr. L. *regula*, ruler]

rail *v.i.* utter abuse. **-raill´ery** *n.* light-hearted banter. [F. *railler*]

rain *n.* moisture falling in drops from the clouds; fall of such drops. **-v.i.** fall as rain. **-v.t.** pour down like rain. **-rain´y** *a.* - **rain´bow** *n.* arch of prismatic colors formed in the sky by the sun's rays. **-rain check** *n.* ticket for a future performance, game *etc.* when one has been postponed by rain. **rain´coat** *n.* light rainproof overcoat. **rain´fall** *n.* quantity of rain falling in given area. [OE. *regn*]

raise *v.t.* set up, rear; lift up; breed, bring into existence; levy, collect; end (a siege). **-n.** rise, *esp.* in salary. [ON. *reisa*]

rake *n.* tool consisting of a long handle with a cross-piece armed with teeth for drawing together hay, *etc.* , or breaking the ground. **-v.t.** draw or break with a rake; sweep or search over; sweep with shot. [OE. *raca*]

rall´y *v.t.* bring together, *esp.* what has been scattered, as a routed army or dispersed troops. **-v.i.** come together; regain health or strength *n.* act of rallying. [F. *rallier*]

ram *n.* male sheep; swinging beam with metal head for battering hydraulic machine; beak projecting from bow of a warship. **-v.t.** beat down; stuff, strike with a ram. [OE. *ramm*]

ram´ble *v.i.* walk without definite route, wander; talk incoherently. **-n.** rambling walk. **-ram´bler** *n.* one who rambles; climbing rose. **-ram´bling** *a.* [ME. *ramen*, roam]

ramp *v.i.* stand on the hind legs. **-n.** slope. **-ramp´ant** *a.* rearing; violent. [F. *ramper* clamber]

ranch *n.* very large farm, *esp.* one where sheep, cattle or horses are produced. **-v.i.** conduct such a form. **-v.i.** conduct one. **ranch´er** *n.* [Sp. *rancho*, row (of huts, *etc.*)]

ran´cid *a.* smelling or tasting like stale fat. **-rancid´ity** *n.* [L. *rancidus*]

ran´dom *n.* **at random**, haphazard. *a.* made or done at random. [OF. *randon*, headlong rush]

range *n.* rank; area, scope, sphere; distance a gun can reach; distance of a mark shot at; place for practicing shooting; kitchen stove. **-v.t.** set in a row; roam. **-v.i.** extend; roam. **-ran´ger** *n.* **range´-finder** *n.* instrument to determine distance of object. [F. *rang*]

rank *n.* row or line; order; social position; high social position; relative place or position. **-v.t.** draw up in a rank, classify. **-v.i.** have rank or place. (F. *rang*). **rank** *a.* growing too thickly or coarsely; offensively strong; vile; flagrant. **rank´ly** *adv.* [OE. *ranc*, insolent]

ransack *v.t.* search thoroughly. [ON. *rann*, house, *soekaj*, seek]

ran´som *n.* release from captivity by payment; amount paid. **-v.t.** pay ransom for. **-ran´somer** *n.* [F. *rancon* fr. L. *redemptio*, buying back]

rant *v.i.* talk, preach, in a loud, bombastic way. **-n.** bombast. **-rant´er** *n.* [O. Du. *ranten*, rave]

rap *n.* smart slight blow. **-v.t.** give a rap to. **-v.i.** [imit. orig.]- **rap** *n.* talk, conversation. **-v.i.** [orig. uncertain]

rape *v.t.* violate; force a person to submit unwillingly to sexual intercourse. **-n.** act of raping. **-ra´pist** *n.* [ME. *rappen*, seize. L. *rapere*, seize] rap'id *a.* quick, swift; speedy. -**rapid'ity** *n.* -**rap'idly** *adv.* [L. *rapidus*]

rapport' *n.* rotation; harmony, sympathy. [F.]

rapt *a.* snatched away; lost in thought; intent. -**rap'ture** *n.* ecstasy. -**rap'turous** *a.* [L. *rapere,* snatch]

rare *a.* uncommon; of uncommon quality. -**rare'bit** *n.* Welsh rabbit, cheese sauce on toast. -**rar'efy** *v.t.* lessen the density of. -**rar'ity** *n.* anything rare. [L. *rarus,* thinly sown]

rare *a.* raw, underdone. [OE. *hrér,* half-cooked]

ras'cal *n.* rogue, knave. -**ras'cally** *a.* **rascal'ity** *n.* [OF. *rascaille.* rabble]

rash *n.* skin eruption. [OF. *rasche*]

rash *a.* hasty, reckless, without due caution. -**rash'ly** *adv.* [Du *rasch* quick]

rasp *n.* coarse file. -*v.t.* scrape with one. -*v.i.* scrape; make a scraping noise, [OF. *raspe*]

rat *n.* small rodent animal; one who deserts his party. -**ratt'y** *a.* (*sl.*) riled. *v.i.* hunt rats; desert one's party. -**rat's-bane** *n.* poison for rats. [OE. *rcet*]

rat'chet *n.* set of teeth on a bar wheel allowing motion in one direction only. [F. *rochet*]

rate *n.* proportion between two things; charge; degree of speed, *etc.* -*v.t.* estimate the value of. -**rat'able** *a.* that can be rated; liable to pay rates. [Med. L. *rata,* fr. *reri, rat-,* think, judge]

rate *v.t.* scold. [OF. *reter,* accuse]

ra'ther *adv.* some extent; in preference. [OE. *hrathe,* quickly]

rat'ify *v.t.* confirm, make valid. **ratifica'tion** *n.* [F. *ratifier*]

ra'ting *n.* (*naut.*) grading of a seaman on ship's books; tonnage-class of racing yacht; amount fixed as a rate. [*rate*]

ra'tio *n.* relative magnitude; proportion. [L. = *reason*]

ra'tion (rash'un) *n.* fixed daily allowance. -*v.t.* supply with, or limit to, rations. [L. *ratio*]

ra'tional *a.* reasonable. -**ra'tionalism** *n.* philosophy which regards reason as the only guide or authority. -**ra'tionalist** *n.* -**ra'tionalize** *v.t.* explain away by reasoning. -**rational'ity** *n.* -**ra'tionally** *adv.* [L. , fr. *veri, rat-,* think, judge]

rat'tle *v.i.* give out a succession of short sharp sounds, as of shaking small stones in a box. -*v.t.* cause to sound thus; (*sl.*) irritate, make angry. -*n.* the sound; instrument for making it; set of horny rings in a rattlesnake's tail. -**rat'tle-snake** *n.*

poisonous snake that makes a rattling noise with its tail. [imit. orig.]

rauc'ous *a.* hoarse; harsh-sounding. [L. *raucus*]

rav'age *v.t.* lay waste. -*n.* destruction and pillage; devastation. [F.]

ra'ven *n.* black bird of the crow family. [OE. *hroefn*]

rav'en *v.t.* and *i.* seek prey or plunder. -**rav'enous** *a.* very hungry. [OF. *ravine* -L. *rapina,* plunder]

ravine' *n.* narrow gorge worn by running water. [F. fr. L. *rapina*]

rav'ish *v.t.* carry off, sweep away; commit rape upon (a woman); enrapture. **rav'ishment** *n.* [F. *ravir* fr. L. *rapere,* snatch]

raw *a.* uncooked; not manufactured; crude, inexperienced, uncultivated; stripped of skin; sensitive; chilly. [OE. *hreaw*]

ray *n.* single line or narrow beam of light, heat, *etc.*; any of a set of radiating lines. *v.i.* radiate. (OF. *rai,* fr. L. *radius*]

raze *v.t.* destroy completely; level to the ground; wipe out, delete. [F. *raser,* fr. L. *radere, ras-,* scrape]

raz'or *n.* an instrument for shaving. -**razor-bill** *n.* bird, a kind of auk. [F. *raser,* fr. L. *radere, ras-,* scrape]

re, in re *prep.* in the matter of. [L.]

re- *prefix* makes compounds with meaning of, again, *e.g.* **readdress'** *v.t.* address afresh. -**recap'ture** *v.t.* capture again. These are not given where the meaning and derivation may easily be found from the simple word. [L.]

reach *v.t.* succeed in touching; arrive at. -*v.i.* stretch out the hand; extend. -*n.* act of reaching; grasp, scope; stretch of river between two bends, (OE. *roecan,* stretch out]

react'*v.i.* act in return or opposition or towards a former state. -**reac'tion** *n.* **reac'tionary** *n.* one advocating backward movement, in politics, *etc.* -*a.* of or inclined to such reaction. -**rea'gent** *n.* chemical substance that reacts with another and is used to detect the presence of the other. [*act*]

read *v.t.* look at and understand written or printed matter; interpret mentally; learn by reading; read and utter. -*v.i.* be occupied in reading; find mentioned in reading. -**read'able** *a.* that can be read with pleasure. [OE. *roedan,* make out]

read'y (red'i) *a.* prepared, prompt. **read'iness** *n.* -**read'ily** *adv.* [OE. *gero-ode*]

re'al *a.* existing in fact; happening; actual;

of property, consisting of land and houses. **-re'alism** n. regarding things as they are; artistic treatment with this outlook. **- re'alist** n. **-realist'ic** a. **real'ity** n. real existence. **-re'alize** v. t. make real; convert into money. **realiza'tion** n. **-re'ally** adv. **-real estate'** n. immovable property, as houses etc. **-real'tor** n. real estate agent. **re'alty** n. real estate. [F. reel, fr. L. res, thing]

realm (relm) n. kingdom, province, sphere. [OF. reame, fr. L. regimen]

reap v.i. cut grain. -v.t. cut (grain). **reap'er** n. [OE. repan]

rear n. back part. **-rear'-guard** n. troops protecting rear of an army. [arrear]

rear v.t. set on end; build up; breed, bring up. -v.i. rise on the hind feet. [OE. roeran, raise]

reas'on (-z-) n. ground or motive; faculty of thinking; sensible or logical view. -v.i. think logically in forming conclusions. v.t. persuade by logical argument (into doing, etc.). **-reas'onable** a. sensible, not excessive, suitable; marked by logic. [F. raison, fr. L. ratio]

reassure' v.t. calm, give confidence to. [assure]

re'bate n. discount. -v.t. diminish; allow as discount. [F. rabattre]

rebel' v.i. revolt, take arms against the ruling power. **-reb'el** n. one who rebels; one resisting authority. **-a.** in rebellion. **'rebell'ion** n. organized open resistance to authority. [L. rebellare]

rebound' v.t. drive back. -v.i. spring back; re-echo; recoil. -n. [bound]

rebuke' v.t. reprove, reprimand, find fault with. -n. act of rebuking. [OF. rebuchier, repulse]

re'bus n. riddle in which words are represented by pictures standing for the syllables, etc. [L. = 'by things']

rebut' v.t. force back, refute evidence etc. **-rebutt'al** [F. rebouter]

recapitulate v.t. state again briefly. **- recapitula'tion** n. (L. recapitulare- capitulum, chapter]

recede' v.t. go back. **-rece'ding** a. going, sloping, backward. [L. recedere]

receipt' n. written acknowledgment of money received; fact of receiving or being received; recipe. **-receive'** v.t. take, accept, get; experience. [L. recipere, recept-, fr. capere, take]

re'cent a. that has lately happened, new, fresh. **-re'cently** adv. [L. recens]

receptacle n. containing vessel, place or space. **-recep'tion** n. receiving; manner of receiving; formal receiving of guests. **- recep'tionist** n. one who receives (hotel) guests or clients. **receptive** a. able or quick to receive, esp. impressions. **-receptiv'ity** n. [L. recipere, receive]

re'cess n. vacation or holiday; niche or alcove; secret hidden place. [recede]

recidivist n. one who relapses into crime. [L. recidere, fall back]

re'cipe (res'i-pe) n. directions for cooking a dish, prescription. [L. recipere, receive]

recipient a. that can or does receive. n. that which receives. [L. recipere, receive]

reciprocal a. in return, mutual. **recip'rocally** adv. **-recip'rocate** v.i. move backwards and forwards. -v.t. give in return, give and receive mutually. [L. reciprocus]

recite' v.t. repeat aloud, esp. to an audience. **-reci'tal** n. narrative; musical performance by one person. **-recita'tion** n. [L. recitare]

reck'on v.t. count; include; consider. -v.i. make calculations, cast accounts. **reck'oner** n. [OE. gerecenian]

reclaim' v.t. bring back (from wrong); make fit for cultivation. **-reclaim'able** a. **-reclama'tion** n. reformation; regaining, as of land from the sea. [L. reclamare, call back]

recline' v.i. sit or lie with back supported on a slope; repose. [L. reclinare]

recluse' a. living in complete retirement. -n. hermit. [L. reclusus]

recognize v.t. know again; treat as valid; notice. **-recogni'tion** n. **-recogni'zable** a. [L. recognoscere]

recoil' n. rebound, esp. of a gun when fired; act of recoiling. -v.i. draw or spring back. [F. reculer]

recollect' v.t. call back to mind, remember. **-recollec'tion** n. [L. recolligere, recollect- collect again]

recommend' v.t. entrust; present as worthy of favor or trial; make acceptable. **- recommenda'tion** n. [F. recommander. cp. command, commend]

reconcile v.t. bring back into friendship; adjust, settle, harmonize. [L. reconciliare]

reconnoiter (-ter) v.t. survey the position of an enemy, strange district, etc. -v.i. make a reconnaissance. **reconnaissance** n. such survey. [OF. reconnoitre (F. reconnoitre) recognize]

reconstruct' v.t. rebuild. **- reconstruc'tion** n. a rebuilding; rebuilding of a country, its trade, etc., after war. [construct]

record' v.t. put down in writing. **rec'ord**

n. a being recorded; document or other thing that records, *e.g.,* gramophone record; best recorded achievement. **record'er** *n.* a person or thing that records; type of flute. **record'ing** *n.* art of registering sounds for reproduction. [L. *recordari*, get by heart]

recount' *v.t.* tell in detail. -*n.* second count (of votes, *etc.*) [OF, *reconter*]

recoup' *v.t.* recompense; indemnify. [F. *recouper*, cut back]

recourse' *n.* resorting to for help. [L, *recurrere, recurs-*, run back]

recov'er (-kuv) *v.t.* get back. -*v.i.* get back health. [F. *recouvrir*, fr. L. *recuperare*]

rec'reate *v.t.* restore. -*v.i.* take recreation. **-recrea'tion** *n.* agreeable or refreshing occupation. **-rec'reative** *a.* [L. *recreare*, make again]

recriminate *v.i.* make a counter charge or mutual accusation. [L. *crimen*, charge, crime]

recruit' (-oot) *n.* newly-enlisted soldier; one newly joining a society. -*v.i.* enlist, *v.t.* enlist fresh soldiers, *etc.*; recover health. **-recruit'ment** *n.* [OF. *recrue*, reinforcement]

rectangle *n.* four-sided figure with four right-angles. **-rectang'ular** *a.* [L. *rectus*, right, straight]

rect'ify (-fi) *v.t.* put right, purify; (*elec.*) change from alternate to direct current. [L. *rectus*, right]

rect'um *n.* the final section of the large intestine. [L. *rectus*]

recumbent *a.* lying down; reclining. [L. *recumbere*, to lie down]

recuperate *v.t.* and *i.* to restore, be restored from illness. losses, *etc.* [L. *recuperate*, to recover]

recur' *v.i.* go or come back in mind; happen again. [L. *recurrere*, run back]

red *a.* of a color varying from crimson to orange and seen in blood, rubies, glowing fire, *etc.*; (politics) communist. -*n.* the color. [OE. *read*]

redeem' *v.t.* ransom, atone for; save: fulfill (a promise); make good use of (time). -**the Redeem'er** Jesus Christ [L. *redimere, redempt-*]

red'olent *a.* scented with, diffusing the fragrance, odor of. **-red'olence** *n.* [F.]

reduce *v.t.* bring down, lower, lessen; bring by force or necessity to some state or action. -*v.i.* slim. [L. *reducere, reduct-*, lead back]

redundant *a.* superfluous, unnecesary; become deprived of a job. **-redundancy** *n.* [L. *redundare*, overflow]

reef *n.* part of a sail which can be rolled up to reduce the area; ridge of rock near the surface of the sea; lodge of auriferous quartz. -*v.t.* take in a reef of. [ON. *rif*, reef, rib]

reek *n.* strong smell or smoke. -*v.i.* smoke, emit fumes. [OE. *reocan*, to smoke]

reel *n.* winding apparatus; cylinder for winding cotton, *etc.*, on; act of staggering. -*v.t.* wind on a reel. -*v.i.* stagger away. [OE. *hreol*]

refer' *v.t.* trace or ascribe to; submit for decision; send to for information. -*v.i.* have relation, allude. **-ref'erable** *a.* **referee'** *n.* umpire; arbitrator. **-ref'erence** *n.* **-referen'dum** *n.* submitting of a question to a whole body of voters. [L. *referre*, carry back]

refine' *v.t.* purify. **-refi'nery** *n.* place where sugar, *etc.*, is refined. [F. *raffiner*]

reflect' *v.t.* throw back, *esp.* rays of light; cast (discredit, fame, etc.), upon. -*v.i.* meditate. **-reflec'tion, reflex'ion** *n.* **-reflect'ive** *a.* **-reflect'or** *n.* a polished surface for reflecting light, *etc.* **-re'flex** *a.* reflected, bent back; of muscular action, involuntary. **-reflex'ive** *a.* in grammar, describes a verb denoting the agent's action on himself. [L. *reflectere*, bend back]

reform *v.t.* and *i.* amend, improve. -*n.* amendment, improvement. [L. *reformare*, reshape]

refrain' *n.* chorus of a song. [F.]

refrain' *v.i.* abstain from. -*v.t.* check. [L. *refrenare*, bridle]

refresh' *v.t.* give freshness to. **-refresher** *n.* **-refresh'ment** *n.* that which refreshes, *esp.* food or drink. [F. *rafraichir-frais*, fresh]

refrig'erate (-j-) freeze, cool. **-refrig'erator** *n.* apparatus for cooling or freezing. [L. *frigus, frigerare, frigerat-*, cold]

ref'uge *n.* shelter, protection. **-refugee'** *n. one who seeks refuge, esp. in a foreign country.* [L. *refugium*, fr. *fugere*, flee]

refund' *v.t.* pay back; restore. -*n.* refunder *n.* [L. *refundere*, pour back]

refuse' (-z) *v.t.* and *i.* decline. **-ref'use** (-s) *a.* discarded. -*n.* rubbish, useless matter. **-refu'sal** *n.* [L. *refusare*]

re'gal *a.* of, or like, a king. **-rega'lia** *n. pl.* insignia of royalty, as used at a coronation, *etc.* [L. *regales*, fr. *rex, reg-*, king]

regale' *v.t.* and *i.* feast. [F. *régaler*]

regard' *v.t.* look at; consider (as); heed; relate to. -*n.* look; particular respect; esteem. -*pl.* expression of goodwill. **-regard'ing** *prep.* concerning. **-regard'less** *a.* [F. *regarder*]

regen'erate *v.t.* and *i.* cause spiritual rebirth, reform morally; reproduce, recreate, reorganize. [*generate*]

reg'imen *n.* prescribed system of diet. [L.]

regiment *n.* an organized body of troops as a unit of an army. -**regiment'al** *a.* of a regiment. -*n.* in *pl.* uniform. [F. *régiment*]

re'gion (-jun) *n.* area, district. [L. *regio, region-,* fr. *regere,* rule]

reg'ister (-j-) *n.* written record; compass of a voice; device for registering. -*v.t.* set down in writing; enter in a register; express. -*v.i.* make a visible impress. - **registrar'** *n.* keeper of a register. - **registra'tion** *n.* -**reg'istry** *n.* registering; place where registers are kept. [F. *registre*]

regress *n.* passage back; ability to pass back. -**regress'ive** *a.* passing back. salon *n.* returning, retrogression. [L. *re,* back, *gradi,* step]

regret' *v.t.* grieve for the loss of, or on account of-*n.* grief for something done or left undone or lost. -**regret'ful** *a.* -**regrett'able** *a.* (F. *regretter*]

reg'ular *a.* done according to rule; habitual; living under rule; belonging to the standing army. -*n.* regular soldier. -**regular'ity** *n.* -**reg'ulate** *v.t.* adjust; put under rule. -**regula'tion** *n.* rule; law; ordinance. -**reg'ulator** *n.* [L. *regularis,* fr. *regula,* rule]

rehabilitate *v.t.* restore to reputation or former physical state. -**rehabilita'tion** *n.* (L. *habilitare,* make fit]

reign (rai)) *n.* royal power; dominion; supremacy; period of a sovereign's rule. -*v.i.* be sovereign. [L. *regnum*]

reimburse' *v.t.* pay back, refund (expenses, *etc.*). [F. *rembourser,* fr. *bourse,* purse]

rein *n.* narrow strap attached to the bit to check or guide a horse. -*v.t.* check or manage with reins. [OF. *reine,* fr. L. *retinere,* hold back]

reinforce' *v.t.* strengthen, *esp.* by sending fresh men. [F. *reinforcer*]

reiterate *v.t.* repeat over and over again. -**reitera'tion** *n.* [*iterate*]

reject' *v.t.* refuse, put aside; decline. **rejec'tion** *n.* [L. *rejacere, reject-,* throw back]

rejoice' *v.t.* and *i.* make or be joyful. [F. *rejouir, rejouiss-,*]

rejoin' *v.t.* say in answer. -**rejoin'der** *n.* answer; response. [F. *réjoindre*]

relapse' *v.i.* fall back, into evil, illness, *etc.* -*n.* [L. *relabi, relaps-,* slip back]

relate' *v.t.* narrate, recount; establish relation between; have reference or relation to. -**rela'tion** *n.* narration, narrative; correspondence, connection; connection by blood or marriage. -**rel'ative** *a.* dependent on relation to something else not absolute; have reference or relation to. -*n.* relative word or thing; one connected by blood or marriage. -**relativ'ity** *n.* Einstein's theory in physics that motion or velocity is relative, not absolute, and that time is a correlate of space. [F. *relater*]

relax' *v.t.* make loose or slack. -*v.i.* become loosened or slack; become more friendly. -**relaxa'tion** *n.* relaxing; recreation. [L. *laxus,* loose]

re'lay *n.* set of fresh horses to replace tired ones; gang of men, supply of material, *etc.* , used similarly; (radio) broadcast relayed from another station. *v.t.* pass on broadcast thus. [F. *relais*]

release' *v.t.* give up, surrender, set free. -*n.* a releasing; written discharge. [OF. *relaissier*]

relent' *v.i.* give up harsh intention, become less severe. [L. *lentus,* slow]

rel'evant *a.* having to do with the matter in hand; pertinent. -**rel'evance** *n.* [L. *relevare,* raise up]

rel'ic *n.* something remaining as a memorial of a saint, *etc.*; a thing kept as a memento. -*pl.* dead body; remains, surviving traces. -**rel'ict** *n.* a widow. [L. *relinquere, relict-,* to leave]

relief' *n.* alleviation or end of pain, distress, *etc.*; money or food given to victims of a disaster, poverty, *etc.*; release from duty; one who relieves another; projection of a carved design from a surface; distinctness, prominence. [OF. *relief* fr. *relever*]

relieve' *v.t.* bring or give relief to; set free; free (a person or duty) by taking his place. [F. *relever,* raise up]

reli'gion (-ijun) *n.* system of faith and worship. [L. *religio*]

relinquish (-inkw-) *v.t.* give up. [L. *relinquere*]

reluctant *a.* unwilling. -**reluct'ance** *n.* [L. *reluctari,* struggle against]

rely' *v.i.* depend (on). -**reli'able** *a.* trustworthy. [L. *religare,* bind together]

remain' *v.i.* stay or be left behind; continue. -**remaind'er** *n.* rest, what is left after substraction. [L. *remanere*]

remark' *v.t.* take notice of; say. -*v.* i, make a remark (on). -*n.* observation, comment. -**remark'able** *a.* noteworthy, unusual. [F. *remarquer*]

rem'edy *n.* means of curing, counteracting or relieving a disease, trouble, *etc.* -*v.t.* put right. [L. *remedium*]

remem'ber *v.t.* retain in or recall to the

memory. -*v.i.* have in mind. **-remem'-brance** *n.* [L. *memor*, mindful]

remind' (-mind) *v.t.* put in mind (of). -**remind'er** *n.* [mind]

reminisc'ence *n.* remembering; thing recollected. **-reminis'cent** *a.* reminding. [L. *reminisce*, remember]

remiss' *a.* negligent. **-remiss'ly** *adv.* -**remit'** *v.t. forgive, not to exact, give up; slacken.* -*v.i.* slacken, give up. remissible *a.* **-remis'sion** *n.* **-remit'tance** *n.* a sending of money; money sent. [L. *remittere*, *remiss*-, send back, slacken]

remorse' *a.* regret and repentance. -**remorse'ful** *a.* **-remorse'fully** *adv.* **remorse'less** *a.* pitiless. [L. *remordere*, *remors*-, bite again]

remote' *a.* far away; distant in time or place. **-remote'ly** *adv.* [L. *removere*, *remot*-]

remove' *v.t.* take away or off. *v.i.* go away; change residence. **-remo'val** *n.* removable *a.* [L.]

renaissance *n.* revival, rebirth, *esp.* revival or learning in the 14th-16th centuries. [F. *renaissance*, fr. L. *nasci*, be born]

re'nal *a.* of the kidneys. [L. *renalis*]

rend'er *v.t.* give in return, deliver up; submit, present; portray, represent; melt down. **-rendi'tion** *n.* surrender; translation. [F. *rendre*]

rendezvous *n.* meeting; meeting-place. -*v.i.* meet, come together. [F.]

renege' *v.i.* revoke at cards; back out; renounce. [L. *negare*, deny]

renounce' *v.t.* give up, cast off. -*v.i.* in cards, fail to follow suit. **-renuncia'tion** *n.* [F. *renoncer*, fr. L. *renuntiare*, protest against]

ren'ovate *v.t.* restore, repair. [L. *renovare-novus*, new]

rent *n.* payment for the use of land or buildings. -*v.t.* hold as a tenant; lease; hire -**rent'al** *n.* sum payable as rent. [F. *rente*, income]

rent *n.* tear. [obs. *rent* = *rend*]

repair' *v.i.* resort, betake oneself (to). [OF. *repairier*, fr. Late L. *repatriare*, go home, return to one's country]

repair' *v.t.* mend. -*n.* mend. **-repair'able** *a.* **-repara'tion** *n.* a repairing; amends, compensation. [L. *reparare*, fr. *parare*, prepare]

repeal' *v.t.* annul, cancel. -*n.* act of repealing, [appeal]

repeat' *v.t.* say or do again, reproduce. **repeat'edly** *adv.* **-repeat'er** *n.* **-repeti'-tion** *n.* [L. *repetere*, *repetit*-, try again]

repel' *v.t.* drive back, ward off, refuse. **repell'ent** *a.* [L. *repellere*]

repent' *v.i.* feel penitence; feel regret for a deed or omission. -*v.t.* feel regret for. [F. *se repentir*]

repercussion *n.* recoil; echo; indirect effect. [percussion]

repertory *n.* store; repertoire. **repertory the'ater**, theater with a permanent company and a stock of plays. [L. *repertorium*]

replace' *v.t.* put back; fill up with a substitute for. **-replace'ment** *n.* [place]

replay *v.t.* to repeat an action or process, game or match; show a videotape of a portion of a televised event. -*n.* an act or instance or repeating an action.

reply' *v.t.* and *i.* answer. -*n.* answer. (F. *replier*, fold back]

report' *v.i.* relate; take down in writing; make or give an account of-, name as an offender. -*v.i.* make a report. -*n.* rumor; account or statement; repute; bang. -**report'er** *n.* one who reports, *esp.* for a newspaper. [L. *reportare*, bring back]

repose' *v.i.* take rest. -*v.t.* give rest to; put (trust, etc.). -*n.* rest. **-repos'itory** *n.* store or shop. [F. *reposer*]

represent' *v.t.* call up by description or portrait; make out to be; act, play, symbolize; act as deputy for; stand for. [F. *reprosenter*]

repress' *v.t.* keep down or under. [L. *reprimere*, *repress*-, press back]

reprieve' *v.t.* suspend the execution of (condemned person); a reprieving or warrant for it. [for earlier *repry*, fr. F. *repris*, taken back]

rep'rimand *n.* sharp, rebuke. -*v.t.* rebuke sharply. [F. *reprimande*, fr. *réprimer*, repress]

reprint' *v.t.* print again. -*n.* book, publication reprinted. [print]

reproach' *v.t.* scold, rebuke. -*n.* scolding or upbraiding; expression of this; thing bringing discredit. **-reproach'ful** *a.* [F. *reprocher*]

reproduce' *v.t.* produce anew; produce a copy of, bring new individuals into existence. **-reproduct'ive** *a.* [*produce*]

rep'tile *n.* cold-blooded air-breathing vertebrate with horny scales or plates, such as a snake, lizard, tortoise, *etc.* **-reptil'ian** *a.* [L. *reptiles- repere*, creep]

repub'lic *n.* state in which the supremacy of the people or its elected representatives is formally acknowledged. [L. *res publica*, common weal]

repulse' *v.t.* drive back; rebuff. [L. *repellere*, *repuls*-,]

repute' *v.t.* reckon, consider. -*n.* reputation, credit. -**reputa'tion** *n.* what is generally believed about a character; good fame. -**rep'utable** *a.* of good repute. [L. *reputare,* consider, weigh]

request' *n.* asking; thing asked for. -*v.t.* ask. [OF. requester]

require' *v.t.* demand; want, need. **require'ment** *n.* -**req'uisite** (-zit) *a.* needed. -*n.* something necessary. **requisition** *n.* formal demand, usually for military supplies, etc-*v.t.* demand by an order of requisition; press into service. [L. *requirere,* requisite,]

res'cue *v.t.* save, deliver. -*n.* rescuing. **res'cuer** *n.* [OF. *resourre]*

research' *n.* investigation, *esp.* scientific study to try to discover facts. -**research'er** *n.* [search]

resem'ble (-z-) *v.t.* be like. -**resem'blance** *n.* [F. *ressembler]*

resent' (-z-) *v.t.* show or feel indignation at, retain bitterness about. [F. *ressentir]*

reserve' (-z-) *v.t.* hold back, set apart, keep for future use. -*n.* something reserved; part of an army only called out in emergency; reticence, concealment of feelings or friendliness. -*pl.* troops in support. [L. *reseruare,* keep back]

reservoir *n.* receptacle for liquid, *esp.* a large one built for storing water. [F. reservoir]

reside' (-z-) *v.i.* dwell. -**res'idence** *n.* dwelling; house. -**res'idency** *n.* act or time of dwelling in a place. -**res'ident** *a.* and *n.* -**residen'tial** *a.* (L. *residere,* fr. *sedere,* sit]

res'idue (-z-) *n.* what is left. [L. *residuum]*

resign' (-zin) *v.t.* give up—*v.i.* give up an office, employment, *etc.* -**resigned'** *a.* content to endure. -**resigna'tion** *n.* resigning; being resigned. [L. *resignare,* unseal]

resist' (-z-) *v.t.* withstand. -*v.i.* oppose. [L. *resistere]*

res'olute *a.* resolved; fixed in purpose. **res'olutely** *adv.* -**resolu'tion** *n.* a resolving; fixed determination; firmness; formal proposal put before a meeting. [resolve]

resolve' *v.t.* break up into parts, disintegrate; dissolve, disperse; solve (a problem); decide, determine; (*mus.*) follow a discord by a concord. -**resolved'** *a.* firm; set on a course of action. [F., L. *resolvers, resolut-,* loose]

resort' (-z-) *v.i.* have recourse; frequent. -*n.* recourse; frequented place. [F. *ressortir,* rebound, go back]

resource' *n.* skill in devising means. -*pl.* means of supplying a want; stock that can be drawn on, means of support. -

resource'ful *a.* -**resource'-** fully *adv.* [F. *ressource]*

respect' *v.t.* defer to, treat with esteem. esteem; point or aspect. -**respect'able** *a.* worthy of respect. -**respect'ive** *a.* several, separate. -**respect'ively** *adv.* [L. *respicere, respect-,* look back at]

res'pite *n.* delay; breathing space; suspension of capital sentence; reprieve; suspension of labor. -*v.t.* grant respite to; reprieve; relieve by resting. [L. *respectus,* respect]

resplendent *a.* brilliant, shining. -**resplend'ence** *n.* [L. *resplendere,* shine]

respond' *v.i.* answer; act in answer. -**respond'ent** *a.* replying. -*n.* one who answers; defendant. -**response'** *n.* answer. -responsible *a.* liable to answer for something; of good credit or position. -**responsibil'ity** *n.* -**respon'sive** *a.* [L. *responders,* response,]

rest *n.* repose; freedom from exertion or activity; pause; supporting appliance; *v.i.* take rest; be supported. -*v.t.* give rest to; place on a support. -**rest'ful** *a.* **rest'less** *a.* [OE. *roest]*

rest *n.* remainder. -*v.i.* be left over. [F. *reste-* L. *restare,* remain]

restaurant *n.* eating-house. **restauranteur'** *n.* keeper of one. [F.]

restore' *v.t.* build up again, repair, renew; re-establish; give back. **restoration** *n.* -**restor'ative** *a.* restoring. -*n.* medicine to strengthen, *etc.* [L, *restaurare, restaurat-,* repair]

restrict' *v.t.* limit, bound. -**restric'tion** *n.* -**restrict'ive** *a.* [L. *restringere,* restrict]

result' (-z-) *v.i.* follow as a consequence, end. -*n.* effect, outcome. -**result'ant** *a.* [L. *resultare,* leap back]

resume' *v.t.* begin again; summarize. -**ré'umé** *n.* summary. -**resump'tion** *n.* a resuming. -**resump'tive** *a.* [L. *resumere, resumpt-,* take back]

resurge' *v.i.* rise again. -**resur'gent** *a.* [L. *resurgere]*

resurrect' *v.t.* restore to life. **ressurec'tion** *n.* rising again; revival. [L. *resurrec resurgere.* resurrect-]

re'tail *n.* sale in small quantities. -*v.t.* sell in small quantities; recount. -*adv.* by retail. -**re'tailer** *n.* [OF. *retailler,* cut up]

retain' *v.t.* keep; engage services of retain'er *n.* fee to retain a lawyer, or other professional person; follower of a nobleman, *etc.* [L. *retinere,* hold back]

retaliate *v.t.* and *i.* repay in kind. [L. *retaliare, retaliate,* fr. *talis,* like, such]

retard' *v.t.* make slow or late. **retard-**

a'tion *n.* [I, . *retardate, tardus,* slow]

ret'icent *a.* reserved in speech, not communicative. -ret'icence *n.* [L. *reticere,* fr. *tacere,* be silent]

ret'ina *n.* sensitive layer at the back of the eye. [Med. L.]

retire' *v.i.* withdraw; give up office or work: go away; go to bed. -*v.t.* cause to retire. -retired' *a.* that has retired from office, *etc.* -retire'ment *n.* -reti'ring *a.* unobtrusive, shy. [F. *retirer,* pull back]

retort' *v.t.* repay in kind; reply; hurl back (a charge, *etc.*). -*n.* thing done or said as vigorous reply or repartee; vessel with a bent neck used for distilling. [L. *retorquere,* retort-, twist back]

retract' *v.t.* draw back; recant. -*v.i.* recant. -retracta'tion *n.* [L. *retrahere. retract-,* draw back]

retreat' *n.* act of, or military signal for, retiring; sunset call on a bugle, *etc;* place of seclusion. -*v.i.* retire. [F. *retraite,* fr. *retraire,* draw back]

retribution *n.* recompense, *esp.* for evil deed; vengeance. [L. *retributio* payment]

retrieve' *v.t.* bring in: regain; restore; rescue from a bad state. [F. *retrouver,* find again]

retro-, backward. [L.] -ret'rograde *a.* going backwards, reverting reactionary. -retrogres'sion *n.* -retrogress'ive *a.* -ret'rospect *n.* a looking back, survey of the past.

retrovirus *n. pl* -retroviruses any of a group of viruses that use RNA and reverse transcriptase to encode information and which cause cancers, AIDS, leukemia, etc.

return *v.i.* go or come back. -*v.t.* give or send back report officially; report as being elected; elect. [F. *retourner.* -L. *tornare,* turn]

rev *n, (sl.)* abbrev. of revolution (of engine)-rev up *v.t.* and *i.* cause (engine) to quicken speed; speed up.

reveal' *v.t.* make known; disclose. revela'tion *n.* what is revealed. *esp.* by divine inspiration. [L. *revelare,* draw back the veil, *velum*]

revenge' *v. refl.* avenge oneself-*v.t.* make retaliation for; avenge. -*n.* a revenging, desire for vengeance; act that satisfies this. [OF. *revengier,* fr. L. *revindicare*]

rev'enue *n.* income, *esp.* of a state or institution; receipts; profits. [L. *revenière,* come back]

reverberate *v.t.* and *i.* echo or throwback. -reverbera'tion *n.* [L. *reverberare,* beat back]

reverse' *v.t.* turn upside down or the other way round; change completely. -*n.* opposite or contrary; side opposite the obverse; defeat. *a.* opposite, contrary, revers'al *n.* -revers'ible *a.* -revert' *v.i.* return to a former state; come back to a subject. [L. *vertere, vers-,* turn]

review *n.* revision; survey, inspection, *esp.* of massed military forces; critical notice of a book, *etc.*; periodical with critical articles, discussion of current events, *etc.* -*v.t.* hold, make, or write, a review of -review'er *n.* writer of reviews. [F. *revue,* fr. *revoir,* see again, revise]

revile' *v.t.* abuse, reproach. [OF. *reviler*]

revise' *v.t.* look over and correct. revi'ser *n.* -revi'sion *n.* . [L. *revisere*]

revive' *v.i.* come back to life, vigor, *etc.* *v.t.* bring back to life, vigor, use *etc.* revi'val *n.* a reviving, *esp.* of religious fervor. [L. *viuere,* live]

revoke' *v.t.* annul. -*v.i.* at cards, to fail to follow suit though able to. -*n.* at cards, an act of revoking. [L. *revocare,* call back]

revolt' *v.i.* rise in rebellion; feel disgust. -*v.t.* affect with disgust. -*n.* rebellion. -revolt'ing *a.* disgusting, horrible. [F. *révolter*]

revolve' *v.i.* turn round, rotate. -*v.t.* rotate; meditate upon. -revolu'tion *n.* rotation or turning round; turning or spinning round; great change; the violent overthrow of a system of government. -revolu'tionary *a.* and *n.* -revolu'tionize *v.t.* -revol'ver *n.* repeating pistol with a revolving cartridge-magazine. [L. *revoluere, revolut-*]

revulsion *n.* sudden violent change of feeling; strong distaste. [L. *revulsio*]

reward' (-word) *v.t.* pay, or make return, for service, conduct, *etc-n.* recompense or return. [ONF. *rewarder*]

rhap'sody *n.* enthusiastic or highflown composition. -rhapsod'ic *a.* -rhap'sodist *n.* (G. *rhapsodia,* piece of epic verse for one recital]

rhetoric *n.* art of effective speaking or writing; artificial or exaggerated language. -rhetor'ical *a.* -rhetori'cian *n.* [G. *rhetor,* orator]

rhinovirus *n. pl.* -rhinoviruses any of a large group of picornaviruses which are the cause of the common cold and other respiratory diseases.

rhizosphere *n.* The region of soil immediately surrounding and influenced by the roots of the plant. -rhizospheric *a.*

rhom'bus, rhomb *n.* equilateral but not right-angled parallelogram, diamond or lozenge. [G. *rhombus,* thing that can be twirled]

rhyme *n-* identity of sounds at ends of lines of verse, or in words, word or syllable identical in sound to another; verse marked by rhyme; *v.t.* use (word) to make rhymes. [F. *rime*, fr. G. *rhythmos*, rhythm]

rhythm (riTHm) *n.* measured beat or flow, *esp,* of words, music, *etc.* [G. *rhythmos*]

rib *n.* one of the curved bones springing from the spine and making the framework of the upper part of the body; curved timber of the framework of a boat. *-v.t.* furnish or mark with ribs. [OE. *ribb*]

ribb'on, rib'and *n.* narrow band of fine fabric. [OF. *riban*]

ribcage *n.* cagelike enclosure of the chest formed by the rigs and their connecting bones.

ribosomal RNA *n.* type of ribonucleic acid that is a basic, permanent component of the ribosomes and plays a major part in protein synthesis. [*abbr.* **rRNA**]

rice *n.* white seeds of an Eastern plant, used as food; the plant. **-rice'-paper** *n.* fine Chinese paper. [F. *riz*]

rich *a.* wealthy; fertile; abounding in some product or material; valuable; of food, containing much fat or sugar; mellow; amusing. [OE. *rice*, powerful, rich]

rick'ets *n.* disease of children marked by softening of bones, bowlegs, *etc.* [orig. uncertain]

rid *v.t.* clear, relieve of **-ridd'ance** *n.* [ON. *rythja*, to clear (land)]

rid'dle *n.* question made puzzling to test the ingenuity of the hearer, enigma; puzzling fact, thing, or person. *-v.i.* speak in or make riddles. [OE. *roedels*]

ride *v.i.* go on horseback or in a vehicle; lie at anchor; float lightly. *-n.* journey on a horse or other animal or in any vehicle; road for riding on horseback. **-ri'der** *n.* one who rides; supplementary clause; mathematical problem on a given proposition. **-ri'derless** *n.* [OE. *ridan*]

ridge *n.* line of meeting of two sloping surfaces; long narrow hill; long narrow elevation on a surface. *-v.t.* form into ridges. [OE. *hyrcg*, spine, back]

ridiculous *a.* deserving to be laughed at, absurd, foolish. **-rid'icule** *v.t.* laugh at, hold up as ridiculous. *-n.* treatment of a person or thing as ridiculous. [L. *ridiculus-ridere*, laugh]

ri'fle *v.t.* search and rob; make spiral grooves in (gun-barrel, *etc.*). *-n.* firearm with a long barrel. **-ri'fling** *n.* arrangement of grooves in a gun barrel. [F. *rifler*]

rift *n.* a crack, split. **-rift'-vall'ey** *n.* (*geol.*) subsistence between two faults. [ON. *ript*]

rig *v.t.* provide (a ship) with spars, ropes, *etc.*; equip; set up, *esp.* as a makeshift. *-n.* way a ship's masts and sails are arranged; costume; style of dress; apparatus for drilling oil and gas. **-rigg'ing** *n.* spars and ropes of a ship. [orig. uncertain]

right *a.* straight; just; proper; true; correct; genuine. **-right side,** side of a person which is to the east when he faces north, opposite of left. *-v.t.* bring back to a vertical position; do justice to. *-v.i.* come back to a vertical position-*n.* what is right, just, or due. *-adv.* straight; properly; very; on or to the right side. **-righteous** (ri-chus) *a.* just, upright. **-right'-hand man,** subordinate chiefly relied on. [OE. *riht*]

ri'gid *a.* stiff; harsh; unyielding. **rigid'ity** *n.* **-ri'gidly** *adv.* [L. *rigidus*]

rig'or *n.* harshness, severity, strictness; sense of chill and shivering. **-rig'orous** *a.* [L. *rigor*]

rile *v.t.* make angry. [earlier *roil*, disturb, fr. OF. *rouil*, mud]

rim *n.* outer ring of a wheel; edge, border. **-rim'less** *a.* [OE. *rima*]

ring *n.* small circle of gold, *etc.* , *esp.* as worn on the finger; any circular appliance, band, coil, rim, *etc.*; circle of persons. *-v.t.* put a ring round. [OE. *hring*]

ring *v.i.* give out a clear resonant sound, as a bell; resound. *-v.t.* cause (a bell) to sound. *-n.* a ringing. [OE. *hringan*]

rink *n.* sheet of ice for skating; floor for roller-skating. [Sc.]

rinse *v.t.* clean by putting in and emptying out water; wash lightly. *-n.* a rinsing. [F. *rincer*]

ri'ot *n.* tumult, disorder; loud revelry; unrestrained indulgence or display. *-v.i.* make or engage in a riot; brawl. **-ri'otous** *a.* **-ri'otously** *adv.* [F. *riotte*]

rip *v.t.* cut or tear away, slash, rend. *-n.* rent or tear, broken water, as in tide-rip. [of Teutonic orig.]

ripe *a.* matured, ready to be reaped, eaten, *etc.* **-ri'pen** *v.i.* and *t.* [OE.]

rip'ple *v.i.* flow or form into little waves. *-v.t.* form ripples on. *-n.* slight wave or ruffling of surface. [rip]

rise *v.i.* get up; move upwards; reach a higher level; appear above the horizon; adjourn. *-n.* rising; upslope; increase; beginning. [OE. *risan*]

risk *n.* danger. *-v.t.* venture. [F. *risque*]

rite *n.* a formal practice or custom, *esp.* religious. **-rit'ual** *a.* concerning rites. *-n.* prescribed order or book of rites. [L. *ritus*]

ri'val *n.* one that competes with another for favor, success, *etc.* *-v.t.* vie with. *a.* in the position of a rival. -ri'valry n. emulation; competition. (L. rivalis]

riv'er n. large stream of water. riv'erbead n. spring, source, of a river. riv'er basin n. land that is drained by a river and its tributaries. -riv'er-horse n. hippopotamus. [F. rivière]

riv'et n. bolt for fastening plates of metal together, the end being put through the holes and then beaten flat. -v.t. fasten with rivets; clinch; (fig.) fascinate, enthrall. [F.]

road n. track or way prepared for passengers, vehicles, etc.; direction, way; roadstead. [OE. rad, riding]

roam v.t. and i. wander about, rove. [orig. uncertain]

roar n. loud deep hoarse sound as of a lion, thunder, voice in anger, etc. -make such sound. -v.t. utter in roaring voice, shout out. [OE. rarian]

rob v.t. plunder, steal from. -robb'er n. -robb'ery n. [OF. rober]

robe n. long outer garment. -v.t. dress. v.i. put on robes or vestments. (F.]

rob'in n. brown red-breasted bird of the thrush family. -robin-red'-breast n. [Robin]

ro'bot n. automated machine, esp. performing functions in a human manner; automaton, mechanical slave. -ro'botics n. science or technology of designing, building, and using robots; robot dancing. [Czech, fr. Karel Kapek's play, R.U.R. (Rossum's Universal Robots)]

rock n. stone; large rugged mass of stone; hard toffee. -rockery, rock-garden n. mound or grotto of stones or rocks for plants in a garden. -rock'y a. [F. roche]

rock v.i. sway to and fro. -v.t. cause to do this. -rock'er n. curved piece of wood, etc., on which a thing may rock; rocking chair. -rock mus'ic n. pop music developing from the rock-and-roll idiom. [OE. rocoian]

rock'et n. self-propelling device powered by burning of explosive contents, used as firework, for display, signalling, line carrying, weapon etc.; vehicle propelled by rocket engine, as weapon or carrying spacecraft. -v.i. move fast, esp. upwards, as rocket -rock'etry n. [It. rocchetta, dim. of rocca, distaff]

rod n. slender, straight round bar, wand, stick or switch; birch or cane; measure a pole). [OE. rood]

ro'dent a. gnawing. -n. gnawing animal, e.g. rat, hare etc. [L. rodere, gnaw]

ro'deo n. gathering of cattle to be branded or marked; exhibition of skill in steer wrestling, and bronco riding etc. [Mex. -Sp.]

roe n. mass of eggs in a fish. [of Teutonic origin]

rogue n. rascal, knave; sturdy beggar; mischief-loving person or child wild beast of savage temper living apart from its herd. [orig. uncertain]

roll n. piece of paper, etc., rolled up; list or catalogue; small loaf-v.t. move by turning over and over; wind round; smooth out with a roller. -v.i. move by turning over and over; move or sweep along; of a ship, swing from side to side. -roll-call n. calling out of a list of names, e.g. as in schools, army. -roll'er n. cylinder used for pressing or smoothing, supporting something to be moved, winding something on etc. [F. rouler, fr. L. rotula, dim. of rota, wheel]

Ro'man a. of Rome or the Church of Rome. -Roman type, plain upright letters, ordinary script of printing. -Roman figures, letters, V, X, L, C, D, M, used to represent numbers in the manner of the Romans. [L. Romanus, fr. Roma, Rome]

roof n. outside upper covering of a building; (aircraft) flying height limit. v.t. put a roof on, be a roof over. -roof-garden n. garden on a flat roof. [OE. hrol]

rook'ie n. (sl.) raw recruit. [recruit]

room n. space; space enough; division of a house. -room'ing house n. building divided into separate rooms for rent. -room'y a. having plenty of space. [OE. rum]

roost n. perch for fowls; henhouse. v.i. perch. -roost'er n. barnyard cock. [OE. hrost]

root n. part of a plant that grows down into the earth and conveys nourishment to the plant; source, origin; original or vital part. -v.t. cause to take root; pull by the roots. -v.i. take root. [ON. rot]

rope n. thick cord. -v.t. secure or mark off with a rope. -ro'py a. sticky and stringy. -rope-dancer n. tight-rope performer. -rope'-trick n.ndian vanishing trick. -rope'-walk n. long shed for rope-spinning. -rope'-walk'er n. walker on the tight rope, an acrobat. [OE. rap]

rose n. beautiful flower of many varieties rose-bush; perforated flat nozzle for a hose, etc.; pink color-a. of this color. -rosa'ceous a. like a rose, of rose family. ro'sary n. string of beads for keeping count of prayers, form of prayer. -ro'sery n. rose-garden. [L. rose]

rot v.t. and i. decompose naturally. -n. decay, putrefaction; disease of sheep; nonsense. -rott'en a. decomposed; corrupt. [OE, rotian]

ro'tary *a.* of movement, circular. **rotate'** *v.i.* move round a center or on a pivot. -*v.t.* cause to do this. [L. *rota*, wheel]

rote *n.* by rote, by memory without understanding. [orig. uncertain]

ro'tor *n.* rotating part of machine or apparatus, *e.g.* dynamo, turbine, *etc.* [L. *rota*, wheel]

rough (ruf), *a.* not smooth, of irregular surface; violent, boisterous; lacking refinement; approximate; in a preliminary form. -*v.t.* make rough; plan out approximately. -*n.* disorderly ruffian; rough state; (*golf*) rough ground adjoining the fairway. -rough'age *n.* bulky, unassimilated portion of food promoting proper intestinal action. **-rough'-house** *n.* indoor brawl. [OE. ruh]

round (rownd) *a.* spherical or cylindrical or circular or nearly so; roughly correct; large; plain. -*adv* with a circular or circuitous course. -*n.* something round in shape; rung; movement in a circle; recurrent duties; customary course, as of a postman or military patrol; cartridge for a firearm. -*prep.* about; on all sides of. *v.t.* make round; get round. -*v.i.* become round. **-round-trip** *n.* journey to a place and back again, *usu.* by the same route. **round'-up** *n.* driving of cattle together; arresting of criminals. [F. *rond*]

route *n.* road, way. [F.]

routine' *n.* regular course; regularity of procedure. [F. fr. *route*]

row *n.* number of things in a straight line. [OE. *raw*]

row *v.i.* propel a boat by oars. -*v.t.* propel by oars. -*n.* spell of rowing. [OE. *rowan*]

row *n.* uproar; dispute. [orig. uncertain]

roy'al *a.* of, worthy of, befitting, patronized by, a king or queen; splendid. **-roy'alist** *n.* supporter of monarchy. **-roy'alty** *n.* royal dignity or power; royal persons; payment to an owner of land for the right to work minerals, or to an inventor for use of his invention; payment to an author based on sales. [F. fr. L. *regalia*, fr. *rex. reg*-, king]

rub *v.t.* subject to friction; pass the hand over; abrade, chafe; remove by friction. *v.i.* come into contact accompanied by friction, become frayed or worn with friction. **-rub'bing** *n.* [orig. obscure]

rubb'er *n.* coagulated sap of rough, elastic consistency, of certain tropical trees; piece of rubber *etc.* used for erasing. -*a.* made of rubber. [orig. obscure]

rubb'er *n.* series of three games at various card games; series of an odd number of games or contests at various games; two out of three games won. [orig. uncertain]

rubb'ish *n.* refuse, waste material; trash, nonsense. [orig. uncertain]

rub'ble *n.* irregular pieces of stone, brick, *etc.*; masonry made of this. [orig. uncertain. c.f. rubbish]

rudd'er *n.* flat piece hinged to the stern of a ship, boat, airplane *etc.* to steer by. [OE. *rothor*, steering oar]

rude *a.* primitive; roughly made; uneducated; uncivil. [L. *rudis,* rough]

rue *v.t.* and *i.* regret; repent; lament; suffer for. -*n.* repentance. [OE. *hreowan*]

rug *n.* thick woolen wrap; floor-mat, of shaggy or thick-piled surface. **-rugg'ed** *a.* rough, broken; furrowed; unpolishable; harsh. [of Scand. orig.]

ru'in *n.* downfall; fallen or broken state; decay, destruction. -*pl.* ruined buildings, *etc.* -*v.t.* reduce to ruins; bring to decay or destruction, spoil; cause loss of fortune to. [L. *ruina,* fr. *ruere,* rush down]

rule *n.* a principle or precept; what is usual; government; strip of wood, *etc.* , for measuring length. -*v.t.* govern, decide. **-ru'ler** *n.* one who governs; strip of wood, *etc.* , for measuring or drawing straight lines. [OF. *reule,* fr. L. *reguila-regere,* govern]

rum'ble *v.i.* make a noise as of distant thunder, a heavy cart moving along, *etc.* -*n.* such noise. [imit. orig.]

ru'minate *v.i.* chew and cud; meditate. **-ru'minant** *a.* cud-chewing. -*n.* cud-chewing animal. [L. *ruminari,* chew the cud]

ru'mor *n.* hearsay, common talk; current but unproved statement, usually rather vague. -*v.t.* put round as a rumor. [L. *rumor,* noise]

rump *n.* tail-end; buttocks. [ME. *rumpe*]

run *v.i.* move rapidly on the legs -*n.* act or spell of running, rush; tendency, course; space for keeping chickens. **-runn'er** *n.* **-runner-up** *n.* next after winner in a contest. **-run'way** *n.* pathway made by animals to and from feeding ground or water; level stretch of ground for aircraft landing and taking off. [OE. *rinnan*]

rup'ture *n.* breaking or breach; hernia. -*v.t.* and *i.* break or burst. [L. *rupture,* fr. *rumpere,* break]

ru'ral *a.* of the country; rustic. **-ru'rally** *adv.* [L. *ruralis,* fr. *rus, rur*-, country]

rush *n.* plant with a slender pithy stem growing in marshes, *etc.*; the stems as a material for baskets. [OE. *rysc*]

rush *v.t.* impel or carry along violently and rapidly; take by sudden assault. -*v.i.* move violently or rapidly. -*n*. a rushing; pressure of business affairs. [AF. *russher*, OF-*ruser*, drive back]

rust *n*. reddish-brown coating formed on iron by oxidation and corrosion; disease of plants. -*v.i.* and *v.t.* contract or affect with rust. **-rust'y** *a*. **-rust'less** *a*. **-rust'proof** a, [OE.]

rut *n*. periodical sexual excitement of the male deer and certain other animals. *v.i.* be under the influence of this. [F., fr. L. *rugire*, roar]

rut n. furrow made by a wheel; settled habit or way of living. **-rutt'y** *a*. [F. *rotate*, way, track, *etc*.]

rye *n*. grain used as fodder or for bread; plant bearing it.; whiskey made from it-**rye-bread** *n*. **rye-grass** *n*. kinds of grass cultivated for fodder. [OE. *ryge*]

S

Sabb'ath *n*. Jewish Sunday or seventh day, *i.e.* Christian Saturday. [Heb. *shabbath*]

sa'ber (-her) *n*. cavalry sword, slightly curved. -*v.t.* strike with one. [F.]

sacc'harin(e) *a*. pertaining to sugar. -*n*. extremely sweet substance from coal tar. [F., fr. G. *sakcharon*, sugar]

sack *n*. large bag, usually of some coarse textile material; (*sl*.) dismissal. -*v.t.* pillage (a captured town, *etc*.); (*sl*.) dismiss. -**sack'-cloth** *n*. coarse fabric used for sacks. **-sacking** *n*. material used for sacks. [Heb. *saq*]

sacrament *n*. one of certain ceremonies of the Christian Church, *esp*. the Eucharist. -**sacrament'al** *a*. [L. *sacramentum*]

sa'cred *a*. dedicated, regarded as holy. -**sa'credly** *adv*. [OF. *sacrer*-, L. *sacer*, sacred]

sac'rifice *n*. making of an offering to a god; thing offered; giving something up for the sake of something else; act of giving up; thing so given up as a sacrifice. -*v.t.* offer as sacrifice. **-sacrifi'cial** *a*. pert. to sacrifice. [OF.]

sacrilege *n*. violation of something sacred. **-sacrile'gious** *a*. [F. fr. L. *sacer*, holy]

sad *a*. sorrowful; deplorably bad; of color; dull, sober. **-sad'ly** *adv*. **-sadd'en** *v.t.* [OE. *sced*, sated]

sad'dle *n*. rider's seat to fasten on a horse, or form part of a bicycle, *etc*. ; part of a shaft; joint of mutton or venison; ridge of a hill. -*v.t.* put a saddle on. **-sadd'le-bag** *n*. bag hung from horse's or bicycle saddle. [OE. *sadol*]

sa'dism (-a-) *n*. psychological perversion involving delight in cruelty; (*colloq*.) love of cruelty. [Marquis de *Sade*, 1740-1814]

safa'ri *n*. (party) making overland (hunting) trip, *esp*. in Africa. [*Swahili*]

safe *a*. uninjured, out of danger; not involving risk; cautious; trustworthy. -*n*. strong box; ventilated cupboard for meat, *etc*. **-safe'ly** *adv*. **-safe'ty** *n*. **-safecon'duct** *n*. passport or permit to pass somewhere. **-safe'-guard** *n*. protection. -*v.t.* protect. -**safety-valve** *n*. valve allowing escape of excess steam *etc*.; outlet for emotion. [F. *sauf*, fr. L *salvos*]

sag *v.i.* sink in the middle, hang sideways or curve downwards under pressure. [of Teut. orig.]

sa'ga *n*. medieval tale of Norse heroes; any such long tale of events. [ON. cp. *saw*]

sage *a*. wise, discreet. -*n*. very wise man. **-sage'ly** *adv*. [F., fr. L. *sapere*, be wise]

Sagitta'rius *n*. (The Archer) 9th sign of Zodiac, operative Nov. 22-Dec. 20; southern constellation. [L. *Sagitta*, arrow]

sail *n*. piece of canvas stretched to catch the wind for propelling a ship; windcatching appliance forming the arm of a windmill; ships collectively; act of sailing. -*v.i.* travel by water; begin a voyage. -*v.t.* navigate. **-sail'board** *n*. craft used for windsurfing, consisting of a molded board like a surfboard, to which a mast bearing a single sail is attached by a swivel joint. **-sail'or** *n*. [OE. *segl*]

saint *adj*. holy; title of a canonized person. -*n*. one who has been canonized. **-saint'ly** *adj*. **-saint'ed** *a*. canonized; sacred. -**saint'liness** *n*. **-St. Bernard** *n*. kind of large dog used to rescue travellers in the snow. *n*. **-St. Vitus's dance** *n*. chores. [F., fr. L. *sanctus*, consecrated]

sake *n*. for the sake of, on behalf of, to please or benefit, or get, or keep. [OE. *sacu*, dispute at law]

sal'ad *n*. uncooked vegetables as food; lettuce or other plant suitable for this use. [F. *salade*]

sala'mi, *n*. highly-spiced sausage. [It.]

sal'ary *n*. fixed payment of persons employed in non-manual or non-mechanical work. **-sal'aried** *a*. [L. *solarium*, soldiers' pay]

sale *n*. a selling; special disposal of stock at low prices; auction. **-sales'man** *n*. shop assistant or traveler. **-sales'manship** *n*. **-sale'price** *n*. special price at a sale. [OE. *sala*]

sa'line *n*. fruit salt. -*a*. salty. [L. *salinus*]

sali'va *n*. liquid which forms in the mouth. **-sali'vary** *a*. [L.]

sall'ow n. kind of willow. [OE. sealh]

sall'ow a. of a sickly yellow or pale in color. [OE. sato]

sall'y v.i. rush; set out. -n. a rushing out, esp. from a fort; an outburst; witty remark. [F. saillir, rush]

salm'on (sam'-) n. large silvery-scaled fish with orange-pink flesh valued as food; color of its flesh. -a. of this color. [OF. aulmon, fr. L. salmon]

sal'on (-ong) n. drawing-room; reception graced by celebrities. [F.]

saloon' n. large reception room; public dining-room; principal cabin or sitting-room in a passenger ship; Pullman car on a railway; public place where liquor is sold and consumed. [F. salon]

salt (solt) n. sodium chloride, a substance which gives sea-water its taste; chemical compound of an acid and a metal. -a. preserved with, or full of, or tasting like, salt. -v.i. preserved with salt; put salt on. -salt'ern n. salt works. -salt'ing n. area of low ground regularly inundated with salt water. -sailt'y a. -salt'ness n. -salt'-cellar n. small vessel for salt on the table. -salt lake n. inland lake of high salinity resulting from inland drainage in an arid area of high evaporation. -salt marsh n. area of marshy ground that is intermittently inundated with salt water or that retains pools or rivulets of salt or brackish. -salt'peter n. potassium nitrate used in gunpowder. [OE. sealt]

sal'utary n. wholesome, resulting in good. [L. salutaris]

salute' v.t. greet with words or sign. -v.i. perform a military salute. -n. word or sign by which one greets another: prescribed motion of the arm as a mark of respect to a superior, etc., in military usage. -saluta'tion n. [L. salus, salut-, health]

sal'vage n. payment for saving a ship from danger; act of saving a ship or other property from danger; property or materials so saved. [OF.]

salva'tion n. fact or state of being saved. -salva'tionist n. member of religious group, Salvation Army. -salve v. save from peril. [L. salvus, safe]

salve n. healing ointment. -v.i. anoint with such. [OE. sealf]

same a. identical, not different, unchanged, unvarying. -same'ness n. monotony. [ON. samr]

sa'mite (sa-) n. medieval heavy silk stuff. [OF. samit]

sam'pan n. Chinese boat, sculled from stern, usu. with a sail and a cabin made of

mats. (Chin. sam, three, pan, board]

sam'phire n. herb found on rocky coasts; St. Peter's wort; sea-feud. [F. Saint-Pierre, St. Peter]

sam'ple n. specimen. -v.i. take or give a sample of. -sam'pler a. beginner's exercise in embroidery. [for ME. essample]

sanatoriums n. establishment for the treatment of invalids, esp, by therapy and diet; health resort. [L.]

sanc'tify v.t. set apart as holy; free from sin. -sanctifica'tion n. -sanctimo'nious a. making a show of piety. -sanc'tity n. saintliness, sacredness; inviolability. -sanc'tuary n. holy place; place where a fugitive was safe from arrest or violence. -sanc'tum n. sacred place or shrine; person's private room. [L. sanctus, holy]

sanc'tion n. penalty or reward following the breaking or observing of a law; treaty; permission with authority; countenance given by custom. -n.pl. boycott or other coercive measure, esp. by one state against another regarded as having violated a law, right etc. -v.i. allow or authorize. [L. sanctus, holy]

sand n. powdery substance made by the wearing down of rock. -pl. stretches or banks of this, usually forming a seashore. -v.t. cover or mix with sand. -sand'stone n. rock composed of sand. -sand'bag n. bag filled with sand or earth and used in fortification. -sand'paper n. paper with sand stuck on it for scraping or polishing wood, etc. -sand'piper n. longlegged wading bird. etc. -sand'y a. [OE.]

san'dal n. shoe consisting of a sole attached by straps. [G. sandalon]

sand'wich n. two slices of bread with meat or other substance between. -v.t. insert between two other different things. [Earl of Sandwich (d. 1792)]

sane a. of sound mind, sensible. -san'ity n. [L. sanus, healthy]

san'guine (sang-gwin) a. hopeful or confident; florid. [L. sanguis, sanguin-, blood]

san'itary a. promoting health by protection against dirt, etc. -sanitar'ium n. sanatorium. -sanita'tion n. improving of sanitary conditions. [L. Sanitas]

Sans'krit n. ancient classical language of India. [Sans. Sam, together, kr. make]

San'ta Claus' in nursery folk lore, giftbringer of Christmas Eve, riding over the roofs in a sled drawn by reindeer. [Du. Sint Klaas, St. Nicholas]

sap n. juice of plants. -sap'ling n. young tree. [OE. scep]

sap *n.* covered trench approaching a besieged place or enemy trench. -*v.t.* construct such trenches. -*v. i.* undermine; destroy insidiously. **-sapp'er** *n.* one who saps; Royal Engineer. [It. *zappa*, spade]

Sapph'ic *a.* of Sappho, Grecian poetess; verse of 3 lines of 5 feet each, followed by line of 2 feet. -*n.* sapphic verse. [*Sappho*]

sapph'ire (saf-) *n.* blue precious stone. [G. *sappheiros*]

sarcasm *n.* bitter or wounding ironic remarks; such remarks; power of using them. **-sarcast'ic** *a.* **-sarcast'ically** *adv.* [G. *sarkasmos*]

sarcophagus *n.* stone coffin; stone used for it. [G. *sarkophagos*]

sard, sar'dius *n.* precious stone, variety of chalcedony. [*Sardis* in Lydia]

sardine' *n.* small fish of herring family, usually packed in oil. [F.]

sardon'ic *a.* of a smile or laughter, bitter, scornful. [L. *sardonius*]

sa'ri *n.* Hindu woman's outer garment, a long straight piece of cotton, silk. [Hind.]

sarong' *n.* skirtlike garment worn in Asian and Pacific countries. [Malay, *sarung*]

sash *n.* frame forming a window, usually sliding up or down. [F. *chdssis*]

sash *n.* scarf wound around the body. [Arab. *shash*]

Sa'tan *n.* the devil. [Low L.]

sat'chel *n.* small bag, or bag for school books. (L. *saccellus*, a small sack)

sate *v.t.* gratify to the full; glut. [earlier *sade*, make sad]

sat'ellite *n.* in astronomy, planet revolving round another; man-made projectile orbiting a planet; person or country dependent on another. [L. *satellites*, *pl.*]

satiate *v.t.* satisfy to the full; surfeit. -**sa'tiable** *a.* **-satia'tion** *n.* **-sati'ety** *n.* feeling of having had too much. [L. *satiare-satis*, enough]

sat'in *n.* silk fabric with a glossy surface. **-sateen'** *n.* glossy cotton or woolen fabric. **-sat'inwood** *n.* ornamental wood of a tropical tree. **-sat'iny** *a.* [F., from It. *seta*, silk]

sat'ire (-Ir) *n.* composition in which vice or folly, or a foolish person, is held up to ridicule; use of ridicule or sarcasm to expose vice and folly. **-satir'ic, satirica** *a.* **-sat'irist** *n.* **-sat'irize** *v.t.* [L. *satura*, poetic medley]

sat'isfy *v.t.* content, meet the wishes of, pay, fulfill, supply adequately; convince; be sufficient. **-satisfac'tion** *n.* **-satisfac'tory** *a.* [L. *satisfacere*]

saturate *v.t.* soak thoroughly; cause to dissolve a maximum amount. **-satura'tion** *n.*

-sat'uration point *n.* point at which no more (people, things, ideas, *etc.*) can be absorbed, accommodated, used. etc; in chemistry, the point at. which no more solute can be dissolved in a solution or gaseous material absorbed in a vapor. [L. *saturate*]

Sat'urday *n.* seventh day of the week. Jewish Sabbath. [*Saturn*]

Sat'urn *n.* Roman god; one of the major planets. **-sat'urnine** *a.* gloomy; sluggish in temperament. **-saturn'alia** *n.* ancient festival of Saturn; noisy orgy or revel. [L. *Saturnus*, god of agricultura]

sat'yr (-r) *n.* woodland god, part man and part goat. **-satyr'ic** *a.* [G. *satyros*]

sauce *n.* liquid added to food to give relish. -*v.t.* add sauce to. **-sauce'pan** *n.* cooking-pot. **-sau'cy** *a.* impudent, cheeky. **-sau'cily** *adv.* [F.]

sau'cer *n.* curved plate put under a cup, *etc.*, to catch spilt liquid. [OF. *saussiere*]

saunter *v.i.* walk in leisurely manner, stroll. -*n.* leisurely walk or stroll. [AF. *sauntrer*, adventure]

sausage *n.* minced meat enclosed in a tube of thin membrane. **-saus'age-meat** *n.* [F. *saucisse*]

sau'té *a.* fried lightly and quickly. [F.]

savage *a.* uncivilized, primitive; wild. -*n.* member of a savage tribe, barbarian. *v.t.* attack with trampling, biting. **sav'agery** *n.* **-sav'agely** *adv.* [F. *sauvage*, fr. L. *silva*, wood]

sav'ant *n.* learned man. [F.]

save *v.t.* rescue, preserve; keep for the future, lay by; prevent the need of. -*v.i.* lay by money. -*prep.* except. *conj.* but. -**sa'ving** *a.* frugal. -*n.pl.* what is saved, laid by. **-sa'vior** *n.* deliverer or redeemer; Christ. [F. *sauver*, fr. L. *saluare*]

savoir-faire' (-war-fer') *n.* tact; knowing what to do. **-savoir-vivre'** *n.* knowledge of polite usages; social adequacy; good breeding. [F.]

sa'vor *n.* characteristic taste. -*v.i.* smack of -**sa'vory** *a.* having an appetizing taste or smell. -*n.* savory dish at beginning or end of dinner; aromatic mint. [L. *sapor*]

savoy' *n.* variety of cabbage. [*Savoy*]

saw *n.* old saying, maxim. [OE. *sagu*]

saw *n.* tool for cutting wood, *etc.* toothed. -*v.t.* cut with a saw. -*v.i.* make the movements of sawing. **-saw'dust** *n.* fine wood dust made in sawing. **-saw'fish** *n.* fish armed with a toothed snout. **-saw'mill** *n.* one for mechanical sawing of timber. -**saw'pit** *n.* pit in which one of wielders of two-handed saw stands. **-saw'yer** *n.*

workman who saws timber. [OE. *saga*]

sax'horn *n.* instrument of the trumpet class. **-sax'ophone** *n.* large instrument like a clarinet. [invented by C. J. *Sax*, a Belgian (d. 1865)]

say *v.t.* utter or deliver with the speaking voice; state; express; take as an example or as near enough; deliver an opinion. -*n.* what one has to say; chance of saying it; share in a decision. **-say'ing** *n.* maxim, proverb. [OE. *secgan*]

scab' *n.* crust formed over a wound; skin disease; disease of plants; somebody who works while his colleagues are on strike. **scabb'y** *a.* **-scab'land s** *pl.n.* type of terrain consisting of bare rock surfaces deeply channelled by glacial floodwaters. [ON. *skabbi*]

scabb'ard *n.* sheath for sword or dagger. [OF. *escalberc*]

scald (skold) *v.t.* injure with boiling liquid or steam; clean with boiling water. -*n.* injury by scalding. [ONF. *escaider*, fr. L. *calidus*, hot]

scald (skold) *n.* ancient Scandinavian poet. [ON. *skaid*]

scale *n.* pan of a balance; weighing instrument. -*v.t.* weigh in scales; have the weight of. [ON. *skal*, bowl]

scale *n.* one of the plates forming the outer covering of fishes and reptiles; thin flakes. -*v.t.* remove the scales from. -*v.i.* come off in scales. **-sca'ly** *a.* **-sca'liness** *n.* [OF. *escale*, husk]

scale *n.* series of musical notes, degrees, or graduations; steps of graduating measuring instrument; relative size, ratio of enlarging or reduction (*e.g.* in a map, *etc.*). -*v.t.* climb; attack with ladders. [L. *scala*, ladder]

sca'lene *a.* of a triangle, having its three sides unequal. [G. *skalenos*]

scallion *n.* variety of shallot; green onion. [L. *cepa Ascalonia*, onion of Ascalon]

scall'op *n.* edible shellfish; edging in small curves imitating the edge of a scallop shell. -*v.t.* shape in this way; cook in a scallop shell or a dish resembling one. [OF. *escalope*, shell]

scalp *n.* skin and hair of the top of the head. -*v.t.* cut off the scalp of; reprimand severely. [contr. of *scallop*]

scalper *n.* small surgical knife. **-scal'per** *n.* engraver's gouge. [L. *scalpere*, cut]

scamp'er *v.i.* run about; run hastily from place to place. -*n.* scampering. [fr. *scamp*, rascal]

scan *v.t.* look at carefully; measure or read (verse) by its metrical feet; examine,

search by systematically varying the direction or a radar or sonar beam; glance over quickly. -*n.* **-scann'er** *n.* one that scans. **-scan'sion** *n.* analysis or metrical structure of verse. [L. *scandere*, climb]

scand'al *n.* malicious gossip; feeling that something is an outrage or cause of discussion; thing causing such feeling. **scan'dalize** *v.t.* shock. **-scan'dalous** *a.* outrageous; disgraceful. **-scan'dalmonger** *n.* one who spreads malicious rumors. [G. *skandalon*, cause of stumbling]

scanner *n.* (*compute.*) input device that reads symbols, codes, text, or graphics, by passing a light or laser beam over them.

scant *a.* barely sufficient; not sufficient. -*v.t.* put on short allowance; supply grudgingly. **-scant'y** *a.* **-scant'ily** *adv.* **-scantiness** *n.* [ON. *skamt*, short]

scape *n.* and *v.t.* (*arch.*) escape. **-scape'goat** *n.* person unwillingly bearing blame due to others. **-scape'grace** *n.* incorrigible fellow. [*escape*]

scap'ula *n.* shoulder-blade. **-scap'ular** *a.* of the shoulder. **-scap'ulary** *n.* small shoulder-garment worn as badge of a religious order. [L.]

scar *n.* mark left by a healed wound, burn or sore. -*v.t.* mark with a scar. -*v.i.* heal with a scar. [ON. *scarth*, cleft]

scar *n.* rocky face of hillside. [ON. *sker*, skerry]

scarce *a.* hard to find; existing or available in insufficient quantity. **-scarce'ly** *adv.* only just; not quite. **scarce'ness** *n.* **-scar'city** *n.* [OF. *escars*]

scare *v.t.* frighten. -*n.* fright or panic. **-sca'ry** *a.* timid. [ON. *skirra*]

scarf *n.* scarfs, scarves, *pl.* long narrow strip of material to put round neck, shoulders, *etc.* [OE. *scearfe*, piece]

scarf *v.t.* join two timbers. [Sw. *scarfa*]

scarify *v.t.* scratch or cut slightly all over; criticize mercilessly. **-scarifica'tion** *n.* [L. *scarificare*]

scar'let *n.* brilliant red color; cloth or clothing of this color, *esp.* military uniform. -*a.* of this color. **-scar'let fe'ver** *n.* infectious fever with a scarlet rash. [Pers. *saqirtat*, broadcloth]

scathe (-TH) *n.* injury. -*v.t.* injure, especially by withering up. **-scathe'less** *a.* unharmed. [ON. *skatha*]

scatter *v.t.* throw or put here and there; sprinkle. -*v.i.* disperse. **-scatt'er-brained** *a.* giddy, thoughtless. [orig. uncertain]

scav'enger *n.* one employed in cleaning streets, removing refuse, *etc.* **-scav'enge**

v.t. clean (streets). *-v.i.* work as a scavenger; originally a kind of Customs Inspector. [OF. *escauuer*, inspect]

scene (sen) *n.* place of the action of a novel, play, *etc.*; place of any action; subdivision of a play; view; episode; stormy conversation, *esp.* with display of temper. - **sce'nery** *n.* stage scenes; natural features of a district. **-sce'nic** *a.* picturesque; of, or on, the stage. **-scenar'io** *n.* written version of a play to be produced by cinematograph. [L. *scena*]

scent (a-) *v.t.* track by smell; detect; give a perfume to. *-n.* smell; liquid perfume. [F. *sentir*, smell]

scep'ter (s-) *n.* ornamental staff as a symbol of royal power; royal or imperial dignity. [G. *skeptron*, staff]

sched'ule (sk-) *n.* plan or procedure of a project; list; timetable. *-v.t.* enter in a schedule; plan to occur at a certain time. [Late L. *scedula*, small scroll]

sche'ma *n.* image to aid the process of thought; synopsis; diagrammatic outline. **-schemat'ic** *a.* [*scheme*]

scheme (sk-) *n.* plan or design; project; list or table; outline or syllabus. *-v.i.* make plans, especially as a secret intrigue. *-v.t.* plan, bring about. **-schema** *n.* (*compute.*) logical structure, plan, or method by which data are organized in a database system. **-sche'mer** *n.* **-sche'ming** *a.* plotting, intriguing. [G. *schema*, form]

schis'm (sizm) *n.* division in a church or party. **-schismat'ic** *n.* and *a.* **-schis'mat'ical** *a.* [G. *schisma*, cleft]

schist (shist) *n.* crystalline rock which splits into layers. **-schist'ose** *a.* [G. *schiotos*, split stone]

schizophrenia *n.* split personality; dementia præcox, a mental disorder. **-schizophren'ic** *a.* [G. *schizein*, cleave, *phren*, mind]

school *n.* institution for teaching or for giving instruction in any subject; buildings of such institution; time of lessons; group of thinkers, writers, artists, *etc.*, with principles or methods in common. *-v.t.* educate; bring under control, train. - **school'man** *n.* medieval philosopher. **-schol'ar** *n.* one taught in a school; one quick to learn; learned person; person holding a scholarship. **-schol'arly** *a.* - **schol'arship** *n.* learning; prize or grant to a student for payment of school or college fees. **-scholast'ic** *a.* relating to schools or schoolmen; pedantic. [G. *schole*, leisure; place for discussion]

school (sk-) *n.* shoal (of fish, whales, *etc.*). [Du. *school*, crowd]

schooner (sk-) *n.* ship having fore and aft sails or two or more masts. [orig. uncertain]

sciatica (si-) *n.* pain in the sciatic nerve. **-sciat'ic** *a.* of the hip. [Low L.]

science *n.* systematic knowledge; investigation of this; any branch of study concerned with a body of observed material facts. **-scientif'ic** *a.* **-scientif'ically** *adv.* - **sci'entist** *n.* [L. *scientia*, knowledge]

scimitar (a-) *n.* short, single-edged curved sword. [F. *cimeterre*]

scintilla (a-) *n.* spark. **-scin'tillate** *v.i.* sparkle. **-scintilla'tion** *n.* [L.]

scissors (siz'-) *n. pl.* **cutting instrument of two blades pivoted together so that the edges slip over each other. [OF.** *cisoires*]

sclerosis *n.* hardening of bodily organs, tissues *etc.* [G. *skleros*, hard] [*See* **arteriosclerosis**]

scoff (sk-) *n.* taunt; mocking words. *-v.i.* jeer, mock. **-scoff'er** *n.* **-scoffing'ly** *adv.* [of Teut. orig.]

scold (sk-) *n.* nagging woman. *-v.i.* find fault noisily. *-v.t.* rebuke. [ON. *skald,* poet, later lampooner]

sconce *n.* bracket candlestick on a wall. [orig. screened lantern. OF. *esconce*]

scone (skon) *n.* round griddle cake. [SC. fr. Du. *schoonbrot*, fine bread]

scoop *n.* article for ladling; kind of shovel; tool for hollowing out. *-v.t.* ladle out; hollow out or rake in with a scoop; exclusive news-story. [of Teut. orig.]

scoot *v.i.* (*sl.*) move off quickly. **-scoot'er** *n.* toy consisting of small platform with two wheels and a guiding handle, to carry one person. [Sw. *skjuta*, shoot (v.i.)]

scope *n.* range of activity or applications room, play. [It. *scopo*, target]

scorch *v.t.* burn the surface of. *-v.i.* be burnt on the surface. **-scorched' earth' policy** (of a retreating army) of laying waste as it goes. [orig. uncertain]

score *n.* group or set of twenty; cut, notch, stroke, or mark; written or printed piece of orchestral music; tally; reason; sake; number of points made in a game, measure of weight, 20 lbs. *-v.i.* notch or mark; cross out; record; make (points) in a game. *-v.i.* achieve a success. **-scor'er** *n.* [ON. *skor*, notch]

scorn *n.* contempt, derision. [OF. *escarnir*]

scorp'ion *n.* small lobster-shaped animal with a sting at the end of its jointed tail. **-Scorpio** *n.* 8th sign of the zodiac, which sun enters about 22nd October. [L. *scorpio*]

scot *n.* payment or a person's share of it. -**scot-free'** *a.* free from payment, punishment, *etc.* [ON. *skot*]

Scot *n.* native of Scotland. -**Scott'ish** *a.* (also **Scotch, Scots**). -**Scots'man** *n.* -**scott'icism** *n.* Scottish turn of speech. **Scotch** *n.* or Scotland; Scotch whiskey. **Scotch' terrier,** short-legged, long-bodied rough terrier. [OE. *Scottas* (*pl.*), Irishmen]

scoun'drel *n.* villain. -**scound'relly** *a.* [orig. uncertain]

scour *v.t.* clear or polish by rubbing; clear out. [OF. *escurer*]

scourge (skurj) *n.* whip or lash; an evil pest or plague. -*v.t.* flog. [OF. *escorgiee*]

scout *n.* man sent out to reconnoiter; ship used for reconnoitering; small fast airplane; Boy Scout or Girl Scout. -*v.i.* go out or act as a scout. [OF. *escoute*]

scow *n.* large flat-bottomed boat. [Du. *schouw*]

scowl *v.t.* frown gloomily or sullenly. -*n.* gloomy frown. [of Scand. orig.]

scram *v.i.* to clear off, to depart hurriedly (when unwanted) [U.S. *slang*]

scram'ble *v.i.* move along or up by crawling, climbing, *etc.*, struggle with others for; cook (eggs) by stirring them, when broken, in the pan. -*n.* scrambling; disorderly proceeding. [orig. uncertain]

scrap *n.* small detached piece of fragment; fight, quarrel. -**scrapp'y** *a.* -**scrap'-book** *n.* book in which scraps, cuttings are pasted. (ON. *skrap*]

scrape *v.t.* rub with something sharp; clean or smooth in this way; rub with harsh noise. -*v.i.* make an awkward bow. -*n.* act or sound of scraping; awkward situation, *esp.* one resulting from an escapade. -**scra'per** *n.* [OE. *scrapian*]

scratch *v.t.* score or mark a narrow surface wound with claws, nails, or anything pointed; make marks on with pointed instruments; remove from a list. *v.i.* use claws or nails. -*n.* wound or mark or sound made by scratching; line or starting point. -*a.* got together at short notice; impromptu. -**scratch'ily** *a.* [mixture of earlier *scrat* and *crotch*, both of Teut. orig.]

scrawl *v.t.* write or draw untidily. -*n.* something scrawled; careless writing. [orig. uncertain]

scream *v.i.* utter a piercing cry; whistle or hoot shrilly. -*n.* shrill piercing cry; (*sl.*) something ludicrous. -**scream'er** *n.* [imit. orig.]

screech *v.i.* and *n.* scream. -**screechowl** *n.* barn-owl. [earlier *scratch*, of imit. orig.]

screen *n.* piece of furniture to shelter from heat, light, draught or observation; anything used for such purpose; sheet or board to display cinema pictures, *etc.*, wooden or stone partition in a church. -*v.t.* shelter or hide; protect from detection; sift, assort, as coal; examine a person's political antecedents. [OF. *escren*]

screw *n.* cylinder with a spiral ridge running round it, outside or inside; ship's propeller; turn of a screw; twist; miser; worn-out horse. -*v.t.* fasten with a screw; press or stretch with a screw; obtain by pressure, extort; work by turning, twist round. [OF. *escroue*]

scrib'ble *v.t.* wrote or draw carelessly. *v.i.* write or draw carelessly; make meaningless marks with a pen or pencil. -*n.* something scribbled. [*scribe*]

scribe *n.* writer; copyist; author. [L. *scribere*, write]

scrimmage *n.* scuffle. [*skirmish*]

scrimp *v.t.* and *i.* make short or scanty; limit; straiten. -**scrimp'y** *a.* scanty. [OE. *scrimpan*]

scrip *n.* small wallet. [OF. escrepe]

scrip *n.* certificate of holding stocks or shares. [for *subscription* (receipt)]

script *n.* handwriting; written characters. -**script'ure** *n.* sacred writings; the Bible. -**script'ural** *adv.* [L. *scribere, script-,* write]

scrivener *n.* copyist or clerk. [L. *scribere, script-,* write]

scroll *n.* roll or parchment of paper; list; ornament shaped like a scroll of paper. [OF. *escrou*]

scrounge' (-ow-) *v.t.* and *i.* (*sl.*) pinch; cadge. -**scroung'er** *n.* [orig. unknown]

scrub *v.t.* clean with a hard brush and water. -*n.* a scrubbing. -**scrubb'ing-brush** *n.* [obs. Du. *schrubben*]

scruff *n.* nape (of neck). [of Teut. orig.]

scrum'mage, scrum *n.* in Rugby football, close skirmish between opposing forwards. [var. of *scrimmage*]

scru'ple *n.* small weight; feeling of doubt about a proposed action; conscientious objection. -*v.i.* hesitate. -**scru'pulous** *a.* extremely conscientious, thorough; attentive to small points of conscience. -**scrupulos'ity** *n.* [L. *scrupulus,* small sharp stone]

scru'tiny *n.* investigation, official examination of votes; searching look. -**scrutineer'** *n.* *examiner of votes. scrutinize v.t* . examine closely. **scru'table** *a.* [L. *scrutari,* examine closely]

scuf'fle *v.i.* struggle at close quarters. -*n.*

confused struggle. [Sw. *skuffa*, push]

scull *n.* oar used for the stern of a boat; short oar used in pairs. *-v.t.* and *i.* propel or move by means of a scull or sculls. [orig. unknown]

sculpture *n.* art of forming figures in relief or solid; product of this art. *-v.t.* represent, by sculpture. [L. *sculpere, sculpt-*, carve]

scum *n.* froth or other floating matter on a liquid; waste part of anything. [OF. *escume*]

scurrilous *a.* coarse or indecent language. *-scurril'ity* *n.* [L. *scurrilis*]

scurr'y *v.i.* run hastily. *-n.* bustling haste. [orig. uncertain]

scur'vy *n.* disease due to lack of fresh vegetable food. *-a.* afflicted with the disease; mean, low, contemptible. [*scurg*]

scut'tle *v.i.* rush away. [freq. of *scud*]

scut'tle *n.* lidded opening in the side or deck of a ship. *-v.i.* make a hole in a ship, *esp.* to sink it, or to salve the cargo. [OF. *escoutile*, hatchway]

scythe (sith) *n.* mowing implement consisting of a long curved blade swung by a bent handle held in both hands. *-v.t.* cut with a scythe. [OE. *sithe*]

sea *n.* mass of solid water covering most of the earth; broad tract of this; waves; swell. *-sea'board* *n.* coast. *-sea'-cow* *n.* dugong. *-sea'-dog* *n.* old sailor. **seafaring** *a.* occupied in sea voyages. **sea-gull** *n.* gull. *-sea-horse* *n.* fabulous sea-monster; walrus; warm-water fish remarkable for its horse-like head. *-sea'man* *n.* sailor. *-sea'weed* *n.* plant growing in the sea. *-sea'worthy* *a.* in a fit condition to put to sea. *-sea'plane* *n.* amphibious aircraft. *-sea'power*, nation's naval strength. *-sea ur'chin* *n.* marine annual with globular body enclosed in rigid, spine-covered shell. [OE. *sce*]

seal *n.* amphibious marine animal with flippers as limbs, of which some varieties have valuable fur. *-v.i.* hunt seals. **seal'skin** *n.* skin or fur of seals. *-seal'er* *n.* man or ship engaged in sealing. [OF. *seolh*]

seal *n.* piece of metal or stone engraved with a device for impression on wax, *etc.*, impression made by this (on letters, documents, *etc.*) *-v.t.* affix a seal to; ratify; mark with a stamp as evidence of some quality; keep close, or secret; settle, as doom. *-seal'ing wax* *n.* [OF. *seet*, fr. L. *sigillum*, seal]

seam *n.* line of junction of two edges, *e.g.*, of two pieces of cloth, or two planks; thin layer of stratum. *-v.t.* mark with furrows or wrinkles. [OE.]

sé'ance *n.* session of a public body; meeting of Spiritualists. [F.]

sear *v.t.* scorch or brand with a hot iron; deaden. IOE. *seartan*]

search *v.t.* look over or through in order to find something: probe into. *-v.i.* explore. look for something. *-n.* act of searching; quest. *-search'ing* *a.* keen thorough. *-search'light* *n.* electric arelight which sends a concentrated beam in any desired direction. *-search-warrant* *n.* authorization enabling police to search house *etc.*, [F. *chercher*]

seas'on *n.* one of the four divisions of the year associated with a type of weather and a stage of agriculture: proper time; period during which something happens, grows, is active, *etc.* *-v.t.* bring into sound condition; flavor with salt or condiments, *etc.* *-seas'onable* *a.* suitable for the season. *-seas'onal* *a.* depending on, or varying with seasons. *-seas'oning* *n.* flavoring materials. [F. *saison*, fr. L. *satio*, sowing]

seat *n.* thing made or used for sitting on: manner of sitting (of riding, *etc.*); right to sit (*e.g.*, in a council, etc,); sitting part of the body; locality of a disease, trouble, *etc.*, country house. *-v.t.* make to sit; provide sitting accommodation for. [ON. *salti*]

sec'ant *a.* cutting. *-n* . line that cuts another; (*trig.*) line from center of a circle through one end of an arc, cutting the tangent from the other end. [L. *secare*, cut]

secede' *v.i.* withdraw from a federation, *etc.* *-seces'sion* *n.* *-seces'sionist* *n.* [L. *secedere, secess-*, go apart]

seclude' *v.t.* guard from, remove from sight or resort, *-seclu'sion* *n.* [L. *secludere, seclus-*, shut away]

sec'ond *a.* next after the first. *-n.* person or thing coming second; one giving aid, *esp.* assisting a principal in a duel; sixtieth part of a minute. *-v.t* . support further; support (a motion in a meeting) so that discussion may be in order. *-sec'ondly* *adv.* *-sec'ondary* *a.* subsidiary, or of less importance; of education, coming between primary and university stages. *-sec'ondarily* *adv.* *-sec'onder* *n.* *-sec'ondhand'* *a.* buy after use by a previous owner, not original. *-sec'ond-rate* *a.* inferior, mediocre. *-sec'ond sight'*, faculty of prophetic vision. [L. *secundus*]

se'cret *a.* kept or meant to be kept from general knowledge; hidden. *-n.* something kept secret. *-se'cretly* *adv.* **se'crecy** *n.* a keeping or being kept secret; ability to keep secrets. *-se'cretive* *a.* uncommunicative. *-se'cretiveness* *n.* [L. *secretus*, separated]

sec'retary *n*. one employed by another to deal with papers and correspondence, keep records, prepare business, *etc.*; official in charge of certain departments of government. -**secreta'rial** *a*. -**secretar'iat** *n*. body of officials led by a secretary; body of secretaries. -**sec'retaryship** *n*. [Med. L. *secretarius*]

secrete' *v.t*. hide; of a gland, *etc.*, collect and supply a particular substance in the body. [L. *secernere, secret-*, to put apart]

sect *n*. party within a church; religious denomination. -**sect'ary** *n*. -**secta'rian** *a*. [L. *sequi, sect-*, follow]

sec'tion *n*. cutting; part cut off, drawing of anything as if cut through. -**sec'tional** *a*. -**sec'tor** *n*. a part of a circle enclosed by two radii and the arc which they cut off, a sub-division of the front occupied by an army. [L. *secare, sect-*, cut]

sec'ular *a*. wordly; lay; not monastic; lasting for, or occurring once in, an age- **sec'ularist** *n*. one who would exclude religion from schools. -**sec'ularism** *n*. **sec'ularize** *v.t*. transfer from religious to lay possession or use. -**seculariza'tion** *n*. [L. *secularis*, fr. *seculurn*, age, century]

secure' *a*. safe; free from care; firmly fixed. -*v.t*. make safe; free (a creditor) from risk of loss; make firm; gain possession of. -**secure'ly** *adv*. -**secu'rity** *n*. [L. *secur-us*]

sedate' *a*. calm, collected, serious. **sedate'ly** *adv*. -**sed'ative** *a*. soothing. -*n*. soothing drug. -**sed'entary** *a*. sitting much; done in a chair. [L. *sedere*, sit]

sed'iment *n*. matter which settles to the bottom of liquid. [L. *sedimentum-sedere*, sit]

sedi'tion *n*. talk or speech urging to rebellion. -**sedi'tious** *a*. [L. *seditio*, a going apart]

seduce *v.t*. lead astray, persuade to commit some sin or folly; induce (a woman) to surrender her chastity. -**seduc'tion** *n*. -**seduct'ive** *a*. alluring, winning. [L. *seducere, seduct-*, lead away]

see *v.t*. perceive with the eyes or mentally; find out, reflect; come to know; interview. -*v.i*. perceive; understand. -**seer** *n*. prophet. -**see'ing** *conj*. since. [OE. *seon*]

see *n*. diocese and work of a bishop. [OF. *sie*, fr. L. *sedere*, sit]

seed *n*. reproductive germs of flowering plants; one grain of this; such grains saved or used for sowing; offspring. -*v.i*. produce seed. -*v.t*. sow with seed. -**seed'ling** *n*. young plant raised from seed. [OE. *soed*]

seek *v.t*. make search or enquiry for. -*v.i*. search. [OE. *secant*]

seem *v.i*. appear (to be or to do). - **seem'ingly** *adv*. -**seem'ly** *a*. becoming and proper. -**seem'liness** *n*. [ON. *soma*]

seep *v.i*. oak through; ooze. [OE. *sipean*]

seer. *See* see.

see'saw *n*. game in which children sit at opposite ends of a plank supported in the middle and swing up and down, plank used for this. -*v.i*. move up and down. [redupl. on *saw*]

seethe *v.t*. boil, cook or soak in hot liquid. -*v.i*. be agitated or in confused movement. [OE. *seothan*, boil]

seg'ment *n*. piece cut off, section; part of a circle cut off by a straight line. [L. *segmentum*]

segregate *v.t*. set apart from the rest. - **segrega'tion** *n*. [L. *segregate*, remove from the flock, *grex, greg-*]

segue (-gwi) *v.i*. proceed from one section or piece of music to another without a break; (imperative) play on without pause; a musical direction. *n*. practice or an instance of playing music in this way. [It. *seguire*, follow]

seine (son) *n*. large upright fishing net. [F.]

seis'm (sizm) *n*. earthquake. -**seis'mic** *a*. of earthquakes. -**seis'micity** *n*. seismic activity; the phenomenon of earthquake activity or the occurrence of artificially produced earth tremors. -**seis'mograph** *n*. instrument to record earthquakes. - **seismol'ogy** *n*. science of earthquakes. [G. *seismos*, earthquake]

seize *v.t*. grasp; lay hold of; perceive. - **seiz'able** *a*. -**seiz'ure** *n*. a seizing; sudden illness. [F. *saisir*]

sel'dom *adv*. rarely. [OE. *seldan*]

select' *v.t*. pick out, choose. -*a*. choice, picked; exclusive. -**selec'tion** *n*. -**select'or** *n*. [L. *seligere, select-*]

self *pron*. selves *pl*. is used to express emphasis or a reflexive usage. -*a*. of a color, uniform, the same throughout. -*n*. one's own person or individuality. -**self- deceit**, -**deception** *n*. deceiving oneself , **self- denial** *n*. unselfishness, denying oneself pleasure. -**self-evident** *a*. explaining itself without proof- **self'ish** *a*. concerned unduly over personal profit or pleasure, lacking consideration for others. -**self'ishly** *adv*. -**self'less** *a*. - **self'contained'** *a*. complete in itself, *(of a person)* reserved. -**self-possessed'** *a*. calm, composed. -**self-righteous** *a*. smug, believing oneself better than others. -**self'-**same *a*. very same. -**self-seeking** *a*. striving for one's own advancement only. -**self-sufficient** *a*. independent of others, presumptuous. self-will *n.* obstinacy. [OE.]

sell *v.t.* hand over for a price; betray or cheat; of an idea *etc.* promote it with 'sales talk'. *-v.i.* find purchasers. *-n.* (*sl.*) disappointment. **-sell'er** *n.* [OE. *sellan*]

seman'tic *a.* concerned with the meanings of words. *- n.pl.* science of the meanings of words. [G. *seinantikos*, significant]

semaphore *n.* post with movable arm or arms used for signaling; system of signaling by human or mechanical arms. [G. *sema*, sign, *phoros*, bearing]

sem'blance *n.* appearance; image; likeness. [F. *sembler*, seem]

seme'ster *n.* university or college half-year course; one of the two, or three, divisions of the school year. [L. *semestris*-six months (course)]

semi- *prefix.* half as in **sem'ibreve** *n.* musical note half the length of a breve. **sem'icircle** *n.* half a circle. **-semicir'cular** *a.* **-semico'lon** *n.* punctuation mark (;} **sem'iquaver** *n.* musical note half the length of a quaver. **-sem'itone** *n.* musical half note. **-sem'i-detach'ed** *a.* of a house, joined to another on one side only. **-sem'ifi'nal** *a.* and *n.* last but one (match) of series. [L. *semi*, half]

semiconductor *n.* (*compute.*) solid state electronic switching device that performs functions similar to an electronic tube. **semiconductor memory** *n.* memory system containing thousands of microscopic transistors and instructions manufactured on a chip of silicon.

seminal *a.* pert. to semen or seed; reproductive; capable of developing; influential. [L. *semen*, seed]

seminary *n.* school or college, *esp.* for priests. [L. *seminarium*, seed plot]

Semi'tic *a.* of Semites. (Jews, Arabs *etc.*) of their languages; the languages. [G. *Sem*, *Shem*]

semolin'a *a.* hard grains left after the sifting of flour, used for puddings *etc.* [L. *simila*, wheatmeal]

sen'ate *n.* upper council of a state, university, *etc.* **-sen'ator** *n.* **-senator'ial** *a.* [L. *senatus*, council of old men]

send *v.t.* cause to go or be conveyed; despatch; discharge. [OE. *setidan*]

sen'eschal *n.* steward or major domo of medieval castle. [OF.]

se'nile *a.* showing the weakness of old age. **-senil'ity** *n.* [L. *senex*, old]

se'nior *a.* older; superior in rank or standing. *-n.* an elder person; a superior. **senior'ity** *n.* [L. compar. of *senex*, old]

sense *n.* any of the bodily functions of perception or feeling; sensitiveness ofany or all of these faculties; ability to perceive, mental alertness; consciousness; meaning; coherence, intelligible meaning. **sensa'tion** *n.* operation of a sense, feeling; excited feeling or state of excitement; exciting event. **-sensa'tional** *a.* **sensa'tionalism** *n.* **-sense'less** *a.* **sense'lessly** *adv.* **-sen'sible** *a.* that can be perceived by the senses; aware, mindful; considerable; appreciable; reasonable, wise. **-sensibly** *adv.* **-sensibil'ity** *n.* delicacy of perception, feeling. **-sen'sitive** *a.* open to or acutely affected by external impressions; easily affected or altered; responsive to slight changes. **-sen'sitively** *adv.* **-sen'sitiveness** *n.* **sensitize** *v.t.* make sensitive, *esp.* to make (photographic film, *etc.*) sensitive to light. **-senso'rial, sen'sory** *a.* pert to senses, sensation. **sen'sual** *a.* depending on the senses only and not on the mind; given to the pursuit of pleasure of sense, self-indulgent; licentious. **-sen'suous** *a.* stimulating or apprehended by the senses. [L. *sensus*, fr. *sentire*, feel]

sen'tence *n.* judgment passed on criminal by court or judge; combination of words which is complete as expressing thought. *-v.t.* condemn. **-senten'tial** *a.* of sentence. [L. *sentire*, feel]

sentiment *n.* a mental feeling; emotion; tendency to be moved by feeling rather than reason; verbal expression of feeling. **-sentiment'al** *a.* **-sentiment'alist** *n.* **sentimental'ity** *n.* [Fr., fr. L. *sentire*, feel]

sentinel *n.* sentry. [F. *sentinelle*]

sent'ry *n.* soldier on watch. [fr. *sanctuary*, place of safety, shelter for a watchman]

sep'arate *v.t.* put apart; occupy a place between. *-v.i.* withdraw, become parted from. *a.* disconnected, apart. **-sep'arator** *n.* that which separates, *esp.* an apparatus for separating cream from milk. [L. *separare*]

se'pia *n.* brown pigment made from a fluid secreted by the cuttle fish. *-a.* of this color. [G. = cuttlefish]

sept'-, [L. *septem*, seven] **-Septem'ber** *n.* ninth month (seventh in the Roman reckoning). **-septenn'ial** *a.* occurring every seven years. **-septent'rional** *a.* northern. **-septet(te)** *n.* music for seven instruments or voices. **-septuagena'rian** *n.* person in his seventies. **-sept'uagint** *n.* the Greek version of the Old Testament. [L. *septem*, seven]

sep'tic *a.* causing or caused by blood poisoning or putrefaction. **-sep'sis** *n.* septic state. [G. *septikos*]

sep'ulcher (-ker) *n.* tomb. **-sepul'chral** *a.*

-sep'ulture n. burial. [L. sepulcrum-sepelire, sepult-, bury]

se'quel n. consequence or continuation. -se'quent a. following. -se'quence n. connected series, succession. [L. sequelasequi, follow]

sequest'er v.t. seclude. -sequest'rate v.t. confiscate; divert to satisfy claims against its owner. [L. sequestrate, put in safe keeping]

se'quin n. ornamental metal disk on dresses, etc.; formerly, a Venetian gold coin. [It. zecchino, fr. zecca, mint]

sequoi'a n. kind of giant conifers of California. [Cherokee chief Sequoiah]

sere a. dried up, withered. [OE. sear]

serenade' n. music sung or played at night below a person's window, esp. by a lover. -v.t. entertain with a serenade. [It. serenata, fr. sereno, open air]

serene' a. calm, tranquil. -serene'ly a. -seren'ity n. [L. serenus]

serf n. one of a class of laborers bound to, and transferred with, land. -serf'dom n. [L. servus, slave]

serg'eant (sarj-ant) n. non-commissioned officer; police officer; officer at a law court. -serg'eant-at-arms n. ceremonial official responsible for discipline. -sergeant-ma'jor n. highest non-commissioned officer. [F. sergent, fr. L. serviens, servient-, serving]

serial output n. (compute.) form of output in which the characters are printed letter by letter. opp. parallel output.

ser'ies a. sequence, succession, set. -se'rial a. of and forming a series; published in instalments. -se'rialize v.t. n. serial story or publication. -seria'tim adv. one after another. [L.]

ser'if n. fine cross-line finishing off stroke of letter, as for example at the top and base of H. [orig. uncertain]

serious a. earnest, sedate, thoughtful; not jesting; of importance. -se'riously adv. [L. serius, heavy]

ser'mon n. discourse of religious instruction or exhortation spoken or read from a pulpit; any similar discourse. -ser'monize v.i. talk like a preacher; compose sermons. [L. sermo, sermon-, discourse]

serp'ent n. snake; kind of firework; obsolete wind instrument. -serp'entine a. like or shaped like a serpent or snake; tortuous. [L. serpere, creep]

serra'ted a. notched like a saw. -serra'tion n. [L. serra, saw]

ser'ried a. in close order, press shoulder to shoulder. [F. serrer, lock]

ser'um (se-r-) n. watery animal fluid, esp. a thin part of blood as used for inoculation. -ser'ous a. [L. = whey]

serve v.i. work under another; carry out duties; be a member of a military unit; be useful or suitable or enough; in tennis, start play by striking the ball. -v.t. work for, attend on, help to food; supply something; be useful to; contribute to; deliver formally; treat in a specified way. ser'vant n. personal or domestic attendant. -ser'vice n. state of being a servant; work done for and benefit conferred on another; military, naval, air-force duty; set of dishes, etc. -ser'viceable a. useful or profitable. -ser'vitude n. bondage or slavery. [L. servire]

ser'vice n. a tree like a mountain ash with a pear-shaped fruit. [L. sorbus]

se'same n. eastern plant whose seeds yield gingili-oil. o'pen se'same, magic formula to gain entrance. [G.]

ses'sion n. meeting of a court, etc.; continuous series of such meetings. -ses'sional a. [L. sessio, fr. sedere, sess-, sit]

set v.t. cause to sit, put in place; fix, point, put up; make ready; put to music; put in position. etc. -v.i. of the sun, to go down, become firm or fixed; have a directions. deliberate; formal, arranged beforehand; unvarying. -n. a setting; tendency; habit. [OE. settan]

set n. number of things or persons associated as being similar or complementary or used together, etc.; (tennis) series of games. [OF. sette, sect]

settee' n. couch. [var. of settle]

sett'er n. breed of dog which sets (crouches) on scenting game. (e.g., Gordon, Irish, English)[set]

set'tle n. bench with a back and arms. [OE. setl]

set'tle v.t. put in order; establish, make firm or secure or quiet; decide upon; bring (a dispute, etc.), to an end; pay. -v.i. come to rest; subside; become clear; take up an abode; come to an agreement. [OE. setlan, fix]

sev'en a. and n. cardinal number, next after six. -sev'enth a. ordinal number. -sev'enth heav'en, state of supreme bliss. [OE. soefon]

sev'er v.t. separate, divide; cut off. -v.i. divide. -sev'erance n. -sev'eral a. separate; individual; some, a few. -pron. a few. -sev'erally adv. [F. seurer, wean, fr. L. separate]

severe' (-ear) a. strict; rigorous; simple

and austere; hard to do or undo. **severe'ly**
adv. **sever'ity** *n*. [L. *severus*]

sew *v.t*. join with thread. -*v.i*. be occupied
in sewing. [OE *seowian*]

sew'er (sia-) *n*. underground drain to
remove waste water and refuse. -**sew'age**
n. the refuse. [OE. *esseveur*]

sex *n*. state of being male or female; males
or females collectively; sexual intercourse. -**sex'ism** *n*. discrimination on the
basis of sex. -**sex'ist** *a*. and *n*. -**sex'ual** *a*.
sexually *adv*. [L. *sexus*]

sext'ant *n*. instrument with a graduated arc
of a sixth of a circle to measure angles,
altitudes of a heavenly body, *etc*. [L. *sex-
tans*, sixth part]

sextet' *n*. (*mus*.) composition for six
voices, instruments; the singers, players.
[L. *sex*, six]

shabb'y *a*. poorly dressed; faded, worn;
dishonorable. [OE. *sceabb*, scab]

shack' *n*. hut, cabin. [*shake*]

shac'kle *n*. fetter; manacles; link to join
two pieces of chain, *etc*.; anything that
hampers. -*v.t*. fetter or hamper. [OE.
scacul, bond]

shade *n*. partial darkness; darker part of
anything; depth of color; tinge; shelter or
a place sheltered from light, heat, *etc*.;
ghost. -*v.t*. screen from light, darken; represent shades in a drawing. -**shad'ow** *n*.
patch of shade; dark figure projected by
anything that intercepts rays of light. -*v.t*.
cast a shadow over; follow and watch
closely. -**shad'owy** *a*. -**sha'dy** *a*. [OE.
sceadu, shadow]

shaft (-a-) *n*. straight rod, stem, or handle;
one of the bars between which a horse is
harnessed; entrance boring of a mine;
revolving rod for transmitting power. [OE.
sceaft, shaft of spear]

shag *n*. matted wool or hair; cloth with a
long nap; fine cut tobacco. -**shagg'y** *a*.
[OE. *sceacga*, head of hair]

shake *v.i*. tremble, totter, vibrate. -*v.t*.
cause to shake. -*n*. act of shaking; vibration; jolt. -**sha'ky** *a*. -**sha'kily** *adv*. -
shake'-down *n*. make-shift bed, as of hay
or straw. [OE. *sceancan*]

shall *v. aux*. makes compound tenses to express obligation, command, condition or
intention. [OE. *sceal*]

shallot' *n*. small onion. [F. *échalotte*]

shall'ow *a*. not deep. -*n*. shallow place,
shoal, sandbank. [ep. *shoal*]

sham *n*. imitation, counterfeit. -*a*. imitation. -*v.t*. and *i*. pretend; feign (sickness).
[orig. uncertain]

sha'man *n*. priest of shamanism;

medicine man of similar religion. [Russ.
fr. *Tungus*]

shamb'les *n.pl*. messy, disorderly thing or
place; slaughter-house [OE. *sceamel*,
bench]

shame *n*. emotion caused by consciousness of something wrong or dishonoring
in one's conduct or state; cause of disgrace.
v.t. cause to feel shame; disgrace.
shame'faced *a*. (earlier shame-fast) shy.
-**shame'less** *a*. bold, immodest. [OE.
sceamu]

shampoo' *v.t*. wash (*esp*. hair) with something forming a lather in rubbing. *n* . any
of various preparations of liquid soap for
washing hair, carpets *etc*. [Hind. *sharnpo*,
kind of massager]

sham'rock *n*. trefoil plant taken as the
emblem of Ireland. [Ir. *searnrog*]

shanghai' *v.t*. drug (sailor) and convey on
board ship for service; force or trick someone into doing something. [*Shanghai*,
China]

shank *n*. the lower leg; the shinbone; the
stem of a thing. [OE. sceanca, leg]

shant'y *n*. hut; ramshackle or temporary
house. [F. *chantier*, workshop]

shant'y *n*. sailor's song with chorus sung
by crew at work. [*See* **chanty**]

shape *n*. external form or appearance;
mold or pattern. -*v.t*. give shape to; mold,
fashion, make. -**shape'less** *a*. -**shape'ly** *a*.
well-proportioned. [OE. *gesceap* *n*.; *sciep-
pan v*.]

shard *n*. broken fragment, *esp*. of earthenware. [OE. *sceard*]

share *n*. blade of a plough [OE. *scear*]

share (sher) *n*. portion; dividend. -*v.t*. give
or allot a share. -*v.i*. take a share. -
share'holder *n*. holder of shares in a company *etc*. [OE. *scearu*, cutting or division]

shark *n*. large, *usu*. predatory, sea fish;
grasping person; sharper. [orig. unknown]

sharp *a*. having a keen edge or fine point;
apt, keen; brisk; harsh; dealing cleverly but
unfairly; shrill; strongly marked, *esp*. in
outline. -*n*. in music, a note half a tone
above the natural pitch. -**sharp'ly** *adv*.
sharp'en *v.t*. -**sharp'er** *n*. swindler. -
sharp'ness *n*. -**sharp'-shooter** *n*. marks-
man. -**sharp'-set** *a*. hungry, ravenous.
[OE. *scearp*]

shatt'er *v.t*. break in pieces. -*v.i*. fly in
pieces. [var. of *scatter*]

shave *v.t*. pare away; cut close, *esp*. the hair
of the face or head; graze. -*v.i*. shave
oneself. -*n*. shaving; narrow escape. -
sha'ver *n*. (*sl*.) youngster. [OE. *sceafan*,
scrape]

shawl *n*. square of fabric mainly used to cover the shoulders. [Pers. *shal*]

she *pron.* third person singular feminine pronoun. [OE. *seo*]

she′a-butt′er *n*. butter derived from W. African shea-tree. [native, *shea*]

sheaf *n*. bundle, *esp*. corn. [OE. *sceaf*]

shear *v.t.* cut through; clip or cut; clip the hair or wool from. -*n*. in *pl*. cutting implement like a large pair of scissors; scissor-shaped erection of beams used as a crane. -**shear′er** *n*. -**shear′water** *n*. sea bird of the petrel family. [OE. *scieran*]

sheath *n*. close-fitting cover, *esp*. for a knife or sword; scabbard. -**sheathe** *v.t.* put into a sheath. [OE. *scceth*]

shed *n*. roofed shelter used as a store or workshop. [var. of *shade*]

shed *v.t.* cast off, scatter, throw off, divide. -*n*. dividing ridge; hair-parting. [OE. *sceadan*, divider]

sheen *n*. gloss, brightness, luster. **sheen′y** *a*. [OE. *sciene*, beautiful]

sheep *n*. ruminant animal with a heavy coat of wool. -**sheep′ish** *a*. shy, awkwardly bashful. [OE. *sceap*]

sheer *a*. pure; perpendicular. [OE. *scir*, pure, bright]

sheer *v.i.* deviate from a course. -**sheer off′**, avoid, leave. [var. of *shear*, divide]

sheet *n*. large piece of linen, *etc*., to cover a bed; broad piece of any thin material; large expanse. -*v.t.* cover with a sheet. [OE. *sciete*]

sheet *n*. rope fastened to the corner of a sail. -**sheet′-anchor** *n*. large anchor used only in an emergency. [OE. *sceata*]

shelf *n*. board fixed horizontally (on a wall, *etc*.), on which to put things; underwater ledge. -**shelve** *v.t.* put on a shelf: put off, slope. [LG. *schelf*]

shell *n*. hard outer case of an animal, fruit, *etc*.; explosive projectile; inner coffin; outer part of a structure left when the interior is removed. -*v.t.* take a shell from, or from a shell; fire at with shells. **shell-fish** *n*. sea-animal covered in shell. -**shell′-shock** *n*. nervous or mental disorder caused by shock from bursting shells, bombs, *etc*. [OE. *sciell*]

shelt′er *n*. place or structure giving protection; protection. -*v.t.* give protection to, screen. -*v.i.* take shelter. [orig. uncertain]

shep′herd (shep′-erd) *n*. man who tends sheep. -**shep′herdess** *fem*. [OE. *sceaphirde*, sheep herd]

sher′bet *n*. oriental drink of sugar, water and fruit juices. [Pers.]

sher′iff *n*. county or city officer; chief law-enforcement officer. -**sher′iffdom**, **sher′iff-ship** *n*. office, area of jurisdiction of sheriff. [OE. *scirgerefa*, shire reeve]

sherr′y *n*. Spanish wine. [wine of *Seres* (now Jerez)]

shield *n*. plate of armor carried on the left arm; protective covering. -*v.t.* cover, screen. [OE. *scield*]

shift *v.t.* move, remove. -*v.i.* remove; change position. -*n*. evasion; expendient; relay of workmen; time of their working; removal; formerly, a woman's undergarment. -**shift′less** *a*. lacking in resource or character. -**shift′y** *a*. shuffling, full of evasions. -**shift′iness** *n*. [OE. *sciftan*, arrange]

shill′ing *n*. formerly, British silver coin = twelve pence. [OE. *scilling*]

shimm′er *v.i.* shine with faint quivering light. -*n*. such light; glimmer. [OE. *seymrian*, shine]

shin *n*. front of the lower leg. -*v.i.* climb with arms and legs. [OE. *scinu*]

shine *v.i.* give out or reflect light. -*n*. brightness. -**shi′ny** *a*. [OE. *scinan*]

shin′gle *n*. flat piece of wood used as a tile. -*v.t.* cover with shingles; name board; cut (a woman's hair) close. [L. *scindula*, for *scandula*]

shin′gle (-ng-gl) *n*. pebbles on the shore, of river, sea. [fr. *chink*]

shin′gles (-ng-glz) *n*. disease with eruptions often forming a belt round the body; herpes. [L. *cingula*, belt]

shin′ty *n*. game like hockey played by the Scots and Irish. [orig. uncertain]

ship *n*. large sea-going vessel. -*v.t.* put on or send in a ship. -*v.i.* embark; take service in a ship. -*v.i.* -**ship′ment** *n*. act of shipping; goods shipped. -**shipp′ing** *n*. ships collectively. -**ship′shape** *a*. orderly, trim. [OE. *scip*]

shire *n*. county. [OE. *scir*, district]

shirk *v.t.* evade, try to avoid (duty, etc). -**shirk′er** *n*. [orig. uncertain]

shirt *n*. undergarment for the upper part of the body; blouse. [OE. *seyrte*]

shiv′er *n*. splinter. -*v.t.* shatter. -*v.i.* split into pieces. [ME. *scifre*]

shiv′er *v.i.* tremble, usually with cold or fear. -*n*. act or state of shivering. [orig. uncertain]

shoal *n*. sandbank or bar, shallow; school of fish. -*v.i.* become shallow; collect in a shoal. [OE. *sceald*]

shock *v.t.* horrify, scandalize. -*n*. violent or damaging blow; collision. -**shock′er** *n*. sensational novel. -**shock′ing** *a*. [F. *choquer*]

shock *n*. mass of hair. *a*. shaggy. (obs. *shock-dog*, fr. OE. *scucca*, demon]

shod'dy *n*. cloth made of mixed old and new wool. *-a*. worthless, second-rate, of poor material. [orig. unknown]

shoe *n*. covering for the foot, like a boot, but not enclosing the ankle; metal rim or curved bar put on a horse's hoof, various protective plates or undercoverings. *-v.t.* provide with shoes. **-shoe' black** *n*. one who polishes shoes. **-shoe'horn** *v.t*. implement to ease heel into shoe. [OE. *scoh*]

shoot *v.i*. move swiftly and suddenly; let off a gun, bow, *etc*.; go after game with a gun; sprout. *-v.t.* pass quickly under or along; dump; discharge; kill or wound with a missile. *-n*. act of shooting; expedition to shoot; young branch or stem. **-shoot'ing** *n*. area where game is preserved. [OE. *sceotan*]

shop *n*. place where goods are made, or bought and sold. *-v.i.* visit shops. **shop'lifter** *n*. one who steals from a shop. **-shop'-steward** *n*. trade union representative of factory workers, *etc*. in negotiating with employers. **shop'walker** *n*. overseer who directs customers to various departments. [F. *schoppe*, booth]

shore *n*. edge of the sea, or large lake. [Du. *schor*]

shore *n*. *prop*, *esp*. for a ship on the slips. *-v.t.* prop. [orig. uncertain]

short *a*. having little length: brief, hasty: friable. *-n*. in *pl*. short trousers coming to. and open at, the knee; underpants of a similar style. *-adv*. abruptly. **-short'age** *a*. deficiency. **-short'en** *v.t.* and *i*. **short'bread** *n*. rich cookie made with butter. **-short'coming** *n*. failing, fault, defect. **-short'hand** *n*. method of rapid writing by signs or contractions. **-short'ly** *adv*. soon; briefly. **-short waves** *n*. (wireless) waves between 10 and 50 meters. [OE. *sceort*]

shot *n*. act of shooting, shooter; missile; lead in small pellets; bill at a tavern; film sceiie. *-a*. woven so that the color is different according to the angle of the light. [OE. *sceot*]

shoul'der *n*. part of a body to which an arm or foreleg is attached; support or bracket. *-v.t.* put on one's shoulder. *-v.t.* make a way by pushing. **-shoulder'blade** *n*. shoulder bone; clavicle. [OE. *sculdor*]

shout *n*. loud cry. *-v.i.* utter one. *-v.t.* utter with a very loud voice. [orig. uncertain]

shove *v.t.* and *n*. push. [OE. *scufan*]

shov'el (-uv-) *n*. broad spade with a long or short handle. *-v.t.* lift or move with a

shovel. [OE. *scofl*]

show *v.t.* expose to view, point out; guide; accord (favor, *etc*.,). *-v.i.* appear. be visible. *-n*. something shown; display, spectacle. **-show'down** *n*. disclosure of true state of things. **-show'man** *n*. **-show'off.** display. [OE. *sceau, ian*, look at]

show'er *n*. short fall of rain; anything coming down like rain. *-v.t.* and *i*. rain. **show'ery** *a*. [OE. *scur*]

shred *n*. fragment, torn strip. *-v.t.* break or tear to shreds. [OE. *scread*]

shrew *n*. animal like a mouse; malicious person: scold. **-shrewd** *a*. intelligent, crafty; coming near the truth. [OE. *screawa*, shrewmouse]

shriek *v.t.* and *i*. and *n*. (to utter) a loud. piercing cry of alarm, pain, *etc*. [imit. orig.]

shrill *a*. piercing, sharp in tone. **-shril'ly** *adv*. [imit. orig.]

shrimp *n*. small crustacean of lobster shape. *-v.i.* go catching shrimps. **shrimp'er** *n*. [orig. uncertain]

shrine *n*. case for relics; altar; chapel; temple. [L. *scrinium*, coffer]

shrink *v.i.* become smaller; retire, flinch. *-v.t.* make shrink. **-shrink'age** *n*. [OE. *scrincan*]

shriv'el *v.i.* shrink and wrinkle. *-v.t.* wither up; scorcb. [orig. uncertain]

shroud *n*. sheet for a corpse; covering. *-pl*. set of ropes to a masthead. *-v.t.* put a shroud on; screen, wrap up (fig.) conceal. [OE. *scrud*, garment]

shrub *n*. woody or bushy plant. **-shrubb'y** *a*. **-shrubb'ery** *n*. plantation of shrubs, part of a garden filled with them. [OE. *scrybb*]

shrub *n*. drink of fruit juice, rum, *etc*. [Arab. *sharab*]

shrug *v.i.* raise and narrow the shoulders. as a sign of disdain, *etc*. *-v.t.* move (the shoulders) thus. *-n*. shrugging. [orig. unknown]

shudd'er *v.i.* tremble violently, *esp*. with horror. *-n*. shuddering. **-shudd'ering** *a*. [of Tent. orig.]

shuf'fle *v.i.* move the feet without lifting them; act evasively. *-v.t.* mix (cards); (with off) evade, pass to another. Also *n*. [orig. uncertain]

shun *v.t.* avoid. [OE. *scrunian*]

shunt *v.t.* move (a train) from one line to another; push aside; switch over. [orig. uncertain]

shut *v.t.* and *i*. close. **-shutt'er** *n*. movable screen for a window usually hinged to the frame. [OE. *scyttan*]

shut'tle *n*. instrument which threads the wool between the threads of the warp in weaving; similar appliance in a sewing machine; airplane, bus etc. traveling to and fro over a short distance. -**shuttlecock** n. cork with cup-shaped fan of feathers stuck in it for use with battledore or badminton racquet. [OE. scytel, missile]

shy a. timid, bashful, awkward in company; reluctant. -v. i. start back in sudden fear; show sudden reluctance. -n. sudden start of fear by a horse. -**shy'ly** adv. -**shy'ness** n. [OF. eschif]

sib'ilant a. having a hissing sound. -n, speech sound with a hissing effect. [L. sibilare, whistler]

sicc'ate v.t. dry. -**sicc'ative** a. drying. [L. siccare, siccat-, dry]

sick a. affected by disease or ill health; tired of; disgusted. -**sick'en** v.t. and i. **sick'ly** a. -**sick'ness** n. -**sick'bay** n. on a ship, etc., place for treating the sick. IOE. seoc]

side n. one of the surfaces of an object, esp. upright inner or outer surface; either surface of a thing having only two; part of the body that is to the right or left; region nearer or farther than, or right or left of, a dividing line, etc. ; one of two parties or sets of opponents. -v.i. take up the cause of. -**side'arms** n. pl. weapons worn at the side. -**side'board** n. piece of furniture for holding dishes, etc., in a dining room. -**side'kick** n. person closely associated with another, usu. as subordinate. -**side'long** adv. obliquely. -**side'walk** n. paved walkway for pedestrians at the side of a street. -**side'ways** adv. -**si'ding** n. track added at the side of a railway. -**si'dle** v.i. edge along. -**side'show** n. (auxiliary) fairground show. -**side'track** v.t. shunt; divert. -**side'slip** n. skid. [OE.]

sider'eal a. relating to the stars. [L. sidus, sider-, constellation]

siege n. a besieging of a town or fortified place. [F. siege, seat, siege]

sierr'a n. mountain drawn with saw-like ridges. (Sp.]

siest'a n. rest or sleep in the afternoon. [Sp. = sixth (hour)]

sieve (siv) n. utensil with network or a perforated bottom for sifting. -**sift** v.t. separate coarser portion from finer; solid from liquid. [OE. site]

sigh v.i. utter a long audible breath. -n. such a breath. [OE. sican]

sight (sit) n. faculty of seeing; a seeing; something seen; device (on a rifle, etc.) for guiding the eye; (sl.) large number. -v.t. catch sight of; adjust sights of. -**sight'less** a. -**sight'ly** a. good to look at. [OE. sihth, from seon, see]

sign (sin) n. movement, mark, or indication to convey some meaning; spoor, trail. -v.t. put one's signature to. -v.i. make a sign or gesture; affix a signature. -**sign'-post** n. post supporting a signboard, esp. to show the way at cross roads. -**sign'board** (sin-) n. board with some device or inscription. [L. signum]

sig'nal n. sign to convey an order, etc., semaphore, esp. on a railway. -v.t. make signals to. -v.i. give orders, etc., by signals. -a. remarkable, striking. -**sig'nally** adv. -**sig'nalize** v.t. make notable. [L. signalis]

signature n. person's name written by himself; act of writing it. -**sig'natory** n. one of those who sign a document. **sig'nature tune'**, tune announcing a particular performer, radio feature, etc. [L. signore, signat-]

sig'nify v.t. mean; to intimate. -v.i. to be of importance. -**signif'icant** a. expressing the importance. -**signif'icantly** adv. -**significance** n. -**significa'tion** n. the meaning. [L. signum, sign]

si'lence n. stillness, absence of noise; refraining from speech. -v.t. make silent. -**si'lent** a. -**si'lencer** n. expansion chamber in internal combustion engine., minimizing sound of exhaust; device to deaden report of firearm. [L. silentium]

silhouette' n. portrait or picture cut from black paper or done in solid black on white; outline of an object seen against the light. [E. de Silhouette, French politician (d. 1767)]

sil'icon n. non-metallic base of silica. **sil'ica** n. mineral found in rock-crystal, quartz, etc. -**sil'icon chip** n. tiny wafer of silicon forming an integrated circuit in a computer. -**silico'sis** n. stonemason's disease caused by inhaling silicia-dust. [L. silex, sitic-, flint]

silk n. fiber made by the larvae of certain moths; thread or fabric made from this. -**silk'en** a. -**silk'y** a. -**silk'iness** adv. -**silk'ily** a. [OE. seole]

sill n. slab of wood or stone at bottom of a door or window. [OE. syll]

sill'y a. foolish; weak in intellect. -**sill'iness** n. [OE. gescelig, happy]

si'lo n. pit or tower for storing fodder or grain; underground missile launching site. -**si'lage** n . the fodder, etc . [Sp.]

silt n. mud deposited by water. -v.t. and i. fill with silt. [orig. uncertain]

Silu'rian a./n. (of) division of Palaeozoic rocks before Devonian. [L. Silurs, ancient Welsh tribe]

sil'van a. wooded; rural. [L. silua, wood]

sil'ver *n.* white precious metal; things made of it; silver coins. -*v.t.* coat with silver. -**sil'very** *a.* -**sil'ver-fish** *n.* small wingless insect, the spring-tail. [OE. *siolfor*]

sim'ian *a.* of apes; ape-like. -*n.* ape; any kind of monkey. [L. *simia*, ape]

sim'ilar *a.* resembling, like. -**sim'ilarly** *adv.* -**similar'ity** *n.* likeness. -**simile** (sim-i-li) *n.* (*rhet.*) comparison, *esp.* in poetry. -**simil'itude** *n.* outward appear ance; guise. [L. *similis*]

simm'er *v.t.* and *i.* keep or be just bubbling or just below boiling point; be in a state of suppressed anger or laughter. [imit. orig.]

sim'per *v.i.* smile in a silly or affected way. [orig. uncertain]

sim'ple *a.* plain; straightforward; ordinary, mere. -**sim'ply** *adv.* -**sim'pleton** *n.* foolish person. [L. *simplus*]

sim'ulate *v.t.* pretend to be. -**simulac'rum** *n.* -**simulac'ra** *pl.* shadowy likeness; unreal thing. -**simula'tion** *n.* [L. *simulare*, make like]

simultaneous *a.* occurring at the same time. [L. *simmul*, at the same time]

sin *n.* transgression against divine or moral law, *esp.* one committed consciously; conduct or state of mind of a habitual or unrepentant sinner. -*v.i.* commit sin. -**sin'ful** *a.* of the nature of sin; guilty of sin. -**sin'fully** *a.* -**sinn'er** *n.* [OE. *synn*]

since *adv.* from then till now; subsequently; ago. -*prep.* at some time subsequent to. -*conj.* from the time that; seeing that. [earlier *sithens*, OE. *siththan*, after that]

sincere' *a.* not assumed or merely professed; actually moved by or feeling the apparent motives; straightforward. -**sincere'ly** *adv.* -**sincer'ity** *n.* honesty of purpose; frankness. [L. *sincerus*, pure]

sine (sin) *abbrev.* **sin** (sin) *n.* (trigonometry) in a right-angled triangle the sine of an acute angle is the ratio of its opposite side to the hypotenuse. [L. *sinus*, a bay]

si'necure *n.* office with pay, but no duties. [orig. a church benefice without cure of souls; L. *sine cure*]

sin'ew *n.* tendon. -*pl* . muscles, strength; mainstay or motive power. -**sin'ewy** *a.* [OE. *sinu*]

sing *v.i.* utter musical sounds. -*v.t.* utter (words) with musical modulation; celebrate in song or poetry. -**sing'er** *n.* one who, or that which, sings. [OE. *singan*]

singe (-nj) *v.t.* burn the surface of. -*n.* act or effect of singeing. [OE. *sengan*, make to hiss]

sin'gle (-ng-gl) *a.* one only; alone, separate; unmarried; formed of only one part, fold, *etc.* -*v.t.* pick (out). -**singlet** (-ng-gl-) *n.* undergarment. -**sin'gleton** *n.* single thing; only card of a suit in a hand. -**sin'gly** *adv.* -**sin'gular** *a.* unique; remarkable; odd; denoting one person or thing. -*n.* word in singular. [L. *singuli*, one at a time]

Sinhalese, Singhalese *a.* of people living mainly in Sri Lanka. [Sans. *Sinhalam*, Ceylon]

sin'ister *a.* evil-looking; wicked; ill omened; in heraldry, on the left-hand side. [L. = on the left hand]

sink *v.i.* become submerged in water; drop, give way, decline. -*v.t.* cause to sink; make by digging out; invest. -*n.* receptacle for washing up with a pipe for carrying away waste water; ditch or tunnel for carrying off sewage; place where evil, corruption collects. -**sink'er** *n.* weight used to sink line. [OE. *sincan*]

sin'uous *a.* curving, winding -**sin'uously** *adv.* -**sinuos'ity** *n.* [L. *sinuosus*]

si'nus *n.* an opening; a hollow; a recess in the shore; a bay; (*surg* .) a cavity in a bone or other part; an abscess with a small orifice (**si'nuses, si'nusi** *pl.*) [L. *sinus*, a curve]

sip *v.t.* and *i.* drink in very small draughts. -*n.* portion of liquid sipped. -**sipp'er** *n.* [var. of *sup*]

si'phon *n.* bent tube for drawing off liquids; bottle with a tape at the top through which liquid is forced by pressure of gas inside. (G. = tube)

sir *n.* title of a knight or baronet (with Christian name and surname); public or respectful form of address. [*sire*]

si'ren *n.* legendary female monster supposed to lure sailors to destruction; fog signal; air-raid or fire signal. [L.]

sir'loin *n.* upper part of a loin of beef. [OF. *surloigne*, over loin]

sis'ter *n.* daughter of the same parents or having a common parent. *a.* closely related, exactly similar. -**sis'terly** *a.* -**sis'terhood** *n.* relation of sister; order or band of women. -**sis'ter-in-law** *n.* sister of a husband or wife; wife of a brother. [ON. *systir*]

sit *v.i.* rest on the lower part of the body as on a chair, seat oneself; hold a session; incubate. -*v.t.* sit upon (horse). -**sitt'ing** *n.* act of sitting down or being seated; session, meeting; posing for artist; church seat. [OE. *sittan*]

site *n.* place, situation, plot of ground for,

or with, a building. -sit'uate, sit'uated a.
placed. -situa'tion n. place or position;
employment or post; state of affairs. [L.
situs, place]

six a. and n. cardinal number one more than
five. -sixth a. ordinal number. -n. sixth
part. -six'pence n. sum of six pence; silver
coin of this value. -six'penny a. costing
sixpence. [OE. siex]

size n. bigness, dimensions. -v.t. sort or estimate by size. [for assize]

size n. substance resembling glue. -v.t. coat
or treat with size. [F. assise]

sizz'le v.i. hiss as when frying. -n. hissing
sound; great heat. -sizz'ling a. [imit. orig.]

skate n. flat fish. [ON. skata]

skate n. steel blade with a framework to
attach it to a boot, for gliding over ice. -v.i.
glide on skates. [Du. schaats]

skel'eton n. bones of an animal. -skel'eton
key', key used for picking locks —
skel'eton in the cupboard, hidden domestic secret. [G. = dried up]

sketch n. rough drawing; brief account;
essay, etc. . -v.t. make a sketch of. -v.i.
practice sketching. -sketch'y a. rough, unfinished. [Du. schets]

skew v.i. move obliquely. -a. slanting,
oblique. [OF. escuer]

skew'er n. pin to fasten meat together. v.i.
pierce or fasten with a skewer. [orig. un-
certain]

ski n. long runner fastened to the foot for
sliding over snow. -v.i. slide on skis.
[Norw.]

skid n. drag for a wheel; side-slip. -v.t.
apply a skid to. -v.i. of a wheel, slip without
revolving, slip sideways. [orig. uncertain]

skiff n. small boat. [F. esquif]

skill n. practical ability, cleverness. [ON,
skil, distinction]

skill'et n. pan with long handle; small
cauldron. [ON. skjola, pail]

skim v.t. rid of floating matter; remove
from the surface of a liquid; move over
lightly and rapidly; read in this way. -v.i.
move thus. [OF. escumer]

skin n. outer covering, esp. of an animal or
fruit. -v.t. remove the skin of. -skinn'y a.
thin. -skin'flint n. miser, niggard. [ON.
skinn]

skip v.i. leap lightly; jump a rope as it is
swung under one. -v.t. pass over. -n. act of
skipping. [orig. uncertain]

skipp'er n. captain of a ship. [Du. scipper,
fr. scip, ship]

skirm'ish n. fight between small parties,
small battle. -v.i. fight slightly or irregularly. [F. escarmouche]

skirt n. lower part of a woman's dress,
coat, etc., outlying part. -v.t. border; go
round. [ON. skyrta]

skit n. satire or caricature. -skitt'ish a. frisky, frivolous. [orig. uncertain]

skulk v.i. sneak out of the way; lurk;
malinger. -skulk'er n. [Nor. skulka, to
lurk]

skull n. bony case enclosing the brain.
[orig. uncertain]

skunk n. small N. American animal like a
weasel, which defends itself by emitting
an evil-smelling fluid; mean fellow. [N.
Amer. Ind. segankw]

sky n. apparent canopy of the heavens;
heavenly regions. -sky-lark n. lark; prank.
-sky-light n. window in roof; sky-scraper
n. very tall building. -sky'-writing n.
smoke writing executed in the sky by an
airplane. [ON. = cloud]

slab n. thick broad piece. [orig. uncertain]

slack a. loose, sluggish, not busy. -n. loose
part. -v.t. mix (lime) with water. -v.i. be idle
or lazy. -slack'ly adv . slack'en v.t. and i.
[OE. sloec]

slack n. small coal. slack'-water n. ebb-
tide. [Ger. schlacke, dross]

slacks n. pl. loose trousers for men or
women. [fr. slack a. q.v.]

slag n. dross of melted metal; spongy volcanic lava. -v.i. to form into slag. [Ger.
schlacke, dross]

slake v.i. moderate. -v.t. quench; slack
(time). [OE. slacian]

slam v.t. shut noisily; dash down. -v.i. shut
with a bang. -n. noisy shutting or other
bang. [imit. orig.]

slander n. false or malicious statement
about a person. -v.t. utter such statement.
-slan'derer n. -slan'derous a. [F.
esclandre, fr. L. scandal, scandal]

slang n. colloquial language. -v.t. scold
violently. [orig. uncertain]

slant (-a-) v.t. and i. and n. slope; idea;
viewpoint. v. in a slanting manner. - a.
sloping, oblique. [orig. uncertain]

slap n. blow with the open hand or a flat
instrument. -v.t. strike thus. -slap'-dash a.
careless, rash, slipshod. adv. -slap'stick
(comedy) n. rough knockabout comedy,
farce. [imit. orig.]

slash v.t. gash; lash. -n. gash; cutting
stroke. [orig. uncertain]

slat n. narrow strip of wood or metal; thin,
flat stone. [OF. esclat]

slate n. kind of stone which splits easily in
flat sheets; piece of this for covering a roof
or for writing on. -v.t. cover with slates.
[var. of slat]

slaught'er *n.* killing *v.t.* kill. - **slaught'erous** *a.* -**slaught'er-** *n.* place for killing animals for food. [ON. *site*, butcher's meat]

slave *n.* captive, person without freedom or personal rights. -*v.i.* work like a slave. -**sla'very** *n.* -**sla'vish** *a.* -**sla'ver** *n.* person or ship engaged in slave traffic. [*slav*]

slay *v.t.* kill. -**slay'er** *n.* [OE. *stean*]

sledge, sledge-ham'mer *n.* heavy blacksmith's hammer. [OE. *sleog*]

sledge, sled *n.* carriage on runners for sliding on snow; toboggan. -*v.t.* and *i.* [Du. *slede*]

sleep *n.* unconscious state regularly occurring in men and animals. -*v.i.* take rest in sleep, slumber. -**sleep'er** *n.* one who sleeps; sleeping-car. -**sleep'less** *a.* **sleep'iness** *n.* -**sleep'y** *a.* -**sleep'ily** *adv.* -**sleep'ing-sick'ness** *n.* tropical African disease spread by tsetse fly. -**sleep-walker** *n.* one who walks in sleep, somnambulist. [OE. *slcepan*]

sleet *n.* partly-thawed snow-flakes. -*v.i.* rain sleet. [orig. uncertain]

sleeve *n.* part of a garment covering the arm. -**sleeve'less** *a.* [OE. *slicfe*]

sleigh (sla) *n.* sledge. [Du. *sleet*]

sleight (slit) *n.* dexterity. -**sleight'-of-hand** ' *n.* conjuring. [OE. *sleegth*]

slender *a.* slim, slight, small. [orig. uncertain]

sleuth *n.* track; bloodhound; relentless tracker; detective. [ON. *sloth*, track]

slice *n.* thin flat piece cut off. -*v.t.* cut into slices. [OF. *esclice*]

slick *a.* smooth; smooth-tongued; smart. -*adv.* deftly. -*v.t.* make glossy. -**slick'er** *n.* waterproof [OE. *slycian*, sleek]

slide *v.i.* slip smoothly along. -*v.t.* cause to slide. -*n.* a sliding track on ice made for or by sliding; sliding part of mechanism. - **slide'-rule** *n.* ruler with sliding graduated scale to simplify calculations. -**sli'ding scale'**, scale of *e.g.* wages, which varies in ratio to the variations of another factor. -**sli'der** *n.* sliding part of a machine *etc.* [OE. *slidan*]

slight (-it) *a.* slim, slender; not substantial; trifling. -*v.t.* disregard; neglect. -*n.* indifference; act of discourtesy. -**slight'ly** *adv.* [ON. *slettr*]

slim *a.* thin, slight; crafty. -*v.i.* reduce, grow thinner. [Du. = *crafty*]

slime *n.* sticky mud. -**sli'my** *a.* -**sli'miness** *n.* [OE. *slim*]

sling *n.* pocket with a string attached at each end for hurling a stone; hanging bandage for a wounded limb; any rope, belt, *etc.*, for hoisting or carrying weights. -*v.t.* throw; hoist or swing by means of a rope. [ON. *slyngua*]

slink *v.i.* move stealthily (*p.t.* and *pp.*, slunk, *pres. p.* **slinking**). [OE. *slincan*, creep]

slip *n.* twig cut for grafting or planting; long narrow strip; landing place; slope on which ships are built; leash; mistake; act of slipping. -*v.i.* lose one's foothold. -*v.t.* cause to slip; put on or off easily or gently; release (a dog). -**slipp'er** *n.* light shoe for indoor use. -**stipp'ery** *a.* so smooth as to cause slipping or to be difficult to hold or catch. -**slip'shod** *a.* slovenly, careless. - **slip'-way** *n.* sloping launching-way with one end under water. [OE. *slipor*, slippery]

slit *v.t.* cut open, sever. -*a.* cut, torn. -*n.* straight narrow cut. [OE. *slitan*]

slith'er *n.* slip or splinter of wood; long strip. -*v.t.* divide into long, thin or very small pieces. -*v.i.* split; become split off. [OE. *slifan*, split]

slo'gan *n.* Scottish Highland war-cry; catchword, motto. [Gael. *sluagh-ghairm*, army cry]

sloop *n.* one-masted cutter-rigged vessel; small warship. [Du. *sloep*]

slop *n.* dirty liquid; semi-liquid food. -*v.t.* spill or splash. -*v.i.* spill. -**slopp'y** *a.* (*sl.*) weakly sentimental. [OE. *sloppe*]

slope *n.* slant, upward or downward inclination. -*v.t.* move obliquely. -*v.t.* place slanting; (*sl.*) abscond; stroll off. [OE. *aslupan*, slip away]

slot *n.* narrow hole, depression; slit for coins in, *e.g.*, stamp machine. -*v.i.* make a slot or slots in. -**slotted** *a.* (OE. *esclot*]

sloth *n.* sluggishness; sluggish S. Amer. animal. -**sloth'fully** *a.* idle; unwilling to exert oneself. [fr. *slow*]

slouch *n.* stooping, or shambling walk. -*v.i.* walk in this way. -*v.t.* pull down (a hat). [orig. uncertain]

slough (-ow) *n.* bog. [OE. *sloh*]

slough (-uf) *n.* skin shed by a snake; dead tissue from a sore. -*v.i.* of such tissue to be shed. -*v.t.* shed (skin). [of Scand. orig.]

slow *a.* moving at a low rate of speed; behindhand; dull. -*v.i.* slacken speed. - **slow'ly** *adv.* -**slow'ness** *n.* [OE. *slaw*, sluggish]

sludge *n.* slush, sewage. [*slush*]

slug *n.* land snail with no shell; lazy fellow. -**slugg'ard** *n.* -**slugg'ish** *a.* slow moving; lazy. -**slugg'ishness** *n.* [of Scand. orig.]

sluice *n.* sliding gate or door to control a flow of water. -*v.t.* pour water over; drench. [OF. *escluse*]

slum *n*. squalid street or neighborhood. -*v.i.* visit slums. [orig. unknown]

slum´ber *v.i.* sleep. -*n.* sleep. -**slumbrous** *a.* sleepy, inducing slumber. [OE. *sluma*]

slump *v.i.* of prices, *etc*., to fall suddenly or heavily. -*n.* such fall. [imit.]

slur *v.t.* pass over lightly; depreciate. -*n.* slight. [orig. uncertain]

slut *n.* a dirty untidy woman. -**slutt´tish** *a.* [orig. uncertain]

sly *a.* cunning, wily; done with artful dexterity. -**sly´ly** *adv.* -**sly´ness** *n.* -on the **sly´**, surreptitiously. [ON. *slcegr*]

smack *n.* taste, flavor. -*v.i.* taste (of). [OE. *smcec*]

small (-awl) *a.* little. -**small´ness** *n.* - **small´pox** *n.* contagious disease. - **small´talk** *n.* polite conversation. [OE. *smcel*]

smart *a.* brisk; clever; trim, well dressed; fashionable. -*v.i.* be very painful; suffer acutely. -*n.* sharp pain. [OE. *smeortan*, to be painful]

smash *v.t.* shatter; dash. -*v.i* break. -*n.* heavy blow; wrecked state; accident wrecking vehicles. [fr. *mash*]

smattering *n.* superficial knowledge. - **smatt´er** *v.i.* have a smattering. -**smatt´er** *n.* [orig. unknown]

smear *v.t.* rub with grease, *etc*. -*n.* mark made thus. [OE. *smeoru*, fat]

smell *v.t.* perceive by the nose. -*v.i.* use the nose; give out an odor. -*n.* odor; faculty of perceiving odors by the nose. [orig. unknown]

smelt *v.t.* extract metal from ore. - **smelt´ing-fur´nace** *n.* [obs. Du. *smelten*]

smile *v.i.* assume a pleased or amused expression. -*n.* act of smiling. [orig. uncertain]

smirch *v.t.* make dirty; soil; dishonor. -*n.* mark, blot; stain. [orig. uncertain]

smirk *v.i.* smile affectedly. -*n.* such smile. [OE. *smearcian*]

smite *v.t.* strike; attack; affect, *esp*. with love. [OE. *smitan*, smear]

smith *n.* worker in iron, *etc*. -**smith´y** (-TH-) *n.* his workshop. [OE.]

smock *n.* loose garment with the upper part gathered. -*v.t.* gather by diagonal lines of sewing. -**smock´-frock** *n.* laborer's smock. [OE. *smoc*]

smog *n.* mixture of smoke and fog. [*smoke*, *fog*]

smoke *n.* cloudy mass of suspended particles that rises from fire or anything burning; spell of tobacco smoking. -*v.i.* give off smoke; inhale and expel the smoke of burning tobacco. -*v.t.* expose to smoke (*esp*. in curing fish, *etc*.); consume (tobacco) by smoking. -**smo´ker** *n.* -**smo´ky** *a.* -*n.* smoked haddock. -**smo´kily** *adv.* - **smokestack** *n.* funnel, chimney, from a steam boiler *etc*. -**smoke-screen** *n.* in warfare, cloud of smoke to conceal activities of ships or troops. [OE. *smoca*]

smol´der *v.i.* burn slowly without flame. [orig. uncertain]

smooth (-TH) *a.* not rough, even of surface; plausible. -*v.t.* make smooth. quieten. -**smooth´ly** *adv.* [OE. *smoth*]

smoth´er (-uTH-) *n.* dense smoke, spray, foam, *etc*. -*v.t.* suffocate, suppress. -*v.i.* be suffocated. [OE. *smorian*]

smudge *n.* smear, dirty mark. -*v.t.* make a dirty mark on. [orig. uncertain]

smug *a.* self-satisfied, complacent. - **smug´ly** *adv.* [Low Ger. *smuk*, neat]

smug´gle *v.t.* bring into a country without payment of legal customs duties. - **smugg´ler** *n.* [LG. *smuggeln*]

smut *n.* piece of soot, black particle of dirt; disease of grain; lewd or obscene talk. -*v.t.* blacken, smudge. -**smutt´y** *a.* [Low Ger.]

snack *n.* light meal. -**snack´-bar** *n.* bar, counter, for this. [dial. *snack*, bite]

snag *n.* stump, *esp*. a tree-trunk in a river; any obstacle or impediment. [ON. *snagi*, point]

snail *n.* slow-moving mollusk with a shell, common in gardens. [OE. *sncegel*]

snake *n.* long scaly limbless reptile. - **sna´ky** *a.* [OE. *snaca*]

snap *v.i.* make a quick bite or snatch. -*v.t.* snatch or bite; break abruptly; photograph. -*n.* quick sharp sound; bite; break; photograph. -**snap´shot** *n.* instantaneous photography; print of this; shot without deliberate aim. [Du. *snappen*]

snare *n.* noose used as a trap. -*v.t.* catch with one. [ON. *snara*]

snarl *n.* growling sound made by an angry dog. -*v.i.* make this sound; grumble. [imit. orig.]

snarl *n.* tangle. [fr. *snare*]

snatch *v.i.* make a quick grab or bite (at). -*v.t.* seize, catch. -*n.* grab; short spell. [cp. *snack*]

sneak *v.i.* slink. -*n.* mean or treacherous person. [OE. *snican*, creep]

sneer *v.i.* smile, speak or write scornfully. -*n.* a sneering. [orig. uncertain]

sneeze *v.i.* emit breath with a sudden convulsive spasm and noise. -*n.* sneezing. [OE. *fneosan*]

snick´er *v.t.* snigger, giggle. [imit.]

sniff *v.i.* draw in breath through the nose with a sharp hiss; express disapproval, *etc*., by sniffing. -*v.t.* take up through the nose, smell. -*n.* a sniffing. [imit. orig.]

snip *v.t.* cut, cut bits off. -*n.* bit cut off, small cut. -**snipp'et** *n.* shred, fragment. [Du. *snippen*]

snipe *n.* long-billed marsh-bird. -*v.i.* shoot at enemy individuals from cover. *v.t.* hit by so shooting. -**sni'per** *n.* [ON. *snipe*]

sniv'el *v.i.* sniff to show real or sham emotion, *esp.* sorrow. [OE. *snyflan*]

snob *n.* one who judges by social rank or wealth rather than merit. -**snobb'ery** *n.* -**snobb'ish** *a.* -**snobb'ishly** *adv.* [orig. uncertain]

snoop *v.i.* pry, sneak around. -**snoop'er** *n.* [Du. *snoepen*]

snooze *v.i.* take a short sleep, be half asleep. -*n.* nap. [orig. unknown]

snore *v.i.* make noises with the breath when asleep. -*n.* act of snoring. [imit. orig.]

snort *v.i.* make a noise by driving breath through the nostrils; show defiance; contempt. -*n.* such noise. [imit. orig.]

snout *n.* nose of an animal. [OE. *snut*]

snow *n.* frozen vapor which falls in flakes. -(*sl.*) cocaine. -*v.i.* it snows, snow is falling. -*v.t.* let fall or throw down like snow; cover with snow. -**snow-line** *n.* elevation above which snow does not melt. -**snow'y** *a.* [OE. *snow*]

snub *v.t.* mortify or repress intentionally; rebuke. -*n.* snubbing. -**snub'nose** *n.* turned-up stumpy nose. [ON. *snubba*, rebuke]

snuff *n.* charred candle-wick; powdered tobacco for inhaling through the nose; act of snuffing. -*v.t.* free (a candle) from snuff; put out; draw up or through the nostrils. *v.i.* draw air or snuff into the nose. [cp. *sniff*]

snug *a.* cosy; trim. -**snug'ly** *adv.* -**snugg'ery** *n.* cosy room. -**snuggle** *v.i.* nestle. [orig. uncertain]

so *adv.* in such manner; very; the case being such. -*conj.* therefore; in case that. [OE. *swa*]

soak *v.i.* lie in a liquid. -*v.t.* steep, make throughly wet. -*n.* a soaking. [OE. *socian*]

soap *n.* compound of alkali and oil used in washing. -*v.t.* apply soap to. -**soap'stone** *n.* soft kind of rock, steatite. -**soap'y** *a.* [OE. *sape*]

soar *v.i.* to fly high. [F. *essorer*]

sob *v.i.* catch the breath, *esp.* in weeping. -*n.* sobbing. -**sob'-stuff** *n.* cheap pathos. [imit.]

so'ber *a.* temperate; subdued; not drunk. -*v.t.* and *i.* make or become sober. -**so'berly** *adv.* -**sobri'ety** *n.* [L. *sobrius*]

socc'er *n.* association football, game between two teams of eleven players using a round ball which is kicked from one to another in order to score goals between goalposts. [fr. association football]

so'cial *a.* living in communities; relating to society; sociable. -**so'cially** *adv.* -**so'ciable** *a.* inclined to be friendly, of ready companionship. -**sociabil'ity** *n.* -**so'ciably** *adv.* -**soci'ety** *n.* companionship; living associated with others; those so living; fashionable people collectively; association or club. -**sociol'ogy** *n.* social science. -**so'cialism** *n.* policy aiming at ownership of means of production and transport, *etc.*, by the community. -**so'cialist** *n.* -**socialist'tic** *a.* [L. *socius*, companion]

sock *n.* short stocking; inner sole, formerly, light shoe worn by actors in comedy; hence, comedy. [L. *soccus*]

sock *v.t.* (*sl.*) hit, punch. [orig. unknown]

sock'et *n.* hole for something to fit into. [AF. *soket*, spear-head]

sod *n.* flat piece of earth with grass; a turf. [orig. uncertain]

so'da *n.* alkali. -**so'da-water** *n.* water charged with gas. [It. -L. *solids*, firm]

sodd'en *a.* soaked; like dough; of ground, boggy. [orig. *pp.* of *seethe*]

so'dium *n.* a metallic element found in soda, salt and other compounds. [Latinized from *soda*]

sod'omy *n.* unnatural sexual intercourse, *esp.* between males; anal intercourse. [*Sodom* (Gen. xviii)]

so'fa *n.* long padded seat with a back and one or two ends. [F.]

soft *a.* yielding easily to pressure; not hard; not loud; mild; easy; subdued; over-sentimental. -**soft'ly** *adv.* -**soft'en** (sofn) *v.t.* and *i.* [OE. *softe*]

sogg'y *a.* soaked, soden, marshly; damp and heavy. [orig. uncertain]

soil *n.* earth, ground. [L. *solum*]

soil *v.t.* and *i.* make or become dirty. -*n.* dirt; sewage. [F. *souiller*]

so'lace *n.* and *v.t.* comfort; consolation in distress. [L. *solari*, comfort]

so'lan *n.* large sea-bird like a goose; gannet. [orig. uncertain]

so'lar *a.* of the sun. -**sola'rium** *n.* sunroom. -**so'lar hea'ting** *n.* heat radiation from the sun collected by heat-absorbing panels through which water is circulated. -**so'lar pan'el** *n.* a panel exposed to radiation of heat from the sun, used for heating water or, when mounted with solar cells, to produce electricity direct, *esp,* for powering instruments in satellites. -

so'lar pow'er *n.* heat radiation from the sun converted to electrical energy by specially designed steam boilers and turbogenerators. -**so'lar sys'tem**, system of planets, *etc.* revolving round the sun. -**so'lar plex'us**, nerve network at pit of stomach. [L. *sol*, sun]

sol'der (sōl-, sol-, sod-) *n.* an easily melted alloy used for joining metal. -*v.t.* to join with it. -**sol'dering-iron** *n.* [L. *solidare*, to make solid]

sol'dier *n.* one serving in an army. -*v.i.* serve in the army. -**sol'dierly** *a.* -**sol'diery** *n.* troops.[F. *solde*, pay]

sole *n.* flat of the foot; under part of a boot or shoe, *etc.* -*v.t.* supply with a sole. [F. fr. L. *solea*]

sole *a.* only, unique; single. -**sole'ly** *adv.* only; singly. [L. *solus*]

sol'emn (-M) *a.* serious, grave; formal; impressive. -**sol'emnly** *adv.* -**solem'nity** *n.* -**sol'emnize** *v.t.* celebrate, perform; make solemn. -**solemniza'tion** *n.* [L. *sollemnis*, appointed]

soli'cit (-lis'-) *v.t.* urge; request; entice. -**solicita'tion** *n.* -**soli'citor** *n.* one who solicits; lawyer. -**soli'citous** *a.* anxious. -**solicitude** *n.* [L. *sollicitare*]

sol'id *a.* not hollow; compact; substantial; unanimous. -*n.* body of three dimensions. -**sol'idly** *adv.* -**solid'ity** *n.* -**solid'ify** *v.t.* and *i.* -**solidifica'tion** *n.* -**solidar'ity** *n.* united state. [L. *solidus*]

solid-state circuit *See* semiconductor.

soliloquy *n.* talking with oneself. -**solil'oquize** *v.i.* [Late L. *soliloquium*]

solitaire' *n.* single precious stone set by itself; game for one. [L. *solus*, alone]

solitary *a.* alone, single. -*n.* hermit. -**sol'itude** *n.* [L. *solitarius*]

so'lo *n.* music for one performer; a solo part; motor-bicycle without sidecar. -**so'loist** *n.* -**so'lo flight'**, flight by one person alone. (F.]

sol'stice *n.* period of the year when the sun is overhead at one of the tropics. -**solsti'tial** *a.* [L. *solstitium*]

solve *v.t.* work out, clear up, find the answer of. -**sol'uble** *a.* capable of solution. -**solubil'ity** *n.* -**solu'tion** *n.* answer to a problem; a dissolving; liquid with something dissolved in it. -**sol'vable** *a.* -**sol'vent** *a.* able to pay debts, having more assets than liabilities. -*n.* liquid with a power of dissolving. -**sol'vency** *n.* state of being able to pay one's debts. [L. *solvere, solut-*, loosen]

som'ber *a.* dark or gloomy. -**som'berly** *adv.* -**somberness** *n.* (F.]

sombre'ro *n.* wide-brimmed felt hat worn in Mexico. [Sp.]

some (sum) *pron.* portion, quantity. -*a.* one or other; amount of; certain; approximately; **some'body** *n.* -**some'how** *adv.* -**some'thing** *n.* -**some'time** *a.* former. -*adv.* formerly; at some (past or future) time. -**some'times** *adv.* on occasion. -**some'what** *n.* something. -*adv.* to some extent, rather. -**some'where** *adv.* [OE. *sum*]

somersault (sum-) *n.* tumbling head over heels. [F. *soubresant*]

somnolent *a.* sleepy. -**som'nolence** *n.* [L. *somnus*, sleep]

son *n.* male child. -**son'-in-law** *n.* daughter's husband. [OE. *sunu*]

sona'ta (-d-) *n.* piece of music in several movements, mainly for a solo instrumental. -**sonati'na** *n.* short and simple sonata. [It.]

song *n.* singing; poem for singing; notes of certain birds. -**song'ster** *n.* -**song'-stress** *fem.* [OE.]

so'nic *a.* of sound waves. [L. *sonus*, sound]

sonnet *n.* fourteen-line poem with a rhyme system. -**sonneteer'** *n.* [F.]

sonor'ous *a.* giving out deep sound, resonant. -**son'orously** *adv.* -**sonor'ity** *n.* [L. *sonorus-sonare*, sound]

soon *adv.* before long; early; without delay. [OE. *sona*, at once]

soot *n.* black substance formed from smoke. -**soot'y** *a.* [OE. *sot*]

soothe *v.t.* calm, soften; please with soft words. -**sooth'ing** *a.* -**sooth'ingly** *adv.* [OE. *sothian*, show to be true]

sop *n.* piece of bread, *etc.*, soaked in liquid; bribe; something to quieten. -*v.t.* steep in water *etc.* [OE. *sopp*]

sophist *n.* captious reasoner. -**soph'ism** *n.* specious argument. -**sophist'ical** *a.* -**soph'istry** *n.* -**sophisticate** *v.t.* make artificial, spoil, falsify. -**sophistic'ation** *n.* [G. *sophisma*] -**sophistication** *n.* [G. *sophisms*]

soprano *n.* highest voice in women and boys; singer with this voice; musical part for it. [It.]

sor'cerer *n.* wizard. -**sor'ceress** *fem.* -**sor'cery** *n.* witchcraft.[F. *soreier*]

sor'did *a.* mean, squalid. -**sor'didly** *adv.* -**sor'didness** *n.* [L. *sordidus*]

sore *a.* painful; distressed. *adv.* grievously. -*n.* sore place, ulcer or boil, *etc.* -**sore'ness** *n.* -**sore'ly** *adv.* [OE. *sar*]

soror'ity *n.* club of women, *esp.* a women's student organization formed chiefly for social purposes, *etc.* [L. *soror*, sister] sorr'ow *n.* pain of mind, grief. -*v.i.* grieve. -sorr'owful *a.* -sorr'owfully *adv.* [OE. *sorh*]

sorr'y *a.* distressed; mean, poor. -sorr'ily *adv.* [OE. *sarig*]

sort *n.* kind or class. -*v.t.* classify. -sort'er *n.* [L. *sors, sort-*, share, lot]

sort'ie *n.* sally by besieged forces. [F.]

SOS *n.* letters of Morse Code sent as an appeal for help by ship at sea; a broadcast appeal for a relative of one dangerously ill; an urgent appeal.

sou'fflé *n.* dish made with whisked white-of-egg. [F.]

soul *n.* spiritual part of a human being; person. -soul'ful *a.* expressing elevated feeling. -soul'less *a.* mean, prosaic. -soul food *n.* food, as yams *etc.*, traditionally eaten by southern black Americans. -soul mate *n.* person for whom one has deep affinity. -soul music *n.* type of Black music resulting from addition of jazz and gospel to urban blues style. [OE. *sawol*]

sound *n.* that which is heard; meaningless noise. -*v.i.* make a sound. -*v.t.* cause to sound. -sound'ing *n.* act of sounding; an ascertained depth. [L. *sonus*]

sound *a.* in good condition; solid; of good judgment. -sound'ly *adv.* . thoroughly. [OE. *gesund*, healthy]

sound *n.* channel or strait. (ON. *sund*]

sound *v.t.* find the depth of -*v.i.* find the depth of water. [F. *sonder*]

soup *n.* liquid food made by boiling meat or vegetables. [F. *souse*]

sour *a.* acid; peevish. -*v.t.* and *i.* make or become sour. -sour'ly *adv.* -sour'ness *n.* -sour'dough *n.* leaven; old timer. [OE. *sur*]

source *n.* spring; origin. [F.]

south *n.* cardinal point opposite the north; region, or part of a country, *etc.*, lying to that side. *a.* that is towards the south. *adv.* . towards the south. south'erly (suTH-) *a.* -south'ern (suTH-) *a.* -south'wards *a.* and *adv.* -south'wester, sou'-wester *n.* waterproof hat. [OE. *suth*]

souvenir *n.* memory; keepsake. [F.]

sovereign (sov'rin) *n.* king or queen; ruler; formerly, gold coin *a.* supreme; efficacious. -sov'ereignty *n.* [OF. *soverain*]

soviet' *n.* council, *esp.* of soldiers and workmen, in Russia, forming basis of Russian national government. [Russ.]

sow *n.* female of the swine. [OE. *sugu*]

sow *v.i.* scatter seed. -*v.t.* scatter or deposit (seed); spread abroad. -sow'er *n.* [OE. *sawan*]

soy'a-bean *n.* Eastern edible bean. -soy'a-flour *n.* flour made from it. -soy sauce *n.* salty, dark brown sauce made from fermented soya beans, used *esp.* in Chinese cookery. [Jap. *shoyu*]

space *n.* extent; period; area; expanse; expanse of the universe; empty place. *v.t.* place at intervals. -spa'cious *n.* roomy. [F. *espace*, fr. L. *spatium*]

spade *n.* tool for digging. [OE. *spadu*]

spades *n.pl.* suit at cards. -*sing.* card of this suit. [Sp. *espada*, sword]

spaghetti (-get'-) *n.* dried wheat-paste in long narrow tubes, thinner than macaroni. [It.]

span *n.* space from thumb to little finger as a measure; extent or space; the stretch of an arch, *etc.*; (airplane) distance between wingtips; team of oxen. -*v.t.* stretch over; measure with the hand; harness or yoke. -spann'er *n.* tool for gripping the nut of a screw. [OE. *spann*]

spaniel *n.* dog with long ears and hair. [OF. *espagneul*, 'Spanish']

spank *v.i.* move with vigor or spirit. -spank'ing *a.* brisk; fine, big. -spank'er *n.* fast-going horse, ship, *etc.* [Dan. *spanke*, strut]

spank *v.t.* slap with the flat of the hand, *esp.* in chastising children. [imit.]

spar *n.* pole, *esp.* as part of a ship's rigging. [On. *sparri*]

spar *v.i.* box; make boxing motions; dispute, *esp.* in fun. [orig. uncertain]

spare *a.* additional, in reserve, not in use. -*v.t.* leave unhurt; abstain from using; do without; give away. spar'ing using little; economical. -spar'ingly *adv.* [OE. *sparian*]

spark *n.* small glowing or burning particle; trace; electric spark igniting explosive mixture in car cylinder. -*v.i.* emit sparks. -spar'kie *v.i.* glitter. [OE. *spearca*]

sparr'ow *n.* small brownish bird, common in towns. [OE. *spearswa*]

sparse *a.* thinly scattered. -sparse'ly *adv.* [L. *spargere, spars-*, scatter]

spar'tan *a.* hardy; frugal. [*Sparta*]

spas'm (-zm) *n.* convulsive muscular contraction. -spasmod'ic *a.* of the nature of a spasm; jerky; intermittent; disjointed. -spa'stic *a.* of, like spasms, spasmodic. [G. *spasmos*]

spat *n.* usu. pl. short gaiter. [short for *spatter-dash*, shield against splashes]

spatt'er *v.t.* splash, cast drops over. -*v.i.* fall in drops. -*n.* slight splash. -spatt'er-dash *n.* protection against splashes. [Du. *spatten*, burst]

spat'ula *n.* broad blade, used for mixing paint, *etc.* [L.]

spawn *n*. eggs of fish. -*v.i.* of fish, to cast eggs. [OF. *espandre*, shed]

speak *v.i.* utter words; converse; deliver a discourse. -*v.t.* utter; communicate with (apassingwith). [OE. *sprecan*]

spear *n*. long pointed weapon, pike. -*v.t.* pierce with a spear. -**spear'-side** *n*. male side of family *pl*. distaff-side. [OE. *spere*]

spe'cial (spesh-) *a*. beyond the usual; particular, individual; distinct; limited. -**spe'cially** *adv*. -**spe'cialist** *n*. one who devotes himself to a special subject or branch of a subject. -**spe'cialism** *n*. -**spe'cialize** *v.i.* be a specialist. -*v.t.* make special. -**special'ty** *n*. special product, characteristic, *etc*. [L. *species*, kind, appearance]

spe'cies *n*. class; sub-division; sort or kind. [L.]

specific *a*. characteristic of a thing or kind; definite; specially efficacious for something. -**specif'ically** *adv*. -**spe'cify** (-fi) *v.t.* state definitely or in detail. -**specifica'tion** *n*. detailed description. [L. *species*, kind, appearance]

spe'cimen *n*. individual example; part used to typify a whole. [L. *specimen*]

speck *n*. small spot, particle. -*v.t.* spot. -**spec'kle** *n*. and *v*. speck. -**spec'kled** *a*. -**speck'less** *a*. spotless [OE. *specca*]

spectacle *n*. show; thing exhibited. -*pl*. arrangement of lenses to help defective sight. -**spectac'ular** *a*. -**specta'tor** *n*. one who looks on. [L. *specere, spect-*, look]

spec'ter *n*. ghost; threatening image. [L. *spec'trum*, vision]

spectrum *n*. -**spec'tra** *pl*. colored band into which a beam of light can be decomposed. -**spec'toscope** *n*. instrument for decomposing light and examining spectra. [L.]

speculate *v.i.* make theories or guesses; engage in risky commercial transactions. -**spec'ulator** *n*. -**spec'ulative** *a*. -**specula'tion** *n*. [L. *speculatus*]

spec'ulum *n*. a mirror; a reflector of polished metal, *esp*. such as that used in reflecting-telescopes. [L. *speculum*, a mirror; *specere*, to look at]

speech *n*. act or faculty of speaking words; language; conversation; discourse. -**speechify** *v.i.* make a speech. -**speech'less** *a*. [OE. *sprxc*]

speed *n*. swiftness; rate of progress. -*v.i.* move quickly; succeed. -*v.t.* further; expedite; bid farewell to. -**speedom'eter** *n*. instrument to show the speed of a moving vehicle. -**speed'y** *a*. -**speed'ily** *adv*. -**speed'way** *n*. track for racing. [OE. *spxd*]

spell *n*. magic formula; enchantment. -**spell'-bound** *a*. entranced. [OE.]

spell *n*. turn of work, *etc*.; bout. [OE. *spelian*, act for]

spell *v.t.* read letter by letter; give the letters of in order. [OF. *espeler*]

speller *n*. zinc. [orig. unknown]

spend *v.t.* lay out; disburse; employ. -**spend'thrift** *n*. wasteful person, prodigal. -**spend'er** *n*. [L. *expendere*, pay]

sperm *n*. animal seed; spawn of fishes, frogs. [G. *sperma*]

sphere *n*. globe; range, province. -**spher'ical** *a*. -**sphe'roid** *n*. body nearly a sphere in shape. [G. *sphaira*, ball]

sphinx *n*. statue, half woman, half lion; enigmatic person. [G. *Sphingx*]

spice *n*. aromatic or pungent vegetable substance; spices collectively; trace. -*v.t.* season with spices. -**spi'cy** *a*. piquant. -**spi'cily** *adv*. [OF. *espice*]

spick and span *a*. new and neat. [*spick, spike*, and ME. *span-new*, ON. *span-nyr*, chip-new]

spi'der *n*. animal which spins a web to catch its prey. -**spi'dery** *a*. [ME. *spithre*, fr. OE. *spinnam*, spin]

spig'ot *n*. peg for a hole in a cask. [orig. uncertain]

spike *n*. ear (of corn, *etc*.); sharp-pointed piece of metal, wood, nail. -*v.t.* drive a spike into, supply with spikes, fasten with spikes. [L. *spica*]

spill *n*. splinter or twist of paper for use as a taper. [OE. *speld*, torch]

spin *v.t.* twist into thread; revolve rapidly. -*v.i.* make thread; revolve rapidly. -*n*. rapid run or ride; spinning. -**spin'dle** *n*. rod or axis for spinning. -**spinn'er** *n*. -**spin'ster** *n*. one who spins. [OE. *spinnan*]

spin'ach (-ij) *n*. edible green vegetable. [OF. *espinage*]

spine *n*. thorn; various things like this; backbone. -**spi'nal** *a*. [L. *spina*]

spin'et *n*. instrument like a small harpsichord. [OF. *espiente*]

spin'ster *n*. unmarried woman. [*spin*]

spire *n*. pointed steeple on church or other building; peak, plant, *etc*., of this form. -*v.t.* and *i*. shoot up; furnish into a spire. [OE. *spir*, sprout, shoot]

spire *n*. coil. -**spi'ral** *n*. continuous curve round a cylinder, like the thread of a screw. -*a*. of this form. -**spi'rally** *adv*. [G. *speira*, coil]

spir'it *n*. soul; ghost; essential character or meaning; courage, liveliness; frame of mind; liquid got by distillation, *esp*. an alcoholic one. -*v.t.* carry away mysteriously.

-**spir′itual** *a.* hymn, *esp.* of Black Americans. -**spir′itually** *adv.* -**spir′itless** *a.* -**spir′ituality** *n.* -**spir′itualism, spir′- itism** *n.* belief that the spirits of the dead can communicate with living people. - **spiritualist, spir′itist** *n.* -*spir′ituous a.* alcoholic. [L. *spiritus*, fr. *spirare*, breathe]

spirt *v.t.* and *i.* send or come out in jet. -*n.* jet. [orig. uncertain]

spit *n.* sharp metal rod to put through meat for roasting; sandy point projecting into the sea. -*v.t.* thrust through; impale. [OE. *spitu*]

spit *v.i.* eject saliva. -*v.t.* eject from the mouth. -*n.* a spitting; saliva. -**spit′tle** *n.* saliva. -**spittoon′** *n. vessel to spit into. [OE. spittan]*

spit *n.* spadeful; depth of a spade blade as measure of depth for digging. [OE. *spittan*]

spite *n.* malice. -*v.t.* thwart. -**spite′ful** *a.* -**spite′fully** *adv.* [*despite*]

splash *v.t.* spatter liquid over. -*v.i.* dash, scatter (of liquids). -*n.* sound or result of splashing. -**splash′board** *n.* mudguard. [imit. orig.]

spleen *n.* organ in the abdomen; irritable or morose temper. -**splenet′ic** *a.* melancholy, irritable. [G. *splen*]

splen′did *a.* magnificent, gorgeous; illustrious; excellent. -**splen′didly** *adv.* -**splen′dor** *n.* [L. *splendidus*]

splice *v.t.* join by interweaving strands; join (wood) by overlapping. -*n.* spliced joint. [Du. *splitsen*]

splint *n.* rigid strip of material for holding a broken limb in position. -**splin′ter** *n.* split-off fragment, chip. -*v.i.* break into fragments. [Du.]

split *v.t.* and *i.* break asunder; (*sl.*) give away (a secret, *etc.*). -*n.* crack or fissure. [Du. *splitten*]

splurge *n.* ostentatious display. -*v.i.* [orig. unknown]

spoil *v.t.* damage. or injure; pillage; damage the manners or behavior of by indulgence. -*v.i.* go bad. -*n.* booty. [L. *spoliate*]

spoke *n.* radial bar of a wheel; rung of ladder. -**spoke′shave** *n.* tool for shaping wood. [OE. *spaca*]

spokesman *n.* one deputed to speak for others. [*speak*]

sponge (-unj) *n.* marine growth used to absorb liquids. -*v.t.* wipe with a sponge. -*v.i.* live craftily at the expense of others. - **spon′gy** *a.* [L. *spongia*]

spon′sor *n.* guarantor; patron; one who provides financial backing for an enterprise, *usu.* in return for publicity; one who answers for an infant at baptism; surety. [L.]

spontaneous *a.* of one's own accord; involuntary; impulsive; self-produced; self motivated. -**spontane′ity** *n.* - **sponta′neously.** *adv.* [L. *spontaneous*]

spoof *n.* card game; hoax, trick. -*v.f.* [mod. *coinage*]

spook *n.* ghost; specter. [Du.]

spool *n.* reel. [Du. *spoel*]

spoon *n.* implement with a shallow bowl at the end of a handle for carrying food to the mouth, *etc.* -*v.t.* transfer with a spoon. [OE. *spon*, chip]

spoor *n.* trail of a wild beast. [Du.]

sporad′ic *a.* occurring at intervals or in small numbers. [G. *sporadikos-sporas, sporad-*, scattered]

spore *n.* tiny organ of reproduction in plants and protozoa. [G. *spora*, seed]

sport *n.* pastime; merriment; (*sl.*) one prepared to take a risk, a sporting chance- *v.i.* amuse onself, take part in a game. *etc.* -**sport′ive** *a.* playful. -**sports′man** *n.* one who hunts, shoots, *etc.* -**sports′manship** *n.* [for *disport*]

spot *n.* small mark or stain; place. -*v.t.* mark with spots; detect. -**spot′less** *a.* - **spot′lessly** *adv.* -**spot′light** *n.* light thrown on one part of the stage. -**spott′ed dog** *n.* (*sl.*) plum-pudding. [ON. *spotti*]

spouse *n.* husband or wife. [OF. *espouse*, fr. L. *sponsus*, promised]

spout *v.t.* and *i.* pour out. -*n.* projecting tube for pouring a liquid; copious discharge. [orig. uncertain]

sprain *n.* and *v.t.* wrench or twist (of muscle, *etc.*). [OF. *espreindre*, press out]

sprawl *v.i.* lie or toss about awkwardly.- *n.* sprawling position. [OE. *spreawlian*]

spray *n.* water, *etc.*, flying in small, fine drops. -*v.t.* sprinkle with spray. [LG. *sprei*]

spread (-ed) *v.t.* stretch out; scatter. -*v.i.* become spread.-*n.* extent. -**spreader** *n.* - **spread′-eagle** *v.t.* tie up with outstretched arms and legs. [OE. *spraedan*]

spreadsheet *n.* (*compute.*) form of computer program that manipulates information and displays it in the form of an electronic ledger; accounting tables.

spright′ly *a.* lively, brisk. [fr. *sprite*]

spring *v.i.* leap; appear; crack. - *v.t.* produce unexpectedly. - *n.* flow of water from the earth; first season of the year; leap; recoil; piece of coiled or bent metal with much resilience. - **spring′bok** *n.* S. African antelope. - **spring′-tide** *n.* high tide at new or full moon. [OE. *springan*]

sprin′kle (-ng-kl) *v.t.* scatter small drops

on. - **sprink'ler** n. [OE sprengan]

sprint v.i. run a short distance at great speed. - n. such run or race. - **sprint'er** n. [of Scand. orig.]

sprout v.i. put forth shoots, spring up. - n. shoot. [OE. spurtan]

spruce n. variety of fir. - a. neat in dress. [earlier pruce, fr. Pruce, Prussia]

spry a. active; lively, gay. [orig. unknown]

spud n. small spade-like implement for cutting roots of weeds, etc.; (sl.) potato. [orig. uncertain]

spur n. pricking instrument attached to a horseman's hell; projection on the leg of a cock; projecting mountain range; stimulus. - v.t. apply spurs to; urge. - v.i. ride hard. [OE. sporu]

spurious a. sham. [L. spurius]

spurn v.t. reject with scorn. - **spurn'ing** n. [OE. spornan, kick]

spurt n. a short sudden effort, esp. in a race. - v.i. gush. [var. of spirt]

sput'ter v.t. and i. and n. splutter. [imit. orig.]

spy n. one who enters hostile territory to observe and report. - v.i. act as a spy. - v.t. catch sight of. [OF. espie]

squab (-ob) n. unfledged bird; sofa cushion. - a. clumsy; squat. [imit. orig.]

squab'ble n. petty noisy quarrel. - v.i. engage in one. [imit. orig.]

squad (-od) n. small party, esp. of soldiers. - **squad'ron** n. division of a cavalry regiment or of a fleet, or of an air force. [F. escouade]

squal'id a. mean and dirty, as slums. - **squal'or** n. [L. squalidus]

squall (-awl) n. scream; sudden gust of wind. - v.i. scream. [imit. orig.]

squan'der (-on-) v.t. spend wastefully. [orig. uncertain]

square n. equilateral rectangle; area of this shape; product of a number multiplied by itself; instrument for drawing right angles. - a. square in form honest. - **square meal** n. a substantial meal consisting of enough food to satisfy. - v.t. make square; find the square of; pay; bribe. - v.i. fit, suit. - **square'ly** adv. - **square'-rigg'ed** a. having chief sails square on horizontal yards at right angles to keel. [OF. esquarre, fr. L. ex-quadra]

squash (-osh) v.t. crush flat or to pulp. - n. crowd; game (squash rackets) played with rackets and a rubber ball inside a specially constructed enclosed space. [OF. esquasser]

squash n. gourd-like vegetable [Amer. Ind. asquash]

squat (-ot) v.i. sit on the heels. - a. short and thick. - **squatt'er** n. one who settles on land without title. [OF. esquati, fr. quatir, press flat]

squaw n. N. American Indian wife or woman. [N. Amer. Ind. squa]

squeak v.i. make a short shrill sound. - n. such sound. - **squeak'er** n. one who betrays an accomplice. [imit. orig.]

squeal n. long squeak. - v.i. make one; turn informer. [imit. orig.]

squeam'ish a. easily made sick; over-scrupulous. [AF. escoymos]

squeeze v.t. press; subject to extortion. - n. a squeezing. [OE. cwiesan]

squid n. cuttle-fish. [var. of squirt]

squint v.i. have the eyes turned in different directions. - n. this affection of the eyes; glance. [earlier asquint, of uncertain orig.]

squirm v.i. and n. wriggle. [imit. orig.]

squirr'el n. small graceful animal living in trees and having a large bushy tail. [OF. escureul]

squirt v.t. and i. eject, be ejected, in a jet. - n. instrument for squirting; small rapid stream. [orig. uncertain]

stab v.i. pierce with a pointed weapon. - v.i. strike with such weapon. - n. wound so inflicted. [Gael. stob, stake]

sta'ble n. building for horses. - v.t. put into one. [L. stabulum, stall]

sta'ble a. firmly fixed; resolute. - **sta'bly** adv. - **stabil'ity** n. - **sta'bilize** v.t. and i. [L. stabilis]

stack n. pile or heap, esp. of hay or straw; tall chimney. - v.t. pile in a stack. [ON. stak-kr, haystack]

sta'dium n. (sta'dia pl.) sportsground; arena. [G. stodion]

staff n. (staffs, staves pl.), pole; body of officers or workers; five lines on which music is written. [OE. stæf]

stag n. male deer. [OE. stagga]

stage n. raised floor or platform; platform of a theater; dramatic art or literature, scene of action; point of development; stopping-place on a road, distance between two of them. - v.t. put (a play) on the stage. - **sta'gy** a. theatrical. - **stage'-coach** n. public passenger coach running between stages. - **stage'-fright** n. nervousness before an audience. [OE. estage]

stagg'er v.i. walk or stand unsteadily. - v.t. shock; spread (e.g. holidays) over a period to prevent overlapping. - n. act of staggering. [ON. stakra]

stag'nate v.i. to cease to flow, be motionless. - **stag'nant** a. - **stagna'tion** n. [L. stagnum, pool]

staid *a.* of sober and quiet character. [for *stayed*]

stain *v.t.* and *i.* discolor, soil. -*n.* spot or mark; blemish. [for *distain*, OF. *desteindre*]

stair *n.* set of steps, *esp.* as part of a house. -**stair'case** *n.* [OE. *stager*]

stake *n.* sharpened stick or post; money wagered or contended for; martyrdom. -*v.t.* secure or mark out with stakes; wager-. [OE. *stoca*]

stalactite *n.* deposit of lime like an icicle on roof of a cave. -**stal'agmite** *n.* similar deposit on floor. [G. *stalaktos*, dropping; *stalagmos*, a dropping]

stale *a.* old, lacking freshness. -*n.* urine of horses. -*v.i.* of horses, make water. -**stale'mate** *n.* in chess, a draw through one player being unable to move. [OF. *estale*, spread out]

stalk (-awk) *v.i.* steal up to game; walk in a stiff and stately manner. -*v.t.* steal up to. -*n.* a stalking. [OF. *stealcian*]

stall (-awl) *n.* compartment in a stable; erection for the display and sale of goods; seat in the chancel of a church; front seat in a theater, *etc.* -*v.t.* put in a stall. -*v.i.* stick fast; of an airplane, lose flying speed. [OE. *steall,* standing place, *esp.* for cattle]

stallion (stal'-yun) *n.* uncastrated male horse. [OF. *estalon*]

stal'wart *a.* strong, sturdy, brave. -*n.* stalwart person. -**stal'wartness** *n.* [OE. *stoelwierthe*, serviceable]

sta'men *n.* male organ of a flowering plant. [L. = fibre]

stamina *n. pl.* powers of endurance; vigor, vitality. [L. *stamen*, warp, thread]

stamm'er *v.s.* speak with repetitions of syllables, stutter. -*v.t.* utter thus. -*n.* habit of so speaking. [OE. *stamerian*]

stamp *v.i.* put down a foot with force. -*v.t.* impress a mark on; affix a postage stamp. -*n.* stamping with the foot; imprinted mark; appliance for marking; piece of gummed paper printed with a device as evidence of postage, *etc.*; character. [ME. cp. OE. *stempan*]

stampede' *n.* sudden frightened rush, *esp.* of a herd of cattle, crowd, *etc.* -*v.t.* and *i.* put into, take part in, a stampede. [Sp. *estampido*]

stance *n.* (golf, *etc.*) position, stand; site. [Scot.]

stand *v.i.* have an upright position; be situated; become or remain firm or stationary; be a symbol of, *etc.* -*v.t.* set upright; endure. -*n.* stoppage, a holding firm; something on which a thing may be placed; structure for spectators to stand on for better view. -**stand'ing** *n.* position (in society, *etc.*). [OE. *standan*]

stand'ard *n.* flag; weight or measure to which others must conform; degree, quality; post, *e.g.* lamp-post. -**stand'ardize** *v.t.* [OF. *estendard,* royal banner]

stan'za *n.* group of lines of verse. [It.]

sta'ple *n.* U-shaped piece of metal with pointed ends to drive into wood for use as a ring; main commodity; the fiber of wool. [OE. *stapol*, post]

star *n.* shining celestial body seen as a twinkling point of light; asterisk (*); celebrated player; medal or jewel, *etc.*, of the apparent shape of a star. -*v.t.* adorn with stars; to mark with an asterisk (*). -**star-gazer** *n.* astrologer; astronomer. [OE. *steorra*]

starboard *n.* right-hand side of a ship looking forward. -*a.* of, or on, this side. -*v.t.* put (the helm) to starboard. [OE. *steorbord,* steer side (the steering oar being worked on this side)]

starch *n.* substance forming the main food element in bread, potatoes, *etc.*, and used, mixed with water, for stiffening linen, *etc.* -*v.t.* stiffen with it. [OE. *stearc*, rigid]

stare *v.i.* looked fixedly at; be prominent or obvious. -*v.t.* abash by staring at. -*n.* a staring. [OE. *starian*]

stark *a.* stiff, downright. *adv* . quite (*e.g.* in stark-mad). [OE. *stearc*, hard, strong]

start *v.i.* make a sudden movement; begin, *esp.* a journey. -*v.t.* begin; set going. -*n.* abrupt movement; advantage of less distance to run in a race. [OE. *styrtan*]

star'tle *v.t.* give a fright to. -**start'ling** *a.* -**start'lingly** *adv.* [OE. *steartlian*]

starve *v.i.* suffer from cold, hunger; die of hunger. -*v.t.* kill or distress with lack of food, warmth, or other necessary thing. -**starve'ling** *n.* starving person. -**starvation** *n.* [OE. *steorfan*, di]

state *n.* condition; politically organized community; rank; pomp. -*v.t.* express in words; fix. -**state'ly** *a.* dignified. -**statement** *n.* expression in words; account. -**states'man** *n.* one able in managing the affairs of a state. -**states'manship** *n.* his art. -**state'room** *n.* separate cabin on a ship. [L. *status*, state, fr. *stare*, stand]

stat'ic *a.* motionless, at rest; dealing with forces in equilibrium. -*n.* in *pl.* the branch of physics studying such forces. [G. *statikos*, causing to stand]

sta'tion *n.* place where a thing stops or is placed; position in life; stopping place for trains. -*v.t.* put in a position. -**sta′tionary** *a.* not moving or not intended to be moved. [L. *statio-stare, stat-*, stand]

sta′tioner *n.* one who deals in writing materials, *etc.* -**sta′tionery** *n.* his wares. [orig. tradesman with a *station*]

statist′ics *n.pl.* numerical facts collected systematically and arranged; study of them. -**statisti′cian**, *n.* one who deals with statistics. -**statist′ic** *a.* -**statist′ically** *adv.* [fr. obs. *statist*, politician]

stat′us *n.* solid carved or cast image of a person, *etc.* -**stat′uary** *n.* statues collectively. -**statuesque′** *a.* like a statue. -**statuette′** *n.* small statue. [L. *status*]

stature *n.* height (of a person). [F.]

sta′tus *n.* position, rank, 'standing'; position of affairs. [L.]

stat′ute *n.* a written law. -**stat′utory** *a.* [L. *statuere, statut-*, set up]

staunch, stanch *v.t.* stop a flow [of blood] from. -*a.* trustworthy, loyal. [OF. *estancher*, stop a flow; *estanche*, watertight]

stay *v.t.* stop. -*v.i.* remain; sojourn; pause. -*n.* a remaining or sojourning. -**stay′-in-strike,** strike in which strikers stay in their place of work. [OF. *ester*, fr. L., *stare*, stand]

stay *n.* support, prop; rope supporting a mast, *etc.* -*pl.* corsets. -*v.t.* prop or support. [OE. *stay*]

stead (-ed) *n.* in stead, in place; in good stead, of service. -**stead′y** *a.* firm; regular; temperate. -**stead′ily** *adv.* -**stead′fast** *a.* firm, unyielding. -**stead′fastly** *adv.* -**steadiness** *n.* [OE. *stede*, position, place]

steak (stak) *n.* slice of meat, fish for grilling, *etc.* [ON. *steik*, roast on a spit]

steal *v.i.* rob; move silently. -*v.t.* take without right or leave. -**stealth** (stelth) *n.* secrecy; slinking way. -**stealth′y** *a.* -**stealth′ily** *adv.* [OE. *stelan*]

steam *n.* vapor of boiling water. -*v.t.* cook or treat with steam. -*v.i.* give off steam; rise in vapor; move by steam power. -**steam′er** *n.* vessel for cooking or treating with steam; steam-propelled ship. -**steam′-engine,** engine worked by steam power. [OE.]

steel *n.* hard and malleable metal made by mixing carbon in iron; tool or weapon of steel. -*v.t.* harden. -**steel′y** *a.* [OE. *stele*]

steep *a.* having an abrupt or decided slope. -*n.* steep place. -**steep′ly** *adv.* [OE. *steep*, lofty]

steep *v.t.* soak. [orig. uncertain]

stee′ple *n.* church tower with a spire. **steeplechase** *n.* cross-country horse-race over obstacles. [OE. *stepel*]

steer *v.t.* guide, direct the course of. -*v.i.* direct one's course. -**steer′age** *n.* effect of a helm; part of a ship allotted to the passengers paying lowest fare. -**steers′man** *n.* one who steers a ship. -**steer′ing- wheel** *n.* [OE. *stieran*]

steer *n.* young male ox, bullock. [OE. *steor*, bullock]

stem *n.* stalk; trunk; part of a word to which inflectional endings are added; foremost part of a ship. [OE. *stemm*]

stem *v.t.* check. [ON. *stemma*]

stench *n.* evil smell. [OE. *stenc*]

sten′cil *v.t.* paint with figures, *etc.*, by passing a brush over a pierced plate. -*n.* the plate; pattern made. [orig. uncertain]

stenog′raphy *n.* shorthand writing. [G. *stenos*, narrow]

step *v.i.* move and set down a foot. -*v.t.* measure in paces; set up (a mast). -*n.* act of stepping; mark made by the foot; measure, act, stage in a proceeding; board, rung, *etc.*, to put the foot on; degree in a scale; mast socket. -**step′-dance** *n.* solo dance with intricate steps. [OE. *stæppan*]

stepchild *n.* child of a husband or wife by a former marriage. -**stepfather** *n.* -**step′mother** *n.* -**step′brother** *n.* -**step′sister** *n.* [OE. *steop-*, orphaned]

ster′eophonic *a.* (of sound reproduction) using two or more separate microphones to feed two or more loudspeakers through separate channels in order to give spatial effect to sound. -**ster′eo** *a.* /n.* (of, for) stereophonic sound system. [G. *stereos*, solid, *phone*, sound]

ster′eoscope *n.* instrument in which two pictures taken at different viewpoints are combined into one image with an effect of solidity. -**stereoscop′ic** *a.* [G. *stereos*, solid]

ster′eotype *n.* plate for printing cast from set-up type; something monotonously familiar, conventional, predictable. -*v.t.* make a stereotype from; make into an empty formula. [G. *stereos*, solid]

ster′ile *a.* barren; free from disease germs. -**ster′ilize** *v.t.* -**ster′ilizer** *n.* apparatus to destroy germs. [L. *sterilis*]

ster′ling *a.* of standard value or purity; of solid worth; in British coin. [AF. *esterling*]

stern *a.* severe, strict. -**stern′ly** *adv.* -**stern′ness** *n.* [OE. *stierne*]

stern *n.* after part of a ship; rump, tail, of an animal. [ON. *stjorn*, steering]

stet *v.t.* "let it stand", proof-reader's direction to cancel previous alteration. [L.]

steth′oscope *n.* instrument for listening to the action of the heart or lungs. [G. *stethos*, chest]

steve'dore *n.* one who loads or unloads ships. [Sp. *estivador*, wool-packer]

stew *v.t.* and *i.* cook slowly in a closed vessel. *-n.* food so cooked. **-stew'pan** *n.* [OF. *estuve*, hot bath]

steward *n.* one who manages another's property; attendant on a ship's passengers; official managing a race-meeting assembly, *etc.* **-stew'ardess** *fem.* [OE. *stigweard*, majordomo]

stick *v.t.* jab, stab, fix, fasten. *-v.i.* adhere, project, come to a stop, *etc.* *-n.* rod. **-stick'y** *a.* adhesive, viscous. [OE. *stician*, pierce]

stiff *a.* rigid; awkward, difficult. [OE. *stil*]

sti'fle *v.t.* smother. [earlier *stuffle*; OF. *estouffer*]

stig'ma *n.* brand, mark. **-stig'matize** *v.t.* mark out, brand with disgrace. [G.]

stile *n.* arrangement of steps for climbing a fence. [OE. *stigel*]

stilett'o *n.* small dagger. [It.]

still *a.* motionless, noiseless. *-v.t.* quiet. *-adv.* to this time; yet; even. **-still'ness** *n.* **-still'y** *a.* quiet. **-still'born** *a.* born dead. **-still life** *n.* painting of inanimate objects. [OE. *stille*]

still *n.* apparatus for distilling, *esp.* spirits. **-still'-room** *n.* housekeeper's storeroom. [for *distil*]

stilt *n.* one of a pair of poles with footrests for walking raised from the ground. **stilt'ed** *a.* stiff in manner, pompous [Du. *stelt*]

Stil'ton *n.* kind of cheese. [made famous by an inn at *Stilton*, England]

stim'ulus *n.* something that rouses to activity. **-stim'ulate** *v.t.* rouse up, spur. **-stim'ulant** *a.* producing a temporary increase of energy. *-n.* drug, *etc.*, doing this. [L. = goad]

sting *v.t.* thrust a sting into; cause sharp pain to. *-v.i.* be affected with sharp pain. *-n.* pointed weapon, often poisoned, of certain insects and animals; thrust, wound, or pain of one. **-stin'gy** (-ji) *a.* miserly. [OE. *stingan*, pierce]

stink *v.i.* give out a strongly offensive smell. *-n.* such smell. [OE. *stincan*]

stint *v.t.* keep on short allowance. *-n.* limitation of supply or effect. [OE. *styntan*, blunt]

stipend *n.* salary. **-stipend'iary** *a.* receiving a stipend. *-n.* stipendiary magistrate. [L. *stipendium*]

stipulate *-v.i.* insist on, mention in making a bargain. **-stipula'tion** *n.* **-stip'ulator** *n.* [L. *stipulari*, stipulate]

stir *v.t.* set or keep in motion. *-v.i.* begin to move, be out of bed. *-n.* commotion. **-stir'-**

cra'zy *a.* (*sl.*) mentally disturbed as a result of being in prison or otherwise confined. [OE. *styrian*]

stirr'up *n.* metal loop hung from a strap, support to the foot of a horseman. **-stirr'up-cup** *n.* drink given to a departing rider. [OE. *stigrap*, mount rope]

stitch *n.* movement of the needle in sewing; its result in the work; sharp pain in the side *v.t.* and *i.* sew. **-stitch'ery** *n.* [OE. *stice*, puncture]

stoat *n.* ermine. [orig. unknown]

stock *n.* stump or post; stem; handle or piece to hold by; lineage; animals, materials, *etc.*, requisite for farming trade; supply; broth used as a foundation of soup; various sweet-smelling flowers; money invested in a concern. *pl.* frame of timber supporting a ship while building; frame with holes to confine the feet of offenders. *-v.t.* supply with, or keep, a stock. **-stockbroker** *n.* agent for buying and selling shares in companies. **-stock exchange'** *n.* where stocks are bought and sold; association of stockbrokers. **-stock'piling** *n.* **-stock'still** *a.* motionless. [OE. *stoc*, trunk]

stockade' *n.* enclosure of stakes. *-v.t.* surround with a stockade. [F. *estocade*]

stock'ing *n.* close-fitting covering for leg and foot; anything resembling this. [for *nether stock*, lower hose]

stod'gy *a.* heavy, dull, indigestible. **-stodge** *n.* heavy food. [orig. uncertain]

sto'ic *n.* philosopher holding virtue to be the highest good and teaching indifference to pleasure and pain; person of great selfcontrol. **-sto'ic, sto'ical** *a.* **-sto'ically** *adv.* **-sto'icism** *n.* [G. *stoa*, the Porch where Zeno taught this philosophy]

stole *n.* priestly vestment; a long robe reaching to the feet; women's long scarf of fur or fabric. [G.]

stol'id *a.* hard to excite; phlegmatic; dull. **-stol'idly** *adv.* **-stolid'ity** *n.* [L. *stolidus*]

stom'ach (-mak) *n.* bag forming the chief digestive organ; appetite; inclination. *-v.t.* put up with. [G. *stomachos*, gullet]

stone *n.* piece of rock; rock; gem; hard seed of a fruit; weight = 14 lbs. *-v.t.* throw stones at; free (fruit) from stones. **-stone'-blind'** *a.* quite blind. **-stone' ware** *n.* heavy common pottery. **sto'ny** *a.* **-sto'nily** *adv.* [OE. *stan*]

stonewall *v.i.* obstruct (government) business; play slow defensive game. [*stone* and *wall*]

stool *n.* chair with no back; place for evacuating the bowels; what is evacuated. [OE. *stol*, throne]

stoop *v.i.* lean forward or down. -*n.* stooping carriage of the body. [OE. *stupian*, bow]

stop *v.t.* fill up; check, bring to a halt. -*v.i.* cease, stay. -*n.* a stopping or being stopped; punctuation mark; set of organ pipes; lever for putting it in action. -**stopp´er** *n.* a plug for closing a bottle. -**stop´over** *n.* stop at an intermediate point during a journey. -**stop´watch** *n.* watch with hands which can be stopped for exact timing of races. [OE. *stoppian*, to plug]

store *n.* abundance; stock; place for keeping goods. -*pl.* stocks of goods, provisions, *etc.* -*v.t.* stock, furnish, keep. -**stor´age** *n.* [OF. *estorer*, fr. L. *instaurare*, provide]

stork *n.* wading bird. [OE. *store*]

storm *n.* violent wind or disturbance of the atmosphere; assault on a fortress. -*v.t.* take by storm. -*v.i.* rage. -**storm´y** *n.* [OE.]

stor´y *n.* tale; account; horizontal division of a building; plot of book or play; (*sl.*) lie. -**stor´ied** *a.* celebrated in tales. [L. *historia*]

stout *a.* sturdy; fat. -*n.* kind of beer. [OF. *estout*, proud, fierce]

stove *n.* apparatus for cooking, warming a room, *etc.* [Du.]

stow *v.t.* pack away. -**stow´age** *n.* -**stow´away** *n.* one who hides himself on a ship to obtain passage. [OE. = place]

strad´dle *v.i.* spread the legs wide. -*v.t.* bestride something in this way. [fr. OE. *straed-stridan*, stride]

strag´gle *v.i.* stray, get dispersed. -**strag´gler** *n.* [orig. uncertain]

straight [strat] *a.* without bend; honest; level; in order. -*n.* straight state or part. *adv.* direct. -**straight´en** *v.t.* and *i.* -**straightfor´ward** *a.* open, frank; simple. -**straightfor´wardly** *adv.* - **straightway** *adv.* at once. [ME. *streght*, *p.p.* of *stretch*]

strain *v.t.* stretch tightly; stretch to the full or to excess; filter. -*v.i.* make great effort. -*n.* stretching force; violent effort; injury from being strained; burst of music or poetry; tone of speaking or writing. -**strain´er** *n.* filter. [OF. *estreindre*, fr. L. *stringers*]

strain *n.* breed or race. [OE. *strean*]

strait *a.* narrow, strict. -*n.* channel of water connecting two larger areas. *pl.* position of difficulty or distress. **straitlaced** *a.* puritanical. -**straitjacket** *n.* jacket to confine the arms of maniacs, *etc.* [OF. *estreit*, fr. L. *strictus*]

strait´en *v.t.* make straight, narrow; distress *esp.* by poverty. [OE. *estreit*]

strand *n.* one of the strings or wires making up a rope. [OF. *estran*, rope]

strange (-anj) *a.* unaccustomed, singular. -strangely *adv.* -**strange´ness** *n.* -**stra´nger** *n.* unknown person; a foreigner; one unaccustomed (to). [OF. *estrange*, fr. L. *extraneus*, -extra, beyond]

stran´gle (-ng-gl) *v.t.* kill by squeezing the windpipe. -**strangula´tion** *n.* [L. *strangulate*, strangulat-]

strap *n.* strip of leather or metal. -*v.t.* fasten with a strap; beat with one. **strapp´ing** *a.* tall and well-made. **strap´hanger** *n.* one who travels in crowded buses, trains, clinging to strap. [var. of *strop*]

stratagem *n.* artifice in war; a trick, device. -**strat´egy** *n.* art of handling troops, ships, *etc.*, to the best advantage. **strat´egist** *n.* -**strate´gic** *n.* [G. *stratagema*, piece of generalship]

stra´tum *n.* (**strata** *pl.*) layer. -**stra´tify** *v.t.* arrange things. -**stratifica´tion** *n.* -**stra´tosphere** *n.* high layer of atmosphere, with constant temperature. [L.]

straw *n.* dry cut stalks of corn. -**straw´berry** *n.* creeping plant producing a red fruit; the fruit. [OE. *streow*]

stray *v.i.* wander, get lost. -*a.* strayed; occasional. -*n.* stray animal, person (as in waits and strays). [*astray*]

streak *n.* long line, band. -*v.t.* mark with streaks. -**streak´y** *a.* [OE. *strica*]

stream *n.* flowing body of water, or other liquid. -*v.i.* flow; run with liquid; float or wave in the air. -**stream´er** *n.* ribbon to stream in the air. [OE.]

street *n.* road in a town or village with houses at the side. -**street´car** *n.* vehicle on rails for transporting passengers, *usu.* in a city. -**street´wise** *a.* attuned to and adept at surviving in an urban, poor and often criminal environment. also **street-smart** *a.* [Late L. *strata*]

strength *n.* power. -**strength´en** *v.t.* and *i.* [OE. *strengthu*]

stren´uous *a.* energetic, earnest. -**stren´uously** *adv.* [L. *strenuus*]

stress *n.* strain; impelling force; effort; emphasis. -*v.t.* emphasize; put mechanical stress on. [OF. *estrecier* and for *distress*]

stretch *v.t.* tighten, pull out; reach out; exert to the utmost. -*v.i.* reach; have elasticity. -*n.* stretching or being stretched; expanse; spell. -**stretch´er** *n.* person or thing that stretches; bar in a boat for a rower's feet; appliance on which an injured person can be carried. -**stretch´marks** *n.pl.* marks that remain visible on the abdomen after its distension in pregnancy. [OE. *streccan*]

strew *v.t.* scatter over a surface. [OE. *strewian*]

strict *a.* defined; without exception; stern, not lax or indulgent. **-strict'ly** *adv.* **strict'ness** *n.* **-stric'ture** *n.* critical remark; morbid contraction. [L. *stringers, strict-,* tighten]

stride *v.i.* walk with long steps. **-v.t.** pass over with one step. **-n.** step, or its length. [OE. *stridan*]

strident *a.* harsh in tone. **-strid'ulous** *a.* emitting a grating sound. **-stridor** *n.* harsh sound in breathing. [L. *stridere,* creak]

strife *n.* conflict; discord. [OF. *estrif*]

strike *v.t.* hit. **-v.i.** hit; cease work in order to enforce a demand. **-n.** such stoppage of work. **-stri'ker** *n.* **-stri'king** *a.* noteworthy. [OE. *strican*]

string *n.* fine cord; row or series; gut, *etc.* cord of a musical instrument. **-v.t.** tie with or thread on string. **-pl.** stringed instruments. **-string'y** *a.* fibrous. [OE. *streng*]

stringent *a.* strict. **-strin'gency** *n.* **string'gently** *adv.* [L. *stringers,* tighten]

strip *v.t.* lay bare, take the covering off. **-v.t.** take off one's clothes. **-n.** long narrow piece. **-strip'ling** *n.* youth **com'ic strip,** in a newspaper, strip of small pictures telling a story. [OE. *stripan,* plunder]

stripe *n.* narrow mark or band; blow with a scourge. [of. LG. orig.]

strive *v.i.* try hard, struggle. [*strife*]

stroke *n.* blow, attack of paralysis, apoplexy; mark of a pen; completed movement in a series; rower sitting nearest the stern; act of stroking. **-v.t.** set the time in rowing; pass the hand lightly over. [OE. *stracian*]

stroll *v.i.* walk in a leisurely or idle or rambling manner. **-n.** leisurely walk. [orig. uncertain]

strong *a.* powerful, earnest; forceful; pronounced, *e.g.,* a strong flavor. **stron'gest** *a.* (superl.). **-strong'hold** *n.* fortress. **-strong'ly** *adv.* [OE. *strong*]

structure *n.* construction, building, something made of various pieces. **-struc'tural** *a.* **-struc'turally** *adv.* [L. *struere, struct-,* build]

strug'gle *v.i.* contend, fight; proceed or work with difficulty and effort. **-n.** contest, effort. [orig. uncertain]

strum *v.t.* and *i.* play piano, guitar, *etc.,* idly or inefficiently. [imit.]

strut *v.i.* walk affectedly or pompously. **-n.** such gait. **-strut'ting** *n.* and *a.* [OE. *strutian,* stick out stiffly]

strut *n.* rigid support, usually set obliquely. **-v.t.** stay with struts. [orig. uncertain]

stub *n.* tree-stump; end of a cigar, *etc.* **-v.t.** strike (one's toe) on an obstruction. **-**

stub'bed *a.* [OE. *stubb*]

stub'ble *n.* stumps of cut grain. [L. *stipula,* dim. of *stipes,* stalk]

stubb'orn *a.* unyielding, obstinate. [*stub*]

stucc'o *n.* and *v.t.* plaster. (It.)

stud *n.* movable double button; nail with large head sticking out; boss. **-v.t.** set with studs. [OE. *studu,* post]

stud *n.* set of horses kept for breeding. [OE. *stod*]

stud'y *n.* effort to acquire knowledge; subject of this; room to study in; sketch. **-v.t.** make a study of; try constantly to do. **-v.i.** be engaged in learning. **-stu'dent** *n.* one who studies. **-stu'dio** *n.* workroom of an artist, photographer, *etc.,* building where film, television or radio shows are made, broadcast, *etc.* **-stu'dious** *a.* **stu'diously** *adv.* [L. *studere,* be zealous]

stuff *n.* material, fabric. **-v.t.** stop or fill up. **-v.i.** eat greedily. **-stuffy** *a.* lacking fresh air. [OE. *estoffe,* fr. L. *stuppa,* tow]

stum'ble *v.i.* trip and nearly fall; slip. *n.* **-stumbling** *a.* **-stum'bling block** *n.* obstacle. [ME. *stomelen*]

stump *n.* remnant of a tree, *etc.* when the main part has been cut away; one of the uprights of the wicket at cricket. **-v.i.** walk noisily. **-v.t.** walk heavily; confuse, puzzle; tour making speeches. **-stump'y** *a.* **-stump'orator** *n.* traveling speaker (as using tree-stumps for platforms). [of Teut. orig.]

stun *v.t.* knock senseless. [OF. *estoner,* astonish]

stunt *n.* spectacular effort or feat. [orig. uncertain]

stunt *v.t.* check the growth of. **-stunt'ed** *a.* dwarfed. [OE. *stunt,* dull]

stupendous *a.* amazing. [L. *stupendus*]

stu'pid *a.* slow-witted, dull. **-stupid'ity** *n.* **-stu'pidly** *adv.* [L. *stupidus*]

stu'por *n.* dazed state; torpor. [L. *stupor*]

stur'dy *a.* robust, strongly built. **-stur'dily** *adv.* **-stur'diness** *n.* [OF. *estordi,* reckless]

stutt'er *v.i.* and *t.* speak with difficulty, *esp.* with repetition of initial consonants; stammer. **-n.** act or habit of stuttering. [frequentative of obs. *stut*]

sty *n.* place to keep pigs in. [OE. *stig*]

sty, stye *n.* inflammation on the eyelid. [OE. *stigend*]

style *n.* manner of writing, doing, etc, ; designation; sort; superior manner or quality; pointed instrument for writing on waxed tablets. **-v.t.** designate. **-sty'lish** *a.* fashionable. **-sty'lishly** *adv.* **-sty'list** *n.* one cultivating style in literary or other execution. **-sty'listics** *n.* a branch of linguistics concerned with the study of characteristic choices in use of language, *esp.* literary language, as regards sound, form, or vocabulary. [L. *stilus*]

suave *a.* smoothly polite. [L. *suavis*, sweet]

sub- *prefix*, meaning under, in lower position, *etc.* Often used separated as abbreviation for the whole compound, *e.g.*, 'sub'= a subscription. [L.]

subcommittee *n.* section of a committee functioning separately. committee **subdivide'** *v.t.* divide again. -*v.i.* separate. -**subdivis'ion** *n.* [*divide*]

subdue' *v.t.* overcome; tame; tone down. [OF. *souduire*, fr. L. *subducere*]

sub'ject *a.* liable to, owing allegiance. subject to, conditional upon. -*n.* one owing allegiance; that about which something is predicated; conscious self; topic, theme. -**subject'** *v.t.* make liable, or cause to undergo. -**subject'ive** *a.* relating to the self; displaying an artist's individuality. -**subjectiv'ity** *n.* [L. *subicere*, subject]

sub'jugate *v.t.* conquer. [L. *jugum*, yoke]

subjunc'tive *n.* mood used mainly in conditional clauses. -*a.* in or of that mood. [L. *jungere*, *junct*-, join]

sublet' *v.t.* of a tenant, let to another the whole or part of what he himself has rented. [*let*]

sublime' *a.* inspiring awe. -**sub'limate** *v.t.* purify; heat into vapor and allow to solidify again. -*n.* sublimated substance. -**sublima-tion** *n.* purification of *e.g.* an emotion. -**sublime'ly** *adv.* -**sublim'ity** *n.* [L. *sublimis*, lofty]

sub'marine *a.* below the surface of the sea. -*n.* warship that can operate under water. [*marine*]

submerge' *v.t.* place under water. -*v.i.* go under. -also **submerse'**-**submersion** *n.* -**submers'ible** *a.* -*n.* submarine. [L. *mergere*, *mers*-, dip]

submit' *v.t.* put forward for consideration; surrender. -*v.i.* surrender; urge. **submiss'ive** *a.* -**submis'sion** *n.* [L. *mittere*, *miss*-, put]

subord'inate *a.* of lower rank or importance. -*n.* one under the orders of another. -*v.t.* make or treat as subordinate. [L. *ordinare*, set in order]

suborn' *v.t.* bribe to do evil. -**subornation** *n.* [L. *subornare*. equip secretly]

subpoe'na *n.* writ requiring attendance at a court of law. -*v.t.* summon by one. [L. *sub pcena*, under penalty (first words of the writ)]

subscribe' *v.t.* write one's name at the end of a document; assent; pay or promise to pay (a contribution). -**subscri'ber** *n.* -**subscription** *n.* [L. *scribere, script*-, write]

subsequent *a.* later; coming after. -**sub'sequence** *n.* -**sub'sequently** *adv.* [L. *sequi*, follow]

subside' *v.i.* sink, settle; come to an end. -**sub'sidence** *n.* [L. *subsidere*, settle]

sub'sidy *n.* money granted, *e.g.*, by the state to an industry, or by one state to another. -**sub'sidize** *v.t.* pay a grant to. -**subsid'iary** *a.* supplementing. [*subsidium*, aid]

subsist' *v.i.* exist. -**subsist'ence** *n.* being; livelihood. -**subsist'ence allow'ance**, allowance for living expenses in special circumstances. [L. *sistere*, stand]

substance *n.* matter; particular kind of matter: chief part, essence; wealth. -**substan'tial** *a.* solid, big, important. -**substan'tially** *adv.* -**substantial'ity** *n.* -**substantiate** *v.t.* bring evidence for. -**substantia'tion** *n.* -**sub'stantive** *a.* having independent existence. -*n.* noun. [L. *substare*, stand under, be present]

substitute *n.* thing or person put in place of another. -*v.t.* put in exchange for. [L. *statuere*, appoint]

subterfuge *n.* evasion, lying excuse. [L. *fugere*, flee]

subterranean *a.* underground. -**subterra'neously** *adv.* [L. *terra*, earth]

sub'tile *a.* delicate, rare, tenuous; acute. -**sub'tilty** *n.* fineness; dialectic nicety; acuteness. [L. *subtilistela*, web]

subtle (sut'l) *a.* ingenious, clever; acute; crafty; tenuous. -**subt'ly** *adv.* -**subt'lety** *n.* [L. *subtilis*, fine woven]

subtract' *v.t.* take away a part. -**subtrac'tion** *n.* [L. *trahere, tract*-, draw]

sub'urb *n.* outlying part of a city. -**suburb'an** *a.* [L. *urbs*, city]

subvert' *v.t.* overthrow; corrupt. -**subver'sive** *a.* -**subver'sion** *n.* [L. *vertere, vers*-, turn]

sub'way *n.* underground passage, railway, roadway. [OE. *weg*]

succeed' (-ks-) *v.t.* follow, take the place of-*v.i.* follow; accomplish a purpose. **success'** *n.* accomplishment, attainment; issue, outcome. -**success'ful** *a.* -**success'fully** *adv.* -**succes'sion** *n.* a following; series; a succeeding. -**success'ive** *a.* -**success'ively** *adv.* -**success'or** *n.* [L. *succedere*, success-]

succinct' *a.* terse, concise. -**succinct'ly** *adv.* -**succinct'ness** *n.* [L. *succingere, succinct*-, gird up]

succ'or *v.t.* and *n.* help. [L. *succurrere*]

succ'ulent *a.* juicy. **-succ'ulence** *n.* [L. *succulentus-succus,* juice]

succumb' (-kum) *v.i.* yield; die. [L. *succumbere,* lie down under]

such *a.* of the kind, quality or degree mentioned; of the same kind. [OE. *swile*]

suck *v.t.* draw into the mouth; roll in the mouth. *-n.* a sucking. **-suck'er** *n.* person or thing that sucks; organ or appliance which adheres by suction; (*sl.*) mug, dupe. **-suc'kle** *v.t.* feed from the breast. **-suck'ling** *n.* unweaned child. **-suc'tion** *n.* drawing in or sucking, *esp.* of air. [OE. sucan]

sudd'en *a.* done or occurring unexpectedly, abrupt. **-sudd'enly** *adv.* **-sudd'enness** *n.* [F. *soudain*]

suds *n.pl.* froth of soap and water. [orig. Du. *sudde,* ooze]

sue *v.t.* seek justice from. *-v.i.* make application or entreaty. [F. *suivre,* follow]

suet *n.* hard animal fat. [OF. *sicu,* fr. L. *sebum,* tallow]

suff'er *v.t.* undergo; permit. *-v.i.* undergo pain, hurt, *etc.* **-suff'erable** *a.* **-suff'erance** *n.* toleration. **-sufferer** *n.* **-suff'ering** *n.* trouble, distress. [F. *souffrir*]

suffice' *v.i.* be enough. *-v.t.* meet the needs of. **-suffi'cent** *a.* enough. **-suffi'ciency** *n.* [L. *sufficere*]

suffix *n.* letter or syllable added to the root word. [L. *suffigere,* suffix, fix under]

suff'ocate *v.t.* kill by stopping breathing. *-v.i.* feel suffocated. **-suffoca'tion** *n.* [L. *suffocate,* suffocate]

suff'rage *n.* vote or right of voting. **-suff'ragist** *n.* one claiming a right of voting. **-suffragette'** *n.* militant woman suffragist. [L. *suffragium*]

suffuse' *v.t.* well up and spread over. **-suffu'sion** *n.* [L. *suffundere,* suffus-]

su'gar (shoog-) *n.* sweet crystalline vegetable substance. *-v.t.* sweeten with it. **-su'gary** *a.* [Arab. *sukkar*]

suggest' *v.t.* propose; call up the idea of. **-suggest'ible,** **suggestive** *a.* **-suggest'ively** *adv.* **-sugges'tion** *n.* [L. *suggerere,* suggest-]

suicide *n.* one who kills himself intentionally; self-murder. **-suici'dal** *a.* **suici'dally** *adv.* [Mod. L. *suicidium,* fr. *ccedere,* kill]

suit *n.* action at law; petition; courtship; set, *esp.* of outer clothes; one of the four sets in a pack of cards. *-v.t.* go with, be adapted to; meet the desires of, make fitting, *etc.* *-v.i.* be convenient. **-suit'able** *a.* fitting, convenient. **-suit'ably** *adv.* **-suitabil'ity** *n.* **-suite** *n.* set of things going or used together, *esp.* furniture; retinue. **-suit'or** *n.* one who sues; wooer. **-suit'case**

n. portable traveling-case for clothes, *etc.* [F. *suite*]

sul'fate *n.* salt of sulfuric acid. [L.]

sul'fur *n.* pale-yellow non-metallic element. **-sul'furous** *a.* **-sulfu'ric** *a.* **sulfu'reous** *a.* [L.]

sull'en *a.* resentful, ill-humored; dismal. **-sull'enly** *adv.* [var. of *solemn*]

sull'y *v.t.* stain, tarnish. [F. *souiller*]

sul'tan *n.* Mohammedan sovereign. **sulta'na** *n.* mother, wife, daughter of a sultan; small kind of raisin. [Arab.]

sul'try *a.* hot and close. **-sul'triness** *n.* [obs. *v. sulter,* var. of *swelter*]

sum *n.* amount, total; arithmetical problem. *-v.t.* add up. **-summ'ary** *a.* done quickly. *-n.* abridgement or statement of the chief points of a longer document, speech, *etc.* **-summ'arily** *adv.* **summ'arize** *v.t.* **-summa'tion** *n.* an adding up. **-sum up,** recapitulate. [F. *somme,* L. *summa*]

summ'er *n.* second season. *-v.i.* pass the summer. **-summ'ery** *a.* [OE. *sumor*]

summ'it *n.* top; peak. [F. *sommet*]

summ'on *v.t.* demand the attendance of, call on; gather up (energies, *etc.*). **summ'ons** *n.* call, authoritative demand. [L. *summonere*]

sump'tuary *a.* regulating expenditure, **sumptuous** *a.* lavish, magnificent. **sumptuously** *adv.* **-sump'tuousness** *n.* [L. *sumptus,* expense]

sun *n.* luminous body round which the earth revolves; its rays. *-v.t.* expose to the sun's rays. **-Sun'belt** *n.* the Southern states of the U. S. *a.* **-Sun'day** *n.* first day of the week. **-sun'down, sun'set** *n.* action of the sun dropping below the horizon at the end of the day; the time at which it does this **sun'flower** *n.* plant with large golden flowers like pictures of the sun. **-sunn'y** *a.* **-sun'less** *a.* **-sun'bathing** *n.* exposure of the body to sun's rays. **-sun'rise, sun'up** *n.* action of the sun rising above the horizon at the beginning of the day, the time at which it does this. **-sun'stroke** *n.* collapse from excessive exposure to the sun. [OE. *sunne*]

sun'dae *n.* ice-cream with fruit, nuts, *etc.* [orig. uncertain]

sup *v.t.* take by sips. *-v.i.* take supper. *-n.* sip of liquid. [OE. *supan*]

su'per- *prefix,* makes compounds with meaning of above, in excess, *e.g.* superabundant *a.* excessively abundant, superhuman *a.* more than human. *etc .* These are not given where the meaning and derivation may easily be found from the simple word. [L. *super,* above]

superann'uate *v.t.* pension off, or discharge as too old. **-superannua'tion** *n.* [L. *annus*, year]

superb' *a.* splendid, grand, impressive. superb'ly *adv.* [L. *superbus*, haughty]

supercil'ious *a.* indifferent and haughty. **-superciliously** *adv.* **-supercil'iousness** *n.* [L. *supercilium*, eyebrow]

superfi'cial *a.* of or on a surface; without depth. **-superficial'ity** *n.* [L., fr. *facies*, face]

super'fluous *a.* extra, unnecessary. [L. *superfluere*, overflow]

superintend' *v.t.* have charge of or look. [L. *intenders*, attend to]

supe'rior *a.* upper, higher in position or rank or quality; showing a consciousness of being so. **-superior'ity** *n.* [L.]

super'lative *a.* of or in the highest degree. **-***n.* superlative degree of an adjective or adverb. [L. *superlativus*]

su'perman *n.* ideal man, of an ideal and higher type; person of extraordinary powers. [trans. of Ger. *Ubermensch*]

supernat'ural *a.* above nature; occult; miraculous; spiritual. **-supernat'urally** *adv.* [*natural*]

supernu'merary *a.* in excess of the normal number. **-***n.* supernumerary person or thing. [L. *numerus*, number]

supersede' *v.t.* set aside; supplant; take the place of **-superses'sion** *n.* [L. *supersedere*, *supersess* -, be superior to]

supersonic *a.* of waves of greater frequency than sound; faster than sound. [L. *sonus*, sound]

superstition *n.* religion or opinion or practice based on a belief in luck or magic. **-supersti'tious** *a.* **-supersti'tiously** *adv.* [L. *superstitio*]

supervise *v.t.* superintend. **-supervi'sion** *n.* **-supervi'sor** *n.* [L. *videre, vis*-, see]

su'pine *a.* indolent; negligent; inactive. [L. *supinus*, lying on one's back]

supp'er *n.* last meal of the day when dinner is not the last. **-supp'erless** *a.* [F. *souper*, fr. LG. *supen*, sup]

supplant' *v.t.* take the place of, *esp.* unfairly. **-supplant'er** *n.* [L. *supplantare*, trip up]

sup'ple *a.* pliable; lithe; compliant. **-***v.t.* **sup'ply** *adv.* **-sup'pleness** *n.* [L. *supplex*]

supp'lement *n.* something added to fill up, supply a deficiency. **-***v.t.* add to. **supplement'al** *a.* **-supplement'ary** *a.* [L. *supplere*, fill up]

supp'licate *v.t.* and *i.* beg humbly. **-supplica'tion** *n.* **-supp'licatory** *a.* **supp'liant** *a.* petitioning. **-***n.* petitioner. [L. *supplicate*, fr. *plicare*, bend]

supply' *v.t.* furnish; *s* ubstitute for. **-***n.* a supplying, substitute; stock, store. [L. *supplere*, fill up]

support' *v.t* . hold up; assist; sustain. **-***n.* a supporting or being supported, or means of support. **-support'able** *a.* tolerable. **-support'er** *n.* adherent. [L. *supportare*, fr. *portare*, carry]

suppose' *v.t.* assume as a theory; take for granted; accept as likely. **-suppo'sable** *a* . **-supposi'tion** *n.* **-supposi'tious** *a.* sham. [F. *supposer*]

suppress' *v.t.* put down, restrain, keep or withdraw from publication. **-suppres'sion** *n.* [L. *supprimere*, suppress-]

supreme' *a.* highest. **-supreme'ly** *adv.* **-suprem'acy** *n.* [L. *supremus*]

sure *a.* certain; trustworthy; strong, secure. **-***adv.* certainly. **-sure'ly** *adv.* **-sure'ty** *n.* certainty; one who makes himself responsible for the obligations of another. [F. *sur*, fr. L. *securus*]

surf *n.* foam of breaking waves on a beach. **-surf'y** *a.* **-surfing** *n.* sport of riding the incoming waves on a surfboard. [orig. uncertain]

sur'face (-fis) *n.* outside face of a body; plane; top, visible side; lifting or controlling surface of an plane. [F.]

sur'feit (-fit) *n.* excess. **-***v.t.* and *i.* feed to excess. [F. *surfaire*, overdo]

surge *v.i.* move in large waves. **-***n.* a great wave. [L. *surgere*, rise]

sur'geon (-in) *n.* medical expert who performs operations. **-sur'gery** *n.* treatment by operation; doctor's consulting room. **-surg'ical** *a.* **-sur'gically** *adv.* [F. *chirurgien*, fr. G. *cheirourgos*, lit. hand worker]

sur'ly *a.* morose, ill-tempered. [fr. *sir-ly*, orig. like an arrogant master]

surmise' *v.t.* and *i.* and *n.* guess. [OF. fr. *surmettre*, accuse]

surmount' *v.t.* get over, overcome. **surmount'able** *a.* [F. *surmonter*]

sur'name *n.* family name. [*name*]

surpass' *v.t.* outdo. [F. *surpasser*]

sur'plice (-plis) *n.* loose white vestment worn by clergy and choristers. **sur'pliced** *a.* [OF. *surpeli* s]

sur'plus *n.* what remains over or in excess. *a* . excess. [F.]

surprise' *n.* what takes unawares; emotion roused by being taken unawares; a taking unawares. **-***v.t.* cause surprise to. **-surprising** *a.* [OF., fr. *surprendre*, lit. overtaken]

surre'alism *n.* movement in the creative arts, which endeavors to express the subjective and subconscious. **-surreal** *a.* of the world of the subconscious; dreamlike. -**surrealist** n. [*real*]

surren'der v.t. hand over. -v.i. yield. -n. act of surrendering. [OF. *surrendre*, hand over]

surreptitious a. done secretly or steathily. -**surrepti'tiously** adv. [L. *subripere*, snatch]

surr'ogate n. deputy, *esp*. of a bishop. -a. -**surr'ogate** motherhood or surrogacy n. role of a woman who bears a child on behalf of a couple unable to have a child, either by articial insemination from the man or implantation of an embryo from the woman. -**surr'ogate moth'er** n. [L. *surrogatus*]

surround' v.t. be or come all round. -n. border. [OF. *suronder*, overflow]

surveill'ance n. close watching. [F. *veiller*, fr. L. *vigilare*, watch]

survey' v.t. view; measure or map (land). -**sur'vey** n. a surveying. -**survey'or** n. [OF. *veir*, fr. L. *videre*, see]

survive' v.t. outlive; come alive through. -v.i. continue to live or exist. **survi'val** n. -**surviv'alist** n. person who believes in ensuring personal survival of a catastrophic event by arming himself and often by living in the wild. **sur'viv'atism** n. -**survi'vor** n. [L. *supervivere*, overlive]

suscep'tible a. sensitive; impressionable. -**susceptibil'ity** n. [L. *suscipere, suscept-*, receive]

suspect' v.t. have an impression of the existence or presence of, be inclined to believe; doubt the innocence of. a . of suspected character. -n. (sus'-) suspected person. -**suspi'cion** n. a suspecting or being suspected. -**suspi'cious** a. **suspiciously** adv. [L. *suspicere, suspect-*, lit. look up at]

suspend' v.t. hang up; sustain in fluid; cause to cease for a time, keep inoperative. -**suspend'er** n. -**suspend'-ers** n.pl. straps for supporting trousers, skirt *etc.* . -**suspense'** n. *state of uncertainty.* -**suspen'sion** n. state of being hung up, or debarred. -**suspensory** a. [L. *suspendare*, suspense]

sus'tain v.t. keep or hold up; endure; confirm. -**sustain'able** a. -**sus'tenance** n. food. -**sustenta'tion** n. maintenance. [OF. *sostenir*, fr. L. *sustinere*, hold up]

su'ture n. act of joining together, as the exterior parts of a wound; the seam or joint that unites two bones, *esp*. of the skull. -v.t. to stitch up. [L. *sutura, -suere*, to sew]

svelte a. lithe, slender. [F.]

swab (-ob) n. mop; pad of surgical wool. -v.t. clean with a swab. -**swabb'er** n. [orig. uncertain]

swad'dle (-od-) v.t. swathe. -**swadd'ling bands** (-clothes) n.pl. clothes in which an infant is swathed. [fr. *swathe*]

swagg'er v.i. strut; talk boastfully. -n. strutting gait; boastful or overconfident manner. [orig. uncertain]

swall'ow n. migratory bird with a skimming flight. [OE. *swealwe*]

swall'ow (-ol-o) v.t. cause or allow to pass down the gullet. -n. an act of swallowing. [OE. *swelgan*]

swamp (-omp) n. bog. -v.t. entangle in a swamp; overwhelm, flood. -**swamp'y** a. [of LG. orig. cp. *sump*]

swan (-on) n. large water bird with graceful curved neck. -**swan'-song** n. fabled song of swan before its death; last work of poet, musician. [OE.]

swank n. (sl.) brag; display. -v.i. show off. -**swank'y** a. [Sc.]

swap, swop v.t. and i. and n. (sl.) exchange. (ME. *swappen*]

swarm n. large cluster of insects; vast crowd. -v.i. of bees, to emigrate in a swarm; gather in larger numbers. [OE. *swearm*]

swarm v.i. climb grasping with hands and knees. [orig. uncertain]

swash'buckler n. swaggerer; blustering braggart. [obs. *swack*, strike]

swasti'ka n. form of cross with arms bent at right-angles. [Sanskrit *swastika*, fortunate]

swathe v.t. cover with wraps or bandages. [OE. *swathian*]

sway v.i. swing unsteadily. -v.t. make to do this; govern; wield. -n. swaying motion; government. [LG. *swajen*, swing in the wind]

swear v.t. promise on oath; cause to take an oath. -v.i . use profane oaths. [OE. *swerian*]

sweat (swet) n. moisture oozing from the skin. -v.i. exude sweat; toil. -v.t. cause to sweat; employ at wrongfully low wages. -**sweat'er** n. woolen jersey. [OE. *swcetan*]

sweep v.i. pass quickly or magnificently; extend in a continuous curve. -v.t. clean with a broom; carry impetuously. -n. sweeping motion; wide curve; range; act of cleaning with a broom; long oar; one who cleans chimneys. [OE. *swapan*]

sweep'stake n. gamble in which the winner takes the stakes contributed by all. [*sweep* and *stake*]

sweet a. tasting like sugar; agreeable; tuneful; in good condition. -n. sweet part; **sweetmeat**. -pl. sweet dishes at table; delights. -**sweet'bread** n. animal's pancreas as food. -**sweet'-brier** n. wild rose. -**sweetmeat** *n.* piece of confectionery. -**sweetheart** *n.* lover. -**sweetpea'** *n.* plant of the pea family with bright flowers. [OE. *swete*]

swell *v.i.* expand. -*v.t.* cause to expand. -*n.* act of swelling or being swollen; heave of the sea after a storm; mechanism in an organ to vary the volume of sound. [OE. *swellan*]

swelt'er *v.i.* be oppressive, or oppressed, with heat. [OE. *sweltan*, die]

swerve *v.i.* swing round, change direction during motion; deviate. -*n.* a swerving. [OE. *sweorfan*]

swift *a.* rapid, quick, ready. -*n.* bird like a swallow. -**swift'ly** *adv.* [OE.]

swill *v.t.* pour water over or through; drink greedily. -*v.i.* drink greedily. -*n.* a rinsing; liquid food for pigs. [OE. *swillan*, wash]

swim *v.i.* support and move oneself in water; float; be flooded; have a feeling of dizziness. -*v.t.* cross by swimming. -*n.* spell of swimming. -**swimm'er** *n.* [OE. *swimman*]

swind'ler *n.* cheat. -**swin'dle** *v.t.* and *i* and *n.* cheat. [Ger. *schwindler*]

swine *n.* pig. -**swine'herd** *n.* [OE. *swin*]

swing *v.i.* move to and fro, *esp.* as a suspended body; revolve; (*sl.*) be hanged. -*v.t.* cause to swing; suspend. -*n.* an act of swinging; a seat hung to swing on. [OE. *swingan*]

swipe *n.* sweeping blow. -*v.t.* give a sweeping blow to; (*sl.*) steal. [var. of *sweep*]

swirl *v.i.* move with an eddying motion. -*v.t.* cause to do this. -*n.* such motion. [of Scand. orig.]

swish *v.i.* swing a rod, *etc.*, with an audible hissing sound; move with a similar sound. -*v.t.* swing cane thus. -*n.* the sound; stroke with a cane, *etc.* [imit.]

switch *n.* flexible stick or twig; mechanism to complete or interrupt an electric circuit, *etc.*; on railway, two movable rails for transferring locomotive or train from one set of tracks to another. -*v.t.* strike with a switch; affect (current, *etc.*) with a switch; swing round abruptly. -**switch'back** *n.* short railway in steep undulations as a fairground amusement. -**switch'blade** *n.* pocket-knife with a spring-operated blade which opens at the release of a button. -**switch'board** *n.* board with switches to connect telephones, *etc.* [orig. uncertain]

swiv'el *n.* mechanism of two parts which can resolve the one on the other. -*v.t.* and *i.* turn on a swivel. [OE. *swifan*, revolve]

swoop *v.i.* come down like a hawk. -*n.* an act of swooping. [OE. *swapan*, sweep]

swop *v.i.* barter, exchange. -*n.* (orig. strike hands in bargaining.) [imit.]

sword (sord) *n.* weapon, long blade for cutting or thrusting. -**sword'-fish** *n.* fish with a long sharp upper jaw. -**sword'play** *n.* fencing. [OE. *sweord*]

sycamore *n.* tree allied to maple and plane. [G. *sykomoros*]

sycophant *n.* flatterer. -**sycophant'ic.** *a.* -**syc'ophancy** *n.* obsequiousness. [G. *sykophantes*, informer]

syllable *n.* division of a word as a unit for pronunication. -**syllab'ic** *a.* [G. *syliambanein*, take together]

syll'abus *n.* programme; outline. [by a misunderstanding for G. *sittube*, label of a parchment]

syllogism (-j-) *n.* form of logical reasoning consisting of two premises and a conclusion. -**syllogist'ic** *a.* [G. *syllogismos*, reckoning together]

sylph *n.* sprite. [coined by Paracelsus]

sym'bol *n.* sign; thing representing or typifying something. [G. *symbolon*, token]

symmetry *n.* proportion between parts, balance of arrangement between two sides; regularity. [G. *symmetria*, fr. *metron*, measure]

sympathy *n.* feeling for another in pain, *etc.*; sharing of emotion, interest, desire, *etc.* [G. *sympatheia*, fr. *pathos*, feeling]

symphony *n.* (*mus.*) important composition, in several movements, for full orchestra. [G. *phone*, sound]

sympo'sium *n.* drinking party; friendly discussion; set of magazine articles by various writers on the same subject. [G. *symposion*, fr. *posis*, drinking]

symp'tom *n.* sign, token; change in the body indicating its health or disease. **symptomat'ic** *a.* [G. *sympotoma*]

synagogue *n.* Jewish congregation; its meeting-place. [G. *synagoge*, assembly]

synch'ronize *v.t.* make agree in time. -*v.i.* happen at the same time. [G. *synchronlein*]

syn'cope (*pl.*) *n.* fainting; syncopated spelling, *etc.* -**syn'copate** *v.t.* shorten by the omission of an interior element (in words, music, *etc.*) -**syncopa'tion** *n.* [G. *synkope*, dashing together]

synd'rome *n.* symptoms occurring together in a disease. [G. *syn*, together, *dramein*, run]

syn'onym *n.* word with the same meaning as another. -**synon'ymous** *a.* -**synonym'ity** *n.* [G. *synonymso*]

synop'sis *n.* a summary. -**synop'tic** *a.*

having the same viewpoint. [G. *synopsis, seeing together*]

syn'tax *n.* part of grammar treating of the arrangement of words. -**syntact'ic** *a.* - **syntact'ically** *adv.* [G. *syntaxis*, arrangement together]

synth'esis *n.* a putting together, combination *esp.* of ideas, theories, *etc.* - **syn'thesize** *v.t.* [G. *synthesis*]

synthet'ic *a.* (*colloq.*) artificial. -**synthetically** *adv.* [G. *sunthetikos*]

syph'ilis *n.* infectious venereal disease. - **syphilit'ic** *a.* [coined (1530) by a doctor of Verona]

syringe' *n.* instrument for drawing in liquid by a piston and forcing it out in a fine stream or spray; squirt; (*med.*) injecting instrument. -*v.t.* spray with a syringe. [G. *syrinx*, shepherd's pipe, reed]

syr'up *n.* thick solution of sugar; treacle, *etc.* -**syr'upy** *a.* [Arab. *sharab*, fr. *shariba*, drink]

sys'tem *n.* complex whole; organization; method; classification. -**systemat'ic** *a.* methodical. -**systemat'ically** *adv.* - **sys'tematize** *v.t.* reduce to system. [G. *systems*, what stands together]

sys'tole *n.* shortening of long syllable; contraction of heart and arteries for expelling blood and carrying on circulation. - **systol'ic** *a.* contracting; of systole. [G. *syn*, together, *stellein*, place]

T

tab *n.* tag, label, short strap; bill, check; surveillance. [orig. uncertain]

tabernacle *n.* tent or booth; religious meeting-house. [L. *taberna*, hut]

ta'ble *n.* piece of furniture consisting mainly of a flat board supported by legs, brackets, *etc.*, about three feet from the ground; tablet; food; set of facts or figures arranged in lines or columns. -*v.t.* lay on a table. -**ta'ble-cloth** *n.* cloth of linen, *etc.*, to cover table at mealtimes. -**tab'ular** *a.* shaped or arranged like a table. -**tab'ulate** *v.t.* arrange (figures, facts, *etc.*) in tables. -**tabula'tion** *n.* [L. *tabula*]

tab'leau *n.* -**tab'leaux** *pl.* dramatic situation. [*table*]

tab'loid *n.* illustrated popular newspaper with brief sensational headlines. -concentrated, very short. [Trademark]

taboo' *n.* setting apart of a thing as sacred or accursed; ban or prohibition. *a.* put under a taboo. -*v. t.* to put under a taboo. [Polynesian]

tac'it (tas'-) *a.* implied but not spoken. **tac'itly** *adv.* -**tac'iturn** *a.* talking little,

habitually silent. -**taciturn'ity** *n.* [L. *tacere*, be silent]

tack *n.* small nail; long loose stitch; rope at the corner of a sail; course of a ship obliquely to windward. -*v. t.* nail with tacks; stitch lightly; beat to windward with tacks; change from one tack to another. [ONF. *toque*, fastening]

tack *n.* food. -**hard tack**, ship's biscuit. [for *tackle*]

tac'kle *n.* equipment, apparatus, *esp.* lifting appliances with ropes. -*v.t.* take in hand; grip. [LG. *takel*]

tact *n.* skill in dealing with people or situations. -**tact'ful** *a.* -**tact'less** *a.* **tact'fully** *adv.* -**tact'lessly** *adv.* **tact'ile** *a.* of or relating to the sense of touch. [L. *tactus-tangere, tact-*, touch]

tactics *n. pl.* art of handing troops or ships in battle; science of strategy. **tact'ical** *a.* -**tacti'cian** *n.* [G. *la taktika*, matters of arrangement]

tad'pole *n.* young frog in the tailed stage. [ME. *taddepol*, 'toad-head']

tag *n.* ragged end; pointed end of lace, *etc.* [of Scand. orig.]

tail *n.* projecting continuation of the backbone at the hinder end of an animal; any tail-like appendage. -**tailed** *a.* -**tail'less** *a.* -**tail'spin** *n.* spiral dive of airplane. [OE. *taegel*]

tail'or *n.* maker of outer clothing. [F. *tailleur*, tailor, cutter]

taint *n.* stain; infection; moral infection. *v.t.* stain slightly; corrupt. -*v. i.* become corrupted. [for *attaint*]

take *v.t.* grasp, get hold of, get; receive, assume, adopt; accept; understand; consider; carry or conduct; captivate. -*v. i.* be effective. -**take'-off** *n.* of a plane, *etc.*, rise from the ground. [ON. *taka*]

talc *n.* white or green mineral of soapy feel; powder made from it. [Arab. *talq*]

tale *n.* story; number, count. [OE. *talu*, speech, number]

tal'ent *n.* natural ability or power; ancient weight or money. [L. *talenturn*, money of account]

tal'isman *n.* object supposed to have magic powers. -**talisman'ic** *a.* [G. *telesma*, payment, religious rite]

talk (tawk) *v.i.* speak or converse. -*v.t.* express in speech; use (a language); discuss. -*n.* speech; conversation; rumor. -**talkative** *a.* [fr. *tale*]

tall *a.* high; of great stature; (*sl.*) of a story, to be taken with a pinch of salt. [OE. *getoel*, swift, prompt]

tall'y *n.* notched rod for keeping accounts;

account so kept; reckoning. -v.t. record by a tally. -v. i. agree, correspond. [F. *tailler*, cut]

Tal'mud *n.* collection of volumes containing Jewish civil and canonical law. - Talmud'ic *a.* [Heb. *talmud*, instruction]

tal'on *n.* claw. [F. = *heel*]

tame *a.* not wild; domesticated: unexciting, uninteresting. -v.t. make tame. [OE. *tam*]

tamp'er *v.i.* interfere (with) improperly; meddle. [var. of *temper*]

tan *n.* crushed oak-bark; color of this. *v.t.* make into leather; make brown. tann'in *n.* astringent substance got from oak-bark, *etc.* [of Celt. orig.]

tan'dem *adv.* one behind the other. -n. vehicle with two horses one behind the other; bicycle for two riders one behind the other. [L. = *at length*]

tan'gent (-j-) *a.* touching, meeting without cutting. -n. line tangent to a curve. -tangen'tial *a.* -tangen'tially *adv.* [L. *tangere, tangent-*, touch]

tangent (tan'-jent) abbrev. tan *n.* (*trigonometry*) in a right-angled triangle, the tangent of an acute angle is the ratio of the perpendicular to the base. [fr. L. *tangere*, to touch]

tangerine' *n.* kind of small orange. [F. Tanger, Tangiers]

tan'gible *a.* that can be touched; definite. -tangibil'ity *n.* [L. *tangibilis*]

tan'gle *v.t.* twist together in a muddle. -n. tangled mass, kind of edible seaweed. [orig. uncertain]

tank *n.* storage vessel for liquids, *esp.* a large one; (*mil.*) heavily armed and armored tracked vehicle used in modern warfare. -tank'er *n.* vessel designed to carry petroleum in bulk. [Port, *tanque*]

tan'ner *n.* one who tans; (*sl.*) sixpence. tannery *n.* place where hides are tanned. [OE. *tannere*]

tantalize *v. t.* torment by presenting and then taking away something desired. [fr. punishment of Tantalus, king of Phrygia]

tantamount *a.* equivalent in value or signification; equal. [L. *tantus*, so great, and E. *amount*]

tan'trum *n.* outburst of temper. [orig. unknown]

tap *n.* hollow plug for drawing off liquid; valve with a handle to regulate or stop the flow of a fluid in a pipe, *etc.* -v. t. put a tap in; draw off. [OE. *tæppa*]

tap *v. t.* strike lightly but with some noise. -n. slight blow or rap. [imit.]

tape *n.* narrow long strip of fabric, paper,

etc. -tape'worm *n.* flat worm parasitic on animals. IOE. *teeppa*]

ta'per *n.* long wick covered with wax; thin candle. -v.i. become gradually thinner towards one end. -v.t. make thus. [OE. *tapur*]

tap'estry *n.* fabric decorated with woven designs in colors. [F. *tapisserie*]

tar *n.* thick black liquid distilled from coal, resinous wood, *etc.* -v.t. coat with tar. - tarr'y *a.* [OE. *teru*]

tarantula *n.* large, poisonous spider of Southern Europe. [Taranto, in Italy]

tard'y *a.* slow, behindhand. -tard'ily *adv.* -tard'iness *n.* [L. *tardus*, late]

tar'get *n.* mark to aim at in shooting; small shield. [ON. *targa*, shield]

tar'iff *n.* list of charges. [It. *tariffa*]

tar'nish *v.t.* discolor (*esp.* metal). -v.i. become stained, lose shine. -n. discoloration. [F. *ternir*, become dull, dingy]

tarpaulin *n.* canvas treated with tar or oil. [ME. *palyoun*, canopy]

tart *n.* open pie of fruit, *etc.*; small covered fruit pie. [F. *tarte*]

tart *a.* sour. [OE. *teart*, severe]

tart'an *n.* woollen cloth woven in a pattern of stripes crossing at right angles. [OF. *tartarin*, rich fabric imported through Tartary]

task *n.* piece of work set or undertaken. -v.t. put a task on, take to task, to reprove. -task'master *n.* [ONF. *tasque*, fr. L. *taxare*, appraise]

tass'el *n.* bunch of threads on a knob as an ornament. [OF. = 'little heap']

taste *v.t.* perceive or try the flavor of, eat or drink; experience. -v.i. have a flavor. *n.* small quantity; flavor; judgment in matters of beauty, style, *etc.* -taste'ful *a.* - taste'fully *adv.* -taste'less *a.* [OF. *taster*, touch, handle]

tatt'er *n.* rag-tatterdema'lion *n.* ragged fellow. [of Teut. orig.]

tat'tle *v.i.* gossip; talk idly; give away secrets. -n. [Flem. *tateln.* stammer]

tattoo' *n.* beat of drum and bugle-call; military spectacle, earlier *taptoo*: lights out, or closing time for taverns. [Du. *tap toe*, 'shut the tap to']

tattoo' *v.t.* mark the skin in patterns, *etc.*, by pricking and filling the punctures with coloring matter. -n. mark so made. [Polynesian]

taunt *n.* reproach, insulting words. -v.t. insult, reproach bitterly. [OF. *tanter*]

Taur'us *n.* the Bull, 2nd sign of the zodiac, which sun enters on 21st April. [L.]

taut *a.* drawn tight. [orig. uncertain]

tav'ern *n*. inn or ale-house. [F. *taverner* fr. L. *taberna*, hut]

taw'dry *a*. showy but cheap and without taste. **-taw'drily** *adv*. [St. Audrey's fair (Oct. 17th) where trinkets were sold]

tawn'y *a*. yellowish-brown. *-n*. this color. [F. *tanné*, tanned]

tax *v.t*. exact a contribution to the cost of government; examine accounts; put a burden or strain on. *-n*. charge imposed; a burden. **-taxa'tion** *n*. **-tax'able** *a*. **tax'-payer** *n*. [L. *taxare*, reckon]

tax'i- (cab) *n*. motor-cab for hire with driver. **-tax'i** *v.i*. go in a taxi; (of an airplane) run along the ground under its own power. *-pres. part*. **-tax'ying**. **taxim'eter** *n*. instrument for measuring the time and distance to reckon the charge for a cab fitted with it. [abbrev. of **taximeter**. *See* tax]

tax'idermy *n*. art of stuffing animals. **taxi'dermist** *n*. [fr. G. *taxis*, arrangement, and *derma*, skin]

tea *n*. dried leaves of a plant cultivated in China, India, *etc*.; infusion of it as a beverage; various herbal infusions; afternoon meal at which tea is served. [Du. *thee* (fr. Chin.)]

teach *v.t*. instruct; impart knowledge of, direct; discipline. *-v.i*. act as teacher. **teach'er** *n*. [OE. *toecan*]

teak *n*. East Indian tree; the very hard wood obtained from it. (Malayalam *tekka*]

teal *n*. small water-fowl allied to the duck. [orig. uncertain]

team *n*. set of animals, players of a game, *etc*., associated in an activity. **-team'ster** *n*. one who drives a team of draught animals; driver of a motortruck, *esp*. as an occupation. [OE.]

tear *n*. drop of fluid in, or failing from, the eye. **-tear'ful** *a*. **-tear'less** *a*. **-tear'drop** *n*. **-tear'-stained** *a*. **-tear'-gas** *n*. irritant gas causing watering of the eyes. [OE.]

tear *v.t*. pull apart, rend. *-v.i*. become torn; rush. *-n*. rent. [OE. *teran*]

tease *v.t*. pull apart the fibers of, torment; irritate. *-n*. one who torments. **-teas'ing** *a*. [OE. *toesan*]

teat *n*. nipple of a female breast; artificial substitute for this. [F. *tette*]

technical (tek-) *a*. of or used in an art, *esp*. an industrial art; belonging to a particular art. **-technical'ity** *n*. state of being technical; that which is technical. **-tech'nically** *adv*. **-technique'** *n*. method of performance. **techni'cian** *n*. **-technol'ogy** *n*. systematic knowledge of industrial arts. **technol'ogist** *n*. [G. *techne*, art, craft]

te'dium *n*. boredom or quality of boring. **-te'dious** *a*. wearisome. **-te'diously** *adv*. [L. *toedium*, fr. *toedere*, weary]

tee *n*. (*golf*) small peg or sand-heap from which the ball is played off at each hole. [orig. unknown]

teem *v.i*. abound with, swarm, be prolific. [OE. *tieman*]

teens *n. pl*. years of youth, between 12 and 20. **-teen'ager** *n*.

teethe (-TH) *v.i*. cut teeth. [fr. *teeth*]

tel- *prefix*, at a distance. [G. = far off] **-telecommunications** *n* transmission of data signals in digital, audio, or video form. **-tel'egraph** *n*. apparatus for sending messages mechanically to a distance, as by semaphore, electricity, *etc*. *-v.t*. and *i*. communicate by telegraph. **-tel'egram** *n*. message sent by telegraph. **-telekine'sis** *n*. motion caused by spirit or psychic force. **-telep'athy** *n*. action of one mind on another at a distance. **-telepath'ic** *a*. **-telepath'ically** *adv*. **-tel'ephone** *n*. apparatus for communicating sound to a distance. *-v. t*. and *i*. communicate or speak by telephone. **tel'escope** *n*. instrument of lenses to see things more clearly at a distance. **telescop'ic** *a*. **-televi'sion** *n*. seeing at a distance by the use of wireless transmission.

tell *v.t*. narrate, make known; count. *-v. i*. give an account; be of weight or importance. **-tell'er** *n*. **-tell'ing** *a*. effective. **-tell'tale** *a*. indicating, betraying (secrets, *etc*.). *-n*. teller of secrets. **-tell'off** *v.t*. berate. [OE. *tellan*]

temp'er *v.t*. harden; bring to proper condition; restrain, moderate. *-n*. degree of hardness of steel, *etc*.; mental constitution, frame of mind; anger, *esp*. in noisy outburst. **-temp'erament** *n*. mental constitution. **-temperament'al** *a*. **temperament'ally** *adv*. **-temp'erate** *a*. showing or practicing moderation. **temp'erance** *n*. moderation, self-restraint **-temp'erately** *adv*. **-temp'erature** *n*. degree of heat or coldness. [L. *temperate*, proportion duly]

temp'est *n*. violent storm. **-tempest'uous** *a*. **-tempest'uously** *adv*. [L. *tempestas*, weather, storm]

template *n*. pattern or guide. (*compute*.) plastic cutout used for drawing computer flowcharting symbols.

tem'ple *n*. building for worship, or to house a deity. [L. *templum*]

tem'ple *n*. flat part on either side of the head above the cheekbone. [L. *temporal* pl.]

tem'po n. (*music*) time, rate; rhythm. [It.]

temp'oral a. relating to time, or to this life or world; secular. **-temporal'ity** n.

temp'orary a. lasting or used only for a time [L. *tempus, tempor-,* time]

tempt v.t. try; try to persuade, *esp.* to evil. **-tempt'er** n. **-temptress** n. *fem.* **tempta'tion** n. [OF. *tempter,* fr. L. *temptare,* test]

ten n. and a. cardinal number next after nine. **-tenth** a. ordinal number. **tenth'ly** adv. [OE. *tien*]

tenacious a. holding fast. **-tenac'ity** n. [L. *tenax-tenere,* hold]

ten'ant n. one who holds lands or house, *etc.,* on a rent, or lease. [F. fr. L. *tenere,* hold]

tend v.t. take care of. **-tend'er** n. vessel attending a larger one; carriage for fuel and water attached to a locomotive. [for *attend*]

tend v.i. incline; make in direction of **tend'ency** n. **-tend'er** v. t. offer. -n. offer; what may legally be offered in payment. [L. *tendere,* stretch]

tend'er a. delicate, soft; fragile; gentle, loving, affectionate. **-tend'erly** adv. **tend'erness** n. **-tend'erfoot** n. new comer on plains; novice. **-tend'er loin** n. undercut of sirloin; (*sl.*) district of a city known for vice, corruption *etc.* [F. *tendre,* fr. L. *tener*]

tend'on n. sinew attaching a muscle to a bone, *etc.* [G. *tenon,* sinew]

tend'ril n. slender curling stem by which a climbing plant attaches itself to anything. [F. *tendre,* stretch]

ten'ement n. piece of land or a house; part of a house forming a separate dwelling; block of flats. [L. *tenere,* hold]

ten'nis n. game in which a ball is struck between players on opposite sides of a net in a covered court; variation of this played on a grass or other court (also called lawn tennis). [F. *tenez,* take; (called by the server)]

ten'on n. tongue on the end of a piece of wood, *etc.,* to fit into a mortise. [F.]

ten'or n. meaning; trend; male voice between alto and bass, music for this; singer with this voice. [L.]

tense n. modification of a verb to show time of action, *etc.* **-ten'sity** n. [OF. *tens,* fr. L. *tempus,* time]

tense a. stretched tight. **-ten'sile** a. capable of being stretched. **-ten'sion** n. stretching or strain when stretched; mental strain. [L. *tendere, tens-, tent-,* stretch]

tent n. portable shelter of canvas. **tent'pole** n. **-tent'-peg** n. [F. *tente,* fr. L. *tendere,* stretch]

tentacle n. feeler. **-tent'ative** a. done as a trial. -n. attempt. **-tent'atively** adv. [L. *tentare,* try]

tenuous a. thin. [L. *tenuitas-tenuis,* slender]

tepee' n. American Indian skin-tent. [Sioux = *dwelling*]

tep'id a. moderately warm; lukewarm. [L. *tepidus*]

tequila n. strong Mexican liquor. [Tequila, district of Mexico]

term n. limit or end; fixed day for regular payment, *e.g.* rent; period during which courts sit, schools are open, *etc.* **-pl.** conditions, mutual relationship; word or expression. **-v.t.** name. **-term'inal** a. at or forming an end. -n. terminal part or structure. **-term'inate** v.t. bring to an ena. -v.i. come to an end. **-termina'tion** n. study of terms; set of technical terms or vocabulary. **-terminolo'gical** (-j-) a. **term'inus** n. finishing point; station at the end of a railway. [L. *terminus,* limit]

ter'mite n. the so-called white ant. [L. *termes,* woodworm]

tern n. sea-bird allied to the gull. [Ice. *therna*]

tertiary a. in threes; proceeding in threes. [L. *terni,* three each]

Terpsich'ore n. Muse of dancing. [G.]

terrace n. raised level place, level cut out of a hill; row or street of uniform houses. **-v.t.** form into a terrace. [F. *terasse,* fr. *terre,* earth]

terr'ain n. a region or tract of land; ground considered in relation to, *e.g.* , military operations. [F.]

terrest'rial a. of the earth; of land. [L. *terrestris,* fr. *terra,* earth]

terr'ible a. causing fear; (call.) excessive. **-terr'ibly** adv. **-terrif'ic** a. terrible, awesome. **-terrif'ically** adv. **terr'ify** v.t. frighten. **-terr'or** n. state of great fear. **terr'orize** v. t. force or oppress by fear. **terrorism** n. **-terr'orist** n. [L. *terrere,* frighten]

terr'ier n. small dog of various breeds, orig. for following a quarry into a burrow. [F., fr. *terre,* earth]

territory n. region; land subject to a ruler. **-territo'rial** a. relating to a territory. [L. *territorium*]

ter'tiary a. third. [L. *tertius,* third]

test n. means of trial. **-v.** t. try, put to the proof. **-test pi'lot** n. pilot who flies aircraft of new design to test performance in air. **-test tube** n. narrow cylindrical glass vessel used in scientific experiments. [OF. *test,* pot]

test'ament *n.* will; one of the two divisions of the Bible. **-testament'ary** *a.* **-test'ate** *a.* that has left a will. [L. *testamentum*]

test'icle *n.* male genital organ. [L. *testiculus*]

test'ify *v.i.* bear witness. *-v.t.* bear witness to. **-test'imony** *n.* evidence. **testimo'nial** *n.* certificate of character, ability, *etc.*; gift by a number of persons to express their regard for the recipient. [L. *testis*, witness]

test'y *a.* irritable, short-tempered. [OF. *testif*, heady, obstinate]

tet'anus *n.* lockjaw; rigidity of some or all muscles. [G. *tetanos*, muscular spasm]

teth'er *v. t.* tie up (a horse, *etc.*), with a rope. *-n.* rope or chain for fastening a grazing animal; limit of endurance (end of one's tether). [ON. *tjothr*]

tet'ragon *a.* figure with four angles and four sides. **-tetrag'onal** *a.* **-tetrahe'dron** *n.* solid contained by four plane faces. [G. *tetra*, four]

Teuton'ic *a.* of, pert. to, Germanic race, *e.g.* Germans, Scandinavians, English. [L. *Teutonicus*, from the Teutones]

text *n.* actual words of a book, passage, *etc.*; main body of a literary work; letterpress; passage from the Scriptures, *etc.*, *esp.* as the subject of a discourse. **-text'book** *n.* manual of instruction. **-text editing** *v.t.* procss of changing, adding, or deleting material on a computer. **-text'ual** *a.* of or in a text. [L. *textus-texere*, text-, weave]

text'ile *a.* woven; capable of being woven; relating to weaving. *-n.* a woven fabric. [L. *textilis*]

text'ure *n.* the character or structure of a textile fabric. [L. *texere, text-*, weave]

than (TH-) *conj.* and *prep.* introduces second part of a comparison. [OE. *thanne*]

thank *v.t.* give thanks to, express gratitude to. **-thanks** *n. pl.* words of gratitude. **-thank'ful** *a.* feeling grateful. **-thankless** *a.* having or bringing no thanks. [OE *thanc*]

that (TH-) *a.* demonstrates or particularizes. *fem. pron.* particular thing meant. *-adv.* as. *-rel. pron.* which, who. *-conj.* introduces noun or adverbial clauses. [OE. *thcet*]

thatch *v. t.* roof (a house) with straw or similar material. *-n.* straw used in thatching. [OE. *thœc*, roof]

thaw *v.t.* and *i.* melt. *-n.* a melting (of frost, *etc.*). [OE. *thawian*]

the (TH-) is the definite article. [that]

the'ater *n.* place where plays are performed; drama or dramatic works generally; surgical operating room. **theat'rical** *a.* of or for the theater; showy, spectacular. **-theat'rically** *adv.* **-theat'ricals** *n. pl.* amateur dramatic performances. [G. *theatron*]

theft *n.* stealing. [OF. *thiefth*]

their (THir) *a.* *-pron.* belonging to them. [ON. *theirra*]

them *pron.* objective case of they; those persons or things. [ON. *theim*]

theme *n.* subject of a composition; essay. [G. *theme*, proposition]

then (TH-) *adv.* at that time; next; that being so. [OE. *thanne*]

theol'ogy *n.* science treating of God. **-theoc'racy** *n.* government by God. **-theocrat'ic** *a.* [G. *theos*, god]

the'orem *n.* proposition which can be demonstrated by argument. **-the'ory** *n.* supposition to account for something; system of rules and principles; rules and reasoning, *etc.*, as distinguished from practice. [G. *theorems*, proposition to be proved]

theos'ophy *n.* any of various ancient and modern systems of esoteric philosophy by which the soul may attain to knowledge of, and ultimate union with, the universal spirit. [G. *theosophos*, wise in the things of God]

therapeu'tic *a.* relating to healing. *-n.* in *pl.* art of healing. **-ther'apy** *n.* curative treatment. [G. *therapeutikos*]

there (TH-) *adv.* in that place, to that point. **-there'fore** *adv.* in consequence, that being so. [OE. *thcer*]

ther'mal *a.* of or pertaining to heat. **-therm** *n.* unit of heat; unit of 1,000 calories. **-ther'mic** *a.* thermal. **-thermom'eter** *n.* instrument to measure temperature. **-thermomet'ric** *a.* [G. *therme*, heat]

therm'ostat *n.* automatic regulator of temperature. **-thermostat'ic** *a.* [G. *thermos*, hot]

thesaur'us *n.* treasury; storehouse; *esp.* a collection of words and phrases; a lexicon or encyclopedia. [L. -G. *thesauros*, *tithenae*, place]

the'sis *n.* proposition; dissertation. [G.]

thes'pian *a.* of the drama. [*Thespis*, founder of Greek drama]

they *pron.* third person plural pronoun. [ON. *their*]

thick *a.* having great thickness, not thin; dense, crowded; viscous; foggy. **-thick'ly** *adv.* **-thick'en** *v. t.* and *i.* **-thick'ness** *n.* dimension of anything measured through it, at right angles to the length and breadth.

-**thick′et** *n.* thick growth of small trees.
-**thick′set** *a.* set closely together; sturdy and solid in limbs and frame. [OE. *thicce*]

thief *n.* thieves *pl.* one who steals. **thieve** *v.t.* and *i.* steal. [OE. *theof*]

thigh *n.* upper part of the leg above the knee. [OE. *theoh*]

thim′ble *n.* metal cover for the fingertip in sewing. [OE. *thymel*, fr. thumb]

thin *a.* not thick; of little density; loose, not closely packed. -*v.t.* and *i.* make or become thin. -**thin′ness** *n.* [OE. *thynne*]

thing *n.* material object; any possible object of thought. [OE. = assembly for deliberation; affairs; matters]

think *v.i.* have one's mind at work; reflect; hold an opinion. -*v.t.* conceive or consider in the mind. -**think′er** *n.* [OE. *thencan*]

third *a.* ordinal number corresponding to three. -*n.* third part. -**third degree′**, drastic police methods to make a prisoner 'talk'. [ver. of *thrid*, fr. three]

thirst *n.* feeling caused by lack of drink. *v. i.* feel the lack of drink. -**thirst′y** *a.* **thirst′ily** *adv.* [OE. *thurst*]

thirteen′ *a.* and *n.* number, three and ten. -**thirt′y** *n.* and *a.* number, three times ten. [OE. *threotyne; thritig*]

this, these *pl.* -*dem. a.* and *pron.* denotes a thing or person near, or just mentioned, *etc.* [OE.]

this′tle (-*sl*) *n.* prickly plant with a purple flower. [OE. *thistel*]

thong *n.* narrow strip of leather. -*v.t.* sew with thongs. [OE. *thwang*, strap]

thor′ax *n.* part of the body between neck and belly. [G. = breastplate]

thorn *n.* prickle on a plant; bush noted for its thorns. -**thorn′y** *a.* [OE.]

thor′ough *a.* complete, painstaking. -**thor′oughly** *adv.* -**thor′oughbred** *a.* of pure breed. -*n.* purebred animal, *esp.* horse. -**thor′oughfare** *n.* road or passage open at both ends; right of way. [var. of *through*]

those *a.* and pron. *pl.* of that. [OE. *thas*]

thou *pron.* (*arch.*) second person singular pronoun. [OE. *thu*]

though *conj.* in spite of the fact that. -*adv.* for all that. [OE. *theah*]

thought (thawt) *n.* process of thinking; what one thinks; a product of thinking; meditation. -**thought′ful** *a.* engaged in meditation; considerate. -**thought′less** *a.* careless, heedless, inconsiderate. [OE. *thoht*]

thou′sand (-z-) *a.* and *n.* cardinal number, ten hundreds. [OE. *thusend*]

thrash, thresh *v.t.* of corn, *etc.*, beat out the grains of. -**thrash** *v.t.* beat, whip. [OE. *threscan*]

thread (-ed) *n.* fine cord; yarn; ridge cut spirally on a screw. -*v.t.* put a thread into; put on a thread; pick (one's way, *etc.*). **thread′bare** *a.* worn, with the nap rubbed off. [OE. *thrced*]

threat (-et) *n.* announcement of what the speaker intends to do if his orders or wishes are not complied with. -**threat′en** *v.t.* and *i.* utter threats against. **threat′ening** *a.* menacing. [OE. *pressure*]

three *n.* and *a.* cardinal number, one more than two. [OE. *threo*]

threshold (-old) *n.* the bar of stone or wood forming the bottom of the framework of a door. [OE. *therscold*, fr. *therscask*, tread]

thrift *n.* saving, economy. [fr. thrive]

thrill *v.t.* send -a nervous tremor of emotion through. -*v. i.* feel one. -*n.* such emotional tremor. -**thrill′er** *n.* (*sl.*) sensational story. -**thrill′ing** *a.* exciting. [OE. *thyrlian*, pierce]

thrive *v. i.* grow well; flourish, prosper. [ON. *thrifa*, grasp]

throat *n.* front of the neck; either or both of the passages through it. -**throat′y** *a.* of voice, hoarse. [OE. *throte*]

throb *v. i.* beat or quiver strongly. -*n.* a throbbing. [orig. uncertain]

thrombosis *n.* formation of a bloodclot in artery or vein. (G. *thrombos*, clot]

throne *n.* seat of state, *esp.* of a king. *v. t.* place on a throne. [G. *thronos*]

throng *n. v.t.* , and *i.* crowd. [OE. *gethrana*, fr. *thringan*, press]

throt′tle *v.t.* and *i.* strangle. [fr. *throat*]

through *prep.* from end to end of, *adv.* from end to end; to the end. **throughout′** *adv.* in every part. -*prep.* in every part of [OE. *thurh*]

throw *v.t.* fling; bring down. -*n.* an act or distance of throwing. -**throw′back** *n.* reversion to an ancestral type. [OE. *thrawan*, to twist]

thrush *n.* throat and mouth disease of children; foot disease of horses. [orig. uncertain]

thrust *v. t.* push, stab, drive. -*v. i.* lunge, stab; push one's way. -*n.* lunge or stab with sword, *etc.* [ON. *thrysta*]

thud *n.* dull heavy sound, as of a brick falling on earth. -*v. i.* make a thud. [imit. orig.]

thug *n.* one of a body of Indian assassins in early 19th c.; cutthroat; ruffian. [Hind.]

thumb *n.* short thick finger, the one which can be opposed to the others. -*v.t.* handle or dirty with the thumb. **thumb′tack** *n.*

tack with a large flat head for pressing into a surface with the thumb. [OE. *thuma*]

thump *v.t.* strike heavily. -*n.* dull heavy blow; sound of one. [imit.]

thunder *n.* loud noise accompanying lightning. -*v.i.* of thunder, to sound. -*v. t.* utter loudly. -**thun'derbolt** *n.* lightning flash as agent of destruction. -**thun'dery** *a.* -**thun'derous** *a.* [OE. *thunor*]

Thurs'day *n.* fifth day of the week. [OE. *thunresdaeg*, day of Thor or thunder]

thus *adv.* in this way; therefore. [OE.]

thwart *v.t.* foil, frustrate. *adv.* across. [ON. *thuert*, across]

thwart *n.* seat for a rower across a boat. [OE. *thofte*, rower's bench]

thy'roid (gland) *n.* ductless gland at front of neck; chief cartilage of larynx. [G. *thyreos*, shield, *eidos*, form]

tiar'a *n.* jeweled head-ornmanent. [G.]

tib'ia *n.* shin-bone; flute. [L.]

tic *n.* spasmodic twitch in the muscles of the face; tic douloureux. [F.]

tick *n.* mite in hair or fur. [Teut. orig.]

tick *n.* mattress case. [G. *theke*, case]

tick *n.* slight sound as of a watch movement; -*v.i.* make the sound; small mark -*v.t.* mark with a tick. [imit.]

tick *n.* (*sl.*) credit. -**give tick**, sell on credit. [ticket]

tick'et *n.* card or paper entitling to admission, travel, *etc.*; label. -*v.t.* attach a label to. [F. *étiquette*, label]

tickle *v.i.* itch. -*v.t.* make itch with light touches, *etc.* -**tick'lish** *a.* sensitive to tickling; requiring care or tact in handling. [orig. uncertain]

tide *n.* season or time; rise and fall of the sea happening twice each lunar day; stream. -*v.i.* tide over, get over or surmount. -*v.t.* enable someone to do this. -**ti'dal** *a.* of or resembling a tide. [OE. *tid*, time]

ti'dings *n.* news; happenings; a report. [fr. *betide*]

ti'dy *a.* orderly, neat. -*v.t.* put in order. [orig.]

tie *v.t.* fasten, bind; restrict. -*n.* that with which anything is bound; cravat; bond; drawn game with equal points; match. [OE. *teag n.*; *tigan v.*]

tier *n.* row, rank, *esp.* rising in a series. [F. *tirer*, draw]

ti'ger *n.* large carnivorous animal with striped coat. -**ti'gress** *fem.* [G. *tigris*]

tight *a.* firm; tense, taut; fitting close; not allowing the passage of water, *etc.*; (*colloq.*) drunk. -**tights** *n. pl.* tight-fitting elastic garments. -**tight'en** *v.t.* and *i.* **tight'ly** *adv.* [ON. *thettr*, watertight]

tile *n.* slab of baked clay, porcelain, *etc. v.t.* cover with tiles. [L. *tegula*]

till *n.* drawer for money in a shop. [orig. uncertain]

tilt *v.t.* cultivate. -**till'er** *n.* lever to move a rudder of a boat. [OF. *telier*, weaver's beam]

tilt *n.* canvas cover or hood for a wagon; stern-sheets of boat, *etc.* [orig. uncertain]

tilt *v.t.* and *i.* slope, slant. -*n.* inclination from the vertical. [OE. *tealt*, unsteady]

tilt *v.i.* take part in a medieval combat with lances, joust. -*n.* combat for mounted men with lances. [orig. uncertain]

tim'ber *n.* wood for building, *etc.* **tim'bered** *a.* made or partly made of wood. [OE. = house or material suitable to make one]

time *n.* existence as a succession of states; hour; duration; period; point in duration. -*v. t.* choose or note the time of. -**time'ly** *a.* seasonable. -**time'ous** *a.* opportune, seasonable. -**time'piece** *n.* watch or clock. [OE. *tima*]

tim'id *a.* diffident; lacking courage. [L. *timidus*, fr. *timere*, fear]

tin *n.* malleable white metal; vessel of tin or tinned iron. -*v. t.* coat with tin; put in a tin, *esp.* for preserving (food). -**tinn'y** *a.* of sound, light and unmusical, like clash of tin. [OE.]

tin'der *n.* dry easily-burning material used to catch a spark from flint and steel. [OE. *tynder-tendan*, kindle]

tine *n.* tooth, spike of fork, antler, harrow, *etc.* [OE. *tind*]

tinge *v.t.* color or flavor slightly. -*n.* slight trace. [L. *tingere*, dye]

tink'er *n.* mender of pots and pans. -*v.i.* work in clumsy or amateur fashion. [fr. noise of his work]

tin'kle *v.i.* give out a series of light sounds like a small bell. -*v. t.* cause to do this. -*n.* sound or action of this. [imit.]

tin'sel *n.* thin metal plates, cord, *etc.* , for decoration; anything sham and showy. [F. *étincelle*, spark]

tint *n.* color; tinge. -*v. t.* dye, give a tint to. [L. *tingere*, dye]

ti'ny *a.* very small. [orig. uncertain]

tip *n.* slender or pointed end of anything; piece of metal, leather, *etc.* , protecting or softening a tip. -*v.t.* put a tip on. **tip'staff** *n.* sheriffs officer, who carried a tipped staff. -**tip'toe** *v.i.* walk on one's toes. -**tiptop'** *a.* of the best quality or highest degree. [of Teut. orig.]

tip *n.* small present of money; piece of useful private information. -*v.t.* give a tip to.

-tip′ster *n.* one who sells tips about races. [orig. a *cant* word]

tip *v.t.* upset. *-v.i.* topple over. *-n.* place for tipping carts, emptying out rubbish, *etc.* **-tip′-cat** *n.* game in which a spindle of wood is struck into the air by hitting one of the pointed ends with a stick; the piece of wood struck. [orig. type. of unknown orig.]

tip′sy *a.* drunk or partly drunk. [fr. *tip*, upset]

tirade′ *n.* long speech, generally vigorous and hostile; harangue. [It. *tirata*, volley]

tire *n.* and *v.* attire; rim of metal, rubber, *etc.*, round a wheel. *-v.t.* put one on. [attire]

tire *v.i.* become weary or fatigued. *-v.t.* fatigue. **-tire′some** *a.* wearisome, irritating. [OE. *tiorian*, exhaust]

tiss′ue *n.* fine woven fabric *esp.* of gold or silver; substance of an animal body, of a plant *etc.* **-tiss′ue-paper** *n.* very thin paper. [F. *tissu*, woven]

titan′ic *a.* huge, gigantic. [G. *Titanes*, family of giants]

tit′illate *v.t.* tickle, stimulate agreeably. **titilla′tion** *n.* [L. *titillare*]

tі′tle *n.* heading, name of a book; name, appellation; legal right or document proving it. **-tit′le-deed** *n.* document confirming ownership. **-ti′tle-page** *n.* page at beginning of book bearing title, author's name and publishers' imprint. [L. *titulus*]

tit′ular *a.* so in name or title only; held by virtue of a title. [*See* **title**]

to *prep.* towards, in the direction of, as far as; used to introduce a comparison, ratio, indirect object, infinitive mood, *etc. -adv.* to the required or normal state or position. **-to-do′** *n.* fuss, commotion. [OE.]

toad *n.* animal like a frog. **-toad′stool** *n.* fungus like a mushroom, but usually poisonous. **-toad′y** *n.* one who fawns or curries favor unworthily. *-v.i.* do this. **toad′-eater** *n.* sycophant. [OE. *tadige*]

toast *v.t.* brown at the fire; warm; drink the health of. *-n.* slice of bread browned at the fire; a health; person toasted. **toast′master** *n.* one whose duty is to announce toasts at a banquet. [OF. *toster*, fr. L. *torrere, tort*-, parch]

tobacco *n.* plant of which the leaves are used for smoking; prepared leaves. [Sp. *taboco*]

today′ *n.* this day; present time. *-adv.* on this day. [*to* and *day*]

toddle *v.i.* walk with unsteady short steps. *-n.* a toddling. **-todd′ler** *n.* little child. [orig. uncertain]

toe *n.* digit of the foot. *-v. t.* reach or touch with the toe. [OE. *ta*]

to′ga *n.* mantle of a Roman citizen. [L.]

togeth′er *adv.* in company, simultaneously. [OE. *togoedere*]

togs *n. pl. (sl.)* clothes. [L. *toga*]

toil *v.i.* labor. *-n.* heavy work or task. **toil′some** *a.* **-toil′-worn** *a.* [OF. *touillier*, fr. L. *tudiculare*, stir]

toil′et *n.* process of dressing; articles used in this; manner of doing it, style of dress; dressing-table; cover for it; lavatory. [F. *toilette*]

toils *n. pl.* nets for catching game. [F. *toile*, fr. L. *tela*, cloth, web]

tol′erate *v.i.* put up with. **-tol′erant** *a.* disinclined to interfere with others ways or opinions. **-tol′erance** *n.* **tol′erantly** *adv.* [L. *tolerare*]

toll *n.* tax, *esp.* for the use of a bridge or road. **-toll-gate.** [OE.]

toll *v.t.* make (a bell) ring slowly at regular intervals; announce a death thus. *-v.i.* ring thus. *-n.* action or sound of tolling. [obs. *toll*, draw, pull]

toma′to *n.* plant with bright red yellow, fruit; the fruit, [Mex. *tomatl*]

tomb *n.* grave or monument over one. [G. *tymbos*, funeral mound]

tom′boy *n.* romping boyish girl. [*Tom* and *boy*]

tome *n.* volume, large ponderous book, [G. *tomos*]

tomorr′ow *n.* day after to-day. *adv.* on the next day after this one. [*morrow*]

ton (tun) *n.* measure of weight, 20 cwt.; unit of a ship's carrying capacity. **tonn′age** *n.* carrying capacity; charge per ton; ships. [var. of *tun*]

tondo *n.* round painting, carved relief, or other work of art.

tongs (-z) *n. pl.* large pincers, *esp.* for handling coal, *etc.* [OE. *tang*]

tongue (tung) *n.* muscular organ inside the mouth, used for speech, taste, *etc.*; various things shaped like this; speech; language. [OE. *tunge*]

tonight′ *n.* this night; the coming night. *-adv.* on this night. [night]

ton′sil *n.* gland at the side of the throat. **ton′sillitis** *n.* inflammation of the tonsils. [L. *tonsillce pl.*]

too *adv.* in addition; in excess, more than enough; also. [stressed form of **to**]

tool *n.* implement or appliance for mechanical operations. *-v.t.* work on with a tool. [OE. *tol*]

tooth *n.* teeth *pl.* ivory process of the jaw; anything resembling this. **-tooth′some** *a.* pleasant to eat. [OE. *toth*]

top *n.* highest part; platform on a ship's mast. *-v.t.* cut off, put on, pass, or reach, a top. **-top'hole** *a.* (*sl.*) first-rate **top'most** *a.* [OE.]

top *n.* toy which spins on a point. [orig. uncertain]

to'paz *n.* precious stone of various colors; humming bird. [G. *topazos*]

top'ic *n.* subject of a discourse or conversation. **-top'ical** *a.* of a topic; up-to-date, having news value. [G. *topos*, place]

topography *n.* description of a place; its features. **-topograph'ic** *a.* **-topograph'ically** *adv.* **-topog'rapher** *n.* [G. *topos*, place]

top'ple *v. i.* fall over. [top]

torch *n.* twist of bemp, *etc.*, soaked in tar or oil to burn as a portable light. **torch'light** *n.* **-torch'bearer** *n.* [F. *torche*]

toreador' *n.* bull-fighter, *esp.* one who fights on horseback. [Sp.]

tor'ment *n.* suffering or agony of body or mind. **-torment'** *v.t.* afflict; tease. **torment'or** *n.* [L. *tormentum*]

torna'do *n.* whirlwind; violent storm. [Sp. *tronada*, fr. *tronar*, to thunder]

torpe'do *n.* cigar-shaped missile filled with explosives and propelling itself underwater by compressed air engines after discharge from a ship. *-v.t.* strike or sink with a torpedo. **-torpe'do-boat** *n.* [usually destroyer] [L. = *numbness*; cramp-fish]

tor'pid *a.* sluggish, dormant. **-torpid'ity** *n.* **-tor'por** *n.* torpid state. [L. *torpere*, be torpid]

torque *n.* collar or like ornament of twisted gold or metal; in mechanics, rotating or twisting forces. [L. *torquire*, twist]

torr'ent *n.* rushing stream. **-torren'tial** *a.* [L. *torrens, torrent-*, boil]

torr'id *a.* hot, scorching; dried up with heat. [L. *torrere*, burn or boil]

tor'sion *n.* twist. [L, *torquere*, twist]

tort *n.* breach of legal duty. [F.]

tort'uous *a.* winding, twisting, not straightforward. [L. *torquere*, twist]

tor'toise *n.* four-footed reptile covered with a shell of horny plates. [Late L. *tortuca*]

tort'ure *n.* infliction of severe pain. *-v. t.* subject to torture. **-tort'urer** *n.* **tort'ure-chamber** *n.* [L. *torquere*, twist]

toss *v. t.* throw up or about. *-v. i.* be thrown, or fling oneself, about. *-n.* act of tossing. **-toss'pot** *n.* toper. [orig. uncertain]

tot *n.* very small thing; small quantity, *esp.* of a drink; tiny child. [orig. uncertain]

tot *v.t.* add up. *-v.i.* (with up) amount to. *-n.* addition sum. [orig. uncertain]

to'tal *n.* whole amount. *-a.* complete, entire. *-v. t.* add up; amount to. **-total'ity** *n.* **-totaliza'tor** *n.* machine which registers total **totalita'rian** *a.* of a government, in complete control of the nation's resources. [L. *totus*, all]

to'tem *n.* tribal badge or emblem, usually an animal. **-totem'ic** *a.* [N. Amer. Ind., hereditary emblem]

tatter *v. i.* walk unsteadily, begin to fall [orig. uncertain]

touch (tuch) *v.t.* put the hand on, come into contact with; reach; move the feelings of (*sl.*) borrow from. *-v.i.* call; (with on) refer to. *-n.* a touching; slight blow, stroke, contact, amount, *etc.* [F. *toucher*]

touch'y (tuch'-) *a.* over-sensitive, easily offended. [earlier *tetchy*, fr. OF. *entechio*]

tough (tuf) *a.* strong and pliable, not brittle; sturdy; difficult; needing effort to bite. **tough'ness** *n.* **-tough'en** *v.t. and i.* [OE. *toh*]

toupee' *n.* false hair, wig. [F.]

tour *n.* a traveling round. *-v.t.* travel through. *-v.i.* travel. **-tour'ist** *n.* one who travels for pleasure. [F. fr. *tourner*, turn]

tournament *n.* a meeting for knightly contests; a meeting for games or athletic contests. **-tour'ney** *n.* a tournament. [F. *tournoyer*, fr. *tourner*, turn]

tourniquet *n.* bandage which can be tightened by twisting a crosspiece put through it to stop bleeding. [P.]

tow *v.t.* drag at the end of a reopen. a towing, being towed; vessel in tow. **tow'age** *n.* [OE. *togian*, draw]

tow'ard *a.* docile (also **tow'ardly**). **towards'** (tordz) *prep.* in the direction of. (also toward'). [OE. *toweard*]

tow'el *n.* cloth for wiping off moisture after washing. **-tow'eling** *n.* material used for towels. [OF. *touaille*]

tow'er *n.* tall building or part of a building; fortress. *-v.i.* rise aloft, stand very high. [F. *tour*, fr. L. *turris*]

town *n.* collection of dwellings, *etc.* larger than a village. **-town'ship** *n.* division of a county. [OE. *tun*, homestead]

tox'ic *a.* poisonous, due to poison. **toxi'city, toxication** *n.* **-toxicol'ogy** *n.* science of poisons. **-tox'in** *n.* poison, *usu.* of bacterial origin. [G. *taxikon*, arrow poison]

toy *n.* plaything. *-v.i.* act idly, trifle. [Du. *tuig*, tools]

trace *n.* chain or strap by which a horse pulls a vehicle; track left by anything; indication; minute quantity. *-v. t.* follow the course or track of, find out; make a plan of, draw. [L. *trahere, tract-*, draw]

trache'a *n.* windpipe. **-trache'al, trach-e'an** *a.* [L. *trachia*]

track *n.* mark or line of marks, left by the passage of anything; path; course. *v.t.* follow up the track of, *esp.* in hunting. [F. *trac*]

tract *n.* space of land, *etc.* , area. [L. *tractus*, a stretching out]

tract *n.* pamphlet, *esp.* a religious one. **tract'ate** *n.* treatise. [L. *tractare*, handle]

trac'tion *n.* action of drawing. **trac'tion-engine** *n.* steam or motor engine for drawing; steam-roller. **tract'or** *n.* self-propelling agricultural implement, *e.g.*, plow. **-tract'orfeed** *n.* in computer technology, the automatic movement of a continuous roll of edge-perforated paper through the platen of the printer. [L. *trahere, tract-*, draw]

trade *n.* commerce, traffic; practice of buying and selling; any profitable pursuit; those engaged in a trade. *-v.i.* engage in trade. *-v.t.* buy and self-, barter. **trade'mark** *n.* distinctive mark on a maker's goods. **-tra'der** *n.* **-trades'man** *n.* shopkeeper; mechanic. **-trade-u'nion** *n.* society of workmen for protection of their interests. **-trade'wind** *n.* wind blowing constantly towards the equator in certain parts of the globe. [LG. *cognate* with tread]

tradition *n.* body of beliefs, facts, *etc.*, handed down from generation to generation without being reduced to writing; process of handing down, **-tradi'tional** *a.* **-tradi'tionally** *adv.* [L. *traditio* a handing over]

traffic *n.* passing to and fro of pedestrians, vehicles, *etc.*, in a road or street, *etc.*; trade. *-v.i.* trade. **-trafficker** *n.* trader. [F. *trafic*]

trag'edy (-j-) *n.* drama showing the ruin or downfall of the principal character, dealing with the sorrowful or terrible side of life; this type of drama. **-trag'ic** *a.* of, or in the manner of, tragedy; (journalism) disastrous; appalling. **-trag'ically** *adv.* **-trage'dian** *n.* player in tragedy; **tragicom'edy** *n.* play with both tragic and comic elements. [G. *tragoidia-* lit. 'goat-song']

trail *v.t.* drag behind one; follow the track of. *-v.i.* be drawn behind; hang loosely. *n.* thing that trails; back end of a guncarriage; track or trace. **-trail'er** *n.* road vehicle drawn by an automobile, *esp.* one that is designed to serve as a dwelling, office *etc.* when parked; film scenes shown as preliminary advertisement for a cinema film. [OF. *irainer*, tow]

train *v.t.* cause to grow in a particular way; educate, instruct, exercise; aim (a gun). *-v.i.* follow a course of training, *esp.* to achieve physical fitness for athletics. *n.* trailing part of a dress; body of attendants; fuse or trail of powder to a mine; line of railway vehicles joined to a locomotive; collection of vehicles, *etc.*, *esp.* in military use. **-trainee'** *n.* person being trained. [F. *trainer*, drag]

trait *n.* distinguishing characteristic. [F. = line, stroke, feature]

trait'or *n.* one who betrays or is guilty of treason. [L. *traditor*, fr. *tradere*, hand over]

trajectory *n.* line of flight of a projectile. [L. *trajicere, traject-*, cast across]

tramp *v.i.* walk heavily, travel on foot, *esp.* as a vagabond or for pleasure. *-v.t.* cross on foot. *-n.* an act of tramping; walk; vagabond; cargo-boat. **-tram'ple** *v.t.* tread under foot. [of Teut. orig.]

trampoline *n.* tough canvas sheet stretched horizontally with elastic cords *etc.* over frame for gymnastic, acrobatic use. [It. *trampoline*, springboard]

trance (-a-) *n.* state of suspended consciousness, *esp.* from rapture or ecstasy; catalepsy. [F. *transe*; (orig. passage from life to death)]

tran'quil (*a.* calm, quiet. **tran'quilly** *adv.* **-tranquil'ity, tranquill'ity** *n.* **-tranquil'ize, tranquillize** *v.t.* **-tranquil'izer, tranquillizer** *n.* one that tranquilizes; drug used to reduce anxiety. [L. *tranquillus*]

trans- *prefix*, across, through, beyond. [L.] **-transact'** *v.t.* carry on or through; conduct (an affair, *etc.*). -transac'tion *n.* **-transcend'** *v.t.* exceed, surpass. transcend'ent *a.* **-transcend'ence** *n.* **transcendent'al** *a.* surpassing experience; super-natural; abstruse. **-trancendent'alism** *n.* **-transcribe'** *v.t.* copy out. **-trans'cript** *n.* copy. **-transfer'** *v.t.* make over; move from one place to another. **trans'fer** *n.* a transferring or being transferred. **-transform'** *v.t.* change the shape or character of. **-transforma'tion** *n.* **-transform'er** *n.* (*elec.*) apparatus for transforming voltage of alternating current. **-transgress'** *v.t.* break (a law); sin. **-tran'sient** *a.* passing away. **-tran'sience** *n.* **-tran'sit** *n.* passage, crossing. **-transi'tion** *n.* change from one state to another. **-translate'** *v.t.* move (a bishop) from one see to another; turn from one language into another. **-transla'tion** *n.* **transla'tor** *n.* **-translu'cent** *a.* letting light pass, semi-transparent **-translu'cent** *n.* **transmit'** *v.t.* send or cause to pass to another place, person, *etc.* **-transmute'** *v.t.* change in form, properties, or nature. **-transmuta'tion** *n.* **-transpar'ent** *a.* letting light pass without distortion, that can be

seen through distinctly; obvious. -
transpire' v.t. exhale. -v.i. exhale; come to
be known. **transpira'tion** n. **-transplant'**
v.t. move and plant again in another place.
-transplanta'tion n. **-transport'** v.t. convey from one place to another; carry into
banishment; enrapture. **-trans'port** n.
means of conveyance; ships, vehicles, etc-
, used in transporting stores; ship so used.
-transpose' v.t. change the order of, interchange; put music into a different key.
transom n. cross-piece; lintel. [corrupt. of
F. traversin, crosspiece]

trap n. snare, contrivance for catching
game, etc.; movable covering for an opening, esp. through a ceiling, etc.; two-
wheeled carriage; arrangement of pipes to
prevent escape of gas, etc. -v.t. catch,
entrap. **-trap'door** n. door in a floor or
roof. **-trapp'er** n. [OE. troeppe]

trap v.t. ornamental coverings usu. for a
horse. **-trapp'ings** n. pl. caparison; equipment, ornaments. [F. drop, cloth]

trapeze' horizontal bar suspended from
two ropes. [L. trapezium]

trash n. worthless refuse; rubbish. **trash'y**
a. **-trash'iness** n. [orig. uncertain]

trau'ma n. wound, injury; shock. -
traumat'ic a. [G. = wound]

trav'ail v.i. labor or be in labor. -n. toil;
pains of childbirth. [F. = work]

trav'el v.i. journey. -v. t. journey through.
-n. journeying. -pl .account of traveling.
-trav'eler n. **-trav'elogue** n. travel talk or
film. [var. of travail]

trav'erse v.t. cross, go through or over; oppose. [F. traverser]

trav'esty n. comic imitation. -v. t. ridicule
by a travesty. [F. travestir, disguise]

trawl n. net dragged along the bottom of
the sea. -v. i. fish with one. **-trawl'er** n.
trawling vessel. [OF. trailler, drag]

tray n. shallow flat receptacle used for
holding or carrying small articles; any
similar utensil of metal, plastic, wicker-
work, etc. [OE. trig]

treachery n. deceit, betrayal.
treach'erous a. **-treach'erously** adv. [F.
tricherie, OF. trecherie, trickery]

tread v. t. set foot on. -v. i. walk. n. a tread-
ing; fashion of walking; upper surface of
a step, tyre, etc. **-trea'dle** n. lever worked
by the foot to turn a wheel. [OE. tredan]

trea'son n. treachery; breaking allegiance.
-trea'sonable a. constituting treason. -
trea'sonous a. [F. trahison, fr. L. tradition
handing over]

treas'ure (trezh-) n. riches, stored wealth
or valuables. -v.t. prize; store up.

treas'urer n. official in charge of funds.
treas'ury n. place for funds or treasure,
esp. of a state; govt. dept. in charge of the
public revenue. [G. thesauros]

treat v.t. deal with, act towards; apply
remedies to. -v.i. negotiate. -n. entertainment, pleasure given. **-treat'ise** n. book on
a given subject. **-treat'ment** n. [F. traiter,
fr. L. tractare, handle]

treat'y n. contract between states. [OF.
traiter fr. L. tractare]

tre'ble (treb'l) a. threefold. -n. soprano
voice; part of music for it; singer with such
voice. -v.t. and i. increase three-fold.
treb'ly adv. [L. triplus]

tree n. large perennial plant with a woody
trunk; beam. [OE. treow]

tree stucture n. (compute.) database format using master records, linked to several
subordinate records, each of which is
linked to only one master record.

trek v.i. journey by bullock-wagon; journey overland. [Du. trekken, drag]

trellis n. lattice or grating of light bars
fitted crosswise. -v.t. screen or supply with
trellis. [F. treillis]

trem'ble v.i. quiver, shake. -n. a trembling.
[L. tremere, quake]

tremen'dous a. causing fear or awe; vast,
immense. [L. tremere, quake]

trem'or n. a trembling. **-trem'ulous** a.
quivering easily; timorous. [L. tremere,
quake]

trench v.t. cut grooves or ditches in. -v. i.
infringe. -n. long narrow ditch, esp. as a
shelter in war. **-trench'ant** a. cutting, incisive. **-trench'er** n. wooden plate. **trench'-
erman** n. hearty eater. [F. trancher, to cut]

trend v.i. have a general direction. -n.
direction or tendency. **-trend'setter** n. person or thing that creates, or may create, a
new fashion. **-trend'setting** a. **-trendy** a.
very fashionable; faddish. [OE. trendan]

trepidation n. state of alarm; trembling
from fear. [L. trepidatio]

tres'pass n. wrongdoing; wrongful entering on another's land. -v. i. commit
trespass. [OF. trespasser, pass across]

tress n. lock of hair. (F. tresse)

tres'tle (-sl) n. bar fixed on pairs of spreading legs and used as a support. [OF. trestel,
fr. L. transtrum, crosspiece]

triangle n. plane figure with three angles
and three sides; percussion instrument. -
triang'ular a. [L. triangulum]

tribe n. race or subdivision of a race of
people. **-tri'bal** a. [L. tribus]

tribula'tion n. misery, trouble, affliction.
[L. tribulare, oppress]

trib'une *n.* popular leader; speaker's platform; bishop's throne. **-tribu'nal** *n.* lawcourt; bench of judges, *etc.* [L. *tribunus*, protector of the commons]

trib'ute *n.* tax paid by one state to another; speech or act of homage. **trib'utary** *a.* paying tribute; auxiliary. *n.* stream flowing into another. [L. *tributum*]

trick *n.* stratagem; feat of skill or cunning; cards played in one round. *-v.t.* cheat. - **trick'ery** *n.* **-trick'ster** *n.* **trick'sy** *a.* sportive; deceptive; crafty. **trick'y** *a.* crafty; ticklish. [ONF. *trique*]

trick *v.t.* deck, attire. (Celt. orig.]

trickle *v.i.* flow slowly or in drops. [for *strickle*, fr. *strike*, in sense of flow]

tri- prefix. three. [L. fr. *tres*, or G. *treis*, three] **-tri'color** *a.* three colored. *-n.* tricolor flag, *esp.* the French one. **tri'cycle** *n.* vehicle like a bicycle, but with three wheels. **-tri'dent** *n.* three-pronged fork. - **trienn'ial** *a.* happening every, or lasting, three years.

tri'fle *n.* insignificant thing or matter; pudding of sponge-cake, whipped cream, *etc.* *-v.i.* act or speak idly. **-tri'fling** *a.* unimportant. **-tri'fler** *n.* [OF. *trufle*, mockery]

trigg'er *n.* catch which releases a spring, *esp.* to fire a gun, *etc.* [earlier tricker, Du. , *trekker*, fr. *trekken*, pull]

trigonom'etry *n.* branch of mathematics dealing with the relations of the sides and angles of triangles. **trigonomet'rical** *a.* - **trigonom'eter** *n.* [fr. G. *trigonon*, triangle]

trill *v.i.* sing with a quavering voice. sing lightly. *-n.* such singing. [It; *trillare*, of imit. orig.]

tril'ogy *n.* series of three related dramas or novels. [G. *trilogia*, series of three tragedies]

trim *v.t.* prune; adjust, put in good order. *-v.i.* shuffle, act as a timeserver. *n.* order, state of being trimmed. *a.* neat, smart; in good order. [OE. *trymman*, arrange, make firm]

trinitrotol'uene (*abbrev.* **TNT**) *n.* a high explosive. [nitric acid, toluene]

trin'ity *n.* state of being threefold; three persons of the Godhead. **-trinitar'ian** *n.* and *a.* [L. *trinitas*]

trink'et *n.* small ornament for the person. [orig. uncertain]

trio. *See* **triple.**

trip *v. i.* run lightly, skip; stumble. *-v. t.* cause to stumble. *-n.* light step; stumble; journey, excursion. [OF. *triper*, dance]

tripe *n.* stomach of a ruminant animal prepared for food; (*sl.*) rubbish. [F. *entrails*]

trip'le *a.* threefold. *-v. t.* and *i.* treble. **trip'ly** *adv.* **-trip'let** *n.* three of a kind. **tri'o** *n.* group of three; music for three performers, *etc.* **-tri'partite** *a.* having three parts. **-trip'licate** *a.* three-fold. *v.t.* make threefold. *-n.* state of being triplicate; one of a set of three copies. **triplica'tion** *n.* **-tri'pod** *n.* stool or stand, *etc.*, with three feet. **-trip'tych** *n.* carving or picture in three compartments. [L. fr. *tres*, three]

tri'sect *v.t.* to divide into three (usually equal) parts. **-trisection** *n.* [L. fr. *tres*, three, *secare, sectu*, to cut]

trite *a.* hackneyed; worn out. [L. *tritus*, to rub]

tri'umph *n.* great success, victory; exultation. *-v.i.* achieve great success or victory; exult. **-triumph'ant** *a.* **-triumph'al** *a.* [L. *triumphus*]

triv'et *n.* an iron bracket or stand for putting a pot or kettle on. [OE. *trefet* fr. L. *tripes, triped-*, tripod]

triv'ial *a.* commonplace, trifling. **triviality** *n.* (L. *trivialis*]

troll *v. t.* pass (cup) round; sing heartily. [orig. uncertain]

troll *n.* diminutive supernatural being in Scandinavian mythology. [ON.]

troll'ey *n.* form of small truck; pole and wheel by which a tramcar collects power from overhead wire. **-trolley bus** *n.* an omnibus which is similarly powered. [orig. uncertain]

trom'bone *n.* large brass wind-instrument of which one part slides in and out of the other. [It.]

troop *n.* crowd of persons or animals; unit of cavalry. *-pl.* soldiers. *-v.i.* move in a troop. **-troop'er** *n.* a cavalry-soldier; state policeman. [F. *troupe*]

tro'phy *n.* memorial of a victory, in war, sport, the chase, *etc.* [F. *trophée*]

trop'ic *n.* either of two circles in the heavens or round the earth where the sun seems to turn at a solstice. *-pl.* hot regions between the tropics. **-trop'ical** *a.* [*trope*]

troposphere *n.* lowest layer of Earth's atmosphere bounded by stratosphere. [G. *trope*, turning, *sphaira*, sphere]

trot *v.i.* of a horse, move at medium pace, lifting the feet in diagonal pairs; of a person, *etc.*, run easily with short strides. *-n.* action of trotting; a brisk, steady pace. - **trott'er** *n.* horse which trots; (*sl.*) foot; pig, sheep's foot for eating. [F. *trotter*]

troth *n.* faith. [var. of *truth*]

trou'ble (trub'l) *v.t.* disturb, afflict. *-v.i.* be agitated or disturbed. *-n.* disturbance, agitation; inconvenience; distress; confusion. **-troub'lous** a. **-troub'lesome** a. [F. trouper]

trough (trof) n. long open vessel; hollow between two waves. [OE. trog]

trounce v. t. beat severely, thrash. **trouncing** n. [orig. uncertain]

troupe n. company of actors, acrobats, etc. **-troup'er** n. [F.]

trou'sers n. pl. two-legged outer garment with legs reaching to the ankles. [earlier trouse, Gael. triuohas]

trousseau n. outfit of clothing, esp. for a bride. [F.]

trout n. freshwater fish esteemed as food. [OE. truht]

trow v.i. trust; believe. [OE. treowian, trust]

trow'el n. small tool like a spade for spreading mortar, lifting plants, etc. [Late L. truella, small ladle]

tru'ant n. one absent from duty without leave, esp. a child so absent from school. [F. truand, vagabond]

truce n. temporary cessation of fighting. [pl. of OE. treow, agreement]

truck v.t. and i. barter; exchange. **-n.** barter; payment of workmen in goods; (colloq.) rubbish. **-truck farm** n. small farm specializing in growing vegetables for market. [F. troquer]

truck n. open vehicle for heavy goods; kind of barrow; disk at a masthead. **-v. t.** transport by truck. [G. trochileia, pulley]

truc'ulent a. ferocious, inclined to fight, belligerent. [L. truculentus]

trudge v.i. walk laboriously. **-n.** laborious walk. [earlier truss, pack (off)]

true a. in accordance with facts; faithful; exact, correct. **-truth** (-oo-) n. state of being true; something that is true. **-tru'ism** n. self-evident truth. **tru'ly** adv. **-truth'ful** a. **-truth'fully** adv. [OE. treow, faith]

truf'fle n. edible fungus growing underground. [OF. truffe]

trump n. card of a suit temporarily ranking above the others. **-v.t.** take (a trick) with a trump. **-v.i.** trump up, get up, fabricate. [earlier triumph]

trum'pery a. showy, but worthless. **-n.** worthless finery. [F. tromperie, deceit]

trum'pet n. metal wind instrument like a horn. **-v.i.** blow a trumpet or make a sound like one. **-v. t.** proclaim. . [F. trompette]

truncate v.t. cut short. [L. truncare, truncate, fr. truncus, trunk]

trunk n. main stem of a tree; person's body without or excluding the head and limbs; box for clothes, etc.; elephant's or other proboscis. [OF. tronc, L. truncus, trunk]

truss v.t. fasten up, tie up. **-n.** support; bundle (of hay, etc.). [F. trousser, pack]

trust n. confidence, firm belief, property held for another; state of being relied on; combination of producers to do away with competition and keep up prices. **-v. t.** rely on, believe in. **-trustee'** n. one legally holding property on another's behalf. **trustee'ship** n. **-trust'ful** a. **-trust'worthy** a. **-trust'y** a. [ON. traust]

truth. See true.

try v.t. test; conduct a judicial enquiry; attempt; cause to suffer. **-v. i.** attempt something, endeavor. **-n.** attempt. **-tri'al** n. **-try-sail** n. small fore-and-aft sail set with gaff, storm sail. [F. trier, to sift]

tryst n. appointment to meet. [OF. tristre, hunting station]

Tsar. See Czar.

tset'se n. small African fly carrying germ of sleeping-sickness. [Bechuana]

tub n. open wooden vessel like the bottom half of a barrel; bath. **-v.t. and i.** bathe. [Du. tobbe]

tube n. pipe, long narrow hollow cylinder. **-tu'bular** a. [L. tubus]

tu'ber n. swelling on the roots of certain plants, e.g. potato. **-tu'berous** a. [L. lump]

tu'bercle n. granular small tumor in consumptive lungs, etc., **-tuber'cular** a. **tuberculo'sis** n. disease, esp. of the lung, marked by the presence of tubercles and a characteristic bacillus, esp. consumption of the lungs. [L. tuberculum, dim. of tuber, lump]

tu'berose n. plant with tuberous root and sweet-scented, creamy flowers. [L. tuberose, tuberous]

tuck v. t. gather or stitch in folds; draw or roll together. **-n.** stitched fold; food, esp. dainties eaten by schoolboys. [orig. tug, OE. tucian, illtreat]

Tues'day n. third day of the week. [OE. Tiwesdoeg, day of Tiw, Teutonic god of war]

tuft n. bunch of feathers, threads, etc. knot; cluster. [F. touffe]

tug v. t. pull hard or violently. **-n.** violent pull; steamship used to tow other vessels. [orig. obscure]

tui'tion n. teaching. [L. twitio]

tu'lip n. plant of the lily family with bright bell-shaped flowers. [OF. tulipe, fr. Pers. dulband, turban]

tum'ble v. i. fall; turn somersaults. **-v. t.** throw down; rumple. **-n.** fall; somersault. **-tum'bler** n. acrobat; round-bottomed drinking-glass; variety of pigeon. [OE. tumbian, dance]

tu'mid *a.* swollen, distended. [L. *tumere,* to swell]

tu'mor *n.* abnormal growth on the body. [L. *tumere,* to swell]

tu'mult *n.* uproar, commotion; confusion of mind. -**tumult'uous** *a.* [L. *tumultus,* fr. *tumere,* swell]

tun *n.* large cask. [OE. *tunne*]

tun'dra *n.* flat, treeless, marshy plains of *n.* Russia and Siberia. [Lapp]

tune *n.* melody; concord; adjustment of a musical instrument. -*v. t.* put in tons. **tune'ful** *a.* -**tune'fully** *adv.* -**tu'ner** *n.* [var. of *tone*]

tung'sten *n.* rare metal with high melting-point. -**tung'stic** *a.* [Sw. *tung,* heavy, *sten,* stone]

tu'nic *n.* short military coat; garment of similar shape. [L. *tunics*]

tunn'el *n.* artificial underground passage. -*v.t.* and *i.* make a tunnel (through). -**tunn'eler** *n.* [OF. *tonel,* dim. of ME. *tonne,* tun]

tur'ban *n.* man's headdress made by coiling a length of material round a cap or the head. -**tur'banned** *a.* [Pers. *dulband*]

tur'bid *a.* muddy, thick. -**turbid'ity** *n.* [E. *turbare,* disturb]

tur'bine *n.* kind of water-wheel; rotary steam or gas engine. [F.]

tur'bulent *a.* riotous, in commotion. [F. -L. *turbulentus*]

tureen' n. dish for soup. [earlier *terreen,* F. *terrine,* earthenware pot]

turf *n.* short grass with the earth bound to it by the matted roots; sod. -*v. t.* lay with turf. [OE. = *sod,* peat]

tur'key *n.* large bird reared for food. [Turkey-cock, orig. the guinea-fowl, the present bird being American]

tur'moil *n.* confusion and bustle; disturbance; agitation. [orig. uncertain]

turn *v.t.* make move round or rotate; shape on a lathe; change, reverse, alter position of, *etc.* -*v.i.* move round; change; become, *etc.* -*n.* act of turning; walk; rotation; part of a rotation; performance; inclination; *etc.* **turn'key** *n.* jailer. -**turn'over** *n.* act of turning over; in business, amount of money changing hands; kind of pie with top flapped over. -**turn'pike** *n.* gate across a road where tolls are paid, toll gate; toll road, or one formerly maintained as one; main road. -**turn'stile** *n.* revolving gate for controlling admission of people. -**turn'table** *n.* revolving platform. [L. *tornare,* fr. *tornus,* lathe]

turn'ip *n.* plant with a round root used as a vegetable or fodder. [*turn* and OE. *næp,* L. *napus*]

turp'entine *n.* resin got from certain trees; oil or spirit made from this. [L. *terebinthina,* resin of the terebinth]

turp'itude *n.* baseness. [L. *turpitudo*]

tur'quoise *n.* opaque blue precious stone. [F. = Turkish]

turr'et *n.* small tower; revolving tower for a gun on a ship, tank or fort. [OF. *tourete,* dim. of *tour,* tower]

tur'tle *n.* common wild dove. [OE.]

tur'tle *n.* sea-tortoise; its shell. -**turn'tur'tle,** capsize. -**tur'tleneck** *n.* closefitting turnover collar; sweater with such a collar. [corrupt. of F. *tortue,* tortoise]

tusk *n.* long pointed tooth sticking out from a mouth. -**tusk'er** *n.* animal with tusks fully developed. [OE. *tux*]

tus'sle *n.* struggle. -*v.i.* [dial *touse*]

tu'telage *n.* guardianship. -**tu'telary** *a.* protecting. [L. *tutela*]

tu'tor *n.* person giving lessons privately, or to individuals in a college; guardian. **tutor'ial** *a.* [L. , fr. *tueri, tut-,* see to]

tuxe'do *n.* semi-formal dinner jacket. [Tuxedo Park, N. Y.]

twain *a.* two. -*n.* a pair, couple; two persons or things. [OE. *twegen*]

twang *n.* ringing sound as of plucked string. -*v. i.* and *t.* make, cause to make, such sound. [imit.]

tweak *v.t.* pinch and twist or pull. -*n.* act of tweaking. [OE. *twiccian*]

tweed *n.* rough-surfaced woolen cloth, usually of mixed colors. [for *tweel,* var. of *twill*]

tweez'ers *n. pl.* small forceps or pincers. [earlier *tweeses, pl.* of obs. *twee,* F. *étui,* case for instruments]

twelve *n.* and *a.* cardinal number, two more than ten. -**twelfth** *a.* ordinal number. -**twelve'month** *n.* year. [OE. *twelf*]

twent'y *n.* and *a.* cardinal number, twice ten. -**twent'ieth** *a.* ordinal number. [OE. *twentig*]

twice *adv.* two times. [OE. *twiges*]

twig *n.* small branch. [OE.]

twi'light *n.* half light after sunset or before dawn. [*twi-,* two]

twill *n.* fabric woven so as to have a surface of parallel diagonal ridges. *v.t.* weave thus. [OE. *twili*]

twin *n.* one of a pair, *esp.* of children born together. -*a.* being a twin. [OE. *twinn,* twofold]

twine *v.t.* and *i.* twist or coil round. -*n.* string. [OE. *twin*]

twinge *n.* momentary sharp pain; (fig.) qualm, as of conscience. [OE. *twengan v.*]

twin´kle *v.i.* shine with dancing or quivering light. -*n.* twinkling; flash; gleam of amusement in eyes or face. -**twink´ling** *n.* instant. [OE. *twinclian*]

twirl *v.t.* and *i.* turn or twist round quickly, spin round. [orig. uncertain]

twist *v.t.* and *i.* make or become spiral, by turning with one end fast. -*n.* a twisting; something twisted. [OE.]

twitch *v.i.* give a momentary sharp pull; jerk. -*v.t.* pull at thus. -*n.* such pull or jerk; spasmodic jerk. [OE. *twiccian*, pluck]

twitt´er *v.i.* of birds, utter a succession of tremulous sounds. -*n.* such succession of notes. [imit.]

two *n.* and *a.* cardinal number, one more than one. -**two-faced** *a.* having two faces; insincere. -**two´fold** *adv.* and *a.* [OE. *two*]

tycoon´ *n.* important business man. [Jap. *taikum*, great prince]

tym´panums *n.* ear-drum. -**tympan´ic** *a.* of or like a drum. [L. fr. G.]

type *n.* class; characteristic build; specimen, block bearing a letter used for printing; such pieces collectively; state of being set up for printing. -*v.t.* print with a typewriter. -**type´writer** *n.* keyed writing machine. -**ty´pist** *n.* -**typ´ical** *a.* **typically** *adv.* -**typ´ify** *v.t.* serve as a type or model of -**typog´raphy** *n.* art of printing; style of printing.

typhoon´ *n.* violent cyclonic hurricane. [Chin. *tai fung*, big wind]

ty´phus *n.* contagious fever. [G. *typhos*, vapour]

ty´rant *n.* oppressive or cruel ruler. **tyrann´ical** *a.* [G. *tyrannos*, absolute ruler]

U

ubiq´uity *n.* a being everywhere at the same moment. **ubiquitous** *a.* [L. *ubique*, everywhere]

U´-boat *n.* German submarine. [Ger. *unterseeboot*, under-sea boat]

udd´er *n.* mammary gland or milk-bag of a cow, *etc.* [OE. uder]

ug´ly *a.* unpleasing or repulsive to the sight; ill-omened; threatening. -**ug´liness** *n.* [ON. *uggligr*, fr. *uggr*, fear]

ukulele *n.* four-stringed guitar. [Hawaiian]

ul´cer *n.* open sore. -**ul´cerate** *v. i.* form an ulcer. -*v.t.* make ulcerous. -**ul´cerous** *a.* -**ulcera´tion** *n.* [L. *ulcus*, *ulcer*-]

ul´ster *n.* **man´s, woman´s,** long caped overcoat. [*Ulster*]

ulterior *a.* situated beyond; beyond what appears. [L., compar. of *ultra*, beyond, on the other side]

ultimate *a.* last, farthest. -**ult´imately** *adv.* -**ultima´tum** *n.* final proposal the rejection of which causes war. -**ult´imo** *adv.* in last month. [L. *ultimus*, superl. of *ultra*, beyond]

ultramarine´ *a.* beyond the sea. *n.* blue pigment. -**ultramont´ane** *a.* south of or beyond the Alps; favorable to the absolute authority of the Pope. **ultrason´ics** *n.* science of waves beyond the frequency of sound. -**ultravi´olet** *a.* beyond the violet (of rays of the spectrum). [L. *ultra*, beyond]

um´ber *n.* dark brown pigment. [It. (*terra d´*) ombra, shadow (earth)]

umbilical *a.* of the navel. -**umbil´icus** *n.* [L. *umbilicus*]

um´brage *n.* sense of injury, offense. **umbrage´ous** *a.* shady. [L. *umbra*, shadow]

umbrella *n.* a light folding circular cover of silk, *etc.*, on a steel framework, carried in the hand to protect against rain. [L. *umbra*, shadow]

um´pire *n.* person chosen to decide a question; person chosen to decide disputes and enforce the rules in a game. -*v.i.* act as umpire in. -*v.i.* act as umpire. [ME. *nomper*, fr. F. *non pair*, not equal (*i. e.*, odd man called in when arbitrators disagreed)]

ump´teen *n.* (*sl.*) indefinite number, quite a lot. [*umpty*, morse for dash]

un- *prefix.* makes compounds negativing the idea of the simple words, *e.g.* -**unarmed´** *a.* not armed. -**unfast´en** *v.t.* loosen or remove the fastening. **untruth´** *n.* lie. These are only given where the meaning or derivation cannot easily be found from the simple word. [OE.]

unan´imous *a.* of one mind, agreeing. [L. *unanimus* -*unus*, one, *animus*, mind]

unassum´ing *a.* modest, not bold or forward. [*an-* and L. *assumere*]

uncann´y *a.* weird, mysterious. -**uncann´iness** *n.* [OE. *can*, know]

un´cate *a.* hooked. [L. *uncus*, hook]

unc´le *n.* brother of a father or mother; husband of an aunt. [F. oncle, fr. L. *avunculus*, uncle on mother's side]

uncon´scious *a.* not knowing, unaware; insensible. -*n.* hidden or repressed part of thought. [*un-* and L. *conscius*]

uncouth´ *a.* clumsy, without ease or polish. -**uncouth´ly** *adv.* -**uncouth´ness** *n.* [OE. *uncuth*, unknown]

unc´tion *n.* anointing; soothing words or thought; fervor of words or tone; imitation of this; affected enthusiasm. **-unc'tuous** a. full of unction; greasy. [L. *unctio*, fr. *ungere, unct-*, anoint]

un'der *prep.* below, beneath; bound by, included in; in the time of. *-adv.* in a lower place or condition *-a.* lower. **underbred'** a. ill-bred. **-und'er-carriage** n. landing structure of aircraft. **undercharge'** v.t. charge less than the proper amount. *-n.* too low a charge. **underhand'** a. unfair, sly. **-underhung'** a. *with the lower part projecting beyond the upper.* **-un'derling** n. subordinate. **underneath'** adv. below. *-prep.* under. **underpass'** n. road or passage for traffic or pedestrians which passes underneath a highway or railroad. **undershirt'** n. collarless garment for wearing underneath a shirt. **-un'der-shot** a. moved by water passing under. **-un'der strapper** n. underling, subordinate. **un'dertow** n. current beneath surface moving in a different direction from surface current; back-wash; and numerous other compounds of *under* which need no explanation. [OE. *under*]

undergrad'uate n. university student who has not yet taken a degree. [*graduate*]

und'erground a. subterranean; secret **-go und'erground**, of a political organization, continue its activities in secret. *-n.* **underground railway.** [*ground*]

understand v.t. see the meaning of, infer; take for granted. *-v. i.* be informed. *-p. p.* **understood.** **-understand'ing** n. intelligence. [OE. *understanan*]

understudy v.t. study an actor's part so as to be able to take his place in emergency. *-n.* one who does this. [*study*]

undertake' v.t. make oneself responsible for; enter upon a task, *etc.* [ME. *undertaken*]

un'dertaker n. one who undertakes; one who manages funerals. [*under* and *take*]

un'derwrite v.t. agree to pay, take up shares in, *e.g.*, in marine insurance, *etc.* [trans. of *subscriber*]

un'dulate v.i. move in waves or like waves. **-undula'tion** n. **-un'dulatory** a. [L. *unda*, wave]

undu'ly adv. too much, excessively, wrongly, improperly. [*due*]

unfrock' v.t. strip a monk, priest, of his gown, *i.e.*, his office. [*frock*]

ungain'ly a. awkward, uncouth, clumsy [ON. *gegn*, convenient]

uxi'guent n. an ointment. **-ung'uentary** a. [L. *unguentum*]

unhinge' v.t. take from hinges; unbalance, *esp.* mentally. [*hinge*]

u'nicorn n. a fabulous animal like a horse, with a single long horn. [L. *unicorns*, fr. *cornu*, horn]

uni- prefix one. [L. *unus*, one]

u'niform a. not changing, unvarying; conforming to the same standard or rule. *-n.* uniform dress worn by members of the same body, *e.g.*, soldiers, nurses, *etc.* **u'niformly** adv. **-uniform'ity** n. [L. *uniformis*]

unify v.t. bring to unity or uniformity. **unifica'tion** n. [Med. L. *unificare*]

u'nion n. joining into one; state of being joined; result of being joined; federation. combination of societies, *etc.*; trade union. **-u'nionist** n. supporter of union. **u'nionism** n. [F.]

unique' a. being the only one of its kind. [F. fr. L. *unicus*]

u'nison n. agreement, harmony; sounding at the same pitch. [L. *uni and sonus*]

u'nit n. single thing or person; standard quantity. **-unitar'ian** n. member of a Christian body that denies the doctrine of the Trinity. **-unitar'ianism** n. [L. *unus*]

unite' v.t. join into one, connect. *-v.i.* become one, combine. **-u'nity** n. state of being one; harmony. **-Uni'ted Nations Organization** organization founded in 1945 for maintaining peace and settling international difficulties by arbitration. [L. *unire, -itus*, to unite]

universe n. whole of creation, all existing things. **-univer'sal** a. relating to all things or all men; applying to all members of a community. **-univer'sally** adv. **universal'ity** n. [L. *universus*, lit. 'turned to one', *unus*]

university n. educational institution for study, examination and conferment of degrees in all or most of the important branches of learning. [L. *universitas*]

unkempt' a. of rough or uncared-for appearance. [OE. *cemban*, comb]

unless' *conj.* if not, except when; save. [for *on less*]

unru'ly a. badly behaved, ungovernable; turbulent. [*rule*]

until' prep. up to the time of. *conj.* to the time that; with a negative, before. [*See* till]

un'to prep. to. [*See* to]

untouchable n. Hindu below the caste level. *-a.* [*touch*]

untoward' a. inconvenient; inopportune. [arch. toward, propitious]

unwield'y a. large and cumbersome; difficult to handle. [*wield*]

up adv. in or to a higher position, a source, an activity, *etc.*; quite. *-prep.* to or towards the source, *etc.* -**up'ward** *a.* and *adv.* -**up'wards** *adv.* [OE.]

up- *prefix* makes compounds mostly of obvious meaning, *e.g.*, **upbringing** *n.* bringing up. -**uphold'** *v.t.* hold up, support, *etc.*

upbraid' *v.t.* scold, reproach; reprove severely. -**upbraid'ing** *n.* abuse, reproach. -**upbraid'ingly** *adv.* [orig. uncertain]

upholsterer *n.* one who provides carpets, hangings, or covers chairs, *etc.* **upholst'er** *v.t.* to put coverings on, supply carpets, *etc.* -**upholst'ery** *n.* [earlier *upholder,* in ME. a broker]

upon' *prep.* on. [OE. *uppon*]

upp'er *a.* higher, situated above. -*n.* upper part of a boot or shoe. [up]

upp'ish *a.* self-assertive. [up]

up'right *a.* erect; honest, just. -*n.* thing standing upright, *e. g.*, post in a framework. [right]

up'roar *n.* tumult, disturbance. **uproar'ious** *a.* -**uproar'iously** *adv.* [Du. *oproer,* stirring up]

upset' *v. t.* overturned. overturned. -*n.* an upsetting; trouble. -**up'set price** *n.* price below which goods at auction may not be sold. [set]

up'shot *n.* outcome, conclusion, final result. [orig. *deciding shot*]

up'start *n.* one suddenly raised to wealth, power, *etc.* [start]

ura'nium *n.* hard white radioactive metal. [*Uranus,* planet]

urbane' *a.* polished, courteous. **urban'ity** *n.* -**ur'ban** *a.* relating to a town or city. [L. *urbanus,* of a city, urbs]

urch'in *n.* sea urchin; hedgehog; mischievous boy; boy or youngster. [F. *hérisson,* fr. L. *ericius,* hedgehog]

urge *v.t.* drive on; entreat or exhort earnestly. -*n.* strong impulse. -**ur'gent** *a.* pressing; needing attention at once; importunate. -**ur'gently** *adv.* -**ur'gency** *n.* (L. *urgere*]

urine *n.* fluid secreted by the kidneys. **u'ric** *a.* -**u'ric a'cid** *n.* -**u'rinate** *v. t.* discharge urine. -**u'rinal** *n.* . place for urinating. [L. *urina*]

urn *n.* vase with a foot and usually a rounded body. [L. *urna*]

ur'sine *a.* of, like, a bear. [L. *ursus,* bear]

us *pron.* obj. case of *we.* [OE.]

use *n.* employment, applications to a purpose; profit, serviceableness; need to employ; habit. -**use** *v. t.* employ, avail oneself of, accustom. -**u'sable** (-z-) *a.* **u'sage** (-s-) *n.* act of using; custom; customary way of using. -**use'ful** (-s-) *a.* - **use'fully** *adv.* -**usefulness** *n.* **use'less** *a.* -**use'lessly** *adv.* -**use'lessness** *n.* -**u'sual**

(-z-) *a.* habitual, ordinary. -**u'sually** *adv.* [L. *usus,* use]

ush'er *n.* doorkeeper, one showing people to seats, *etc.*; formerly an underteacher. *v.t.* introduce, announce. [F. *huissier,* fr. L. *ostiarius-stium,* door]

usurp' *v.t.* seize wrongfully. -**usurp'er** *n.* -**usurpa'tion** *n.* [L. *usurpare*]

u'sury (-z-) *n.* lending of money at excessive interest; such interest. **u'surer** *n.* -**usu'rious** *a.* [L. *usura*]

utensil *n.* vessel or implement, *esp.* in domestic use. [L. *utensilis,* fr. *uti,* use]

u'terus *n.* womb. -**u'terine** *a.* [L.]

utility *n.* usefulness; useful thing. *a.* serviceable. -**utilita'rianism** *n.* doctrine that the morality of actions is to be tested by their utility, *esp.* that the greatest good of the greatest number should be the sole end of public action. **utilita'ria** *a.* -**u'tilize** *v. t.* make use of. -**utiliza'tion** *n.* [L. *utilitas,* fr. *uti,* use]

ut'most *a.* extreme, farthest. -*n.* one's best endeavor. [OE. *ut,* out]

Uto'pia *n.* imaginary state with perfect political, social, conditions or constitution. -**Uto'pian** *a.* visionary. [Sir T. More's imaginary country (in book published 1516), fr. G. *ou,* not, *topos,* place]

utt'er *a.* complete, total. -**utt'erly** *adv.* [OE. *uttera,* compar. of *ut,* out]

utt'er *v.t.* express, emit audibly; put in circulation. -**utt'erance** *n.* uttering; expression in words; spoken words. [ME. *uttren,* fr. *adv.* utter]

u'vula *n.* pendent fleshy part of the soft palate. -**u'vular** *a.* [Med. L. dim. of *uva,* bunch of grapes]

uxorious *a.* excessively fond of one's wife. [L. *uxorius,* fr. *uxor,* wife]

V

vacate' *v.t.* quit, leave empty. -**va'cant** *a.* unoccupied; without thought, empty. **va'cantly** *adv.* -**va'cancy** *n.* emptiness; situation unoccupied. -**vaca'tion** *n.* act of vacating; scheduled period when school is suspended; period away from work or home for recreation. [L. *vacare,* be empty]

vac'cinate (-ks-) *v.t.* inoculate with vaccine *esp,* as a protection against smallpox. -**vaccina'tion** *n.* -**vac'cinator** *n.* -**vac'cine** *n.* virus of cowpox. [L. *vacca,* cow]

va'cillate (vas'-) *v.i.* waver. -**vacilla'tion** *n.* [L. *vacillate,* vacillate]

vac'uum *n.* place devoid of matter; place from which air has been practically exhausted. -**vac'uous** *a.* vacant. **vacu'ity** *n.* -**vac'uum clean'er,** suction cleaner for sweeping, dusting, *etc.* [L. *vacuus*, empty]

vademe′cum *n.* manual, pocket companion. [L. = go with me]

vag′abond *a.* having no fixed dwelling. -*n.* wanderer; idle scamp. **vag′abondage** *n.* [L. *vagari*, wander]

vagar′y *n.* freak; unaccountable proceeding. -(*pl.*) **vagar′ies**. (prob. fr. L. *vagare*, to wander]

va′grant *n.* tramp. -*a.* on tramp; wandering idly. -**va′grancy** *n.* [OF. *walcrer*, wander]

vague *a.* indefinite; not distinct; mentally unprecise. -**vague′ly** *adv.* **vague′ness** *n.* [L. *vagus*, wandering]

vain *a.* worthless, useless; conceited; foolish. -**va′nity** *n.* [L. *vanus*, empty]

vainglo′ry *n.* self-glorification from vanity. -**vainglo′rious** *a.* [*vain* and *glory*]

val′ance *n.* short curtain round a bedstead, above window-curtains, *etc.* **val′anced** *a.* [orig. uncertain]

vale *n.* valley. [L. *vallis*]

valedic′tion *n.* farewell. -**valedic′tory** *a.* [L. *valedicere*, *valedict-*, say farewell]

va′lences, va′lency *n.* combining power of element or atom. [L. *valere*, be strong]

val′entine *n.* picture, set of verses, *etc.*, sent to a sweetheart on the 14th February; sweetheart chosen on that day. [Saint Valentine]

valer′ian *n.* flowering herb used in medicine. [F. *valériane*]

val′et *n.* manservant looking after his master's clothes, *etc.* [F.]

valetudinary *a.* sickly. -**valetudina′rian** *n.* person obliged or disposed to live the life of an invalid. [L. *valetudinarius*, fr. *valetudo*, state of health]

Valhall′a *n.* in Scandinavian mythology, place of immortality for heroes slain in battle. [ON. *valr*, slain, *holl*, hall]

valiant *a.* brave. [F. *vaillant*]

val′id *a.* sound; binding in law. **valid′ity** *n.* -**val′idate** *v. t.* [L. *validus*, strong]

valise′ *n.* traveling bag. [F.]

vall′ey *n.* (**vall′eys** *pl.*) low area between hills. [F. *vallee*]

val′or (-er) *n.* personal bravery or courage. -**val′orous** *a.* [OF. *valour*]

val′ue *n.* worth, price; equivalent. -*v. t.* to estimate a value of; to care for. - **val′uable** *a.* capable of being valued; of great value. -*n.* a valuable thing. **valua′tion** *n.* - **val′ueless** *a.* -**val′uer** *n.* [L. *valere*, be worth]

valve *n.* device to control the passage of a fluid, gas, *etc.*, through a pipe; thermionic valve (*q.v.*). -**val′vular** *a.* [L. *valva*, leaf of folding door]

vamp *n.* upper leather of a shoe. -*v.t.* and *i.* (*music*) improvise an accompaniment. [OF. *avanpie* (i. e. *avant pied*) part of the shoe covering the front of foot]

vamp′ire *n.* blood-sucking animal, person, ghost *etc.*; (*sl.*) person who preys on others. -**vamp** *n.* (*sl.*) a flirt. (Slav. *vampir*]

van *n.* leading division of an army or fleet. -**van′guard** *n.* [F. *avant-garde*, fr. *avant*, in front]

van *n.* covered road or rail vehicle, *esp.* for goods. [short for *caravan*]

vandalism *n.* barbarous destruction of works of art *etc.*; malicious destruction or defacement of property. -**vandal** *n.* -**vandalize** *v.t.* [L. *Vandalus*, Vandal]

vanill′a *n.* plant of the orchid kind; extract of this for flavoring. [Sp. *vainilla*, small pod]

van′ish *v.i.* disappear. [L. *evanescere*, fr. *vanus*, empty]

van′ity *n.* worthless pleasure or display; conceit of one's appearance, ability, *etc.* [L. *vanitas*, *-atis*]

van′quish *v.t.* conquer. [OF. *vainquir*, fr. L. *vincere*]

van′tage (va-) *n.* advantage, *esp.* in lawn tennis; condition favoring success. [AF. *vantage*]

vap′id *a.* flat, dull, insipid; savorless. **vapid′ity** *n.* [L. *vapidus*]

va′por (-er) *n.* gaseous form of a substance more familiar as liquid or solid; steam or mist; invisible moisture in the air. -**va′porize** *a.* turn into vapor, fine mist. -**va′porous** *a.* [L. *vapor*]

var′icose *a.* of a vein, morbidly dilated. [L. *varicosus-varix*, dilated vein]

var′nish *n.* resinous solution put on a surface to make it hard and shiny. -*v.t.* apply varnish to. [F. *vernis*]

var′y (var′-i) *v.t.* change. -*v.i.* be changed; become different. -**var′iable** *a.* -**variabil′ity** *n.* -**var′iance** *n.* state of discord. -**var′iant** *a.* different. -*n.* different form. -**varia′tion** *n.* -**var′iegate** *v.t.* diversify by patches of different colors. **variegation** *n.* -**vari′ety** *n.* state of being varied or various; varied assortment; sort or kind. -**var′ious** *a.* manifold, diverse, of several kinds. [L. *varius*, various]

vase *n.* vessel, jar. -**vas′cular** *a.* of, or having, vessels for conveying sap, blood, *etc.* [L. *vas*, with dim. *vasculum*]

Vas′eline *n.* brand of petroleum which is a transparent yellowish semi-solid substance used in ointments, pomades, as a lubricant, *etc.* [Trademark]

vass′al *n.* holder of land by feudal tenure;

dependant. -vass'alage n. (F.)

vast a. very large. -vast'ly adv. vast'ness n. [L. vastus]

vat n. large tub. [OE. foet, cask]

Vat'ican n. collection of buildings, including the palace of the Pope, at Rome; the papal authority. [L. Mons Vaticanus, a hill in Rome]

vaudeville n. popular song, light theatrical production interspersed with comic songs; variety concert. [from F. Vau (Val) de Vire, in Normandy]

vault n. arched roof; arched apartment; cellar. -v.t. build with an arched roof. [L. voluta, turned]

vault v.i. spring or jump with the hands resting on something. -v. t. jump over in this way. -n. such jump. [F. volter]

vaunt v.i. boast. -v.t. boast of. -n. boast. [F. vanter]

veal n. calf flesh used as food. [OF. veel, fr. L. vitulus, calf]

vedette' n. mounted sentinel. [F.]

veer v.i. change direction (e.g. wind); change one's opinion. [F. virer]

veer v.t. (naut.) slacken or let out (rope). [Du vieren]

veg'etable (-j-) a. of, from, or concerned with, plants. -n. plant, esp. one used for food. -vegeta'rian n. one who does not eat meat. -vegeta'rianism n. -veg'etate v. i. live the life of a plant. vegeta'tion n. plants collectively; the plants growing in a place; process of plant growth. [L. vegetus, lively, flourishing]

ve'hement a. forcefully eager, impetuous. -ve'hemently adv. -ve'hemence n. (L. vehemens]

ve'hicle n. carriage, cart, or other conveyance on land; means of expression; liquid which serves as medium for medicinal substances, etc. -vehic'ular a. [L. vehiculum, fr. vehere, carry]

veil n. piece of material to cover the face and head; pretext. -v.t. cover with, or as with, a veil. [L. velum]

vein n. tube in the body taking blood to the heart; rib of a leaf or insect's wing; fissure in rock filled with ore; streak. -v. t. mark with streaks. -ve'nous a. [L. vena]

veld (felt) n. (S. Africa) open country, thinly wooded grassland. [Du. veld, field]

vell'um n. parchment of calf skin prepared for writing on or bookbinding. [L. vitulus]

veloc'ipede (-os'-) n. early bicycle without pedals, moved by striking the feet on the ground. [F.]

velo'city n. speed, rate of speed. [L. velax, veloc-, swift]

velours n. kind of hatter's plush; fabric resembling velvet. [F.]

vel'vet n. silk fabric with a thick, short pile. -vel'vety a. smoothly soft like velvet. -velveteen' n. cotton fabric resembling velvet. (L. villus, nap]

ve'nal a. guilty of taking, prepared to take, bribes. -venal'ity n. [L. veaalis, fr. venum, that which is for sale]

vend v.t. sell; peddle. -vend'or n. vend'ible a. [L. vendere]

vendetta' n. blood-feud. [It.]

veneer' v.t. to cover with a thin layer of finer wood. -n. such covering. [earlier fineer, Ger. furnieren]

ven'erable a. worthy of reverence; aged; hallowed by age. -ven'erate v. t. -veneration n. [L. venerari, worship]

vene'real a. from, or connected with, sexual intercourse. [L. venereus, fr. venus, vener-, love]

vene'tian-blind n. window blind of thin slats of wood, slanted to admit light and air. [Venice]

ven'geance n. revenge, retribution for wrong done. -venge'ful a. -venge'fully adv. [F. veneer, fr. L. vindicate]

ve'nial a. pardonable. -venial'ity n. [L. venia, pardon]

ven'ison n. flesh of deer as food. [F. venaison, L. venatio, hunting]

ven'om n. poison, esp. of a snake; spite. ven'omous a. [L. venenum]

vent n. small hole or outlet. -v. t. give outlet to (e.g. air, one's feelings, etc.) [F.]

ventilate v.t. supply with fresh air; bring into discussion. -vent'ilator n. ventila'tion n. [L. ventilare, fan]

ventricle n. cavity or hollow in the body, esp. in the heart or brain. -ventric'ular a. [L. venter, belly]

ventril'oquist n. one who can so speak that the sounds seem to come from some other person or place. -ventril'oquism n. -ventrilo'quial a. [ventricle]

ven'ture n. undertaking of a risk, speculation. -v.t. risk. -v.i. dare; have courage to do something or go somewhere. -ven'turesome a. -vent'urous a. [ME. aventure, adventure]

ven'ue n. district in which a case is tried; meeting place; scene (of some event). [Med. L. vicinetum, area from which a jury was summoned]

vera'cious a. truthful. -vera'city (-as'-) n. [L. verax, verac-]

veran'da, veran'dah n. open gallery or portico at the side of a house. [Port. veranda]

verb *n.* part of speech which asserts or declares. **-verb'al** *a.* of, by, or relating to, words. **-verb'ally** *adv.* **-verba'tim** *adv.* word for word. **-verb'iage** *n.* excess of words. **-verbose'** *a.* wordy. **-verbos'ity** *n.* [L. *verbum*, word]

ver'dant *a.* green. **-verd'ure** *n.* greenery. [OF. *verd*, green, fr. L. *viridis*]

ver'dict *n.* decision of a jury; opinion reached after examination of facts, *etc.* [OF. *veir dit*, true word]

verdigris' *n.* green rust on copper. [OF. *vert de Grece*, Greek green]

verge *n.* edge, brink. **-ver'ger** *n.* bearer of a wand of office; usher in a church. [L. *virga*, wand]

verge *v.i.* be on the border of, come close to. [L. *vergere*, turn]

ver'ify *v.t.* prove or confirm the truth of. **-verifi'able** *a.* **-verifica'tion** *n.* **ver'itable** *a.* true, genuine. **-ver'itably** *adv.* **-ver'ity** *n.* truth. **-ver'ily** *adv.* truly. **-verisimil'tude** *n.* appearance of truth. [L. *verus*, true]

vermicell'i *n.* Italian pasta of flour, *etc.*, made in long thin tubes. [It.]

verm'icide *n.* substance to destroy worms. **-verm'iform** *a.* shaped like a worm. **-verm'ifuge** *n.* substance to drive out worms. [L. *vermis*, worm]

vermil'ion *n.* bright red color or pigment. *-a.* of this color. [L. *vermiculus*, dim. of *vermis*, worm]

ver'min *n.* injurious animals, parasites, *etc.* **-ver'minous** *a.* [L. *vermis*, worm]

ver'mouth *n.* liqueur of wormwood. [L. *vermis*, worm]

vernacular *a.* of language, idiom, *etc.*, of one's own country *n.* mother tongue; homely speech. [L. *vernaculus*, domestic]

vern'al *a.* of spring. [L. *ver*, spring]

vernier *n.* small sliding scale for obtaining fractional parts of the subdivisions of a graduated scale. [Vernier, F. mathematician (d. 1637)]

vers'atile *a.* capable of dealing with many subjects. **-versatil'ity** *n.* [F.]

verse *n.* line of poetry; short division of a poem or other composition. **-ver'sify** *v. t.* turn into verse. *-v.i.* to write verses. **versifica'tion** *n.* [OE. *fers*]

versed *a.* skilled; proficient. [F. *versé*]

ver'sion *n.* a translation; an account or description. [L. *vertere*, translate]

ver'so *n.* back of an object; left-hand page. [L. *vertere*, *vers-*, turn]

ver'sus *prep.* against. [L.]

vert'ebra *n.* single section of a backbone. **-vert'ebrate** *a.* having a backbone. **-vert'ebral** *a.* [L.]

vert'ex *n.* **-vert'ices** *pl.* summit. [L. *vertex, -icis*, summit]

vert'ical *a.* upright; overhead. [fr. L. *vertere*, to turn]

verti'go *n.* giddiness. **-verti'ginous** *a.* dizzy. [L.]

verve *n.* inspired enthusiasm; life, vigor, *esp.* in creative work, [F.]

ver'y *a.* true, real. *adv.* extremely, to a great extent. [OF. *verai*, true]

ves'icle *n.* small blister, bubble, or cavity. **-vesic'ular** *a.* (L. *vesica*, bladder]

ves'pers *n. pl.* evening church service. [L. *vesper*, evening star]

vess'el *n.* any utensil or appliance for containing, *esp.* for liquids; ship. [OF. *vaissel*, fr. L. *vas*, vase]

vest *n.* sleeveless garment worn beneath s suit coat, waistcoat. *-v.t.* endow. *-v.i.* be in a person's authority. **-vest'ment** *n.* robe or official garment. **-vest'ry** *n.* room attached to a church for keeping vestments, holding meetings, *etc.* **-vest'ure** *n.* clothing, a covering. [L. *vestis*, garment]

vest'ige *n.* trace or mark. [L. *vestigium*, footprint]

vet'eran *n.* person who has served a long time, *esp.* a soldier with much service. [L. *veteranus*]

veterinary *a.* of, or for, the diseases of domestic animals. **-vetinar'ian** *n.* one skilled in the medical treatment of animals. *n.* [L. *veterinarius*]

ve'to *n.* power of rejecting a piece of legislation, or preventing it from coming into effect; any prohibition. *-v. t.* enforce a veto against; forbid with authority. [L. = I forbid]

vex *v.t.* annoy or distress. **-vexa'tion** *n.* vexatious *a.* **-vexed** *a.* annoyed; much discussed. [L. *vexare*, shake]

vi'able *a.* born alive, capable of living and growing; practicable. [L. *vita*, life]

vi'aduct *n.* bridge over a valley for road or rail. [L. *via*, way]

vi'al, phi'al *n.* small glass bottle for holding liquids. [G. *phiale*, flat vessel]

vi'brate *v.i.* move to and fro rapidly and continuously, oscillate, quiver. *-v.t.* cause to do this. **-vibra'tion** *n.* **-vibra'tor** *n.* **vibra'tory** *a.* **-vi'brant** *a.* [L. *vibrare*, shake]

vic'ar *n.* clergyman; deputy. [L. *vicarius*, substitute]

vice *n.* fault or blemish; evil or immoral habit or practice. **-vi'cious** *a.* **-vi'ciously** *adv.* [L. *vitium*]

vice - *prefix.* **-vicere'gent** *n.* holder of delegated authority. **-vice'roy** *n.* ruler acting for a king in a province or dependency.

-vicere'gal *a.* -vice'reine *n. fem.* viceroy's wife. -viceroy'alty *n.* [L. = in place of]

vice ver'sa *adv.* other way round. [L.]

vicinity *n.* neighborhood. [L. *vicinitas vicinus,* neighborhood]

victim *n.* person or animal killed as a sacrifice; one injured by accident or so that an object may be gained by another. - vic'timize *v.t.* make a victim of- victimiza'tion *n.* [L. *victima*]

vic'tor *n.* conqueror or winner. -vic'tory *n.* winning of a battle, *etc.* -victor'ious *a.* -victor'iously *adv.* [L.]

victual *n.* (*usu.* in *pl.*) food. -*v. t.* supply with food. *v.i.* obtain supplies [L. *victualia,* fr. *vivere, vict-,* live]

vid'eo *a.* relating to vision or the transmission or production of television image. -*n.* apparatus for recording television programs and viewing pre-recorded video tapes. -vid'eophone *n.* telephonic device in which there is both verbal and visual communication between parties. vid'eo tape *n.* magnetic tape on which to record images for use in the video machine. [L. *videre,* to see]

vie *v.i.* contend, enter into competition. [OF. *envier,* challenge]

view *n.* survey by eyes or mind; picture; scene; opinion; purpose, -*v. t.* took at, examine, survey. -viewless *a.* invisible- [F. *vue*]

vig'il (-j-) *n.* a keeping awake, a watch; eve of a feast day. -vig'ilant *a.* vig'ilance *n.* [L. *vigilia,* watchfulness]

vig'or (-ger) *n.* force, strength, activity. vig'orous *a.* -vig'orously *adv.* [L. *vigor-vigere,* be strong]

vile *a.* base, mean, bad. -vil'ify *v.t.* speak ill of. -vilifica'tion *n.* [L. *vilis*]

vill'a *n.* country or suburban house. (L. *manor*]

vill'age *n.* assemblage of dwellings in the country. -vill'ager *n.* dweller in a village. [L. *villa,* manor]

vill'ain (-in) *n.* feudal serf (also vill'ein); scoundrel. -vill'ainous *a.* -vill'ainy *n.* [Low L. *villanus*]

vim *n.* (*sl.*) vigor, force, energy. [L. *vis.* strength]

vinaigrette' *n.* savory sauce, *esp.* for salads; small bottle of smelling salts. [F.]

vin'dicate *v. t.* establish the truth or merit of, clear of charges. -vindica'tion *n.* - vin'dicator *n.* -vin'dicatory *a.* vindic'tive *a.* revengeful; inspired by resentment. [L. *vindicate,* avenge]

vine *n.* climbing plant which bears grapes: -vine'yard *n.* vine farm, or plantation of vines. -vi'nery *n.* greenhouse for grapes. -vi'nous *a.* of, or due, to wine. -vin'tage *n.* gathering of the grapes; the yield; wine of a particular year. -vint'ner *n.* dealer in wine. [L. *vinum,* wine]

vine'gar *n.* an acid liquid got from wine and other alcoholic liquors. [F. *vinaigre,* fr. *aigre,* sour]

vi'ol *n.* medieval instrument like a violin. -violin' *n.* fiddle. -vi'ola *n.* tenor fiddle. -violoncell'o (-chel'-) *n.* large bass violin. -violin'ist *n.* -violoncell'ist *n.* [F. *viole*; It. *viola*]

vi'ola *n.* single-colored variety of pansy. [L. = *violet*]

vi'olate *v.t.* outrage, desecrate; infringe. - viola'tion *n.* -vi'olator *n.* [L. *violare, violate-*]

vi'olent *a.* of great force; marked by, or due to, extreme force of passion or fierceness. -vi'olence *n.* -vi'olently *adv.* [F.]

vi'olet *n.* plant with a small bluish purple flower; the flower; color of it. -*a* of this color. [L. *viola*]

vi'per *n.* venomous snake. [L. *vipera*]

vir'gin *n.* girl or woman who has not had sexual intercourse with a man. -*a.* chaste unsullied; fresh, untilled (of land). vir'ginal *a.* -*n.* kind of harpsichord. virgin'ity *n.* [L. *virgo, virgin-*]

Vir'go *n.* the Virgin, 6th sign of the zodiac, which sun enters about 22nd August. [L.]

vir'ile *a.* manly; strong; procreative. vir'ility *n.* (L. *virilis,* fr. vir, man]

virtu' *n.* artistic excellence, objects of art or antiquity collectively. [It. *virtu,* virtue]

vir'tue *n.* moral goodness; good quality; inherent power. -vir'tual *a.* so in effect though not in name. -vir'tually *adv.* vir'tuous *a.* morally good; chaste. vir'tuously *adv.* -virtuo'so *n.* one with special skill in a fine art. -virtuos'ity *n.* such a skill. [L. *virtus*]

vi'rus *n.* poison; disease, infection. vir'ulent *a.* poisonous; bitter, malignant. virulently *adv.* -vir'ulence *n.* [L.]

vi'sa *n.* endorsement on passport to show that it has been examined, [F.]

vis'age (-z-) *n.* face; expression. [F.]

vise *n.* appliance with a screwjaw for holding things while working on them. (F. *vis.,* screw]

vis'cera *n. pl.* internal organs; entrails. - vis'ceral *a.* [L.]

viscid *a.* sticky, of a consistency like treacle. -vis'cose *n.* form of cellulose used in making rayon. -vis'cous *a.* viscid. - viscid'ity *n.* -viscos'ity *n.* [L. *viscum,* birdlime]

vis'ion *n.* sight. **-vis'ionary** *a.* unpractical, dreamy. *-n.* one full of fancies. **-vis'ible** *a.* that can be seen. **visibil'ity** *n.* **-vis'ibly** *adv.* **-vis'ual** *a.* of sight. **-vis'ual dis'play u'nit** (*abbrev.* **VDU**) *n.* screen attached to a computer on which the information is displayed. **vis'ualize** *v.t.* make visible; form a mental image of. **-visualization** *n.* [L. *videre, vis-,* see]

vis'it *v. t.* go, or come, and see. *-n.* a visiting. **-vis'itor** *n.* **-vis'itant** *n.* visitor. **-visita'tion** *n.* formal visit or inspection; affliction or plague. [vision]

vi'sor *n.* movable front part of a helmet covering the face. [F. *visière,* fr. *vis,* face]

vista *n.* view, *esp.* between trees. [It., fr. *videre,* see]

vi'tal *a.* necessary to, or affecting life. **vi'tally** *adv.* **-vital'ity** *n.* life, vigor. **vi'talize** *v.t.* give life to. [L. *vita,* life]

vitamin *n.* factor in certain foodstuffs regarded as essential to life and health. [L. *vita,* life]

vit'treous *a.* of glass; glassy. **-vit'rify** *v.t.* and *i.* [L. *vitrum,* glass]

vit'riol *n.* sulfuric acid; caustic speech. **vitriol'ic** *a.* [Low L. *vitreous*]

vituperate *v.t.* abuse in words, revile. *-v.i.* use abusive language. **vitupera'tion** *n.* **vitu'perative** *a.* [L. *vituperate,* vituperate, fr. *vitium,* fault]

vivacious *a.* lively, animated, gay. **viva'city** *n.* [L. *vivax, vivac-,* fr. *vivere,* live]

vivid *a.* bright, intense; clear, lively, graphic. **-viv'idly** *adv.* **-viv'ify** *v. t.* animate, inspire. [L. *vividus*]

viviparous *a.* bringing forth young alive. [L. *vivus,* alive, *parere,* bring forth]

vivisection *n.* dissection or experiment on living bodies of animals, *etc.* **viv'isector** *n.* [L. *virus,* alive, *secare,* cut]

vix'en *n.* female fox; spiteful woman. **vix'enish** *a.* [OE. *fem.* of fox]

vocable *n.* word. **-vocab'ulary** *n.* list of words; stock of words used. [L. *vocabulum,* fr. *vocare,* call]

vo'cal *a.* of, with, or giving out, voice. **vo'calist** *n.* singer. **-vo'cally** *adv.* **vo'calize** *v.t.* utter with the voice. **-voca'tion** *n.* calling. [L. *vox,* voice]

vocif'erate *v.t.* and *i.* shout. **-vocif'erous** *a.* shouting, noisy. **-vocifera'tion** *n.* [L. *vox,* voice]

vod'ka *n.* Russian spirit distilled from rye. [Russ. dim. of *voda,* water]

vogue *n.* fashion. [F.]

voice *n.* sound given out by a person in speaking or singing, *etc.*; quality of the sound; expressed opinion; share in a discussion; verbal forms proper to relation of subject and action. *-v. t.* give utterance to. **-voice'less** *a.* (F. *voix,* fr. L. *vox, voc-*]

void *a.* empty. *-n.* empty space. *-v.t.* empty out. [OF. *voit*]

voile *n.* thin cotton fabric. [F.]

vol'atile *a.* evaporating quickly; lively. **volatil'ity** *n.* **-volat'ilize** *v.t.* and *i.* [L. *volatilis,* flying]

volca'no *n.* mountain with a hole through which lava, ashes, smoke, *etc.,* are discharged. **-volcan'ic** *a.* [L. *Vulcanus,* Vulcan (whose forge was supposed to be below Etna)]

voll'ey *n.* simultaneous discharge of weapons or missiles; rush of oaths, questions, *etc.* in sport, kick, stroke at moving ball before it hits the ground. *-v.t.* discharge in a volley. *-v.i.* fly in a volley. **-voll'eyball** *n.* team game where a large ball is hit by hand over a high net. [F. *volée,* flight, orig. at tennis]

volt'age *n.* electromotive force measured in volts. **-volt** *n.* unit of electromotive power. [A. Volta, 1745-1827]

voluble *a.* with incessant or abundant speech. **-volubil'ity** *n.* **-vol'ubly** *adv.* [L. *volvere, volut-,* roll]

vol'ume *n.* book, or part of a book, bound; mass; bulk, space occupied. **-volu'minous** *a.* bulky, over ample. [L. *volumen*]

voluntary *a.* having, or done by, free will. *-n.* organ solo in a church service. **vol'untarily** *adv.* **-volunteer'** *n.* one who offers service, joins a force, *etc.,* of his own free will. *-v.i.* offer oneself. [L. *voluntas,* wish, will]

voluptuous *a.* of or contributing to the pleasures of the senses. **-volup'tuary** *n.* one given to luxury and sensual pleasures. [L. *voluptas,* pleasure]

vom'it *v.t.* eject from the stomach through the mouth. *-v.t.* be sick. *-n.* matter vomited. [L. *vomere,* vomit-]

voracious *a.* greedy, ravenous. **-vora'city** *n.* **voraciously** *adv.* [L. *vorax, vorac-*]

vor'tex *n.* **vortices** *pl.* whirlpool; whirling motion. [L.]

vote *n.* formal expression of a choice; individual pronouncement, or right to give it, in a question or election; result of voting; that which is given or allowed by vote. *v.i.* give a vote. *-v. t.* grant or enact by vote. **-vo'ter** *n.* [L. *votum, vow*]

vouch *v.i.* vouch for, make oneself responsible for. *-v. t.* guarantee. **-vouch'er** *n.* document proving the correctness of an item in accounts. **-vouchsafe'** *v.i.* condescend to grant or do something. [OF. *vochier*]

vow *n.* solemn promise, *esp.* a religious one. -*v.t.* promise or threaten by vow, [F. *væu*, fr. L. *vovere*, *vot*-]

vow'el *n.* vocal sound pronounced without stoppage or friction of the breath; letter standing for such sound. [F. *voyelle*, fr. L. *vocalis* (*littera*), vocal (letter)]

voy'age *n.* journey, *esp.* a long one, by water. -*v.i.* make a voyage. [F]

vulcanize *v.t.* treat (rubber) with sulfur at a high temperature. -**vul'canite** *n.* rubber so hardened. -**vulcanization** *n.* [Vulcan; See **volcano**]

vul'gar *a.* of the common people; common; coarse, not refined; offending against good taste. -**vulga'rian** *n.* vulgar fellow, *esp.* a rich one. -**vul'garly** *adv.* **vul'garism** *n.* word or construction used only by the uneducated. -**vutgar'ity** *n.* **vul'garize** *v.t.* make vulgar or too common. -**vulgariza'tion** *n.* -**vul'gar fractions** common fraction, as distinct from decimals. -**vul'gar tongue'**, vernacular. [L. *vulgaris*, fr. *vulgus*, common people]

Vul'gate *n.* 4th cent. Latin version of the Bible made by St. Jerome [L. *vulgatus*]

vulnerable *a.* not proof against wounds; offering an opening to criticism, *etc.* [L. *vulnerare*, wound]

vul'pine *a.* of foxes; foxy; crafty, cunning. [L. *vulpinus*, of the fox, *vulpes*]

vul'ture *n.* large bird which feeds on carrion. [L. *vultur*]

W

wad (wod) *n.* small pad of fibrous material, used *esp.* to pack charge in a gun; money, notes. -*v. t.* line, pad, stuff, *etc.*, with a wad. -**wadd'ing** *n.* stuffing. [orig. unknown]

wad'dle *v.i.* walk like a duck. [wade]

wade *v.i.* walk through something that hampers movement, *esp.* water. -**wa'der** *n.* person or bird that wades; high waterproof boot. [OE. *wadan*]

wad'i *n.* dry bed of a stream. [Arab.]

wafer *n.* thin cake or biscuit; the Host; disk of paste for fastening papers. -*v. t.* fasten with a wafer. -**waf'fle** *n.* kind of pancake. -**waffle-iron** *n.* [Du. *wafel*]

waft *v.t.* convey smoothly through air or water. -*n.* breath of wind, odor, etc, [orig. uncertain]

wag *v.t.* cause to move to and fro. -*v.i.* shake, swing. -*n.* merry fellow (orig. waghalter, rascal). -**wagg'ery** *n.* -**wagg'ish** *a.* -**wag'tail** *n.* small bird with a wagging

tail. [OE. *wagian*]

wage *n.* payment for work done (usu. in *pl.*). -*v. t.* carry on. -**wa'ger** *n.* and *v.t.* and *i.* bet. [ONF. *wage*, for *gage*, pledge]

wag'on *n.* four-wheeled vehicle for heavy loads. -**wag'oner** *n.* -**wagonette'** *n.* four-wheeled horse carriage with lengthwise seats. [Du. *wagen*, carriage]

waif *n.* homeless person, *esp.* a child. **waifs and strays**, the homeless destitute; odds and ends. [ONF.]

wail *n.*, *v.t.* and *i.* lament. [ON. *væla*]

wains'cot *n.* wooden lining of the walls of a room, *esp.* oak. -*v.t.* line thus. [LG. *wagenschot*]

waist *n.* part of the body between hips and ribs; various central parts. **waistcoat** *n.* sleeveless garment worn under a coat. [ME. *waste*, growth, fr. *wax*, grow]

wait *v.t.* await. -*v.i.* be expecting, attend; serve at table. -*n.* act of waiting; carol singer. -**wait'er** *n.* attendant on guests in restaurant, hotel, *etc.* -**wait'ress** *fem.* [ONF. *waitier*, lurk, lie in ambush]

waive *v.t.* forgo; renounce (a right, claim). (ONF. *waiver*, renounce)

wake *v.i.* rouse from sleep. -*v.t.* rouse from sleep; stir up. -*n.* watch by a dead person; holiday. -**wa'ken** *v.t.* wake. **wake'ful** *a.* [OE. *waccian*]

wake *n.* track left by a ship, airplane, *etc.*, track. (Du. *wak*)

walk (wawk) *v. i.* move on the feet at an ordinary pace; cross by walking. -*v. t.* cause to walk. -*n.* slowest gait of animals; occupation or career; path, *etc.* for walking; spell of walking for pleasure, *etc.* -**walk'er** *n.* -**walk'way** *n.* pedestrian passage, *usu.* suspended *e.g.* between buildings. [OE. *wealean*, roll]

Walkman *n.* small portable cassette recorder with light headphones. [Trademark]

wall (wawl) *n.* structure of brick, stone, *etc.*, serving as a fence, side of a building, *etc.*; surface of one. -*v.t.* supply with a wall; block up with a wall. -**wall'flower** *n.* sweet smelling garden flower, often growing on walls. [L. *vallum*]

wall'et (wol-) *n.* small bag; pocketbook for paper-money, *etc.* [var. of *wattle*]

wall'op *v.t.* beat, flog. -*n.* beating, blow; (*sl.*) draught beer. [ONF. *waloper*]

wall'ow *v.i.* roll in mire, water, *etc.* -*n.* act of wallowing. [OE. *wealwian*]

wal'nut (wawl-) *n.* large nut with a crinkled shell splitting easily into two halves; the tree. [OE. *wealh*, foreign]

wal'rus (wol-) *n.* large seal-like sea

animal with long tusks. [Dan. *hvalros*]

waltz (wawlts) *n.* dance. *-v. i.* dance it. [Ger. *walzer-watzen,* roll]

wam'pum *n.* strings of shells, beads, used by N. American Indians as money. [N. Amer. Ind.]

wan (won) a. pale, sickly-complexioned, faint-looking. [OE. *wann,* lurid]

wand'er (won-) *v.i.* roam; ramble; deviate from one's path; be delirious. [OE. *wandrian*]

wanderlust *n.* travel urge. [Ger.]

wane *v.i.* and *n.* decline. [OE. *wanian*]

wang'le *v.t.* manipulate, manage in a skillful way. [orig. uncertain]

want (wont) *n., v.t.* and *i.* lack. [ON. *vant]*

want'on (won-) *a.* unrestrained; playful; dissolute; without motive. *-v.i.* frolic. *-n.* wanton person. [ME. *wanto-wen*]

war *n.* fighting between nations; state of hostility. *-v.i.* make war. **-war'fare** *n.* hostilities. **-war'like** *a.* **-war'monger** *n.* spreader of war propaganda. **war'paint** *n.* paint, adornments assumed by N. American Indians before battle. **war'ship** *n.* naval vessel of any type used in warfare. **-warr'ior** *n.* fighter. [ONF. *werre,* F. *guerre*]

war'ble (wor-) *v.i.* sing with trills. **warb'ler** *n.* [ONF. *werbler*]

ward (wawrd) *n.* guardianship; minor under care of a guardian; division of a city, or hospital, *etc. -pl.* indentations of the bead of a key or lock. *-v.t.* guard. **ward'er** *n.* prison keeper. **-ward'ress** *fem.* **ward'ship** *n.* **-ward'robe** *n.* piece of furniture for hanging clothes in. **ward'room** *n.* officers' mess on a warship. **-ward'en** *n.* president or governor. **-ward'enship** *n.* [OE. weard, ONF. *warder,* F. *garder*]

ware *n.* goods; articles collectively. **ware'house** *n.* store-house; large commercial establishment. [OE. *waru*]

ware *a.* on guard. *-v. t.* beware; keep clear of. **-wa'riness** *n.* suspicious care, caution. [OE. *woer*]

war'lock *n.* wizard, sorcerer. [OE. *waer,* truth, compact, *leogan,* to lie]

warm *a.* moderately hot; ardent. *-v.t.* and *i.* heat. **-warm'ly** *adv.* **warm'th** *n.* [OE. *wearm*]

warn *v.t.* caution, put on guard. **-warn'ing** *n.* [OE. warnian]

warp *n.* lengthwise threads in a loom; rope. *-v.t.* twist; move by a rope fastened to a buoy. *-v.i.* become twisted. [OE. *weorpan,* throw]

warr'ant *n.* authority; document giving authority. *-v.t.* authorize; guarantee.

warr'anty *n.* justification, guarantee. [ONF. *warant,* F. *garant*]

warr'en *n.* ground occupied by rabbits. [ONF. *warenne,* F. *garenne*]

wart (wort) *n.* hard growth on the skin. **-wart'y** *a.* [OE. *wearte*]

war'y *a.* cautious; watchful; on the defensive. **-war'ily** *adv.* [fr. *ware*]

wash (wosh) *v.t.* clean with liquid; carry along with a rush of water; color lightly. *v.i.* wash oneself-, stand washing. *-n.* an act of washing; clothes washed at one time; sweep of water, *esp.* set up by moving ship; thin coat of color. **-wash'er** *n.* one who or that which washes; ring put under a nut. **-wash'y** *a.* diluted. **wash'out** *n. (sl.)* failure, ineffectual effort. **-wash-stand** *n.* stand holding basin and waterjug. [OE. *wascan*]

wasp *n.* striped stinging insect resembling a bee. **-wasp'ish** *a.* irritable; spiteful. [OE. *wæsp, wæps*]

waste *v. t.* expend uselessly, use extravagantly; lay desolate. *-v. i.* dwindle; pine away. *-a.* wasted; desert. *-n.* what is wasted; act of wasting; desert. **-wast'age** *n.* **-waste'ful** *a.* **-waste'fully** *adv.* **wast'er** *n.* **-waste'ful** *a.* **-waste'fully** *adv.* **-wast'er** *n.* **-wast'rel** *n.* useless person, profligate. [ONF. *waster,* F. *gâter,* fr. L. *vastare,* destroy]

watch (woch) *n.* state of being on the lookout; spell of duty; pocket clock. *-v. t.* observe closely; guard. *-v. i.* be on watch, be wakeful. **-watch'ful** *a.* **-watch'fully** *adv.* **-watch'man** *n.* **-watch'keeper** *n.* officer of the watch. **-watch'maker** *n.* **watch'word** *n.* rallying-cry. [OE. *wæcce*]

wat'er *n.* transparent tasteless liquid, the substance of rain, rivers, *etc.,* transparency of a gem. *-v. t.* put water on or into; cause to drink. *-v.i.* take in or obtain water. **wat'erfall** *n.* fall of water (river, stream) over a perpendicular drop. **-wat'er-logged** *a.* soaked, filled with water so as to be unseaworthy. **-wat'ermark** *n.* mark made in paper during manufacture and visible on holding the paper to the light. **wat'erproof** *a.* not letting water through. *-n.* waterproof garment. **-watertight** *a.* [OE. *wæter*]

watt (wot) *n.* unit of electric power. [J. Watt, engineer (d. 1819)]

wave *v.i.* move to and fro; beckon; have an undulating shape. *-v. t.* move to and fro; give the shape of waves; express by waves. *-n.* act or gesture of waving; ridge and trough on water, *etc.;* vibration. **wa'vy** *a.* **-wa'vily** *adv.* [OE. *wafian,* brandish]

wa'ver *v.i.* hesitate, be irresolute. **wa'verer** *n.* [fr. *wave*]

wax *n.* yellow plastic material made by bees; this or similar substance used for sealing, making candles, *etc.* -*v.t.* put wax on. -**wax′works** *n. pl.* display of figures modelled in wax. [OE. *weax*, beeswax]

way *n.* track; direction; method. **way′farer** *n.* traveler, *esp.* on foot. **waylay′** *v.t.* lie in wait for. -**way′ward** *a.* capricious, perverse. -**way′wardly** *adv.* -**way′wardness** *n.* [OE. *weg*]

we *pron.* first person plural, pronoun. I and others. [OE.]

weak *a.* lacking strength. -**weak′ly** *a.* weak; sickly. -**weak′ly** *adv.* -**weak′en** *v.t.* and *i.* -**weak′ling** *n.* feeble creature. -**weak′ness** *n.* [ON. *vickr*]

weal *n.* well-being. [OE. *wela*]

weald *n.* open or wooded country; the Weald, formerly wooded, between the N. and S. Downs, England. [OE. *weald*]

wealth (welth) *n.* riches; abundance. -**wealth′y** *a.* [OE. *weld*]

wean *v.t.* accustom to food other than mother's milk. -**wean′ling** *n.* newly weaned child. [OE. *wenian*, accustom]

weap′on (wep′n) *n.* implement to fight with. [OE. *woepen*]

wear *v.t.* carry on the body; show consume. -*v.i.* last; become impaired by use. -*n.* act of wearing; impairment; things to wear. -**wear′er** *n.* -**wear′ing** *a.* exhausting. [OE. *woerian*]

wear′y *a.* tired. -*v.t.* and *i.* tire. **wear′ily** *adv.* -**wear′iness** *n.* -**wear′isome** *a.* [OE. *werig*]

weas′el (-z-) *n.* small animal related to the ferret, *etc.* [OE. *wesle*]

weath′er (weTH-) *n.* atmospheric conditions. -*a.* towards the wind. -*v.t.* affect by weather; sail to windward of, come safely through. -**weath′ercock** *n.* revolving vane to show which way the wind blows. [OE. *weder*]

weave *v.t.* form in texture or fabric by interlacing. -*v.i.* make by crossing. threads, *etc.*, thread one's way (among). *n.* texture. -**weav′er** *n.* [OE. *wefan*]

web *n.* woven fabric; net spun by a spider; membrane between the toes of waterfowl. [OE. *webb*]

wed *v.t.* marry; to unite closely. -**wedd′ing** *n.* marriage. -**wed′lock** *n.* marriage. [OE. *weddian*]

wedge *n.* piece of material sloping to an edge. -*v.t.* fasten or split with a wedge; stick by compression or crowding. [OE. *wecg*]

Wed′nesday *n.* fourth day of the week. [OE. *wodnesdoeg*, day of Woden, or Odin]

wee *a.* small, little, tiny. [ME. *we*, bit]

weed *n.* plant growing where it is not desired. -*v.t.* and *i.* pull out weeds. -**weed′y** *a.* [OE. *weod*, herb]

weeds *n. pl.* widow's mourning garments. [OE. *woed*, garment]

week *n.* period of seven days. -**week′ly** *a.* happening, done, *etc.*, once a week. -**week′ly** *adv.* once a week, (OE. *wicu*]

ween *v.i.* think, imagine. [OE. *wenan*]

weep *v.i.* shed tears. -*v.t.* lament. -**weep′ing-** **will′ow,** willow with drooping boughs. (OE. *wepan*]

wee′vil *n.* beetle harmful to grain, *etc.* [OE. *wifel*, beetle]

weigh *v.t.* find the weight of, raise, as in weigh anchor. -*v.i.* have weight. **weight** *n.* force exerted by the earth on a body; heavy mass; object of known mass for weighing; importance. -*v.t.* add a weight to. -**weight′y** *a.* -**weight′ily** *adv.* [OE. *wegan*, carry]

weird *a.* unearthly. [OE. *wyrd*, fate]

wel′come *a.* received gladly. -*n.* kindly greeting. -*v.t.* receive gladly or hospitably. [*well* and *come*]

weld *v.t.* unite (hot metal) by hammering or compressing; unite closely. -*n.* welded joint. [var. of *well*]

wel′fare *n.* well-being; prosperity. [*well* and *fare*]

well *adv.* in good manner or degree. -*a.* in good health; suitable. -**well-being** *n.* health and contentment; prosperity. **well-bred** *a.* polite, mannerly; (of horse) coming from good stock. [OE. *wel*]

well *n.* deep hole for water; spring. -*v. i.* flow out or up. [OE. *wiella*]

Welsh *a.* of Wales. -*n.* language, or people, of Wales. [OE. *wcelisc*, foreign]

welsh, welch *v.t.* and *i.* (of bookmaker) abscond without paying debts. -**welsh′er** *n.* [uncertain]

welt *n.* seam; leather rim put on a boot-upper for the sole to be attached to; wale. -*v.t.* provide a shoe with a welt; thrash. [orig. uncertain]

went *v.i. p.t.* of go. [*wend*]

wer′wolf, were′wolf *n.* human being able to turn into a wolf. [OE. *werwulf*, man-wolf]

Wes′leyan *a.* of Wesley or the Church founded by him. -*n.* member of that church. [J. Wesley (d. 1791)]

west *n.* part of the sky where the sun sets; part of a country, *etc.*, lying to this side. *a.* that is toward this region. *adv.* to the west. -**west′erly** *a.* -**west′ward** *a.* and *adv.* -**west′wards** *adv.* -**west′ern** *a.* [OE.]

wet *a.* having water or other liquid on a surface or being soaked in it; rainy. -*v.t.*

make wet. -*n.* moisture, rain. -**wet' blankets** damping influence. -**wet nurse,** nurse who suckles a child not her own. [OE. *woot*]

whack *v.t.* hit, *esp.* with a stick. -*n.* such a blow. [imit.]

whale *n.* large fish-shaped sea animal. -**whale'bone** *n.* springy substance from the upper jaw of certain whales. -**wha'ler** *n.* man or ship employed in hunting whales. [OF. *hwœl*]

wharf (hworf) *n.* quay for loading and unloading ships. [OE. *hwerf*, shore]

what (hwot) *pron.* which thing? that which. -*a.* which. -**whatev'er** *pron.* anything which; of what kind it may be. **whatsoev'er** *a.* [OE. *hwcet*]

wheat *n.* cereal plant with thick four-sided seed-spikes, of which bread is chiefly made. -**wheat'en** *a.* [OE. *hwœte*]

wheel *n.* circular frame or disk with spokes revolving on an axle. -*v.t.* convey by wheeled apparatus or vehicles; cause to turn or change direction. -*v.i.* revolve; change direction. -**wheel'-barrow** *n.* barrow with one wheel. -**wheel'wright** *n.* maker or repairer of wheels. [OE. *kweol*]

wheeze *v.i.* to breathe with difficulty and noise. -*n.* (*sl.*) joke; trick. -**wheez'y** *a.* [ON. *hvœsa*, hiss]

whelp *n.* pup or cub. -*v.i.* and *t.* produce whelps. [OE. *hwelp*]

when *adv.* at what time. -*conj.* at the time. -**whenev'er** *adv.* and *conj.* at whatever time. [OE. *hwœnne*]

where *adv.* and *conj.* at what place. **whereas'** *conj.* considering that, while, on the contrary. -**where'fore** *adv.* why. *conj.* consequently. -**wherev'er** *adv.* at whatever place. -**where'withal** *n.* means; resources. [OE. *hwar*]

whet *v.t.* sharpen. -**whet'stone** *n.* stone for sharpening tools. [OE. *hwettan*]

wheth'er (-TH-) *a.* and *pron.* which of the two. -*conj.* introduces first of two alternatives, of which second may be expressed or implied. [OE. *hwœther*]

which *a.* asks for a selection from alternatives. -*pron.* which person or thing; thing 'who.' [OE. *kwilc*]

while *n.* space of time. -*conj.* in the time that. -*v.t.* pass (*time*, usually idly). **whilst** *adv.* [OE. *hwil*]

whim *n.* caprice, fancy. -**whim'sical** *a.* delicately fanciful. -**whimsical'ity** *n.* [orig. uncertain]

whim'per *v.i.* cry or whine softly. **whim'pering** *v.i.* cry or whine softly. **whim'pering** *a.* such cry. [imit.]

whine *n.* long-drawn wail. *v.i.* make one. [OE. *hwinan*]

whip *v.t.* apply a whip to; thrash; lash. *v.i.* dart. -*n.* lash attached to a stick for urging or punishing. -**whip'cord** *n.* thin hard cord. -**whip-hand** *n.* superiority, advantage. -**whipp'er-snapper** *n.* small child; insignificant person. [orig. uncertain]

whirl *v.t.* and *i.* swing rapidly round. -*n.* whirling movement. -**whirl'igig** *n.* spinning toy. -**whirl'pool** *n.* circular current. -**whirl'wind** *n.* wind whirling round a forward-moving axis. [ON. *hvirfill*, ring]

whisk *v.t.* and *i.* brandish, sweep, or beat lightly. -*n.* light brush; flapper; egg-beating implement. -**whisk'er** *n.* hair of a man's face. [of Teut. orig.]

whiskey *n.* spirit distilled from various grains. [for *usquebaugh*, Ir. *uisge beatha*, water of life]

whisp'er *v.t.* and *i.* speak with rustling breath instead of voice. -*n.* such speech. [OE. *hwisprian*]

whist *n.* card game. [var. of *whisk*]

whis'tle (-sl) *n.* sound made by forcing the breath through rounded and nearly closed lips; any similar sound; instrument to make it. -*v.i.* make such sound. -*v.t.* utter or summon, *etc.*, by whistle. **whis'tler** *n.* [OE. hwistle]

white *a.* of the color of snow; pale; light in color. -*n.* color of snow; white pigment; white part. -**white-ant** *n.* termite. **white'bait** *n.* small edible fish. -**white drugs** *n. pl.* harmful narcotics; dope. **white elephant** *n.* useless or incongruous gift. -**White House** *n.* executive department of the U.S. government; official residence of the president of the U.S. in Washington D.C. -**whi'ten** *v.t.* and *i.* -**white'ness** *n.* **white-paper** *n.* government report on any recent investigation. [OE. *hwit*]

whith'er (-TH-) *adv.* to what place. **whithersoev'er** *adv.* [OE. *hwider*]

whit'tle *v.t.* cut or carve with a knife; pare away. [OE. *thwitan*, cut]

who *pron.* (*obj.* whom) relative and interrogative pronoun, always referring to persons. -**whoev'er** *pron.* any one or everyone that. [OE. *hwa*]

whole (h-) *a.* complete; healthy; all. -*n.* complete thing or system. -**who'lly** *adv.* **whole'sale** *n.* sale of goods by large quantities. -*a.* dealing by wholesale; extensive. -**whole'saler** *n.* -**whole'some** *a.* producing a good effect, physically or morally. [OE. *hal*, hale, uninjured]

whoop *v.t.* and *i.* and *n.* about. -**whoop'ing-cough** *n.* disease marked by a whooping breath. [F. *houper*]

whore (h-) *n.* prostitute. [ON. *hora*]

whose *pron.* possess. of who, which. [OE. *hwces-hwa*, who]

why *adv.* and *conj.* for what cause; wherefore. *-interj.* of surprise, *etc.* *-n.* the reason or purpose of anything. [OE. *hwi*]

wick'ed *a.* evil, sinful. -wick'edly *adv.* - wick'edness *n.* [ME. *wikke*, feeble]

wide *a.* broad; far from the mark. **wi'den** *v.t.* and *i.* -wide'ly *adv.* -width *n.* -wide'- awake' *a.* alert. *-n.* kind of soft felt hat. [OE. *wid*]

wid'ow *n.* woman whose husband is dead and who has not married again. *v. t.* make a widow of -wid'ower *n.* man whose wife has died and who has not married again. -wid'owhood *n.* [OE. *wydewa*]

wife *n.* wives *pl.* woman married to a man. -wife'ly *a.* [OE. *wif*, woman]

wig *n.* artificial hair for the head. [for *periwig* -O Du. *peruyk*]

wild (wild) *a.* not tamed or domesticated; not cultivated (as wildflowers); savage; excited, rash. -wild'ly *adv.* -wild'ness *n.* -wil'derness *a.* desert. -wild fire *n.* burning liquid used formerly in sea-fights, Greek fire. -like wild'fire *adv.* very quickly. [OE. *wilde*]

wile *n.* trick. -wi'ly *a.* artful. [OE. *wil*]

will *v. aux.* forms moods and tenses indicating intention or conditional result. *v.i.* have a wish. *-v.t.* wish intend, purpose; leave as a legacy. *-n.* faculty of deciding what one will do; purpose, wish; directions written for disposal of property after death. -will'ing *a.* ready; given cheerfully. - will'ingly *adv.* -will'ingness *n.* -will'y- nill'y *adv.* willing or unwilling. [OE. *willan*]

will'ow *n.* tree such as the weeping willow with long thin flexible branches; its wood. -will'owy *a.* lithe and slender. **will'ow patterns** famous pattern on china *etc.*, illustrating a Chinese legend. [OE. *welig*]

wilt *v.i.* droop; fade; go limp. *-v.t.* make to wilt. [orig. uncertain]

win *v.t.* get by labor or effort; reach; allure; be successful in. *-v.i.* be successful. - winn'er *n.* [OE. *gewinaan*]

wind *n.* air in motion; breath. -(wind) *v.t.* sound by blowing. -wind'fall (-awl) *n.* fallen fruit; piece of good luck. - wind'jamm'er *n.* sailing ship. -wind'mill *n.* mill worked by sails. -wind'surfing *n.* sport of sailing standing up on a sailboard that is equipped with a mast, sail, and wishbone boom; boardsailing. -wind'y *a.* exposed to winds; (*sl.*) timid, fearful. -

wind'ward (-ord) *n.* side towards the wind. [OE.]

wind *v.i.* twine; vary from a direct course. *-v.t.* twist round, wrap; make ready for working by tightening a spring. -wind'lass *n.* machine which hauls or hoists by wrapping rope round an axle. [OE. *windan*]

win'dow *n.* hole in a wall (with or without glass), to admit light. [ON. *vindauge*, wind-eye]

wine *n.* fermented juice of the grape, or other fruit. [OE. *win*, fr. L. *vinum*]

wing *n.* limb a bird uses in flying; flight; lateral extension; plane. *v.t.* cross by flight; supply with wings; disable. *-v.i.* fly. [ON. *voengr*, wing]

win'ter *n.* fourth season. *-v. i.* pass the winter. *-v. t.* tend during winter. -win'try *a.* -win'ter-green *n.* evergreen plant; flavoring obtained from oil extracted from the plant. -win'ter quarters *n. pl.* quarters for troops during winter. [OE.]

wipe *v.t.* rub so as to clean. *-n.* a wiping. [OE. *wipian*]

wire *n.* metal drawn into the form of cord; (*coll.*) telegram. *-v. t.* provide, catch, fasten with, wire; send by telegraph. **wi'ry** *a.* like wire, tough. -wire'tap *v.t.* and *i.* make a connection to a telegraph or telephone wire in order to obtain information secretly. [OE. *wir*]

wise *a.* sagacious; having intelligence and knowledge. -wis'dom *n.* -wise'ly *adv.* wis'dom-tooth', large back-tooth cut in one's later 'teens. [OE. *wis*]

wish *v.i.* have a desire. *-v. t.* desire. *-n.* desire or thing desired. -wish'ful *a.* **wish'ful think'ing,** beliefs colored by one's wishes. [OE. *wyscan*]

wit *n.* sense; intellect; ingenuity in connecting amusingly incongrous ideas; person gifted with this power. -witt'y *a.* - witt'ily *adv.* -witt'icism *n.* witty remark. -witt'ingly *adv.* on purpose. [OE. *witt*, fr. *witan*, know]

witch *n.* woman said to be endowed with black-magical powers. [OE. *wicca*]

with *prep.* in company or possession of-, against; in relation to; through. -withal' *adv.* also, likewise. -withdraw' *v. t.* and *i.* draw back, retire. -withdraw'al *n.* - withhold' *v. t.* keep, hold back, restrain. -within' *prep.* and *adv.* in, inside. -without' *adv.* outside. *-prep.* lacking. -withstand *v.t.* oppose. [OE.]

withe, with'y *n.* tough, flexible twig, willow. [OE. *withthe*]

with'er *v.i.* fade. *-v.t.* cause to fade; blight. [var. of *weather*]

with'ers *n. pl.* ridge between a horse's shoulder-blades. [OE. *withre*, resistance]

wit'ness *n.* testimony; one who sees something; one who gives testimony. *-v.i.* give testimony. *-v.t.* see; attest; see and sign as having seen. [OE *witnes*, evidence]

wiz'ened *a.* shriveled, dried up, withered. [OE. *wisnian*, wither]

wobb'le *v.i.* shake, be unsteady. *-n.* swaying movement. [L. Ger. *wabbeln*]

woe *n.* grief. **-woe'begone** *a.* sorrowful. - **woe'ful** *a.* **-woe'fully** *adv.* [OE. wa]

wolf (woolf) *n.* wolves *pl.* wild beast allied to the dog. [OE. *wull*]

wom'an *n.* **wom'en** *pl.* adult human female; female sex.[OE. *wifmann*, *wife-man*, female]

womb *n.* female organ of conception and gestation, the uterus. [OE. *wamb*, belly]

won'der (wun-) *n.* marvel; emotion excited by an amazing or unusual thing. *v.i.* feel this emotion. **-won'derful** *a.* **won'derfully** *adv.* **-won'drous** *a.* **won'drously** *adv.* **-won'derment** *n.* [OE. *wundor*]

wont *n.* custom. **-wont'ed** *a.* habitual. [OE. *gewun*, usual]

woo *v.t.* court, seek to marry. **-woo'er** *n.* **-woo'ing** *n.* and *a.* [OE. *wogian*]

wood *n.* tract of land with growing trees; substance of trees, timber. **-wood'en** *a.* **wood'y** *a.*. **-wood'-cut** *n.* engraving on wood. **-wood'land** *n.* woods, forest. - **wood'pecker** *n.* bird which searches tree-trunks for insects. **-wood'winds** *n. pl.* clarinet, oboe, *etc.*, in an orchestra. [OE. *wudu*, forest]

woof *n.* threads that cross the warp in weaving, the weft. [OE. *owef*]

wool *n.* soft hair of the sheep and certain other animals. **-wool'en** *a.* **-wooll'y** *a.* [OE. *wull*]

word (wurd) *n.* single symbol used in speaking or writing, a unit of speech; information; promise. *-v.t.* express in words. **-word'y** *a.* **-word'ily** *adv.* [OE.]

work (wurk) *n.* labor; task; something made or accomplished. *-pl.* factory. *-v. i.* cause to operate; make, shape. *-v.i.* apply effort; labor; operate; ferment; be engaged in a trade, profession, *etc.* **-work'able** *a.* **-work'er** *n.* **-work'house** *n.* institution for paupers. **-work'man** *n.* manual worker. - **work'manship** *n.* skill of a workman; way a thing is finished, style. **-work'shop** *n.* place where things are made. **-work'top** *n.* a surface in a kitchen, often of heat resistant laminated plastic, that is used for food preparation. [OE. *woerc*]

world (wurld) *n.* universe; sphere of existence; mankind; society. **-world'ly** *a.* engrossed in temporal pursuits. [OE. *weorold*]

worm (wurm) *n.* small limbless creeping creature, shaped like a snake; thread of a screw. *-v. i.* crawl. *-v. t.* work (oneself) in insidiously; extract (a secret) craftily. **worm'eaten** *a.* eaten by worms; old, out-of-date. [OE. *wyrm*, serpent]

worr'y (wur'i) *v.t.* seize or shake with teeth; trouble, harass. *-v.i.* be unduly concerned. *-n.* useless care or anxiety. **worry'ing** *a.* [OE. *wyrgan*, strangle]

worse *a.* and *adv.* comparative of bad or badly. **-worst** *a.* and *adv.* superlative of bad or badly. **-wors'en** *v. t.* and *i.* [OE. *wiersa*]

wor'ship *n.* reverence, adoration. *-v.t.* adore; love and admire. [OE. *weorthscipe*, 'worth-ship']

wort *n.* plant, herb; infusion of malt before fermentation. [OE. *wyrt*]

worth (wurth) *a.* having value specified; meriting. *-n.* merit, value. **-wor'thy** (-TH-) *a.* **-wor'thily** *adv.* **-wor'thiness** *n.* - **worth'less** *a.* [OE. *weorth*]

wound *n.* injury, hurt by cut, stab, *etc. -v.t.* inflict a wound on; pain. **-wound'ing** *a.* [OE. *wund*]

wraith *n.* apparition of a person seen shortly before or after death. [ON. *vörthr*, guardian]

wrap *v.t.* cover, *esp.* by putting something round; put round. *-n.* loose garment; covering. **-wrapp'er** *n*; [earlier *wiap*, of uncertain orig.]

wrath *n.* anger. [OE. = *angry*]

wreak *v.t.* inflict (vengeance, *etc.*). [OE. *wrecan*, avenge]

wreck *n.* destruction of a ship by accident; wrecked ship; ruin; something ruined. *-v.t.* cause the wreck of. **-wreck'age** *n.* [OE. *wræc*, fr. *wrecan*, drive]

wren *n.* very small brown bird, allied to the goldcrest. [OE. *wrenna*]

wrench *n.* violent twist; tool for twisting or screwing. *-v.t.* twist; distort; seize forcibly. [OE. *wrenc*, trick]

wrest *v.t.* take by force; twist violently. *n.* tool for tuning a harp, *etc.* **-wres'tle** (-sl) *v.i.* contend by grappling and trying to throw down. **-wres'tler** *n.* [OE. *wræstan*]

wretch *n.* miserable creature. **-wretch'ed** *a.* miserable; worthless. **-wretch'edness** *n.* **-wretch'edly** *adv.* [OE. *wræcca*, outcast]

wright *n.* workman, maker, *e.g.* wheelwright. [OE. *wyrhta*, worker]

wring *v.t.* twist, squeeze, compress; extort; pain. [OE. *wringan*]

wrist *n.* joint between the hand and the arm. **-wrist′let** *n.* band worn on the wrist. **-wrist-watch′** *n.* watch worn on wrist. [OE]

write *v.i.* mark paper, *etc.*, with the symbols which are used to represent words or sounds; compose; send a letter. *v.t.* set down in words; compose; communicate in writing. **-writ** *n.* a formal or legal document. **-wri′ter** *n.* penman; author. [OE. *writan*]

writhe *v.i.* twist or roll body about, as in pain; to squirm (with shame, *etc.*) [OE. *writhan*]

wrong *a.* not right or good or suitable. *n.* that which is wrong; harm; evil. *-v.t.* do wrong to. **-wrong′ly** *adv.* **-wrong′ful** *a.* **-wrong′fully** *adv.* [OE. *wrang*, injustice]

wrung′ *p.p.* and *p.t.* of wring.

wry *a.* turned to one side, distorted. [OE. *wrigian*, twist]

wyandotte *n.* breed of domestic fowls. [name of Amer. Ind. tribe]

X

X-rays′ *n. pl.* invisible short-wave rays used in surgery to take photographs of the bones, etc., inside the human frame. [X = the unknown]

xanth′ic (zan-) *a.* yellowish. **-xanth′ism** *n.* a condition of skin, fur, or feathers in which yellow coloration predominates. [G. *xanthos*, yellow]

xantipp′e *n.* shrewish woman, scold. [wife of Socrates]

xen′on *n.* gaseous element of the atmosphere. [G. *zenos*, stranger]

xenopho′bia *n.* morbid fear of strangers. [G. *zenos*, stranger]

xy′lograph *n.* wood-engraving, impression from wood-block. **-xylog′raphy** *n.* wood-engraving. **- xylog′rapher** *n.* wood-engraver. **-xylograph′ic** *a.* pert. to xylography. [G. *xylon*, wood, *graphein*, write]

xy′lonite (zi) *n.* celluloid.

xylophone *n.* musical instrument of wooden bars which vibrate when struck. [G. *xylon*, wood]

xy′lorimba (zi) *n.* large xylophone with an extended range of five octaves. [fr. *xylophone* and *marimba*]

Y

yacht (yot) *n.* light vessel for racing or pleasure. *-v.i.* cruise or race in a yacht. **yachts′man** *n.* [Du. *jacht*]

yak *n.* long-haired Tibetan ox. [Tibetan]

yam *n.* tropical plant with large edible tuber, the sweet potato. [Senegalese *nyami*, eat]

Yank′ee *n.* inhabitant of U.S.A. *esp.* of New England, or of the Northern States. *-a.* belonging to U.S.A. [orig. uncertain]

yard *n.* unit of measure, 36 inches; that length of anything; spar slung across a ship's mast to extend sails. **-yard′arm** *n.* either half of a long slender beam or pole used to support a square sail. [OE. *gierd*, rod]

yard *n.* piece of enclosed ground around a building [OE. *geard*]

yarn *n.* spun thread of fiber prepared for weaving, knitting, *etc.*; tale. *-v. i.* tell a tale. [OE. *gearn*]

yawn *v.i.* gape; open the mouth wide, *esp.* in sleepiness. *-n.* the act of yawning. [OE. *ganian*]

year *n.* time taken by one revolution of the earth round the sun, about 365¼ days; twelve months. **-year′ling** *n.* animal one year old. **-year′ly** *adv.* every year, once a year. *-a.* happening, *etc.*, once a year. [OE. *gear*]

yearn (yern) *v. i.* feel a longing or desire. [OE. *giernan*]

yeast *n.* substance used as a fermenting agent, *esp.* in raising bread. **-yeast′y** *a.* frothy, fermenting. [OE. *gist*]

yell *v.i.* cry out in a loud shrill tone. *-n.* loud, shrill cry. [OE. *gellan*]

yell′ow *a.* of the color of lemons, gold, *etc.* *-n.* this color-, *-a.* (*fig.*) envious, jealous. *-(coll.)* cowardly. **-yell′ow fever** *n.* acute infectious disease of tropical Amer. and W. Africa. **-yell′owhammer** *n.* yellow bunting. **-yell′ow press′** sensational journalism. **-yell′ow rain** *n.* a type of yellow precipitation described in parts of S.E. Asia and alleged by some to be evidence of chemical warfare. [OE. *geoly*]

yes *interj.* affirms or consents, gives an affirmative answer. **-yes′man** *n.* servile person who never dares to disagree. [OE. *gese*]

yesterday *n.* day before today. [OE. *giestrandæg*]

yet *adv.* now, still; hitherto. *conj.* but, at the same time, nevertheless, however. [OE. *giet*]

yew *n.* evergreen tree with dark leaves; its wood. [OE. *iw*]

Yidd′ish *n.* Jewish dialect of corrupt Hebrew, German and other elements. [Ger. *jüdisch*, Jewish]

yield *v.t.* give or return as food; give up, surrender. *-v.i.* produce; surrender, give way. -*n.* amount produced; profit, or result. [OE. *gieldan*, pay]

yog'urt, yogh'urt *n.* thick, custard-like preparation of curdled milk. [Turk. *yoghurt*]

yoke *n.* wooden bar put across the necks of two animals to hold them together and to which a plow, *etc.*, may be attached; various objects like a yoke in shape or use; bond or tie. -*v.t.* put a yoke on; couple, unite. [OE. *geoc*]

yolk *n.* yellow part of an egg. [OE. *geoloca*, fr. *geolu*, yellow]

you *pron.* plural of the second person pronoun, but used also as a singular. (OE. *eow*]

young (yung) *a.* not far advanced in growth, life or existence, not yet old; vigorous. -*n.* offspring. -**young'ster** *n.* child, *esp.* an active or lively boy. [OE. *geong*]

your *pron.* belonging to you. -**yours** *pron.* -**yourself** *pron.* [OE. *eower*]

youth *n.* state or time of being young; state before adult age; young person; young people. -**youth'ful** *a.* [OE. *geogoth*]

yule *n.* Christmas festival. -**yule-log** *n.* -**yule-tide** *n.* [OE. *geol*]

yuppie *n.* wealthy young person. -*a.* [fr. *young up*wardly-mobile *p*rofessional]

Z

za'ny *n.* clown. [It. Giovanni, John]

zeal *n.* fervor, keenness. -**zeal'ous** *a.* -**zeal'ously** *adv.* -**zeal'ot** *n.* fanatic. [G. *zeros*]

ze'bra *n.* striped animal like a horse, native of Africa. [Port.]

Zen *n.* Japanese school of Buddhism teaching contemplation and meditation. *a.* [Jap.]

zen'ith *n.* point of the heavens directly above an observer. [Arab. *samt*, a road]

zeph'yr (zefer) *n.* west wind; gentle breeze. [G. *zephyros*, west wind]

ze'ro *n.* nothing; figure 0; point on a graduated instrument from which positive and negative quantities are reckoned. **ze'ro hour** in military operations, time from which each item on the program is at an interval stated. [It., fr. Arab. *sifr*, cipher]

zest *n.* relish. -**zest'ful** *a.* -**zest'fully** *adv.*

[F. = slice of lemon peel for flavoring]

zig'zag *n.* line bent by a series of angles. -*a.* forming a zigzag. -*adv.* with a zigzag course. -*v. i.* move along in a zigzag course. [F.]

zinc *n.* white metal. -*v.t.* coat with it [Ger. *zink*]

zinn'ia *n.* plant allied to the aster, with brightly colored flowers. [J. G. Zinn (d. 1759)]

Zi'on *n.* (hill in) ancient Jerusalem; Israel; the people of Israel; Christianity; paradise. -**Zi'onism** *n.* movement to found and support a Jewish homeland in Palestine. -**Zi'onist** *n.* advocate of this. [Heb. *tsiyon*, hill]

zip code *n.* five-figure number used in postal addresses designed to facilitate delivery of mail. [fr. *z*one *i*mprovement *p*lan]

zip'per *n.* quick-fastening device for clothes. [imit.]

zir'con *n.* mineral, Ceylon stone, varieties of which include jocinth and jargoon. -**zircon'ic** *a.* [Arab. *zarquin*]

zo'diac *n.* imaginary belt of the heavens outside which the sun, moon, and chief planets do not pass and divided crosswise into twelve equal areas (signs of the zodiac), each named after a constellation. -**zo'diacal** *a.* [G. *zodiakos*, fr. *zoon*, animal (the constellations being named mainly after animals)]

zone *n.* girdle; encircling band; any of the five belts into which the tropics and the arctic and antarctic circles divide the earth. -**zo'ning** *n.* town-planning according to zonal areas, residential, *etc.* [G.]

zool'ogy *n.* natural history of animals. -**zoolo'gical** *a.* -**zool'ogist** *n.*

zoo *n.* short for zoological gardens, place where wild animals are kept for show. -**zo'olite** *n.* fossil animal. **zo'ophyte** *n.* plant-like animal, *e.g.* a sponge. [G. *zoos*, living]

zy'gote *n.* fertilized egg cell. [G. *zygon*, yoke]

zymot'ic *a.* of, or caused by, fermentation; of a disease, due to multiplication of germs introduced into the body from outside. [G. *zimotikos*, fr. *zume*, leaven]

Thesaurus

How to Use a Thesaurus

If you have never used a thesaurus before, you are in for an unique experience. In some ways, it is like a dictionary, but there are no definitions given. Instead a thesaurus gives you *alternative* words.

First, you will learn the correct spelling of the word. Then, you will be given an extensive selection of choices that you can use instead of the primary word. These are synonyms, and providing a series of similar alternative words is what a thesaurus is all about.

When the first thesaurus was published by Peter Mark Roget, the primary purpose of his book was to provide the reader with synonyms for a word. In addition, his goal was to provide the reader with a tool that would offer a wide range of words that could be used as a substitute to the original concept. His book, however, was somewhat more complicated than this one, since it presented not only the *synonyms*, but *expressions* that were pertinent to the ideas of seventeenth century philosophy and science.

In this thesaurus, the words are presented in alphabetical order, just like a dictionary, to help you quickly find the words you need. However, these are not just synonyms, but the words are presented on the basis of grammatical type—nouns, verbs, adverbs, adjectives, etc. Whether you are a student, a writer, a businessperson, a player of word games, or someone who just enjoys reading, this book will provide you with a wealth of synonyms to increase your word power.

One word of caution: you will note that not all of the words presented as synonyms are completely and identically interchangeable alternatives for the primary word. Instead, by presenting the richness of the language, you will have access to a broader choice of words. Somewhere in those extensive choices you will find those words that can best express your intended meaning.

It is interesting to note that most lexicographers recognize the fact that there are no true synonyms. Although many words may mean the same thing, they each may have slightly different meanings. Something that is odd may be *abnormal* as well as *peculiar*, but these are not the same words. Something odd may also be *uncommon*, and that still does not carry the same meaning. Therefore, as we have mentioned above, choose your words carefully.

In addition, we have also provided you with many foreign words, but those that have come into popular or common usage. These, too, will enhance your writing skills, and provide an often "colorful" alternative to your original word.

Finally, we have taken care to include important and current words and synonyms, but these were purely editorial decisions. You may take exception to the words we have included or excluded. If you don't find the word you are looking for, or don't agree with our selection of choices, we suggest you consult a dictionary, where you will certainly find the words to your liking, and hopefully, those that will satisfy your need.

We hope you **enjoy** (*appreciate, delight in, dig, experience, have, like, make a meal of, own, posses, rejoice in, relish, revel in, savor, take pleasure in, use*) using this thesaurus.

A

abandon v. abdicate, cede, desert, desist, discontinue, ditch, drop, evacuate, forgo, forsake, give up, jilt, leave, leave behind, leave in the lurch, quit, relinquish, renounce, repudiate, resign, surrender, vacate, waive, withdraw from, yield. n. dash, recklessness, unrestraint, wantonness, wildness.

abate v. alleviate, appease, attenuate, decline, decrease, deduct, diminish, discount, dwindle, ease, ebb, fade, fall off, lessen, let up, mitigate, moderate, quell, rebate, reduce, relive, remit, sink, slacken, slow, subside, subtract, taper off, wane, weaken.

abbreviate v. abridge, abstract, clip, compress, condense, contract, curtail, cut, digest, epitomize, lessen, reduce, shorten, shrink, summarize, trim, truncate.

abet v. aid, assist, back, condone, connive, egg on, encourage, goad, help, incite, promote, prompt, sanction, second, spur, succor, support, sustain, uphold, urge.

ability v. adeptness, adroitness, aptitude, capability, capacity, competence, deftness, dexterity, expertise, expertness, facility, faculty, flair, genius, gift, knack, know-how, power, proficiency, qualification, savoir-faire, savvy, skill, strength, talent, touch.

able adj. accomplished, adept, adequate, adroit, capable, clever, competent, deft, dexterous, effective, efficient, experienced, expert, fit, fitted, gifted, ingenious, masterful, masterly, powerful, practiced, proficient, qualified, skillful, skilled, strong, talented.

abolish v. abrogate, annihilate, annul, blot out, cancel, destroy, do away with, eliminate, end, eradicate, expunge, exterminate, extinguish, invalidate, nullify, obliterate, overthrow, quash, repeal, repudiate, rescind, revoke, stamp out, suppress, terminate, vitiate, void.

about prep. adjacent to, around, beside, circa, concerning, encircling, encompassing, in respect to, in the matter of, near, nearby, on, over, re, referring to, regarding, relative to, surrounding, with regard to, with respect to.

above prep. atop, before, beyond, exceeding, higher than, in excess of, on top of, over, surpassing, upon. adv. aloft, atop, earlier, overhead, supra.

abroad adv. about, at large, away, circulating, current, elsewhere, extensively, far, far and wide, forth, in circulation, in foreign parts, out, out-of-doors, outside, overseas, publicly, widely.

absent adj. absent-minded, absorbed, abstracted, away, bemused, blank, daydreaming, distracted, faraway, gone, heedless, inattentive, lacking, missing, not present, oblivious, out, preoccupied, truant, unavailable, unaware, unconscious, vacant, vague, wanting.

absolute adj. actual, autocratic, autonomous, complete, decisive, definite, entire, exact, indubitable, omnipotent, perfect, positive, precise, pure, supreme, sure, total, unambiguous, unequivocal, utter.

absolve v. acquit, clear, deliver, discharge, emancipate, exculpate, excuse, exempt, exonerate, forgive, free, justify, let off, liberate, loose, pardon, ransom, redeem, release, remit, set free, shrive, vindicate.

abstain v. avoid, cease, decline, deny, desist, eschew, forbear, forgo, give up, keep from, refrain, refuse, reject, renounce, resist, shun, stop, swear off, withhold.

abstract adj. abstruse, conceptual, generalized, hypo-thetical, indefinite, philosophical, subtle, theoretical, unrealistic. n. abridgment, abstractive, compendium, digest, epitome, résumé, summary, synopsis. v. abbreviate, abridge, condense, detach, digest, extract, outline.

absurd adj. anomalous, comical, crazy, daft, derisory, fantastic, farcical, foolish, funny, humorous, idiotic, illogical, implausible, incongruous, irrational, laughable, ludicrous, meaningless, nonsensical, paradoxical, preposterous, ridiculous, risible, senseless, silly, stupid, unreasonable, untenable.

abundant adj. ample, bounteous, bountiful, copious, exuberant, filled, full, generous, in plenty, lavish, luxuriant, overflowing, plenteous, plentiful, prodigal, profuse, rank, rich, superabundant, teeming, uberous, unstinted, well-provided, well-supplied.

abuse v. batter, damage, defame, denigrate, disparage, exploit, harm, hurt, injure, insult, libel, malign, maltreat, manhandle, misuse, molest, oppress, revile, scold, slander, smear, spoil, swear at, take advantage of, upbraid, vilify, violate, vituperate, wrong.

accent n. accentuation, articulation, beat, cadence, emphasis, enunciation, force, ictus, inflection, intensity, intonation, modulation, pitch, pronunciation, pulsation, pulse, rhythm, stress, thesis, timbre, tonality, tone.

accept v. abide by, accede, acknowledge, acquiesce, admit, adopt, affirm, agree to, approve, assume, believe, bow to, concur with, cooperate with, get, have, jump at, obtain, receive, recognize, secure, stand, stomach, suffer, swallow, take, take on, tolerate, undertake, wear, yield to.

acceptable *adj.* adequate, admissible, agreeable, all right, conventional, correct, delightful, desirable, done, grateful, gratifying, moderate, passable, pleasant, pleasing, satisfactory, standard, suitable, tolerable, unexceptionable, unobjectionable, welcome.

access *n.* admission, admittance, approach, avenue, course, door, entering, entrance, entrée, entry, gateway, increase, ingress, key, onset, passage, passageway, path, road, upsurge.

accident *n.* blow, calamity, casualty, chance, collision, contingency, contretemps, crash, disaster, fate, fluke, fortuity, fortune, happenstance, hazard, luck, misadventure, miscarriage, mischance, misfortune, mishap, pile-up, serendipity, shunt.

acclaim *v.* announce, applaud, approve, celebrate, cheer, clap, commend, crown, declare, eulogize, exalt, extol, hail, honor, laud, praise, salute, welcome.

accommodate *v.* acclimatize, accustom, adapt, adjust, afford, aid, assist, attune, billet, board, cater for, comply, compose, conform, domicile, entertain, fit, furnish, harbor, harmonize, help, house, lodge, modify, oblige, provide, put up, quarter, reconcile, serve, settle, shelter, supply.

accompany *v.* attend, belong to, chaperon, coexist, coincide, complement, conduct, consort, convoy, escort, follow, go with, occur with, squire, supplement, usher.

accomplish *v.* achieve, attain, bring about, bring off, carry out, compass, complete, conclude, consummate, discharge, do, effect, effectuate, engineer, execute, finish, fulfill, manage, obtain, perform, produce, realize.

accord *v.* agree, allow, assent, concede, concur, confer, conform, correspond, endow, fit, give, grant, harmonize, jibe, match, present, render, suit, tally, tender, vouchsafe. *n.* accordance, agreement, assent, concert, congruence, correspondence, harmony, rapport, symmetry, sympathy, unanimity, unity.

accordingly *adv.* appropriately, as a result, as requested, consequently, correspondingly, ergo, hence, in accord with, in accordance, in consequence, properly, so, suitably, therefore, thus.

accumulate *v.* accrue, agglomerate, ag-

gregate, amass, assemble, build up, collect cumulate, gather, grow, hoard, increase, multiply, pile up, stash, stockpile, store.

accurate *adj.* authentic, careful, close, correct, exact, factual, faithful, faultless, just, letter-perfect, mathematical, meticulous, minute, nice, perfect, precise, proper, regular, right, rigorous, scrupulous, sound, spot-on, strict, true, truthful, unerring, veracious, well-aimed, well-directed, well-judged, word-perfect.

accuse *v.* allege, arraign, attaint, attribute, blame, censure, charge, cite, criminate, delate, denounce, impeach, impugn, impute, incriminate, indict, inform, against, recriminate, tax.

ache *v.* agonize, covet, crave, desire, grieve, hanker, hunger, hurt, itch, long, mourn, need, pain, pine, smart, sorrow, suffer, throb, twinge, yearn. *n.* anguish, craving desire, grief, hunger, hurt, itch, longing, misery, mourning, need, pain, pang, pining, pounding, smart, smarting, soreness, sorrow, suffering, throb, throbbing, yearning.

achieve *v.* accomplish, acquire, attain, bring about, carry out, compass, complete, consummate, do, earn, effect, effectuate, finish, fulfill, gain, get, manage, obtain, perform, procure, produce, reach, realize, score, strike, succeed, win.

acid *adj.* acerbic, acidulous, acrid, astringent, biting, bitter, caustic, corrosive, cutting, harsh, hurtful, ill-natured, incisive, mordant, morose, pungent, sharp, sour, stinging, tart, trenchant, vinegary, vitriolic.

acknowledge *v.* accede, accept, acquiesce, address, admit, affirm, agree to, allow, answer, attest, avouch, concede, confess, confirm, declare, endorse, grant, greet, hail, notice, own, profess, react to, recognize, reply to, respond to, return, salute, vouch for, witness, yield.

acquaint *v.* accustom, advise, announce, apprize, brief, disclose, divulge, enlighten, familiarize, inform, notify, reveal, tell.

acquiesce *v.* accede, accept, agree, allow, approve, assent, comply, concur, conform, consent, defer, give in, submit, yield.

acquire *v.* achieve, amass, appropriate, attain, buy, collect, cop, earn, gain, gather, get, net, obtain, pick up, procure, realize, receive, secure, win.

acquit *v.* absolve, bear, behave, clear, comport, conduct, deliver, discharge, dismiss, exculpate, excuse, exonerate, free, fulfill, liberate, pay, pay off, perform, release, relieve, repay, reprieve, satisfy, settle, vindicate.

acrid *adj.* acerbic, acid, acrimonious, astringent, biting, bitter, burning, caustic, cutting, harsh, incisive, irritating, malicious, mordant, nasty, pungent, sarcastic, sardonic, sharp, stinging, tart, trenchant, venomous, virulent, vitriolic.

act *n.* accomplishment, achievement, decree, deed, enterprise, feigning, make-believe, maneuver, operation, performance, pose, posture, pretense, stance, undertaking. *v.*

action *n.* achievement, act, activity, battle, clash, combat, conflict, contest, deed, encounter, endeavor, energy, engagement, enterprise, exercise, exploit, feat, fight, fighting, force, fray, litigation, motion, move, movement, operation, performance, undertaking, warfare, work.

active *adj.* acting, activist, alert, animated, assiduous, bustling, busy, diligent, energetic, engaged, enterprising, enthusiastic, forceful, hard-working, industrious, involved, lively, occupied, on the go, on the move, spirited, sprightly, spry, vibrant, vigorous, vital, zealous.

actual *adj.* absolute, authentic, bona fide, certain, concrete, confirmed, current, definite, existent, factual, genuine, indisputable, legitimate, live, living, material, physical, positive, present, real, realistic, substantial, tangible, true, truthful, unquestionable, verified, veritable.

adapt *v.* acclimatize, accommodate, adjust, alter, apply, change, comply, conform, convert, customize, familiarize, fashion, fit, habituate, harmonize, match, metamorphose, modify, prepare, proportion, qualify, re-fashion, remodel, shape, suit, tailor.

add *v.* adjoin, affix, amplify, annex, append, attach, augment, combine, compute, count, include, join, reckon, subjoin, sum up, superimpose, supplement, tack-on, tote up, total.

adequate *adj.* able, acceptable, capable, commensurate, competent, condign, efficacious, enough, fair, fit, passable, presentable, requisite, respectable, satisfactory, serviceable, sufficient, suitable, tolerable.

adhere *v.* abide by, agree, attach, cement, cleave, cleave to, cling, coalesce, cohere, combine, comply with, fasten, fix, follow, fulfill, glue, heed, hold, hold fast, join, keep, link, maintain, mind, obey, observe, paste, respect, stand by, stick, stick fast, support, unite.

adjust *v.* acclimatize, accommodate, accustom, adapt, alter, arrange, balance, change, coapt, compose, concert, con-

form, convert, dispose, fix, harmonize, modify, order, proportion, reconcile, rectify, redress, regulate, remodel, reshape, set, settle, shape, temper, tune.

administer *v.* apply, assign, conduct, contribute, control, direct, dispense, dispose, distribute, execute, give, govern, head, lead, manage, officiate, organize, oversee, perform, preside over, provide, regulate, rule, run, superintend, supervise, supply.

admirable *adj.* choice, commendable, creditable, deserving, estimable, excellent, exquisite, fine, laudable, meritorious, praiseworthy, rare, respected, superior, valuable, wonderful, worthy.

admire *v.* adore, applaud, appreciate, approve, esteem, iconize, idolize, laud, praise, prize, respect, revere, value, venerate, worship.

admission *n.* acceptance, access, acknowledgement, affirmation, allowance, concession, declaration, disclosure, divulgence, entrance, entrée, entry, exposé, granting, inclusion, ingress, initiation, introduction, owning, profession, revelation.

admit *v.* accept, acknowledge, adhibit, affirm, agree, allow, allow to enter, avow, concede, confess, declare, disclose, divulge, give access, grant, initiate, introduce, intromit, let, let in, permit, profess, receive, recognize, reveal, take in.

admonish *v.* advise, berate, caution, censure, check, chide, counsel, enjoin, exhort, forewarn, rebuke, reprehend, reprimand, reproach, reprove, scold, upbraid, warn.

adopt *v.* accept, affect, appropriate, approve, assume, back, choose, embrace, endorse, espouse, follow, foster, maintain, ratify, sanction, select, support, take in, take on, take up.

adoration *n.* admiration, esteem, estimation, exaltation, glorification, honor, idolatry, idolization, love, magnification, reverence, veneration, worship.

adore *v.* admire, cherish, dote on, esteem, exalt, glorify, honor, idolatrize, idolize, love, magnify, revere, reverence, venerate, worship.

advantage *n.* account, aid, asset, assistance, benefit, blessing, convenience, dominance, edge, gain, good, help, hold, interest, lead, leverage, precedence, profit, purchase, service, start, superiority, sway, upper-hand, use, usefulness, utility, welfare.

adventure *n.* chance, contingency, enterprise, experience, exploit, hazard, incident, occurrence, risk, speculation, undertaking, venture.

adverse *adj.* antagonistic, conflicting, contrary, counter, counter-productive, detrimental, disadvantageous, hostile, hurtful, injurious, inopportune, negative, opposing, opposite, reluctant, repugnant, unfortunate, unfriendly, unlucky, unwilling.

adversity *n.* affliction, bad luck, blight, calamity, catastrophe, contretemps, disaster, distress, hard times, hardship, ill-fortune, ill-luck, mischance, misery, misfortune, mishap, reverse, sorrow, suffering, trial, tribulation, trouble, woe, wretchedness.

advertise *v.* advise, announce, apprize, blazon, broadcast, bruit, declare, display, flaunt, herald, inform, make known, notify, plug, praise, proclaim, promote, promulgate, publicize, publish, puff, push, tout, trumpet.

advice *n.* admonition, caution, communication, counsel, direction, do's and don'ts, guidance, help, information, injunction, instruction, intelligence, memorandum, notice, notification, opinion, recommendation, suggestion, view, warning, wisdom, word.

advise *v.* acquaint, apprize, bethink, caution, commend, counsel, enjoin, forewarn, guide, inform, instruct, make known, notify, recommend, report, suggest, teach, tell, tutor, urge, warn.

affair *n.* activity, adventure, amour, business, circumstance, concern, connection, episode, event, happening, incident, interest, liaison, matter, occurrence, operation, organization, party, proceeding, project, question, reception, relationship, responsibility, romance, subject, topic, transaction, undertaking.

affect[1] *v.* act on, agitate, alter, apply to, attack, bear upon, change, concern, disturb, grieve, grip, impinge upon, impress, influence, interest, involve, melt, modify, move, overcome, penetrate, pertain to, perturb, prevail over, regard, relate to, seize, soften, stir, strike, sway, touch, transform, trouble, upset.

affect[2] *v.* adopt, aspire to, assume, contrive, counterfeit, fake, feign, imitate, pretend, profess, put on, sham, simulate.

affected *adj.* afflicted, agitated, altered, changed, concerned, damaged, distressed, gripped, hurt, impaired, impressed, influenced, injured, melted, moved, perturbed, smitten, stimulated, stirred, swayed, touched, troubled, upset.

affection *n.* amity, attachment, care, desire, devotion, favor, feeling, fondness, friendliness, good will, inclination, kindness, liking, love, partiality, passion,

penchant, predilection, predisposition, proclivity, propensity, regard, tenderness, warmth.

affirm *v.* assert, asseverate, attest, aver, avouch, avow, certify, confirm, corroborate, declare, depose, endorse, maintain, pronounce, ratify, state, swear, testify, witness.

afraid *adj.* aghast, alarmed, anxious, apprehensive, cowardly, diffident, distrustful, faint-hearted, fearful, frightened, intimidated, nervous, regretful, reluctant, scared, sorry, suspicious, timid, timorous, tremulous, unhappy.

after *prep.* afterwards, as a result of, behind, below, following, in consequence of, later, post, subsequent to, subsequently, succeeding, thereafter.

again *adv.* afresh, also, anew, another time, au contraire, besides, conversely, da capo, de integro, de novo, ditto, encore, furthermore, in addition, moreover, on the contrary, on the other hand, once more.

against *prep.* abutting, across, adjacent to, athwart, close up to, confronting, contra, counter to, facing, fronting, hostile to, in contact with, in contrast to, in defiance of, in exchange for, in opposition to, in the face of, on, opposed to, opposing, opposite to, resisting, touching, versus.

agent *n.* actor, agency, author, cause, channel, delegate, deputy, emissary, envoy, executor, factor, force, functionary, instrument, intermediary, middleman, mover, negotiator, operative, operator, representative, substitute, surrogate, vehicle, worker.

aggravate *v.* annoy, exacerbate, exaggerate, exasperate, harass, hassle, heighten, incense, increase, inflame, intensify, irk, irritate, magnify, needle, nettle, peeve, pester, provoke, tease vex, worsen.

aggression *n.* aggressiveness, antagonism, assault, attack, bellicosity, belligerence, combativeness, destructiveness, encroachment, hostility, impingement, incursion, injury, intrusion, invasion, jingoism, militancy, offence, offensive, onslaught, provocation, pugnacity, raid.

agile *adj.* active, acute, adroit, alert, brisk, clever, fleet, flexible, limber, lissome, lithe, lively, mobile, nimble, prompt, quick, quick-witted, sharp, smart, sprightly, spry, supple, swift.

agitate *v.* alarm, arouse, beat, churn, confuse, convulse, discompose, disconcert, disquiet, distract, disturb, excite, ferment, flurry, fluster, incite, inflame, perturb, rattle, rock, rouse, ruffle, shake, stimulate, stir, toss, trouble, unnerve, unsettle, upset, work up, worry.

agree v. accede, accord, acquiesce, admit, allow, answer, assent, chime, coincide, comply, concede, concord, concur, conform, consent, consort, contract, correspond, cotton, covenant, engage, fit, fix, get on, grant, harmonize, jibe, match, permit, promise, side with, square, suit, yield.

agreement[1] n. acceptance, accord, accordance, compact, compatibility, compliance, concert, conformity, congruence, congruity, correspondence, harmony, resemblance, similarity, suitableness, sympathy, unanimity, union.

agreement[2] n. arrangement, bargain, compact, concordat, contract, covenant, deal, pact, settlement, treaty, understanding.

aid v. abet, accommodate, assist, befriend, ease, encourage, expedite, facilitate, favor, help, oblige, promote, serve, subsidize, succor, support, sustain. n. a leg up, assistance, assistant, benefit, contribution, donation, encouragement, favor, help, helper, patronage, prop, relief, service, sponsorship, subsidy, subvention, succor, support, supporter.

ail v. afflict, annoy, be indisposed, bother, decline, distress, droop, fail, irritate, languish, pain, pine, sicken, trouble, upset, weaken, worry.

aim v. address, aspire, attempt, design, direct, endeavor, head for, intend, plan, point, propose, purpose, resolve, seek, set one's sights on, sight, strive, take aim, target, train, try, want, wish, zero in on. n. ambition, aspiration, course, desire, direction, dream, end, goal, hope, intent, intention, mark, motive, object, objective, plan, purpose, scheme, target, wish.

aimless adj. chance, desultory, directionless, erratic, feckless, frivolous, goalless, haphazard, irresolute, pointless, purposeless, rambling, random, stray, undirected, unguided, unmotivated, unpredictable, vagrant, wayward.

air n. ambience, appearance, atmosphere, aura, breeze, character, demeanor, effect, manner, melody, mood, puff, quality, strain, theme, tune, waft, whiff, wind, zephyr.

aisle n. alleyway, ambulatory, corridor, division, gangway, lane, passage, passageway, path, walkway.

alarm v. agitate, daunt, dismay, distress, frighten, give (someone) a turn, panic, scare, startle, terrify, terrorize, unnerve.

alert adj. active, agile, attentive, brisk, careful, circumspect, heedful, lively, nimble, observant, on the ball, on the lookout, on the qui vive, perceptive, prepared, quick, ready, sharp-eyed, sharp-witted, spirited, sprightly, vigilant, wary, watchful, wide-awake.

alias n. assumed name, false name, nickname, nom de guerre, nom de plume, pen name, pseudonym, soubriquet, stage name.

alive adj. active, alert, animate, animated, awake, breathing, brisk, cheerful, eager, energetic, existent, existing, extant, functioning, having life, in existence, in force, life-like, live, lively, living, operative, quick, real, spirited, sprightly, spry, subsisting, vibrant, vigorous, vital, vivacious, zestful.

allegiance n. adherence, constancy, devotion, duty, faithfulness, fealty, fidelity, friendship, homage, loyalty, obedience, obligation, support.

allot v. allocate, apportion, appropriate, assign, budget, designate, dispense, distribute, earmark, grant, mete, render, set aside, share out.

allow v. accord, acknowledge, acquiesce, admit, allocate, allot, apportion, approve, assign, authorize, bear, brook, concede, confess, deduct, endure, give, give leave, grant, let, own, permit, provide, put up with, remit, sanction, spare, stand, suffer, tolerate.

almost adv. about, all but, approaching, approximately, as good as, close to, just about, nearing, nearly, not far from, not quite, practically, towards, virtually, well-nigh.

alone adj., adv. abandoned, apart, by itself, by oneself, deserted, desolate, detached, discrete, isolated, just, lonely, lonesome, on one's own, only, peerless, separate, simply, single, single-handed, singular, sole, solitary, unaccompanied, unaided, unassisted, unattended, uncombined, unconnected, unequaled, unescorted, unique, unparalleled, unsurpassed.

also adv. additionally, along with, and, as well, as well as, besides, ditto, further, furthermore, in addition, including, moreover, plus, therewithal, to boot, too.

alter v. adapt, adjust, amend, bushel, castrate, change, convert, diversify, emend, metamorphose, modify, qualify, recast, reform, remodel, reshape, revise, shift, take liberties with, transform, transmute, transpose, turn, vary.

alternate v. alter, change, fluctuate, interchange, intersperse, reciprocate, rotate, substitute, take turns, transpose, vary. *adj.* alternating, alternative, another, different, every other, every second, reciprocating, reciprocative, rotating, second, substitute.

alternative *n.* back-up, choice, option, other, preference, recourse, selection, substitute. *adj.* alternate, another, different, fall-back, fringe, other, second, substitute, unconventional, unorthodox.

although *conj.* admitting that, albeit, conceding that, even if, even though, granted that, howbeit, notwithstanding, though, while.

altitude *n.* elevation, height, loftiness, stature, tallness.

altogether *adv.* absolutely, all in all, all told, as a whole, collectively, completely, entirely, fully, generally, in all, in general, in sum, in toto, on the whole, perfectly, quite, thoroughly, totally, utterly, wholesale, wholly.

always *adv.* aye, consistently, constantly, continually, endlessly, eternally, ever, everlastingly, evermore, every time, forever, in perpetuum, invariably, perpetually, regularly, repeatedly, unceasingly, unfailingly, without exception.

amaze *v.* alarm, astonish, astound, bewilder, confound, daze, disconcert, dismay, dumbfound, electrify, flabbergast, floor, shock, stagger, startle, stun, stupefy, surprise, wow.

ambition *n.* aim, aspiration, avidity, craving, design, desire, dream, drive, eagerness, end, enterprise, goal, hankering, hope, hunger, ideal, intent, longing, object, objective, purpose, push, striving, target, wish, yearning, zeal.

ambush *n.* ambuscade, concealment, cover, hiding, hiding-place, retreat, shelter, snare, trap, waylaying. *v.* ambuscade, bushwhack, ensnare, entrap, surprise, trap, waylay.

amend *v.* adjust, alter, ameliorate, better, change, correct, emend, enhance, fix, improve, mend, modify, qualify, rectify, redress, reform, remedy, repair, revise.

amid *conj.* amidst, among, amongst, in the middle of, in the midst of, in the thick of, surrounded by.

among *prep.* amid, amidst, amongst, between, in the middle of, in the midst of, in the thick of, midst, mongst, surrounded by, together with, with.

amount *n.* addition, aggregate, bulk, entirety, expanse, extent, lot, magnitude, mass, measure, number, quantity, quantum, quota, sum, sum total, supply, total, volume, whole.

amuse *v.* absorb, beguile, charm, cheer, cheer up, delight, disport, divert, engross, enliven, entertain, enthrall, gladden, interest, occupy, please, recreate, regale, relax, slay, tickle.

amusing *adj.* charming, cheerful, cheering, comical, delightful, diverting, droll, enjoyable, entertaining, facetious, funny, gladdening, hilarious, humorous, interesting, jocular, jolly, killing, laughable, lively, ludicrous, merry, pleasant, pleasing, risible, sportive, witty.

analysis *n.* anatomy, assay, breakdown, dissection, dissolution, division, enquiry, estimation, evaluation, examination, explanation, exposition, interpretation, investigation, judgment, opinion, reasoning, reduction, resolution, review, scrutiny, separation, sifting, study, test.

analyze *v.* anatomize, assay, break down, consider, dissect, dissolve, divide, estimate, evaluate, examine, interpret, investigate, judge, reduce, resolve, review, scrutinize, separate, sift, study, test.

anesthetic *n.* analgesic, anodyne, narcotic, opiate, painkiller, palliative, sedative, soporific, stupefacient, stupefactive.

angel *n.* archangel, backer, benefactor, cherub, darling, divine messenger, fairy godmother, guardian spirit, ideal, paragon, principality, saint, seraph, supporter, treasure.

anger *n.* annoyance, antagonism, bad blood, bile, bitterness, choler, dander, displeasure, dudgeon, exasperation, fury, gall, indignation, ire, irritability, irritation, monkey, outrage, passion, pique, rage, rancor, resentment, spleen, temper, vexation, wrath.

angry *adj.* aggravated, annoyed, antagonized, bitter, burned up, choked, disgruntled, displeased, enraged, exasperated, furious, heated, hot, incensed, indignant, infuriated, irascible, irate, ireful, irked, irritable, irritated, mad, miffed, needled, nettled, outraged, passionate, provoked, raging, riled, tumultuous, uptight, wrathful, wroth.

anguish *n.* agony, angst, anxiety, desolation, distress, dole, dolor, grief, heartache, heartbreak, misery, pain, pang, rack, sorrow, suffering, torment, torture, tribulation, woe, wretchedness.

animate *v.* activate, arouse, embolden, encourage, energize, enliven, excite, fire, galvanize, goad, impel, incite, inspire, inspirit, instigate, invest, invigorate, irradiate, kindle, move, quicken, reactivate, revive, revivify, rouse, spark, spur, stimulate, stir, suffuse, urge, vitalize, vivify.

annex v. acquire, add, adjoin, affix, append, appropriate, arrogate, attach, connect, conquer, expropriate, fasten, incorporate, join, occupy, purloin, seize, subjoin, tack, take over, unite, usurp. n. addendum, additament, addition, adjunct, appendix, attachment, supplement.

announce v. advertise, blazon, broadcast, declare, disclose, divulge, intimate, leak, make known, notify, proclaim, promulgate, propound, publicize, publish, report, reveal, state.

annoy v. aggravate, anger, badger, bore, bother, bug, chagrin, contrary, displease, disturb, exasperate, gall, get, harass, harm, harry, hip, irk, irritate, madden, molest, needle, nettle, peeve, pester, pique, plague, provoke, rile, ruffle, tease, trouble, vex.

answer n. acknowledgment, defense, explanation, outcome, plea, rebuttal, reciprocation, rejoinder, reply, response, retort.

anxiety n. angst, anxiousness, apprehension, care, concern, craving, desire, disquiet, distress, dread, dysthymia, eagerness, foreboding, keenness, misgiving, nervousness, restlessness, solicitude, suspense, tension, torment, torture, uneasiness, watchfulness, worry.

anxious adj. afraid, apprehensive, avid, careful, concerned, desirous, distressed, disturbed, eager, expectant, fearful, fretful, impatient,keen, nervous, on tenterhooks, restless, solicitous, taut, tense, tormented, tortured, troubled, uneasy, unquiet, watchful, worried, yearning.

apartment n. accommodation, chambers, compartment, condominium, flat, living quarters, lodgings, maisonette, pad, penthouse, quarters, room, rooms, suite, tenement.

aperture n. breach, chink, cleft, crack, eye, eyelet, fissure, foramen, gap, hole, interstice, opening, orifice, passage, perforation, rent, rift, slit, slot, space, vent.

apology n. acknowledgment, apologia, confession, defense, excuse, explanation, extenuation, justification, palliation, plea, semblance, substitute, travesty, vindication.

appall v. alarm, astound, daunt, disconcert, disgust, dishearten, dismay, frighten, harrow, horrify, intimidate, outrage, petrify, scare, shock, terrify, unnerve.

apparent adj. clear, conspicuous, declared, discernible, distinct, evident, indubitable, manifest, marked, noticeable, obvious, on paper, open, ostensible, outward, overt, patent, perceptible, plain,

seeming, specious, superficial, unmistakable, visible.

appeal[1] n. application, entreaty, imploration, invocation, petition, plea, prayer, request, solicitation, suit, supplication. v. address, adjure, apply, ask, beg, beseech, call, call upon, entreat, implore, invoke, petition, plead, pray, refer, request, resort to, solicit, sue.

appeal[2] n. allure, attraction, attractiveness, beauty, charisma, charm, enchantment, fascination, interest, magnetism, winsomeness. v. allure, attract, charm, draw, engage, entice, fascinate, interest, invite, lure, please, tempt.

appear v. act, arise, arrive, attend, be published, bob up, come into sight, come into view, come out, come to light, crop up, develop, emerge, enter, issue, leak out, look, loom, materialize, occur, perform, play, rise, seem, show, show up, surface, take part, transpire, turn out, turn up.

appearance n. advent, air, arrival, aspect, bearing, brow, cast, character, coming, demeanor, emergence, expression, face, favor, form, front, guise, illusion, image, impression, look, manner, mien, physiognomy, pres-ence, pretense, seeming, semblance, show.

append v. add, adjoin, affix, annex, attach, conjoin, fasten, join, subjoin, tack on.

appetite n. appetency, craving, demand, desire, eagerness, hankering, hunger, inclination, keenness, liking, longing, orexis, passion, predilection, proclivity, propensity, relish, stomach, taste, willingness, yearning, zeal, zest.

appliance n. apparatus, contraption, contrivance, device, gadget, implement, instrument, machine, mechanism, tool.

apply[1] v. adhibit, administer, appose, assign, bring into play, bring to bear, direct, employ, engage, execute, exercise, implement, ply, practice, resort to, set, use, utilize, wield.

apply[2] v. appertain, be relevant, fit, have force, pertain, refer, relate, suit.

apply[3] v. anoint, cover with, lay on, paint, place, put on, rub, smear, spread on, use.

apply[4] v. appeal, ask for, claim, indent for, inquire, petition, put in, request, requisition, solicit, sue.

apply[5] v. address, bend, buckle down, commit, concentrate, dedicate, devote, direct, give, persevere, settle down, study, throw.

appointment n. allotment, arrangement, assignation, assignment, choice, choosing, commissioning, consultation, date, delegation, election, engagement, installation, interview, job, meeting, naming, nomination, office, place, position, post, rendezvous, selection, session, situation, station, tryst.

appreciate v. acknowledge, admire, be sensible of, be sensitive to, cherish, comprehend, dig, do justice to, enjoy, esteem, estimate, know, like, perceive, prize, realize, recognize, regard, relish, respect, savor, sympathize with, take kindly to, treasure, understand, value.

apprehend[1] v. arrest, bust, capture, catch, collar, detain, get, grab, nab, nick, pinch, run in, seize, take.

apprehend[2] v. appreciate, believe, comprehend, conceive, consider, discern, grasp, imagine, know, perceive, realize, recognize, see, twig, understand.

apprehensive adj. afraid, alarmed, anxious, concerned, disquieted, distrustful, disturbed, doubtful, fearful, mistrustful, nervous, solicitous, suspicious, uneasy, worried.

approach v. advance, approximate, be like, come close, come near to, draw near, meet, near, resemble, sound out, undertake. n. access, advance, application, arrival, attitude, entrance, gesture, manner, modus operandi, overture, procedure, resemblance, technique, way.

approve v. accede to, accept, acclaim, admire, adopt, advocate, agree to, allow, applaud, appreciate, authorize, back, concur in, confirm, consent to, countenance, endorse, esteem, favor, like, mandate, OK, pass, permit, praise, ratify, recommend, regard, respect, sanction, second, support, take, kindly to, uphold, validate.

aptitude n. ability, aptness, bent, capability, capacity, cleverness, disposition, facility, faculty, flair, gift, inclination, intelligence, knack, leaning, penchant, predilection, proclivity, proficiency, proneness, propensity, quickness, talent, tendency.

area n. arena, bailiwick, ball-park, breadth, canvas, compass, department, district, domain, environs, expanse, extent, field, locality, neighborhood, part, patch, portion, province, range, realm, region, scope, section, sector, size, sphere, stretch, terrain, territory, tract, width, zone.

argue v. altercate, bicker, claim, contend, convince, debate, disagree, discuss, display, dispute, evidence, feud, fight, haggle, hold, imply, indicate, maintain, persuade, plead, prevail upon, prove, quarrel, question, reason, squabble, suggest, talk into, wrangle.

arid adj. baked, barren, boring, colorless, desert, desiccated, dreary, dry, dull, empty, flat, infertile, lifeless, monotonous, parched, spiritless, sterile, tedious, torrid, uninspired, uninteresting, unproductive, vapid, waste, waterless.

arise v. appear, ascend, begin, climb, come to light, commence, crop up, derive, emanate, emerge, ensue, flow, follow, get up, go up, grow, happen, issue, lift, mount, occur, originate, proceed, result, rise, set in, soar, spring, stand up, start, stem, tower, wake up.

arm[1] n. appendage, authority, bough, brachium, branch, channel, department, detachment, division, estuary, extension, firth, inlet, limb, offshoot, projection, section, sector, sound, strait, sway, tributary, upper limb.

arm[2] v. accouter, ammunition, array, brace, equip, forearm, fortify, furnish, gird, issue with, outfit, prepare, prime, protect, provide, reinforce, rig, steel, strengthen, supply.

arrange v. adjust, align, array, categorize, class, classify, collocate, concert, construct, contrive, coordinate, design, determine, devise, dispose, distribute, fettle, file, fix, form, group, lay out, marshal, methodize, order, organize, plan, position, prepare, project, range, rank, regulate, schedule, set out, settle, sift, sort, sort out, stage-manage, style, swing, systematize, tidy, trim.

arrangement[1] n. adjustment, agreement, alignment, array, battery, classification, compact, compromise, construction, deal, design, display, disposition, form, grouping, layout, line-up, marshaling, method, modus vivendi, order, ordering, organization, plan, planning, preparation, provision, ranging, rank, schedule, scheme, settlement, set-up, spacing, structure, system, tabulation, taxis, terms.

arrangement[2] n. adaptation, harmonization, instrumentation, interpretation, orchestration, score, setting, version.

arrest v. apprehend, bust, capture, catch, check, collar, delay, detain, engross, fascinate, halt, hinder, hold, impede, inhibit, nab, prevent, restrain, retard, seize, slow, stop, suppress.

arrival n. accession, advent, appearance, approach, caller, comer, coming, entrance, entrant, happening, landfall, newcomer, occurrence, visitant, visitor.

arrive v. alight, appear, attain, befall, come, enter, fetch, get to the top, happen, land, make it, materialize, occur, reach, show, show up, succeed, turn up.

art *n.* adroitness, aptitude, artifice, artistry, artwork, craft, craftiness, craftsmanship, cunning, dexterity, draftsmanship, drawing, expertise, facility, finesse, knack, knowledge, mastery, meth-od, painting, sculpture, skill, trade, trick, trickery, virtu, virtuosity, visuals, wiliness.

article *n.* account, bit, clause, commodity, composition, constituent, count, detail, discourse, division, element, essay, feature, head, heading, item, matter, object, paper, paragraph, part, particular, piece, point, portion, report, review, section, story, thing, unit.

artificial *adj.* affected, assumed, bogus, contrived, counterfeit, ersatz, factitious, fake, false, feigned, forced, hyped up, imitation, insincere, made-up, manmade, mannered, manufactured, meretricious, mock, phony, plastic, pretended, pseudo, sham, simulated, specious, spurious, synthetic, unnatural.

artist *n.* colorist, craftsman, draftsman, expert, maestro, master, painter, portraitist, portrait-painter, sculptor, water-colorist.

ascend *v.* climb, float up, fly up, go up, lift off, move up, rise, scale, slope upwards, soar, take off, tower.

ashamed *adj.* abashed, apologetic, bashful, blushing, chagrined, confused, conscience-stricken, crestfallen, discomfited, discomposed, distressed, embarrassed, guilty, hesitant, humbled, humiliated, modest, mortified, prudish, red in the face, redfaced, reluctant, remorseful, self-conscious, shamefaced, sheepish, shy, sorry, unwilling.

ask *v.* appeal, apply, beg, beseech, bid, catechize, claim, clamor, crave, demand, enquire, entreat, implore, importune, indent, interrogate, invite, order, petition, plead, pray, press, query, question, quiz, request, require, seek, solicit, sue, summon, supplicate.

asleep *adj.* benumbed, comatose, dead to the world, dormant, dozing, fast asleep, inactive, inert, napping, numb, reposing, sleeping, slumbering, snoozing, sound asleep, unconscious.

aspect *n.* air, angle, appearance, attitude, bearing, condition, countenance, demeanor, direction, elevation, exposure, expression, face, facet, feature, look, manner, mien, outlook, physiognomy, point of view, position, prospect, scene, side, situation, standpoint, view, visage.

aspire *v.* aim, crave, desire, dream, hope, intend, long, purpose, pursue, seek, wish, yearn.

assail *v.* abuse, assault, attack, belabor, berate, beset, bombard, charge, criticize, encounter, fall upon, impugn, invade, lay into, malign, maltreat, pelt, revile, set about, set upon, strike, vilify.

assault *n.* aggression, attack, blitz, charge, incursion, invasion, offensive, onset, onslaught, raid, storm, storming, strike. *v.* assail, attack, beset, charge, fall on, hit, invade, lay violent hands on, set upon, storm, strike.

assemble *v.* accumulate, amass, build, collect, compose, congregate, construct, convene, convocate, convoke, erect, fabricate, flock, forgather, gather, group, join up, levy, make, manufacture, marshal, meet, mobilize, muster, muster (up), piece, rally, round up, set up, summon, together.

assembly *n.* agora, assemblage, caucus, collection, company, conclave, concourse, conference, congregation, congress, convention, crowd, fabrication, fitting, flock, gathering, group, manufacture, mass, meeting, multitude, rally, reception, setting up, soiree, synod, throng.

assert *v.* advance, affirm, allege, asseverate, attest, aver, avouch, avow, claim, contend, declare, defend, dogmatize, insist, lay down, maintain, predicate, press, profess, promote, pronounce, protest, state, stress, swear, testify to, thrust forward, uphold, vindicate.

assertion *n.* affirmance, affirmation, allegation, asseveration, attestation, averment, avowal, claim, contention, declaration, dictum, gratis, dictum, ipse dixit, predication, profession, pronouncement, statement, vindication, vouch, word.

assess *v.* appraise, compute, consider, demand, determine, estimate, evaluate, fix, gauge, impose, investigate, judge, levy, rate, reckon, review, size up, tax, value, weigh.

assist *v.* abet, accommodate, aid, back, benefit, bestead, boost, collaborate, cooperate, enable, expedite, facilitate, further, help, rally round, reinforce, relieve, second, serve, succor, support, sustain.

associate *v.* accompany, affiliate, ally, combine, confederate, connect, consort, couple, fraternize, hang around, join, mingle, mix, pair, relate, socialize, unite, yoke. *n.* affiliate, ally, assistant, bedfellow, collaborator, colleague, companion, comrade, confederate, coworker, fellow, follower, friend, leaguer, partner, peer, sidekick.

assume *v.* accept, acquire, adopt, affect, appropriate, believe, deduce, embrace, imagine, infer, opine, postulate, premise, presume, presuppose, pretend to, put on, seize, sham, suppose, surmise, suspect, take, undertake.

attach v. add, adhere, affix, annex, append, articulate, ascribe, assign, associate, attract, attribute, belong, bind, captivate, combine, connect, couple, fasten, fix, impute, join, link, place, put, relate to, secure, stick, tie, unite, weld.

attain v. accomplish, achieve, acquire, arrive at, bag, compass, complete, earn, effect, gain, get, grasp, net, obtain, procure, reach, realize, reap, secure, touch, win.

attitude n. affectation, air, approach, aspect, bearing, carriage, condition, demeanor, disposition, feeling, manner, mien, mood, opinion, outlook, perspective, point of view, pose, position, posture, stance, view.

authentic adj. accurate, actual, authoritative, bona fide, certain, dependable, actual, faithful, genuine, honest, kosher, legitimate, original, pure, real, reliable, simon-pure, true, true-to-life, trustworthy, valid, veracious, veritable.

author n. architect, begetter, composer, creator, designer, fabricator, fashioner, father, forger, founder, framer, initiator, inventor, maker, mover, originator, paperstainer, parent, pen, penman, planner, prime mover, producer, volumist, writer.

authoritative adj. accurate, approved, authentic, authorized, commanding, decisive, definitive, dependable, factual, faithful, learned, legitimate, magis-terial, masterly, official, reliable, sovereign, true, trustworthy, truthful, valid, veritable.

avarice n. acquisitiveness, covetousness, greed, greediness, miserliness, niggardliness, parsimoniousness, penny-pinching, penuriousness, stinginess, tight-fistedness.

average n. mean, mediocrity, medium, midpoint, norm, par, rule, run, standard.

aware adj. acquainted, alive to, appreciative, apprized, attentive, cognizant, conscious, conversant, enlightened, familiar, heedful, informed, knowing, knowledgeable, mindful, observant, on the ball, sensible, sharp, shrewd.

awe n. admiration, amazement, apprehension, astonishment, dread, fear, respect, reverence, terror, veneration, wonder, wonderment.

awful adj. abysmal, alarming, atrocious, august, dire, dread, dreadful, fearful, fearsome, frightful, ghastly, gruesome, harrowing, horrendous, horrible, shocking, solemn, spine-chilling, terrible, tremendous, ugly, unpleasant.

B

baby n. babe, child, infant, suckling, tiny, toddler, youngling. adj. diminutive, dwarf, Lilliputian, little, midget, mini, miniature, minute, pygmy, small, tiny, toy, wee.

back¹ v. advocate, assist, boost, buttress, champion, countenance, countersign, encourage, endorse, favor, finance, sanction, second, side with, sponsor, subsidize, support, sustain, underwrite.

back² n. backside, end, hind part, hindquarters, posterior, rear, reverse, stern, tail, tail end, verso. adj. end, hind, hindmost, posterior, rear, reverse, tail.

back³ v. backtrack, recede, recoil, regress, retire, retreat, reverse, withdraw.

back⁴ adj. delayed, earlier, elapsed, former, outdated, overdue, past, previous, prior, superseded.

backing n. accompaniment, advocacy, aid, assistance, championing, championship, encouragement, endorsement, favor, funds, grant, helpers, moral support, patronage, sanction, seconding, sponsorship, subsidy, support.

bad adj. ailing, base, corrupt, dangerous, defective, deficient, disastrous, distressing, evil, fallacious, faulty, gloomy, grave, harmful, harsh, ill, imperfect, incorrect, inferior, naughty, offensive, putrid, rancid, rotten, sad, sick, sinful, spoilt, terrible, unsatisfactory, vile, wicked, wrong.

bag v. acquire, appropriate, capture, catch, commandeer, corner, gain, get, grab, kill, land, obtain, reserve, shoot, take, trap. n. carrier, container, grab-bag, grip, gripsack, handbag, haversack, holder, pack, poke, rucksack, sack, satchel, shoulderbag, totebag, valise.

bail n. bond, guarantee, guaranty, pledge, security, surety, warranty.

bald adj. bald-headed, bare, barren, bleak, depilated, direct, downright, exposed, forthright, glabrous, hairless, naked, outright, peeled, plain, severe, simple, stark, straight, straightforward, treeless, unadorned, uncompromising, uncovered, undisguised, unvarnished.

balloon v. bag, belly, billow, blow up, bulge, dilate, distend, enlarge, expand, inflate, puff out, swell.

ballot n. election, plebiscite, poll, polling, referendum, vote, voting.

ban v. banish, bar, debar, disallow, exclude, forbid, interdict, ostracize, outlaw, prohibit, proscribe, restrict, suppress. n. boycott, censorship, condemnation, curse, denunciation, embargo, prohibition, proscription, restriction, stoppage, suppression, taboo.

band¹ *n.* bandage, binding, bond, chain, cord, fascia, manacle, ribbon, shackle, strap, strip, swath, tape, tie.

band² *n.* association, body, clique, club, combo, company, coterie, crew, ensemble, flock, gang, group, herd, horde, orchestra, party, range, society, troop, waits. *v.* affiliate, ally, amalgamate, collaborate, consolidate, federate, gather, group, join, merge, unite.

banish *v.* ban, bar, blacklist, debar, deport, discard, dislodge, dismiss, dispel, eject, eliminate, eradicate, evict, exclude, excommunicate, exile, expatriate, expel, get rid of, ostracize, oust, outlaw, remove, shut out, transport.

bar *n.* barricade, barrier, batten, check, crosspiece, deterrent, determent, hindrance, impediment, obstacle, obstruction, paling, pole, preventive, rail, railing, rod, shaft, stake, stanchion, stick, stop. *v.* ban, barricade, blackball, bolt, debar, exclude, fasten, forbid, hinder, latch, lock, obstruct, preclude, prevent, prohibit, restrain, secure.

bare *adj.* austere, bald, barren, basic, blank, defoliate, defoliated, denuded, empty, essential, explicit, exposed, hard, lacking, literal, mean, naked, napless, nude, open, peeled, plain, poor, scanty, scarce, severe, sheer, shorn, spare, stark, stripped, unclad, unclothed, uncovered, undressed, vacant, void, wanting.

barely¹ *adv.* almost, hardly, just, scarcely, sparingly, sparsely.

barely² *adv.* explicity, nakedly, openly, plainly.

bargain *n.* agreement, arrangement, compact, contract, discount, giveaway, negotiation, pact, pledge, promise, reduction, snip, steal, stipulation, transaction, treaty, understanding. *v.* agree, barter, broke, buy, contract, covenant, deal, dicker, haggle, negotiate, promise, sell, stipulate, trade, traffic, transact.

barren *adj.* arid, boring, childless, desert, desolate, dry, dull, empty, flat, fruitless, infertile, jejune, lackluster, pointless, profitless, stale, sterile, unbearing, unfruitful, uninspiring, uninteresting, unproductive, unprolific, unrewarding, useless, vapid, waste.

barrier *n.* bail, bar, barricade, blockade, boom, boundary, bulkhead, check, difficulty, ditch, drawback, fence, fortification, handicap, hindrance, hurdle, impediment, limitation, obstacle, obstruction, railing, rampart, restriction, stop, stumbling-block, transverse, wall.

base¹ *n.* basis, bed, bottom, camp, center, core, essence, foundation, fundamental, headquarters, heart, home, key, pedestal, root, source, starting-point,, substructure, underpinning.

base² *adj.* abject, contemptible, corrupt, counterfeit, depraved, disgraceful, disreputable, dog, evil, groveling, humble, ignoble, ignominious, immoral, infamous, low, lowly, low-minded, mean, menial, miserable, paltry, pitiful, poor, scandalous, servile, shameful, slavish, sordid, sorry, valueless, vile, villainous, vulgar, wicked, worthless, wretched.

base³ *adj.* adulterated, alloyed, artificial, bastard, counterfeit, debased, fake, forged, fraudulent, impure, inferior, pinchbeck, spurious.

basic *adj.* central, elementary, essential, fundamental, important, indispensable, inherent, intrinsic, key, necessary, primary, radical, root, underlying, vital.

batter *v.* abuse, assault, bash, beat, belabor, bruise, buffet, crush, dash, deface, demolish, destroy, disfigure, distress, hurt, injure, lash, maltreat, mangle, manhandle, mar, maul, pelt, pound, pummel, ruin, shatter, smash, thrash, wallop.

battle *n.* action, affray, attack, campaign, clash, combat, conflict, contest, controversy, crusade, debate, disagreement, dispute, encounter, engagement, fight, fray, hostilities, row, skirmish, strife, struggle, war, warfare.

bearing *n.* air, application, aspect, attitude, behavior, carriage, comportment, connection, course, demeanor, deportment, direction, import, manner, mien, poise, posture, presence, reference, relation, relevance, significance.

bearings *n.* aim, course, direction, inclination, location, orientation, position, situation, track, way, whereabouts.

beat¹ *v.* bang, batter, bludgeon, bruise, buffet, cane, flog, hammer, hit, knock, lash, lay into, pelt, pound, punch, strike, thrash, whip. *n.* blow, hit, lash, punch, shake, slap, strike, swing, thump. *adj.* exhausted, fatigued, tired, wearied, worn out, zonked.

beat² *v.* best, conquer, defeat, excel, hammer, outdo, outrun, outstrip, overcome, overwhelm, slaughter, subdue, surpass, trounce, vanquish.

beat³ *v.* flutter, palpitate, patter, pound, pulsate, pulse, quake, quiver, race, shake, throb, thump, tremble, vibrate. *n.* accent, cadence, flutter, measure, meter, palpitation, pulsation, pulse, rhyme, stress, throb, time.

beautiful *adj.* alluring, appealing, attractive, beau, beauteous, belle, charming, comely, delightful, exquisite, fair, fine, good-looking, gorgeous, graceful, handsome, lovely, pleasing, pulchritudinous, radiant, ravishing, stunning.

because *conj.* as, by reason of, for, forasmuch, in that, inasmuch as, on account of, owing to, since, thanks to.

becoming *adj.* appropriate, attractive, charming, comely, decent, flattering, graceful, pretty, proper, seemly, suitable, tasteful, worthy.

before *adv.* ahead, earlier, formerly, in advance, in front, previously, sooner.

beg *v.* beseech, crave, desire, entreat, implore, importune, petition, plead, pray, request, require, scrounge, solicit, sponge on, supplicate, touch.

begin *v.* activate, actuate, appear, arise, commence, crop up, dawn, emerge, happen, inaugurate, initiate, instigate, introduce, originate, prepare, set about, set in, spring, start.

beginning *n.* birth, commencement, embryo, establishment, germ, inception, introduction, onset, opening, origin, preface, prelude, seed, source, start, starting point.

behavior *n.* action, actions, bearing, carriage, comportment, conduct, dealings, demeanor, deportment, doings, functioning, habits, manner, manners, operation, performance, reaction, response, ways.

behind *prep.* after, backing, causing, following, for, initiating, instigating, later than, responsible for, supporting. *adv.* after, afterwards, behindhand, following, in arrears, in debt, in the wake of, next, overdue, subsequently. *n.* ass, backside, bottom, butt, buttocks, derriere, fanny, posterior, prat, rear, rump, seat, sit-upon, tail, tush.

belief *n.* assurance, confidence, conviction, credence, credit, credo, creed, doctrine, dogma, expectation, faith, feeling, ideology, impression, intuition, ism, judgment, notion, opinion, persuasion, presumption, principle, principles, reliance, sureness, surety, tenet, theory, trust, view.

belligerent *adj.* aggressive, antagonistic, argumentative, bellicose, bullying, combative, contentious, forceful, militant, pugnacious, quarrelsome, violent, warlike, warring.

belonging *n.* acceptance, affinity, association, attachment, closeness, compatibility, fellow-feeling, fellowship, inclusion, kinship, link, linkage, loyalty, rapport, relationship.

below *adv.* beneath, down, infra, lower, lower down, under, underneath. *prep.* inferior to, lesser than, subject to, subordinate to, under, underneath, unworthy of.

belt[1] *n.* area, band, cincture, cingulum, cummerbund, district, girdle, girth, layer, region, sash, strait, stretch, strip, swathe, tract, waistband, zone, zonule. *v.* circle, encircle, girdle, ring, surround.

beneath *adv.* below, lower, lower down, under, underneath. *prep.* below, inferior to, infra dig(nitatem), lower than, 'neath, subject to, subordinate to, unbefitting, under, underneath, unworthy of.

benefit *n.* advantage, aid, asset, assistance, avail, blessing, boon, favor, gain, good, help, interest, profit, service, use, welfare.

beside *prep.* abreast of, abutting on, adjacent, bordering on, close to, near, neighboring, next door to, next to, overlooking, upsides with.

besides *adv.* additionally, also, as well, extra, further, furthermore, in addition, into the bargain, moreover, otherwise, to boot, too, withal. *prep.* apart from, in addition to, other than, over and above.

betray *v.* abandon, beguile, corrupt, deceive, delude, desert, disclose, discover, divulge, double cross, dupe, entrap, expose, give away, inform on, jilt, reveal, seduce, sell down the river, sell out, show, tell, testify against, turn state's evidence.

between *prep.* amidst, among, amongst, betwixt, inter-, mid.

beyond *prep.* above, across, apart from, away from, before, further than, out of range, out of reach of, over, past, remote from, superior to, yonder.

big *adj.* adult, altruistic, beefy, benevolent, boastful, bombastic, bulky, burly, buxom, colossal, considerable, corpulent, elder, elephantine, eminent, enormous, extensive, gargantuan, generous, gigantic, gracious, great, grown, grown-up, heroic, huge, hulking, immense, important, influential, large, leading, lofty, magnanimous, main, mammoth, man-sized, massive, mature, mighty, noble, paramount, ponderous, powerful, prime, principal, prodigious, prominent, serious, significant, sizable, spacious, stout, substantial, titanic, tolerant, unselfish, valuable, vast, voluminous, weighty.

bigot *n.* chauvinist, dogmatist, fanatic, racist, religionist, sectarian, sexist, zealot.

blade *n.* dagger, edge, knife, rapier, scalpel, sword.

blame *v.* accuse, admonish, censure, charge, chide, condemn, criticize, disapprove, find fault with, rebuke, reprimand, reproach, reprove, upbraid.

blank *adj.* apathetic, bare, deadpan, empty, expressionless, featureless, impassive, lifeless, plain, staring, uncomprehending, vacant, vacuous, vague, void, white.

bleak *adj.* bare, barren, cheerless, chilly, cold, colorless, depressing, desolate, dismal, dreary, empty, gloomy, joyless, somber, unsheltered, weather-beaten, windswept, windy.

blessed *adj.* adored, beatified, blissful, contented, divine, endowed, favored, fortunate, glad, hallowed, happy, holy, joyful, joyous, lucky, prosperous, revered, sacred, sanctified.

blockade *n.* barricade, barrier, encirclement, obstruction, restriction, siege, stoppage.

bluff¹ *n.* bank, brow, cliff, crag, escarp, escarpment, foreland, headland, height, knoll, peak, precipice, promontory, ridge, scarp, slope. *adj.* affable, blunt, candid, direct, downright, frank, genial, good-natured, hearty, open, outspoken, plainspoken, straightforward.

bluff² *v.* bamboozle, blind, deceive, defraud, delude, fake, feign, grift, hoodwink, humbug, lie, mislead, pretend, sham. *n.* buster, boast, braggadocio, bravado, deceit, deception, fake, feint, fraud, grift, humbug, idle boast, lie, pretence, sham, show, subterfuge, trick.

boast *v.* blow, bluster, bounce, brag, claim, crow, exaggerate, exhibit, show off, strut, swagger, talk big, trumpet, vaunt. *n.* avowal, brag, claim, joy, pride, swank, treasure, vaunt.

bold *adj.* adventurous, audacious, brash, brave, brazen, confident, courageous, daring, fearless, gallant, heroic, intrepid, jazzy, lively, loud, outgoing, prominent, shameless, showy, striking, valiant, valorous, venturesome, vivid.

boom¹ *v.* bang, blare, blast, crash, explode, resound, reverberate, roar, roll, rumble, sound, thunder. *n.* bang, blast, burst, clang, clap, crash, explosion, reverberation, roar, rumble, thunder.

boom² *v.* develop, escalate, expand, explode, flourish, gain, go from strength to strength, grow, increase, intensify, prosper, spurt, strengthen, succeed, swell, thrive. *n.* advance, boost, development, escalation, expansion, explosion, gain, growth, improvement, increase, jump, spurt, upsurge, upturn.

border *n.* borderline, bound, boundary, bounds, brim, brink, circumference, confine, confines, demarcation, edge, fringe, frontier, hem, limit, limits, lip, list, march,

margin, perimeter, periphery, rand, rim, screed, selvage, skirt, surround, trimming, valance, verge. *adj.* boundary, dividing, frontier, marginal, perimeter, separating, side.

bore¹ *v.* burrow, countermine, drill, gouge, mine, penetrate, perforate, pierce, sap, sink, thrill, tunnel, undermine.

bore² *v.* annoy, bother, bug, fatigue, irk, irritate, jade, pester, tire, trouble, vex, weary, worry. *n.* annoyance, bind, bother, drag, dullard, headache, nuisance, pain, pain in the neck, pest, trial, vexation, vieux jeu, yawn.

bound¹ *adj.* bandaged, beholden, cased, certain, chained, committed, compelled, constrained, destined, doomed, dutybound, fastened, fated, fixed, forced, held, liable, manacled, obligated, obliged, pinioned, pledged, required, restricted, secured, sure, tied, tied up.

bound² *v.* bob, bounce, caper, frisk, gambol, hurdle, jump, leap, lope, lunge, pounce, prance, skip, spring, vault. *n.* bob, bounce, caper, dance, frisk, gambol, jump, leap, lope, lunge, pounce, prance, scamper, skip, spring, vault.

bow¹ *v.* accept, acquiesce, bend, bob, capitulate, comply, concede, conquer, consent, crush, curtsey, defer, depress, droop, genuflect, give in, incline, kowtow, nod, overpower, stoop, subdue, subjugate, submit, surrender, vanquish, yield. *n.* acknowledgement, bending, bob, curtsey, genuflection, inclination, kowtow, nod, obeisance, salaam, salutation.

bow² *n.* beak, head, prow, rostrum, stem.

bowl¹ *n.* basin, container, cruse, dish, pan, porringer, receptacle, sink, tureen, vessel.

bowl² *n.* jack, wood. *v.* fling, hurl, pitch, revolve, roll, rotate, spin, throw, trundle, whirl.

bowl³ *n.* amphitheater, arena, auditorium, coliseum, field, ground, hall, hippodrome, stadium.

box¹ *n.* bijou, carton, case, casket, chest, coffer, coffin, container, coop, fund, pack, package, portmanteau, present, receptacle, trunk. *v.* case, encase, pack, package, wrap.

box² *v.* buffet, butt, clout, cuff, fight, hit, punch, slap, sock, spar, strike, thwack, wallop, whack, wham. *n.* blow, buffet, clout, cuff, punch, slap, stroke, thump, wallop, wham.

brag *v.* bluster, boast, crow, swagger, talk big, trumpet.

brave *adj.* audacious, bold, courageous, daring, fearless, gallant, heroic, indomitable, intrepid, stalwart, stoic, unafraid, valiant, valorous.

brawl *n.* affray, altercation, argument, battle, clash, disorder, dispute, dog-fight, Donnybrook, fight, fracas, fray, free-for-all, melee, quarrel, row, ruckus, rumpus, scrap, squabble, tumult, uproar, wrangle.

brief *adj.* abrupt, blunt, brusque, compressed, concise, curt, fleeting, hasty, momentary, passing, quick, sharp, short-lived, succinct, swift, temporary, terse. *v.* advise, direct, explain, fill in, guide, inform, instruct, prepare, prime.

bright *adj.* ablaze, astute, blazing, brainy, brilliant, clever, dazzling, flashing, glaring, gleaming, glistening, illuminated, intelligent, joyful, lively, perceptive, quick, radiant, resplendent, sharp, shining, smart, sparkling, splendid, sunny, vivid.

brink *n.* bank, border, boundary, brim, edge, extremity, fringe, limit, lip, marge, margin, point, rim, skirt, threshold, verge, waterside.

brisk *adj.* active, agile, alert, allegro, bracing, bright, bustling, busy, crank, crisp, effervescing, energetic, exhilarating, expeditious, fresh, invigorating, keen, lively, nimble, nippy, no-nonsense, prompt, quick, refreshing, sharp, snappy, speedy, spirited, sprightly, spry, stimulating, vigorous.

broad *adj.* all-embracing, ample, blue, capacious, catholic, coarse, comprehensive, eclectic, encyclopedic, enlightened, expansive, extensive, far-reaching, general, generous, gross, improper, inclusive, indecent, indelicate, large, roomy, spacious, square, sweeping, tolerant, universal, unlimited, unrefined, vast, voluminous, vulgar, wide, wide-ranging, widespread.

broken *adj.* burst, crushed, defeated, demoralized, destroyed, faulty, fractured, fragmented, hesitating, incomplete, intermittent, out of order, ruptured, severed, shattered, subdued, tamed, vanquished.

brush[1] *n.* broom, sweeper. *v.* buff, burnish, caress, clean, contact, graze, paint, polish, rub, scrape, shine, stroke, sweep, touch, wash.

brush[2] *n.* brushwood, bushes, ground cover, scrub, shrubs, thicket, undergrowth.

brush[3] *n.* clash, conflict, confrontation, encounter, fight, fracas, incident, run-in, scrap, skirmish, tussle.

bud *n.* embryo, germ, shoot, sprig, sprout. *v.* burgeon, develop, grow, shoot, sprout.

bulky *adj.* big, colossal, cumbersome, enormous, heavy, hefty, huge, hulking, immense, large, mammoth, massive, massy,

ponderous, substantial, voluminous, weighty.

burn *v.* blaze, brand, cauterize, char, combust, consume, flame, flare, flash, flicker, fume, glow, ignite, incinerate, kindle, light, scorch, simmer, singe, smoke, smolder, sting, tingle, toast.

busy *adj.* active, assiduous, brisk, diligent, employed, energetic, engaged, engrossed, exacting, full, fussy, hectic, industrious, inquisitive, interfering, lively, meddlesome, meddling, nosy, occupied, officious, persevering, prying, restless, slaving, stirring, strenuous, tireless, tiring, troublesome, versant, working. *v.* absorb, bother, concern, employ, engage, engross, immerse, interest, occupy.

buy *v.* acquire, bribe, corrupt, fix, get, obtain, procure, purchase, square, suborn. *n.* acquisition, bargain, deal, purchase.

by *prep.* along, beside, near, next to, over, past, through, via. *adv.* aside, at hand, away, beyond, close, handy, near, past.

bypass *v.* avoid, circumvent, ignore, neglect, outflank. *n.* detour, ring road.

C

cab *n.* hack, minicab, taxi, taxicab.

cabin *n.* berth, chalet, compartment, cot, cottage, crib, deck-house, hove, hut, lodge, quarters, room, shack, shanty, shed.

calamity *n.* adversity, affliction, cataclysm, catastrophe, desolation, disaster, distress, downfall, misadventure, mischance, misfortune, mishap, reverse, ruin, scourge, tragedy, trial, tribulation, woe, wretchedness.

calculate *v.* aim, cipher, compute, consider, count, determine, enumerate, estimate, figure, gauge, intend, judge, plan, rate, reckon, value, weigh, work out.

calculating *adj.* canny, cautious, contriving, crafty, cunning, designing, devious, manipulative, politic, scheming, sharp, shrewd, sly.

call *v.* announce, appoint, arouse, assemble, awaken, bid, christen, collect, consider, contact, convene, convoke, cry, declare, decree, denominate, designate, dub, elect, entitle, estimate, gather, hail, invite, judge, label, muster, name, ordain, order, phone, proclaim, rally, regard, rouse, shout, style, summon, telephone, term, think, waken, yell. *n.* announcement, appeal, cause, claim, command, cry, demand, excuse, grounds, hail, invitation, justification, need, notice, occasion, order, plea, reason, request, right, ring, scream, shout, signal, summons, supplication, urge, visit, whoop, yell.

calm *adj.* balmy, collected, composed, cool, dispassionate, equable, halcyon, impassive, imperturbable, laid back, mild, pacific, passionless, peaceful, placid, quiet, relaxed, restful, sedate, self-collected, self-possessed, serene, smooth, still, tranquil, unapprehensive, unclouded, undisturbed, unemotional, uneventful, unexcitable, unexcited, unflappable, unmoved, unperturbed, untroubled, windless.

candidate *n.* applicant, aspirant, competitor, contender, contestant, entrant, nominee, possibility, runner, solicitant, suitor.

capital¹ *adj.* cardinal, central, chief, controlling, essential, excellent, find, first, first-rate, foremost, great, important, leading, main, major, overruling, paramount, preeminent, primary, prime, principal, splendid, superb, upper-case.

capital² *n.* assets, cash, finance, finances, financing, fonds, funds, investment(s), means, money, principal, property, resources, stock, wealth, wherewithal.

care *n.* affliction, anxiety, attention, burden, carefulness, caution, charge, circumspection, concern, consideration, control, custody, direction, disquiet, forethought, guardianship, hardship, heed, interest, keeping, leading-strings, management, meticulousness, ministration, pains, perplexity, pressure, protection, prudence, regard, responsibility, solicitude, stress, supervision, tribulation, trouble, vexation, vigilance, ward, watchfulness, woe, worry.

careful *adj.* accurate, alert, attentive, cautious, chary, circumspect, concerned, conscientious, discreet, fastidious, heedful, judicious, meticulous, mindful, painstaking, particular, precise, protective, prudent, punctilious, scrupulous, softly-softly, solicitous, thoughtful, thrifty, vigilant, wary, watchful.

careless *adj.* absent-minded, casual, cursory, derelict, forgetful, heedless, hit-or-miss, inaccurate, incautious, inconsiderate, indiscreet, irresponsible, lackadaisical, messy, neglectful, negligent, nonchalant, offhand, perfunctory, regardless, remiss, slap-dash, slipshod, sloppy, thoughtless, uncaring, unconcerned, unguarded, unmindful, unstudied, unthinking.

caress *v.* cuddle, embrace, fondle, hug, kiss, pet, rub, stroke, touch. *n.* cuddle, embrace, fondle, hug, kiss, pat, stroke.

case¹ *n.* box, cabinet, canister, capsule, carton, chest, container, cover, covering, crate, envelope, holder, receptacle, suitcase, trunk. *v.* encase, enclose, skin.

case² *n.* argument, circumstances, condition, context, contingency, dilemma, event, example, illustration, instance, occasion, occurrence, plight, point, position, predicament, situation, specimen, state, thesis. *v.* investigate, reconnoiter.

case³ *n.* action, argument, cause, dispute, lawsuit, proceedings, process, suit, trial.

cast¹ *v.* abandon, add, allot, appoint, assign, bestow, calculate, categorize, choose, chuck, compute, deposit, diffuse, distribute, drive, drop, emit, figure, fling, forecast, form, found, give, hurl, impel, launch, lob, model, mold, name, pick, pitch, project, radiate, reckon, reject, scatter, select, set, shape, shed, shy, sling, spread, throw, thrust, toss, total. *n.* air, appearance, complexion, demeanor, fling, form, lob, look, manner, mien, quality, semblance, shade, stamp, style, throw, thrust, tinge, tone, toss, turn.

cast² *n.* actors, artistes, characters, company, dramatis personae, entertainers, performers, players, troupe.

casual *adj.* accidental, apathetic, blasé, chance, contingent, cursory, fortuitous, incidental, indifferent, informal, insouciant, irregular, lackadaisical, negligent, nonchalant, occasional, offhand, perfunctory, random, relaxed, serendipitous, stray, unceremonious, uncertain, unconcerned, unexpected, unforeseen, unintentional, unpremeditated.

cease *v.* call a halt, call it a day, conclude, culminate, desist, die, discontinue, end, fail, finish, halt, pack in, poop out, refrain, stay, stop, terminate.

celebrate *v.* bless, commemorate, commend, emblazon, eulogize, exalt, extol, glorify, honor, keep, laud, live it up, observe, perform, praise, proclaim, publicize, rejoice, reverence, solemnize, toast, wassail, whoop it up.

center *n.* bull's-eye, core, crux, focus, heart, hub, mid, middle, mid-point, nucleus, pivot. *v.* cluster, concentrate, converge, focus, gravitate, hinge, pivot, revolve.

certain *adj.* ascertained, assured, bound, conclusive, confident, constant, convinced, convincing, decided, definite, dependable, destined, determinate, established, express, fated, fixed, incontrovertible, individual, indubitable, ineluctable, inescapable, inevitable, inexorable, irrefutable, known, one, particular, plain, positive, precise, regular, reliable, resolved, satisfied, settled, some, special, specific, stable, steady, sure, true, trustworthy, undeniable, undoubted, unequivocal, unfailing, unmistakable, unquestionable, valid.

certify *v.* ascertain, assure, attest, authentic, authorize, aver, avow, confirm, corroborate, declare, endorse, evidence, guarantee, notify, show, testify, validate, verify, vouch, witness.

character[1] *n.* attributes, bent, caliber, cast, complexion, constitution, disposition, feature, honor, individuality, integrity, kidney, make-up, nature, peculiarity, personality, physiognomy, position, quality, rank, rectitude, reputation, stamp, status, strength, temper, temperament, type, uprightness.

character[2] *n.* card, customer, eccentric, fellow, guy, individual, joker, oddball, oddity, original, part, person, persona, portrayal, role, sort, type.

character[3] *n.* cipher, device, emblem, figure, hieroglyph, ideogram, ideograph, letter, logo, mark, rune, sign, symbol, type.

cheat *v.* baffle, bamboozle, check, chisel, deceive, defeat, defraud, deprive, double-cross, dupe, finagle, fleece, foil, fool, frustrate, fudge, hoax, hocus, hoodwink, mislead, prevent, queer, rip off, screw, short-change, skin, swindle, thwart, touch, trick, trim, victimize. *n.* artifice, bilker, cheater, chouse, deceit, deceiver, deception, dodger, double-crosser, extortioner, fraud, grifter, impostor, imposture, knave, rogue, shark, sharp, swindle, swindler, trickery, trickster, welsher.

check[1] *v.* compare, confirm, examine, give the onceover, inspect, investigate, monitor, note, probe, research, scrutinize, study, test, verify. *n.* audit, examination, inspection, investigation, research, scrutiny, tab, test.

check[2] *v.* arrest, bar, blame, bridle, chide, control, curb, damp, delay, halt, hinder, impede, inhibit, limit, obstruct, pause, rebuke, repress, reprimand, reprove, restrain, retard, scold, stop, thwart. *n.* blow, constraint, control, curb, damp, damper, disappointment, frustration, hindrance, impediment, inhibition, limitation, obstruction, rejection, restraint, reverse, setback, stoppage.

cheerful *adj.* animated, blithe, bright, bucked, buoyant, cheery, chipper, contented, enlivening, enthusiastic, eupeptic, gay, genial, glad, gladsome, happy, hearty, jaunty, jolly, jovial, joyful, joyous, light-hearted, lightsome, light-spirited, merry, optimistic, perky, pleasant, sparking,

sprightly, sunny, upbeat, winsome.

chiefly *adv.* especially, essentially, for the most part, generally, mainly, mostly, predominantly, primarily, principally, usually.

choice *n.* alternative, choosing, decision, dilemma, discrimination, election, espousal, opting, option, pick, preference, say, selection, variety. *adj.* best, dainty, elect, élite, excellent, exclusive, exquisite, hand-picked, nice, plum, precious, prime, prize, rare, select, special, superior, uncommon, unusual, valuable.

chore *n.* burden, duty, errand, job, stint, task, trouble.

circle *n.* area, assembly, band, bounds, circumference, clique, disc, enclosure, field, group, orbit, perimeter, revolution, ring, round, set, society, sphere.

circumference *n.* border, boundary, bounds, circuit, edge, extremity, fringe, limits, margin, outline, perimeter, periphery, rim, verge.

civil *adj.* accommodating, affable, civic, civilized, complaisant, courteous, courtly, domestic, home, interior, internal, internecine, lay, municipal, obliging, polished, polite, political, refined, secular, temporal, urbane, well-bred, well-mannered.

claim *v.* affirm, allege, arrogate, ask, assert, challenge, collect, demand, exact, hold, insist, maintain, need, profess, request, require, state, take, uphold. *n.* affirmation, allegation, application, assertion, call, demand, insistence, petition, pretension, privilege, protestation, request, requirement, right, title.

clarify *v.* cleanse, define, elucidate, explain, gloss, illuminate, purify, refine, resolve, shed/throw light on, simplify.

classic *adj.* abiding, ageless, archetypal, best, characteristic, chaste, consummate, deathless, definitive, enduring, established, excellent, exemplary, finest, first-rate, ideal, immortal, lasting, master, masterly, model, quintessential, refined, regular, restrained, standard, time-honored, traditional, typical, undying, usual.

classify *v.* arrange, assort, catalog, categorize, codify, digest, dispose, distribute, file, grade, pigeon-hole, rank, sort, systematize, tabulate.

clear *adj.* apparent, bright, coherent, comprehensible, distinct, empty, evident, explicit, free, guiltless, innocent, lucid, manifest, obvious, positive, pronounced, pure, sharp, sunny, translucent, unambiguous, unquestionable. *v.* absolve, acquit, clarify, clean, emancipate, erase, excuse, exonerate, free, liberate, refine, unclog, vindicate.

climax *n.* acme, apogee, culmination, head, height, high point, highlight, orgasm, peak, summit, top, zenith.

clip¹ *v.* crop, curtail, cut, dock, pare, prune, shear, shorten, snip, trim.

clip² *v.* box, clout, cuff, hit, knock, punch, slap, smack, sock, thump, wallop, whack.

clip³ *n.* gallop, lick, rate, speed.

clip⁴ *v.* attach, fasten, fix, hold, pin, staple.

close¹ *v.* bar, block, cease, choke, clog, cloture, complete, conclude, confine, connect, cork, couple, culminate, discontinue, end, fill, finish, fuse, grapple, join, lock, mothball, obstruct, plug, seal, secure, shut, stop, terminate, unite, wind up.

close² *adj.* adjacent, adjoining, airless, confined, congested, crowded, earnest, hard by, impending, intimate, near, nearby, oppressive, packed, reserved, reticent, secret, stifling, suffocating, tight, tight-fisted, uncommunicative.

cloth *n.* dishcloth, duster, fabric, facecloth, material, rag, stuff, textiles, tissue, towel.

clumsy *adj.* awkward, blundering, bumbling, bungling, crude, ham-handed, inept, rough, uncoordinated, ungraceful, unwieldy.

collection *n.* accumulation, anthology, assortment, compilation, conglomeration, crowd, group, hoard, stockpile.

colorful *adj.* bright, brilliant, distinctive, graphic, intense, interesting, jazzy, kaleidoscopic, lively, motley, multicolored, parti-colored, picturesque, psychedelic, rich, stimulating, unusual, variegated, vibrant, vivid.

comely *adj.* attractive, beautiful, fair, good-looking, handsome, lovely, pleasing, pretty, wholesome, winsome.

comfort *v.* alleviate, assuage, cheer, console, ease, encourage, enliven, gladden, hearten, inspirit, invigorate, reassure, refresh, relieve, solace, soothe, strengthen.

command *v.* bid, charge, compel, direct, dominate, enjoin, govern, head, lead, manage, order, reign over, require, rule, supervise, sway.

commence *v.* begin, embark on, inaugurate, initiate, open, originate, start.

commend *v.* acclaim, applaud, approve, commit, compliment, extol, praise, recommend.

common *adj.* commonplace, communal, conventional, familiar, hackneyed, ordinary, pedestrian, plain, prevailing, regular, routine, standard, trite, universal, usual, vulgar, widespread.

compete *v.* battle, challenge, contend, contest, duel, emulate, fight, oppose, rival, strive, struggle, tussle, vie.

competence *n.* ability, adequacy, appropriateness, aptitude, capability, capacity, expertise, facility, fitness, proficiency, skill, suitability, technique.

complete *v.* accomplish, achieve, cap, clinch, close, conclude, consummate, crown, discharge, do, effect, end, execute, finalize, finish, fulfill, perfect, perform, realize, settle, terminate, wind-up.

compromise *v.* adapt, adjust, agree, arbitrate, bargain, concede, make concessions, negotiate, retire, retreat, settle.

compute *v.* assess, calculate, count, enumerate, estimate, evaluate, figure, measure, rate, reckon, sum, tally, total.

computer *n.* adding machine, analog computer, calculator, data processor, digital computer, mainframe, processor, word processor.

conceal *v.* bury, camouflage, cloak, cover, disguise, dissemble, hide, keep, dark, mask, obscure, screen, secrete, shelter, sink, smother, submerge, suppress, veil.

concede *v.* accept, acknowledge, admit, allow, cede, confess, forfeit, grant, own, recognize, relinquish, sacrifice, surrender, yield.

conceive *v.* appreciate, apprehend, believe, comprehend, contrive, create, design, develop, devise, envisage, fancy, form, formulate, germinate, grasp, imagine, invent, originate, produce, project, purpose, realize, suppose, think, understand, visualize.

concern *n.* affair, anxiety, business, care, consideration, corporation, distress, enterprise, interest, involvement, job, organization, relevance, responsibility, stake, task, uneasiness, worry.

concerning *prep.* about, apropos of, as regards, germane to, in regard to, in the matter of, re, regarding, relating to, relevant to, respecting, touching, with reference to, with regard to.

conclude *v.* accomplish, assume, cease, clinch, close, complete, consummate, culminate, decide, deduce, determine, effect, end, establish, finish, fix, gather, infer, judge, opine, reckon, resolve, settle, suppose, surmise, terminate.

conduct *v.* accompany, acquit, act, administer, attend, bear, behave, carry, chair, comport, control, convoy, demean, deport, direct, escort, govern, guide, handle, lead, manage, orchestrate, organize, pilot, regulate, run, solicit, steer, supervise, transact, usher.

confidential *adj.* classified, close, closed, faithful, familiar, hush-hush, in camera, intimate, private, privy, secret, tête-à-tête, trusted, trustworthy, trusty.

confine *v.* bind, bound, cage, chamber, circumscribe, constrain, cramp, crib, enclose, immure, imprison, incarcerate, inhibit, intern, keep, keep prisoner, limit, mew, repress, restrain, restrict, shackle, shut up, thirl, trammel.

confirm *v.* approve, assure, attest, authenticate, back, buttress, clinch, corroborate, endorse, establish, evidence, fix, fortify, homologate, prove, ratify, reinforce, sanction, settle, strengthen, substantiate, support, validate, verify, witness to.

conflict *v.* battle, clash, collide, combat, contend, contest, contradict, differ, disagree, fight, interfere, oppose, strive, struggle, war, wrangle.

conform *v.* accommodate, accord, adapt, adjust, agree, assimilate, comply, correspond, follow, harmonize, match, obey, quadrate, square, suit, tally, yield.

confront *v.* accost, address, beard, brave, challenge, defy, encounter, face, front, oppose.

confuse *v.* baffle, befuddle, bewilder, confound, disconcert, disorientate, fluster, maze, mix up, mystify, nonplus, perplex, puzzle, upset.

congregate *v.* accumulate, assemble, bunch, clump, cluster, collect, concentrate, conglomerate, convene, converge, convoke, crowd, flock, foregather, gather, mass, meet, muster, rally, rendezvous, throng.

connect *v.* affix, ally, associate, cohere, combine, concatenate, couple, fasten, join, link, relate, unite.

consent *v.* accede, acquiesce, admit, agree, allow, comply, concede, concur, yield.

consequently *adv.* accordingly, consequentially, ergo, hence, inferentially, necessarily, subsequently, therefore, thus.

considerate *adj.* attentive, charitable, circumspect, concerned, discreet, forbearing, gracious, kind, kindly, mindful, obliging, patient, tactful, thoughtful, unselfish.

consistent *adj.* agreeing, compatible, congruous, constant, dependable, harmonious, persistent, regular, steady, unchanging, uniform.

conspire *v.* cabal, collude, confederate, contrive, cooperate, devise, hatch, intrigue, maneuver, plot, scheme, treason.

contact *v.* approach, call, get hold of,

notify, phone, reach, ring.

contaminate *v.* adulterate, befoul, corrupt, debase, defile, infect, pollute, sully, taint, tarnish.

contempt *n.* condescension, contemptuousness, contumely, derision, despite, disdain, disgrace, dishonor, disregard, disrespect, humiliation, loathing, mockery, neglect, scorn, shame, slight.

content *n.* burden, capacity, essence, gist, ideas, load, matter, meaning, measure, significance, size, subject, matter, substance, text, thoughts, volume.

contented *adj.* cheerful, comfortable, complacent, content, glad, gratified, happy, placid, pleased, relaxed, satisfied, serene, thankful.

contest *n.* affray, altercation, battle, combat, competition, conflict, controversy, debate, discord, dispute, encounter, fight, game, match, olympiad, set-to, shock, struggle, tournament, trial, *v.* argue, against, challenge, compete, contend, debate, deny, dispute, doubt, fight, litigate, oppose, question, refute, strive, vie.

contradict *v.* belie, challenge, contravene, controvert, counter, counteract, deny, disaffirm, dispute, gainsay, impugn, negate, oppose.

contrast *v.* compare, differ, differentiate, discriminate, distinguish, oppose, set off.

contribute *v.* add, afford, bestow, conduce, donate, furnish, give, help, kick in, lead, provide, subscribe, supply, tend.

controversy *n.* altercation, argument, contention, debate, disagreement, discussion, dispute, dissension, polemic, quarrel, squabble, strife, war of words, wrangle, wrangling.

conventional *adj.* accepted, arbitrary, bourgeois, common, commonplace, copybook, correct, customary, decorous, expected, formal, habitual, hackneyed, hidebound, nomic, normal, ordinary, orthodox, pedestrian, prevailing, prevalent, proper, prosaic, regular, ritual, routine, run-of-the-mill, standard, stereotyped, straight, stylized, traditional, unoriginal, uptight, usual, wonted.

conversation *n.* chat, chitchat, colloquy, communication, communion, confab, confabulation, conference, converse, dialogue, discourse, discussion, exchange, gossip, intercourse, interlocution, powwow, tête-à-tête.

convict *v.* attaint, condemn, imprison, sentence. *n.* con, criminal, culprit, felon, jailbird, lag, malefactor, prisoner.

cool *adj.* aloof, apathetic, calm, chilly,

composed, deliberate, frigid, imperturbable, laid-back, level-headed, lukewarm, placid, pleasant, relaxed, reserved, self-possessed, stand-offish, together, unexcited, urbane. *v.* abate, allay, assuage, calm, chill, dampen, freeze, lessen, moderate, quiet, refrigerate, temper.

cooperate *v.* abet, aid, assist, collaborate, conspire, help, play along, play ball.

copy *v.* ape, borrow, counterfeit, crib, duplicate, echo, emulate, facsimile, follow, imitate, mimic, mirror, parrot, photocopy, plagiarize, replicate, reproduce, simulate, transcribe.

correct *v.* adjust, admonish, amend, blue-pencil, chasten, chastise, chide, debug, discipline, rectify, reform, reprimand, reprove, right.

correspond *v.* accord, agree, answer, coincide, communicate, complement, concur, conform, correlate, dovetail, fit, harmonize, match, square, tally, write.

cost *n.* amount, charge, damage, deprivation, detriment, disbursement, expenditure, expense, figure, harm, hurt, injury, loss, outlay, payment, penalty, price, rate, sacrifice, worth.

council *n.* assembly, board, cabinet, committee, congress, panel, parliament, syndicate, synod.

counsel *v.* admonish, advise, advocate, caution, direct, exhort, guide, instruct, recommend, suggest, urge, warn.

courage *n.* boldness, bravery, daring, fearlessness, fortitude, grit, guts, heroism, mettle, nerve, spirit, spunk, valor.

courteous *adj.* affable, civil, courtly, debonair, elegant, gallant, gracious, polished, polite, refined, respectful, urbane, well-bred, well-mannered.

covert *adj.* clandestine, concealed, disguised, dissembled, hidden, private, secret, sneaky, stealthy, subreptitious, surreptitious, ulterior, under the table, underhand, unsuspected, veiled.

cower *v.* cringe, crouch, flinch, grovel, quail, shake, shiver, shrink, skulk, tremble.

creed *n.* articles, belief, canon, credo, doctrine, dogma, faith, persuasion, principles, tenets.

criminal *n.* con, convict, crook, culprit, delinquent, felon, jail-bird, law-breaker, malefactor, offender, sinner, transgressor. *adj.* bent, corrupt, crooked, culpable, felonious, illegal, immoral, indictable, lawless, malfeasant, nefarious, scandalous, senseless, unlawful, wrong.

critic *n.* analyst, animadverter, arbiter, attacker, authority, carper, caviler, censor,

censurer, commentator, connoisseur, detractor, expert, expositor, fault-finder, judge, knocker, pundit, reviewer, reviler, vilifier.

crooked[1] *adj.* bent, corrupt, crafty, criminal, deceitful, discreditable, dishonest, dishonorable, dubious, fraudulent, illegal, knavish, nefarious, questionable, shady, shifty, treacherous, underhand, unethical, unlawful, unprincipled, unscrupulous.

crooked[2] *adj.* angled, askew, asymmetric, awry, bent, bowed, crank, cranky, crippled, curved, deformed, deviating, disfigured, distorted, irregular, lopsided, misshapen, off-center, slanted, slanting, tilted, tortuous, twisted, twisting, uneven, warped, zigzag.

cruel *adj.* barbarous, brutal, callous, cold-blooded, fierce, harsh, heartless, inhuman, merciless, murderous, ruthless, sadistic, savage, unfeeling, unmerciful, vicious.

cultivate *v.* aid, cherish, court, develop, elevate, encourage, enrich, farm, fertilize, forward, foster, further, harvest, help, improve, patronize, plant, plow, polish, prepare, promote, pursue, refine, school, support, tend, till, train, work.

cunning *adj.* adroit, arch, artful, astute, canny, crafty, deep, deft, devious, dexterous, foxy, guileful, imaginative, ingenious, knowing, leery, sharp, shifty, shrewd, skilful, sneaky, subtle, tricky, vulpine, wily.

curious *adj.* bizarre, exotic, extraordinary, inquisitive, interested, mysterious, nosy, novel, peculiar, puzzling, searching, unconventional, unorthodox, unusual, wonderful.

cursory *adj.* brief, careless, casual, desultory, fleeting, hasty, hurried, offhand, passing, perfunctory, quick, rapid, slapdash, slight, summary, superficial.

curve *v.* arc, arch, bend, bow, coil, hook, inflect, spiral, swerve, turn, twist, wind. *n.* arc, bend, camber, curvature, half-moon, incurvation, loop, trajectory, turn.

cut *v.* abbreviate, abridge, carve, castrate, cleave, condense, contract, delete, dissect, divide, edit, engrave, excise, hack, harvest, hew, incise, nick, pare, part, prune, reduce, saw, scissor, sever, slash, slice, split, trim, truncate, whittle, wound.

cynical *adj.* contemptuous, derisive, distrustful, ironic, mephistophelian, mephistophilic, mocking, mordant, pessimistic,, sarcastic, sardonic, skeptical, scoffing, scornful, sharp-tongued, sneering.

D

dab v. blot, daub, pat, stipple, swab, tap, touch, wipe. n. bit, dollop, drop, fingerprint, fleck, flick, pat, peck, smear, smidgen, smudge, speck, spot, stroke, tap, touch, trace.

damage n. destruction, detriment, devastation, harm, hurt, impairment, injury, loss, mischief, mutilation, scathe, suffering. v. deface, harm, hurt, impair, incapacitate, injure, mar, mutilate, play havoc with, play hell with, ruin, spoil, tamper with, weaken, wreck.

damp n. clamminess, dampness, dankness, dew, drizzle, fog, humidity, mist, moisture, vapor, wet. adj. clammy, dank, dewy, dripping, drizzly, humid, misty, moist, muggy, sodden, soggy, wet. v. allay, check, chill, cool, curb, dampen, depress diminish, discourage, dull, inhibit, moderate, restrain, stifle, wet.

dance v. frolic, gambol, hoof it, hop, jig, prance, rock, skip, spin, stomp, sway, swing, tread a measure, whirl. n. ball, hop, kick-up, knees-up, prom, shindig, social.

danger n. hazard, insecurity, jeopardy, liability, menace, peril, precariousness, risk, threat, trouble, venture, vulnerability.

dark adj. angry, black, bleak, cheerless, cloudy, concealed, cryptic, deep, dim, dingy, dismal, drab, dusky, ebony, forbidding, foul, gloomy, glowering, glum, grim, hidden, horrible, ignorant, indistinct, joyless, lightless, midnight, morbid, morose, murky, mysterious, mystic, obscure, ominous, overcast, pitch-black, scowling, secret, shadowy, shady, sinful, sinister, somber, sullen, sunless, swarthy, unenlightened, vile, wicked.

date¹ n. age, epoch, era, period, point in time, stage, time.

date² n. appointment, assignation, engagement, escort, friend, meeting, partner, rendezvous, steady, tryst.

dead¹ adj. apathetic, barren, boring, breathless, cold, deceased, defunct, departed, dull, exhausted, extinct, flat, frigid, glassy, glazed, gone, inactive, inanimate, indifferent, inert, inoperative, insipid, late, lifeless, lukewarm, numb, obsolete, paralyzed, perished, spent, spiritless, stagnant, stale, sterile, stiff, still, tasteless, tired, torpid, unemployed, uninteresting, unprofitable, unresponsive, useless, vapid, wooden, worn out.

dead² adj. absolute, complete, downright, entire, outright, perfect, thorough, total, unqualified, utter. adv. absolutely, completely, entirely, exactly, perfectly, quite, totally.

deal v. allot, apportion, assign, bargain, bestow, dispense, distribute, divide, dole out, give, mete out, negotiate, reward, sell, share, stock, trade, traffic, treat. n. agreement, amount, arrangement, bargain, buy, contract, degree, distribution, extent, hand, pact, portion, quantity, round, share, transaction, understanding.

dear adj. beloved, cherished, close, costly, darling, esteemed, expensive, familiar, favorite, high-priced, intimate, loved, overpriced, precious, pric(e)y, prized, respected, treasured, valued.

death n. annihilation, bane, bereavement, cessation, curtains, decease, demise, departure, destruction, dissolution, downfall, dying, end, eradication, exit, expiration, extermination, extinction, fatality, finish, grave, loss, obliteration, passing, quietus, release, ruin, ruination, undoing.

debate v. argue, cogitate, consider, contend, contest, controvert, deliberate, discuss, dispute, meditate on, mull over, ponder, question, reflect, revolve, ruminate, weigh, wrangle.

debt n. arrears, bill, claim, commitment, debit, due, duty, indebtedness, liability, obligation, score, sin.

deceit n. abuse, artifice, blind, cheat, cheating, chicanery, craftiness, cunning, deceitfulness, deception, duplicity, fake, feint, fraud, fraudulence, guile, hypocrisy, misrepresentation, pretense, ruse, sham, shift, slyness, stratagem, subterfuge, swindle, treachery, trick, trickery, underhandedness, wile.

deceive v. abuse, bamboozle, beguile, betray, camouflage, cheat, cog, con, delude, diddle, disappoint, dissemble, double-cross, dupe, entrap, fool, gag, hoax, impose upon, lead on, mislead, outwit, swindle.

decide v. adjudge, adjudicate, , choose, conclude, decree, determine, dijudicate, elect, end, fix, judge, opt, purpose, reach a decision, resolve, settle.

decisive adj. absolute, conclusive, critical, crucial, crunch, decided, definite, definitive, determinate, determined, fateful, final, firm, forceful, forthright, incisive, influential, momentous, positive, resolute, significant, strong-minded, supreme, trenchant.

declare v. affirm, announce, assert, attest, aver, avouch, avow, certify, claim, confess, confirm, convey, disclose, maintain, manifest, nuncupate, proclaim, profess, pronounce, reveal, show, state, swear, testify, validate, witness.

decline¹ *v.* balk, decay, decrease, degenerate, deteriorate, droop, dwindle, ebb, fade, fall, fall off, flag, forgo, languish, lessen, shrink, sink, turn down, wane, weaken, worsen.

decline² *v.* descend, dip, sink, slant, slope. *n.* brae, declination, declivity, descent, deviation, dip, divergence, hill, incline, obliqueness, obliquity, slope.

decorate¹ *v.* adorn, beautify, bedeck, color, deck, do up, embellish, enrich, furbish, grace, impearl, ornament, paint, paper, prettify, renovate, tart up, trick out, trim, wallpaper.

decorate² *v.* bemedal, cite, crown, garland, honor.

decoy *n.* attraction, bait, ensnarement, enticement, inducement, lure, pretence, roper (-in), trap. *v.* allure, attract, bait, beguile, deceive, draw, ensnare, entice, entrap, inveigle, lead, lure, seduce, tempt.

decrease *v.* abate, ablate, contract, curtail, cut down, decline, diminish, drop, dwindle, ease, fall off, lessen, lower, peter out, reduce, shrink, slacken, slim, subside, taper, wane.

dedicate *v.* address, assign, bless, commit, consecrate, devote, give over to, hallow, inscribe, offer, pledge, present, sacrifice, sanctify, set apart, surrender.

deep *adj.* abstruse, acute, astute, bass, booming, bottomless, broad, canny, cryptic, cunning, dark, designing, devious, esoteric, extreme, far, rave, great, hidden, immersed, insidious, intense, learned, lost, low, low-pitched, obscure, penetrating, preoccupied, profound, rapt, rich, sagacious, scheming, secret, shrewd, sonorous, strong, unfathomable, vivid, wide, wise, yawning.

defeat *v.* beat, best, conquer, crush, disappoint, down, foil, frustrate, overpower, overthrow, overwhelm, quell, repulse, rout, ruin, subdue, thwart, trounce, vanquish. *n.* beating, conquest, disappointment, discomfiture, failure, overthrow, rebuff, repulse, reverse, rout, setback, thwarting, trouncing, vanquishment, Waterloo.

defect *n.* absence, blemish, bug, default, deficiency, error, failing, fault, flaw, frailty, hamartia, imperfection, inadequacy, lack, mistake, shortcoming, spot, taint, want, weakness. *v.* apostatize, break faith, desert, rebel, revolt.

defend *n.* assert, bulwark, champion, contest, cover, endorse, espouse, fortify, guard, justify, maintain, plead, preserve, protect, safeguard, screen, secure, shelter, shield, speak up for, stand, by, stand up for, support, sustain, uphold, vindicate, watch over.

defer¹ *v.* adjourn, delay, hold over, postpone, procrastinate, prorogue, protract, put off, put on ice, shelve, suspend, waive.

defer² *v.* accede, bow, capitulate, comply, give way, kowtow, respect, submit, yield.

define *v.* bound, characterize, circumscribe, delimit, delimitate, delineate, demarcate, describe, designate, detail, determine, explain, expound, interpret, limit, mark out, outline, specify, spell out.

definite *adj.* assured, certain, clear, clearcut, decided, determined, exact, explicit, express, fixed, guaranteed, marked, obvious, particular, positive, precise, settled, specific, substantive, sure.

definition¹ *n.* clarification, delimitation, delineation, demarcation, description, determination, elucidation, explanation, exposition, interpretation, outlining, settling.

definition² *n.* clarity, clearness, contrast, distinctness, focus, precision, sharpness.

defunct *adj.* dead, deceased, departed, expired, extinct, gone, inoperative, invalid, kaput, non-existent, obsolete, passé.

defy *v.* baffle, beard, beat, brave, challenge, confront, contemn, dare, defeat, despise, disregard, elude, face, flout, foil, frustrate, provoke, repel, repulse, resist, scorn, slight, spurn, thwart, withstand.

delicate *adj.* choice, dainty, deft, detailed, diplomatic, discreet, discriminating, elegant, exquisite, faint, fine, flimsy, fragile, frail, graceful, hazardous, minute, pastel, precarious, precise, prudish, pure, refined, risky, savory, scrupulous, sensible, sensitive, sickly, skilled, slender, slight, soft, squeamish, sticky, subdued, subtle, tactful, tender, ticklish, touchy, weak.

delicious *adj.* agreeable, ambrosial, ambrosian, appetizing, charming, choice, dainty, delectable, delightful, enjoyable, entertaining, exquisite, flavorsome, luscious, mouthwatering, palatable, pleasant, pleasing, savory, scrumptious, tasty, toothsome, yummy.

delight *n.* bliss, ecstasy, enjoyment, felicity, gladness, gratification, happiness, heaven, joy, jubilation, pleasure, rapture, transport.

deliver *v.* acquit, administer, aim, announce, bear, bring, carry, cart, cede, commit, convey, deal, declare, direct, discharge, dispense, distribute, emancipate, feed, free, give, give forth, give up, grant, hand over, inflict, launch, liberate, loose, make over, pass, present, proclaim, pronounce, publish, ransom, read, redeem, release, relinquish, rescue, resign, save, strike, supply, surrender, throw, transfer, transport, turn over, utter, yield.

demand v. ask, call for, challenge, claim, exact, expect, inquire, insist on, interrogate, involve, necessitate, need, order, question, request, require, take, want.

demean v. abase, condescend, debase, degrade, deign, descend, humble, lower, stoop.

demeanor n. air, bearing, behavior, carriage, comportment, conduct, deportment, manner, mien, port.

demolish v. annihilate, bulldoze, consume, defeat, destroy, devour, dilapidate, dismantle, down, eat, flatten, gobble, gulp, guzzle, knock down, level, overthrow, overturn, pull down, pulverize, raze, ruin, tear down, undo, wreck.

demonstrate[1] v. describe, display, establish, evidence, evince, exhibit, explain, expound, illustrate, indicate, manifest, prove, show, substantiate, teach, testify to.

demonstrate[2] v. march, parade, picket, protest, rally, sit in.

den n. cave, cavern, cloister, cubby-hole, earth, haunt, hide-away, hide-out, hole, lair, retreat, sanctuary, sanctum, set(t), shelter, study.

deny v. abjure, begrudge, contradict, decline, disaffirm, disagree with, disallow, disavow, discard, disclaim, disown, disprove, forbid, gainsay, negative, oppose, rebuff, recant, refuse, refute, reject, renounce, repudiate, revoke, traverse, turn down, veto, withhold.

depart v. absent oneself, decamp, deviate, differ, digress, disappear, diverge, escape, exit, go, leave, levant, make off, migrate, quit, remove, retire, retreat, set forth, stray, swerve, take one's leave, toddle, vanish, vary, veer, withdraw.

dependable adj. certain, conscientious, faithful, gilt-edged, honest, reliable, responsible, steady, sure, trustworthy, trusty, unfailing.

depict v. caricature, characterize, delineate, describe, detail, draw, illustrate, limn, narrate, outline, paint, picture, portray, render, reproduce, sculpt, sketch, trace.

deposit[1] v. drop, dump, lay, locate, park, place, precipitate, put, settle, sit. n. accumulation, alluvium, deposition, dregs, hypostasis, lees, precipitate, sediment, silt.

deposit[2] v. amass, bank, consign, depone,

entrust, file, hoard, lodge, reposit, save, store. n. bailment, down payment, installment, money, part payment, pledge, retainer, security, stake, warranty.

depress v. burden, cheapen, chill, damp, daunt, deject, depreciate, devaluate, devalue, devitalize, diminish, discourage, dishearten, enervate, exhaust, flatten, hip, impair, lessen, level, lower, oppress, overburden, press, reduce, sadden, sap, squash, tire, undermine, upset, weaken, weary.

depression[1] n. blues, decline, dejection, despair, despondency, doldrums, dolefulness, downheartedness, dullness, dumps, examination, gloominess, glumness, hard times, heart-heaviness, hopelessness, inactivity, low spirits, lowness, mal du siècle, megrims, melancholia, melancholy, recession, sadness, slump, stagnation, vapors.

depression[2] n. basin, bowl, cavity, concavity, dent, dimple, dint, dip, dish, excavation, fossa, fossula, fovea, foveola, hollow, hollowness, impression indentation, pit, sag, sink, umbilicus, valley.

deprive v. amerce, bereave, denude, deny, despoil, dispossess, divest, expropriate, mulct, rob, starve, strip.

descend v. alight, arrive, assail, assault, attack, condescend, degenerate, deign, derive, deteriorate, develop, dip, dismount, drop, fall, gravitate, incline, invade, issue, leap, originate, plummet, plunge, pounce, proceed, raid, sink, slant, slope, spring, stem, stoop, subside, swoop, tumble.

describe v. characterize, define, delineate, depict, detail, draw, enlarge on, explain, express, illustrate, mark out, narrate, outline, portray, present, recount, relate, report, sketch, specify, tell, trace.

desert[1] n. solitude, vacuum, vast, void, waste, wasteland, wilderness, wilds. adj. arid, bare, barren, desolate, dry, infertile, lonely, solitary, sterile, uncultivated, uninhabited, unproductive, untilled, waste, waterless, wild.

desert[2] v. abandon, abscond, apostatize, backslide, betray, decamp, deceive, defect, forsake, give up, jilt, leave, leave in the lurch, maroon, quit, rat on, relinquish, renounce, resign, strand, vacate.

desert[3] n. come-uppance, demerit, deserts, due, guerdon, meed, merit, payment, recompense, remuneration, requital, retribution, return, reward, right, virtue, worth.

design n. aim, arrangement, blueprint, composition, configuration, conformation, construction, contrivance, draft, figure, form, goal, guide, intent, meaning, model, objective, outline, pattern, plan, plot, project, prototype, scheme, shape, sketch, structure, style, target, undertaking. *v.* aim, conceive, construct, create, describe destine, develop, devise, draft, draw, draw up, fashion, form, intend, invent, make, mean, model, originate, outline, plan, project, propose, purpose, scheme, shape, sketch, structure, tailor, trace.

designate *v.* allot, appoint, assign, bill, call, characterize, choose, christen, deem, define, delegate, denominate, denote, depute, describe, docket, dub, earmark, entitle, indicate, label, name, nickname, nominate, select, show, specify, stipulate, style, term, ticket, title.

desire *v.* ask, aspire to, beg, covet, crave, desiderata, entreat, fancy, hanker after, hunger for, importune, lack, long for, need, request, solicit, want, wish for, yearn for, *n.* appeal, appetite, ardor, aspiration, covetousness, craving, cupidity, entreaty, greed, lasciviousness, lechery, libido, longing, lust, lustfulness, need, passion, petition, request, want, wish, yearning, yen.

desist *v.* abstain, break off, cease, come to a halt, discontinue, end, forbear, give over, give up, halt, leave off, pause, peter out, refrain, remit, stop, suspend.

despise *v.* abhor, condemn, deplore, deride, detest, disdain, dislike, disregard, ignore, loathe, revile, scorn, slight, spurn, undervalue, vilipend.

despondent *adj.* blue, broken-hearted, dejected, depressed, despairing, disconsolate, discouraged, disheartened, dispirited, doleful, down, downcast, downhearted, gloomy, glum, hopeless, inconsolable, low, low-spirited, melancholy, miserable, morose, mournful, overwhelmed, sad, sorrowful, wretched.

destitute *adj.* bankrupt, beggared, bereft, deficient, depleted, deprived, devoid of, distressed, down and out, impecunious, impoverished, indigent, innocent of, insolvent, lacking, necessitous, needy, penniless, penurious, poor, poverty-stricken, strapped, wanting.

destroy *v.* annihilate, break, canker, crush, demolish, destruct, devastate, dismantle, dispatch, eliminate, eradicate, extinguish, extirpate, gut, kill, level, nullify, overthrow, ravage, raze, ruin, sabotage, scuttle, shatter, slay, slight, smash, thwart, torpedo, undermine, undo, vaporize, waste, wreck, zap.

detail *n.* aspect, attribute, complexity, complication, component, count, elaborateness, elaboration, element, fact, factor, feature, ingredient, intricacy, item, meticulousness, nicety, particular, particularity, point, refinement, respect, specify, specificity, technicality, thoroughness, triviality. *v.* allocate, appoint, assign, catalog, charge, commission, delegate, delineate, depict, depute, describe, detach, enumerate, individualize, itemize, list, narrate, particularize, portray, recount, rehearse, relate, send, specify.

detect *v.* ascertain, catch, descry, discern, disclose, discover, distinguish, find, identify, note, notice, observe, perceive, recognize, reveal, scent, sight, spot, spy, track down, uncover, unmask.

determine *v.* affect, arbitrate, ascertain, certify, check, choose, conclude, control, decide, detect, dictate, direct, discover, elect, end, establish, finish, fix, govern, guide, identify, impel, impose, incline, induce, influence, intend, lead, learn, modify, ordain, point, purpose, regulate, resolve, rule, settle, shape, terminate, undertake, verify.

develop *v.* advance, amplify, augment, begin, bloom, blossom, branch out, breed, broaden, commence, contract, cultivate, diversify, elaborate, enlarge, ensue, establish, evolve, expand, flourish, follow, form, generate, grow, happen, invent, make headway, mature, move on, originate, progress, promote, prosper, result, ripen, sprout, start, unfold.

development *n.* advancement, blossoming, change, detail, elaboration, event, evolution, expansion, growth, happening, improvement, increase, issue, maturation, maturity, occurrence, outcome, phenom-enon, progress, progression, promotion, refinement, result, ripening, situation, spread, unfolding, unraveling, up-building, upshot.

devilish *adj.* accursed, black-hearted, damnable, demoniac, demoniacal, diabolic, diabolical, execrable, fiendish, hellish, impious, infernal, iniquitous, mischievous, monstrous, nefarious, satanic, wicked.

devise *v.* arrange, compass, compose, conceive, concoct, construct, contrive, design, excogitate, forge, form, formulate, frame, imagine, invent, plan, plot, prepare, project, scheme, shape.

devote *v.* allocate, allot, apply, appropriate, assign, commit, consecrate, dedicate, enshrine, give oneself, pledge, reserve, sacrifice, set apart, set aside, surrender.

devour v. absorb, annihilate, bolt, consume, cram, destroy, dispatch, down, eat, engulf, feast on, feast one's eyes on, gobble, gorge, gormandize, gulp, guzzle, polish off, ravage, relish, revel in, spend, stuff, swallow, waste, wolf.

die v. breathe one's last, croak, decay, decease, decline, depart, desire, disappear, dwindle, ebb, end, expire, fade, finish, kick the bucket, languish, lapse, long for, pass, pass away, pass over, perish, peter out, sink, stop, subside, succumb, suffer, vanish, wane, wilt, wither, yearn.

difference n. argument, change, clash, conflict, contrast, controversy, debate, deviation, disagreement, discordance, discrepancy, disparateness, disparity, dispute, dissimilarity, distinctness, divergence, diversity, exception, idiosyncrasy, particularity, peculiarity, quarrel, remainder, rest, strife, tiff, unlikeness, variation, variety, wrangle.

different adj. altered, assorted, at odds, atypical, bizarre, contrasting, deviating, disparate, dissimilar, distinct, divers, diverse, inconsistent, manifold, many, miscellaneous, multifarious, numerous, peculiar, rare, several, singular, special, strange, sundry, uncommon, unconventional, unique, unusual, varied, various.

difficult adj. abstract, arduous, burdensome, complex, complicated, dark, delicate, formidable, hard, herculean, intricate, involved, knotty, laborious, onerous, painful, perplexing, perverse, problematic, rigid, sticky, stiff, straitened, strenuous, stubborn, thorny, ticklish, tiresome, toilsome, tough, troublesome, trying, unmanageable, uphill, wearisome.

difficulty v. arduousness, awkwardness, complication, dilemma, distress, hang-up, hardship, hurdle, impediment, laboriousness, mess, obstacle, opposition, pain, pitfall, plight, predicament, problem, protest, quandary, scruple, spot, strain, straits, strenuousness, stumbling-block, trial, tribulation, trouble, vexed, question.

dig[1] v. burrow, delve, drive, excavate, go into, gouge, graft, grub, hoe, investigate, jab, mine, penetrate, pierce, poke, probe, prod, punch, quarry, research, scoop, search, spit, thrust, till, tunnel. n. aspersion, barb, crack, cut, gibe, insinuation, insult, jab, jeer, poke, prod, punch, quip, sneer, taunt, thrust, wisecrack.

dig[2] v. adore, appreciate, be into, enjoy, fancy, follow, get a kick out of, get off on, go a bundle on, go for, go overboard about, groove, have the hots for, like, love, understand, warm to.

dignity n. courtliness, decorum, elevation, eminence, excellence, glory, grandeur, gravity, greatness, hauteur, honor, importance, loftiness, majesty, nobility, nobleness, pride, propriety, rank, respectability, self-esteem, self-importance, self-respect, solemnity, standing, stateliness, station, status.

diminish v. abate, bate, belittle, cheapen, contract, curtail, cut, deactivate, decline, decrease, demean, depreciate, devalue, dwindle, ebb, fade, lessen, lower, peter out, recede, reduce, retrench, shrink, shrivel, sink, slacken, subside, taper off, wane, weaken.

dip v. bathe, decline, descend, droop, drop, duck, dunk, fade, fall, immerse, plunge, rinse, sag, scoop, slope, slump, spoon, subside, tilt. n. basin, concoction, decline, depression, dilution, dive, fall, hole, hollow, immersion, incline, infusion, lowering, mixture, plunge, preparation, sag, slip, slope, slump, soaking, solution, suspension, swim.

direct[1] v. address, administer, advise, aim, bid, case, charge, command, conduct, control, dictate, dispose, enjoin, fix, focus, govern, guide, handle, indicate, instruct, intend, label, lead, level, mail, manage, mastermind, mean, order, oversee, point, regulate, route, rule, run, send, show, stage-manage, superintend, superscribe, supervise, train, turn.

direct[2] adj. absolute, blunt, candid, categorical, downright, explicit, express, face-to-face, first-hand, frank, head-on, honest, immediate, man-to-man, matter-of-fact, non-stop, open, outright, outspoken, personal, plain, plain-spoken, point-blank, shortest, sincere, straight, straightforward, through, unambiguous, unbroken, undeviating, unequivocal, uninterrupted.

direction n. address, administration, aim, approach, bearing, bent, bias, charge, command, control, course, current, drift, end, government, guidance, label, leadership, line, management, mark, order, orientation, oversight, path, proclivity, purpose, road, route, superintendence, superscription, supervision, tack, tendency, tenor, track, trend, way.

dirty adj. angry, base, beggarly, begrimed, bitter, blue, clouded, contemptible, corrupt, cowardly, crooked, cruddy, dark, despicable, dishonest, dull, filthy, foul, grubby, ignominious, illegal, indecent, low-down, maculate, mean, messy, miry, mucky, nasty, obscene, off-color, polluted, pornographic, salacious, scruffy, scurvy, shabby, sluttish, smutty, soiled, sordid, squalid, sullied, treacherous, unclean, unfair, unscrupulous, vile, vulgar.

disability *n.* affliction, ailment, complaint, defect, disablement, disorder, disqualification, handicap, impairment, impotency, inability, incapacitation, incapacity, incompetency, infirmity, malady, unfitness, weakness.

disable *v.* cripple, damage, debilitate, disenable, disqualify, enfeeble, hamstring, handicap, immobilize, impair, incapacitate, invalidate, lame, paralyze, prostrate, unfit, unman, weaken.

disagree *v.* altercate, argue, bicker, bother, clash, conflict, contend, contest, contradict, counter, depart, deviate, differ, discomfort, dissent, distress, diverge, fall out, hurt, nauseate, object, oppose, quarrel, run counter to, sicken, spat, squabble, take issue with, tiff, trouble, upset, vary, wrangle.

disappear *v.* cease, dematerialize, depart, dissolve, ebb, end, escape, evanesce, evaporate, expire, fade, flee, fly, go, pass, perish, recede, retire, scarper, vamoose, vanish, wane, withdraw.

disappoint *v.* baffle, balk, chagrin, dash, deceive, defeat, delude, disconcert, disenchant, disgruntle, dishearten, disillusion, dismay, dissatisfy, fail, foil, frustrate, hamper, hinder, let down, miff, sadden, thwart, vex.

disaster *n.* accident, act of God, blow, calamity, cataclysm, catastrophe, curtains, debacle, misfortune, mishap, reverse, ruin, ruination, stroke, tragedy, trouble.

discard *v.* abandon, cashier, cast aside, dispense with, dispose of, ditch, drop, dump, jettison, leave off, reject, relinquish, remove, repudiate, scrap, shed.

discharge *v.* absolve, accomplish, acquit, carry out, detonate, disburden, discard, dismiss, dispense, drum out, eject, emit, empty, execute, expel, explode, exude, fire, free, fulfill, give off, gush, honor, leak, liberate, meet, oust, pardon, pay, perform, release, relieve, remove, sack, satisfy, set off, settle, shoot, unburden, unload, vent, void, volley.

disciple *n.* acolyte, adherent, apostle, believer, convert, devotee, follower, learner, partisan, proselyte, pupil, student, supporter, votary.

disconnect *v.* cut off, detach, disengage, divide, part, separate, sever, uncouple, unhitch, unhook, unlink, unplug, unyoke.

discontinue *v.* abandon, break off, cancel, cease, drop, end, finish, halt, interrupt, pause, quit, stop, suspend, terminate.

discourage *v.* abash, awe, check, chill, cow, curb, damp, dampen, dash, daunt, deject, demoralize, deprecate, depress, deter, discountenance, disfavor, dishearten, dismay, dispirit, dissuade, frighten, hinder, inhibit, intimidate, overawe, prevent, put off, restrain, scare, unman, unnerve.

discover *v.* ascertain, conceive, contrive, descry, design, detect, determine, devise, dig up, discern, disclose, espy, find, invent, learn, light on, locate, notice, originate, perceive, pioneer, realize, recognize, reveal, see, spot, suss out, uncover, unearth.

discreet *adj.* careful, cautious, circumspect, considerate, delicate, diplomatic, discerning, guarded, judicious, politic, prudent, reserved, sagacious, sensible, softly-softly, tactful, wary.

discretion *n.* acumen, care, carefulness, caution, choice, circumspection, consideration, diplomacy, discernment, heedfulness, inclination, judgment, judiciousness, liking, maturity, mind, option, pleasure, predilection, preference, prudence, responsibility, sagacity, tact, volition, wariness, will, wisdom, wish.

discriminating *adj.* acute, astute, critical, cultivated, discerning, discriminant, fastidious, particular, perceptive, selective, sensitive, tasteful.

discrimination[1] *n.* bias, bigotry, favoritism, inequity, intolerance, Jim Crow, prejudice, unfairness.

discuss *v.* argue, confer, consider, consult, converse, debate deliberate, examine, lay heads together, rap.

disease *n.* affection, affliction, ailment, blight, cancer, canker, complaint, condition, contagion, contamination, disorder, distemper, epidemic, epizootic, idiopathy, ill-health, illness, indisposition, infection, infirmity, malady, malaise, murrain, pest, plague, sickness, upset.

disgrace *n.* aspersion, attaint, baseness, blemish, blot, contempt, defamation, degradation, discredit, disesteem, disfavor, dishonor, disrepute, dog-house, ignominy, infamy, obloquy, odium, opprobrium, reproach, scandal, shame, slur, stain, stigma.

disguise *v.* camouflage, cloak, conceal, cover, deceive, dissemble, dissimulate, dress up, explain away, fake, falsify, fudge, hide, mask, misrepresent, screen, secrete, shroud, veil.

disgust *v.* displease, nauseate, offend, outrage, put off, repel, revolt, scandalize, sicken.

dish *n.* bowl, fare, food, plate, platter, ramekin, recipe.

dishonor *v.* abase, blacken, corrupt, debase, debauch, defame, defile, deflower, degrade, demean, discredit, disgrace, disparage, pollute, rape, ravish, seduce, shame, sully.

dislike *n.* animosity, animus, antagonism, antipathy, aversion, detestation, disapprobation, disapproval, disgust, disinclination, displeasure, distaste, enmity, hatred, hostility, loathing, repugnance.

dismiss *v.* ax, banish, bounce, bowler-hat, cashier, chuck, disband, discharge, discount, dispel, disperse, disregard, dissolve, drop, fire, free, give (someone) the push, lay off, let go, oust, reject, release, relegate, remove, repudiate, sack, send packing, set aside, shelve, spurn.

disobedient *adj.* contrary, contumacious, defiant, disorderly, forward, insubordinate, intractable, mischievous, naughty, obstreperous, refactory, unruly, wayward, wilful.

disorder *n.* affliction, ailment, brawl, chaos, clamor, clutter, commotion, complaint, confusion, disarray, disease, disorganization, disturbance, fight, fracas, irregularity, jumble, malady, mess, muddle, quarrel, riot, rumpus, shambles, sickness, tumult, untidiness, uproar.

disorganized *n.* chaos, confusion, disordered, haphazard, jumbled, muddled, shuffled, topsy-turvy, unmethodical, unorganized, unregulated, unsifted, unsorted, unstructured, unsystematic, unsystematized.

disparage *v.* belittle, criticize, decry, defame, degrade, denigrate, deprecate, depreciate, deride, derogate, detract from, discredit, disdain, dishonor, dismiss, malign, minimize, ridicule, run down, scorn, slander, traduce, underestimate, underrate, undervalue, vilify, vilipend.

dispatch¹ *v.* accelerate, conclude, discharge, dismiss, dispose of, expedite, finish, hasten, hurry, perform, quicken, settle,

dispatch² *v.* consign, express, forward, remit, send, transmit. *n.* account, bulletin, communication, document, instruction, item, letter, message, missive, news, piece, report, story.

dispense *v.* administer, allocate, allot, apply, apportion, assign, deal out, direct, disburse, discharge, distribute, dole out, enforce, except, excuse, execute, exempt, exonerate, implement, let off, measure, mete out, mix, operate, prepare, release, relieve, reprieve, share, supply, undertake.

disperse *v.* broadcast, circulate, diffuse, disappear, disband, dismiss, dispel, disseminate, dissipate, dissolve, distribute, drive off, evanesce, melt away, rout, scatter, separate, spread, stew, vanish.

displeasure *n.* anger, annoyance, disapprobation, disapproval, discontent, disfavor, dudgeon, huff, indignation, irritation, offense, pique, resentment, vexation, wrath.

dispose *v.* actuate, adapt, adjust, align, arrange, array, bias, condition, determine, dispone, distribute, fix, group, incline, induce, influence, lay, lead, marshal, motivate, move, order, place, position, predispose, prompt, put, range, rank, regulate, set, settle, situate, stand, tempt.

disprove *v.* answer, confute, contradict, controvert, discredit, explode, expose, invalidate, negate, rebut, refute.

dispute *v.* altercate, argue, brawl, challenge, clash, contend, contest, contradict, controvert, debate, deny, discuss, doubt, gainsay, impugn, litigate, moot, oppugn, quarrel, question, spar, squabble, traverse, wrangle.

disqualify *v.* debar, disable, disentitle, incapacitate, invalidate, preclude, prohibit, rule out, unfit.

disregard *v.* brush aside, cold-shoulder, contemn, despise, discount, disdain, disobey, disparage, ignore, laugh off, make light of, neglect, overlook, pass over, pooh-pooh, slight, snub, turn a blind eye to.

disrespectful *adj.* bad-tempered, cheeky, contemptuous, discourteous, impertinent, impolite, impudent, insolent, insulting, irreverent, rude, uncivil, unmannerly.

dissect *v.* analyze, anatomize, break down, dismember, examine, explore, inspect, investigate, pore over, scrutinize, study.

dissolve *v.* break up, crumble, decompose, destroy, diffuse, disappear, discontinue, disintegrate, disorganize, disperse, dissipate, divorce, dwindle, end, evaporate, fade, flux, fuse, liquefy, loose, melt, overthrow, perish, ruin, separate sever, soften, suspend, thaw, vanish, wind up.

distant *adj.* abroad, afar, aloof, apart, ceremonious, cold, cool, disparate, dispersed, distinct, faint, far, faraway, farflung, far-off, formal, haughty, indirect, indistinct, isolated, obscure, outlying, out-of-the-way, remote, removed, reserved, restrained, reticent, scattered, separate, slight, stand-offish, stiff, unapproachable, uncertain, unfriendly, withdrawn.

distinct *adj.* apparent, clear, clear-cut, decided, definite, detached, different, discrete dissimilar, evident, individual, lucid, manifest, marked, noticeable, obvious, palpable, patent, plain, recognizable, separate, several, sharp, unambiguous, unconnected, unmistakable, well-defined.

distinction¹ *n.* characteristic, contradistinction, contrast, difference, differential, differentiation, discernment, discrimination, dissimilarity, distinctiveness, division, feature, individuality, mark, nuance, particularity, peculiarity, , penetration, perception, quality, separation.

distinction² *n.* account, celebrity, consequence, credit, eminence, excellence, fame, glory, greatness, honor, importance, merit, name, note, prestige, prominence, quality, rank, renown, reputation, repute, significance, superiority, worth.

distinguish *v.* ascertain, categorize, celebrate, characterize, classify, decide, determine, differentiate, dignify, discern, discriminate, honor, immortalize, individualize, judge, know, make out, mark, perceive, pick out, recognize, see, separate, signalize, tell, tell apart.

distort *v.* bend, bias, buckle, color, contort, deform, disfigure, falsify, garble, misrepresent, misshape, pervert, skew, slant, torture, twist, warp, wrench, wrest, wring.

distract *v.* agitate, amuse, beguile, bewilder, confound, confuse, derange, discompose, disconcert, disturb, divert, engross, entertain, faze, harass, madden, occupy, perplex, puzzle, sidetrack, torment, trouble.

distress *n.* adversity, affliction, agony, anguish, anxiety, calamity, depravation, destitution, difficulties, discomfort, grief, hardship, heartache, indigence, katzenjammer, misery, misfortune, need, pain, pauperism, poverty, privation, sadness, sorrow, strait(s), suffering, torment, torture, trial, trouble, woe, worry, wretchedness.

distribute *v.* administer, allocate, allot, apportion, arrange, assign, assort, bestow, carve up, categorize, circulate, class, classify, convey, deal, deliver, diffuse, dish out, dispense, disperse, dispose, disseminate, divide, dole, file, give, group, hand out, mete, scatter, share, spread, strew.

disturb *v.* affray, agitate, alarm, annoy, bother, concuss, confound, confuse, derange, disarrange, discompose, disorder, disorganize, disrupt, distract, distress, excite, fluster, harass, interrupt, muddle, perturb, pester, rouse, ruffle, shake, startle, trouble, unsettle, upset, worry.

diverse *adj.* assorted, different, differing,

discrete, disparate, dissimilar, distinct, divergent, diversified, heterogeneous, manifold, many, miscellaneous, multifarious, multiform, numerous, separate, several, some, sundry, unlike, varied, various, varying.

divert *v.* amuse, avert, beguile, deflect, delight, detract, distract, entertain, gratify, hive off, recreate, redirect, regale, sidetrack, switch, tickle.

divide *v.* alienate, allocate, allot, apportion, arrange, bisect, , break up, categorize, classify, cleave, cut, deal out, detach, disconnect, dispense, distribute, disunite, divvy, estrange, grade, group, part, partition, portion, segment, segregate, separate, sever, share, shear, sort, split, subdivide, sunder.

divine *adj.* angelic, beatific, beautiful, blissful, celestial, consecrated, exalted, excellent, glorious, godlike, heavenly, holy, marvelous, mystical, perfect, rapturous, religious, sacred, sanctified, spiritual, splendid, superhuman, superlative, supernatural, supreme, transcendent, transcendental, wonderful.

divorce *n.* annulment, breach, break, break up, decree nisi, dissolution, rupture, separation, severance, split-up. *v.* annul, cancel, disconnect, dissever, dissociate, dissolve, disunite, divide, part, separate, sever, split up, sunder.

do *v.* accomplish, achieve, act, carry out, cause, complete, create, deceive, discharge, dupe, effect, end, execute, fix, fleece, hoax, implement, make, manage, organize, perform, prepare, present, proceed, produce, put on, render, resolve, satisfy, serve, solve, suffice, suit, swindle, travel, trick, undertake, visit, work, work out.

docile *adj.* amenable, biddable, complaisant, compliant, ductile, manageable, obedient, obliging, pliable, pliant, submissive, teachable, tractable, unprotesting, unquestioning.

dock¹ *n.* boat-yard, harbor, marina, pier, quay, water-front, wharf. *v.* anchor, berth, drop anchor, join up, land, link up, moor, put in, rendezvous, tie up, unite.

dock² *v.* clip, crop, curtail, cut, decrease, deduct, diminish, lessen, reduce, shorten, subtract, truncate, withhold.

doctor *n.* clinician, general practitioner, internist, medic, medical officer, medical practitioner, physician, pill(s).

doctrine *n.* belief, canon, concept, conviction, creed, dogma, ism, opinion, precept, principle, teaching, tenet.

document *n.* certificate, deed, form, instrument, paper, parchment, record, report. *v.* authenticate, back, certify, cite, corroborate, detail, enumerate, instance, list, particularize, prove, substantiate, support, validate, verify.

dodge *v.* avoid, dart, deceive, duck, elude, equivocate, evade, fend off, fudge, hedge, parry, shift, shirk, shuffle, side-step, swerve, swing the lead, trick. *n.* chicane, contrivance, device, feint, machination, maneuver, ploy, ruse, scheme, stratagem, subterfuge, trick, wheeze, wile.

dogma *n.* article, article of faith, belief, conviction, credo, creed, doctrine, opinion, precept, principle, , teaching, tenet.

domain *n.* area, authority, bailiwick, business, concern, demesne, department, discipline, dominion, empire, estate, field, jurisdiction, kingdom, lands, orbit, pidgin, policies, power, province, realm, region, scope, specialty, sphere, sway, territory.

dominate *v.* bestride, control, direct, domineer, dwarf, eclipse, govern, have-the-whip hand, keep under one's thumb, lead, master, monopolize, outshine, overbear, overlook, overrule, overshadow, predominate, prevail, rule, tyrannize.

domineering *adj.* arrogant, authoritarian, autocratic, bossy, coercive, despotic, dictatorial, harsh, high-handed, imperious, iron-handed, magisterial, masterful, oppressive, overbearing, severe, tyrannical.

donate *v.* bequeath, bestow, chip in, confer, contribute, cough up, fork out, give, impart, present, proffer, subscribe.

done *adj.* acceptable, accomplished, advised, agreed, completed, concluded, consummated, conventional, cooked, cooked to a turn, de rigueur, depleted, drained, ended, executed, exhausted, fatigued, finished, OK, over, perfected, proper, ready, realized, settled, spent, terminated, through, used up.

double *adj.* bifold, coupled, diploid, doubled, dual, duple, duplex, duplicate, paired, twice, twin, twofold. *v.* duplicate, enlarge, fold, geminate, grow, increase, magnify, multiply, repeat. *n.* clone, copy, counterpart, dead ringer, dead spit, duplicate, fellow, image, impersonator, lookalike, mate, replica, ringer, spitting image, twin.

doubt *v.* be dubious, be uncertain, demure, discredit, distrust, fear, fluctuate, hesitate, mistrust, query, question, scruple, suspect, vacillate, waver.

doubtless *adv.* apparently, assuredly, certainly, clearly, indisputably, most likely, of course, ostensibly, out of question,

precisely, presumably, probably, seemingly, supposedly, surely, truly, undoubtedly, unquestionably, without doubt.

drab *adj.* cheerless, colorless, dingy, dismal, dreary, dull, flat, gloomy, gray, lackluster, mousy, shabby, somber, uninspired, vapid.

draft¹ *v.* compose, delineate, design, draw, draw up, formulate, outline, plan, sketch. *n.* abstract delineation, outline, plan, protocol, rough, sketch, version.

draft² *n.* bill, check, order, postal order.

draft³ *n.* cup, current, dose, dragging, drawing, drench, drink, flow, haulage, influx, movement, portion, potation, puff, pulling, quantity, traction.

drag *v.* crawl, creep, dawdle, draw, hale, haul, inch, lag, linger, loiter, lug, pull, schlep, shamble, shuffle, straggle, sweep, tow, trail, tug, yank. *n.* annoyance, bore, bother, brake, drogue, nuisance, pain, pest, pill.

drain *v.* bleed, consume, deplete, discharge, dissipate, dry, effuse, empty, evacuate, exhaust, exude, leak, milk, ooze, quaff, remove, sap, seep, strain, swallow, tap, tax, trickle, use up, weary, withdraw

drama *n.* acting, crisis, dramatics, dramatization, dramaturgy, excitement, histrionics, kabuki, melodrama, play, scene, show, spectacle, stage-craft, theater, theatricals, Thespian art, turmoil.

draw¹ *v.* allure, attenuate, attract, borrow, breathe in, bring forth, choose, deduce, delineate, depict, derive, design, drag, drain, elicit, elongate, engage, entice, entrain, evoke, extend, extort, extract, get, haul, induce, infer, influence, inhale, inspire, invite, lengthen, make, map out, mark out, outline, paint, pencil, persuade, pick, portray, puff, pull, respire, select, sketch, stretch, suck, take, tow, trace, tug, unsheathe.

draw² *v.* be equal, be even, be neck and neck, dead-heat, tie. *n.* dead-heat, deadlock, impasse, stalemate, tie.

dread *v.* cringe at, fear, flinch, quail, shrink from, shudder, shy, tremble. *n.* alarm, apprehension, aversion, awe, dismay, disquiet, fear, fright, funk, heebie-jeebies, horror, misgiving, terror, trepidation, worry.

dream *n.* ambition, aspiration, beauty, daydream, delight, delusion, design, desire, fantasy, goal, hallucination, hope, illusion, imagination, joy, marvel, notion, phantasm, pipedream, pleasure, reverie, speculation, trance, treasure, vagary, vision, wish. *v.* conjure, daydream, envisage, fancy, fantasize, hallucinate, imagine, muse, think, visualize.

drench *v.* douse, drown, flood, immerse, inundate, saturate, soak, souse, steep, wet.

dress *n.* apparel, attire, clothing, costume, garb, garments, habit, outfit, robe, suit, togs, vestment. *v.* adjust, adorn, apparel, arrange, attire, clothe, deck, decorate, don, drape, embellish, fit, furbish, garb, groom, habit, ornament, prepare, put on, rig, robe, set, straighten, tend, treat, trim.

drill[1] *v.* coach, discipline, exercise, instruct, practice, rehearse, teach, train, tutor. *n.* coaching, discipline, exercise, instruction, practice, preparation, repetition, training, tuition.

drill[2] *v.* bore, penetrate, perforate, pierce, puncture. *n.* awl, bit, borer, gimlet.

drink *v.* absorb, booze, carouse, drain, gulp, guzzle, imbibe, indulge, partake of, quaff, revel, sip, swallow, swig, swill, tank up, tipple, water. *n.* alcohol, ambrosia, beverage, booze, dose, dram, draught, glass, liquor, potion, refreshment, slug, snifter, snort, spirits, swig, swizzle, tipple, toss, tot.

drive *v.* actuate, bear, coerce, compel, constrain, dash, dig, direct, force, goad, guide, hammer, handle, harass, herd, hurl, impel, manage, motivate, motor, oblige, operate, overburden, overwork, plunge, press, prod, propel, push, ram, ride, rush, send, sink, spur, stab, steer, task, tax, thrust, travel, urge. *n.* action, advance, ambition, appeal, campaign, crusade, determination, effort, energy, enterprise, excursion, get-up-and-go, hurl, initiative, jaunt, journey, motivation, outing, pressure, push, ride, run, spin, surge, trip, turn, vigor, vim, zip.

drop *n.* abyss, bead, bubble, chasm, cut, dab, dash, decline, declivity, decrease, descent, deterioration, downturn, driblet, drip, droplet, fall, falling-off, glob, globule, lowering, mouthful, nip, pearl, pinch, plunge, precipice, reduction, shot, sip, slope, slump, spot, taste, tear, tot, trace, trickle. *v.* abandon, cease, chuck, decline, depress, descend, desert, diminish, discontinue, disown, dive, dribble, drip, droop, fall, forsake, give up, jilt, kick, leave, lower, plummet, plunge, quit, reject, relinquish, remit, renounce, repudiate, sink, stop, terminate, throw over, trickle, tumble.

drown *v.* deaden, deluge, drench, engulf, extinguish, flood, go under, immerse, inundate, muffle, obliterate, overcome, overpower, overwhelm, silence, sink, stifle, submerge, swallow up, swamp, wipe out.

drug *n.* depressant, dope, medicament, medication, medicine, Mickey, Mickey Finn, narcotic, opiate, physic, poison, potion, remedy, stimulant. *v.* anesthetize, deaden, dope, dose, drench, knock out, load, medicate, numb, poison, stupefy, treat.

drunk *adj.* a sheet (three sheets) in the wind, blind, bottled, canned, cockeyed, corked, corny, drunken, inebriated, intoxicated, liquored, lit up, loaded, lushy, muddled, obfuscated, pickled, plastered, shickered, sloshed, soaked, sottish, soused, stewed, stoned, tanked up, tiddly, tight, tipsy, up the pole, well-oiled, wet.

dull *adj.* apathetic, blank, blunt, boring, dead, dense, depressed, dimwitted, dismal, drab, dreary, dry, edgeless, faded, featureless, flat, humdrum, insipid, lackluster, listless, monotonous, muted, opaque, overcast, passionless, plain, prosaic, stodgy, subdued, tedious, thick, tiresome, unexciting, uninteresting, vacuous, vapid.

duplicate *adj.* corresponding, geminate, identical, matched, matching, twin, twofold. *n.* carbon copy, copy, facsimile, match, photocopy, replica, reproduction.

duplicity *n.* artifice, chicanery, deceit, deception, dishonesty, dissimulation, double-dealing, falsehood, fraud, guile, hypocrisy, mendacity, perfidy, treachery.

duty *n.* allegiance, assignment, business, calling, charge, chore, customs, debt, deference, devoir, due, engagement, excise, function, impost, job, levy, loyalty, mission, obedience, obligation, office, onus, province, respect, responsibility, reverence, role, service, tariff, task, tax, toll, work.

dying *adj.* at death's door, declining, disappearing, ebbing, expiring, fading, failing, final, going, in articulo mortis, in extremis, moribund, mortal, not long for this world, obsolescent, passing, perishing, sinking, vanishing.

dynamic *adj.* active, driving, electric, energetic, forceful, go-ahead, go-getting, high-powered, lively, powerful, self-starting, spirited, vigorous, vital, zippy.

E

eager *adj.* agog, anxious, ardent, athirst, avid, desirous, earnest, enthusiastic, fervent, fervid, greedy, gung-ho, hot, hungry, impatient, intent, keen, longing, raring, unshrinking, vehement, yearning, zealous.

early *adj.* advanced, forward, matutinal, prehistoric, premature, primeval, primitive, primordial, undeveloped, untimely, young. *adv.* ahead of time, beforehand, betimes, in advance, in good time, prematurely, too soon.

earn *v.* acquire, attain, bring in, collect, deserve, draw, gain, get, gross, make, merit, net, obtain, procure, rate, realize, reap, receive, warrant, win.

ease *n.* affluence, aplomb, calmness, comfort, composure, content, contentment, deftness, dexterity, easiness, effortlessness, enjoyment, facileness, facility, flexibility, freedom, happiness, informality, insouciance, leisure, liberty, naturalness, nonchalance, peace, peace of mind, poise, quiet, quietude, readiness, realization, repose, rest, restfulness, serenity, simplicity, solace, tranquility, unaffectedness, unconstrained, unreservedness.

easy *adj.* a piece of cake, a pushover, accommodating, affable, calm, carefree, casual, child's play, clear, comfortable, contented, easy-going, effortless, facile, gentle, graceful, gracious, leisurely, lenient, liberal, light, manageable, mild, moderate, natural, open, painless, peaceful, permissive, pleasant, quiet, relaxed, satisfied, simple, smooth, soft, straightforward, tolerant, tranquil, uncomplicated, yielding.

ebb *v.* abate, decay, decline, decrease, degenerate, deteriorate, diminish, drop, dwindle, fade away, fall away, fall back, flag, flow back, go out, lessen, peter out, recede, reflow, retire, retreat, retrocede, shrink, sink, slacken, subside, wane, weaken, withdraw.

effect *n.* action, aftermath, clout, conclusion, consequence, drift, effectiveness, efficacy, efficiency, enforcement, essence, event, execution, fact, force, fruit, impact, implementation, import, impression, influence, issue, meaning, operation, outcome, power, purport, purpose, reality, result, sense, significance, strength, tenor, upshot, use, validity, vigor, weight, work. *v.* accomplish, achieve, actuate, cause, complete, consummate, create, effectuate, execute, fulfill, initiate, make, perform, produce, wreak.

efficient *adj.* able, adept, businesslike, capable, competent, economic, effective, effectual, powerful, productive, proficient, ready, skilful, streamlined, well-conducted, well-ordered, well-regulated, workmanlike.

effort *n.* accomplishment, achievement, application, attempt, creation, deed, endeavor, energy, essay, exertion, feat, force, go, job, labor, molimen, nisus, pains,

power, product, production, shot, stab, strain, stress, stretch, striving, struggle, toil, travail, trouble, try, work.

elated *adj.* animated, blissful, cheered, delighted, ecstatic, euphoric, excited, exhilarated, exultant, gleeful, joyful, joyous, jubilant, on the high ropes, over the moon, overjoyed, pleased, proud, roused.

elect *v.* adopt, appoint, choose, designate, determine, opt for, pick, prefer, select, vote. *adj.* choice, chosen, designate, designated, elite, hand-picked, picked, preferred, presumptive, prospective, select, selected, to be.

eliminate *v.* annihilate, bump off, cut out, delete, dispense with, dispose of, disregard, do away with, drop, eject, eradicate, exclude, expel, expunge, exterminate, extinguish, get rid of, ignore, kill, knock out, liquidate, murder, omit, reject, remove, rub out, slay, stamp out, take out, terminate, waste.

embrace *v.* accept, clasp, comprehend, comprise, contain, cover, cuddle, enclose, encompass, enfold, grab, grasp, hold, hug, include, incorporate, squeeze, take up, welcome.

emotion *n.* affect, agitation, ardor, excitement, feeling, fervor, passion, perturbation, reaction, sensation, sentiment, vehemence, warmth.

emotional *adj.* affecting, ardent, demonstrative, emotive, enthusiastic, excitable, exciting, feeling, fervent, fervid, fiery, heart-warming, heated, hot-blooded, impassioned, moved, moving, overcharged, passionate, pathetic, poignant, responsive, roused, sensitive, sentimental, stirred, stirring, susceptible, tear-jerking, temperamental, tempestuous, tender, thrilling, touching, volcanic, warm, zealous.

empty *adj.* absent, aimless, banal, bare, blank, bootless, cheap, clear, deserted, desolate, destitute, expressionless, famished, frivolous, fruitless, futile, hollow, hungry, idle, inane, ineffective, insincere, insubstantial, meaningless, purposeless, ravenous, senseless, silly, starving, superficial, trivial, unfed, unfilled, uninhabited, unoccupied, unreal, unsatisfactory, vacant, vacuous, vain, valueless, void, waste, worthless.

encounter *v.* chance upon, clash with, combat, come upon, confront, contend, cross swords with, engage, experience, face, fight, grapple with, happen on, meet, rencounter, run across, run into, strive, struggle.

encourage *v.* abet, advance, advocate, aid,

animate, boost, buoy up, cheer, comfort, console, egg on, embolden, favor, forward, foster, further, hearten, help, incite, inspire, inspirit, promote, rally, reassure, rouse, second, spirit, spur, stimulate, strengthen, succor, support, urge.

end *n.* aim, annihilation, aspiration, attainment, bit, bound, boundary, butt, cessation, close, closure, completion, conclusion, consequence, consummation, culmination, curtain, death, demise, design, destruction, dissolution, doom, downfall, drift, edge, ending, expiration, expiry, extent, extermination, extinction, extreme, extremity, finale, fine, finis, finish, fragment, goal, intent, intention, issue, left-over, limit, object, objective, outcome, part, pay-off, piece, point, portion, purpose, reason, remainder, remnant, resolution, responsibility, result, ruin, ruination, scrap, share, side, stop, stub, termination, terminus, tip, upshot, wind-up.

endorse *v.* adopt, advocate, affirm, approve, authorize, back, champion, confirm, countenance, countersign, favor, indorse, ratify, recommend, sanction, sign, subscribe to, superscribe, support, sustain, undersign, vouch for, warrant.

endure *v.* abide, bear, brave, brook, cope with, experience, go through, hold, last, live, permit, persist, prevail, put up with, remain, stand, stay, stick, stomach, submit to, suffer, support, survive, sustain, swallow, tolerate, undergo, weather, withstand.

enemy *n.* adversary, antagonist, competitor, foe, foeman, opponent, Philistine, rival, the opposition.

engage *v.* absorb, activate, affiance, agree, allure, apply, appoint, arrest, assail, attach, attack, attract, bespeak, betroth, bind, book, busy, captivate, catch, charm, charter, combat, commission, commit, contract, covenant, draw, embark, employ, enamor, enchant, encounter, energize, engross, enlist, enrol, enter, fascinate, fit, fix, gain, grip, guarantee, hire, interact, interconnect, interlock, involve, join, lease, meet, mesh, obligate, oblige, occupy, operate, partake, participate, pledge, practice, prearrange, preoccupy, promise, rent, reserve, retain, secure, take on, tie up, undertake, vouch, vow, win.

enhance *v.* amplify, augment, boost, complement, elevate, embellish, escalate, exalt, heighten, improve, increase, intensify, lift, magnify, raise, reinforce, strengthen, swell.

enjoy *v.* appreciate, delight in, dig, experience, have, like, make a meal of, own, possess, rejoice in, relish, revel in, savor, take pleasure in, use.

enmity *n.* acrimony, animosity, animus, antagonism, antipathy, aversion, bad blood, bitterness, feud, hate, hatred, hostility, ill-will, invidiousness, malevolence, malice, malignity, rancor, spite, venom.

enormous *adj.* abominable, astronomic(al), atrocious, Brobdingnagian, colossal, cyclopean, depraved, disgraceful, evil, excessive, gargantuan, gigantic, gross, heinous, herculean, huge, hulking, immense, jumbo, leviathan, mammoth, massive, monstrous, mountainous, nefarious, odious, outrageous, prodigious, titanic, tremendous, vast, vicious, vile, villainous, wicked.

enter *v.* arrive, begin, board, commence, embark upon, enlist, enrol, inscribe, insert, introduce, join, list, log, note, offer, participate, participate in, penetrate, pierce, present, proffer, record, register, set about, set down, sign up, start, submit, take down, take up, tender.

enterprise *n.* activity, adventure, adventurousness, alertness, audacity, boldness, business, company, concern, daring, dash, drive, eagerness, effort, endeavor, energy, enthusiasm, essay, establishment, firm, get-up-and-go, gumption, imagination, initiative, operation, plan, program, project, push, readiness, resource, resourcefulness, spirit, undertaking, venture, vigor, zeal.

entertain *v.* accommodate, amuse, charm, cheer, cherish, conceive, consider, contemplate, countenance, delight, divert, fête, foster, harbor, hold, imagine, lodge, maintain, occupy, please, ponder, put up, recreate, regale, support, treat.

entrance[1] *n.* access, admission, admittance, appearance, arrival, atrium, avenue, beginning, commencement, debut, door, doorway, entrée, entry, gate, ingress, initiation, inlet, introduction, opening, outset, passage, portal, start.

entrance[2] *v.* bewitch, captivate, charm, delight, enchant, enrapture, enthrall, fascinate, gladden, hypnotize, magnetize, mesmerize, ravish, spellbind, transport.

entreat *v.* appeal to, ask, beg, beseech, conjure, crave, enjoin, exhort, implore, importune, invoke, petition, plead with, pray, request, sue, supplicate.

environment *n.* ambience, atmosphere, background, conditions, context, domain, element, entourage, habitat, locale, medium, milieu, scene, setting, situation, surroundings, territory.

epoch *n.* age, date, epocha, era, period, time.

equal *adj.* able, adequate, alike, balanced, capable, commensurate, competent, corresponding, egalitarian, equable, equivalent, even, even-handed, evenly-balanced, evenly-matched, evenly-proportioned, fair, fifty-fifty, fit, identical, impartial, just, level-pegging, like, matched, proportionate, ready, regular, sufficient, suitable, symmetrical, tantamount, the same, unbiased, uniform, unvarying, up to.

equilibrium *n.* balance, calm, calmness, collectedness, composure, cool, coolness, counterpoise, equanimity, equipoise, evenness, poise, rest, self-possession, serenity, stability, steadiness, symmetry.

equity *n.* disinterestedness, equality, equitableness, even-handedness, fair play, fair-mindedness, fairness, honesty, impartiality, integrity, justice, justness, objectivity, reasonableness, rectitude, righteousness, uprightness.

era *n.* age, century, cycle, date, day, days, eon, epoch, generation, period, stage, time.

erase *v.* blot out, cancel, cleanse, delete, efface, eliminate, eradicate, expunge, get rid of, obliterate, remove, rub out.

erect *adj.* elevated, engorged, firm, hard, perpendicular, pricked, raised, rigid, standing, stiff, straight, taut, tense, tumescent, upright, upstanding, vertical.

err *v.* blunder, deviate, fail, go astray, lapse, misapprehend, misbehave, miscalculate, misjudge, mistake, misunderstand, offend, sin, slip up, stray, stumble, transgress, trespass, trip up, wander.

errand *n.* assignment, charge, commission, duty, job, message, mission, task.

error *n.* blunder, boner, delinquency, delusion, deviation, erratum, fallacy, fault, faux pas, flaw, inaccuracy, lapse, malapropism, miscalculation, misconception, mistake, offense, omission, oversight, slip-up, transgression, trespass, wrong, wrongdoing.

escort *n.* aide, attendant, beau, bodyguard, chaperon, companion, company, convoy, entourage, gigolo, guard, guardian, guide, partner, pilot, procession, protection, protector, retinue, safeguard, squire, suite, train. *v.* accompany, chaperon, chum, company, conduct, convoy, guard, guide, lead, partner, protect, shepherd, squire, usher.

establish *v.* affirm, attest to, authenticate, authorize, base, certify, confirm, constitute, corroborate, create, decree, demonstrate, enact, ensconce, entrench, fix, form, found, ground, implant, inaugurate, install, institute, introduce, invent, lodge, ordain, organize, plant, prove, radicate, ratify, root, sanction, seat, secure, set up, settle, show, start, station, substantiate, validate, verify.

eternal *adj.* abiding, ceaseless, changeless, constant, deathless, durable, endless, enduring, everlasting, illimitable, immortal, immutable, imperishable, incessant, indestructible, infinite, interminable, lasting, limitless, never-ending, perennial, permanent, perpetual, timeless, unceasing, unchanging, undying, unending, unextinguishable, unremitting.

ethical *adj.* commendable, conscientious, correct, decent, fair, fitting, good, honest, honorable, just, meet, moral, noble, principled, proper, right, righteous, seemly, upright, virtuous.

even *adj.* abreast, alongside, balanced, calm, coequal, commensurate, comparable, composed, constant, cool, disinterested, dispassionate, drawn, equable, equal, equalized, equitable, even-tempered, fair, fair and square, fifty-fifty, flat, fluent, flush, horizontal, identical, impartial, impassive, imperturbable, just, level, level-pegging, like, matching, metrical, monotonous, neck and neck, on a par, parallel, peaceful, placid, plane, proportionate, quits, regular, rhythmical, serene, side by side, similar, smooth, square, stable, steady, straight, symmetrical, tied, tranquil, true, unbiased, unbroken, undisturbed, unexcitable, unexcited, uniform, uninterrupted, unprejudiced, unruffled, unvarying, unwavering, well-balanced.

ever *adv.* always, at all, at all times, at any time, ceaselessly, constantly, continually, endlessly, eternally, everlastingly, evermore, for ever, in any case, in any circumstances, incessantly, on any account, perpetually, unceasingly, unendingly.

evidence *n.* affirmation, attestation, betrayal, confirmation, corroboration, data, declaration, demonstration, deposition, documentation, grounds, hint, indication, manifestation, mark, pledge, proof, sign, substantiation, suggestion, testimony, token, voucher, witness.

evil *adj.* adverse, bad, base, calamitous, corrupt, cruel, deadly, depraved, dire, disastrous, ghastly, grim, harmful, heinous, hurtful, immoral, malevolent, malicious, malignant, nefarious, noxious, offensive, painful, poisonous, putrid, reprobate, ruinous, sinful, sorrowful, ugly, unfortunate, unspeakable, vicious, vile, villainous, wicked, woeful, wrong.

exact *adj.* accurate, blow-by-blow, care-

example 291 express

ful, close, correct, definite, detailed, explicit, express, factual, faithful, faultless, finicky, flawless, identical, letter-perfect, literal, methodical, meticulous, nice, orderly, painstaking, particular, perfectionist, precise, punctilious, right, rigorous, scrupulous, severe, specific, square, strict, true, unambiguous, unequivocal, unerring, veracious, very, word-perfect.

example *n.* admonition, archetype, case, case in point, caution, citation, exemplar, exemplification, ideal, illustration, instance, lesson, mirror, model, occurrence, paradigm, paragon, parallel, pattern, praxis, precedent, prototype, sample, specimen, standard, type, warning.

excel *v.* beat, better, cap, eclipse, exceed, outclass, outdo, outperform, outrank, outshine, outstrip, overshadow, pass, predominate, shine, stand out, surmount, surpass, top, transcend, trump.

except *prep.* apart from, bar, barring, besides, but, except for, excepting, excluding, exclusive of, leaving out, less, minus, not counting, omitting, other than, save, saving. *v.* ban, bar, debar, disallow, eliminate, exclude, leave out, omit, pass over, reject, rule out.

exclude *v.* anathematize, ban, bar, blackball, blacklist, bounce, boycott, debar, disallow, eject, eliminate, embargo, evict, except, excommunicate, expel, forbid, ignore, include out, interdict, keep out, leave out, omit, ostracize, oust, preclude, prohibit, proscribe, refuse, reject, remove, repudiate, rule out, shut out, veto.

exclusive *adj.* absolute, closed, complete, discriminative, entire, esoteric, fashionable, full, limited, monopolistic, private, restricted, restrictive, select, selective, sole, total, undivided, unique, unshared, whole.

excuse *v.* absolve, acquit, apologize for, condone, defend, discharge, exculpate, exempt, exonerate, explain, extenuate, forgive, free, ignore, indulge, justify, let off, liberate, mitigate, overlook, palliate, pardon, release, relieve, sanction, spare, tolerate, vindicate, warrant, wink at. *n.* alibi, apology, defense, disguise, evasion, exculpation, exoneration, expedient, explanation, extenuation, grounds, justification, make-shift, mitigation, mockery, palliation, parody, plea, pretense, pretext, put-off, reason, semblance, shift, substitute, subterfuge, vindication.

execute¹ *v.* behead, crucify, decapitate, decollate, electrocute, guillotine, hang, kill, liquidate, put to death, shoot.

execute² *v.* accomplish, achieve, administer, complete, consummate, deliver, discharge, dispatch, do, effect, effectuate, enact, enforce, expedite, finish, fulfill, implement, perform, prosecute, realize, render, seal, serve, sign, validate.

exempt *v.* absolve, discharge, dismiss, except, excuse, exonerate, free, let off, liberate, make an exception of, release, relieve, spare.

exhibit *v.* air, demonstrate, disclose, display, evidence, evince, expose, express, flaunt, indicate, manifest, offer, parade, present, reveal, show, showcase, sport.

exonerate *v.* absolve, acquit, clear, discharge, dismiss, except, excuse, free, justify, liberate, pardon, release, relieve, vindicate.

expand *v.* amplify, augment, bloat, blow up, branch out, broaden, develop, diffuse, dilate, distend, diversify, elaborate, embellish, enlarge, expatiate, expound, extend, fatten, fill out, flesh out, grow, heighten, increase, inflate, lengthen, magnify, multiply, open, outspread, prolong, protract, snowball, spread, stretch, swell, thicken, unfold, unfurl, unravel, unroll, wax, widen.

expect *v.* anticipate, assume, await, bank on, bargain for, believe, calculate, conjecture, contemplate, count on, demand, envisage, forecast, foresee, hope for, imagine, insist on, look for, look forward to, predict, presume, project, reckon, rely on, require, suppose, surmise, think, trust, want, wish.

explore *v.* analyze, case, examine, inspect, investigate, probe, prospect, reconnoiter, research, scout, scrutinize, search, survey, tour, travel, traverse.

expose *v.* air, betray, bring to light, denounce, detect, disclose, display, divulge, endanger, exhibit, hazard, imperil, jeopardize, manifest, present, reveal, risk, show, uncover, unearth, unmask, unveil, wash one's dirty linen in public.

express *v.* articulate, assert, asseverate, bespeak, communicate, conceive, convey, couch, declare, denote, depict, designate, disclose, divulge, embody, enunciate, evince, exhibit, extract, force out, formulate, indicate, intimate, manifest, phrase, pronounce, put, put across, represent, reveal, say, show, signify, speak, stand for, state, symbolize, tell, testify, utter, verbalize, voice, word. *adj.* accurate, categorical, certain, clear, clear-cut, definite, direct, distinct, especial, exact, explicit, fast, high-speed, manifest, non-stop, outright, particular, plain, pointed, precise, quick, rapid, singular, special, speedy, stated, swift, unambiguous, unqualified.

extend v. advance, amplify, attain, augment, bestow, broaden, confer, continue, develop, dilate, drag out, draw out, elongate, enhance, enlarge, expand, give, grant, hold out, impart, increase, last, lengthen, offer, present, proffer, prolong, protract, pull out, reach, spin out, spread, stretch, supplement, take, uncoil, unfold, unfurl, unroll, widen, yield.

exterminate v. abolish, annihilate, destroy, eliminate, eradicate, massacre, wipe out.

extinct adj. abolished, dead, defunct, doused, ended, exterminated, extinguished, gone, inactive, lost, obsolete, out, quenched, terminated, vanished, void.

extol v. acclaim, applaud, celebrate, commend, cry up, eulogize, exalt, glorify, laud, magnify, praise, puff.

extraordinary adj. amazing, bizarre, curious, exceptional, fantastic, marvelous, notable, noteworthy, odd, outstanding, particular, peculiar, phenomenal, rare, remarkable, significant, singular, special, strange, striking, surprising, uncommon, uncontemplated, unfamiliar, unheard-of, unimaginable, unique, unprecedented, unusual, unwonted, weird, wonderful.

extreme adj. acute, deep-dyed, dire, double-dyed, downright, drastic, egregious, exaggerated, exceptional, excessive, exquisite, extraordinary, extravagant, fanatical, faraway, far-off, farthest, final, great, greatest, harsh, high, highest, immoderate, inordinate, intemperate, intense, last, maximum, out-and-out, outermost, outrageous, radical, red-hot, remarkable, remotest, rigid, severe, sheer, stern, strict, supreme, terminal, ultimate, ultra, unbending, uncommon, uncompromising, unconventional, unreasonable, unusual, utmost, utter, uttermost, worst, zealous.

extricate v. clear, deliver, disembroil, disengage, disentangle, free, liberate, release, relieve, remove, rescue, withdraw.

eye n. appreciation, belief, discernment, discrimination, eyeball, judgment, mind, opinion, optic, orb, peeper, perception, recognition, taste, viewpoint. v. contemplate, examine, eye up, gaze at, glance at, inspect, look at, make eyes at, observe, ogle, peruse, regard, scan, scrutinize, stare at, study, survey, view, watch.

F

fable n. allegory, apologue, fabrication, fairy story, falsehood, fantasy, fib, fiction, figment, invention, legend, lie, myth, narrative, old wives' tale, parable, romance, saga, story, tale, tall story, untruth, yarn.

fabric n. cloth, constitution, construction, foundations, framework, infrastructure, make-up, material, organization, structure, stuff, textile, texture, web.

fabricate v. assemble, build, coin, concoct, construct, create, devise, erect, fake, falsify, fashion, feign, forge, form, frame, invent, make, manufacture, shape, trump up.

façade n. appearance, cloak, cover, disguise, exterior, face, front, frontage, guise, mask, pretense, semblance, show, veil, veneer.

face n. air, appearance, aspect, assurance, boldness, cheek, confidence, countenance, disguise, display, effrontery, exterior, facade, facet, features, front, grimace, image, impudence, kisser, look, mask, reputation, scowl, self-respect, semblance, side, smirk, surface, visage. v. clad, coat, confront, cover, deal with, encounter, experience, finish, front, give in to, meet, oppose, overlook, surface, tackle, veneer.

fact n. act, actuality, certainty, circumstance, datum, deed, detail, event, fait accompli, feature, gospel, happening, incident, item, occurrence, particular, point, reality, specific, truth.

factual adj. accurate, authentic, circumstantial, close, correct, credible, detailed, exact, faithful, genuine, literal, objective, precise, real, straight, sure, true, unadorned, unbiased, veritable.

fad n. affectation, craze, crotchet, fancy, fashion, mania, mode, rage, trend, vogue, whim.

fail v. abandon, cease, come to grief, conk out, crack up, crash, cut out, decline, desert, die, disappoint, droop, dwindle, fade, fall, flop, flub, flunk, fold, forget, forsake, founder, fudge, give out, give up, go bankrupt, go bust, go to the wall, go under, gutter, languish, lay an egg, let down, miscarry, misfire, miss, miss one's trip, neglect, omit, peter out, plow, sink, smash, underachieve, underperform, wane, weaken.

fair¹ adj. adequate, all right, average, beauteous, beautiful, bonny, bright, clean, clement, cloudless, comely, decent, disinterested, dispassionate, dry, equal, equitable, even-handed, favorable, fine, handsome, honest, honorable, impartial, just, lawful, legitimate, lovely, mediocre, middling, moderate, not bad, objective, OK, on the level, passable, pretty, proper, reasonable, respectable, satisfactory, so-

so, square, sunny, sunshiny, tolerable, trustworthy, unbiased, unclouded, unprejudiced, upright, well-favored.

fair² *adj.* blond(e), fair-haired, fair-headed, flaxen, light, tow-headed.

fake *v.* affect, assume, copy, counterfeit, fabricate, feign, forge, phony, pretend, put on, sham, simulate. *n.* charlatan, copy, forgery, fraud, hoax, imitation, imposter, mountebank, phony, reproduction, sham, simulation. *adj.* affected, artificial, assumed, bastard, bogus, counterfeit, ersatz, false, forged, hyped up, imitation, mock, phony, pretended, pseudo, reproduction, sham, simulated, spurious.

fall *v.* abate, backslide, become, befall, capitulate, cascade, chance, collapse, come about, come to pass, crash, decline, decrease, depreciate, descend, die, diminish, dive, drop, drop down, dwindle, ebb, err, fall away, fall off, fall out, flag, give in, give up, give way, go astray, go down, happen, incline, keep over, lapse, lessen, measure one's length, meet one's end, perish, pitch, plummet, plunge, push, resign, settle, sin, sink, slope, slump, stumble, subside, succumb, surrender, take place, topple, transgress, trespass, trip, trip over, tumble, yield, yield to temptation.

false *adj.* artificial, bogus, concocted, counterfeit, deceitful, deceptive, dishonest, dishonorable, disloyal, duplicitous, erroneous, ersatz, fake, fallacious, faulty, feigned, fictitious, forged, fraudulent, hypocritical, imitation, improper, inaccurate, incorrect, inexact, lying, mendacious, misleading, mistaken, mock, perfidious, pseudo, sham, simulated, spurious, synthetic, treacherous, treasonable, trumped-up, two-faced, unfaithful, unfounded, unreal, unreliable, unsound, untrue, untrustworthy, untruthful, wrong.

fame *n.* celebrity, credit, eminence, esteem, glory, honor, illustriousness, kudos, name, prominence, renown, reputation, repute, stardom.

family *n.* ancestors, ancestry, birth, blood, brood, children, clan, class, classification, descendants, descent, dynasty, extraction, folk, forebears, forefathers, genealogy, genre, group, house, household, issue, kin, kind, kinsmen, kith and kin, line, lineage, network, offspring, parentage, pedigree, people, progeny, race, relations, relatives, sept, stirps, strain, subdivision, system, tribe.

famous *adj.* acclaimed, celebrated, conspicuous, distinguished, eminent, excellent, famed, glorious, great, honored, illustrious, legendary, lionized, notable, noted, prominent, remarkable, renowned, signal, well-known.

fan¹ *v.* aggravate, agitate, aircondition, aircool, arouse, blow, cool, enkindle, excite, impassion, increase, provoke, refresh, rouse, stimulate, stir up, ventilate, whip up, winnow, work up. *n.* air-conditioner, blower, extractor fan, flabellum, propeller, vane, ventilator.

fan² *n.* adherent, admirer, aficionado, buff, devotee, enthusiast, fiend, follower, freak, groupie, lover, rooter, supporter, zealot.

far *adv.* a good way, a long way, afar, considerably, decidedly, deep, extremely, greatly, incomparably, miles, much.

fare¹ *n.* charge, cost, fee, passage, passenger, pick-up, price, traveler.

fare² *n.* board, commons, diet, eatables, food, meals, menu, provisions, rations, sustenance, table, victuals.

fare³ *v.* be, do, get along, get on, go, go on, happen, make out, manage, proceed, prosper, turn out.

fashion *n.* appearance, attitude, craze, custom, cut, demeanor, description, fad, figure, form, guise, haute couture, jet set, latest, line, look, make, manner, method, mode, model, mold, pattern, rage, shape, sort, style, trend, type, usage, vogue, way.

fast¹ *adj.* accelerated, brisk, fleet, flying, hasty, hurried, mercurial, nippy, quick, rapid, spanking, speedy, swift, winged.

fast² *adj.* close, constant, fastened, firm, fixed, fortified, immovable, impregnable, lasting, loyal, permanent, secure, sound, staunch, steadfast, tight, unflinching, unwavering.

fast³ *adj.* dissipated, dissolute, extravagant, immoral, intemperate, licentious, loose, profligate, promiscuous, rakish, reckless, self-indulgent, wanton, whorish, wild.

fast⁴ *v.* abstain, diet, go hungry, starve. *n.* abstinence, diet, fasting, starvation, xerophagy.

fat *adj.* abdominous, beefy, corpulent, fatty, fertile, fleshy, flourishing, greasy, gross, heavy, lucrative, obese, overweight, paunchy, plump, portly, pot-bellied, profitable, prosperous, pudgy, rotund, round, solid, stout, thriving, tubby.

fatal *adj.* baleful, baneful, calamitous, catastrophic, deadly, destructive, disastrous, final, incurable, killing, lethal, malignant, mortal, pernicious, ruinous, terminal, vital.

father *n.* ancestor, architect, author, begetter, confessor, creator, dad, daddy, elder, forebear, forefather, founder, genitor, governor, inventor, leader, maker, old boy, old man, originator, pa, padre, papa, pappy, parent, pastor, pater, paterfamilias, patriarch, patron, pop, poppa, pops, predecessor, priest, prime mover, procreator, progenitor, senator, sire. *v.* beget, conceive, create, dream up, engender, establish, found, get, institute, invent, originate, procreate, produce, sire.

favor *n.* acceptance, approbation, approval, backing, badge, benefit, bias, boon, championship, courtesy, decoration, esteem, favoritism, friendliness, gift, good turn, goodwill, grace, indulgence, keepsake, kindness, knot, love-token, memento, obligement, partiality, patronage, present, regard, rosette, service, smile, souvenir, support, token.

favorite *adj.* best-loved, choice, dearest, esteemed, favored, pet, preferred.

fear *n.* agitation, alarm, anxiety, apprehension, apprehensiveness, awe, bogey, bugbear, concern, consternation, cravenness, danger, dismay, disquietude, distress, doubt, dread, foreboding(s), fright, funk, heart-quake, horror, likelihood, misgiving(s), nightmare, panic, phobia, phobism, qualms, reverence, risk, solicitude, specter, suspicion, terror, timidity, tremors, trepidation, unease, uneasiness, veneration, wonder, worry.

feast *n.* banquet, barbecue, beanfeast, beano, binge, blow-out, carousal, carouse, celebration, delight, dinner, enjoyment, entertainment, festival, fête, gala day, gaudy, gratification, holiday, holy day, pleasure, repast, revels, saint's day, spread, treat. *v.* delight, eat one's fill, entertain, gladden, gorge, gormandize, gratify, indulge, overindulge, regale, rejoice, stuff, stuff one's face, thrill, treat, wine and dine.

feature *n.* article, aspect, attraction, attribute, character, characteristic, column, comment, draw, facet, factor, hallmark, highlight, innovation, item, lineament, mark, peculiarity, piece, point, property, quality, report, special, specialty, story, trait. *v.* accentuate, emphasize, headline, highlight, play up, present, promote, push, recommend, show, spotlight, star.

feed *v.* augment, bolster, cater for, dine, eat, encourage, fare, foster, fuel, graze, grub, nourish, nurture, pasture, provide for, provision, strengthen, subsist, supply, sustain, victual. *n.* banquet, feast, fodder, food, forage, meal, nosh, pasturage, pasture, provender, repast, silage, spread, tuck-in, victuals.

feel *v.* appear, believe, caress, consider, deem, empathize, endure, enjoy, experience, explore, finger, fondle, fumble, go through, grope, handle, have, have a hunch, hold, intuit, judge, know, manipulate, maul, notice, observe, paw, perceive, reckon, resemble, seem, sense, sound, stroke, suffer, take to heart, test, think, touch, try, undergo.

feeling *n.* affection, air, ambience, appreciation, apprehension, ardor, atmosphere, aura, compassion, concern, consciousness, emotion, empathy, feel, fervor, fondness, heat, hunch, idea, impression, inclination, inkling, instinct, intensity, mood, notion, opinion, passion, perception, pity, point of view, presentiment, quality, sensation, sense, sensibility, sensitivity, sentiment, sentimentality, suspicion, sympathy, touch, understanding, vibes, vibrations, view, warmth.

fertile *adj.* abundant, fat, fecund, flowering, fruit-bearing, fruitful, generative, lush, luxuriant, plenteous, plentiful, potent, productive, prolific, rich, teeming, uberous, virile, yielding.

festive *adj.* carnival, celebratory, cheery, convivial, cordial, gala, gay, gleeful, happy, hearty, holiday, jolly, jovial, joyful, joyous, jubilant, merry, mirthful, rollicking, sportive, uproarious.

feud *n.* animosity, antagonism, argument, bad blood, bickering, bitterness, conflict, contention, disagreement, discord, dispute, dissension, enmity, estrangement, faction, feuding, grudge, hostility, ill will, quarrel, rivalry, row, strife, variance, vendetta.

fight *v.* altercate, argue, assault, battle, bear arms against, brawl, clash, close, combat, conduct, conflict, contend, contest, dispute, do battle, engage, exchange blows, fence, feud, grapple, joust, lock horns, oppose, prosecute, quarrel, resist, scrap, scuffle, skirmish, spar, squabble, struggle, take the field, tilt, wage war, war, withstand, wrangle, wrestle. *n.* action, affray, altercation, argument, battle, belligerence, bout, brawl, brush, clash, combat, conflict, contest, courage, dispute, dissension, duel, encounter, engagement, free-for-all, hostilities, joust, quarrel, resistance, riot, row, rumble, scrap, scuffle, struggle, tenacity, tussle, war.

file¹ *v.* abrade, burnish, furbish, grate, hone, pare, plane, polish, rasp, refine, rub (down), sand, scour, scrape, shape, shave, smooth, trim, whet.

file² *n.* column, line, list, procession, queue, row, stream, string, trail, train. *v.* march, parade, stream, trail, troop.

fill *v.* assign, charge, clog, crowd, engage, glut, gorge, inflate, load, permeate, pervade, sate, satiate, satisfy, saturate, seal, soak, stuff, suffuse, supply, surfeit, swell, take up.

fine[1] *adj.* acceptable, admirable, agreeable, beautiful, clear, delicate, dry, elegant, excellent, exceptional, exquisite, first-class, fragile, honed, lovely, magnificent, pleasant, pure, satisfactory, slender, splendid, suitable, sunny, tasteful, virtuoso.

fine[2] *v.* amerce, mulct, penalize, punish, sting. *n.* amercement, damages, forfeit, forfeiture, mulct, penalty, punishment.

finish *v.* accomplish, achieve, annihilate, cease, complete, conclude, consummate, culminate, defeat, destroy, dispose of, empty, end, exterminate, finalize, kill, overcome, polish, put an end to, rout, ruin, smooth, stop, terminate, texture, veneer, wind up.

firm[1] *adj.* abiding, braced, cast-iron, cemented, compressed, concentrated, definite, dense, dogged, enduring, fastened, fixed, grounded, hard, immovable, inflexible, motionless, obdurate, reliable, resolute, rigid, robust, secure, settled, solid, stable, steady, substantial, sure, taut, tight, unmoved, unshakable, unwavering, unyielding.

firm[2] *n.* association, business, company, concern, conglomerate, corporation, enterprise, establishment, house, institution, organization, outfit, partnership, set-up, syndicate.

fit[1] *adj.* able, able-bodied, appropriate, apt, becoming, blooming, capable, commensurate, competent, condign, convenient, correct, deserving, due, eligible, equipped, expedient, hale, hale and hearty, healthy, in the pink, prepared, proper, satisfactory, seemly, sound, strapping, sturdy, suitable, trained, trim, well, well-suited, worthy.

fit[2] *n.* access, attack, bout, burst, caprice, convulsion, eruption, explosion, fancy, humor, mood, outbreak, outburst, paroxysm, seizure, spasm, spell, storm, surge, whim.

fix[1] *v.* adjust, agree on, anchor, bind, cement, conclude, connect, correct, define, determine, direct, establish, fasten, install, limit, maneuver, mend, place, position, prearrange, repair, resolve, seat, secure, settle, stabilize, stick, tidy, tie.

fix[2] *n.* dose, hit, injection, jag, score, shot, slug.

flame *v.* beam, blaze, burn, flare, flash, glare, glow, radiate, shine. *n.* affection, ardor, beau, blaze, brightness, enthusiasm, fervency, fervor, fire, flake, heartthrob, intensity, keenness, light, lover, passion, radiance, sweetheart, warmth, zeal.

flat[1] *adj.* even, horizontal, lamellar, level, leveled, low, outstretched, planar, prone, prostrate, reclining, recumbent, smooth, spread-eagled, supine, uniform. *n.* lowland, marsh, morass, moss, mud flat, plain, shallow, shoal, strand, swamp.

flat[2] *adj.* bored, boring, burst, collapsed, dead, deflated, depressed, dull, empty, flavorless, insipid, jejune, lackluster, lifeless, monotonous, pointless, prosaic, punctured, spiritless, stale, tedious, uninteresting, unpalatable, vapid, watery, weak.

flattery *n.* adulation, backscratching, blandishment, blarney, bootlicking, butter, cajolement, cajolery, eulogy, fawning, flannel, fulsomeness, ingratiation, obsequiousness, servility, soap, soft soap, sugar, sweet talk, sycophancy, sycophantism, taffy, toadyism, unctuousness.

flavor *n.* aroma, aspect, character, essence, extract, feel, feeling, flavoring, hint, odor, piquancy, property, quality, relish, savor, savoriness, seasoning, smack, soupçon, stamp, style, suggestion, tang, taste, tastiness, tinge, tone, touch, zest, zing. *v.* contaminate, ginger up, imbue, infuse, lace, leaven, season, spice, taint.

flee *v.* abscond, avoid, beat a hasty retreat, bolt, bunk (off), cut and run, decamp, depart, escape, fly, get away, leave, make off, make oneself scarce, scarper, scram, shun, skedaddle, split, take flight, take it on the lam, take off, take to one's heels, vamoose, vanish, withdraw.

fleet[1] *n.* argosy, armada, flotilla, navy, squadron, task force.

fleet[2] *adj.* expeditious, fast, flying, light-footed, mercurial, meteoric, nimble, quick, rapid, speedy, swift, velocipede, winged.

flexible *adj.* accommodating, adaptable, adjustable, agreeable, amenable, bendable, biddable, complaisant, compliant, discretionary, docile, double-jointed, ductile, elastic, gentle, limber, lissome, lithe, loose-limbed, manageable, mobile, open, plastic, pliable, pliant, responsive, springy, stretchy, supple, tensile, tractable, variable, willowy, yielding.

flourish[1] *v.* advance, bloom, blossom, boom, burgeon, develop, do well, flower, get on, grow, increase, mushroom, progress, prosper, succeed, thrive, wax.

flourish[2] *v.* brandish, display, flaunt, flutter, parade, shake, sweep, swing, swish, twirl, vaunt, wag, wave, wield. *n.*

arabesque, brandishing, ceremony, decoration, display, embellishment, fanfare, ornament, parade, show.

flow v. arise, bubble, cascade, circulate, course, deluge, derive, emanate, emerge, flood, glide, gush, originate, proceed, rush, spring, spurt, stream, teem, well, whirl.

fluent adj. articulate, easy, effortless, eloquent, facile, flowing, fluid, glib, mellifluous, natural, ready, smooth, smooth-talking, voluble, well-versed.

fly v. abscond, bolt, clear out, dart, dash, disappear, escape, flee, flutter, get away, hightail it, hurry, light out, pilot, race, retreat, run for it, rush, scamper, soar, speed, sprint, take off, vamoose, wing.

foe n. adversary, antagonist, enemy, foeman, ill-wisher, opponent, rival.

fold v. bend, clasp, close, collapse, crash, crumple, dog-ear, enclose, enfold, entwine, envelop, gather, hug, intertwine, pleat, ply, wrap, wrap up.

fond adj. absurd, adoring, affectionate, amorous, caring, credulous, deluded, devoted, doting, empty, foolish, indiscreet, indulgent, loving, naive, over-optimistic, sanguine, tender, uxorious, vain, warm.

food n. aliment, ambrosia, board, bread, cheer, chow, comestibles, commons, cooking, cuisine, diet, eatables, eats, edibles, fare, feed, fodder, foodstuffs, forage, grub, larder, meat, menu, nosh, nourishment, nutriment, nutrition, pabulum, pap, provend, provender, provisions, rations, refreshment, scoff, stores, subsistence, sustenance, table, tack, tucker, viands, victuals, vittles.

fool v. act up, bamboozle, bluff, deceive, delude, hoax, hoodwink, joke, kid, mislead, pretend, string along, swindle, take in, trifle.

foolish adj. absurd, brainless, crazy, daft, half-witted, idiotic, idle-headed, ill-advised, imbecilic, imprudent, incautious, indiscreet, inept, ludicrous, mad, moronic, nonsensical, ridiculous, senseless, simple-minded, stupid, unwise, witless.

forbid v. ban, block, contraindicate, debar, deny, disallow, exclude, hinder, inhibit, interdict, outlaw, preclude, prevent, prohibit, proscribe, refuse, rule out, veto.

force v. bulldoze, coerce, compel, constrain, drag, drive, exact, extort, impel, impose, lean on, make, necessitate, obligate, oblige, press, pressure, pressurize, prize, propel, push, strong-arm, thrust, urge, wrench, wring.

foreign adj. adventitious, alien, borrowed, distant, exotic, external, extraneous, extrinsic, imported, incongruous, irrelevant, outlandish, outside, overseas, remote, strange, uncharacteristic, unfamiliar, unknown, unrelated.

forever adv. always, ceaselessly, constantly, continually, endlessly, eternally, everlastingly, evermore, for all time, for good and all, for keeps, in perpetuity, in saecula saeculorum, incessantly, interminably, permanently, perpetually, persistently, till the cows come home, till the end of time, unremittingly, world without end.

forget v. discount, dismiss, disregard, fail, ignore, lose sight of, neglect, omit, overlook, think no more of.

forgive v. absolve, acquit, condone, exculpate, excuse, exonerate, let off, overlook, pardon, remit, shrive.

formidable adj. alarming, appalling, arduous, awesome, challenging, colossal, dangerous, daunting, difficult, frightening, frightful, great, huge, impressive, intimidating, menacing, onerous, overwhelming, terrifying, threatening.

forte n. aptitude, bent, gift, long suit, skill, specialty, strength, strong point, talent.

fortunate adj. advantageous, auspicious, blessed, bright, convenient, encouraging, favorable, favored, felicitous, fortuitous, golden, happy, helpful, lucky, opportune, profitable, promising, propitious, prosperous, providential, rosy, serendipitous, successful, timely, well-off, well-timed.

foul adj. abhorrent, abominable, contaminated, crooked, despicable, detestable, dirty, disagreeable, disgusting, fetid, filthy, gross, impure, loathsome, low, malodorous, nasty, nauseating, nefarious, offensive, polluted, profane, putrid, rank, repulsive, revolting, rotten, smutty, squalid, stinking, tainted, unsportsmanlike, vile, vulgar, wet, wicked, wild.

fragile adj. breakable, brittle, dainty, delicate, feeble, fine, flimsy, frail, frangible, infirm, insubstantial, slight, weak.

fragrant adj. aromatic, balmy, odoriferous, odorous, perfumed, redolent, sweet, sweet-scented, sweet-smelling.

frail adj. breakable, brittle, decrepit, delicate, feeble, flimsy, fragile, infirm, insubstantial, puny, slight, tender, vulnerable, weak.

frank adj. artless, blunt, candid, direct, downright, forthright, four-square, free, honest, ingenuous, open, outright, outspoken, plain, plain-spoken, simple-hearted, sincere, straight, straightforward, transparent, truthful, unconcealed, undisguised, unreserved, unrestricted.

fraud¹ *n.* artifice, cheat, chicane, chicanery, craft, deceit, deception, double-dealing, duplicity, fake, forgery, guile, hoax, humbug, imposture, sham, sharp practice, spuriousness, swindling, swiz, swizzle, take-in, treachery, trickery.

fraud² *n.* bluffer, charlatan, cheat, counterfeit, double-dealer, hoaxer, impostor, malingerer, mountebank, phony, pretender, pseud, quack, swindler.

frequent¹ *adj.* common, commonplace, constant, continual, customary, everyday, familiar, habitual, incessant, numerous, persistent, recurrent, recurring, regular, reiterated, repeated, usual.

frequent² *v.* associate with, attend, crowd, hang about, hang out at, haunt, haunt about, patronize, resort, visit.

fresh *adj.* added, additional, alert, artless, auxiliary, blooming, bold, bouncing, bracing, brazen, bright, brisk, callow, cheeky, chipper, clean, clear, cool, crisp, crude, dewy, different, disrespectful, energetic, extra, fair, familiar, flip, florid, forward, further, glowing, green, hardy, healthy, impudent, inexperienced, innovative, insolent, inventive, latest, lively, modern, modernistic, more, natural, new, novel, original, raw, recent, refreshed, refreshing, renewed, rested, restored, revived, rosy, spanking, sparkling, spick, sprightly, spry, stiff, supplementary, sweet, unspoiled, untrained, untried, up-to-date, vigorous, vital, vivid, warm, wholesome, young, youthful.

fright *n.* alarm, apprehension, consternation, dismay, dread, fear, horror, mess, monstrosity, panic, quaking, scare, scarecrow, shock, sight, spectacle, sweat, terror, the shivers, trepidation.

fruitful *adj.* abundant, advantageous, beneficial, copious, effective, fecund, feracious, fertile, flush, gainful, plenteous, plentiful, productive, profitable, profuse, prolific, rewarding, rich, spawning, successful, teeming, uberous, useful, well-spent, worthwhile.

fulfill *v.* accomplish, achieve, answer, carry out, complete, conform to, execute, implement, perform, realize, satisfy.

full *adj.* abundant, ample, brimming, complete, comprehensive, copious, detailed, exhaustive, extensive, filled, jammed, loaded, orotund, packed, plentiful, replete, satiated, satisfied, saturated, sufficient, uncut, unedited, unexpurgated.

funny *adj.* a card, a caution, a scream, absurd, amusing, comic, comical, entertaining, farcical, hilarious, humorous, jocular, jolly, peculiar, perplexing, puzzling, queer, riotous, silly, slapstick, strange, suspicious, unusual, weird, witty.

fury *n.* anger, desperation, ferocity, fierceness, force, frenzy, impetuosity, intensity, ire, madness, passion, power, rage, savagery, severity, tempestuousness, turbulence, vehemence, violence, wax, wrath.

future *n.* expectation, futurity, hereafter, outlook, prospects.

G

gab *v.* babble, blabber, chatter, drivel, gossip, jaw, prattle, talk, yak.

gag¹ *v.* choke, choke up, curb, disgorge, gasp, heave, muffle, muzzle, puke, quiet, retch, silence, spew, stifle, still, stop up, suppress, throttle, throw up, vomit.

gag² *n.* funny, hoax, jest, joke, one-liner, pun, quip, wisecrack, witticism.

gaiety *n.* animation, blitheness, celebration, cheerfulness, effervescence, elation, exhilaration, festivity, high spirits, hilarity, joyousness, light-heartedness, liveliness, merriment, mirth, revelry, sparkle, sprightliness, vivacity.

gain *v.* achieve, acquire, advance, arrive at, attain, avail, bag, bring in, capture, clear, collect, come to, earn, enlist, gather, get, get to, glean, harvest, improve, increase, make, net, obtain, pick up, procure, produce, profit, progress, reach, realize, reap, secure, win, win over, yield.

game¹ *n.* adventure, amusement, contest, diversion, entertainment, frolic, fun, lark, merriment, merry-making, pastime, recreation, romp, scheme, sport, strategy, tactic, tournament, trick, undertaking.

game² *n.* animals, bag, flesh, game-birds, meat, prey, quarry, spoils.

game³ *adj.* bold, brave, courageous, dauntless, desirous, disposed, dogged, eager, fearless, gallant, gamy, heroic, inclined, interested, intrepid, persevering, persistent, plucky, prepared, ready, resolute, spirited, spunky, unflinching, valiant, valorous, willing.

game⁴ *adj.* bad, crippled, deformed, disabled, gouty, hobbling, incapacitated, injured, lame, maimed.

gang *n.* band, circle, clique, club, company, core, coterie, crew, crowd, group, herd, horde, lot, mob, pack, party, ring, set, shift, squad, team, troupe.

gap *n.* blank, breach, break, chink, cleft, crack, cranny, crevice, diastema, difference, disagreement, discontinuity, disparateness, disparity, divergence, divide, hiatus, hole, inconsistency, interlude, intermission, interruption, interspace, interstice, interval, lacuna, lull, opening, pause, recess, rent, rift, space, vacuity, void.

gather v. accumulate, amass, assemble, collect, congregate, convene, deduce, enfold, garner, glean, harvest, hoard, hold, hug, increase, infer, pile up, reap, round up, stockpile, surmise, understand.

generous adj. abundant, ample, beneficent, benevolent, big-hearted, bounteous, bountiful, charitable, copious, disinterested, free, full, good, high-minded, lavish, liberal, lofty, magnanimous, munificent, noble, open-handed, overflowing, plentiful, princely, rich, soft-boiled, soft-hearted, ungrudging, unresentful, unselfish, unsparing, unstinted, unstinting.

give v. accord, administer, admit, allow, announce, award, bend, bestow, break, cause, cede, collapse, commit, communicate, concede, confer, consign, contribute, deliver, demonstrate, devote, display, do, emit, engender, entrust, evidence, fall, furnish, grant, hand, hand over, impart, indicate, issue, lead, lend, make, make over, manifest, notify, occasion, offer, pay, perform, permit, present, produce, proffer, pronounce, provide, publish, recede, render, retire, set forth, show, sink, state, supply, surrender, vouchsafe, yield.

glad adj. animated, blithe, cheerful, cheering, cheery, delighted, delightful, gleeful, happy, jocund, jovial, joyful, joyous, merry, overjoyed, pleasant, pleased.

glance¹ v. browse, dip, flip, gaze, glimpse, leaf, look, peek, peep, riffle, scan, skim, thumb, touch on, view. n. allusion, coup d'oiel, gander, glimpse, look, mention, once over, peek, peep, reference, squint, view.

glance² v. bounce, brush, cannon, carom, coruscate, flash, gleam, glimmer, glint, glisten, glitter, graze, rebound, reflect, ricochet, shimmer, shine, skim, twinkle.

gleam n. beam, brightness, brilliance, coruscation, flash, flicker, glimmer, glint, gloss, glow, hint, inkling, luster, ray, sheen, shimmer, sparkle, splendor, suggestion, trace. v. coruscate, flare, flash, glance, glimmer, glint, glisten, glitter, glow, scintillate, shimmer, shine, sparkle.

glee n. cheerfulness, delight, elation, exhilaration, exuberance, exultation, fun, gaiety, gladness, gratification, hilarity, jocularity, jollity, joviality, joy, joyfulness, joyousness, liveliness, merriment, mirth, pleasure, sprightliness, triumph, verve.

glint v. flash, gleam, glimmer, glitter, reflect, shine, sparkle, twinkle. n. flash,

gleem, glimmer, glimmering, glitter, shine, sparkle, twinkle, twinkling.

globe n. ball, earth, orb, planet, round, sphere, world.

gloom n. blackness, blues, cloud, cloudiness, damp, dark, darkness, dejection, depression, desolation, despair, despondency, dimness, downheartedness, dullness, dusk, duskiness, gloominess, glumness, low spirits, melancholy, misery, murk murkiness, obscurity, sadness, shade, shadow, sorrow, twilight, unhappiness, woe.

goal n. aim, ambition, aspiration, design, destination, destiny, end, grail, intention, limit, mark, object, objective, purpose, target.

good adj. able, accomplished, adept, adroit, agreeable, ample, approved, approving, beneficent, beneficial, benevolent, calm, capable, choice, clear, clever, competent, complete, congenial, considerate, decorous, dependable, efficient, enjoyable, ethical, excellent, exemplary, fair, favorable, first-rate, gracious, gratifying, great, helpful, honest, honorable, humane, kind, kindly, large, legitimate, long, loyal, mannerly, merciful, meritorious, mild, moral, nice, noble, nourishing, nutritious, obedient, pleasing, pleasurable, polite, positive, praiseworthy, precious, presentable, professional proficient, profitable, proper, propitious, rattling, real, reliable, right, righteous, safe, salubrious, salutary, satisfactory, satisfying, seemly, serviceable, sizeable, skilful, skilled, solid, sound, special, splendid, substantial, sufficient, suitable, sunny, super, superior, sustaining, talented, tested, thorough, tranquil, true, trustworthy, useful, valid, valuable, virtuous, wholesome, worthwhile, worthy.

govern v. administer, allay, bridle, check, command, conduct, contain, control, curb, decide, determine, direct, discipline, guide, influence, inhibit, lead, manage, master, order, oversee, pilot, preside, quell, regulate, reign, restrain, rule, steer, subdue, superintend, supervise, sway, tame, underlie.

gracious adj. accommodating, affable, amenable, amiable, beneficent, benevolent, chivalrous, considerate, courteous, hospitable, indulgent, kind, obliging, polite, refined.

grand adj. A1, admirable, chief, dignified, elevated, eminent, exalted, excellent, fine, first-class, glorious, grandiose, great, highest, illustrious, imposing, impressive, large, leading, lofty, magnificent, main, monumental, opulent, palatial, regal, splendid, sumptuous, super, superb, supreme, wonderful.

grant *v.* accede to, accord, acknowledge, admit, agree to, allocate, allot, allow, apportion, assign, award, bestow, cede, concede, confer, consent to, convey, deign, dispense, donate, give, impart, permit, present, provide, transfer, transmit, vouchsafe, yield.

grateful *adj.* appreciative, aware, beholden, indebted, mindful, obligated, obliged, sensible, thankful.

gratitude *n.* acknowledgment, appreciation, awareness, gratefulness, indebtedness, mindfulness, obligation, recognition, thankfulness, thanks.

greed *n.* acquisitiveness, anxiety, avidity, covetousness, craving, cupidity, desire, eagerness, edacity, gluttony, gormandizing, gourmandism, gormandize, greediness, hunger, insatiability, insatiableness, itchy palm, land-hunger, longing. plutolatry, rapacity, ravenousness, selfishness, voraciousness, voracity.

grief *n.* ache, affliction, agony, anguish, bereavement, glow, burden, dejection, distress, dole, grievance, heartache, heartbreak, misery, mournfulness, pain, regret, remorse, sadness, sorrow, suffering, tragedy, trial, woe.

grim *adj.* adamant, cruel, dour, fierce, forbidding, formidable, gruesome, harsh, horrible, morose, repellent, resolute, ruthless, severe, sinister, stern, sullen, surly, terrible, unpleasant.

gross¹ *adj.* apparent, arrant, bawdy, bestial, big, blatant, blue, boorish, broad, brutish, bulky, callous, coarse, crass, crude, egregious, fat, foul, heavy, heinous, huge, impure, indecent, large, lewd, obscene, offensive, rank, shocking, tasteless, uncouth, vulgar.

gross² *adj.* aggregate, all-inclusive, complete, entire, inclusive, total, whole. *v.* accumulate, aggregate, bring, earn, make, rake in, take, total.

grounds¹ *n.* acres, area, country, district, domain, estate, fields, gardens, habitat, holding, land, park, property, realm, surroundings, terrain, territory, tract.

grounds² *n.* account, argument, base, basis, call, cause, excuse, factor, foundation, inducement, justification, motive, occasion, premise, pretext, principle, rationale, reason, score, vindication.

grounds³ *n.* deposit, dregs, grouts, lees, precipitate, precipitation, sediment, settlings.

grow *v.* advance, arise, augment, become,

branch out, breed, broaden, burgeon, cultivate, develop, diversify, enlarge, evolve, expand, extend, farm, flourish, flower, germinate, get, heighten, improve, increase, issue, mature, multiply, nurture, originate, produce, progress, proliferate, propagate, prosper, raise, ripen, rise, shoot, spread, spring, sprout, stem, stretch, succeed, swell, thicken, thrive, turn, vegetate, wax, widen.

guarantee *n.* assurance, attestation, bond, certainty, collateral, covenant, earnest, endorsement, guaranty, insurance, oath, pledge, promise, security, surety, testimonial, undertaking, voucher, warranty, word, word of honor. *v.* answer for, assure, avouch, certify, ensure, insure, maintain, make certain, make sure of, pledge, promise, protect, secure, swear, underwrite, vouch for, warrant.

guard *v.* beware, conserve, cover, defend, escort, keep, look out, mind, oversee, patrol, police, preserve, protect, safeguard, save, screen, secure, sentinel, shelter, shield, supervise, tend, ward, watch. *n.* attention, backstop, barrier, buffer, bulwark, bumper, care, caution, convoy, custodian, defense, defender, escort, guarantee, heed, lookout, minder, pad, patrol, picket, precaution, protection, protector, rampart, safeguard, screen, security, sentinel, sentry, shield, vigilance, wall, warder, wariness, watch, watchfulness, watchman.

guess *v.* assume, believe, conjecture, estimate, fancy, fathom, feel, guesstimate, hazard, hypothesize, imagine, intuit, judge, opine, penetrate, predict, reckon, solve, speculate, suppose, surmise, suspect, think, work out. *n.* assumption, belief, conjecture, fancy, feeling, guesstimate, hypothesis, intuition, judgment, notion, opinion, prediction, reckoning, shot (in the dark), speculation, supposition, surmise, suspicion, theory.

gutter *n.* channel, conduit, ditch, drain, duct, pipe, sluice, trench, trough, tube.

H

habit¹ *n.* accustomedness, addiction, assuetude, bent, constitution, convention, custom, dependence, disposition, fixation, frame of mind, habitude, inclination, make-up, manner, mannerism, mode, mores, nature, obsession, practice, proclivity, propensity, quirk, routine, rule, second nature, tendency, usage, vice, way, weakness, wont.

habit² *n.* apparel, attire, clothes, clothing,

dress, garb, garment, habiliment.

hack¹ *v.* bark, chop, cough, cut, gash, haggle, hew, kick, lacerate, mangle, mutilate, notch, rasp, slash. *n.* bark, chop, cough, cut, gash, notch, rasp, slash.

hack² *adj.* banal, hackneyed, mediocre, pedestrian, poor, stereotyped, tired, undistinguished, uninspired, unoriginal.

hand *n.* ability, agency, aid, applause, art, artistry, assistance, calligraphy, clap, daddle, direction, fist, flipper, handwriting, help, influence, mitt, ovation, palm, part, participation, paw, penmanship, script, share, skill, support. *v.* aid, assist, conduct, convey, deliver, give, guide, help, lead, offer, pass, present, provide, transmit, yield.

harass *v.* annoy, badger, bait, beleaguer, bother, distress, disturb, exasperate, exhaust, fatigue, harry, hassle, hound, perplex, persecute, pester, plague, tease, tire, torment, trash, trouble, vex, wear out, weary, worry.

hard *adj.* acrimonious, actual, arduous, backbreaking, bitter, burdensome, cold, compact, complex, complicated, cruel, definite, disagreeable, disastrous, distressing, exhausting, fatiguing, forceful, grievous, grim, hostile, impenetrable, implacable, intolerable, laborious, obdurate, plain, powerful, puzzling, resentful, rigid, severe, solid, stern, stiff, stony, strong, stubborn, tough, undeniable, unjust, unkind, unpleasant, uphill, violent, wearying.

harm *n.* abuse, damage, detriment, disservice, evil, hurt, ill, immorality, impairment, iniquity, injury, loss, mischief, misfortune, scathe, sin, sinfulness, vice, wickedness, wrong.

harmful *adj.* baleful, baneful, damaging, deleterious, destructive, detrimental, disadvantageous, evil, hurtful, injurious, noxious, pernicious, pestiferous, pestilent, scatheful.

harmless *adj.* gentle, innocent, innocuous, innoxious, inoffensive, nontoxic, safe, scatheless, unharmed, uninjured, unobjectionable, unscathed.

hate *v.* abhor, abominate, despise, detest, dislike, execrate, loathe, spite.

head *n.* apex, boss, brain, captain, chief, chieftain, commander, crown, director, forefront, front, intellect, intelligence, leader, manager, master, mastermind, principal, promontory, rise, skull, source, start, summit, top, vanguard, vertex.

heal *v.* alleviate, ameliorate, balsam, compose, conciliate, cure, harmonize, mend, patch up, physic, reconcile, regenerate, remedy, restore, salve, settle, soothe, treat.

healthy *adj.* active, beneficial, blooming, bracing, fine, fit, flourishing, good, hale (and hearty), hardy, healthful, hearty, hygienic, in fine feather, in fine fettle, in fine form, in good condition, in good shape, in the pink, invigorating, nourishing, nutritious, physically fit, robust, salubrious, salutary, sound, strong, sturdy, vigorous, well, wholesome.

hearty *adj.* active, affable, ample, ardent, cordial, eager, earnest, ebullient, effusive, energetic, enthusiastic, exuberant, genial, genuine, hale, hardy, jovial, nourishing, robust, sound, stalwart, strong, substantial, true, vigorous, wholehearted.

heat *n.* ardor, excitement, fervor, fever, fury, hotness, intensity, passion, sizzle, sultriness, swelter, vehemence, violence, warmness, warmth, zeal.

height *n.* acme, altitude, apex, apogee, ceiling, climax, crest, crown, culmination, degree, dignity, elevation, eminence, exaltation, extremity, grandeur, highness, hill, limit, loftiness, maximum, mountain, ne plus ultra, peak, pinnacle, prominence, stature, summit, tallness, top, ultimate, utmost, uttermost, vertex, zenith.

help¹ *v.* abet, abstain, aid, alleviate, ameliorate, assist, avoid, back, befriend, bestead, control, cooperate, cure, ease, eschew, facilitate, forbear, heal, hinder, improve, keep from, lend a hand, mitigate, prevent, promote, rally round, refrain from, relieve, remedy, resist, restore, save, second, serve, shun, stand by, succor, support, withstand.

helpful *adj.* accommodating, adjuvant, advantageous, beneficent, beneficial, benevolent, caring, considerate, constructive, cooperative, favorable, fortunate, friendly, kind, neighborly, practical, productive, profitable, serviceable, supportive, sympathetic, timely, useful.

helpless *adj.* abandoned, debilitated, defenseless, dependent, destitute, disabled, exposed, feeble, forlorn, friendless, impotent, incapable, incompetent, infirm, paralyzed, powerless, unfit, unprotected, vulnerable, weak.

herd *n.* assemblage, canaille, collection, cowherd, crowd, crush, drove, flock, herdboy, herdsman, horde, mass, mob, multitude, populace, press, rabble, riffraff, shepherd, swarm, the hoi polloi, the masses, the plebs, throng, vulgus.

heritage *n.* bequest, birthright, deserts, due, endowment, estate, history, inheritance, legacy, lot, past, patrimony, record, share, tradition.

hide *v.* abscond, bury, cache, camouflage,

cloak, conceal, cover, disguise, earth, eclipse, ensconce, go to ground, go underground, hole up, keep dark, lie low, mask, obscure, occult, screen, secret, shadow, shelter, shroud, stash, suppress, take cover, veil, withhold.

hint v. allude, imply, indicate, inkle, innuendo, insinuate, intimate, mention, prompt, suggest, tip off.

hire v. appoint, book, charter, commission, employ, engage, lease, let, rent, reserve, retain, sign up, take on.

history n. account, annals, antecedents, antiquity, autobiography, biography, chronicle, chronology, days of old, days of yore, genealogy, memoirs, narration, narrative, olden days, recapitulation, recital, record, relation, saga, story, tale, the past.

hobby n. avocation, diversion, pastime, pursuit, recreation, relaxation, sideline.

holocaust n. annihilation, carnage, conflagration, destruction, devastation, extermination, extinction, flames, genocide, immolation, inferno, mass murder, massacre, pogrom, sacrifice, slaughter.

holy adj. blessed, consecrated, dedicated, devout, divine, evangelical, evangelistic, faithful, god-fearing, godly, good, hallowed, perfect, pious, pure, religious, righteous, sacred, sacrosanct, saintly, sanctified, sanctimonious, spiritual, sublime, unctuous, venerable, venerated, virtuous.

honest adj. above-board, authentic, bona fide, decent, direct, fair, forthright, genuine, impartial, legitimate, on the level, real, reputable, scrupulous, sincere, straight, true, trustworthy, trusty, truthful, upright, veracious, virtuous.

hope n. ambition, anticipation, aspiration, assumption, assurance, belief, confidence, conviction, desire, dream, expectancy, expectation, faith, hopefulness, longing, optimism, promise, prospect, wish.

hospitable adj. accessible, amenable, amicable, approachable, bountiful, congenial, convivial, cordial, friendly, gemutlich, generous, genial, gracious, kind, liberal, liv(e)able, openminded, receptive, responsive, sociable, tolerant, welcoming.

hostile adj. adverse, alien, antagonistic, anti, antipathetic, bellicose, belligerent, contrary, illdisposed, inhospitable, inimical, malevolent, opposed, opposite, rancorous, unfriendly, ungenial, unkind, unpropitious, unsympathetic, unwelcoming, warlike.

hue n. aspect, cast, character, color, complexion, dye, light, nuance, shade, tincture, tinge, tint, tone.

hug v. cherish, clasp, cling to, cuddle, embrace, enclose, enfold, follow, grip, hold, lock, nurse, retain, skirt, squeeze. n. clasp, clinch, cuddle, embrace, squeeze.

humane adj. beneficent, benevolent, benign, charitable, civilizing, clement, compassionate, forbearing, forgiving, gentle, good, good-natured, human, humanizing, kind, kind-hearted, kindly, lenient, loving, magnanimous, merciful, mild, sympathetic, tender, understanding.

humiliate v. abase, abash, bring low, chagrin, chasten, confound, crush, debase, deflate, degrade, discomfit, discredit, disgrace, embarrass, humble, mortify, shame, subdue, undignify.

humor n. amusement, banter, caprice, comedy, conceit, disposition, farce, fun, funniness, gags, jesting, jocularity, jokes, joking, quirk, temperament, vein, whim, wise-cracks, wit, witticisms, wittiness.

hunger n. appetence, appetite, craving, desire, emptiness, famine, greediness, hungriness, itch, lust, rapacity, ravenousness, starvation, voracity, yearning, yen.

hurry v. accelerate, belt, bustle, dash, dispatch, expedite, fly, get a move on, goad, hasten, hightail it, hump, hustle, jump to it, look lively, move, pike, quicken, rush, scoot, scurry, scuttle, shake a leg, shift, speed up, step on it, step on the gas, urge.

hurt v. abuse, ache, afflict, annoy, bruise, burn, damage, disable, distress, grieve, harm, impair, injure, maim, pain, sadden, smart, spoil, sting, throb, tingle, torture, upset, wound.

hypothesis n. assumption, conjecture, guess, postulate, premise, premiss, presumption, proposition, starting-point, supposition, theory, thesis.

I

idea n. abstraction, belief, clue, concept, design, doctrine, end, essence, estimate, guess, hypothesis, impression, interpretation, judgement, notion, opinion, perception, scheme, suggestion, surmise, suspicion, teaching, theory, thought, viewpoint, vision.

ideal n. archetype, epitome, example, image, model, paradigm, paragon, perfection, prototype, standard, type.

identify v. catalog, classify, detect, diagnose, distinguish, finger, know, label, make out, name, pick out, pinpoint, place, recognize, single out, specify, spot, tag.

identity n. accord, coincidence, correspondence, empathy, existence, individuality, oneness, particularity, personality, quiddity, rapport, sameness, self, selfhood, singularity, unanimity, uniqueness, unity.

idiom *n.* colloquialism, expression, idiolect, idiotism, jargon, language, locution, parlance, phrase, regionalism, set phrase, style, talk, turn of phrase, usage, vernacular.

idle *adj.* abortive, dormant, frivolous, fruitless, futile, good-for-nothing, inactive, indolent, lackadaisical, lazy, purposeless, shiftless, slothful, unemployed, useless, vain, worthless.

idol *n.* beloved, darling, deity, favorite, fetish, god, graven image, hero, icon, image, joss, ju-ju, mumbo-jumbo, pet, pin-up, superstar.

idolize *v.* admire, adore, apotheosize, deify, dote on, exalt, glorify, hero-worship, iconize, lionize, love, revere, reverence, venerate, worship.

ignorant *adj.* clueless, dense, green, gross, half-baked, idealess, ill-informed, illiterate, ill-versed, inexperienced, innocent, innumerate, insensitive, know-nothing, naïve, nascent, oblivious, pig-ignorant, stupid, thick, unacquainted, unaware, unconscious, uncultivated, uneducated, unenlightened, uninformed, uninitiated, uninstructed, unknowing, unlearned, unlettered, unread, unscholarly, unschooled, untaught, untrained, untutored, unwitting.

ignore *v.* blink, cold-shoulder, cut, disregard, neglect, omit, overlook, pass over, pay no attention to, pigeon-hole, reject, set aside, shut one's eyes to, slight, take no notice of, turn a blind eye to, turn a deaf ear to, turn one's back on.

ill *adj.* ailing, diseased, frail, indisposed, infirm, laid up, out of sorts, queasy, sick, under the weather, unhealthy.

illegal *adj.* actionable, banned, black-market, contraband, criminal, felonious, forbidden, illicit, outlawed, pirate, prohibited, proscribed, unauthorized, unconstitutional, under-the-counter, unlawful, unlicensed, wrongful, wrongous.

illustrate *v.* adorn, clarify, decorate, demonstrate, depict, draw, elucidate, emphasize, exemplify, exhibit, explain, illuminate, instance, interpret, ornament, picture, show, sketch.

ill *adj.* ailing, diseased, frail, indisposed, infirm, laid up, out of sorts, queasy, sick, under the weather, unhealthy.

illegal *adj.* actionable, banned, black-market, contraband, criminal, felonious, forbidden, illicit, outlawed, pirate, prohibited, proscribed, unauthorized, un-

constitutional, under-the-counter, unlawful, unlicensed, wrongful, wrongous.

illustrate *v.* adorn, clarify, decorate, demonstrate, depict, draw, elucidate, emphasize, exemplify, exhibit, explain, illuminate, instance, interpret, ornament, picture, show, sketch.

image *n.* appearance, conceit, concept, conception, counterpart, dead ringer, Doppelgänger, double, effigies, effigy, eidolon, facsimile, figure, icon, idea, idol, impression, likeness, perception, picture, portrait, reflection, replica, representation, semblance, similitude, simulacrum, spit, spitting image, statue, trope.

imagine *v.* apprehend, assume, believe, conceive, conceptualize, conjecture, conjure up, create, deduce, deem, devise, dream up, envisage, envision, fancy, fantasize, frame, gather, guess, ideate, infer, invent, judge, picture, plan, project, realize, scheme, suppose, surmise, suspect, take it, think, think of, think up, visualize.

imitate *v.* affect, ape, burlesque, caricature, clone, copy, copycat, counterfeit, do, duplicate, echo, emulate, follow, follow suit, forge, impersonate, mimic, mirror, mock, monkey, parody, parrot, personate, repeat, reproduce, send up, simulate, spoof, take off, travesty.

immature *adj.* adolescent, babyish, callow, childish, crude, green, immatured, imperfect, inexperienced, infantile, jejune, juvenile, premature, puerile, raw, under-age, undeveloped, unfinished, unfledged, unformed, unripe, unseasonable, untimely, young.

immediate *adj.* actual, adjacent, close, contiguous, current, direct, existing, extant, instant, instantaneous, near, nearest, neighboring, next, on hand, present, pressing, primary, prompt, proximate, recent, unhesitating, up-to-date, urgent.

immense *adj.* colossal, elephantine, enormous, giant, herculean, huge, jumbo, large, mammoth, massive, titanic, tremendous, vast.

immoral *adj.* abandoned, bad, corrupt, debauched, degenerate, depraved, dishonest, dissolute, evil, foul, impure, indecent, iniquitous, lecherous, lewd, licentious, nefarious, obscene, pornographic, profligate, reprobate, sinful, unchaste, unethical, unprincipled, unrighteous, unscrupulous, vicious, vile, wanton, wicked, wrong.

immortal *adj.* abiding, ambrosial, constant, deathless, endless, enduring, eternal, everlasting, imperishable, incorruptible, indestructible, lasting, perennial, perpetual, timeless, undying, unfading, unforgettable.

impartial *adj.* detached, disinterested, dispassionate, equal, equitable, evenhanded, fair, just, neutral, nondiscriminating, nonpartisan, objective, open-minded, unbiased, uncommitted, unprejudiced.

impasse *n.* blind alley, cul-de-sac, dead end, deadlock, halt, nonplus, stalemate, stand-off, standstill.

impending *adj.* approaching, brewing, coming, forthcoming, imminent, looming, menacing, near, threatening.

imperfection *n.* blemish, blot, blotch, crack, defect, deficiency, dent, failing, fallibility, fault, flaw, foible, frailty, glitch, inadequacy, incompleteness, insufficiency, peccadillo, shortcoming, stain, taint, weakness.

impersonate *v.* act, ape, caricature, do, imitate, masquerade as, mimic, mock, parody, personate, pose as, take off.

implore *v.* ask, beg, beseech, crave, entreat, importune, plead, pray, solicit, supplicate, wheedle.

imply *v.* betoken, connote, denote, entail, evidence, hint, import, indicate, insinuate, intimate, involve, mean, point to, presuppose, require, signify, suggest.

important *adj.* basic, eminent, essential, far-reaching, foremost, grave, heavy, high-level, high-ranking, influential, key, keynote, large, leading, material, meaningful, momentous, notable, noteworthy, on the map, outstanding, powerful, preeminent, primary, prominent, relevant, salient, seminal, serious, signal, significant, substantial, urgent, valuable, valued, weighty.

impossible *adj.* absurd, hopeless, impracticable, inadmissible, inconceivable, insoluble, intolerable, ludicrous, outrageous, preposterous, unacceptable, unachievable, unattainable, ungovernable, unobtainable, unreasonable, untenable, unthinkable, unworkable.

impress *v.* affect, emboss, emphasize, engrave, excite, fix, grab, imprint, inculcate, indent, influence, inspire, instill, make one's mark, mark, move, namedrop, print, slay, stamp, stand out, stir, strike, sway, touch, wow.

improve *v.* advance, ameliorate, amend, augment, better, correct, culture, develop, embourgeoise, enhance, gentrify, help, increase, look up, meliorate, mend, mend one's ways, perk up, pick up, polish, progress, rally, recover, rectify, recuperate, reform, rise, touch up, turn over a

new leaf, turn the corner, up, upgrade.

impulsive *adj.* hasty, headlong, impetuous, instinctive, intuitive, passionate, precipitant, precipitate, quick, rash, reckless, spontaneous, unconsidered, unpredictable, unpremeditated.

in effect actually, effectively, essentially, for practical purposes, in actuality, in fact, in reality, in the end, in truth, really, to all intents and purposes, virtually, when all is said and done.

in spite of despite, notwithstanding.

inaccurate *adj.* careless, defective, discrepant, erroneous, faulty, imprecise, in error, incorrect, inexact, loose, mistaken, out, unfaithful, unreliable, unrepresentative, unsound, wide of the mark, wild, wrong.

inadequate *adj.* defective, deficient, faulty, imperfect, inapt, incapable, incommensurate, incompetent, incomplete, ineffective, ineffectual, inefficacious, inefficient, insubstantial, insufficient, leaving a little/a lot/much to be desired, meager, niggardly, scanty, short, sketchy, skimpy, sparse, unequal, unfitted, unqualified, wanting.

inaugurate *v.* begin, christen, commence, commission, consecrate, dedicate, enthrone, han(d)sel, induct, initiate, install, instate, institute, introduce, invest, kick off, launch, open, ordain, originate, set up, start, start off, usher in.

incessant *adj.* ceaseless, constant, continual, continuous, endless, eternal, everlasting, interminable, never-ending, nonstop, perpetual, persistent, relentless, unbroken, unceasing, unending, unrelenting, unremitting, weariless.

incident *n.* adventure, affair(e), brush, circumstance, clash, commotion, confrontation, contretemps, disturbance, episode, event, fight, happening, mishap, occasion, occurrence, scene, skirmish.

incinerate *v.* burn, char, cremate, reduce to ashes.

incite *v.* abet, animate, drive, egg on, encourage, excite, foment, goad, impel, inflame, instigate, prompt, provoke, put up to, rouse, set on, solicit, spur, stimulate, stir up, urge, whip up.

inconsiderate *adj.* careless, imprudent, indelicate, insensitive, intolerant, rash, rude, self-centered, selfish, tactless, thoughtless, unconcerned, ungracious, unkind, unthinking.

inconsistent *adj.* at odds, at variance, capricious, changeable, conflicting, contradictory, contrary, discordant, discrepant, erratic, fickle, incoherent, incompatible, incongruous, inconstant, irreconcilable, irregular, unpredictable, unstable, unsteady, variable, varying.

incorrect *adj.* erroneous, false, faulty, flawed, inaccurate, inappropriate, inexact, mistaken, out, specious, untrue, wrong.

increase *v.* add to, advance, amplify, augment, build up, develop, enhance, escalate, expand, extend, heighten, inflate, intensify, magnify, multiply, proliferate, snowball, swell.

incredible *adj.* absurd, amazing, astonishing, astounding, extraordinary, fabulous, farfetched, great, implausible, impossible, improbable, inconceivable, inspired, marvelous, preposterous, prodigious, superb, superhuman, unbelievable, unimaginable, unthinkable, wonderful.

indefinite *adj.* ambiguous, confused, doubtful, equivocal, evasive, general, ill-defined, imprecise, indeterminate, indistinct, inexact, loose, obscure, uncertain, unclear, undecided, undefined, undetermined, unfixed, unfocus(s)ed, unformed, unformulated, unknown, unlimited, unresolved, unsettled, vague.

independent *adj.* absolute, autarchical, autocephalous, autogenous, autonomous, bold, crossbench, free, individualistic, liberated, nonaligned, one's own man, self-contained, self-determining, self-governing, self-reliant, self-sufficient, self-supporting, separate, separated, sovereign, unaided, unbiased, unconnected, unconstrained, uncontrolled, unconventional, unrelated, upon one's legs.

indignant *adj.* angry, annoyed, disgruntled, exasperated, fuming, furibund, furious, heated, huffy, in a paddy, in a wax, incensed, irate, livid, mad, marked, miffed, peeved, provoked, resentful, riled, scornful, sore, waxy, wrathful, wroth.

indirect *adj.* ancillary, backhanded, circuitous, circumlocutory, collateral, contingent, crooked, devious, incidental, meandering, mediate, oblique, rambling, roundabout, secondary, slanted, subsidiary, tortuous, unintended, wandering, winding, zigzag.

indulge *v.* baby, coddle, give in to, gratify, humor, pamper, pander to, spoil, yield to.

inept *adj.* absurd, awkward, bungling, back-handed, clumsy, fatuous, futile, gauche, improper, inappropriate, inapt, incompetent, inexpert, infelicitous, irrelevant, maladroit, malapropos, meaningless, ridiculous, unfit, unhandy, unskillful, unworkmanlike.

inexperienced *adj.* amateur, callow, fresh,

green, immature, inexpert, innocent, nascent, new, raw, unaccustomed, unacquainted, unbearded, unfamiliar, unpractical, unpracticed, unschooled, unseasoned, unskilled, unsophisticated, untrained, untraveled, untried, unused, unversed, verdant.

infect *v.* affect, blight, canker, contaminate, corrupt, defile, enthuse, influence, inject, inspire, pervert, poison, pollute, taint, touch, vitiate.

infer *v.* assume, conclude, conjecture, construe, deduce, derive, extract, extrapolate, gather, presume, surmise, understand.

infinite *adj.* absolute, bottomless, boundless, countless, enormous, eternal, everlasting, fathomless, illimitable, immeasurable, immense, incomputable, inestimable, inexhaustible, interminable, limitless, measureless, never-ending, numberless, perpetual, stupendous, total, unbounded, uncountable, uncounted, unfathomable, untold, vast, wide.

inform[1] *v.* acquaint, advise, apprise, brief, clue up, communicate, enlighten, fill in, illuminate, impart, instruct, intimate, leak, notify, teach, tell, tip off, wise up.

inform[2] *v.* animate, characterize, endue, fill, illuminate, imbue, inspire, invest, irradiate, light up, permeate, suffuse, typify.

information *n.* advises, blurb, briefing, bulletin, clues, communique, data, databank, database, dope, dossier, enlightenment, facts, gen, illumination, info, input, instruction, intelligence, knowledge, low-down, message, news, notice, report, tidings, word.

ingenuous *adj.* artless, candid, childlike, frank, guileless, honest, innocent, open, plain, simple, sincere, trustful, trusting, unreserved, unsophisticated.

ingredient *n.* component, constituent, element, factor, part.

inhabit *v.* abide, bide, dwell, habit, live, lodge, make one's home, occupy, people, populate, possess, reside, settle, settle in, stay, take up one's abode, tenant.

inherent *adj.* basic, characteristic, congenital, connate, essential, fundamental, hereditary, immanent, inborn, inbred, inbuilt, ingrained, inherited, innate, instinctive, intrinsic, native, natural.

inheritance *n.* accession, bequest, birthright, descent, heredity, heritage, legacy, patrimony, succession.

initial *adj.* beginning, early, embryonic, first, formative, inaugural, inauguratory, inceptive, incipient, infant, introductory, opening, original, primary.

injure *v.* abuse, aggrieve, blemish, blight, break, cripple, damage, deface, disable, disfigure, disserve, harm, hurt, ill-treat, impair, maim, maltreat, mar, ruin, scathe, spoil, tarnish, undermine, vandalize, vitiate, weaken, wound, wrong.

injury *n.* abase, annoyance, damage, damnification, detriment, disservice, evil, grievance, harm, hurt, ill, impairment, injustice, insult, lesion, loss, mischief, prejudice, ruin, scathe, trauma, vexation, wound, wrong.

innocent *adj.* artless, benign, blameless, faultless, guileless, guiltless, harmless, honest, immaculate, naive, natural, pure, spotless, stainless, unblemished, virginal, well-intentioned, well-meaning.

inquire *v.* ask, catechize, delve, enquire, examine, explore, inspect, interrogate, investigate, look into, probe, query, quest, question, reconnoiter, scout, scrutinize, search.

insane *adj.* barmy, batty, bizarre, bonkers, brainsick, cracked, crackers, crazed, cuckoo, daft, delirious, demented, deranged, distracted, disturbed, fatuous, foolish, idiotic, impractical, irrational, irresponsible, loony, loopy, lunatic, mad, manic, mental, mentally ill, non compos mentis, nuts, nutty, preposterous, psychotic, queer, schizoid, schizophrenic, screwy, senseless, stupid, touched, unbalanced, unhinged.

insecure *adj.* afraid, anxious, apprehensive, dangerous, defenseless, diffident, exposed, expugnable, flimsy, frail, hazardous, insubstantial, jerry-built, loose, nervous, perilous, precarious, pregnable, rickety, rocky, shaky, uncertain, unconfident, uneasy, unguarded, unprotected, unsafe, unshielded, unsound, unstable, unsteady, unsure, vulnerable, weak, wobbly, worried.

insight *n.* acumen, acuteness, apprehension, awareness, comprehension, discernment, grasp, ingenuity, intelligence, intuition, intuitiveness, judgment, knowledge, observation, penetration, perception, percipience, perspicacity, sensitivity, shrewdness, understanding, vision, wisdom.

insincere *adj.* artificial, canting, deceitful, deceptive, devious, dishonest, disingenuous, dissembling, dissimulating, double-dealing, duplicitous, evasive, faithless, false, hollow, hypocritical, lipdeep, lying, mendacious, perfidious, phony, pretended, synthetic, two-faced, unfaithful, ungenuine, untrue, untruthful.

insinuate *v.* allude, get at, hint, imply, indicate, innuendo, intimate, suggest.

insist *v.* assert, asseverate, aver, claim, contend, demand, dwell on, emphasize, harp on, hold, maintain, persist, reiterate, repeat, request, require, stand firm, stress, swear, urge, vow.

inspect *v.* audit, check, examine, give the once-over, investigate, look over, oversee, peruse, reconnoiter, scan, scrutinize, search, study, superintend, supervise, survey, vet, visit.

instal(l) *v.* consecrate, ensconce, establish, fix, inaugurate, induct, instate, institute, introduce, invest, lay, locate, lodge, ordain, place, plant, position, put, set, set up, settle, site, situate, station.

instance² *n.* advice, application, behest, demand, entreaty, exhortation, importunity, impulse, incitement, initiative, insistence, instigation, pressure, prompting, request, solicitation, urging.

instant *n.* flash, jiffy, juncture, minute, mo, moment, occasion, point, second, shake, split second, tick, time, trice, twinkling, two shakes. *adj.* convenience, direct, fast, immediate, instantaneous, on-the-spot, precooked, prompt, quick, rapid, ready-mixed, split-second, unhesitating, urgent.

instinct *n.* ability, aptitude, faculty, feel, feeling, flair, gift, gut feeling, gut reaction, id, impulse, intuition, knack, nose, predisposition, proclivity, sixth sense, talent, tendency, urge.

institute¹ *v.* appoint, begin, commence, constitute, create, enact, establish, fix, found, inaugurate, induct, initiate, install, introduce, invest, launch, open, ordain, organize, originate, pioneer, set up, settle, start.

institute² *n.* custom, decree, doctrine, dogma, edict, law, maxim, precedent, precept, principle, regulation, rescript, rule, tenet, ukase.

institute³ *n.* academy, association, college, conservatory, foundation, guild, institution, organization, poly, polytechnic, school, seminary, society.

instruct *v.* acquaint, advise, apprise, bid, brief, catechize, charge, coach, command, counsel, direct, discipline, drill, educate, enjoin, enlighten, ground, guide, inform, mandate, notify, order, school, teach, tell, train, tutor.

insult *v.* abuse, affront, call names, fling/throw mud at, give offense to, injure, libel, miscall, offend, outrage, revile, slag, slander, slight, snub, vilify, vilipend.

insure *v.* assure, cover, guarantee, indemnify, protect, underwrite, warrant.

intelligent *adj.* acute, alert, apt, brainy, bright, clever, deep-browed, discerning, enlightened, instructed, knowing, penetrating, perspicacious, quick, quick-witted, rational, razor-sharp, sharp, smart, thinking, well-informed.

intend *v.* aim, consign, contemplate, design, destine, determine, earmark, have a mind, mark out, mean, meditate, plan, project, propose, purpose, scheme, set apart.

intent *adj.* absorbed, alert, attentive, bent, committed, concentrated, concentrating, determined, eager, earnest, engrossed, fixed, hell-bent, industrious, intense, mindful, occupied, piercing, preoccupied, rapt, resolute, resolved, set, steadfast, steady, watchful, wrapped up.

intercourse¹ *n.* association, commerce, communication, communion, congress, connection, contact, conversation, converse, correspondence, dealings, inter-communication, traffic, truck.

intercourse² *n.* carnal knowledge, coition, coitus, copulation, embraces, intimacy, love-making, sex, sexual relations, venery.

interest *n.* activity, advantage, affair, affection, attention, attentiveness, attraction, authority, bag, benefit, business, care, claim, commitment, concern, consequence, curiosity, diversion, finger, gain, good, hobby, importance, influence, investment, involvement, line of country, matter, moment, note, notice, participation, pastime, portion, preoccupation, profit, pursuit, regard, relaxation, relevance, right, share, significance, stake, study, suspicion, sympathy, weight.

interfere *v.* block, butt in, clash, collide, conflict, hamper, handicap, hinder, impede, intervene, intrude, meddle, obstruct, tamper.

interval *n.* break, delay, distance, entr'acte, gap, hiatus, in-between, interim, interlude, intermission, interspace, interstice, meantime, meanwhile, opening, pause, period, playtime, rest, season, space, spell, term, time, wait.

intimate¹ *v.* allude, announce, communicate, declare, hint, impart, imply, indicate, insinuate, state, suggest, tell.

intimate² *adj.* as thick as thieves, bosom, cherished, close, confidential, cozy, dear, deep, deep-seated, detailed, exhaustive, friendly, gremial, informal, innermost, internal, near, palsy-walsy, penetrating, personal, private, privy, profound, secret, warm.

intimidate *v.* alarm, appall, browbeat, bulldoze, bully, coerce, cow, daunt, dishearten, dismay, dispirit, frighten, lean on, overawe, psych out, put the frighteners on, scare, subdue, terrify, terrorize, threaten.

intrigue¹ *v.* attract, charm, fascinate, interest, puzzle, rivet, tantalize, tickle one's fancy, titillate.

intrigue² *n.* affair, amour, cabal, chicanery, collusion, conspiracy, double-dealing, intimacy, knavery, liaison, machination, machination(s), maneuver, manipulation, plot, romance, ruse, scheme, sharp practice, stratagem, string-pulling, trickery, wheeler-dealing, wile, wire-pulling. *v.* connive, conspire, mach-inate, maneuver, plot, scheme.

introduce *v.* acquaint, add, advance, air, announce, begin, bring in, bring up, broach, commence, conduct, establish, familiarize, found, inaugurate, initiate, inject, insert, institute, interpolate, interpose, launch, lead in, lead into, moot, offer, open, organize, pioneer, preface, present, propose, put forward, put in, recommend, set forth, start, submit, suggest, throw in, ventilate.

intrude *v.* aggress, butt in, encroach, infringe, interfere, interrupt, meddle, obtrude, trespass, violate.

invade *v.* assail, assault, attack, burst in, come upon, descend upon, encroach, enter, fall upon, infest, infringe, irrupt, occupy, overrun, overspread, penetrate, pervade, raid, rush into, seize, swarm over, violate

invalid¹ *adj.* ailing, bedridden, disabled, feeble, frail, ill, infirm, invalidish, poorly, sick, sickly, valetudinarian, valetudinary, weak.

invalid² *adj.* baseless, fallacious, false, ill-founded, illogical, incorrect, inoperative, irrational, nugatory, null, null and void, unfounded, unscientific, unsound, untrue, void, worthless.

invent *v.* coin, conceive, concoct, contrive, cook up, create, design, devise, discover, dream up, fabricate, formulate, frame, imagine, improvise, make up, originate, think up, trump up.

inventory *n.* account, catalog, equipment, file, list, listing, record, register, roll, roster, schedule, stock.

investigate *v.* consider, enquire into, examine, explore, go into, inspect, look into, probe, scrutinize, search, see how the land lies, sift, study.

invisible *adj.* concealed, disguised, hidden, imperceptible, inappreciable, inconspicuous, indiscernible, infinitesimal, microscopic, out of sight, unperceivable, unseeable, unseen.

invite *v.* allure, ask, ask for, attract, beckon, beg, bid, bring on, call, court, draw, encourage, entice, lead, provoke, request, seek, solicit, summon, tempt, welcome.

involve *v.* absorb, affect, associate, bind, commit, comprehend, comprise, compromise, concern, connect, contain, cover, draw in, embrace, engage, engross, entail, grip, hold, implicate, imply, include, incorporate, incriminate, inculpate, mean, mix up, necessitate, number among, preoccupy, presuppose, require, rivet, take in, touch.

irate *adj.* angered, angry, annoyed, enraged, exasperated, fuming, furibund, furious, gusty, in a paddy, incensed, indignant, infuriated, ireful, irritated, livid, mad, piqued, provoked, riled, up in arms, waxy, worked up, wrathful, wroth.

ire *n.* anger, annoyance, choler, displeasure, exasperation, fury, indignation, passion, rage, wax, wrath.

irk *v.* aggravate, annoy, bug, disgust, distress, gall, get, get to, irritate, miff, nettle, peeve, provoke, put out, rile, rub up the wrong way, ruffle, vex, weary.

irrational *adj.* aberrant, absurd, alogical, brainless, crazy, demented, foolish, illogical, injudicious, insane, mindless, muddle-headed, nonsensical, preposterous, raving, senseless, silly, unreasonable, unreasoning, unsound, unstable, unthinking, unwise, wild.

irregular *adj.* abnormal, anomalistic(al), anomalous, asymmetrical, broken, bumpy, capricious, craggy, crooked, disconnected, disorderly, eccentric, erratic, exceptional, extraordinary, extravagant, fitful, fluctuating, fragmentary, haphazard, holey, immoderate, improper, inappropriate, inordinate, intermittent, jagged, lop-sided, lumpy, occasional, odd, patchy, peculiar, pitted, queer, quirky, ragged, random, rough, serrated, shifting, spasmodic, sporadic, uncertain, unconventional, unequal, uneven, unofficial, unorthodox, unprocedural, unpunctual, unsteady, unsuitable, unsymmetrical, unsystematic, unusual, variable, wavering.

irrelevant *adj.* alien, extraneous, foreign, immaterial, impertinent, inapplicable, inapposite, inappropriate, inapt, inconsequent, inessential, peripheral, tangential, unapt, unconnected, unnecessary, unrelated.

irresponsible *adj.* carefree, careless, feather-brained, feckless, flighty, footloose, giddy, hare-brained, harum-scarum, heedless, ill-considered, immature, lighthearted, madcap, negligent, rash, reckless, scatterbrained, shiftless, thoughtless, undependable, unreliable, untrustworthy, wild.

irritate *v.* acerbate, aggravate, anger, annoy, bedevil, bother, bug, chafe, embroil, enrage, exacerbate, exasperate, faze, fret, get on one's nerves, get to, give the pip, gravel, harass, incense, inflame, infuriate, intensify, irk, needle, nettle, offend, pain, peeve, pester, pique, provoke, put out, rankle, rile, rouse, rub, ruffle, vex.

isolate *v.* abstract, cut off, detach, disconnect, divorce, exclude, identify, insulate, keep apart, ostracize, pinpoint, quarantine, remove, seclude, segregate, separate, sequester, set apart.

issue¹ *n.* affair, argument, concern, controversy, crux, debate, matter, point, problem, question, subject, topic.

issue² *n.* announcement, broadcast, circulation, copy, delivery, dispersal, dissemination, distribution, edition, emanation, flow, granting, handout, impression, installment, issuance, issuing, number, printing, promulgation, propagation, publication, release, supply, supplying, vent. *v.* announce, broadcast, circulate, deal out, deliver, distribute, emit, give out, mint, produce, promulgate, publicize, publish, put out, release, supply.

issue³ *n.* conclusion, consequence, culmination, denouement, effect, end, finale, outcome, pay-off, product, result, termination, upshot. *v.* arise, burst forth, debouch, emanate, emerge, flow, leak, originate, proceed, rise, spring, stem.

issue⁴ *n.* brood, children, descendants, heirs, offspring, progeny, scions, seed, young.

itemize *v.* count, detail, document, enumerate, instance, inventory, list, mention, number, overname, particularize, record, specify, tabulate.

itinerant *adj.* ambulatory, drifting, journeying, migratory, nomadic, peripatetic, rambling, roaming, rootless, roving, traveling, vagabond, vagrant, wandering, wayfaring.

itinerary *n.* circuit, course, journey, line, plan, program, route, schedule, tour.

J

jab *v.* dig, elbow, jag, lunge, nudge, poke, prod, punch, push, shove, stab, tap, thrust.

jacket *n.* case, casing, coat, cover covering, envelope, folder, jerkin, mackinaw, sheath, shell, skin, wrap, wrapper, wrapping.

jackpot *n.* award, big time, bonanza, kitty, pool, pot, prize, reward, stakes, winnings.

jail *n.* borstal, bridewell, brig, calaboose, can, cells, clink, cooler, coop, custody, guardhouse, hoos(e)gow, house of correction, inside, jailhouse, jankers, jug, lock-up, nick, pen, penitentiary, pokey, prison, quod, reformatory, slammer, stir, tollbooth. *v.* confine, detail, immure, impound, imprison, incarcerate, intern, lock up, quod, send down.

jangle *v.* chime, clank, clash, clatter, jar, jingle, rattle, upset, vibrate. *n.* cacophony, clang, clangor, clash, din, dissonance, jar, racket, rattle, reverberation, stridency, stridor.

janitor *n.* caretaker, concierge, custodian, door-keeper, doorman, janitress, porter.

jar *v.* agitate, annoy, clash, convulse, disagree, discompose, disturb, grate, grind, interfere, irk, irritate, jangle, jolt, nettle, offend, quarrel, rasp, rattle, rock, shake, upset, vibrate. *n.* clash, disagreement, discord, dissonance, grating, irritation, jangle, jolt, quarrel, rasping, wrangling.

jealous *adj.* anxious, apprehensive, attentive, careful, covetous, desirous, emulous, envious, green, green-eyed, grudging, guarded, heedful, invidious, mistrustful, possessive, proprietorial, protective, resentful, rival, solicitous, suspicious, vigilant, wary, watchful, zealous.

jerk¹ *n.* bounce, jog, jolt, lurch, pluck, pull, shrug, throw, thrust, tug, tweak, twitch, wrench, yank. *v.* bounce, flirt, jigger, job, jolt, jounce, lurch, peck, pluck, pull, shrug, throw, thrust, tug, tweak, twitch, wrench, yank.

jerk² *n.* bum, clod, clown, creep, dimwit, dolt, dope, fool, halfwit, idiot, klutz, ninny, prick, schlep, schmo, schmuck, twit.

job *n.* activity, affair, assignment, calling, career, craft, duty, employment, enterprise, livelihood, lot, message, occupation, position, post, profession, pursuit, role, share, trade, undertaking, venture, vocation, work.

jog¹ *v.* activate, arouse, bounce, jar, jerk, joggle, jolt, jostle, jounce, nudge, poke, prod, prompt, push, remind, rock, shake, shove, stimulate, stir. *n.* jerk, jiggle, jolt, nudge, poke, prod, push, reminder, shake, shove.

jog² *v., n.* bump, canter, dogtrot, jogtrot, lope, lumber, pad, run, trot.

join *v.* abut, accompany, accrete, add, adhere, adjoin, affiliate, amalgamate, annex, append, associate, attach, border, border on, butt, cement, coincide, combine, conglutinate, conjoin, conjugate, connect, couple, dock, enlist, enrol, enter, fasten, knit, link, march with, marry, meet, merge, reach, sign up, splice, team, tie, touch, unite, verge on, yoke.

joke *n.* buffoon, butt, clown, conceit, frolic, fun, funny, gag, guy, hoot, jape, jest, lark, laughing-stock, play, pun, quip, quirk, sally, simpleton, sport, target, whimsy, wisecrack, witticism, yarn, yell. *v.* banter, chaff, clown, deride, fool, frolic, gambol, jest, kid, laugh, mock, quip, ridicule, spoof, taunt, tease, wisecrack.

journey *n.* career, course, excursion, expedition, eyre, itinerary, jaunt, odyssey, outing, passage, peregrination, pilgrimage, progress, ramble, route, tour, travel, trek, trip, voyage, wanderings.

joy *n.* blessedness, bliss, charm, delight, ecstasy, elation, exaltation, exultation, felicity, festivity, gaiety, gem, gladness, gladsomeness, glee, gratification, happiness, hilarity, jewel, joyance, joyfulness, joyousness, pleasure, pride, prize, rapture, ravishment, satisfaction, transport, treasure, treat, triumph, wonder.

judge *n.* adjudicator, alcalde, arbiter, arbiter, arbitrator, assessor, authority, beak, connoisseur, critic, Daniel, deemster, doomster, elegantiarum, evaluator, expert, hakim, justice, justiciar, justiciary, Law Lord, magistrate, mediator, moderator, pundit, referee, umpire, virtuoso, wig. *v.* adjudge, adjudicate, appraise, appreciate, arbitrate, ascertain, assess, conclude, condemn, consider, criticize, decide, decree, determine, dijudicate, discern, distinguish, doom, esteem, estimate, evaluate, examine, find, gauge, mediate, opine, rate, reckon, referee, review, rule, sentence, sit, try, umpire, value.

judgment *n.* acumen, appraisal, arbitration, assessment, assize, award, belief, common sense, conclusion, conviction, damnation, decision, decree, decreet, deduction, determination, diagnosis, discernment, discretion, discrimination, doom, enlightenment, estimate, expertise, fate, finding, intelligence, mediation, misfortune, opinion, order, penetration, perceptiveness, percipience, perspicacity, prudence, punishment, result, retribution, ruling, sagacity, sense, sentence, shrewdness, taste, understanding, valuation, verdict, view, virtuosity, wisdom.

jump¹ *v.* bounce, bound, caper, clear, dance, frisk, frolic, gambol, hop, hurdle, jig, leap, pounce, prance, skip, spring, vault. *n.* bounce, bound, capriole, curvet, dance, frisk, frolic, ho, leap, pounce, prance, saltation, skip, spring, vault.

jump² v. avoid, bypass, digress, disregard, evade, ignore, leave out, miss, omit, overshoot, pass over, skip, switch. n. breach, break, gap, hiatus, interruption, interval, lacuna, lapse, omission, saltation, switch.

jump³ v. advance, appreciate, ascend, boost, escalate, gain, hike, increase, mount, rise, spiral, surge. n. advance, ascent, augmentation, boost, escalation, increase, increment, mounting, rise, upsurge, upturn.

jump⁴ v. flinch, jerk, jump out of one's skin, leap in the air, quail, recoil, resile, shrink, start, wince. n. jar, jerk, jolt, lurch, quiver, shiver, shock, spasm, start, swerve, twitch, wrench.

jump⁵ n. barricade, barrier, fence, gate, hedge, hurdle, impediment, obstacle, pons asinorum, rail.

jumpy adj. agitated, anxious, apprehensive, discomposed, edgy, fidgety, jittery, nervous, nervy, restive, restless, shaky, tense, tremulous, uneasy.

just adj. accurate, apposite, appropriate, apt, blameless, condign, conscientious, correct, decent, deserved, disinterested, due, equitable, even-handed, exact, fair, fair-minded, faithful, fitting, four-square, good, honest, honorable, impartial, impeccable, irreproachable, justified, lawful, legitimate, merited, normal, precise, proper, pure, reasonable, regular, right, righteous, rightful, sound, suitable, true, unbiased, unimpeachable, unprejudiced, upright, virtuous, well-deserved.

justice n. amends, appositeness, appropriateness, compensation, correction, dharma, equitableness, equity, fairness, honesty, impartiality, integrity, justifiableness, justness, law, legality, legitimacy, nemesis, penalty, propriety, reasonableness, recompense, rectitude, redress, reparation, requital, right, rightfulness, rightness, satisfaction.

justify v. absolve, acquit, condone, confirm, defend, establish, exculpate, excuse, exonerate, explain, forgive, legalize, legitimize, maintain, pardon, substantiate, support, sustain, uphold, validate, vindicate, warrant.

juvenile n. adolescent, boy, child, girl, halfling, infant, kid, minor, young person, youngster, youth.

K

keen adj. acid, acute, anxious, ardent, assiduous, astute, avid, biting, brilliant, canny, caustic, clever, cutting, devoted, diligent, discerning, discriminating, eager, earnest, ebullient, edged, enthusiastic, fervid, fierce, fond, forthright, impassioned, incisive, industrious, intense, intent, mordant, penetrating, perceptive, perfervid, perspicacious, piercing, pointed, pungent, quick, razorlike, sagacious, sapient, sardonic, satirical, scathing, sedulous, sensitive, sharp, shrewd, shrill, tart, trenchant, wise, zealous.

keep¹ v. accumulate, amass, carry, collect, conserve, control, deal in, deposit, furnish, garner, hang on to, heap, hold, hold on to, maintain, pile, place, possess, preserve, retain, stack, stock, store.

keep² v. be responsible for, board, care for, defend, feed, foster, guard, have charge of, have custody of, look after, maintain, manage, mind, nourish, nurture, operate, protect, provide for, provision, safeguard, shelter, shield, subsidize, support, sustain, tend, victual, watch, watch over. n. board, food, livelihood, living, maintenance, means, nourishment, nurture, subsistence, support, upkeep.

keep³ v. arrest, block, check, constrain, control, curb, delay, detain, deter, hamper, hamstring, hinder, hold, hold back, hold up, impede, inhibit, interfere with, keep back, limit, obstruct, prevent, restrain, retard, shackle, stall, trammel, withhold.

keg n. barrel, butt, cask, drum, firkin, hogshead, puncheon, round, tun, vat.

key n. answer, clue, code, crib, cue, digital, explanation, glossary, guide, index, indicator, interpretation, lead, means, pointer, secret, sign, solution, table, translation. adj. basic, cardinal, central, chief, core, crucial, decisive, essential, fundamental, hinge, important, leading, main, major, pivotal, principal, salient.

kill v. abolish, annihilate, assassinate, beguile, bump off, butcher, cancel, cease, deaden, defeat, destroy, dispatch, do away with, do in, do to death, eliminate, eradicate, execute, exterminate, extinguish, extirpate, fill, finish off, halt, kibosh, knock off, knock on the head, liquidate, mar, martyr, massacre, murder, neutralize, nip in the bud, nullify, obliterate, occupy, pass, pip, put to death, quash, quell, rub out, ruin, scotch, slaughter, slay, smite, smother, spoil, stifle, still, stop, suppress, top, veto, vitiate, while away, zap. n. climax, conclusion, coup de grâce, death, deathblow, denouement, dispatch, end, finish, mop-up, shoot-out.

killing n. big hit, bonanza, coup, fortune, gain, hit, lucky break, profit, smash, success, windfall, winner.

killing³ *adj.* absurd, amusing, comical, funny, hilarious, ludicrous, side-splitting, uproarious.

kind¹ *n.* brand, breed, category, character, class, description, essence, family, genus, habit, ilk, kidney, manner, mold, nature, persuasion, race, set, sort, species, stamp, style, temperament, type, variety.

kind² *adj.* accommodating, affectionate, altruistic, amiable, amicable, avuncular, beneficent, benevolent, benign, benignant, bonhomous, boon, bounteous, bountiful, brotherly, charitable, clement, compassionate, congenial, considerate, cordial, courteous, diplomatic, fatherly, friendly, generous, gentle, giving, good, gracious, hospitable, humane, indulgent, kind-hearted, kindly, lenient, loving, mild, motherly, neighborly, obliging, philanthropic, propitious, sisterly, soft-boiled, soft-hearted, sweet, sympathetic, tactful, tender-hearted, thoughtful, understanding.

kink *n.* bend, coil, complication, corkscrew, crick, crimp, defect, dent, difficulty, entanglement, flaw, hitch, imperfection, indentation, knot, loop, tangle, twist, wrinkle. *v.* bend, coil, crimp, curl, tangle, twist, wrinkle.

kiss *v.* buss, neck, peck, salute, smooch.

knife *n.* blade, carver, cutter, dagger, flick-knife, jackknife, machete, pen-knife, pocket-knife, skene, switchblade, whittle. *v.* cut, impale, lacerate, pierce, rip, slash, stab, wound.

knock¹ *v.* buffet, clap, cuff, ding, hit, knobble, (k)nubble, punch, rap, slap, smack, smite, strike, thump, thwack. *n.* blow, box, chap, clip, clout, con, cuff, hammering, rap, slap, slam, vilify, vilipend. *n.* blame, censure, condemnation, criticism, defeat, failure, rebuff, rejection, reversal, setback, stricture.

knock² *v.* abuse, belittle, carp, cavil, censure, condemn, criticize, deprecate, disparage, find fault, run down, slam, vilify, vilipend. *n.* blame, censure, condemnation, criticism, defeat, failure, rebuff, rejection, reversal, setback, stricture.

knot *v.* bind, entangle, entwine, knit loop, secure, tangle, tether, tie, weave.

know *v.* apprehend, comprehend, discern, distinguish, experience, fathom, identify, intuit, ken, learn, make out, notice, perceive, realize, recognize, see, tell, undergo, understand, wist.

knowledge *n.* ability, acquaintance, acquaintanceship, apprehension, book learning, booklore, cognition, cognizance, comprehension, consciousness, discernment, education, enlightenment, erudition, familiarity, grasp, information, instruction, intelligence, intimacy, judgment, learning, notice, recognition, scholarship, schooling, science, wisdom.

knowledgeable adj. acquainted, aware, bright, cognizant, conscious, conversant, educated, erudite, intelligent, learned, lettered, scholarly, well-informed.

kudos n. acclaim, applause, distinction, esteem, fame, glory, honor, laudation, laurels, plaudits, praise, prestige, regard, renown, repute.

L

label *n.* badge, brand, categorization, characterization, classification, company, description, docket, epithet, mark, marker, sticker, tag, tally, ticket, trademark. *v.* brand, call, categorize, characterize, class, classify, define, describe, designate, docket, dub, identify, mark, name, stamp, tag.

labor¹ *n.* chore, drudgery, effort, employees, exertion, grind, job, labor, laborers, pains, painstaking, sweat, task, toil, undertaking, work, workers, workmen.

labor² *n.* birth, childbirth, contractions, delivery, labor pains, pains, parturition, throes, travail. *v.* dwell on, elaborate, overdo, overemphasize, overstress, strain.

lace¹ *n.* crochet, filigree, mesh-work, netting, open-work, tatting.

lace² *n.* bootlace, cord, lanyard, shoelace, string, thong, tie. *v.* attach, bind, close, do up, fasten, intertwine, interweave, interwork, string, thread, tie.

lace³ *v.* add to, fortify, intermix, mix in, spike.

laceration *n.* cut, gash, injury, maim, mutilation, rent, rip, slash, tear, wound.

lack *n.* absence, dearth, deficiency, deprivation, destitution, emptiness, insufficiency, need, privation, scantiness, scarcity, shortage, shortcoming, shortness, vacancy, void, want.

lad *n.* boy, chap, fellow, guy, juvenile, kid, schoolboy, stripling, youngster, youth.

lady *n.* dame, damsel, gentlewoman, madam(e), matron, noblewoman, woman.

lag *v.* dawdle, delay, hang back, idle, linger, loiter, mosey, saunter, shuffle, straggle, tarry, trail.

land *n.* country, countryside, dirt, district, earth, estate, farmland, fatherland, ground, grounds, loam, motherland, nation, property, province, real estate, realty, region, soil, terra firma, territory, tract. *v.* alight, arrive, berth, bring, carry, cause, come to rest, debark, deposit, disembark, dock, drop, end up, plant, touch down, turn up, wind up.

language *n.* argot, cant, conversation, dialect, diction, discourse, expression, idiolect, idiom, interchange, jargon, lingo, lingua franca, parlance, parole, patois, phraseology, phrasing, speech, style, talk, terminology, tongue, utterance, vernacular, vocabulary, wording.

large *adj.* abundant, ample, big, broad, bulky, capacious, colossal, comprehensive, considerable, copious, colossal, enormous, extensive, full, generous, giant, gigantic, goodly, grand, grandiose, great, huge, immense, jumbo, king-sized, liberal, man-sized, massive, monumental, plentiful, roomy, sizeable, spacious, spanking, substantial, sweeping, swinging, tidy, vast, wide.

last[1] *adj.* aftermost, closing, concluding, conclusive, definitive, extreme, final, furthest, hindmost, latest, rearmost, remotest, terminal, ultimate, utmost.

last[2] *v.* abide, carry on, continue, endure, hold on, hold out, keep (on), perdure, persist, remain, stand up, stay, survive, wear.

late[1] *adj.* behind, behind-hand, belated, delayed, dilatory, last-minute, overdue, slow, tardy, unpunctual.

late[2] *adj.* dead, deceased, defunct, departed, ex-, former, old, past, preceding, previous.

lately *adv.* formerly, here-to-fore, latterly, recently.

latitude *n.* breadth, clearance, compass, elbowroom, extent, field, freedom, indulgence, laxity, leeway, liberty, license, play, range, reach, room, scope, space, span, spread, sweep, width.

laugh *v.* cachinnate, chortle, chuckle, crease up, fall about, giggle, guffaw, snicker, snigger, split one's sides, te(e)hee, titter.

launch *n.* begin, cast, commence, discharge, dispatch, embark on, establish, fire, float, found, inaugurate, initiate, instigate, introduce, open, project, propel, send off, set in motion, start, throw.

lay *v.* advance, allay, alleviate, allocate, allot, appease, apply, arrange, ascribe, assess, assign, assuage, attribute, bet, burden, calm, charge, concoct, contrive, deposit, design, devise, dispose, encumber, establish, gamble, hatch, hazard, impose, impute, leave, locate, lodge, offer, organize, place, plan, plant, plot, posit, position, prepare, present, put, quiet, relieve, risk, saddle, set, set down, set out, settle, soothe, spread, stake, still, submit, suppress, tax, wager, work out.

lazy *adj.* dormant, drowsy, idle, inactive, indolent, inert, languid, languorous, lethargic, shiftless, slack, sleepy, slobby, slothful, slow, slow-moving, sluggish, somnolent, torpid, work-shy.

leach *v.* drain, extract, filter, filtrate, osmose, percolate, seep, strain.

lead *v.* antecede, cause, command, conduct, direct, dispose, draw, escort, exceed, excel, experience, govern, guide, have, head, incline, induce, influence, live, manage, outdo, outstrip, pass, persuade, pilot, precede, preside over, prevail, prompt, spend, steer, supervise, surpass, transcend, undergo, usher.

leak *n.* aperture, chink, crack, crevice, disclosure, divulgence, drip, fissure, hole, leakage, leaking, oozing, opening, percolation, perforation, puncture, seepage. *v.* discharge, disclose, divulge, drip, escape, exude, give away, let slip, let the cat out of the bag, make known, make public, make water, ooze, pass, pass on, percolate, reveal, seep, spill, spill the beans, tell, trickle, weep.

lean[1] *v.* bend, confide, count on, depend, favor, incline, list, prefer, prop, recline, rely, repose, rest, slant, slope, tend, tilt, tip, trust.

lean[2] *adj.* angular, bare, barren, bony, emaciated, gaunt, inadequate, infertile, lank, meager, pitiful, poor, rangy, scanty, scraggy, scrawny, skinny, slender, slim, slink(y), spare, sparse, thin, unfruitful, unproductive, wiry.

learn *v.* acquire, ascertain, assimilate, attain, cognize, con, detect, determine, discern, discover, find out, gather, get off pat, grasp, hear, imbibe, learn by heart, master, memorize, pick up, see, understand.

least *adj.* fewest, last, lowest, meanest, merest, minimum, minutest, poorest, slightest, smallest, tiniest.

leave[1] *v.* abandon, allot, assign, bequeath, cause, cease, cede, commit, consign, decamp, depart, deposit, desert, desist, disappear, do a bunk, drop, entrust, exit, flit, forget, forsake, generate, give over, give up, go, go away, hand down, leave behind, levant, move, produce, pull out, quit, refer, refrain, relinquish, renounce, retire, set out, stop, surrender, take off, transmit, will, withdraw.

leave[2] *n.* allowance, authorization, concession, consent, dispensation, exeat, freedom, furlough, holiday, indulgence, liberty, permission, sabbatical, sanction, time off, vacation.

legal *adj.* aboveboard, allowable, allowed, authorized, constitutional, forensic, judicial, juridical, lawful, legalized, legitimate, licit, permissible, proper, rightful, sanctioned, valid, warrantable.

legend *n.* caption, celebrity, cipher, code, device, fable, fiction, folk tale, household name, inscription, key, luminary, marvel, motto, myth, narrative, phenomenon, prodigy, saga, spectacle, story, tale, tradition, wonder.

legible *adj.* clear, decipherable, discernible, distinct, intelligible, neat, readable.

legislation *n.* act, authorization, bill, charter, codification, constitutionalization, enactment, law, law making, measure, prescription, regulation, ruling, statute.

leisure *n.* breather, ease, freedom, holiday, letup, liberty, opportunity, pause, quiet, recreation, relaxation, respite, rest, retirement, spare time, time off, vacation.

lend *v.* add, advance, afford, bestow, confer, contribute, furnish, give, grant, impart, lease, loan, present, provide, supply.

length *n.* distance, duration, elongation, extensiveness, extent, lengthiness, longitude, measure, period, piece, portion, prolixity, protractedness, reach, section, segment, space, span, stretch, tediousness, term.

lessen *v.* abate, abridge, bate, contract, curtail, deaden, decrease, deescalate, degrade, die down, diminish, dwindle, ease, erode, fail, flag, impair, lighten, lower, minimize, moderate, narrow, reduce, shrink, slack, slow down, weaken

lesson n. admonition, assignment, censure, chiding, class, coaching, deterrent, drill, example, exemplar, exercise, homework, instruction, lecture, message, model, moral, period, practice, precept, punishment, reading, rebuke, recitation, reprimand, reproof, schooling, scolding, task, teaching, tutorial, tutoring, warning.

let[1] *v.* agree to, allow, authorize, cause, charter, consent to, empower, enable, entitle, give leave, give permission, give the go-ahead, give the green light, grant, hire, lease, make, permit, rent, sanction, tolerate.

let[2] *n.* check, constraint, hindrance, impediment, interference, obstacle, obstruction, prohibition, restraint, restriction.

level[1] *adj.* aligned, balanced, calm, champaign, commensurate, comparable, consistent, equable, equal, equivalent, even, even-tempered, flat, flush, horizontal, neck and neck, on a par, plain, proportionate, smooth, stable, steady, uniform.

level[2] *v.* admit, avow, come clean, confess, divulge, open up, tell.

leverage *n.* advantage, ascendancy, authority, clout, force, influence, pull, purchase, rank, strength, weight.

libel *n.* aspersion, calumny, defamation, denigration, obloquy, slander, slur, smear, vilification, vituperation.

liberal *adj.* abundant, advanced, altruistic, ample, beneficent, bounteous, bountiful, broad, broadminded, catholic, charitable, copious, enlightened, flexible, free, freehanded, general, generous, handsome, highminded, humanistic, humanitarian, indulgent, inexact, kind, large-hearted, latitudinarian, lavish, lenient, libertarian, loose, magnanimous, munificent, openhanded, open-hearted, permissive, plentiful, profuse, progressive, radical, reformist, rich, tolerant, unbiased, unbigoted, unprejudiced, unstinting.

liberty *n.* authorization, autonomy, carte blanche, dispensation, emancipation, exemption, franchise, free rein, freedom, immunity, independence, latitude, leave, liberation, license, permission, prerogative, privilege, release, right, sanction, self-determination, sovereignty.

license[1] *n.* authorization, authority, carte blanche, certificate, charter, dispensation, entitlement, exemption, freedom, immunity, imprimatur, independence, latitude, leave, liberty, permission, permit, privilege, right, self-determination, warrant.

license[2] *n.* abandon, amorality, anarchy, debauchery, disorder, dissipation, dissoluteness, excess, immoderation, impropriety, indulgence, intemperance, irresponsibility, lawlessness, laxity, profligacy, unruliness.

lick[1] *v.* brush, dart, flick, lap, play over, smear, taste, tongue, touch, wash. *n.* bit, brush, dab, hint, little, sample, smidgeon, speck, spot, stroke, taste, touch.

lick[2] *v.* beat, best, defeat, excel, flog, outdo, outstrip, overcome, rout, slap, smack, spank, strike, surpass, thrash, top, trounce, vanquish, wallop.

lie[1] *v.* dissimulate, equivocate, fabricate, falsify, fib, forswear oneself, invent, misrepresent, perjure, prevaricate. *n.* bounce, caulker, cram, crammer, deceit, fabrication, falsehood, falsification, falsity, fib, fiction, flam, invention, mendacity, plumper, prevarication, stretcher, tar(r)adiddle, untruth, whacker, white lie, whopper.

lie[2] *v.* be, belong, couch, dwell, exist, extend, inhere, laze, loll, lounge, recline, remain, repose, rest, slump, sprawl, stretch out.

life *n.* activity, animation, autobiography, behavior, being, biography, breath, brio, career, conduct, confessions, continuance, course, creatures, duration, élan vital, energy, entity, essence, existence, fauna, flora and fauna, get-up-and-go, go, growth, heart, high spirits, history, memoirs, soul, span, sparkle, spirit, story, the world, this mortal coil, time, verve, viability, vigor, vita, vital flame, vital spark, vitality, vivacity, way of life, wildlife, zest.

lift *v.* advance, ameliorate, annul, appropriate, arrest, ascend, boost, buoy up, cancel, climb, collar, copy, countermand, crib, dignify, disappear, disperse, dissipate, draw up, elevate, end, enhance, exalt, half-inch, heft, hoist, improve, mount, nab, nick, pick up, pilfer, pinch, pirate, plagiarize, pocket, promote, purloin, raise, rear, relax, remove, rescind, revoke, rise, steal, stop, take, terminate, thieve, up, upgrade, uplift, upraise, vanish.

light[1] *n.* beacon, blaze, brightness, brilliance, bulb, candle, cockcrow, dawn, day, daybreak, daylight, daytime, effulgence, flame, flare, flash, glare, gleam, glim, glint, glow, illumination, incandescence, lambency, lamp, lantern, lighter, lighthouse, luminescence, luminosity, luster, match, morn, morning, phosphorescence, radiance, ray, refulgence, scintillation, shine, sparkle, star, sunrise, sunshine, taper, torch, window, Yang.

light[2] *n.* angle, approach, aspect, attitude, awareness, clue, comprehension, context, elucidation, enlightenment, example, exemplar, explanation, hint, illustration, information, insight, interpretation, knowledge, model, paragon, point of view, slant, understanding, viewpoint.

light[3] *adj.* agile, airy, amusing, animated, blithe, buoyant, carefree, cheerful, cheery, crumbly, delicate, delirious, digestible, diverting, dizzy, easy, effortless, entertaining, facile, faint, fickle, flimsy, friable, frivolous, frugal, funny, gay, gentle, giddy, graceful, humorous, idle, imponderous, inconsequential, inconsiderable, indistinct, insignificant, insubstantial, lightfooted, light-headed, light-hearted, lightweight, lithe, lively, loose, manageable, merry, mild, minute, moderate, modest, nimble, pleasing, porous, portable, reeling, restricted, sandy, scanty, simple, slight, small, soft, spongy, sprightly, sunny, superficial, thin, tiny, trifling, trivial, unchaste, undemanding, underweight, unexacting, unheeding, unsteady, unsubstantial, untaxing, volatile, wanton, weak, witty, worthless.

lighten[1] *v.* beacon, brighten, illume, illuminate, illumine, light up, shine.

lighten[2] *v.* alleviate, ameliorate, assuage, brighten buoy up, cheer, disburden, disencumber, ease, elate, encourage, facilitate, gladden, hearten, inspire, inspirit, lessen, lift, mitigate, perk up, reduce, relieve, revive, unload, uplift.

like[1] *adj.* akin, alike, allied, analogous, approximating, cognate, corresponding, equivalent, homologous, identical, parallel, related, relating, resembling, same, similar.

like[2] *v.* admire, adore, appreciate, approve, care to, cherish, choose, choose to, delight in, desire, dig, enjoy, esteem, fancy, feel inclined, go a bundle on, go for, hold dear, love, prefer, prize, relish, revel in, select, take a shine to, take kindly to, want, wish.

limb *n.* appendage, arm, bough, branch, extension, extremity, fork, leg, member, offshoot, part, projection, ramus, spur, wing.

limit *n.* bitter end, border, bound, boundary, brink, ceiling, check, compass, confines, curb, cut-off point, deadline, edge, end, extent, frontier, limitation, maximum, mete, obstruction, perimeter, periphery, precinct, restraint, restriction, rim, saturation point, termination, terminus, terminus a quo, terminus ad quem, threshold, ultimate, utmost, verge. *v.* bound, check, circumscribe, condition, confine, constrain, curb, delimit, delimitate, demarcate, fix, hem in, hinder, ration, restrain, restrict, specify.

limp[1] *v.* dot, falter, halt, hitch, hobble, hop, shamble, shuffle. *n.* claudication, hitch, hobble, lameness.

limp[2] *adj.* debilitated, drooping, enervated, exhausted, flabby, flaccid, flexible, flexile, floppy, hypotonic, lax, lethargic, limber, loose, pliable, pooped, relaxed, slack, soft, spent, tired, toneless, weak, worn out.

line[1] *n.* band, bar, border, borderline, boundary, cable, chain, channel, column, configuration, contour, cord, crease, crocodile, crow's foot, dash, demarcation, disposition, edge, features, figure, filament, file, firing line, formation, front, front line, frontier, furrow, groove, limit, mark, outline, position, procession, profile, queue, rank, rope, row, rule, score, scratch, sequence, series, silhouette, stipe, strand, streak, string, stroke, tail, thread, trail, trenches, underline, wire, wrinkle. *v.* border, bound, crease, cut, draw, edge, fringe, furrow, hatch, inscribe, mark, rank, rim, rule, score, skirt, verge.

line² *n.* activity, approach, area, avenue, axis, belief, business, calling, course, course of action, department, direction, employment, field, forte, ideology, interest, job, line of country, method, occupation, path, policy, position, practice, procedure, profession, province, pursuit, route, scheme, specialism, specialization, specialty, system, track, trade, trajectory, vocation.

line³ *n.* ancestry, breed, family, lineage, pedigree, race, stirps, stock, strain, succession.

link *n.* association, attachment, bond, communication, component, connection, constituent, division, element, joint, knot, liaison, member, part, piece, relationship, tie, tie-up, union. *v.* associate, attach, bind, bracket, catenate, concatenate, connect, couple, fasten, identify, join, relate, tie, unite, yoke.

lip *n.* border, brim, brink, edge, margin, rim, verge.

liquid *n.* drink, fluid, juice, liquor, lotion, potation, sap, solution. *adj.* aqueous, clear, convertible, dulcet, flowing, fluid, limpid, liquefied, mellifluent, mellifluous, melted, molten, negotiable, running, runny, serous, shining, smooth, soft, sweet, thawed, translucent, transparent, watery, wet.

liquidate *v.* abolish, annihilate, annul, assassinate, bump off, cancel, cash, clear, destroy, discharge, dispatch, dissolve, do away with, do in, eliminate, exterminate, finish off, honor, kill, massacre, murder, pay, pay off, realize, remove, rub out, sell off, sell up, settle, silence, square, terminate, wipe out.

list¹ *n.* catalog, directory, enumeration, file, index, inventory, invoice, listing, litany, record, register, roll, schedule, series, syllabus, table, tabulation, tally. *v.* alphabetize, bill, book, catalog, enroll, enter, enumerate, file, index, itemize, note, record, register, schedule, set down, tabulate, write down.

list² *v.* cant, careen, heel, heel over, incline, lean, slope, tilt, tip. *n.* cant, leaning, slant, slope, tilt.

listen *v.* attend, get a load of, give ear, give heed to, hang on (someone's) words, hang on (someone's) lips, hark, hear, hearken, heed, keep one's ears open, lend an ear, mind, obey, observe, pay attention, pin back one's ears, prick up one's ears, take notice.

literal *adj.* accurate, actual, boring, close, colorless, down-to-earth, dull, exact, factual, faithful, genuine, matter-of-fact, plain, prosaic, prosy, real, simple, strict, true, unexaggerated, unimaginative, uninspired, unvarnished, verbatim, word-for-word.

literary *adj.* bookish, cultivated, cultured, erudite, formal, learned, lettered, literate, refined, scholarly, well-read.

litter¹ *n.* clutter, confusion, debris, detritus, disarray, disorder, fragments, jumble, mess, muck, refuse, rubbish, scatter, scoria, shreds, untidiness, wastage. *v.* bestrew, clutter, derange, disarrange, disorder, mess up, scatter, strew.

litter² *n.* brood, family, offspring, progeny, quiverfull, young.

little *adj.* babyish, base, brief, cheap, diminutive, dwarf, elfin, fleeting, hasty, immature, inconsiderable, infant, infinitesimal, insignificant, insufficient, junior, Lilliputian, meager, mean, microscopic, miniature, minor, minute, negligible, paltry, passing, petite, petty, pickaninny, pint-size(d), pygmy, scant, short, short-lived, skimpy, slender, small, sparse, tiny, transient, trifling, trivial, undeveloped, unimportant, wee, young.

live¹ *v.* abide, breathe, continue, draw breath, dwell, earn a living, endure, exist, fare, feed, get along, hang out, inhabit, last, led, lodge, make ends meet, pass, persist, prevail, remain, reside, settle, stay, subsist, survive.

live² *adj.* active, alert, alive, animate, blazing, breathing, brisk, burning, connected, controversial, current, dynamic, earnest, energetic, existent, glowing, hot, ignited, lively, living, pertinent, pressing, prevalent, relevant, sentient, smoldering, topical, unsettled, vigorous, vital, vivid, wideawake.

livelihood *n.* employment, income, job, living, maintenance, means, occupation, subsistence, support, sustenance, work.

lively *adj.* active, agile, alert, animated, astir, blithe, blithesome, breezy, bright, brisk, buckish, bustling, busy, buxom, buzzing, cheerful, chipper, chirpy, colorful, crowded, energetic, eventful, exciting, forceful, frisky, frolicsome, gay, invigorating, keen, lifesome, lightsome, merry, moving, nimble, perky, quick, racy, refreshing, skittish, sparkling, spirited, sprightly, spry, stimulating, stirring, swinging, vigorous, vivacious, vivid, zippy.

livid¹ *adj.* angry, beside oneself, boiling, enraged, exasperated, fuming, furibund, furious, incensed, indignant, infuriated, irate, ireful, mad, outraged, waxy.

livid² *adj.* angry, ashen, black-and-blue, blanched, bloodless, bruised, contused, discolored, doughy, grayish, leaden, pale, pallid, pasty, purple, wan, waxen, waxy.

living *adj.* active, alive, animated, breathing, existing, live, lively, strong, vigorous, vital.

load *n.* affliction, albatross, bale, burden, cargo, consignment, encumbrance, freight, goods, lading, millstone, onus, oppression, pressure, shipment, trouble, weight, worry. *v.* adulterate, burden, charge, cram, doctor, drug, encumber, fill, fortify, freight, hamper, heap, lade, oppress, overburden, pack, pile, prime, saddle with, stack, stuff, trouble, weigh down, weight, worry.

loan *n.* accommodation, advance, allowance, credit, lend-lease, loan translation, loan-word, mortgage, touch. *v.* accommodate, advance, allow, credit, lend, let out, oblige.

loathe *v.* abhor, abominate, despise, detest, dislike, execrate, hate.

locate *v.* detect, discover, establish, find, fix, identify, lay one's hands on, pinpoint, place, put, run to earth, seat, set, settle, situate, track down, unearth.

location *n.* bearings, locale, locus, place, point, position, site, situation, spot, venue, whereabouts.

lock¹ *n.* bolt, clasp, fastening, padlock. *v.* bolt, clasp, clench, close, clutch, disengage, embrace, encircle, enclose, engage, entangle, entwine, fasten, grapple, grasp, hug, join, latch, link, mesh, press, seal, secure, shut, unite, unlock.

lock² *n.* curl, plait, ringlet, strand, tress, tuft.

log¹ *n.* billet, bole, chunk, stump, timber, trunk.

log² *n.* account, chart, daybook, diary, journal, listing, logbook, record, tally. *v.* book, chart, note, record, register, report, tally, write down, write in, write up.

logic *n.* argumentation, deduction, dialectic(s), rationale, rationality, reason, reasoning, sense.

lone *adj.* deserted, isolated, lonesome, one, only, separate, separated, single, sole, solitary, unaccompanied, unattached, unattended.

loneliness *n.* aloneness, desolation, forlornness, friendlessness, isolation, lone-someness, seclusion, solitariness, solitude.

lonely *adj.* abandoned, alone, apart, companionless, destitute, estranged, forlorn, forsaken, friendless, isolated, lonely-heart, lonesome, outcast, out-of-the-way, remote, secluded, sequestered, solitary, unfrequented, uninhabited, untrodden.

long *adj.* dragging, elongated, expanded, expansive, extended, extensive, far-reaching, interminable, late, lengthy, lingering, long-drawn-out, marathon, prolonged, protracted, slow, spread out, stretched, sustained, tardy.

look *v.* appear, behold, consider, contemplate, display, evidence, examine, exhibit, eye, gape, gawk, gaze, get a load of, glance, goggle, inspect, observe, ogle, peep, regard, rubberneck, scan, scrutinize, see, seem, show, stare, study, survey, view, watch. *n.* air, appearance, aspect, bearing, cast, complexion, countenance, demeanor, effect, examination, expression, eyeful, eye-glance, face, fashion, gaze, glance, glimpse, guise, inspection, look-see, manner, mien, observation, once-over, peek, review, semblance, sight, squint, survey, view.

loose¹ *adj.* baggy, crank, diffuse, disconnected, disordered, easy, floating, free, hanging, ill-defined, imprecise, inaccurate, indefinite, indistinct, inexact, insecure, loosened, movable, rambling, random, relaxed, released, shaky, slack, slackened, sloppy, solute, unattached, unbound, unconfined, unfastened, unfettered, unrestricted, unsecured, untied, vague, wobbly.

loose² *adj.* abandoned, careless, debauched, disreputable, dissipated, dissolute, fast, heedless, immoral, imprudent, lax, lewd, libertine, licentious, negligent, profligate, promiscuous, rash, thoughtless, unchaste, unmindful, wanton.

loosen *v.* deliver, detach, free, let go, let out, liberate, release, separate, set free, slacken, unbind, undo, unfasten, unloose, unloosen, unstick, untie.

lose *v.* capitulate, come a cropper, come to grief, consume, default, deplete, displace, dissipate, dodge, drain, drop, duck, elude, escape, evade, exhaust, expend, fail, fall short, forfeit, forget, get the worst of, give (someone) the slip, lap, lavish, leave behind, lose out on, misfile, mislay, misplace, miss, misspend, outdistance, outrun, outstrip, overtake, pass, pass up, shake off, slip away, squander, stray from, suffer defeat, take a licking, throw off, use up, wander from, waste, yield.

loss *n.* bereavement, cost, damage, debit, debt, defeat, deficiency, deficit, depletion, deprivation, destruction, detriment, disadvantage, disappearance, failure, forfeiture, harm, hurt, impairment, injury, losing, misfortune, privation, ruin, shrinkage, squandering, waste, write-off.

lost *adj.* abandoned, abolished, absent, absorbed, abstracted, adrift, annihilated, astray, baffled, bewildered, confused, consumed, corrupt, damned, demolished, depraved, destroyed, devastated, disappeared, disoriented, dissipated, dissolute, distracted, dreamy, engrossed, entranced, eradicated, exterminated, fallen, forfeited, frittered away, irreclaimable, licentious, misapplied, misdirected, mislaid, misplaced, missed, missing, misspent, misused, mystified, obliterated, off-course, off-track, perished, perplexed, preoccupied, profligate, puzzled, rapt, ruined, spell-bound, squandered, strayed, unrecallable, unrecapturable, unrecoverable, untraceable, vanished, wanton, wasted, wayward, wiped out, wrecked.

loud adj. blaring, blatant, boisterous, booming, brash, brassy, brazen, clamorous, coarse, crass, crude, deafening, ear-piercing, ear-splitting, flamboyant, flashy, garish, gaudy, glaring, high-sounding, loud-mouthed, lurid, noisy, offensive, ostentatious, piercing, raucous, resounding, rowdy, showy, sonorous, stentorian, strident, strong, tasteless, tawdry, thundering, tumultuous, turbulent, vehement, vocal, vociferous, vulgar.

love v. adore, adulate, appreciate, cherish, delight in, desire, dote on, enjoy, fancy, hold dear, idolize, like, prize, relish, savor, take pleasure in, think the world of, treasure, want, worship.

lovely *adj.* admirable, adorable, agreeable, amiable, attractive, beautiful, captivating, charming, comely, delightful, enchanting, engaging, enjoyable, exquisite, graceful, gratifying, handsome, idyllic, nice, pleasant, pleasing, pretty, sweet, taking, winning.

lover *n.* admirer, beau, beloved, boyfriend, Casanova, flame, gigolo, girlfriend, mistress, paramour, philanderer, suitor, swain, sweetheart.

loving *adj.* affectionate, amative, amatorial, amatorian, amatorious, amorous, ardent, cordial, dear, demonstrative, devoted, doting, fond, friendly, kind, passionate, solicitous, tender, warm, warm-hearted.

low[1] *adj.* abject, base, base-born, blue, browned off, cheap, coarse, common, contemptible, crude, dastardly, debilitated, deep, deficient, degraded, dejected, depleted, depraved, depressed, despicable, despondent, disgraceful, dishear-

tened, dishonorable, disreputable, down, down in the dumps, downcast, dying, economical, exhausted, fed up, feeble, forlorn, frail, gloomy, glum, gross, humble, hushed, ignoble, ill, ill-bred, inadequate, inexpensive, inferior, insignificant, little, low-born, low-grade, lowly, low-lying, meager, mean, mediocre, meek, menial miserable, moderate, modest, morose, muffled, muted, nasty, obscene, obscure, paltry, plain, plebeian, poor, prostrate, puny, quiet, reasonable, reduced, rough, rude, sad, scant, scurvy, second-rate, servile, shallow, shoddy, short, simple, sinking, small, soft, sordid, sparse, squat, stricken, stunted, subdued, substandard, sunken, trifling, unbecoming, undignified, unhappy, unpretentious, unrefined, unworthy, vile, vulgar, weak, whispered, worthless.

lower[1] *adj.* inferior, insignificant, junior, lesser, low-level, lowly, minor, secondary, second-class, smaller, subordinate, subservient, under, unimportant. *v.* abase, abate, belittle, condescend, couch, curtail, cut, debase, decrease, degrade, deign, demean, demolish, depress, devalue, diminish, discredit, disgrace, downgrade, drop, fall, humble, humiliate, lessen, let down, minimize, moderate, prune, raze, reduce, sink, slash, soften stoop, submerge, take down, tone down.

loyal *adj.* attached, constant, dependable, devoted, dutiful, faithful, honest, patriotic, sincere, staunch, steadfast, true, true-blue, true-hearted, trustworthy, trusty, unswerving, unwavering.

luck *n.* accident, blessing, break, chance, destiny, fate, fluke, fortuity, fortune, godsend, good fortune, hap, happenstance, hazard, jam, joss, prosperity, serendipity, stroke, success, windfall.

lucrative *adj.* advantageous, fecund, fertile, fruitful, gainful, paying, productive, profitable, remunerative, well-paid.

ludicrous *adj.* absurd, amusing, burlesque, comic, comical, crazy, droll, farcical, funny, incongruous, laughable, nonsensical, odd, outlandish, preposterous, ridiculous, risible, silly, zany.

lug *v.* carry, drag, haul, heave, hump, humph, pull, tote, tow, yank.

lull *v.* abate, allay, calm, cease, compose, decrease, diminish, dwindle, ease off, hush, let up, lullaby, moderate, pacify, quell, quiet, down, sedate, slacken, soothe, still, subdue, subside, tranquilize, wane.

luminous *adj.* bright, brilliant, glowing, illuminated, lighted, lit, lucent, luminescent, luminiferous, lustrous, radiant, resplendent, shining, vivid.

lump¹ *n.* ball, bulge, bump, bunch, cake, chuck, chump, chunk, clod, cluster, cyst, dab, gob, gobbet, group, growth, hunch, hunk, (k)nub, (k)nubble, lob, mass, nugget, piece, protrusion, protuberance, spot, swelling, tuber, tumescence, tumor, wedge, wen. *v.* coalesce, collect, combine, consolidate, group, mass, unite.

lump² *v.* bear (with), brook, endure, put up with, stand, stomach, suffer, swallow, take, tolerate.

lunge *v.* bound, charge, cut, dash, dive, fall upon, grab (at), hit (at), jab, leap, pitch into, plunge, poke, pounce, set upon, stab, strike (at), thrust. *n.* charge, cut, jab, pass, pounce, spring, stab, swing, swipe, thrust.

lure *v.* allure, attract, beckon, decoy, draw, ensnare, entice, inveigle, invite, lead on, seduce, tempt, trepan. *n.* allurement, attraction, bait, carrot, come-on, decoy, enticement, inducement, magnet, siren, song, temptation, train.

lurk *v.* crouch, hide, hide out, lie in wait, lie low, prowl, skulk, slink, sneak, snoop.

lush *adj.* abundant, dense, elaborate, extravagant, flourishing, grand, green, juicy, lavish, luxuriant, luxurious, opulent, ornate, overgrown, palatial, plush, prolific, rank, ripe, ritzy, succulent, sumptuous, superabundant, teeming, tender, verdant.

lust *n.* appetence, appetency, appetite, avidity, carnality, concupiscence, covetousness, craving, cupidity, desire, greed, lasciviousness, lechery, lewdness, libido, licentiousness, longing, passion, prurience, randiness, salaciousness, sensuality, thirst, wantonness.

luxury *n.* affluence, bliss, comfort, delight, dolce vita, enjoyment, extra, extravagance, flesh-pots, flesh-pottery, frill, gratification, hedonism, indulgence, milk and honey, nonessential, opulence, pleasure, richness, satisfaction, splendor, sumptuousness, treat, voluptuousness, well-being.

lying *adj.* accumbent, deceitful, dishonest, dissembling, double-dealing, duplicitous, false, guileful, mendacious, perfidious, treacherous, two-faced, untruthful.

lyrical *adj.* carried away, ecstatic, effusive, emotional, enthusiastic, expressive, impassioned, inspired, musical, passionate, poetic, rapturous, rhapsodic.

M

macabre *adj.* cadaverous, deathlike, deathly, dreadful, eerie, frightening, frightful, ghastly, ghostly, ghoulish, grim, grisly, gruesome, hideous, horrible, horrid, morbid, sick, weird.

Machiavellian *adj.* amoral, artful, astute, calculating, crafty, cunning, cynical, deceitful, designing, double-dealing, foxy, guileful, intriguing, opportunist, perfidious, scheming, shrewd, sly, underhand, unscrupulous, wily.

machine *n.* agency, agent, apparatus, appliance, automaton, contraption, contrivance, device, engine, gadget, gizmo, instrument, machinery, mechanism, organization, party, puppet, robot, setup, structure, system, tool, zombie.

mad *adj.* abandoned, aberrant, absurd, agitated, angry, ardent, avid, bananas, bats, batty, berserk, boisterous, bonkers, crackers, crazed, crazy, cuckoo, daft, delirious, demented, deranged, devoted, distracted, dotty, ebullient, enamored, energetic, enraged, enthusiastic, exasperated, excited, fanatical, fond, foolhardy, foolish, frantic, frenetic, frenzied, fuming, furious, gay, have bats in the belfry, hooked, impassioned, imprudent, in a paddy, incensed, infatuated, infuriated, insane, irate, irrational, irritated, keen, livid, loony, loopy, ludicrous, lunatic, madcap, mental, moonstricken, moon-struck, non compos mentis, nonsensical, nuts, nutty, off one's chump, off one's head, off one's nut, off one's rocker, off one's trolley, out of one's mind, possessed, preposterous, psychotic, rabid, raging, raving, resentful, riotous, round the bend, round the twist, screwball, screwy, senseless, unbalanced, uncontrolled, unhinged, unreasonable, unrestrained, unsafe, unsound, unstable, up the pole, waxy, wild, wrathful, zealous.

magic *n.* allurement, black art, charm, conjuring, enchantment, fascination, illusion, legerdemain, magnetism, medicine, necromancy, occultism, prestidigitation, sleight of hand, sorcery, spell, trickery, voodoo, witchcraft, wizardry.

magnanimous *adj.* altruistic, beneficent, big, big-hearted, bountiful, charitable, free, generous, great-hearted, handsome, high-minded, kind, kindly, large-hearted, large-minded, liberal, munificent, noble, open-handed, philanthropic, selfless, ungrudging, unselfish, unstinting.

magnet *n.* appeal, attraction, bait, draw, enticement, lodestone, lure, solenoid.

magnify *v.* aggrandize, aggravate, amplify, augment, blow up, boost, build up, deepen, dilate, dramatize, enhance, enlarge, exaggerate, expand, greaten, heighten, increase, inflate, intensify, lionize, overdo, overemphasize, overestimate, overplay, overrate, overstate, praise.

main¹ *adj.* absolute, brute, capital, cardinal, central, chief, critical, crucial, direct, downright, entire, essential, extensive, first, foremost, general, great, head, leading, mere, necessary, outstanding, paramount, particular, predominant, preeminent, premier, primary, prime, principal, pure, sheer, special, staple, supreme, undisguised, utmost, utter, vital.

main² *n.* cable, channel, conduit, duct, line, pipe.

maintain *v.* advocate, affirm, allege, argue, assert, asseverate, aver, avouch, avow, back, care for, carry on, champion, claim, conserve, contend, continue, declare, defend, fight for, finance, hold, insist, justify, keep, keep up, look after, make good, nurture, observe, perpetuate, plead for, practice, preserve, profess, prolong, provide, retain, stand by, state, supply, support, sustain, take care of, uphold, vindicate.

majestic *adj.* august, awesome, dignified, distinguished, elevated, exalted, grand, grandiose, imperial, imperious, imposing, impressive, kingly, lofty, magisterial, magnificent, monumental, noble, pompous, princely, queenly, regal, royal, splendid, stately, sublime, superb.

make *v.* accomplish, acquire, act, add up to, amount to, appoint, arrive at, assemble, assign, attain, beget, bring about, build, calculate, carry out, catch, cause, clear, coerce, compel, compose, conclude, constitute, constrain, construct, contract, contribute, convert, create, designate, do, dragoon, draw up, drive, earn, effect elect, embody, enact, engage in, engender, establish, estimate, execute, fabricate, fashion, fix, flow, force, forge, form, frame, gain, gar, gauge, generate, get, give rise to, impel, induce, install, invest, judge, lead to, manufacture, meet, mold, net, nominate, oblige, obtain, occasion, ordain, originate, pass, perform, practice, press, pressurize, prevail upon, proceed, produce, prosecute, put together, reach, reckon, render, require, secure, shape, smith(y), suppose, synthesize, take in, tend, think, turn, win.

makeup¹ *n.* cosmetics, greasepaint, paint, powder, war paint, white-face.

makeup² *n.* arrangement, assembly, build, cast, character, complexion, composition, configuration, constitution, construction, disposition, figure, form, format, make, nature, organ- ization, stamp, structure, style, temper, temperament.

malicious *adj.* baleful, bitchy, bitter, catty, despiteful, evil-minded, hateful, ill-natured, injurious, malevolent, malignant, mischievous, pernicious, rancorous, resentful, sham, spiteful, vengeful, venomous, vicious.

malignant *adj.* baleful, bitter, cancerous, cankered, dangerous, deadly, destructive, devilish, evil, fatal, harmful, hostile, hurtful, inimical, injurious, irremediable, malevolent, malicious, malign, pernicious, spiteful, uncontrollable, venomous, vicious, viperous, virulent.

malleable *adj.* adaptable, compliant, impressionable, manageable, plastic, pliable, tractable.

man¹ adult, attendant, beau, bloke, body, boyfriend, cat, chap, employee, fellow, follower, gentleman, guy, hand, hireling, hombre, human, human being, husband, individual, lover, male, man-servant, partner, person, retainer, servant, soldier, spouse, subject, subordinate, valet, vassal, worker, workman. *v.* crew, fill, garrison, occupy, operate, people, staff, take charge of.

man² *n.* Homo sapiens, human race, humanity, humankind, humans, mankind, mortals, people.

manage *v.* accomplish, administer, arrange, bring about, bring off, carry on, command, concert, conduct, contrive, control, cope, cope with, deal with, direct, dominate, effect, engineer, fare, get along, get by, get on, govern, guide, handle, influence, make do, make out, manipulate, muddle through, operate, oversee, pilot, ply, preside over, rule, run, shift, solicit, stage-manage, steer, succeed, superintend, supervise, survive, train, use, wield.

manageable *adj.* amenable, biddable, compliant, controllable, convenient, docile, easy, governable, handy, submissive, tamable, tractable, wieldy.

mandatory *adj.* binding, compulsory, imperative, necessary, obligatory, required, requisite.

maneuver *n.* action, artifice, device, dodge, exercise, gambit, intrigue, machination, move, movement, operation, plan, plot, ploy, ruse, scheme, stratagem, subterfuge, tactic, trick. *v.* contrive, deploy, devise, direct, drive, engineer, exercise, guide, handle, intrigue, jockey, machinate, manage, manipulate, move, navigate, negotiate, pilot, plan, plot, pull strings, scheme, steer, wangle.

manipulate *v.* conduct, control, cook, direct, employ, engineer, gerrymander, guide, handle, influence, juggle with, maneuver, negotiate, operate, ply, shuffle, steer, use, wield, work.

manner *n.* address, air, appearance, approach, aspect, bearing, behavior, brand, breed, category, character, comportment, conduct, custom, demeanor, deportment, description, fashion, form, genre, habit, kind, line, look, means, method, mien, mode, nature, practice, presence, procedure, process, routine, sort, style, tack, tenor, tone, type, usage, variety, way, wise, wont.

mannerism *n.* characteristic, feature, foible, habit, idiosyncrasy, peculiarity, quirk, trick.

manufacture *v.* assemble, build, churn out compose, concoct, construct, cook up, create, devise, fabricate, forge, form, hatch, invent, make, make up, mass-produce, mold, process, produce, shape, think up, trump up, turn out. *n.* assembly, construction, creation, fabrication, formation, making, mass production, production.

many *adj.* abundant, copious, countless, divers, frequent, innumerable, manifold, multifarious, multifold, multitudinous, myriad, numerous, profuse, sundry, umpteen, varied, various, zillion.

march *v.* countermarch, file, flounce, goose-step, pace, parade, slog, stalk, stride, strut, stump, tramp, tread, walk. *n.* advance, career, demo, demonstration, development, evolution, footslog, gait, hike, pace, parade, passage, procession, progress, progression, step, stride, tramp, trek, walk.

margin *n.* allowance, border, bound, boundary, brim, brink, compass, confine, edge, extra, latitude, leeway, limit, marge, perimeter, periphery, play, rand, rim, room, scope, side, skirt, space, surplus, verge.

marine *adj.* maritime, nautical, naval, ocean-going, oceanic, saltwater, sea, seafaring, seagoing.

mark *n.* aim, badge, blaze, blemish, blot, blotch, brand, bruise, character, characteristic, consequence, criterion, dent, device, dignity, distinction, earmark, emblem, eminence, end, evidence, fame, feature, fingermark, footmark, footprint, goal, hallmark, importance, impression, incision, index, indication, influence, label, level, line, lineament, marque, measure, nick, norm, notability, note, noteworthiness, notice, object, objective, pock, prestige, print, proof, purpose, quality, regard, scar, scratch, seal, sign, smudge, splotch, spot, stain, stamp, stand-

ard, standing, streak, symbol, symptom, target, token, trace, track, trail, vestige, yardstick. *v.* appraise, assess, attend, betoken, blemish, blot, blotch, brand, bruise, characterize, correct, denote, dent, distinguish, evaluate, evince, exemplify, grade, hearken, heed, identify, illustrate, impress, imprint, label, list, listen, mind, nick, note, notice, observe, print, regard, remark, scar, scratch, show, smudge, splotch, stain, stamp, streak, take to heart, traumatize, watch.

marriage *n.* alliance, amalgamation, association, confederation, coupling, espousal, link, match, matrimony, merger, nuptials, union, wedding, wedlock.

marry *v.* ally, bond, espouse, get hitched, get spliced, join, jump the broomstick, knit, link, match, merge, spice, tie, tie the knot, unify, unite, wed, wive, yoke.

marvelous *adj.* amazing, astonishing, astounding, beyond belief, breathtaking, excellent, extraordinary, fabulous, fantastic, glorious, great, implausible, improbable, incredible, magnificent, miraculous, phenomenal, prodigious, remarkable, sensational, singular, smashing, spectacular, splendid, stupendous, super, superb, surprising, terrific, unbelievable, unlikely, wonderful, wondrous.

masculine *adj.* bold, brave, butch, gallant, hardy, macho, male, manlike, manly, mannish, muscular, powerful, red-blooded, resolute, robust, stout-hearted, strapping, strong, tomboyish, vigorous, virile.

mass[1] *n.* accumulation, aggregate, aggregation, assemblage, band, batch, block, body, bulk, bunch, chunk, collection, combination, concretion, congeries, conglomeration, crowd, dimension, entirety, group, heap, horde, host, hunk, lion's share, load, lot, lump, magnitude, majority, mob, number, piece, pile, preponderance, quantity, size, stack, sum, sum total, throng, totality, troop, welter, whole. *adj.* across-the-board, blanket, comprehensive, extensive, general, indiscriminate, large-scale, pandemic, popular, sweeping, wholesale, widespread.

mass[2] *n.* communion, eucharist, holy communion, Lord's Supper, Lord's Table.

massacre *v.* annihilate, butcher, decimate, exterminate, kill, mow down, murder, slaughter, slay, wipe out.

master *n.* ace, adept, baas, boss, bwana, captain, chief, commander, controller, dab hand, deacon, director, employer, expert, genius, governor, guide, guru, head, instructor, lord, maestro, manager, overlord, overseer, owner, past master, pedagogue, preceptor, principal, pro, ruler, school-master, skipper, superintendent, swami, teacher, tutor, virtuoso, wizard.

masterpiece *n.* chef d'oeuvre, classic, jewel, magnum opus, masterwork, museum piece, pièce de résistance, tour de force.

match¹ *n.* bout, competition, contest, game, main, test, trial, venue. *v.* compete, contend, oppose, pit against, rival, vie.

match² *n.* affiliation, alliance, combination, companion, complement, copy, counterpart, couple, dead ringer, double, duet, duplicate, equal, equivalent, fellow, like, look-alike, marriage, mate, pair, pairing, parallel, partnership, peer, replica, ringer, rival, spit, spitting image, tally, twin, union. *v.* accompany, accord, adapt, agree, ally, blend, combine, compare, coordinate, correspond, couple, emulate, equal, fit, gee, go together, go with, harmonize, join, link, marry, mate, measure up to, pair, relate, rival, suit, tally, team, tone with, unite, yoke.

match³ *n.* fuse, fusee, light, lucifer, lucifer match, safety match, spill, taper, vesta, vesuvian.

material *n.* body, cloth, constituents, data, element, evidence, fabric, facts, information, literature, matter, notes, stuff, substance, textile, work.

materialize *v.* appear, arise, happen, occur, take shape, turn up.

maternal *adj.* loving, motherly, protective.

matter¹ *n.* affair, amount, argument, body, business, complication, concern, consequence, context, difficulty, distress, episode, event, import, importance, incident, issue, material, moment, note, occurrence, problem, proceeding, purport, quantity, question, sense, significance, situation, stuff, subject, substance, sum, text, thesis, thing, topic, transaction, trouble, upset, weight, worry.

matter² *n.* discharge, purulence, pus, secretion, suppuration. *v.* discharge, secrete.

mature *adj.* adult, complete, due, fit, full-blown, full-grown, fully fledged, grown, grown-up, matured, mellow, nubile, perfect, perfected, reaped, ready, ripe, ripened, seasoned, well-thought-out.

maybe *adv.* haply, happen, perchance, perhaps, possibly.

meal¹ *n.* banquet, barbecue, blow-out, breakfast, brunch, collation, déjeuner, déjeuner à la fourchette, dinner, feast, lunch, luncheon, nosh, nosh-up, petit déjeuner, picnic, repast, scoff, snack, supper, tea, tuck-in.

meal² *n.* farina, flour, grits, oatmeal, powder.

mean¹ *adj.* abject, base, callous, common, contemptible, despicable, disgraceful, hard-hearted, hostile, humble, inconsiderable, inferior, lowly, malicious, miserable, miserly, nasty, near, niggardly, obscure, parsimonious, penurious, petty, pusillanimous, rude, run-down, scrub, scurvy, seedy, selfish, servile, shabby, small-minded, squalid, stingy, tawdry, tight, tight-fisted, vicious, vile, vulgar, wretched.

mean² *v.* adumbrate, aim, aspire, augur, betoken, cause, connote, contemplate, convey, denote, design, desire, destine, drive at, engender, entail, express, fate, fit, foreshadow, foretell, get at, give rise to, herald, hint, imply, indicate, insinuate, intend, involve, lead to, make, match, necessitate, omen, plan, portend, predestine, preordain, presage, produce, promise, propose, purport, purpose, represent, result in, say, set out, signify, spell, stand for, suggest, suit, symbolize, want, wish.

mean³ *adj.* average, halfway, intermediate, medial, median, medium, middle, middling, moderate, normal, standard.

meaning *n.* aim, connotation, construction, denotation, design, drift, end, explanation, force, gist, goal, idea, implication, import, intention, interpretation, matter, message, object, plan, point, purport, purpose, sense, significance, signification, substance, thrust, trend, upshot, validity, value, worth.

measure *n.* act, action, allotment, allowance, amount, amplitude, beat, bill, bounds, cadence, capacity, control, course, criterion, deed, degree, démarche, enactment, example, expedient, extent, foot, gauge, jigger, law, limit, limitation, magnitude, maneuver, means, method, meter, model, moderation, norm, portion, procedure, proceeding, proportion, quantity, quota, range, ration, reach, resolution, restraint, rhythm, rule, scale, scope, share, size, standard, statute, step, system, test, touchstone, verse, yardstick. *v.* admeasure, appraise, assess, calculate, calibrate, choose, compute, determine, estimate, evaluate, fathom, gauge, judge, mark out, measure off, measure out, plumb, quantify, rate, size, sound, step, survey, value, weigh.

meat¹ *n.* chow, comestibles, eats, fare, food, grub, nourishment, nutriment, provisions, rations, sustenance, viands, victuals.

meat² *n.* core, crux, essence, fundamentals, gist, heart, kernel, marrow, nub, nucleus, pith, point, substance.

mechanic *n.* artificer, engineer, machinist, operative, operator, repairman, technician.

medal *n.* award, decoration, gong, honor, medallion, prize, reward, trophy.

meddle *v.* interfere, interlope, interpose, intervene, intrude, mell, pry, put one's oar in, tamper.

mediate *v.* arbitrate, conciliate, incubate, intercede, interpose, intervene, moderate, negotiate, reconcile, referee, resolve, settle, step in, umpire.

medium¹ *adj.* average, fair, intermediate, mean, medial, median, mediocre, middle, middling, midway, standard. *n.* average, center, compromise, golden mean, happy medium, mean, middle, middle ground, midpoint, via media, way.

medium² *n.* agency, avenue, base, channel, excipient, form, instrument, instrumentality, means, mode, organ, vehicle, way.

medium³ *n.* clairvoyant, psychic, spiritualist.

medium⁴ *n.* ambience, atmosphere, circumstances, conditions, element, environment, habitat, influences, milieu, setting, surroundings.

meet *v.* abut, adjoin, answer, assemble, bear, bump into, chance on, collect, come across, come together, comply, confront, congregate, connect, contact, convene, converge, cross, discharge, encounter, endure, equal, experience, face, find, forgather, fulfill, gather, go through, gratify, handle, happen on, intersect, join, link up, match, measure up to, muster, perform, rally, rencounter, run across, run into, satisfy, suffer, touch, undergo, unite.

melancholy *adj.* blue, dejected, depressed, despondent, disconsolate, dismal, dispirited, doleful, down, down in the dumps, down in the mouth, downcast, downhearted, gloomy, glum, heavyhearted, hipped, joyless, low, low-spirited, lugubrious, melancholic, miserable, moody, mournful, pensive, sad, somber, sorrowful, splenific, unhappy, woebegone, woeful.

member *n.* appendage, arm, associate, component, constituent, element, extremity, fellow, initiate, leg, limb, organ, part, portion, representative.

memento *n.* keepsake, memorial, record, relic, remembrance, reminder, souvenir, token, trophy.

memory *n.* celebrity, commemoration, fame, glory, honor, memorial, name, recall, recollection, remembrance, reminiscence, renown, reputation, repute, retention.

menial *adj.* abject, attending, base, boring, degrading, demeaning, dull, fawning, groveling, helping, humble, humdrum, ignoble, ignominious, low, lowly, mean, obsequious, routine, servile, slavish, sorry, subservient, sycophantic, unskilled, vile.

mental¹ *adj.* abstract, cerebral, cognitive, conceptual, ideational, intellectual, noetic, rational, theoretical.

mental² *adj.* crazy, deranged, disturbed, insane, loony, loopy, lunatic, mad, psychiatric, psychotic, unbalanced, unstable.

merchandise *n.* cargo, commodities, freight, goods, produce, products, shipment, staples, stock, stock in trade, truck, vendibles, wares. *v.* carry, deal in, distribute, market, peddle, retail, sell, supply, trade, traffic in, vend.

mercy *n.* benevolence, blessing, boon, charity, clemency, compassion, favor, forbearance, forgiveness, godsend, grace, humanitarianism, kindness, lenience, pity, quarter, relief.

merit *n.* advantage, asset, claim, credit, desert, due, excellence, good, goodness, integrity, justification, quality, right, strong point, talent, value, virtue, worth, worthiness.

merry *adj.* amusing, blithe, blithesome, boon, carefree, cheerful, chirpy, comic, comical, convivial, crank, elevated, facetious, festive, frolicsome, fun-loving, funny, gay, glad, gleeful, happy, heartsome, hilarious, humorous, jocular, jocund, jolly, joyful, joyous, light-hearted, mellow, mirthful, rollicking, saturnalian, sportful, sportive, squiffy, tiddly, tipsy, vivacious.

messenger *n.* agent, ambassador, bearer, carrier, courier, delivery boy, emissary, envoy, errand boy, go-between, harbinger, herald, in-between, internuncio, mercury, nuncio, runner, send, vaunt-courier.

messy *adj.* chaotic, cluttered, confused, dirty, disheveled, disordered, disorganized, grubby, littered, muddled, sloppy, slovenly, unkempt, untidy, yucky.

method *n.* approach, arrangement, course, design, fashion, form, manner, mode, modus operandi, order, orderliness, organization, pattern, plan, planning, practice, procedure, process, program, purpose, regularity, routine, rule, scheme, structure, style, system, technique, way.

middle *adj.* central, halfway, inner, inside, intermediate, intervening, mean, medial, median, mediate, medium, mid, middle-bracket.

might *n.* ability, capability, capacity, clout, efficacy, efficiency, energy, force, heftiness, muscularity, potency, power, powerfulness, prowess, puissance, strength, sway, valor, vigor.

migrate *v.* drift, emigrate, journey, move, roam, rove, shift, travel, trek, voyage, wander.

migratory *adj.* gipsy, itinerant, migrant, nomadic, peripatetic, roving, shifting, transient, transitory, traveling, vagrant, wandering.

mild *adj.* amiable, balmy, bland, clam, clement, compassionate, docile, easy, easygong, equable, forbearing, forgiving, gentle, indulgent, lenient, meek, mellow, merciful, moderate, pacific, passive, peaceable, placid, pleasant, serene, smooth, soft, temperate, tender, tranquil, warm.

militant *adj.* active, aggressive, assertive, belligerent, combating, combative, contending, embattled, fighting, hawkish, pugnacious, vigorous, warring. *n.* activist, aggressor, belligerent, combatant, fighter, partisan, struggler, warrior.

mind[1] *n.* attention, attitude, believe, bent, brains, concentration, desire, disposition, fancy, feeling, genius, gray matter, head, imagination, inclination, inner, intellect, intellectual, intelligence, intention, judgment, leaning, marbles, memory, mentality, notion, opinion, outlook, point of view, psyche, purpose, rationality, reason, recollection, remembrance, sanity, sense, senses, sensorium, sensory, sentiment, spirit, tendency, thinker, thinking, thoughts, understanding, urge, view, will, wish, wits.

mind[2] *v.* care, demur, disapprove, dislike, object, resent, take offense.

mind[3] *v.* adhere to, attend, attend to, be careful, be on one's guard, comply with, ensure, follow, guard, have charge of, heed, keep an eye on, listen to, look after, make certain, mark, note, notice, obey, observe, pay attention, pay heed to, regard, respect, take care, take care of, take heed, tend, watch.

mine[1] *n.* abundance, deposit, excavation, fund, hoard, lode, pit, source, stock, store, supply, treasury, tunnel, vein, wealth. *v.* delve, dig up, excavate, extract, quarry, remove, tunnel, unearth, weaken.

mine[2] *n.* bomb, depth charge, egg, explosive, land mine.

minimum *n.* bottom, least, lowest point, nadir, slightest.

minister *n.* administrator, agent, aide, ambassador, assistant, churchman, clergyman, cleric, delegate, diplomat, divine, ecclesiastic, envoy, executive, officeholder, official, parson, pastor, plenipotentiary, preacher, priest, servant, subordinate, underlying, vicar, vizier. *v.* accommodate, administer, attend, cater to, nurse, pander to, serve, take care of, tend.

minor *adj.* inconsequential, inconsiderable, inferior, insignificant, junior, lesser, light, negligible, paltry, petty, piddling, secondary, second-class, slight, small, smaller, subordinate, trifling, trivial, unclassified, unimportant, younger.

minute[1] *n.* flash, instant, jiff, jiffy, mo, moment, sec, second, shake, tick, trice.

minute[2] *adj.* close, critical, detailed, diminutive, exact, exhaustive, fine, inconsiderable, infinitesimal, itsy-bitsy, Lilliputian, little, meticulous, microscopic, miniature, minimum, minuscule, negligible, painstaking, paltry, petty, picayune, piddling, precise, punctilious, puny, slender, slight, small, tiny, trifling, trivial, unimportant.

misbehave *v.* act up, carry on, get up to mischief, kick over the traces, mess about, muck about, offend, transgress, trespass.

miscalculate *v.* blunder, boob, err, get wrong, misjudge, overestimate, overrate, overvalue, slip up, underestimate, underrate, undervalue.

miscellaneous *adj.* assorted, confused, diverse, diversified, indiscriminate, jumbled, manifold, many, mingled, mixed, motley, multifarious, multiform, promiscuous, sundry, varied, various.

mischief[1] *n.* bane, damage, detriment, devilment, deviltry, disruption, evil, harm, hurt, impishness, injury, misbehavior, misfortune, monkey business, naughtiness, pranks, roguery, roguishness, shenanigans, trouble, waggery, waywardness.

mischief[2] *n.* devil, imp, monkey, nuisance, pest, rapscallion, rascal, rapscallion, rogue, scallywag, scamp, tyke, villain.

miserable *adj.* abject, anguished, contemptible, dejected, deplorable, depressed, despondent, destitute, detestable, dismal, distressed, dolorous, down, downcast, dreary, forlorn, gloomy, glum, heartbroken, ignominious, low, luckless, lugubrious, meager, mean, melancholic, melancholy, mournful, needy, niggardly,

paltry, pathetic, penniless, piteous, pitiable, pitiful, poor, sad, scanty, scurvy, shabby, shameful, sordid, sorrowful, sorrowing, sorry, squalid, starcrossed, stricken, tearful, unhappy, vile, woebegone, worthless, wretched.

misery¹ *n.* abjectness, adversity, affliction, agony, anguish, bale, bane, bitter pill, blow, burden, calamity, catastrophe, cross, curse, depression, desolation, despair, destitution, disaster, discomfort, distress, dole, dolor, extremity, gloom, grief, hardship, heartache, heartbreak, humiliation, indigence, living death, load, melancholia, melancholy, misfortune, mortification, need, oppression, ordeal, penury, poverty, privation, prostration, sadness, sordidness, sorrow, squalor, suffering, torment, torture, trial, tribulation, trouble, unhappiness, want, woe, wretchedness.

misery² *n.* grouch, Jeremiah, Job's comforter, killjoy, moaner, pessimist, prophet of doom, ray of sunshine, sourpuss, spoilsport, Weary Willie, wet blanket, whiner.

misfortune *n.* accident, adversity, affliction, bad luck, blow, buffet, calamity, catastrophe, disaster, failure, grief, hardship, harm, ill-luck, infelicity, loss, misadventure, mischance, misery, mishap, reverse, setback, sorrow, tragedy, trial, tribulation, trouble, woe.

misjudge *v.* miscalculate, mistake, overestimate, overrate, underestimate, undervalue.

mislead *v.* beguile, bluff, deceive, delude, fool, give a bum steer, hoodwink, lead up the garden path, misadvise, misdirect, misguide, misinform, pull the wool over someone's eyes, snow, take for a ride, take in.

miss¹ *v.* avoid, bypass, circumvent, err, escape, evade, fail, forego, jump, lack, leave out, let go, let slip, lose, miscarry, mistake, obviate, omit, overlook, pass over, pass up, sidestep, skip, slip, trip. *n.* blunder, error, failure, fault, fiasco, flop, lack, lacuna, loss, mistake, need, omission, oversight, want.

miss² *v.* grieve for, lack, lament, long for, mourn, need, pine for, regret, sorrow for, want, wish, yearn for.

miss³ *n.* child, damsel, demoiselle, flapper, Fraulein, girl, junior miss, kid, lass, lassie, mademoiselle, maid, maiden, missy, Ms., schoolgirl, spinster, teenager, young thing.

missing *adj.* absent, astray, disappeared, gone, lacking, lost, minus, mislaid, misplaced, strayed, unaccounted-for, wanting.

mistake *n.* aberration, blunder, boner, boob, boo-boo, clinker, corrigendum, erratum, error, fallacy, false move, fault, faux pas, floater, folly, gaffe, gaucherie, goof, howler, inaccuracy, indiscretion, inexactitude, lapse, lapsus, lapsus calami, lapsus linguae, lapsus memoriae, literal, malapropism, misapprehension, miscalculation, misconception, misjudgment, misprint, misprision, mispronunciation, misreading, misspelling, misunderstanding, oversight, scape, slip, slip-up, solecism, tactlessness, trespass. *v.* blunder, confound, confuse, err, get the wrong end of the stick, goof, misapprehend, miscalculate, misconceive, misconstrue, misinterpret, misjudge, misread, misreckon, misunderstand, slip up.

misunderstand *v.* get the wrong end of the stick, get wrong, misapprehend, miscomprehend, misconceive, misconstrue, mishear, misinterpret, misjudge, misread, miss the point, mistake, take up wrong(ly).

mix *v.* allay, alloy, amalgamate, associate, blend, coalesce, combine, commingle, compound, consort, cross, dash, fold in, fraternize, fuse, hobnob, homogenize, incorporate, intermingle, intermix, interweave, join, jumble, mell, merge, mingle, shuffle, socialize, synthesize, unite.

mixture *n.* admixture, alloy, amalgam, amalgamation, association, assortment, blend, brew, coalescence, combination, combine, composite, compost, compound, concoction, conglomeration, cross, fusion, gallimaufry, half-breed, hotchpotch, hybrid, miscegenation, miscellany, mix, mixed bag, mongrel, olio, ollapodrida, pastiche, potpourri, salad, salmagundi, synthesis, union, variety.

mock *v.* ape, baffle, befool, burlesque, caricature, chaff, cheat, counterfeit, debunk, deceive, defeat, defy, delude, deride, disappoint, disparage, dupe, elude, explode, fleer, flout, foil, fool, frustrate, guy, imitate, insult, jeer, lampoon, laugh at, laugh in (someone's) face, laugh to scorn, make fun of, make sport of, mimic, parody, parrot, poke fun at, queer, quiz, ridicule, satirize, scoff, scorn, send up, sneer, take the mickey, taunt, tease, thwart, travesty, twit.

moderate *adj.* abstemious, average, calm, centrist, continent, controlled, cool, deliberate, disciplined, equable, fair, fairish, frugal, gentle, indifferent, judicious, limited, mediocre, medium, middle-of-the-road, middling, mild, modest, nonextreme, ordinary, passable, peaceable, quiet, rational, reasonable, restrained, sensible, sober, soft-shell(ed), so-so, steady, temperate, unexceptional, well-regulated. *v.* abate, allay, alleviate, appease, assuage, blunt, calm, chasten, check, control, curb, cushion, decrease, diminish, dwindle, ease, lessen, mitigate, modify, modulate, pacify, palliate, play down, quiet, regulate, repress, restrain, slake, soften, soft-pedal, subdue, subside, tame, temper, tone down.

modern *adj.* advanced, avant-garde, contemporary, current, emancipated, fashionable, fresh, go-ahead, innovative, inventive, jazzy, late, latest, mod, modernistic, modish, new, newfangled, novel, present, present-day, progressive, recent, stylish, trendy, twentieth-century, up-to-date, up-to-the-minute, with-it.

modest *adj.* bashful, blushing, chaste, chastened, coy, demure, diffident, discreet, fair, humble, limited, maidenly, meek, middling, moderate, ordinary, proper, quiet, reserved, reticent, retiring, seemly, self-conscious, self-effacing, shame-faced, shy, simple, small, timid, unassuming, unexceptional, unpresuming, unpresumptuous, unpretending, unpretentious, verecund.

modify *v.* abate, adapt, adjust, allay, alter, temper, change, convert, improve, lessen, limit, lower, moderate, modulate, qualify, recast, redesign, redo, reduce, refashion, reform, remodel, reorganize, reshape, restrain, restrict, revise, rework, soften, temper, tone down, transform, vary.

moist *adj.* clammy, damp, dampish, dampy, dank, dewy, dripping, drizzly, humid, marshy, muggy, rainy, soggy, swampy, tearful, vaporous, watery, wet, wettish.

mold[1] *n.* arrangement, brand, build, caliber, cast, character, configuration, construction, cut, design, die, fashion, form, format, frame, framework, ilk, kidney, kind, line, make, matrix, model, nature, pattern, quality, shape, sort, stamp, structure, style, template, type. *v.* affect, carve, cast, construct, control, create, design, direct, fashion, fit, forge, form, hew, influence, make, model, sculpt, sculpture, shape, stamp, work.

mold[2] *n.* black, black spot, blight, fungus, mildew, moldiness, must, mustiness, rust.

mold[3] *n.* clods, dirt, dust, earth, ground, humus, loam, soil.

moment[1] *n.* breathing-while, flash, hour, instant, jiff, jiffy, juncture, less than no time, minute, mo, point, second, shake, split second, stage, tick, time, trice, twink, twinkling.

moment[2] *n.* concern, consequence, gravity, import, importance, note interest, seriousness, significance, substance, value, weight, weightiness, worth.

momentary *adj.* brief, elusive, ephemeral, evanescent, fleeting, flying, fugitive, hasty, passing, quick, short, short-lived, temporary, transient, transitory.

money *n.* baksheesh, banco, banknotes, bankroll, boodle, brass, bread, capital, cash, chips, coin, currency, dough, dumps, fat, filthy lucre, fonds, funds, gelt, gold, gravy, greens, hard cash, hard money, legal tender, lolly, loot, mazuma, mint-sauce, money of account, moolah, pelf, readies, ready, money, riches, scrip, shekels, silver, specie, spondulix (spondulicks), stumpy, sugar, the needful, the ready, the wherewithal, tin, wealth.

monkey[1] *n.* ape, primate, simian.

monkey[2] *n.* dupe, fool, imp, jackanapes, laughing-stock, mug, rapscallion, rascal, rogue, scallywag, scamp. *v.* fiddle, fidget, fool, interfere, meddle, mess, play, potter, tamper, tinker, trifle.

monster *n.* abortion, barbarian, basilisk, beast, behemoth, bogeyman, brute, centaur, chimera, cockatrice, colossus, Cyclops, demon, devil, fiend, freak, giant, Gorgon, harpy, hellhound, hippocampus, leviathan, mammoth, monstrosity, mutant, ogre, ogress, prodigy, savage, villain.

monument *n.* ancient monument, antiquity, barrow, commemoration, cross, dolmen, evidence, gravestone, headstone, marker, mausoleum, memento, memorial, obelisk, pillar, record, relic, remembrance, reminder, shaft, shrine, statute, testament, token, tombstone.

mood *n.* blues, caprice, depression, disposition, doldrums, dumps, fit, frame of mind, grumps, humor, melancholy, pique, spirit, state of mind, sulk, temper, tenor, the sulks, vein, whim.

moral *adj.* blameless, chaste, clean-living, decent, equitable, ethical, good, high-minded, honest, honorable, incorruptible, innocent, just, meritorious, moralistic, noble, principled, proper, pure, responsible, right, righteous, square, straight, temperate, upright, upstanding, virtuous.

morale *n.* confidence, espirit de corps, heart, mettle, mood, resolve, self-esteem, spirit, spirits, state of mind, temper.

morality *n.* chastity, conduct, decency, deontology, equity, ethicality, ethicalness, ethics, ethos, goodness, habits, honesty, ideals, integrity, justice, manners, morals, mores, philosophy, principle, principles, probity, propriety, rationale, rectitude, righteousness, standards, tightness, uprightness, virtue.

morbid *adj.* ailing, brooding, corrupt, deadly, diseased, dreadful, ghastly, ghoulish, gloomy, grim, grisly, gruesome, hideous, horrid, hypochondriacal, infected, lugubrious, macabre, malignant, melancholy, neurotic, pathological, peccant, pessimistic, putrid, sick, sickly, somber, unhealthy, unsound, unwholesome, vicious.

more *adj.* added, additional, alternative, extra, fresh, further, increased, new, other, renewed, repeated, spare, supplementary. *adv.* again, better, further, longer.

morsel *n.* atom, bit, bite, crumb, fraction, fragment, grain, modicum, mouthful, nibble, part, piece, scrap, segment, slice, soupçon, taste, tidbit.

mortal *adj.* agonizing, awful, bodily, corporeal, deadly, deathful, dire, earthly, enormous, ephemeral, extreme, fatal, fleshly, grave, great, human, impermanent, implacable, intense, irreconcilable, lethal lethiferious, mortiferous, passing, perishable, relentless, remorseless, severe, sublunary, sworn, temporal, terrible, transient, unrelenting, worldly.

mortified *adj.* abashed, affronted, annoyed, ashamed, chagrined, chastened, confounded, crushed, dead, decayed, deflated, discomfited, displeased, embarrassed, gangrenous, humbled, humiliated, necrotic, put out, put to shame, putrefied, putrid, rotted, rotten, shamed, vexed.

motion *n.* action, change, dynamics, flow, flux, gesticulation, gesture, inclination, kinesics, kinetics, locomotion, mechanics, mobility, motility, move, movement, nod, passage, passing, progress, proposal, proposition, recommendation, sign, signal, submission, suggestion, transit, travel, wave. *v.* beckon, direct, gesticulate, gesture, nod, sign, signal, usher, wave.

motivate *v.* actuate, arouse, bring, cause, draw, drive, encourage, impel, incite, induce, inspire, inspirit, instigate, kindle, lead, move, persuade, prompt, propel, provoke, push, spur, stimulate, stir, trigger, urge.

motive *n.* cause, consideration, design, desire, encouragement, ground(s), impulse, incentive, incitement, inducement, influence, inspiration, intention, mainspring, motivation, object, occasion, purpose, rationale, reason, spur, stimulus, thinking, urge.

mourn *v.* bemoan, bewail, beweep, deplore, grieve, keen, lament, miss, regret, rue, sorrow, wail, weep.

move *v.* activate, actuate, adjust, advance, advise, advocate, affect, agitate, budge, carry, cause, change, cover the ground, decamp, depart, disturb, drift, drive, ease, edge, excite, flit, get, give rise to, go, go away, gravitate, impel, impress, incite, induce, influence, inspire, instigate, jiggle, lead, leave, locomote, make strides, march, migrate, motivate, move house, operate, persuade, proceed, progress, prompt, propel, propose, pull, push, put forward, quit, recommend, relocate, remove, rouse, run, set going, shift, shove, start, stimulate, stir, submit, suggest, switch, take, touch, transfer, transport, transpose, turn, urge, walk. *n.* act, action, deed, démarche, dodge, drift, flit, flitting, go, maneuver, measure, migration, motion, movement, ploy, relocation, removal, ruse, shift, step, stratagem, stroke, tack, tactic, transfer, turn.

movement *n.* act, action, activity, advance, agitation, beat, cadence, campaign, change, crusade, current, development, displacement, division, drift, drive, evolution, exercise, faction, flow, front, gesture, ground swell, group, grouping, innards, machinery, maneuver, measure, mechanism, meter, motion, move, moving, operation, organization, pace, part, party, passage, progress, progression, rhythm, section, shift, steps, stir, stirring, swing, tempo, tendency, transfer, trend, workings, works.

moving *adj.* affecting, ambulant, ambulatory, arousing, dynamic, emotional, emotive, exciting, impelling, impressive, inspirational, inspiring, locomobile, mobile, motile, motivating, movable, pathetic, persuasive, poignant, portable, propelling, running, stimulating, stimulative, stirring, touching, unfixed.

much *adv.* considerably, copiously, decidedly, exceedingly, frequently, greatly, often. *adj.* a lot of, abundant, ample, considerable, copious, great, plenteous, plenty of, sizable, substantial. *n.* heaps, lashings, loads, lots, oodles, plenty, scads.

muddle *v.* befuddle, bewilder, confound, confuse, daze, disarrange, disorder, disorganize, disorient(ate), fuddle, jumble, make a mess of, mess, mix up, mull, perplex, scramble, spoil, stupefy, tangle. *n.* balls up, chaos, clutter, cock-up, confusion, daze, disarray, disorder, disorganization, jumble, mess, mix-up, mull, perplexity, pie, plight, predicament, puddle, snarl-up, tangle.

mug¹ *n.* breaker, cup, flagon, jug, pot, tankard, jug.

mug² *n.* chump, fool, gull, innocent, mark, sap, saphead, simpleton, soft touch, sucker.

mug³ *n.* clock, countenance, dial, face, features, mush, phiz(og), puss, visage.

mug⁴ *v.* attack, bash, batter, beat up, garrote, jump (on), mill, rob, roll, set upon, steal from, waylay.

multiply *v.* accumulate, augment, boost, breed, build up, expand, extend, increase, intensify, proliferate, propagate, reproduce, spread.

multitude *n.* army, assemblage, assembly, collection, commonalty, concourse, congregation, crowd, herd, hive, hoi polloi, horde, host, legion, lot, lots, mass, mob, myriad, people, populace, proletariat, public, rabble, sea, swarm, throng.

mundane *adj.* banal, commonplace, day-to-day, earthly, everyday, fleshly, human, humdrum, material, mortal, ordinary, prosaic, routine, secular, temporal, terrestrial, workaday, worldly.

murder *n.* agony, assassination, bloodshed, butchery, carnage, danger, difficulty, fratricide, hell, homicide, infanticide, killing, manslaughter, massacre, misery, ordeal, parricide, patricide, slaying, trial, trouble. *v.* abuse, assassinate, bump off, butcher, destroy, dispatch, do in, drub, eliminate, hammer, hit, kill, mangle, mar, massacre, misuse, rub out, ruin, slaughter, slay, spoil, thrash, waste.

murderer *n.* assassin, butcher, cut-throat, hitman, homicide, killer, matricide, parricide, patricide, slaughterer, slayer.

muscle *n.* brawn, clout, depressor, force, forcefulness, levator, might, potency, power, sinew, stamina, strength, sturdiness, tendon, weight.

musical *adj.* dulcet, euphonious, harmonious, lifting, lyrical, melodic, melodious, sweet-sounding, tuneful.

mutter *v.* complain, grouch, grouse, grumble, mumble, murmur, rumble.

mutual *adj.* common, communal, complementary, exchanged, interchangeable, interchanged, joint, reciprocal, reciprocated, requited, returned, shared.

myriad *adj.* boundless, countless, immeasurable, incalculable, innumerable, limitless, multitudinous, untold. *n.* army, flood, horde, host, millions, mountain, multitude, scores, sea, swarm, thousands, throng.

mystery *n.* arcanum, conundrum, enigma, problem, puzzle, question, riddle, secrecy, secret.

myth *n.* allegory, delusion, fable, fairy tale, fancy, fantasy, fiction, figment, illusion, legend, old wives' tale, parable, saga, story, superstition, tradition, untruism.

N

nag *v.* annoy, badger, berate, chivvy, goad, harass, harry, henpeck, irritate, kvetch, pain, pester, plague, scold, torment, upbraid, vex. *n.* harpy, harridan, kvetch(er), scold, shrew, tartar, termagant, virago.

naked *adj.* bare, blatant, defenseless, denuded, disrobed, divested, evident, exposed, helpless, in puris in the altogether, in the buff, insecure, manifest, mother-naked, nude, open, overt, patent, plain, simple, skyclad, stark, starkers, stark naked, stripped, unadorned, unarmed, unclothed, unconcealed, uncovered, undisguised, undraped, undressed, unexaggerated, unguarded, unmistakable, unprotected, unqualified, unvarnished, vulnerable.

name *n.* acronym, agnomen, appellation, character, cognomen, compilation, credit, denomination, designation, distinction, eminence, epithet, esteem, fame, handle, honor, moni(c)ker, nickname, note, praise, renown, reputation, repute, sobriquet, stage name, term, title, to-name. *v.* appoint, baptize, bename, betitle, call, choose, christen, cite, classify, cognominate, commission, denominate, designate, dub, entitle, identify, label, mention, nominate, select, specify, style, term, title.

nap¹ *v.* catnap, doze, drop off, drowse, kip, nod, nod off, rest, sleep, snooze. *n.* catnap, forty winks, kip, rest, shuteye, siesta, sleep.

nap² *n.* down, downiness, fuzz, grain, pile, shag, weave.

narcotic *n.* anesthetic, analgesic, drug, opiate, pain-killer, sedative, tranquilizer.

narrate *v.* chronicle, describe, detail, recite, recount, rehearse, relate, repeat, report, set forth, state, tell, unfold.

narrow *adj.* attenuated, avaricious, biased, bigoted, circumscribed, close, confined, constricted, contracted, cramped, dogmatic, exclusive, fine, illiberal, incapacious, intolerant, limited, meager, mean, mercenary, narrow-minded, near, niggardly, partial, pinched, prejudiced, reactionary, restricted, scanty, select, simplistic, slender, slim, small-minded, spare, straitened, tapering, thin, tight, ungenerous.

nasty *adj.* abusive, annoying, bad, bad-tempered, base, critical, dangerous, despicable, dirty, disagreeable, disgusting, distasteful, filthy, foul, gross, horrible, impure, indecent, lascivious, lewd, licentious, loathsome, low-down, malicious, malodorous, mean, mephitic, nauseating, noisome, objectionable, obnoxious, obscene, odious, offensive, painful, polluted, pornographic, repellent, repugnant, ribald, serious, severe, sickening, smutty, spiteful, unappetizing, unpleasant, unsavory, vicious, vile, waspish.

native *adj.* aboriginal, autochthonous, built-in, congenital, domestic, endemic, genuine, hereditary, home, home-born, home-bred, home-grown, home-made, inborn, inbred, indigenous, ingrained, inherent, inherited, innate, instinctive, intrinsic, inveterate, local, mother, natal, natural, original, real, vernacular. *n.* aborigine, citizen, countryman, dweller, indigent, inhabitant, national, resident.

natural *adj.* artless, candid, characteristic, common, congenital, constitutional, essential, everyday, frank, genuine, inborn, indigenous, ingenuous, inherent, innate, instinctive, intuitive, legitimate, logical natal, native, normal, open, ordinary, organic, plain, pure, real, regular, simple, spontaneous, typical, unaffected, unbleached, unforced, unlabored, unlearned, unmixed, unpolished, unpretentious, unrefined, unsophisticated, unstudied, untaught, usual, whole.

naturally *adv.* absolutely, artlessly, as a matter of course, candidly, certainly, customarily, frankly, genuinely, informally, normally, of course, plainly, simply, spontaneously, typically, unaffectedly, unpretentiously.

nature[1] *n.* attributes, category, character, complexion, constitution, cosmos, creation, description, disposition, earth, environment, essence, features, humor, inbeing, kind, make-up, mood, outlook quality, sort, species, style, temper, temperament, traits, type, universe, variety, world.

nature[2] *n.* country, countryside, landscape, natural history, scenery.

naval *adj.* marine, maritime, nautical, sea.

near *adj.* accessible, adjacent, adjoining, akin, allied, alongside, approaching, at close quarters, attached, beside, bordering, close, connected, contiguous, dear, familiar, forthcoming, handy, imminent, impending, in the offing, intimate, looming, near at hand, nearby, neighboring, next, nigh, on the cards, proximal, related, touching.

nearly *adv.* about, all but, almost, approaching, approximately, as good as, closely, just about, not quite, practically, pretty much, pretty well, roughly, virtually, well-nigh.

necessary *adj.* certain, compulsory, de rigueur, essential, fated, imperative, indispensable, ineluctable, inescapable, inevitable, inexorable, mandatory, needed, needful, obligatory, required, requisite, unavoidable, vital.

need *v.* call for, crave, demand, lack, miss, necessitate, require, want. *n.* demand, deprivation, desideratum, destitution, distress, emergency, essential, exigency, extremity, impecuniousness, inadequacy, indigence, insufficiency, lack, longing, necessity, neediness, obligation, paucity, penury, poverty, privation, requirement, requisite, shortage, urgency, want, wish.

needed *adj.* called for, compulsory, desired, essential, lacking, necessary, obligatory, required, requisite, wanted.

needless *adj.* causeless, dispensable, excessive, expendable, gratuitous, groundless, inessential, nonessential, pointless, purposeless, redundant, superfluous, uncalled-for, unessential, unnecessary, unwanted, useless.

needy *adj.* deprived destitute, disadvantaged, impecunious, impoverished, indigent, penniless, penurious, poor, poverty-stricken, underprivileged.

neglect *v.* contemn, disdain, disprovide disregard, forget, ignore, leave alone, let slide, omit, overlook, pass by, pigeonhole, rebuff, scorn, shirk, skimp, slight, spurn.

negligent *adj.* careless, cursory, disregardful, forgetful, inattentive, indifferent, lax, neglectful, nonchalant, offhand, regardless, remiss, slack, thoughtless, uncaring, unmindful, unthinking.

negotiate *v.* adjudicate, arbitrate, arrange, bargain, broker, clear, conciliate, confer, consult, contract, cross, deal, debate, discuss, get past, handle, manage, mediate, parley, pass, settle, surmount, transact, transverse, treat, work out.

neighborhood *n.* community, confines, district, environs, locale, locality, precincts, proximity, purlieus, quarter, region, surroundings, vicinage, vicinity.

nerve *n.* audacity, boldness, bottle, brass, bravery, brazenness, cheek, chutzpah, coolness, courage, daring, determination, effrontery, endurance, energy, fearlessness, firmness, force, fortitude, gall, gameness, grit, guts, hardihood, impertinence, impudence, insolence, intrepidity, mettle, might, pluck, resolution, sauce, spirit, spunk, steadfastness, temerity, vigor, will.

nervous *adj.* agitated, anxious, apprehensive, edgy, excitable, fearful, fidgety, flustered, hesitant, highly strung, highstrung, hysterical, jittery, jumpy, nervy, neurotic, on edge, shaky, tense, timid, timorous, twitchy, uneasy, uptight, weak, windy, worried.

net¹ *n.* drag, dragnet, drift, driftnet, dropnet, lattice, mesh, netting, network, openwork, reticulum, tracery, web. *v.* apprehend, bag, benet, capture, catch, enmesh, ensnare, entangle, nab, trap.

net² *adj.* after tax, clear, final, lowest. *v.* accumulate, bring in, clear, earn, gain, make, obtain, realize, reap, receive, secure.

neurotic *adj.* abnormal, anxious, compulsive, deviant, disordered, distraught, disturbed, maladjusted, manic, morbid, nervous, obsessive, overwrought, unhealthy, unstable, wearisome.

neutral *adj.* colorless, disinterested, dispassionate, dull, even-handed, expressionless, impartial, indeterminate, indifferent, indistinct, indistinguishable, intermediate, nonaligned, noncommittal, nondescript, nonpartisan, unbia(s)sed, uncommitted, undecided, undefined, uninvolved, unprejudiced.

new *adj.* added, advanced, altered, changed, contemporary, current, different, extra, fresh, improved, latest, modern, modernistic, modernized, modish, more, newborn, newfangled, novel, original, recent, redesigned, renewed, restored, supplementary, topical, trendy, ultramodern, unfamiliar, unknowns, unused, unusual, up-to-date, up-to-the-minute, virgin.

news *n.* account, advice, bulletin, communique, disclosure, dispatch, exposé, gen, gossip, hearsay, information, intelligence, latest, leak, release, report, revelation, rumor, scandal, statement, story, tidings, update, word.

next *adj.* adjacent, adjoining, closest, consequent, ensuing, following, later, nearest, neighboring, sequent, sequential, subsequent, succeeding.

nice *adj.* accurate, agreeable, amiable, attractive, careful, charming, commendable, courteous, critical, cultured, dainty, delicate, delightful, discriminating, exact, exacting, fastidious, fine, finical, friendly, genteel, good, kind, likable, meticulous,

neat, particular, pleasant, pleasurable, polite, precise, prepossessing, punctilious, purist, refined, respectable, rigorous, scrupulous, strict, subtle, tidy, trim, virtuous, well-bred, well-mannered.

niche¹ *n.* alcove, corner, cubby, cubbyhole, hollow, nook, opening, recess.

niche² *n.* calling, métier, pigeon-hole, place, position, slot, vocation.

nick¹ *n.* chip, cut, damage, dent, indent, indentation, mark, notch, scar, score, scratch, snick. *v.* chip, cut, damage, dent, indent, mark, notch, scar, score, scratch, snick.

nick² *v.* finger, knap, knock off, lag, pilfer, pinch, snitch, steal.

nil *n.* duck, goose-egg, love, naught, nihil, none, nothing, zero.

nip¹ *v.* bite, catch, check, clip, compress, grip, nibble, pinch, snag, snap, snip, squeeze, tweak, twitch.

nip² *n.* dram, draught, drop, finger, mouthful, peg, portion, shot, sip, slug, snifter, soupçon, sup, swallow, taste.

noise *n.* babble, ballyhoo, blare, clamor, clash, clatter, coil, commotion, cry, din, fracas, hubbub, outcry, pandemonium, racket, row, sound, talk, tumult, uproar.

noisome *adj.* bad, baneful, deleterious, disgusting, fetid, foul, fulsome, harmful, hurtful, injurious, malodorous, mephitic, mischievous, noxious, offensive, pernicious, pestiferous, pestilential, poisonous, putrid, reeking, smelly, stinking, unhealthy, unwholesome.

noisy *adj.* boisterous, cacophonous, chattering, clamorous, deafening, ear-piercing, ear-splitting, loud, obstreperous, piercing, plangent, rackety, riotous, strident, tumultuous, turbulent, uproarious, vocal, vociferous.

nominee *n.* appointee, assignee, candidate, contestant, entrant, protégé, runner.

nonessential *adj.* dispensable, excessive, expendable, extraneous, extrinsic(al), inessential, peripheral, superfluous, supplementary, unimportant, unnecessary.

nonexistent *adj.* chimerical, fancied, fictional, hallucinatory, hypothetical, illusory, imaginary, imagined, immaterial, incorporeal, insubstantial, legendary, missing, mythical, null, unreal.

nonplus *v.* astonish, astound, baffle, bewilder, confound, confuse, discomfit, disconcert, discountenance, dismay, dumbfound, embarrass, flabbergast, flummox, mystify, perplex, puzzle, stump, stun, take aback.

nonsense *n.* absurdity, balderdash, balls, baloney, bilge, blah, blather, bombast, bosh, bull, bunk, bunkum, claptrap, cobblers, crap, double-Dutch, drivel, faddle, fandangle, fatuity, fiddle-de-dee, fiddle-faddle, fiddle-sticks, flapdoodle, folly, foolishness, fudge, gaff, gas and gaiters, gibberish, gobbledygook, hogwash, hooey, inanity, jabberwock(y), jest, ludicrousness, moonshine, no-meaning, piffle, pulp, ridiculousness, rot, rubbish, senselessness, silliness, squish, stuff, stupidity, tar(r)adiddle, tommy-rot, trash, twaddle, twattle, waffle.

normal *adj.* accustomed, acknowledged, average, common, common-or-garden, conventional, habitual, mainstream, natural, ordinary, par for the course, popular, rational, reasonable, regular, routine, run-of-the-mill, sane, standard, straight, typical, usual, well-adjusted.

note *n.* annotation, apostill(e), billet, celebrity, character, comment, communication, consequence, distinction, eminence, epistle, epistolet, fame, gloss, heed, indication, jotting, letter, line, mark, memo, memorandum, message, minute, notice, observation, prestige, record, regard, remark, reminder, renown, reputation, signal, symbol, token. *v.* denote, designate, detect, enter, indicate, mark, mention, notice, observe, perceive, record, register, remark, see, witness.

noted *adj.* acclaimed, celebrated, conspicuous, distinguished, eminent, famous, great, illustrious, notable, notorious, prominent, recognized, renowned, respected, well-known.

notice *v.* descry, detect, discern, distinguish, espy, heed, mark, mind, note, observe, perceive, remark, see, spot.

nourish *v.* attend, cherish, comfort, cultivate, encourage, feed, foster, furnish, harbor, maintain, nurse, nurture, promote, supply, support, sustain, tend.

novel *adj.* different, fresh, imaginative, innovative, new, original, rare, singular, strange, surprising, uncommon, unconventional, unfamiliar, unusual.

novice *n.* amateur, apprentice, beginner, learner, neophyte, newcomer, novitiate, probationer, proselyte, pupil.

now *adv.* at once, at present, directly, immediately, instanter, instantly, next, nowadays, presently, promptly, straightaway, these days.

nude *adj.* au natural, bare, disrobed, exposed, in one's birthday suit, in puris naturalibus, in the altogether, in the buff, naked, starkers, stark naked, stripped, unattired, unclad, unclothed, uncovered, undraped, undressed, without a stitch.

nuisance *n.* annoyance, bore, bother, drawback, inconvenience, infliction, irritation, offense, pain, pest, plague, problem, trouble, vexation.

number[1] *n.* aggregate, amount, character, collection, company, count, crowd, digit, figure, folio, horde, index, integer, many, numeral, quantity, several, sum, throng, total, unit. *v.* account, add, apportion, calculate, compute, count, enumerate, include, inventory, reckon, tell, total.

number[2] *n.* copy, edition, impression, imprint, issue, printing, volume.

numeral *n.* character, cipher, digit, figure, folio, integer, number.

numerous *adj.* abundant, copious, divers, many, multitudinous, myriad, plentiful, profuse, several, sundry.

nutrition *n.* eutrophy, food, nourishment, nutriment, sustenance.

O

oasis *n.* enclave, haven, island, refuge, resting place, retreat, sanctuary, sanctum, watering hole.

oath *n.* affirmation, assurance, avowal, blasphemy, bond, curse, cuss, expletive, imprecation, malediction, pledge, plight, profanity, promise, swearword, vow, word, word of honor.

obedient *adj.* acquiescent, amenable, biddable, compliant, deferential, docile, duteous, dutiful, law-abiding, observant, passive, regardful, respectful, submissive, subservient, tractable, unquestioning, unresisting, well-trained, yielding.

obey *v.* abide by, act upon, adhere to, be ruled by, bow to, carry out, comply, conform, defer (to), discharge, embrace, execute, follow, fulfill, give in, give way, heed, implement, keep, knuckle under, mind, observe, perform, respond, serve, submit, surrender, take orders from, toe the line, yield.

object[1] *n.* aim, article, body, butt, design, end, entity, fact, focus, goal, idea, intent, intention, item, motive, objective, phenomenon, point, purpose, raison d'être, reality, reason, recipient, target, thing, victim, visible.

object[2] *v.* argue, complain, demur, dissent, expostulate, oppose, protest, rebut, refuse, repudiate, take exception.

objective *adj.* calm, detached, disinterested, dispassionate, equitable, evenhanded, fair, impartial, impersonal, judicial, just, open-minded, sensible, sober, unbiased, uncolored, unemotional, unimpassioned, uninvolved, unprejudiced.

oblige *v.* accommodate, assist, benefit, bind, coerce, compel, constrain, do a favor, favor, force, gratify, help, impel, indulge, make, necessitate, obligate, please, require, serve.

obsequious *adj.* abject, cringing, deferential, doughfaced, fawning, flattering, groveling, ingratiating, kneecrooking, menial, oily, servile, slavish, slimy, smarmy, submissive, subservient, sycophantic, toadying, unctuous.

observe *v.* abide by, adhere to, celebrate, commemorate, comment, comply, conform to, contemplate, declare, detect, discern, discover, espy, follow, fulfill, heed, honor, keep, keep an eye on, keep tabs on, mention, mind, monitor, note, notice, obey, opine, perceive, perform, regard, remark, remember, respect, say, scrutinize, see, solemnize, spot, state, study, surveille, survey, view, watch, witness.

obstruct *v.* arrest, bar, barricade, block, check, choke, clog, crab, cumber, curb, cut off, frustrate, hamper, hamstring, hide, hinder, hold, up, impede, inhibit, interfere with, interrupt, mask, obscure, occlude, prevent, restrict, retard, shield, shut off, slow down, stall, stonewall, stop, stuff, thwart, trammel.

obtain¹ *v.* achieve, acquire, attain, come by, compass, earn, gain, get, procure, secure.

obtain² *v.* be in force, be prevalent, be-the-case, exist, hold, prevail, reign, rule, stand.

obvious *adj.* apparent, clear, conspicuous, discernible, distinct, evident, glaring, indisputable, manifest, noticeable, open, open-and-shut, overt, palpable, patent, perceptible, plain, prominent, pronounced, recognizable, self-evident, self-explanatory, straightforward, transparent, unconcealed, undeniable, undisguised, unmistakable, unsubtle, visible.

occasion *n.* affair, call, case, cause, celebration, chance, convenience, event, excuse, experience, ground(s), incident, inducement, influence, instance, justification, moment, motive, occurrence, opening, opportunity, prompting, provocation, reason, time. *v.* bring about, bring on, cause, create, effect, elicit, engender, evoke, generate, give rise to, induce, influence, inspire, lead to, make, originate, persuade, produce, prompt, provoke.

occupy *v.* absorb, amuse, beguile, busy, capture, conquer, cover, divert, dwell in, employ, engage, engross, ensconce oneself in, entertain, establish oneself in, fill, garrison, hold, immerse, inhabit, interest, invade, involve, keep, keep busy, live in, monopolize, overrun, own, permeate, pervade, possess, preoccupy, reside in, seize, stay in, take over, take possession of, take up, tenant, tie up, use, utilize.

occur *v.* appear, arise, be found, be met with, be present, befall, betide, chance, come about, come off, come to pass, crop up, develop, eventuate, exist, happen, intervene, manifest itself, materialize, obtain, result, show itself, take place, transpire, turn up.

ocean *n.* briny, main, profound, sea, the deep, the drink.

odd¹ *adj.* abnormal, atypical, bizarre, curious, deviant, different, eccentric, exceptional, extraordinary, fantastic, freak, freakish, freaky, funky, funny, irregular, kinky, outlandish, peculiar, quaint, queer, rare, remarkable, singular, strange, uncanny, uncommon, unconventional, unexplained, unusual, weird, whimsical.

odd² *adj.* auxiliary, casual, fragmentary, ill-matched, incidental, irregular, leftover, lone, miscellaneous, occasional, periodic, random, remaining, seasonal, single, solitary, spare, sundry, surplus, uneven, unmatched, unpaired, varied, various.

odor *n.* air, aroma, atmosphere, aura, bouquet, breath, emanation, essence, exhalation, flavor, fragrance, perfume, quality, redolence, scent, smell, spirit, stench, stink.

off *adj.* abnormal, absent, bad, below par, canceled, decomposed, disappointing, disheartening, displeasing, finished, gone, high, inoperative, moldy, poor, postponed, quiet, rancid, rotten, slack, sour, substandard, turned, unavailable, unsatisfactory, wrong. *adv.* apart, aside, at a distance, away, elsewhere, out.

offend *v.* affront, annoy, disgruntle, disgust, displease, fret, gall, hip, hurt, insult, irritate, miff, nauseate, outrage, pain, pique, provoke, repel, repulse, rile, sicken, slight, snub, transgress, turn off, upset, vex, violate, wound, wrong.

offense *n.* affront, anger, annoyance, crime, delict, delinquency, displeasure, fault, hard feelings, harm, huff, hurt, indignation, indignity, infraction, infringement, injury, injustice, insult, ire, lapse, misdeed, misdemeanor, needle, outrage, peccadillo, pique, put-down, resentment, sin, slight, snub, transgression, trespass, umbrage, violation, wrath, wrong, wrong-doing.

offer *v.* advance, afford, bid, extend, furnish, give, hold out, make available, move, present, proffer, propose, propound, provide, put forth, put forward, show, submit, suggest, tender, volunteer. *n.* approach, attempt, bid, endeavor, essay, overture, presentation, proposal, proposition, submission, suggestion, tender.

often *adv.* again and again, frequently, generally, habitually, many a time, much, oft, over and over, regularly, repeatedly, time after time, time and again.

ogle *v.* eye, eye up, leer, look, make eyes at, stare.

old *adj.* aboriginal, aged, age-old, ancient, antediluvian, antiquated, antique, archaic, bygone, cast-off, crumbling, dated, decayed, decrepit, done, earlier, early, elderly, erstwhile, ex-, experienced, familiar, former, gray, gray-haired, grizzled, hackneyed, hardened, hoary, immemorial, long-established, long-standing, mature, obsolete, of old, of yore, olden, old-fashioned, one-time, original, out-of-date, outdated, outmoded, over the hill, passé, patriarchal, practiced, prehistoric, previous, primitive, primordial, pristine, quondam, remote, senescent, senile, skilled, stale, superannuated, time-honored, time-worn, traditional, unfashionable, unoriginal, venerable, versed, veteran, vintage, worn-out.

omen *n.* augury, auspice, boding, foreboding, foretoken, indication, portent, premonition, presage, prognostic, prognostication, sign, straw in the wind, warning, writing on the wall.

omit *v.* disregard, drop, edit out, eliminate, exclude, fail, forget, give something a miss, leave out, leave undone, let slide, miss out, neglect, overlook, pass over, pretermit, skip.

omnipotent *adj.* all-powerful, almighty, plenipotent, supreme.

omniscient *adj.* all-knowing, all-seeing, pansophic.

once *adv.* at one time, formerly, heretofore, in the old days, in the past, in times gone by, in times past, long ago, once upon a time, previously.

only *adv.* at most, barely, exclusively, just, merely, purely, simply, solely. *adj.* exclusive, individual, lone, single, sole, solitary, unique.

open *adj.* above-board, accessible, ajar, apparent, available, bare, blatant, conspicuous, evident, expanded, exposed, flagrant, frank, free, gaping, honest, innocent, liberal, natural, navigable, noticeable, obvious, overt, porous, public, receptive, sincere, transparent, unconcealed, unconditional, unobstructed, unoccupied,

unsealed, vacant, visible, wide, wide-open, yawning.

opening *n.* adit, aperture, beginning, birth, breach, break, chance, chasm, chink, cleft, commencement, crack, dawn, fissure, fistula, foramen, gap, hole, inauguration, inception, initiation, interstice, kick-off, launch, launching, occasion, onset, opportunity, orifice, outset, perforation, place, rent, rupture, slot, space, split, start, vacancy, vent, vista.

operate *v.* act, function, go, handle, manage, maneuver, perform, run, serve, use, utilize, work.

opponent *n.* adversary, antagonist, challenger, competitor, contestant, disputant, dissentient, dissident, enemy, foe, objector, opposer, opposition, rival.

opportunity *n.* break, chance, convenience, hour, moment, occasion, opening, scope, shot, time, turn.

oppose *v.* bar, beard, breast, check, combat, compare, confront, contradict, contrary, contrast, contravene, controvert, counter, counter-attack, counterbalance, defy, face, fight, fly in the face of, gainsay, hinder, obstruct, pit against, play off, prevent, resist, stand up to, take a stand against, take issue with, thwart, withstand.

opposite *adj.* adverse, antagonistic, antipodal, antipodean, antithetical, conflicting, contradictory, contrary, contrasted, corresponding, different, differing, diverse, facing, fronting, hostile, inconsistent, inimical, irreconcilable, opposed, reverse, unlike.

opposition *n.* antagonism, antagonist, clash, competition, contraposition, contrariety, counteraction, counter-stand, countertime, counterview, disapproval, foe, hostility, obstruction, opponent, other side, prevention, resistance, rival.

optimistic *adj.* assured, bright, bullish, buoyant, cheerful, idealistic, Panglossian, Panglossic, positive, sanguine, upbeat, Utopian.

option *n.* alternative, choice, election, possibility, preference, selection.

orate *v.* declaim, discourse, harangue, hold forth, pontificate, sermonize, speak, speechify, talk.

ordeal *n.* affliction, agony, anguish, nightmare, pain, persecution, suffering, test, torture, trial, tribulation(s), trouble(s).

order¹ *n.* application, arrangement, array, behest, booking, calm, categorization, chit, classification, codification, command, commission, control, cosmos, decree, dictate, direction, directive, discipline, disposal, disposition, grouping, harmony, injunction, instruction, law, law and order, layout, line, line-up, mandate, method, neatness, ordering, orderliness, ordinance, organization, pattern, peace, placement, plan, precept, progression, propriety, quiet, regularity, regulation, request, requisition, reservation, rule, sequence, series, stipulation, structure, succession, symmetry, system, tidiness, tranquility.

order² *n.* association, breed, brotherhood, cast, caste, class, community, company, degree, family, fraternity, genre, genus, grade, guild, hierarchy, ilk, kind, league, lodge, organization, pecking order, phylum, position, rank, sect, sisterhood, society, sort, species, status, subclass, tribe, type, union.

ordinary *adj.* average, common, common-or-garden, commonplace, established, everyday, familiar, habitual, humdrum, inferior, mediocre, modest, normal, pedestrian, plain, prosaic, routine, standard, stock, typical, unremarkable, usual, wonted, workaday.

organ n. agency, channel, device, element, forum, harmonium, hurdy-gurdy, implement, instrument, means, medium, member, mouthpiece, newspaper, paper, part, process, publication, structure, tool, unit, vehicle, viscus, voice.

organization n. arrangement, assembling, assembly, association, body, business, chemistry, combine, company, composition, concern, confederation, configuration, conformation, consortium, constitution, construction, coordination, corporation, design, disposal, federation, firm, format, formation, formulation, framework, group, grouping, institution, league, makeup, management, method, methodology, organism, outfit, pattern, plan, planning, regulation, running, standardization, structure, structuring, syndicate, system, unity, whole.

organize *v.* arrange, catalog, classify, codify, constitute, construct, coordinate, dispose, establish, form, frame, group, marshal, pigeonhole, regiment, run, see to, set up, shape, structure, systematize, tabulate.

origin *n.* ancestry, base, basis, beginning, beginnings, birth, cause, commencement, creation, dawning, derivation, descent, emergence, etymology, foundation, fountain, genesis, heritage, inauguration, inception, launch, lineage, occasion, origination, outset, parentage, paternity, pedigree, provenance, root, roots, source,

spring, start, stirps, stock, well-spring.

original *adj.* aboriginal, archetypal, authentic, autochthonous, commencing, creative, earliest, early, embryonic, fertile, first, first-hand, fresh, genuine, imaginative, ingenious, initial, innovative, new, novel, opening, primal, primary, primitive, primordial, prototypical, resourceful, rudimentary, seminal, starting.

originate *v.* arise, be born, begin, come, commence, conceive, create, derive, develop, discover, emanate, emerge, establish, evolve, flow, form, formulate, generate, give birth to, inaugurate, initiate, institute, introduce, invent, issue, launch, pioneer, proceed, produce, result, rise, set up, spring, start, stem.

ornament *n.* accessory, adornment, bauble, decoration, embellishment, flower, frill, garnish, gaud, honor, jewel, treasure, trimming, trinket.

other *adj.* added, additional, alternative, auxiliary, contrasting, different, differing, dissimilar, distinct, diverse, extra, fresh, further, more, new, remaining, separate, spare, supplementary, unrelated.

out¹ *adj.* abroad, absent, away, disclosed, elsewhere, evident, exposed, gone, manifest, not at home, outside, public, revealed.

out² *adj.* antiquated, banned, blacked, dated dead, démodé, disallowed, ended, excluded, exhausted, expired, extinguished, finished, forbidden, impossible, not on, old hat, old-fashioned, out of date, passé, square, taboo, unacceptable, unfashionable, used up.

outcome *n.* aftereffect, aftermath, conclusion, consequence, effect, end, end result, issue, payoff, result, sequel, upshot.

outfit¹ *n.* clothes, costume, ensemble, equipment, garb, gear, kit, rig, suit, togs, trappings,

outfit² *n.* business, clan, clique, company, corps, coterie, crew, firm, gang, group, organization, set, setout, set-up, squad, team, unit.

outlaw *n.* bandit, brigand, desperado, fugitive, highwayman, marauder, robber. *v.* ban, banish, bar, condemn, debar, exclude, excommunicate, forbid, illegalize, prohibit, proscribe, waive.

outline *n.* bare facts, configuration, contour, draft, form, frame, framework, plan, profile, résumé, rough, scenario, schema, shape, silhouette, sketch, summary, synopsis, thumbnail sketch, tracing.

outlook *n.* angle, aspect, attitude, forecast, frame of mind, future, panorama, perspective, point of view, prognosis, prospect, scene, slant, vantage point, view, vista.

outside¹ *adj.* exterior, external, extramural, extraneous, extreme, outdoor, outer, outermost, outward, superficial, surface.

outside² *adj.* distant, faint, infinitesimal, marginal, minute, negligible, remote, slight, slim, small, unlikely.

outsmart *v.* beat, best, deceive, dupe, get the better of, outfox, outmaneuver, outperform, outthink, outwit, trick.

outstanding¹ *adj.* ace, arresting, celebrated, distinguished, eminent, excellent, exceptional, extraordinary, great, important, impressive, notable, noteworthy, prominent, remarkable, salient, signal, singular, special, striking, superior, superlative.

outstanding² adj. due, left, ongoing, open, over, owing, payable, pending, remaining, uncollected, undone, unpaid, unresolved, unsettled.

outwit *v.* beat, best, better, cheat, circumvent, deceive, defraud, dupe, get the better of, gull, make a monkey of, outfox, outmaneuver, outsmart, outthink, swindle, trick.

ovation *n.* acclaim, acclamation, applause, bravos, cheering, cheers, clapping, éclat, laudation, plaudits, praises, tribute.

over¹ *adj.* accomplished, bygone, closed, completed, concluded, done with, ended, finished, forgotten, gone, in the past, past, settled up.

over² *prep.* above, exceeding, in charge of, in command of, in excess of, more than, on, on top of, superior to, upon.

overcome *v.* beat, best, better, conquer, crush, defeat, lick, master, overpower, overthrow, overwhelm, prevail, subjugate, surmount, triumph over, vanquish, weather, worst.

overflow *v.* brim over, bubble over, cover, deluge, discharge, drown, flood, inundate, pour over, shower, soak, spill, spray, submerge, surge, swamp, well over. *n.* flood, inundation, overabundance, spill, superfluity, surplus.

overlook *v.* condone, disregard, excuse, forget, forgive, ignore, neglect, omit, pardon, pass, pass over, skip, slight, wink at.

overpower *v.* beat, best, conquer, crush, defeat, floor, immobilize, master, overcome, overthrow, overwhelm, quell, subdue, subjugate, vanquish.

overrun¹ *v.* choke, infest, inundate, invade, occupy, overflow, overwhelm, permeate, ravage, swamp, swarm over.

overseer *n.* boss, chief, foreman, manager, master, super, superintendent, superior, supervisor, surveyor, workmaster.

overthrow *v.* abolish, beat, bring down, conquer, crush, defeat, destroy, dethrone, displace, level, master, oust, overcome, overpower, overturn, subjugate, subvert, topple, unseat, upset, vanquish.

own¹ *adj.* idiosyncratic, individual, inimitable, particular, personal, private.

own² *v.* acknowledge, admit, agree, allow, avow, concede, confess, disclose, enjoy, grant, have, hold, keep, possess, recognize, retain.

P

pace *n.* celerity, clip, gait, lick, measure, momentum, motion, movement, progress, quickness, rapidity, rate, speed, step, stride, tempo, time, tread, velocity, walk. *v.* count, determine, march, mark out, measure, pad, patrol, pound, step, stride, tramp, tread, walk.

pack *n.* assemblage, backpack, band, bunch, bundle, collection, company, crew, crowd, gang, group, haversack, herd, knapsack, load, lot, mob, outfit, package, parcel, rucksack, set, troop, truss. *v.* batch, bundle, burden, charge, compact, compress, cram, crowd, fill, jam, load, package, store, stow, stuff, wedge.

package *n.* agreement, amalgamation, arrangement, bale, box, carton, combination, consignment, container, deal, entity, kit, pack, packet, parcel, proposal, proposition, unit, whole. *v.* batch, box, pack, pack up, packet, parcel, parcel up, wrap, wrap up.

pact *n.* agreement, alliance, arrangement, bargain, bond, cartel, compact, concord, concordat, contract, convention, covenant, deal, entente, league, protocol, treaty, understanding.

pain *n.* ache, affliction, aggravation, agony, anguish, annoyance, bitterness, burden, cramp, discomfort, distress, dole, dolor, drag, grief, gyp, headache, heartache, heartbreak, hurt, irritation, misery, nuisance, pang, pest, smart, soreness, spasm, suffering, tenderness, throb, throe, torment, torture, tribulation, trouble, twinge, vexation, woe, wretchedness. *v.* afflict, aggrieve, agonize, annoy, chagrin, cut to the quick, disappoint, disquiet, distress, exasperate, gall, grieve, harass, hurt, irritate, nettle, rile, sadden, torment, torture, vex, worry, wound, wring.

pair *n.* brace, combination, couple, doublet, doubleton, duo, dyad, match, span, twins, two of a kind, twosome, yoke. *v.* bracket, couple, join, link, marry, match, match up, mate, pair off, put together, splice, team, twin, wed, yoke.

pal *n.* amigo, buddy, chum, companion, comrade, confidant(e), crony, friend, gossip, mate, partner, sidekick, soul mate.

pale *adj.* anemic, ashen, bleached, bloodless, chalky, colorless, dim, faded, faint, pallid, pasty, poor, wan, washed-out, white.

pamper *v.* baby, cocker, coddle, cosset, fondle, gratify, humor, indulge, mollycoddle, mother, overindulge, pet, spoil.

panic *n.* agitation, alarm, consternation, dismay, fear, fright, hassle, horror, hysteria, scare, terror, tizzy, to-do.

pardon *v.* absolve, acquit, amnesty, condone, emancipate, exculpate, excuse, exonerate, forgive, free, let off, liberate, overlook, release, remit, reprieve, respite, vindicate. *n.* absolution, acquittal, allowance, amnesty, compassion, condonation, discharge, excuse, exoneration, forgiveness, grace, humanity, indulgence, mercy, release, remission, reprieval, reprieve.

pare *v.* clip, crop, cut, cut back, decrease, diminish, dock, float, lop, peel, prune, reduce, retrench, shave, shear, skin, trim.

part *n.* area, behalf, bit, branch, business, capacity, cause, character, charge, clause, complement, component, concern, constituent, department, district, division, duty, element, faction, factor, fraction, fragment, function, heft, ingredient, interest, involvement, limb, lines, lot, member, module, neck of the woods, neighborhood, office, organ, particle, partwork, party, piece, place, portion, quarter, region, responsibility, role, scrap, section, sector, segment, share, side, slice, task, territory, tip of the iceberg, unit, vicinity, work. *v.* break, break up, cleave, come apart, depart, detach, disband, disconnect, disjoin, dismantle, disperse, disunite, divide, go, go away, leave, part company, quit, rend, scatter, separate, sever, split, split up, sunder, take leave, tear, withdraw.

partial¹ *adj.* fragmentary, imperfect, incomplete, inexhaustive, limited, part, uncompleted, unfinished.

partial² *adj.* affected, biased, colored, discriminatory, ex parte, influenced, interested, one-sided, partisan, predisposed, prejudiced, tendentious, unfair, unjust.

participant *n.* associate, contributor, cooperator, helper, member, partaker, participator, party, shareholder, worker.

partisan *n.* adherent, backer, champion, devotee, disciple, factionist, follower, guerrilla, irregular, party man, stalwart, supporter, upholder, votary. *adj.* biased, discriminatory, factional, guerrilla, interested, irregular, one-sided, partial,

predisposed, prejudiced, resistant, sectarian, tendentious, underground.

partner *n.* accomplice, ally, associate, bedfellow, buddy, collaborator, colleague, companion, comrade, confederate, consort, copartner, gigolo, helper, helpmate, helpmeet, husband, mate, participant, sidekick, spouse, teammate, wife.

party¹ *n.* assembly, at-home, bash, beanfest, beano, celebration, do, drag, drum, entertainment, fest, festivity, function, gathering, get-together, hoot(e)nanny, housewarming, hurricane, jollification, knees-up, rave-up, reception, rout, shindig, social, soirée, thrash.

party² *n.* alliance, association, band, body, bunch, cabal, caucus, clique, coalition, combination, company, confederacy, contingent, contractor, coterie, crew, defendant, detachment, faction, gang, gathering, group, grouping, individual, junto, league, litigant, participant, person, plaintiff, set, side, squad, team, unit.

passable *adj.* acceptable, adequate, average, fair, mediocre, moderate, OK, so-so, tolerable, unexceptional.

passion *n.* adoration, affection, anger, animation, ardor, attachment, avidity, bug, chafe, concupiscence, craving, craze, dander, desire, eagerness, emotion, enthusiasm, excitement, fancy, fascination, feeling, fervency, fervor, fire, fit, flare-up, fondness, frenzy, fury, heat, idol, indignation, infatuation, intensity, ire, itch, joy, keenness, love, lust, mania, monomania, obsession, outburst, paroxysm, rage, rapture, resentment, spirit, storm, transport, vehemence, verve, vivacity, warmth, wax, wrath, zeal, zest.

passive *adj.* acquiescent, compliant, docile, enduring, impassive, inactive, indifferent, indolent, inert, lifeless, long-suffering, nonparticipating, nonviolent, patient, quiescent, receptive, resigned, submissive, supine, unaffected, unassertive, uninvolved, unresisting.

patrol *n.* defense, garrison, guard, guarding, policing, protecting, sentinel, surveillance, watch, watching, watchman. *v.* cruise, go the rounds, guard, inspect, perambulate, police, range, tour.

pause *v.* break, cease, cut, delay, desist, discontinue, halt, hesitate, interrupt, rest, take a break, take a breather, take five, wait, waver. *n.* abatement, break, breather, caesura, cessation, delay, discontinuance, gap, halt, hesitation, interlude, intermission, interruption, interval, letup, lull, respite, rest, slackening, stay, stoppage, suspension, wait.

pay v. ante, benefit, bestow, bring in, clear, compensate, cough up, disburse, discharge, extend, foot, get even with, give, grant, honor, indemnify, liquidate, meet, offer, pay out, present, produce, proffer, profit, punish, reciprocate, recompense, reimburse, remit, remunerate, render, repay, requite, return, reward, serve, settle, square, square up, yield. n. allowance, compensation, consideration, earnings, emoluments, fee, hire, honorarium, income, payment, recompense, reimbursement, remuneration, reward, salary, stipend, takings, wages.

peak n. acme, apex, apogee, brow, climax, crest, crown, culmination, cuspid, high point, maximum, ne plus ultra, pinnacle, point, summit, tip, top, visor, zenith.

peculiar[1] adj. abnormal, bizarre, curious, eccentric, exceptional, extraordinary, far-out, freakish, funky, funny, odd, offbeat, outlandish, out-of-the-way, quaint, queer, singular, strange, uncommon, unconventional, unusual, way-out, weird.

peculiar[2] adj. appropriate, characteristic, discriminative, distinct, distinctive, distinguishing, endemic, idiosyncratic, individual, local, particular, personal, private, quintessential, restricted, special, specific, unique.

peek v. glance, look, peep, peer, spy. n. blink, gander, glance, glimpse, look, looksee, peep.

pen n. cage, coop, crib, enclosure, fold, hutch, stall, sty. v. cage, confine, coop, corral, crib, enclose, fence, hedge, hem in, hurdle, mew (up), shut up.

perceive v. appreciate, apprehend, be aware of, behold, catch, comprehend, conclude, deduce, descry, discern, discover, distinguish, espy, feel, gather, get, grasp, intuit, know, learn, make out, note, observe, realize, recognize, remark, see, sense, spot, understand.

perfect adj. absolute, accomplished, accurate, adept, blameless, close, complete, completed, consummate, copybook, correct, entire, exact, excellent, experienced, expert, faithful, faultless, finished, flawless, full, ideal, immaculate, impeccable, irreproachable, masterly, model, polished, practiced, precise, pure, right, sheer, skilled, skillful, splendid, spotless, spot-on, strict, sublime, superb, superlative, supreme, true, unadulterated, unalloyed, unblemished, unerring, unimpeachable, unmarred, unmitigated, untarnished, utter, whole.

perfection n. accomplishment, achievement, acme, completeness, completion, consummation, crown, evolution, exactness, excellence, exquisiteness, flawlessness, fulfillment, ideal, integrity, maturity, nonpareil, paragon, perfectness, pinnacle, precision, purity, realization, sublimity, superiority, wholeness.

perform v. accomplish, achieve, act, appear as, bring about, bring off, carry out, complete, depict, discharge, do, effect, enact, execute, fulfill, function, functionate, manage, observe, play, present, produce, pull off, put on, render, represent, satisfy, stage, transact, work.

perhaps adv. conceivably, feasibly, happen, maybe, mayhap, peradventure, perchance, possibly, you never know.

peril n. danger, exposure, hazard, imperilment, insecurity, jeopardy, menace, pitfall, risk, threat, uncertainty, vulnerability.

period n. age, course, cycle, date, days, end, eon, epoch, era, generation, interval, season, space, span, spell, stage, stint, stop, stretch, term, time, turn, while, years.

perish v. collapse, croak, crumble, decay, decline, decompose, decrease, die, disappear, disintegrate, end, expire, fall, molder, pass away, rot, vanish, waste, wither.

permit v. admit, agree, allow, authorize, consent, empower, enable, endorse, endure, give leave, grant, let, warrant.

perpetrate v. carry out, commit, do, effect, enact, execute, inflict, perform, practice, wreak.

perpetual adj. abiding, ceaseless, constant, continual, continuous, deathless, endless, enduring, eternal, everlasting, immortal, incessant, infinite, interminable, lasting, never-ending, never-failing, perennial, permanent, persistent, recurrent, repeated, unceasing, unchanging, undying, unending, unfailing, unflagging, uninterrupted, unremitting, unvarying.

perplex v. baffle, befuddle, beset, bewilder, complicate, confound, confuse, dumbfound, encumber, entangle, gravel, hobble, involve, jumble, mix up, muddle, mystify, nonplus, pother, pudder, puzzle, stump, tangle, thicken, throw.

persist v. abide, carry on, continue, endure, insist, keep at it, last, linger, perdure, persevere, remain, stand fast, stand firm.

person n. being, body, character, customer, human, human being, individual, living soul, party, soul, specimen.

persuade v. actuate, advise, allure, bring round, cajole, coax, convert, convince, counsel, entice, impel, incite, induce, influence, inveigle, lead on, lean on, prevail upon, prompt, satisfy, sway, sweet-talk, talk into, urge, win over.

pertain v. appertain, apply, be appropriate, be part of, be relevant, bear on, befit, belong, come under, concern, refer, regard, relate.

pervade v. affect, charge, diffuse, extend, fill, imbue, infuse, osmose, overspread, penetrate, percolate, permeate, saturate, suffuse.

perverse adj. abnormal, balky, cantankerous, churlish, contradictory, contrary, contumacious, crabbed, cross, crossgrained, cussed, delinquent, depraved, deviant, disobedient, dogged, fractious, forward, head-strong, ill-natured, ill-tempered, improper, incorrect, intractable, intransigent, miscreant, mulish, obdurate, obstinate, peevish, petulant, pigheaded, rebellious, recalcitrant, refractory, spiteful, stubborn, surly, thwart, troublesome, unhealthy, unmanageable, unreasonable, unyielding, uppity, wayward, wilful, wrong-headed, wry.

pest n. annoyance, bane, blight, bore, bother, bug, canker, curse, irritation, nuisance, pain (in the neck), scourge, thorn in one's flesh, trial, vexation.

phantom n. apparition, chimera, eidolon, figment (of the imagination), ghost, hallucination, illusion, manes, phantasm(a), shade, simulacrum, specter, spirit, spook, vision, wraith.

phony adj. affected, assumed, bogus, counterfeit, fake, false, forged, imitation, pseudo, put-on, quack, quack-salving, sham, spurious, trick.

pick v. break into, break open, choose, collect, crack, cull, cut, decide on, elect, embrace, espouse, fix upon, foment, gather, harvest, incite, instigate, opt for, pluck, prize, provoke, pull, screen, select, settle on, sift out, single out, start.

pile[1] n. accumulation, assemblage, assortment, bomb, building, cock, collection, edifice, erection, fortune, heap, hoard, mass, mint, money, mound, mountain, mow, packet, pot, stack, stockpile, structure, wealth. v. accumulate, amass, assemble, build up, charge, climb, collect, crowd, crush, flock, flood, gather, heap, hoard, jam, load up, mass, pack, rush, stack, store, stream.

pile[2] n. bar, beam, column, foundation, pier, piling, pill, post, rib, stanchion, support, upright.

pile[3] n. down, fur, fuzz, fuzziness, hair, nap, plush, shag.

pilgrim n. crusader, traveler, wanderer, wayfarer.

plain adj. apparent, artless, austere, bare, basic, blunt, candid, clear, clinical, common, commonplace, comprehensible, direct, discreet, distinct, downright, even, everyday, evident, flat, forthright, frank, frugal, guileless, homebred, homely, homespun, honest, ill-favored, ingenuous, legible, level, lowly, lucid, manifest, modest, muted, obvious, open, ordinary, outspoken, patent, penny-plain, plane, pure, restrained, self-colored, severe, simple, sincere, smooth, spartan, stark, straightforward, transparent, ugly, unadorned, unaffected, unambiguous, unattractive, unbeautiful, understandable, undistinguished, unelaborate, unembellished, unfigured, unhandsome, unlovely, unmistakable, unobstructed, unornamented, unpatterned, unprepossessing, unpretentious, untrimmed, unvarnished, visible, whole-colored, workaday.

plan n. blueprint, design, diagram, illustration, plot, proposal, scenario, scheme, sketch, strategy, suggestion, system. v. arrange, conspire, contrive, draft, formulate, frame, invent, outline, plot, represent, scheme.

play v. act, bet, caper, challenge, chance, compete, contend, execute, fiddle, fidget, flirt, fool around, frisk, frolic, gamble, gambol, hazard, impersonate, interfere, lilt, participate, perform, personate, portray, punt, represent, revel, risk, rival, romp, speculate, sport, string along, take, take on, take part, take the part of, trifle, vie with, wager.

plead v. adduce, allege, appeal, argue, ask, assert, beg, beseech, crave, entreat, implore, importune, maintain, moot, petition, put forward, request, solicit, supplicate.

pleasant adj. acceptable, affable, agreeable, amiable, amusing, charming, cheerful, cheery, congenial, cool, delectable, delightful, delightsome, engaging, enjoyable, fine, friendly, genial, good-humored, gratifying, likable, lovely, nice, pleasing, pleasurable, refreshing, satisfying, sunshiny, toothsome, welcome, winsome.

please v. amuse, captivate, charm, cheer, choose, content, delight, desire, enchant, entertain, gladden, go for, gratify, humor, indulge, like, opt, prefer, rejoice, satisfy, see fit, suit, think fit, tickle, tickle pink, want, will, wish.

plenty n. abundance, affluence, copiousness, enough, fertility, fruitfulness, fund, heap(s), lots, luxury, mass, masses, milk and honey, mine, mountain(s), oodles, opulence, pile(s), plenitude, plenteousness, plentifulness, plethora, profusion, prosperity, quantities, quantity, stack(s), store, sufficiency, volume, wealth.

plot *n.* action, cabal, conspiracy, covin, design, intrigue, machination(s), narrative, outline, plan, scenario, scheme, story, story line, stratagem, subject, theme, thread. *v.* brew, cabal, calculate, chart, collude, compass, compute, conceive, concoct, conspire, contrive, cook up, design, devise, draft, draw, frame, hatch, imagine, intrigue, lay, locate, machinate, maneuver, map, mark, outline, plan, project, scheme.

plump *adj.* beefy, burly, buxom, chopping, chubby, corpulent, dumpy, embonpoint, endomorphic, fat, fleshy, full, matronly, obese, podgy, portly, roly-poly, rotund, round, stout, tubby, well-upholstered.

plunder *v.* depredate, despoil, devastate, loot, pillage, raid, ransack, ravage, rifle, rob, sack, spoil, steal, strip. *n.* booty, despoilment, ill-gotten gains, loot, pickings, pillage, prey, prize, rapine, spoils, swag.

point *n.* aim, aspect, attribute, burden, characteristic, circumstance, condition, core, crux, degree, design, detail, dot, drift, end, essence, extent, fact, feature, full stop, gist, goal, import, instance, instant, intent, intention, item, juncture, location, mark, marrow, matter, meaning, moment, motive, nicety, nub, object, objective, particular, peculiarity, period, pith, place, position, property, proposition, purpose, quality, question, reason, respect, score, side, site, speck, spot, stage, station, stop, subject, tally, text, theme, thrust, time, trait, unit, use, usefulness, utility. *v.* aim, denote, designate, direct, draw attention to, hint, indicate, level, show, signal, signify, suggest, train.

pointless *adj.* absurd, aimless, bootless, fruitless, futile, inane, ineffectual, irrelevant, meaningless, nonsensical, profitless, senseless, silly, stupid, unavailing, unbeneficial, unproductive, unprofitable, useless, vague, vain, worthless.

poise *n.* aplomb, assurance, calmness, collectedness, composure, cool, coolness, dignity, elegance, equanimity, equilibrium, grace, presence, presence of mind, sangfroid, savoir faire, self-possession, serenity. *v.* balance, float, hang, hold, hover, position, support, suspend.

polish *v.* brighten, brush up, buff, burnish, clean, correct, cultivate, emend, emery, enhance, file, finish, furbish, improve, luster, perfect, refine, rub, rub up, shine, shine up, slick, slicken, smooth, touch up, wax.

pollute *v.* adulterate, befoul, besmirch, canker, contaminate, corrupt, debase, debauch, defile, deprave, desecrate, dirty, dishonor, foul, infect, mar, poison, profane, soil, spoil, stain, sully, taint, violate, vitiate.

ponder *v.* analyze, brood, cerebrate, cogitate, contemplate, consider, deliberate, examine, excogitate, give thought to, incubate, meditate, mull over, muse, puzzle over, ratiocinate, reason, reflect, ruminate over, study, think, weigh.

pool[1] *n.* dub, lake, lasher, leisure pool, mere, pond, puddle, splash, stank, swimming bath, swimming pool, tarn, water hole, watering hole.

pool[2] *n.* accumulation, bank, cartel, collective, combine, consortium, funds, group, jackpot, kitty, pot, purse, reserve, ring, stakes, syndicate, team, trust. *v.* amalgamate, chip in, combine, contribute, merge, muck, put together, share.

poor[1] *adj.* badly off, bankrupt, beggared, beggarly, broke, deficient, destitute, distressed, embarrassed, exiguous, hard up, impecunious, impoverished, in reduced circumstances, inadequate, indigent, insufficient, lacking, meager, miserable, moneyless, necessitous, needy, niggardly, on one's beam-ends, on one's uppers, on the rocks, pauperized, penniless, penurious, pinched, pitiable, poverty-stricken, reduced, scanty, skimpy, skint, slight, sparse, stony-broke, straitened, without means, without the wherewithal.

poor[2] *adj.* bad, bare, barren, below par, depleted, exhausted, faulty, feeble, fruitless, grotty, humble, imperfect, impoverished, inferior, infertile, insignificant, je-june, low-grade, lowly, mean, mediocre, modest, paltry, pathetic, pitiful, plain, ropy, rotten, rubbishy, second-rate, shabby, shoddy, sorry, spiritless, sterile, substandard, third-rate, trivial, unfruitful, unimpressive, unproductive, unsatisfactory, valueless, weak, worthless.

poor[3] *adj.* accursed, cursed, forlorn, hapless, ill-fated, luckless, miserable, pathetic, pitiable, star-crossed, unfortunate, unhappy, unlucky, wretched.

popular *adj.* accepted, approved, celebrated, common, conventional, current, democratic, famous, fashionable, favored, favorite, fêted, general, household, idolized, in, in demand, in favor, liked, lionized, modish, overpopular, overused, prevailing, prevalent, public, sought-after, standard, stock, trite, ubiquitous, universal, vernacular, voguish, vulgar, well-liked, widespread.

portable *adj.* carriageable, compact, convenient, handy, light, lightweight, manageable, movable, transportable.

portray v. act, capture, characterize, delineate, depict, describe, draw, emblazon, encapsulate, evoke, figure, illustrate, impersonate, limn, paint, personate, personify, picture, play, present, render, represent, sketch, suggest.

position n. angle, area, arrangement, attitude, bearings, belief, berth, billet, capacity, character, circumstances, condition, deployment, disposition, duty, employment, function, grade, importance, job, level, locale, locality, location, niche, occupation, office, opinion, outlook, pass, perspective, pinch, place, placement, placing, plight, point, point of view, pose, positioning, post, posture, predicament, prestige, rank, reference, reputation, role, set, setting, site, situation, slant, slot, spot, stance, stand, standing, standpoint, state, station, stature, status, view, viewpoint, where-abouts. v. arrange, array, deploy, dispose, fix, lay out, locate, place, pose, put, range, set, settle, stand, stick.

positive adj. absolute, actual, affirmative, arrant, assertive, assured, authoritative, beneficial, categorical, certain, clear, clear-cut, cocksure, complete, conclusive, concrete, confident, constructive, consummate, convinced, decided, decisive, definite, direct, dogmatic, downright, effective, efficacious, emphatic, explicit, express, firm, forceful, forward-looking, helpful, hopeful, incontestable, incontrovertible, indisputable, irrefragable, irrefutable, open-and-shut, opinionated, optimistic, out-and-out, peremptory, perfect, practical, productive, progressive, promising, rank, real, realistic, resolute, secure, self-evident, sheer, stubborn, sure, thorough, thoroughgoing, uncompromising, undeniable, unequivocal, unmistakable, unmitigated, unquestioning, useful, utter.

possess v. acquire, be endowed with, control, dominate, enjoy, have, hold, obtain, occupy, own, possess oneself of, seize, take, take over, take possession of.

postpone v. adjourn, defer, delay, freeze, hold over, pigeonhole, prorogue, put back, put off, put on ice, shelve, suspend, table, waive.

potency n. authority, capacity, cogency, control, effectiveness, efficaciousness, efficacy, energy, force, headiness, influence, kick, might, muscle, persuasiveness, potential, power, puissance, punch, strength, sway, vigor.

pound¹ v. bang, bash, baste, batter, beat, belabor, bray, bruise, clobber, clomp,

clump, comminute, crush, drum, hammer, march, palpitate, pelt, powder, pulsate, pulse, pulverize, pummel, smash, stomp, strike, strum, thrash, throb, thrum, thud, thump, thunder, tramp, triturate.

pound² n. compound, corral, enclosure, fold, pen, yard.

power n. ability, ascendancy, authority, authorization, brawn, capability, capacity, clout, clutches, command, competence, competency, control, dominance, domination, dominion, efficience, energy, faculty, force, forcefulness, heavy metal, hegemony, imperium, influence, intensity, juice, license, mastery, might, muscle, omnipotence, plenipotence, potency, potential, prerogative, privilege, right, rule, sovereignty, strength, supremacy, sway, teeth, vigor, virtue, vis, voltage, warrant, weight.

practical adj. accomplished, active, applicative, applied, businesslike, common sense, commonsensical, down-to-earth, efficient, empirical, everyday, expedient, experienced, experimental, factual, feasible, functional, hardheaded, hardnosed, material, matter-of-fact, mundane, nuts-and-bolts, ordinary, practicable, pragmatic, proficient, qualified, realistic, seasoned, sensible, serviceable, skilled, sound, trained, unsentimental, useful, utilitarian, workable, workaday, working.

practice¹ n. action, application, business, career, clientele, convention, custom, discipline, frill, dry run, dummy run, effect, exercise, experience, habit, ism, method, mode, modus operandi, operation, patronage, performance, policy, practic, practicalities, practicum, praxis, preparation, procedure, profession, rehearsal, repetition, routine, rule, run-through, study, system, tradition, training, usage, use, vocation, way, wont, work, workout.

practice² v. apply, carry out, discipline, do, drill, enact, engage in, execute, exercise, follow, implement, live up to, observe, perfect, perform, ply, prepare, pursue, put into practice, rehearse, repeat, run through, study, train, undertake, warm up.

pragmatic adj. businesslike, efficient, factual, hard-headed, opportunistic, practical, realistic, sensible, unidealistic, unsentimental, utilitarian.

praise n. acclaim, acclamation, accolade, acknowledgment, adoration, adulation, applause, approbation, approval, bouquet, cheering, comment, commendation, compliment, compliments, congratulation, devotion, encomium, eulogy, extolment, flattery, glory, homage, honor, kudos, laud, laudation, ovation, panegyric, plaudit, puff, rave, recognition, salvos, testimonial, thanks, thanksgiving, tribute, worship.

precise *adj.* absolute, accurate, actual, authentic, blow-by-blow, buckram, careful, ceremonious, clear-cut, correct, definite, delimitative, determinate, distinct, exact, explicit, express, expressis verbis, factual, faithful, fastidious, finical, finicky, fixed, formal, identical, literal, meticulous, minute, nice, particular, prim, punctilious, puritanical, rigid, scrupulous, specific, strict, succinct, unequivocal verbatim, word for word.

predilection *n.* affection, affinity, bent, bias, enthusiasm, fancy, fondness, inclination, leaning, liking, love, partiality, penchant, predisposition, preference, proclivity, proneness, propensity, soft spot, taste, tendency, weakness.

preeminent *adj.* chief, consummate, distinguished, excellent, exceptional, facile princeps, foremost, incomparable, inimitable, leading, matchless, nonpareil, outstanding, paramount, passing, peerless, predominant, prominent, renowned, superior, superlative, supreme, surpassing, transcendent, unequaled, urmatched, unrivaled, unsurpassed.

prefer[1] *v.* adopt, advocate, back, be partial to, choose, desire, elect, endorse, fancy, favor, go for, incline toward, like better, opt for, pick, plump for, recommend, select, single out, support, want, wish, would rather, would sooner.

prefer[2] *v.* bring, file, lodge, place, present, press.

prefer[3] *v.* advance, aggrandize, dignify, elevate, exalt, promote, raise, upgrade.

prejudice[1] *n.* bias, bigotry, chauvinism, discrimination, injustice, intolerance, narrow-mindedness, partiality, partisanship, preconception, prejudgment, racism, sexism, unfairness, viewiness, warp.

prejudice[2] *n.* damage, detriment, disadvantage, harm, hurt, impairment, injury, loss, mischief, ruin, vitiation, wreck.

premature *adj.* abortive, early, embryonic, forward, green, half-formed, hasty, ill-considered, ill-timed, immature, imperfect, impulsive, incomplete, inopportune, over-hasty, precipitate, precocious, preterm, previous, rash, raw, undeveloped, unfledged, unripe, unseasonable, untimely.

prepare *v.* accouter, adapt, adjust, anticipate, arrange, assemble, brace, brief, coach, compose, concoct, construct, contrive, develop, devise, dispose, do one's homework, draft, draw up, dress, equip, fashion, fettle, fit, fit out, fix up, forearm, form, fortify, furnish, get up, gird, groom, instruct, limber up, make, make ready, outfit, plan, practice, predispose, prime, produce, provide, psych up, ready, rehearse, rig out, steel, strengthen, supply, train, trim, warm up.

prescribe *v.* appoint, assign, command, decree, define, dictate, direct, enjoin, fix, impose, lay down, limit, ordain, require, rule, set, set bounds to, specify, stipulate.

present[1] *adj.* at hand, attending, available, contemporary, current, existent, extant, here, immediate, instant, near, ready, there, to hand.

present[2] *v.* acquaint with, adduce, advance, award, bestow, confer, declare, demonstrate, display, donate, entrust, exhibit, expound, extend, furnish, give, grant, hand over, hold out, introduce, mount, offer, pose, produce, proffer, put on, raise, recount, relate, show, stage, state, submit, suggest, tender.

presume *v.* assume, bank on, believe, conjecture, count on, dare, depend on, go so far, have the audacity, hypothesize, infer, make bold, make so bold, posit, postulate, presuppose, rely on, suppose, surmise, take for granted, take it, take the liberty, think, trust, undertake, venture.

pretend *v.* act, affect, allege, aspire, assume, claim, counterfeit, dissemble, dissimulate, fake, falsify, feign, go through the motions, imagine, impersonate, make believe, pass oneself off, profess, purport, put on, sham, simulate, suppose.

prey *n.* booty, dupe, fall guy, game, kill, mark, mug, plunder, quarry, target, victim.

primary *adj.* aboriginal, basic, beginning, best, capital, cardinal, chief, dominant, earliest, elemental, elementary, essential, first, first-formed, first-made, fundamental, greatest, highest, initial, introductory, leading, main, original, paramount, primal, prime, primeval, primitive, primordial, principal, pristine, radical, rudimentary, simple, top, ultimate, underlying.

principal[1] *adj.* capital, cardinal, chief, controlling, dominant, essential, first, foremost, highest, key, leading, main, paramount, preeminent, primary, prime, strongest, truncal.

principal[2] *n.* assets, capital, capital funds, money.

principle *n.* assumption, attitude, axiom, belief, canon, code, conscience, credo, criterion, dictum, doctrine, dogma, duty, element, ethic, formula, fundamental, golden rule, honor, institute, integrity, law, maxim, moral, morality, morals, opinion, precept, principium, probity, proposition, rectitude, rule, scruples, standard, tenet, truth, uprightness, verity.

private *adj.* clandestine, closet, concealed, confidential, exclusive, home-felt, hush-hush, in camera, independent, individual, inside, intimate, intraparietal, inward, isolated, off the record, own, particular, personal, privy, reserved, retired, secluded, secret, separate, sequestrated, solitary, special, unofficial, withdrawn.

prize[1] *n.* accolade, aim, ambition, award, conquest, desire, gain, goal, haul, honor, hope, jackpot, premium, purse, reward, stake(s), trophy, windfall, winnings. *adj.* award-winning, best, champion, excellent, first-rate, outstanding, top, top-notch, winning.

prize[2] *n.* booty, capture, loot, pickings, pillage, plunder, spoils, trophy.

prize[3] *v.* force, jimmy, lever, pry, winkle.

problem *n.* brainteaser, complication, conundrum, difficulty, dilemma, disagreement, dispute, doubt, enigma, no laughing matter, poster, predicament, puzzle, quandary, question, riddle, trouble, vexata quaestio, vexed question. *adj.* delinquent, difficult, intractable, perverse, refractory, uncontrollable, unmanageable, unruly.

procedure *n.* action, conduct, course, custom, form, formula, method, modus operandi, move, operation, performance, plan of action, policy, practice, process, routing, scheme, step, strategy, system, transaction.

proceed *v.* advance, arise, carry on, come, continue, derive, emanate, ensue, flow, follow, go ahead, issue, move on, originate, press on, progress, result, set in motion, spring, start, stem.

procrastinate *v.* adjourn, dally, defer, delay, dillydally, drag one's feet, gain time, play for time, postpone, prolong, protract, put off, retard, stall, temporize.

procreate *v.* beget, breed, conceive, engender, father, generate, mother, produce, propagate, reproduce, sire, spawn.

procure *v.* acquire, appropriate, bag, buy, come by, earn, effect, find, gain, get, induce, lay hands on, obtain, pander, pick up, pimp, purchase, secure, win.

prod *v.* dig, drive, egg on, elbow, goad, impel, incite, jab, motivate, move, nudge, poke, prick, prompt, propel, push, rouse, shove, sup, stimulate, urge. *n.* boost, cue, dig, elbow, jab, nudge, poke, prompt, push, reminder, shove, signal, stimulus.

product *n.* artefact, commodity, concoction, consequence, creation, effect, fruit,

goods, invention, issue, legacy, merchandise, offshoot, offspring, outcome, output, produce, production, result, returns, spinoff, upshot, work, yield.

profess *v.* acknowledge, admit, affirm, allege, announce, assert, asseverate, aver, avow, certify, claim, confess, confirm, declare, enunciate, fake, feign, maintain, make out, own, pretend, proclaim, propose, propound, purport, sham, state, vouch.

profit *n.* a fast buck, advancement, advantage, avail, benefit, boot, bottom line, earnings, emoluments, fruit, gain, gelt, good, graft, gravy, grist, interest, melon, percentage, proceeds, receipts, return, revenue, surplus, takings, use, value, velvet, winnings, yield.

progress *n.* advance, advancement, amelioration, betterment, breakthrough, circuit, continuation, course, development, gain, growth, headway, improvement, increase, journey, movement, passage, procession, progression, promotion, step forward, way.

prohibit *v.* ban, bar, constrain, debar, disallow, forbid, hamper, hinder, impede, interdict, obstruct, outlaw, preclude, prevent, proscribe, restrict, rule out, stop, veto.

project *n.* activity, assignment, conception, design, enterprise, idea, job, occupation, plan, program, proposal, purpose, scheme, task, undertaking, venture, work. *v.* beetle, bulge, calculate, cast, contemplate, contrive, design, devise, discharge, draft, estimate, exert, extend, extrapolate, extrude, fling, forecast, frame, gauge, hurl, jut, launch, map out, outline, overhand, plan, predetermine, predict, propel, prophesy, propose, protrude, purpose, reckon, scheme, shoot, stand out, stick out, throw, transmit.

prolific *adj.* abounding, abundant, bountiful, copious, fecund, fertile, fertilizing, fruitful, generative, luxuriant, productive, profuse, rank, reproductive, rich, teeming, voluminous.

promise *v.* assure, augur, bespeak, betoken, bid fair, contract, denote, engage, guarantee, hint at, indicate, look like, pledge, plight, predict, presage, prophesy, stipulate, suggest, swear, take an oath, undertake, vouch, vow, warrant. *n.* ability, aptitude, assurance, bond, capability, capacity, commitment, compact, covenant, engagement, flair, guarantee, oath, pledge, pollicitation, potential, talent, undertaking, vow, word, word of honor.

promote *v.* advance, advertise, advocate,

aggrandize, aid, assist, back, blazon, boost, champion, contribute to, develop, dignify, elevate, encourage, endorse, espouse, exalt, forward, foster, further, help, honor, hype, kick upstairs, nurture, plug, popularize, prefer, publicize, puff, push, raise, recommend, sell, sponsor, stimulate, support, trumpet, upgrade, urge.

prompt¹ *adj.* alert, brisk, eager, early, efficient, expeditious, immediate, instant, instantaneous, on time, punctual, quick, rapid, ready, responsive, smart, speedy, swift, timely, timeous, unhesitating, willing.

prompt² *v.* advise, assist, call forth, cause, cue, elicit, evoke, give rise to, impel, incite, induce, inspire, instigate, motivate, move, occasion, prod, produce, provoke, remind, result in, spur, stimulate, urge.

prone¹ *adj.* apt, bent, disposed, given, inclined, liable, likely, predisposed, subject, susceptible, tending, vulnerable.

prone² *adj.* facedown, flat, full-length, horizontal, procumbent, prostrate, recumbent, stretched.

pronounce *v.* accent, affirm, announce, articulate, assert, breathe, declaim, declare, decree, deliver, enunciate, judge, proclaim, say, sound, speak, stress, utter, vocalize, voice.

proper *adj.* accepted, accurate, appropriate, apt, becoming, befitting, characteristic, conventional, correct, decent, decorous, established, exact, fit, fitting, formal, genteel, gentlemanly, individual, kosher, ladylike, legitimate, mannerly, meet, orthodox, own, particular, peculiar, personal, polite, precise, prim, prissy, punctilious, refined, respectable, respective, right, sedate, seemly, special, specific, suitable, suited, well-becoming, well-beseeming.

property¹ *n.* acres, assets, belongings, building(s), capital, chattels, effects, estate, freehold, goods, holding, holdings, house(s), land, means, meum et tuum, possessions, real estate, realty, resources, riches, title, wealth.

property² *n.* ability, affection, attribute, characteristic, feature, hallmark, idiosyncrasy, mark, peculiarity, quality, trait, virtue.

prophecy *n.* augury, divination, forecast, foretelling, prediction, prognosis, prognostication, revelation, second sight, soothsaying, vaticination.

prophesy *v.* augur, divine, forecast, foresee, foretell, forewarn, predict, presage, prognosticate, soothsay, vaticinate.

proposal *n.* bid, design, draft, manifesto, motion, offer, outline, overture, plan, platform, presentation, proffer, program, project, proposition, recommendation, scheme, sketch, suggestion, suit, tender, terms.

propose *v.* advance, aim, bring up, design, enunciate, have in mind, intend, introduce, invite, lay before, mean, move, name, nominate, pay suit, plan, pop the question, present, proffer, propound, purpose, put forward, put up, recommend, scheme, submit, suggest, table, tender.

prospect *n.* calculation, chance, contemplation, expectation, future, hope, landscape, likelihood, odds, opening, outlook, panorama, perspective, plan, possibility, presumption, probability, promise, proposition, scene, sight, spectacle, thought, view, vision, vista.

prosper *v.* advance, bloom, boom, burgeon, fare well, flourish, flower, get on, grow rich, make good, progress, succeed, thrive, turn out well.

protest *n.* complaint, declaration, demur, demurral, disapproval, dissent, formal complaint, objection, obtestation, outcry, protestation, remonstrance.

proud *adj.* appreciative, arrogant, august, boastful, conceited, content, contented, disdainful, distinguished, egotistical, eminent, exalted, glad, glorious, grand, gratified, gratifying, great, haughty, high and mighty, honored, illustrious, imperious, imposing, lofty, lordly, magnificent, majestic, memorable, noble, overbearing, pleased, pleasing, presumptuous, prideful, red-letter, rewarding, satisfied, satisfying, self-important, self-respecting, snobbish, snobby, snooty, splendid, stately, stuck-up, supercilious, toffee-nosed, vain.

prove *v.* analyze, ascertain, assay, attest, authenticate, bear out, check, confirm, corroborate, demonstrate, determine, document, establish, evidence, evince, examine, experience, experiment, justify, show, substantiate, suffer, test, try, turn out, verify.

provide *v.* accommodate, add, afford, anticipate, arrange for, bring, cater, contribute, determine, equip, forearm, furnish, give, impart, lay down, lend, outfit, plan for, prepare, present, produce, provision, render, require, serve, specify, state, stipulate, stock up, suit, supply, take measures, take precautions, yield.

prowl *v.* creep, cruise, hunt, lurk, nose, patrol, range, roam, rove, scavenge, search, skulk, slink, sneak, stalk, steal.

prudent *adj.* canny, careful, cautious, circumspect, discerning, discreet, economical, farsighted, frugal, judicious, politic, provident, sagacious, sage, sensible, shrewd, sparing, thrift, vigilant, wary, well-advised, wise, wise-hearted.

pry *v.* delve, dig, ferret, interfere, intrude, meddle, nose, peep, peer, poke, poke one's nose in, snoop.

psyche *n.* anima, awareness, consciousness, individuality, intellect, intelligence, mind, personality, pneuma, self, soul, spirit, subconscious, understanding.

public *adj.* accessible, acknowledged, circulating, civic, civil, common, communal, community, exposed, general, important, known, national, notorious, obvious, open, overt, patent, plain, popular, prominent, published, recognized, respected, social, state, universal, unrestricted, well-known, wide-spread.

pugnacious *adj.* aggressive, antagonistic, argumentative, bellicose, belligerent, choleric, combative, contentious, disputatious, hostile, hot-tempered, irascible, petulant, quarrelsome.

pull *v.* attract, cull, dislocate, drag, draw, draw out, entice, extract, gather, haul, jerk, lure, magnetize, pick, pluck, remove, rend, rip, schlep, sprain, strain, stretch, take out, tear, tow, track, trail, tug, tweak, uproot, weed, whang, wrench, yank.

punish *v.* abuse, amerce, batter, beat, castigate, chasten, chastise, correct, crucify, discipline, flog, give a lesson to, give someone harm, hurt, injure, keelhaul, kneecap, lash, maltreat, manhandle, masthead, misuse, oppress, penalize, rough up, scour, scourge, sort, strafe, trounce.

pure *adj.* absolute, abstract, academic, antiseptic, authentic, blameless, chaste, clean, clear, disinfected, flawless, genuine, germ-free, guileless, high-minded, honest, hygienic, immaculate, innocent, maidenly, modest, natural, neat, pasteurized, perfect, philosophical, real, refined, sanitary, Saturnian, sheer, simple, sincere, snow-white, speculative, spirituous, spotless, stainless, sterile, sterilized, straight, taintless, theoretical, thorough, true, unadulterate, unadulterated, unalloyed, unblemished, uncontaminated, uncorrupted, undefiled, unmingled, unmitigated, unmixed, unpolluted, unqualified, unsoiled, unspoiled, unspotted, unstained, unsullied, untainted, untarnished, upright, utter, virgin, virginal, virtuous, wholesome.

purpose *n.* advantage, aim, ambition, aspiration, assiduity, avail, benefit, constancy, contemplation, decision, dedication, design, determination, devotion, drive, effect, end, firmness, function, gain, goal, good, hope, idea, ideal, intention, motive, object, objective, outcome, persistence, pertinacity, plan, point, principle, profit, project, rationale, reason, resolution, resolve, result, return, scheme, service, single-mindedness, steadfastness, target, tenacity, use, usefulness, utility, view, vision, will, wish, zeal. *v.* aim, aspire, contemplate, decide, design, desire, determine, intend, mean, meditate, plan, propose, resolve.

pursue *v.* accompany, adhere to, aim at, aim for, aspire to, attend, bedevil, beset, besiege, carry on, chase, check out, conduct, continue, course, court, cultivate, desire, dog, engage, in, follow, follow up, go for, gun for, harass, harry, haunt, hold to, hound, hunt, inquire into, investigate, keep on, maintain, perform, persecute, persevere in, persist in, plague, ply, practice, proceed, prosecute, purpose, seek, set one's cap at, shadow, stalk, strive for, tackle, tail, track, trail, try for, wage, woo.

push *v.* advance, bully, coerce, drive, egg on, encourage, force, incite, inveigle, maneuver, persuade, prod, shove, urge.

pushy *adj.* aggressive, ambitious, arrogant, assertive, assuming, bold, bossy, brash, bumptious, forceful, forward, loud, obtrusive, offensive, officious, overconfident, presumptuous, pushing, self-assertive.

puzzle[1] *v.* baffle, bamboozle, beat, bewilder, confound, confuse, fickle, floor, flummox, mystify, nonplus, perplex, pother, stump, worry. *n.* acrostic, anagram, brainteaser, confusion, conundrum, crossword, difficulty, dilemma, enigma, knot, koan, maze, mind-bender, mystery, paradox, poser, problem, quandary, question, rebus, riddle, Sphinx, tickler.

puzzle[2] *v.* brood, cogitate, consider, deliberate, figure, meditate, mull over, muse, ponder, rack one's brains, ratiocinate, reason, ruminate, study, think, wonder, worry.

Q

quack *n.* charlatan, cowboy, empiric, fake, fraud, humbug, impostor, masquerader, mountebank, phony, pretender, pseud, quacksalver, sham, spieler, swindler, trickster, witch doctor. *adj.* bogus, counterfeit, fake, false, fraudulent, phony, pretended, sham, so-called, spurious, supposed, unqualified.

quagmire *n.* bog, everglade, fen, marsh, mire, morass, moss, mudflat, quag, quicksand, slough, swamp.

quake *v.* convulse, heave, jolt, move, pulsate, quail, quiver, rock, shake, shiver, shudder, sway, throb, totter, tremble, vibrate, waver, wobble.

quantity *n.* aggregate, allotment, amount, breadth, bulk, capacity, content, dosage, expanse, extent, greatness, length, lot, magnitude, mass, measure, number, part, portion, proportion, quantum, quota, share, size, spread, strength, sum, total, volume, weight.

quarrel *n.* affray, altercation, argument, beef, bicker, clash, conflict, controversy, debate, discord, dispute, dissension, feud, fight, fray, row, scrap, spat, squabble, tiff, wrangle.

quarry *n.* game, goal, kill, object, objective, prey, prize, target, victim.

quarter¹ *n.* area, direction, district, division, locality, location, neighborhood, part, place, point, position, province, quartier, region, section, sector, side, spot, station, territory, vicinity, zone.

quarter² *n.* clemency, compassion, favor, forgiveness, grace, indulgence, leniency, mercy, pardon, pity.

quarter³ *n.* fourth, quartern, term. *v.* decussate, divide in four, quadrisect.

quarter⁴ *v.* accommodate, bed, billet, board, house, install, lodge, place, post, put up, shelter, station.

queer *adj.* aberrant, abnormal, absurd, anomalous, atypical, bizarre, cranky, crazy, curious, daft, demented, deranged, deviant, disquieting, dizzy, doubtful, droll, dubious, eccentric, eerie, erratic, exceptional, extraordinary, faint, fanciful, fantastic, fey, fishy, freakish, funny, giddy, grotesque, homosexual, idiosyncratic, ill, irrational, irregular, light-headed, mad, mysterious, odd, offbeat, outlandish, outré, peculiar, preternatural, puzzling, quaint, queasy, questionable, reeling, remarkable, rum, screwy, shady, shifty, singular, strange, suspect, suspicious, touched, unaccountable, unbalanced, uncanny, uncommon, unconventional, uneasy, unhinged, unnatural, unorthodox, unusual, unwell, unwonted, weird.

quench *v.* allay, appease, check, cool, crush, damp down, destroy, douse, end, extinguish, overcome, put out, quash, quell, sate, satisfy, silence, slake, smother, snuff out, stifle, suppress.

query *v.* ask, be skeptical of, call in question, challenge, disbelieve, dispute, distrust, doubt, enquire, misdoubt, mistrust, quarrel with, question, suspect.

question *v.* ask, be skeptical of, catechize, challenge, controvert, cross-examine, debrief, disbelieve, dispute, distrust, doubt, enquire, examine, grill, impugn, interpellate, interrogate, interview, investigate, misdoubt, mistrust, oppose, probe, pump, quarrel with, query, quiz, suspect. *n.* argument, confusion, contention, controversy, debate, difficulty, dispute, doubt, dubiety, examination, inquiry, interpellation, interrogation, investigation, issue, misdoubt, misgiving, motion, point, problem, proposal, proposition, quaere, query, quibble, skepsis, subject, theme, topic, uncertainty.

quick *adj.* able, active, acute, adept, adroit, agile, alert, animated, apt, astute, awake, brief, bright, brisk, clever, cursory, deft, dexterous, discerning, energetic, expeditious, express, fast, fleet, flying, hasty, headlong, hurried, immediate, instant, instantaneous, intelligent, keen, lively, nifty, nimble, nippy, penetrating, perceptive, perfunctory, precipitate, prompt, quick-witted, rapid, ready, receptive, responsive, sharp, shrewd, skillful, smart, snappy, speedy, spirited, sprightly, spry, sudden, summary, swift, unhesitating, vivacious, wide-awake, winged.

quiet *adj.* calm, composed, conservative, contemplative, contented, docile, dumb, even-tempered, gentle, hushed, inaudible, isolated, lonely, low, low-pitched, meek, mild, modest, motionless, noiseless, pacific, passive, peaceable, peaceful, placid, plain, private, removed, reserved, restful, restrained, retired, retiring, secluded, secret, sedate, self-contained, sequestered, serene, shy, silent, simple, smooth, sober, soft, soundless, still, subdued, taciturn, thoughtful, tranquil, uncommunicative, undisturbed, uneventful, unexcitable, unexciting, unforthcoming, unfrequented, uninterrupted, unobtrusive, untroubled.

quit *v.* abandon, abdicate, apostatize, cease, conclude, decamp, depart, desert, disappear, discontinue, drop, end, exit, forsake, give up, go, halt, leave, relinquish, renege, renounce, repudiate, resign, retire, stop, surrender, suspend, vamoose, vanish, withdraw.

quite *adv.* absolutely, comparatively, completely, entirely, exactly, fairly, fully, moderately, perfectly, precisely, rather, relatively, somewhat, totally, utterly, wholly.

quota *n.* allocation, allowance, assignment, cut, part, percentage, portion, proportion, quotum, ration, share, slice, whack.

quotation¹ *n.* citation, crib, cutting, excerpt, extract, gobbet, locus classicus, passage, piece, quote, reference, remnant.

quote *v.* adduce, attest, cite, detail, echo, instance, name, parrot, recall, recite, recollect, refer to, repeat, reproduce, retell.

R

race¹ *n.* chase, competition, contention, contest, dash, derby, footrace, marathon, pursuit, quest, rat race, regatta, rivalry, scramble, sprint, steeplechase. *v.* career, compete, contest, dart, dash, fly, gallop, hare, hasten, hurry, run, rush, speed, sprint, tear, zoom.

race² *n.* ancestry, blood, breed, clan, descent, family, folk, house, issue, kin, kindred, line, lineage, nation, offspring, people, progeny, seed, stirps, stock, strain, tribe, type.

rage *n.* agitation, anger, bate, chafe, conniption, craze, dernier cri, enthusiasm, fad, fashion, frenzy, fury, ire, madness, mania, obsession, paddy, passion, style, tantrum, vehemence, violence, vogue, wrath. *v.* chafe, explode, fret, fulminate, fume, inveigh, ramp, rampage, rant, rave, seethe, storm, surge, thunder.

raid *n.* attack, break-in, bust, descent, foray, incursion, inroad, invasion, irruption, onset, onslaught, sally, seizure, sortie, strike, swoop. *v.* attack, bust, descend on, do, forage, foray, invade, loot, maraud, pillage, plunder, ransack, rifle, rush, sack.

rail *v.* abuse, arraign, attack, castigate, censure, criticize, decry, denounce, fulminate, inveigh, jeer, mock, revile, ridicule, scoff, upbraid, vituperate, vociferate.

rain *n.* cloudburst, deluge, downpour, drizzle, fall, flood, hail, mizzle, precipitation, raindrops, rainfall, rains, shower, spate, squall, stream, torrent, volley. *v.* bestow, bucket, deluge, deposit, drizzle, drop, expend, fall, heap, lavish, mizzle, pour, shower, spit, sprinkle, teem.

raise *v.* abandon, activate, advance, aggrandize, aggravate, amplify, arouse, assemble, augment, awaken, boost, breed, broach, build, cause, collect, construct, create, cultivate, develop, discontinue, elate, elevate, emboss, embourgeoise, end, engender, enhance, enlarge, erect, escalate, evoke, exaggerate, exalt, excite, foment, form, foster, father, gentrify, get, grow, heave, heighten, hoist, incite, increase, inflate, instigate, intensify, introduce, kindle, levy, lift, loft, magnify, mass,

mobilize, moot, motivate, muster, nurture, obtain, occasion, originate, pose, prefer, produce, promote, propagate, provoke, rally, rear, recruit, reinforce, relinquish, remove, sky, start, strengthen, sublime, suggest, terminate, up, upgrade, uplift.

rampage *v.* rage, rant, rave, run amok, run riot, run wild, rush, storm, tear. *n.* destruction, frenzy, furor, fury, rage, storm, tempest, tumult, uproar, violence.

rancid *adj.* bad, fetid, foul, fusty, musty, off, putrid, rank, rotten, sour, stale, strong-smelling, tainted.

rancor *n.* acrimony, animosity, animus, antipathy, bitterness, enmity, grudge, hate, hatred, hostility, ill-feeling, ill-will, malevolence, malice, malignity, resentfulness, resentment, spite, spleen, venom, vindictiveness.

random *adj.* accidental, adventitious, aimless, arbitrary, casual, chance, desultory, fortuitous, haphazard, incidental, indiscriminate, purposeless, scattershot, spot, stray, unfocused, unplanned, unpremeditated.

rant *v.* bellow, bluster, cry, declaim, mouth it, rave, roar, shout, slang-whang, spout, vociferate, yell. *n.* bluster, bombast, declamation, diatribe, fanfaronade, harangue, philippic, rhetoric, storm, tirade, vociferation.

rapid *adj.* brisk, expeditious, express, fast, fleet, flying, hasty, headlong, hurried, precipitate, prompt, quick, speedy, swift.

rare *adj.* admirable, choice, curious, excellent, exceptional, exquisite, extreme, few, fine, great, incomparable, infrequent, invaluable, peerless, precious, priceless, recherche, rich, scarce, singular, sparse, sporadic, strange, superb, superlative, uncommon, unusual.

rash¹ *adj.* adventurous, audacious, brash, careless, foolhardy, harebrained, harum-scarum, hasty, headlong, headstrong, heedless, helter-skelter, hotheaded, ill-advised, ill-considered, impetuous, imprudent, impulsive, incautious, indiscreet, injudicious, incipient, madcap, precipitant, precipitate, premature, reckless, slapdash, thoughtless, unguarded, unthinking, unwary, venturesome.

rash² *n.* epidemic, eruption, exanthem(a), flood, hives, nettlerash, outbreak, plague, pompholyx, series, spate, succession, urticaria, wave.

ration *n.* allocation, allotment, allowance, amount, dole, helping, measure, part, provision, quota, share. *v.* allocate, allot, apportion, budget, conserve, control, deal, dispense, distribute, dole, issue, limit, mete, restrict, save, supply.

rational *adj.* balanced, cerebral, cognitive, compos mentis, enlightened, intelligent, judicious, logical, lucid, normal, ratiocinative, realistic, reasonable, reasoning, sagacious, sane, sensible, sound, thinking, well-founded, well-grounded, wise.

ravish *v.* abuse, captivate, charm, deflorate, deflower, delight, enchant, enrapture, entrance, fascinate, outrage, overjoy, rape, spellbind, transport, violate.

ravishing *adj.* alluring, beautiful, bewitching, charming, dazzling, delightful, enchanting, entrancing, gorgeous, lovely, radiant, seductive, stunning.

raw *adj.* abraded, bare, basic, biting, bitter, bleak, bloody, blunt, brutal, callow, candid, chafed, chill, chilly, coarse, cold, crude, damp, frank, freezing, fresh, grazed, green, harsh, ignorant, immature, inexperienced, naked, natural, new, open, organic, piercing, plain, realistic, rough, scraped, scratched, sensitive, skinned, sore, tender, unadorned, uncooked, undisciplined, undisguised, undressed, unfinished, unpleasant, unpracticed, unprepared, unprocessed, unrefined, unripe, unseasoned, unskilled, untrained, untreated, untried, unvarnished, verdant, wet.

raze *v.* bulldoze, delete, demolish, destroy, dismantle, efface, erase, expunge, extinguish, extirpate, flatten, level, obliterate, remove, ruin.

react *v.* acknowledge, act, answer, behave, emote, function, operate, proceed, reply, respond, work.

real *adj.* absolute, actual, authentic, bona fide, certain, dinkum, dinky-di(e), essential, existent, factual, genuine, heartfelt, honest, intrinsic, legitimate, positive, right, rightful, simon-pure, sincere, substantial, substantive, sure-enough, tangible, true, unaffected, unfeigned, valid, veritable.

rear¹ *n.* back, backside, bottom, buttocks, croup, end, hindquarters, posterior, rearguard, rump, stern, tail.

rear² *v.* breed, build, construct, cultivate, educate, elevate, erect, fabricate, foster, grow, hoist, lift, loom, nurse, nurture, parent, raise, rise, soar, tower, train.

reasonable *adj.* acceptable, advisable, arguable, average, believable, credible, equitable, fair, fit, honest, inexpensive, intelligent, judicious, just, justifiable, logical, moderate, modest, OK, passable, plausible, possible, practical, proper, rational, reasoned, right, sane, satisfactory,

sensible, sober, sound, tenable, tolerable, viable, well-advised, well thought-out, wise.

rebel *v.* defy, disobey, dissent, flinch, kick, over the traces, mutiny, recoil, resist, revolt, rise up, run riot, shrink. *n.* apostate, dissenter, heretic, insurgent, insurrectionary, Jacobin, malcontent, mutineer, nonconformist, revolutionary, revolutionist, schismatic, secessionist. *adj.* insubordinate, insurgent, insurrectionary, malcontent(ed), mutinous, rebellious, revolutionary.

recede *v.* abate, decline, decrease, diminish, dwindle, ebb, fade, lessen, regress, retire, retreat, retrogress, return, shrink, sink, slacken, subside, wane, withdraw.

receive *v.* accept, accommodate, acquire, admit, apprehend, bear, collect, derive, encounter, entertain, experience, gather, get, greet, hear, meet, obtain, perceive, pick up, react to, respond to, suffer, sustain, take, undergo, welcome.

recession *n.* decline, depression, downturn, slump, stagflation.

recite *v.* articulate, declaim, deliver, describe, detail, enumerate, itemize, narrate, orate, perform, recapitulate, recount, rehearse, relate, repeat, speak, tell.

reckless *adj.* careless, daredevil, devil-may-care, foolhardy, harebrained, hasty, headlong, heedless, ill-advised, imprudent, inattentive, incautious, indiscreet, irresponsible, madcap, mindless, negligent, precipitate, rash, regardless, tearaway, thoughtless, wild.

recognize *v.* accept, acknowledge, admit, allow, appreciate, approve, avow, concede, confess, grant, greet, honor, identify, know, notice, own, perceive, place, realize, recall, recollect, remember, respect, salute, see, spot, understand.

recover *v.* convalesce, heal, improve, mend, pick up, pull through, rally, recapture, reclaim, recoup, recuperate, redeem, regain, repair, replevy, repossess, restore, retake, retrieve, revive.

recreation *n.* amusement, distraction, diversion, enjoyment, entertainment, exercise, fun, games, hobby, leisure activity, pastime, play, pleasure, refreshment, relaxation, relief, sport.

recur *v.* persist, reappear, repeat, return.

reduce *v.* abate, abridge, bankrupt, break, cheapen, conquer, contract, curtail, cut, debase, decimate, decrease, degrade, demote, deoxidate, deoxidize, depress, diet, dilute, diminish, discount, downgrade, drive, force, humble, humiliate, impair, impoverish, lessen, lower, master, moderate, overpower, pauperize, rebate, ruin, scant, shorten, slake, slash, slenderize, slim, subdue, trim, truncate, vanquish, weaken.

reek v. exhale, fume, hum, pong, smell, smoke, stink.

refine v. chasten, civilize, clarify, cultivate, distill, elevate, exalt, filter, hone, improve, perfect, polish, process, purify, rarefy, spiritualize, sublimize, subtilize, temper.

refrain[1] v. abstain, avoid, cease, desist, eschew, forbear, leave off, quit, renounce, stop, swear off.

refrain[2] n. burden, chorus, epistrophe, melody, song, tune, undersong, wheel.

refresh v. brace, cheer, cool, energize, enliven, freshen, inspirit, jog, prod, prompt, reanimate, reinvigorate, rejuvenate, renew, renovate, repair, replenish, restore, revitalize, revive, revivify, stimulate.

regale v. amuse, captivate, delight, divert, entertain, fascinate, feast, gratify, ply, refresh, serve.

regard v. account, adjudge, attend, behold, believe, concern, consider, deem, esteem, estimate, eye, heed, hold, imagine, interest, judge, mark, mind, note, notice, observe, pertain to, rate, relate to, remark, respect, scrutinize, see, suppose, think, treat, value, view, watch.

regret v. bemoan, bewail, deplore, grieve, lament, miss, mourn, repent, rue, sorrow. n. bitterness, compunction, contrition, disappointment, grief, lamentation, penitence, remorse, repentance, ruefulness, self-reproach, shame, sorrow.

regulate v. adjust, administer, arrange, balance, conduct, control, direct, fit, govern, guide, handle, manage, moderate, modulate, monitor, order, organize, oversee, regiment, rule, run, settle, square, superintend, supervise, systematize, tune.

reimburse v. compensate, indemnify, recompense, refund, remunerate, repay, requite, restore, return, square up.

reject v. condemn, decline, deny, despise, disallow, discard, eliminate, exclude, explode, jettison, jilt, pip, rebuff, refuse, renounce, repel, reprobate, repudiate, repulse, scrap, spike, spurn, veto.

rejoice v. celebrate, delight, exult, glory, joy, jubilate, revel, triumph.

relative adj. allied, applicable, apposite, appropriate, appurtenant, apropos, associated, comparative, connected, contingent, correlative, corresponding, dependent, germane, interrelated, pertinent, proportionate, reciprocal, related, relevant, respective. n. cognate, connection, german, kinsman, kinswoman, relation, sib.

relatively adv. comparatively, fairly, quite, rather, somewhat.

relax v. abate, diminish, disinhibit, ease, ebb, lessen, loosen, lower, mitigate, moderate, reduce, relieve, remit, rest, slacken, soften, tranquilize, unbend, unclench, unwind, weaken.

relent v. acquiesce, capitulate, drop, ease, fall, forbear, give in, melt, relax, slacken, slow, soften, unbend, weaken, yield.

reluctant adj. averse, backward, disinclined, grudging, hesitant, indisposed, loath, loathful, loth, recalcitrant, slow, squeamish, unenthusiastic, unwilling.

rely v. bank, bet, count, depend, lean, reckon, swear by, trust.

remain v. abide, bide, cling, continue, delay, dwell, endure, last, linger, persist, prevail, rest, sojourn, stand, stay, survive, tarry, wait.

remark v. animadvert, comment, declare, espy, heed, mark, mention, note, notice, observe, perceive, reflect, regard, say, see, state. n. acknowledgment, assertion, attention, comment, consideration, declaration, heed, mention, notice, observation, opinion, recognition, reflection, regard, say, statement, thought, utterance, word.

remarkable adj. amazing, conspicuous, distinguished, exceptional, extraordinary, famous, impressive, miraculous, notable, noteworthy, odd, outstanding, phenomenal, preeminent, prominent, rare, signal, singular, strange, striking, surprising, unco, uncommon, unusual, wonderful.

remedy n. antidote, countermeasure, cure, medicine, panacea, relief, restorative, solution, treatment.

remember v. commemorate, place, recall, recognize, recollect, reminisce, retain, summon up, think back.

remit v. abate, alleviate, cancel, decrease, defer, delay, desist, desist from, diminish, dispatch, dwindle, forbear, forward, halt, mail, mitigate, moderate, post, postpone, put back, reduce, relax, repeal, rescind, send, send back, shelve, sink, slacken, soften, stop, suspend, transfer, transmit, wane, weaken. n. authorization, brief, guidelines, instructions, orders, responsibility, scope, terms of reference.

renew v. continue, extend, mend, modernize, overhaul, prolong, reaffirm, recommence, recreate, reestablish, refashion, refit, refresh, refurbish, regenerate, rejuvenate, remodel, renovate, reopen, repair, repeat, replace, replenish, restate, restock, restore, resume, revitalize, transform.

renounce *v.* abandon, abdicate, abjure, abnegate, decline, deny, discard, disclaim, disown, yank, eschew, forgo, forsake, forswear, put away, quit, recant, reject, relinquish, repudiate, resign, spurn.

repeal *v.* abolish, annul, cancel, invalidate, nullify, rescind, revoke, set aside, void, withdraw.

repeat *v.* duplicate, echo, iterate, quote, rebroadcast, recapitulate, recite, redo, rehearse, reiterate, relate, renew, replay, reproduce, rerun, reshow, restate, retell. *n.* duplicate, echo, rebroadcast, recapitulation, reiteration, repetition, replay, reproduction, rerun, reshowing.

repel *v.* check, confront, decline, disadvantage, disgust, fight, hold off, nauseate, offend, oppose, parry, rebuff, refuse, reject, repulse, resist, revolt, sicken, ward off.

repent *n.* atone, bewail, deplore, lament, regret, relent, rue, sorrow.

reply *v.* acknowledge, answer, reciprocate, respond, retort, return, riposte.

report n. account, announcement, article, bang, blast, boom, bruit, character, communication, communique, crack, crash, declaration, description, detail, detonation, discharge, dispatch, esteem, explosion, fame, gossip, hearsay, information, message, narrative, news, noise, note, paper, piece, record, regard, relation, reputation, repute, reverberation, rumor, sound, statement, story, summary, tale, talk, tidings, version, word, write-up. *v.* air, announce, appear, arrive, broadcast, bruit, circulate, come, communicate, cover, declare, describe, detail, document, mention, narrate, note, notify, proclaim, publish, recite, record, recount, relate, relay, state, tell.

represent *v.* act, appear as, be, betoken, delineate, denote, depict, describe, designate, embody, enact, epitomize, equal, evoke, exemplify, exhibit, express, illustrate, mean, outline, perform, personify, picture, portray, produce, render, reproduce, show, sketch, stage, symbolize, typify.

reprimand *n.* admonition, blame, castigation, censure, dressing-down, lecture, rebuke, reprehension, reproach, reprove, scold, slate, tongue-lash, upbraid.

request *v.* ask, ask for, beg, beseech, demand, desire, entreat, importune, petition, pray, requisition, seek, solicit, supplicate. *n.* appeal, application, asking, beg-

ging, call, demand, desire, entreaty, impetration, petition, prayer, representation, requisition, solicitation, suit, supplication.

require *v.* ask, beg, beseech, bid, command, compel, constrain, crave, demand, desire, direct, enjoin, exact, force, instruct, involve, lack, make, miss, necessitate, need, oblige, order, request, take, want, wish.

requirement *n.* demand, desideratum, essential, lack, must, necessity, need, precondition, prerequisite, provision, proviso, qualification, requisite, sine qua non, specification, stipulation, term, want.

rescue *v.* deliver, extricate, free, liberate, ransom, recover, redeem, release, salvage, save.

reside *v.* abide, consist, dwell, exist, inhabit, inhere, lie, live, lodge, remain, settle, sit, sojourn, stay.

resign *v.* abandon, abdicate, cede, forgo, forsake, leave, quit, relinquish, renounce, sacrifice, stand down, surrender, vacate, waive, yield.

resilience *n.* adaptability, bounce, buoyancy, elasticity, flexibility, give, hardiness, plasticity, pliability, recoil, spring, springiness, strength, suppleness, toughness, unshockability.

resist *v.* avoid, battle, check, combat, confront, counteract, countervail, curb, defy, dispute, fight back, forbear, forgo, hinder, oppose, refuse, repel, thwart, weather, withstand.

respect *n.* admiration, appreciation, approbation, aspect, bearing, characteristic, connection, consideration, deference, detail, esteem, estimation, facet, feature, homage, honor, matter, particular, point, recognition, reference, regard, relation, reverence, sense, veneration, way.

response *n.* acknowledgment, answer, comeback, counterblast, feedback, reaction, rejoinder, reply, respond, retort, return, riposte.

rest¹ *n.* base, break, breather, breathing space, breathing time, breathing while, calm, cessation, cradle, doze, halt, haven, holiday, idleness, inactivity, interlude, intermission, interval, leisure, lie-down, lie-in, lodging, lull, motionlessness, nap, pause, prop, refreshment, refuge, relaxation, relieve, repose, retreat, shelf, shelter, shut-eye, siesta, sleep, slumber, snooze, somnolence, spell, stand, standstill, stillness, stop, support, tranquillity, trestle, vacation.

rest² *n.* balance, core, excess, leftovers, majority, others, remainder, remains, remnants, residue, residuum, rump, surplus.

restrict v. bound, circumscribe, confine, constrain, contain, impede, inhibit, limit, regulate, restrain, restringe.

retard v. arrest, brake, check, clog, decelerate, defer, delay, detain, encumber, handicap, hinder, impede, keep back, obstruct, slow, stall.

retreat v. depart, ebb, leave, quit, recede, recoil, retire, shrink, turn tail, withdraw.

retrieve v. fetch, make good, recall, recapture, recoup, recover, redeem, regain, repair, repossess, rescue, restore, return, salvage, save.

return v. answer, choose, communicate, convey, deliver, earn, elect, make, net, pick, reappear, rebound, reciprocate, recoil, recompense, recur, redound, reestablish, refund, reimburse, reinstate, rejoin, remit, render, repair, repay, replace, reply, report, requite, respond, restore, retort, retreat, revert, send, submit, transmit, volley, yield.

reveal v. announce, bare, betray, broadcast, communicate, disbosom, disclose, dismask, display, divulge, exhibit, expose, impart, leak, lift the lid off, manifest, open, proclaim, publish, show, tell, unbare, unbosom, uncover, unearth, unfold, unmask, unshadow, unveil.

revenge n. a dose/taste of one's own medicine, reprisal, requital, retaliation, retribution, revengement, satisfaction, vengeance, vindictiveness. v. avenge, even the score, get one's own back, get satisfaction, repay, requite, retaliate, vindicate.

revere v. adore, defer to, exalt, honor, pay homage to, respect, reverence, venerate, worship.

reverse v. alter, annul, back, backtrack, cancel, change, countermand, hark back, invalidate, invert, negate, overrule, overset, overthrow, overturn, quash, repeal, rescind, retract, retreat, revert, revoke, transpose, undo, upend, upset.

revert v. backslide, lapse, recur, regress, relapse, resume, retrogress, return, reverse.

revise v. alter, amend, change, correct, edit, emend, memorize, modify, recast, reconsider, reconstruct, redo, reexamine, reread, revamp, review, rewrite, study, update.

revive v. animate, awaken, cheer, comfort, invigorate, quicken, rally, reactivate, reanimate, recover, refresh, rekindle, renew, renovate, restore, resuscitate, revitalize, revivify, rouse.

revolt[1] n. breakaway, defection, insurgency, insurrection, jacquerie, mutiny, putsch, rebellion, revolution, rising, secession, sedition, uprising. v. defect, mutiny, rebel, resist, riot, rise.

revolt[2] v. disgust, nauseate, offend, outrage, repel, repulse, scandalize, shock, sicken.

revolution n. cataclysm, change, circle, circuit, coup, coup d'état, cycle, gyration, innovation, insurgency, jacquerie, lap, metamorphosis, mutiny, orbit, putsch, rebellion, reformation, revolt, rising, rotation, round, shift, spin, transformation, turn, upheaval, uprising, volution, wheel, whirl.

revulsion n. abhorrence, abomination, aversion, detestation, disgust, dislike, distaste, hatred, loathing, recoil, repugnance, repulsion.

reward n. benefit, bonus, bounty, come-up(p)ance, compensation, desert, gain, guerdon, honor, meed, merit, payment, payoff, premium, prize, profit, punishment, recompense, remuneration, repayment, requital, retribution, return, wages.

rich adj. abounding, abundant, affluent, ample, bright, copious, costly, creamy, deep, delicious, dulcet, elaborate, elegant, expensive, exquisite, exuberant, fatty, fecund, fertile, fine, flavorsome, flush, fruitful, full, full-bodied, full-flavored, full-toned, gay, gorgeous, heavy, highly flavored, humorous, in the money, intense, juicy, laughable, lavish, loaded, ludicrous, luscious, lush, luxurious, mellifluous, mellow, moneyed, opulent, palatial, pecunious, plenteous, plentiful, plutocratic, precious, priceless, productive, prolific, propertied, property, prosperous, resonant, ridiculous, risible, rolling, savory, sidesplitting, spicy, splendid, strong, succulent, sumptuous, superb, sweet, tasty, uberous, valuable, vibrant, vivid, warm, wealthy, well-heeled, well-off, well-provided, well-stocked, well-supplied, well-to-do.

ridiculous adj. absurd, comical, contemptible, damfool, derisory, farcical, foolish, funny, hilarious, incredible, laughable, laughworthy, ludicrous, nonsensical, outrageous, preposterous, risible, silly, stupid, unbelievable.

right adj. absolute, accurate, admissible, advantageous, appropriate, authentic, balanced, becoming, characteristic, comme il faut, complete, compos mentis, conservative, correct, deserved, desirable, dexter, dextral, direct, done, due, equitable, ethical, exact, factual, fair, favorable, fine, fit, fitting, genuine, good, healthy, honest, honorable, ideal, just, lawful, lucid, moral, normal, opportune, out-

and-out, perpendicular, precise, proper, propitious, rational, reactionary, real, reasonable, righteous, rightful, rightist, rightward, right-wing, sane, satisfactory, seemly, sound, spot-on, straight, suitable, thorough, thoroughgoing, Tory, true, unerring, unimpaired, upright, utter, valid, veracious, veritable, virtuous, well.

rile *v.* anger, annoy, bug, exasperate, gall, get, irk, irritate, miff, nettle, peeve, pique, provoke, put out, upset, vex.

ring¹ *n.* association, band, cartel, cell, circle, circuit, circus, clique, collar, collet, combine, coterie, crew, enclosure, gang, group, gyre, halo, hoop, knot, loop, mob, organization, rink, round, syndicate. *v.* circumscribe, encircle, enclose, encompass, gash, gird, girdle, mark, score, surround.

ring² *v.* bell, buzz, call, chime, clang, clink, peal, phone, resonate, resound, reverberate, sound, tang, telephone, ting, tinkle, tintinnabulate, toll. *n.* buzz, call, chime, clang, clink, knell, peal, phone call, tang, ting, tinkle, tintinnabulation.

rinse *v.* bathe, clean, cleanse, dip, sluice, splash, swill, wash, wet. *n.* bath, dip, dye, splash, tint, wash, wetting.

rise *v.* advance, appear, arise, ascend, buoy, climb, crop up, emanate, emerge, enlarge, eventuate, flow, get up, grow, happen, improve, increase, intensify, issue, levitate, lift, mount, mutiny, occur, originate, progress, prosper, rebel, resist, revolt, slope, slope up, soar, spring, spring up, stand up, surface, swell, tower, volume, wax.

risk *n.* adventure, chance, danger, gamble, hazard, jeopardy, peril, possibility, speculation, uncertainty, venture.

rite *n.* act, ceremonial, ceremony, custom, form, formality, liturgy, mystery, observance, office, ordinance, practice, procedure, ritual, sacrament, service, solemnity, usage, worship.

rival *n.* adversary, antagonist, challenger, collateral, compeer, competitor, contender, contestant, emulator, equal, equivalent, fellow, match, opponent, peer, rivaless.

roam *v.* drift, meander, prowl, ramble, range, rove, squander, stray, stroll, travel, walk, wander.

roar *v.* bawl, bay, bell, bellow, blare, clamor, crash, cry, guffaw, hoot, howl, rumble, shout, thunder, vociferate, yell.

rob *v.* bereave, bunko, cheat, con, defraud, deprive, despoil, dispossess, do, flake, gyp, heist, hold up, loot, mill, pillage, plunder, raid, ramp, ransack, rifle, rip off, roll, sack, sting, strip, swindle.

rock¹ *n.* anchor, boulder, bulwark, cornerstone, danger, foundation, hazard, logan, log(g)an-stone, mainstay, obstacle, pebble, problem, protection, stone, support.

rock² *v.* astonish, astound, daze, dumbfound, jar, lurch, pitch, reel, roll, shake, shock, stagger, stun, surprise, way, swing, tilt, tip, toss, wobble.

rocky *adj.* craggy, flinty, hard, pebbly, rocklike, rough, rugged, stony.

rogue *n.* blackguard, charlatan, cheat, con man, crook, deceiver, devil, fraud, knave, miscreant, mountebank, nasty piece/bit of work, ne'er-do-well, picaroon, rapscallion, rascal, reprobate, scamp, scapegallows, scoundrel, sharper, swindler, vagrant, villain, wag.

romance *n.* absurdity, adventure, affair(e), amour, attachment, charm, color, exaggeration, excitement, fabrication, fairy tale, falsehood, fantasy, fascination, fiction, gest(e), glamour, idyll, intrigue, invention, legend, liaison, lie, love affair, love story, melodrama, mystery, novel, passion, relationship, sentiment, story, tale, tear-jerker. *v.* exaggerate, fantasize, lie, overstate.

romantic *adj.* amorous, charming, chimerical, colorful, dreamy, exaggerated, exciting, exotic, extravagant, fabulous, fairy-tale, fanciful, fantastic, fascinating, fictitious, fond, glamorous, high-flown, idealistic, idyllic, imaginary, imaginative, impractical, improbable, legendary, lovey-dovey, loving, made-up, mushy, mysterious, passionate, picturesque, quixotic, romantical, sentimental, sloppy, soppy, starry-eyed, tender, unrealistic, utopian, visionary, whimsical, wild.

room *n.* allowance, apartment, area, capacity, chamber, chance, compartment, compass, elbow-room, expanse, extent, house-room, latitude, leeway, margin, occasion, office, opportunity, play, range, salon, saloon, scope, space, territory, volume.

roomy *adj.* ample, broad, capacious, commodious, extensive, generous, large, sizable, spacious, voluminous, wide.

root¹ *n.* base, basis, beginnings, bottom, cause, core, crux, derivation, essence, foundation, fountainhead, fundamental, germ, heart, mainspring, more, nub, nucleus, occasion, origin, radicle, radix, rhizome, seat, seed, source, starting point, stem, tuber. *v.* anchor, embed, entrench, establish, fasten, fix, ground, implant, moor, set, sink, stick.

root² *v.* burrow, delve, dig, ferret, forage,

grout, hunt, nose, poke, pry, rummage.

rot v. corrode, corrupt, crumble, decay, decline, decompose, degenerate, deteriorate, disintegrate, fester, go bad, languish, molder, perish, putrefy, ret, spoil, taint. n. balderdash, blight, bosh, bunk, bunkum, canker, claptrap, collapse, corrosion, corruption, decay, decomposition, deterioration, disintegration, drivel, flapdoodle, guff, hogwash, moonshine, mold, nonsense, poppycock, putrefaction, putrescence, rubbish, tommyrot, twaddle.

rotate v. alternate, gyrate, interchange, pirouette, pivot, reel, revolve, spell, spin, switch, swivel, turn, twiddle, wheel.

round adj. ample, annular, ball-shaped, blunt, bowed, bulbous, candid, circular, complete, curved, curvilinear, cylindrical, direct, discoid, disc-shaped, entire, fleshy, frank, full, full-fleshed, globular, mellifluous, orbed, orbicular, orby, orotund, outspoken, plain, plump, resonant, rich, ring-shaped, roly-poly, rotund, rotundate, rounded, solid, sonorous, spheral, spheric, spherical, straight-forward, unbroken, undivided, unmodified, whole.

row¹ n. bank, colonnade, column, file, line, queue, range, rank, sequence, series, string, tier.

row² n. altercation, brawl, castigation, commotion, controversy, dispute, disturbance, donnybrook, dressing-down, falling-out, fracas, fray, fuss, lecture, noise, quarrel, racket, reprimand, reproof, rhubarb, rollicking, rookery, rout, ruckus, ruction, ruffle, rumpus, scrap, shemozzle, shindig, shindy, slanging, match, squabble, talking-to, telling-off, ticking-off, tiff, tongue-lashing, trouble, tumult, uproar.

rude adj. abrupt, abusive, artless, barbarous, blunt, boorish, brusque, brutish, cheeky, churlish, coarse, crude, curt, discourteous, disrespectful, graceless, gross, harsh, ignorant, illiterate, ill-mannered, impertinent, impolite, impudent, inartistic, inconsiderate, inelegant, insolent, insulting, loutish, low, makeshift, oafish, obscene, offhand, peremptory, primitive, raw, rough, savage, scurrilous, sharp, short, simple, startling, sudden, uncivil, uncivilized, uncouth, uncultured, uneducated, ungracious, unmannerly, unpleasant, unpolished, unrefined, untutored, violent, vulgar.

rue v. bemoan, bewail, beweep, deplore, grieve, lament, mourn, regret, repent.

ruler n. commander, emperor, governor, head of state, king, leader, lord, monarch, potentate, prince, princess, queen, sovereign.

run v. abscond, administer, bear, beat it, bleed, bolt, boss, career, carry, cascade, challenge, circulate, clear out, climb, compete, conduct, contend, continue, control, convey, coordinate, course, creep, dart, dash, decamp, depart, direct, discharge, display, dissolve, drive to, escape, extend, feature, flee, flow, function, fuse, gallop, glide, go, gush, hare, hasten, head, hie, hotfoot, hurry, issue, jog, ladder, last, lead, leak, lie, liquefy, lope, manage, maneuver, mastermind, melt, mix, move, operate, oversee, own, pass, perform, ply, pour, print, proceed, propel, publish, race, range, reach, regulate, roll, rush, scamper, scarper, scramble, scud, scurry, skedaddle, skim, slide, speed, spill, spout, spread, sprint, stand, stream, stretch, superintend, supervise, tear, tick, trail, transport, unravel, work.

ruse n. artifice, blind, deception, device, dodge, hoax, imposture, maneuver, play, sham, stall, stratagem, subterfuge, trick, wile.

rush v. accelerate, attack, bolt, capture, career, charge, dart, dash, dispatch, expedite, fly, hasten, hightail it, hotfoot, hurry, hustle, overcome, press, push, quicken, race, run, scour, scramble, scurry, shoot, speed, speed up, sprint, stampede, storm, tear, wallop, w(h)oosh. n. assault, charge, dash, dispatch, expedition, flow, haste, hurry, onslaught, push, race, scramble, speed, stampede, storm, streak, surge, swiftness, tear, urgency. adj. brisk, careless, cursory, emergency, expeditious, fast, hasty, hurried, prompt, quick, rapid, superficial, swift, urgent.

S

sabotage v. cripple, damage, destroy, disable, disrupt, incapacitate, mar, nullify, scupper, subvert, thwart, undermine, vandalize, vitiate, wreck. n. damage, destruction, disablement, disruption, impairment, marring, rattening, subversion, treachery, treason, undermining, vandalism, vitiation, wrecking.

sack¹ v. axe, discharge, dismiss, fire, lay off, make redundant. n. discharge, dismissal, notice, one's books, one's cards, one's marching orders, the ax, the boot, the bum's rush, the chop, the elbow, the push.

sack² v. demolish, depredate, desecrate, despoil, destroy, devastate, lay waste, level, loot, maraud, pillage, plunder, raid, rape, ravage, raze, rifle, rob, ruin, spoil, strip, waste. n. depredation, desecration, despoliation, destruction, devastation, leveling, looting, marauding, pillage, plunder, plundering, rape, rapine, ravage, razing, ruin, waste.

sacred *adj.* blessed, consecrated, dedicated, devotional, divine, ecclesiastical, godly, hallowed, heavenly, holy, inviolable, inviolate, invulnerable, priestly, protected, religious, revered, sacrosanct, saintly, sanctified, secure, solemn, venerable, venerated.

sad *adj.* bad, blue, calamitous, cheerless, chopfallen, crestfallen, crushed, dark, dejected, deplorable, depressed, depressing, desolated, despondent, disastrous, disconsolate, dismal, dispirited, distressed, distressing, doleful, dolesome, doloriferous, dolorific, doughy, dour, downcast, downhearted, drear, dreary, gloomy, glum, grave, grief stricken, grieved, grieving, grievous, heart rending, heavy, heavy-hearted, jaw-fallen, joyless, lachrymose, lamentable, long-faced, low, low-spirited, lugubrious, melancholy, miserable, mournful, moving, painful, pathetic, pensive, piteous, pitiable, pitiful, poignant, regrettable, serious, shabby, sober, sober-minded, somber, sorrowful, sorry, sportless, stiff, tearful, touching, tragic, triste, uncheerful, unfortunate, unhappy, unsatisfactory, upsetting, wan, wistful, woebegone, woeful, wretched.

safe *adj.* alive and will, all right, cautious, certain, circumspect, conservative, dependable, discreet, fool-proof, guarded, hale, harmless, immune, impregnable, innocuous, intact, invulnerable, nonpoisonous, nontoxic, OK, out of harm's way, protected, proven, prudent, pure, realistic, reliable, scatheless, secure, sound, sure, tame, tested, tried, trustworthy, unadventurous, uncontaminated, undamaged, unfailing, unharmed, unhurt, uninjured, unscathed, wholesome.

sage *adj.* astute, canny, discerning, intelligent, judicious, knowing, knowledgeable, learned, perspicacious, politic, prudent, sagacious, sapient, sensible, wise.

saintly *adj.* angelic, beatific, blameless, blessed, blest, celestial, devout, godfearing, godly, holy, immaculate, innocent, pious, pure, religious, righteous, sainted, saintlike, seraphic, sinless, spotless, stainless, upright, virtuous, worthy.

salvage *v.* conserve, glean, preserve, reclaim, recover, recuperate, redeem, repair, rescue, restore, retrieve, salve, save.

salvation *n.* deliverance, escape, liberation, lifeline, preservation, reclamation, redemption, rescue, restoration, retrieval, safety, saving.

sane *adj.* all there, balanced, compos mentis, dependable, judicious, levelheaded, lucid, moderate, normal, rational, reasonable, reliable, right-minded, sensible, sober, sound, stable.

sarcastic *adj.* acerbic, acid, acrimonious, biting, caustic, contemptuous, cutting, cynical, derisive, disparaging, incisive, ironical, mocking, mordant, sardonic, satirical, scathing, sharp, sharp-tongued, sneering, taunting, withering.

satisfactory *adj.* acceptable, adequate, all right, average, competent, fair, fit, OK, passable, proper, sufficient, suitable, tickety-boo, up to the mark.

save *v.* cache, collect, conserve, cut back, deliver, economize, free, gather, guard, hinder, hoard, hold, husband, keep, lay up, liberate, obviate, preserve, prevent, protect, put aside, put by, reclaim, recover, redeem, rescue, reserve, retain, retrench, safeguard, salt away, salvage, screen, shield, spare, squirrel, stash, store.

saying *n.* adage, aphorism, apophthegm, axiom, byword, dictum, gnome, maxim, mot, motto, precept, proverb, remnant, saw, slogan.

scald *v.* blister, burn, sear.

scandal *n.* abuse, aspersion, backbiting, calumniation, calumny, crime, defamation, detraction, dirt, discredit, disgrace, dishonor, embarrassment, enormity, evil, furor, gossip, gossiping, ignominy, infamy, muckraking, obloquy, odium, offense, opprobrium, outcry, outrage, reproach, rumors, shame, sin, slander, stigma, talk, tattle, traducement, uproar, Watergate, wrongdoing.

scant *adj.* bare, deficient, hardly any, insufficient, limited, little, little or no, minimal, sparse.

scarce *adj.* deficient, few, infrequent, insufficient, lacking, rare, scanty, sparse, thin on the ground, uncommon, unusual, wanting.

scare *v.* affright, alarm, appall, daunt, dismay, frighten, intimidate, panic, shock, startle, terrify, terrorize, unnerve.

scene *n.* act, arena, backdrop, background, business, chapter, circumstances, commotion, confrontation, display, disturbance, division, drama, environment, episode, exhibition, focus, fuss, incident, landscape, locale, locality, location, melodrama, milieu, mise en scène, outburst, pageant, panorama, part, performance, picture, place, position, prospect, representation, row, set, setting, show, sight, site, situation, spectacle, spot, stage, tableau, tantrum, to-do, upset, view, vista, where-abouts, world.

scent *n.* aroma, bouquet, fragrance, odor, perfume, smell, spoor, trail, waft, whiff.

scheme *n.* arrangement, blueprint, chart, codification, configuration, conformation, conspiracy, contrivance, dart, design, device, diagram, disposition, dodge, draft, game, idea, intrigue, layout, machinations, maneuver, method, outline, pattern, plan, plot, ploy, procedure, program, project, proposal, proposition, racket, ruse, schedule, schema, shape, shift, stratagem, strategy, subterfuge, suggestion, system, tactics, theory. *v.* collude, conspire, contrive, design, devise, frame, imagine, intrigue, machinate, manipulate, maneuver, mastermind, plan, plot, project, pull strings, pull wires, work out.

scholar *n.* academe, academic, authority, bookworm, egghead, intellectual, pupil, savant, student.

scold *v.* admonish, bawl out, berate, blame, castigate, censure, chide, find fault with, jaw, lecture, nag, rate, rebuke, remonstrate, reprimand, reproach, reprove, take to task, tell off, tick off, upbraid, vituperate, wig.

scowl *v.* frown, glare, glower, grimace, lower. *n.* frown, glare, glower, grimace, moue.

scrap[1] *n.* atom, bit, bite, crumb, fraction, fragment, grain, iota, junk, mite, modicum, morsel, mouthful, part, particle, piece, portion, remnant, shard, shred, sliver, snap, snatch, snippet, trace, vestige, waste, whit. *v.* abandon, ax, break up, cancel, chuck, demolish, discard, ditch, drop, jettison, junk, shed, throw out, write off.

scrap[2] *n.* argument, battle, brawl, disagreement, dispute, dust-up, fight, quarrel, row, ruckus, ruction, rumpus, scuffle, set-to, shindy, squabble, tiff, wrangle.

scream *v.* bawl, clash, cry, holler, jar, roar, screak, screech, shriek, shrill, squeal, wail, yell, help, yowl. *n.* howl, outcry, roar, screak, screech, shriek, squeal, wail, yell, yelp, yowl.

script *n.* book, calligraphy, copy, hand, handwriting, letters, libretto, lines, longhand, manuscript, penmanship, text, words, writing.

search *v.* check, comb, examine, explore, ferret, frisk, inquire, inspect, investigate, look, probe, pry, quest, ransack, rifle, rummage, scour, scrutinize, sift, test. *n.* examination, exploration, going-over, hunt, inquiry, inspection, investigation, pursuit, quest, researches, rummage, scrutiny.

season *n.* division, interval, period, span, spell, term, time. *v.* acclimatize, accustom, anneal, color, condiment, condition, discipline, enliven, flavor, habituate, harden, imbue, insure, lace, leaven, mature, mitigate, moderate, prepare, qualify, salt, spice, temper, toughen, train.

secret *adj.* abstruse, arcane, back door, backstairs, cabalistic(al), camouflaged, clandestine, classified, cloak-and-dagger, close, closet, concealed, conspiratorial, covered, covert, cryptic, deep, discreet, disguised, esoteric, furtive, hidden, hole-and-corner, hush hush, inlay, mysterious, occult, out-of-the-way, private, privy, recondite, reticent, retired, secluded, secretive, sensitive, shrouded, sly, stealthy, tête-à-tête, undercover, underground, underhand, under-the-counter, undisclosed, unfrequented, unknown, unpublished, unrevealed, unseen.

secure *adj.* absolute, assured, certain, conclusive, confident, definite, dependable, easy, fast, fastened, firm, fixed, fortified, immovable, immune, impregnable, on velvet, overconfident, protected, reassured, reliable, safe, sheltered, shielded, solid, stable, steadfast, steady, sure, tight, unassailable, undamaged, unharmed, well-founded.

see *v.* accompany, anticipate, appreciate, ascertain, attend, behold, comprehend, consider, consult, court, date, decide, deem, deliberate, descry, determine, discern, discover, distinguish, divine, encounter, ensure, envisage, escort, espy, experience, fathom, feel, follow, foresee, foretell, get, glimpse, grasp, guarantee, heed, identify, imagine, interview, investigate, judge, know, lead, learn, look, make out, mark, meet, mind, note, notice, observe, perceive, picture, realize, receive, recognize, reflect, regard, show, sight, spot, take, understand, usher, view, visit, visualize, walk, witness.

seek *v.* aim, ask, aspire to, attempt, beg, busk, desire, endeavor, entreat, essay, follow, hunt, inquire, invite, petition, pursue, request, solicit, strive, try, want.

seem *v.* appear, look, look like, pretend, sound like.

select *v.* choose, cull, pick, prefer, single out. *adj.* choice, elite, excellent, exclusive, first-class, first-rate, handpicked, limited, picked, posh, preferable, prime, privileged, rare, selected, special, superior, top, top-notch.

selfish *adj.* egoistic, egotistic, greedy, mercenary, self-centered, self-serving.

sell *v.* barter, cheat, convince, deal in, exchange, handle, hawk, impose on, market, merchandise, peddle, persuade, promote, retail, sell out, stock, surrender, trade, trade in, traffic in, trick, vend.

send v. broadcast, cast, charm, communicate, consign, convey, delight, deliver, direct, discharge, dispatch, electrify, emit, enrapture, enthrall, excite, exude, fire, fling, forward, grant, hurl, intoxicate, move, please, propel, radiate, ravish, remit, shoot, stir, thrill, titillate, transmit.

senile adj. anile, decrepit, doddering, doting, failing, imbecile, senescent.

sense n. appreciation, atmosphere, aura, awareness, brains, clearheadedness, cleverness, consciousness, definition, denotation, direction, discernment, discrimination, drift, faculty, feel, feeling, gist, good, gumption, implication, import, impression, intelligence, interpretation, intuition, judgment, logic, meaning, message, mother wit, perception, point, premonition, presentiment, purport, purpose, quickness, reason, reasonableness, sagacity, sanity, savvy, sensation, sensibility, sentiment, sharpness, significance, signification, substance, tact, understanding, use, value, wisdom, wit(s), worth.

senseless adj. absurd, crazy, illogical, inconsistent, ludicrous, pointless, ridiculous, silly, unreasonable, unwise.

sentimental adj. corny, dewy-eyed, drippy, emotional, gushing, gushy, gutbucket, impressionable, lovey-dovey, maudlin, mawkish, mushy, nostalgic, pathetic, romantic, rosewater, schmaltzy, simpering, sloppy, slush, softhearted, tearful, tear-jerking, tender, too-too, touching, treacly, weepy. Wertherian.

separate v. abstract, bifurcate, departmentalize, detach, disaffiliate, disconnect, disentangle, disjoin, dislink, dispart, dissever, distance, disunite, divaricate, diverge, divide, divorce, eloi(g)n, estrange, exfoliate, isolate, part, part company, rescind, remove, secede, secern, seclude, segregate, sever, shear, split, split up, sunder, uncouple, winnow, withdraw.

serene adj. calm, composed, cool, halcyon, imperturbable, peaceful, placid, tranquil, unclouded, undisturbed, unflappable, unruffled, untroubled.

serve v. act, aid, answer, arrange, assist, attend, avail, complete, content, dance attendance, deal, deliver, discharge, distribute, do, fulfill, further, handle, help, minister to, oblige, observe, officiate, pass, perform, present, provide, satisfy, succor, suffice, suit, supply, undergo, wait on, work for.

set[1] v. adjust, aim, allocate, allot, apply, appoint, arrange, assign, cake, conclude, condense, congeal, coordinate, crystallize, decline, decree, deposit, designate, determine, dip, direct, disappear, embed, establish, fasten, fix, fix up, gelatinize, harden, impose, install, jell, lay, locate, lodge, mount, name, ordain, park, place, plant, plonk, plump, position, prepare, prescribe, propound, put, rectify, regulate, resolve, rest, schedule, seat, settle, sink, situate, solidify, specify, spread, stake, station, stick, stiffen, subside, synchronize, thicken, turn, vanish. n. attitude, bearing, carriage, fit, hang, inclination, mise-en-scène, position, posture, scene, scenery, setting, turn. adj. agreed, appointed, arranged, artificial, conventional, customary, decided, definite, deliberate, entrenched, established, firm, fixed, formal, hackneyed, immovable, inflexible intentional, prearranged, predetermined, prescribed, regular, rehearsed, rigid, routine, scheduled, settled, standard, stereotyped, stock, strict, stubborn, traditional, unspontaneous, usual.

set[2] n. apparatus, assemblage, assortment, band, batch, circle, class, clique, collection, company, compendium, coterie, covey, crew, crowd, faction, gang, group, kit, outfit, sect, sequence, series.

settle v. adjust, agree, alight, appoint, arrange, bed, calm, choose, clear, colonize, compact, complete, compose, conclude, confirm, decide, decree, descend, determine, discharge, dispose, dower, drop, dwell, endow, establish, fall, fix, found, hush, inhabit, land, light, liquidate, live, lower, lull, occupy, ordain, order, pacify, pay, people, pioneer, plant, plump, populate, quell, quiet, quieten, quit, reassure, reconcile, relax, relieve, reside, resolve, sedate, sink, soothe, square, square up, subside, tranquilize.

sever v. alienate, bisect, cleave, cut, detach, disconnect, disjoin, dissever, dissociate, dissolve, dissunder, disunite, divide, estrange, part, rend, separate, split, sunder, terminate.

several adj. assorted, different, discrete, disparate, distinct, divers, diverse, individual, many, particular, respective, separate, single, some, some few, specific, sundry, various.

sex n. coition, coitus, congress, copulation, desire, fornication, gender, intercourse, intimacy, libido, lovemaking, reproduction, screw, sexual intercourse, sexual relations, sexuality, union, venery.

sexual adj. carnal, coital, erotic, gamic, genital, intimate, procreative, reproductive, sensual, sex, sex-related, venereal.

shade *n.* amount, apparition, blind, canopy, color, coolness, cover, covering, curtain, darkness, dash, degree, difference, dimness, dusk, eidolon, ghost, gloaming, gloom, gloominess, gradation, hint, hue, manes, murk, nuance, obscurity, phantasm, phantom, screen, semblance, semidarkness, shadiness, shadow, shadows, shelter, shield, shroud, specter, spirit, stain, suggestion, suspicion, tinge, tint, tone, trace, twilight, umbra, umbrage, variation, variety, veil, wraith. *v.* cloud, conceal, cover, darken, dim, hide, mute, obscure, overshadow, protect, screen, shadow, shield, shroud, veil.

shake *n.* agitation, convulsion, disturbance, instant, jar, jerk, jiffy, jolt, jounce, moment, no time, pulsation, quaking, second, shiver, shock, shudder, tick, trembling, tremor, trice, twitch, vellication, vibration. *v.* agitate, brandish, bump, churn, concuss, convulse, discompose, distress, disturb, flourish, fluctuate, frighten, heave, impair, intimidate, jar, joggle, jolt, jounce, move, oscillate, quake, quiver, rattle, rock, rouse, shimmy, shiver, shock, shudder, split, stir, sway, totter, tremble, twitch, undermine, unnerve, unsettle, upset, vellicate, vibrate, wag, waggle, wave, waver, weaken, wobble.

shape *n.* apparition, appearance, aspect, build, condition, configuration, conformation, contours, cut, dimensions, fettle, figure, form, format, frame, gestalt, guise, health, kilter, likeness, lines, make, model, mold, outline, pattern, physique, profile, semblance, silhouette, state, template, trim. *v.* accommodate, adapt, construct, create, define, develop, devise, embody, fashion, forge, form, frame, guide, make, model, modify, mold, plan, prepare, produce, redact, regulate, remodel.

share *v.* allot, apportion, assign, chip in, distribute, divide, divvy, divvy up, go Dutch, go fifty-fifty, go halves, muck in, partake, participate, split, whack. *n.* a piece of the action, allotment, allowance, contribution, cut, dividend, division, divvy, due, finger, lot, part, portion, proportion, quota, ration, snap, snip, stint, whack.

sharp *adj.* abrupt, acerbic, acicular, acid, acidulous, acrid, acrimonious, acute, alert, apt, artful, astute, barbed, biting, bitter, bright, burning, canny, caustic, chic, chiseled, classy, clear, clear-cut, clever, crafty, crisp, cunning, cutting, discerning, dishonest, distinct, dressy, eager, edged, excruciating, extreme, fashionable, fierce, fit, fly, harsh, honed, hot, hurtful, incisive,

intense, jagged, keen, knife-edged, knifelike, knowing, long-headed, marked, natty, nimble-witted, noticing, observant, painful, penetrating, peracute, perceptive, piercing, piquant, pointed, pungent, quick, quick-witted, rapid, razor-sharp, ready, sarcastic, sardonic, saw-edged, scathing, serrated, severe, sharpened, shooting, shrewd, sly, smart, snappy, snazzy, sour, spiky, stabbing, stinging, stylish, subtle, sudden, tart, trenchant, trendy, unblurred, undulled, unscrupulous, vinegary, violent, vitriolic, waspish, wily.

shatter *v.* blast, blight, break, burst, crack, crush, demolish, destroy, devastate, disable, dumbfound, exhaust, explode, impair, implode, overturn, overwhelm, pulverize, ruin, shiver, smash, split, stun, torpedo, undermine, upset, wreck.

shine *v.* beam, brush, buff, burnish, coruscate, excel, flash, glare, gleam, glimmer, glisten, glitter, glow, luster, polish, radiate, resplend, scintillate, shimmer, sparkle, stand out, star, twinkle. *n.* brightness, burnish, effulgence, glare, glaze, gleam, gloss, glow, lambency, light, luminosity, luster, patina, polish, radiance, sheen, shimmer, sparkle.

shiver *v.* palpitate, quake, quiver, shake, shudder, tremble, vibrate. *n.* flutter, frisson, quiver, shudder, start, thrill, tremble, trembling, tremor, twitch, vibration.

shock *v.* agitate, appall, astound, confound, disgust, dismay, disquiet, horrify, jar, jolt, nauseate, numb, offend, outrage, paralyze, revolt, scandalize, shake, sicken, stagger, stun, stupefy, traumatize, unnerve, unsettle.

short *adj.* abbreviated, abridged, abrupt, blunt, brief, brittle, brusque, compressed, concise, crisp, crumbly, crusty, curt, curtailed, deficient, diminutive, direct, discourteous, dumpy, ephemeral, evanescent, fleeting, friable, gruff, impolite, inadequate, insufficient, lacking, laconic, limited, little, low, meager, momentary, offhand, passing, petite, pithy, poor, sawnoff, scant, scanty, scarce, sententious, sharp, shortened, shorthanded, short-lived, short-term, slender, slim, small, snappish, snappy, sparse, squat, straight, succinct, summarized, summary, tart, terse, tight, tiny, transitory, uncivil, understaffed, unplentiful, wanting, wee.

shout *n.* bay, bellow, belt, call, cheer, cry, roar, scream, shriek, yell. *v.* bawl, bay, bellow, call, cheer, cry, holler, roar, scream, shriek, yell.

show *v.* accompany, accord, assert, attend, attest, bestow, betray, clarify, conduct, confer, demonstrate, disclose, display, divulge, elucidate, escort, evidence, evince, exemplify, exhibit, explain, grant, guide, illustrate, indicate, instruct, lead, manifest, offer, present, prove, register, reveal, teach, usher, witness. *n.* affectation, air, appearance, array, dash, demonstration, display, eclat, elan, entertainment, exhibition, exhibitionism, expo, exposition, extravaganza, façade, fair, flamboyance, gig, illusion, indication, likeness, manifestation, ostentation, pageant, pageantry, panache, parade, performance, pizzazz, plausibility, pose, presentation, pretence, pretext, production, profession, razzle-dazzle, representation, semblance, sight, sign, spectacle, swagger, view.

sick *adj.* ailing, black, blasé, bored, diseased, disgusted, displeased, dog-sick, fed up, feeble, ghoulish, glutted, ill, indisposed, jaded, laid up, morbid, mortified, nauseated, pining, poorly, puking, qualmish, queasy, sated, satiated, sickly, tired, under the weather, unwell, vomiting, weak, weary.

side *n.* airs, angle, arrogance, aspect, bank, border, boundary, brim, brink, camp, cause, department, direction, division, edge, elevation, face, facet, faction, flank, flitch, fringe, gang, hand, insolence, light, limit, margin, opinion, ostentation, page, part, party, perimeter, periphery, position, pretentiousness, quarter, region, rim, sect, sector, slant, stand, standpoint, surface, team, twist, verge, view, viewpoint. *adj.* flanking, incidental, indirect, irrelevant, lateral, lesser, marginal, minor, oblique, roundabout, secondary, subordinate, subsidiary.

sight *n.* appearance, apprehension, decko, display, estimation, exhibition, eye, eyes, eyeshot, eyesight, eyesore, field of vision, fright, gander, glance, glimpse, judgment, ken, look, mess, monstrosity, observation, opinion, pageant, perception, range, scene, seeing, show, spectacle, view, viewing, visibility, vision, vista. *v.* behold, discern, distinguish, glimpse, observe, perceive, see, spot.

sign *n.* augury, auspice, badge, beck, betrayal, board, character, cipher, clue, device, emblem, ensign, evidence, figure, foreboding, forewarning, gesture, giveaway, hint, indication, insignia, intimation, lexigram, logo, logogram, notice, omen, placard, pointer, portent, presage, proof, reminder, representation, rune, signal, signature, signification, signpost, spoor, suggestion, symbol, symptom,

token, trace, trademark, vestige, warning. *v.* autograph, beckon, endorse, gesticulate, gesture, indicate, initial, inscribe, motion, signal, subscribe, wave.

signal *n.* alarm, alert, beacon, beck, cue, flare, flash, gesture, go-ahead, griffin, impulse, indication, indicator, light, mark, OK, password, rocket, sign, tip-off, token, transmitter, waft, warning, watchword. *adj.* conspicuous, distinguished, eminent, exceptional, extraordinary, famous, glorious, impressive, memorable, momentous, notable, noteworthy, outstanding, remarkable, significant, striking. *v.* beckon, communicate, gesticulate, gesture, indicate, motion, nod, sign, telegraph, waft, wave.

silence *n.* calm, numbness, hush, lull, muteness, noiselessness, peace, quiet, speechlessness, stillness, taciturnity, uncommunicativeness.

similar *adj.* alike, analogous, close, comparable, compatible, congruous, corresponding, homogeneous, homogenous, homologous, related, resembling, selflike, uniform.

sin *n.* crime, damnation, debt, error, evil, fault, guilt, hamartia, impiety, iniquity, lapse, misdeed, offense, sinfulness, transgression, trespass, ungodliness, unrighteousness, wickedness, wrong, wrong-doing. *v.* err, fall, fall from grace, go astray, lapse, misbehave, offend, stray, transgress, trespass.

sincere *adj.* artless, bona fide, candid, deep-felt, earnest, frank, genuine, guileless, heartfelt, heart-whole, honest, natural, open, plain-hearted, plainspoken, pure, real, serious, simple, simple-hearted, single-hearted, soulful, straightforward, true, true-hearted, truthful, unadulterated, unaffected unfeigned, unmixed, wholehearted.

singe *v.* blacken, burn, cauterize, char, scorch, sear.

single *adj.* celibate, distinct, exclusive, free, individual, lone, man-to-man, one, onefold, one-to-one, only, particular, separate, simple, sincere, single-minded, singular, sole, solitary, unattached, unblended, unbroken, uncombined, uncompounded, undivided, unique, unmarried, unmixed, unshared, unwed, wholehearted.

site *n.* ground, location, lot, place, plot, position, setting, spot, station. *v.* dispose, install, locate, place, position, set, situate, station.

skill *n.* ability, accomplishment, adroitness, aptitude, art, cleverness, competence, dexterity, experience, expertise, expertness, facility, finesse, handiness, ingenuity, intelligence, knack, proficiency, quickness, readiness, savoir faire, savvy, skillfulness, talent, technique, touch.

skinny *adj*. attenuate(d), emaciated, lean, scagged, scraggy, skeletal, skin-and-bone, thin, twiggy, underfed, undernourished, weedy.

slant *v*. angle, bend, bevel, bias, cant, color, distort, incline, lean, list, shelve, skew, slope, tilt, twist, warp, weight. *n*. angle, attitude, bias, camber, declination, diagonal, emphasis, gradient, incline, leaning, obliquity, pitch, prejudice, rake, ramp, slope, tilt, viewpoint.

slavery *n*. bondage, captivity, enslavement, impressment, serfdom, servitude, subjugation, thrall, yoke.

sleepy *adj*. drowsy, dull, heavy, hypnotic, inactive, lethargic, quiet, slow, sluggish, slumb(e)rous, slumbersome, somnolent, soporific, soporose, torpid.

slender *adj*. acicular, faint, feeble, flimsy, fragile, inadequate, inconsiderable, insufficient, lean, little, meager, narrow, poor, remote, scanty, slight, slim, small, spare, svelte, sylphlike, tenuous, thin, thready, wasp-waisted, weak, willowish, willowy.

slide *v*. coast, glide, glissade, lapse, skate, skim, slip, slither, toboggan, veer.

slit *v*. cut, gash, knife, lance, pierce, rip, slash, slice, split. *n*. cut, fissure, gash, incision, opening, rent, split, tear, vent. *adj*. cut, pertuse(d), rent, split, torn.

slow *adj*. adagio, backward, behind, behindhand, boring, bovine, conservative, creeping, dawdling, dead, dead-and-alive, delayed, deliberate, dense, dilatory, dim, dull, dull-witted, dumb, easy, gradual, inactive, lackadaisical, laggard, lagging, late, lazy, leaden, leisurely, lingering, loitering, long-drawn-out, measured, obtuse, one-horse, plodding, ponderous, prolonged, protracted, quiet, retarded, slack, sleepy, slow-moving, slow-witted, sluggardly, sluggish, stagnant, stupid, tame, tardy, tedious, thick, time-consuming, uneventful, unhasty, unhurried, uninteresting, unproductive, unprogressive, unpunctual, unresponsive, wearisome.

sluggish *adj*. dull, heavy, inactive, indolent, inert, lethargic, lifeless, listless, lymphatic, phlegmatic, slothful, slow, slow-moving, torpid, unresponsive.

slumber *v*. doze, drowse, nap, repose, rest, sleep, snooze.

small *adj*. bantam, base, dilute, diminutive, dwarfish, grudging, humble, illiberal, immature, inadequate, incapacious, inconsiderable, insignificant, insufficient, itsy-bitsy, lesser, limited, little, meager, mean, mignon(ne), mini, miniature, minor, minuscule, minute, modest, narrow, negligible, paltry, petite, petty, pint-size(d), pocket, pocket-sized, puny, pygmean, scanty, selfish, slight, small-scale, tiddl(e)y, tiny, trifling, trivial, undersized, unimportant, unpretentious, wee, young.

smart[1] *adj*. acute, adept, agile, apt, astute, bright, brisk, canny, chic, clever, cracking, dandy, effective, elegant, fashionable, fine, impertinent, ingenious, intelligent, jaunty, keen, lively, modish, natty, neat, nimble, nimble-witted, nobby, pert, pointed, quick, quick-witted, rattling, ready, ready-witted, saucy, sharp, shrewd, smart-alecky, snappy, spanking, spirited, spruce, stylish, swagger, swish, tippy, trim, vigorous, vivacious, well-appointed, witty.

smart[2] *v*. burn, hurt, nip, pain, sting, throb, tingle, twinge. *adj*. hard, keen, nipping, nippy, painful, piercing, resounding, sharp, stinging. *n*. nip, pain, pang, smarting, soreness, sting, twinge.

smell *n*. aroma, bouquet, fragrance, odor, perfume, scent, stench, stink, whiff.

smooth *adj*. agreeable, bland, calm, classy, easy, effortless, elegant, equable, even, facile, fair-spoken, flat, flowing, fluent, flush, frictionless, glassy, glib, glossy, hairless, horizontal, ingratiating, level, levitate, mellow, mild, mirrorlike, peaceful, persuasive, plain, plane, pleasant, polished, regular, rhythmic, serene, shiny, silken, silky, sleek, slick, slippery, smarmy, smug, soft, soothing, steady, suave, tranquil, unbroken, unctuous, undisturbed, uneventful, uniform, uninterrupted, unpuckered, unruffled, unrumpled, untroubled, unwrinkled, urbane, velvety, well-ordered.

smug *adj*. cocksure, complacent, conceited, holier-than-thou, priggish, self-opinionated, self-righteous, self-satisfied, superior, unctuous.

sneak *v*. cower, cringe, grass on, inform on, lurk, pad, peach, sidle, skulk, slink, slip, smuggle, spirit, steal, tell tales. *n*. informer, snake in the grass, sneaker, telltale. *adj*. clandestine, covert, furtive, quick, secret, stealthy, surprise, surreptitious.

snoop *v*. interfere, pry, sneak, spy.

snug *adj*. close, close-fitting, comfortable, comfy, compact, cozy, homely, intimate, neat, sheltered, trim, warm.

sober *adj*. abstemious, abstinent, calm, clearheaded, cold, composed, cool, dark, dispassionate, drab, grave, level-headed, lucid, moderate, peaceful, plain, practical, quiet, rational, realistic, reasonable, restrained, sedate, serene, serious, severe, solemn, somber, sound, staid, steady, subdued, temperate, unexcited, unruffled.

soft *adj.* balmy, bendable, bland, caressing, comfortable, compassionate, cottony, creamy, crumby, cushioned, cushiony, cushy, daft, delicate, diffuse, diffused, dim, dimmed, doughy, downy, ductile, dulcet, easy, easygoing, effeminate, elastic, faint, feathery, feeble-minded, flabby, flaccid, fleecy, flexible, flowing, fluid, foolish, furry, gelatinous, gentle, impressible, indulgent, kind, lash, lax, lenient, liberal, light, limp, low, malleable, mellifluous, mellow, melodious, mild, moldable, murmured, muted, namby-pamby, nonalcoholic, overindulgent, pale, pampered, pastel, permissive, pitying, plastic, pleasant, pleasing, pliable, pulpy, quaggy, quiet, restful, sensitive, sentimental, shaded, silky, silly, simple, smooth, soothing, soppy, spineless, spongy, squashy, subdued, supple, swampy, sweet, sympathetic, temperate, tender, tenderhearted, undemanding, understated, unprotected, velvety, weak, whispered, yielding.

sole *adj.* alone, exclusive, individual, one, only, single, singular, solitary, unique.

solemn *adj.* august, awed, awe-inspiring, ceremonial, ceremonious, devotional, dignified, earnest, formal, glum, grand, grave, hallowed, holy, imposing, impressive, majestic, momentous, pompous, portentous, religious, reverential, ritual, sacred, sanctified, sedate, serious, sober, somber, staid, stately, thoughtful, venerable.

solid *adj.* agreed, compact, complete, concrete, constant, continuous, cubic(al), decent, dense, dependable, estimable, firm, genuine, good, hard, law-abiding, level-headed, massed, pure, real, reliable, sensible, serious, sober, sound, square, stable, stocky, strong, sturdy, substantial, trusty, unalloyed, unanimous, unbroken, undivided, uninterrupted, united, unmixed, unshakable, unvaried, up-right, upstanding, wealthy, weighty, worthy.

solitude *n.* aloneness, desert, emptiness, isolation, loneliness, privacy, reclusiveness, retirement, seclusion, waste, wasteland, wilderness.

sometimes *adv.* at times, from time to time, now and again, now and then, occasionally, off and on, once in a while, otherwise.

soothe *v.* allay, alleviate, appease, assuage, calm, coax, comfort, compose, ease, hush, lull, mitigate, mollify, pacify, quiet, relieve, salve, settle, soften, still, tranquilize.

sorry *adj.* abject, apologetic, contrite, distressed, guilt-ridden, penitent, regretful, remorseful, repentant, sorrowful.

sour *adj.* acerb(ic), acetic, acid, acidulated, acrid, acrimonious, bad, bitter, churlish, crabbed, curdled, cynical, disagreeable, discontented, embittered fermented, grouchy, grudging, ill-natured, ill-tempered, inharmonious, jaundiced, off, peevish, pungent, rancid, rank, sharp, tart, turned, ungenerous, unpleasant, unsavory, unsuccessful, unsweet, unwholesome, vinegarish, vinegary, waspish.

special *adj.* appropriate, certain, characteristic, chief, choice, detailed, distinctive, distinguished, especial, exceptional, exclusive, extraordinary, festive, gala, important, individual, intimate, main, major, memorable, momentous, particular, peculiar, precise, primary, red-letter, select, significant, specialized, specific, uncommon, unique, unusual.

speck *n.* atom, bit, blemish, blot, defect, dot, fault, flaw, fleck, grain, iota, jot, macula, mark, mite, modicum, mote, particle, shred, speckle, spot, stain, title, trace, whit.

speed *n.* acceleration, celerity, dispatch, expedition, fleetness, haste, hurry, lick, momentum, pace, precipitation, quickness, rapidity, rush, swiftness, tempo, velocity. *v.* advance, aid, assist, belt, bomb, boost, bowl along, career, dispatch, expedite, facilitate, flash, fleet, further, gallop, hasten, help, hurry, impel, lick, press on, promote, put one's foot down, quicken, race, rush, sprint, step on it, step on the gas, step on the juice, tear, urge, vroom, zap, zoom.

spell[1] *n.* bout, course, innings, interval, patch, period, season, sting, stretch, term, time, turn.

spell[2] *n.* abracadabra, allure, bewitchment, charm, conjuration, enchantment, exorcism, fascination, glamour, hex, incantation, love charm, magic, open sesame, paternoster, philter, rune, sorcery, trance, weird, witchery.

spicy *adj.* aromatic, flavorsome, fragrant, hot, improper, indelicate, off-color, piquant, pointed, pungent, racy, ribald, risque, savory, scandalous, seasoned, sensational, showy, suggestive, tangy, titillating, unseemly. *n.* bland.

spirit *n.* air, animation, apparition, attitude, backbone, character, disposition, energy, feeling, ghost, humor, life, motivation, outlook, phantom, psyche, purport, purpose, python, quality, resolution, resolve, sense, shade, shadow, soul, sparkle, specter, spook, sprite, temper, temperament, tenor, tone, verve, vigor, vision, vivacity, warmth, water-horse, water nymph, water rixie, water sprite, will, willpower, zeitgeist, zest. *v.* abduct, abstract, capture, carry, convey, kidnap, purloin, remove, seize, snaffle, steal, whisk.

spite *n.* animosity, bitchiness, despite, gall, grudge, hate, hatred, ill nature, malevolence, malice, malignity, pique, rancor, spitefulness, spleen, venom, viciousness.

splinter *n.* chip, flake, fragment, needle, paring, shaving, sliver, spall, spicule. *v.* disintegrate, fracture, fragment, shatter, shiver, smash, split.

split *v.* allocate, allot, apportion, betray, bifurcate, branch, break, burst, cleave, crack, delaminate, disband, distribute, disunite, divaricate, diverge, divide, divulge, fork, gape, grass, halve, inform on, open, parcel out, part, partition, peach, rend, rip, separate, share out, slash, slice up, slit, sliver, snap, spell, splinter, squeal. *n.* breach, break, breakup, cleft, crack, damage, dichotomy, difference, discord, disruption, dissension, disunion, divergence, division, estrangement, fissure, gap, partition, race, rent, rift, rip, rupture, schism, separation, slash, slit, tear. *adj.* ambivalent, bisected, broken, cleft, cloven, cracked, divided, dual, fractured, ruptured, twofold.

spoil *v.* addle, baby, blemish, bugger, butcher, cocker, coddle, cosset, curdle, damage, debase, decay, decompose, deface, despoil, destroy, deteriorate, disfigure, go bad, go off, harm, impair, indulge, injure, jigger, louse up, mar, mildew, mollycoddle, pamper, plunder, putrefy, queer, rot, ruin, screw, spoonfeed, turn, upset, wreck.

spontaneous *adj.* extempore, free, impromptu, impulsive, instinctive, natural, ultroneous, unbidden, uncompelled, unconstrained, unforced, unhesitating, unlabored, unpremeditated, unprompted, unstudied, untaught, voluntary, willing.

spray[1] *v.* atomize, diffuse, douse, drench, scatter, shower, sprinkle, wet. *n.* aerosol, atomizer, drizzle, droplets, foam, froth, mist, moisture, spindrift, spoon-drift, sprinkler.

spray[2] *n.* bough, branch, corsage, garland, shoot, sprig, wreath.

spry *adj.* active, agile, alert, brisk, energetic, nimble, nippy, peppy, quick, ready, sprightly, supple.

squabble *v.* argue, bicker, brawl, clash, dispute, fall out, fight, quarrel, row, scrap, spat, tiff, wrangle. *n.* argument, clash, disagreement, dispute, fight, rhubarb, row, scrap, set-to, spat, tiff.

staid *adj.* calm, composed, decorous, demure, grave, quiet, sedate, selfrestrained, serious, sober, solemn, steady.

stalk[1] *v.* approach, follow, haunt, hunt, march, pace, pursue, shadow, stride, strut, tail, track.

stalk[2] *n.* bole, branch, shoot, spire, stem, sterigma, trunk.

stall *v.* delay, equivocate, hedge, obstruct, prevaricate.

stamp *v.* bet, brand, bray, categorize, characterize, crush, engrave, exhibit, fix, identify, impress, imprint, inscribe, label, mark, mint, mold, pound, print, pronounce, reveal, strike, trample. *n.* attestation, authorization, brand, breed, cast, character, cut, description, earmark, evidence, fashion, form, hallmark, impression, imprint, kind, mark, mold, sign, signature, sort, stomp, type.

stand *v.* abide, allow, bear, belong, brook, continue, cost, countenance, demur, endure, erect, exist, experience, halt, handle, hold, mount, obtain, pause, place, position, prevail, put, rank, remain, rest, rise, scruple, set, stay, stomach, stop, suffer, support, sustain, take, tolerate, undergo, wear, weather, withstand.

standard[1] *n.* average, benchmark, criterion, guide, measure, specification, touchstone, yardstick.

staple *adj.* basic, chief, essential, fundamental, key, leading, main, major, predominant, primary, principle.

stare *v.* gape, gaze, glare, look, watch.

start *v.* begin, commence, establish, initiate, instigate, launch, originate, pioneer.

startle *v.* affray, agitate, alarm, amaze, astonish, astound, electrify, flush, frighten, scare, shock, spook, start, surprise.

starving *adj.* famished, hungering, hungry, ravenous, undernourished.

state *v.* affirm, articulate, assert, asseverate, aver, declare, enumerate, explain, expound, express, formalize, formulate, present, propound, put, report, say, specify, voice. *n.* attitude, bother, case, category, ceremony, circumstances, condition, dignity, display, flap, glory, grandeur, humor, majesty, mode, mood, panic, pass, phase, plight, pomp, position, pother, predicament, shape, situation, spirits, splendor, stage, station, style, tizzy.

stay *v.* abide, adjourn, allay, arrest, check, continue, curb, defer, delay, detain, discontinue, dwell, endure, halt, hinder, hold out, hover, impede, last, linger, live, lodge, loiter, obstruct, pause, prevent, prorogue, remain, reside, restrain, settle, sojourn, stand, stop, suspend, tarry, visit, wait.

steal *v.* appropriate, filch, heist, misappropriate, pilfer, poach, purloin, sneak, swipe.

steep¹ *adj.* abrupt, bluff, excessive, exorbitant, extortionate, extreme, headlong, high, overpriced, precipitous, sheer, stiff, uncalled-for, unreasonable.

steep² *v.* brine, damp, drench, fill, imbrue, imbue, immerse, infuse, macerate, marinate, moisten, permeate, pervade, pickle, saturate, seethe, soak, souse, submerge, suffuse.

steer *v.* conduct, control, direct, govern, guide, pilot.

stem¹ *n.* axis, branch, family, house, line, lineage, peduncle, race, shoot, stalk, stock, trunk.

stem² *v.* check, contain, curb, dam, oppose, resist, restrain, stay, stop, tamp.

step *n.* act, action, advance, advancement, deed, degree, demarche, doorstep, expedient, footfall, footprint, footstep, gait, halfpace, impression, level, maneuver, means, measure, move, pace, phase, point, print, procedure, proceeding, process, progression, rank, remove, round, rung, stage, stair, stride, trace, track, tread, walk. *v.* move, pace, stalk, stamp, tread, walk.

sterile *adj.* abortive, antiseptic, aseptic, bare, barren, disinfected, dry, empty, fruitless, germ-free, infecund, pointless, sterilized, unfruitful, unimaginative, unproductive, unprofitable, unprolific.

stick *v.* adhere, affix, attach, bind, bond, bulge, catch, cement, cleave, cling, clog, deposit, dig, drop, endure, extend, fasten, fix, fuse, glue, gore, hold, insert, install, jab, jam, join, jut, lay, linger, lodge, obtrude, paste, penetrate, persist, pierce, pin, place, plant, plonk, poke, position, prod, project, protrude, puncture, put, put up with, remain, set, show, snag, spear, stab, stand, stay, stomach, stop, store, stuff, take, thrust, tolerate, transfix, weld.

stiff *adj.* arduous, arthritic, artificial, austere, awkward, brisk, brittle, buckram, budge, ceremonious, chilly, clumsy, cold, constrained, creaky, crude, cruel, difficult, drastic, exacting, excessive, extreme, fatiguing, firm, forced, formal, formidable, fresh, graceless, great, hard, har-

dened, harsh, heavy, inelastic, inelegant, inexorable, inflexible, jerky, laborious, labored, mannered, oppressive, pertinacious, pitiless, pompous, powerful, priggish, prim, punctilious, resistant, rigid, rigorous, severe, sharp, solid, solidified, standoffish, starch(y), stark, stilted, strict, stringent, strong, stubborn, taut, tense, tight, toilsome, tough, trying, unbending, uneasy, ungainly, ungraceful, unnatural, unrelaxed, unsupple, unyielding, uphill, vigorous, wooden.

still *adj.* calm, hushed, inert, lifeless, motionless, noiseless, pacific, peaceful, placid, quiet, restful, serene, silent, smooth, stagnant, stationary, stilly, tranquil, undisturbed, unruffled, unstirring.

stingy *adj.* avaricious, cheese-paring, close-fisted, covetous, illiberal, inadequate, insufficient, meager, mean, measly, miserly, near, niggardly, parsimonious, penny-pinching, penurious, save-all, scanty, scrimping, small, tightfisted, ungenerous, ungiving.

stop *v.* arrest, bar, block, break, cease, check, close, conclude, desist, discontinue, end, finish, forestall, frustrate, halt, hinder, impede, intercept, intermit, interrupt, knock off, leave off, lodge, obstruct, pack (it) in, pack up, pause, plug, poop out, prevent, quit, refrain, repress, rest, restrain, scotch, seal, silence, sojourn, stall, staunch, stay, stem, stymie, suspend, tarry, terminate.

story¹ *n.* account, anecdote, article, chronicle, episode, fable, fairy tale, falsehood, feature, fib, fiction, history, legend, lie, myth, narration, narrative, news, novel, plot, recital, record, relation, report, romance, scoop, spiel, tale, untruth, version, yarn.

story² *n.* deck, étage, flight, floor, level, stage, stratum, tier.

straight *adj.* accurate, aligned, arranged, authentic, balanced, blunt, bourgeois, candid, consecutive, conservative, continuous, conventional, decent, direct, downright, equitable, erect, even, fair, forthright, frank, honest, honorable, horizontal, just, law-abiding, level, near, neat, nonstop, normal, orderly, organized, orthodox, outright, perpendicular, plain, plumb, point-blank, pure, reliable, respectable, right, running, settled, shipshape, short, smooth, solid, square, straightforward, successive, sustained, thorough, tidy, traditional, true, trustworthy, unadulterated, undeviating, undiluted, uninterrupted, unmixed, unqualified, unrelieved, unswerving, upright, vertical.

strain¹ v. compress, distend, drive, embrace, endeavor, exert, express, extend, fatigue, filter, injure, labor, overtax, overwork, percolate, pull, purify, restrain, retch, riddle, screen, seep, separate, sieve, sift, sprain, squeeze, stretch, strive, struggle, tauten, tax, tear, tighten, tire, tug, twist, weaken, wrench, wrest, wrick. *n.* anxiety, burden, effort, exertion, force, height, injury, key, pitch, pressure, pull, sprain, stress, struggle, tautness, tension, wrench.

strain² *n.* ancestry, blood, descent, extraction, family, humor, lineage, manner, pedigree, race, spirit, stem, stock, streak, style, suggestion, suspicion, temper, tendency, tone, trace, trait, vein, way.

strange *adj.* abnormal, alien, astonishing, awkward, bewildered, bizarre, curious, disorientated, disoriented, eccentric, eerie, exceptional, exotic, extraordinary, fantastic(al), foreign, funny, irregular, lost, marvelous, mystifying, new, novel, odd, out-of-the-way, peculiar, perplexing, queer, rare, remarkable, remote, singular, sinister, unaccountable, unacquainted, uncanny, unco, uncomfortable, uncommon, unexplained, unexplored, unfamiliar, unheard of, unknown, untired, unversed, weird, wonderful.

street *n.* avenue, boulevard, crescent, drive, expressway, freeway, highway, lane, main drag, parkway, road, roadway, row, terrace, thoroughfare, thruway, turnpike.

strength *n.* advantage, anchor, asset, backbone, brawn, brawniness, cogency, concentration, courage, effectiveness, efficacy, energy, firmness, force, fortitude, health, intensity, lustiness, mainstay, might, muscle, potency, power, resolution, robustness, security, sinew, spirit, stamina, stoutness, sturdiness, toughness, vehemence, vigor, virtue.

stress *n.* accent, accentuation, anxiety, beat, burden, emphasis, emphaticalness, force, hassle, importance, oppression, pressure, significance, strain, tautness, tension, trauma, urgency, weight, worry.

strict *adj.* absolute, accurate, austere, authoritarian, close, complete, exact, faithful, firm, harsh, meticulous, no-nonsense, particular, perfect, precise, religious, restricted, rigid, rigorous, scrupulous, severe, stern, stringent, thoroughgoing, total, true, unsparing, utter, Victorian.

strident *adj.* cacophonous, discordant, grating, harsh, shrill.

strong *adj.* acute, aggressive, athletic, beefy, biting, bold, brave, brawny, bright, brilliant, burly, capable, clear, clear-cut, cogent, compelling, competent, concentrated, convincing, courageous, dazzling, dedicated, deep, deep-rooted, determined, distinct, drastic, durable, eager, effective, efficient, emphasized, excelling, extreme, fast-moving, fervent, fervid, fierce, firm, forceful, forcible, formidable, glaring, great, grievous, gross, hale, hard, hard-nosed, hard-wearing, hardy, heady, healthy, hearty, heavy-duty, herculean, highly flavored, highly seasoned, hot, intemperate, intense, intoxicating, keen, loud, lusty, marked, muscular, nappy, numerous, offensive, overpowering, persuasive, piquant, pithy, plucky, potent, powerful, pungent, pure, rank, redoubtable, reinforced, resilient, resolute, resourceful, robust, self-assertive, severe, sharp, sinewy, sound, spicy, stalwart, stark, staunch, steadfast, stout, stout-hearted, strapping, stressed, sturdy, substantial, telling, tenacious, tough, trenchant, undiluted, unmistakable, unseemly, unyielding, urgent, vehement, violent, virile, vivid, weighty, well-armed, well-built, well-established, well-founded, well-knit, well-protected, well-set, well-versed, zealous.

struggle *v.* agonize, battle, compete, contend, fight, grapple, labor, scuffle, strain, strive, toil, work, wrestle.

stubborn *adj.* bullheaded, difficult, dogged, headstrong, intractable, obstinate, opinionated, pig-headed, unbending.

stumble *v.* blunder, fall, falter, flounder, fluff, hesitate, lurch, reel, slip, stagger, stutter, trip.

stun *v.* amaze, astonish, astound, bewilder, confound, confuse, daze, deafen, dumbfound, flabbergast, overcome, overpower, shock, stagger, stupefy.

sturdy *adj.* athletic, brawny, determined, durable, firm, flourishing, hardy, hearty, husky, lusty, muscular, obstinate, powerful, resolute, robust, secure, solid, stalwart, stench, steadfast, stout, strong, substantial, vigorous, well-built, well-made.

subject *n.* affair, business, case, chapter, citizen, client, dependant, ground, issue, matter, mind, national, object, participant, patient, point, question, subordinate, substance, theme, topic, vassal, victim.

subordinate *adj.* ancillary, auxiliary, dependent, inferior, junior, lesser, lower, menial, minor, secondary, servient, subject, subservient, subsidiary, supplementary.

subside *v.* abate, collapse, decline, decrease, descend, diminish, drop, dwindle, ease, ebb, fall, lessen, lower, moderate, quieten, recede, settle, sink, slacken, slake, wane.

substitute *v.* change, replace, subrogate, swap, switch. *n.* alternate, equivalent, replacement, surrogate. *adj.* acting, alternative, replacement, temporary.

succeed *v.* arrive, ensue, flourish, follow, make good, make it, prosper, result, supervene, thrive, triumph, work.

success *n.* ascendancy, best-seller, celebrity, eminence, fame, fortune, happiness, hit, luck, prosperity, sensation, somebody, star, triumph, VIP, well-doing, winner.

sudden *adj.* abrupt, hasty, hurried, impulsive, prompt, quick rapid, rash, snap, startling, swift, unexpected, unforeseen, unusual.

suffer *v.* ache, agonize, allow, bear, brook, deteriorate, endure, experience, feel, grieve, hurt, let, permit, sorrow, support, sustain, tolerate, undergo.

sufficient *adj.* adequate, competent, effective, enough, satisfactory, sufficing, well-off, well-to-do.

suffocate *v.* asphyxiate, choke, smother, stifle, strangle, throttle.

suggest *v.* advise, advocate, connote, evoke, hint, imply, indicate, inkle, innuendo, insinuate, intimate, move, propose, recommend.

sum *n.* aggregate, amount, completion, culmination, entirety, height, quantity, reckoning, result, score, substance, sum total, summary, tally, total, totality, whole.

summarize *v.* abbreviate, abridge, condense, encapsulate, epitomize, outline, précis, review, shorten, sum up.

summit *n.* acme, apex, apogee, crown, culmination, head, height, peek, pinnacle, point to, zenith.

superior *adj.* admirable, airy, better, choice, condescending, de luxe, disdainful, distinguished, excellent, exceptional, exclusive, fine, first-class, first-rate, good, grander, greater, haughty, high-class, higher, hoity-toity, lofty, lordly, par excellence, patronizing, predominant, preferred, pretentious, prevailing, respectable, snobbish, snooty, snotty, snouty, stuck-up, supercilious, superordinate, surpassing, topflight, top-notch, transcendent, unrivaled, upper, uppish, uppity, upstage, worth.

supervise *v.* administer, conduct, control, direct, general, handle, inspect, keep tabs on, manage, oversee, preside over, run, superintend.

supplant *v.* displace, dispossess, oust, overthrow, remove, replace, supersede, topple, undermine, unseat.

suppose *v.* assume, believe, calculate, conceive, conclude, conjecture, consider, expect, fancy, guess, hypothesize, imagine, infer, judge, opine, posit, postulate, presume, presuppose, pretend, surmise, think.

supreme *adj.* cardinal, chief, consummate, crowning, culminating, extreme, final, first, foremost, greatest, head, highest, incomparable, leading, matchless, nonpareil, paramount, peerless, predominant, preeminent, prevailing, prime, principal, second-to-none, sov-ereign, superlative, surpassing, to, transcendent, ultimate, unbeatable, unbeaten, unsurpassed, utmost, world-beating.

sure *adj.* accurate, assured, bound, certain, clear, confident, convinced, decided, definite, dependable, effective, fast, firm, fixed, foolproof, guaranteed, honest, indisputable, inescapable, inevitable, infallible, irrevocable, persuaded, positive, precise, reliable, safe, satisfied, secure, solid, stable, steadfast, steady, surefire, trustworthy, trusty, undeniable, undoubted, unerring, unfailing, unmistakable, unswerving, unwavering.

surface *n.* covering, façade, face, facet, skin, veneer.

surprise *v.* amaze, astonish, astound, bewilder, confuse, disconcert, dismay, flabbergast, nonplus, stagger, startle, stun. *n.* amazement, astonishment, bewilderment, bombshell, dismay, eye-opener, incredulity, jolt, revelation, shock, start, stupefaction, wonder.

surrender *v.* abandon, capitulate, cede, concede, give in, give up, quit, renounce, resign, submit, succumb, waive, yield.

surreptitious *adj.* clandestine, covert, furtive, secret, sly, sneaking, stealthy.

survive *v.* endure, exist, last, last out, live, live out, live through, outlast, outlive, ride, stay, subsist, weather, withstand.

suspect *v.* believe, call in question, conclude, conjecture, consider, distrust, doubt, fancy, feel, guess, infer, mistrust, opine, speculate, suppose, surmise. *adj.* debatable, dodgy, doubtful, dubious, fishy, questionable, suspicious, unauthoritative, unreliable.

suspicious *adj.* apprehensive, chary, distrustful, dodgy, doubtful, dubious, fishy, incredulous, irregular, jealous, mistrustful, peculiar, queer, questionable, shady, skeptical, suspect, suspecting, unbelieving, uneasy, wary.

swamp n. bog, dismal, everglades, fen, marsh, mire, morass, moss, quagmire, quicksands. v. beset, besiege, capsize, deluge, drench, engulf, flood, inundate, overload, overwhelm, saturate, sink, submerge, waterlog.

swear[1] v. affirm, assert, asseverate, attest, vow, declare, depose, insist, promise, testify, vow, warrant.

swear[2] v. blaspheme, blind, curse, cuss, take the Lord's name in vain.

sweet[1] adj. affectionate, appealing, aromatic, beloved, cherished, darling, engaging, gentle, lovable, saccharine, sugary, syrupy, wholesome.

sweet[2] n. bonbon, candy, comfit, confect, confection, confectionery, sweetie, sweetmeat.

switch v. change, change course, change direction, chop and change, deflect, deviate, divert, exchange, interchange, put, rearrange, replace, shift, shunt, substitute, swap, trade, turn, veer. n. aboutturn, alteration, change, change of direction, exchange, interchange, shift, substitution, swap.

sympathize v. agree, commiserate, condole, empathize, feel for, identify with, pity, rap, respond to, side with, understand.

sympathy n. affinity, agreement, comfort, commiseration, compassion, condolement, condolence, condolences, empathy, fellow feeling, harmony, pity, rapport, tenderness, thoughtfulness, understanding, warmth.

synopsis n. abridgement, abstract, compendium, condensation, digest, epitome, outline, précis, recapitulation, review, sketch, summary, summation.

system n. arrangement, classification, coordination, logic, method, methodicalness, methodology, mode, modus operandi, orderliness, organization, plan, practice, procedure, process, regularity, routine, rule, scheme, structure, systematization, tabulation, taxis, taxonomy, technique, theory, usage.

systematic adj. businesslike, efficient, habitual, intentional, logical, methodical, ordered, orderly, organized, planned, precise, standardized, systematical, systematized, well-ordered, well-planned.

T

tact n. address, adroitness, consideration, delicacy, diplomacy, discernment, discretion, finesse, grace, judgment, perception, prudence, savoir faire, sensitivity, skill, thoughtfulness, understanding.

tactical adj. adroit, artful, calculated, clever, cunning, diplomatic, judicious, politic, prudent, shrewd, skillful, smart, strategic.

take v. abduct, abstract, accept, accommodate, accompany, acquire, adopt, appropriate, arrest, ascertain, assume, attract, bear, believe, betake, bewitch, blight, book, brave, bring, brook, buy, call for, captivate, capture, carry, cart, catch, charm, clutch, conduct, consider, contain, convey, convoy, deduct, deem, delight, demand, derive, detract, do, drink, eat, eliminate, endure, engage, ensnare, entrap, escort, execute, fascinate, ferry, fetch, filch, gather, glean, grasp, grip, guide, haul, have, have room for, hire, hold, imbibe, ingest, inhale, lead, lease, make, measure, misappropriate, necessitate, need, nick, observe, obtain, operate, perceive, perform, photograph, pick, pinch, please, pocket, portray, presume, purchase, purloin, receive, regard, remove, rent, require, reserve, secure, seize, select, stand, steal, stomach, strike, subtract, succeed, suffer, swallow, swipe, thole, tolerate, tote, transport, undergo, understand, undertake, usher, weather, win, withstand, work. n. catch, gate, haul, income, proceeds, profits, receipts, return, revenue, takings, yield.

tale n. account, anecdote, fable, fabrication, falsehood, fib, fiction, legend, lie, märchen, Munchausen, myth, narration, narrative, old wives' tale, relation, report, rigmarole, romance, rumor, saga, spiel, story, superstition, tall story, tradition, untruth, yarn.

talent n. ability, aptitude, bent, capacity, endowment, faculty, feel, flair, forte, genius, gift, knack, long suit, nous, parts, power, strength.

talk v. articulate, blab, blather, chat, chatter, chinwag, commune, communicate, confabulate, confer, converse, crack, gab, gossip, grass, inform, jaw, natter, negotiate, palaver, parley, prate, prattle, rap, say, sing, speak, squeak, squeal, utter, verbalize, witter. n. address, argot, bavardage, blather, blether, causerie, chat, chatter, chinwag, chitchat, clash, claver, colloquy, conclave, confab, confabulation, conference, consultation, conversation, crack, dialect, dialogue, discourse, discussion, dissertation, gab, gossip, harangue, hearsay, jargon, jaw, jawing, language, lecture, lingo, meeting, natter, negotiation, oration, palaver, parley, patois, rap, rumor, seminar, sermon, slang, speech, spiel, symposium, utterance, words.

tangible *adj.* actual, concrete, corporeal, definite, discernible, evident, manifest, material, objective, observable, palpable, perceptible, physical, positive, real, sensible, solid, substantial, tactile, touchable.

tart[1] *n.* pastry, pie, quiche, tartlet.

tart[2] *adj.* acerb, acerbic, acid, acrimonious, astringent, barbed, biting, bitter, caustic, cutting, incisive, piquant, pungent, sardonic, scathing, sharp, short, sour, tangy, trenchant, vinegary.

task *n.* assignment, aufgabe, burden, business, charge, chore, darg, duty, employment, enterprise, exercise, imposition, job, job of work, labor, mission, occupation, pensum, toil, undertaking, work. *v.* burden, charge, commit, encumber, entrust, exhaust, load, lumber, oppress, overload, push, saddle, strain, tax, test, weary.

taste *n.* appetite, appreciation, bent, bit, bite, choice, correctness, cultivation, culture, dash, decorum, delicacy, desire, discernment, discretion, discrimination, drop, elegance, experience, fancy, finesse, flavor, fondness, grace, inclination, judgment, leaning, liking, morsel, mouthful, nibble, nicety, nip, palate, penchant, perception, polish, politeness, predilection, preference, propriety, refinement, relish, restraint, sample, sapor, savor, soupçon, spoonful, style, swallow, tact, tactfulness, tang, tastefulness, tidbit, touch. *v.* assay, degust, degustate, differentiate, discern, distinguish, encounter, experience, feel, know, meet, nibble, perceive, relish, sample, savor, sip, smack, test, try, undergo.

tasteful *adj.* aesthetic, artistic, beautiful, charming, comme il faut, correct, cultivated, cultured, delicate, discreet, discriminating, elegant, exquisite, fastidious, graceful, handsome, judicious, polished, refined, restrained, smart, stylish, well-judged.

tasteless *adj.* barbaric, bland, boring, cheap, coarse, crass, crude, dilute, dull, flashy, flat, flavorless, garish, gaudy, graceless, gross, improper, inartistic, indecorous, indelicate, indiscreet, inelegant, inharmonious, insipid, low, mild, rude, stale, tacky, tactless, tame, tatty, tawdry, thin, uncouth, undiscriminating, uninspired, uninteresting, unseemly, untasteful, vapid, vulgar, watered-down, watery, weak, wearish.

taut *adj.* contracted, rigid, strained, stressed, stretched, tense, tensed, tight, tightened, unrelaxed.

teach *v.* accustom, advise, coach, counsel, demonstrate, direct, discipline, drill, edify, educate, enlighten, ground, guide, impart,

implant, inculcate, inform, instill, instruct, school, show, train, tutor, verse.

tedious *adj.* annoying, banal, boring, deadly, drab, dreary, dreich, dull, fatiguing, humdrum, irksome, laborious, lifeless, long-drawn-out, longsome, longspun, monotonous, prosaic, prosy, soporific, tiring, unexciting, uninteresting, vapid, wearisome.

teem *v.* abound, bear, brim, bristle, burst, increase, multiply, overflow, overspill, produce, proliferate, pullulate, swarm.

temperament *n.* anger, bent, character, constitution, disposition, makeup, outlook, personality, soul, tendency.

temperamental *adj.* capricious, erratic, high-strung, hotheaded, mercurial, moody, passionate, sensitive, touchy, volatile.

tenacious *adj.* adamant, adhesive, clinging, coherent, cohesive, determined, dogged, fast, firm, forceful, gluey, glutinous, inflexible, intransigent, mucilaginous, obdurate, obstinate, persistent, pertinacious, resolute, retentive, single-minded, solid, staunch, steadfast, sticky, strong, strong-willed, stubborn, sure, tight, tough, unshakable, unswerving, unwavering, unyielding, viscous.

tender[1] *adj.* aching, acute, affectionate, affettuoso, amoroso, amorous, benevolent, breakable, bruised, callow, caring, chary, compassionate, complicated, considerate, dangerous, delicate, difficult, emotional, evocative, feeble, fond, fragile, frail, gentle, green, humane, immature, impressionable, inexperienced, inflamed, irritated, kind, loving, merciful, moving, new, painful, pathetic, pitiful, poignant, raw, risky, romantic, scrupulous, sensitive, sentimental, smarting, soft, softhearted, sore, sympathetic, tenderhearted, ticklish, touching, touchy, tricky, vulnerable, warm, warm-hearted, weak, young, youthful.

tender[2] *v.* advance, extend, give, offer, present, proffer, propose, submit, suggest, volunteer. *n.* bid, currency, estimate, medium, money, offer, payment, proffer, proposal, proposition, specie, submissions, suggestion.

tenet *n.* article of faith, belief, canon, conviction, credo, creed, doctrine, dogma, maxim, opinion, precept, presumption, principle, rule, teaching, thesis, view.

tense *adj.* anxious, apprehensive, edgy, electric, exciting, fidgety, jittery, jumpy, moving, nerve-racking, nervous, overwrought, restless, rigid, strained, stressful, stretched, strung up, taut, tight, uneasy, uptight, worrying.

terminate v. abort, cease, close, complete, conclude, cut off, discontinue, drop, end, expire, finish, issue, lapse, result, stop, wind up.

terrify v. affright, alarm, appall, awe, dismay, frighten, horrify, intimidate, petrify, scare, shock, terrorize.

testify v. affirm, assert, asseverate, attest, avow, certify, corroborate, declare, depone, depose, evince, show, state, swear, vouch, witness.

thaw v. defrost, dissolve, liquefy, melt, soften, unbend, warm.

thief n. bandit, burglar, cheat, crook, embezzler, larcenist, mugger, pickpocket, plunderer, robber, shoplifter, swindler.

think v. anticipate, be under the impression, believe, brood, calculate, cerebrate, cogitate, conceive, conclude, consider, contemplate, deem, deliberate, design, determine, envisage, esteem, estimate, expect, foresee, hold, ideate, imagine, intellectualize, judge, meditate, mull over, muse, ponder, presume, purpose, ratiocinate, reason, recall, reckon, recollect, reflect, regard, remember, revolve, ruminate, suppose, surmise. n. assessment, cogitation, consideration, contemplation, deliberation, meditation, reflection.

thoughtful adj. absorbed, abstracted, astute, attentive, canny, careful, caring, cautious, circumspect, considerate, contemplative, deliberate, deliberative, discreet, heedful, helpful, introspective, kind, kindly, meditative, mindful, musing, pensieroso, pensive, prudent, rapt, reflective, ruminative, serious, solicitous, studious, thinking, unselfish, wary, wistful.

thoughtless adj. absentminded, careless, étourdi(e), foolish, heedless, ill-considered, impolite, imprudent, inadvertent, inattentive, inconsiderate, indiscreet, injudicious, insensitive, mindless, neglectful, negligent, rash, reckless, regardless, remiss, rude, selfish, silly, stupid, tactless, uncaring, undiplomatic, unkind, unmindful, unobservant, unreflecting, unthinking.

thrash v. beat, belt, bethump, bethwack, birch, cane, chastise, clobber, crush, defeat, drub, flagellate, flair, flog, hammer, heave, horsewhip, jerk, lam, lambaste, larrup, lather, lay into, leather, maul, overwhelm, paste, plunge, punish, quilt, rout, scourge, slaughter, spank, squirm, swish, tan, thresh, toss, towel, trim, trounce, wallop, whale, whap, whip, writhe.

threaten v. browbeat, bully, foreshadow, impend, imperil, menace, portend, presage, terrorize, warn.

thrifty adj. careful, conserving, economical, frugal, parsimonious, provident, prudent, saving, sparing.

throb v. beat, palpitate, pound, pulsate, pulse, thump, vibrate. n. beat, palpitation, pounding, pulsating, pulsation, pulse, thump, thumping, vibration, vibrato.

through prep. as a result of, because of, between, by, by means of, by reason of, by virtue of, by way of, during, in, in and out, in consequence of, in the middle of, past, thanks to, throughout, using, via. adj. completed, direct, done, ended, express, finished, non-stop, terminated.

throughout adv. everywhere, extensively, ubiquitously, widely.

thrust v. bear, butt, drive, force, impel, intrude, jab, jam, lunge, pierce, plunge, poke, press, prod, propel, push, ram, shove, stab, stick, urge, wedge. n. drive, flanconade, impetus, lunge, momentum, poke, prod, prog, push, shove, stab, stoccado.

tight[1] adj. close, close-fitting, compact, competent, constricted, cramped, dangerous, difficult, even, evenly balanced, fast, firm, fixed, grasping, harsh, hazardous, hermetic, impervious, inflexible, mean, miserly, narrow, near, niggardly, parsimonious, penurious, perilous, precarious, precise, problematic, proof, rigid, rigorous, sealed, secure, severe, snug, sound, sparing, stern, sticky, stiff, stingy, stretched, strict, stringent, taut, tense, ticklish, tightfisted, tough, tricky, trig, troublesome, uncompromising, unyielding, watertight, well-matched, worrisome.

timeless adj. ageless, endless, eternal, everlasting, immortal, permanent, perpetual, persistent, undying.

timely adj. appropriate, judicious, opportune, prompt, punctual, well-timed.

timid adj. afraid, apprehensive, bashful, cowardly, coy, diffident, fainthearted, fearful, henhearted, irresolute, modest, mousy, nervous, pavid, pusillanimous, retiring, shrinking, shy, spineless, timorous.

tired adj. all in, awearied, aweary, beat, bone-weary, bushed, clapped-out, clichéd, conventional, corny, deadbeat, disjaskit, dog-tired, drained, drooping, drowsy, enervated, épuisé(e), exhausted, fagged, familiar, fatigued, flagging, forfairn, forfough(t)en, forjeskit, hackneyed, jaded, knackered, old, outworn, shagged, shattered, sleepy, spent, stale, stock, threadbare, trite, weary, well-worn, whacked, worn out.

toil *n.* application, donkey-work, drudgery, effort, elbow grease, exertion, graft, industry, labor, labor improbus, pains, slog, sweat, travail. *v.* drudge, graft, grind, grub, labor, persevere, plug away, slave, slog, strive, struggle, sweat, tew, work.

toll[1] *v.* announce, call, chime, clang, knell, peal, ring, send, signal, sound, strike, summon, warn.

toll[2] *n.* assessment, charge, cost, customs, damage, demand, duty, fee, impost, inroad, levy, loss, payment, penalty, rate, tariff, tax, tithe, tribute.

tone *n.* accent, air, approach, aspect, attitude, cast, character, color, drift, effect, emphasis, feel, force, frame, grain, harmony, hue, inflection, intonation, klang, manner, modulation, mood, note, pitch, quality, shade, spirit, strength, stress, style, temper, tenor, timbre, tinge, tint, tonality, vein, volume. *v.* blend, harmonize, intone, match, sound, suit.

top *n.* acme, apex, apogee, cap, cover, crest, culmination, high point, meridian, peak, pinnacle, summit, zenith.

topical *adj.* contemporary, current, familiar, newsworthy, popular, relevant, up-to-date, up-to-the-minute.

total *n.* aggregate, all, amount, ensemble, entirety, lot, mass, sum, totality, whole. *adj.* absolute, all-out, complete, comprehensive, consummate, downright, entire, full, gross, integral, out-and-out, outright, perfect, root-and-branch, sheer, sweeping, thorough, thoroughgoing, unconditional, undisputed, undivided, unmitigated, unqualified, utter, whole, whole-hog.

touch *n.* ability, artistry, awareness, bit, blow, brush, caress, characteristic, command, communication, contact, correspondence, dash, deftness, detail, direction, drop, effect, facility, familiarity, feel, feeling, flair, fondling, hand, handiwork, handling, hint, hit, influence, intimation, jot, knack, manner, mastery, method, palpation, pat, pinch, push, skill, smack, smattering, soupçon, speck, spot, stroke, style, suggestion, suspicion, tactility, tap, taste, technique, tig, tincture, tinge, trace, trademark, understanding, virtuosity, way, whiff. *v.* abut, adjoin, affect, attain, border, brush, caress, cheat, compare with, concern, consume, contact, converge, disturb, drink, eat, equal, feel, finger, fondle, graze, handle, hit, hold a candle to, impress, influence, inspire, interest, mark, match, meet, melt, move, palp, palpate, parallel,

pat, pertain to, push, reach, regard, rival, soften, stir, strike, stroke, tap, tat, tinge, upset, use, utilize.

touching *adj.* affecting, emotional, heartbreaking, moving, pathetic, pitiful, poignant, sad, stirring, tender.

touchy *adj.* bad-tempered, captious, crabbed, cross, feisty, grouchy, grumpy, huffy, irascible, irritable, miffy, peevish, pettish, petulant, querulous, quick-tempered, snippety, snuffy, sore, splenetic, surly, testy, tetchy, thin-skinned.

tough *adj.* adamant, arduous, bad, baffling, brawny, butch, callous, cohesive, difficult, durable, exacting, exhausting, firm, fit, had, hard-bitten, hard-boiled, hardened, hard-nosed, hardy, herculean, inflexible, intractable, irksome, knotty, laborious, lamentable, leathery, merciless, obdurate, obstinate, perplexing, pugnacious, puzzling, refractory, regrettable, resilient, resistant, resolute, rigid, rough, ruffianly, rugged, ruthless, seasoned, sever, solid, stalwart, stern, stiff, stout, strapping, strenuous, strict, strong, stubborn, sturdy, tenacious, thorny, troublesome, unbending, unforgiving, unfortunate, unlucky, unyielding, uphill, vicious, vigorous, violent.

ournament *n.* championship, competition, contest, event, joust, lists, match, meeting, series, tourney.

tow *v.* drag, draw, haul, lug, pull, tote, trail, transport, trawl, tug, yank.

toxic *adj.* baneful, deadly, harmful, lethal, morbific, noxious, pernicious, pestilential, poisonous, septic, unhealthy.

tract[1] *n.* area, district, estate, expanse, extent, lot, plot, quarter, region, section, stretch, territory, zone.

tract[2] *n.* booklet, brochure, discourse, disquisition, dissertation, essay, homily, leaflet, monograph, pamphlet, sermon, tractate, treatise.

tragedy *n.* adversity, affliction, blow, calamity, catastrophe, disaster, misfortune, unhappiness.

train *v.* aim, coach, direct, discipline, drill, educate, exercise, focus, guide, improve, instruct, lesson, level, point, prepare, rear, rehearse, school, teach, tutor.

trait *n.* attribute, characteristic, feature, idiosyncrasy, peculiarity, quality, quirk.

transact *v.* accomplish, carry on, carry out, conclude, conduct, discharge, dispatch, do, enact, execute, handle, manage, negotiate, perform, prosecute, settle.

transfer *v.* carry, cede, change, consign, convey, decal, decant, demise, displace, grant, hand over, move, relocate, remove, second, shift, translate, transmit, transplant, transport, transpose. *n.* change, changeover, crossover, decantation, displacement, handover, move, relocation, removal, shift, switch, switch-over, transference, translation, transmission, transposition, virement.

transform *v.* alter, change, convert, metamorphose, reconstruct, remodel, renew, revolutionize, transfigure, translate, transmogrify, transmute, transverse.

transmit *v.* bear, broadcast, carry, communicate, convey, diffuse, dispatch, disseminate, forward, impart, network, radio, relay, remit, send, spread, traject, transfer, transport.

trap *n.* ambush, artifice, bunker, danger, deception, device, gin, hazard, net, noose, pitfall, ruse, snare, spring, springe, springle, stratagem, subterfuge, toils, trapdoor, trepan, trick, trickery, wile. *v.* ambush, beguile, benet, catch, corner, deceive, dupe, enmesh, ensnare, entrap, illaqueate, inveigle, lime, snare, take, tangle, trepan, trick.

treaty *n.* agreement, alliance, bargain, bond, compact, contract, convention, covenant, pact.

tremble *v.* heave, oscillate, quake, quiver, rock, shake, shiver, shudder, teeter, totter, vibrate, wobble, *n.* heartquake, oscillation, quake, quiver, shake, shiver, shudder, tremblement, tremor, vibration.

tremor *n.* agitation, earthquake, quake, quaking, quaver, quavering, quiver, quivering, shake, shaking, shiver, shock, thrill, tremble, trembling, trepidation, trillo, vibration, wobble.

trespass *v.* encroach, err, infringe, injure, intrude, invade, obtrude, offend, poach, sin, transgress, violate, wrong.

tricky *adj.* artful, complicated, crafty, cunning, deceitful, deceptive, delicate, devious, difficult, foxy, risky, scheming, slippery, sly, sticky, subtle, thorny, ticklish, touch-and-go, wily.

trite *adj.* banal, bromidic, clichéd, common, commonplace, corny, dull, hack, hackneyed, Mickey Mouse, ordinary, overworn, pedestrian, routing, run-of-the-mill, stale, stereotyped, stock, threadbare, tired, uninspired, unoriginal, well-trodden, well-worn, worn, worn-out.

trouble *n.* affliction, agitation, ailment, annoyance, anxiety, attention, bother, care, commotion, complaint, concern, danger, defect, difficulty, dilemma, disability, discontent, discord, disease, disorder, disquiet, dissatisfaction, distress, disturbance, effort, exertion, failure, grief, heartache, illness, inconvenience, irritation, labor, malfunction, mess, misfortune, nuisance, pain, pains, pest, pickle, predicament, problem, row, scrape, solicitude, sorrow, spot, strife, struggle, suffering, thought, torment, travail, trial, tribulation, tumult, uneasiness, unrest, upheaval, upset, vexation, woe, work, worry.

true *adj.* absolute, accurate, actual, authentic, bona fide, confirmed, correct, devoted, dutiful, exact, factual, faithful, honest, loyal, precise, right, rightful, true-blue, trustworthy, upright, valid.

trust *n.* affiance, assurance, belief, care, certainty, certitude, charge, confidence, conviction, credence, credit, custody, duty, expectation, faith, fidelity, guard, guardianship, hope, obligation, protection, reliance, responsiblity, safekeeping, trusteeship, uberrima feids.

trustworthy *adj.* authentic, dependable, ethical, foursquare, honest, honorable, level-headed, mature, principled, reliable, responsible, righteous, sensible, steadfast, true, trusty, truthful, upright.

truthful *adj.* accurate, candid, correct, exact, faithful, forthright, frank, honest, literal, naturalistic, plainspoken, precise, realistic, reliable, sincere, sooth, soothfast, soothful, straight, straightforward, true, trustworthy, veracious, veridicous, verist, veristic, veritable.

try *v.* adjudge, adjudicate, afflict, aim, annoy, appraise, attempt, catechize, endeavor, essay, evaluate, examine, experiment, hear, inconvenience, inspect, investigate, irk, irritate, pain, plague, prove, sample, seek, strain, stress, strive, struggle, sate, tax, test, tire, trouble, undertake, upset, venture, vex, wear out, weary. *n.* appraisal, attempt, bash, crack, effort, endeavor, essay, evaluation, experiment, fling, go, inspection, sample, shot, stab, taste, taster, test, trial, whack.

tub *n.* back, barrel, basin, bath, bathtub, bucket, butt, cask, hogshead, keeve, keg, kid, kit, pail, puncheon, stand, tun, vat.

tug *v.* drag, draw, haul, heave, jerk, jigger, lug, pluck, pull, tow, wrench, yank. *n.* drag, haul, heave, jerk, pluck, pull, tow, traction, wrench, yank.

tumble *v.* disorder, drop, fall, flop, jumble, overthrow, pitch, plummet, roll, rumple, stumble, topple, toss, trip up. *n.* collapse, drop, fall, flop, plunge, roll, spill, stumble, toss, trip.

tutor *n.* coach, governor, guardian, guide, guru, instructor, lecturer, master, mentor, preceptor, teacher. *v.* coach, direct, drill, guide, instruct, lecture, teach, train.

tycoon *n.* baron, big cheese, big shot, capitalist, entrepreneur, fat cat, financier, magnate, mogul, plutocrat, potentate.

tyrannize *v.* browbeat, bully, coerce, crush, dictate, domineer, enslave, intimidate, lord it, oppress, subjugate, terrorize.

U

ubiquitous *adj.* all-over, common, commonly encountered, ever-present, everywhere, global, omnipresent, pervasive, universal.

ugly *adj.* dangerous, disagreeable, distasteful, evil, frightful, hideous, homely, menacing, monstrous, offensive, repugnant, repulsive, revolting, sinister, unattractive, unsightly, vile.

unaffected *adj.* aloof, impervious, natural, unimpressed, unmoved, untouched.

unalterable *adj.* final, fixed, immutable, inflexible, permanent, rigid, steadfast, unyielding.

unassuming *adj.* diffident, humble, modest, self-effacing, unobtrusive, unpretentious.

unbearable *adj.* insufferable, insupportable, intolerable, outrageous, unacceptable, unendurable, unspeakable.

unbiased *adj.* disinterested, dispassionate, equitable, evenhanded, fair, fairminded, impartial, independent, just, neutral, objective, open-minded, uncolored, uninfluenced, unprejudiced.

uncertain *adj.* ambiguous, ambivalent, chancy, changeable, conjectural, dicky, doubtful, dubious, erratic, fitful, hazardous, hazy, hesitant, iffy, in the lap of the gods, incalculable, inconstant, indefinite, indeterminate, indistinct, insecure, irregular, irresolute, on the knees of the gods, precarious, problematic, questionable, risky, shaky, slippy, speculative, unclear, unconfirmed, undecided, undetermined, unfixed, unforeseeable, unpredictable, unreliable, unresolved, unsettled, unsure, vacillating, vague, variable, wavering.

uncomfortable *adj.* awkward, bleak, confused, conscience-stricken, cramped, disagreeable, discomfited, discomfortable, discomposed, disquieted, distressed, disturbed, embarrassed, hard, ill-fitting, incommodious, irritating, painful, poky, self-conscious, sheepish, troubled, troublesome, uneasy.

uncommon *adj.* abnormal, atypical, bizarre, curious, distinctive, exceptional, extraordinary, incomparable, infrequent, inimitable, notable, noteworthy, novel, odd, outstanding, peculiar, queer, rare, remarkable, scarce, singular, special, strange, superior, unfamiliar, unparalleled, unprecedented, unusual, unwonted.

unconditional *adj.* absolute, categorical, full, outright, total, unequivocal, unqualified, unreserved, unrestricted, utter, whole-hearted.

uncouth *adj.* awkward, barbarian, barbaric, boorish, clownish, clumsy, coarse, crude, gauche, gawky, graceless, gross, ill-mannered, loutish, lubberly, oafish, rough, rude, rustic, uncivilized, uncultivated, ungainly, unrefined, unseemly, vulgar.

understand *v.* accept, appreciate, apprehend, assume, believe, commiserate, comprehend, conceive, conclude, cotton on, discern, fathom, follow, gather, get, get the message, get the picture, grasp, hear, know, learn, penetrate, perceive, presume, realize, recognize, savvy, see, see daylight, suppose, sympathize, think, tolerate, tumble, twig.

understanding *n.* accord, agreement, appreciation, awareness, belief, comprehension, conclusion, discernment, estimation, grasp, idea, impression, insight, intellect, intellection, intelligence, interpretation, judgment, knowledge, opinion, pact, penetration, perception, reading, sense, view, viewpoint, wisdom. *adj.* accepting, compassionate, considerate, discerning, forbearing, forgiving, kind, kindly, loving, patient, perceptive, responsive, sensitive, sympathetic, tender, tolerant.

undertake *v.* accept, agree, assume, attempt, bargain, begin, commence, contract, covenant, embark on, endeavor, engage, guarantee, pledge, promise, shoulder, stipulate, tackle, try.

undignified *adj.* foolish, improper, inappropriate, indecorous, inelegant, ipetty, unbecoming, unrefined, unseemly, unsuitable.

unequal *adj.* asymmetrical, different, differing, disparate, disproportionate, dissimilar, ill-equipped, ill-matched, inadequate, incapable, incompetent, insufficient, irregular, unbalanced, uneven, unlike, unmatched, variable, varying.

unethical *adj.* dirty, discreditable, dishonest, dishonorable, disreputable, illegal, illicit, immoral, improper, shady, underhand, unfair, unprincipled, unprofessional, unscrupulous, wrong.

unfaithful *adj.* adulterous, deceitful, dishonest, disloyal, faithless, false, fickle, perfidious, two-timing, unreliable, untrue, untrustworthy.

unfavorable adj. adverse, bad, contrary, critical, disadvantageous, discouraging, hostile, ill-suited, inauspicious, infelicitous, inimical, inopportune, low, negative, ominous, poor, threatening, uncomplimentary, unfortunate, unfriendly, unlucky, unpromising, unpropitious, unseasonable, unsuited, untimely, untoward.

ungainly adj. awkward, clumsy, gangling, gauche, gawky, inelegant, loutish, lubberly, lumbering, slouching, uncoordinated, uncouth, unwieldy.

unimportant adj. immaterial, inconsequential, insignificant, irrelevant, lminor, negligible, small-time, trifling, trivial, worthless.

unintentional adj. accidental, fortuitous, inadvertent, involuntary, unconscious, undeliberate, unintended, unpremeditated, unthinking, unwitting.

unique adj. incomparable, inimitable, lone, matchless, nonpareil, one-off, only, peerless, single, sole, solitary, sui generis, unequaled, unexampled, unmatched, unparalleled, unprecedented, unrivaled.

unite v. accrete, ally, amalgamate, associate, band, blend, coadunate, coalesce, combine, confederate, conglutinate, conjoin, conjugate, consolidate, cooperate, couple, fay, fuse, incorporate, join, join forces, league, link, marry, merge, pool, splice, unify, wed.

universal adj. across-the-board, all-embracing, all-inclusive, all-round, catholic, common, ecumenic, ecumenical, entire, general, global, omnipresent, total, ubiquitous, unlimited, whole, widespread, worldwide.

unlucky adj. cursed, disastrous, doomed, hapless, ill-fated, ill-omened, ill-starred, inauspicious, infaust, jinxed, left-handed, luckless, mischanceful, miserable, ominous, unfavorable, unfortunate, unhappy, unsuccessful, untimely, wretched.

unnecessary adj. expendable, needless, redundant, superfluous, unneeded, useless.

unobtrusive adj. inconspicuous, low-key, quiet, restrained, self-effacing, unnoticeable, unostentatious, unpretentious.

unpleasant adj. abhorrent, bad, disagreeable, displeasing, distasteful, god-awful, ill-natured, irksome, nasty, objectionable, obnoxious, repulsive, rocky, sticky, traumatic, troublesome, unattractive, unpalatable.

unreasonable adj. absurd, arbitrary,

biased, blindered, capricious, cussed, erratic, excessive, exorbitant, extortionate, extravagant, far-fetched, foolish, froward, headstrong, illogical, immoderate, inconsistent, irrational, mad, nonsensical, opinionated, perverse, preposterous, quirky, senseless, silly, steep, stupid, thrawn, uncalled-for, undue, unfair, unjust, unjustifiable, unjustified, unwarranted.

unreliable adj. deceptive, delusive, disreputable, erroneous, fair-weather, fallible, false, implausible, inaccurate, inauthentic, irresponsible, mistaken, specious, uncertain, unconvincing, undependable, unsound, unstable, untrustworthy.

unsafe adj. dangerous, exposed, hazardous, insecure, parlous, perilous, precarious, risky, threatening, treacherous, uncertain, unreliable, unsound, unstable, vulnerable.

unsatisfactory adj. deficient, disappointing, inadequate, inferior, insufficient, mediocre, poor, unsuitable, unworthy.

unsightly adj. disagreeable, displeasing, hideous, repellent, repugnant, repulsive, revolting, ugly, unattractive, unpleasant, unprepossessing.

unsteady adj. changeable, dicky, erratic, flickering, flighty, fluctuating, frail, inconstant, infirm, insecure, irregular, precarious, reeling, rickety, shaky, shoogly, skittish, tittupy, tottering, totty, treacherous, tremulous, unreliable, unsafe, unstable, unsteeled, vacillating, variable, volatile, wavering, wobbly.

unsuitable adj. improper, inapposite, inappropriate, iunacceptable, unbecoming, unseemly, unsuited.

unsuspecting adj. childlike, confiding, credulous, green, gullible, inexperienced, ingenuous, innocent, naive, trustful, trusting, unconscious, uncritical, unsuspicious, unwary, unwitting.

untidy adj. bedraggled, chaotic, cluttered, disheveled, disorderly, higgledy-piggledy, jumbled, littered, messy, muddled, ratty, raunchy, rumpled, scruffy, shambolic, slatternly, slipshod, sloppy, slovenly, sluttish, topsy-turvy, unkempt, unsystematic.

untrustworthy adj. capricious, deceitful, devious, dishonest, disloyal, dubious, duplicitous, fair-weather, faithless, false, fickle, fly-by-night, shady, slippery, treacherous, tricky, two-faced, undependable, unfaithful, unreliable, unsafe, untrue, untrusty.

unusual adj. abnormal, anomalous, atypical, bizarre, curious, different, eccentric, exceptional, extraordinary, odd, phenomenal, queer, rare, remarkable, singular, strange, surprising, uncommon, unconventional, unexpected, unfamiliar, unwonted.

unwarranted *adj.* baseless, gratuitous, groundless, indefensible, inexcusable, uncalled-for, unjust, unjustified, unprovoked, unreasonable, vain, wrong.

unyielding *adj.* adamant, determined, firm, hardline, immovable, implacable, inexorable, inflexible, intractable, intransigent, obdurate, obstinate, relentless, resolute, rigid, solid, staunch, steadfast, stubborn, tough, unbending, uncompromising, unrelenting, unwavering.

upkeep *n.* care, expenses, keep, maintenance, operating costs, overhead, preservation, repair, running, subsistence, support, sustenance.

uprising *n.* insurgence, insurgency, insurrection, mutiny, putsch, rebellion, revolt, revolution, rising, sedition, upheaval.

uproar *n.* brawl, clamor, commotion, disorder, furor, noise, outcry, pandemonium, racket, ruckus, rumpus, turmoil.

upset *v.* agitate, bother, capsize, change, conquer, defeat, destabilize, discombobulate, discompose, disconcert, dismay, disorder, disorganize, disquiet, distress, disturb, fluster, grieve, hop, overcome, overset, overthrow, overturn, perturb, ruffle, shake, spill, spoil, tip, topple, trouble, unnerve, unsteady. *n.* agitation, bother, bug, complaint, defeat, disorder, disruption, disturbance, illness, indisposition, malady, purl, reverse, shake-up, shock, sickness, surprise, trouble, upheaval, worry. *adj.* agitate, bothered, capsized, chaotic, choked, confused, disconcerted, dismayed, disordered, disquieted, distressed, disturbed, frantic, gippy, grieved, hurt, ill, messed up, muddled, overturned, overwrought, pained, poorly, qualmish, queasy, ruffled, shattered, sick, spilled, toppled, topsy-turvy, troubled, tumbled, worried.

urgent *adj.* clamorous, cogent, compelling, critical, crucial, eager, earnest, emergent, exigent, immediate, imperative, important, importunate, insistent, instant, intense, persistent, persuasive, pressing, top-priority.

use *v.* apply, bring, consume, employ, enjoy, exercise, exhaust, expend, exploit, handle, manipulate, misuse, operate, ply, practice, spend, treat, usufruct, utilize, waste, wield, work. *n.* advantage, application, avail, benefit, call, cause, custom,

employment, end, enjoyment, exercise, good, habit, handling, help, meaning, mileage, necessity, need, object, occasion, operation, point, practice, profit, purpose, reason, service, treatment, usage, usefulness, usufruct, utility, value, way, wont, worth.

useful *adj.* advantageous, all-purpose, beneficial, convenient, effective, fruitful, general-purpose, handy, helpful, practical, productive, profitable, salutary, serviceable, valuable, worthwhile.

usual *adj.* accepted, accustomed, common, constant, conventional, customary, everyday, expected, familiar, fixed, general, habitual, nomic, normal, ordinary, recognized, regular, routine, standard, stock, typical, unexceptional, wonted.

utilize *v.* adapt, appropriate, employ, exploit, make use of, put to use, resort to, take advantage of, turn to account, use.

utopian *adj.* airy, chimerical, dream, elysian, fanciful, fantastic, ideal, idealistic, illusory, imaginary, impractical, perfect, romantic, unworkable, visionary, wishful.

utter[1] *adj.* absolute, arrant, complete, consummate, dead, downright, entire, out-and-out, perfect, sheer, stark, thorough, thoroughgoing, total, unalleviated, unmitigated, unqualified.

utter[2] *v.* articulate, declare, deliver, divulge, enounce, enunciate, express, proclaim, promulgate, pronounce, publish, reveal, say, sound, speak, state, tell, tongue, verbalize, vocalize, voice.

V

vacancy *n.* accommodation, emptiness, gap, job, opening, opportunity, place, position, post, room, situation, space, vacuity, vacuousness, vacuum, void.

vacant *adj.* absent, absentminded, abstracted, available, blank, disengaged, dreaming, dreamy, empty, expressionless, free, idle, inane, inattentive, incurious, thoughtless, to let, unemployed, unengaged, unfilled, unoccupied, untenanted, unthinking, vacuous, void.

vacate *v.* abandon, depart, evacuate, leave, quit, withdraw.

vacillate *v.* fluctuate, haver, hesitate, oscillate, shilly-shally, shuffle, sway, swither, temporize, tergiversate, waver.

vague *adj.* amorphous, blurred, dim, doubtful, evasive, fuzzy, generalized, hazy, ill-defined, imprecise, indefinite, indeterminate, indistinct, inexact, lax, loose, misty, nebulous, obscure, shadowy, uncertain, unclear, undefined, undetermined, unknown, unspecific, unspecified, woolly.

vain *adj.* affected, arrogant, conceited, egotistical, groundless, narcissistic, pointless, pretentious, self-important, self-satisfied, stuck-up, unavailing, unproductive, useless, worthless.

valiant *adj.* bold, brave, courageous, dauntless, doughty, fearless, gallant, heroic, indomitable, intrepid, plucky, redoubtable, stalwart, staunch, stout, stouthearted, valorous, worthy.

valid *adj.* approved, authentic, binding, bona fide, cogent, conclusive, convincing, efficacious, efficient, genuine, good, just, lawful, legal, legitimate, logical, official, potent, powerful, proper, rational, reliable, sound, substantial, telling, weighty, well-founded, well-grounded.

validate *v.* attest, authenticate, authorize, certify, confirm, corroborate, endorse, legalize, ratify, substantiate, underwrite.

vanish *v.* dematerialize, depart, die out, disappear, disperse, dissolve, evanesce, evaporate, exit, fade, fizzle out, melt, peter out.

vanquish *v.* beat, confound, conquer, crush, defeat, humble, master, overcome, overpower, overwhelm, quell, reduce, repress, rout, subdue, subjugate, triumph over.

variety *n.* array, assortment, brand, breed, category, change, class, collection, difference, discrepancy, diversification, diversity, intermixture, kind, make, manifoldness, many-sidedness, medley, miscellany, mixture, multifariousness, multiplicity, olio, olla podrida, order, potpourri, range, sort, species, strain, type, variation.

various *adj.* assorted, different, disparate, diverse, diversified, miscellaneous, several, sundry, varied.

vast *adj.* astronomical, boundless, capacious, colossal, cyclopean, enormous, extensive, far-flung, fathomless, gigantic, great, huge, illimitable, immeasurable, immense, limitless, mammoth, massive, measureless, monstrous, monumental, never-ending, prodigious, stupendous, sweeping, tremendous, unbounded, unlimited, vasty, voluminous, wide.

veer *v.* change, sheer, shift, swerve, tack, turn, wheel.

venal *adj.* bent, bribable, buyable, corrupt, mercenary, purchasable.

venture *v.* advance, adventure, chance, dare, endanger, hazard, imperil, jeopardize, make bold, presume, put forward, risk, speculate, stake, suggest, take the liberty,

volunteer, wager. *n.* adventure, chance, endeavor, enterprise, fling, gamble, hazard, operation, project, risk, speculation, undertaking.

verdict *n.* adjudication, assessment, conclusion, decision, finding, judgment, opinion, sentence.

versatile *adj.* adaptable, adjustable, all-round, flexible, functional, general-purpose, handy, many-sided, multifaceted, multipurpose, protean, renaissance, resourceful, variable.

veto *v.* ban, blackball, disallow, forbid, interdict, kill, negative, prohibit, reject, rule out, turn down.

vex *v.* afflict, aggravate, agitate, annoy, bother, bug, chagrin, deave, displease, distress, disturb, exasperate, fret, gall, get (to), harass, hump, irritate, molest, needle, nettle, offend, peeve, perplex, pester, pique, plague, provoke, rile, spite, tease, torment, trouble, upset, worry.

vicious *adj.* abhorrent, atrocious, backbiting, bad, barbarous, bitchy, brutal, catty, corrupt, cruel, dangerous, debased, defamatory, depraved, diabolical, fiendish, foul, heinous, immoral, infamous, malicious, mean, monstrous, nasty, perverted, profligate, rancorous, savage, sinful, slanderous, spiteful, unprincipled, venomous, vile, vindictive, violent, virulent, vitriolic, wicked, worthless, wrong.

victimize *v.* bully, cheat, deceive, defraud, discriminate against, dupe, exploit, fool, gull, hoodwink, oppress, persecute, pick on, prey on, swindle, use.

victor *n.* champ, champion, conqueror, first, prizewinner, subjugator, top dog, vanquisher, victor ludorum, victrix, winner.

victory *n.* conquest, laurels, mastery, palm, prize, subjugation, success, superiority, triumph, win.

vigorous *adj.* active, brisk, dynamic, effective, efficient, energetic, enterprising, flourishing, forceful, forcible, full-blooded, hale, heady, healthy, hearty, intense, lively, lusty, mettlesome, powerful, red-blooded, robust, sound, spanking, spirited, stout, strenuous, strong, virile, vital, zippy.

vindication *n.* apology, assertion, defense, exculpation, excuse, exoneration, justification, maintenance, plea, rehabilitation, support, verification.

virgin *n.* bachelor, celibate, damsel, girl, maid, maiden, spinster, vestal, virgo intacta. *adj.* chaste, fresh, immaculate, intact, maidenly, modest, new, pristine, pure, snowy, spotless, stainless, uncorrupted, undefiled, unsullied, untouched, unused, vestal, virginal.

virile *adj.* forceful, husky, lusty, macho, male, manlike, manly, masculine, potent, red-blooded, robust, rugged, strong, vigorous.

vision *n.* apparition, chimera, concept, conception, construct, daydream, delusion, discernment, dream, eyes, eyesight, fantasy, far-sightedness, foresight, ghost, hallucination, idea, ideal, illusion, image, imagination, insight, intuition, mirage, penetration, perception, phantasm, phantasma, phantom, picture, prescience, revelation, seeing, sight, spectacle, specter, view, wraith.

vital *adj.* alive, animate, animated, animating, basic, cardinal, critical, crucial, decisive, dynamic, energetic, essential, forceful, fundamental, generative, imperative, important, indispensable, invigorating, key, life-giving, life-or-death, live, lively, living, necessary, quickening, requisite, significant, spirited, urgent, vibrant, vigorous, vivacious, zestful.

vivacious *adj.* animated, bubbling, bubbly, cheerful, chipper, ebullient, effervescent, frisky, frolicsome, gay, high-spirited, jolly, lighthearted, lively, merry, scintillating, sparkling, spirited, sportive, sprightly, vital.

void *adj.* bare, blank, canceled, clear, dead, drained, emptied, empty, free, inane, ineffective, ineffectual, inoperative, invalid, nugatory, null, tenantless, unenforceable, unfilled, unoccupied, useless, vacant, vain, worthless.

volatile *adj.* airy, changeable, erratic, explosive, fickle, flighty, gay, giddy, hotheaded, hot-tempered, inconstant, lively, mercurial, sprightly, temperamental, unsettled, unstable, unsteady, variable, volcanic.

voluminous *adj.* abounding, ample, big, billowing, bulky, capacious, cavernous, commodious, copious, full, large, massive, prolific, roomy, vast.

vow *v.* affirm, avouch, bename, consecrate, dedicate, devote, maintain, pledge, profess, promise, swear. *n.* avouchment, oath, pledge, promise, troth.

vulgar *adj.* banausic, blue, boorish, cheap and nasty, coarse, common, crude, dirty, flashy, gaudy, general, gross, ill-bred, impolite, improper, indecent, indecorous, indelicate, low, low-life, low-lived, low-minded, low-thoughted, nasty, native, naughty, ordinary, pandemian, plebby, plebeian, ribald, risqué, rude, suggestive,

tacky, tasteless, tawdry, uncouth, unmannerly, unrefined, vernacular.

vulnerable *adj.* accessible, assailable, defenseless, exposed, expugnable, pregnable, sensitive, susceptible, tender, thin-skinned, unprotected, weak, wide open.

W

wacky *adj.* crazy, daft, eccentric, erratic, goofy, irrational, loony, loopy, nutty, odd, screwy, silly, unpredictable, wild, zany.

wad *n.* ball, block, bundle, chunk, hump, hunk, mass, pledget, plug, roll.

wail *v.* bemoan, bewail, complain, cry, deplore, grieve, howl, keen, lament, mewl, moan, ululate, weep, yammer, yowl. *n.* caterwaul, complaint, cry, grief, howl, keen, lament, lamentation, moan, ululation, weeping, yowl.

wait *v.* abide, dally, delay, hang fire, hesitate, hold back, hover, linger, loiter, mark time, pause, remain, rest, stay, tarry.

wallow *v.* bask, delight, enjoy, flounder, glory, indulge, lie, lurch, luxuriate, relish, revel, roll, splash, stagger, stumble, tumble, wade, welter.

want *v.* call for, covet, crave, demand, desiderate, desire, fancy, hanker after, hunger for, lack, long for, miss, need, pine for, require, thirst for, wish, yearn for, yen. *n.* absence, appetite, besoin, craving, dearth, default, deficiency, demand, desideratum, desire, destitution, famine, fancy, hankering, hunger, indigence, insufficiency, lack, longing, necessity, need, neediness, paucity, pauperism, penury, poverty, privation, requirement, scantiness, scarcity, shortage, thirst, wish, yearning, yen.

war *n.* battle, bloodshed, combat, conflict, contention, contest, enmity, fighting, hostilities, hostility, jihad, strife, struggle, ultima ratio regum, warfare.

warm *adj.* affable, affectionate, amiable, amorous, animated, ardent, balmy, calid, cheerful, cordial, dangerous, disagreeable, earnest, effusive, emotional, enthusiastic, excited, fervent, friendly, genial, glowing, happy, hazardous, hearty, heated, hospitable, impassioned, incalescent, intense, irascible, irritable, keen, kindly, lively, loving, lukewarm, passionate, perilous, pleasant, quick, sensitive, short, spirited, stormy, sunny, tender, tepid, thermal, touchy, tricky, uncomfortable, unpleasant, vehement, vigorous, violent, zealous.

warning *n.* admonishment, admonition, advance notice, advice, alarm, alert, augury, caution, caveat, forenotice, foretoken, forewarning, griffin, hint, larum, larum bell, lesson, monition, notice, notification, omen, premonition, presage, prodrome, sign, signal, siren, threat, tip, tip-off, token, vigia, word, word to the wise. *adj.* admonitory, aposematic, cautionary, in terrorem, monitive, monitory, ominous, premonitory, prodromal, prodromic, threatening.

wary *adj.* alert, apprehensive, attentive, cagey, careful, cautious, chary, circumspect, distrustful, guarded, hawkeyed, heedful, leery, on one's guard, on the lookout, on the qui vive, prudent, suspicious, vigilant, watchful, wideawake.

waste *v.* atrophy, blow, consume, corrode, crumble, debilitate, decay, decline, deplete, despoil, destroy, devastate, disable, dissipate, drain, dwindle, eat away, ebb, emaciate, enfeeble, exhaust, fade, fritter away, gnaw, lavish, lay waste, misspend, misuse, perish, pillage, prodigalize, rape, ravage, raze, rig, ruin, sack, sink, spend, spoil, squander, tabefy, throw away, undermine, wane, wanton, wear out, wither. *n.* debris, desert, desolation, destruction, devastation, dissipation, dregs, dross, effluent, expenditure, extravagance, garbage, havoc, leavings, leftovers, litter, loss, misapplication, misuse, mullock, offal, offscouring(s), prodigality, ravage, recrement, refuse, rubbish, ruin, scrap, slops, solitude, spoilage, squandering, sweepings, trash, void, wastefulness, wasteland, wild, wilderness. *adj.* bare, barren, desolate, devastate, dismal, dreary, empty, extra, leftover, superfluous, supernumerary, uncultivated, uninhabited, unproductive, unprofitable, unused, unwanted, useless, wild, worthless.

watch *v.* attend, contemplate, eye, gaze at, guard, keep, keep an eye open, look, look after, look at, look on, look out, mark, mind, note, observe, ogle, pay attention, peer at, protect, regard, see, spectate, stare at, superintend, take care of, take heed, tend, view, wait. *n.* alertness, attention, eye, heed, inspection, lookout, notice, observation, pernoctation, supervision, surveillance, vigil, vigilance, wake, watchfulness.

watchful *adj.* alert, attentive, cautious, circumspect, guarded, heedful, observant, on one's guard, on the lookout, on the qui vive, on the watch, suspicious, unmistaking, vigilant, wary, wideawake.

waver *v.* blow hot and cold, dither, falter, flicker, fluctuate, haver, hesitate, hem and haw, quiver, reel, rock, seesaw, shake, shilly-shally, sway, swither, totter, tremble, undulate, vacillate, vary, waffle, wave, weave, wobble.

weak *adj.* anemic, asthenic, atonic, cowardly, debile, debilitated, decrepit, defenseless, deficient, delicate, diluted, disturbant, dull, effete, enervated, exhausted, exposed, faint, faulty, feeble, fiberless, flimsy, fragile, frail, helpless, hollow, imperceptible, impotent, inadequate, inconclusive, indecisive, ineffective, ineffectual, infirm, insipid, invalid, irresolute, lacking, lame, languid, low, milk-and-water, muffled, namby-pamby, pathetic, poor, powerless, puny, quiet, runny, shaky, shallow, sickly, slight, small, soft, spent, spineless, substandard, tasteless, tender, thin, timorous, toothless, unconvincing, under-strength, unguarded, unprotected, unresisting, unsafe, unsatisfactory, unsound, unsteady, unstressed, untenable, vulnerable, wanting, wasted, watery, weakhearted, weak-kneed, weakly, weak-minded, weak-spirited, wishy-washy.

weaken *v.* abate, adulterate, craze, cut, debase, debilitate, depress, dilute, diminish, disinvigorate, droop, dwindle, ease up, effeminate, effeminize, emasculate, enervate, enfeeble, fade, fail, flag, give way, impair, invalidate, lessen, lower, mitigate, moderate, reduce, sap, soften up, temper, thin, tire, undermine, wane, water down.

weakling *n.* coward, milk-sop, pushover, sissy, softling, underdog, underling, wimp.

weakness *n.* Achilles' heel, debility, deficiency, faintness, fragility, frailty, lack, predilection, proclivity, vulnerability, weak point.

wealth *n.* abundance, affluence, assets, bounty, capital, cash, copiousness, cornucopia, estate, fortune, fullness, funds, golden calf, goods, klondike, lucre, mammon, means, money, opulence, pelf, plenitude, plenty, possessions, profusion, property, prosperity, resources, riches, richness, store, substance.

wear *v.* abrade, accept, allow, annoy, bear, bear up, believe, brook, carry, consume, corrode, countenance, deteriorate, display, don, drain, dress in, endure, enervate, erode, exasperate, exhibit, fall for, fatigue, fly, fray, grind, harass, have on, hold up, irk, last, permit, pester, put on, put up with, rub, show, sport, stand for, stand up, stomach, swallow, take, tax, tolerate, undermine, use, vex, waste, weaken, weary. *n.* abrasion, apparel, attire, attrition, clothes, corrosion, costume, damage, depreciation, deterioration, dress, durability, employment, erosion, friction, garb, garments, gear, habit, mileage, outfit, service, things, use, usefulness, utility, wear and tear.

weary *adj.* all in, arduous, awearied, aweary, beat, bored, dead beat, dead on one's feet, discontented, dog-tired, drained, drooping, drowsy, enervated, enervative, ennuied, ennuyé, exhausted, fagged, fatigued, fed up, flagging, impatient, indifferent, irksome, jaded, knackered, laborious, sick, sick and tired, sleepy, spent, taxing, tired, tiresome, tiring, wayworn, wearied, wearing, wearisome, whacked, worn-out.

weep *v.* bemoan, bewail, blub, blubber, boo-hoo, bubble, complain, cry, drip, exude, greet, keen, lament, leak, moan, mourn, ooze, pipe, pipe one's eye, pour forth, pour out, rain, snivel, sob, tune one's pipes, ululate, whimper, whine.

weigh *v.* bear down, burden, carry weight, consider, contemplate, count, deliberate, evaluate, examine, give thought to, impress, matter, mediate on, mull over, oppress, ponder, ponderate, prey, reflect on, study, tell, think over.

weight *n.* authority, avoirdupois, ballast, burden, clout, consequence, consideration, efficacy, emphasis, force, gravity, heaviness, heft, impact, import, importance, impressiveness, influence, load, mass, millstone, moment, onus, oppression, persuasiveness, ponderance, ponderancy, poundage, power, preponderance, pressure, significance, strain, substance, tonnage, value.

weird *adj.* bizarre, creepy, eerie, eldritch, freakish, ghostly, grotesque, mysterious, odd, outlandish, preternatural, queer, spooky, strange, superlunar, supernatural, uncanny, unco, unearthly, unnatural, witching.

well¹ *n.* bore, cavity, fount, fountain, hole, lift-shaft, mine, pit, pool, repository, shaft, source, spring, water hole, wellspring. *v.* brim over, flood, flow, gush, jet, ooze, pour, rise, run, seep, spout, spring, spurt, stream, surge, swell, trickle.

well² *adv.* ably, abundantly, accurately, adeptly, adequately, admirably, agreeably, amply, approvingly, attentively, capitally, carefully, clearly, closely, comfortably, completely, conscientiously, considerably, correctly, deeply, easily, effectively, efficiently, expertly, fairly, famously, favorably, fittingly, flourishingly, fully, glowingly, graciously, greatly, happily, heartily, highly, intimately, justly, kindly,

nicely, personally, pleasantly, possibly, proficiently, profoundly, properly, prosperously, readily, rightly, satisfactorily, skillfully, smoothly, splendidly, substantially, successfully, sufficiently, suitably, thoroughly, warmly.

wet *adj.* boggy, clammy, damp, dank, drenched, dripping, drizzling, effete, feeble, foolish, humid, ineffectual, irresolute, misty, moist, moistened, namby-pamby, pouring, raining, rainy, saturated, showery, silly, sloppy, soaked, soaking, sodden, soft, soggy, sopping, soppy, soused, spineless, spongy, teeming, timorous, waterlogged, watery, weak, weedy.

whim *n.* caprice, chimera, conceit, concetto, crank, craze, crotchet, fad, fancy, fizgig, flam, freak, humor, impulse, maggot, notion, quirk, sport, urge, vagary, whims(e)y.

whole *adj.* better, complete, cured, entire, faultless, fit, flawless, full, good, hale, healed, healthy, in one piece, intact, integral, integrated, inviolate, mint, perfect, recovered, robust, sound, strong, total, unabbreviated, unabridged, unbroken, uncut, undamaged, undivided, unedited, unexpurgated, unharmed, unhurt, unimpaired, uninjured, unmutilated, unscathed, untouched, well.

wholesome *adj.* advantageous, beneficial, clean, decent, edifying, exemplary, good, healthful, health-giving, healthy, helpful, honorable, hygienic, improving, innocent, invigorating, moral, nice, nourishing, nutritious, propitious, pure, respectable, righteous, salubrious, salutary, sanitary, uplifting, virtuous, worthy.

wide *adj.* ample, away, baggy, broad, capacious, catholic, commodious, comprehensive, diffuse, dilated, distant, distended, encyclopedic, expanded, expansive, extensive, far-reaching, full, general, immense, inclusive, large, latitudinous, loose, off, off-course, off-target, outspread, outstretched, remote, roomy, spacious, sweeping, vast.

wile *n.* artfulness, artifice, cheating, chicanery, contrivance, craft, craftiness, cunning, deceit, device, dodge, expedient, fraud, guile, hanky-panky, imposition, lure, maneuver, ploy, ruse, slyness, stratagem, subterfuge, trick, trickery.

will *n.* aim, attitude, choice, command, decision, declaration, decree, desire, determination, discretion, disposition, fancy, feeling, inclination, intention, mind, option, pleasure, preference, prerogative, purpose, resolution, resolve,

testament, velleity, volition, willpower,
wish, wishes. *v.* bequeath, bid, cause,
choose, command, confer, decree, desire,
determine, devise, direct, dispose of, elect,
give, leave, opt, ordain, order, pass on,
resolve, transfer, want, wish.

willful *adj.* adamant, deliberate, dogged,
intransigent, obstinate, persistent, stubborn, unyielding.

willing *adj.* agreeable, amenable, biddable, compliant, consenting, content,
desirous, disposed, eager, enthusiastic,
favorable, game, happy, inclined, nothing
lo(a)th, pleased, prepared, ready, so-
minded, volitient, willing-hearted.

win *v.* accomplish, achieve, acquire, attain,
bag, capture, catch, collect, come away
with, conquer, earn, gain, get, net, obtain,
overcome, pick up, prevail, procure,
receive, secure, succeed, sweep the board,
triumph.

wind[1] *n.* air, air current, babble, blast,
blather, bluster, boasting, breath, breeze,
clue, current, cyclone, draft, flatulence,
flatus, gab, gale, gas, gust, hint, hot air,
humbug, hurricane, idle talk, inkling, intimation, northeaster, notice, puff, report,
respiration, rumor, sirocco, southwester,
suggestion, talk, tidings, tornado, twister,
typhoon, warning, whisper, williwaw,
windiness, zephyr.

wind[2] *v.* bend, coil, curl, curve, deviate,
encircle, furl, loop, meander, ramble, reel,
roll, serpent, serpentine, serpentinize,
snake, spiral, turn, twine, twist, wreath,
zigzag. *n.* bend, curve, meander, turn,
twist, zigzag.

wisdom *n.* anthroposophy, astuteness, circumspection, comprehension, discernment, enlightenment, erudition, foresight,
intelligence, judgment, judiciousness,
knowledge, learning, penetration,
prudence, reason, sagacity, sapience,
sense, sophia, understanding.

wise *adj.* aware, clever, discerning, enlightened, erudite, informed, intelligent,
judicious, knowing, longheaded, long-
sighted, perceptive, politic, prudent, rational, reasonable, sagacious, sage,
sapient, sensible, shrewd, sound, understanding, well-advised, well-informed.

wish *v.* ask, aspire, bid, command, covet,
crave, desiderate, desire, direct, greet,
hanker, hope, hunger, instruct, long, need,
order, require, thirst, want, whim, yearn,
yen.

withhold *v.* check, conceal, deduct,
detain, hide, keen, keep back, refuse,
repress, reserve, resist, restrain, retain, sit
on, suppress, suspend.

witty *adj.* amusing, brilliant, clever,
comic, droll, epigrammatic, facetious,
fanciful, funny, humorous, sparkling,
waggish, whimsical.

wizard[1] *n.* conjurer, enchanter, mage,
magician, magus, necromancer, occultist,
shaman, sorcerer, sortileger, thaumaturge,
warlock, witch.

wizard[2] *n.* ace, adept, dabster, deacon, expert, genius, hotshot, maestro, master,
prodigy, star, virtuoso, whiz.

wonder *n.* admiration, amaze, amazement, astonishment, awe, bewilderment,
curiosity, fascination, marvel, miracle,
nonpareil, phenomenon, portent, prodigy,
rarity, sight, spectacle, stupefaction,
surprise, wonderment, wunderkind.

wonderful *adj.* admirable, amazing,
astonishing, astounding, awesome, excellent, extraordinary, fantastic, great, incredible, magnificent, outstanding,
phenomenal, remarkable, stupendous, superb, terrific, tip-top, top-hole, topping,
tremendous, unheard-of, wizard, wondrous.

work *n.* achievement, art, assignment,
book, business, calling, chore, commission, composition, craft, creation, darg,
deed, doings, drudgery, duty, effort, elbow
grease, employ, employment, exertion,
graft, grind, handiwork, industry, job,
labor, line, livelihood, métier, occupation,
oeuvre, office, opus, performance, piece,
play, poem, production, profession, pursuit, service, skill, slog, stint, sweat, task,
toil, trade, travail, undertaking, workload,
workmanship.

workable *adj.* doable, effectible, feasible,
possible, practicable, practical, realistic,
viable. *antonym* unworkable.

working *n.* action, functioning, manner,
method, operation, routing, running. *adj.*
active, employed, functioning, going,
laboring, operational, operative, running.
antonyms idle, inoperative, retired, unemployed.

workmanlike *adj.* adept, careful, efficient, expert, masterly, painstaking,
professional, proficient, satisfactory,
skilled, skillful, thorough, workmanly.

workmanship *n.* art, artistry, craft, craftsmanship, execution, expertise, facture,
finish, handicraft, handiwork, manufacture, skill, technique, work.

world *n.* age, area, class, creation, days,
division, domain, earth, environment,
epoch, era, existence, field, globe, human
race, humanity, humankind, kingdom, life,
man, mankind, men, nature, people,
period, planet, province, public, realm,

society, sphere, star, system, terrene, times, universe.

wordly *adj.* ambitious, avaricious, blasé, carnal, cosmopolitan, covetous, earthly, experienced, fleshly, grasping, greedy, knowing, lay, materialistic, mundane, physical, politic, profane, secular, selfish, sophisticated, sublunary, temporal, terrene, terrestrial, unspiritual, urbane, worldly-minded, worldly-wise. *antonym* unworldly.

worn *adj.* attrite, bromidic, careworn, clichéd, drawn, exhausted, fatigued, frayed, hackneyed, haggard, jaded, lined, pinched, played-out, ragged, shabby, shiny, spent, tattered, tatty, threadbare, tired, trite, wearied, weary, wizened, woe-wearied, woe-worn, worn-out. *antonyms* fresh, new.

worried *adj.* afraid, agonized, anxious, apprehensive, bothered, concerned, distracted, distraught, distressed, disturbed, fearful, frabbit, fretful, frightened, ill at ease, ner-vous, on edge, overwrought, perturbed, strained, tense, tormented, troubled, uneasy, unquiet, upset. *antonyms* calm, unconcerned, unworried.

worry *v.* agonize, annoy, attack, badger, bite, bother, brood, disquiet, distress, disturb, faze, fret, get one's knickers in a twist, gnaw at, go for, harass, harry, hassle, hector, importune, irritate, kill, lacerate, nag, perturb, pester, plague, savage, tantalize, tear, tease, torment, trouble, unsettle, upset, vex.

worthy *adj.* admirable, appropriate, commendable, creditable, decent, dependable, deserving, estimable, excellent, fit, good, honest, honorable, laudable, meritorious, praiseworthy, reliable, reputable, respectable, righteous, suitable, upright, valuable, virtuous, worthwhile.

wound *n.* anguish, cut, damage, distress, gash, grief, harm, heartbreak, hurt, injury, insult, laceration, lesion, offense, pain, pang, scar, shock, slash, slight, torment, torture, trauma. *v.* annoy, bless, cut, cut to the quick, damage, distress, gash, grieve, harm, hit, hurt, injure, irritate, lacerate, mortify, offend, pain, pierce, pip, shock, slash, sting, traumatize, wing, wring someone's withers.

wrath *n.* anger, bitterness, choler, displeasure, exasperation, fury, indignation, ire, irritation, passion, rage, resentment, spleen, temper.

write *v.* compose, copy, correspond, create, draft, draw up, inscribe, jot down, pen, record, screeve, scribble, scribe, set down, take down, tell, transcribe.

wrong *adj.* abusive, amiss, askew, awry, bad, blameworthy, criminal, crooked, defective, dishonest, dishonorable, erroneous, evil, fallacious, false, faulty, felonious, funny, illegal, illicit, immoral, improper, in error, in the wrong, inaccurate, inappropriate, inapt, incongruous, incorrect, indecorous, infelicitous, iniquitous, inner, inside, inverse, malapropos, misinformed, mistaken, off-beam, off-target, off-base, opposite, out, out of commission, out of order, reprehensible, reverse, sinful, unacceptable, unbecoming, unconventional, under, undesirable, unethical, unfair, unfitting, unhappy, unjust, unlawful, unseemly, unsound, unsuitable, untrue, wicked, wide of the mark, wrongful.

wry *adj.* askew, aslant, awry, contorted, crooked, deformed, distorted, droll, dry, ironic, mocking, pawky, perverse, sarcastic, sardonic, thrawn, twisted, uneven, warped.

Y

yank *v.* haul, heave, jerk, pull, snatch, tug, wrench.

yap *v.* babble, blather, chatter, go on, gossip, jabber, jaw, prattle, talk, tattle, twattle, ya(c)k, yammer, yatter, yelp, yip.

yard *n.* court, courtyard, garden, garth, hypaethron, quad, quadrangle.

yardstick *n.* benchmark, comparison, criterion, gauge, measure, standard, touchstone.

yarn¹ *n.* abb, fiber, fingering, gimp, lisle, thread.

yarn² *n.* anecdote, cock-and-bull story, fable, fabrication, story, tale, tall story.

yearly *adj.* annual, per annum, per year. *adv.* annually, every year, once a year.

yearn for *v.* ache for, covet, crave, desire, hanker for, hunger for, itch for, languish for, long for, lust for, pant for, pine for, want, wish for, yen for.

yell *v.* bawl, bellow, holler, hollo, howl, roar, scream, screech, shout, shriek, squawl, squeal, whoop, yelp, yowl.

yield¹ *v.* abandon, abdicate, accede, acquiesce, admit defeat, agree, allow, bow, capitulate, cave in, cede, comply, concede, consent, cry quits, give, give in, give way, go along with, grant, knuckle under, part with, permit, relinquish, resign, resign oneself, submit, succumb, surrender, throw in the towel.

yield² *v.* afford, bear, bring forth, bring in, earn, fructify, fructuate, fruit, furnish, generate, give, net, pay, produce, provide, return, supply. *n.* crop, earning, harvest, income, output, proceeds, produce, product, profit, return, revenue, takings.

young *adj.* adolescent, baby, callow, cub, early, fledgling, green, growing, immature, infant, junior, juvenile, little, new, recent, unblown, unfledged, youthful.

youthful *adj.* active, boyish, childish, ephebic, fresh, girlish, immature, inexperienced, juvenescent, juvenile, lively, pubescent, puerile, sprightly, spry, vigorous, vivacious, well-preserved , young. *n.* freshness, juvenileness, juvenility, liveliness, sprightliness, spryness, vigor, vivaciousness, vivacity.

yowl *v.* bay, caterwaul, cry, howl, screech, squall, ululate, wail, yell, yelp. *n.* cry, howl, screech, wail, yell, yelp.

Z

zany *adj.* amusing, clownish, comical, crazy, daft, droll, eccentric, funny, goofy, kooky, loony, madcap, nutty, screwy, wacky.

zealot *n.* bigot, devotee, enthusiast, extremist, fanatic, fiend, freak, maniac, militant.

zenith *n.* acme, apex, apogee, climax, culmination, height, high point, meridian, peak, pinnacle, summit, top, vertex.

zero *n.* bottom, cipher, duck, goose egg, love, nadir, naught, nil, nothing, nought.

zest *n.* appetite, charm, delectation, élan, enjoyment, flavor, gusto, interest, joie de vivre, keenness, kick, peel, piquancy, pungency, relish, rind, savor, smack, spice, tang, taste, zeal, zing.

zone *n.* area, belt, district, region, section, sector, sphere, stratum, territory, tract, zona, zonule, zonulet.

zoo *n.* animal park, aquarium, aviary, menagerie, safari park, zoological gardens.